2003
NOVEL &
SHORT STORY
WRITER'S

1,900+ PLACES TO GET YOUR FICTION INTO PRINT *MARKET*

EDITOR
ANNE BOWLING

ASSISTANT EDITOR
VANESSA LYMAN

WRITER'S DIGEST BOOKS
CINCINNATI, OH

If you are a publisher of fiction and would like to be considered for a listing in the next edition of *Novel & Short Story Writer's Market*, send a SASE (or SAE and IRC) with your request for a questionnaire to *Novel & Short Story Writer's Market*—QR, 4700 East Galbraith Road, Cincinnati OH 45236. Questionnaires received after June 7, 2003, will be held for the 2004 edition.

Editorial Director, Annuals Department: Barbara Kuroff
Supervisory Editor, Annuals Department: Alice Pope

Writer's Digest Books website: www.writersdigest.com
Writer's Market website: www.writersmarket.com.

International Standard Serial Number 0897-9812
International Standard Book Number 1-58297-147-1

Cover design by Matthew DeRhodes.

Attention Booksellers: This is an annual directory of F&W Publications.
Return deadline for this edition is January 15, 2004.

contents at a glance

Contents

RESOURCES

From the Editor

In the past two years, I've had the opportunity to meet with writer's groups in Seattle, Los Angeles, British Columbia, Houston, Oklahoma City, and Writer's Digest Books' hometown of Cincinnati. At bookstore appearances, workshops and conferences, it's been a privilege to meet such a diverse group of dedicated people—genre writers, literary writers, hypertext authors, published and unpublished—all similarly committed to the craft of storytelling. I believe the energy that comes from groups of writers, from five to three hundred, is a force we carry back to the desk, the kitchen table, the laptop or legal pad, to continue the work of fiction writing.

If you don't have plans to meet a with a writers' group this year, consider *Novel & Short Story Writer's Market* your personal connection to the literary community. In this edition we've brought together a strong collection of writers—some bestsellers, some debut novelists—to share the lessons they've learned. **Michael Chabon** discusses the "bloody mess" of editing *The Amazing Adventures of Kavalier & Clay* before it went on to win the Pulitzer Prize; **Tracy Chevalier** (*Girl with a Pearl Earring*) shares secrets for writing strong historical fiction (and withholds others); and **Stewart O'Nan** (*Wish You Were Here*) talks about researching topics from Vietnam to Route 66. First-time novelists **Silas House**, **Tess Uriza Holthe**, **Nicole Krauss** and **Ana Menéndez** discuss the struggles of finding an agent and the joy of seeing that first bound book.

You'll also hear from editors: Hannah Tinti of the new *One Story*, Keith Hood of the new journal *Orchid*, Nancy Zafris of *The Kenyon Review*, Michael Chester of *Glass Tesseract*, and Margaret Marbury of the new Harlequin imprint Red Dress Ink. Says Zafris: "Finding new writers, encouraging them, working on revisions with them, and then bringing them into print, is the most rewarding thing we do."

We will also connect you with markets for your work: here you'll find contacts for nearly 2,000 literary magazines, consumer magazines, zines, online publications, book publishers and small presses, many with specific instructions from editors regarding what they look for in fiction. This year we have also added a section of writing programs across the country, for those of you interested in furthering your formal instruction in craft. And of course, if you are inclined to travel, don't miss our section of conferences. Best wishes for a successful year of writing!

Anne Patterson Bowling.

Anne Patterson Bowling
Editor, *Novel & Short Story Writer's Market*
anne.bowling@fwpubs.com

With many thanks to our community of readers, to the authors who generously share their time and stories, and to our contributors whose work sets the standard: writer and assistant editor Vanessa Lyman, Aaron Abell, Travis Adkins, Will Allison, Nancy Baumgartner, David Borcherding, Cindy Duesing, Jeff Hillard, Kim Kane, Kelly Nickell, Alice Pope, W.E. Reinka, I.J. Schecter, Eric Schwartzberg, Jack Smith, Michelle Taute, Brad Vice and our Writer's Digest Books staff. Thanks also to Scott Turow for his good-natured agreement to a guest appearance in our article "The Five Cardinal Rules of Queries."

The "Quick-Start" Guide to Publishing Your Fiction

To make the most of *Novel & Short Story Writer's Market* you need to know how to use it. And with more than 600 pages of fiction publishing markets and resources, a writer could easily get lost amid the information. This "quick-start" guide will help you wind your way through the pages of *Novel & Short Story Writer's Market*, as well as the fiction publishing process, and emerge with your dream accomplished—to see your fiction in print.

1. Read, read, read.

Read numerous magazines, fiction collections and novels to determine if your fiction compares favorably with work currently being published. If your fiction is at least the same caliber as that you're reading, then move on to step two. If not, postpone submitting your work and spend your time polishing your fiction. Writing and reading the work of others are the best ways to improve craft.

For help with craft and critique of your work:
- You'll find articles on the craft and business aspects of writing fiction in the Craft & Technique section, beginning on page 28 and in the Getting Published section, beginning on page 41.
- If you're thinking about publishing your work online, see the Electronic Publishing section on page 67.
- If you're a genre writer, you will find information in For Mystery Writers, beginning on page 74, For Romance Writers, beginning on page 86 and For Science Fiction/Fantasy & Horror Writers, beginning on page 100.
- You'll find Conference & Workshop listings beginning on page 513.
- You'll find Organizations for fiction writers on page 581.

2. Analyze your fiction.

Determine the type of fiction you write to best target your submissions to markets most suitable to your work. Do you write literary, genre, mainstream or one of many other categories of fiction? There are magazines and presses seeking specialized work in each of these areas as well as numerous others.

For editors and publishers with specialized interests, see the Category Index beginning on page 606.

3. Learn about the market.

Read *Writer's Digest* magazine (F&W Publications, Inc.), *Publishers Weekly*, the trade magazine of the publishing industry, and *Independent Publisher* containing information about small- to medium-sized independent presses. And don't forget the Internet. The number of sites for writers seems to grow daily, and among them you'll find www.writersmarket.com and www.writers digest.com.

4. Find markets for your work.

There are a variety of ways to locate markets for fiction. The periodicals sections of bookstores and libraries are great places to discover new journals and magazines that might be open to your type of short stories. Read writing-related magazines and newsletters for information about new markets and publications seeking fiction submissions. Also, frequently browse bookstore shelves to see what novels and short story collections are being published and by whom. Check acknowledgment pages for names of editors and agents, too. Online journals often have links to the websites of other journals that may publish fiction. And last but certainly not least, read the listings found here in *Novel & Short Story Writer's Market*.

Also, don't forget to utilize the Category Indexes at the back of this book to help you target your fiction to the right market.

5. Send for guidelines.

In the listings in this book, we try to include as much submission information as we can from editors and publishers. Over the course of the year, however, editors' expectations and needs may change. Therefore, it is best to request submission guidelines by sending a self-addressed stamped envelope (SASE). You can also check the websites of magazines and presses which usually contain a page with guideline information. You can find updated guidelines of many of the markets listed here at www.writersdigest.com. And for an even more comprehensive and continually updated online markets list, you can obtain a subscription to www.writersmarket.com by calling 1-800-448-0915.

6. Begin your publishing efforts with journals and contests open to beginners.

If this is your first attempt at publishing your work, your best bet is to begin with local publications or those you know are open to beginning writers. Then, after you have built a publication history, you can try the more prestigious and nationally distributed magazines. For markets most open to beginners, look for the ❑ symbol preceding listing titles. Also, look for the ◢ symbol that identifies markets open to exceptional work from beginners as well as work from experienced, previously published writers.

7. Submit your fiction in a professional manner.

Take the time to show editors that you care about your work and are serious about publishing. By following a publication's or book publisher's submission guidelines and practicing standard submission etiquette, you can better ensure your chances that an editor will want to take the time to read your work and consider it for publication. Remember, first impressions last, and a carelessly assembled submission packet can jeopardize your chances before your story or novel manuscript has had a chance to speak for itself. For help with preparing submissions read The Business of Fiction Writing, beginning on page 58.

8. Keep track of your submissions.

Know when and where you have sent fiction and how long you need to wait before expecting a reply. If an editor does not respond by the time indicated in his market listing or guidelines, wait a few more weeks and then follow up with a letter (and SASE) asking when the editor anticipates making a decision. If you still do not receive a reply from the editor within a reasonable amount of time, send a letter withdrawing your work from consideration and move on to the next market on your list.

9. Learn from rejection.

Rejection is the hardest part of the publication process. Unfortunately, rejection happens to every writer, and every writer needs to learn to deal with the negativity involved. On the other hand, rejection can be valuable when used as a teaching tool rather than a reason to doubt yourself and your work. If an editor offers suggestions with his or her rejection slip, take those comments into consideration. You don't have to automatically agree with an editor's opinion of your work. It may be that the editor has a different perspective on the piece than you do. Or, you may find that the editor's suggestions give you new insight into your work and help you improve your craft.

10. Don't give up.

The best advice for you as you try to get published is be persistent, and always believe in yourself and your work. By continually reading other writers' work, constantly working on the craft of fiction writing and relentlessly submitting your work, you will eventually find that magazine or book publisher that's the perfect match for your fiction. And, *Novel & Short Story Writer's Market* will be here to help you every step of the way.

GUIDE TO LISTING FEATURES

Below you will find an example of the market listings contained in *Novel & Short Story Writer's Market*. Also included are call-outs identifying the various format features of the listings. (For an explanation of the symbols used, see the front and back covers of this book.)

ICONS FOR EASY REFERENCE

WHAT KIND OF FICTION THEY BUY

COMMENTS FROM THE NSSWM EDITOR

PUBLICATION PROFILE

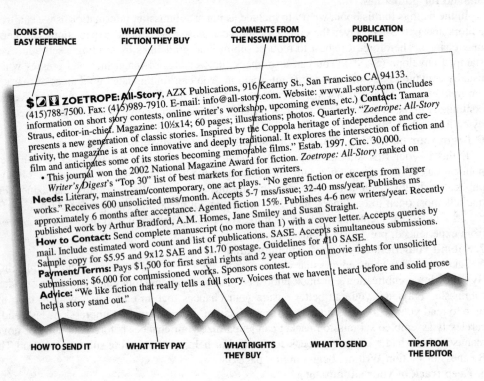

$ ☑ ❏ **ZOETROPE: All-Story**, AZX Publications, 916 Kearny St., San Francisco CA 94133. (415)788-7500. Fax: (415)989-7910. E-mail: info@all-story.com. Website: www.all-story.com (includes information on short story contests, online writer's workshop, upcoming events, etc.) **Contact:** Tamara Straus, editor-in-chief. Magazine: 10½x14; 60 pages; illustrations; photos. Quarterly. "*Zoetrope: All-Story* presents a new generation of classic stories. Inspired by the Coppola heritage of independence and creativity, the magazine is at once innovative and deeply traditional. It explores the intersection of fiction and film and anticipates some of its stories becoming memorable films." Estab. 1997. Circ. 30,000.

• This journal won the 2002 National Magazine Award for fiction. *Zoetrope: All-Story* ranked on *Writer's Digest*'s "Top 30" list of best markets for fiction writers.

Needs: Literary, mainstream/contemporary, one act plays. "No genre fiction or excerpts from larger works." Receives 600 unsolicited mss/month. Accepts 5-7 mss/issue; 32-40 mss/year. Publishes ms approximately 6 months after acceptance. Agented fiction 15%. Publishes 4-6 new writers/year. Recently published work by Arthur Bradford, A.M. Homes, Jane Smiley and Susan Straight.

How to Contact: Send complete manuscript (no more than 1) with a cover letter. Accepts queries by mail. Include estimated word count and list of publications. SASE. Accepts simultaneous submissions. Sample copy for $5.95 and 9x12 SAE and $1.70 postage. Guidelines for #10 SASE.

Payment/Terms: Pays $1,500 for first serial rights and 2 year option on movie rights for unsolicited submissions; $6,000 for commissioned works. Sponsors contest.

Advice: "We like fiction that really tells a full story. Voices that we haven't heard before and solid prose help a story stand out."

HOW TO SEND IT   **WHAT THEY PAY**   **WHAT RIGHTS THEY BUY**   **WHAT TO SEND**   **TIPS FROM THE EDITOR**

Writing Fiction

Tracy Chevalier Breathes Life into History

BY ANNE BOWLING

Something in Highgate Cemetery, outside London, spoke loud and clear to Tracy Chevalier. Whether it was romance of the crowded, crumbling monuments, or ropes of overgrown ivy in the Victorian graveyard, she's not sure. But she was haunted by the place, and "fell in love with it," she says. "I wanted to set a novel there."

To write her novels, Chevalier immerses herself in the past, and it's a place she's very happy in. Her *Girl with a Pearl Earring* (Dutton)—which was a bestseller as both hardcover and trade paperback—was set in seventeenth century Delft. Her latest novel, *Falling Angels*, studies two families at the turn of the twentieth century, as England moved from the strict conventions of Victorian rule to a more liberal Edwardian era.

"I like writing about the past—I feel more comfortable exploring it than I do the present," she says. "Today's world is a strange place that I don't entirely understand. I don't mind living in it, but I don't feel I need to write about it."

Critics have almost universally praised

Tracy Chevalier

Photo © Jerry Bauer

Chevalier's evocation of setting and period, and that's an aspect of her writing she takes beyond scholarly research. For *Girl with a Pearl Earring*, inspired by a work by Dutch artist Johannes Vermeer, she took a painting class, and for *Falling Angels* Chevalier did volunteer work in Highgate Cemetery. Her upcoming title is centered on medieval tapestries, now housed in a Paris museum, and she plans to learn the weaving craft herself.

"A reader recently told me she loved how Griet in *Girl* boiled her cap in potato peelings to starch it," she says. "I was glad, because I spent some time finding that out. Those little historical details are so important, because they add verisimilitude to a book. If I get those things right, the reader will trust me with the bigger issues." To the question of where she allows herself liberties, she replies with a wily, "ho, ho—those are my secrets!"

Chevalier may have picked up some of her "secrets" at the University of East Anglia in Norwich, England, where in 1993 she earned her MFA in creative writing, after years of frustra-

---

ANNE BOWLING *is editor of* Novel & Short Story Writer's Market. *This interview appeared originally in* Writer's Digest.

tion as an editor for a reference book publisher. "I wrote at night and on weekends very sporadically," she says, "and sometimes it took me a year to finish a story." Her year of study gave her deadlines, a critical audience, "and most of all the expectation that I would write all day, every day," she says. "In terms of craft, I wouldn't say it helped me any more than simply writing for a year would. But that's a lot . . . I can see it in my novels, the improvement in craft over time simply because the more I do it the more I learn what works and what doesn't."

"I think the hardest part is finding a way of telling the story that matches the story itself," Chevalier says. "For a book to really work, form and function must go hand in hand, just like with buildings, as any decent architect will tell you."

Writing her first novel *The Virgin Blue*, published in 1997 in the UK and scheduled for U.S. release next year, was also a learning opportunity, Chevalier says, although more in process than in craft. "The main lesson I learned was to write the thing straight through, get it down, and then go back and revise. I didn't do that with *The Virgin Blue*—I'd get halfway through and discover something through research and think 'oh my God, this changes everything! Gotta go back and write it again,' " she says. "It took me much longer to write as a result, and I put myself through a lot of unnecessary agony."

Writing *Girl with a Pearl Earring*, Chevalier says, was an entirely different story. Lying in bed one morning, her eyes resting on a poster of the Vermeer painting she had always loved, it came to her. Within three days Chevalier had the whole story worked out, she says. With that book, "I learned that it is better to know the ending early on rather than to be unsure—then you know what you're aiming for and can arc the story towards that end," she says. "I was absolutely clear about *Girl* from the start, not just the ending, but the length, feel and sound of the book. It came out in one long write, then I went back and revised."

Stylistically, *Falling Angels* was not quite as cooperative. Chevalier wrote nearly the entire book—with its seven lead characters, both adults and children—in third person, realizing late in the process that the point of view wasn't working. As a remedy, she reworked the manuscript using a multiple first-person point of view, and "now I think of style as its strongest point," she says.

"I think the hardest part is finding a way of telling the story that matches the story itself," Chevalier says. "For a book to really work, form and function must go hand in hand, just like with buildings, as any decent architect will tell you."

In order to conserve time for writing, and revision, Chevalier has worked with an agent since publication of *The Virgin Blue*—using the agency's expertise to get her manuscripts in the publisher's door and into the hands of the right editor. Once the manuscript is placed, the arrangement becomes one of mediation, which is "essential when working on a book," she says. "If I am not happy about something, it's much easier for everyone if the agent discusses it with the editor. They also have a much better sense of what I'm worth than I do, and know what kind of deal to ask for . . . I would be lost without them."

To find that first agent, she suggests, "call literary agencies and ask the receptionist if there are any agents just starting out—they are far more likely to be actively seeking clients than established agents, will answer you more quickly, and may well work harder for you."

Michael Chabon: Trust the Process

BY KELLY NICKELL

"I like to say there are three things that are required for success as a writer: talent, luck, discipline," says Michael Chabon. "It can be in any combination, but there's nothing you do to influence the first two. Discipline is the one element of those three things that you can control, and so that is the one that you have to focus on controlling. You just have to hope and trust in the other two."

Chabon won't credit discipline alone with his winning the Pulitzer Prize in 2001 for his novel *The Amazing Adventures of Kavalier & Clay.* But he will say the experience was thrilling. "It was very exciting," Chabon says of the moment he heard the news. "There was lots of leaping and screaming going on in my house. It was really definitely one of the most fun days in my life so far."

For Chabon, 38, success came early with the 1988 release of *The Mysteries of Pittsburgh.* The book, which he originally wrote for his master's thesis while at the University of California at Irvine, became a bestseller and pushed the then-twentysomething author to the forefront of literary up-and-comers.

Michael Chabon

Photo © Patty Williams

In the years that followed *Mysteries,* however, Chabon's hope and trust were challenged. After the 1991 publication of his second book, the short story collection *A Model World and Other Stories,* he went to work on what was to be his next novel, *Fountain City.* But, after a five-and-a-half-year odyssey of scrapped drafts, revisions and frustrations, Chabon had to stop.

"I was just starting another draft of that book, and I thought, 'You know, I really don't want to do this anymore. I can't do this.' "

So, he put the manuscript aside, and gave himself a six-week break to work on "this other thing about a teacher and his student." Six weeks turned into seven months, and from those seven months came the bestseller *Wonder Boys*—which also went on to become an award-winning film.

Ultimately, the adversity that was *Fountain City*—which remains unfinished—proved crucial to the successful completion of *The Amazing Adventures of Kavalier & Clay.*

"I went through some very difficult periods with *Kavalier & Clay*—periods that were uncomfortably reminiscent of my experience with *Fountain City*—where I felt like I had lost my way," he says. "I didn't really know what I was trying to say, or why I was writing it, or why I had

---

KELLY NICKELL *is an editor for* Writer's Digest Books, *and former features editor for* Writer's Digest *magazine.*

ever thought in a million years that I would be able to write a book like that."

Despite such doubts, Chabon drew on past experiences and immersed himself in his own creative process. The novel, which took four and a half years to finish, follows two Jewish cousins who create their own comic book in New York City in the late '30s and '40s. The novel's breadth is ever-reaching: the "Golden Age" of comic books, a young New York City, the role of Antarctica in WWII, Jewish mysticism, self-reinvention, Houdini-esque feats. Put simply, it's complex. And it wasn't easy to sustain. As with his previous books, he began *Kavalier & Clay* without an outline, instead preferring a more "organic approach" that allows characters and themes to develop and reveal themselves naturally.

"It's really about the discovery for me," he says. "It's about the mystery of where I'm going and what I'll find when I get there. So, I sort of operated in the first draft without a map, as it were. Then I began in subsequent drafts to hone the story and really figure out where I was going in terms of plot, and to get a greater thematic sense of the story—like the theme of escape, for example, which is very strong in the novel."

"I went through some very difficult periods with Kavalier & Clay—where I felt like I had lost my way. I didn't really know . . . why I had ever thought in a million years that I would be able to write a book like that."

It's this unrestrained process of discovery—though Chabon says it often produces "completely useless" material—that allows the author to revel in creating life from the unknown and the nonexistent. And, in each evolving draft, the story's path becomes more defined as distractions and unnecessary story lines are cut away.

In the end, Chabon estimates he cut some 250 pages from the novel, relying on his own instincts, as well as on input from various readers—including his wife, mystery writer Ayelet Waldman. But, cutting from such an intricate novel required precision.

"There was a lot of repair work that needed to be done—some of the things that I cut were worked very deeply into the fabric of the novel, and it was kind of a bloody mess to get them out of there," he says.

For a novel that, at times, plagued Chabon with self-doubt and hesitation, the rewards have been great. And the influence of self-discipline is perhaps most evident. "I think, looking back at it now—especially when they're calling and saying they're going to give you the Pulitzer Prize for it—it's very satisfying just to think that I stuck with it and that I pulled it off, even though many times in the course of writing it, it really looked like I wasn't going to be able to."

Chabon's personal schedule is as hectic as ever. He's currently at work on a children's novel, *Summerland*, as well as a screenplay version of *Kavalier & Clay*. Although the projects were in the works prior to his Pulitzer win, Chabon says he's not nervous about starting a new novel in his "post-Pulitzer era."

"I love beginning things," he says. "When it's all fresh and new, and I know exactly how I want it to be, and it's going to be splendid and beautiful—that's a great feeling. It's from that point on that it's downhill.

"As soon as you begin to write it, you start to veer away from that shining example, and corruptions enter the process. It never comes out the way you thought it was going to."

The father of three young children and a self-proclaimed night owl, Chabon writes from 10 p.m. to 4 a.m., Sunday through Thursday. It's a schedule he sticks to without exception, and it punctuates his basic ideology: "Keep a regular schedule, and write at the same time every day for the same amount of time. That's it. That is the sum total of my wisdom."

Bonnie Jo Campbell Makes Shift from Story to Novel Writing

BY WILL ALLISON

Like many novelists, Bonnie Jo Campbell first found success as a short-story writer. Her collection, *Women & Other Animals* (University of Massachusetts Press, 1999), won the AWP Award for Short Fiction and has since been reprinted in paperback (Simon & Schuster, 2002) and translated into German. Her second book is a novel, *Q Road* (Scribner, 2002). In making the transition from story writing to novel writing, the key for Campbell was staying interested in her material.

"It was surprising to work month after month, year after year with the characters and still the story wasn't done," says Campbell, who lives with her husband near Kalamazoo, Michigan. "I didn't get tired of it, though. It was kind of like being married, waking up with the same guy, morning after morning. If you like the guy or the story well enough, you don't mind."

The novel, like much of Campbell's fiction, draws heavily on her life. *Q Road* is set in rural Michigan, where Campbell grew up on a small farm. She's now working on more stories, essays, and two other novels. One of

Bonnie Jo Campbell

Photo © Christopher Magson

those novels, she says, is about "a mathematics department gone wild." In addition to a BA in philosophy and an MFA in creative writing, Campbell holds a BA in math education and an MA in math.

Her other novel-in-progress involves a present-day circus. Campbell once traveled with the Ringling Brothers and Barnum & Bailey Circus selling snow cones, an experience already reflected in several of her short stories. Some of her other stories draw upon her work as president of Goulash Tours Inc., in which she has organized and led adventure tours in Russia and the Baltics, and all the way south to Romania and Bulgaria.

Here, Campbell discusses the shift from writing short stories to writing novels, and the challenges and rewards inherent in both forms.

WILL ALLISON *is former editor-at-large for* Zoetrope: All-Story, *former executive editor of* Story, *and former editor of* Novel & Short Story Writer's Market. *He is also a staff member at the Squaw Valley Community of Writers and the recipient of a 2000 Ohio Arts Council grant for fiction.*

How did writing a novel compare to writing your story collection?

For some reason I had expected the novel wouldn't take as long as the collection, but it ended up taking about the same amount of time, three years. That makes sense, I guess, since they're both about the same length.

My novel has some of the elements of a collection of short stories, lots of point-of-view shifts, so sometimes working on the different parts felt something like working on short stories. But then I had to also be making sure all those parts were working together.

Which form suits you best?

Oh gosh, I like them both. And though you're not supposed to both be married and date, you are allowed to write both short stories and novels.

Short stories allow you to experiment, try out new forms and voices. You can tell a short story using a weird point of view (such as that of a baby or a psychopath), whereas that point of view would become tiresome to write or read after five or ten pages. In a short story you can focus on an image or just play around. If I want to write a story about a woman who is losing her mind because she's pregnant, I don't have to go to the doctor with her or meet her husband. I can just leave her sitting on the edge of her bed, swollen up and losing her mind. And if I write a bad story, so what? It's just a few bad pages. Now if I write a bad novel, that's a lot of lost time to lament.

Why risk losing that much time if you could be writing stories instead?

Because short stories are easier, it is tempting to not bother with a novel, but writing a novel made my life better, forced me to make connections between one human situation—a kind of love triangle that inspired me to tell the story—and the community in which these people live, and even to American society at large. I found a lot more meaning in the novel than I ever could have found in a short story.

And then there are the practical aspects about writing a novel. Publishers and readers prefer them, and that's an incentive to write them—a lot of why I write is because I like to be read.

I feel lucky that I'm able to write anything that anybody wants to read, and if they want novels, then, by golly, I'll try to put together novels for them. If they want another one, I'll write them another one, starting right now. That doesn't mean I'll stop writing short stories or essays.

Did you find yourself cannibalizing stories for the novel, or vice versa?

Flannery O'Connor made some of her short stories into novel chapters. I can't imagine doing that, but I ended up using a lot of themes from my collection in my novel. I wanted to do more with a girl with a gun (as in "Shotgun Wedding"), a girl living on her own (as in "The Fishing Dog,"), and a really cranky self-sufficient mother (as in "Bringing Home the Bones"). I continue to be interested in beauty and ugliness, in rivers and the land rising up from rivers, and so all those things appear in the novel as well as in the stories. And now that I think of it, some of the ideas for those short stories came out of essays that I wrote even earlier. That makes me a kind of recycler, I guess.

What made you think you could write a novel?

I love reading novels and admire novelists, so I've been so flattered when someone said of one of my short stories, "Oh, I was sad it was over, I wish it were a novel." Maybe a few stories from my collection could have developed into novels, but when I wrote them I wasn't ready to write a novel. I figured I'd better learn how to write with short stories. When I got inspired to write *Q Road*, I think I was in the mood to have a novel, just like one of those girls who marries the guy she's with just because she's in the mood to be married.

When I first shared the basic plot with a novelist friend of mine, Jaimy Gordon, she said, "That sounds like another one of your short stories." But I knew I wanted to stretch it out, roll around in the story the way my dog rolls around on a dead animal. The central emotion at the heart of *Q Road*—love, of course—sustained me through all 300 pages, and somehow I knew from the beginning that it would.

You weren't daunted?

Though I'll never be an opera star or a gymnast, I like to entertain the idea I can do most anything. When I initially talked to my editor on the phone, before she bought the novel (an early draft), I told her that I could castrate pigs with a penknife and factor polynomials in my head. In convincing her I could work this novel into something good, I guess I convinced myself.

Also, I guess I wanted to prove to myself I had the stuff to produce a novel; that was kind of like why I got my master's degree in mathematics. I wanted to prove I was smart enough.

What inspired you to write this particular novel, *Q Road*?

Unfortunately I can't tell people about the real-life spark that ignited the idea for this novel, because that gives away a surprise in the book. But the general idea was my interest in the shrinking farmland around my hometown. As in many places in the Great Lakes States, farmland is disappearing, and it's hard for anybody to hold onto a big chunk of land nowadays; the diminishing rewards of farming make farmers tempted to sell to developers.

Did you keep the same writing schedule when you began work on the novel?

When I initially got the idea for *Q Road*, I was still working on short stories for my collection— at the time I called it my MFA project. I committed myself to writing three pages a day on the novel, just whatever came to mind. I did that for 50 days and then called that my first draft. It was an awfully rough piece of work, but having a beginning, a middle, and an end gave me a lot of confidence.

What's your schedule?

I generally write in the hours between breakfast and lunch—yes, my meals are even more important to me than my writing—and I have kept that schedule ever since I took my first writing class in 1994. I usually have a few different projects in the works, so that if I get tired of one story, I can work on another or on an essay. I avoid writer's block that way.

Generally, I write in the mornings, but for a while, when I wasn't employed, I also took up evening writing. In the morning I'm fresh from dreamland, and writing is as natural as eating breakfast. By evening, though, I've heard way too much radio news, have talked to a dozen people, have worried about my mother's livestock problems and my bachelor brother's girl troubles, so I have to work myself into the right mood to write. I lit candles, put on weird Celtic music or even New Age stuff I'd never listen to at any other time.

To be honest, my life was quite fabulous when I was writing mornings and evenings. I do worry that someday, left to my own devices, I might just give up real life for writing. My husband would probably find that a bit dull.

How do you decide whether any given material is better suited for long fiction or short?

That's like asking what sort of men are better suited for marriage—you follow your heart and your instincts and then hope for the best.

The central material for a novel might be no bigger than the central material for a short story to start with, but in the novel that material should connect to a more complex web of material. Most of my favorite novels go beyond individual circumstance and make some comment about how the world works, how things really are. Maybe we can't all be as wise as the great novelists, but if we keep writing and rewriting, any of us can eventually come up with something pretty smart.

One reviewer wrote of *Women and Other Animals*, "The stories are unrelated, but eventually emerge as a sort of inbred family tree." In writing those stories, did you think of them as parts of a unified whole, or did they exist independent of one another until they were collected in the book?

I didn't set out to write a collection. The stories in *Women & Other Animals* were the first ones I ever wrote; I felt lucky to just get them figured out and finished, let alone published as a collection. They are pretty much all set in a town like Comstock, Michigan, so that helps glue them together; I wrote them in a relatively short period of time, in the three years I worked on my MFA, and I was surrounded by the same people in that time, so maybe they all come from one frame of mind. I guess I'm a sort of poster child for MFA writing programs.

Reviewers have been kind to me, and sometimes their reviews are works of art as much as any of my stories. One reviewer said I presented "domestic situations where Martha Stewart would fear to tread," and I liked that. My new novel would definitely make Martha a little queasy.

In working with editors, did you find that you received more editorial input on stories, or on your novel? Or did it vary more by editor than by form?

As far as literary magazines go, few of them are really able to offer editing assistance. *Story* did, and *Southern Review* a little and *Mid-American Review*. Literary magazine editors are over-worked, and they change regularly, so mostly they can either accept or reject a story, and don't have time to do much else. *Kiosk* was very helpful with a story they published and with one they rejected but which later won an award when I took their suggestions for revision. I probably ought to track that editor down and buy him a beer.

Because I was working on my MFA when I wrote the stories, I had the benefit of a workshop and wonderful professors—that is a kind of editorial help that often goes unacknowledged. After University of Massachusetts Press accepted the book, however, the editor, Bruce Wilcox, pretty much said they'd publish them however I wanted.

As for the novel, my agent and I sold an early draft to a publisher, with the understanding that I'd revise, and so I got editorial help at various stages; each time I sent it to Sarah McGrath I got some direction. At first it was big stuff, such as, "Cut this character" and "You don't need all that bird information." Later it was smaller details, such as phrasing and length of focus. Though I wasn't in writing workshops while I wrote my novel, my writer pals generously read and provided editorial support as well.

I'm one of those rare people who love to be edited. I love editors. I love other people looking at my work and sharing their thoughts. What a luxury!

Will you go back to stories next, or try another novel?

Both. I'm working on a couple novels now, one about a mathematics department gone wild and another about a present-day circus, and I haven't decided yet which one gets to be first. Also I'm trying to finish up enough stories for a collection. And essays. People in my family like my essays better than my stories because my essays are funnier—I come from one of those families that loves to laugh.

(For more on Bonnie Jo Campbell, visit her Web site at www.bonniejocampbell.com.)

Stewart O'Nan: Write Not What You Know, But What You Want to Know

BY BRAD VICE

"Like Joanna Scott says, I don't write what I know. I write toward what I want to know. I start from a place of total ignorance." This is Stewart O'Nan's motto. And out of ignorance, O'Nan has managed to acquire enough knowledge to publish seven books in under ten years. Unlike many writers who seem to rehash prefab plots or manufacture characters as cartoons of previous creations, O'Nan has had the courage to try something new with each book. His characters struggle to survive in myriad hostile environs, both physical and emotional.

Stewart O'Nan

From the battlefields of Vietnam in *The Names of the Dead* (Doubleday); to the backwoods of nineteenth century Wisconsin in *A Prayer for the Dying* (Henry Holt); to the dangerous blacktop of Route 66 filled with murderous teens hopped up on crystal meth in *The Speed Queen* (Doubleday); O'Nan prefers the adventure of learning something new to the comfort of tried-and-true themes and settings, even at the expense of a reliable readership. Finding readers has never been as much of a concern for the author as building a fictive world that will attract them. "Each book seems to appeal to different people, and that's okay with me."

O'Nan's current title, *Wish You Were Here* (Grove Press), is yet another departure for the experimental author. Called O'Nan's "finest and deepest novel to date," by *The New York Times* (and "an epic about nothing" by one of O'Nan's friends), that title provides a snapshot of a family dealing with personal demons set over the course of a summer house vacation.

Who could deny that O'Nan has made good on the promises of his early career? Tobias Wolff selected O'Nan's short story collection *In the Walled City* (University of Pittsburgh Press) for the Drue Heinz Prize in 1993, claiming that the author had the ability to "delve into the lives and souls of an astonishing range of characters." Shortly after the 1994 publication of his first novel *Snow Angels* (Doubleday), O'Nan was selected by *Granta* as one of the 20 Best Young American Novelists. But it is not fame that motivates the former aerospace engineer.

"My books have sold well, but never well enough for anyone to have any expectations as to my next project. No one is whispering in my ear, saying, 'this one needs to be bigger or move

BRAD VICE *has published fiction in* The Georgia Review, The Southern Review, The Atlantic Monthly, New Stories from the South *and* Best New American Voices. *He teaches creative writing at Mississippi State University in Starkville.*

faster.' There's a lot of freedom in not being too well-known. My wife, Trudy, says that I write the novels just so I can do the research. It's like this new novel I'm working on. I was reading a lot of books about prison, specifically about people in relationships with prisoners, but I didn't know why. Sometimes what you write about finds you."

Here O'Nan discusses his diverse body of work, his passion and methods for research, and how he turns the results into compelling fiction.

Your most recent book, *Wish You Were Here*, is a kind of summery piece about a week-long family vacation in a cabin by a lake. Does that kind of domestic setting require heavy research?

My ambition was to write a book in the vein of Virginia Woolf's *To the Lighthouse*. Also, I think I'm drawing from Alice Munro and William Maxwell. The novel is kind of like a 500-page haiku; I'm trying to capture a fleeting moment in time. The events recorded in the book are the moments that the family will remember after their time together is over. Most of my research involved photography, as one of the characters is a photographer and I wanted to know not only about his occupation, but how he would see the world. Now that the book is over, I still have subscriptions to seven photography magazines.

You were an engineer before you quit to become a writer. Did you always want to write or was that something that came later?

I always read: comics, sci-fi, horror. I visited the library often as a kid. I spent a lot of time with books, but I was good at math and liked it. My father was an engineer and so was my grandfather. I didn't think seriously about writing—I went to aerospace in college and worked for Grumman on Long Island. It was a good job, very interesting. Actually my first year out of school was in the Reagan recession and all I could get was a job at a muffler shop. After a year I told them, "I'm quitting to be a writer." They looked at me like I was from outer space.

You were writing by this time?

Yeah, at about 23 or so. I'd come home after work, take a six pack of beer down to the basement and bang away at stories. By the end of my stint at Grumman, I was going to the library to research and read during my lunch hour. At work, I'd go to the bathroom and read a novel for 20 minutes in one of the stalls. Finally my wife Trudy said, "Look, you're not spending any time with me. You aren't playing with the kids. All you do is read and write. Why don't you try to make a living at this rather than have it hog all your spare time?"

That's when you moved to Cornell to get an MFA. Is that also where you wrote your story collection *In the Walled City*?

Well, I'd say two-thirds of that was done by the time I got there. I wrote three books in four years, though. I wrote a book I eventually called *About a Girl*, but there is a version in the Cornell library entitled *End of Memory*. It's a virtual reality book and everybody, at the time, said these things can't happen. Ha! Now it's horribly out of date. I wrote *A World Away* and *Snow Angels* there too. I even began *The Names of the Dead*.

Back up a second. Many writers today grow up writing in creative writing workshops. What was it like for you in a writing class after being out in the world for so long?

Well, it was the first time I had a lot of time on my hands. Lots of people there were older. I was just reading good stuff. Reading new writers I'd never heard of like Margaret Atwood, Tim O'Brien, William Maxwell. *Snow Angels* is very much inspired by Maxwell's *So Long, See You Tomorrow*. It has a first person narrator that turns into a third-person omniscient narrator who looks back in time, but still possesses the obsessions of the first person. But even before I went to school, I spent a lot of time at the library—checking out books I had never even heard of. Lots of records, too, jazz like Coltrane. I felt like I had a lot of catching up to do after college.

You said you did more research for *The Names of the Dead* than any of your other books. What did that entail?

The book started off concentrating on the protagonist Larry's father, a doctor and a World War II vet who was losing his memory. For awhile it was a love story about him and his housekeeper, the one who takes care of him. Then Larry showed up in the narrative and I remember I got to this sentence—"But he had been a Vietnam vet, and things had not gone well between them." I stopped. Wait. I had to ask myself, what does that mean? Just because he went to Vietnam, does that mean he has to be screwed up? So I wrote a short story about Larry—that's a method I use to learn things about a character—and I began to think this might be a father/son novel. I wrote a long section of the book and realized it was just Larry, in the present and his past in Vietnam. I didn't know anything about Vietnam. Cornell has a massive collection of first person accounts, hundreds and hundreds of them, part of their Southeast Asian collection.

When I started to talk to vets, I had questions about simple stuff like platoon size and chain of command. Later I moved to Oklahoma to teach and there was kind of a tradition there of military people who retired and went into education. They were very helpful. Near the end of the book, I went to the McDowell writers' colony. I met a poet who asked me what I was working on, and I told him I was writing a novel about a combat medic in Vietnam. As it turns out, I had used his oral history as part of my research. He read the entire novel. I was very flattered when he told me that he thought I didn't need to change anything.

There are so many books about Vietnam? Did any of them show you what you didn't want to do?

One reason I wrote *Names of the Dead* was because I don't think anybody had told the story of the vet back home. There are a ton of combat novels but few good ones. Tim O'Brien is great, but O'Brien is a very philosophical writer, often writing about ideas or intellectual categories. He plays games and has fun. I wanted to go deeper. What does this experience mean on a personal level? Do all these rap sessions Larry has with his fellow vets really help him? I don't know. I look back on that book now and see things I could have done better. I could have been more selective here or executed better there.

Do you ever feel overwhelmed by your research? How about your past as an engineer? Does that help you with your selection process? Does it help you to conceptualize a plot?

Yes. The first thing you learn as an engineer is that numbers lie. It took me a while longer to learn that language lies too. But I know how to sort through a massive amount of raw data and cut to what's important. When I begin to get overwhelmed, I know how to color-code files and cross-reference. As far as the writing goes, plot is more poetic for me. I have to go by feel.

Your next book was *Speed Queen*, a book that was originally entitled *Dear Stephen King*. Your narrator is a death-row drug addict dictating her story into a tape recorder, so Stephen King can write her biography. What did you have to learn to write that book?

I was still in Oklahoma when I started writing *The Speed Queen*. I spent a lot of time on the road, out on Route 66, which has a weird subculture of muscle cars and fast food. I wanted to write a real 'my generation, sex, drugs, and rock 'n roll' kind of book. I wrote fast. At the time my knowledge of crystal meth culture was very limited. But one thing I learned is that people will tell you anything. I set up interviews with my students from night school. I said, "If any of you know anything about fast food, drugs, or prison, I'd like to talk." I interviewed people out on the Route 66. After the book was published, I got a nice letter from a Leavenworth inmate, telling me how to make and distribute meth. The guy who wrote the letter kind of wanted me to know more about the mechanics of drugs. I wished I'd had that letter when I started. But in a way it was just as well because after I wanted to write a book fast. Gail Godwin once said she wanted a book she could roll out of bed and write. So she wrote a kind of diary book, a day one, day two sort of thing. I kept asking myself, how does one write like Stephen King? How does one put together the set-up, build up, pay-off kind of novel? Once I made a list of King's questions, everything fell into place.

I've heard that your novel *A Prayer for the Dying* was inspired by *Wisconsin Death Trip*, a collection of local Wisconsin newspaper articles from the nineteenth century that show a regional, maybe national, obsession with arson, epidemic, murder, suicide, and madness. You managed to fit all these things into your novel as well.

I wanted to do two things with *A Prayer for the Dying*. One, I wanted to write something that was remote in time and space. I didn't want to do too much research, so I created a place where nobody could call me on anything. I also wanted to write a book like Albert Camus's *The Plague*.

After I came across *Wisconsin Death Trip*, I had all the elements I needed: diphtheria, murder, fire. Halfway through the book I found out that there really was a fire. I read a book about the Peshtigo Fire, but that was about it.

You wrote about fire again in your nonfiction book *The Circus Fire*, in which you gave an account of a 1944 Ringling Brothers and Barnum & Bailey big top fire that killed 167 people. How do you research an event like that, one that presumably little has been written on?

Of my books, I worked hardest on *Circus Fire*, except for maybe *Names of the Dead*. I didn't want to get too poetic. I didn't want it to be "creative nonfiction." I wanted the facts to be able to speak for themselves. To get those facts, I talked to over 200 people before it was all over. On Thanksgiving week, 1998, I put an ad in the paper requesting anyone who knew something about the fire to call me. I had an unbelievable number of people contact me in the first few days, most just to say, "I didn't go to the circus that day, but I was supposed to." Most big institutions have their own publicity people now, and so I contacted Ringling Brothers. A public relations person informed me that there is a circus museum in Wisconsin where they keep all their own records. That was a lucky thing for me. If you're not lucky enough to live near a museum dedicated to your subject, living near a state capitol is the next best thing. You can find police and fire records, health department records, court transcripts, tax maps, old phone directories, everything. With *Circus Fire*, I discovered the invaluable resources of historical societies. I found the Circus Historical Society to be extremely knowledgeable and also very passionate about the subject. I mean, these people are fans. The Circus Model Builders Club would get into debates as to the color scheme of a particular wagon, or its placement outside the big top.

Do you find that you're still interested in the research you began on your other books?

With the best of it, you continue. I'm still into Vietnam. I'm still into the muscle cars. I am still learning more stories about the circus fire. It's just like the people you write about, they become a part of you.

Jeff Shaara

Jeff Shaara: Bringing Alive the Stories of History

BY W.E. REINKA

Writing was the last profession Jeff Shaara expected to pursue. After all, his late father, Michael Shaara, was a writer. Jeff witnessed his father's frustrations—pain over rejection, the financial difficulties of a mid-list novelist, writer's block, the stress of balancing one's own writing career against teaching demands. Why should he put himself through the same misery? Jeff went off to college, majored in criminology and eventually became a coins and precious metals dealer.

But, through an odd series of events no novelist would dare to plot, Jeff Shaara turned out to follow in the footsteps of his father as a writer of historical fiction. Which means he now understands something else about his father, namely why his dad used to emphasize "show, don't tell" to his writing classes at Florida State.

"I despise those days when I have to write a page explaining what happened rather than taking the reader there," Shaara says. "I struggle against it but sometimes it's unavoidable. Otherwise, I'd have a 1,000-page book and my publisher would scream. If I have a choice between explaining something that Ben Franklin did or taking the reader along with Ben to see it happen, I'd much rather do the second. It's easier to do the first."

Narrative takes the book out of the hands of the characters and gives it back to the author. That's not what Shaara wants. He wants his stories told by the people who made history—the characters in his novels, in other words.

Whatever era of history Shaara focuses on, he selects about four key historical characters to carry the tale. Each chapter is headed with the character's name to identify the focus character to the reader, though the narrative remains in the third person. His father, Michael Shaara, used that technique in the Pulitzer Prize-winning *The Killer Angels* when he traced the Battle of Gettysburg through the eyes of participants. The technique is a departure from most historical fiction where the author places a fictional focus character in a historical setting—think Stephen Crane's *Red Badge of Courage* or, more recently, Stephen Harrigan's *Gates of the Alamo*.

Telling tales from both sides of historical conflicts is another technique Shaara picked up from his father. His own Civil War novels, *Gods and Generals* and *The Last Full Measure* serve as prequel and sequel, respectively, to his father's classic. In them, Shaara takes the perspective of, among others, Grant and Chamberlain for the Union, and Lee and Jackson for the Confederacy. Likewise, in *Gone for Soldiers*, a novel of the 1847 Mexican War, we see through the eyes of General Antonio Lopez de Santa Anna as well as through the United States' key figures. Finally, in his twin books on the American Revolution, *Rise to Rebellion* and *The Glorious Cause*, British Lt. Gen. Thomas Gage weighs in as do more familiar American patriots.

Novelists often say that good plots start with good characters. Using real people as characters, Shaara offers new perspectives on known events. "We already know how the Civil War turned out. We know what happened when they signed the Declaration of Independence. My job is to give you that story in a way you have not seen it before. The reader may be surprised, not by

W.E. REINKA, *who writes frequently about books and authors, contributes to magazines and newspapers nationwide.*

the ending or the event but by how it happened, by the passion that went into it, and by what it was like for the characters themselves."

Passion and characters—therein lie some tales. That's how Shaara got away from his Civil War base (his Mexican War book grew out of his Civil War research) and plunged into the American Revolution. "The first thing that occurred to me is that you've got all these guys signing this document, the Declaration of Independence. By putting their signatures on that piece of paper, every one of these fellows put their neck in a noose. They committed treason—formally, officially, on paper. My God, what went into that? That's got to be a story."

"If the story is interesting and worth my time, I'll start with a couple of general histories, just to get the facts straight. It's important that the facts are straight, that the fundamental history is right. It's also through that process that I figure out who I'm going to go with as my principal characters."

Once Shaara narrows down his focus characters, he reads diaries, letters, battle reports, memoirs—any original sources he can find that speak in the voices of his characters. Those original sources lead him to the voices of his characters. "I do all my reading and all my research before I type the first word. I'll make notes, not so much about what's in the books but more like 'Look at chapter such and such for a good description from Nathaniel Greene of Valley Forge.' Then when I'm in the process of writing, I'll go back and double check, particularly when I quote something, to make sure I quote accurately. The story is in my head before I ever try to write it. My research is not so much the painstaking historical accounts of what happened. It's really hearing the voices of the characters. I have to hear the voice of Robert E. Lee or George Washington or Benjamin Franklin before I can get into that character's mind and tell you their story. That's the key to my research—to get the voice and words of my characters."

Sometimes research involves a bit of detective work. "There may not be a diary from George Washington but almost anyone who ever got a letter from him saved it. We do not have, for example, a great many of Benjamin Franklin's ruminations around the Revolutionary period because he stopped his autobiography at a much earlier time, and yet we have an enormous number of articles and essays that he wrote. Franklin also wrote to important people all over Europe and the States and those letters were saved."

Sometimes Shaara has to change plans. "I anticipate finding information on a character who intrigues me and the information simply isn't there or the character is not as interesting as I thought." Before he started his books on the American Revolution, he anticipated using Thomas Paine as one of his focus characters. Though Paine's writings greatly influenced the Revolution, Shaara did not find him personally engaging. "On the other hand, someone may emerge in research who proves fascinating. That might surprise me and I hope it surprises the reader. It's fun to surprise the reader with an unfamiliar character. Winfield Scott, a name many people have never heard of, is one of the most fascinating military characters in American history."

Given that Winfield Scott commanded the U.S. forces during the Mexican War, it's easy to see why he was selected to help tell *Gone for Soldiers*. In contrast, Abigail Adams practically jumped into the American Revolution books.

"John Adams was pretty much of a given. Then when I got into the letters between John and Abigail Adams, her letters were every bit as interesting—sometimes more interesting—than his. She was very opinionated and way ahead of her time in the way that women tended to look at the world. At a time when women were forbidden by law from receiving a college education, Abigail Adams was self-educated. She read all the classics and just about any other book."

Shaara recognizes the responsibility of trying to personify fictionally mythical figures in the pages of his novels. One Virginia reader once angrily demanded, "How dare you put words in the mouth of Robert E. Lee?" Yet, by the time Shaara starts to write his novel, he is comfortable. "One of the things I'm proud of is feeling comfortable to the point where I am putting words in the mouths of the characters. If the words don't ring true to me, they won't ring true to the reader. That gets back to research. If we don't have documentation that Lee said such and such to Longstreet at this point in time, we know that he could have. The characterization is accurate. This is what was happening and this is Lee, the man, the character. Therefore, this is what he could have or should have been thinking. If I'm not comfortable with it, I won't write it."

Gone for Soldiers includes an extraordinary scene where young Captain Robert E. Lee of the United States Army is serving in Mexico in 1847 and is ordered by General Winfield Scott to search for a passage around the flank of the Mexican forces. In a memorable scene, Lee and a young lieutenant almost stumble onto the enemy and hurriedly take cover. Lee spends hours hiding under a log. Shaara takes us through his process in writing that scene: "The event is real. The specifics of the event, the Mexican soldiers coming around Lee and the young lieutenant who was with him—all of that is documented. When Lee went back to camp, he wrote a report on his mission to General Scott. That report remains in the archives at West Point and provides the nuts and bolts of the scene.

"But did Lee's left leg go to sleep when he was trapped under the log like I portrayed it? Well, it could have. That's the key. Everything that happened to Lee under that log—lying on the rock that cut into his backbone; having a spider walk down his leg; having the Mexican soldier bend down to drink from the spring within eyesight of Lee and not seeing him; feeling the pistol at his belt, knowing he can get off a few shots before they get him; having the log actually move because a Mexican is sitting on it; daydreaming about his father—imagine hours and hours in that situation—the stinging needles in his leg when he finally crawled out of the log and his immense relief at seeing that young lieutenant appear because he didn't know what happened to him. All of that is license. That's where being a writer comes in."

"We already know how the Civil War turned out. We know what happened when they signed the Declaration of Independence. My job is to give you that story in a way you have not seen it before. The reader may be surprised, not by the ending or the event but by how it happened, by the passion that went into it, and by what it was like for the characters themselves."

Though Shaara uses artistic license to flesh out details of scenes like Lee under the log, he painstakingly avoids anachronisms. That avoidance extends to speech as well as to physical objects. After all, if he's going to put words in a mythic character's mouth, he wants them to be words the character might have used. "My enormous Random House dictionary has word origins in it. It tells me when a word was put into use. For example, I would not write 'Franklin knew this would put him in the spotlight.' Ben Franklin didn't know what a spotlight was. That's a theatrical term that came into use in the 1890s. I will not have a character using a word he did not know."

Likewise, Shaara feels it would be anachronistically unfair to judge historical figures by twenty-first century standards. "I won't put words in the mouths of characters because of a modern symbol or concept, what I call the 'Xena the Warrior Princess syndrome.' George Washington never asked himself how he could farm Mt. Vernon without slaves. That was not a question anyone was asking. It's easy to paint a portrait of these characters with a modern brush. I won't do that. It's not to say everyone was wonderful. Was Benjamin Franklin a perfect human being? Of course not, but his accomplishments far outweighed his foibles. Benedict Arnold was a hero to America before he ever committed treason. Let's tell both sides. Let's get away from judgments."

His insistence on accuracy and the need to hear the characters' voices is why Shaara won't use a research assistant. He must know the material firsthand before it goes in his books. Occasionally, he errs. "A great many people are watching and paying attention to minute details. Once in a while I hear from someone. I think it's wonderful that people care that much. When I do slip up, I fix it before the paperback edition."

It's a wonder that Shaara is doing any of this. After his father, Michael Shaara, died at 59, Jeff, still a coin dealer, took control of his father's estate. Among other things, he found the unpublished manuscript for *The Love of the Game*, a baseball novel that Jeff arranged to get published and then sold feature film rights to Universal. During this time, screenwriter-director Ron Maxwell was adapting Michael Shaara's *The Killer Angels* into the movie *Gettysburg*. Jeff got to know Maxwell during the filming. The film made *The Killer Angels* a bestseller 19 years after its original publication.

Shaara notes: "After *The Killer Angels* became a phenomenal success, Ron Maxwell said 'Wouldn't it be wonderful to continue the story in both directions?' I thought as a concept that sounded like a great idea. I had no idea that I would be the one to write it. I gave it some thought and about a week later I called Ron back telling him that this is something I would like to try to do. Maybe there was something inside me that wanted to complete the work my father would have completed himself. After all, Michael Shaara earned the right to follow up the success of his own work with a prequel and a sequel. Yet he never had the opportunity.

"The question I get more than any other," says Shaara, "is 'How did you sit down and write when you had never written before?' I wish I had a good answer, other than to say that I approached writing with no fear because I had no expectations. The whole idea was for me to do the research and create a story that Ron Maxwell could adapt for a screenplay. It was never to be a book. Well, Ballantine Books, which had *The Killer Angels* as a number one bestseller heard about what I was doing and wanted to take a look at it. What I did not expect is that they would call me back and say 'We don't care if it's a movie, we like the book. We think you're a writer. We think you should do more of this and we would like you to do the sequel.' That phone call changed my life. Now, five books later, working on a sixth, I'm a writer. That's something that would have surprised my father. Certainly it has surprised me. It's a second lifetime."

Shaara goes out of his way to acknowledge how fortunate he's been in his writing career. It's not just lip service—his father's struggles remain firmly in his memory. He knows his life-changing phone call was unique. Yet he also feels that aspiring historical novelists don't need a father's coattails or serendipitous movie tie-ins to achieve success.

"My books work as good stories. I no longer have to follow in my father's footsteps in order to have people pick up my books. People simply enjoy a good story. If you're honest with your characters and get the history right, if you tell a good story—it doesn't matter what genre you're in—you'll attract an audience."

Premiere Voices

BY MICHELLE TAUTE

Every writer dreams of the breakthrough year. You finish your novel. Find an agent. A publisher bites. So how do you make the leap from aspiring writer to published author? The truth is that there are as many paths to publication as there are writers. You won't find any hard-and-fast rules that link your life choices with a six-figure book advance, but you can increase the odds with a lot of hard work and dedication.

We talked with four first-time authors about their roads to success. Despite drastically different backgrounds and career paths, they all found their way to the elusive breakthrough year. Read on to find out what advice and insight they have to offer those still trying to knock down the wall.

SILAS HOUSE
Clay's Quilt, Ballantine Books

Before publishing *Clay's Quilt*, Silas House spent his days delivering mail in rural Kentucky. He composed his debut novel in his head as he went from house to house and typed up the day's work after his two daughters went to bed each night. "Straight out of college I went to work as a newspaper journalist, but I came home and didn't want to write," he says. "Becoming a mail carrier really helped me as a writer."

Photo © Lisa J. Parker

Silas House

House credits his job with giving him the quiet time he needed to think about his novel and helping him become more descriptive. He observed thunderstorms and snowstorms close up and had the privilege of listening to people's life stories at the mailbox. The writer's time at the keyboard didn't start until 10 p.m., and it sometimes stretched until 2 a.m. During those late-night sessions, House focused on getting down the story he'd composed during the day and avoided revisions until the entire book was complete. The hard work eventually paid off. *Clay's Quilt* received the Kentucky Fiction Prize and was nominated for the Appalachian Book of the Year.

The novel chronicles the life of Clay Sizemore, a young man who's lived in Appalachia his entire life. Raised by relatives after the death of his mother at age four, Clay struggles with the unanswered questions surrounding his mother's murder. This central conflict was culled from a formative experience in House's own childhood.

"When I was 11 years old my uncle was murdered in a shoot-out," House says. "While writing I wasn't really aware that was what I was writing about. It was sort of a catharsis for me." Besides this part of his personal history, the novel draws heavily on House's ties to Appalachia. The book has been credited with breaking down stereotypes about the region, and readers from small towns across the country have found it captures the true flavor of rural life. "I just wanted to represent an authentic look at what I knew," he says. "I wanted to show the way people really were."

With his family commitments and full-time job, it took House three years to write *Clay's*

MICHELLE TAUTE (*michelletaute@hotmail.com*) *is a freelance writer and editor based in Cincinnati, Ohio. She's written for* Natural Home, HOW, I.D. *and* The Artist's Magazine.

Quilt and another three years to sell it. He started the publishing process by finding out who the agents were for his six favorite authors. Then he sent a copy of his manuscript to each person and hoped for the best. While he eventually received several offers to represent the book, House didn't land an agent for two years. "I went with the one who I thought loved the work," he says. It took that agent 11 months to sell the book.

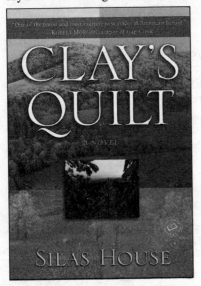

"I encourage beginning writers to learn about the industry as much as possible," House says. "In the long run it will really help your art." In his own writing life, House gained much of his knowledge about the business end of publishing from conferences and workshops. It gave him the opportunity to form a network with other writers and often boosted his creativity. He also learned which agents took his style of writing and what the submission process would be like. Another important stepping stone for House was entering writing competitions. "Publishers were as concerned with the contests I had won as much as the places I had been published," he says.

About eight months after *Clay's Quilt* came out, House was able to quit his job as a mail carrier. He believes it's possible to make a living as a writer if you're willing to be creative. Besides working on his second and third novels, House writes a variety of freelance magazine articles, teaches writing workshops and contributes to NPR. His best advice for struggling writers is to be determined. "I think if you're truly a writer you have that drive and ambition," he says. "Each rejection you receive will make you more determined."

NICOLE KRAUSS

Man Walks Into a Room, Doubleday

When she started writing *Man Walks Into a Room*, Nicole Krauss was dating a fiction writer who had yet to be published. That's part of the reason she initially kept the project a secret. "I felt like I was doing something illegal and stepping on someone's toes," she says. "It's almost as if to say what you're writing about takes away the excitement. It's no longer as mysterious and private."

Her debut novel was published in May 2002 and follows the life of Samson Greene, an English professor who loses 24 years of memory after the removal of a brain tumor. "Memory absolutely tells us who we are," Krauss says. "There's a way in which we're all amnesiacs. The strange thing is not what we remember but what we forget. The truth is that our mind picks and chooses narratives. They tell us who we are and who we think we are." In the book, Samson struggles to reconnect with his wife Anna and regain any sense of his personal history.

Photo © Joyce Ravid

Nicole Krauss

Already an accomplished writer in the realms of poetry and criticism, Krauss made the switch to novels shortly after finishing a lengthy documentary project for the BBC. "When it was done I felt sort of empty," she says. "I'm a person who's happier when I have something on my desk every day. It was a less tortured existence." The experience changed Krauss's expectations about what she would write and she soon committed herself to a novel.

"I was really rigorous about my schedule," she says. "I would get up at 6:30 or 7, make coffee and sit at my computer." Krauss readily admits, however, that working every day included a lot of staring out the window and thinking about her novel. "I definitely revised a lot as I went," she says. "When I sat down in the morning I would reread almost from the beginning. Every time I did it, I would polish and correct. I must have read that book a hundred times."

While she didn't have a full-time job, Krauss earned money by tutoring high-school kids in the evenings and taking on freelance research projects and book reviews. She also spent a lot of time reading contemporary American fiction. "I changed how I read for awhile," she says. "It became more like 'let me see technically what is going on in these pages.'" The process helped Krauss figure out how to handle plot, character and dialogue—things she hadn't conquered in the realm of poetry.

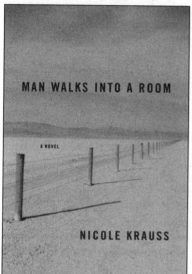

When she was about halfway through the book, Krauss left her home in New York City to spend a month at the Yaddo artist's colony in Saratoga Springs, New York. It proved to be a valuable catalyst for her productivity as well as her eventual road to publication. After a reading another writer approached her and said "you have to talk to my agent," Kraus says. "I eventually called that agent because I wanted Anne Carson (another of the agent's writers) at a reading series I was organizing." On the phone she mentioned the referral and got an invitation to send the novel-in-progress. The agent wanted to represent Krauss based on the unfinished manuscript, and months later he sold the book a few days after completion. "It was kind of a blessed experience," she says.

Krauss looks back on the year she spent writing the book with a romantic eye. "I am really a happy novel writer," she says. "I liked living with this story in my life."

TESS URIZA HOLTHE

When the Elephants Dance, Crown Publishing

First-time author Tess Uriza Holthe has been compared to such famous writers as Amy Tan and Gabriel García Márquez. Her novel, *When the Elephants Dance*, mixes magical realism with Filipino history to paint a picture of the embattled country during World War II. The title is drawn from these opening lines: "Papa explains the war like this: 'When the elephants dance, the chickens must be careful. The great beasts, as they circle one another, shaking the trees and trumpeting loudly, are the Amerikanos and the Japanese as they fight. And our Philippine Islands? We are the small chickens.'"

The daughter of Filipino immigrants, Holthe grew up in San Francisco listening to stories told by her father and grandmother during marathon mahjong games. "Writing started out as a hobby," she says. "My parents wanted me to do something stable, like be a lawyer or accountant." Holthe attended Golden Gate University and was

Tess Uriza Holthe

Photo © Stephanie Mohan

working as an accountant in northern California when she signed up for a writing class. One of the first assignments was to write about a family myth. "I'd made a list of 10 myths and I said jokingly 'I could write a book about this.'"

This fertile source material eventually turned into *When the Elephants Dance*. Holthe created an informal writing group with several of her classmates and began writing the book after work. She wrote six days a week for anywhere from five minutes to five hours at a time. "It was for the joy of actually writing," she says. "I sat in for the long haul, thinking I might get a short story published in a magazine. It was nice because I didn't have the pressure of 'this has to be published.' "

Her novel is based in part on the experiences of her father, running from stray bullets and land mines to survive the month-long Battle for Manila in 1945. It focuses on a patchwork collection of family and neighbors who hide in a cellar to avoid Japanese soldiers. Holthe uses three main narrators to share with her readers the battle for survival and the stories her characters tell each other. It took a year and a half to finish the book.

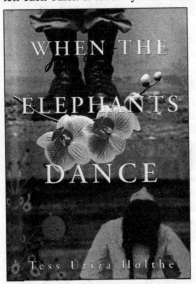

On the recommendation of a friend, Holthe attended the Maui Writers Conference. "I signed up to meet a bunch of agents, thinking I'd lay the groundwork this year and have something to present next year," she says. "I got some interest from agents and sent the manuscript to the woman I really made a connection with." Shortly after, Holthe went to Las Vegas for the weekend with her husband and inadvertently unplugged the answering machine. When she got back to work on Monday, she had two e-mails from the agent.

"I feel like a Disney character because everything turned out so right," she says. Holthe line edited the book with her agent and once it was sold, she did three revisions with her editor over a four-month period. After receiving a 12-page editorial letter, she addressed the concerns point-by-point, fleshing out some parts and paring down others. Now she's hard at work on her second novel but is keeping the details secret—even from her husband.

"My writing group members are the only ones who know what the story is right now," she says. "I show them anything I have." Holthe's group serves as an invaluable support and feedback mechanism for her work. They meet every Wednesday night and take turns bringing dinner. "It's funny because for a while my husband talked about moving," she says. "I said 'we can't, my writing group is here.' "

ANA MENÉNDEZ

In Cuba I was a German Shepherd, Grove Press

At age 27 Ana Menéndez found herself burned out with her journalism career. "I got into newspapers when I was very young," she says. "*The Miami Herald* hired me at 21. I thought it was a way to write and get paid for it." The work ultimately became less fulfilling than Menéndez wanted, and she began applying to graduate writing programs with an eye toward exploring her creativity.

"I would get up early in the morning and study for the GRE," she says. "Then I would come home dead tired and bang out stories." Those early pieces of fiction landed her a fellowship at New York University, where she would complete her first short-story collection. *In Cuba I was a German Shepherd* draws heavily from her experiences as the daughter of Cuban immigrants and as a newspaper reporter covering Havana. Menéndez skillfully weaves together stories that give her readers a glimpse into the humor and heartbreak unique to Cuban Americans.

Ana Menéndez

Photo © Amy Williams

While she didn't have many expectations about graduate school, Menéndez found the structure and deadlines helpful after the discipline of the newsroom. "It's very hard to put in the hours on my own," she says. "They were expecting my short stories next week." Now that she's working independently, Menéndez misses the structure of the writing program and struggles to keep a set schedule as she works on her first novel. "I'm at least halfway through, but it's in rough form and needs a lot of work," she says. "What I actually love is to do a lot of revisions."

With no concrete goals for her post-graduate school writing career, Menéndez thought she would join her husband in India, where he works as a bureau chief for the *Los Angeles Times*, and freelance a few articles. The move to publish her fiction came after a professor suggested she submit what became the title story for her collection to *Zoetrope All-Story*. She got a rejection letter that said 'we like your story but it doesn't have a plot,' but a few months later the magazine reversed the decision. The story went on to win a Pushcart Prize and appear in *Best New American Voices*.

Menéndez loosely had an agent through a friend of a friend, but he wasn't very enthusiastic about her work. It was her thesis advisor who suggested she could put together a collection of her stories. Things began to take off after another agent read her story in *Best New American Voices*. Menéndez shared her other stories with the agent, and the collection and a follow-up novel were sold within two weeks. After the sale, she spent a lot of time working with her editor at Grove Press. "We sat many times in her office going page by page and even line by line at times," she says. "She asked pointed questions that prompted good changes." Menéndez especially appreciated the sensitivity of the editing process compared to the journalism world.

"I was very lucky," she says of her publishing experience. "There are incredible writers out there who toil for years and years without publication. It's all very arbitrary." She's certainly not content, however, to be a one-book writer. Menéndez is still working on her first novel and has no plans to return to journalism any time soon. "I don't feel like an author yet," she says. "I feel like I need more than one book to claim that exalted title."

Lightning in a Bottle: Five Rules for Metaphors and Similes

BY I.J. SCHECTER

Metaphors and similes have become such common parts of our everyday language that we hardly notice them. The problem student in your class is a "bad apple"; the miscreant in your family, a "black sheep." Trying to find the contact lens you dropped is like "searching for a needle in a haystack." A person in your office may be trying to "butter up" the boss to secure a promotion. The boss may be making him "jump through hoops" to get one. And so on.

Metaphors and similes are two sides of the same coin. Their common purpose is to make a concept or image more powerful by figuratively comparing it to something else. Just in case you've forgotten the distinction you were forced to memorize in ninth-grade English, here's a refresher: similes involve the use of the words "like," "as" and "so" to accomplish this goal ("His voice was like a fine wine"), while metaphors make the comparison absolute ("His voice was honey to her insides"). It's that simple.

Handled judiciously, metaphors and similes can be powerful tools in the writer's arsenal. Misused, they can serve as distractions. Here are five guidelines for creating metaphors and similes that will help make your story stand out from the rest.

Keep your comparisons short and simple— no need to use a rifle when a pistol will do

Metaphors and similes don't need to be long or elaborate to pack a punch. Consider the way Ann-Marie McDonald describes a thug in her novel *Fall On Your Knees*:

> Frances looks up at Boutros. Concrete with eyeballs.

Or Mordecai Richler's take on a group of snobby women in *On Snooker*:

> The suits were monitored by a patrol of formidable wives, not so much dressed as upholstered.

Or Alice Munro's portrayal of awkward teenage romance in her story "Baptizing":

> He put a finger against one of my nipples as if he was testing a thorn.

All three cases demonstrate the aim of metaphors and similes: to quickly illuminate a story, like shining a flashlight on the page and then switching it off.

Here are two examples of similes in Margaret Atwood's *The Blind Assassin* that describe the narrator's relationship with her mother:

> Her love for us was a given—solid and tangible, like a cake. The only question was which of us was going to get the bigger slice.

I.J. SCHECTER *is a freelance writer of fiction and essays. His latest book, a collection of short stories, is titled* The Bottom of the Mug. *His nonfiction frequently appears in* Novel & Short Story Writer's Market.

Even if love was underneath it all, there was a great deal piled on top, and what would you find when you dug down? Not a simple gift, pure gold and shining; instead, something ancient and possibly baneful, like an iron charm rusting among old bones. A talisman of sorts, this love, but a heavy one; a heavy thing for me to carry around with me, slung on its iron chain around my neck.

From both examples—the second one combining both metaphor and simile—we get a clear idea about this relationship, but you probably agree that the first one does a better job of it, and in many fewer words. Whereas the longer paragraph presents a flurry of thoughts and images, the shorter one comes off like a quick, hard jab—efficient, unexpected, and impossible to dodge.

Be sure all your metaphors and similes can meet the minimum requirement—they should be able to pass muster

Used deftly, metaphors and similes become glittering, unexpected jewels that readers encounter along the path of your story; used clumsily, they become rocks that readers trip over. But how do you decide whether a comparison is helping or hindering your story?

To make the final cut in a manuscript, a metaphor or simile should be able to fill two criteria: integrity (it makes sense, can stand on its own, and doesn't clash with anything around it) and value (it adds something significant that would otherwise be lost).

You can apply the test for integrity by asking whether the metaphor or simile satisfies the three C's: coherence, comfort and consistency.

First, coherence—will the figurative comparison make sense to a reader? The best way to understand what coherence means is to think about the most obvious example of incoherence: the dreaded mixed metaphor. As Sam Malone put it in an episode of *Cheers*, "It's not fair to get someone's engine all revved up and then yank the carpet out from under them." Though they make for memorable sitcom lines, incompatible images do not serve stories well. Remember, the goal of metaphors and similes is to lend instant clarity to a certain character, place, idea or object. A coherent metaphor or simile will make a reader nod with recognition.

Keep in mind the cardinal rule: every word should serve to advance the story. Is a specific comparison there because it elucidates some person or object, or because you liked the way it sounded and couldn't bring yourself to take it out? Answer honestly and you'll see the result: a tight, nimble manuscript clipping along with powerful momentum.

Second, comfort—does the metaphor or simile have enough breathing room? It's easy—and dangerous—to fall in love with figurative speech. Force yourself to be discriminating. The best authors strike an engaging balance by sprinkling their manuscripts with enough comparisons to enhance the story but not so many that a reader feels inundated. When numerous metaphors and similes are banging around together within close proximity, though each may be strong on its own, the overall effect is often one of dilution. When you look at a jar stuffed with marbles, nothing compels you to remember any specific one. But a single cat's eye will certainly draw your attention. So a metaphor, or simile, if it deserves to be there in the first place, also deserves room to be noticed.

Finally, consistency—the tone of your metaphors and similes should be congruent with the type of piece you are writing. Think of your story as a piece of music. Metaphors and similes represent the harmony; they subtly enhance the theme without disturbing it. In a tender romance, for instance, the language should be soft and graceful. "She wore a necklace whose pearls were like hailstones" is an example of a simile that doesn't fit. Comparing the pearls to something gentler will keep your reader in the environment you've established instead of suddenly introducing a new one.

Consistency is especially important in historical pieces. In a Civil War story, for example, the effect of the simile, "he wore his love like a neon sign," would be to temporarily jolt a reader out of the setting—and once readers have been bumped out, it's not always easy to lure them back in.

Here's a metaphor for an adulterous relationship from Herman Wouk's *War and Remembrance*:

> Forbidden fruit has its brown spots, but these are not seen in the dusky glow of appetite;
> one has to bite and taste the unpleasant mush.

Wouk's sober, literate tone reflectes the voice that permeates the rest of his World War II epic—serious, meditative, atmospheric. Compare Wouk's metaphor to the following simile, again from *Fall On Your Knees*, in which a Lebanese character reflects on hearing her native Arabic:

> What a relief from the chill of English, which is exactly like immersing your tongue in
> ice water.

The characters in *Fall On Your Knees* are driven by unbending ideas about the world, and the language used to tell their story is appropriately terse and direct, mirroring the characters' rigid perspectives. As you edit your manuscripts, watch for metaphors and similes that suddenly inject a different voice and try to adapt them. If a certain comparison resists being tailored, it belongs in another manuscript.

Be sure all of your metaphors and similes have a reason for being there—each one should bring something to the table

Once a metaphor or simile has demonstrated integrity, it must be scrutinized again—for value. Here you must ask yourself whether the manuscript loses something if the comparison is removed. This can be established with another simple test. Read the sentence or passage containing the metaphor or simile. Then read it again, this time leaving out the comparison. If the same amount of information is conveyed in both versions, the metaphor or simile is probably redundant. But if the stripped-down version suddenly seems to be lacking substance, your metaphor or simile deserves its rightful place.

Let's go back to the example of the pearl necklace. Is a comparison for the size of the pearls truly necessary? If you're trying to develop the character as an ostentatious socialite, perhaps. But if you've already established this character and done it well, a reader should be able to envision the type of pearls automatically.

Here's a simile used by Tennessee Williams in his story "Portrait of a Girl in Glass":

> The door came timidly open and there she stood in a dress from Mother's wardrobe, a
> black chiffon ankle-length and high-heeled slippers on which she balanced uncertainly like
> a tipsy crane of melancholy plumage.

In William's masterful hands, we come to know this girl—a piteous mix of vulnerability and insecurity—through just a few words. Let's see how the same sentence reads with the simile removed:

> The door came timidly open and there she stood in a dress from Mother's wardrobe, a black chiffon ankle-length and high-heeled slippers.

The writing is still lovely, but something in the description of this character has clearly been lost. The metaphor therefore has value.

Once a metaphor or simile has passed the dual test of integrity and value, allow yourself to trust that it will do its job. In other words, resist the urge to pile on more figurative description out of concern that your reader still may not get it. Let's look again at Ann-Marie McDonald's description of the thug named Boutros as "concrete with eyeballs." Suppose she had written the following instead:

> Frances looks at Boutros. Concrete with eyeballs. A man built like a linebacker and twice as mean. He looked to be the kind of man who broke people's arms for sport, like a child absently snapping twigs.

Does the added description help us understand Boutros any better? No. Those three words tell us all we need to know. Like concrete, he's thick, opaque and immovable. And like an entity inhabited entirely by eyeballs, he's frightening.

As you review your manuscript, subject each metaphor and simile to the integrity-value test. If you feel that doesn't work, simply keep in mind the cardinal rule: every word should serve to advance the story. Is a specific comparison there because it elucidates some person or object, or because you liked the way it sounded and couldn't bring yourself to take it out? Answer honestly and you'll see the result: a tight, nimble manuscript clipping along with powerful momentum.

Don't let yourself get away with easy metaphors and similes—like cliches, they're a dime a dozen

When you catch yourself writing something like, "He was her knight in shining armor," "His heart was racing like a thoroughbred's," or "They were two peas in a pod," take a step back. Demand something new of yourself, even if it means placing a temporary flag in the spot to return to later. Readers will appreciate the effort you've made to come up with something they haven't pictured before, and your story will receive a spark in exactly the spot you want.

Certain objects or images will demand more of your creativity because they've been so often used as metaphoric fodder. It may seem, for example, that there just isn't any new way to describe the experience of love. But take heart (pardon the pun). Consider the following figurative comparison, in which different writers address various aspects of love—from the realization of it:

> Knowing it was like running into a wall of heat, his head and hands pushing right through it.
>
> Carol Shields, *Larry's Party*

—to its loss:

> Their relationship had run out like a phonograph record; their chitchat was the last scratching of the needle.
>
> Herman Wouk, *War and Remembrance*

—from the love of something abstract (the desert):

> He had an affection for it that grew out of awe at our stark order . . . like a joyous undergraduate who respects silent behavior in a library.
>
> Michael Ondaatje, *The English Patient*

—to something more tangible:

> As she spoke she changed in some provocative way, seemed suddenly drenched in eroticism as a diver rising out of a pool gleams like chrome with a sheet of unbroken water for a fractional moment.

E. Annie Proulx, The Shipping News

—and from shared, crackling sexuality:

> It was tense as electricity, the force fed on resistance, rushing through wires of metal stretched tight; it was tense as water made into power by the restraining violence of a dam.

Ayn Rand, The Fountainhead

—to reflections on the physical act itself:

> In bed, only an hour and a half before, we had been unconvincing somehow, as though there lay between our mucous membranes a fine dust or grit, or its mental equivalent, but as tangible as beach sand.

Ian McEwan, Enduring Love

Practice constantly—keep your nose to the grindstone

Metaphors and similes are coy animals, and sometimes they need to be coaxed out of hiding. Are you struggling for an image to liven up your story in a particular spot? Have you searched high and low without success? Use the world around you to practice. Take a stroll, pausing to describe the things you see—a tree, a car, a group of squirrels nibbling at chestnuts—by expressing them as things other than themselves. Do this out loud so you can hear how the comparisons sound. Remember, the point of this exercise is to get into the habit of creating. Don't worry if what comes out of your mouth sounds ridiculous. Often, it will take nine mediocre attempts to find the metaphor or simile that makes you say, "Nailed it."

We all know that writing stories is hard. Finding interesting ways to describe things can be even harder. Creating metaphors and similes is a specific skill, like using proper grammar, developing characters, or building a narrative arc, and it demands both patience and determination. Keep at it, practicing as often as possible, and soon metaphors and similes will begin to flow from your pen like . . . let's see . . . hmm. I can't seem to think of anything that would work well here.

Can you?

Great Novels Start with Great Beginnings

BY DAVID MORRELL

You've done your research. You've made decisions about structure and viewpoint. Now it's time to write the first sentence, the first paragraph, the first page . . .

At this moment, if your stomach shivers and your mind balks with indecision, don't worry—it's natural. It happens to me at the start of every project. No matter how many years I've been writing, I still have to remind myself that this is only my first draft and that it's okay to make mistakes. I'll make hundreds of corrections before I'm ready to submit the manuscript. For now, all that matters is surrendering to the idea and getting those initial words on the page.

Do I know how the plot is going to end before I start writing? Only to a limited extent. Yes, I have a basic sense of how everything will proceed, but I don't know many specifics, and I prefer it that way. After all, the reason I'm writing is that an idea for a story has possessed me and I have an uncontrollable urge to dramatize it. In effect, I'm telling the story to myself. I'm eager to learn how it turns out. If I knew all the details, if there wasn't the possibility of surprises, I'd soon get bored.

I once had an idea for a novel's opening that so excited me I started writing without any sense of its middle and end. The book was called *The Fraternity of the Stone*, and to this day I smile when I think of the book's setup. A mysterious man whom we know nothing about except that he has a deadly past and that his name is Drew MacLane has taken refuge in a hermit monastery in Vermont. He lives alone in a spartan room. His only contact with the outside world is a slot through which an unseen person slides him a tray of food each day. For six years, he has used this deprivation to try to atone for unnamed violent sins that he has committed.

The only thing that makes Drew feel human is a mouse that comes to visit him. Drew has named him Stuart Little (from E.B. White's story). Each day, he gives the mouse a piece of bread. As the novel begins, Drew tosses a crust to Stuart, then closes his eyes and prays before eating. When he opens his eyes, he looks down at Stuart, surprised to find the mouse on its side, unmoving.

Drew stares at the dead mouse for several long seconds. Was Stuart old? Did he have a

DAVID MORRELL *is the best-selling author of more than 15 novels, including the 1972 title* First Blood, *which introduced the character Rambo and was the basis for the hit movie. He is a former professor of American literature at the University of Iowa, and his most recent novel* Long Shot *was published in 2002 by Warner Books. This article appeared originally in* Lessons from a Lifetime of Writing *(Writer's Digest Books).*

sudden heart attack? Drew considers that as a possibility, keeps staring at the dead mouse, and finally looks from the bread Stuart was eating to the bread that he himself was about to eat. Instincts that he has struggled to subdue for the previous six years take control. Wracked by conflicting emotions, he stands, approaches the door to the outside corridor, breaks his hermit's vow, leaves his cell, and discovers that the entire monastery has been poisoned, the kitchen staff shot to death.

As an execution team searches each cell, Drew fights his way out of the monastery and vows to learn who ordered the attack. After six years of atonement, he's forced to use his hated former skills, entering an alien world in which everything seems a threat. Drew and I both faced that alien world together. I had no idea what he would do next, where he would go, what contacts from his previous life he would ask for help. I smiled when I wondered what Drew's reaction would be to learning who was president and all the other cultural changes that had occurred. I couldn't wait to go with him on his quest.

Eventually, one idea led to another, and soon I realized how *The Fraternity of the Stone* would need to end. But on page one, all I had was my enthusiasm for the novel's initial scenes. For other books, I've had a definite idea from the start about how they needed to proceed. The point is, every instance is different. Each first page is a new adventure. Let your enthusiasm be your guide.

A few general rules do need to be followed, however. They all have to do with the people who'll be reading your story. I'm not talking about a mythical ideal reader, not your spouse, not your best friend, not the members of your writing group. When you start your first sentence, your first paragraph, your first page, the readers you have to keep in mind are your agent and your editor. If you believe what you see in the movies, agents and editors have bushels of time to conduct fascinating discussions with authors, tell them how brilliant they are, and generally be sensitive and literary. Sometimes, they have editing pencils stuck behind their ears. Almost always, they carry little bitty manuscripts that look suspiciously like the 115-page scripts for the movies in which they're impersonating agents or editors. They spend a lot of time at book-publishing parties and glamorous luncheons.

When people in the book business see this nonsense on the screen, they shake their heads in dismay or weep with laughter. Parties? Gala publishing events? Ha. Let me tell you about my current editor, Rick Horgan, at Warner Books. He's around 40. He has a wife and three children. He lives in Westchester County (to raise kids away from New York). He gets up at 5:30 A.M., exercises, dresses, catches a ninety-minute train into the city, arrives at his office around 8:30, and has staff meetings all morning. Covers need to be chosen. Budgets have to be decided. The next year's publishing schedule has to be worked out. After this tedium, Rick eats an efficient lunch with an author or an agent, has more staff meetings all afternoon, catches the 7:00 train, arrives home around 8:30, has dinner with his family, and . . .

Do you notice anything missing in this schedule? When on Earth does Rick have time to read manuscripts? The answer is, on the train and on weekends. And the manuscripts he's hauling around aren't those dinky 115-page things you see actors-pretending-to-be-editors carry in the movies. Many of them are gut-busting 800-page monsters. Put yourself in Rick's place. You've got a spouse and three children. You want to spend time with them on the weekend, but you've also got to read those manuscripts. You want desperately for those manuscripts to be worth the effort, but you know from experience that most of them are going to waste your time. How many pages of tediousness are you going to allow an author before you cram a manuscript back into its box? A hundred pages? Not damned likely. *Fifty* pages? Don't make me laugh. *Twenty* pages. Now we're approaching reality. Unless the book is by a proven author, the editor is going to allow the writer 20 pages at best to do something of interest. After that, bye-bye manuscript. All those fabulous touches that the author worked so hard to put into the climax? They're never going to get read if the book doesn't announce that it's worth reading from the start.

Many years ago, I was asked to be a judge for the Mystery Writers of America best-novel

Edgar award (so called because Edgar Allan Poe invented the mystery story). I was promised that at most I'd have to look at about 50 books. But day after day, the UPS driver plodded to my door with his arms full of book boxes that eventually totaled around 300. Desperate for a filing system, I arranged laundry baskets throughout the living room, labeling them "new," "awful," "maybe," and "wonderful." Faced with so much to read, I quickly learned how an editor must feel. In fact, the 300 books littering my living room were nothing compared to the *thousands* of manuscripts that come to most publishing houses each year. Decisions have to be made. In a hurry.

Thus, as one of the Edgar judges, I started by conscientiously reading every book from cover to cover. Even if some of them bored me to death. There had to be *something* good in even the worst of them, I thought. But as the deadline approached for submitting my choices and as *more* books arrived on my doorstep, I stopped reading after 50 pages if a novel still hadn't grabbed my attention. By definition, an Edgar-winning book shouldn't be a chore to read, I reminded myself. In a few cases, I tossed a book into the "awful" basket after five pages. On one memorable occasion, this was a novel's first sentence.

He strolled, leisurely, into the park.

I stared at that sentence for a long time. Is there any other way to stroll except leisurely? I asked myself. Why would a writer begin a novel on such a lethargic redundant note? Strolled? And why the commas to emphasize "leisurely"? I turned to page two where a character let out "a blood-curdling scream." (I swear to God.) I frisbeed the book into the "awful" basket.

Common sense tells us that the first sentence, the first paragraph, and the first page are where a book makes its strongest impression. Then why would anyone, especially an unknown author desperate to make an impression, begin a book with a page of listless description? Or an ordinary day in the life of the main character? Imagine that you're in a crowd, trying to get someone's attention. You've got to jump higher, wave stronger, and shout louder than everybody else. That doesn't mean you need to begin with "The shotgun blast blew the groom's head apart, spewing blood and brain all over the white dresses of the flower girls at the wedding." That might be more waving and shouting than an editor would appreciate. As Gene Kelly says in *Singin' in the Rain*, "Dignity, always dignity." But at least, my shotgun example is better than the put-me-to-sleep "He strolled, leisurely, into the park." (Love those commas.)

I recommend that beginning novelists go to a large bookstore once a month, the kind that has a huge section of novels marked "new releases." Read the first sentence/paragraph/page of every one of them. Don't pay attention to the type of novel it is. Mystery, romance, thriller, mainstream. Makes no difference. What you're trying to identify is writing that, because of tone or incident or whatever, grabs your attention. You'll be amazed at how many first pages don't manage the job. But we're not interested in those. What we care about are the ones that *do* grab our attention. Without imitating, use them as examples. Raise your standards. Keep remembering my editor trying to read manuscripts on the noisy train or on the weekend when he'd much rather be with his family. Above all, pay attention to first sentences. The following are some of my favorites.

In the late summer of that year we lived in a house in a village that looked across the river and the plain to the mountains.

Ernest Hemingway, *A Farewell to Arms*

This is the saddest story I have ever heard.

Ford Madox Ford, *The Good Soldier*

Whether I shall turn out to be the hero of my life, or whether that station will be held by anybody else, these pages must show.

Charles Dickens, *David Copperfield*

Last night I dreamt I went to Manderley again.

Daphne du Maurier, *Rebecca*

I had the story, bit by bit, from various people, and, as generally happens in such cases, each time it was a different story.

Edith Wharton, *Ethan Frome*

When he was nearly thirteen, my brother Jem got his arm badly broken at the elbow.

Harper Lee, *To Kill a Mockingbird*

Many years later, as he faced the firing squad, Colonel Aureliano Buendía was to remember that distant afternoon when his father took him to discover ice.

Gabriel García Márquez, *One Hundred Years of Solitude*

Call me Ishmael.

Herman Melville, *Moby-Dick*

For an extensive list of great first sentences, see Georgianne Ensign's *Great Beginnings: Opening Lines of Great Novels* (HarperCollins). What they all have in common is a directness that confidently draws the reader into the narrative, promising a special experience.

First *paragraphs* ought to have a similar impact, also. Have a look at Geoffrey Household's incomparable opening to the literate thriller *Rogue Male*.

I cannot blame them. After all, one doesn't need a telescopic sight to shoot boar and bear; so that when they came on me watching the terrace at a range of 550 yards, it was natural enough that they should jump to conclusions.

What's going on here? I want to know. Why was the narrator watching the house with a rifle and a telescopic sight? Who caught him? What did they do to him? In these few brief sentences, a host of urgent questions has controlled me.

Here's another great first paragraph. One of the qualities I most admire about it is that the author, knowing his obligation to capture the reader, has created a tone that could just as easily begin a thriller as it does a classic mainstream, socially conscious novel.

I am an invisible man. No, I am not a spook like those who haunted Edgar Allan Poe; nor am I one of your Hollywood-movie ectoplasms. I am a man of substance, of flesh and bone, fiber and liquids—and I might even be said to possess a mind. I am invisible, understand, simply because people refuse to see me.

Ralph Ellison, *Invisible Man*

I could keep providing examples. Instead, I encourage you to supply your own favorites. Without imitating, use them as your model. Try to write first sentences and paragraphs that create the same tingle that you felt when you first read your own favorite openings. Once you have a distinctive first sentence/paragraph/page, maintain that tone. Keep imagining a very busy, intelligent, experienced editor or agent who would love nothing better than to acknowledge that you've written a masterpiece. The task is, from the start, to get that reader's attention.

In this regard, I try to keep in mind something that Donald E. Westlake once told me. Don is an amazingly versatile productive writer who is perhaps best known for a character named Dortmunder in a series of comic-caper novels, a subgenre that Don invented (*The Hot Rock*, *Bank Shot*), and who under the name of Richard Stark has written several intense novels about a professional thief named Parker. I'm one of many writers who admire the Parker books for their economy, directness, and hard-boiled impact. Here are some randomly selected first sentences:

When a fresh-faced guy in a Chevy offered him a lift, Parker told him to go to hell.

Point Blank (A.K.A. *The Hunter*)

When he didn't get any answer the second time he knocked, Parker kicked the door in.

The Split

When the knock came at the door, Parker was just turning to the obituary page.

The Jugger

When the car stopped rolling, Parker kicked out the rest of the windshield and crawled through onto the wrinkled hood.

Backflash

The pattern should be obvious. With a few exceptions in the more-than-twenty Stark/Parker books, all begin with a dynamic "when" clause. Further, *every* book has the same four-part structure. Sections one, two, and four are from Parker's limited third-person viewpoint. Section three is always from the third-person viewpoint of Parker's antagonist. The series has a remarkable consistency of form. It feels unique.

One evening years ago, at the start of my career, Don advised me to think about writing in the following context. A hundred novels are on a table. Someone has ripped off the covers so that we don't know who wrote the books. The names of famous characters have been changed. There's no explicit indicator to identify who's responsible. Nothing except the writer's tone, his or her approach, the quality of the story and the prose. As we go through these books, Don maintained, we'll soon discover that most of them feel alike, even though each has been written by a different person. It's as if a lot of the authors are imitating each other. We put those that feel alike at one end of the table. By the time we finish reading the hundred books, 95 are at one end, and five (the distinctive ones) are at the other. Our task, Don said, is to be among those five.

How did I apply this advice to myself? The answer goes back to Stirling Silliphant and *Route 66*. That show was unusual because it combined two elements that we normally don't find together. On the one hand, it was an adventure program whose action could be extreme. In the opening episode, "Black November," for example, a fight in a sawmill came brutally close to a buzz saw. In another episode, "Most Vanquished, Most Victorious," the two main characters had to fight an L.A. street gang, who attacked them swinging bicycle chains.

But on the other hand, the same episode that featured the buzz saw also had long literate speeches that alluded to *Hamlet* and talked about existential loneliness. The second episode in the series was about a female captain of a shrimp boat in the Gulf of Mexico. The plot was patterned after Shakespeare's *The Taming of the Shrew* and paraphrased a quote from that play as its title, "A Lance of Straw." The third episode, set in New Orleans, evoked the mood of Tennessee Williams. About an outbreak of lethal parrot fever, the script was titled "The Swan Bed," with overtones of Leda and the Swan as well as the ugly duckling. "The Stone Guest" was about a mining disaster and had numerous allusions to Mozart's *Don Giovanni*. Sartre, Ionesco, and Spinoza were alluded to in other episodes. Frequently, speeches held disguised poetry and went on for several minutes. One memorable speech lasted an entire act.

On television, there had never been anything like *Route 66*, and there has never been anything like its combination of action and literacy since then. In retrospect, I realize that the program's preoccupation with philosophers and writers is what made me go to college and eventually get a doctorate in literature. In my teenage letter to Silliphant, I had said that I wanted to become him. But as I aged (and as I've said many times in these pages), I understood that imitation wasn't the way to go. My goal was to take what I'd learned from Silliphant and make it my own.

Thus I set myself the task of writing thrillers that would appeal to the men and women with whom I'd worked in various factories, people with a general education who were grateful for distraction from the tedium of their jobs. The action and suspense in my novels was for them. Simultaneously, I thought of the graduate students and professors I knew at Penn State and the

University of Iowa, specialists who weren't satisfied with a book if it didn't feel artistic. My goal is to try to appeal to both sets of readers.

In *Testament*, I peppered the text with allusions to Poe, Melville, Hemingway, Faulkner, just about any American author I admired. I named the main character Reuben Bourne after a character in a Hawthorne story, "Roger Malvin's Burial," which is about guilt and retribution, themes in the novel. I named two policeman Webster and Ford after two well-known seventeenth-century British dramatists, one of whom wrote *The Duchess of Malfi*, a revenge drama (*Testament* is about revenge). I didn't emphasize these allusions. Embedding them so they wouldn't interfere with the narrative, I hoped that they would add a resonance, however.

In *Last Reveille*, I used a historical detail (a bullet stopped a clock during Pancho Villa's historic raid on Columbus, New Mexico) to split time. Thus I started two succeeding chapters with the same sentence: "The rider took the bullet in the neck and toppled." Having marked that point in time, I then led the action in two separate simultaneous directions. I thought of this technique as a sort of cubism on the page. (A troubled reader wrote to tell me, with regret, that the book's printer had repeated a sentence by mistake.)

The Brotherhood of the Rose begins in the Middle Ages with the story of Eloise and Abelard. *Burnt Sienna* is filled with allusions to Dante and Beatrice. But I bury the literary part of my thrillers so that they're not overtly self-conscious, so that a reader who wants nothing more than thrills won't be distracted. Meanwhile, another kind of reader who needs a literary approach will be pleasantly surprised. This combination is something that I never would have tried if it hadn't been for Silliphant, and yet the way I do it is different from the poetry that Silliphant employed, not to mention that I'm writing books while he wrote for television and the movies.

Similarly, *you* have to learn how to adapt the approaches of writers who've inspired you so that you move onward, creating something new. Use your singular background to create themes and approaches unique to you, even though you might have been inspired by other writers. In the end, a first-class you is better than a secondhand version of somebody else. Write books that can't be clumped with a bunch of similar ones. If an editor hasn't seen anything like your writing before, you have a good chance of getting a favorable reading. Of course, some editors are as trendy as some writers and don't see a value in something that isn't part of a current fashion. There's nothing you can do about that. Just keep remembering that first sentence I hated so much. Don't stroll, leisurely, into the park.

Subject Matters: With Fiction as with Food, Fresh is Better

BY WILL ALLISON

What Justice Potter Stewart once said about porn is also true of literary fiction: It's hard to define, but we know it when we see it. Even if we can't agree on a definition of literary fiction, we do know that its literariness has to do with the way in which a story is told rather than what the story is about.

This is an important distinction for writers who aspire to publish stories in prestigious literary magazines and in the few glossies that still bother with short fiction. To have a shot at publication in these venues, your story must achieve a certain level of literary quality. It doesn't matter if your story has the world's most fascinating theme or ingenious plot; if the writing—the form, style and language—isn't up to snuff, you'll find no takers among editors of so-called serious fiction.

But let's say your story is up to snuff. Whether it's accepted for publication still depends upon the editor's taste, the competition, the magazine's current needs and other factors over which you have no control. There is, however, one often overlooked factor that you can control: the story's subject matter.

While it's true a literary short story can tackle just about any subject and still be literary, that doesn't mean all subjects are created equal. What you choose to write about may make the difference between a byline in your favorite quarterly or a rejection slip.

STALE TALES

When I worked at *Story*, a quarterly literary magazine that ceased publication with its Winter 2000 issue, we received about 20,000 manuscripts each year. As you can imagine, certain subjects, themes and types of stories cropped up again and again.

Most popular were coming-of-age stories, usually told from the perspective of an adolescent protagonist, often in first person. We also received a lot of troubled-family stories, especially those involving the death (or the aftermath of the death) of a parent or child. Other troubled-family stories examined the effects of divorce and often featured single mothers bringing home inappropriate men or traveling cross-country with their hapless children and spending time in nondescript hotel rooms.

We also saw a fair number of stories whose protagonists were writers or predictably quirky Southern types who spent a lot of time on their porches. There were stories about lottery winners and stories about characters meeting homeless people who changed their lives. A disproportionate number of stories were set in New York City and in Boston. And then there were looking-for-love stories, those tales that chronicled the difficulties of dating and often included scenes in coffee shops.

Is there anything wrong with such subject matter? Of course not. Many of the stories published each year (including many that end up in prize anthologies) traffic in pretty similar material.

WILL ALLISON *is former editor-at-large for* Zoetrope: All-Story, *former executive editor of* Story, *and former editor of* Novel & Short Story Writer's Market. *He is also a staff member at the Squaw Valley Community of Writers and the recipient of a 2000 Ohio Arts Council Grant for fiction.*

And after all, the prevalence of these stories comes as no surprise. The death of a family member, one's passage into adulthood, these are heavy-duty experiences, so of course we're inclined to write about them.

Nevertheless, if you're writing stories that deal with familiar subject matter, you should know that, when it comes to publication, you might be making things harder for yourself. In a sense, you're choosing to compete more directly with similar stories that fill every editor's slush pile. Also, you're inviting editors to make more direct comparisons between your story and others they've published. For example, if a writer sent a coming-of-age tale to *Story*, and it didn't measure up to, say, Chris Adrian's "High Speeds" or Aimee Bender's "The Healer," I was apt to figure, why bother? But if a writer sent a story unlike any I'd seen, it didn't have to go up against the greats; it had the advantage of being its own yardstick.

What's overly familiar to one editor may seem quite fresh to another, as each editor brings to the slush pile a unique reading history. Still, by reading plenty of literary magazines and story collections, you can get a general sense of what ground hasn't been covered, what has, and what's been thoroughly trampled by the scribbling masses.

THINK FRESH

The good news is that you can increase your chances of catching an editor's eye by writing stories that deal with fresh subject matter (or that deal with familiar subjects in fresh ways). Your subject matter needn't be outlandish or outrageous, merely out of the ordinary—themes, characters, settings, milieus and dramatic problems that haven't been done to death.

Put yourself in the editor's shoes. One day you receive a hundred stories in the mail. Of those, perhaps five are publishable. Of those five, two really strike your fancy. One is the brilliant story of a man who loses his father to lung cancer, and the other is the brilliant story of a man who loses his father (literally loses sight of him) on a scuba diving trip in an abandoned rock quarry. You are equally moved by both stories. Problem is, you have only one slot left in the magazine. In the previous issue, you published a brilliant story about a woman who loses her mother to breast cancer, but you've never before seen a father-son-scuba-diving drama. Which one are you going to accept?

THE ROAD LESS TRAVELED

What's overly familiar to one editor may seem quite fresh to another, as each editor brings to the slush pile a unique reading history. Still, by reading plenty of literary magazines and story collections, you can get a general sense of what ground hasn't been covered, what has, and what's been thoroughly trampled by the scribbling masses.

So next time you sit down to write a story, ask yourself: What stories have I read that deal with similar subjects in similar ways? If you can come up with two or three examples, odds are you're headed into familiar territory. That's no reason to stop (anyway, many writers will tell you their subjects choose them, not vice versa), but it is worth knowing.

In most walks of life, the road less traveled is usually the tougher route, but when it comes to selecting subject matter for your short stories, that road may turn out to be your quickest path to publication.

Swimming Naked in the Sea of Publication

BY VANESSA LYMAN

"It's a little like saying 'George Clooney, my boyfriend,' and meaning it," says Stacy Sims on the acceptance of her first novel, *Swimming Naked*. "Amazing, but surreal."

In October of 2001, Sims submitted a cover letter, two sample chapters, a synopsis and an endorsement to six different agents. Mid-December, Deborah Schneider at Gelfman Schneider asked to see the entire manuscript. On January third, Schneider called, agreeing to represent Sims's work. On the twenty-third of the same month, Sims's novel went to auction, garnering a book deal with Viking by the close of the day.

This is unbelievably fast. This is surreal, a fairy tale, amazing. This . . . this is like "George Clooney, my boyfriend."

Photo © Photosmith 2002

Stacy Sims

Auctioning a first novel, even from a writer who has never published any fiction at all, is not unheard of, though certainly not the norm. And such auctions, when they do occur, very rarely fail—numbers sometimes become prohibitively high for a publisher, but usually an author walks away with a hefty advance and good word of mouth.

In other words, it's every first novelist's "well-I-can-dream,-can't-I?" wish.

Let's backtrack a bit: how'd she get from there to here?

Though she'd dabbled in creative writing, Sims had never had any fiction published. Nonfiction, sure; two articles in *Northern Ohio Life*, a few pieces in her college newspaper, but no fiction.

"I always imagined myself to be a writer, but in the same way, for ten years, I imagined myself to be someone who worked out and I didn't do anything at all," Sims admits. Now a certified Pilates instructor with her own recently opened studio, she's brought reality up to speed.

Sims was told, " 'Writers write,' and I was pretty sure that didn't mean me," she says. When she finally did sit down to write in earnest, Sims brought an image with her. "A friend of mine told me about when she was little, going on vacation with her mother to the beach, how her mother wore this black bathing suit and these dark sunglasses and smoked a cigarette—there was this moment of recognition. There was someone different inside your mother than who you've come to know as your mother."

When she'd finished writing, it felt like she had a scene, one which set up that moment of recognition between a young girl and her mother. The young girl would develop into Lucy Greene, the protagonist of *Swimming Naked*. The manuscript chronicled Lucy Greene's relationship with her mother over the years. "Within fairly short order, I understood what I wanted to happen in terms of the structure of the novel—going back and forth between past and present, point of view and interweaving . . . I'm lucky I didn't sit down one day, hands poised to write 'my

---

VANESSA LYMAN *is assistant editor for* Novel & Short Story Writer's Market *and* Poet's Market.

novel,' " she says, intoning the last words with a wry twist. "That would have been a lot of pressure. It just evolved into a bit more."

She confesses that for the first three months she worked on it, she couldn't bring herself to admit to writing a novel. But after six months of squeezing time in for writing, mostly on weekends and days off, she decided to commit to it. Sims left her position at a design firm to finish the manuscript. She took on a few freelance writing and marketing jobs and began to teach Pilates, since she could no longer afford lessons and teacher certification meant free instruction. "I loved the combination," Sims says. "Writing in the morning and then getting out of my head to teach somebody to do something with their body. It's something that still is meaningful to me, rather than trying to get excited about marketing something."

Throughout the writing of *Swimming Naked*, Sims kept it loose. "I didn't set rigid rules for myself. It works for some people, to write every day from this time to this time. I really just gave myself freedom for thought; writing and thinking are sort of the same thing. By the time I get to the typ—uh, the word processor, it's just getting it out; I just gave myself the freedom to do it when it felt like the right time to do it."

Sims describes this method as intuitive and adds, "I never sat down without something to say."

Once she'd committed to it, she wrote for several hours three or four days a week until her first draft of 317 pages felt like something worth showing to readers. Sims selected her initial audience carefully. One friend, a woodcut artist, read a great deal of fiction and could tell her when "something didn't ring true." Another reader was a local poet and filmmaker and another, Susan Andrews Grace, was a Canadian poet and creative writing teacher who Sims corresponded with but hadn't met. "I knew enough to know it was well-written," Sims says slowly, "so it was a tricky thing to figure out what I was asking them to do. I wasn't looking for a line edit, I was looking for an overall response." Her readers came through with their advice, certainly, but even more so in the validation and encouragement they gave Sims.

Opening up to friends and family came next. Though the reactions varied in focus, they didn't in intensity. "There were very different and very *personal* responses to the characters—'I was so mad when she did this,' and 'I couldn't believe when this happened,' which I thought was a good sign." Sims couldn't address everyone's reactions without watering down the book, so she focused on a few criticisms and clarified a character or smoothed a rough patch of dialogue. "The only thing I majorly revised was the first chapter," she says. "It was plain old too long. I was saying the same thing about the characters over and over again. That chapter got edited substantially before I sent it out."

She adds, "I still believe it could be a tighter manuscript, but I felt it was ready to get into the hands of an editor—one person to work with."

Submission: "Baffling, baffling process"

Sims had researched manuscript format early on, because that was something she didn't want to tangle with twice. But as for submitting to agents, she says, "I sort of assumed that I would figure those steps when the manuscript was ready. I figured I was clever enough to handle it, but when I finished writing, which was the most important part, I didn't see anything that dealt with this stage."

She did read somewhere that writers get agent recommendations from other writers. So Sims, being resourceful, approached other writers. She rolls her eyes as she admits, "And they wouldn't tell me their agents."

Using phrases like "smoke and mirrors" and "baffling, baffling process" and "impenetrable," Sims describes researching the world of agents. Eventually, Sims targeted six likely candidates, four from the Internet, one suggested by a friend in New York and the last, a former classmate of another friend, who ultimately asked to see the manuscript.

"It was so weird not to be able to call and ask someone how this works. I tried to be as respectful as I could, using what I learned about the industry from various guides. Even sending two chapters, I said, 'If I broke some huge rule, I've done it for a reason','' she says. "Mainly because the narrator in the book alternates between being a grown woman and being a child so I wanted them to get a sense of her at both ages."

Despite her efforts and careful considerations, she received her share of rejections. "Three, literally not even on a whole sheet of paper. It was like half a piece of paper, Xeroxed." She did receive a really nice letter from one agent, who had obviously paid attention to the package of material Sims had submitted, but it was a polite 'No, thank you,' nonetheless.

Then, in mid-December, Deborah Schneider of Gelfman Schneider called asking to see the rest of the manuscript. It would probably take Schneider two or three months to get back in touch, she said, so Sims settled in to wait.

"In my mind, she was going to be my inside track to 'Great letter, sucky chapters' or 'It's fine, I'm not interested. Send it to these 8,000 people,' so I was *delighted* when she ended up wanting to represent me. I didn't want to send out 60 packages in the beginning, but I would have."

On January third, only a few weeks after shipping off the entire manuscript of *Swimming Naked*, Schneider called and accepted Sims as a new client. And she'd be taking the book to auction.

With the auction scheduled for January twenty-fourth, Sims had just enough time to worry a lot. "I was trying so hard to not freak out but I was freaking out just a little, and then I read the manuscript again." The butterflies calmed as Sims reread what she'd written. "It gave me comfort. *This* is what this is about and I'm really happy with it." She distracted herself with some freelance work and waited for the auction.

When the round of phone calls finally stopped, *Swimming Naked* was sold to Viking, to be edited by Molly Stern and released in May 2003.

Keeping in touch with New York

Sims wanted to meet everyone involved, so after the deal was closed, she flew to New York. "These people would be really important to my life," Sims explains. "We went to lunch and talked a little about the book but mostly we talked about other stuff. Deborah was so competent, so good at what she does, I felt like I was in good hands."

Then she went to the Viking offices to meet her editor. "Molly's great, she's just really enthusiastic."

The entire situation, however, was a little overwhelming. "It's not as though I didn't understand what was happening, but walking into Viking and seeing all the titles in the bookcases and the titles in her office, that was a pretty big deal, because I wasn't being sent down the hall to work with some other division."

The meeting between the two women lasted about an hour, covering generalities for the most part, but Sims had accomplished what she's set out to do. "They have very, very busy lives and in the publishing cycle, my book was far out for them. I think it was just a good idea for them to see me and know who I am. This way, if I feel like something needs attention, hopefully I won't register as that pesky, annoying writer from Cincinnati."

Sims left New York with the idea of having two distinct jobs to do, "One as author and one as writer. There will be times when I'm called on to do the job of the author, which is the book tour, the interviews, the business side of it . . . I'm fairly interested in that; it'll be a fun time and I'm confident enough to take part in that activity. It's almost like, if I do a good job as the author two percent of the time, it'll allow me to live the other ninety-eight percent of the time as a writer, which looks a whole lot like the life I led before I became the 'author,' '' she says, smiling. "Which is, I get up, I make my own toast, I have my coffee—you know, it sort of separates this all out."

Foreign rights, film rights . . .

Sims's current situation satisfies her; with *Swimming Naked* in a good home with a nurturing editor and all those negotiable rights carefully shepherded by her agent, Sims has reason to be assured. "I'm somewhat curious about what's going to happen and how," she says of the rights she retained. "But it has really no bearing on my day to day life. We don't really talk about what's going to happen; if it happens then we have something to talk about."

Recently for example, Sims received a preemptive offer from Holland for foreign rights. The advance would be in euros. "I don't even know what that is!" she laughs. She's confident that her agent will explain what the offer means and whether or not she can use those euros to buy a new computer printer.

Sims won't need to ask Schneider why her book found such a quick market with the Dutch, though. "My friend told me that family dysfunction is huge in Holland."

In addition to foreign rights, it's likely someone will approach Sims concerning film rights; *Swimming Naked* is a strongly visual book—relying in part on a snapshot motif—so an extension to film feels like a natural next step. And then there are all those other rights . . .

Right now, Sims is focused not on the rights for *Swimming Naked*, but on her next novel. "My head is really more in my second novel," she admits. "I have those glasses on now, I look at the world with this other character's lenses, not with Lucy's so much. But when it's time to go back and revisit, I'll be really happy."

Swimming Naked: An Agent's Take

What attracted you to the *Swimming Naked* manuscript? Was it professional, or maybe unusual in some way?

From the opening pages, I was taken in by her characters, her mastery and her confidence as a writer. This was no typical first novel; it was convincing, moving, compelling and the work of a mature writer. I usually know within the first few pages if a novel is working, and whether it's something I want to represent.

Less than two months after sending you her manuscript, she had a book deal with Viking. That was fast . . .

It was fast. It is far more common for a first work of literary or serious fiction to take some time to find the right home. Publishers are looking for books with obvious marketing hooks, name brands and bestseller potential. It is harder to market beautiful writing on its own merit, especially if the story isn't big, sensational, or "high concept." In Stacy's case, her novel had both beautiful writing and a great story.

Why did *Swimming Naked* go to auction? That's incredibly unusual for a debut novel, right?

As I said before, *Swimming Naked* had everything going for it. Publishers are hungry for good material and I thought this novel had potential. Additionally, an auction stirs the adrenaline a bit: it causes more excitement, good word of mouth, makes the book more of an event.

How did you arrange the auction? Were publishers selected based on certain criteria? How many publishers were involved in the bidding?

Every publishing house has a host of editors, all with different tastes, sensibilities and fields of expertise. I chose editors from 15 different imprints whom I considered ideal for this kind of literary/commercial fiction and would know how to publish it well. Five publishers called to say they loved the book; by auction day, two were bidding.

How are auctions done? By phone, e-mail?

By phone, in rounds. The agent determines the terms and rules of the auction and invites bids. In this case, I was offering the U.S. and Canadian publication rights only (all foreign and ancillary rights reserved to the author). Then each editor takes turns topping the previous bid until one of them can or will not bid anymore.

Now that the book is sold, how involved are you with the publication process?

The publisher is the final arbiter of all decisions about the book's publication, but I consult with the editor on each step of the process, from jacket design, cover copy and quotes, to marketing and promotional plans. Additionally, the sale to a U.S. publisher is only the first of what can be many: to UK and foreign publishers for translation, to the movies, to magazines, to audio publishers. As well, I oversee all royalty payments, from all sources. An agent is involved for the life of the book.

A Tale of Two Start-Ups

BY CINDY DUESING

It's fortunate when two writers, both on the path to publication, meet up and form a working friendship. But it could be called serendipitous when a writer and editor, both on the starting block of their publishing careers, find each other through the slush pile. New Jersey author Bonnie Glover had yet to have a short story published when she sent her work to Michael Chester, editor of the literary journal Glass Tesseract. *For his part, Chester was still "gradually learning" what shape his publication would take as he sifted through stacks of submissions. Here's the story of how the match was made, and how they're getting their respective careers up and running.*

BONNIE GLOVER
Writer

New Jersey author Bonnie Glover juggles her roles as wife, full-time mother and mediation consultant as she works toward her dream of becoming an established writer. Last year, Glover realized the first part of that dream when her short story, "The Demise of Queenie Monroe," appeared in *Glass Tesseract*, a California-based literary journal edited and published by Michael Chester. This marked her first publication, but if talent, persistence and enthusiasm have anything to do with it, it won't be her last.

Glover's "Queenie" is a cautionary tale about a lusty old woman preparing to meet Death, and the deal she tries to work out with him. The plot has an unexpected twist, employs magic realism, and springs from the writer's ethnic heritage.

Bonnie Glover

Photo © Motophoto

"There is an undercurrent of superstition—folktales of conjure-women and the like—that is so embedded in the African-American culture, it's really true for us," Glover says. "My stories are about how we as a people relate to those superstitions. They're about more than just what's going on at the surface."

"Queenie" is earthy in tone and use of language, and it's this quality that draws readers into the story and keeps them reading. Says Glover, "When I write, I like to get down to the essence of people, to get down to the essence of me. I have to be true to myself, or else it's flat. I'd have to describe my style as hedonistic—by that, I mean it's wild. Think 1920s and bathtub gin and all that."

CINDY DUESING *is a freelance writer and former editor of* WritersMarket.com. *Her work has appeared in* Writer's Digest *and* Personal Journaling *magazines, as well as* Photographer's Market, Artist's & Graphic Designer's Market, Children's Writer's & Illustrator's Market *and* Guide to Literary Agents.

Glover tried to write more conventionally. In fact, she submitted such a story to Chester before she sent him "Queenie," but he turned it down, saying it was "too civilized." That reinforced her theory that she shouldn't worry about changing her style to match what's out there. "Go with what your gut feeling is, with what makes you happiest to write," she advises. "If you're lucky, the words will write themselves."

Glover first attempted creative writing in sixth grade, when she penned a short story, aptly titled "Rebel Melissa." She was a voracious reader with a vivid imagination, but circumstances didn't allow much time to devote to her craft. Her mother was bedridden and her father died when she was 16, which meant that practical matters took precedence over indulging in her passion. She eventually married and became a successful attorney, making a home with her husband and children in St. Petersburg, Florida, and living the life of a suburban soccer mom. But something was missing.

"Going to law school was a means to an end," says Glover. "My work as an attorney was very important, and I had a great boss, but I was feeling kind of stuck because I wasn't being creative. I had no way to express myself."

The situation changed, however, after Glover's youngest son was born. She became very ill, and her doctors didn't think she was going to make it. But she survived, and the experience forced her to take stock of her life. "I resolved to do all the things I said I wanted to do but had put off for one reason or another—particularly writing. And once I started paying attention to it, it began to blossom."

So Glover switched to working as a part-time consultant to devote more time to her writing at home. It's proven to be less stressful, she says, but it's still not easy. In between doing her consulting work and running kids around all day, she looks over projects in progress and revises and edits them. Then, when everyone's gone to bed, she stays up late working on original material. "I have that late-night disease," she says. "It's the only way to get things done. Plus, my friends are very good about not calling me during the day. I tell them 'I'll call you when I'm free.' "

A trip to the Florida Suncoast Writer's Conference paid off for Glover when she met an editor who critiqued "Queenie" and made recommendations. Says Glover, "She really liked the story, so I asked her if she knew of any publications that are open to new writers. She suggested I send it to Michael Chester at *Glass Tesseract*.

"He made it so easy for me. He didn't have a lot of revisions, but what he suggested were things I'd had in mind all along. We're still e-mailing and sharing our writing. We talk about fiction-writing techniques, and he explains things that, as a writer, I haven't been exposed to. His feedback has been so helpful."

Now that she's seen her first story in print, Glover is following up with several projects, including a short-story collection (which she's currently shopping around to agents) and a novel, *The Tale of Joe Willie Walker*. She listens to music when she works, immersing herself and "writing to the beat." She also finds that her consulting work teaching conflict-resolution skills gives her a wealth of information about people, personalities and incidents that helps keep her writing fresh.

"You're not just a writer," she explains, "you're a spectator. And with fiction in particular, you'll see something and put your own spin on it. I think of it as lying within a lie in order to tell a big truth."

In talking with Glover and listening to her enthusiasm and easy laugh, it would seem that very little gets her down. After all, this is a woman who gets excited about going to the post office and buying "fifty million stamps," putting the manuscript in the envelope, and sending it off to the publisher. But like most writers, she's had her share of discouragement.

"For me, the hardest part isn't the rejection," she states matter-of-factly. "I've learned not to take it personally. It's the waiting for a reply! But my answer to that is to go home after I mail one manuscript and start on the next one—and be thankful that there *is* a next one."

Glover plans to enroll in an MFA program in the future, but until then, she sets a curriculum of sorts for herself, reading good literature and books on the craft of writing to keep herself motivated. "I'll read stuff like *Chicken Soup for the Writer's Soul* or Stephen King's *On Writing*. I love learning that Jack London was rejected 4,000 times before he was published. It helps me feel like I'm on my way. And when I read stories in *The New Yorker*, I keep thinking, 'that will be me one of these days. . . .' "

In the end, though, Glover doesn't write for the accolades or the money. "It's for the need to tell, the need to express myself," she says. "Having time to write is having it all. Time to write is the most valuable thing you have."

MICHAEL CHESTER
Editor

In some ways, Bonnie Glover and editor Michael Chester are a lot alike—both had definite goals for their writing, and both were willing to take action to make it happen. For Chester, it began with a poem he'd written in early 1999. Chester submitted it to the *Boston Review*, and fared better than most writers by getting a hand-written reply from the poetry editor. She complimented him on the poem, saying it had come very close to the mark. However, they weren't in need of any more writing at that time. She also told him her preference of the two versions he'd submitted, which he found very helpful. Encouraged by his near-success, Chester sent the poem to several other literary magazines, but all he received were standard rejection letters.

Michael Chester

Photo © Camilla DeSelms

"I was sure that this poem was better than others of mine that had been accepted for publication," Chester says. "This reminded me of how whimsical the processes of acceptance and rejection were. It wasn't exactly news to me, because I'd been writing stories and poems for a long time, with many more rejections than acceptances—but the contrast in those responses brought it home with special force."

At that point, it occurred to him that the only way he would see that poem published would be to start his own literary magazine. Explains Chester: "That momentary impulse alone wouldn't have set me on this path. Even I would have enough sense not to launch a magazine for the sake of my own poem. But, trailing along in the wake of that impulse, sort of like a freighter behind a pilot boat, was my realization that I had friends who were outstanding writers and poets—some of them published, some not. I realized that I could put together a selection of really good artistic works—and the prospect excited me."

The first issue of *Glass Tesseract* launched in the spring of 2001. Chester initially relied on submissions from his writer friends, because "they did terrific work and because hardly anyone else had heard of the magazine." He adds, "As time went by, and as more and more submissions came in, I found that I was immersed in the writings of people whom I'd never met, many of them also authors of terrific capabilities. By providing a medium for the works of all these people, I felt a lot of artistic fulfillment—a feeling of orchestrating the multi-faceted work of many artists."

Besides being exciting, wading through the increased submissions also proved to be more daunting than originally expected. Chester had at first envisioned *Tesseract* as a biannual publication, but in order to give himself and his staff some breathing room, he changed that specification to once or twice a year. "I liked the free, irregular spirit of that—and so, in its third year of publication, 2003, *Glass Tesseract* will appear in a single summer issue. I hope that we'll be biannual most years—but I will take each year as it comes."

The print version of *Glass Tesseract* has a small circulation that is steadily growing, but its biggest readership is on the web at www.glasstesseract.com, where it experiences some 4,000 hits per year. At any given time, 9-12 short stories and poems are featured in the Selections menu. These are changed at irregular intervals, but authors and readers can access a particular piece during "off" times by going to its URL, which means, says Chester, "works that we publish 'stay published.' "

When asked what kind of fiction his journal is open to, Chester says, "We aren't dedicated to any special kind of fiction. Rather than operating from an *a priori* set of criteria, we are ourselves gradually learning what *Glass Tesseract* is like from the works that we instinctively accept. From observation, I would say that our tastes tend to be unconventional. We have published stories that deal sensitively with people's interactions . . . stories that are jauntily and outspokenly sexual . . . stories that are laced with darkness and fatality . . . stories that are abstract, mysterious, or steeped in magic realism. Someone observed once that we are 'on the edge'—and, without trying to define exactly what that means, I think it sounds right."

This description, of course, fits author Bonnie Glover's writing style perfectly. Glover submitted a story to Chester in June of 2001. Chester says: "When I received Bonnie Glover's story, 'The Demise of Queenie Monroe,' I passed it to one of our consulting editors, Isabelle Hannich-who strongly recommended it to me. Then, as I read it, I was drawn to its comedy, its vivid, eccentric characters, and its sheer irreverence. It came through to me as a natural and spontaneous work of art. In working with Bonnie, I always feel the vitality and energy that she puts into her writing—and this has been enlivening to me as an editor."

Chester's passion for helping writers get their work out there has caused somewhat of a dilemma for him. In the beginning, he set for himself the goal of responding to each author personally. "I think a writer's work deserves that," he explains. "That worked fine at first, as a light scattering of manuscripts arrived. But when the avalanche of submissions came, I found that I was working full time writing critical essays, and falling further and further behind in my response time. And finally I knew that what I was trying to do was impossible. Now, sometimes I will write a few lines of comment if something very specific occurs to me—or if something in the work that I'm declining appealed to me very much. I wish that I could answer everyone personally."

When looking over submissions, Chester has a very clear idea of what he wants to see. "I feel that many stories fail because they read like documentaries. As a reader, I don't want to be told what the characters are like or what their conflicts are. I want to be flung right into the middle of the story. I may not know right away who is speaking, who is thinking, or who is even present. But, like a movie viewer, I will gradually find out. Also I think it's good to establish the protagonist's main passion or goal very early. And, in addition, it's important for any writer to learn to use language well, paying attention to every nuance—even in the boldest, most direct narratives."

But even the best writers will have their work rejected by editors who are overwhelmed, or who just don't have much interest in the subject matter. This, Chester says, is where a writer needs to be persistent and believe in his or her own abilities. "Every editor is just a person with reading biases. But the better the writing and the more editors receive it, the better your chances are in this harsh lottery.

"What can a writer do? Keep developing your style. Be alert to the world around you and to your own past for material that can be transformed into fiction. Take criticisms seriously—don't dismiss them—yet don't take them on faith either. And write a lot—first to develop your style—and secondly to give yourself more chances to be read. If you have 20 stories out to publishers, then the chance that one will break through the fierce, statistical wall is better than if you have only two or three in the mail."

What Happens After the Contract Is Signed?

BY WALTER C. HUNT

If you, as an author, sit with a group of readers for any length of time, someone will eventually ask the question, "How long did it take you to get published?"

Walter Hunt

Here's what I tell them: "It depends on how you measure it; 10 weeks, 14 years or 18 months." I wrote my science fiction novel, *The Dark Wing*, in first-draft form in about ten weeks in 1986-87. It was released in serial form—it was 66 episodes sent out by e-mail to friends.

I made some additions and changes based on suggestions from my original editor to get the book ready for submission. That's how the 14 years comes into the story; I submitted *The Dark Wing* several times with no success—to Ace, to Baen, and to Warner, among others. It wasn't that publishers and editors didn't like the writing; it was usually a matter of numbers or a question of placement ("We like the book but it isn't what we're doing right now"). I waited 14 years for the same editor to get to a position at science fiction publisher Tor Books. With contract in hand in late May 2000, my editor told me that it would appear in December 2001—18 months from then.

I was surprised. Eighteen months seemed like a long lead time. I'd been working on my manuscript for many years, and didn't think it needed much to be completed. Nonetheless, that was the scheduled release date. As it turned out Tor needed that amount of time and so did I. With a "finished" book that I'd worked on for years, I went through five edit passes between the contract date and the release date.

EDITING THE BOOK
First edit: characters and commas

I have always had a few too many commas in my prose. Everyone has to have an Achilles' heel, after all. I took a printed copy of my manuscript and sat in my blue armchair. I went at it with a pen, looking to smooth out rough spots and remove some of those pesky commas. In addition, I made up three lists as I went through the book: a list of every character, every space ship, and every location I mentioned. This was for consistency; in particular, my editor told me that a character list was essential for the copy editor—without it, the first occurrence of any character would establish any salient facts about it. It's amazing how many characters a writer invents for one scene or mentions in passing in one paragraph.

Science fiction writing might well require more attention to this sort of detail—with the universe as your canvas, there seem to be more possibilities for changes of setting. Moreover,

---

WALTER C. HUNT *has been an active writer since school days. His first novel,* The Dark Wing, *was published by Tor Books in 2001; his second,* The Dark Path *is scheduled for 2002 publication. He is married with one daughter.*

the places you describe aren't exactly Boston or Paris—at least not the Boston or Paris we know in the early twenty-first century. Settings should be fully realized, but whatever is written, it has to be consistent in its presentation. As I worked through the manuscript, I noted descriptions of places I mentioned to make sure of this. Even the best intentions aren't always successful. I'd located Langley Base, the Headquarters of Imperial Intelligence, on Callisto, Jupiter's moon, but towards the end of the editing process, I found one instance in the manuscript where I'd put it on Ganymede. Score one for multiple edit passes.

Second edit: editor's choice (general)

My editor provided me with two pages of general commentary on the book. He'd seen the book in various versions and had bought what he'd last seen, but had an idea of what needed to be done to make the book more marketable, more coherent, and more compelling. With this in hand, I took my marked-up manuscript and looked for ways to improve the book according to these instructions. It forced me to look at it as my editor did—looking for things that he felt were needed. This was an interesting exercise, since I'd never looked at my writing except as its author.

Third edit: editor's choice (specific)

With all of the first and second edit changes incorporated into the manuscript, I sent it along to the editor. There were 562 pages in the draft, and it seemed like there was a mark or change on every page. This can be interpreted in two ways. On one hand, it can be disheartening for a writer to look up from his manuscript and see that much editing—what does it say about the quality of the original writing? On the other hand, it means that no page has been overlooked.

My editor's comments on this version of the manuscript were more specific, listing places where material had to be added or deleted. This pass was fine tuning, and I focused my attention on the passages he had highlighted. During this editing pass, I wrote more new material than I had previously done, but only where the editor had indicated. Other than a few passages where he didn't like my turn of phrase, the effort was directed at revising and adding material rather than deleting it. I'm not sure whether that derives from the subject matter; science fiction is sometimes "far enough out" that some leeway may be given to the author.

When I was finished with this pass, my editor accepted the final manuscript. This is significant, because upon acceptance the editor's (and therefore the publisher's) authority over content mostly disappears. New writers should defy their publisher at their peril, but after the manuscript is accepted, no one will make the author change anything. The copy editor doesn't have the authority of the editor, but the next step is still very important.

Fourth edit: copy edit

Once the manuscript is accepted, it is sent to a copy editor. This is an underappreciated profession; the copy editor's job is to prepare the book for typesetting, and to look for stylistic and consistency problems. The only emphasis permitted the writer is underlining; the copy editor follows an accepted style guide (such as *The Chicago Manual of Style*) to convert those underlines to bold or italic.

A good copy editor asks not only punctuation or grammar but also context questions. For example, my book had an alien race with a part verbal, part gestural language. All through the manuscript, I saw laborious noting of alien spellings and alien terminology. She had to distinguish between esGa'uYal (evil servants of the Deceiver, the zor aliens' adversary god) and esHara'y (those whose deeds are evil, but who do not serve the Deceiver directly) and naZora'i (those who are not zor, i.e., humans). I had a very good copy editor.

The copy editor returned six closely-written pages of questions and notes, along with an alphabetical summary of every important word in the book—names of things, terms, and so forth. She was supplied with my list of characters, and she noted a few places where I had overlooked a reference. An author is responsible for addressing these questions, but he can choose to leave something alone if he feels that it's correct. Copy editors aren't always right.

Fifth edit: page proofs

After the copy edit is done, the author has one more chance to find problems in the typeset page proofs. In addition to picking up typos and things you might have overlooked, it's important to look for places where the typeset manuscript differs from the last manuscript sent to the publisher. Don't laugh, but I had a long scene with breaks in perspective, and the typeset manuscript dropped several, running them all together. I found them by reading the page proofs with the final copy editor's draft beside it. As with every other editing pass, I looked at every page.

WHY DO IT?

From the time a writer starts to work on a project until the time it's sold, the objective is to get the contract. The publisher, the editor, and the writer have one basis on which to evaluate the writing: the submitted draft that the writer writes, the editor evaluates, and the publisher buys.

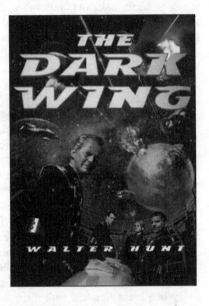

Ask a writer what he thinks of the manuscript he's trying to sell, and he'll tell you that he likes it a lot—it's the culmination of hours/weeks/months/years of work, it's an artistic triumph, it's the best he can make it. The last opinion is the most important one, to which I can certainly attest: after years trying to sell my book I had reached the conclusion that I had done the best job I could. After the last rejection I told myself that I wasn't going to change a punctuation mark until I was paid to do it.

Editors offer input on a piece of writing for a variety of reasons. Obviously, grammatical changes and corrections are necessary; any piece can be improved by attention to coherence and consistency. Only writers much more stubborn than myself would turn aside such advice.

Past those areas, though, there are other changes an editor might make. I had an assurance from my editor; he liked the book I wrote, and didn't want it to be something it wasn't. His editorial comments and suggestions were intended to make my book a better one. New writers should trust experienced editors who know the market and what makes a book successful. That doesn't mean surrendering to every suggestion the editor makes, but listening is important. In general, the further you go in the editing process, the more confidence you should have that the writing is solid.

SUMMING UP

In the final analysis, it's remarkable how much is required to take "the best you can make it" to a final edition, words on paper. In my opinion, it's much better to work in this environment—after the contract—because you're working toward a known goal (the finished manuscript) with an editor who is hopefully experienced and helpful. Without the goal and the editor, it's possible that revision could make the writing worse and move you away from the goal.

As a new writer, I suspect that I was given more guidance than a much more seasoned writer might have received. I am also confident that I (and my work) needed that attention. The ideas are good, the writing is good. It takes a lot of effort to get yourself published, and a lot of effort to bring the published product to completion. With *The Dark Wing* published and out on shelves, and *The Dark Path* under contract and in the middle of Editing Step 1, I have now seen the entire process. Though I'm one book more experienced, I still qualify as a new writer; thus, the majority of the cycle is still ahead of me. In truth, I can hardly wait.

Foot in the Door: The Five Cardinal Rules of Queries

BY I.J. SCHECTER

When it comes to query letters, you've heard every piece of advice under the sun. Don't make it too short, but don't make it too long. Be persuasive but not ingratiating. Sell the story, but don't trumpet the writing. Use plain paper and standard margins. Don't spray perfume on the page, enclose a twenty-dollar bill, or promise to set the editor up with your sister.

All this well-intentioned advice can be boiled down to five essential rules. Before you slip that next query into the mailbox, ask yourself whether it satisfies each of the guidelines below. If you answer yes five times, run, do not walk, to the nearest post office. If the answer to even one of the five is no, force yourself to get it right before sealing that envelope.

1. Stick to the point

Queries that are "clean, clear and crisp" stand a much better chance of being considered, says Iris Tupholme, editor-in-chief of HarperCollins Canada. That means your job in a query is to present the relevant facts in an original way—not to be mistaken for playing coy or confusing an editor by withholding key details.

Let's pretend it's 1987. A former prosecutor, you've written what you feel is a pretty solid courtroom suspense/murder mystery. Competition in this genre, of course, is fierce at the best of times. Furthermore, this is your first shot at a novel; your only other significant writing credit is an account of your first year at Harvard Law School. You're going to need a dazzling query just to avoid having your sample chapters transferred directly to the circular file.

Let's assume you start out with the following:

To Whom It May Concern:

Rusty Sabich, Kindle County's longtime chief deputy prosecutor, has been asked to investigate the murder of one of his colleagues, Carolyn Polhemus. What Raymond Horgan, Sabich's boss, doesn't know is that Carolyn and Rusty had been lovers.

As Rusty nears 40, both his marriage and his career seem stalled. His energies focus on his son, and his desperate, unhappy love for Carolyn. The investigation fuels his fantasies, but he makes little progress in finding the killer. When his boss loses his bid for re-election, Rusty suddenly, incredibly, finds himself on trial for Carolyn's murder. He is a trial lawyer on trial.

My high-suspense novel, *Presumed Innocent*, promises to keep readers on the edge of their seats by exploring the above circumstances and answering the question of whether Rusty Sabich indeed killed Carolyn Polhemus. Enclosed for your consideration are three sample chapters and an outline. Please let me know if you are interested in seeing the full manuscript.

Sincerely,

Scott Turow

I.J. SCHECTER *is a freelance writer of fiction and essays. His latest book, a collection of short stories, is titled* The Bottom of the Mug. *His nonfiction appears frequently in* Novel & Short Story Writers Market.

The plot here sounds interesting, but it's difficult to tease out the main thrust because of the letter's lack of focus. Is this novel about the murder? Rusty's relationship with his son? His boss's political campaigning?

Let's look at which elements of the story are critical. A prosecutor has been asked to investigate the murder of a woman with whom he had a clandestine affair. Then he somehow ends up on trial for the murder. So the point of this story is a simple "Whodunit?" All other implied questions—how and why Rusty has become a suspect, whether he did it, whether he'll be convicted—are driven by, and subordinate to, that one question. Everything else in this query should be jettisoned. If an editor is interested enough to start reading, secondary information will be revealed as the story unfolds.

If you find yourself mentioning anything not directly relevant to the story, break out the red pen, summon that self-discipline you've nurtured over the years, and start cutting.

2. Identify the nerves

The "nerves" of your story are the parts that make it more interesting than the next. You may have written a great family saga, but what are the unique elements that will make an editor start reading? Is the family's simple farm life really a front for a gambling ring? Are the matriarch and patriarch actually brother and sister? Does the family live on a shoestring but own real estate in Manhattan? Whatever the nerves, they should be at the heart of your query letter.

Say you're seeking sponsorship for a lemonade stand. Everyone else on your street is planning to open one also. There are two things that make your stand distinctive: first, you're selling your lemonade for three cents a cup versus the going rate of five cents, and second, Britney Spears has agreed to be your guest spokesperson once a week. In your letter to potential sponsors, you aren't going to mention the tablecloth you'll be using, the refreshing taste of your lemonade, or your streetfront location. Each of these things may contribute to your stand's potential success, but none of them are the key reasons people will patronize your stand over any other. Your comparatively low price and your celebrity guest are the nerves, so that's where your focus should lie.

What are the nerves of *Presumed Innocent*? Not the murder on its own, since many novels involve murders. Not the affair on its own, because sex finds its way into lots of books. The nerves of this manuscript are twofold. First, Rusty Sabich is asked to investigate his ex-lover's murder. That's a definite nerve—a plot element not found in other books. Turow goes one better by throwing an additional twist at his protagonist: Rusty becomes a suspect in the investigation he was asked to conduct. Now it's truly a story we haven't seen before, and when Turow makes the claim that his novel is unique, he's telling the truth.

Let's alter the letter, focusing on the nerves:

To Whom It May Concern:

Forty years old, unhappy in his marriage and his career as Kindle County's longtime chief deputy prosecutor, Rusty Sabich's energies are still wrapped around his desperate, unhappy love for Carolyn Polhemus, an ex-colleague. When Carolyn is found murdered, Rusty is the logical choice to conduct the investigation. What Raymond Horgan, Rusty's boss, doesn't know is that Carolyn and Rusty had been lovers. Caught up in unrequited feelings and fueled by the investigation, Rusty makes little progress in finding the killer. And when his boss loses his re-election bid, Rusty suddenly, incredibly, finds himself on trial for Carolyn's murder. He is a trial lawyer on trial.

My high-suspense novel, *Presumed Innocent*, promises to keep readers on the edge of their seats by exploring the above circumstances and answering the question of whether Rusty Sabich indeed killed Carolyn Polhemus.

Numerous entertaining murder mysteries have shown up on bookshelves in the past several years. I hope you'll agree, however, that none of them share the plot turns of *Pre-*

sumed Innocent. Enclosed for your consideration are three sample chapters and an outline. Please let me know if you are interested in seeing the full manuscript.

Sincerely,

Scott Turow

Now the letter emphasizes the nerves right away while still managing to integrate other provocative details. For example, we know Carolyn's murder is somehow related to Raymond Horgan's re-election bid, but that piece of information serves as an accent to the meal rather than the meal itself.

3. Always remember less is more

A good query letter is like a good horror movie: rather than aiming to shock, it aims to grab you by the lapels and not let go. Just as a good director allows the concept, rather than his own style, to be prominent, a good query writer knows that the story, rather than the writing, comes first.

Your goal is not for an editor to exclaim, "Oh my God!", since extreme reactions are a) often elicited by exaggerated claims and b) like a sugar high, temporary. The right query will make an editor hold the letter in his hand, lean back in his chair, and say, "Now *that's* interesting."

Think about a party you've been at when, after gaping initially at the decked-out model who swept in, you couldn't get your mind off that person standing in the corner—the one whose look was somehow compelling, though you couldn't say exactly how or why. Though you'd seen lots of other model-types before—all impressive but essentially indistinguishable from one another—there was just something about this other person. You want your letter to be that person: an idea that winds its way into the editor's mind and sticks, rather than a torpedo that blows the editor out of the water and is quickly forgotten.

In our current query letter for *Presumed Innocent*, we're showing a few too many cards. We'd be wise to follow the maxim, "The suggestive is more appealing than the revealed." An editor wants to know the basic facts of a story while having his curiosity aroused at the same time.

That means we ought to perform some addition by subtraction. Do we need to explain that a man who's cheated has an unhappy marriage? No. Is Rusty's age going to influence whether an editor picks up the manuscript? No. Even naming multiple characters bogs the letter down. Let's trim a little and re-order some elements:

To Whom It May Concern:

Rusty Sabich, Kindle County's longtime chief deputy prosecutor, has been asked to investigate the murder of an ex-colleague, Carolyn Polhemus. What his boss doesn't know is that Rusty and Carolyn had been lovers.

Caught up in unrequited feelings and fueled by the investigation, Rusty makes little headway. When his boss loses a bitter re-election bid, Rusty suddenly, incredibly, finds himself on trial for Carolyn's murder.

Numerous entertaining murder mysteries have shown up on bookshelves in the past several years. I hope you'll agree, however, that none of them share the plot turns of my high-suspense novel *Presumed Innocent*, which promises to keep readers on the edge of their seats by answering the question of who killed Carolyn Polhemus.

Enclosed for your consideration are three sample chapters and an outline. Please let me know if you are interested in seeing the full manuscript.

Sincerely,

Scott Turow

Our letter has become leaner and meaner. Consider that most publishing houses receive hundreds of manuscripts every week. The point of a query letter is not the query itself—it is *to get the editor to page one of your manuscript* and to do it as quickly as possible. That's why you need to dump any ballast. Let the query establish the tease; your manuscript will fill in the blanks with swift prose, vivid descriptions and crackling dialogue.

4. Show evidence of research

It's not good enough in today's competitive environment simply to insist that your story will be a hit with readers. You must make a case for one of two scenarios: 1) that the market hasn't seen anything like this before (a story about iguanas taking over the world, for example), or 2) that stories like yours are reliably popular (say, a Harlequin-type romance). In the case of *Presumed Innocent*, we might want to add a note about the solid track record of murder mysteries and suspense novels, referring to specific titles if appropriate. Ideally, mention successful titles the specific publisher has put out recently.

If you have expertise that qualifies you to write on the subject, say so. If not, don't worry about it, and do not fabricate information. To our query we should add our background as a former U.S. prosecutor, since that lets an editor know we're familiar with the ins and outs of the legal system and we've experienced the true drama and emotional impact of the courtroom.

Finally, part of demonstrating research is addressing your query to a specific individual. Under no circumstances should you allow yourself to address a query generically—that promises a direct route to the slush pile or, worse, the garbage. With manuscripts coming in droves to virtually any publisher open today, "To Whom It May Concern" just doesn't cut it.

Don't be intimidated by this part of the process. Often all it takes is a single call to the publisher's switchboard. The name you get doesn't have to be an editor's. More likely you'll be given that of an editorial assistant, which is just fine (and perhaps better, since an enthusiastic assistant holds more direct influence over an editor than even the best query).

Observing each of these points, let's adjust our letter again:

Dear Editor Smith:

Rusty Sabich, Kindle County's longtime chief deputy prosecutor, has been asked to investigate the murder of an ex-colleague, Carolyn Polhemus. What his boss doesn't know is that Rusty and Carolyn had been lovers.

Caught up in unrequited feelings and fueled by the investigation, Rusty makes little headway. When his boss loses a bitter re-election bid, Rusty suddenly, incredibly, finds himself on trial for Carolyn's murder.

Numerous entertaining murder mysteries have shown up on bookshelves in the past several years. I hope you'll agree, however, that none of them compare to my high-suspense novel *Presumed Innocent*, whose frequent plot turns, along with the historical success of novels in the suspense genre, promise to keep readers on the edge of their seats by answering the question of who killed Carolyn Polhemus.

A former U.S. prosecutor, I am well qualified to write this novel. I am intimately familiar with the very real drama of the courtroom as well as the ploys and tricks involved in any trial.

Enclosed for your consideration are three sample chapters and an outline. Please let me know if you are interested in seeing the full manuscript.

Sincerely,

Scott Turow

Now we're getting somewhere. But there's one more thing.

5. Make sure it's as good as it can be

Patience, of course, is the thorn in every writer's side. When the instinct hits and the words have flooded onto the page, we want more than anything to get the manuscript out there before fear of rejection takes over.

Taking the time to polish your query, however, is as important as taking the time to polish the manuscript. The query is your foot in the door, your key to the suite, your electronic passcard, your secret handshake. Excited as you are to have completed that potential bestseller, don't shoot yourself in the foot by letting it go out the door with a sub-par introduction.

Our query letter is now pretty solid, but it can still be improved in a few areas. In particular, no form of self-congratulations should ever be allowed into a query, so we are not going to promise that this novel will "keep readers on the edge of their seats." If we didn't think it would, we wouldn't be submitting it. Nor are we going to proclaim it a "high-suspense" novel; the editor will decide how much suspense there is. Some other tweaking will help give the letter a little more zing as well:

Dear Editor Smith:

Rusty Sabich, Kindle County's longtime chief deputy prosecutor, has been asked to investigate the murder of an ex-colleague, Carolyn Polhemus. What his boss doesn't know is that Rusty and Carolyn were lovers.

Tormented by unrequited feelings, his desperate obsession fueled by the investigation, Rusty makes little headway. When his boss loses a bitter re-election bid, Rusty suddenly, incredibly, finds himself charged with Carolyn's murder. He is forced to put everything he loves and values on trial—including his own life.

The many successful murder mysteries of the past several years point to the ongoing popularity of this genre. I hope you'll agree that my courtroom suspense novel, *Presumed Innocent*, would make an entertaining addition to the field. Having spent years as a U.S. attorney, I am intimately familiar with the intense drama of life in the courtroom as well as the depths to which prosecutors will sink.

Enclosed for your consideration are three sample chapters and an outline. Please let me know if you are interested in seeing the full manuscript.

Sincerely,

Scott Turow
Encl.

Now we've got a concise, forceful letter that sticks to the point, highlights the nerves, doesn't go over the top, and includes evidence of research.

I know what you're thinking: "But how do I know when it's as good as it can be? If all writers waited until they thought their work was perfect before sending it out, nothing would ever be submitted."

That's true. But it's also true that each of us has a voice—constantly resented because of its infuriating honesty—that tells us when something hasn't reached that mysterious level of self-acceptability. We love this voice because it also tells us when we've nailed it, like a friend who cared too much not to tell the truth. Bounce your queries off others, sure. Workshop your drafts in writers' groups, absolutely. But more than any other source, trust that voice. It will tell you when your query is "perfect" enough.

Once it is, get that manuscript in the mail—and hopefully, your foot in the door.

The Business of Fiction Writing

It's true there are no substitutes for talent and hard work. A writer's first concern must always be attention to craft. No matter how well presented, a poorly written story or novel has little chance of being published. On the other hand, a well-written piece may be equally hard to sell in today's competitive publishing market. Talent alone is just not enough.

To be successful, writers need to study the field and pay careful attention to finding the right market. While the hours spent perfecting your writing are usually hours spent alone, you're not alone when it comes to developing your marketing plan. *Novel & Short Story Writer's Market* provides you with detailed listings containing the essential information you'll need to locate and contact the markets most suitable for your work.

Once you've determined where to send your work, you must turn your attention to presentation. We can help here, too. We've included the basics of manuscript preparation, along with a compilation of information on submission procedures and approaching markets. In addition we provide information on setting up and giving readings. We also include tips on promoting your work. No matter where you're from or what level of experience you have, you'll find useful information here on everything from presentation to mailing to selling rights to promoting your work—the "business" of fiction.

APPROACHING MAGAZINE MARKETS

While it is essential for nonfiction markets, a query letter by itself is usually not needed by most magazine fiction editors. If you are approaching a magazine to find out if fiction is accepted, a query is fine, but editors looking for short fiction want to see *how* you write. A cover letter can be useful as a letter of introduction, but it must be accompanied by the actual piece. Include basic information in your cover letter—name, address, a brief list of previous publications—if you have any—and two or three sentences about the piece (why you are sending it to *this* magazine or how your experience influenced your story). Keep it to one page and remember to include a self-addressed, stamped envelope (SASE) for reply. See the Sample Short Story Cover Letter on page 60.

Agents: Agents are not usually needed for short fiction and most do not handle it unless they already have a working relationship with you. For novels, you may want to consider working with an agent, especially if marketing to publishers who do not look at unsolicited submissions. For more on approaching agents and listings of agents willing to work with beginning and established writers, see our Literary Agents section beginning on page 117. For information on over 500 agencies, see *Guide to Literary Agents* (Writer's Digest Books).

APPROACHING BOOK PUBLISHERS

Some book publishers do ask for queries first, but most want a query plus sample chapters or an outline or, occasionally, the complete manuscript. Again, make your letter brief. Include the essentials about yourself—name, address, phone number and publishing experience. Include only the personal information related to your story. Show that you have researched the market with a few sentences about why you chose this publisher. See the Sample Book Query Cover Letter on page 61.

THE SAMPLE COVER LETTER

A successful cover letter is no more than one page (20 lb. bond paper), single spaced with a double space between paragraphs, proofread carefully, and neatly typed in a standard typeface (not script or italic). The writer's name, address and phone number appear at the top, and it is addressed, ideally, to a specific editor. (If the editor's name is unavailable, address to "Fiction Editor.")

The body of a successful cover letter contains the name and word count of the story, the reason you are submitting to this particular publication, a short overview of the story, and some brief biographical information, especially when relevant to your story. Mention that you have enclosed a self-addressed, stamped envelope or postcard for reply. Also let the editor know if you are sending a disposable manuscript that doesn't need to be returned. (More and more editors prefer disposable manuscripts that save them time and save you postage.) When sending a computer disk, identify the program you are using. Remember, however, that even editors who appreciate receiving your story on a disk usually also want a printed copy. Finally, don't forget to thank the editor for considering your story.

BOOK PROPOSALS

A book proposal is a package sent to a publisher that includes a cover letter and one or more of the following: sample chapters, outline, synopsis, author bio, publications list. When asked to send sample chapters, send up to three *consecutive* chapters. An **outline** covers the highlights of your book chapter by chapter. Be sure to include details on main characters, the plot and subplots. Outlines can run up to 30 pages, depending on the length of your novel. The object is to tell what happens in a concise, but clear, manner. A **synopsis** is a very brief description of what happens in the story. Keep it to two or three pages. The terms synopsis and outline are sometimes used interchangeably, so be sure to find out exactly what each publisher wants.

MANUSCRIPT MECHANICS

A professionally presented manuscript will not guarantee publication. But a sloppy, hard-to-read manuscript will not be read—publishers simply do not have the time. Here's a list of suggested submission techniques for polished manuscript presentation:
- **Use white, 8½×11 bond paper,** preferably 16 or 20 lb. weight. The paper should be heavy enough so it will not show pages underneath it and strong enough to take handling by several people.
- **Type your manuscript** on a computer using a laser or ink jet printer, or on a typewriter using a new ribbon.
- **Proofread carefully.** An occasional white-out is okay, but don't send a marked-up manuscript with many typos. Keep a dictionary, thesaurus and stylebook handy and use the spellcheck function of your computer.
- **Always double space and leave a 1¼ inch margin** on all sides of the page.
- **For a short story manuscript,** your first page should include your name, address and phone number (single-spaced) in the upper left corner. In the upper right, indicate an approximate word count. Center the name of your story about one-third of the way down, skip two or three lines and center your byline (byline is optional). Skip three lines and begin your story. On subsequent pages, put last name and page number in the upper right hand corner.
- **For book manuscripts,** use a separate cover sheet. Put your name, address and phone number in the upper left corner and word count in the upper right. Some writers list their agent's name and address in the upper right (word count is then placed at the bottom of the page). Center your title and byline about halfway down the page. Start your first chapter on the next page. Center the chapter number and title (if there is one) one-third of the way down the page. Include your last name and page number in the upper right of this page and each page to follow. Start each chapter with a new page.
- **Include a word count.** If you work on a computer, chances are your word processing program can give you a word count. If you are using a typewriter, there are a number of ways to count

SAMPLE SHORT STORY COVER LETTER

Jennifer Williamson
8822 Rose Petal Ct.
Norwood OH 45212

June 22, 2003

Rebecca Rossdale
Young Woman Magazine
4234 Market St.
Chicago IL 60606

Dear Ms. Rossdale,

As a teacher and former assistant camp director I have witnessed many a summer romance between teens working at camp. One romance in particular touched me because the young people involved helped each other through a very difficult summer. It inspired me to write the enclosed 8,000-word short story, "Summer Love," a love story about two teens, both from troubled families, who find love and support while working at a camp in upstate New York.

I think the story will fit nicely into your Summer Reading issue. My publishing credits include stories in *Youth Today* and *Sparkle* magazines as well as publications for adults. I am also working on a historical romance.

I look forward to hearing from you.

Sincerely,

Jennifer Williamson
(513)555-5555

Encl.: Manuscript
SASE

SAMPLE BOOK QUERY COVER LETTER

Bonnie Booth
1453 Nuance Blvd.
Norwood OH 45212

December 18, 2003

Ms. Thelma Collins
Bradford House Publishing
187 72nd St., Fifth Floor
New York NY 10101

Dear Ms. Collins,

I am a published mystery writer whose short stories have appeared in *Modern Mystery* and *Doyle's Mystery Magazine.* I am also a law student and professional hair designer and have brought these interests together in *Only Skin Deep*, my 60,000-word novel set in the glamorous world of beauty care, featuring hair designer to the stars and amateur detective Norma Haines.

In *Only Skin Deep*, Haines is helping put together the state's largest hair design show when she gets a call from a friend at the local police station. The body of famed designer Lynette LaSalle has been found in an Indianapolis motel room. She's been strangled and her legendary blonde mane has been shaved off. Later, when the bodies of two other designers are discovered also with shaven heads, it's clear their shared occupation is more than a coincidence.

Your successful series by Ann Smythe and the bestseller *The Gas Pump Murders*, by Marc Crawford, point to the continued popularity of amateur detectives. *Only Skin Deep* would make a strong addition to your line.

Sincerely,

Bonnie Booth
(513)555-5555

Encl.: three sample chapters
synopsis
SASE

the number of words in your piece. One way is to count the words in five lines and divide that number by five to find an average. Then count the number of lines and multiply to find the total words. For long pieces, you may want to count the words in the first three pages, divide by three and multiply by the number of pages you have.

• **Always keep a copy.** Manuscripts do get lost. To avoid expensive mailing costs, send only what is required. If you are including artwork or photos, but you are not positive they will be used, send photocopies. Artwork is hard to replace.

• **Suggest art where applicable.** Most publishers do not expect you to provide artwork and some insist on selecting their own illustrators, but if you have suggestions, please let them know. Magazine publishers work in a very visual field and are usually open to ideas.

• **Enclose a self-addressed, stamped envelope (SASE)** if you want a reply or if you want your manuscript returned. For most letters, a business-size (#10) envelope will do. Avoid using any envelope too small for an 8½×11 sheet of paper. For manuscripts, be sure to include enough postage and an envelope large enough to contain it.

• **Consider sending a disposable manuscript** that saves editors time and saves you money. If you are requesting a sample copy of a magazine or a book publisher's catalog, send an envelope big enough to fit.

• **When sending electronic (disk or modem) submissions,** *contact the publisher first for specific information and follow the directions carefully.* Always include a printed copy with any disk submission. *Fax or e-mail your submissions only with prior approval of the publisher.*

• **Keep accurate records.** This can be done in a number of ways, but be sure to keep track of where your stories are and how long they have been "out." Write down submission dates. If you do not hear about your submission for a long time—about three weeks to one month longer than the reporting time stated in the listing—you may want to contact the publisher. When you do, you will need an accurate record for reference.

MAILING TIPS
When mailing short correspondence or short manuscripts:
• Fold manuscripts under five pages into thirds and send in a business-size (#10) envelope.
• Mail manuscripts five pages or more unfolded in a 9×12 or 10×13 envelope.
• Mark envelopes in all caps, FIRST CLASS MAIL or SPECIAL FOURTH CLASS MANU-SCRIPT RATE.
• For return envelope, fold it in half, address it to yourself and add a stamp or, if going to a foreign country, International Reply Coupons (available at the main branch of your local post office).
• Don't send by certified mail. This is a sign of an amateur and publishers do not appreciate receiving unsolicited manuscripts this way.
• For the most current postage rates, visit the United States Postal Service online at www.usps.com.

When mailing book-length manuscripts:
FIRST CLASS MAIL over 11 ounces (@ 65 8½× 11 20 lb.-weight pages) automatically becomes **PRIORITY MAIL.**

METERED MAIL may be dropped in any post office box, but meter strips on SASEs should not be dated.

The Postal Service provides, free of charge, tape, boxes and envelopes to hold up to two pounds for those using PRIORITY and EXPRESS MAIL.

Requirements for mailing FOURTH CLASS and PARCEL POST have not changed.

Main branches of local banks will cash foreign checks, but keep in mind payment quoted in our listings by publishers in other countries is usually payment in their currency. Also note reporting time is longer in most overseas markets. To save time and money, you may want to include a return postcard (and IRC) with your submission and forgo asking for a manuscript to be returned. If you live in Canada, see "Canadian Writers Take Note" on page 593.

RIGHTS

Know what rights you are selling. The Copyright Law states that writers are selling one-time rights (in almost all cases) unless they and the publisher have agreed otherwise. A list of various rights follows. Be sure you know exactly what rights you are selling before you agree to the sale.
• **Copyright** is the legal right to exclusive publication, sale or distribution of a literary work. As the writer or creator of a written work, you need simply to include your name, date and the copyright symbol © on your piece in order to copyright it. Be aware, however, that most editors today consider placing the copyright symbol on your work the sign of an amateur and many are even offended by it.

To get specific answers to questions about copyright (but not legal advice), you can call the Copyright Public Information Office at (202)707-3000 weekdays between 8:30 a.m. and 5 p.m. EST. Publications listed in *Novel & Short Story Writer's Market* are copyrighted *unless* otherwise stated. In the case of magazines that are not copyrighted, be sure to keep a copy of your manuscript with your notice printed on it. For more information on copyrighting your work see *The Copyright Handbook: How to Protect and Use Written Works* by Stephen Fishman (Nolo Press, 1992).

Some people are under the mistaken impression that copyright is something they have to send away for, and that their writing is not properly protected until they have "received" their copyright from the government. The fact is, you don't have to register your work with the Copyright Office in order for your work to be copyrighted; any piece of writing is copyrighted the moment it is put to paper. Registration of your work does, however, offer some additional protection (specifically, the possibility of recovering punitive damages in an infringement suit) as well as legal proof of the date of copyright.

Registration is a matter of filling out an application form (for writers, that's generally Form TX) and sending the completed form, a nonreturnable copy of the work in question and a check for $30 to the Library of Congress, Copyright Office, Register of Copyrights, 101 Independence Ave. SE, Washington DC 20559-6000. If the thought of paying $30 each to register every piece you write does not appeal to you, you can cut costs by registering a group of your works with one form, under one title for one $30 fee.

Most magazines are registered with the Copyright Office as single collective entities themselves; that is, the individual works that make up the magazine are *not* copyrighted individually in the names of the authors. You'll need to register your article yourself if you wish to have the additional protection of copyright registration.

For more information, visit the United States Copyright Office, Library of Congress, online at www.copyright.gov.
• **First Serial Rights**—This means the writer offers a newspaper or magazine the right to publish the article, story or poem for the first time in any periodical. All other rights to the material remain with the writer. The qualifier "North American" is often added to this phrase to specify a geographical limit to the license.

When material is excerpted from a book scheduled to be published and it appears in a magazine or newspaper prior to book publication, this is also called first serial rights.
• **One-time Rights**—A periodical that licenses one-time rights to a work (also known as simultaneous rights) buys the *nonexclusive* right to publish the work once. That is, there is nothing to stop the author from selling the work to other publications at the same time. Simultaneous sales would typically be to periodicals without overlapping audiences.
• **Second Serial (Reprint) Rights**—This gives a newspaper or magazine the opportunity to print an article, poem or story after it has already appeared in another newspaper or magazine. Second serial rights are nonexclusive—that is, they can be licensed to more than one market.
• **All Rights**—This is just what it sounds like. All Rights means a publisher may use the

manuscript anywhere and in any form, including movie and book club sales, without further payment to the writer (although such a transfer, or *assignment*, of rights will terminate after 35 years). If you think you'll want to use the material later, you must avoid submitting to such markets or refuse payment and withdraw your material. Ask the editor whether he is willing to buy first rights instead of all rights before you agree to an assignment or sale. Some editors will reassign rights to a writer after a given period, such as one year. It's worth an inquiry in writing.

• **Subsidiary Rights**—These are the rights, other than book publication rights, that should be covered in a book contract. These may include various serial rights; movie, television, audiotape and other electronic rights; translation rights, etc. The book contract should specify who controls these rights (author or publisher) and what percentage of sales from the licensing of these sub rights goes to the author.

• **Dramatic, Television and Motion Picture Rights**—This means the writer is selling his material for use on the stage, in television or in the movies. Often a one-year option to buy such rights is offered (generally for 10% of the total price). The interested party then tries to sell the idea to other people—actors, directors, studios or television networks, etc. Some properties are optioned over and over again, but most fail to become dramatic productions. In such cases, the writer can sell his rights again and again—as long as there is interest in the material. Though dramatic, TV and motion picture rights are more important to the fiction writer than the nonfiction writer, producers today are increasingly interested in nonfiction material; many biographies, topical books and true stories are being dramatized.

• **Electronic Rights**—These rights cover usage in a broad range of electronic media, from online magazines and databases to CD-ROM magazine anthologies and interactive games. The editor should specify in writing if—and which—electronic rights are being requested. The presumption is that unspecified rights are kept by the writer.

Compensation for electronic rights is a major source of conflict between writers and publishers, as many book publishers seek control of them and many magazines routinely include electronic rights in the purchase of print rights, often with no additional payment. Alternative ways of handling this issue include an additional 15% added to the amount to purchase first rights to a royalty system based on the number of times an article is accessed from an electronic database.

PROMOTION TIPS

Everyone agrees writing is hard work whether you are published or not. Yet, once you arrive at the published side of the equation the work changes. Most published authors will tell you the work is still hard but it is different. Now, not only do you continue working on your next project, you must also concern yourself with getting your book into the hands of readers. It becomes time to switch hats from artist to salesperson.

While even bestselling authors whose publishers have committed big bucks to promotion are asked to help in promoting their books, new authors may have to take it upon themselves to plan and initiate some of their own promotion, sometimes dipping into their own pockets. While this does not mean that every author is expected to go on tour, sometimes at their own expense, it does mean authors should be prepared to offer suggestions for promoting their books.

Depending on the time, money and the personal preferences of the author and publisher, a promotional campaign could mean anything from mailing out press releases to setting up book signings to hitting the talk-show circuit. Most writers can contribute to their own promotion by providing contact names—reviewers, home-town newspapers, civic groups, organizations—that might have a special interest in the book or the writer.

Above all, when it comes to promotion, be creative. What is your book about? Try to capitalize on it. For example, if you've written a mystery whose protagonist is a wine connoisseur, you might give a reading at a local wine-tasting or try to set something up at one of the national wine events. For more suggestions on promoting your work see *The Writer's Guide to Promotion & Publicity*, by Elane Feldman (Writer's Digest Books).

About Our Policies

We occasionally receive letters asking why a certain magazine, publisher or contest is not in the book. Sometimes when we contact a listing, the editor does not want to be listed because they: do not use very much fiction; are overwhelmed with submissions; are having financial difficulty or have been recently sold; use only solicited material; accept work from a select group of writers only; do not have the staff or time for the many unsolicited submissions a listing may bring.

Some of the listings do not appear because we have chosen not to list them. We investigate complaints of unprofessional conduct in editors' dealings with writers and misrepresentation of information provided to us by editors and publishers. If we find these reports to be true, after a thorough investigation, we will delete the listing from future editions. See Important Listing Information on page 115 for more about our listing policies.

If a listing appeared in our book last year but is no longer listed, we list it in the General Index, beginning on page 656, with a code explaining why it is not listed. The key to those codes is given in the introduction to the General Index. Sometimes the listing does not appear because the editor did not respond in time for our press deadline, or it may not appear for any of the reasons previously mentioned above.

There is no charge to the companies that list in this book. Listings appearing in *Novel & Short Story Writer's Market* are compiled from detailed questionnaires, phone interviews and information provided by editors, publishers and awards directors. The publishing industry is volatile and changes of address, editor, policies and needs happen frequently. To keep up with the changes between editors of the book, we suggest you check the monthly Markets columns in *Writer's Digest*. Also check the market information on the *Writer's Market* website at www.writersmarket.com, or on the *Writer's Digest* website at www.writersdigest.com.

Club newsletters and small magazines devoted to helping writers also list market information. For those writers with access to online services, several offer writers' bulletin boards, message centers and chat lines with up-to-the-minute changes and happenings in the writing community. Many magazine and book publishers offer updated information for writers on their websites. Check individual listings for those website addresses.

We rely on our readers, as well, for new markets and information about market conditions. Write us if you have any new information or if you have suggestions on how to improve our listings to better suit your writing needs.

Specialized Markets

From the Editor's Chair: *Kenyon Review*'s David Lynn on Moving Online

BY DAVID LYNN

Electronic or online publishing is already a fact of life, no more a matter of debate than, well, the moveable type it threatens to replace. The final hurdles to bits and bytes being a perfectly acceptable replacement for printed pages will be cleared in a year or two, perhaps less. By that I largely have in mind the development of comfortably readable and portable screens. Few people, myself included, want to read lengthy fiction or more than a few poems at a time on current computer screens. But ebooks are coming, and they will be more attractive, lighter, less costly, easier to read—of that we can be certain.

Will printed pages disappear entirely? I don't think so. Publishing books, magazines, even small literary journals has become amazingly efficient. It simply isn't all that expensive to produce type on paper. And many of us will prefer, always I suspect, the tactile pleasures of carrying, of browsing, of poring over a paper page. But over time this increasingly will be a somewhat indulgent pleasure for a limited market. Independent or institutionally supported presses will continue to produce relatively small numbers of books, limited editions that will be attractive, sought after, admired, and enjoyed.

Indeed, this trend towards smaller, regional presses is already happening, driven not so much by the Internet but by the collapse of literary values in New York-based and international publishing. For the multinational corporations that now own and control those large publishing houses, all that matters is profit. Not just adequate or handsome profit, as in the past, but the greatest possible profit, right down to every pinched penny. Poetry, short stories, ambitious literary novels, are growing rarer and rarer on the lists of those houses, the great old names of publishing. Editors pay enormous advances to snare, and spend millions on promoting, the latest blockbusters in mystery, sci fi, and romance, not to mention self-help and sexy diets.

It's presses such as Graywolf and Copper Canyon and Wesleyan and Arkansas, and on and on, that have taken up some of the slack. They are the ones now producing the most exciting new writing, the writing that matters and that shapes us. These and many other small presses produce wonderfully high quality and attractive printed books that also contain first-rate literature.

Yet the small presses face many great challenges, from scraping by on terribly frugal budgets, seeking foundation grants, looking for financial backers, to the practical dilemmas of cracking into national distribution. It is very, very hard to get a book from a little-known publisher into bookstores across the nation. And, of course, the major distributors are themselves increasingly owned by the same corporations as the large publishing houses (not to mention tie-ins with movie and television production companies as well).

It may be that online publishing or other functions of the Internet will help independent presses solve the challenges of wide promotion and distribution. Books may be printed to order

DAVID LYNN *is editor of* The Kenyon Review. *This essay was reprinted from* Without Covers: literary magazines @ the digital edge *(Purdue University Press) with permission of the author.*

(this is already happening); promotions may find creative new initiatives not controlled by the expense of major magazines and catalogues; and, if the book itself ultimately disappears into a cyberspace version, distribution will no longer require shipping a physical object from one place to another.

So far I've failed to mention the rather separate dilemma facing the world of literary magazines, which is my own particular bailiwick. Such magazines have always faced a precarious existence, surviving from hand to mouth, issue to issue, one step ahead of the debt collector. For over a hundred years it's been a simple fact of life that, while literally hundreds of small literary magazines exist at any one moment in the U.S. alone, every year many of them fade from view and memory, while others appear, fresh and invigorating. It's that very freshness, that unexpectedness that has really created a reason for such magazines to exist. They play a role that no other institution can, bringing fresh writers to the fore, offering new editorial visions, moving on.

Even *The Kenyon Review* was forced to close its doors for a decade in the '70s, though many people continue to claim with ferocious passion that they've got an unbroken series of issues on their shelves, including that period as well. And *KR* was nearly shut down again in 1994 because of financial pressures. Since then, we've spent nearly as much time cutting expenses, creating a board of trustees, and launching an endowment campaign as gathering the finest writing from around the world. I believe we've managed to do both.

"There has been a veritable explosion of literary ventures on the Internet. The Internet allows both a straightforward electronic version of conventional magazines and more innovative possibilities, such as works that exploit hypertext, random structures, and text/art hybrids that aren't possible in printed formats."

We provide a weekly feature highlighting one short story or poem from the most recent issue of *The Kenyon Review*, and plan an even stronger web presence in the future. I think this move anticipates other magazines following suit. Many other journals are turning to the Web, viewing it as a complement to their traditional publication, as a source of new possibilities, or as a financial alternative to traditional print.

As long as I'm editor, and I trust well beyond that, however, *The Kenyon Review* will continue to be printed conventionally as well. For me the artifact is a significant part of the pleasure, the experience of reading the poems, and stories, and essays we have gathered together.

But many magazines may not have the luxury of both an online and print format. Institutions are increasingly chary of financing literary magazines—it's hard to quantify just what they receive as a return on their "investment." Greater status? More applications from hopeful students? Increased funding? Academic administrators face straitened budgets of their own and are skeptical about dedicating hefty sums to publications that reach a very limited audience. Editors of independent magazines all too often must dip into their own pockets, and rarely are those pockets comfortably deep. Small wonder, then, that many more magazines than usual have shut up shop over the past couple of years, both famous names and lesser ones.

On the other hand, there has been a veritable explosion of literary ventures on the Internet. E-zines already exist in countless forms and venues, from those mounted by small reading groups in cities or small towns or individual writing workshops, undergraduate endeavors, to sophisticated sites that have sufficient funding for creative enterprise. The Internet allows both a straightforward electronic version of conventional magazines, publishing stories, poems, etc., and more innovative possibilities, such as works that exploit hypertext, random structures, and text/art hybrids that aren't possible in printed formats. Other sites offer specially tailored features. One particularly popular site, for example, is *Poetry Daily*, which publishes a different poem from a new book or magazine every day. Many people have their computers set to default at *Poetry Daily* when they go online. There are many other examples.

Online sites also offer the great advantage of essentially unlimited capacity at very little cost. They can make vast quantities of material available to viewers, either free or for a charge. One new venture is hoping to act as a storehouse for all the short stories ever published. Others already offer work published in hundreds of magazines for sale as individual pieces. The thorny issue of copyright is spinning out of control, and authors rightly worry about their creative work being exploited. Organizations such as the Council of Literary Magazines and Small Presses and Poets and Writers are beseiged by requests for advice from their members, and they are scrambling for coherent policy and response. This will be one of the hottest, most vexing areas of the Internet in years to come. Of that I'm certain.

Another critical issue has to do with one traditional role of a literary magazine: editorial selectivity. In traditional publishing at all levels, editors make decisions about what gets included between the covers and what doesn't. They are exercising their professional judgment. The reputation of their magazine or small press rests on the reliability, more or less, of such judgments. Readers generally have a pretty good idea of what they are in for when they pick up certain magazines or books from reputable presses. Authors who give in to the (often understandable) temptation of vanity presses sacrifice a credibility in the larger community for the sake of seeing their work in print.

But how will this work on the Web? Who will call the editorial shots? How will an intelligent reader know? These aren't little questions. It may be that the greatest challenge to literature and publishing on the Web will simply be the overwhelming-ness of it all. How can one choose intelligently among all the possibilities crying for our attention? How can we avoid the deluge of sites and links and navigational opportunities? While some readers will slowly develop a map of the Web that suits their tastes and judgment, "bookmarking" sites to which they want to return regularly, others will continue to trust the editorial judgments of magazines and small presses, and larger presses too, for that matter. Of course, this is also a false distinction, at least at this early stage of electronic development: many of us already exist with a foot in cyberspace while the other rests comfortably and securely propped on the couch, as we carefully thumb from one printed page to the next.

(See the Insider Report with *Kenyon Review* Fiction Editor Nancy Zafris on page 191.)

Print on Demand: The Pros and Cons

BY JEFF HILLARD

In this new millennium, writers are gravitating toward new outlets for publishing their fiction. One recent, innovative publishing opportunity is called Print On Demand (POD), and it's gaining momentum. Just as kinks exist in traditional publishing, there are certainly risks in choosing a POD publisher, but a number of writers are finding the risks worth taking.

POD publishing meets the twenty-first century demands of getting out a book quickly and into the hands of readers. Traditional publishing, whether it occurs in New York or with a small publisher, just doesn't offer the abbreviated turnaround time as POD does. Also, competition among writers to catch the eye of an agent or publisher is intense, so a writer must find a way to gain an edge. Knowing that competition is grueling, writers may want to supply a market readership with their book as soon as possible. A POD book has the possibility of reaching readers' hands within weeks or a few months, as opposed to the typical year (or longer) turn-around time in traditional publishing.

The major differences between POD and traditional publishing involve printing costs, format, and timely book production. The long, costly process of printing a book on a traditional rolling press that uses materials such as "book plates," film separation equipment, and ink is still intact in major publishing houses. POD publishing, however, circumvents the high costs of using plates and ink by using a digital printer which lays ink directly onto the pages in a pattern determined by a computer code.

While traditional publishers have the flexibility to create different size formats and books, POD technology does not. The POD publisher is always keeping costs as low as possible, and that means POD books are limited to two sizes: $5\frac{1}{2} \times 8\frac{1}{2}$ or 6×9. Keeping these printing costs low by digitizing the text and limiting the format enables the POD publisher to produce a book quickly—usually within weeks.

Another big difference between POD and traditional publishers rests in the terms of a contract. Contracts vary among POD publishers, although almost without exception traditional publishers typically want "exclusive" contracts, guaranteeing them very specific terms and rights. With POD, however, the writer retains most all control over rights—in a "non-exclusive" manner— because the publisher is not as concerned over the editorial or marketing quality of a manuscript. It strives only to sell the book, and is paid per copy sold. The POD publisher makes none of the investments of a traditional publisher, which ultimately gives the writer more control over the process.

The POD contract usually consists of four areas: rights and exclusivity; pricing and royalties; warranties; and termination clause. Additional services like editing, proofreading, or design generally cost extra. With non-exclusive rights the author may, for instance, be allowed to sell book club rights and keep all book club revenue if the chance arises. With non-exclusive rights, the author will likely own the copyright outright and be able to terminate the production contract when he or she desires.

It is always wise for prospective POD authors to consult a literary attorney in going over the

JEFF HILLARD *is a poet, fiction writer, journalist and past contributor to* Novel & Short Story Writer's Market. *The author of four books of poems, he is associate professor of English at the College of Mount St. Joseph in Cincinnati, Ohio.*

contract before authorizing a book's production. Most POD contracts are more simple and accessible than traditional publishing house contracts. Still, an author is hiring a publisher to do work, thus it makes sense to be cautious and not to forge ahead without analyzing a contract.

Assuming you know the ground rules and want to proceed with a POD arrangement, here are the primary advantages and disadvantages to taking that route. A huge benefit of POD is that the author has two choices: he can settle with POD as the conduit for any present or future books, or POD-publish a book with the intent of showing it to an agent or editor at a traditional publishing house. In the POD publishing world, if you want a major publisher to read your work, you can supply an editor or agent with the "book" itself. The old adage that your manuscript—if it's of superior quality—could eventually find a traditional publishing house can now be revised to substitute the word "book" for "manuscript." There could be an advantage to supplying an editor with a book instead of a manuscript—again, if the *writing* attracts an editor's attention. Still, there are never guarantees that any agent or editor will read a POD publication in front of any other intriguing manuscript.

POD is, of course, self-publishing and a first cousin to vanity publishing, yet without the tag of "vanity" attached to it. Although a writer pays a POD publisher to publish a manuscript, the writer essentially has three distinct advantages in using POD over other "bulk-publishing" vanity presses: first, the payment for production of a book is far less; secondly, by ordering copies "per demand" or request, the writer doesn't need to worry about boxes of unsold books gathering dust in storage; and thirdly, the writer can exercise total control over a book's promotion and marketing. This third advantage even gives an edge to POD over traditional publishing, when one considers how little energy publishers today often exert on promoting book, or how quickly they can let books go out of print.

POD publishers want a writer to see the book's production happen quickly, which is an advantage to the writer because the final editing stage of the book can be expedited in a matter of days or weeks, once the book is digitized and printed for proofreading. When POD publishers first surfaced in the late 1990s, turnaround production time for a book was approximately two months. Now, a few years later, production time averages four to six weeks, sometimes less. With several notable POD publishers such as iUniverse, GreatUnpublished.com and 1stBooks, production takes three to four weeks for small books of 50 to 150 pages.

If a writer uses a POD publisher and does not mind the strict limitations on the book's size and "computerized-print" appearance, that's not a disadvantage. But POD publishers are also limited in their ability to reproduce a good deal of artwork in a book, which could be a disadvantage to a writer who expects a lot of photographs or art to accompany text. Still, with POD, color-coded pages appear as high quality, and the paper is not run through the press more than once—contrary to that of the traditional offset press, meaning pages are set up on "plates" so that the press can do bulk or "gang press" printings.

Here are two more major advantages: the digital component in POD ensures that a book never goes out of print, since it's stored as a file. And the printing cost of a single POD book usually ranges between $5 and $12. A book's pricing, depending on the number of pages, may range between $6.50 (60-90 pages) to $25 (400-plus pages). So with the buyer's price less than those generated by traditional houses, consumers may be more likely to purchase them.

Obviously, the ultimate goal of a writer who publishes is to sell books, and the bookstore is a key marketing strategy. But many bookstores have yet to embrace the accessibility of a POD book. There are three major reasons why bookstores shy away from stocking POD books: the unpredictability of the writing quality, the POD book's promotional potential, and the fact that POD books are *non*-returnable to the publisher.

Here's how it works: an author pays a POD publisher to print "on demand/request" one or multiple orders for her book. The customer then *prepays* a POD order and only the number of books ordered will be printed. In very few exceptions is there any inventory or shelving of the book at larger (for instance, chain) bookstores. That's one drawback because browsers won't be able to find a POD book unless through word-of-mouth or intense advertising. An author may have a slight chance at getting an independent bookstore to carry copies of a book, but even that's a dubious proposition, according to numerous POD authors.

Despite the difficulty of getting POD books onto bookstore shelves, the reasons writers go with a POD publisher are numerous, and they tend to be personal.

In the POD publishing world, if you want a major publisher to read your work, you can supply an editor or agent with the "book" itself. The old adage that your manuscript—if it's of superior quality— could eventually find a traditional publishing house can now be revised to substitute the word "book" for "manuscript."

When novelist David Brody decided to publish his first novel, *Unlawful Deeds*, with iUniverse (then known as toExcel), he had a game plan. He first studied all aspects of the fledgling POD industry and became comfortable with iUniverse's contract. He paid the publisher $99, which included costs for formatting and cover design. The publisher handled the ISBN, placing it in Brody's name. He and iUniverse did not pursue copyright registration, because by law copyright occurs immediately once a book is published. The novel did not incur other fees, so Brody could devote other money he saved toward marketing.

Brody had high expectations for his legal thriller, one of which was to use the novel in hope of landing a major traditional publisher for his second novel, *Blood on the Tribe* (which he recently completed). Another expectation involved his marketing plan, one that he could control and give total attention to. And obviously his greatest expectation was to sell copies of his novel—on demand.

Unlawful Deeds was published in late 2000. Brody's relationship with iUniverse was "a positive one," he says. He felt iUniverse put effort into both the production and the promotion of his novel, since the publisher, in its infancy stage, would succeed when an author succeeds. Brody's contract stipulated that he would receive 20 percent of gross sales of the novel; on the average, with the book priced at $16.95, he netted $2.20 for each book sold.

At the same time, iUniverse's growing pains caused a few glitches that affected Brody's novel in terms of on-demand publishing and shipping time. To him, it seemed like "instead of 'print on demand,' it was sometimes 'print weeks after demand'," he says. Still, iUniverse's contract allowed Brody full rights when he optioned the novel to a movie producer.

Brody urges authors to look carefully at distribution issues in the contract. In his experience, POD publishers that have good relations with major distributors like Ingram, Baker & Taylor, and Partners offer the best chance to a writer seeking wider marketing of a book. "Bookstores like to buy from distributors they deal with on a regular basis," he says, "not directly from POD publishers."

Because *Unlawful Deeds* was set in Boston, where Brody lives, he knew the significance of creating a media campaign that stressed the local interest of the novel. He was basically "100 percent responsible for marketing" his novel, and yet an unexpected thing happened: when *Unlawful Deeds* began selling extremely well regionally, he says, iUniverse took a more active role promoting the book.

Brody realized at the onset that writing the novel would nearly take a backseat to promotional demands. He sent out press releases to local papers. He sent copies of his novel to a plethora of online book review sites. He made himself available to local book groups, which he found through libraries and bookstores. When readers began requesting the novel at a few bookstores, the stores "grew tired of special ordering it one at a time," he says, and ordered bulk copies.

Now, months later, Brody's success with his first novel has landed him an agent who is representing his second legal thriller, *Blood on the Tribe*.

Brody's experience shows that POD publishing can be advantageous to the writer, but it's not without residual drawbacks. The chance that a customer will find your POD book on a bookstore's shelves is highly unlikely. The chance that you, the writer, may spend perhaps more time promoting your book than writing it is not exaggerated. The chance for others to know about your book depends solely on your personal goal for the book: you may want two people to read it, or you may want thousands to know it exists. Either way, the POD industry is becoming a viable means for writers to pursue their individual goals for a book.

Brody compares his experience with POD publishing to leaping—hopefully—from the minor leagues to the major league of traditional publishing. "POD publishing is a great way to break in to the game," he says. "And if your book is good, people will notice. You'll have a much easier time finding a traditional publisher for a re-release of your book, or for publication of your next book. And even if the book is not a commercial success, the comments and criticisms you get from readers should help you improve your writing skills."

S.J. Rozan: Defining Space in Fiction

BY W.E. REINKA

Mystery writer S.J. Rozan stocks more varieties of tea in her kitchen than the Empress of China. But she drinks only Fortnum and Mason Queen Anne tea when writing. If you see her with a cup, it means that she's already had her morning shower and walk, two other parts of her writing ritual. No doubt if you're smelling that Queen Anne tea, you're also hearing classical music playing softly in the background. The tea remains the same but the music changes with each book. Rozan chooses only one or two classical pieces, endlessly repeated, to get her through each book.

"There's a Benjamin Brittain piano and cello sonata that is so *No Colder Place*," she recalls. "Hearing it brings the book back." When she uses private eye Lydia Chin as her narrator, Rozan listens to Peking Opera or music played on the erhu, a Chinese two-stringed instrument. Rozan relishes writing rituals. "You need to get yourself 'surrounded.' You need to get yourself in a writing place in order to have the freedom to wander around in that place and that place has to be defined."

S.J. Rozan

Defining space is what Rozan did before she started writing her award-winning Lydia Chin/ Bill Smith private eye series. She worked full-time as an architect. In spite of the fact that her most recent title, *Reflecting the Sky* (St. Martin's), was predicted by *Publishers Weekly* to be her "break-out book" in a starred review, Rozan still puts in about 15 hours a week at the architectural office, specializing in historic restorations.

"You can't work less than 15 hours and convince anyone you're really working for them. They lean so far over backwards for me at my office that I feel like a real churl whenever I consider leaving."

Architects work from blueprints. "Everything, everything is on paper. Builders come to me and say 'you didn't need to put that down, we would've known.' But you can't take the chance." That must mean that Rozan carefully outlines every whodunnit down to the last paragraph in advance. Just the opposite. She works without an outline. "I could never do that in construction," she says with a nervous laugh as she considers the consequences of builders following their whims. But she finds that outlining fiction would confine her.

W.E. REINKA, *who writes frequently about books and authors, contributes to magazines and newspapers nationwide.*

"I usually type the first sentence of a novel long before I should. However, I do have an idea of the setting—fashion world or construction, for instance—and the theme, such as the difference between who you are and who you say you are. Once I have the theme, I expect the book to head in the right direction. It's kind of like you're in New York, and you get in the car and want to get to L.A. You know L.A. is to the Southwest and you head in the Southwest direction. You'll get there eventually. I start a book knowing where I want to end up and sort of the direction." Although she never has worked from an outline, she understands that many other writers need them. "Half the writers I know write with an outline and half without an outline. We're all aghast at the other half."

Following the general direction of her theme keeps her characters and writing fresh. "Characters come alive as you write them. They interact with other characters and react to events in their own way, just like real people. For me, describing everything about the book in advance turns the characters into chess pieces. You find you've assigned them tasks that the person you created would never do. Conversely, by letting characters do what they will, when you're done, the book is alive."

The same way that characters evolve a little at a time, Rozan evolved gradually as a writer. "As a kid, I always wanted to be a writer. Then, growing up, I got bamboozled into the idea that real people didn't become writers, the same way real people didn't join the circus. Somewhere I got the idea you had to have a career and do something useful. Architecture had always interested me, though not in the same passionate way as writing. Of course, real people do join the circus and real people do become writers."

After eight years as an architect, Rozan had such a great job that she knew it wasn't the job that was causing her unhappiness. Finally, she listened when the little voice inside her head said, 'Weren't we going to write a book?'

That little voice was drawn, in turn, to the voice in private eye novels. "That alienated voice over, the person who already knows that the war is over and the good guys lost. That's the voice I wanted, a voice that elicited social commentary and moral ambiguity."

"I found that no one wants to know you on weekend mornings. If you start to write at eight on Saturday morning, you can work until noon before anyone cares. I also would write an hour or two here and there in the evenings. In an hour you can write three hundred words. If you do that often enough, you've got a book."

Rozan is a beautifully descriptive writer with two vibrant central characters. Yet she's not tempted to take on literary fiction. "I don't see a difference between crime novels and other novels. The rap you can put on crime fiction is that there is such a large appetite for it that there's a lower threshold for what's published than in literary fiction. The 'great American novel' has been written a number of times. *Moby Dick* was one. *The Long Goodbye*, by Raymond Chandler, was another. More recently Margaret Atwood—okay, she's Canadian—wrote *The Blind Assassin*, which is a great novel and a great crime novel."

No matter how flexible they were down at the office, Rozan couldn't immediately cut down to 15 hours a week because of a little voice in her head. She had to write first. "I found that no one wants to know you on weekend mornings. If you start to write at eight on Saturday morning, you can work until noon before anyone cares. I also would write an hour or two here and there in the evenings. In an hour you can write three hundred words. If you do that often enough, you've got a book.

"When people asked me to weekend lunch, I'd say 'after twelve.' The important thing is to keep at it—when you don't feel well, when you don't know what to write. I don't have time for writer's block. I learned that from architecture. You can't just tell the client 'I'm uninspired.' Your client expects drawings on time, inspired or not. That's not to say that I don't spend a lot of time looking at the screen. But I never say the hell with it, I'm going to go do the dishes. You're not going to get published just because you keep writing. But you're never going to get published if you stop writing."

Making time to write wasn't the only thing she had to learn when she started her new career. She'd never been a private eye and here she was writing about them. "I made friends with Patrick Picciarelli. He's a private eye and writer himself who used to be a cop. Most PIs, you buy them a beer and you're fine. Pat actually buys me beers. I run stuff, especially guns and procedural things, by him. I do sometimes have mistakes pointed out afterwards. I also get things pointed out that aren't wrong," she says with a laugh. "I subscribe to *PI Magazine* and read a number of books written by private investigators about their careers."

Rozan alternates between focus characters and narrators with each novel. Lydia Chin is first generation Chinese American who lives in New York's Chinatown. She has one foot in contemporary American culture, the other foot in the Chinese culture of her parents. Bill Smith, Chin's private eye partner, is the alternate narrator. He is a cigarette smoking, beer-drinking white male who softens his belly-scratching image with a reverential dedication to classical piano.

Books and websites may have helped train Rozan in the ways of private investigators, but how can she pull off series characters with backgrounds different from her own? "I am pretty sure I get it right. You can learn a lot through research and just observing people. I check things with my Chinese friends. I felt great when a Chinese guy came up to me at a reading and asked, 'Do you know my mother?'

"As for Bill Smith, I don't know why I'm comfortable with him. Lydia, at least, is a girl. Maybe I just absorbed the quintessential male PI from books and movies. I've never been a particularly feminine woman. I grew up climbing trees and jumping off rocks. I'm a feminist but men are not the enemy as far as I'm concerned. If people say I failed to capture others' experience, I can talk about that. But that I shouldn't do it from the get-go? That I can't buy."

Rozan maintains that she's really doing what every writer does—working from imagination. "Can I only write about Jewish women? Jewish women from the Bronx? I suppose there are some people who won't read me because I'm neither Chinese nor a man. Politically, I see the point of the argument—people talk about colonization. I don't have a real answer to the political point except that writing is not a political act in that sense. It's a political act in a much more subversive sense. If I can put Lydia across and get readers to think of her as a real person rather than as a dragon lady or inscrutable mystical presence, then politically I think that's good."

Tamar Myers: Do Not Reject Rejection

BY NANCY E. BAUMGARTNER

When Tamar Myers was a child, slogging along primitive roads in the Belgian Congo, her idea of adventure was getting to school without being eaten by a wild animal. She never imagined that someday she would be titillating the appetites of mystery buffs with her talent as a writer.

Her Pennsylvania Dutch Mystery Series (New American Library) has satisfied readers who are hungry for the caustic wit and irreverent style of the series' protagonist, Magdalena Yoder. Magdalena is an Amish-Mennonite sleuth who runs a bed-and-breakfast in the mythical town of Hernia, Pennsylvania. Myers also writes the Charlotte Antique Mystery Series (Avon), in which a more mannerly, sophisticated main character, Abigail Timberlake, owns an upscale antique shop called the Den of Antiquity.

"Magdalena is one side of my personality, Abigail the other. Mag is 'Tamar Uncensored' and Abby is me with manners," says Myers,

Tamar Myers

who recently finished the eleventh book in the Pennsylvania Dutch Series and the ninth in the Charlotte Antique Series. The first eight books in the antiques series takes place in Charlotte, North Carolina, but recently Myers changed the setting to Charleston because she says the city is "a story in itself."

Myers' life in the Congo as the daughter of missionaries provided rich and unusual experiences for the budding writer. She grew up eating elephant, hippopotamus, and even monkey. Attending a boarding school that was two days away by truck occasionally required splashing through crocodile-infested waters to reach the school. She coped with the dangers of cobras, deadly green mambas, and voracious armies of driver ants that ate every animal (and human) that didn't get out of their way. By age ten, she had finished her first book. "Of course it wasn't published, but I knew then I either wanted to paint or write," she says.

When she was 16, her family returned to America and Myers underwent severe culture shock. "I didn't know how to dial a telephone, cross a street at a stoplight, or use a vending machine," she says. Although she had endured deadly African wildlife, she wasn't prepared for college-style criticism. As an art major, her first drawing efforts brought harsh critical review from a professor. Convinced she could not withstand criticism, she switched her major to writing where—she imagined—a less castigating environment existed. So while continuing undergraduate and graduate study, she continued to write and submit work to publishers.

"I kept finding the manuscript packages ending up back at my door. I was naive enough to believe I might get a positive response in those packages. I didn't know any positive response

NANCY E. BAUMGARTNER *has been a freelance writer and journalist for 25 years. Her feature stories and columns have been published in regional newspapers and national magazines. She is the author of* Cogan House Township-The 1900s *and works as a literary agent with The Omnibus Multimedia Agency in Williamsport, Pennsylvania.*

would come by phone," Myers says. "I would tear open the packages only to read the standard rejection letter, and I'd be crushed. After 10 or 11 years of writing and receiving standard turn-downs, I got my first rejection that was in any way personal. I had set the novel in Tennessee and the editor, who had lived in that area, remembered a particular road in the story. He also wrote that they 'loved the humor but it was uneven.'

"I did not take the hint that the editor was saying I couldn't decide whether to make the book dramatic or humorous," she says. "I could have improved my chances of getting published much earlier and would have profited by listening to what that editor was trying to tell me."

Finally, Myers made a contract with herself that if she were not published by age 45 she would give up writing. Eight months shy of that deadline, Myers was told by an agent at a writers' conference that he loved her work and would "represent" two of her novels for $150 each. "I didn't realize that charging for such a service was a sign the agent was bogus. Although my husband had reservations about the deal, it seemed like a boost of confidence to me. I came home from the conference all excited."

About that same time she got another rejection letter from another manuscript she'd sent out. This time the message from the editor said, "Too short, too international, nice writing." Myers says: "I clamped on to those two words, 'nice writing' and began to edit the book. I lengthened it, made it fit one setting, and sent it back to the same editor," she says. Then one day a phone call came from that editor. "She said, 'I love your book and I want to buy three of them,'" Myers recalls.

While negotiating the contractual maze for her first book *Too Many Crooks Spoil the Broth*, Myers realized the need for an agent and contacted Nancy Yost of Lowenstein Associates. Yost remains her agent for the Pennsylvania Dutch Series as well as the Charlotte Mystery Series, which was subsequently proposed by Avon.

"They wanted a mystery set in the antiques' business. Timeliness is everything and you have to act fast to take advantage of those windows of opportunity. I had the characters and plot ideas back to Avon in about a day," she says. Myers envisioned the owner of the Den of Antiquity dashing through books with titles like the upcoming *Splendor in the Glass* (August 2002) and *Tiles and Tribulations* (May 2003).

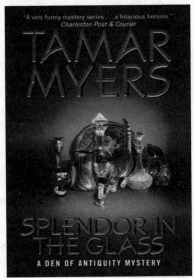

Myers is known for the quirky, theme-driven titles of her books which marketing departments love because they attract readers' attention. "The titles are what sell the books. They are closely guarded secrets until I have the story completed," says Myers, whose contract guarantees she gets to choose each title. It was Myers' idea to use food and folksy, familiar phrases as basic elements in the Pennsylvania Dutch Series that has generated titles like *Gruel and Unusual Punishment* and *Custard's Last Stand*.

"Writing makes me hungry," she explains. "It uses up energy and I look forward to lunch or a snack. I had not read any other food-based mysteries at the time I started writing these, and I thought it would be very clever to do one and to include a recipe every fifth chapter. And I'm superstitious about that. They can't go anywhere except at the end of the fifth chapter."

Writing two series simultaneously requires a disciplined, focused routine. "I write one book completely, take about three days and begin the other book in the other series. During that time off I reread the last book in the series I'm doing next. That puts me back in the voice of the character. I know the main characters in each series better than I know my own siblings because I spend more time with them than with my family."

Myers writes five days a week from 9 a.m to 5:30 p.m, during which she produces about 1,000 words. "My personal style is to edit as I'm going, because in writing humor one line depends on the line before it. I build it line by line and edit, edit, edit. At the end of the day, basically, I have something that is ready to send to an editor. Once the book is done it takes only two or three days to make final revisions. I think this works well for humor but I also think it would work in any genre."

She describes her writing style as "more excavating than creating." Myers says: "I allow my subconscious to uncover what is already there. Letting yourself be receptive and going with the muses, God, inspiration, whatever you call it. I believe it is all there and you just have to let it come out. I let it bubble to the surface and my writing has gotten so much easier and better."

Although Myers uses humor as the framework for her stories, they are constructed on a foundation of more serious issues which the author addresses with subtlety. "I like to explore themes of tolerance, forgiveness, and that someone can change. I think it is better to do it in a subliminal way than to beat people over the head. I don't like to preach. I think one can instruct better by entertaining than by lecturing," she says.

At a keynote address Myers gave to the 2002 Pennwriter's Conference in Harrisburg, Pennsylvania, she told of her 23-year struggle to get published. "Persistence is what you need," she told her audience. "Look hard at your own work. Learn from constructive criticism. Not all criticism is valid but there is a fine line between the self confidence you need to be a writer and the humility you need to evaluate criticism and make the writing better. Critique groups are helpful, but I recommend those based on a specific genre. I also tell writers that they must take criticism and roll it over and, if it is valid, use it. My motto is taken from Kenny Rogers' *The Gambler*, 'you have to know when to hold 'em and know when to fold 'em'."

Myers does not plan to "fold 'em" anytime soon. She is working on what she hopes will be a break-out novel, and whose particulars she's guarding as closely as the titles of her next three series books.

James Lee Burke: The Story is Already Written

BY W.E. REINKA

Spend any time with James Lee Burke and you'll soon realize that this gentle, self-effacing man consciously tries to be consistent with a higher spiritual plane in thought, word and deed.

Odd that such a gentle man would provide some of the starkest (and finest) crime fiction of his generation. Now over 60, Burke has two Edgar Awards on his trophy shelf for Best Novel of the Year from the Mystery Writers of America. The first Edgar came for his 1989 novel, *Black Cherry Blues*, the second for *Cimarron Rose* in 1997. Appropriately enough, that makes one Edgar each for Burke's two ongoing series.

In 2002, *Jolie Blon's Bounce* became the twelfth installment in Burke's first and longest running series which revolves around Dave Robicheaux, a police detective and bait shop owner in New Iberia, Louisiana. Robicheaux is a classic flawed protagonist, a Vietnam veteran whose own violent and alcoholic past gives him common ground with the bad guys he tracks as well as constant motivation in his own imperfect quest for redemption.

Edgar-winning *Cimarron Rose* starts defense attorney Billy Bob Holland's series. Holland works out of Deaf Smith, Texas. Like Robicheaux, ghosts from his past (Holland was a Texas Ranger) still haunt him. His knack for following clients into trouble keeps tension tight as his adventures outside the courtroom are more likely to free his clients than pleadings before a judge.

These days, Burke publishes a new book every year and Hollywood money has fattened his bank account. To borrow one of his favorite metaphors, his career is in "tall cotton."

But life wasn't always so sweet. After being teased with success (he published three books early on), he hit a period which he once summarized as a time when "I couldn't sell ice water in hell." For 13 years—from 1972 to 1985—Burke was unable to publish in hardcover. To this day, he says, "I have no explanation for that period. I wrote many short stories and a number of novels. Most eventually got into print. Several manuscripts came out of that period that did not become publishable in themselves but they formed the material for the trilogy of *The Neon Rain*, *Heaven's Prisoners*, and *Black Cherry Blues*. So out of failure eventually came success."

Burke will tell you that when one is in "tall cotton," friends are easy to come by. One's true friends are those who stay close when our lives are not so lush. Take Philip Spitzer, Burke's literary agent. During that gap in hardcover sales, Spitzer watched one book, *The Lost Get Back Boogie*, get rejected, sometimes virulently, 111 times. Still he stuck by Burke through that long period of short cotton. "Short cotton? Heck, I wasn't even a seedpod," Burke says with a roaring laugh. Ironically, *The Lost Get Back Boogie* was later nominated for a Pulitzer Prize. In turn, Burke has stayed loyal to those who stood by him. Not only is Spitzer still his agent, Burke is still married after 42 years to the same woman who endured those tough times with him. Likewise, he's had the same editor for years.

Just as tough times measure one's true friends, Burke concedes that publishing droughts measure one's commitment to writing. "It is discouraging having people tell you you're short,

W.E. REINKA, *who writes frequently about books and authors, contributes to magazines and newspapers nationwide.*

fat, stupid and got beat on by an ugly stick at birth. But I relearned an old lesson during those 13 years, namely that you do it a day at a time. You write for the love of your art. Every writer knows in his heart that he has a reason for writing. A writer wants to convey to the reader his vision of history. We try to tell the truth in perfect fashion as we see it.''

Despite phrases like "truth in perfect fashion," one might presume that Burke's self-efface-ment would carry over to his writing. That he might point out that he is, after all, "only" a mystery writer, that category fiction is "merely" escapist entertainment, and not high art.

"Every real artist knows ultimately that artistic talent is a votive gift. It comes from somewhere else. The day he abuses it, becomes cavalier or contemptuous or arrogant with it, that is the day it's given to someone else. I've never seen that not to be true."

But James Lee Burke doesn't except himself or his mystery-writing colleagues when he uses terms like "art" or "artist." He is not self-deprecating because he believes that artistic talent—in whatever form—is a gift from God and Burke won't trivialize the Higher Power he sees behind the universe. In place of writing with an outline, he prays. "I pray before I write because I believe the gift comes from outside myself. The story is already written and a writer discovers it in an incremental way. If there's any moment in the week when I see things perfectly clearly inside my work, it's at mass during the consecration. It's like seeing a match struck in a dark room."

Burke is certain the divine muse is not unique to him. He cites how a drunken Jack Kerouac was having a rambling conversation with critic Bruce Cook. "Suddenly Kerouac seemed to have this moment of clarity when he stopped and, out of the blue, said 'You know what your art is? Your art is your Holy Ghost blowing through your soul.' " Burke pauses before adding his own reflection. "Every real artist knows ultimately that artistic talent is a votive gift. It comes from somewhere else. The day he abuses it, becomes cavalier or contemptuous or arrogant with it, that is the day it's given to someone else. I've never seen that not to be true."

Part of Burke's artistic vision is condemning the evil he sees in society. "The stories in my books deal with violence in a very miniscule basis." That may sound strange coming from a writer who sometimes portrays creepy torturers pushing the borders of the bad guy bell curve. But Burke means that heinous individual crimes are miniscule compared to institutional violence. "Violence in this country is a way of life. I often hear people comment about violence in films, violence in books, but my heavens, we export enormous amounts of weaponry all over the world. It's a great evil that robs the poor. We're constructing our doomsday machine. If people wring their hands over violence in art, it's somewhat disingenuous."

The mimetic impulse to write about violence and other aspects of the human condition, not the clever unraveling of elaborate whodunnit puzzles, drives Burke's mysteries. Although his two series heroes both solve crimes, Burke concedes, "I don't know that much about law enforce-ment. If you know your subject matter—which is the nature of people—it doesn't matter what vocational role they occupy. That becomes irrelevant. It's the human story that makes it work. We still watch *Hamlet*, 400 years after it was written, to learn about ourselves, not Elizabethan England. The best book I ever read was Eusebius of Caesarea's *Church History*. My God, the Romans are us. Nothing has changed."

In writing about the human condition, Burke's artistic well provides a wealth of past jobs to draw from, including the "Darwinian environment" of East Los Angeles in the early '60s where he was a social worker. "I lived in a slum. I was privy to an underside most of us are not privy to—gangs and narcotics and people tearing each day from the earth with their fingernails."

His dialogue may reflect speech patterns he overhead on Houston buses or conversations with Kentucky moonshiners. "A good writer learns to be a good listener. The poetry of English is all around us, it's a matter of hearing it. I've read where probably only ten percent of what people say is significant. Writers learn to listen for that ten percent."

Asked if listening to others' profanity, which Burke generally avoids in his personal speech, helps inspire him when a character like Robicheaux sidekick, Clete Purcel, cusses in pithy word pictures, he answers with a laugh. "No one's asked me that before. But that's part of listening. It so happens that when I was just 19, I went to a Louisiana writer's conference to hear Pulitzer Prize winner MackInlay Kantor on 'The Lost Art of Profanity in Literature.' His point was that profanity is an art form because it's the most effective element in the English language. It's monosyllabic, visceral with an iambic cadence. It's a primitive means of acquiring magic. Bang your thumb with a hammer and you swear to make the pain go away."

While Burke struggled for literary success through some of those jobs, he developed work habits that might help other developing writers. He remembers when he was only 20 years old, working on a seismographic crew out in the Gulf of Mexico, when he would alternate working offshore for ten days with five days back home. "I made a rule then that I still follow: Never let a manuscript sit idle for more than 36 hours. I'd come in off the Gulf and clean out my mailbox, collecting all my rejection slips. Then I'd put them all in clean envelopes and send them right out again."

Another of his many jobs was teaching writing at Wichita State University, so he's read a lot of beginners' manuscripts. But when asked about tips he might pass along to writers, Burke doesn't bother with mechanical advice. He reverts, instead, to the spiritual impetus behind art. "Far more numerous people will criticize or denigrate than will encourage or praise. Learn not to take them seriously. Boos and catcalls always come from the fifty-cent seats. Once you know you have the gift, you never compromise. Don't work for money or fame. If you do, you'll have neither. Write whatever you write as well as you can. Put it in the mail and let God be the measure of it. In other words, take care of the bailiwick of the artist—your own creative talent. Creativity is the one area of human experience that allows us to step inside the province of God. Once you're in that cathedral, it becomes a very private place. But there's another presence there. It's that force, that power that gave us vision that others do not possess. It seems like a vanity and terrible presumption but, in his heart, every writer feels that there's a divine fire he gets to share in. It's the greatest gift on earth. Who cares if we're rejected?"

Mystery Markets
Appearing in This Book

Below is a list of mystery markets appearing in this edition of *Novel & Short Story Writer's Market*. For complete information—including who to contact and how to submit your mystery short story or novel manuscript—turn to the page number provided.

Book Publishers

Resources for Mystery Writers

Below is a list of invaluable resources specifically for mystery writers. For more information on the magazines and organizations listed below, check the General Index and the Publications of Interest and Organizations sections of this book. To order any of the Writer's Digest Books titles or to get a consumer book catalog, call 1-800-448-0915. You may also order Writer's Digest Books selections through www.writersdigest.com, Amazon.com, or www.barnesandnoble.com.

MAGAZINES:

- *Mystery Readers Journal*, Mystery Readers International, P.O. Box 8116, Berkeley CA 94707.
- *Writer's Digest*, 4700 East Galbraith Rd., Cincinnati OH 45236. Website: www.writersdigest.com

BOOKS:

Howdunit series (Writer's Digest Books):

- *Private Eyes: A Writer's Guide to Private Investigators*
- *Missing Persons: A Writer's Guide to Finding the Lost, the Abducted and the Escaped*
- *Deadly Doses: A Writer's Guide to Poisons*
- *Cause of Death: A Writer's Guide to Death, Murder & Forensic Medicine*
- *Scene of the Crime: A Writer's Guide to Crime Scene Investigation*
- *Body Trauma: A Writer's Guide to Wounds and Injuries*
- *Just the Facts, Ma'am: A Writer's Guide to Investigators and Investigation Techniques*
- *Rip-off: A Writer's Guide to Crimes of Deception*

Other Writer's Digest books for mystery writers:

- *The Criminal Mind, A Writer's Guide to Forensic Psychology*
- *Howdunit*
- *Writing Mysteries: A Handbook by the Mystery Writers of America*
- *You Can Write a Mystery*
- *Writing the Thriller*

ORGANIZATIONS & ONLINE:

- The Mystery Writers' Forum. Website: www.zott.com/mysforum/.
- Mystery Writers of America, 17 E. 47th St., 6th Floor, New York NY 10017. Website: www.mysterywriters.org.
- The Private Eye Writers of America, 4342 Forest DeVille Dr., Apt. H, St. Louis MO 63129. Website: http://hometown.aol.com/rrandisi/myhomepage/writing.html.
- Sisters in Crime, P.O. Box 442124, Lawrence KS 66044-8933. Website: www.sistersincrime.org.

Red Dress Ink: Hip Novels for Urban Women

BY DAVID BORCHERDING

Ask someone in publishing about Red Dress Ink and you'll most likely hear the term "chick lit"—books about the foibles of hip, young, urban women. *Bridget Jones's Diary*-type stuff.

You might also hear that it's an imprint of Harlequin Enterprises, which may surprise you. These new trade paperbacks bear little resemblance to the frillier, more pastel romances. From the covers of Ariella Papa's *On the Verge* or Sarah Mlynowski's *Milkrun*, you wouldn't suspect the books are even related to their mass-market cousins; the designs are fun and stylish and just a little bit sexy. These are not books you'll have to disguise when you read them on the subway.

"Right now we really want to be known as an author-led, trade paperback, quality program," says Margaret Marbury, editor of Red Dress Ink. "We're buying the best possible books we can get out hands on."

Red Dress Ink saw the publication of its debut novel, Melissa Senate's *See Jane Date*, in November of 2001. The idea behind the relative newcomer to the publishing field is to market books that appeal to twenty- and thirtysomething hip, urban women. And so far, according to Marbury, they seem to be hitting the mark. "I have to say, this has been more successful than I ever imagined. We've had an amazing response. People are buying the books."

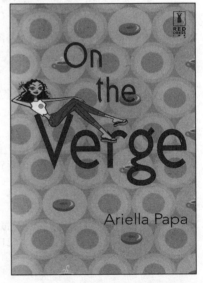

Novels in the Red Dress line are trade paperbacks priced at around $13. Although the submission guidelines say manuscripts should run between 95,000 and 110,000 words, Marbury says authors should really shoot for 85,000 to 105,000 words because the books are heavy on dialogue, which takes up more space on the page. The average initial print run is 45,000, and they plan to release one new novel per month.

The stories aren't romances, but rather edgy, hip tales of young women's adventures in the big city. Thus, Red Dress books are most often compared to Helen Fielding's *Bridget Jones's Diary* or Melissa Bank's *The Girl's Guide to Hunting and Fishing*. Marbury says those comparisons are useful as examples of the kinds of books she's looking for, but she doesn't want mere carbon copies. The manuscripts she buys are books that "imitate the feeling you get when you read *Bridget Jones's Diary*—the feeling of being familiar and relating to this person and saying, 'I've been there, I've totally been there.' And liking her enough despite her flaws that you want to keep going. You cheer for her because you want good things to happen for her by the end of that book, in the same way that you want good things to happen

---

DAVID BORCHERDING *is a Cincinnati-based freelance writer and editor of* Romance Writers Sourcebook, *published by Writer's Digest Books.*

for yourself and your friends. It's that feeling of hope at the end that *Bridget Jones's Diary* delivers."

In like manner, Red Dress books are also ultimately upbeat. "The upbeat ending could be that you know she's not going to throw in the towel," Marbury explains. "She's got things around her that make her happy, and they don't necessarily have to be a man or a fabulous job. It could just be that she's content right now. She's navigated herself to a place where she's happy." Marbury doesn't rule out a romantic ending, however. "Some books just warrant that. You just want it to happen. But they're not romances in the conventional sense, because in many of the books it's not about the guy; it's about something else that's going on in the heroine's life."

Despite what comparisons to Fielding and Bank might make you think, Red Dress novels are not about women who have one bad date after another. Rather, they cover all aspects of being young and female and urban. *Fashionistas*, by Lynn Messina, tells the tale of a woman at a New York fashion magazine who gets drawn into a disastrous plot to oust the editor-in-chief. *Spanish Disco*, by Erica Orloff, is about a celebrity editor sent to Sanibel Island, Florida, to coax another novel out of a Hemingway-like author. Although dating happens in these stories, it is not the focal point.

The heroine, however, is the focal point. Red Dress heroines must be hip and sassy. They can drink or smoke or curse. They don't mind casual sex; sometimes, Mr. Right Now has to stand in until Mr. Right comes along. And if Mr. Right takes his own sweet time, that's fine, too; these women are more concerned with friends and family and career. They want to find themselves before they find a husband. "It's not a cookie-cutter character," says associate editor Farrin Jacobs in an interview on the Red Dress website. "We don't just want the same type of woman in each book. She does have to have a certain attitude; she has to be dynamic. That goes without saying. But beyond that, anything goes. She could fall in love or not fall in love. She could find the perfect career or decide that she's not ready to strap herself down to a job. Red Dress Ink books will be about the journey, no matter what that journey is."

Marbury says she looks for books that she can believe in, that feel authentic. "I want tell-it-like-it-is, realistic stories, stories that reflect real life. A lot of the books I see don't seem real. They feel like the writer made the story up in her head. They seem fake. I don't feel like I'm getting the real experience or the real thing. So the author either hasn't portrayed her character effectively enough, she doesn't *know* the character she's trying to portray well enough, or she's writing about something that isn't close to her or known to her."

Marbury won't buy a manuscript if it doesn't have that authentic feel. She also doesn't want manuscripts in which the scenes are overly descriptive. "Many of writers blow up a scene for too long," she says. "They'll give little stage directions, they'll have their characters walking here and putting cups down. Every single move the characters make, they feel like they have to take the readers through. Authors get so focused in, they lose the thread of the story. Obviously, you can't ignore certain things. But on the other hand, there are greater points and more compelling parts of a story than that. With really good writers, you don't notice their writing so much. You're into the story, and the writing doesn't ever get in the way."

When the writing does get in the way, Marbury often gets bored. "The main reason I get bored is because I see these writers have the problem where the story hasn't evolved or hasn't become compelling enough even to them. They can't focus on the main bulk of it and really portray the characters without doing these things that get in the way and keep you from getting to what the story's about. I'm not saying don't pay attention to details; just pay attention to the right details and ignore the others."

Cardboard dialogue is another thing that causes Marbury to reject manuscripts. Each character in Red Dress books should have his or her own voice. Many times, this isn't the case, and Marbury finds that the author has "five different characters speaking, but it all sounds like one character."

Even though the books are aimed at hip, young, big city girls, Red Dress novels don't necessarily have to be set in New York, Los Angeles, or Chicago. "It's really not as much about the locale as it is about the attitude," explains Marbury. "We're talking about today's modern young woman. That's the key. It doesn't matter where it's set."

Marbury's ideal book has compelling characters, strong writing and an original story—one that will keep her turning the pages. "Editors read so much, we get a little bit jaded. It's frustrating when you're spending time reading stuff that you don't like. I just want authors to give me a reason to turn the page. And if they don't give me that reason, I'm quitting by page 20." She cites *Fashionistas* as an example of a "dream book" that has all of the above. "It's very clever, very fast paced. Very different, in terms of plot and story. You really immerse yourself into the life of this character. You respect her integrity. And it's just really good; it's fun. You feel like you're in New York, you feel like you're at this place, you feel like you're working at this magazine [where the heroine works]. So the writing is there, the story is original, and the characters are completely compelling. You just want to turn the pages as fast as you can."

With those criteria in mind and a limit to publish only 12 books per year, Marbury has to be very selective. "I'm looking for a rainbow of books that fall into this genre, but yet I still need books that are incredible, that really do fulfill the same things that the readers of these types of books are hoping to get when they pick up the book." While that means she can't stray too far from certain expectations, she is still willing to take risks. In fact, she says some of the books coming out in the late 2002-early 2003 season verge on being considered literary novels. Marbury says she balances these with the more traditional books by staggering their release to make sure two less-traditional books aren't released back-to-back. "You can offer something that's vastly different from the month before, and then you may go back to something a little more familiar. So for me, it's all about balance. Taking risks, yet balancing it with your known commercial story."

Taking a close look at the Red Dress Ink website (www.reddressink.com) will give you a sense of the kind of balance Marbury is looking for. One of the best publishing websites out there, the Red Dress site has a wealth of information about the audience it's targeting. In addition to the usual—plugs for the books, interviews with the authors, submission guidelines, chat rooms, etc.—the site also features some interesting, informative and just plain fun features. There's even a free monthly story to whet your appetite. Oh, and don't forget to check out the interviews with Marbury and Jacobs.

It's quite possible the website alone will leave you panting to write for Red Dress. Fortunately, Marbury is very open to new writers. Even though she's flooded with submissions, she's still looking for manuscripts that excite her. "That's one of my challenges. I take on a lot of brand-new writers," she says. "That's the nature of this type of fiction, of women's fiction." Because Red Dress books are geared more toward the twenty- and thirtysomethings, it attracts younger writers who might not have much experience in publishing. "Many of them don't have much writing history—if any. I have people that write for magazines and are freelance writers, but they've never done full-length fiction. And that's the exciting part of it. Any editor will tell you that the best part of their job is acquiring great new books."

See the listing for Red Dress Ink in the Book Publishers section, page 439.

Categorizing Romance: Easy Once You Get the Hang of It

BY SUSAN MEIER

Tammy Hoag, Sandra Brown, Nora Roberts and Lisa Gardner. If these names sound familiar to you, it's because they regularly appear on *The New York Times*, *Publishers Weekly*, and *USA Today* bestseller lists with their remarkable suspense and mainstream novels. But did you know all of these women began their careers as category romance authors? And why not? Category romance is a segment of the highest selling genre in publishing.

Statistics show romance generated $1.37 billion in sales in 2000, and that romance fiction comprised 55.9% of all popular paperback fiction sold in North America. With this established and stable audience, publishers and authors alike constantly seek to please and keep readers.

So . . . what is it, exactly?

If you want to succeed as a category romance writer, you must first do a little legwork. What is category romance? How does it differ from single title romance? Who produces it? Why is it so popular with readers? Why is it such a good foot in the door?

Susan Meier

Photo © Cover Studios

The romance website www.cataromance.com, designed and maintained by a conglomerate of romance readers and writers, defines category romance as: "Books in a line or imprint which have been written to very specific publisher guidelines which include length (all books are printed at the same pre-determined number of pages) and style/tone/sensuality level (each category carries a promise to the reader, and those expectations are clearly stated in the guidelines)."

This sharply contrasts with single title romances, which—like categories—are typically set in contemporary times but place no restriction on style, tone or sensuality level. A reader purchasing a single title romance has no preconceived ideas concerning the level of sensuality or violence, and no assumptions about the story except that it will include a romance, though that romance might not be the book's main focus.

SUSAN MEIER *is the author of over 20 romance novels for Silhouette. She is a frequent workshop speaker on such topics as self-editing, analyzing the books you read, time management, and goal setting. Visit her web page at www.susanmeier.com.*

Single title romances run the gamut from family saga to erotica. Longer, more detailed story lines allow single title authors to throw in a dash of whichever subgenre they choose. A romantic suspense can include elements of humor, or a family saga can be based on a mystery. With no boundaries to this genre, love scenes can be graphic or mild and violence can be in your face or off stage, story dependent.

The single title portion of the romance market evolved from the readers' wish for longer, more complex story lines populated by more complicated characters. At the same time, many category romance authors were eager to create longer, more involved stories with more engaging characters. For this reason single title authors frequently emerge from category romance.

Reading between the lines

But authors also move within the category lines themselves, and category publishers are always actively recruiting new writers to replace authors who have grown within the industry. Which makes category romance a very good foot in the door to the largest market in publishing.

Category romance is very straightforward. Publishers Harlequin and Silhouette divide their offerings into lines which are clearly distinguished by level or degree of sensuality, word count, style, and tone. Each line represents a specific kind of story and promises a certain level of sensuality.

Predictability is the hallmark of the subgenre—not for the purpose of furthering stereotypes or to take advantage of market trends, but to provide readers with a fulfilling experience by repeating familiar story lines with new twists, turns and unexplored avenues of emotion in popular themes.

And they know what they'll get. Readers looking for suspense with their romance know to choose Silhouette Intimate Moments or Harlequin Intrigue. Readers looking for comedy choose lighthearted Harlequin Duets. Those seeking a higher degree of sensuality choose Silhouette Desire or Harlequin Blaze and Temptation, which are the steamier reads.

There's no confusion here; a reader of romantic suspense won't leave the store with a traditional title (unless she was trying something different, of course). Covers, titles and back cover blurbs are created in such a way as to clearly signal its contents. Provided an author did her job—wrote well and hit the right marks along the way—the reader's expectations will be met. When the reader returns to the bookstore later, she knows she can count on this particular line to satisfy her for a few hours and she'll head straight for that series.

Word count also plays a part in the success of category romance sales. A reader looking for an entire night's entertainment has different needs than a reader stealing away for an hour or two with a book. Category romance readers know on sight (those series markers again) which books will take more time and emotional energy and can easily gauge their purchases based upon their needs.

A woman facing a three-hour wait during her husband's surgery will be looking for something totally different than a woman planning to entertain herself for three hours on a beach. Yet each woman can satisfactorily fill those three hours with a category romance novel. She can grab the appropriate book from the shelf based on the easily identified story tone, style and sensuality level, and she's almost guaranteed the satisfying story she wants. It's an easy task.

Psst! Got an easy tip for you

If you are a writer interested in breaking into the category romance market, the publishers have made your task easy, too. While single title publishers leave the doors wide open for style, sensuality level and even story type, category romance publishers distribute tip sheets detailing the requirements for their lines.

Tip sheets for both Harlequin and Silhouette lines can be acquired through eHarlequin, the official website for Harlequin and Silhouette books or writers can send a SASE to the Harlequin/ Silhouette offices. Each line's tip sheet contains the name of the senior editor, the required book length and a paragraph describing the level of sexual tension as well as the types of stories that appeal most to readers of the line. Pay attention to the tip sheets; they're a great tool.

If you're looking at the tip sheets online, you might want to browse the rest of eHarlequin. There are all kinds of useful features like editor interviews, author facts and writing how-tos. Category romance publishers go out of their way to provide the information, tips and tools to help aspiring authors, opening the publishing door, so to speak, so that the most serious writers can get at least a foot inside.

For as valuable as the tip sheets and websites are, editors also advise would-be authors to read, because there is no better way to not only identify the current markets and trends, but also to identify the line that appeals to you as a writer. The best way to discover your particular forte is to read a little bit of everything before you make any decisions.

After sampling from each line, you'll understand exactly what the tip sheets mean when they say that the lines differ in terms of length as well as level or degree of sensuality, emotion and plot. A 50,000-word Silhouette Romance, for instance, typically has a lower degree of sensuality, a high degree of emotion, fewer plot twists and turns and no subplot—if only because the word count is too low to support an overabundance of plot twists and/or subplots. Read a Silhouette Romance and then follow up with a longer, more complex Silhouette Special Edition or Harlequin Superromance. The differences will leap out at you.

As you read, really be honest about which line appeals to you, and also about which line would support your abilities. If you tend to write lengthy stories, it might not be exactly easy for you to limit yourself to a story in 50,000 words. If you plan to use one of the basic plots like marriage of convenience, secret baby or bodyguard for an 80,000-word Special Edition, are you confident you're able to write something fresh or unusual enough to sustain a longer manuscript?

How did she *do* that?

Reading through the lines doesn't merely help you decide what to write but also *how* to write. Every time you thumb through a book by a multi-published category author, you should consider yourself as an apprentice to that author; if you're doing your job and reading closely, you are witnessing everything she did to make that book in your hands publishable. The trick to discovering the author's secrets is to focus on the positive, looking for what the author did right, what appealed to you about the story and what elements of the plot made you turn the page, eager to read on.

Learn from the books already on the shelves by targeting a specific author (or authors) and studying the way her writing evolved over the course of her career. By scouring used bookstores, you can start at the beginning of your chosen author's career with one of her first books and compare that book to her most recent releases. When you compare an earlier release to a current release, the improvements are usually obvious. This is a quick way to see what writing improvements pushed her up the ladder to success.

Take your study one step further by investigating the order in which she made her writing improvements. In the beginning of her career, she probably focused on writing the book. Keep reading her work and you'll notice when she masters the ability to juggle two or three hundred pages of "stuff " and starts to get tricky. It's interesting to see the order in which each individual author begins to get tricky. Sometimes the writing itself gets better. Sometimes characters improve. Sometimes sexual tension spikes to new heights. Sometimes the author's story lines get better. It's fun to watch someone improve by reading her body of work. Plus, as you begin to recognize the different ways your chosen author improved, you should also begin to recognize things you could be doing better in your own work.

But don't stick with the superstars. Make a point of following a bread-and-butter author— someone who has worked within one specific line for several years, who typically writes and releases three or four books for that line each year. Which generally means she attracts readers.

Lots of people read her books or she wouldn't be doing four a year for the same line. If you want to write for that line, do what she's doing. If her books are funny, write funny. If her books are deeply emotional, make yours deeply emotional. If her books contain unexpected plot twists, give your plot some tweaking.

The point of your career in category romance is to become the best you can be by matching your talents, crafting abilities and likes and dislikes to the already existing lines. If you choose the right line, study the market and the craft, and model not only the best, but also the bread-and-butter writers, you have a good shot at getting your name on the cover of one of the books in the most popular genre in the industry.

(See listings in the Book Publishers section for these category romance lines: Harlequin American Romance, Harlequin Blaze, Harlequin Duets, Harlequin Intrigue, Harlequin Presents, Harlequin Romance, Harlequin Special Releases, Harlequin Superromance, Harlequin Temptation, Silhouette Desire, Silhouette Intimate Moments, Silhouette Romance, Silhouette Special Edition, Silhouette Special Releases, and Steeple Hill.)

Emotionally Speaking: Romance Fiction in the Twenty-First Century

BY JENNIFER CRUSIE

Romance fiction is the most popular, elastic, exciting, and creative genre in publishing today, but it's also the hardest kind of fiction to write. All you have to do is convince the modern, jaded, ironic reader that your heroine and hero have not only fallen in love and surmounted all the barriers in their path, but that their love is unconditional and will last throughout time. You must, in short, give your reader not only good narrative, but also great emotional satisfaction. If you're up to the challenge, there are three things you'll need to know.

Jennifer Crusie

Photo © Sigrid Estrada

Know the genre and how you're going to fit into it

A romance is a love story with an optimistic, emotionally cathartic ending which means that a romance can be anything you want as long as the main plot

1. traces a struggle to develop a committed relationship
2. through the unabashed exploration of emotion on the page that
3. ends optimistically.

If your story is about two people who have no problems except for an almost pathological inability to communicate, try another genre. If your lovers don't have real problems that cause a believable struggle, there's no emotional catharsis when they finally commit at the end. And romance is about emotional catharsis.

If your story is about interesting people who have real problems that are written with irony and distance, you're not our kind of people. Irony and distance kill emotional involvement and reader identification, and without involvement and identification, there's no emotional catharsis when the lovers finally commit in the end. And romance is about emotional catharsis.

If your story has interesting characters who have real problems that are written with great passion, but your story ends tragically, we feel your pain, but go someplace else. Dying is easy, commitment is hard, and romance has no room for writers who weasel out by killing people off or leaving them to yearn hopelessly for lost passion. Romance is about optimistic, life-affirming emotional catharsis.

JENNIFER CRUSIE *is the author of* Tell Me Lies, Welcome to Temptation, Fast Women, *and* Faking It, *all from St. Martin's, as well as a number of Harlequin category romances. She's currently working on her sixth novel for St. Martin's Press,* Bet Me.

But understanding the definition isn't enough; you have to read widely in the genre to understand the subtleties therein. If you're a lifetime romance reader, you're way ahead of the game because you know the subgenre you like to read which in turn is probably the subgenre you want to write. If you're not a lifelong reader, you'll have to do your research and narrow down the kind of romance you're interested in. Historical, contemporary, suspense, comedy, inspirational, paranormal, fantasy, the genre is so elastic and so broad that you can write almost any kind of book as long as the central plot is an emotionally true love story, but every subgenre makes its own peculiar demands and you ignore them at your peril.

When you've read at least two dozen titles in a specific subgenre published in the last two years (romance changes radically with the times), analyze what it was in the books that kept you turning the pages and made them satisfying reading experiences for you; that is, find the "good parts." Don't bother trying to analyze them for some non-existent formula or to find what works for "the average romance reader." There is no formula and no average romance reader. You're writing new, original stories for a reader who is exactly like you, only a little bit smarter; always write up to your audience in romance, not down.

Then when you've discovered those aspects of that subgenre that you want to keep, think about the aspects you wanted that weren't there, the things that would have made the stories even better, the characters or actions or themes that you want to read but couldn't find. I loved the wit and romance of Jane Austen and Georgette Heyer, but they weren't contemporary. I loved the angry internal monologues of Dorothy Parker, but she wrote anti-romance. I loved the contemporary romance of Susan Elizabeth Phillips, but her heroines weren't mean enough. I loved romance, but nobody was writing the edgy, angry feminist love stories I wanted to read.

The combination of what you love in your romance reading and what you can't find in your romance reading defines the romance you want to write.

You need to know how to write the story

Romance as a genre is character-based; your characters must have strong motivations for what they do, especially for why they fall in love. If your hero takes one look at the size of the heroine's breasts, and your heroine takes one look at the size of the hero's bank account, and they fall instantly in love, that's not just lazy characterization, that's lousy romance writing. The psychology of the characters will dictate how and why they fall in love, and their growth as human beings will dictate whether or not the reader believes they'll stay in love. That's why, along with researching the genre, it's a good idea to research the psychology, anthropology, and biology of romantic love (a good place to start is Erich Fromm's *The Art of Loving*).

But fully realized characters aren't enough; those characters have to struggle through conflict. Early romances often cast the hero and heroine as antagonists, the I-hate-you-I-hate-you-I-love you story. As the genre grew more sophisticated, this plot began to look as dumb as it sounds. It also makes for weak plots: since a strong conflict ends in a fight to the death (literally or psychologically), casting your hero and heroine as opposite numbers makes it almost impossible to achieve a satisfying ending. Either they compromise to save the relationship, leaving the book with a fizzle of a climax, or one destroys the other, leaving the relationship in shambles. It is possible to make this latter plot work if the destruction creates a phoenix-like transformation in the one who's destroyed, but it's extremely hard to bring off in a genre that's already difficult to write.

Making both the heroine and hero protagonists and giving them a strong antagonist to defeat together not only allows for that fight-to-the-death ending; it fosters the relationship because people who struggle together against a common enemy in pursuit of a common goal form a strong emotional bond.

That conflict, echoed in the struggle to know and trust each other as the relationship develops, must be played out in action. There's a misconception that characters in romance novels don't have to do much besides fall in love and then think about it, and this misconception has led to a lot of interminable scenes where the heroine (less often the hero) sits and ponders her delight/misery/confusion/desire/rage. While some internal monologue is essential, it's a weak characterization and plot device because most thought is rationalization and review. Readers like to see emotion played out in movement on the page because they know that action is character. (If somebody says, "I love animals," and then kicks a kitten, which do you believe—the dialogue or the act? Readers feel the same way.) All that internal monologue is also death to pacing: pages of long paragraphs (as opposed to pages of dialogue and action) become the parts readers skip.

"In most creative writing programs, the unspoken rule is that if you must err, err on the icy side because it's better to be too ironic and detached than to be too emotional and melodramatic. This is playing it safe, and every creative writing teacher who implies this should be slapped. Writing is not about playing it safe, it's about taking risks to put the truth on the page. And the truth in romance is that love makes hot, embarrassing fools of us all."

Finally, you have to write those fully realized characters in active plots that are emotionally true and evident. Every writer walks a fine line between melodrama and detachment, between embarrassing hot and boring cold. In most creative writing programs, the unspoken rule is that if you must err, err on the icy side because it's better to be too ironic and detached than it is to be too emotional and melodramatic. This is playing it safe, and every creative writing teacher who implies this should be slapped. Writing is not about playing it safe, it's about taking risks to put the truth on the page. And the truth in romance is that love makes hot, embarrassing fools of us all. The brave writer is not the one who cowers behind irony, leaving her reader unsatisfied in the cold; she's the one who strikes boldly into burning emotion, drawing her reader into the warmth of catharsis and satisfaction. If you don't have the guts to write emotion, don't try romance: love is no subject for wimps.

So the way to write romance is to

- write fascinating protagonists who fall believably in love and
- struggle to form a relationship and grow as people and partners
- while contending with fascinating antagonists in pursuit of a goal that is vital to them
- in a well-written emotional narrative that shows the conflict in action on the page
- and concludes in a satisfying, optimistic, and psychologically plausible ending that convinces the reader that the hero and heroine will be together until death does them part.

I told you it wasn't easy.

You need to know the romance industry

Publishing is a very strange industry, a place where perception is reality, the landscape changes daily, and an unwary writer can become a nice snack for a publishing house. This is particularly true in romance writing, because the genre has traditionally garnered so little respect and because it has traditionally been written by women (these two things are not unrelated).

So the first thing a romance writer should do is join Romance Writers of America. One of the largest writers' organizations in the country and one of the very few that welcomes the unpublished author, RWA publishes the *Romance Writers' Report*, a monthly magazine with industry news and advice articles; supports several Internet links for writers on topics such as industry, craft, and promotion; holds a national conference that is heavily attended by editors and agents; runs contests for both published (the Rita) and unpublished (the Golden Heart) romance writers; vets new publishers to make sure they can provide authors with viable career options (that is, they sell books); publishes position papers on topics such as contracts, agents, and electronic publishing; maintains a website on the romance genre (www.rwanational.com) and generally keeps tabs on the industry at large and in detail.

Then, with your book written and RWA's education, networking and advocacy behind you, research the market again, this time with the purpose of finding the best market for this particular book. Go back to the books that inspired you and find out who edited them. (You can call the publisher to find out, or ask online on the RWA links; somebody will have the information there.) In your query letter, tell the editor that you really enjoyed the book she edited, then pitch your story to her in two or three sentences that make the characters sound fascinating and their struggle new and different in terms that evoke her emotions. Since you both have the same tastes in reading material, chances are she'll like your book, too. If she turns you down, go to the next novel you liked and query that editor.

The important thing to remember is to do this research after your book is written. The dumbest thing an author can do is find out what's selling at the moment—the hot trend—and then write to that. In an impossible-dream-best-case scenario, the book only takes six months to write, an editor buys it after only six months of submitting, it's on the shelves a year later. So, the book won't hit the market for two years after the author spotted the trend at which point she's not even a wannabe anymore. The smartest thing an author can do is start the trend and be the one everybody else emulates. If you're writing the book that you want to read, the book you have to write, and everybody else is following you, your books will always be the truest and the most exciting. And readers notice that.

If all of this sounds difficult, it is. But it's not impossible; the *Romance Writers' Report* lists an average of half a dozen first sales every month, and the romance market is booming. Even so, it's a market that only embraces true believers. If you really love and respect the genre, and you're willing to work hard to learn your craft, and you're brave enough to take huge emotional risks on the page, you, too, can have an optimistic, emotionally satisfying ending.

Welcome to romance writing. You're going to love it.

Romance Markets Appearing in This Book

Below is a list of romance markets appearing in this edition of *Novel & Short Story Writer's Market*. For complete information—including who to contact and how to submit your romance short story or novel manuscript—turn to the page number provided.

Resources for Romance Writers

Below is a list of invaluable resources specifically for romance writers. For more information on the magazines and organizations listed below, check the General Index and the Publications of Interest and Organizations sections of this book. To order any of the Writer's Digest Books titles or to get a consumer book catalog, call 1-800-448-0915. You may also order Writer's Digest Books selections through www.writersdigest.com, Amazon.com or www.barnesandnoble.com.

MAGAZINES:
- *Romance Writers Report*, Romance Writers of America, 3707 FM 1960 West, Suite 555, Houston TX 77014. (281)440-6885. Fax: (281)440-7510. E-mail: info@rwanational. com.
- *Romantic Times Magazine*, 55 Bergen St., Brooklyn NY 11201. (718)237-1097. Website: www.romantictimes.com.
- *Writer's Digest*, 4700 East Galbraith Rd., Cincinnati OH 45236. Website: www.writersdig est.com.

BOOKS:
- *How To Write Romances (Revised and Updated)*, Writer's Digest Books.
- *Keys to Success: A Professional Writer's Career Handbook*, Attention: Handbook, Romance Writers of America, 3707 FM 1960 West, Suite 555, Houston TX 77014-1023. (281)440-6885, ext. 21. Fax: (281)440-7510. E-mail: info@rwanational.com.
- *Writing Romances: A Handbook by the Romance Writers of America*, Writer's Digest Books.
- *You Can Write a Romance*, Writer's Digest Books.

ORGANIZATIONS & ONLINE
- Romance Writers of America, Inc. (RWA), 3703 FM 1960 West, Suite 555, Houston TX 77068. (281)440-6885, ext. 21. Fax: (281)440-7510. E-mail: info@rwanational.com. Website: www.rwanational.com.
- Romance Writers of America regional chapters. Contact National Office (address above) for information on the chapter nearest you.
- Romance Central website: romance-central.com. Offers workshops and forum where romance writers share ideas and exchange advice about romance writing.
- www.writersmarket.com.
- www.writersdigest.com.

Telling the Old Stories, and Making Up the New Ones

BY BARBARA CHEPAITIS

When people ask me where my story ideas come from, I'll often tell them what professor and poet Judy Johnson taught me in a class on myth and folktale—there's only one story. We just keep telling it in endless variation. People think I'm being humble when I say that sort of thing. Actually, as St. Theresa said, humility is truth; I'm just being honest.

There are story patterns. We repeat them endlessly. Moreover, this is good. And moreover, this may be especially visible in the realm of science fiction, which tends to carry the Mythic energy of our era, since twenty-first century folk believe in science and technology as a saving force.

I might never have noticed the connection, except that when I was in graduate school I started a storytelling trio called The Snickering Witches. We were all writers, so our motto was we tell the old stories, and make up the new ones. The first half of the motto meant learning and telling a wealth of stories that spanned many cultures and times. The second half, for me, meant writing a series of science fiction novels. Combining these two elements at one time allowed me to see the infinite variety of some very standard patterns in stories old and new.

Barbara Chepaitis

Photo © Leif Zurmuhlen Photographer

Though I saw the storytelling as a sort of sidebar to my writing life, it wasn't long before I fell head over heels in love with both medium and material. There were tropes and characters in these magical old stories that defied logical explanation, yet had the feel of truth. Dreamlike, the images haunted me even when I had no idea what they meant. They hit my old brain, where all the good stuff resonates.

And what I tumbled to quickly was that these old stories, cleaned through the teeth of many generations of tellers, had a lot to teach about writing. Within folktales there were a closet full of skeletons to hang modern flesh on for both plot and character. After a little study, I realized that I wasn't the only writer, and certainly not the only science fiction writer, to get this.

When Rodenberry latched onto the idea of putting a bunch of people on the Starship Enterprise and tossing them into space, he was recreating the Odyssey (Greece), Malduin (Celtic Isles), The Magic Brocade (China), and many other stories that send their heroes out into the world, to boldly go.

This may be the most obvious example, but a quick study gives plenty more. There is the

BARBARA CHEPAITIS *is author of* These Dreams *and* Feeding Christine *(both mainstream novels), as well as* The Fear Principle, The Fear of God, *and* Learning Fear, *a science fiction series.*

Underworld Journey as taken by Persephone, the Goddess Innana and others. It's mirrored in contemporary fiction by, believe it or not, *Silence of the Lambs*, where Clarice Starling goes down, down, down to face Hannibal Lecter, then Buffalo Bill and finally, of course, her own fear because ultimately that's what the Underworld Journey story is about. Though Thomas Harris probably never heard of Innana, he certainly knew the story of another Paschal Lamb, and whatever you believe in religious terms, the story of Christ is a prime example of an Underworld Journey.

Then, there is the hero story of, for instance, Luke Skywalker, which mirrors the Hero Twins of Navajo legend, who also go through a lot of trouble to locate the paternal force. Then again, there must be obstacles, or else it's a vacation, not a heroic journey.

There is Heinlien's *Stranger in a Strange Land*, and Tolkien's *Lord of the Rings*, and there are all the folktales about the youngest, seemingly weakest and most foolish, daughter or son, who is also the only one able to complete the required task. Indeed, it is exactly what everyone calls foolish about them that sees them through.

The point of all this is that we need to retell this stuff. Each generation must learn these lessons in a way that connects specifically to their time and issues. For our times, science fiction and horror are often the medium of re-telling. These genres represent some fundamentally modern (or is that post-modern?) beliefs. A lot of people who have serious questions about the existence of God—and those who don't—believe most firmly in science, technology and, alas, the possibility of the horrific. While the technology of magic needed no explanation in the Middle Ages, the magic of technology needs no explanation in our day. When Mr. Scott says he'll just Recapitulate the Whoositz into the Technobabble, we believe him without question.

Therefore, science fiction and horror genres can carry magic for us in a way we might not allow mainstream stories to do. And genres tend to be patterned, so they take on the patterning of folktale more readily. In fact, we are set up to expect patterns in genres. In mainstream fiction, we may not be.

Having said that, let me contradict myself and say that folktale and myth are also useful and present in mainstream literature. Read my mainstream novel *Feeding Christine* and you'll see exactly what I mean. Think about Cinderella, and *Memoirs of a Geisha* or *Pretty Woman*. Hero stories, and *Angela's Ashes*. Patterns may not be followed exactly—in fact, some of the pleasure may be in deliberately breaking them—but there's something about the people in these stories, an archetypal quality to their journeys.

Are you getting the idea? Does the word ubiquity come to mind? Okay, then. The next question is "So what? How does this knowledge serve me?" The answer, of course, is that it depends. It depends on what you're writing, and how you tend to write it.

If you struggle with narrative structure and plot, a useful exercise is deliberately translating folktales into modern forms. If the nuance of character is your nemesis, correlating your character to one in folktale or myth can help. Jungians claim that these characters are archetypes—bundles of energy that existed long before writing, which still ring true because they connect to our deepest imaginings, yearnings and fears.

They also say that each character in a folktale is a piece of our psyche, trying to achieve wholeness by integrating with other pieces, which is why there's so often a marriage at the end. It's not really about the benefits of wedlock, but about the male and female within one's self working together for the common good, at last.

Whether you believe that or not, there are certain figures whose outlines are familiar to us all. The King. The Trickster. The Wise Woman. The Witch. Though these figures may seem one-sided as portrayed by Disney, if you read the folktales that generated them, they are often riddled with moral ambiguity and complexity. The Witch is terrifying, but she has something to teach. The King's power is large, but he is limited. The Trickster's chaos creates a better world.

Knowing this, you may want to ask yourself if you have a King/Queen, Witch/Warlock, Trickster, Hero or Fool among your imaginary friends. If so, are they dealing with their issues, integrating well, and do they follow or break the patterns we've seen them in before?

Over time, you might even begin to see your own issues emerging in the particular problems and complexities you make your characters face—not that you have issues, of course, and if you did, you'd certainly never ever work them out in your writing. This is all purely an intellectual exercise. Ahem. Let's just move right along.

You can make choices about whether you want to try variations on these tropes, or work against them to create something jarring. If *Silence of the Lambs* worked with the pattern, *Hannibal* worked against. That can be fun, too.

What you do also depends on how you write. For myself, I'm not rational when I'm writing. Ask my family or friends. For instance, when I wrote *The Fear Principle*, *The Fear of God*, and *Learning Fear*, I wasn't asking if my protagonist and Archetypal Wild Woman, Jaguar Addams, was up to Jungian snuff. I just danced with her energy, recognizing it as special and rather large, hoping to successfully transfer it to the page. I put my analytical mind on hold, in deference to image, emotion, sound and fury.

But when I edit, I do like to think, so at that point I'm asking myself where I might be sticking to or breaking the rules of the Mythic world.

I'll also use the old stories when I feel a little stuck in a piece. I find it helpful when I'm in a writing hole to ask myself what story I'm retelling. What archetypes, what tropes, what magic is here? Knowing this can lead me to solutions.

In *The Finite Heart*, a screenplay I wrote with my partner, Steve Sawicki, we were well into the third draft when I began to feel as if one of the main characters, Paul Ryder, was flat in some way that was small and subtle, but crucial—you know the feeling. I re-read it to see what folktale it most closely resembled. Only then did I recognize the Camelot elements in the thing. Though the world of this screenplay doesn't resemble anything vaguely Arthurian in physical set-up, time or place, the psychological factors were all there. Paul Ryder was facing the classic Arthurian dilemma of how political systems are often defeated by the complexities of the human heart.

Huh. Who knew my brain would spit that out? On the last draft, we took advantage of this, highlighting his emotional arc as he became aware of the limits of perfection. For me, it's in editing that these things become apparent.

This may not be true for you. Some writers I know actually believe writing is a rational process. I let them have their fantasies. If that's yours, you might want to walk through the old patterns in a detailed, more conscious way as you write.

Now, here's one last morsel of thought.

The motto of my storytelling trio—'We tell the old stories and make up the new ones'—is from a Seneca tale about where stories come from. In it, the Story Stone tells a little boy all the original stories of creation. When she's done, the boy is terribly disappointed because he loves stories so much he just wants more and more.

But she's told him all the old stories, and though he must remember them and tell them always, now he must also go and make up the new ones.

Boldly go, and do the same.

Teri Jacobs: At Home in Horror

BY ALICE POPE

Along with writing, author Teri A. Jacobs has a great love of creating decadent desserts. Raspberry torte, blueberry lemon pound cake, Grand Marnier brownies, meringue bones, eyeball truffles, graveyard cake. In baking, as in life, Jacobs seems to have a gift for balancing the sweet and the gruesome, assuming the roles of both a stay-at-home suburban mom and author of horror. "My mother-in-law wonders how someone so bubbly and bright can be so dark in her writing," says Jacobs, whose first novel, *The Void* was released by Leisure Books in 2002. "Others wonder how a mother of two can be so dark and disturbing."

Jacobs says her style of writing could be described as "lush, dense, poetic, imagery-laden, visceral, purple. But I'd call it livid, like a bruise." Here's what *Publishers Weekly* says about *The Void*: "Alternating between the real world and the netherworld of Xibalba, a hellish realm where demons torture unfortunate souls, Teri Jacobs's debut novel covers the gamut of gruesome ways to die. And there are many, which this book describes with blood-curdling clarity."

Photo © Bob Meyer

Teri A. Jacobs

Before penning *The Void*, Jacobs amassed an impressive list of credits in just a few years, publishing more than 20 stories in anthologies and magazines such as *Dark Testament*, *The Bible of Hell* (from which her story "The Darker Deceit" has been nominated for the Pushcart Prize), *Decadence 1 & 2*, *Divas of Darkness*, *Gothic.net*, and *Flesh & Blood Magazine*. She's sold about 75 percent of the stories she's written and was first published at age 13.

A champion of horror writing, Jacobs jumps to the defense of her genre to critics who find horror without artistic merit as literature. "Right, Dante never wrote about Hell; Shakespeare never wrote about witches or ghosts or murder; Milton never wrote about scores of fallen angels and paradise lost; Conrad never wrote about the heart of darkness; Poe never was the master of dread."

Here Jacobs talks about horror, and even scarier topics like self promotion and book signings. She tells how she found her editor at Leisure, discusses the value of networking, and even gives us a glimpse into her bedroom.

ALICE POPE *is supervisory editor of Writer's Digest Books annuals division, and editor of* Children's Writer's & Illustrator's Market.

What is horror?

Horror is not a genre but an emotion and an experience. Any literature that evokes a deep, resonating feeling of dread or terrible awe is horror. Any form that evokes the use of myth and other supernatural elements and expounds upon drama and tragedy is horror. Sophocles' "Oedipus Rex" is sublime horror—a man who accidentally kills his father and unknowingly marries his mother, who finds his mother dead from hanging herself in shame of her deed, who gouges out his own eyes, crying "No more, no more shall you look on the misery about me, The horrors of my own doing!"

People assume horror fiction resembles the B-rate gore-fest movies, and this has degraded respect for the horror label. Publishers reinforce this image by smacking clownish-creepish art on the covers. And as a whole, the horror genre suffers because it isn't being touted as serious work. But, horror deals with how ordinary characters deal with extraordinary situations, and nothing is more serious than the survival of humankind, the world, and all its goodness.

How did you hook up with your editor at Leisure?

I cheated. I met Don D'Auria, the editor of Leisure Books, at a World Horror Convention and had the fortune to sit near him on the hour-long shuttle ride to the airport. I drilled the poor man for information about his tastes in books and in horror, what types of submissions he'd seen too much of, what he'd like to see, etc. Armed with this information, I tailored my first novel to match his interests. I pitched *The Void* at the next convention, and the rest snowballed into approval of the proposal and acceptance of the completed manuscript within three months of submission.

What conventions do you regularly attend? Why is attendance at these events important to an author's career?

Since 1998, I have attended the World Horror Convention every year. Its location varies, but I've traveled to Atlanta, Denver, Seattle, Chicago and will go to Kansas City in 2003 and London in 2004. I've also enjoyed the Stoker Award banquets for the last three years. This summer I'll attend Dragon*Con for the first time and plan on hitting a future World Fantasy Convention.

I believe conventions boost a writer's career because you meet the editors, other writers (established, mid-list, newcomer . . . connections every one), and fans and step into the light as a face instead of merely a name. People respond to people, not names, not biographies, not websites, not fan clubs. As a perk, you'll edge off the slush pile, establish yourself as part of the writing community, make long-lasting friendships, and soak in all the advice and support your spongy mind can handle. And it's a lot of fun.

Your first book signing was a group signing in New York. What did you learn from it?

After the Barnes & Noble put 15 horror authors in the back, in the music section of all places, I learned that the general consensus in the publishing business is that the genre should be swept under the rug. Luckily, fans found us and the signing went well. Only one copy of *The Void* was left! Horror may stay in the dark but will never die.

What's your advice to other first-time novelists in regard to marketing and promotion?

I would suggest all new authors, after signing their first contracts, find out what their publishers (and agents, if they have one) will provide in the way of marketing. Every house differs. The first thing an author needs for the book is quotes or blurbs for the jacket and the inside praise page. For *The Void*, I made all the personal contacts with the authors/editors and supplied the uncorrected proof.

Next in the course is advance critic reviews. The galleys are used for this since an actual book has yet to be produced. Some publishers/authors have the galleys professionally bound before they present them to reviewers; however, Leisure Books sent out the unbound galleys and *Publishers Weekly* still previewed the work in their mass market notes. I wished I had researched which publications reviewed galleys and had copies made and sent to them for advance reviews. The more reviews, the more padded and impressive your press kit will be.

Which brings me to the third directive. Contact every local media source (keep meticulous records), spark their interest in you and your novel, and follow-up on every lead. Once you have author copies of your book, send one to every suitable reviewer your publisher has excluded (as a member of the Horror Writers Association, I had access to a comprehensive list of reviewers—use your organizations to your advantage). Free publicity is the name of this challenging game.

My last bit of advice—join writers', garden, church, golf, dance, any and all groups. It might go against the grain of being a reclusive writer, but if the public, the potential audience, doesn't know about your book, then your book might sit on the stores' shelves gathering dust instead of fans.

Can you tell me about the novel you're currently working on?

I finished my second novel, *Shadow of Jezebel*, and am currently editing the style down for Leisure Books. *Shadow of Jezebel* is a gothic novel, darkly beautiful, despairing and heavy in horror. It begins with the Grigori, fallen angels, escaping their prison in Heaven. These are the Seraphim that disobeyed God, sought relations with human women and fathered the Nephilim, the race of giants which gorged upon all the beasts and men, which were annihilated by the Archangels and God's Flood. Now, the Grigori want to bring back their sons and force Rani into becoming the mother host of horrors. The novel involves Rani's sorrow and terror—the murder of one infant son, the monstrous and unnatural incubation of another son, and the threats of her son's murderer, who wants her as dead as her boy.

After I edit the second manuscript, I'll return to my third novel, *Virtu in Flesh*, but will give nothing more than it deals with an artist, his paintings, and the seductive evil which escapes from the frames.

Do you ever scare or disturb yourself when you're writing?

I rarely scare myself. Although, when I proofed *The Void* at night all alone in the house, I did get the creeps. More often a particular scene will disturb me, not always because of the extreme graphic nature but sometimes because of the emotional impact. When I write about matters of the heart, especially the vulnerable, painful and broken aspects, it's as if I'm living, or even possibly reliving, the hurt. Quite disturbing for someone like me who denies her sensitivities.

You have an unusual stained glass window in your house. Will you describe it?

In my bedroom, a half-round stained glass window pictures a nighttime cemetery scene—storm-violet sky, pearly full moon, eerie streaks of clouds, old stone grave markers, wrought iron fence with blood-red roses intertwined. The main figure of the glass is the Grim Reaper. He seems as if he's coming through the glass, his sickle thrust forward, intent on taking souls.

Virginia Woolf says every woman needs a room of her own. My bedroom, although shared with my husband at night, is mine during the day when I write. I have all my mythology books, my creepy painted wooden masks, paintings of angels of death and pagan gods, and the stained glass. Elements of fantasy and horror, always inspiring the darker side of me.

Greg Bear, On the 'New Frontier' of Storytelling

BY W.E. REINKA

Science fiction writer Greg Bear has enjoyed a lot of accolades as a bestselling author—multiple Hugo and Nebula Awards, science consultant to PBS, member of the National Citizens Advisory Council on Space Policy, lecturer to the FBI, scholar and researcher into varied scientific and cultural subjects. However, the compliment he might most enjoy is "storyteller."

Once a college English major, he says "Quite often when we come out of academics, we're taught about style, theme and symbols but we're not taught much about simple storytelling. Let me tell you, for writers, the hardest of all of these things is 'simple' storytelling, telling a tale that someone wants to read to the end. Most readers don't give a damn about style, they care only about the story and readability."

He cites Leo Tolstoy's "sprawling panoramas of history" to make his point. "Daubed with war, adultery, peasants, yearning women and wild men—subject came first, not effect, not what today could be called mood, form or style."

Greg Bear

Bear has obviously thought a lot about his craft and profession and, in discussing literature and writing, he sounds professorial himself. He elucidates how "soft" science fiction usually involves a distortion of possibilities that's more attitudinal than "hard" science fiction and how, traditionally, the "hardest" science fictions are those based on physics or astronomy—mathematically dependent sciences. Some critics are reluctant to give up their spaceships and see biological sciences as being somewhat lower on the scale than astrophysics. Bear disagrees. "I regard biology as even harder to understand than physics."

While many readers would categorize the bulk of his work as "hard" science fiction, Bear doesn't see himself as being much different than any other novelist. "I've always tried to write convincing fiction. If you write a regular mainstream novel in a realistic form, you get your facts straight. And if you write a novel that's set in the future you get as many of your facts straight as you possibly can."

After writing novels and stories based upon physics earlier in his career, Bear has focused on the biological sciences since the publication of *Blood Music* (Arbor House). Last year, he followed the Nebula Award-winning *Darwin's Radio* (Del Rey) with a biological thriller, *Vitals* (Del Rey), and he plans to stay in that territory with the forthcoming *Darwin's Children*. In many ways, biology—genetic engineering and the like—is this century's new scientific frontier

W.E. REINKA, *who writes frequently about books and authors, contributes to magazines and newspapers nationwide.*

the way that space travel represented the frontier in the last century. These days, Bear isn't writing about distant galaxies 500 years in the future. He's writing about what is happening, or could happen—the line is blurred—here and now with all the societal and ethical considerations that accompany uncharted territory. Therefore, beyond biology, he relies on sociological and psychological sciences to make his stories more convincing.

Just as Bear hates to see people diminish one science at the expense of another, he detests the snobbism that diminishes science fiction relative to other literature. He tries to embrace all good literature, regardless of its so-called genre. In discussing how many modern short stories don't seem to have a point, he is as likely to cite a literary touchstone like James Joyce's *Dubliners* as the works of Ray Bradbury. Bear puts it this way, "Any science fiction, even Wells's, is stealth literature—it flies beneath the establishment's radar."

Greg Bear began flying under the establishment's radar when he was 15 and got a story published in *Famous Science*. He was already well read. "My influences come from all over the territory as long as they involve the fantastic and imagination. At the age of seven, I was scared watching a Ray Harryhausen movie called *20 Million Miles to Earth* and the Monster from Venus came out of my bedroom wall at night and threatened to eat me. I screamed and said, 'Hey that's for me. That's what I want to do to other people.' It wasn't just the fright. It was the incredible excitement involved in watching this peculiar beast or reading comic books and wondering 'Gosh, how could you do that?' I read all sorts of things—Tom Swift and Edgar Rice Burroughs, eventually Ray Bradbury and E.E. "Doc" Smith. After that, Brian Aldiss, Isaac Asimov and Robert Heinlein. The first legitimate science fiction novel I ever read was Robert Heinlein's *Red Planet*. I didn't just read science fiction. Any thick book appealed to me. That's how I got introduced to Tolkien. By the time I got to college, I had a pretty good grounding in literature."

Before he entered college, Bear was writing, drawing and experimenting with movie special effects. He remains avidly interested in movie effects and has even illustrated some of his own books.

"I started going to science fiction conventions, hanging out with writers and listening to what they had to say. That's still possible today for a kid of 16 or 17 or 18. Science fiction is a fairly accepting community, open to someone who shows little signs of intelligence or enthusiasm. What do writers need to get the conversation going but enthusiastic kids hanging around listening to them?"

The teenage writer began observing other writers. "By hanging around listening and watching how writers behaved, I learned what I liked and what I didn't like about what they did. My mentor essentially became Ray Bradbury." Later Bear met his eventual father-in-law, science fiction legend Poul Anderson. "Poul Anderson seemed a very civilized, kind and intelligent man. I took bits and pieces from various parts of writers' careers and said to myself, 'That's what probably I should be doing.' I slowly put together a kind of voice. Early on, I was more derivative. At 14 years old, I was writing an Edgar Rice Burroughs pastiche or trying to figure out Star Trek screenplays."

The successful writer who remembers hanging around famous writers as a kid tries to be accessible himself. Leave a message at www.gregbear.com and chances are you'll get a personal answer. Bear grimaces when writers act in any way other than what comes naturally and he positively rails against contrived coolness. "If you think being a writer is cool, you've probably already lost the battle."

So if being cool isn't what it takes to be a writer, what does it take?

"The simplest answer is that you have to write. Set time aside each day, even if it's only a half an hour. If you write just a page or half a page a day, at the end of the year you'll have the substantial portion of a novel. Sometimes writers spend too much time trying to imitate the successes that are all around them and that becomes derivative. Focus on what you have to say.

You really do have to find out what's inside of you that's worth the 'beer money' of the reader audience, as my father-in-law, Poul Anderson, used to put it.

"When you're looking for that thing inside yourself that's valuable, I say, 'Write about what you love and write about what scares you.' If you can be honest about those things, you'll have a story because you'll have the conflict and you'll have the unresolved problem that you'll have to deal with. If you're writing about what you love, you might have stories that are perfectly resolved and quite happy. If you're writing about what scares you, you may sometimes have a story that's not quite resolved. If you write about what you love and if what you love scares you, then you may have the 'great American novel.' "

Bear warns beginning writers about getting stagnant. "Don't just sit down and write one story or one novel endlessly year after year after year. The perfection of one story will not advance your career. If you take the Ray Bradbury technique and focus on short stories, you should probably write a story every week."

"Put your work aside, put it in the cave and wrap it in a moist cloth and see if it ferments and becomes wonderful. Pull out your work after it's cooled down in your mind. Then take a look at it and revise it. The white-hot heat of writing can sometimes lead to spontaneous and immaculate genius but very seldom. Revising is the real art in writing."

Weekly writing does not mean rushed writing. "Put your work aside, put it in the cave and wrap it in a moist cloth and see if it ferments and becomes wonderful. Pull out your work after it's cooled down in your mind. Then take a look at it and revise it. The white-hot heat of writing can sometimes lead to spontaneous and immaculate genius but very seldom. Revising is the real art in writing."

Only after the story is revised and rearranged to the writer's satisfaction, should it be shown around. "When you have a manuscript commented upon, wisdom is knowing when not to take advice. Your instincts have to rule. If an editor tells you something needs to be changed, you may want to change that story. But if the change completely ruins the story for you, you may want to move to another editor or publisher."

Bear's own work is sometimes a process of self-discovery. "Quite often after I develop a story, I then find out what's important to me in the story and I emphasize those aspects. Your voice is emphasizing what's important to you. When your prose style comes naturally, when it's the way you write and the way you talk and sometimes almost the way you walk, sometimes that's a natural genius. That sort of natural voice extends over many bestselling writers and indicates that they're true storytellers."

True storytellers? It takes one to know one.

Science Fiction/Fantasy & Horror Markets Appearing in This Book

Below is a list of science fiction, fantasy, and horror markets appearing in this edition of *Novel & Short Story Writer's Market*. For complete information—including who to contact and how to submit your manuscript—turn to the page number provided.

Magazines (Horror)

Magazines (Science Fiction)

Book Publishers (Fantasy)

Book Publishers (Horror)

Book Publishers (Science Fiction)

Resources for Science Fiction/ Fantasy & Horror Writers

Below is a list of invaluable resources specifically for science fiction and fantasy writers. For more information on the magazines and organizations listed below, check the General Index and the Publications of Interest and Organizations sections of this book. To order any of the Writer's Digest Books titles or to get a consumer book catalog, call 1-800-448-0915. You may also order Writer's Digest Books selections through www.writersdigest.com, Amazon.com, or www.barnes andnoble.com.

MAGAZINES:
- *Locus*, P.O. Box 13305, Oakland CA 94661. E-mail: locus@locusmag.com.
- *Science Fiction Chronicle*, P.O. Box 022730, Brooklyn NY 11202-0056. (718)643-9011. Fax: (718)522-3308. E-mail: sf_chronicle@compuserve.com.
- *Writer's Digest*, 4700 East Galbraith Rd., Cincinnati OH 45236. Website: www.writersdigest. com.

BOOKS:
Science Fiction Writing series (Writer's Digest Books)
- *Aliens and Alien Societies: A Writer's Guide to Creating Extraterrestrial Life-forms*
- *Time Travel: A Writer's Guide to the Real Science of Plausible Time Travel*

Other Writer's Digest books for science fiction/fantasy & horror writers:
- *Worlds of Wonder, How to Write Science Fiction and Fantasy* (Gerrold)
- *How to Write Science Fiction & Fantasy*
- *The Craft of Writing Science Fiction That Sells*
- *How to Write Tales of Horror, Fantasy & Science Fiction*
- *Science Fiction and Fantasy Writer's Sourcebook, 2nd Edition*
- *The Writer's Complete Fantasy Reference*
- *Writing Horror*

ORGANIZATIONS & ONLINE:
- Science Fiction & Fantasy Writers of America, Inc., P.O. Box 877, Chestertown MD 21620. E-mail: execdir@sfwa.org. Website: www.sfwa.org/.
- Con-Tour: www.con-tour.com.
- Books and Writing Online: www.interzone.com/Books/books.html.
- www.writersmarket.com.
- www.locusmag.com.

The Markets

Important Listing Information

- Listings are not advertisements. Although the information here is as accurate as possible, the listings are not endorsed or guaranteed by the editor of *Novel & Short Story Writer's Market*.
- *Novel & Short Story Writer's Market* reserves the right to exclude any listing that does not meet its requirements.

Key to Symbols and Abbreviations

- **N** New listing in all sections
- Canadian listing
- International listing
- Parent company, subsidiary, or division of major book publishing house
- **A** Agented material only
- Online publication
- Award-winning publication
- **$** Market pays money
- Accepts no submissions
- Actively seeking beginning writers
- Seeking new and established writers
- Prefers working with established writers, mostly referrals
- Only handles specific types of work
- • Comment by editor of *Novel & Short Story Writer's Market*

ms—manuscript; **mss**—manuscripts

SASE—self-addressed, stamped envelope

SAE—self-addressed envelope

IRC—International Reply Coupon, for use on reply mail from other countries

(See Glossary for definitions of words and expressions used in writing and publishing.)

Complaint Procedure

If you feel you have not been treated fairly by a listing in *Novel & Short Story Writer's Market*, we advise you to take the following steps:

- First try to contact the listing. Sometimes one phone call or a letter can quickly clear up the matter.
- Document all your correspondence with the listing. When you write to us with a complaint, provide the details of your submission, the date of your first contact with the listing and the nature of your subsequent correspondence.
- We will enter your letter into our files and attempt to contact the listing.
- The number and severity of complaints will be considered in our decision whether or not to delete the listing from the next edition.

Literary Agents

Many publishers are willing to look at unsolicited submissions but most feel having an agent is to the writer's best advantage. In this section we include 50 + agents who specialize in fiction, or publish a significant amount of fiction. These agents were also selected because of their openness to submissions from writers.

The commercial fiction field is intensely competitive. Many publishers have smaller staffs and less time. For that reason, more book publishers are relying on agents for new talent. Some publishers are even relying on agents as "first readers" who must wade through the deluge of submissions from writers to find the very best. For writers, a good agent can be a foot in the door—someone willing to do the necessary work to put your manuscript in the right editor's hands.

It would seem today that finding a good agent is as hard as finding a good publisher. Yet those writers who have agents say they are invaluable. Not only can a good agent help you make your work more marketable, an agent acts as your business manager and adviser, keeping your interests up front during and even after contract negotiations.

Still, finding an agent can be very difficult for a new writer. If you are already published in magazines, you have a better chance than someone with no publishing credits. (Many agents routinely read periodicals searching for new writers.) Although many agents do read queries and manuscripts from unpublished authors without introduction, referrals from their writer clients can be a big help. If you don't know any published authors with agents, you may want to attend a conference as a way of meeting agents. Some agents even set aside time at conferences to meet new writers.

All the agents listed here have said they are open to working with new, previously unpublished writers as well as published writers. Most do not charge a fee to cover the time and effort involved in reviewing a manuscript or a synopsis and chapters.

USING THE LISTINGS

It is especially important when contacting these busy agents that you read individual listings carefully before submitting anything. The first information after the company name includes the address and phone, fax and e-mail address (when available). **Member Agents** gives the names of individual agents working at that company (specific types of fiction an agent handles are indicated in parenthesis after that agent's name). The **Represents** section lists the types of fiction the agency works with. Reading the **Recent Sales** gives you the names of writers an agent is currently working with and, very importantly, publishers the agent has placed manuscripts with. **Writers' Conferences** identifies conferences an agent attends (and where you might possibly meet that agent). **Tips** presents advice directly from the agent to authors.

MIRIAM ALTSHULER LITERARY AGENCY, 53 Old Post Rd. N., Red Hook NY 12571. (845)758-9408. Fax: (845)758-3118. **Contact:** Miriam Altshuler. Estab. 1994. Member of AAR. Represents 40 clients. Currently handles: 45% nonfiction books; 45% novels; 5% story collections; 5% juvenile books.
- Ms. Altshuler has been an agent since 1982.

Represents: Novels, short story collections, juvenile books. **Considers these fiction areas:** Literary; mainstream/contemporary; multicultural; thriller.

How to Contact: Query with SASE. Prefers to read materials exclusively. No e-mail or fax queries. Considers simultaneous queries. Responds in 2 weeks to queries; 3 weeks to mss. Returns materials only with SASE. Obtains most new clients through recommendations from others.

Terms: Agent receives 15% commission on domestic sales; 20% commission on foreign sales. No written contract. Charges clients for overseas mailing, photocopies, overnight mail when requested by author.

Writers' Conferences: Bread Loaf Writers' Conference (Middlebury VT, August).

MARCIA AMSTERDAM AGENCY, 41 W. 82nd St., New York NY 10024-5613. (212)873-4945. **Contact:** Marcia Amsterdam. Estab. 1970. Signatory of WGA. Currently handles: 15% nonfiction books; 70% novels; 5% movie scripts; 10% TV scripts.

• Prior to opening her agency, Ms. Amsterdam was an editor.

Represents: Novels. **Considers these fiction areas:** Action/adventure; detective/police/crime; horror; mainstream/ contemporary; mystery/suspense; romance (contemporary, historical); science fiction; thriller; westerns/frontier; young adult.

How to Contact: Submit outline, 3 sample chapter(s), SASE. Responds in 1 month to queries.

Recent Sales: *Rosey in the Present Tense*, by Louise Hawes (Walker); *Flash Factor*, by William H. Lovejoy (Kensington). *Movie/TV MOW script(s) optioned/sold: Mad About You*, by Jenna Bruce (Columbia Tristar TV).

Terms: Agent receives 15% commission on domestic sales; 20% commission on foreign sales; 10% commission on dramatic rights sales. Offers written contract, binding for 1 year. Charges clients for extra office expenses, foreign postage, copying, legal fees (when agreed upon).

Tips: "We are always looking for interesting literary voices."

LORETTA BARRETT BOOKS INC., 101 Fifth Ave., New York NY 10003. (212)242-3420. Fax: (212)807-9579. **Contact:** Loretta A. Barrett or Nick Mullendore. Estab. 1990. Member of AAR. Represents 90 clients. Currently handles: 60% nonfiction books; 40% novels.

• Prior to opening her agency, Ms. Barrett was vice president and executive editor at Doubleday for 25 years.

Represents: Novels. **Considers these fiction areas:** Action/adventure; confession; contemporary issues; detective/ police/crime; ethnic; family saga; feminist; gay/lesbian; glitz; historical; humor/satire; literary; mainstream/contemporary; mystery/suspense; psychic/supernatural; religious/inspirational; romance; spiritual; sports; thriller.

O-¬ This agency specializes in general interest books. No children's or juvenile.

How to Contact: Query with SASE. No e-mail or fax queries. Considers simultaneous queries. Responds in 1 month to queries. Returns materials only with SASE.

Recent Sales: *A Lady First*, by Letitia Baldrige (Viking); *The Singularity is Near*, by Ray Kurzweil (Viking); *Flesh Tones*, by MJ Rose (Ballantine Books); *The Lake of Dead Languages*, by Carol Goodman (Ballantine Books); *The Bad Witness*, by Laura Van Wormer (Mira Books).

Terms: Agent receives 15% commission on domestic sales; 20% commission on foreign sales. Offers written contract. Charges clients for shipping and photocopying.

Writers' Conferences: San Diego State University Writer's Conference; Maui Writer's Conference.

MEREDITH BERNSTEIN LITERARY AGENCY, 2112 Broadway, Suite 503A, New York NY 10023. (212)799-1007. Fax: (212)799-1145. Estab. 1981. Member of AAR. Represents 100 clients. 20% of clients are new/ unpublished writers. Currently handles: 50% nonfiction books; 50% novels.

• Prior to opening her agency, Ms. Bernstein served in another agency for 5 years.

Member Agents: Meredith Bernstein; Elizabeth Cavanaugh.

Represents: Novels. **Considers these fiction areas:** Literary; mystery/suspense; romance; women's fiction.

O-¬ This agency does not specialize, "very eclectic."

How to Contact: Query with SASE. No e-mail or fax queries. Considers simultaneous queries. Obtains most new clients through recommendations from others, conferences, also develops and packages own ideas.

Recent Sales: *The Botox Book*, by Dr. Michael Kane (St. Martin's); *No More Knee Pain*, by Dr. George Kessler (Berkley).

Terms: Agent receives 15% commission on domestic sales; 20% commission on foreign sales. Charges clients $75 disbursement fee/year.

Writers' Conferences: Southwest Writers Conference (Albuquereque, August); Rocky Moutnain Writers' Conference (Denver, September); Golden Triangle (Beaumont TX, October); Pacific Northwest Writers Conference; Austin League Writers Conference; Willamette Writers Conference (Portland, OR); Lafayette Writers Conference (Lafayette, LA); Surrey Writers Conference (Surrey, BC.); San Diego State University Writers Conference (San Diego, CA).

BOOKENDS, LLC, 136 Long Hill Rd., Gillette NJ 07933. (908)604-2652. E-mail: editor@bookends-inc.com. Website: www.bookends-inc.com. **Contact:** Jessica Faust or Jacky Sach. Estab. 1999. Represents 50 clients. 60% of clients are new/unpublished writers. Currently handles: 50% nonfiction books; 50% novels.

• Prior to opening their agency, Ms. Faust and Ms. Sach worked at such publishing houses as Berkley, Penguin Putnam, Macmillan and IDG.

Member Agents: Jessica Faust (mysteries, romance, relationships, business, finance, pets, general self-help); Jacky Sach (suspense thrillers, mysteries, literary fiction, spirituality, pets, general self-help).

Represents: Novels. **Considers these fiction areas:** Contemporary issues; detective/police/crime; ethnic; family saga; feminist; glitz; historical; literary; mainstream/contemporary; mystery/suspense; romance; thriller.

O-¬ BookEnds specializes in genre fiction and personality driven nonfiction. Actively seeking romance, mystery, women's fiction, literary fiction and suspense thrillers. For nonfiction, relationships, business, general self-help, women's interest, parenting, pets, spirituality, health and psychology. Does not want to receive children's books, screenplays, science fiction, poetry, technical/military thrillers.

How to Contact: Submit outline, 3 sample chapter(s). Considers simultaneous queries. Responds in 6 weeks to queries; 10 weeks to mss. Returns materials only with SASE. Obtains most new clients through recommendations from others, solicitations, conferences.

Recent Sales: Sold 40 titles in the last year. *Women at Ground Zero*, by Mary Carouba and Susan Hagen (Alpha); *Soapmaking: A Magickal Guide*, by Alicia Grosso (Career Press); *Streetwise Guide to Publicity*, by Sandra Beckwith (Adams Media); *Managing your Parents' Money*, by Sharon Burns, Ph.D., and Dr. Ray Laforge (McGraw-Hill); *And a Hard Rain Fell*, by John Ketwig (Sourcebooks); *Pills for Pets*, by Debra Eldredge (Kensington Books); *Drawing for Dummies*, by Brenda Hodinnott (Hungry Minds).

Terms: Agent receives 15% commission on domestic sales; 20% commission on foreign sales. Offers written contract. Charges clients for photocopying, messenger, cables, overseas postage, long-distance phone calls, copies of the published book when purchases for subsidiary rights submissions. Expenses will not exceed $150.

Writers' Conferences: Central Florida Romance Writers Conference (Orlando FL, September); Emerald Coast Writers Conference (Seattle WA, October 2002).

Tips: "When submitting material be sure to include any information that might be helpful to the agent. In your query letter you should include the title of the book, your name, your publishing history and a brief 1 or 2 sentence description of the book. Also be sure to let the agent know if you see this book as part of a series and if you've already begun work on other books. Once an agent has expressed interest in representing you it is crucial to let her know who has seen your book and even supply copies of any correspondence you've had with prospective editors."

CURTIS BROWN LTD., 10 Astor Place, New York NY 10003-6935. (212)473-5400. Also: 1750 Montgomery St., San Francisco CA 94111. (415)954-8566. **Contact:** Perry Knowlton, chairman; Timothy Knowlton, CEO; Peter L. Ginsberg, president. Member of AAR; signatory of WGA.

Member Agents: Laura Blake Peterson; Ellen Geiger; Emilie Jacobson, vice president; Maureen Walters, vice president; Virginia Knowlton (literary, adult, children's); Timothy Knowlton (film, screenplays, plays; Marilyn Marlow, executive vice president; Ed Wintle (film, screenplays, plays); Mitchell Waters; Elizabeth Harding; Douglas Stewart; Kristen Manges; Dave Barber (translation rights).

Represents: Novels, short story collections, novellas, juvenile books, poetry books. **Considers these fiction areas:** Action/adventure; comic books/cartoon; confession; contemporary issues; detective/police/crime; erotica; ethnic; experimental; family saga; fantasy; feminist; gay/lesbian; glitz; gothic; hi-lo; historical; horror; humor/satire; juvenile; literary; mainstream/contemporary; military/war; multicultural; multimedia; mystery/suspense; New Age; occult; picture books; plays; poetry; poetry in translation; psychic/supernatural; regional; religious/inspirational; romance; science fiction; short story collections; spiritual; sports; thriller; translation; westerns/frontier; young adult; women's.

How to Contact: Query with SASE. Prefers to read materials exclusively. No unsolicited mss. No e-mail or fax queries. Responds in 3 weeks to queries; 5 weeks to mss. Obtains most new clients through recommendations from others, solicitations, conferences.

Recent Sales: This agency prefers not to share information on specific sales.

Terms: Offers written contract. Charges for photocopying, some postage. "There are no office fees until we sell a manuscript."

MARIA CARVAINIS AGENCY, INC., 1350 Avenue of the Americas, Suite 2905, New York NY 10019. (212)245-6365. Fax: (212)245-7196. E-mail: mca@mariacarvainisagency.com. **Contact:** Maria Carvainis, president; Frances Kuffel, executive vice president. Estab. 1977. Member of AAR, Authors Guild, ABA, MWA, Novelists Inc., RWA; signatory of WGA. Represents 70 clients. 10% of clients are new/unpublished writers. Currently handles: 34% nonfiction books; 65% novels; 1% poetry.

- Prior to opening her agency, Ms. Carvainis spent more than 10 years in the publishing industry as a senior editor with Macmillan Publishing, Basic Books, Avon Books (where she worked closely with Peter Mayer), and Crown Publishers. Ms. Carvainis has served as a member of the AAR Board of Directors and AAR Treasurer, as well as serving as chair of the AAR Contracts Committee. She presently serves on the AAR Royalty Committee.

Member Agents: Frances Kuffel (Executive Vice President); Anna Del Vecchio (Contracts Associate); Moira Sullivan (Editorial Associate); Elise Shin (Editorial Assistant).

Represents: Novels. **Considers these fiction areas:** Historical; literary; mainstream/contemporary; mystery/suspense; romance; thriller; young adult; middle grade.

   O— Does not want to receive science fiction or children's.

How to Contact: Query with SASE. Responds in 1 week to queries; 3 months to mss. Obtains most new clients through recommendations from others, conferences, 60% from conferences/referrals; 40% from query letters.

Recent Sales: *The Crush*, by Sandra Brown (Warner Books); *The Guru Guide to Money Management*, by Joseph H. Boyett and Jimmie T. Boyett (John Wiley and Sons); *Trophy Widow*, by Michael Kahn (TOR/Forge); *Paint it Black*, by P.J. Parrish (Kensington); *A Summer to Remember*, by Mary Balogh (Delacorte); *The Floating World*, by Cynthia Gralla (Ballantine Books); *His Wicked Promise*, by Samantha James (Morrow/Avon); *The Airedale Heiress*, by Lee Charles Kelley (Morrow/Avon). Other clients include Other clients include Sue Erikson Boland, Pam Conrad, Phillip DePoy, Carlos Dews, FDNY Emerald Society Pipes & Drums, Cindy Gerard, Fred Haefle, Hugo Mager, Kristine Rolofson, Janet Mansfield Soares, Charlie Smith, Peter Stark, Ernest Suarez.

Terms: Agent receives 15% commission on domestic sales; 20% commission on foreign sales. Offers written contract, binding for 2 years on a book-by-book basis. Charges clients for foreign postage, bulk copying.

Writers' Conferences: BEA; Frankfurt Book Fair.

CASTIGLIA LITERARY AGENCY, 1155 Camino Del Mar, Suite 510, Del Mar CA 92014. (858)755-8761. Fax: (858)755-7063. **Contact:** Julie Castiglia. Estab. 1993. Member of AAR, PEN. Represents 50 clients. Currently handles: 55% nonfiction books; 45% novels.
Member Agents: Winifred Golden; Julie Castiglia.
Represents: Novels. **Considers these fiction areas:** Contemporary issues; ethnic; literary; mainstream/contemporary; mystery/suspense; women's (especially).
    O-π Does not want to receive horror, screenplays or academic nonfiction.
How to Contact: Query with SASE. No fax queries. Responds in 2 months to mss. Returns materials only with SASE. Obtains most new clients through recommendations from others, solicitations, conferences.
Recent Sales: Sold 25 titles in the last year. *Ready to Roll*, by Doug Keister(Viking Penguin); *Red Tile Style*, by Arrel Gellner(Penguin); *West of Kabul, East of New York*, by Tamim Ansary (Farrar, Straus & Giroux).
Terms: Agent receives 15% commission on domestic sales; 25% commission on foreign sales. Offers written contract; 6-week notice must be given to terminate contract. Charges clients for Fed Ex or Messenger.
Writers' Conferences: Southwestern Writers Conference (Albuquerque NM, August); National Writers Conference; Willamette Writers Conference (OR); San Diego State University (CA); Writers at Work (Utah); Austin Conference (TX).
Tips: "Be professional with submissions. Attend workshops and conferences before you approach an agent."

RUTH COHEN, INC. LITERARY AGENCY, P.O. Box 2244, La Jolla CA 92038-2244. (858)456-5805. **Contact:** Ruth Cohen. Estab. 1982. Member of AAR, Authors Guild, Sisters in Crime, RWA, SCBWI. Represents 45 clients. 15% of clients are new/unpublished writers. Currently handles: 60% novels; 40% juvenile books.
    ● Prior to becoming an agent, Ms. Cohen served as directing editor at Scott Foresman & Company (now HarperCollins).
Represents: Novels (adult), juvenile books. **Considers these fiction areas:** Ethnic; historical; juvenile; literary; mainstream/contemporary; mystery/suspense; picture books; young adult.
    O-π This agency specializes in "quality writing in contemporary fiction, women's fiction, mysteries, thrillers and juvenile fiction." Does not want to receive poetry, westerns, film scripts or how-to books.
How to Contact: Submit outline, 1 sample chapter(s). Does not accept fax or e-mail queries. Accepts simultaneous queries. Responds in 3 weeks to queries. Returns materials only with SASE. Obtains most new clients through recommendations from others, solicitations.
Recent Sales: This agency prefers not to share information on specific sales.
Terms: Agent receives 15% commission on domestic sales; 20% commission on foreign sales. Offers written contract, binding for 1 year. Charges for foreign postage, phone calls, photocopying submissions and overnight delivery of mss when appropriate.
Tips: "As the publishing world merges and changes, there seem to be fewer opportunities for new writers to succeed in the work that they love. We urge you to develop the patience, persistence and preseverance that have made this agency so successful. Prepare a well-written and well-crafted manuscript, and our combined best efforts can help advance both our careers."

CORNERSTONE LITERARY, INC., 4500 Wilshire Blvd., 3rd floor, Los Angeles CA 90010. (323)930-6039. Fax: (323)930-0407. Website: www.cornerstoneliterary.com. **Contact:** Helen Breitwieser. Estab. 1998. Member of AAR; Author's Guild. Represents 40 clients. 75% of clients are new/unpublished writers.
    ● Prior to founding her own boutique agency, Ms. Breitwieser was a literary agent at The William Morris Agency.
Represents: Novels, short story collections. **Considers these fiction areas:** Detective/police/crime; erotica; ethnic; family saga; glitz; historical; humor/satire; literary; mainstream/contemporary; multicultural; mystery/suspense; New Age; romance; thriller.
    O-π Actively seeking first fiction, literary. Does not want to receive science fiction, westerns, children's books, poetry, screenplays, fantasy, gay/lesbian, horror.
How to Contact: Query with SASE. Responds in 2 weeks to queries; 2 months to mss. Returns materials only with SASE. Obtains most new clients through recommendations from others.
Recent Sales: Sold 42 titles in the last year. *Last Breath*, by Rachel Lee (Warner); *Cold Silence*, by Danielle Girard (NAL). Other clients include Stan Diehl, Elaine Coffman, Carole Matthews, Kayla Perrin, Candice Proctor.
Terms: Agent receives 15% commission on domestic sales; 20% commission on foreign sales. Offers written contract, binding for 1 year; 60-day notice must be given to terminate contract.
Tips: "Don't query about more than one manuscript."

CRAWFORD LITERARY AGENCY, 94 Evans Rd., Barnstead NH 03218. (603)269-5851. Fax: (603)269-2533. E-mail: CrawfordLit@att.net. **Contact:** Susan Crawford. Estab. 1988. Represents 40 clients. 10% of clients are new/unpublished writers. Currently handles: 50% nonfiction books; 50% novels.
Member Agents: Susan Crawford; Lorne Crawford (commercial fiction); Scott Neister (scientific/techno thrillers); Kristen Hales (parenting, psychology, New Age, self help).
Represents: Novels (commercial fiction). **Considers these fiction areas:** Action/adventure; mystery/suspense; thriller (medical).

O→ This agency specializes in celebrity and/or media-based books and authors. Actively seeking action/adventure stories, medical thrillers, suspense thrillers, self-help, inspirational, how-to and women's issues. Does not want to receive short stories, poetry.

How to Contact: Query with SASE. Considers simultaneous queries. Responds in 3 weeks to queries. Returns materials only with SASE. Obtains most new clients through recommendations from others, solicitations, conferences.

Recent Sales: Sold 42 titles in the last year. *Handy at Home*, by Richard Karn and George Mair (St. Martin's Press); *Float Like a Butterfly and Sting Like a Bee*, by Maryum Ali (Beyond Words). Other clients include John Travolta, Kat Carney, Cal Morris,MD, Mimi Donaldson, Linda Seger.

Terms: Agent receives 15% commission on domestic sales; 20% commission on foreign sales. Offers written contract, binding for 90 days; 100% of business is derived from commissions on ms sales.

Writers' Conferences: International Film & Television Workshops (Rockport ME); ; Maui Writers Conference.

Tips: "Keep learning to improve your craft. Attend conferences and network."

◐ **DARHANSOFF & VERRILL LITERARY AGENTS**, 236 W. 26th St., Suite 802, New York NY 10001. (917)305-1300. Fax: (917)305-1400. Estab. 1975. Member of AAR. Represents 120 clients. 10% of clients are new/ unpublished writers. Currently handles: 25% nonfiction books; 60% novels; 15% story collections.

Member Agents: Liz Darhansoff; Charles Verrill; Leigh Feldman.

Represents: Novels, short story collections. **Considers these fiction areas:** Literary.

O→ Specializes in literary fiction.

How to Contact: Obtains most new clients through recommendations from others.

Recent Sales: *At Home in Mitford*, by Jan Karon (Viking); *Cold Mountain*, by Charles Frazier (Atlantic Monthly Press). Other clients include Arthur Golden.

◐ **JOAN DAVES AGENCY**, 21 W. 26th St., New York NY 10010. (212)685-2663. Fax: (212)685-1781. **Contact:** Jennifer Lyons, director. Estab. 1960. Member of AAR. Represents 100 clients. 10% of clients are new/unpublished writers.

Represents: Novels. **Considers these fiction areas:** Ethnic; family saga; gay/lesbian; literary; mainstream/contemporary.

O→ This agency specializes in literary fiction and nonfiction, also commercial fiction.

How to Contact: Query with SASE. No e-mail or fax queries. Considers simultaneous queries. Responds in 3 weeks to queries; 6 weeks to mss. Returns materials only with SASE. Obtains most new clients through recommendations from others, solicitations.

Recent Sales: Sold 70 titles in the last year. *Confessions of a Dangerous Mind*, by Chuck Barris (Miramax); *Complete Works of Isaac Babel*, ed. by Nathalie Babel (W.W. Norton); *Red Ribbons and the Broken Memory Tree*, by April Reynolds (Henry Holt).

Terms: Agent receives 15% commission on domestic sales; 20% commission on foreign sales. Offers written contract, binding for per-book basis; 100% of business is derived from commissions on ms sales. Charges for office expenses.

Tips: "A few queries translate into representation."

◐ **LIZA DAWSON ASSOCIATES**, 240 W. 35th St., Suite 500, New York NY 10001. (212)465-9071 or (212)629-9212. **Contact:** Liza Dawson, Rebecca Kurson, Caitlin Blasdell. Member of AAR, MWA, Women's Media Group. Represents 50 clients. 10% of clients are new/unpublished writers. Currently handles: 60% nonfiction books; 40% novels.

• Prior to becoming an agent, Ms. Dawson was an editor for 20 years, spending 11 years at William Morrow as vice president and 2 at Putnam as executive editor. Ms. Kurson was an associate editor at Farrar Straus; Ms. Blasdell was a senior editor at HarperCollins and Avon.

Member Agents: Liza Dawson; Rebecca Kurson (science, women's issues, narrative nonfiction, literary fiction); Caitlin Blasdell (science fiction, business books, commercial fiction).

Represents: Novels. **Considers these fiction areas:** Ethnic; family saga; historical; literary; mystery/suspense; regional; thriller.

O→ This agency specializes in readable literary fiction, thrillers, mainstream historicals and women's fiction, academics, historians, business, journalists and psychology. "My specialty is shaping books and ideas so that a publisher will respond quickly." Actively seeking talented professionals. Does not want to receive westerns, sports, computers, juvenile.

How to Contact: Query with SASE. Responds in 3 weeks to queries; 6 weeks to mss. Obtains most new clients through recommendations from others, conferences.

Recent Sales: Sold 40 titles in the last year. *Darjeeling*, by Bharti Kirchner (St. Martin's); *Wild Mothers*, (Algonquin); *My Mother's Island*, by Marnie Mueller (Curbstone); *Life or Debt*, by Stacy Johnson (Ballantine); *The Summer of My Greek Taverna*, by Tom Stone (Simon & Schuster); *Poker Nation*, by Andy Bellin (HarperCollins).

Terms: Agent receives 15% commission on domestic sales; 20% commission on foreign sales. Offers written contract. Charges clients for photocopying and overseas postage.

Writers' Conferences: Pacific Northwest Book Conference (Seattle, July).

Reading List: Reads *The Sun, New York Review of Books, The New York Observer, Utne Reader*, and *The Wall Street Journal* to find new clients.

Tips: "Please include a detailed bio with any query letter, let me know somehow that you've done a little research, that you're not just interested in any agent but someone who is right for you."

ETHAN ELLENBERG LITERARY AGENCY, 548 Broadway, #5-E, New York NY 10012. (212)431-4554. Fax: (212)941-4652. E-mail: agent@ethanellenberg.com. Website: www.ethanellenberg.com. **Contact:** Ethan Ellenberg, Michael Psaltis. Estab. 1983. Represents 80 clients. 10% of clients are new/unpublished writers. Currently handles: 25% nonfiction books; 75% novels.
- Prior to opening his agency, Mr. Ellenberg was contracts manager of Berkley/Jove and associate contracts manager for Bantam.

Member Agents: Michael Psaltis (serious and commercial nonfiction, including science, health, popular culture, cooking, current events, politics, business, memoir and other unique projects; and commercial and literary fiction); Ethan Ellenberg.

Represents: Novels. **Considers these fiction areas:** Fantasy; romance; science fiction; thriller; women's.
- This agency specializes in commercial fiction, especially thrillers, romance/women's fiction and specialized nonfiction. "We also do a lot of children's books." For children's books: Send introductory letter (with credits, if any), up to 3 picture book mss, outline and first 3 chapters for longer projects, SASE. Actively seeking commercial and literary fiction, children's books, break-through nonfiction. Does not want to receive poetry, short stories, westerns, autobiographies.

How to Contact: For fiction: Send introductory letter (with credits, if any), outline, first 3 chapters and SASE. For nonfiction: Send query letter and/or proposal, 1 sample chapter if written. No fax queries. Accepts e-mail queries, no attachments. Considers simultaneous queries. Responds in 10 days to queries; 1 month to mss. Returns materials only with SASE.

Recent Sales: Has sold over 100 titles in the last 3 years.; *On Punk's Wing*, by Ward Carroll (Dutton); *Shadow of the Warrior*, by Marcus Wynne (Tor Books); *The Tentmaker*, by Clay Reynolds (Berkley); *The Rover*, by Mel Odom (Tor Books); *Angelica*, by Sharon Shinn (Ace Books); *Reckless Embrace*, by Madeline Baker (Leisure Books); *Bliss River*, by Thea Devine (Kensington); *Just Beyond Tomorrow*, by Beatrice Small (Kensington); *My Friend Rabbit*, by Eric Rohmann (Millbrook Press); *A Taste of the Season*, by Diane Worthington (Chronicle Books); *Yoga Mini-Book* series, by Elaine Gavalas (Fireside/Simon & Schuster).

Terms: Agent receives 15% commission on domestic sales; 10% commission on foreign sales. Offers written contract. Charges clients for "direct expenses only limited to photocopying, postage, by writer's consent only."

Writers' Conferences: RWA National; Novelists, Inc.; and other regional conferences.

Tips: "We do consider new material from unsolicited authors. Write a good clear letter with a succinct description of your book. We prefer the first three chapters when we consider fiction. For all submissions you must include SASE for return or the material is discarded. It's always hard to break in, but talent will find a home. Check our website for complete submission guidelines. We continue to see natural storytellers and nonfiction writers with important books."

GELFMAN SCHNEIDER LITERARY AGENTS, INC., 250 W. 57th St., New York NY 10107. (212)245-1993. Fax: (212)245-8678. **Contact:** Jane Gelfman, Deborah Schneider. Estab. 1981. Member of AAR. Represents 150 clients. 10% of clients are new/unpublished writers.

Represents: Novels. "We represent adult, general, hardcover fiction and nonfiction, literary and commercial, and some mysteries." **Considers these fiction areas:** Literary; mainstream/contemporary; mystery/suspense.
- Does not want to receive romances, science fiction, westerns or children's books.

How to Contact: Query with SASE. No e-mail queries. Accepts simultaneous queries. Responds in 1 month to queries; 2 months to mss. Obtains most new clients through recommendations from others.

Terms: Agent receives 15% commission on domestic sales; 20% commission on foreign sales. Offers written contract. Charges clients for photocopying, messengers and couriers.

THE GISLASON AGENCY, 219 Main St. SE, Suite 506, Minneapolis MN 55414-2160. (612)331-8033. Fax: (612)332-8115. E-mail: gislasonbj@aol.com. Website: www.thegislasonagency.com. **Contact:** Barbara J. Gislason, literary agent. Estab. 1992. Member of Minnesota State Bar Association, Art & Entertainment Law Section (former chair), Internet Committee, Minnesota Intellectual Property Law Association Copyright Committee (former chair). Also a member of SFWA, MWA, RWA, Sisters in Crime, University Film Society (board member), Neighborhood Justice (board member) and American Academy of Acupuncture and Oriental Medicine (advisory board member). 80% of clients are new/unpublished writers. Currently handles: 25% nonfiction books; 75% novels.
- Ms. Gislason became an attorney in 1980, and continues to practice Art & Entertainment Law. She has been nationally recognized as a Leading American Attorney and a SuperLawyer.

Member Agents: Adam Kintopf (senior editor); Deborah Sweeney (fantasy, science fiction); Kellie Hultgren (fantasy, science fiction); Lisa Higgs (Romance); Ally Ohlson (nonfiction); Kris Olson (mystery).

Represents: Novels. **Considers these fiction areas:** Fantasy; mainstream/contemporary; mystery/suspense; romance; science fiction; thriller (legal).
- Do not send personal memoirs, poetry, screenplays or children's books.

How to Contact: Fiction: Query with synopsis, first 3 chapters and SASE. Nonfiction: Query with proposal and sample chapters; published authors may submit complete ms. Responds in 2 months to queries; 3 months to mss. Obtains most new clients through recommendations from others, conferences, *Guide to Literary Agents*, *Literary Market Place* and other reference books.

Recent Sales: *Historical Romance # 4*, by Linda Cook (Kensington); *Dancing Dead*, by Deborah Woodworth (Harper-Collins); *Autumn World*, by Joan Verba, et al (Dragon Stone Press).

Terms: Agent receives 15% commission on domestic sales; 20% commission on foreign sales. Offers written contract, binding for 1 year with option to renew. Charges clients for photocopying and postage.

Writers' Conferences: Romance Writers of America; Midwest Fiction Writers; University of Wisconsin Writer's Institute. Also attend state and regional writers conferences.

Tips: "Cover letter should be well written and include a detailed synopsis (if fiction) or proposal (if nonfiction), the first three chapters and author bio. Appropriate SASE required. We are looking for a great writer with a poetic, lyrical or quirky writing style who can create intriguing ambiguities. We expect a well-researched, imaginative and fresh plot that reflects a familiarity with the applicable genre. If submitting nonfiction work, explain how the submission differs from and adds to previously published works in the field. Scenes with sex and violence must be intrinsic to the plot. Remember to proofread, proofread, proofread. If the work was written with a specific publisher in mind, this should be communicated. In addition to owning an agency, Ms. Gislason practices law in the area of Art and Entertainment and has a broad spectrum of entertainment industry contacts."

◖ SANFORD J. GREENBURGER ASSOCIATES, INC., 55 Fifth Ave., New York NY 10003. (212)206-5600. Fax: (212)463-8718. Website: www.greenburger.com. **Contact:** Heide Lange. Estab. 1945. Member of AAR. Represents 500 clients.

Member Agents: Heide Lange; Faith Hamlin; Beth Vesel; Theresa Park; Elyse Cheney; Dan Mandel; Julie Barer.

Represents: Novels. **Considers these fiction areas:** Action/adventure; contemporary issues; detective/police/crime; ethnic; family saga; feminist; gay/lesbian; glitz; historical; humor/satire; literary; mainstream/contemporary; mystery/suspense; psychic/supernatural; regional; sports; thriller.

   0→ Does not want to receive romances or westerns.

How to Contact: Query with SASE. Considers simultaneous queries. Responds in 3 weeks to queries; 2 months to mss.

Recent Sales: Sold 200 titles in the last year. This agency prefers not to share information on specific sales. Other clients include Andrew Ross, Margaret Cuthbert, Nicholas Sparks, Mary Kurcinka, Linda Nichols, Edy Clarke and Peggy Claude Pierre, Brad Thor, Dan Brown, Sallie Bissell.

Terms: Agent receives 15% commission on domestic sales; 20% commission on foreign sales. Charges for photocopying, books for foreign and subsidiary rights submissions.

⊕ ◖ GREGORY AND COMPANY AUTHORS' AGENTS, (formerly Gregory and Radice Authors' Agents), 3 Barb Mews, London W6 7PA, England. 020-7610-4676. Fax: 020-7610-4686. E-mail: info@gregoryandcompany.co.uk. Website: www.gregoryandcompany.co.uk. **Contact:** Jane Gregory, sales; Broo Doherty, editorial; Jane Barlow/Claire Morris, rights. Estab. 1987. Member of Association of Authors' Agents. Represents 60 clients. Currently handles: 10% nonfiction books; 90% novels.

   ● Prior to becoming an agent, Ms. Gregory was Rights Director for Chatto & Windus.

Member Agents: Jane Gregory (sales); Broo Doherty (editorial); Jane Barlow/Claire Morris (rights).

Represents: Novels. **Considers these fiction areas:** Action/adventure; detective/police/crime; historical; humor/satire; literary; mainstream/contemporary; multicultural; romance; thriller.

   0→ "Jane Gregory is successful at selling rights all over the world, including film and television rights. As a British agency we do not generally take on American authors." Actively seeking well-written, accessible modern novels. Does not want to receive horror, science fiction, fantasy, children's books, scripts, poetry.

How to Contact: Query with SASE, or submit outline, 3 sample chapters, SASE. Considers simultaneous queries. Returns materials only with SASE. Obtains most new clients through recommendations from others, conferences.

Recent Sales: Sold 100 titles in the last year. *Tokyo*, by Mo Hayder (Bantam UK/Doubleday USA); *Distant Echo*, by Val McDermid (HarperCollins UK/St. Martin's Press NY); *Fox Evil*, by Minette Walters (McMillan UK/Putnam USA); *Hello Bunny*, by Laura Wilson (Orion UK/Bantam USA); *Out of the Dark* by Natasha Cooper (Simon & Schuster UK/St. Martin's Press USA).

Terms: Agent receives 15% commission on domestic sales; 20% commission on foreign sales. Offers written contract; 3-month notice must be given to terminate contract. Charges clients for photocopying of whole typescripts and copies of book for submissions.

Writers' Conferences: CWA Conference (United Kingdom, Spring); Dead on Deansgate (Manchester, Autumn); Bouchercon (location varies, Autumn).

◖ JILL GROSJEAN LITERARY AGENCY, 1390 Millstone Rd., Sag Harbor NY 11963-2214. (631)725-7419. Fax: (631)725-8632. E-mail: JILL6981@aol.com. Website: www.hometown.aol.com/JILL6981/myhomepage/index.html. **Contact:** Jill Grosjean. Estab. 1999. Represents 19 clients. 100% of clients are new/unpublished writers. Currently handles: 1% nonfiction books; 99% novels.

   ● Prior to becoming an agent, Ms. Grosjean was manager of an independent bookstore. She also worked in publishing and advertising.

Represents: Novels. **Considers these fiction areas:** Contemporary issues; historical; humor/satire; literary; mainstream/contemporary; mystery/suspense; regional; romance; thriller.

   0→ This agency offers some editorial assistance (i.e., line-by-line edits). Actively seeking literary novels and mysteries. Does not want to receive any nonfiction subjects not indicated above.

How to Contact: Query with SASE. Considers simultaneous queries. Responds in 1 week to queries; 1 month to mss. Returns materials only with SASE. Obtains most new clients through recommendations from others, solicitations.

Recent Sales: *I Love You Like a Tomato*, by Marie Giordano (Forge Books); *Nectar*, by David C. Fickett (Forge Books); *Spectres in the Smoke*, by Tony Broadbent (Thomas Dunne); *Free Bird*, by Greg Garrett (Kensington); *The Smoke*, by Tony Broadbent (Thomas Dunne).

Terms: Agent receives 15% commission on domestic sales; 20% commission on foreign sales. No written contract. Charges clients for photocopying, mailing expenses; writers reimbursed for office fees after the sale of ms.

Writers' Conferences: Book Passages Mystery Writer's Conference (Corte Madera CA, July).

REECE HALSEY NORTH, 98 Main St., #704, Tiburon CA 94920. (415)789-9191. E-mail: info@reecehalseynorth.com. Website: www.reecehalseynorth.com or www.kimberleycameron.com. **Contact:** Kimberley Cameron. Estab. 1995. Member of AAR. Represents 40 clients. 30% of clients are new/unpublished writers. Currently handles: 30% nonfiction books; 70% novels.

Member Agents: Kimberley Cameron (Reece Halsey North); Dorris Halsey (by referral only, LA office).

Represents: Novels. **Considers these fiction areas:** Action/adventure; contemporary issues; detective/police/crime; ethnic; family saga; historical; horror; literary; mainstream/contemporary; mystery/suspense; science fiction; thriller; women's.

> **O—** This agency specializes in mystery, literary and mainstream fiction, excellent writing. The Reece Halsey Agency has an illustrious client list largely of established writers, including the estate of Aldous Huxley and has represented Upton Sinclair, William Faulkner and Henry Miller. Ms. Cameron has a Northern California office and all queries should be addressed to her at the Tiburon address.

How to Contact: Query with SASE. No e-mail or fax queries. Considers simultaneous queries. Responds in 1 month to queries; 3 months to mss. Obtains most new clients through recommendations from others, solicitations.

Recent Sales: *Jinn*, by Matthew Delaney (St. Martin's Press); *Final Epidemic*, by Earl Merkel (Dutton-NAL); *Sea Room*, by Norman Gautreau; *The Modern Gentleman*, by Phineas Mollod and Jason Tesauro.

Terms: Agent receives 15% commission on domestic sales. Offers written contract, binding for 1 year. Requests 8 copies of ms if representing an author.

Writers' Conferences: BEA; Maui Writers Conference; San Diego State University; Pacific Northwest; Cape Cod.

Reading List: Reads *Glimmer Train*, *The Sun*, *Zyzzyva* and *The New Yorker* to find new clients. Looks for "writing that touches the heart."

Tips: "Please send a polite, well-written query and include a SASE with it! You may also include the first ten pages of the manuscript."

THE JOY HARRIS LITERARY AGENCY, INC., 156 Fifth Ave., Suite 617, New York NY 10010. (212)924-6269. Fax: (212)924-6609. E-mail: gen.office@jhlitagent.com. **Contact:** Joy Harris. Member of AAR. Represents 100 clients. Currently handles: 50% nonfiction books; 50% novels.

Member Agents: Leslie Daniels; Stéphanie Abou; Alexia Paul (associate member).

Represents: Novels. **Considers these fiction areas:** Action/adventure; comic books/cartoon; confession; contemporary issues; detective/police/crime; ethnic; experimental; family saga; feminist; gay/lesbian; glitz; hi-lo; historical; humor/satire; literary; mainstream/contemporary; military/war; multicultural; multimedia; mystery/suspense; New Age; picture books; poetry; poetry in translation; regional; religious/inspirational; short story collections; spiritual; sports; thriller; translation; women's.

> **O—** Does not want to receive screenplays.

How to Contact: Query with outline/proposal, SASE. Considers simultaneous queries. Responds in 2 months to queries. Obtains most new clients through recommendations from clients and editors.

Recent Sales: Sold 15 titles in the last year. This agency prefers not to share information on specific sales.

Terms: Agent receives 15% commission on domestic sales; 20% commission on foreign sales. Charges clients for some office expenses.

NATASHA KERN LITERARY AGENCY, P.O. Box 2908, Portland OR 97208-2908. (503)297-6190. Website: www.natashakern.com. **Contact:** Natasha Kern. Estab. 1986. Member of RWA, MWA, SinC.

> **●** Prior to opening her agency, Ms. Kern worked as an editor and publicist for New York publishers (Simon & Schuster, Bantam, Ballantine). "This agency has sold over 500 books."

Member Agents: Natasha Kern; Ruth Widener.

Represents: Adult commercial fiction. **Considers these fiction areas:** Ethnic; feminist; historical; mainstream/contemporary; mystery/suspense; religious/inspirational; romance (contemporary, historical); thriller (medical, scientific, historical).

> **O—** This agency specializes in commercial fiction and nonfiction for adults. "A full service agency." Does not represent sports, true crime, scholarly works, coffee table books, war memoirs, software, scripts, literary fiction, photography, poetry, short stories, children's, horror, fantasy, genre science fiction, stage plays or traditional Westerns.

How to Contact: Query with SASE, include submission history, writing credits, how long ms is. For fiction: send 2-3 page synopsis and 3-5 first pages. For nonfiction: overview, describe market and how ms is different/better than similar works, author bio and ms length. See Web site before querying. No e-mail or fax queries. Considers simultaneous queries. Responds in 3 weeks to queries.

Recent Sales: Sold 53 titles in the last year. *Firstborn*, by Robin Lee Hatcher (Tyndale); *Bone Mountain*, by Eliot Pattison (St. Martin's Press); *The Diamond Conspiracy*, by Nick Kublicki (Sourcebooks).
Terms: Agent receives 15% commission on domestic sales; 20% commission on foreign sales; 15% commission on dramatic rights sales.
Writers' Conferences: RWA National Conference, MWA National Conference and many regional conferences.
Tips: "Our idea of a Dream Client is someone who participates in a mutually respectful business relationship, is clear about needs and goals, and communicates about career planning. If we know what you need and want, we can help you achieve it. A dream client has a storytelling gift, a commitment to a writing career, a desire to learn and grow, and a passion for excellence. We want clients who are expressing their own unique voice and truly have something of their own to communicate. This client understands that many people have to work together for a book to succeed and that everything in publishing takes far longer than one imagines. Trust and communication are truly essential."

HARVEY KLINGER, INC., 301 W. 53rd St., Suite 21-A, New York NY 10019. (212)581-7068. Fax: (212)315-3823. E-mail: klingerinc@aol.com. **Contact:** Harvey Klinger. Estab. 1977. Member of AAR. Represents 100 clients. 25% of clients are new/unpublished writers. Currently handles: 50% nonfiction books; 50% novels.
Member Agents: Jenny Bent (literary fiction; commercial women's fiction; memoir; narrative nonfiction; self help/pop psychology); David Dunton (popular culture, with a speciality in music-related books; literary fiction; crime novels; thrillers); Wendy Silbert (narrative nonfiction; historical narrative nonfiction; politics; history; biographies; memoir; literary ficiton; business books; culinary narratives); Lisa Dicker, associate agent (literary fiction; sports; narrative nonfiction).
Represents: Novels. **Considers these fiction areas:** Action/adventure; detective/police/crime; family saga; glitz; literary; mainstream/contemporary; mystery/suspense; thriller.
  O─¬ This agency specializes in "big, mainstream contemporary fiction and nonfiction."
How to Contact: Query with SASE. No phone queries. Accepts e-mail queries. No fax queries. Responds in 2 months to queries; 2 months to mss. Obtains most new clients through recommendations from others.
Recent Sales: Sold 30 titles in the last year. *Swan Place*, by Augusta Trobaugh (Dutton); *Fund Your Future*, by Julie Stav (Berkley); *Auriel Rising*, by Elizabeth Redfern (Putnam); *A Love Supreme*, by Ashley Kahn (Viking); *Idiot Girls' Action Adventure Guide*, by Laurie Notaro; *Inside Medicine*, by Kevin Soden and Christine Dumas; *Where I Work and Other Stories*, by Ann Cummins (Houghton Mifflin); *Thirty Years of Shame*, by Mark Kemp (Free Press). Other clients include Barbara Wood, Terry Kay, Barbara De Angelis, Jill Conner Browne, Michael Farquhar, Greg Bottoms, Jeremy Jackson, Pamela Berkman, Jonetta Rose Barras, Paul Russell.
Terms: Agent receives 15% commission on domestic sales; 25% commission on foreign sales. Offers written contract. Charges for photocopying mss, overseas postage for mss.

THE KNIGHT AGENCY, P.O. Box 550648, Atlanta GA 30355. (404)816-9620. E-mail: knightagency@msn.com. Website: www.knightagency.net. **Contact:** Lisa Payne, manuscript coordinator. Estab. 1996. Member of AAR, RWA, Authors Guild. Represents 65 clients. 40% of clients are new/unpublished writers. Currently handles: 50% nonfiction books; 50% novels.
Member Agents: Deidre Knight (president, agent); Pamela Harty (agent); Lisa Wessling Payne (agency associate).
Represents: Novels. **Considers these fiction areas:** Literary; mainstream/contemporary (commercial); romance (contemporary, paranormal, romantic suspense, historical, inspirational); women's.
  O─¬ "We are looking for a wide variety of fiction and nonfiction. In the nonfiction area, we're particularly eager to find personal finance, business investment, pop culture, self-help/motivational and popular reference books. In fiction, we're always looking for romance; women's fiction; commercial fiction."
How to Contact: Query with SASE. Accepts e-mail queries; no attachments Considers simultaneous queries. Responds in 3 weeks to queries; 3 months to mss.
Recent Sales: Sold approximately 65 titles in the last year. *Dark Highlander*, by Karen Marie Moning (Bantam Dell); *The Healing Quilt*, by Lauraine Snelling (WaterBrook Press).
Terms: Agent receives 15% commission on domestic sales; 20-25% commission on foreign sales. Offers written contract, binding for 1 year; 30-day notice must be given to terminate contract. Charges clients for photocopying, postage, overnight courier expenses. "These are deducted from the sale of the work, not billed upfront."
Tips: "At the Knight Agency, a client usually ends up becoming a friend."

● **IRENE KRAAS AGENCY**, 256 Rancho Alegre Rd., Santa Fe NM 87508. (505)438-7715. Fax: (505)438-7783. Estab. 1990. Represents 30 clients. 75% of clients are new/unpublished writers. Currently handles: 100% novels.
Represents: Novels (adult). **Considers these fiction areas:** Action/adventure; detective/police/crime; mystery/suspense; science fiction; thriller (psychological).
  O─¬ This agency specializes in adult fiction. Actively seeking "books that are well written with commercial potential." Does not want to receive romance, short stories, plays or poetry.
How to Contact: Submit cover letter, first 50 pages, SASE; must include return postage and/or SASE. No e-mail or fax queries. Considers simultaneous queries. Returns materials only with SASE.
Recent Sales: *Night Blooming*, by Chelsea Quinn Yarbro (Warner); *Goblin Wood*, by Hilari Bell (Harper/Avon); *Farsala Trilogy*, by Hilari Bell (Simon & Schuster); *Edge of the Sword Trilogy*, by Rebecca Tingle (Putnam); *Patriots in Petticoats*, by Shirley Raye Redmond (Random); *No Place Like the Chevy*, by Janet Lee Cary (Atheneum). Other clients include Denise Vitola, Duncan Long, Shirley-Raye Redmond, Torry England.

Terms: Agent receives 15% commission on domestic sales. Offers written contract, binding for 1 year. Charges clients for photocopying and postage.

Writers' Conferences: Southwest Writers Conference (Albuquerque); Pacific Northwest Conference (Seattle); Vancouver Writers Conference (Vancouver BC); Austin Writers Workshop; Wilamette Writers' Group.

MICHAEL LARSEN/ELIZABETH POMADA LITERARY AGENTS, 1029 Jones St., San Francisco CA 94109-5023. (415)673-0939. E-mail: larsenpoma@aol.com. Website: www.Larsen-Pomada.com. **Contact:** Mike Larsen or Elizabeth Pomada. Estab. 1972. Member of AAR, Authors Guild, ASJA, PEN, WNBA, California Writers Club. Represents 100 clients. 40-45% of clients are new/unpublished writers. Currently handles: 70% nonfiction books; 30% novels.
- Prior to opening their agency, Mr. Larsen and Ms. Pomada were promotion executives for major publishing houses. Mr. Larsen worked for Morrow, Bantam and Pyramid (now part of Berkley), Ms. Pomada worked at Holt, David McKay, and The Dial Press.

Member Agents: Michael Larsen (nonfiction); Elizabeth Pomada (narrative nonfiction, books of interest to women).

Represents: Novels. **Considers these fiction areas:** Action/adventure; contemporary issues; detective/police/crime; ethnic; experimental; family saga; fantasy; feminist; gay/lesbian; glitz; historical; humor/satire; literary; mainstream/contemporary; mystery/suspense; religious/inspirational; romance (contemporary, gothic, historical).
- O—ₜ "We have very diverse tastes. We look for fresh voices and new ideas. We handle literary, commercial and genre fiction, and the full range of nonfiction books." Actively seeking commercial and literary fiction. Does not want to receive children's books, plays, short stories, screenplays, pornography, poetry or stories of abuse.

How to Contact: Query with SASE, first 10 pages of completed novel and two page synopsis, SASE. For nonfiction, send title, promotion plan and proposal done according to our plan (See brochure and website.). No e-mail or fax queries. Responds in 2 months to queries.

Recent Sales: Sold 15 titles in the last year. *Night Whispers*, by Pam Chun (Sourcebooks); *Marketing for Free*, by Jay C. Levinson (Houghton Mifflin); *Snoopy's Guide to the Writing Life*, introduction by Barnaby Conrad and foreward by Monte Schulz (Writer's Digest); *Fox on the Rhine*, by Michael Dobson and Doug Niles (Tor)

Terms: Agent receives 15% commission on domestic sales; 20% (30% for Asia) commission on foreign sales. May charge for printing, postage for multiple submissions, foreign mail, foreign phone calls, galleys, books, and legal fees.

Writers' Conferences: Book Expo America; Santa Barbara Writers Conference (Santa Barbara); Maui Writers Conference (Maui); ASJA.

Tips: "If you can write books that meet the needs of the marketplace, and you can promote your books, now is the best time ever to be a writer. We must find new writers to make a living so we are very eager to hear from new writers whose work will interest large houses and nonfiction writers who can promote their books. Please new writers whose work will interest large houses and nonfiction writers who can promote their books. Please send a SASE for a free 16-page brochure and a list of recent sales."

◖ THE LITERARY GROUP, 270 Lafayette St., 1505, New York NY 10012. (212)274-1616. Fax: (212)274-9876. E-mail: fweimann@theliterarygroup.com. Website: www.theliterarygroup.com. **Contact:** Frank Weimann. Estab. 1985. Represents 200 clients. 65% of clients are new/unpublished writers. Currently handles: 50% nonfiction books; 50% fiction.

Member Agents: Frank Weimann (fiction, nonfiction); Andrew Stuart (nonfiction); Priya Ratneshwar (fiction).

Represents: Novels. **Considers these fiction areas:** Action/adventure; contemporary issues; detective/police/crime; ethnic; family saga; fantasy; feminist; horror; humor/satire; mystery/suspense; psychic/supernatural; romance (contemporary, gothic, historical, regency); sports; thriller; westerns/frontier.
- O—ₜ This agency specializes in nonfiction (true crime, military, history, biography, sports, how-to).

How to Contact: Query with SASE, outline, 3 sample chapter(s). Prefers to read materials exclusively. Responds in 1 week to queries; 1 month to mss. Returns materials only with SASE. Obtains most new clients through referrals, writers' conferences, query letters.

Recent Sales: Sold 80 titles in the last year. *Inside Delta Force*, by Eric Haney; *The Greater Good*, by William Casey Moreton; *The Dead Room*, by Robert Ellis; *It's Only a Game*, by Terry Bradshaw. Other clients include James Bradley, Victoria Gotti, Judith Lansdowne.

Terms: Agent receives 15% commission on domestic sales; 15% commission on foreign sales. Offers written contract; 30-day notice must be given to terminate contract.

Writers' Conferences: Detroit Women's Writers (MI); Kent State University (OH); San Diego Writers Conference (CA); Maui Writers Conference (HI); Austin Writers' Conference (TX).

◖ LITWEST GROUP, LLC, 379 Burning Tree Court, Half Moon Bay CA 94019. (650)726-3969. Fax: (650)726-4925. E-mail: linda@litwest.com. Website: www.litwest.com. **Contact:** Linda Mead. Represents 160 clients. 45% of clients are new/unpublished writers. Currently handles: 75% nonfiction books; 25% novels; TV, movie, Internet projects revolving around the book.
- Prior to opening the agency, Ms. Ellis was in academia, Mr. Preskill was in law and Ms. Mead and Ms. Boyle were in publishing.

Member Agents: Linda Mead (business, personal improvement, memoir); Nancy Ellis (mystery/suspense/thriller, religion/spiritual, parenting, psychology, science); Rob Preskill (men's, thrillers, sports, literary); Katie Boyle (literary, women's issues, pop-culture, religion/spirituality).

Represents: Novels. **Considers these fiction areas:** Contemporary issues; detective/police/crime; ethnic; family saga; feminist; historical; humor/satire; literary; mainstream/contemporary; multicultural; mystery/suspense; religious/inspirational; sports; thriller.

○━ "We are multi-faceted." Actively seeking all subjects. Does not want to receive science fiction, horror, western.
How to Contact: Query with SASE, outline, 3 sample chapter(s). Considers simultaneous queries. Responds in 1 month to queries; 2 months to mss. Returns materials only with SASE. Obtains most new clients through recommendations from others, solicitations, conferences.
Recent Sales: *Stone Soup for the World*, by Marianne Larned (Crown); *The Acne Cure*, by Stephen Dubrow, Ph.D. and Brenda Adderly (Redale); *The Nature of Music*, by Maureen McCarthy Draper (Riverhead/Penguin/Putnam); *Esther Stories*, by Peter Orner (Houghton Mifflin). Other clients include Woodleigh Marx Hubbard, Jennifer Openshaw, Jed Diamond, Dr. Jay Gordon, Dr. Arthur White, Eric Harr, Brad Herzog, Martin Yan, Lyn Webster-Wilde, Larraine Segil, Bobby Unser.
Terms: Agent receives 15% commission on domestic sales; 20% commission on foreign sales. Offers written contract; 60-days notice must be given to terminate contract. Charges for postage and photocopying.
Writers' Conferences: Maui Writers Conference (Maui HI, Labor Day); San Diego State University Writers' Conference (San Diego CA, January); William Saroyan Writers Conference (Fresno CA, March); Santa Barbara (June) and many others.
Tips: "Clarity and precision about your work also helps the agent process."

LIVINGSTON COOKE, 457A Danforth Ave., Suite 201, Toronto Ontario M4K 1P1, Canada. (416)406-3390. Fax: (416)406-3389. E-mail: livcooke@idirect.ca. **Contact:** Elizabeth Griffen. Estab. 1992. Represents 200 clients. 30% of clients are new/unpublished writers. Currently handles: 50% nonfiction books; 30% novels; 10% movie scripts; 10% TV scripts.
● Prior to becoming an agent, Mr. Cooke was the publisher of Seal Books Canada.
Member Agents: David Johnston (film rights, literary fiction/nonfiction); Dean Cooke (literary fiction, nonfiction).
Represents: Novels. **Considers these fiction areas:** Juvenile; literary.
○━ Livingston Cooke represents some of the best Canadian writers in the world. "Through our contacts and sub-agents, we are building an international reputation for quality. Curtis Brown Canada is jointly owned by Dean Cooke and Curtis Brown New York. It represents Curtis Brown New York authors in Canada." Does not want to receive genre fiction (science fiction, fantasy, mystery, thriller, horror).
How to Contact: Query with SASE. Accepts e-mail and fax queries. Considers simultaneous queries. Responds in 1 month to queries; 6 weeks to mss. Returns materials only with SASE. Obtains most new clients through recommendations from others.
Recent Sales: Sold 40 titles and sold 4 scripts in the last year. *Clara Callan*, by Richard B. Wright (Harperflamingo Canada); *Stanley Park*, by Timothy Taylor (Knopf Canada); *Your Mouth is Lovely*, by Nancy Richler (Harper Collins); *Spirit Cabinet*, by Paul Quarrinton (Grove/Atlantic); *Lazarus and the Hurricane*, by S. Charton/T. Swinton (St. Martin's Press); *Latitudes of Melt*, by Joan Clark (Knopf Canada); *Possesing Genius: The Bizarre Odyssey of Eintein's Brain*, by Caroline Abraham (Penguin Canada, St. Martin's Press); *Englishman's Boy*, by Guy Vanderhaeghe (Minds Eye); *Lazarus and the Hurricane*, by T. Swinton and S. Chaiton (Universal/Beacon). Other clients include Margaret Gibson, Richard Scrimger, Tony Hillerman, Robertson Davies, Brian Moore.
Terms: Agent receives 15% commission on domestic sales; 20% commission on foreign sales. Offers written contract. Charges clients for postage, photocopying, courier.

LOWENSTEIN ASSOCIATES, 121 W. 27th St., Suite 601, New York NY 10001. (212)206-1630. Fax: (212)727-0280. **Contact:** President: Barbara Lowenstein. Estab. 1976. Member of AAR. Represents 150 clients. 20% of clients are new/unpublished writers. Currently handles: 60% nonfiction books; 40% novels.
Member Agents: Barbara Lowenstein (president); Nancy Yost (agent); Eileen Cope (agent); Norman Kurz (business affairs); Dorian Karchmar (associate member).
Represents: Novels. **Considers these fiction areas:** Contemporary issues; detective/police/crime; erotica; ethnic; feminist; gay/lesbian; historical; literary; mainstream/contemporary; mystery/suspense; romance (contemporary, historical, regency); thriller (medical).
○━ This agency specializes in health, business, spirituality, creative nonfiction, literary fiction, commercial fiction, especially suspense, crime and women's issues. "We are a full-service agency, handling domestic and foreign rights, film rights, and audio rights to all of our books."
How to Contact: Query with SASE. Prefers to read materials exclusively. For fiction, send outline and first chapter. No unsolicited mss. Responds in 6 weeks to queries. Returns materials only with SASE. Obtains most new clients through recommendations from others, solicitations, conferences.
Recent Sales: Sold 75 titles in the last year. *Secrets of the Baby Whisperer*, by Tracy Hogg and Melinda Blau (Ballantine); *Insect Dreams*, by Marc Estrin (Putnam/Blue Hen); *Murad Magic!*, by Dr. Howard Murad (St. Martin's). Other clients include Ishmael Reed, Deborah Crombie, Leslie Glass, Stephanie Laurens, Dr. Grace Cornish, Stephen Raleigh Byler, Harriet Scott Chessman, Camron Wright, Tim Cahill, Gina Nahai, Kevin Young.
Terms: Agent receives 15% commission on domestic sales; 20% commission on foreign sales. Offers written contract, binding for book by book basis. Charges for large photocopy batches and international postage.
Writers' Conferences: Malice Domestic; Bouchercon.
Tips: "Know the genre you are working in and READ!"

DONALD MAASS LITERARY AGENCY, 160 W. 95th St., Suite 1B, New York NY 10025. (212)866-8200. **Contact:** Donald Maass, Jennifer Jackson or Michelle Brummer. Estab. 1980. Member of AAR, SFWA, MWA, RWA. Represents over 100 clients. 5% of clients are new/unpublished writers. Currently handles: 100% novels.

● Prior to opening his agency, Mr. Maass served as an editor at Dell Publishing (NY) and as a reader at Gollancz (London). He is the current president of AAR.

Member Agents: Donald Maass (mainstream, literary, mystery/suspense, science fiction); Jennifer Jackson (commercial fiction, especially romance, science fiction, fantasy, mystery/suspense); Michelle Brummer (fiction: literary, contemporary, feminist, science fiction, fantasy, romance).

Represents: Novels. **Considers these fiction areas:** Detective/police/crime; fantasy; historical; horror; literary; mainstream/contemporary; mystery/suspense; psychic/supernatural; romance (historical, paranormal, time travel); science fiction; thriller; women's.

○━ This agency specializes in commercial fiction, especially science fiction, fantasy, mystery, romance, suspense. Actively seeking "to expand the literary portion of our list and expand in romance and women's fiction." Does not want to receive nonfiction, children's or poetry.

How to Contact: Query with SASE. Returns material only with SASE. Considers simultaneous queries. Responds in 2 weeks to queries; 3 months to mss.

Recent Sales: Sold over 100 titles in the last year. *No Graves as Yet*, by Anne Perry (Ballantine); *Griffone*, by Nalo Hopkinson (Warner Aspect).

Terms: Agent receives 15% commission on domestic sales; 20% commission on foreign sales.

Writers' Conferences: *Donald Maass*: World Science Fiction Convention; Frankfurt Book Fair; Pacific Northwest Writers Conference; Bouchercon and others; *Jennifer Jackson*: World Science Fiction and Fantasy Convention; RWA National and others; *Michelle Brummer*: ReaderCon; Luna Con; Frankfurt.

Tips: "We are fiction specialists, also noted for our innovative approach to career planning. Few new clients are accepted, but interested authors should query with SASE. Subagents in all principle foreign countries and Hollywood. No nonfiction or juvenile works considered."

MANUS & ASSOCIATES LITERARY AGENCY, INC., 375 Forest Ave., Palo Alto CA 94301. (650)470-5151. Fax: (650)470-5159. E-mail: manuslit@manuslit.com. Website: www.manuslit.com. **Contact:** Jillian Manus. Also: 445 Park Ave., New York NY 10022. (212)644-8020. Fax (212)644-3374. **Contact**: Janet Manus. Estab. 1985. Member of AAR. Represents 75 clients. 30% of clients are new/unpublished writers. Currently handles: 55% nonfiction books; 40% novels; 5% juvenile books.

● Prior to becoming agents, Jillian Manus was associate publisher of two national magazines and director of development at Warner Bros. and Universal Studios; Janet Manus has been a literary agent for 20 years.

Member Agents: Jandy Nelson (self-help, health, memoirs, narrative nonfiction, literary fiction, multicultural fiction, thrillers); Stephanie Lee (self-help, memoirs, dramatic nonfiction, commercial literary fiction, multicultural fiction, quirky/edgy fiction).

Represents: Novels. **Considers these fiction areas:** Literary; mainstream/contemporary; multicultural; mystery/suspense; romance; thriller; women's; Southern fiction; quirky/edgy fiction.

○━ This agency specializes in commercial literary fiction, narrative nonfiction, thrillers, health, pop psychology, women's empowerment. "Our agency is unique in the way that we not only sell the material, but we edit, develop concepts and participate in the marketing effort. We specialize in large, conceptual fiction and nonfiction, and always value a project that can be sold in the TV/feature film market." Actively seeking high-concept thrillers, commercial literary fiction, women's fiction, celebrity biographies, memoirs, multicultural fiction, popular health, women's empowerment, mysteries. Does not want to receive horror, romance, science fiction/fantasy, westerns, young adult, children's, poetry, cookbooks, magazine articles. Usually obtains new clients through recommendations from editors, clients and others; conferences; and unsolicited materials.

How to Contact: Query with SASE. If requested, submit outline, 2-3 sample chapter(s). Accepts e-mail and fax queries. Considers simultaneous queries. Responds in 2 months to queries; 6 weeks to mss. Returns materials only with SASE. Obtains most new clients through recommendations from others, solicitations, conferences.

Recent Sales: *Lily Dale: The Town that Talks to the Dead*, by Christine Wicker (Harper Collins); *Avoiding Prison and Other Noble Vacation Goals*, by Wendy Dale (Crown); *Within These Walls: Memoirs of a Death House Chaplain*, by Carol Pickett with Carlton Stowers (St. Martin's); *Beyond Choice*, by Alexander Sanger(Public Affairs); *Geisha: A Life*, by Mineko Iwasaki with Rande Brown (Pocket Books). Other clients include Dr. Lorraine Zappart, Marcus Allen, Carlton Stowers, Alan Jacobson, Ann Brandt, Dr. Richard Marrs, Mary Loverde, Lisa Huang Fleishman, Judy Carter, Daryl Ott Underhill, Glen Kleier, Andrew X. Pham, Lalita Tademy, Frank Baldwin, Katy Robinson, K.M. Soehnlein, Joelle Fraser, Fred Luskin, Jim Schutze.

Terms: Agent receives 15% commission on domestic sales; 20-25% commission on foreign sales. Offers written contract, binding for 2 years; 60 days notice must be given to terminate contract. Charges for photocopying and postage.

Writers' Conferences: Maui Writers Conference (Maui HI, Labor Day); San Diego Writer's Conference (San Diego CA, January); Willamette Writers Conference (Willamette OR, July).

Tips: "Research agents using a variety of sources, including *LMP*, guides, *Publishers Weekly*, conferences and even acknowledgements in books similar in tone to yours."

L. PERKINS ASSOCIATES, 5800 Arlington Ave., Riverdale NY 10471. (718)543-5344. Fax: (718)543-5354. E-mail: lperkinsagency@yahoo.com. **Contact:** Lori Perkins. Estab. 1990. Member of AAR. Represents 50 clients. 10% of clients are new/unpublished writers.

- Ms. Perkins has been an agent for 18 years. Her agency has an affiliate agency, Southern Literary Group. She is also the author of *The Insider's Guide to Getting an Agent* (Writer's Digest Books).

Represents: Novels. **Considers these fiction areas:** Fantasy; horror; literary (dark); science fiction.

- All of Ms. Perkins's clients write both fiction and nonfiction. "This combination keeps my clients publishing for years. I am also a published author so I know what it takes to write a book." Actively seeking a Latino *Gone With the Wind* and *Waiting to Exhale,* and urban ethnic horror. Does not want to receive "anything outside of the above categories, i.e., westerns, romance."

How to Contact: Query with SASE. Considers simultaneous queries. Responds in 6 weeks to queries; 3 months to mss. Returns materials only with SASE. Obtains most new clients through recommendations from others, solicitations, conferences.

Recent Sales: Sold 100 titles in the last year. *The Illustrated Ray Bradbury*, by Jerry Weist (Avon); *The Poet in Exile*, by Ray Manzarek (Avalon); *Behind Sad Eyes: The Life of George Harrison*, (St. Martin's Press).

Terms: Agent receives 15% commission on domestic sales; 20% commission on foreign sales. No written contract. Charges clients for photocopying.

Writers' Conferences: San Diego Writer's Conference; NECON; BEA; World Fantasy.

Tips: "Research your field and contact professional writers' organizations to see who is looking for what. Finish your novel before querying agents. Read my book, *An Insider's Guide to Getting an Agent* to get a sense of how agents operate."

PINDER LANE & GARON-BROOKE ASSOCIATES, LTD., 159 W. 53rd St., Suite 14E, New York NY 10019-6005. (212)489-0880. E-mail: pinderl@interport.com. **Contact:** Robert Thixton. Member of AAR; signatory of WGA. Represents 30 clients. 20% of clients are new/unpublished writers. Currently handles: 25% nonfiction books; 75% novels.

Member Agents: Nancy Coffey (contributing agent); Dick Duane; Robert Thixton.

Represents: Novels. **Considers these fiction areas:** Contemporary issues; detective/police/crime; family saga; fantasy; gay/lesbian; literary; mainstream/contemporary; mystery/suspense; romance; science fiction.

- This agency specializes in mainstream fiction and nonfiction. Does not want to receive screenplays, TV series teleplays or dramatic plays.

How to Contact: Query with SASE. No unsolicited mss. Responds in 3 weeks to queries; 2 months to mss. Obtains most new clients through referrals, queries.

Recent Sales: Sold 20 titles in the last year. *Diana & Jackie - Maidens, Mothers & Myths*, by Jay Mulvaney (St. Martin's Press); *The Sixth Fleet* (series), by David Meadows (Berkley); *Dark Fires*, by Rosemary Rogers (Mira Books).

Terms: Agent receives 15% commission on domestic sales; 30% commission on foreign sales. Offers written contract, binding for 3-5 years.

Tips: "With our literary and media experience, our agency is uniquely positioned for the current and future direction publishing is taking. Send query letter first giving the essence of the ms and a personal or career bio with SASE."

JODIE RHODES LITERARY AGENCY, 8840 Villa La Jolla Dr., Suite 315, La Jolla CA 92037-1957. (858)625-0544. Fax: (858)625-0544. **Contact:** Jodie Rhodes, president. Estab. 1998. Member of AAR. Represents 50 clients. 60% of clients are new/unpublished writers. Currently handles: 60% nonfiction books; 35% novels; 5% middle to young adult books.

- Prior to opening her agency, Ms. Rhodes was a university level creative writing teacher, workshop director, published novelist and Vice President Media Director at the N.W. Ayer Advertising Agency.

Member Agents: Jodie Rhodes, president; Clark McCutcheon (fiction); Bob McCarter (nonfiction).

Represents: Novels, juvenile books. **Considers these fiction areas:** Contemporary issues; ethnic; family saga; historical; juvenile; literary; mainstream/contemporary; mystery/suspense; thriller; young adult; women's.

- Actively seeking "writers passionate about their books with a talent for richly textured narrative, an eye for details, and a nose for research." Nonfiction writers must have recognized credentials and expert knowledge of their subject matter. Does not want to receive erotica, horror, fantasy, romance, science fiction.

How to Contact: Query with brief synopsis, first 30 to 50 pages and SASE. No e-mail or fax queries. Considers simultaneous queries. Responds in 10 days to queries. Returns materials only with SASE. Obtains most new clients through recommendations from others, agent sourcebooks.

Recent Sales: *Eyes of a Child*, by Robert Clark (Random House); *Dying to be Thin*, by Tara and Linda Rio (Rodale); *Sapphire's Grave*, by Hilda Highgate (Doubleday).

Terms: Agent receives 15% commission on domestic sales; 20% commission on foreign sales. Offers written contract; 30-day notice must be given to terminate contract. Charges clients for fax, photocopying, phone calls and postage. "Charges are itemized and approved by writers upfront."

Writers' Conferences: Southern California Writers Conference (San Diego, mid-February); SDSU Writers Conference (San Diego, mid-January); Los Angeles Writers' Conference (Los Angeles, mid-October).

Tips: "Think your book out before you write it. Do your research, know your subject matter intimately, write vivid specifics, not bland generalities. Care deeply about your book. Don't imitate other writers. Find your own voice. We never take on a book we don't believe in, and we go the extra mile for our writers. We welcome talented new writers. We hold monthly weekend clinics on how to write a query letter and weekly writing workshops for area writers."

ANGELA RINALDI LITERARY AGENCY, P.O. Box 7877, Beverly Hills CA 90212-7877. (310)842-7665. Fax: (310)837-8143. E-mail: ARinaldilitagcy@aol.com. **Contact:** Angela Rinaldi. Estab. 1994. Member of AAR. Represents 50 clients. Currently handles: 50% nonfiction books; 50% novels.
  • Prior to opening her agency, Ms. Rinaldi was an editor at New American Library, Pocket Books and Bantam, and the Manager of Book Development for *The Los Angeles Times*.
Represents: Novels. **Considers these fiction areas:** Literary; mainstream/contemporary.
  O—¬ Actively seeking commercial and literary fiction. Does not want to receive scripts, category romances, children's books, westerns, science fiction/fantasy and cookbooks.
How to Contact: For fiction: Send the first 3 chapters, brief synopsis, SASE. For nonfiction: Query with SASE first or send outline/proposal, SASE. Do not send metered mail as SASE. Considers simultaneous queries. Please advise if this is a multiple submission. Responds in 6 weeks to queries. Returns materials only with SASE.
Recent Sales: *Stepwives: Ten Steps to Help Ex-wives and Stepmothers*, by Lynne Oxhorn, Louise Oxhorn, and Marjorie Krausz (Simon & Schuster); *Zen Golf Mastering the Mental Game*, by Dr. Joseph Parent (Doubleday); *Who Moved My Cheese?*, by Dr. Spencer Johnson (Putnam); *Breach of Confidence*, by Eben Paul Perison (NAL/Signet);
Terms: Agent receives 15% commission on domestic sales; 20% commission on foreign sales. Offers written contract. Charges clients for photocopying if client doesn't supply copies for submission.

B.J. ROBBINS LITERARY AGENCY, 5130 Bellaire Ave., North Hollywood CA 91607-2908. (818)760-6602. Fax: (818)760-6616. E-mail: robbinsliterary@aol.com. **Contact:** (Ms.) B.J. Robbins. Estab. 1992. Member of Board of Directors, PEN American Center West. Represents 40 clients. 50% of clients are new/unpublished writers. Currently handles: 50% nonfiction books; 50% novels.
Member Agents: Rob McAndrews (commercial fiction).
Represents: Novels. **Considers these fiction areas:** Contemporary issues; detective/police/crime; ethnic; literary; mainstream/contemporary; mystery/suspense; sports; thriller.
How to Contact: Submit 3 sample chapter(s), outline/proposal, SASE. No e-mail or fax queries. Considers simultaneous queries. Responds in 2 weeks to queries; 6 weeks to mss. Returns materials only with SASE. Obtains most new clients through conferences, referrals.
Recent Sales: Sold 15 titles in the last year. *Please, Please, Please*, by Renee Swindle (Dial Press); *Katie.com*, by Katherine Tarbox (Dutton); *Quickening*, by Laura Catherine Brown (Random House/Ballantine); *Snow Mountain Passage*, by James D. Houston (Knopf); *The Last Summer*, by John Hough, Jr. (Simon & Schuster).
Terms: Agent receives 15% commission on domestic sales; 20% commission on foreign sales. Offers written contract; 3-month notice must be given to terminate contract. 100% of business is derived from commissions on ms sales. Charges clients for postage and photocopying only. Writers charged for fees only after the sale of ms.
Writers' Conferences: Squaw Valley Fiction Writers Workshop (Squaw Valley CA, August); Maui Writers Conference(Maui HI); SDSU Writers Conference (San Diego CA, January).

JANE ROTROSEN AGENCY LLC, 318 E. 51st St., New York NY 10022. (212)593-4330. Fax: (212)935-6985. E-mail: firstinitiallastname@janerotrosen.com. Estab. 1974. Member of AAR, Authors Guild. Represents over 100 clients. Currently handles: 30% nonfiction books; 70% novels.
Member Agents: Jane R. Berkey; Andrea Cirillo; Annelise Robey; Margaret Ruley; Kara Cesare (director of English-language sub-rights); Perry Gordijn (director of translation rights).
Represents: Novels. **Considers these fiction areas:** Action/adventure; detective/police/crime; family saga; historical; horror; mainstream/contemporary; mystery/suspense; romance; thriller; women's.
How to Contact: Query with SASE. By referral only. No e-mail or fax queries. Responds in 2 months to mss. Responds in 2 weeks (to writers who have been referred by a client or colleague). Returns materials only with SASE.
Recent Sales: Sold 140 titles in the last year. This agency prefers not to share information on specific sales.
Terms: Agent receives 15% commission on domestic sales; 20% commission on foreign sales. Offers written contract, binding for 3-5 years; 60-day notice must be given to terminate contract. Charges clients for photocopying, express mail, overseas postage, book purchase.

THE PETER RUBIE LITERARY AGENCY, 240 W. 35th St., Suite 500, New York NY 10001. (212)279-1776. Fax: (212)279-0927. E-mail: peterrubie@prlit.com. Website: www.prlit.com. **Contact:** Peter Rubie or June Clark. Estab. 2000. Member of AAR. Represents 130 clients. 30% of clients are new/unpublished writers.
  • Prior to opening his agency, Mr. Rubie was a founding partner at Perkins, Rubie & Associates and the fiction editor at Walker and Co.
Member Agents: June Clark (New Age, pop culture, gay issues); Peter Rubie (crime, science fiction, fantasy, literary fiction, thrillers, narrative nonfiction, history, commercial science, music).
Represents: Novels. **Considers these fiction areas:** Action/adventure; detective/police/crime; ethnic; fantasy; gay/lesbian; historical; literary; science fiction; thriller.
How to Contact: Query with SASE. Accepts e-mail queries. No fax queries. Responds in 2 months to queries; 3 months to mss. Returns materials only with SASE. Obtains most new clients through recommendations from others.

Recent Sales: Sold 30 titles in the last year. *The Emperor and the Wolf*, by Stuart Galbraith (Faber and Faber); *Unfinished Business*, by Harlon Ullman (Kensington); *No One Left Behind*, by Amy Yarsinske (Dutton/Signet); *Toward Rational Exuberance* (Farrar, Straus & Giroux); *On Night's Shore*, by Randall Silvis (St. Martin's Press); *Jewboy*, by Allan Kauffman (Fromm); *Einstein's Refrigerator*, by Steve Silverman (Andrews McMeel); *Hope's End*, by Stephen Chambers (TOR).

Terms: Agent receives 15% commission on domestic sales; 20% commission on foreign sales. Offers written contract. Charges clients for photocopying and some foreign mailings.

Tips: "We look for writers who are experts and have an outstanding prose style. Be professional. Read *Publishers Weekly* and genre-related magazines. Join writers' organizations. Go to conferences. Know your market, and learn your craft. Read Rubie's books *The Elements of Storytelling* (Wiley) and *The Writer's Market FAQs*(Writer's Digest Books). Go to our Web site for up-to-date information on clients and sales."

RUSSELL & VOLKENING, 50 W. 29th St., #7E, New York NY 10001. (212)684-6050. Fax: (212)889-3026. **Contact:** Timothy Seldes. Estab. 1940. Member of AAR. Represents 140 clients. 20% of clients are new/unpublished writers. Currently handles: 45% nonfiction books; 50% novels; 3% story collections; 2% novellas.

Member Agents: Timothy Seldes (nonfiction, literary fiction).

Represents: Novels, short story collections, novellas. **Considers these fiction areas:** Action/adventure; detective/police/crime; ethnic; literary; mainstream/contemporary; mystery/suspense; picture books; sports; thriller.

　O→ This agency specializes in literary fiction and narrative nonfiction.

Recent Sales: *Back when We Were Grownups*, by Anne Tyler (Knopf); *Warriors of God*, by James Reston Jr. (Doubleday); *No Certain Rest*, by Jim Lehrer (Random House).

Terms: Agent receives 15% commission on domestic sales; 20% commission on foreign sales. Charges clients for "standard office expenses relating to the submission of materials of an author we represent, e.g., photocopying, postage."

Tips: "If the query is cogent, well written, well presented and is the type of book we'd represent, we'll ask to see the manuscript. From there, it depends purely on the quality of the work."

WENDY SHERMAN ASSOCIATES, INC., 450 Seventh Ave., Suite 3004, New York NY 10123. (212)279-9027. Fax: (212)279-8863. E-mail: wendy@wsherman.com. **Contact:** Wendy Sherman. Estab. 1999. Member of AAR. Represents 30 clients. 30% of clients are new/unpublished writers. Currently handles: 50% nonfiction books; 50% novels.

　• Prior to becoming an agent, Ms. Sherman worked for Aaron Priest Agency and was vice president, executive director of Henry Holt, associate publisher, subsidary rights director, sales and marketing director.

Member Agents: Jessica Lichtenstein (suspense); Wendy Sherman.

Represents: Novels. **Considers these fiction areas:** Literary; women's.

　O→ "We specialize in developing new writers as well as working with more established writers. My experience as a publisher has proven to be a great asset to my clients."

How to Contact: Query with SASE, or send outline/proposal, 1 sample chapter. All unsolicited mss returned unopened. Considers simultaneous queries. Responds in 1 month to queries. Returns materials only with SASE. Obtains most new clients through recommendations from others.

Recent Sales: Sold 14 titles in the last year. *Real Love*, by Greg Baer, Ph.D. (Penguin Putnam); *The Cloud Atlas*, by Liam Callanan (Delacorte). Other clients include D.W. Buffa, Nani Power, Sarah Stonich, Alan Eisenstock, Howard Bahr, Lundy Bancroft, Lise Friedman, Tom Schweich, Suzanne Chazin.

Terms: Agent receives 15% commission on domestic sales; 20% commission on foreign sales. Offers written contract. Charges for photocopying of ms, messengers, express mail services, etc. (reasonable, standard expenses).

JEFFREY SIMMONS LITERARY AGENCY, 10 Lowndes Square, London SWIX 9HA, England. (020)7235 8852. Fax: (020)7235 9733. **Contact:** Jeffrey Simmons. Estab. 1978. Represents 43 clients. 40% of clients are new/unpublished writers. Currently handles: 60% nonfiction books; 40% novels.

　• Prior to becoming an agent, Mr. Simmons was a publisher and he is also an author.

Represents: Novels. **Considers these fiction areas:** Action/adventure; confession; detective/police/crime; family saga; literary; mainstream/contemporary; mystery/suspense; thriller.

　O→ This agency seeks to handle good books and promising young writers. "My long experience in publishing and as an author and ghostwriter means I can offer an excellent service all round, especially in terms of editorial experience where appropriate." Actively seeking quality fiction, biography, autobiography, showbiz, personality books, law, crime, politics, world affairs. Does not want to receive science fiction, horror, fantasy, juvenile, academic books, specialist subjects (i.e., cooking, gardening, religious).

How to Contact: Submit sample chapter, outline/proposal, IRCs if necessary, SASE. Prefers to read materials exclusively. Responds in 1 week to queries; 1 month to mss. Obtains most new clients through recommendations from others, solicitations.

Recent Sales: Sold 16 titles in the last year. *War of the Windsors*, by Picknett, Prince and Prior (Mainstream); *Town Without Pity*, by Don Hale (Century); *Only Fools and Horses*, by Richard Webber (Orion).

Terms: Agent receives 10-15% commission on domestic sales; 15% commission on foreign sales. Offers written contract, binding for lifetime of book in question or until it becomes out of print.

Tips: "When contacting us with an outline/proposal, include a brief biographical note (listing any previous publications, with publishers and dates). Preferably tell us if the book has already been offered elsewhere."

STEELE-PERKINS LITERARY AGENCY, 26 Island Lane, Canandaigua NY 14424. (716)396-9290. Fax: (716)396-3579. E-mail: pattiesp@aol.com. **Contact:** Pattie Steele-Perkins. Member of AAR, RWA. Currently handles: 100% Romance and mainstream women's fiction.

Represents: Novels. **Considers these fiction areas:** Mainstream/contemporary; multicultural; romance; women's.

O→ Actively seeking romance, women's fiction and multicultural works.

How to Contact: Submit outline, 3 sample chapter(s), SASE. Considers simultaneous queries. Responds in 6 weeks to queries. Returns materials only with SASE. Obtains most new clients through recommendations from others, queries/solicitations.

Recent Sales: This agency prefers not to share information on specific sales.

Terms: Agent receives 15% commission on domestic sales. Offers written contract, binding for 1 year; 30-day notice must be given to terminate contract.

Writers' Conferences: National Conference of Romance Writers of America; Book Expo America Writers' Conferences.

Tips: "Be patient. E-mail rather than call. Make sure what you are sending is the best it can be."

THE SUSIJN AGENCY, 820 Harrow Road, London NW10 5JU, England. (020) 8968 7435. Fax: 0044 (207)580-8626. E-mail: info@thesusijnagency.com. Website: www.thesusijnagency.com. **Contact:** Laura Susijn. Estab. 1998. Currently handles: 15% nonfiction books; 85% novels.

● Prior to becoming an agent, Ms. Susijn was a rights director at Sheil Land Associates and at Fourth Estate Ltd.

Member Agents: Laura Susijn

Represents: Novels. **Considers these fiction areas:** Literary.

O→ This agency specializes in international works, selling world rights, representing non-English language writing as well as English. Emphasis on cross-cultural subjects. Self-help, romance, sagas, science fiction, screenplays.

How to Contact: Submit outline, 2 sample chapter(s). Accepts e-mail and fax queries. Considers simultaneous queries. Responds in 2 months to queries. Returns materials only with SASE. Obtains most new clients through recommendations from others, via publishers in Europe and beyond.

Recent Sales: Sold 120 titles in the last year. *Gone*, by Helena Echlin (Secker and Warburg, UK); *Daalder*, by Philibert Schogt (4 Walls 8 Windows); *Prisoner in a Red Rose Chain*, by Jeffrey Moore (Weidenfeld & Nicholson); *Smell*, by Radhika Jha (Quartet Books); *The Formula One Fanatic*, by Koen Vergeer (Bloomsbury); *A Mouthful of Glass*, by Henk Van Woerden (Granta); *Fragile Science*, by Robin Baker (Macmillan); *East of Acre Lane*, by Alex Wheatle (Fourth Estate). Other clients include Vassallucci, Podium, Atlas, De Arbeiderspers, Tiderne Skifter, MB Agency, Van Oorschot

Terms: Agent receives 15% commission on domestic sales; 15-20% commission on foreign sales. Offers written contract; 6 weeks notice must be given to terminate contract. Charges clients for photocopying, buying copies only if sale is made.

THE VINES AGENCY, INC., 648 Broadway, Suite 901, New York NY 10012. (212)777-5522. Fax: (212)777-5978. E-mail: jv@vinesagency.com. Website: www.vinesagency.com. **Contact:** James C. Vines, Paul Surdi, Ali Ryan, Gary Neuwirth. Estab. 1995. Member of Authors' Guild; signatory of WGA. Represents 52 clients. 20% of clients are new/unpublished writers. Currently handles: 50% nonfiction books; 50% novels.

● Prior to opening his agency, Mr. Vines served as an agent with the Virginia Barber Literary Agency.

Member Agents: James C. Vines (quality and commercial fiction and nonfiction); Gary Neuwirth; Paul Surdi (women's fiction, ethnic fiction, quality nonfiction); Ali Ryan (women's fiction and nonfiction, mainstream).

Represents: Novels. **Considers these fiction areas:** Action/adventure; contemporary issues; detective/police/crime; ethnic; experimental; family saga; feminist; gay/lesbian; historical; horror; humor/satire; literary; mainstream/contemporary; mystery/suspense; occult; psychic/supernatural; regional; romance (contemporary, historical); science fiction; sports; thriller; westerns/frontier; women's. **Considers these script subject areas:** Action/adventure; comedy; detective/police/crime; ethnic; experimental; feminist; gay/lesbian; historical; horror; mainstream; mystery/suspense; romantic comedy; romantic drama; science fiction; teen; thriller; western/frontier.

O→ This agency specializes in mystery, suspense, science fiction, women's fiction, ethnic fiction, mainstream novels, screenplays, teleplays.

How to Contact: Submit outline, 3 sample chapter(s), SASE. Accepts e-mail and fax queries. Considers simultaneous queries. Responds in 2 weeks to queries; 1 month to mss. Returns materials only with SASE. Obtains most new clients through query letters, recommendations from others, reading short stories in magazines, soliciting conferences.

Recent Sales: Sold 48 titles and sold 5 scripts in the last year. *The Bottoms*, by Joe R. Lansdale; *The Surrendered Single*, by Laura Doyle; *America the Beautiful*, by Moon Unit Zappa (Scribner); *The Power of the Dog*, by Don Winslow; *Getting Our Breath Back*, by Shawne Johnson; *This Bitter Earth*, by Bernice McFadden.

Terms: Agent receives 15% commission on domestic sales; 25% commission on foreign sales. Offers written contract, binding for 1 year; 30 days notice must be given to terminate contract. 100% of business is derived from commissions on ms sales. Charges clients for foreign postage, messenger services, photocopying.

Writers' Conferences: Maui Writer's Conference.

Tips: "Do not follow up on submissions with phone calls to the agency. The agency will read and respond by mail only. Do not pack your manuscript in plastic 'peanuts' that will make us have to vacuum the office after opening the package containing your manuscript. Always enclose return postage."

WRITERS HOUSE, 21 W. 26th St., New York NY 10010. (212)685-2400. Fax: (212)685-6550. Estab. 1974. Member of AAR. Represents 440 clients. 50% of clients are new/unpublished writers. Currently handles: 25% nonfiction books; 40% novels; 35% juvenile books.

Member Agents: Albert Zuckerman (major novels, thrillers, women's fiction, important nonfiction); Amy Berkower (major juvenile authors, women's fiction, art and decorating, psychology); Merrilee Heifetz (quality children's fiction, science fiction and fantasy, popular culture, literary fiction); Susan Cohen (juvenile and young adult fiction and nonfiction, Judaism, women's issues); Susan Ginsburg (serious and popular fiction, true crime, narrative nonfiction, personality books, cookbooks); Michele Rubin (serious nonfiction); Robin Rue (commercial fiction and nonfiction, YA fiction); Jennifer Lyons (literary, commercial fiction, international fiction, nonfiction and illustrated); Jodi Reamer (juvenile and young adult fiction and nonfiction, adult commercial fiction, popular culture); Simon Lipskar (literary and commercial fiction, narrative nonfiction); Nicole Pitesa (juvenile and young adult fiction, literary fiction); Steven Malk (juvenile and young adult fiction and non-fiction).

Represents: Novels, juvenile books. **Considers these fiction areas:** Action/adventure; comic books/cartoon; confession; contemporary issues; detective/police/crime; erotica; ethnic; experimental; family saga; fantasy; feminist; gay/lesbian; glitz; gothic; hi-lo; historical; horror; humor/satire; juvenile; literary; mainstream/contemporary; military/war; multicultural; multimedia; mystery/suspense; New Age; occult; picture books; plays; poetry; poetry in translation; psychic/supernatural; regional; religious/inspirational; romance; science fiction; short story collections; spiritual; sports; thriller; translation; westerns/frontier; young adult; women's.

○─┐ This agency specializes in all types of popular fiction and nonfiction. Does not want to receive scholarly, professional, poetry, plays or screenplays.

How to Contact: Query with SASE. No e-mail or fax queries. Responds in 1 month to queries. Obtains most new clients through recommendations from others.

Recent Sales: Sold 200-300 titles in the last year. *Next*, by Michael Lewis (Norton); *Art of Deception*, by Ridley Pearson (Hyperion); *Report from Ground Zero*, by Dennis Smith (Viking); *The Villa*, by Nora Roberts (Penguin/Putnam); *Captain Underpants*, by Dan Pilkey (Scholastic). Other clients include Francine Pascal, Ken Follett, Stephen Hawking, Linda Howard, F. Paul Wilson, Neil Gaiman and Laurel Hamilton.

Terms: Agent receives 15% commission on domestic sales; 20% commission on foreign sales. Offers written contract, binding for 1 year. Agency charges fees for copying manuscripts and proposals and overseas airmail of books.

Tips: "Do not send mss. Write a compelling letter. If you do, we'll ask to see your work."

ZACHARY SHUSTER HARMSWORTH, 1776 Broadway, Suite 1405, New York NY 10019. (212)765-6900. Fax: (212)765-6490. E-mail: e.harmsworth@zshliterary.com. Website: www.zshliterary.com. Also: Boston Office: 729 Boylston St., 5th Floor. Phone: (617)262-2400, Fax: (617)262-2468. **Contact:** Esmond Harmsworth; Scott Gold (NY). Estab. 1996. Represents 125 clients. 20% of clients are new/unpublished writers. Currently handles: 45% nonfiction books; 45% novels; 5% story collections; 5% scholarly books.

● "Our principals include two former publishing and entertainment lawyers, a journalist and an editor/agent." Lane Zachary was an editor at Random House before becoming an agent.

Member Agents: Esmond Harmsworth (commercial and literary fiction, history, science, adventure); Todd Shuster (narrative and prescriptive nonfiction, biography, memoirs); Lane Zachary (biography, memoirs, literary fiction); Jennifer Gates (literary fiction, nonfiction).

Represents: Novels. **Considers these fiction areas:** Contemporary issues; detective/police/crime; ethnic; feminist; gay/lesbian; historical; literary; mainstream/contemporary; mystery/suspense; thriller.

○─┐ This agency specializes in journalist-driven narrative nonfiction, literary and commercial fiction. Actively seeking narrative nonfiction, mystery, commercial and literary fiction, memoirs, history, biographies. Does not want to receive poetry.

How to Contact: Query with SASE, submit 50 page sample of ms. No e-mail or fax queries. Considers simultaneous queries. Responds in 3 months to mss. Obtains most new clients through recommendations from others, solicitations, conferences.

Recent Sales: Sold 40-50 titles in the last year. *All Kinds of Minds*, by Mel Levine (Simon & Schuster) #1 New York Times bestseller. Other clients include Leslie Epstein, David Mixner.

Terms: Agent receives 15% commission on domestic sales; 20% commission on foreign sales. Offers written contract, binding for 1 work only; 30 days notice must be given to terminate contract. Charges clients for postage, copying, courier, telephone. "We only charge expenses if the manuscript is sold."

Tips: "We work closely with all our clients on all editorial and promotional aspects of their works."

[N] ⬤ SUSAN ZECKENDORF ASSOC. INC., 171 W. 57th St., New York NY 10019. (212)245-2928. **Contact:** Susan Zeckendorf. Estab. 1979. Member of AAR. Represents 15 clients. 25% of clients are new/unpublished writers. Currently handles: 50% nonfiction books; 50% novels.

● Prior to opening her agency, Ms. Zeckendorf was a counseling psychologist.

Represents: Novels. **Considers these fiction areas:** Detective/police/crime; ethnic; historical; literary; mainstream/contemporary; mystery/suspense; thriller.

○─┐ Actively seeking mysteries, literary fiction, mainstream fiction, thrillers, social history, parenting, classical music, biography. Does not want to receive science fiction, romance. "No children's books."

How to Contact: Query with SASE. No e-mail or fax queries. Considers simultaneous queries. Responds in 10 days to queries; 3 weeks to mss. Returns materials only with SASE.

Recent Sales: Sold 2 titles in the last year. *How to Write a Damn Good Mystery*, by James N. Frey (St. Martin's); *Moment of Madness*, by Una-Mary Parker (Headline).

Terms: Agent receives 15% commission on domestic sales; 20% commission on foreign sales. Charges for photocopying, messenger services.

Writers' Conferences: Central Valley Writers Conference; The Tucson Publishers Association Conference; Writer's Connection; Frontiers in Writing Conference (Amarillo TX); Golden Triangle Writers Conference (Beaumont TX); Oklahoma Festival of Books (Claremont OK); Mary Mount Writers Conference.

Tips: "We are a small agency giving lots of individual attention. We respond quickly to submissions."

Literary Agents Category Index

Agents listed in the preceeding section are indexed below according to the categories of fiction they represent. Use it to find agents who handle the specific kind of fiction you write. Then turn to those listings in the alphabetical Literary Agents section for complete contact and submission information.

Rhodes Literary Agency, Jodie
Robbins Literary Agency, B.J.
Rubie Literary Agency, The Peter
Russell and Volkening
Vines Agency, Inc., The
Writers House
Zachary Shuster Harmsworth
Zeckendorf Assoc. Inc., Susan

Experimental
Brown Ltd., Curtis
Harris Literary Agency, Inc., The Joy
Larsen/Elizabeth Pomada Literary Agents, Michael
Vines Agency, Inc., The
Writers House

Family Saga
Barrett Books Inc., Loretta
BookEnds, LLC
Brown Ltd., Curtis
Cornerstone Literary, Inc.
Daves Agency, Joan
Dawson Associates, Liza
Greenburger Associates, Inc., Sanford J.
Halsey North, Reece
Harris Literary Agency, Inc., The Joy
Klinger, Inc., Harvey
Larsen/Elizabeth Pomada Literary Agents, Michael
Literary Group, The
LitWest Group, LLC
Pinder Lane & Garon-Brooke Associates, Ltd.
Rhodes Literary Agency, Jodie
Rotrosen Agency, LLC, Jane
Simmons Literary Agency, Jeffrey
Vines Agency, Inc., The
Writers House

Fantasy
Brown Ltd., Curtis
Ellenberg Literary Agency, Ethan
Gislason Agency, The
Larsen/Elizabeth Pomada Literary Agents, Michael
Literary Group, The
Maass Literary Agency
Perkins Associates, L.
Pinder Lane & Garon-Brooke Associates, Ltd.
Rubie Literary Agency, The Peter
Writers House

Feminist
Barrett Books Inc., Loretta
BookEnds, LLC
Brown Ltd., Curtis
Greenburger Associates, Inc., Sanford J.
Harris Literary Agency, Inc., The Joy
Kern Literary Agency, Natasha
Larsen/Elizabeth Pomada Literary Agents, Michael
Literary Group, The
LitWest Group, LLC
Lowenstein Associates
Vines Agency, Inc., The
Writers House
Zachary Shuster Harmsworth

Glitz
Barrett Books Inc., Loretta
BookEnds, LLC
Brown Ltd., Curtis
Cornerstone Literary, Inc.
Daves Agency, Joan
Greenburger Associates, Inc., Sanford J.
Harris Literary Agency, Inc., The Joy
Klinger, Inc., Harvey
Larsen/Elizabeth Pomada Literary Agents, Michael
Lowenstein Associates
Pinder Lane & Garon-Brooke Associates, Ltd.
Rubie Literary Agency, The Peter
Vines Agency, Inc., The
Writers House
Zachary Shuster Harmsworth

Hi-Lo
Brown Ltd., Curtis
Harris Literary Agency, Inc., The Joy
Writers House

Historical
Barrett Books Inc., Loretta
BookEnds, LLC
Brown Ltd., Curtis
Carvainis Agency, Inc., Maria
Cohen, Inc. Literary Agency, Ruth
Cornerstone Literary, Inc.
Dawson Associates, Liza
Greenburger Associates, Inc., Sanford J.
Gregory and Company Authors' Agents
Grosjean Literary Agency, Jill
Halsey North, Reece
Harris Literary Agency, Inc., The Joy
Kern Literary Agency, Natasha
Larsen/Elizabeth Pomada Literary Agents, Michael
LitWest Group, LLC
Lowenstein Associates
Maass Literary Agency
Rhodes Literary Agency, Jodie
Rotrosen Agency, LLC, Jane
Rubie Literary Agency, The Peter
Vines Agency, Inc., The
Writers House
Zachary Shuster Harmsworth
Zeckendorf Assoc. Inc., Susan

Horror
Amsterdam Agency, Marcia
Brown Ltd., Curtis
Halsey North, Reece
Literary Group, The
Maass Literary Agency
Perkins Associates, L.
Rotrosen Agency, LLC, Jane
Vines Agency, Inc., The
Writers House

Humor/Satire
Barrett Books Inc., Loretta
Brown Ltd., Curtis
Cornerstone Literary, Inc.
Greenburger Associates, Inc., Sanford J.

Literary Magazines

This section contains markets for your literary short fiction. Although definitions of what constitutes "literary" writing vary, editors of literary journals agree they want to publish the "best" fiction they can acquire. Qualities they look for in fiction include creativity, style, flawless mechanics, and careful attention to detail in content and manuscript preparation. Most of the authors writing such fiction are well-read and well-educated, and many are students and graduates of university creative writing programs.

Please also review our new Online Markets section, page 301, for electronic literary magazines. At a time when paper and publishing costs rise while funding to university presses continues to be cut or eliminated, electronic literary magazines are helping generate a publishing renaissance for experimental as well as more traditional literary fiction. These electronic outlets for literary fiction also benefit writers by eliminating copying and postage costs and providing the opportunity for much quicker responses to submissions. Also notice that some magazines with websites give specific information about what they offer on their websites, including updated writer's guidelines and sample fiction from their publications.

STEPPING STONES TO RECOGNITION

Some well-established literary journals pay several hundred or even several thousand dollars for a short story. Most, though, can only pay with contributor's copies or a subscription to their publication. However, being published in literary journals offers the important benefits of experience, exposure, and prestige. Agents and major book publishers regularly read literary magazines in search of new writers. Work from among these journals is also selected for inclusion in annual prize anthologies such as *The Best American Short Stories, Prize Stories: The O. Henry Awards, Pushcart Prize: Best of the Small Presses*, and *New Stories from the South: The Year's Best*.

You'll find most of the well-known prestigious literary journals listed here. Many, including *Carolina Quarterly* and *Ploughshares*, are associated with universities, while others such as *The Paris Review* are independently published.

SELECTING THE RIGHT LITERARY JOURNAL

Once you have browsed through this section and have a list of journals you might like to submit to, read those listings again, carefully. Remember that this is information editors present to help you in submitting work that fits their needs. The "Quick Start" Guide to Publishing Your Fiction, starting on page 2, will guide you through the process of finding markets for your fiction.

This is the only section in which you will find magazines that do not read submissions all year long. Whether limited reading periods are tied to a university schedule or meant to accommodate the capabilities of a very small staff, those periods are noted within listings. The staffs of university journals are usually made up of student editors and a managing editor who is also a faculty member. These staffs often change every year. Whenever possible, we indicate this in listings and give the name of the current editor and the length of that editor's term. Also be aware that the schedule of a university journal usually coincides with that university's academic year, meaning that the editors of most university publications are difficult or impossible to reach during the summer.

FURTHERING YOUR SEARCH

It cannot be stressed enough that reading the listings for literary journals is only the first part of developing your marketing plan. The second part, equally important, is to obtain fiction guidelines and read the actual journal you'd like to submit to with great care. Reading copies of these journals helps you determine the fine points of each magazine's publishing style and sensibility. There is no substitute for this type of hands-on research.

Unlike commercial periodicals available at most newsstands and bookstores, it requires a little more effort to obtain some of the magazines listed here. The super chain bookstores are doing a better job these days of stocking literaries and you can find some in independent and college bookstores, especially those published in your area. You may, however, need to send for a sample copy. We include sample copy prices in the listings whenever possible. In addition to reading your sample copies, pay close attention to the **Advice** section of each listing. There you'll often find a very specific description of the style of fiction editors at that publication prefer.

Another way to find out more about literary magazines is to check out the various prize anthologies and take note of journals whose fiction is being selected for publication there. Studying prize anthologies not only lets you know which magazines are publishing award-winning work, but it also provides a valuable overview of what is considered to be the best fiction published today. Those anthologies include:

• *Best American Short Stories*, published by Houghton Mifflin, 222 Berkeley St., Boston MA 02116.

• *New Stories from the South: The Year's Best*, published by Algonquin Books of Chapel Hill, P.O. Box 2225, Chapel Hill NC 27515.

• *Prize Stories: The O. Henry Awards*, published by Doubleday/Anchor, 1540 Broadway, New York NY 10036.

• *Pushcart Prize: Best of the Small Presses*, published by Pushcart Press, Box 380, Wainscott NY 11975.

At the beginnings of listings, we include symbols to help you in narrowing your search. Keys to those symbols can be found on the inside front and back covers of this book.

ACM, (ANOTHER CHICAGO MAGAZINE), Left Field Press, 3709 Kenmore, Chicago IL 60613. E-mail: editors@anotherchicagomag.com. Website: www.anotherchicagomag.com (includes guidelines, contest information, subscription information). Editor: Barry Silesky. **Contact:** Sharon Solwitz, fiction editor. Magazine: 5½×8½; 200-220 pages; "art folio each issue." Estab. 1977.
Needs: Contemporary, ethnic, experimental, feminist, gay, lesbian, literary, prose poem and translations. No religious, strictly genre or editorial. Receives 300 unsolicited fiction mss each month. **Publishes 10 new writers/year.** Recently published work by Stuart Dybek and Steve Almond. Also publishes creative nonfiction.
How to Contact: Unsolicited mss acceptable with SASE. "Send only one story (unless you work short, less than five pgs.) then we'll read two. We encourage cover letters." Publishes ms 6-12 months after acceptance. Sample copies are available for $8 ppd. Responds in 5 months. Accepts multiple submissions. Receives small press collections.
Payment/Terms: Pays small honorarium when possible, contributor's copies and 1 year subscription. Acquires first North American serial rights.
Advice: "Support literary publishing by subscribing to at least one literary journal—if not ours another. Get used to rejection slips, and don't get discouraged. Keep introductory letters short. Make sure manuscript has name and address on every page, and that it is clean, neat and proofread. We are looking for stories with freshness and originality in subject angle and style, and work that encounters the world and is not stuck in its own navel."

ADVOCATE, PKA'S PUBLICATION, PKA Publications, 301A Rolling Hills Park, Prattsville NY 12468. (518)299-3103. Tabloid: 9⅜×12¼; 32 pages; newsprint paper; line drawings; b&w photographs. "Eclectic for a general audience." Bimonthly. Estab. 1987. Publishes 12,000 copies.
Needs: Adventure, contemporary, ethnic, experimental, fantasy, feminist, historical, humor/satire, juvenile (5-9 years), literary, mainstream, mystery/suspense, prose poem, regional, romance, science fiction, senior citizen/retirement, sports, western, young adult/teen (10-18 years). "Currently looking for equine (horses) stories, poetry, art, photos and cartoons. The *Gaited Horse Newsletter* is currently published within the pages of *PKA's Advocate*. Nothing religious, pornographic, violent, erotic, pro-drug or anti-environment." Receives 60 unsolicited mss/month. Accepts 6-8 mss/issue; 36-48 mss/year. Publishes ms 4 months to 1 year after acceptance. Length: 1,000 words preferred; 1,500 words maximum. Also publishes poetry. Sometimes critiques rejected mss.

How to Contact: Send complete ms with cover letter. Responds in 2 weeks to queries; 2 months to mss. SASE. No simultaneous submissions; "no work that has appeared on the Internet." Sample copy for $4 (US currency for inside US; $5.25 US currency for Canada). Writers guidelines for SASE.

Payment/Terms: Pays contributor's copies. Acquires first rights.

Advice: "The highest criterion in selecting a work is its entertainment value. It must first be enjoyable reading. It must, of course, be original. To stand out, it must be thought provoking or strongly emotive, or very cleverly plotted. Will consider only previously unpublished works by writers who do not earn their living principally through writing."

AETHLON, East Tennessee State University, Box 70, 683, Johnson City TN 37614-0683. (423)439-5994. E-mail: morefiel@etsu.edu. **Contact:** John Morefield, fiction editor. Magazine: 6×9; 180-240 pages; photos. "Theme: Literary treatment of sport. We publish articles on that theme, critical studies of author's treatment of sport and original fiction and poetry with sport themes. Most of our readers are academics." Biannual. Estab. 1983. Circ. 800.

Needs: Sport. "No fantasy, science fiction, mystery, nostalgia, trick endings, novel excerpts or horror. Stories must have a sport-related theme and subject; otherwise, we're wide open." Receives 15-20 fiction mss/month. Accepts 6-10 fiction mss/issue; 12-20 fiction mss/year. Publishes ms "about 1 year" after acceptance. **Publishes 2-3 new writers/ year.** Published work by James Hinton, Michael Hollister, Leonard Blumenschine and a translation of a story by the Uruguayan writer Juan Carlos Onneti. Length: 500-7,500 words; average length: 2,500-5,000 words. Also publishes literary essays, literary criticism, poetry. Sometimes critiques rejected mss.

How to Contact: Send complete ms and brief cover letter with 1-2 lines for a contributor's note. Responds in 6 months. SASE in size to fit ms. No simultaneous or electronic submissions. Final copy must be submitted on disk (WordPerfect). Sample copy for $12.50. Reviews novels and short story collections. Send books to Prof. Joe Dewey, Dept. of English, University of Pittsburgh-Johnstown, Johnstown PA 15601.

Payment/Terms: Pays 1 contributor's copy and 5 offprints.

Advice: "We are looking for well-written, insightful stories. The only criterion is literary excellence. A story should begin immediately to develop tension or conflict. It should have strong characters and a well-drawn setting. Don't be afraid to be experimental. Take more care with your manuscript. Please send a legible manuscript free of grammatical errors. Be willing to revise."

$ AGNI, Creative Writing Program, Boston University, 236 Bay State Rd., Boston MA 02215. (617)353-7135. Fax: (617)353-7134. E-mail: agni@bu.edu. Website: www.bu.edu/Agni (includes writer's guidelines, names of editors, short fiction, poetry and interviews with authors). **Contact:** Sven Birkerts, editor. Magazine: 5½×8½; 300 pages; 55 lb. booktext paper; recycled cover stock; art portfolios. "Eclectic literary magazine publishing first-rate poems and stories." Biannual. Estab. 1972.

● Founding editor Askold Melnyczuk won the 2001 Nora Magid Award for Literary Editing; work from *Agni* has been selected regularly (and in 2002) for inclusion in both *Pushcart Prize* and *Best American Short Stories* anthologies.

Needs: Stories, prose poems and translations. "No science fiction or romance." Receives more than 250 unsolicited fiction mss/month. Accepts 2-3 mss/issue, 4-6 mss/year. Reading period October 1 through February 15 only. **Publishes 30 new writers/year.** Recently published work by Chitra Divakaruni, Ilan Stavans, Joyce Carol Oates, Tom Bissell and John J. Clayton.

How to Contact: Send complete ms with SASE and cover letter listing previous publications. Accepts simultaneous submissions but not e-mail. Responds in 4 months. Sample copy for $10.

Payment/Terms: Pays $10/page up to $150, 2 contributor's copies and one-year subscription. Pays on publication for first North American serial rights. Sends galleys to author.

Advice: "Read *Agni* carefully to understand the kinds of stories we publish. Read everything, classics, literary journals, bestsellers. People need to read and subscribe to the magazines before sending their work. It's important for artists to support the arts."

THE AGUILAR EXPRESSION, 1329 Gilmore Ave., Donora PA 15033-2228. (724)379-8019. **Contact:** Xavier F. Aguilar, editor. Magazine: 8½×11; 10-16 pages; 20 lb. bond paper; illustrations. "We are open to all writers of a general theme—something that may appeal to everyone." Semiannual. Estab. 1989. Circ. 150.

Needs: Adventure, ethnic/multicultural, experimental, horror, mainstream/contemporary, mystery/suspense (romantic suspense), romance (contemporary). "No religious or erotic stories. Want more current social issues." Receives 15 unsolicited mss/month. Accepts 1-2 mss/issue; 2-4 mss/year. Publishes ms 1 month to 1 year after acceptance. **Publishes 2-4 new writers/year (90% of works published are by new writers).** Published work by Ken Bennet. Length: 750-1,500 words; average length: 1,000 words. Also publishes poetry.

How to Contact: Send complete ms with cover letter. Responds in 1 month. Send a disposable copy of ms with SASE for reply. "We do not return any manuscripts and discard rejected works. If we decide to publish, we contact within 30 days." No simultaneous submissions. Sample copy for $6. Guidelines for first class stamp.

Payment/Terms: Pays 2 contributor's copies for lead story; additional copies at a reduced rate of $3. Acquires one-time rights. Not copyrighted. Write to publication for details on contests.

Advice: "We would like to see more social issues worked into fiction."

$ ALASKA QUARTERLY REVIEW, University of Alaska—Anchorage, 3211 Providence Dr., Anchorage AK 99508. (907)786-6916. E-mail: ayaqr@uaa.alaska.edu. Website: www.uaa.alaska.edu/aqr. **Contact:** Ronald Spatz, fiction editor. Magazine: 6×9; 260-300 pages; 60 lb. Glatfelter paper; 12 pt. C15 black ink or four-color; varnish cover stock; photos on cover only. *AQR* "publishes fiction, poetry, literary nonfiction and short plays in traditional and experimental styles." Semiannual. Estab. 1982. Circ. 2,500.

Needs: Contemporary, experimental, literary, prose poem, translations. "If the works published in *Alaska Quarterly Review* have certain characteristics, they are these: freshness, honesty, and a compelling subject. What makes a piece stand out from the multitude of other submissions? The voice of the piece must be strong—idiosyncratic enough to create a unique persona. We look for the demonstration of craft, making the situation palpable and putting it in a form where it becomes emotionally and intellectually complex. One could look through our pages over time and see that many of the pieces published in *Alaska Quarterly Review* concern everyday life. We're not asking our writers to go outside themselves and their experiences to the absolute exotic to catch our interest. We look for the experiential and revelatory qualities of the work. We will, without hesitation, champion a piece that may be less polished or stylistically sophisticated, if it engages me, surprises me, and resonates for me. The joy in reading such a work is in discovering something true. Moreover, in keeping with our mission to publish new writers, we are looking for voices our readers do not know, voices that may not always be reflected in the dominant culture and that, in all instances, have something important to convey." Receives 200 unsolicited fiction mss/month. Accepts 7-13 mss/issue, 15-24 mss/year. Does not read mss May 10-August 25. Length: not exceeding 100 pages. **Publishes 6 new writers/year.** Recently published work by Ben Brooks, Courtney Angela Brkic, Nicholas Montemarano, Edna Ziesk and Edith Pearlman. Publishes short shorts.

How to Contact: Send complete mss with SASE. Accepts queries by e-mail. Simultaneous submissions "undesirable, but will accept if indicated." Responds in 2-3 months "but during peak periods a reply may take up to 6 months." Publishes ms 6 months to 1 year after acceptance. Sample copy for $6.

Payment/Terms: Pays 1 contributor's copy and a year's subscription. Pays $50-200 honorarium when grant funding permits. Acquires first rights.

Advice: "Professionalism, patience, and persistence are essential. One needs to do one's homework and know the market. The competition is very intense, and funding for the front-line journals is generally inadequate, so staffing is low. It takes times to get a response, and rejections are a fact of life. It is important not to take the rejections personally, and also to know that editors make decisions for better or worse, and they make mistakes too. Fortunately there are many gatekeepers. *Alaska Quarterly Review* has published many pieces that had been turned down by other journals—including pieces that then went on to win national awards. We also know of instances in which pieces *Alaska Quarterly Review* rejected later appeared in other magazines. We haven't regretted that we didn't take those pieces. Rather, we're happy that the authors have made a good match. Disappointment should *never* stop anyone. Will counts as much as talent, and new writers need to have confidence in themselves and stick to it."

$ **AMBIT, Poetry/Art/Short Fiction,** 17 Priory Gardens, London, N6 5QY, United Kingdom. Website: www.ambitmag.co.uk (includes writer's guidelines, names of editors, short fiction, subscription info). Editor: Martin Bax. **Contact:** Geoff Nicholson, J.G. Ballard, fiction editors. Magazine: 240cm×170cm; 100 pages; removable cover; illustrations; photos. Publishes "avant-garde material; short stories only, no novels." Quarterly. Estab. 1959. Circ. 3,000.

Needs: Erotica, ethnic/multicultural, experimental, contemporary, translations. "No fantasy/horror/science fiction. No genre fiction." Receives 80 unsolicited mss/month. Accepts 5 mss/issue; 20 mss/year. Publishes ms up to 1 year after acceptance. Agented fiction under 1%. **Publishes 10 new fiction writers/year.** Published work by Victor Anant, John Berger, Heather Reyes and Sophie Frank. Length: 1,000-5,000 words; average length: 3,000 words. Also publishes poetry.

How to Contact: Send 1-2 stories. Responds in 3 months. "No crits given." Send SASE with UK stamps or IRCs for reply, return of ms. Sample copy for $16. Guidelines free.

Payment/Terms: Pays approximately £5/printed page and 2 contributor's copies; additional copies $12. Acknowledgment if reprinted. Pays on publication. Not copyrighted.

Advice: Chooses a ms for publication "if it involves you straight away. Know how to edit your own work and remember your readers are not patient and do not know you. Also, U.S. stamps have no value outside the U.S. International Reply Coupons, endorsed, please."

AMERICAN LITERARY REVIEW, University of North Texas, P.O. Box 311307, Denton TX 76203-1307. (940)565-2755. Fax: (940)565-4355. E-mail: brodman@unt.edu. Website: www.engl.unt.edu/alr/ (includes excerpts, covers, subscription information, writer's guidelines, contest details). **Contact:** Barb Rodman, fiction editor. Magazine: 7×10; 128 pages; 70 lb. Mohawk paper; 67 lb. Wausau Vellum cover. "Publishes quality, contemporary poems and stories." Semiannual. Estab. 1990. Circ. 900.

Needs: Mainstream and literary only. "No genre works." Receives 50-75 unsolicited fiction mss/month. Accepts 4-8 mss/issue; 8-16 mss/year. Reading period: September 1-April 1. Publishes ms within 2 years after acceptance. Recently published work by Dana Johnson, Bill Roorbach, Cynthia Shearer, Mark Jacobs and Sylvia Watanabe. Length: less than 7,500 words. Critiques or comments on rejected mss when possible. Also accepts poetry and essays.

How to Contact: Send complete ms with cover letter. Responds in 2-3 months. SASE. Accepts simultaneous submissions. Sample copy for $8. Guidelines free.

Payment/Terms: Pays in contributor's copies. Acquires one-time rights.

Advice: "We would like to see more short shorts and stylistically innovative and risk-taking fiction. We like to see stories that illuminate the various layers of characters and their situations with great artistry. Give us distinctive character-driven stories that explore the complexities of human existence." Looks for "the small moments that contain more than at first appears possible, that surprise us with more truth than we thought we had a right to expect."

AMERICAN WRITING; A Magazine, Nierika Editions, 4343 Manayunk Ave., Philadelphia PA 19128. **Contact:** Alexandra Grilikhes, editor. Magazine: 8½×5½; 96 pages; matte paper and cover stock; photos. "We publish new writing that takes risks with form, point of view, language, ways of perceiving. We are interested in the voice of the loner, the artist as shaman, the powers of intuition, exceptional work of all kinds." Semiannual. Estab. 1990. Circ. 2,500.

Needs: Contemporary, excerpted novel, ethnic/multicultural, experimental, feminist, gay, lesbian, literary, translations. "We're looking for more literary, experimental, contemporary writing—writing that drives you to write it. No mainstream, romance, genre fiction, stories about sports." Receives 350 unsolicited mss/month. Accepts 4-5 mss/issue; 25 mss/year. Does not read mss June, December, January. Publishes ms 6-12 months after acceptance. Agented fiction less than 1%. **Publishes 4-6 new writers/year.** Published work by Cris Mazza, Pam Ryder, Saikat Mazumdor, Anne Spollen. Length: 5,000 words maximum; average length: 3,500 words. Publishes short shorts. Also publishes literary essays, personal essays, literary criticism, poetry. Critiques or comments on rejected mss "when there is time."

How to Contact: Send complete ms with a brief cover letter. Include brief bio and list of publications if applicable. "No full-length books. Send one ms at a time." Responds in 6 weeks-4 months. Send SASE for reply, return of ms or send a disposable copy of ms. Accepts simultaneous submissions. Sample copy for $6; guidelines for #10 SASE.

Payment/Terms: Pays 2 contributor's copies. Acquires first or one-time rights.

Advice: "We look for intensity, vision, voice, imaginative use of language, freshness, craft, sophistication; stories that delve. Read not just current stuff, but the old masters—Dostoyevsky, Chekhov and Hesse. Learn about subtlety and depth. Reading helps you to know who you are as a writer, writing makes you more that person, if you're lucky. Read one or two issues of the magazine *carefully.*"

ANCIENT PATHS, A Journal of Christian Art and Literature, Skylar Burris, publisher. E-mail: skylar.burris@gte.net. Website: http://ancientpaths.LiteratureClassics.com (includes guidelines, sample literature, online special issues not in print version, resources for writers, trivia, editor's background, etc.). **Contact:** Skylar H. Burris, editor. Magazine: digest size; 40 pages; 20 lb. plain white paper; cardstock cover; illustrations. "*Ancient Paths* is a literary magazine for thinking Christians as well as non-Christians who are open to traditional ideas and values. We publish fiction with subtle religious themes. Our goal is not evangelistic, but rather artistic in nature. We provide a forum for quality work often overlooked by secular markets." Semiannual. Estab. 1998. Circ. 150.

Needs: Christian fiction but need not be explicit. Fantasy (Christian), historical, humor/satire, literary, mainstream, mystery/suspense (Christian), religious (general religious/literary, religious fantasy, religious mystery/suspense), science fiction (Christian), western (Christian). "No angels, no avant garde. We are open to considering all genres listed; however, we favor literary fiction over genre-specific works, but we will occasionally publish genre-specific works. We do not want preachy, didactic works with obvious morals; prefer narration in past tense." Receives 5-10 unsolicited mss/month. Accepts 3-6 mss/issue; 6-12 mss/year. Publishes ms up to 6 months after acceptance. Recently published work by Larry Marshall Sams, Maureen Stirsman and Chris Williams. Length: 500-2,500 words; average length: 2,000 words. Publishes short shorts. Average length: 1,000 words. Also publishes book reviews and poetry. Often comments on rejected mss.

How to Contact: Send complete ms with a cover letter. Accepts submissions by e-mail. Include estimated word count. Responds in 5 weeks to mss. Send SASE for return of ms or send a disposable copy of ms and #10 SASE for reply only. Accepts simultaneous, previously published and multiple submissions (two at a time). Sample copy for $3. Guidelines for SASE, e-mail or on website. Reviews novels, short story collections and nonfiction books of interest to writers. Send review copies to Skylar Burris.

Payment/Terms: Pays $2 and 1 contributor's copy; additional copies $3.50. Pays on publication for one-time rights and electronic rights (optional). Sometimes sends galleys to author, if time permits. Not copyrighted.

Advice: "We look for fluid prose, intriguing characters, substantial themes in fiction manuscripts."

ANTHOLOGY MAGAZINE, Anthology Inc., P.O. Box 4411, Mesa AZ 85211-4411. (480)461-8200. E-mail: info@anthology.org. Website: www.anthology.org (includes writer's guidelines, editors' names, interviews, fiction not included in print version, staff information, contest information, links). **Contact:** Elissa Harris. Magazine: 8½×11; 28 pages; 20 lb. paper; colored bristol cover; illustrations. "*Anthology* is a small press literary magazine focused on making the written word accessible to the general public. We do not focus on any specific genre, rather we publish works on their own merit." Bimonthly. Estab. 1994. Circ. 1,000.

Needs: Fantasy (space fantasy, sword and sorcery), literary, mainstream, psychic/supernatural/occult, science fiction. "No graphic horror or erotica." Receives 45-50 unsolicited mss/month. Accepts 2-3 mss/issue; 12-18/year. Publishes mss 10-12 months after acceptance. **Publishes 5-10 new writers/year.** Recently published work by Brett Van Emst, Anne Lind, Sean Reagan and Frank Andreotti. Length: 500-5,000 words; average length 3,500 words. Publishes short shorts. Also publishes literary essays and poetry.

How to Contact: Send complete ms with cover letter. Responds in 10-12 weeks. Accepts simultaneous and multiple submissions. Sample copy for $3.95. Guidelines for SASE, by e-mail or on website. Reviews novels, short story collections and books of interest to writers. Send copies to Attn: Exegisis.

Payment/Terms: Pays in contributor's copies; additional copies $2. Pays on publication for first North American serial rights, one time rights and electronic rights. Sponsors contest.

Advice: "We look for good storytelling and good writing. We look for a polished manuscript that is not filled with typos or grammatical errors. Don't send us what you think we want to see—send us what you feel is your best work."

$ ◨ ◎ ◐ **ANTIETAM REVIEW**, Washington County Arts Council, 41 S. Potomac St., Hagerstown MD 21740-5512. (301)791-3132. Fax: (240)420-1754. **Contact:** Winnie Wagaman, managing editor. Magazine: 8½×11; 54-68 pages; glossy paper; light card cover; photos. A literary magazine of short fiction, poetry and black-and-white photographs. Annual. Estab. 1982. Circ. 1,800.

• Work published in *Antietam Review* has been included in the *Pushcart Prize* anthology and *Best American Short Stories*. The magazine also received a grant from the Maryland State Arts Council and Washington County Arts Council.

Needs: Condensed/excerpted novel, contemporary, ethnic, experimental, feminist, literary and prose poem. Wants more contemporary, ethnic, experimental. "We read from September 1 through February 1. No horror, romance, inspirational, pornography." Receives about 100 unsolicited mss/month. Buys 8-10 mss/year. Publishes ms 2-3 months after acceptance. **Publishes 2-3 new writers/year.** Published work by Marc Bookman, Tom Glenn, Richard Plant, Dee Cameron, Ace Boggess, Luke Tennis and Jamie Holland. Length: 3,000 words average. Also publishes poetry.

How to Contact: "Send ms and SASE with a cover letter. Let us know if you have published before and where." Accepts queries by e-mail. Include estimated word count, 1-paragraph bio and list of publications. Responds in 2-4 months after deadline. "If we hold a story, we let the writer know. Occasionally we critique returned ms or ask for rewrites." Sample copy for $8. Back issue $6. Guidelines for SASE.

Payment/Terms: "We believe it is a matter of dignity that writers and poets be paid. We pay $100/story and $25/poem, plus 2 copies." Buys first North American serial rights. Sends galleys to author if requested.

Advice: "We seek high-quality, well-crafted work with significant character development and shift. We seek no specific theme. We look for work that is interesting, involves the reader, and teaches us a new way to view the world. A manuscript stands out because of its energy and flow. Most of our submissions reflect the times (i.e., the news, current events) more than industry trends. We also seek a compelling voice, originality, magic. We now require *accepted* stories to be put on disk by the author to cut down on printing costs. We are seeing an increase of first-person narrative stories."

◼◼ **$** ◨ **THE ANTIGONISH REVIEW**, St. Francis Xavier University, P.O. Box 5000, Antigonish, Nova Scotia B2G 2W5 Canada. (902)867-3962. Fax: (902)867-5563. E-mail: TAR@stfx.ca. Website: www.antigonishreview.com. **Contact:** Allan Quigley, editor. Literary magazine for educated and creative readers. Quarterly. Estab. 1970. Circ. 800.

Needs: Literary, contemporary, prose poem, translations. "No erotic or political material." Accepts 6 mss/issue. Receives 50 unsolicited fiction mss each month. **Published new writers within the last year.** Published work by Arnold Bloch, Richard Butts and Helen Barolini. Length: 1,000-6,000 words. Sometimes comments briefly on rejected mss.

How to Contact: Send complete ms, double spaced with bio, SASE (with IRC) and cover letter. ("U.S. postage not acceptable".) No simultaneous submissions. Accepts electronic (disk compatible with WordPerfect/IBM and Windows) submissions. Prefers hard copy with disk submission. Responds in 4-6 months. Publishes ms 4-8 months after acceptance. Sample copy for $5. Guidelines free.

Payment/Terms: Pays $50 for stories. Authors retain copyright. Pays on publication for first serial rights.

Advice: "Learn the fundamentals and do not deluge an editor."

$ ◨ **ANTIOCH REVIEW**, Box 148, Yellow Springs OH 45387-0148. (937)769-1365. Website: www.antioch.edu/review (includes guidelines, awards, authors, titles and excerpts of current and upcoming issue, history of the Review, subscription info). Editor: Robert S. Fogarty. Associate Editor: Nolan Miller. **Contact:** Fiction Editor. Magazine: 6×9; 128 pages; 50 lb. book offset paper; coated cover stock; illustrations "seldom." "Literary and cultural review of contemporary issues, and literature for general readership." Quarterly. Estab. 1941. Circ. 5,100.

Needs: Literary, contemporary, experimental, translations. "No children's, science fiction or popular market." Accepts 5-6 mss/issue, 20-24 mss/year. Receives approximately 275 unsolicited fiction mss each month. Does not read mss June 1-September 1. Approximately 1-2% of fiction agented. **Publishes 1-2 new writers/year.** Published work by Gordon Lish, Jean Ross Justice, Peter LaSalle, Sylvia Foley, Josie Milliken, Teresa Svoboda, Joseph Caldwell, Richard Stern, Emily Cerf and Carolyn Osborn. Length: generally under 8,000 words.

How to Contact: Send complete ms with SASE, preferably mailed flat. Responds in 2 months. Publishes ms 6-9 months after acceptance. Sample copy for $6. Guidelines for SASE.

Payment/Terms: Pays $10/page and 2 contributor's copies; $3.90 for extras. Pays on publication for first and one-time rights (rights returned to author on request).

Advice: "Our best advice, always, is to *read* the *Antioch Review* to see what type of material we publish. Quality fiction requires an engagement of the reader's intellectual interest supported by mature emotional relevance, written in a style that is rich and rewarding without being freaky. The great number of stories submitted to us indicates that fiction still has great appeal. We assume that if so many are writing fiction, many must be reading it."

◨ **APOSTROPHE: University of South Carolina Beaufort Journal of the Arts**, 801 Carteret St., Beaufort SC 29902. (843)521-4100. Fax: (843)521-4100. E-mail: ellenmalphrus@aol.com. Editor: Sheila Tombe. **Contact:** Ellen Malphrus, fiction editor. "*Apostrophe* seeks excellence in writing for the thoughtful reader." Magazine: 8×5; 70 pages. Annual. Estab. 1996. Circ. 250-300.

Needs: Literary. Does not want anything "poorly written" or "in bad taste." Receives 3 unsolicited mss/month. Accepts 3-4 mss/issue. Does not read mss "during semester." Publishes ms 1-2 months after acceptance. **Publishes 3 new writers/year.** Recently published work by Evan Balkan, Mary Atwell and John Hughes. Publishes short shorts. Also publishes literary essays, literary criticism, poetry. Sometimes comments on rejected mss.

How to Contact: Send complete ms with a cover letter. Include short bio. Responds in 2 weeks to queries; 10 months to mss. Send SASE for reply, return of ms or send a disposable copy of ms. Accepts simultaneous submissions and reprints. Sample copy for $3, 8×5 SAE and 2 first-class stamps. Guidelines free for letter-size SASE.
Payment/Terms: Pays 2 contributor's copies; additional copies $5. Not copyrighted.
Advice: Looks for "excellent prose style; nothing trite or clichéd; nothing 'crafted' à la college fiction writing course. Don't be afraid to ignore your writing instructors, when appropriate. We prefer thoughtful construction; artful phrasing; maturity. Don't rely on anyone to teach you. Write to learn."

N **⊕** **AQUARIUS**, Flat 4, Room-B, 116 Sutherland Ave., Maida-Vale, London W92QP England. Phone: 0171-289-4338. Editor: Eddie Linden. Semiannual. Estab. 1969. Circ. 3,000.
Needs: Humor/satire, literary, prose poem and serialized/excerpted novel. Receives 1,000 unsolicited mss/month. Length: 1,000 words minimum. "The next issue is on the work of the writers W.S. Graham and George Baker whose biography has just been published."
Payment/Terms: Payment is by agreement. Sample copy in UK £6 plus postage and packing; in US $18 plus $3 postage.

◖ **ARKANSAS REVIEW, A Journal of Delta Studies**, Department of English and Philosophy, P.O. Box 1890, Arkansas State University, State University AR 72467-1890. (501)972-3043. Fax: (501)972-3045. E-mail: delta@astate. edu. Website: www.clt.astate.edu/arkreview (includes guidelines, names of editors, ordering information, tables of contents). Editor: William M. Clements. **Contact:** Tom Williams, fiction editor. Magazine: 8¼×11; 64-100 pages; coated, matte paper; matte, 4-color cover stock; illustrations; photos. Publishes articles, fiction, poetry, essays, interviews, reviews, visual art evocative of or responsive to the Mississippi River Delta. Triannual. Estab. 1996. Circ. 700.
Needs: Regional short stories, literary essays, literary criticism. "No genre fiction. Must have a Delta focus." Receives 30-50 unsolicited mss/month. Accepts 2-3 mss/issue; 5-7 mss/year. Publishes ms 6-12 months after acceptance. Agented fiction 1%. **Publishes 3-4 new writers/year.** Published work by Chalana Oueles, Deborah Elliott Deutschmann, Mark Sindecuse and Craig Black. Also publishes literary essays and poetry. Always comments on rejected mss.
How to Contact: Send complete ms with cover letter. Accepts queries/mss by e-mail and fax. Include bio. Responds in 1 week to queries; 4 months to mss. Send SASE for reply, return of ms or send a disposable copy of ms. Sample copy for $7.50. Guidelines free for #10 SASE.
Payment/Terms: Pays 5 contributor's copies; additional copies for $5. Acquires first North American serial rights.
Advice: "We publish new writers in every issue. We look for distinguished, mature writing, surprises, a perfect ending and a story that means more than merely what went on in it. We don't like recognizable imitations of currently fashionable writers."

◖ **THE ARMCHAIR AESTHETE**, Pickle Gas Press, 31 Rolling Meadows Way, Penfield NY 14526. (716)388-6968. E-mail: bypaul@netacc.net. **Contact:** Paul Agosto, editor. Magazine: 5½×8½; 40-65 pages; 20 lb. paper; 110 lb. card stock color cover. "*The Armchair Aesthete* seeks quality writing that enlightens and entertains a thoughtful audience (ages 9-90) with a 'good read.'" Quarterly. Estab. 1996. Circ. 100.
Needs: Adventure, fantasy (science fantasy, sword and sorcery), historical (general), horror, humor/satire, mainstream/contemporary, mystery/suspense (amateur sleuth, cozy, police procedural, private eye/hardboiled, romantic suspense), science fiction (soft/sociological), westerns (frontier, traditional). "No racist, pornographic, overt gore; no religious or material intended for or written by children." Receives 90 unsolicited mss/month. Accepts 13-18 mss/issue; 60-80 mss/year. Publishes ms 3-9 months after acceptance. Agented fiction less than 5%. **Publishes 10-15 new writers/year.** Recently published work by Teresa Bourgeoise, Hilary James Liberty and Valerie Corderman. Length: 3,000 words maximum; average length: 2,000 words. Publishes short shorts. Also publishes poetry. Sometimes comments on rejected mss.
How to Contact: Send complete ms with a cover letter. Include estimated word count, 50-100 word bio and list of publications. Accepts submissions by e-mail and on disk. Responds in 2-3 weeks to queries; 1-3 months to mss. Send SASE for reply, return of ms or send a disposable copy of ms. Accepts simultaneous, multiple, reprint and electronic submissions. Sample copy for $3 and 2 first-class stamps. Guidelines free for #10 SASE. Reviews novels and short story collections.
Payment/Terms: Pays 1 contributor's copy; additional copies for $3 (pay to P. Agosto, editor). Pays on publication for one-time rights.
Advice: "Clever, compelling storytelling has a good chance here. We look for a clever plot, thought-out characters, something that surprises or catches us off guard. Write on innovative subjects and situations. Submissions should be professionally presented and technically sound."

READ 'THE BUSINESS OF FICTION WRITING' section for information on manuscript preparation, mailing tips, rights and more.

$ ✉ ARTFUL DODGE, Dept. of English, College of Wooster, Wooster OH 44691. (330)263-2332. Website: www.wooster.edu/artfuldodge (includes writer's guidelines, editors' bios, interviews with authors, subscription information, history of the magazine). Editor-in-Chief: Daniel Bourne. **Contact:** Ron Antonucci, fiction editor. Magazine: 100 pages; illustrations; photos. "There is no theme in this magazine, except literary power. We also have an ongoing interest in translations from Central/Eastern Europe and elsewhere." Biannual. Estab. 1979. Circ. 1,000.

Needs: Experimental, literary, prose poem, translations. "We judge by literary quality, not by genre. We are especially interested in fine English translations of significant contemporary prose writers. Translations should be submitted with original texts." Receives 40 unsolicited fiction mss/month. Accepts 5 mss/year. Published fiction by Edward Kleinschmidt, Robert Mooney, David Surface, Leslie Pietrzyk and Zbigniew Herbert; and interviews with Tim O'Brien, Lee Smith, Michael Dorris and Stuart Dybek. **Published 1 new writer within the last year.** Length: 10,000 words maximum; 2,500 words average. Also publishes literary essays, literary criticism, poetry. Occasionally critiques rejected mss.

How to Contact: Send complete ms with SASE. Do not send more than 30 pages at a time. Responds in 1 week-8 months. No simultaneous or reprint submissions. Sample copies are $5 for older issues; $7 for current issues. Guidelines for #10 SASE.

Payment/Terms: Pays 2 contributor's copies and honorarium of $5/page, "thanks to funding from the Ohio Arts Council." Acquires first North American serial rights.

Advice: "If we take time to offer criticism, do not subsequently flood us with other stories no better than the first. If starting out, get as many *good* readers as possible. Above all, read contemporary fiction and the magazine you are trying to publish in."

○ ARTISAN, a journal of craft, P.O. Box 157, Wilmette IL 60091. (847)673-7246. E-mail: artisanjnl@aol.com. **Editor:** Joan Daugherty. Tabloid: 8½×11; 36 pages. "The philosophy behind *artisan* is that anyone who strives to express themselves through their craft is an artist and artists of all genres can learn from each other." Published 3 times/year. Estab. 1995. Circ. 200.

Needs: "We love to see 'literary' stories that can still appeal to a general audience—stories that are well-written and sophisticated without being stuffy. Nothing sexually or violently graphic with foul language unless it clearly contributes to the story." Receives 50 unsolicited mss/month. Accepts 6-8 mss/issue; 25 mss/year. Publishes ms 6-8 months after acceptance. Published work by Amy Branson, Laura Durnell, Arthur Franz and Gregory Wolos. Length: 4,000 words maximum; average length: 2,000 words. Publishes short shorts. Also publishes literary essays, literary criticism, poetry. Sometimes comments on rejected mss.

How to Contact: Send complete ms with brief cover letter. Include estimated word count. Responds in 1 month to queries; up to 8 months to mss. SASE for reply and send a disposable copy of ms. Accepts electronic submissions (e-mail or ASCII). Sample copy for $6. Guidelines for #10 SASE. Guidelines also posted on the Internet at members.aol.com/artisanjnl.

Payment/Terms: Pays 2 contributor's copies; additional copies $5. Acquires first rights.

Advice: "There are very few, if any, original stories left to tell. The difference is how you choose to tell them. Show us fresh use of language, character and story line. Make it personal."

Ⓝ AURA LITERARY ARTS REVIEW, University of Alabama at Birmingham, 135 HUC, 1530 3rd Ave. S, Birmingham AL 35294-1150. (205)934-3216. E-mail: aura@popmail.com. **Contact:** Christopher Giganti, editor-in-chief. Literary magazine: 6×9; 140 pages; artwork. Semiannual. Estab. 1974. Circ. 500.

Needs: Experimental, historical, humor/satire, literary, novel excerpts, regional. "No horror, adventure, shock art, feminist, memoir. No mss longer than 10,000 words." Publishes ms 3-4 months after acceptance. **Publishes 25-30 new writers/year.** Recently published work by Jason Aaron, Danny Gamble and Adam Vines. Length: 100-5,000 words; average length: 2,000 words. Publishes short shorts.

How to Contact: Send complete ms with cover letter. Include brief bio. Responds ASAP to queries. Accepts submissions on disk. Send SASE for return of ms or send disposable copy of ms and #10 SASE for reply only. Accepts multiple submissions. Guidelines for SASE.

Payment/Terms: Pays 2 contributor's copies; additional copies $6. Acquires one-time rights.

● AXE FACTORY REVIEW, Cynic Press, P.O. Box 40691, Philadelphia PA 19107. **Contact:** Joseph Farley, editor. Magazine: 11×17 folded to 8½×11; 30-60 pages; 20 lb. stock paper; 70 lb. stock cover; illustrations; photos on occasion. "We firmly believe that literature is a form of (and/or expression/manifestations of) madness. We seek to spread the disease called literature. We will look at any genre. But, we search for the quirky, the off-center, the offensive, the annoying, but always the well-written story, poem, essay." Biannual. Estab. 1986. Circ. 200.

Needs: Adventure, comics/graphic novels, erotica, ethnic/multicultural (Asian), experimental, fantasy (space fantasy, sword and sorcery), feminist, gay, historical, horror (dark fantasy, futuristic, psychological, supernatural), humor/satire, lesbian, literary, mainstream, military/war, mystery/suspense, New Age, psychic/supernatural/occult, regional (Philadelphia area), religious (general religious, inspirational, religious mystery/suspense), romance, science fiction (hard science/technological, soft/sociological, cross genre), thriller/espionage, translations, western (frontier saga, traditional). "We would like to see more hybrid genres, literary fantasy/science fiction, Beat writing. No genteel professional gibberish." Receives 20 unsolicited mss/month. Accepts 1-2 mss/issue; 3 mss/year. Publishes ms 6-12 months after acceptance. Recently published work by Tim Gavin and Michael Hafer. Length: 500-5,000 words; average length: 3,000 words. Publishes short shorts. Also publishes literary essays, literary criticism and poetry. Often comments on rejected mss.

How to Contact: Send complete ms with a cover letter. Include brief bio, list of publications and discuss why you write/philosophy. Responds in 6 weeks. Send SASE (or IRC) for return of ms. Accepts simultaneous, previously published and multiple submissions. Sample copy for $8. Reviews novels, short story collections and nonfiction books of interest to writers. Send review copies to Joseph Farley.

Payment/Terms: Pays 1-2 contributor's copies; additional copies $8. Pays on publication for one-time and anthology rights.

Advice: "In fiction we look for a strong beginning, strong middle, strong end; memorable characters; and most importantly language, language, language."

🌀 **THE BALTIMORE REVIEW**, Baltimore Writers' Alliance, P.O. Box 410, Riderwood MD 21139. (410)377-5265. Fax: (410)377-4507. E-mail: hdiehl@bcpl.net. Website: www.baltimorewriters.org (includes guidelines, info about Baltimore Writers' Alliance, and subscription and sample copy information). Editor: Barbara Diehl. **Contact:** Fiction Editor. Magazine: 6×9; 128 pages; 60 lb. paper; 10 pt. CS1 gloss film cover. Showcase for the best short stories and poetry by writers in the Baltimore area and beyond. Semiannual. Estab. 1996.

Needs: Ethnic/multicultural, experimental, literary, mainstream/contemporary. "No science fiction, westerns, children's, romance, etc." Accepts 8-12 mss/issue; 16-24 mss/year. Publishes ms 1-9 months after acceptance. **Publishes "at least a few" new writers/year.** Published work by Roberta Murphy, Pearl Canick Solomon and Tristan Davies. Length: short shorts to 6,000 words maximum; average length: 3,000 words. Also publishes poetry.

How to Contact: Send complete ms with a cover letter. Include estimated word count, brief bio and list of publications. Responds in 1-3 months. Send SASE for reply, return of ms or send a disposable copy of ms. Accepts simultaneous submissions. No e-mail or fax submissions.

Payment/Terms: Pays 2 contributor's copies. Pays on publication for first North American serial rights.

Advice: "We look for compelling stories and a masterful use of the English language. We want to feel that we have never heard this story, or this voice, before. Read the kinds of publications you want your work to appear in. Make your reader believe, and care."

🌀 **BARBARIC YAWP**, Bone World Publishing, 3700 County Rt. 24, Russell NY 13684-3198. (315)347-2609. Editor: John Berbrich. **Contact:** Nancy Berbrich, fiction editor. Magazine: digest-size; 60 pages; 24 lb. paper; matte cover stock. "We publish what we like. Fiction should include some bounce and surprise. Our publication is intended for the intelligent, open-minded reader." Quarterly. Estab. 1997. Circ. 120.

Needs: Adventure, experimental, fantasy (science, sword and sorcery), historical, horror, humor/satire, literary, mainstream/contemporary, psychic/supernatural/occult, regional, religious/inspirational, science fiction (hard, soft/sociological). Wants more humor, satire and adventure. "We don't want any pornography, gratuitous violence or whining." Receives 30-40 unsolicited mss/month. Accepts 10-12 mss/issue; 40-48 mss/year. Publishes ms within 6 months after acceptance. **Publishes 4-6 new writers/year.** Recently published work by Mark Spitzer, Jon Boilard and Karl Koweski. Length: 1,200 words maximum; average length: 600 words. Publishes short shorts. Also publishes literary essays, literary criticism, poetry. Often comments on rejected mss.

How to Contact: Send complete ms with a cover letter. Include estimated word count, brief bio and list of publications. Responds in 2 weeks to queries; 4 months to mss. Send SASE for reply, return of ms or send a disposable copy of ms. Accepts simultaneous submissions, multiple submissions and reprints. Sample copy for $3. Guidelines for #10 SASE.

Payment/Terms: Pays 1 contributor's copy; additional copies $3. Acquires one-time rights.

Advice: "We are primarily concerned with work that means something to the author, but which is able to transcend the personal into the larger world. Send whatever is important to you. We will use Yin and Yang. Work must hold my interest and be well-crafted. Read, read, read; write, write, write—then send us your best. Don't get discouraged. Believe in yourself. Take risks. Do not fear rejection."

🔘 **BATHTUB GIN**, Pathwise Press, P.O. Box 2392, Bloomington IN 47402. (812)339-7298. E-mail: charter@bluemarble.net. Website: www.bluemarble.net/~charter/btgin.htm (includes guidelines, news, links and catalogue). Editor: Chris Harter. **Contact:** Fiction Editor. Magazine: 8½×5½; 60 pages; recycled 20-lb. paper; 80-lb. card cover; illustrations; photos. "*Bathtub Gin* is looking for work that has some kick to it. We are very eclectic and publish a wide range of styles. Audience is anyone interested in new writing and art that is not being presented in larger magazines." Semiannual. Estab. 1997. Circ. 150.

Needs: Condensed/excerpted novel, experimental, humor/satire, literary. "No horror, science fiction, historical unless they go beyond the usual formula." Want more experimental fiction. Receives 20 unsolicited mss/month. Accepts 2-3 mss/issue. Does not read mss September 15-December 1 and March 15-July 1; "we publish in mid-October and mid-April." **Publishes 10 new writers/year.** Published work by Melissa Frederick and Allen Purdy. Length: 10 double-spaced pages maximum. Publishes short shorts. Also publishes literary essays, literary criticism, poetry. Often comments on rejected ms.

How to Contact: Send complete ms with a cover letter. Include estimated word count, 3-5 line bio. Accepts queries by e-mail. Responds in 1-2 months. Send SASE for reply, return of ms or send a disposable copy of ms. Accepts simultaneous, reprint and electronic submissions (modem). Sample copy for $5 with 6×9 SAE and 4 first-class stamps. Guidelines for #10 SASE. Reviews novels and short story collections.

Payment/Terms: Pays 1 contributor's copy; discount on additional copies. Rights revert to author upon publication.

Advice: "We are looking for writing that contains strong imagery, is complex, and is willing to take a chance with form and structure."

BEACON STREET REVIEW, 120 Boylston St., Emerson College, Boston MA 02116. E-mail: beaconstreetreview@hotmail.com. Website: www.emerson.edu/beaconstreetreview. **Contact:** Prose Editor. Editors change each year. Magazine: 5½×8½; 100 pages; 60 lb. paper. The *Beacon Street Review*, a journal of new prose and poetry, is published twice a year by students in the graduate writing, literature and publishing department of Emerson College. Biannual. Estab. 1986. Circ. 1,500.

Needs: Literary. Receives 200 mss/year. Accepts 5-10 mss/issue; 10-20 mss/year. Publishes ms 1-2 months after acceptance. Length: 25 pages maximum. Publishes short shorts. Also publishes nonfiction and poetry. Sometimes comments on rejected mss.

How to Contact: Send complete ms with a cover letter. Include name, phone, address, e-mail and title of each submission on a separate sheet. Manuscripts must be free of all personal identification. Send 4 copies of each ms in 12 point font with normal margins. Include SASE. Include estimated word count and bio. Reading periods are October for the Fall issue and February for the Spring issue. Send disposable copy of ms. Accepts simultaneous submissions with notification. Sample copy for $6 with #10 SASE. Guidelines free for SASE.

Payment/Terms: Pays 3 contributor's copies; additional copies $2. Pays on publication for one-time rights. Sponsors Editor's Choice Award of $100.

BEGINNINGS PUBLISHING, A Magazine for the Novice Writer, Beginnings Publishing, P.O. Box 92, Shirley NY 11967-1525. (631)205-5542. E-mail: Jeanineb@optonline.net. Website: www.scbeginnings.com. **Contact:** Jeanine Boisits, fiction editor. Magazine: 8½×11; 46 pages; illustrations; photographs. "*Beginnings* publishes only beginner/novice writers." Semiannual. Estab. 1999. Circ. 1,500.

• *Beginnings* ranked on *Writer's Digest*'s "Top 30" list of best markets for fiction writers.

Needs: Literary, mainstream, mystery/suspense, romance, science fiction, western. "No erotica, horror." Accepts 10 mss/issue; 20/year. Does not read mss during January and April. Publishes mss 6 months after acceptance. **Publishes 100 percent new writers/issue.** Recently published work by Freada Dillon, Rich Jordan and Lois Peterson. Maximum length: 3,000 words; average lenth: 2,500 words. Publishes short shorts. Also publishes poetry. Sometimes comments on rejected mss.

How to Contact: Send complete mss with cover letter. Include estimated word count and bio. Responds to queries in 3 weeks; mss in 2 months. Send disposable copy of ms and SASE for reply only. Accepts simultaneous and previously published submissions. Sample copy for $4. Guidelines for SASE, e-mail or on website.

Payment/Terms: Pays 1 contributor's copy; additional copies $3. Pays on publication for first rights.

Advice: "Originality is a plus! Read the magazine first."

BELLOWING ARK, A Literary Tabloid, P.O. Box 55564, Shoreline WA 98155. (206)440-0791. Editor: R.R. Ward. **Contact:** Fiction Editor. Tabloid: 11½×17½; 28 pages; electro-brite paper and cover stock; illustrations; photos. "We publish material which we feel addresses the human situation in an affirmative way. We do not publish academic fiction." Bimonthly. Estab. 1984. Circ. 650.

• Work from *Bellowing Ark* appeared in the *Pushcart Prize* anthology.

Needs: Contemporary, literary, mainstream, serialized/excerpted novel. "No science fiction or fantasy." Receives 700-1,000 unsolicited fiction mss/year. Accepts 2-5 mss/issue; 10-20 mss/year. Time varies, but publishes ms not longer than 6 months after acceptance. **Publishes 10-50 new writers/year.** Recently published work by David Ross, Shelley Uva, Tanyo Ravicz, Susan Montag and E.R. Romaine. Length: 3,000-5,000 words average ("but no length restriction"). Publishes short shorts. Also publishes literary essays, literary criticism, poetry. Sometimes critiques rejected mss.

How to Contact: No queries. Send complete ms with cover letter and short bio. "Prefer cover letters that tell something about the writer. Listing credits doesn't help." No simultaneous submissions. Responds in 6 weeks to mss. SASE. Sample copy for $3, 9×12 SAE and $1.26 postage.

Payment/Terms: Pays in contributor's copies. Acquires one-time rights only.

Advice: "*Bellowing Ark* began as (and remains) an alternative to the despair and negativity of the Workshop/Academic literary scene; we believe that life has meaning and is worth living—the work we publish reflects that belief. Learn how to tell a story before submitting. Avoid 'trick' endings—they have all been done before and better. *Bellowing Ark* is interested in publishing writers who will develop with the magazine, as in an extended community. We find *good* writers and stick with them. This is why the magazine has grown from 12 to 32 pages."

BELOIT FICTION JOURNAL, Box 11, 700 College St., Beloit College WI 53511. (608)363-2577. E-mail: heatherskyler@hotmail.com. Editor-in-Chief: Clint McCown. **Contact:** Heather Skyler, managing editor. Literary magazine: 6×9; 250 pages; 60 lb. paper; 10 pt. C1S cover stock; illustrations; photos on cover; ad-free. "We are interested in publishing the best contemporary fiction and are open to all themes except those involving pornographic, religiously dogmatic or politically propagandistic representations. Our magazine is for general readership, though most of our readers will probably have a specific interest in literary magazines." Annual. Estab. 1985.

• Work first appearing in *Beloit Fiction Journal* has been reprinted in award-winning collections, including the *Flannery O'Connor* and the *Milkweed Fiction Prize* collections, and has won the Iowa Short Fiction award.

Needs: Contemporary, literary and mainstream. Wants more experimental and short shorts. Would like to see more "stories with a focus on both language and plot, unusual metaphors, and vivid characters. No pornography, religious dogma, science fiction, horror, political propaganda or genre fiction." Receives 400 unsolicited fiction mss/month. Accepts 20 mss/year. Replies take longer in summer. Reads mss August 1-December 1. Publishes ms within 9 months after acceptance. **Publishes 3 new writers/year.** Recently published work by Rick Bass, A. Mannette Ansay, Gary Fincke, David Harris Ebenbach, Anne Panning and David Milofsky. Length: 250-10,000 words; average length: 5,000 words. Sometimes critiques rejected mss.

How to Contact: Send complete ms with cover letter to Heather Skyler. Responds in 2 weeks to queries; 2 months to mss. SASE for ms. Accepts simultaneous submissions if identified as such. No fax, e-mail or disk submissions. Sample copy for $14; back issues $7. Guidelines for #10 SASE.

Advice: "Many of our contributors are writers whose work we had previously rejected. Don't let one rejection slip turn you away from our—or any—magazine."

◐ BERKELEY FICTION REVIEW, 10 Eshleman Hall, University of California, Berkeley CA 94720. (510)642-2892. E-mail: nmwright@uclink4.berkeley.edu. Website: www.OCF.Berkeley.EDU/~bfr/ (includes guidelines, contest info and short fiction). **Contact:** Natalie Wright and Elisha Cohen, editors. Magazine: 5½×8½; 180 pages; perfect-bound; glossy cover; some b&w art; photographs. "The mission of *Berkeley Fiction Review* is to provide a forum for new and emerging writers as well as writers already established. We publish a wide variety of contemporary short fiction for a literary audience." Annual. Estab. 1981. Circ. 1,000.

Needs: Contemporary/mainstream, literary, experimental. "Quality, inventive short fiction. No poetry or formula fiction." Receives 60 unsolicited mss/month. Accepts 10-20 mss/issue. **Publishes 15-20 new writers/year.** Published work by Donna Storey, Ruthanne Wiley and Steve Tomasula. Also publishes short shorts. Occasionally comments on rejected mss.

How to Contact: Send complete ms to "Editor" with very brief cover letter and SASE. Usually reports in 3-4 months, longer in summer. Accepts simultaneous and multiple submissions. Sample copy for $9.50. Guidelines for SASE.

Payment/Terms: Pays 1 contributor's copy. Acquires first rights. Sponsors short story contest with $100 first prize. Entry fee: $6. Send SASE for guidelines.

Advice: "Our criteria is fiction that resonates. Voices that are strong and move a reader. Clear, powerful prose (either voice or rendering of subject) with a point. Unique ways of telling stories—these capture the editors. Work hard, don't give up. Don't let your friends or family critique your work. Get someone honest to point out your writing weaknesses, and then work on them. Don't submit thinly veiled autobiographical stories; it's been done before—and better. With the proliferation of computers, everyone thinks they're a writer. Not true, unfortunately. The plus side though is ease of transmission and layout and the diversity and range of new work."

◐ BIBLIOPHILOS, A Journal for Literati, Savants, Bibliophiles, Amantes Artium, and Those Who Love Animals, 200 Security Building, Fairmont WV 26554-2834. (304)366-8107. Editor: Gerald J. Bobango, Ph.D. **Contact:** Fiction Editor. Literary magazine: 5½×8; 68-72 pages; white glossy paper; illustrations; photos. Magazine "for literate persons who are academically and scholastically oriented, focused on the liberal arts, one-third fiction. Nonfiction includes criticism, history, art, music, theology, philosophy, economics. In fiction we look for that which shows the absurdity of our slavish devotion to technology and all-encompassing big government; that which is not politically correct; that which exposes the egregious dumbing down of education; traditional pre-1960 American values." Estab. 1981. Circ. 400.

Needs: Adventure, ethnic, family saga, historical (general, US, Eastern Europe), horror (psychological, supernatural), humor/satire, literary, mainstream/contemporary, military/war, mystery/suspense (police procedural, private eye/hard-boiled, courtroom), regional (New England, Middle Atlantic), romance (gothic, historical, regency period), short story collections, thriller/espionage, translations, western (frontier saga, traditional), Civil War, US ethnic history, immigration, 19th century politics. "No science fiction, high tech; no gay or lesbian material, drug culture stuff, or material full of gratuitous obscenities; nothing single-spaced. We would like to see more fiction about man ignoring technology and being better off for doing so; man triumphing over machines." Receives 40 unsolicited mss/month. Accepts 5-6 mss/issue; 25-30 mss/year. Publishes ms up to 1 year after acceptance. **Publishes 2-3 new writers/year.** Recently published work by Douglas E. Scholen, John A. Broussard, Marvin D. Resnick and Martha Johnson. Length: 1,500-3,000 words. Also publishes literary essays, literary criticism and poetry. Often comments on rejected ms.

How to Contact: Query with clips of published work. Include bio, SASE and $5.25 for sample issue. Responds in 2 weeks to queries. Accepts simultaneous submissions. Sample copy for $5.25. Guidelines for SASE. Reviews novels, short story collections and nonfiction books of interest to writers. Send books to editor.

Payment/Terms: Pays subscription to magazine and 2 contributor's copies; sometimes in cash; additional copies $5. Acquires first North American serial rights.

Advice: "Use correct English, correctly written and punctuated. No jargon, cant, or short-cut language. Type the manuscript on a typewriter, not on a word-processor or computer and you'll have an advantage over other contributors from the start. Scholarly magazines and journals are becoming a rarity. If you use 'feel' rather than 'think' as your verb of choice, better look elsewhere."

▣ ◐ ▼ BIG MUDDY: A JOURNAL OF THE MISSISSIPPI RIVER VALLEY, Southeast Missouri State University Press, MS2650 English Dept., Southeast MO State University, Cape Girardeau MO 63701. Website: www2.semo.edu/swartwout/muddy.html (includes writer's guidelines, editors, excerpts). **Contact:** Susan Swartwout, editor. Magazine: 8½×5½ perfect-bound; 100 pages; acid-free paper; color cover stock; layflat lamination; illustrations; photos. "*Big Muddy* explores multidisciplinary, multicultural issues, people, and events mainly concerning the ten-state area that borders the Mississippi River, by people who have lived here, who have an interest in the area, or who know the River Basin. We publish fiction, poetry, historical essays, creative nonfiction, environmental essays, biography, regional events, photography, art, etc." Semiannual. Estab. 2001. Circ. 500.

* *Big Muddy* was *Small Press Review*'s "Best Pick" in magazines—2001.

Needs: Adventure, ethnic/multicultural, experimental, family saga, feminist, historical, humor/satire, literary, mainstream, military/war, mystery/suspense, regional (Mississippi River Valley; Midwest), translations. "No romance, fantasy or children's." Receives 50 unsolicited mss/month. Accepts 2-4 mss/issue. Publishes ms 6 months after acceptance. Recently published work by John Mort, Colleen McElroy, Anna Leahy and Jim Elledge. Publishes short shorts. Also publishes literary essays, literary criticism and poetry.

How to Contact: Send complete ms with cover letter and brief bio. Responds in 10 weeks to mss. Send SASE for return of ms or send a disposable copy of ms and #10 SASE for reply only. Accepts multiple submissions. Sample copy for $6. Guidelines for SASE, e-mail, fax or on website. Reviews novels, short story collections and nonfiction books of interest to writers. Send review copies to Susan Swartwout, editor.

Payment/Terms: Pays 2 contributor's copies; additional copies $5. Acquires first North American serial rights.

Advice: "In fiction manuscripts we look for clear language, avoidance of clichés except in necessary dialogue, a *fresh* vision of the theme or issue. Find some excellent and honest readers to comment on your work-in-progress and final draft. Consider their viewpoints carefully. Revise."

N ⊘ ◎ BILINGUAL REVIEW, Hispanic Research Center, Arizona State University, Box 872702, Tempe AZ 85287-2702. (602)965-3867. E-mail: kvhbrp@asu.edu. **Editor-in-Chief:** Gary D. Keller. Scholarly/literary journal of US Hispanic life: poetry, short stories, other prose and short theater. Magazine: 7×10; 96 pages; 55 lb. acid-free paper; coated cover stock. Published 3 times/year. Estab. 1974. Circ. 2,000.

Needs: US Hispanic creative literature. "We accept material in English or Spanish. We publish original work only—no translations." US Hispanic themes only. Receives 50 unsolicited fiction mss/month. Accepts 3 mss/issue; 9 mss/year. Publishes ms an average of 1 year after acceptance. **Published work of new writers within the last year.** Published work by Ernestina N. Eger, Leo Romero, Connie Porter and Nash Candelaria. Also publishes literary criticism on US Hispanic themes, poetry. Often critiques rejected mss.

How to Contact: Send 2 copies of complete ms with SAE and loose stamps. Accepts queries by e-mail. Responds in 1-2 months. Accepts simultaneous and high-quality photocopied submissions. Sample copy for $8. Reviews novels and short story collections.

Payment/Terms: Pays 2 contributor's copies; 30% discount for extras. Acquires all rights (50% of reprint permission fee given to author as matter of policy).

Advice: "We do not publish literature about tourists in Latin America and their perceptions of the 'native culture.' We do not publish fiction about Latin America unless there is a clear tie to the United States (characters, theme, etc.)."

⊘ THE BITTER OLEANDER, 4983 Tall Oaks Dr., Fayetteville NY 13066-9776. (315)637-3047. Fax: (315)637-5056. E-mail: bones44@ix.netcom.com. Website: www.bitteroleander.com. **Contact:** Paul B. Roth, editor. Zine specializing in poetry and fiction: 6×9; 128 pages; 55 lb. paper; 12 pt. CIS cover stock; photos. "We're interested in the surreal; deep image; particularization of natural experiences." Semiannual. Estab. 1974. Circ. 1,500.

Needs: Experimental, new age/mystic/spiritual, translations. "No pornography; no confessional; no romance." Receives 100 unsolicited mss/month. Accepts 1-2 mss/issue; 2-4 mss/year. Does not read mss in July. Publishes ms 4-6 months after acceptance. Published work by Isabella Ripota, T.R. Healy and John Shepley. Publishes short shorts. Length: 2,500 words. Also publishes literary essays, poetry. Always comments on rejected ms.

How to Contact: Send complete ms with a cover letter. Include estimated word count, 50-word bio and list of publications. Responds in 1 week to queries; 1 month to mss. Send SASE for reply, return of ms. Sample copy for $8, 7×10 SAE with 4 first-class stamps. Guidelines for #10 SASE.

Payment/Terms: Pays 1 contributor's copy; additional copies $8. Acquires first rights.

Advice: "If within the first 100 words my mind drifts, the rest rarely makes it. Be yourself and listen to no one but yourself."

○ ◎ BLACK LACE, BLK Publishing Co., P.O. Box 83912, Los Angeles CA 90083-0912. (310)410-0808. Fax: (310)410-9250. E-mail: newsroom@blk.com. Website: www.blacklace.org. Editor: Alycee Lane. **Contact:** Fiction Editor. Magazine: 8⅛×10⅞; 48 pages; book stock; color glossy cover; illustrations; photos. "*Black Lace* is a lifestyle magazine for African-American lesbians. Published quarterly, its content ranges from erotic imagery to political commentary." Estab. 1991. Member, COSMEP.

Needs: Ethnic/multicultural, lesbian. "Avoid interracial stories or idealized pornography." Accepts 4 mss/year. Published work by Nicole King, Wanda Thompson, Lynn K. Pannell, Sheree Ann Slaughter, Lyn Lifshin, JoJo and Drew Alise Timmens. Publishes short shorts. Also publishes literary essays, literary criticism, poetry.

How to Contact: Query first with clips of published work or send complete ms with a cover letter. Should include bio (3 sentences). Send a disposable copy of ms. No simultaneous submissions. Accepts electronic submissions. Sample copy for $7. Guidelines free.

Payment/Terms: Pays 2 contributor's copies. Acquires first North American serial rights and right to anthologize.

Advice: *Black Lace* seeks erotic material of the highest quality. The most important thing is that the work be erotic and that it feature black lesbians or themes. Study the magazine to see what we do and how we do it. Some fiction is very romantic, other is highly sexual. Most articles in *Black Lace* cater to black lesbians between these two extremes."

⊕ ◯ **THE BLACK MOUNTAIN REVIEW,** Black Mountain Press, P.O. Box 9, Ballyclare, Co. Antrim BT390JW N. Ireland. Website: www.blackmountainreview.com. **Contact:** Editor. Magazine: A5; approximately 100 pages. "We publish short fiction with a contemporary flavour for an international audience." Semiannual. Estab. 1999.

Needs: Ethnic/multicultural (general), experimental, historical (literary), literary, regional (Irish), religious (general religious, inspirational), romance (literary), science fiction (literary), translations. Publishes ms up to 5 months after acceptance. **Publishes many new writers/year.** Recently published work by Cathal O Searcaigh, Michael Longley and Brian Keenan. Length: up to 3,000 words maximum; average length: 1,500-3,000 words. Publishes short shorts. Average length: 500-2,000 words. Also publishes literary essays, literary criticism and poetry. Sometimes comments on rejected mss.

How to Contact: Send complete ms with disk/e-mail in Word .txt format. Include estimated word count, brief bio and list of publications. Responds in 2 months to queries; 4 months to mss. Send SASE (or IRC) for return of ms or send a disposable copy of ms and #10 SASE for reply only. Accepts multiple submissions. Sample copy for $4.50. Guidelines for SASE or by e-mail. Reviews novels, short story collections and nonfiction books of interest to writers. Send review copies to the editor.

Payment/Terms: Pays 1 contributor's copy; additional copies $4.50. Pays on publication for one-time rights.

Advice: "We look for literary quality. Write well."

$ ◯ ▼ **BLACK WARRIOR REVIEW,** Box 862936, Tuscaloosa AL 35486-0027. (205)348-4518. E-mail: bwr@ ua.edu. Website: webdelsol.com/bwr (includes writer's guidelines, names of editors, samples, contributor index and online ordering). Editor-in-Chief: Ander Monson. **Contact:** Tommy Zurhellen, fiction editor. Magazine: 6×9; 200 pages; illustrations; photos. "We publish contemporary fiction, poetry, reviews, essays, photography and interviews for a literary audience. We strive to publish the most compelling, best written work that we can find." Semiannual. Estab. 1974. Circ. 2,000.

● Work that appeared in the *Black Warrior Review* has been included in the *Pushcart Prize* anthology, *The Year's Best Fantasy & Horror, Harper's Magazine, Best American Short Stories, Best American Poetry* and in *New Short Stories from the South.*

Needs: Contemporary, literary, short and short-short fiction. Want "work that is conscious of form, good experimental writing, short-short fiction, writing that is more than competent—that sings. No genre fiction please." Receives 200 unsolicited fiction mss/month. Accepts 5 mss/issue, 10 mss/year. Approximately 5% of fiction is agented. **Publishes 5 new writers/year.** Published work by Cynthia Riede, John Russell, Drew Perry and Rick Bass. Length: 7,500 words maximum; average length: 2,000-5,000 words. Occasionally critiques rejected mss. Unsolicited novel excerpts are not considered unless the novel is already contracted for publication.

How to Contact: Send complete ms with SASE (1 story per submission). Accepts simultaneous submissions if noted. Responds in 4 months. Publishes ms 2-5 months after acceptance. Sample copy for $8. Guidelines for SASE. Reviews novels and short story collections. "We read year-round."

Payment/Terms: Pays up to $100 per story and 2 contributor's copies. Pays on publication.

Advice: "We look for attention to the language, freshness, honesty, a convincing and sharp voice. Also, send us a clean, well-printed, typo-free manuscript. Become familiar with the magazine prior to submission. We're increasingly interested in considering good experimental writing and in reading short-short fiction."

Ⓝ ◯ **THE blue REVIEW,** Corba Press, 23 Berkeley Dr., Athens OH 45701. (740)592-6072. E-mail: editors@corba press.com. Website: www.corbapress.com (includes submission guidelines and information about current and upcoming publications). **Contact:** Paul Hina and A. Scott Britton, editors. Magazine: 5½×8½; 30 pages; 24 lb. paper; colored cover stock. "*The blue Review* has been created for those of us who have grown tired of the modern literary conventions. Our *Review* has been invented to perpetuate subversive and mindful literary works that would otherwise fall through the cracks of an increasingly less tolerant publishing community. The current celebrated literature has its focus on writer-as-entertainer, which belittles the once highly regarded art form of writing. *The blue Review* is here to supply the writer-as-artist with the voice that has, for far too long, been absent from bookstores and many prominent small press publications." Quarterly. Estab. 2002. Circ. 100.

Needs: Experimental, historical, humor/satire, literary. "No mainstream or genre fiction. No pornography." Receives 30 unsolicited mss/month. Accepts 3 mss/issue; 12 mss/year. Publishes ms 6 months after acceptance. **Publishes 10 new writers/year.** Length: 8,000 words maximum; average length: 4,000 words. Publishes short shorts. Average length: 500 words. Also publishes literary essays and poetry. Sometimes comments on rejected mss.

How to Contact: "No cover letters. No queries. E-mail submissions only." Include estimated word count. Responds in 4-6 weeks to mss. Accepts simultaneous, previously published and multiple submissions. Sample copy for $3 plus $1 s&h. Guidelines on website.

Payment/Terms: Pays 1 contributors copy; additional copies $2. Acquires first rights. Not copyrighted.

Advice: "We look for stories that feel like they are being told for the first time. It is important to display fresh ideas and eccentric characters in interesting, absurd, or surreal, situations. Don't be ashamed to express your unspeakable thoughts on paper. Don't be afraid of ideas just because they seem unpopular or unfashionable."

◯ ◎ **BLUELINE,** English Dept., SUNY, Potsdam NY 13676. (315)267-2043. E-mail: blueline@potsdam.edu. Website: www.potsdam.edu/engl/bluelinedefault.html (includes calls, tables of contents for previous issues). Editor: Rick Henry. **Contact:** Fiction Editor. Magazine: 6×9; 200 pages; 70 lb. white stock paper; 65 lb. smooth cover stock;

illustrations; photos. "*Blueline* is interested in quality writing about the Adirondacks or other places similar in geography and spirit. We publish fiction, poetry, personal essays, book reviews and oral history for those interested in the Adirondacks, nature in general, and well-crafted writing." Annual. Estab. 1979. Circ. 400.

Needs: Adventure, contemporary, humor/satire, literary, prose poem, regional, reminiscences, oral history, nature/outdoors. No urban stories or erotica. Receives 8-10 unsolicited fiction mss/month. Accepts 6-8 mss/issue. Does not read January-August. Publishes ms 3-6 months after acceptance. **Publishes 2 new writers/year.** Published work by Joan Connor, Laura Rodley and Ann Mohin. Length: 500-3,000 words; average length: 2,500 words. Also publishes literary essays, poetry. Occasionally critiques rejected mss.

How to Contact: Send complete ms with SASE, word count and brief bio. Accepts submissions by e-mail. Submit mss September through November 30. Responds in January. Accepts simultaneous submissions. Sample copy for $6. Guidelines for 5×10 SASE.

Payment/Terms: Pays 1 contributor's copy; charges $7 each for 3 or more extra copies. Acquires first rights.

Advice: "We look for concise, clear, concrete prose that tells a story and touches upon a universal theme or situation. We prefer realism to romanticism but will consider nostalgia if well done. Pay attention to grammar and syntax. Avoid murky language, sentimentality, cuteness or folksiness. We would like to see more good fiction related to the Adirondacks and more literary fiction and prose poems. If manuscript has potential, we work with author to improve and reconsider for publication. Our readers prefer fiction to poetry (in general) or reviews. Write from your own experience, be specific and factual (within the bounds of your story) and if you write about universal features such as love, death, change, etc., write about them in a fresh way. Triteness and mediocrity are the hallmarks of the majority of stories seen today."

◑ BOGG, A Magazine of British & North American Writing, Bogg Publications, 422 N. Cleveland St., Arlington VA 22201-1424. (703)243-6019. **Contact:** John Elsberg, US editor. Magazine: 6×9; 68-72 pages; 70 lb. white paper; 70 lb. cover stock; line illustrations. "American and British poetry, prose poems, experimental short 'fictions,' reviews, and essays on small press." Published "two or three times a year." Estab. 1968. Circ. 850.

Needs: Very short experimental fiction and prose poems. "We are always looking for work with British/Commonwealth themes and/or references." Receives 25 unsolicited fiction mss/month. Accepts 1-2 mss/issue; 3-6 mss/year. Publishes ms 3-18 months after acceptance. **Publishes 25-50 new writers/year.** Recently published work by Karen Rosenberg, J. Wesley Clark, Christopher Chambers and T. Gilgore Splake. Length: 300-500 words. Also publishes literary essays, literary criticism. Occasionally critiques rejected mss.

How to Contact: Query first or send ms (2-6 pieces) with SASE. Accepts submissions on disk. Responds in 1 week to queries; 2 weeks to mss. Sample copy for $3.50 or $4.50 (current issue). Reviews novels and short story collections.

Payment/Terms: Pays 2 contributor's copies; reduced charge for extras. Acquires one-time rights.

Advice: "We look for voice and originality. Read magazine first. We are most interested in prose work of experimental or wry nature to supplement poetry, and are always looking for innovative/imaginative uses of British themes and references."

◑ BOOKPRESS, The Newspaper of the Literary Arts, The Bookery, 215 N. Cayuga St., Ithaca NY 14850. (607)277-2254. Fax: (607)275-9221. E-mail: bookpress@thebookery.com. Website: www.thebookery.com/bookpress (includes current issue, credits and archives). **Contact:** Jack Goldman, editor-in-chief. Newspaper: 12-16 pages; newsprint; illustrations and photos. Contains book reviews, analysis, fiction and excerpts from published work. Monthly. Estab. 1991. Circ. 12,000.

Needs: Condensed/excerpted novel, feminist, gay, historical, lesbian, literary, regional. No new age. Publishes special fiction issues or anthologies. Receives 10-12 unsolicited mss/month. Accepts 0-2 mss/issue. Does not read during the summer. Publishes ms 1-3 months after acceptance. **Publishes 5-10 new writers/year.** Published work by J. Robert Lennon, Brian Hall and Robert Sward. Length: 4,000 words maximum; average length: 2,000 words. Also publishes literary essays, literary criticism and poetry.

How to Contact: Send complete ms with a cover letter. Also include on disk in Microsoft Word or .rif format. Submissions accepted via e-mail. Include 3-sentence bio. Responds in 1 month to mss. Send SASE for return of ms. Accepts simultaneous submissions. Sample copy and guidelines free. Reviews novels or short story collections. Send books to editor.

Payment/Terms: Pays free subscription to newspaper.

Advice: "Send a brief, concise cover letter. No overwriting or overly cerebral academic work. The author's genuine interest and passion for the topic makes for good work."

$◑ BOULEVARD, Opojaz Inc., PMB 325, 6614 Clayton Rd., Richmond Heights MO 63117. (314)862-2643. Website: www.richardburgin.com (includes writer's guidelines, sample contents, writing contest information, excerpts from the magazine, etc.). **Contact:** Richard Burgin, editor. Magazine: 5½×8½; 150-250 pages; excellent paper; high-quality cover stock; illustrations; photos. "*Boulevard* tries to attain a meaningful balance between creative writing and critical reflection. We strive to publish the best contemporary fiction and other forms of literature regardless of the writer's particular aesthetics. We are open to many kinds of writing excellence and believe there is only one school that counts—the school of talent." Published 3 times/year. Estab. 1986. Circ. about 3,500.

Needs: Contemporary, experimental, literary. Upcoming theme: Music issue (January 2003). "No erotica, science fiction, westerns, romance, childrens stories—anything whose first purpose is not literary." Wants to see more "work that is moving and intelligent with an original vision." Receives over 600 mss/month. Accepts about 10 mss/issue. Does not accept manuscripts between April 1 and October 1. Publishes ms less than 1 year after acceptance. Agented fiction

⅓-¼. Length: 8,000 words maximum; average length: 5,000 words. Publishes short shorts. **Publishes 10 new writers/ year.** Recently published work by Joyce Carol Oates, Elizabeth Tallent, Josip Novakovich and Jonathan Baumbach. Also publishes literary essays, literary criticism, poetry. Sometimes critiques rejected mss and recommends other markets.

How to Contact: Send complete ms with cover letter. Accepts mss on disk. Responds in 2 weeks to queries; 2 months to mss. SASE for reply. Accepts simultaneous and multiple submissions. Sample copy for $8 and SAE with 5 first-class stamps.

Payment/Terms: Pays $150-500 and contributor's copies; charges for extras. Acquires first North American serial rights. Does not send galleys to author unless requested.

Advice: "We pick the stories that move us the most emotionally, stimulate us the most intellectually, are the best written and thought out. Don't write to get published—write to express your experience and vision of the world."

$ **BRAIN, CHILD, The Magazine for Thinking Mothers**, March Press, P.O. Box 1161, Harrisonburg VA 22803. (540)574-2379. E-mail: editor@brainchildmag.com. Website: www.brainchildmag.com (includes excerpts, guidelines, mission statement, editorial staff info, subscription info). **Contact:** Jennifer Niesslein and Stephanie Wilkinson, co-editors. Magazine: 7¾×10; 60-100 pages; 80 lb matte cover; illustrations; photos. "*Brain, Child* is a quarterly magazine spotlighting women's own experience of motherhood. Instead of focusing on childrearing tips and techniques, like most parenting publications, our writers explore the more personal transformations that motherhood brings. Each issue is packed with essays, in-depth features, humor, reviews, news and fiction, plus superb art, photography, cartoons and more." Quarterly. Estab. 2000. Circ. 12,000. Member, IPA.
  ● *Brain, Child* was winner of *Utne Reader*'s 2001 Best of the Alternative Press Award in Personal Life category, and nominated for general excellence.

Needs: Literary, mainstream. Receives about 50 unsolicited mss/month. Accepts 1 ms/issue; 4 mss/year. Publishes ms 6 months after acceptance. Published work by Anne Tyler, Barbara Lucy Stevens and Jane Smiley. Length: 1,000-5,000 words; average length: 2,500 words. Will consider short shorts but prefer longer pieces. Also publishes literary essays. Sometimes comments on rejected mss.

How to Contact: Send complete ms with a cover letter. Accepts submissions by e-mail (be sure to copy and paste the ms into the body of the e-mail). Include estimated word count, brief bio and list of publications. Responds in 6 weeks to queries; 10 weeks to mss. Send SASE (or IRC) for return of ms or send a disposable copy of ms and #10 SASE for reply only. Accepts previously published work and multiple submissions (no more than 2 at once). Sample copy for $5 ("we *strongly* encourage familiarity with the magazine"). Guidelines for SASE or on website. Reviews novels, short story collections and nonfiction books of interest to mothers.

Payment/Terms: "Our fees vary, depending on a number of considerations. In general, though, payment is modest for now." Pays on publication for electronic rights and the right to include the piece in a *Brain, Child*/March Press anthology, should one ever happen. Sends galleys to author.

Advice: "We only publish fiction with a strong motherhood theme. But, like every other publisher of literary fiction, we look for well-developed characters, a compelling story, and an ending that is as strong as the rest of the piece."

THE BRIAR CLIFF REVIEW, Briar Cliff University, 3303 Rebecca St., Sioux City IA 51104-0100. (712)279-5477. E-mail: currans@briarcliff.edu. Website: www.briarcliff.edu/bcreview (includes writer's guidelines, contest guidelines, previous contest winners and their winning poems/short stories and cover artwork). Managing Editor: Tricia Currans-Sheehan. **Contact:** Phil Hey, fiction editor. Magazine: 8½×11; 80 pages; 70 lb. Finch Opaque cover stock; illustrations; photos. "*The Briar Cliff Review* is an eclectic literary and cultural magazine focusing on (but not limited to) Siouxland writers and subjects. We are happy to proclaim ourselves a regional publication. It doesn't diminish us; it enhances us." Annual. Estab. 1989. Circ. 750.

Needs: Ethnic/multicultural, feminist, historical, humor/satire, literary, mainstream/contemporary, regional. "No romance, horror or alien stories." Accepts 5 mss/year. Reads mss only between August 1 and November 1. Publishes ms 3-4 months after acceptance. **Publishes 10-14 new writers/year.** Published work by J. Annie MacLeod, Christine Phillips, John Lofy, Ken Wheaton, Jacob Appel, Laura Wilson, Cynthia Gregory and Josip Novakovich. Length: 2,500-4,000 words; average length: 3,000 words. Also publishes literary essays, literary criticism and poetry. Sometimes comments on rejected mss.

How to Contact: Send complete ms with a cover letter. Include estimated word count, bio and list of publications. Responds in 4-5 months to mss. Send a SASE for return of ms. Accepts electronic submissions (disk). Accepts simultaneous submissions. Sample copy for $10 and 9×12 SAE. Guidelines free for #10 SASE. Reviews novels and short story collections.

Payment/Terms: Pays 2 contributor's copies; additional copies available for $5. Acquires first rights

Advice: "So many stories are just telling. We want some action. It has to move. We prefer stories in which there is no gimmick, no mechanical turn of events, no moral except the one we would draw privately."

BRILLIANT CORNERS, A Journal of Jazz & Literature, Lycoming College, Williamsport PA 17701. (570)321-4279. Fax: (570)321-4090. E-mail: feinstei@lycoming.edu. **Contact:** Sascha Feinstein, editor. Journal: 6×9; 100 pages; 70 lb. Cougar opaque, vellum, natural paper; photographs. "We publish jazz-related literature—fiction, poetry and nonfiction." Semiannual. Estab. 1996. Circ. 1,200.

Needs: Condensed/excerpted novel, ethnic/multicultural, experimental, literary, mainstream/contemporary, romance (contemporary). Receives 10-15 unsolicited mss/month. Accepts 1-2 mss/issue; 2-3 mss/year. Does not read mss May 15-September 1. Publishes ms 4-12 months after acceptance. Very little agented fiction. Publishes short shorts. Also publishes literary essays, literary criticism and poetry. Rarely comments on rejected mss.

How to Contact: Send complete ms with a cover letter. Include 1-paragraph bio and list of publications. Responds in 2 weeks to queries; 1-2 months to mss. SASE for return of ms or send a disposable copy of ms. Accepts unpublished work only. Sample copy for $7. Reviews novels and short story collections. Send books to editor.

Payment/Terms: Pays 2 contributor's copies. Acquires first North American serial rights. Sends galleys to author when possible.

Advice: "We look for clear, moving prose that demonstrates a love of both writing and jazz. We primarily publish established writers, but we read all submissions carefully and welcome work by outstanding young writers."

N **⬤** **BRYANT LITERARY REVIEW**, Bryant College, 1150 Douglas Pike, Faculty Suite F, Smithfield RI 02917. (401)232-6740. Fax: (401)232-6270. E-mail: rpitt@bryant.edu. Website: http://web.bryant.edu/~blr (includes tables of contents, submission guidelines, sample poems). **Contact:** Tom Chandler. Magazine: 6×9; 125 pages; photos. Annual. Estab. 2000. Circ. 2,400. Member, CLMP.

Needs: Adventure, ethnic/multicultural, experimental, family saga, fantasy, feminist, historical, humor/satire, literary, mainstream, military/war, mystery/suspense, New Age, psychic/supernatural/occult, regional, science fiction, thriller/espionage, translations, western. "No novellas or serialized novels; only short stories." Receives 200 unsolicited mss/year. Accepts 7 mss/issue. Does not read mss January through August. Publishes ms 4-5 months after acceptance. **Publishes 1-2 new writers/year.** Recently published work by Lyzette Wanzer, K.S. Phillips and Richard N. Bentley. Length: 5,000 words maximum. Publishes short shorts. Also publishes poetry.

How to Contact: Send complete ms with a cover letter and brief bio. Responds in 1 week to queries; 6 weeks to mss. Send a disposable copy of ms and #10 SASE for reply only. Accepts simultaneous submissions. Sample copy for $8. Guidelines for e-mail or on website.

Payment/Terms: Pays 2 contributors copies; additional copies $8. Pays on publication.

⬤ **BUTTON, New England's Tiniest Magazine of Poetry, Fiction & Gracious Living**, P.O. Box 26, Lunenburg MA 01462. E-mail: buttonx26@aol.com. Website: www.moonsigns.net (includes history of magazine, honor roll of contributors). Editor: S. Cragin. **Contact:** W.M. Davies, fiction editor. Magazine: 4×5; 34 pages; bond paper; color cardstock cover; illustrations; photos. "*Button*'s designed as a vehicle of gracious living. *Button* attempts to reflect a world you'd want to live in." Annual. Estab. 1993. Circ. 1,500.

Needs: Literary. "No genre fiction, science fiction, techno-thriller." Wants more of "anything Herman Melville, Henry James or Betty MacDonald would like to read." Receives 20-40 unsolicited mss/month. Accepts 1-2 mss/issue; 3-5 mss/year. Publishes ms 3-9 months after acceptance. Published work by Ralph Lombreglia, Michele Chalfoun, They Might Be Giants and Lawrence Millman. Length: 500-2,500 words. Also publishes literary essays, poetry. Sometimes comments on rejected ms "if it shows promise."

How to Contact: Request guidelines. Send ms with bio, list of publications and advise how you found magazine. Responds in 1 month to queries; 2-4 months to mss. SASE. Sample copy for $2. Guidelines for SASE. Reviews novels and short story collections. Send book to editor.

Payment/Terms: Pays honorarium and multiple free subscriptions to the magazine. Pays on publication for first North American serial rights. Sends galleys to author if there are editorial changes. "Chats up your brilliance to a wide and varied circle of acquaintances."

Advice: "What makes a manuscript stand out? Flannery O'Connor once said, 'Don't get subtle till the fourth page,' and I agree. We look for interesting, sympathetic, believable characters and careful setting. I'm really tired of stories that start strong and then devolve into dialogue uninterrupted by further exposition. Also, no stories from a mad person's POV unless it's really tricky and skillful. Advice to prospective writers: continue to read at least ten times as much as you write. Read the best, and read intelligent criticism if you can find it. *No beginners please.* Please don't submit more than once a year—it's more important that you work on your craft rather than machine-gunning publications with samples, and don't submit more than 3 poems in a batch (this advice goes for other places, you'll find . . .)."

$ **⬤** **BYLINE**, Box 5240, Edmond OK 73083-5240. (405)348-5591. E-mail: mpreston@bylinemag.com. Website: www.bylinemag.com (includes writer's guidelines, names of editors, contest list and rules, ad rates and sample article from magazine). Editor-in-Chief: Marcia Preston. **Contact:** Carolyn Wall, fiction editor. Monthly magazine "aimed at encouraging and motivating all writers toward success, with special information to help new writers. Articles center on how to write better, market smarter, sell your work." Estab. 1981.

Needs: Literary, genre, general fiction. Receives 100-200 unsolicited fiction mss/month. "Do not want to see erotica or explicit graphic content. No science fiction or fantasy." Accepts 1 ms/issue; 11 mss/year. **Published many new writers within the last year.** Published work by Julie Weary and Virginia Reiser. Length: 2,000-4,000 words. Also publishes poetry and articles.

How to Contact: Send complete ms with SASE. Accepts simultaneous submissions, "if notified. For us, no cover letter is needed." Responds in 6-12 weeks. Publishes ms an average of 3 months after acceptance. Sample copy for $4. Guidelines for #10 SASE.

Payment/Terms: Pays $100 and 3 contributor's copies. Pays on acceptance for first North American rights.

Advice: "We look for good writing that draws the reader in; conflict and character movement by story's end. We're very open to new writers. Submit a well-written, professionally prepared ms with SASE. No erotica or senseless violence; otherwise, we'll consider most any theme. We also sponsor short story and poetry contests. Read what's being published. Find a good story, not just a narrative reflection. Keep submitting."

CAIRN, St. Andrews College Press, 1700 Dogwood Mile, Laurinburg NC 28352. (910)277-5310. Fax: (910)277-5020. E-mail: press@sapc.edu. Website: www.sapc.edu/sapress.html (includes catalogue, readings, competitions, selections, guidelines). **Contact:** Fiction Editor. Magazine: 50-60 lb. paper, digital printing. "*Cairn* is a nonprofit, student-run literary magazine which seeks to publish established writers and talented students together. We occasionally publish collections by authors published in *Cairn*." Estab. 1969. Member, CLMP and AWP.
Needs: Literary, short story collections. **Publishes 15-20 new writers/year.** "We're looking for original, quirky, imaginative short fiction with real human insight."
How to Contact: Submit complete ms with cover letter. Accepts submissions by e-mail, disk and fax. Include estimated word count and brief bio. Send disposable copy of ms with SASE for reply only. Responds in 3-4 weeks. Accepts simultaneous submissions (with notice).
Payment/Terms: Pays 2 contributor's copies.
Advice: "Read a copy of *Cairn* to get a feel for what we publish, and follow guidelines closely."

CALLALOO, A Journal of African-American and African Diaspora Arts and Letters, Dept. of English, TAMU 4227, Texas A&M University, College Station TX 77843. (979)458-3108. Fax: (979)458-3275. E-mail: callaloo@tamu.edu. Website: http://callaloo.tamu.edu (includes links to *Callaloo* online, writer's guidelines, sample issues, copyright information and editorial information). Editor: Charles H. Rowell. **Contact:** Ginger Thornton, managing editor. Magazine: 7×10; 250 pages. Quarterly. "Devoted to publishing fiction, poetry, drama of the African diaspora, including North, Central and South America, the Caribbean, Europe and Africa. Visually beautiful and well-edited, the journal publishes 3-5 short stories in all forms and styles in each issue." Estab. 1976. Circ. 2,000.
   ● One of the leading voices in African-American literature, *Callaloo* has received NEA literature grants. Several pieces every year are chosen for collections of the year's best stories, such as *Beacon's Best*. John Wideman's "Weight" from *Callaloo* won the 2000 O. Henry Award.
Needs: Contemporary, ethnic (black culture), feminist, historical, humor/satire, literary, prose poem, regional, science fiction, serialized/excerpted novel, translations. Also publishes poetry and drama. "No romance, confessional. Would like to see more experimental fiction, science fiction and well-crafted literary fiction particularly dealing with the black middle class, immigrant communities and/or the black South." Accepts 3-5 mss/issue; 10-20 mss/year. Length: 50 pages double-spaced maximum. **Publishes 5-10 new writers/year.** Recently published work by Charles Johnson, Ernest Gaines, John Edgar Wideman, Jamaica Kincaid, Percival Everett and Patricia Powell.
How to Contact: Submit complete ms in triplicate and cover letter with name, mailing address, e-mail address, if possible and loose stamps. Accepts queries by e-mail and fax. Responds in 2 weeks to queries; 6 months to mss. Accepts multiple submissions (maximum 2). Previously published work accepted "only as part of a special issue or if solicited." Sample copy for $10.
Payment/Terms: Pays in contributor's copies. Acquires some rights. Sends galleys to author.
Advice: "We look for freshness of both writing and plot, strength of characterization, plausibility of plot. Read what's being written and published, especially in journals such as *Callaloo*."

CALYX, A Journal of Art & Literature by Women, Calyx, Inc., P.O. Box B, Corvallis OR 97339. (541)753-9384. Fax: (541)753-0515. E-mail: calyx@proaxis.com. Director: Margarita Donnelly. **Contact:** Beverly McFarland, senior editor. Magazine: 6×8; 128 pages per single issue; 60 lb. coated matte stock paper; 10 pt. chrome coat cover; original art. Publishes prose, poetry, art, essays, interviews and critical and review articles. "*Calyx* exists to publish fine literature and art by women and is committed to publishing the work of all women, including women of color, older women, working class women, and other voices that need to be heard. We are committed to discovering and nurturing beginning writers." Biannual. Estab. 1976. Circ. 6,000.
Needs: Receives approximately 1,000 unsolicited prose and poetry mss when open. Accepts 4-8 prose mss/issue, 9-15 mss/year. Reads mss October 1-December 15; submit only during this period. Mss received when not reading will be returned. **Publishes 10-20 new writers/year.** Published work by M. Evelina Galang, Chitrita Banerji, Diana Ma and Catherine Brady. Length: 5,000 words maximum. Also publishes literary essays, literary criticism, poetry.
How to Contact: Send ms with SASE and bio. Accepts requests for guidelines by e-mail. Accepts simultaneous submissions. Responds in 8 months to mss. Publishes ms an average of 8 months after acceptance. Sample copy for $9.50 plus $2 postage. Guidelines available for SASE. Reviews novels, short story collections, poetry and essays.
Payment/Terms: "Combination of payment, free issues and 1 volume subscription."
Advice: Most mss are rejected because "the writers are not familiar with *Calyx*—writers should read *Calyx* and be familiar with the publication. We look for good writing, imagination and important/interesting subject matter."

CAMBRENSIS, 41 Heol Fach, Cornelly, Bridgend, Mid-Glamorgan, CF33 4LN Wales. Editor: Arthur Smith. **Contact:** Fiction Editor. Quarterly. Circ. 500.
Needs: "Devoted solely to the short story form, featuring short stories by writers born or resident in Wales or with some Welsh connection; receives grants from the Welsh Arts' Council and the Welsh Writers' Trust; uses artwork—cartoons, line-drawings, sketches etc." Length: 2,500 words maximum.

How to Contact: Writer has to have some connection with Wales. SAE and IRCs or similar should be enclosed with "air mail" postage to avoid long delay.

Payment/Terms: Writers receive 3 copies of magazine. Send IRCs for a sample copy. Subscriptions via Blackwell's Periodicals, P.O. Box 40, Hythe Bridge Street, Oxford, OX1 2EU, UK or Swets & Zeitlinger B V, P.O. Box 800, 2160 S Z Lisse, Holland.

CAPERS AWEIGH, Cape Breton Poetry & Fiction, Capers Aweigh Press, 19 Cliff St., Glace Bay, Nova Scotia B1A 1B3 Canada. (902)849-0822. E-mail: capersaweigh@hotmail.com. Editor: John MacNeil. **Contact:** Fiction Editor. Magazine: 5×8; 80 pages; bond paper; Cornwall-coated cover. "*Capers Aweigh* publishes poetry and fiction of, by and for Cape Bretoners." Publication frequency varies. Estab. 1992. Circ. 500.

Needs: Adventure, ethnic/multicultural, fantasy, feminist, historical, humor/satire, literary, mainstream, contemporary, mystery/suspense, psychic/supernatural/occult, regional, science fiction. List of upcoming themes available for SASE. Receives 2 unsolicited mss/month. Accepts 30 mss/issue. Publishes ms 9 months after acceptance. Published work by C. Fairn Kennedy and Shirley Kiju Kawi. Length: 2,500 words. Publishes short shorts. Also publishes literary criticism, poetry. Sponsors contests only to Cape Bretoners fiction writers.

How to Contact: Query first. Send SASE for reply or send a disposable copy of ms. Accepts electronic submissions (IBM). Sample copy for $4.95 and 6×10 SAE.

Payment/Terms: Pays free subscription to the magazine and 1 contributor's copy; additional copies for $4.95. Acquires first North American serial rights. Sends galleys to author.

$ THE CAPILANO REVIEW, 2055 Purcell Way, North Vancouver, British Columbia V7J 3H5 Canada. (604)984-1712. E-mail: tcr@capcollege.bc.ca. Website: www.capcollege.bc.ca/dept/TCR (includes guidelines, excerpts and complete bibliography of 25 years worth of contributors). **Contact:** Sharon Thesen, editor. Magazine: 6×9; 90-120 pages; book paper; glossy cover; perfect-bound; visual art. Magazine of "fresh, innovative art and literature for literary/artistic audience." Triannual. Estab. 1972. Circ. 900.

Needs: Experimental, literary and drama. "No traditional, conventional fiction. Want to see more innovative, genre-blurring work." Receives 80 unsolicited mss/month. Accepts 1 ms/issue; 3-5 mss/year. **Published new writers within the last year.** Recently published work by Michael Turner, Lewis Buzbee and George Bowering. Length: 4,000 words average. Also publishes literary essays, poetry.

How to Contact: Send complete ms with cover letter and SASE or IRC. Include 2- to 3-sentence bio and brief list of publications. Responds in 2-4 months to mss. Send SASE or IRCs for return of ms. Accepts multiple submissions (2 maximum). Sample copy for $9 (Canadian). "No U.S. postage please—we cannot use it."

Payment/Terms: Pays $50-200, 2 contributor's copies and one-year subscription. Pays on publication for first North American serial rights.

Advice: "We are looking for exceptional, original style; strong thematic content; innovation and quality writing. We would like to see more postmodern; cross-genre fiction. Read several issues before submitting and make sure your work is technically perfect."

THE CARIBBEAN WRITER, The University of the Virgin Islands, RR 02, Box 10,000—Kingshill, St. Croix, Virgin Islands 00850. (340)692-4152. Fax: (340)692-4026. E-mail: qmars@uvi.edu. Website: www.Caribbean Writer.com (includes writer's guidelines and excerpts from past publications). Editor: Erika J. Waters. **Contact:** Quilin B. Mars, managing editor. Magazine: 6×9; 304 pages; 60 lb. paper; glossy cover stock; illustrations; photos. "*The Caribbean Writer* is an international magazine with a Caribbean focus. The Caribbean should be central to the work, or the work should reflect a Caribbean heritage, experience or perspective." Annual. Estab. 1987. Circ. 1,500.

● Work published in *The Caribbean Writer* has received a Pushcart Prize and Quenepon Award.

Needs: Contemporary, historical (general), humor/satire, literary, mainstream and prose poem. Receives 800 unsolicited mss/year. Accepts 60 mss/issue. Also accepts poetry, essays, translations, plays. **Publishes approximately 20% new writers/year.** Recently published work by Cecil Gray, Virgil Suarez and Opal Palmer Adisa.

How to Contact: Send complete ms with cover letter. Accepts queries/mss by e-mail and on disk. "Blind submissions only. Send name, address and title of manuscript on separate sheet. Title only on manuscript. Manuscripts will not be returned unless this procedure is followed." SASE (or IRC). Accepts simultaneous and multiple submissions. Sample copy for $7 and $4 postage.

Payment/Terms: Pays 2 contributor's copies. Acquires one-time rights. Annual prizes for best story ($400); for best poem ($300); $200 for first publication; best work by Caribbean author ($500); best work by Virgin Islands author ($200).

Advice: Looks for "work which reflects a Caribbean heritage, experience or perspective."

CAROLINA QUARTERLY, Greenlaw Hall CB #3520, University of North Carolina, Chapel Hill NC 27599-3520. (919)962-0244. Fax: (919)962-3520. E-mail: cquarter@unc.edu. Website: www.unc.edu/depts/cqonline (includes writer's guidelines, current contents, index to past contributors). **Contact:** Tara Powell, editor-in-chief. Literary journal: 70-90 pages; illustrations. Publishes fiction for a "general literary audience." Triannual. Estab. 1948. Circ. 900-1,000.

● Work published in *Carolina Quarterly* has been selected for inclusion in *Best American Short Stories*, in *New Stories from the South: The Year's Best*, and *Best of the South*.

Needs: Literary. "We would like to see more short/micro-fiction and more stories by minority/ethnic writers." Receives 150-200 unsolicited fiction mss/month. Accepts 4-5 mss/issue; 14-16 mss/year. Does not read mss June-August. Pub-

insider report

Forty years between stories

Doug Rennie

Writing fiction, Doug Rennie says, had always seemed "too daunting, the idea of looking at a blank piece of paper and creating a story." Surely, he thought, one must have the "entire story in mind" before actually composing. But in 1991, when Rennie retired from teaching history in the California public schools and became a fulltime freelance writer, he was ready to give it a real shot.

For the first time in his life.

Rennie had to get his "prose sea legs" first, by writing for a number of local publications—health/fitness features, book reviews, pop culture pieces. Soon he began a rather lucrative stint as a columnist for *Runner's World*, with a circulation of over a half million. A collection of these pieces, *Runner's World on the Road*, was recently published by Rodale Press.

Rennie's first love, though, remains fiction. Way back in the fifth grade he penned his first story; 42 years actually passed until he wrote his next, "Tell Me You Ain't Mad"—one of his first published stories picked up by *Sycamore Review*. Now, he's written over 100 stories, with three dozen in print. *Badlands*, his first story collection, was published by Creative Arts Books in the summer of 2002.

So what made the difference? What spurred him on in his fiction writing career after such a long wait?

Taking a couple of fiction writing classes through the Oregon Writers Workshop helped Rennie land his very first publication, "Baptism," in the *Chicago Tribune Magazine*, with a hefty check for $750. But it wasn't just the money or prestige from publication that inspired Rennie to write. A course called "Turning Your Life into Fiction," taught by Andrea Carlisle ("a local writer and a damn good one," Rennie says) sparked his imagination. He found Carlisle "challenging and nurturing at the same time." He gained a sense of what fiction is about—and what it's not about. Carlisle warned her students not to keep writing about their own lives, experiences, needs.

"She stressed that writing only autobiographical fiction holds you down like gravity," Rennie says. "Your imagination would never take flight, never soar. You would end up writing the same stories over and over again." This idea stuck—becoming a watchword for his fiction. "Too few writers ever get beyond autobiography," Rennie says. " 'Write what you know' becomes 'write what you remember' or 'write what happened to you.' " As Rennie sees it, "You *can* use what you see, what you hear, what you remember, but only as a starting point, and not as a template for the entire story. There's a difference between creating a story and merely recording the past."

A "heavy-duty reader since boyhood," Rennie continues to read widely, and like most, he has his models, those who exemplify what he considers the best in fiction—among them John

Cheever, Richard Yates, Robert Stone, T.C. Boyle, Paul Theroux, Lorrie Moore, and Tim O'Brien. His chief influence is Raymond Carver; Rennie admires "the way Carver's stories always leave you disturbed in some way you really cannot clearly identify, how you always feel that there is something more going on than what you're reading about, something beneath the surface unspoken but very much *there*, that often gives his stories a kind of subtly sinister quality I love. I think I try to do some of the same things, sometimes consciously, in my own stories."

The elements that produce such good fiction, Rennie firmly believes, are the classic qualities of all good narration: strong character and a compelling story line. Characters don't have to be likable, just interesting. "Is there a more intriguing character in recent memory than Hannibal Lechter? Or how about the Misfit in 'A Good Man is Hard to Find'?" It's not important that we find anyone likable in a story, says Rennie—it's the riveting characters that make it happen. "It makes a better story, though, if the character is in some way morally ambiguous, one you can't simply label 'good' or 'bad.' "

As to the nature of story itself—the contours of the plot, the essential thrust of the narrative—British novelist Graham Swift's definition of good storytelling answers to Rennie's own needs: "the relating of something strange." In Rennie's stories, this means "a story that takes me to places I've never been or even imagined, and/or inside of characters unlike any others I've known." Good stories retain this element of strangeness to the end—and then some. Rennie prizes "that ending that extends the story beyond the last line, forces the reader to think 'Okay, what just happened here?' "

Perhaps it's this element of the strange that causes Doug Rennie's stories to become "edgy, sometimes bizarre, even creepy." In "Tell Me," a young boy sorts out his father's love in the midst of drunkenness and violence. The story's Sunday morning setting moves from tavern to a nearby stream fed by a spring. Beauty, ugliness, hate, and love all get mixed up. It was his first serious attempt at literary fiction, and it was admired greatly by Carlisle. It also heralded the edgy nature of Rennie's future work: the way his stories dig down, ask uncomfortable questions. Human existence, in Rennie's stories, is plagued by any number of things gone awry—marked by moral flaws, failings. One example is "Breckenridge," dealing with the moral issue of omission—the "things not done that have moral implications. Because of what happens in the story—and what does not—it's one of my most disturbing stories," he says.

When Rennie turns to his background in history, "a powerful, consistent source of story material," he is once again likely to ask unnerving questions. "I've always been morbidly intrigued by the fact that there was no such thing as a parachute in World War I. What happened, then, if your fragile little biplane was going down? Not much of a leap from there to 'Norman Spring, 1917,' a very sad little story," he says. In this story, the historical material provides the story's dramatic core. Sometimes, though, the history connection is oblique, as in a story like "Tobruk," where an overbearing husband ruthlessly tromps his wife at a board game—improving his dark gaming with tactical war information from the History Channel.

As any writer knows, gathering the materials is at least half the battle. Rennie gets many of his ideas on "solitary runs or long bike rides." Ideas "will surface unexpectedly, sometimes just a kernel—other times almost an entire story." "Irian Jaya," published in *American Fiction*, began when Rennie was breaking on a long, strenuous bike ride. "I really think there is something to the theory that intense exercise, a totally non-intellectual endeavor, somehow frees up the right brain." In his essay "Founding a Fiction Factory," Rennie spells out a process that's really worked for him: single lines for "launch pads"; "pod stories," or stories that provide the nuclei of what will some day, perhaps, be fully developed pieces; several stories in the oven at all-times—so that one isn't stuck in the "creative horse latitudes," facing the all too common writer's block.

One great discovery, says Rennie, was that "writing scenes was a semi-breakthrough, one that freed me up and ultimately produced many stories. Before this, unless I had more or less an entire story in mind, I found it almost impossible to sit down and write anything."

Rennie does not count himself a "natural" writer, one "for whom the process comes easily—I don't have that 'z' writer chromosome that the lucky ones have." His problem is not one of finding time, the complaint of many writers; for Rennie writing is often simply a "grind." Rennie believes that one solution is to gain self-confidence, a sense of oneself as a writer: "It does take some intellectual courage to stare at a blank screen and start making things up."

—Jack Smith

lishes ms an average of 4 months after acceptance. **Publishes 1-2 new writers/year.** Published work by Clyde Edgerton, Barry Hannah and Doris Betts. Length: 7,000 words maximum; no minimum. Also publishes short shorts, literary essays, poetry. Occasionally critiques rejected mss.
How to Contact: Send complete ms with cover letter and SASE to fiction editor. Accepts queries by phone and fax. No simultaneous submissions. Responds in 4-5 months. Sample copy for $5; writer's guidelines for SASE.
Payment/Terms: Pays in contributor's copies. Acquires first rights.

N 🖉 ◎ **CAYO, A Chronicle of Life in the Keys**, P.O. Box 1352, Key West FL 33041. (305)296-4286. **Contact:** Alyson Matley, editor. Magazine: 8½×11; 40-48 pages; glossy paper; 70 lb. cover stock; illustrations; photos. Magazine on Keys-related topics or by Keys authors. Quarterly. Estab. 1993. Circ. 1,000.
Needs: Condensed/excerpted novel, experimental, literary, regional. Receives 4-5 unsolicited mss/month. Accepts 2-3 mss/issue; 8-12 mss/year. Published work by Alma Bond, Robin Shanley and Lawrence Ferlinghetti. Length: 800-3,000 words; average length: 3,000 words. Publishes short shorts. Also publishes literary essays, poetry. Often comments on rejected mss.
How to Contact: Send complete ms with a cover letter. Include bio and list of publications with submission. Responds in 6 weeks to queries; 3 months to mss. Send SASE for reply, return of ms or send a disposable copy of ms. Accepts simultaneous, reprint and electronic (ASCII text on disk) submissions. Sample copy for $4. Guidelines for #10 SASE.
Payment/Terms: Pays in contributor's copies. Acquires one-time rights.
Advice: "The story has to stand on its own and move the reader."

N $ **CENTURY**, Century Publishing, P.O. Box 336, Hastings-on-Hudson NY 10706. E-mail: editor@centurymag.com. Website: www.centurymag.com (includes excerpts, writer's guidelines, online order form). **Contact:** Robert Killheffer, editor. Literary Magazine: 6×9; 96-112 pages; acid free. "We seek to publish the broadest range of imaginative or speculative fiction, ranging from science fiction, fantasy, magic realism, surrealism, and even mainstream fiction that has a quirky, offbeat sensibility." Semiannual. Estab. 1995. Circ. 2,000.
Needs: Experimental, fantasy, feminist, historical, horror, literary, science fiction. Receives 200 unsolicited mss/months. Accepts 6-7 mss/issue; 12-14 mss/year. Publishes ms 12-18 months after acceptance. Agented fiction 7%. **Publishes 1-2 new writers/year.** Published work by F. Brett Cox, Greer Gilman, and Ben Miller. Length: 250-20,000 words; average length: 6,000 words. Publishes short shorts. Sometimes comments on rejected mss.
How to Contact: Send complete ms with cover letter. Include estimated word count and list of publications. Responds in 2 months to mss. Send SASE for return of ms or send disposable copy of ms and #10 SASE for reply only. Sample copy for $7. Guidelines for SASE.
Payment/Terms: Pays 4¢/word and 5 contributor's copies; additional copies $3.60. Pays on acceptance for First World English and non-exclusive reprint rights. Sends galleys to author.
Advice: "Read lots of every kind of work, but most importantly, take a look at at least one issue of our magazine to get a sense of our tastes."

N 🖉 **CHAFFIN JOURNAL**, English Department, Eastern Kentucky University, Case Annex 467 EKU, Richmond KY 40475-3102. (854)622-3080. E-mail: robert.witt@eku.edu. **Contact:** Robert Witt, editor. Magazine: 8×5½; 120-130 pages; 70 lb. paper; 80 lb. cover. "We publish fiction on any subject; our only consideration is the quality." Annual. Estab. 1998. Circ. 150.
Needs: Ethnic/multicultural, experimental, family saga, feminist, gay, historical, humor/satire, lesbian, literary, mainstream, regional (Appalachia). "No erotica, fantasy." Receives 3-4 unsolicited mss/month. Accepts 6-8 mss/year. Does

not read mss November 1 through May 31. Publishes ms 6 months after acceptance. **Publishes 2-3 new writers/year.** Recently published work by Meredith Sue Willis, Raymond Abbott, Marjorie Bixler and Chris Helvey. Maximum length: 10,000 words; average length: 5,000 words.

How to Contact: Send complete ms with cover letter. Include estimated word count and brief bio. Responds to queries in 1 week; mss in 3 months. Send SASE for return of ms. Accepts simultaneous and multiple submissions. Sample copy for $5. Guidelines for SASE or by e-mail.

Payment/Terms: Pays 1 contributor's copy; additional copies $5. Pays on publication for one time rights. Sponsors contest.

Advice: "All manuscripts submitted are considered."

$ CHAPMAN, 4 Broughton Place, Edinburgh EH1 3RX Scotland. **Contact:** Joy Hendry, fiction editor. Phone: (+44)131 557 2207. Fax: (+44)131 556 9565. E-mail: editor@chapman-pub.co.uk. Website: www.chapman-pub.co.uk (includes samples from current issues, guidelines, catalog). "*Chapman*, Scotland's quality literary magazine, is a dynamic force in Scotland, publishing poetry, fiction, criticism, reviews; articles on theatre, politics, language and the arts. Our philosophy is to publish new work, from known and unknown writers, mainly Scottish, but also worldwide." Quarterly. Circ. 2,000. Publishes 4-6 stories/issue. Estab. 1970.

Needs: Literary, Scottish/international. "No horror, science fiction." **Publishes 25 new writers/year.** Published work by Quim Monzo, Dilys Rose, Leslie Schenck. Length: 1,000-6,000 words.

How to Contact: Include SAE and return postage (or IRC) with submissions.

Payment/Terms: Pays by negotiation. Sample copy available for £5 (includes postage).

Advice: "Keep your stories for six months and edit carefully. We seek challenging work which attempts to explore difficult/new territory in content and form, but lighter work, if original enough, is welcome."

$ THE CHARITON REVIEW, Truman State University, Kirksville MO 63552. (816)785-4499. Fax: (816)785-7486. Editor: Jim Barnes. **Contact:** Fiction Editor. Magazine: 6×9; approximately 100 pages; 60 lb. paper; 65 lb. cover stock; photographs on cover. "We demand only excellence in fiction and fiction translation for a general and college readership." Semiannual. Estab. 1975. Circ. 700.

Needs: Literary, contemporary, experimental, translations. Accepts 3-5 mss/issue; 6-10 mss/year. **Published new writers within the last year.** Published work by Ann Townsend, Glenn DelGrosso, Paul Ruffin and X.J. Kennedy. Length: 3,000-6,000 words. Also publishes literary essays, poetry. Critiques rejected mss when there is time.

How to Contact: Send complete ms with SASE. No book-length mss. No simultaneous submissions. Responds in less than 1 month to mss. Publishes ms an average of 6 months after acceptance. Sample copy for $5 with SASE. Reviews novels and short story collections.

Payment/Terms: Pays $5/page up to $50 maximum and contributor's copy on publication; additional copies for $5.50. Acquires first North American serial rights; rights returned on request.

Advice: "Do not ask us for guidelines: the only guidelines are excellence in all matters. Write well and study the publication you are submitting to. We are interested only in the very best fiction and fiction translation. We are not interested in slick material. We do not read photocopies, dot-matrix, or carbon copies. Know the simple mechanics of submission—SASE, no paper clips, no odd-sized SASE, etc. Know the genre (short story, novella, etc.). Know the unwritten laws. There is too much manufactured fiction; assembly-lined, ego-centered personal essays offered as fiction."

$ THE CHATTAHOOCHEE REVIEW, Georgia Perimeter College, 2101 Womack Rd., Dunwoody GA 30338-4497. (770)551-3019. Website: www.chattahoochee-review.org. Managing Editor: Jo Ann Yeager Adkins. **Contact:** Lawrence Hetrick, editor. Magazine: 6×9; 150 pages; 70 lb. paper; 80 lb. cover stock; illustrations; photos. Quarterly. Estab. 1980. Circ. 1,250.

● Fiction from *The Chattahoochee Review* has been included in *Best New Stories of the South*.

Needs: Literary, mainstream. "No juvenile, romance, science fiction." Receives 900 unsolicited mss/year. Accepts 5 mss/issue. **Published new writers within the last year.** Published work by Merrill Joan Gerber, Mary Ann Taylor-Hall, Anthony Grooms and Greg Johnson. Length: 2,500 words average. Also publishes creative nonfiction, interviews with writers, poetry reviews, poetry. Sometimes critiques rejected mss.

How to Contact: Send complete ms with cover letter, which should include sufficient bio for notes on contributors' page. Responds in 2-4 months. SASE. May consider simultaneous submission "reluctantly." Sample copy for $6. Fiction and poetry guidelines available on request. Reviews novels and short story collections.

Payment/Terms: Pays $20/page fiction; $15/page nonfiction; $50/poem. Acquires first rights.

Advice: "Arrange to read magazine before you submit to it." Known for publishing Southern regional fiction.

CHICAGO QUARTERLY REVIEW, Monadnock Group Publishers, 517 Sherman Ave., Evanston IL 80906. (719)633-9794. E-mail: lawlaw58@aol.com. **Contact:** Syed Haider, Jane Lawrence and Lisa McKenzie, editors. Magazine: 6×9; 125 pages; illustrations; photos. "*CQR* was begun by a group of writers who felt there were too few venues for quality work that did not conform to preordained criteria. We continue to publish examples of solid writing not in thrall to any particular school of thought or aesthetics." Quarterly. Estab. 1994. Circ. 300.

Needs: Literary. Does not want "any work that is easily categorized, academic, obtuse or self-impressed." Receives 20-30 unsolicited mss/month. Accepts 6-8 mss/issue; 8-16 mss/year. Publishes ms up to 1 year after acceptance. Agented fiction 10%. **Publishes 3 new writers/year.** Recently published work by Jim Mezzanote, D.E. Laczi and Charles Rose. Length: 5,000 words maximum; average length: 2,500 words. Publishes short-shorts. Average length: 1,000 words. Also publishes literary essays and poetry. Sometimes comments on rejected mss.

How to Contact: Send complete ms with a cover letter. Include estimated word count and brief bio. Responds in 2 months to queries; 6 months to mss. Send a disposable copy of ms and #10 SASE for reply only. Accepts simultaneous and multiple submissions. Sample copy for $9.

Payment/Terms: Pays 1 contributor's copy; additional copies $6. Pays on publication for one-time rights.

Advice: "The writer's voice ought to be clear and unique, and should explain something of what it means to be human. We want well-written stories that reflect an appreciation for the rhythm and music of language; work that shows passion and commitment to the art of writing."

$ ◨ CHRYSALIS READER, Journal of the Swedenborg Foundation, The Swedenborg Foundation, 320 N. Church St., West Chester PA 19380-3213. (610)430-3222. Send mss to: Rt. 1, Box 4510, Dillwyn VA 23936. (804)983-3021. **Editor:** Carol S. Lawson. Book series: 7½×10; 192 pages; archival paper; coated cover stock; illustrations; photos. "A literary magazine centered around one theme per issue. Publishes fiction, essays and poetry for intellectually curious readers interested in spiritual topics." Biannual. Estab. 1985. Circ. 3,000.

Needs: Fiction (leading to insight), contemporary, experimental, historical, literary, mainstream, mystery/suspense, science fiction, spiritual, sports. No religious, juvenile, preschool. Upcoming theme: "Spiritual Wellness" (October 2002). Receives 50 mss/month. Accepts 15-20 mss/issue; 20-40 mss/year. Publishes ms within 2 years of acceptance. Published work by Robert Bly, Larry Dossey and John Hitchcock. Length: 2,000-3,500 words. Also publishes literary essays, literary criticism, chapters of novels, poetry. Sometimes critiques rejected mss and recommends other markets.

How to Contact: Query first and send SASE for guidelines. Responds in 2 months. SASE. No simultaneous, reprinted or in-press material. Sample copy for $10. Guidelines for #10 SASE.

Payment/Terms: Pays $75-250 and 5 contributor's copies. Pays on publication for one-time rights. Sends galleys to author.

Advice: Looking for "1. *Quality*; 2. appeal for our audience; 3. relevance to/illumination of an issue's theme."

$ ◨ CIMARRON REVIEW, Oklahoma State University, 205 Morrill Hall, Stillwater OK 74074-0135. (405)744-9476. E-mail: cimarronreview@hotmail.com. Website: cimarronreview.okstate.edu. **Contact:** Toni Graham, Andrea Koenig, fiction editors. Magazine: 6×9; 120 pages. "Poetry and fiction on contemporary themes; personal essay on contemporary issues that cope with life in the 20th century, for educated literary readers. We work hard to reflect quality. We are eager to receive manuscripts from both established and less experienced writers that intrigue us by their unusual perspective, language, imagery and character." Quarterly. Estab. 1967. Circ. 500.

Needs: Literary and contemporary. "Would like to see more language-aware writing. No collegiate reminiscences, science fiction or juvenilia." Accepts 5-6 mss/issue, 20-24 mss/year. **Publishes 8 new writers/year.** Published work by Jose Saramago, Adam Braver, Jonathan Ames and Robert Olen Butler. Also publishes literary essays, literary criticism, poetry.

How to Contact: Send complete ms with SASE. "Short cover letters are appropriate but not essential, except for providing *CR* with the most recent mailing address available." No simultaneous submissions. Responds in 3 months to mss. Publishes ms within 1 year after acceptance. Sample copy with SASE and $7. Reviews novels, short story collections, and poetry collections.

Payment/Terms: Pays $50 for each prose piece. Acquires first North American serial rights only.

Advice: "Don't try to pass personal essays off as fiction. Short fiction is a genre uniquely suited to the modern world. *CR* seeks an individual, innovative style that focuses on contemporary themes."

◨ CITY PRIMEVAL: Narratives of Urban Reality, P.O. Box 30064, Seattle WA 98103. (206)440-0791. Editor: David Ross. **Contact:** Fiction Editor. Magazine: 6×9; 72 pages; 60 lb. paper; card cover stock; illustrations; photos. *City Primeval* "features work in the new genre: urban narrative." Quarterly. Estab. 1995. Circ. 200.

Needs: Adventure, literary, military/war, mystery/suspense, thriller/espionage. Receives 75-150 unsolicited mss/month. Accepts 6-10 mss/issue; 36-60 mss/year. Publishes ms 3-6 months after acceptance. **Publishes 6-10 new writers/year.** Published work by Robin Sterns, Robert R. Ward, P.F. Allen, Susan Montag and Diane Trzcinski. Length: 5,000 words average; 10,000 words maximum. Publishes short shorts. Also publishes literary essays and poetry. Sometimes comments on or critiques rejected ms.

How to Contact: Send complete ms with a cover letter. Include 6-12 line bio. Responds to mss in 6 weeks. Send SASE for return of ms. No simultaneous submissions. Sample copy for $5. Guidelines for SASE.

Payment/Terms: Pays 1 contributor's copy. Pays on publication for first North American serial rights.

Advice: "Must meet editorial requirements—request guidelines before submitting. Know the market."

Ⓝ ◨ ◨ ◎ THE CLAREMONT REVIEW, The Contemporary Magazine of Young Adult Writers, The Claremont Review Publishers, 4980 Wesley Rd., Victoria, British Columbia V8Y 1Y9 Canada. (250)658-5221. Fax: (250)658-5387. E-mail: editor@theClaremontReview.com. Website: www.theClaremontReview.com. **Contact:** Susan Field (business manager), Bill Stenson, Susan Stenson, Janice McCachen, Kim LeMieux and Susan Field, editors. Magazine: 6×9; 110-120 pages; book paper; soft gloss cover; b&w illustrations. "We are dedicated to publishing emerging young writers aged 13-19 from anywhere in the English-speaking world, but primarily Canada and the U.S." Biannual. Estab. 1992. Circ. 700.

Needs: Young adult/teen ("their writing, not writing for them"). "No science fiction, fantasy." Plans special fiction issue or anthology. Receives 20-30 unsolicited mss/month. Accepts 10-12 mss/issue; 20-24 mss/year. Publishes ms 3

months after acceptance. **Publishes 100 new writers/year.** Recently published work by Allisan Chan, Laura Ishiguro and Jason Tsai. Length: 5,000 words maximum; 1,500-3,000 words preferred. Publishes short shorts, prose and poetry. Always comments on rejected mss.
How to Contact: Send complete ms with cover letter. Include 2-line bio, list of publications and SASE. Responds in up to 3 months. Accepts multiple submissions. Sample copy for $8.
Payment/Terms: Pays 1 contributor's copy on publication for first North American and one-time rights. Additional copies for $6.
Advice: Looking for "good concrete narratives with credible dialogue and solid use of original detail. It must be unique, honest and a glimpse of some truth. Send an error-free final draft with a short covering letter and bio; please, read us first to see what we publish."

THE CLIMBING ART, 6390 E. Floyd Dr., Denver CO 80222-7638. Phone/fax: (303)757-0541. E-mail: rmorrow@dnvr.uswest.net. Editor: Ron Morrow. **Contact:** Fiction Editor. Magazine: 5½×8½; 150 pages; illustrations; photos. "*The Climbing Art* publishes literature, poetry and art for and about the spirit of climbing." Annual. Estab. 1986. Circ. 1,200.
Needs: Adventure, condensed/excerpted novel, ethnic/multicultural, experimental, fantasy, historical, literary, mainstream/contemporary, mystery/suspense, regional, science fiction, sports, translations. "Will accept religious articles that are related to climbing, and rhyme is fine." Receives 50 unsolicited mss/month. Accepts 4-6 mss/issue; 10-15 mss/year. Publishes ms up to 1 year after acceptance. Agented fiction 10%. **Publishes 25-30 new writers/year.** Published work by Reg Saner, Robert Walton and Gary Every. Length: 500-10,000 words. Publishes short shorts. Also publishes literary essays, literary criticism, poetry. Sometimes comments on rejected mss. Sometimes sponsors contests.
How to Contact: Send complete ms with a cover letter. Include estimated word count, 1-paragraph bio and list of publications. Accepts queries/mss by fax or e-mail. Responds in 1 month to queries; 2-8 weeks to mss. SASE. Accepts simultaneous and electronic submissions. Sample copy $4. Reviews novels and short story collections.
Payment/Terms: Pays free subscription and 2 contributor's copies; additional copies for $4. Acquires one-time rights.
Advice: Looks for knowledge of subject matter and love of the sport of climbing. "Read several issues first and make certain the material is related to climbing and the spirit of climbing. We have not seen enough literary excellence."

$ COLORADO REVIEW, English Department, Colorado State University, Fort Collins CO 80523. (970)491-5449. E-mail: creview@colostate.edu. Website: www.coloradoreview.com. Editor: David Milofsky. **Contact:** Fiction Editor. Literary journal: 224 pages; 60 lb. book weight paper. Triquarterly. Estab. 1966. Circ. 1,300.
Needs: Contemporary, ethnic, experimental, literary, mainstream. "No genre fiction." Receives 600 unsolicited fiction mss/month. Accepts 3-4 mss/issue. **Published new writers within the last year.** Published work by T. Alan Broughton, Erin Flanagan, Ann Hood and Robert Boswell. Length: under 6,000 words. Does not read mss May-August. Also publishes personal essays, book reviews, poetry.
How to Contact: Send complete ms with SASE (or IRC) and brief bio with previous publications. Responds in 3 months. Publishes ms 6-12 months after acceptance. Sample copy for $10. Reviews novels and poetry or short story collections.
Payment/Terms: Pays $5/printed page for fiction; 2 contributor's copies; extras for $6. Pays on publication for first North American serial rights. "We assign copyright to author on request." Sends proofs to author.
Advice: "We are interested in manuscripts that show craft, imagination, and a convincing voice. If a story has reached a level of technical competence, we are receptive to the fiction working on its own terms. The oldest advice is still the best: persistence. Approach every aspect of the writing process with pride, conscientiousness—from word choice to manuscript appearance."

CONCHO RIVER REVIEW, Angelo State University, English Dept., Box 10894 ASU Station, San Angelo TX 76904. (915)942-2273, ext. 230. Fax: (915)942-2208. E-mail: me.hartje@angelo.edu. **Contact:** Mary Ellen Hartje, fiction editor. Magazine: 6½×9; 100-125 pages; 60 lb. Ardor offset paper; Classic Laid Color cover stock; b&w drawings. "We publish any fiction of high quality—no thematic specialties—*contributors must be residents of Texas or the Southwest generally.*" Semiannual. Estab. 1987. Circ. 300.
Needs: Contemporary, ethnic, historical, humor/satire, literary, regional and western. "No erotica; no science fiction." Receives 10-15 unsolicited mss/month. Accepts 3-6 mss/issue; 8-10 mss/year. Publishes ms 4 months after acceptance. **Publishes 4 new writers/year.** Published work by Gordon Alexander, Riley Froh, Gretchen Geralds and Kimberly Willis Holt. Length: 1,500-5,000 words; average length: 3,500 words. Also publishes literary essays, poetry.
How to Contact: Send complete ms with SASE; cover letter optional. Responds in 3 weeks to queries; 3-6 months to mss. Send disk copy upon acceptance. Accepts simultaneous submissions (if noted). Sample copy for $4. Guidelines for #10 SASE. Reviews novels and short story collections. Books to be reviewed should be sent to Dr. James Moore.
Payment/Terms: Pays in contributor's copies; $5 charge for extras. Acquires first rights.
Advice: "We prefer a clear sense of conflict, strong characterization and effective dialogue."

CONFLUENCE, Ohio Valley Literary Group Inc., P.O. Box 336, Belpre OH 45714-0336. (304)295-6599. E-mail: confluence1989@yahoo.com. Website: www.marietta.edu/~eng/confluence.html (includes writer's guidelines, names of editors). **Contact:** Dr. Beverly Hogue or Sandra Tritt. Magazine: 5½×8½; 100 pages; 60 lb. paper; card stock cover; illustrations. "We publish quality short stories, essays and poetry in collaboration with Marietta College." Annual. Estab. 1989. Circ. 1,000.

Needs: Ethnic/multicultural, literary, mainstream, regional. "No children's/juvenile or young adult." Receives 12 unsolicited mss/month. Accepts 4 mss/year. "We'd accept more if we received more quality fiction." Does not read mss February through August. Publishes ms 9 months after acceptance. **Publishes 6 new writers/year.** Recently published work by R.G. Cantalupo, Mary Winters, Virgil Suarez and D. James Smith. Maximum length: 5,000 words; average length: 3,000 words. Publishes short shorts. Also publishes literary essays and poetry. Often comments on rejected mss.

How to Contact: Send complete ms with cover letter. Accepts submissions by e-mail and on disk. Include estimated word count, brief bio and list of publications. Responds to queries in 3 weeks; mss in up to 7 months. Send SASE for return of ms, or send disposable copy of ms and SASE for reply only. Accepts multiple submissions. Sample copy for $6.50. Guidelines for SASE or by e-mail.

Payment/Terms: Pays 3 contributor's copies; additional copies $4.50. Pays on publication for one time rights. Sponsors contest.

Advice: "We consider overall quality. We look for well-rounded characters, consistent point of view, precise wording, setting integrated into plot, dialogue that moves the plot forward, and so on. Read current short stories, avoid cliches and passive voice, and join a critique group which offers honest evaluation."

$ ◻ ▯ CONFRONTATION, English Dept., C.W. Post of Long Island University, Brookville NY 11548. (516)299-2720. Fax: (516)299-2735. Editor: Martin Tucker. **Contact:** Jonna Semeiks, associate editor. Magazine: 6×9; 250-350 pages; 70 lb. paper; 80 lb. cover; illustrations; photos. "We like to have a 'range' of subjects, form and style in each issue and are open to all forms. Quality is our major concern. Our audience is made up of literate, thinking people; formally or self-educated." Semiannual. Estab. 1968. Circ. 2,000.

● *Confrontation* has garnered a long list of awards and honors, including the Editor's Award for Distinguished Achievement from CCLP and NEA grants. Work from the magazine has appeared in numerous anthologies including the *Pushcart Prize, Best Short Stories* and *O. Henry Prize Stories*.

Needs: Literary, contemporary, prose poem, regional and translations. "No 'proselytizing' literature or genre fiction." Accepts 30 mss/issue; 60 mss/year. Receives 400 unsolicited fiction mss each month. Does not read June-September. Approximately 10-15% of fiction is agented. **Publishes 20-30 new writers/year.** Recently published work by Susan Vreeland, Lanford Wilson, Carol Berge and Sallie Bengham. Length: 500-4,000 words. Publishes short shorts. Also publishes literary essays, poetry. Critiques rejected mss when there is time. Sometimes recommends other markets.

How to Contact: Send complete ms with SASE. "Cover letters acceptable, not necessary. We accept simultaneous submissions but do not prefer them." Accepts diskettes if accompanied by computer printout submissions. Responds in up to 2 months to mss. Publishes ms 6-12 months after acceptance. Sample copy for $3. Reviews novels, short story collections, poetry and literary criticism.

Payment/Terms: Pays $20-250 and 1 contributor's copy; half price for extras. Pays on publication for all rights "with transfer on request to author."

Advice: "We look for literary merit. Keep trying."

◖ ▯ CONNECTICUT REVIEW, Connecticut State University System, SCSU 501 Crescent St., New Haven CT 06515. (203)392-6737. Fax: (203)248-5007. E-mail: ctreview@southernct.edu. **Contact:** Dr. Vivian Shipley, editor. Magazine: 6×9; 202 pages; white/heavy paper; glossy/heavy cover; color and b&w illustrations and photos; artwork. "*Connecticut Review* presents a wide range of cultural interests that cross disciplinary lines. The editors invite the submission of academic articles of general interest, thesis-oriented essays, translations, short stories, plays, poems, and interviews." Semiannual. Estab. 1968. Circ. 4,000. Member, CELJ, CLMJ.

● Work published in *Connecticut Review* has won the Pushcart Prize and inclusion in *Best American Poetry, Best American Short Stories 2000*. *CR* has also received the Phoenix Award for Significant Editorial Achievement, and 2001 National Public Radio's Award for Literary Excellence.

Needs: Literary. "Content must be suitable for circulation to libraries and high schools." Receives 250 unsolicited mss/month. Accepts 6 mss/issue; 12 mss/year. Does not read mss June-August. Publishes ms 1 year after acceptance. **Publishes 6-8 new writers/year.** Recently published work by John Searles, Michael Schiavone, Norman German, Tom Williams and Paul Ruffin. Length: 2,000-4,000 words. Publishes short shorts. Also publishes literary essays and poetry.

How to Contact: Send complete ms with a cover letter. Include estimated word count, brief bio, list of publications and 2 copies of mss. Responds in 4 months to queries. Send a disposable copy of ms and #10 SASE for reply only. Accepts simultaneous submissions. Sample copy for $6. Guidelines for SASE.

Payment/Terms: Pays 2 contributor's copies; additional copies $6. Pays on publication for first rights. Sends galleys to author.

◖ COTTONWOOD, Box J, 400 Kansas Union, University of Kansas, Lawrence KS 66045-2115. (785)864-2516. Fax: (785)864-4298. E-mail: tlorenz@ukans.edu. **Contact:** Tom Lorenz, fiction editor. Magazine: 6×9; 100 pages; illustrations; photos. "*Cottonwood* publishes high quality prose, poetry and artwork and is aimed at an audience that appreciates the same. We have a national scope and reputation while maintaining a strong regional flavor." Semiannual. Estab. 1965. Circ. 500.

Needs: "We publish only literary prose and poetry." Receives 25-50 unsolicited mss/month. Accepts 5-6 mss/issue; 10-12 mss/year. Publishes ms 6-18 months after acceptance. Agented fiction 10%. **Publishes 1-3 new writers/year.**

Published work by Connie May Fowler, Oakley Hall and Cris Mazza. Length: 1,000-8,000 words; average length: 2,000-5,000 words. Publishes short shorts. Length: 1,000 words. Sometimes publishes literary essays; publishes literary criticism, poetry.

How to Contact: Send complete ms with a cover letter or submit through agent. Include 4-5 line bio and brief list of publications. Responds in up to 6 months. SASE for return of ms. Accepts simultaneous submissions. Sample copy for $8.50, 9×12 SAE and $1.90. Reviews novels and short story collections. Send books to review editor at our Cottonwood address.

Payment/Terms: Pays 1 contributor's copy; additional copies $6.50. Pays on publication for one-time rights.

Advice: "We're looking for depth and/or originality of subject matter, engaging voice and style, emotional honesty, command of the material and the structure. *Cottonwood* publishes high quality literary fiction, but we are very open to the work of talented new writers. Write something honest and that you care about and write it as well as you can. Don't hesitate to keep trying us. We sometimes take a piece from a writer we've rejected a number of times. We generally don't like clever, gimmicky writing. The style should be engaging but not claim all the attention for itself."

CRAB CREEK REVIEW, P.O. Box 840, Vashon WA 98070. (206)463-5668. Website: www.crabcreekreview.org. **Contact:** Eleanor Lee, Harris Levinson, Laura Sinai and Terri Stone, editors. Magazine: 6×9 paperbound; 80-112 pgs., line drawings. "Magazine publishing poetry, short stories, and cover art for an audience interested in literary, visual and dramatic arts and in politics." Published twice yearly. Estab. 1983. Circ. 450.

Needs: Contemporary, humor/satire, literary and translations. No confession, erotica, horror, juvenile, preschool, religious/inspirational, romance or young adult. Receives 100 unsolicited mss/month. **Published new writers within the last year.** Recently published work by David Lee, Derek Sheffield, Mary Jane Grinstead and Webb Harris Jr. Length: 1,200-6,000 words; average length: 3,000 words. Publishes short shorts.

How to Contact: Send complete ms with short list of credits. Responds in 2-4 months. SASE. No simultaneous submissions. Sample copy for $5. *Anniversary Anthology* $3.

Payment/Terms: Pays 2 contributor's copies; $4 charge for extras. Acquires first rights. Rarely buys reprints.

Advice: "We appreciate 'sudden fictions.' Type name and address on each piece. Enclose SASE. Send no more than one story in a packet (except for short shorts—no more than three, ten pages total). Know what you want to say and say it in an honest, clear, confident voice."

$ 🖉 🍷 CRAB ORCHARD REVIEW, A Journal of Creative Works, Southern Illinois University at Carbondale, English Department, Faner Hall, Carbondale IL 62901-4503. (618)453-6833. Fax: (618)453-8224. Website: www.siu.edu/~crborchd (includes contest information and guidelines). Prose Editor: Carolyn Alessio. **Contact:** Jon Tribble, managing editor. Magazine: 5½×8½; 275 pages; 55 lb. recycled paper, card cover; photo on cover. "We are a general interest literary journal published twice/year. We strive to be a journal that writers admire and readers enjoy. We publish fiction, poetry, creative nonfiction, fiction translations, interviews and reviews." Estab. 1995. Circ. 1,800.

● Crab Orchard Review has won an Illinois Arts Council Literary Award for prose fiction by Ricardo Cortez Cruz (2001).

Needs: Excerpted novel, ethnic/multicultural, literary, translations. No science fiction, romance, western, horror, gothic or children's. Wants more novel excerpts that also work as stand alone pieces. List of upcoming themes available on website. Receives 300 unsolicited mss/month. Accepts 10-15 mss/issue, 20-25 mss/year. Reads during summer only for special issues. Publishes ms 9-12 months after acceptance. Agented fiction 1%. Published work by Tim Parrish, Gordon Weaver, Garnett Kilberg Gohen, Ellen Slezak and Gina Ochsner. **Publishes 1 new writer/year.** Length: 1,000-6,500 words; average length: 2,500 words. Also publishes literary essays and poetry. Rarely comments on rejected mss.

How to Contact: Send complete ms with a cover letter. "No queries necessary." Include brief bio and list of publications. Responds in 3 weeks to queries; up to 9 months to mss. Send SASE for reply, return of ms. Accepts simultaneous submissions. Sample copy for $6. Guidelines for #10 SASE. Reviews books, small press and university press anthologies and story collections only. Reviews done in house by staff only. No outside reviews. Send review copies to Managing Editor Jon Tribble.

Payment/Terms: Pays $100 minimum; $15/page maximum, 2 contributor's copies and a year's subscription. Acquires first North American serial rights.

Advice: "We look for well-written, provocative, fully realized fiction that seeks to engage both the reader's senses and intellect. Don't submit too often to the same market, and don't send manuscripts that you haven't read over carefully. Writers can't rely on spell checkers to catch all errors. Always include a SASE. Read and support the journals you admire so they can continue to survive."

CRAZYHORSE, College of Charleston, Dept. of English, 66 George St., Charleston SC 29424. (843)953-7740. Email: crazyhorse@cofc.edu. **Contact:** Editors. Literary magazine: 8¾×8¼; 150 pages; illustrations; photos. "Crazyhorse publishes writing of fine quality regardless of style, predilection, subject. Editors are especially interested in original writing that engages in the work of honest communication." Semiannual. Estab. 1961. Circ. 1,000. Raymond Carver called Crazyhorse "an indispensable literary magazine of the first order."

Needs: All fiction of fine quality. Receives 50-100 unsolicited mss/month. Accepts 8-10 mss/issue; 16-20 mss/year. Publishes ms 6-12 months after acceptance. Recently published work by W.D. Wetherell, Paul Zimmer and Lisa Burnell. Length: 35 pages; average length: 15 pages. Publishes short shorts. Also publishes literary essays and poetry.

How to Contact: Send complete ms with cover letter. Include brief bio and list of publications. Responds in 1 week to queries; 5 weeks to mss. Send SASE for return of ms or disposable copy of ms and #10 SASE for reply only. Accepts simultaneous submissions. Sample copy for $7. Guidelines for SASE or by e-mail.

Payment/Terms: Pays 2 contributor's copies; additional copies $5. Acquires first North American serial rights. Sends galleys to author. Sponsors contest; guidelines available for e-mail.

Advice: "Write to explore subjects you care about. Clarity of language; subject is one in which something is at stake."

THE CREAM CITY REVIEW, University of Wisconsin-Milwaukee, Box 413, Milwaukee WI 53201. (414)229-4708. E-mail: creamcity@csd.uwm.edu. Website: www.uwm.edu/dept/english/creamcity.html (includes writer's guidelines, names of editors, table of contents from past issues, cover art scanned and magazine's history). Editor-in-Chief: Karen Auvinen. **Contact:** Steve Nelson, fiction editor. Editors rotate. Magazine: 5½×8½; 200-300 pages; 70 lb. offset/perfect-bound paper; 80 lb. cover stock; illustrations; photos. "General literary publication—an eclectic and electric selection of the best fiction we can find." Semiannual (September and January). Estab. 1975. Circ. 2,000.

Needs: Ethnic, experimental, literary, prose poem, regional, translations. "Would like to see more quality fiction. No horror, formulaic, racist, sexist, pornographic, homophobic, science fiction, romance." Receives approximately 300 unsolicited fiction mss each month. Accepts 6-10 mss/issue. Does not read fiction or poetry April 2-August 31. **Publishes 10 new writers/year.** Recently published work by Diane Glancey, Nina de Gramont, Kate Braverman, Luis Alberto Urrea, Simon Ortiz, George Makana Clark and Pete Fromm. Length: 1,000-10,000 words. Publishes short shorts. Also publishes literary essays, literary criticism, poetry.

How to Contact: Send complete ms with SASE. Accepts simultaneous and multiple submissions if notified and submissions on disk. Responds in 6 months. Hosts annual fiction contest September 1-November 1. Send one story up to 25 pages, $10 contest fee and SASE for results only to: Fiction Contest/TCCR/UWM-Dept. of English, Box 413, Milwaukee WI 53201. Sample copy for $5 (back issue), $8 (current issue). Reviews novels and short story collections.

Payment/Terms: Pays one-year subscription. Acquires first rights. Sends galleys to author. Rights revert to author after publication.

Advice: "The best stories are those in which the reader doesn't know what is going to happen or what the writer is trying to do. Avoid formulas. Surprise us with language and stunning characters."

CROSSCONNECT, P.O. Box 2317, Philadelphia PA 19103. (215)898-5324. Fax: (215)898-9348. E-mail: xconnect@ccat.sas.upenn.edu. Website: ccat.sas.upenn.edu/xconnect. **Editor:** David Deifer. "*CrossConnect* publishes tri-annually on the World Wide Web and annually in print, with the best of our Web issues, plus nominated work from editors in the digital literary community. *xconnect: writers of the information age* is a nationally distributed, full color, journal sized book." 5½×8½; trade paper; 200 pages.

Needs: Literary and experimental fiction. "Our mission—like our name—is one of connection. *CrossConnect* seeks to promote and document the emergent creative artists as well as established artists who have made the transition to the new technologies of the Information Age." **Publishes 25 new writers/year.** Recently published work by Bob Perelman, Paul Hoover and Yusef Komunyakaa.

How to Contact: Electronic and traditional submissions accepted. "We prefer your submissions be cut and pasted into your mail readers and sent to us. No attached files unless requested." Send complete ms (up to three stories) with cover letter and short bio. Accepts previously published and simultaneous submission. Rarely comments on rejections.

Payment/Terms: Pays 1 contributor's copy for use in print version. Author retains all rights. Regularly sends prepublication galleys.

Advice: "Persistence."

CUTBANK, English Dept., University of Montana, Missoula MT 59812. (406)243-6156. E-mail: cutbank@selway.umt.edu. Website: www.umt.edu/cutbank (includes writer's guidelines, names of editors, interviews with authors and excerpts). **Contact:** Fiction Editor. Editors change each year. Magazine: 5½×8½; 115-130 pages. "Publishes serious-minded and innovative fiction and poetry from both well known and up-and-coming authors." Semiannual. Estab. 1973. Circ. 600.

Needs: "Innovative, challenging, well-written stories." No "science fiction, fantasy or unproofed manuscripts." Receives 200 unsolicited mss/month. Accepts 6-12 mss/year. Does not read mss April 15-August 15. Publishes ms up to 6 months after acceptance. **Publishes 4 new writers/year.** Recently published work by Dan Barden and Todd Pierce. Length: 40 pages maximum. Also publishes literary essays, literary criticism, poetry. Occasionally critiques rejected mss.

How to Contact: Send complete ms with cover letter, which should include "name, address, publications." Responds in 4 months to mss. SASE. Accepts simultaneous submissions. Sample copy for $4 (current issue $6.95). Guidelines for SASE. Reviews novels and short story collections. Send books to fiction editor.

MARKET CONDITIONS are constantly changing! If you're still using this book and it is 2004 or later, buy the newest edition of *Novel & Short Story Writer's Market* at your favorite bookstore or order from Writer's Digest Books by calling 1-800-448-0915.

Payment/Terms: Pays 2 contributor's copies. Rights revert to author upon publication, with provision that *Cutbank* receives publication credit.

Advice: "Strongly suggest contributors read an issue. We have published stories by Kevin Canty, Chris Offutt and Pam Houston in recent issues, and like to feature new writers alongside more well-known names. Send only your best work."

THE DALHOUSIE REVIEW, Dalhousie University, Halifax, Nova Scotia B3H 3J5 Canada. (902)494-2541. Fax: (902)494-3561. E-mail: dalhousie.review@dal.ca. Website: www.dal.ca/~dalrev (includes guidelines, subscription information, journal history and excerpts). **Contact:** Dr. Ronald Huebert, editor. Magazine: 15cm×23cm; approximately 140 pages; photographs sometimes. Publishes articles, book reviews, short stories and poetry. Published 3 times a year. Circ. 400.

Needs: Literary. Length: 5,000 words maximum. Also publishes essays on history, philosophy, etc., and poetry. Recently published work by Melissa Hardy, Kim Bridgford, Eugene Dubnov and Shalom Camenietzki.

How to Contact: Send complete ms with cover letter. SASE (Canadian stamps or IRCs). Sample copy for $10 (Canadian) including postage. Occasionally reviews novels and short story collections.

$ DAN RIVER ANTHOLOGY, P.O. Box 298, Thomaston ME 04861. (207)354-0998. Fax: (207)354-8953. E-mail: cal@americanletters.org. Website: www.americanletters.org (includes writer's guidelines, catalogue). **Contact:** R. S. Danbury III, editor. Book: 5½×8½; 180 pages; 60 lb. paper; gloss 10 pt. full-color cover. For general/adult audience. Annual. Estab. 1984. Circ. 600.

Needs: Adventure, contemporary, ethnic, experimental, fantasy, historical, horror, humor/satire, literary, mainstream, prose poem, psychic/supernatural, regional (contemporary and historical), romance, science fiction, senior citizen/retirement, suspense/mystery and western; "virtually anything but porn, evangelical, juvenile. Would like to see more first-person adventure." Receives 150 unsolicited fiction mss each submission period (January 1 through March 31). "We generally publish 12-15 pieces of fiction." Reads "mostly in April." Length: 800-2,500 words; average length: 2,000-2,400 words. Also publishes poetry.

How to Contact: *Charges reading fee: $1 for poetry; $3 for prose* (cash only, no checks). Send complete ms with SASE. Responds by May 15 each year. No simultaneous submissions. Nothing previously published. Sample copy for $13.95 paperback, $59.95 cloth, plus $3.25 shipping. Guidelines for #10 SASE or on website.

Payment/Terms: Pays approximately $4/page, minimum *cash advance on acceptance* against royalties of 10% of all sales attributable to writer's influence: readings, mailings, autograph parties, etc., plus up to 50% discount on copies, plus other discounts to make total as high as 73%. Buys all rights.

Advice: "Know your market. Don't submit without reading guidelines."

DESCANT, Descant Arts & Letters Foundation, P.O. Box 314, Station P, Toronto, Ontario M5S 2K9. (416)593-2557. Fax: (416)593-9362. E-mail: descant@web.net. Website: www.descant.on.ca (includes guidelines, editors' names, excerpts and subscription information). **Contact:** Karen Mulhallen, editor. Quarterly literary journal. Estab. 1970. Circ. 1,200. Member, CMPA.

• *Descant* has received the Canadian National Magazine Award in various categories, including fiction.

Needs: Ethnic/multicultural, experimental, feminist, gay, historical, humor/satire, lesbian, literary. No gothic, religious, beat. **Publishes 14 new writers/year.** Recently published work by Andrew Pyper, Douglas Gloner and Judith McCormack. Also publishes poetry and literary essays. Submit seasonal material 4 months in advance.

How to Contact: Send complete ms with cover letter. Sample copy for $8.50. Guidelines for SASE.

Payment/Terms: Pays $100 (Canadian); additional copies $8. Pays on publication.

Advice: "Familiarize yourself with our magazine before submitting."

$ DOUBLETAKE, 55 Davis Square, Somerville MA 02144-2908. (617)591-9389. E-mail: dtmag@doubletakemagazine.org. Website: www.doubletakemagazine.org (includes guidelines, limited contents, links to DoubleTake Summer Documentary Institute and other related things). **Contact:** Albert LaFarge, deputy editor. "We strive to present storytelling in its many guises—visual and in words."

Needs: "Realistic fiction in all of its variety; it's very unlikely we'd ever publish science fiction or gothic horror, for example. "We would like to see more fiction distinguished by literary excellence and a rare voice." Recently published work by David Leavitt, Charles Baxter, Richard Bausch and Jose Saramago. **Publishes more than 10 new writers/year.** Buys 12 mss/year. Length: 3,000-8,000 words.

How to Contact: Send complete ms with cover letter. Accepts simultaneous submissions. Responds in 3 months to mss. Sample copy for $12. Guidelines for #10 SASE.

Payment/Terms: Pays "competitively." Pays on publication for worldwide first rights.

Advice: "Use a strong, developed narrative voice. Don't attempt too much."

$ DOWNSTATE STORY, 1825 Maple Ridge, Peoria IL 61614. (309)688-1409. E-mail: ehopkins@prairienet.org. Website: www.wiu.edu/users/mfgeh/dss (includes guidelines, names of editors, short fiction and reviews). **Contact:** Elaine Hopkins, editor. Magazine: includes illustrations. "Short fiction—some connection with Illinois or the Midwest." Annual. Estab. 1992. Circ. 500.

Needs: Adventure, ethnic/multicultural, experimental, historical, horror, humor/satire, literary, mainstream/contemporary, mystery/suspense, psychic/supernatural/occult, regional, romance, science fiction, westerns. "No porn." Wants more political fiction. Accepts 10 mss/issue. Publishes ms up to 1 year after acceptance. Length: 300-2,000 words. Publishes short shorts. Also publishes literary essays.

How to Contact: Send complete ms with a cover letter. Responds "ASAP." SASE for return of ms. Accepts simultaneous submissions. Sample copy for $8. Guidelines for SASE.

Payment/Terms: Pays $50 maximum. Pays on acceptance for first rights.

THE EDGE CITY REVIEW, Reston Review, Inc., 10912 Harpers Square Court, Reston VA 20191. E-mail: ecreds@earthlink.net. Website: www.edge-city.com. **Contact:** T.L. Ponick, editor. Magazine: 8½×11; 44-52 pages; 60 lb. paper; 65 lb. color cover. "We publish Formalist poetry, well-plotted artistic or literary fiction, literary essays and book reviews. No left-wing screeds, please." Triannual. Estab. 1994. Circ. 500.

Needs: Humor/satire, literary, serialized novel. "We see too much fiction that's riddled with four-letter words and needless vulgarity." Receives 20 unsolicited mss/month. Accepts 1-2 mss/issue; 3-6 mss/year. Publishes ms 6-8 months after acceptance. Length: 1,500-3,000 words; average length: 2,000 words. Also publishes literary essays, literary criticism, poetry. Sometimes comments on rejected ms.

How to Contact: Send complete ms with a cover letter. Include estimated word count, 25-50 word bio, list of publications. Responds in 1 month to queries; 4-6 months to mss. Send SASE for reply, return of ms or send a disposable copy of ms. Accepts electronic submissions (disk or modem). Sample copy for $6. Reviews novels and short story collections. "No 'chapbooks' or self-published, please."

Payment/Terms: Pays 2 contributor's copies; additional copies $5. Acquires first North American serial rights. Sponsors contest; watch for announcements in major publications.

Advice: "We are looking for character-based fiction. Most fiction we receive does not grow out of its characters—but finely wrought characters, fully realized, are what we want to see."

ELYSIAN FIELDS QUARTERLY: The Baseball Review, P.O. Box 14385, St. Paul MN 55114-0385. (651)644-8558. E-mail: info@efqreview.com. Website: www.efqreview.com (includes ordering capabilities, back issues, affiliated products, sample stories, distribution information, e-mail addresses of staff and links). **Contact:** Tom Goldstein, editor. Magazine: 6×9; 96 pages; 60 lb. paper; gloss/varnish cover; illustrations; and photos. *Elysian Fields Quarterly* is "unique because nobody covers baseball the way that we do, with such an offbeat, irreverent manner and yet with full appreciation for the game." Quarterly. Estab. 1992. Circ. 2,325.

Needs: "Any fiction piece about baseball will be considered. We do not want to see general fiction that tries to be a baseball story by making tangential connections to baseball, but in reality is not a fiction piece about baseball." Receives 4-5 unsolicited mss/month. Accepts 5-6 mss/issue; 20-30/year. Publishes ms 3-9 months after acceptance. **Publishes 10-12 new writers/year.** Recently published work by Kelly Candaele, Alvin Greenberg and Mikhail Horowitz. Word length: 2,000-3,000 words average; 1,000 words minimum; 4,000 words maximum. Does not generally publish short shorts "but we don't rule out any good writing." Length: 750 words. Also publishes literary essays, literary criticism and poetry. Very rarely comments on or critiques rejected ms.

How to Contact: Send complete ms with a cover letter. Accepts inquiries by e-mail. "E-mail submissions should be properly formatted in readable attachments." Include 50-word bio. Responds in 4 months. Send SASE for reply, return of ms or send a disposable copy of ms. "Will occasionally consider" simultaneous and reprint submissions. Sample copy for $7.50. Guidelines free. "We review baseball books and novels of interest to our readership."

Payment/Terms: Pays 4 contributor's copies; additional copies $5. Acquires one-time rights and the right to reprint in any anthologies. Sponsors contest: Dave Moore Award for the "most important baseball book."

Advice: "Originality, creativity, believability—is it truly a baseball story? We do not pay attention to industry trends; we just try to publish good writing, irrespective of what is being published elsewhere."

N **EM, literary asylum for grads & undergrads,** Blue Barnhouse, P.O. Box 194672, San Francisco CA 94119-4672. E-mail: emliterary@aol.com. Website: www.emliterary.org. **Contact:** Fiction Editor. Magazine: size, number of pages and type of paper vary; hardbound, perfect binding; illustrations. "We exclusively publish the work of creative writing students from universities across the nation because we feel they have been unduly underrepresented in the literary world." Semiannual. Estab. 2001. Circ. 500.

Needs: Ethnic/multicultural, experimental, literary. "No translations. We do not want to see any work by anyone who is not a university student studying creative writing." Receives 50 unsolicited mss/month. Accepts 5-8 mss/issue; 10-16 mss/year. Publishes ms 6-8 months after acceptance. **Publishes 10-20 new writers/year.** Recently published work by Jerome Edwards, Tom Demarchi and Mukta Sumbrari. Length: "anything over 8,000 words is likely to be excerpted;" average length: 4,000 words. Publishes short shorts. Average length: 200 words. Also publishes literary essays and poetry. Sometimes comments on rejected mss.

How to Contact: Send complete ms with a cover letter. Include brief bio and status as a student. Responds in 2 weeks to queries; 6 months to mss. Send SASE for return of ms or send a disposable copy of ms and #10 SASE for reply only. Accepts simultaneous and multiple submissions. Sample copy for $6. Guidelines for SASE, e-mail or on website.

Payment/Terms: Pays 1 contributor's copy; charge for additional copies varies. Acquires first North American serial, electronic and anthology rights. Sends galleys to author.

EMPLOI PLUS, DGR Publication, 1256 Principale North St., #203, L'Annonciation, Quebec J0T 1T0 Canada. Phone/fax: (819)275-3293. **Contact:** Daniel G. Reid, fiction editor. Magazine: 7×8½; 12 pages; illustrations; photos. Bilingual (French/English) magazine publishing Canadian and American authors. Every 2 or 3 years. Estab. 1990. Circ. 500.

Needs: Serialized novel. Published work by Robert Biro and D.G. Reid. Also publishes poetry.

How to Contact: *Closed to unsolicited submissions.* Sample copy free.

$ ☑ 💡 EPOCH MAGAZINE, 251 Goldwin Smith Hall, Cornell University, Ithaca NY 14853-3201. (607)255-3385. Fax: (607)255-6661. Senior Editor: Joseph Martin. **Contact:** Michael Koch, editor. (Submissions should be sent to Michael Koch). Magazine: 6×9; 128 pages; good quality paper; good cover stock. "Top level fiction and poetry for people who are interested in good literature." Published 3 times a year. Estab. 1947. Circ. 1,000.

  ● Work originally appearing in this quality literary journal has appeared in numerous anthologies including *Best American Short Stories, Best American Poetry, Pushcart Prize, The O. Henry Prize Stories, Best of the West* and *New Stories from the South*.

Needs: Literary, contemporary and ethnic. "No genre fiction. Would like to see more Southern fiction (Southern US)." Accepts 15-20 mss/issue. Receives 500 unsolicited fiction mss each month. Does not read in summer (April 15-September 15). **Publishes 3-4 new writers/year.** Recently published work by Antonya Nelson, Doris Betts and Heidi Jon Schmidt. Length: no limit. Also publishes personal essays, poetry. Critiques rejected mss when there is time. Sometimes recommends other markets.

How to Contact: Send complete ms with SASE. No simultaneous submissions. Responds in 1 month to mss. Publishes ms an average of 6 months after acceptance. Sample copy for $5.

Payment/Terms: Pays $5-10/printed page and contributor's copies. Pays on publication for first North American serial rights.

Advice: "Read the journals you're sending work to."

◐ EUREKA LITERARY MAGAZINE, 300 E. College Ave., Eureka College, Eureka IL 61530-1500. (309)467-6336. E-mail: llogsdon@eureka.edu. Editor: Loren Logsdon. **Contact:** Jane S. Groeper, fiction editor. Magazine: 6×9; 120 pages; 70 lb. white offset paper; 80 lb. gloss cover; photographs (occasionally). "We seek to be open to the best stories that are submitted to us. We do not want to be narrow in a political sense of the word. Our audience is a combination of professors/writers and general readers." Semiannual. Estab. 1992. Circ. 500.

Needs: Adventure, ethnic/multicultural, experimental, fantasy (science), feminist, historical, humor/satire, literary, mainstream/contemporary, mystery/suspense (private eye/hardboiled, romantic), psychic/supernatural/occult, regional, romance (historical), science fiction (soft/sociological), translations. Would like to see more "good social science fiction stories, good ghost stories. We try to achieve a balance between the traditional and the experimental. We do favor the traditional, though. We look for the well-crafted story, but essentially any type of story that has depth and substance to it—any story that expands us as human beings and celebrates the mystery and miracle of the creation. Make sure you have a good beginning and ending, a strong voice, excellent use of language, good insight into the human condition, narrative skill, humor—if it is appropriate to the subject. No drug or drinking stories of any kind, stories with gratuitous violence or stories with heavy propaganda." Receives 30 unsolicited mss/month. Accepts 4 mss/issue; 8-9 mss/year. Does not read mss mainly in late summer (August). **Publishes 5-6 new writers/year.** Recently published work by Jane Guill, Forrest Robinson, Ray Bradbury and Wendell Mayo. Length: 7,000-8,000 words; average length: 4,500 words. Publishes short shorts. Also publishes poetry.

How to Contact: Send complete ms with a cover letter. Should include estimated word count and bio (short paragraph). Accepts submissions by e-mail and on disk. Responds in 1 week to queries; 4 months to mss. Send SASE for reply, return of ms or send a disposable copy of ms. Accepts simultaneous and multiple submissions. Sample copy for $7.50.

Payment/Terms: Pays free subscription to the magazine and 2 contributor's copies. Acquires first rights or one-time rights.

Advice: "We look for expert storytelling technique; a powerful statement about the human condition; eloquent or effective use of language—metaphor, imagery, description. Find a copy of the magazine and read it before submitting your work. Order a copy if you can."

◐ EVANSVILLE REVIEW, University of Evansville, 1800 Lincoln Ave., Evansville IN 47722. (812)488-1114. E-mail: evansvillereview@yahoo.com. **Contact:** Erica Schmidt, editor. Editors change every 1-2 years. Magazine: 6×9; 180 pages; 70 lb. white paper; glossy full color cover; perfect bound. Annual. Estab. 1990. Circ. 2,500.

Needs: "We're open to all creativity. No discrimination. All fiction, screenplays, nonfiction, poetry, interviews, photo essays and anything in between." No children or young adult. List of upcoming themes available for SASE. Receives 1,000 unsolicited mss/year. Does not read mss February-August. Agented fiction 2%. **Publishes 15 new writers/year.** Recently published work by Arthur Miller, Christopher Bigsby, Julia Kasdorf, Vivian Shipley, Dale Ray Phillips and Reginald Gibbons. Also publishes literary essays, poetry.

How to Contact: Send complete ms with a cover letter, e-mail or fax. Include 150 word or less bio and list of publications. Responds in 2 weeks to queries; 3 months to mss. Send SASE for reply, return of ms or send a disposable copy of ms. Accepts simultaneous and reprint submissions. Sample copy for $5. Guidelines free.

Payment/Terms: Pays 2 contributor's copies. Pays on publication for one-time rights. Sends galleys to author if requested. Not copyrighted.

Advice: "Because editorial staffs roll over every 1-2 years, the journal always has a new flavor."

✂ $ ☑ 💡 EVENT, Douglas College, Box 2503, New Westminster, British Columbia V3L 5B2 Canada. Fax: (604)527-5095. E-mail: event@douglas.ba.ca. Website: http://event.douglas.bc.ca/event (includes guidelines, contest information, contents and author information, names of editors). Editor: Cathy Stonehouse. **Contact:** Christine Dewar, fiction editor. Assistant Editor: Ian Cockfield. Magazine: 6×9; 136 pages; quality paper and cover stock. "Primarily a literary magazine, publishing poetry, fiction, reviews, creative nonfiction; for creative writers, artists, anyone interested in contemporary literature." Triannual. Estab. 1971. Circ. 1,250.

● Fiction originally published in *Event* has been included in *Best Canadian Stories*, and the publication was nominated for a Western Magazine Award in 2000.

Needs: Literary, contemporary, feminist, humor, regional. "No technically poor or unoriginal pieces." Receives approximately 100 unsolicited fiction mss/month. Accepts 6-8 mss/issue. **Publishes 2-3 new writers/year.** Recently published work by Leon Rouke, Bill Gaston and Annabel Lyon. Length: 5,000 words maximum. Also publishes poetry and creative nonfiction.

How to Contact: Send complete ms, bio and SAE with Canadian postage or IRC. Responds in 1-4 months to mss. Publishes ms 6-12 months after acceptance. Sample copy for $5.

Payment/Terms: Pays $22/page and 2 contributor's copies. Pays on publication for first North American serial rights.

Advice: "We're looking for a strong, effective point of view; well-handled and engaging characters, attention to language and strong details."

N @ EXHIBITION, A Journal of Visual and Literary Arts, Bainbridge Island Arts & Humanities Council, 221 Winslow Way West, Bainbridge Island WA 98110. (206)842-7901. E-mail: exhibitioneditor@aol.com. Website: www.artshum.org/exhibition (includes writer's guidelines, images of past covers, etc.). **Contact:** Jennifer Scott. Magazine: 8½×11; 32-40 pages; illustrations; photographs. "*Exhibition* is published by Bainbridge Island Arts & Humanities Council, a nonprofit organization whose mission is to create an environment on Bainbridge Island where the arts and humanities can flourish." Semiannual. Estab. 1985. Circ. 300.

Needs: Historical, humor/satire, literary, mainstream, regional (Pacific Northwest focus). "No erotica, religious, children's." Receives 5 unsolicited mss/month, "would like to receive more fiction." Accepts 0-5 mss/issue. Publishes ms 3 months after acceptance. Publishes short shorts. Also publishes literary essays and poetry. Sometimes comments on rejected mss.

How to Contact: Send complete ms with cover letter. Include brief bio (with information about the writer's connection to our region and other information), and list of publications. Responds to queries in 1 month; ms in 6 months. Send SASE for return of ms or disposable copy of ms with SASE for reply only. Accepts previously published submissions (if indicated) and multiple submissions (up to 3 stories at a time). Sample copy for $7. Guidelines for SASE, by e-mail or on website.

Payment/Terms: Pays 1 contributor's copy; additonal copies $7. Pays on publication for first North American serial rights.

Advice: "We look for quality work relevant to our primary audience—people who live or work on Bainbridge Island and care about it. Our readers are passionate about the arts and humanities and have strong commitments to community and the natural world. Send work you think they'll love."

N @ FAULTLINE, Journal of Art and Literature, Dept. of English & Comparative Literature, University of California, Irvine, Irvine CA 92697-2650. (949)824-1573. E-mail: faultline@uci.edu. Managing Editors: Lorene Delany-Ullman and Lance Uyeda. **Contact:** Lance Uyeda, fiction editor. Editors change in September each year. Literary magazine: 6×9; 105 pages; illustrations; photos. "We publish the very best of what we receive. Our interest is quality and literary merit." Annual. Estab. 1992.

Needs: Literary fiction of up tp 20 pages. "Novel excerpts are fine, but they should be self-contained. No sci-fi, mystery, westerns or romance." Receives 20-30 unsolicited mss/month. Accepts 6 mss/year. Does not read mss June-September. Publishes ms within 9 months after acceptance. Agented fiction 10-20%. **Publishes 30-40% new writers/ year.** Recently published work by Maile Meloy, Susan Emerling, Ben Miller and Joan Frank. Length: any. Publishes short shorts. Also publishes literary essays, poetry. Sometimes comments on rejected ms.

How to Contact: Send complete ms with a cover letter. Include estimated word count, 1-paragraph bio and list of publications. Responds in 2 weeks to queries; up to 4 months to mss. Send SASE for reply, return of ms or send a disposable copy of ms. Accepts simultaneous submissions. Sample copy for $5. Guidelines for business-size envelope.

Payment/Terms: Pays 2 contributor's copies. Pays on publication for one-time rights.

Advice: "Our commitment is to publish the best work possible from well-known and emerging authors as well as those who have been affiliated with UCI's esteemed graduate studies program."

@ @ FEMINIST STUDIES, 0103 Taliaferro, University of Maryland, College Park MD 20742. (301)405-7415. Fax: (301)405-8395. E-mail: femstud@umail.umd.edu. Website: www.feministstudies.org. Editor: Claire G. Moses. **Contact:** Shirley Lim, fiction editor. Magazine: journal-sized; about 200 pages; photographs. "Scholarly manuscripts, fiction, book review essays for professors, graduate/doctoral students; scholarly interdisciplinary feminist journal." Triannual. Estab. 1974. Circ. 7,500.

Needs: Contemporary, ethnic, feminist, gay, lesbian. Receives about 20 poetry and short story mss/month. Accepts 2-3 mss/issue. "We review fiction twice a year. Deadline dates are May 1 and December 1. Authors will receive notice of the board's decision by June 15 and January 15, respectively." Published work by Bell Chevigny, Betsy Gould Gibson and Joan Jacobson. Sometimes comments on rejected mss.

How to Contact: Send complete ms with cover letter. No simultaneous submissions. Sample copy for $15. Guidelines free.

Payment/Terms: Pays 2 contributor's copies and 10 tearsheets. Sends galleys to authors.

$ @ ▼ FICTION, % Dept. of English, City College, 138th St. & Convent Ave., New York NY 10031. (212)650-6319/650-6317. E-mail: fictionmagazine@yahoo.com. Website: www.fictioninc.com. **Contact:** Mark J. Mirsky, editor. Managing Editor: Rosemary Farrell. Magazine: 6×9; 150-250 pages; illustrations; occasionally photos. "As the name implies, we publish *only* fiction; we are looking for the best new writing available, leaning toward the unconventional. *Fiction* has traditionally attempted to make accessible the unaccessible, to bring the experimental to a broader audience." Biannual. Estab. 1972. Circ. 4,000.

● Stories first published in *Fiction* have been selected for inclusion in the *Pushcart Prize* and *Best of the Small Presses* anthologies.

Needs: Contemporary, experimental, humor/satire, literary and translations. "No romance, science-fiction, etc." Receives 200 unsolicited mss/month. Accepts 12-20 mss/issue; 24-40 mss/year. Does not read mss May-October. Publishes ms up to 1 year after acceptance. Agented fiction 10-20%. Published work by Joyce Carol Oates, Robert Musil and Romulus Linney. Length: 5,000 words maximum. Publishes short shorts. Sometimes critiques rejected mss and recommends other markets.

How to Contact: Send complete ms with cover letter. Responds in approximately 3 months to mss. SASE. Accepts simultaneous submissions, but please advise. Sample copy for $5. Guidelines for SASE.

Payment/Terms: Minimum payment per contributor is $114. Acquires first rights.

Advice: "The guiding principle of *Fiction* has always been to go to terra incognita in the writing of the imagination and to ask that modern fiction set itself serious questions, if often in absurd and comic voices, interrogating the nature of the real and the fantastic. It represents no particular school of fiction, except the innovative. Its pages have often been a harbor for writers at odds with each other. As a result of its willingness to publish the difficult, experimental, unusual, while not excluding the well known, *Fiction* has a unique reputation in the U.S. and abroad as a journal of future directions."

 **THE FIDDLEHEAD**, University of New Brunswick, Campus House, Box 4400, Fredericton, New Brunswick E3B 5A3 Canada. (506)453-3501. Website: www.lib.unb.ca/texts/fiddlehead. Editor: Ross Leckie. **Contact:** Mark A. Jarman, fiction editor. Magazine: 6×9; 104-128 pages; ink illustrations; photos. "No criteria for publication except quality. For a general audience, including many poets and writers." Quarterly. Estab. 1945. Circ. 1,000.

Needs: Literary. No non-literary fiction. Receives 100-150 unsolicited mss/month. Buys 4-5 mss/issue; 20-40 mss/year. Publishes ms up to 1 year after acceptance. Small percent agented fiction. **Publishes 30 new writers/year.** Published work by Eric Miller, Tony Steele and A.F. Moritz. Length: 50-3,000 words average. Publishes short shorts. Occasionally critiques rejected mss.

How to Contact: Send complete ms with cover letter. Send SASE and *Canadian* stamps or IRCs for return of mss. No simultaneous submissions. Responds in 6 months. Sample copy for $10 (US). Reviews novels and short story collections—*Canadian only*.

Payment/Terms: Pays $20 (Canadian)/published page and 1 contributor's copy. Pays on publication for first or one-time rights.

Advice: "Less than 5% of the material received is published."

FIRST CLASS, Four-Sep Publications, P.O. Box 12434, Milwaukee WI 53212. E-mail: christopherm@four-sep.com. Website: www.four-sep.com (includes all information regarding Four-Sep Publications). **Contact:** Christopher M, editor. Magazine: 4¼×11; 60+ pages; 24 lb./60 lb. offset paper; craft cover; illustrations; photos. "*First Class* features short fiction and poetics from the cream of the small press and killer unknowns—mingling before your very hungry eyes. I publish plays, too." Biannual. Estab. 1995. Circ. 200-400.

Needs: Erotica, literary, mainstream, science fiction (soft/sociological), post-modern. "No religious or traditional poetry, or 'boomer angst'—therapy-driven self loathing." Receives 35-50 unsolicited mss/month. Accepts 4-6 mss/issue; 10-12 mss/year. Publishes ms 1 month after acceptance. **Publishes 10-15 new writers/year.** Published work by Gerald Locklin, John Bennett and B.Z. Niditch. Length: 5,000-8,000 words; average length: 2,000-3,000 words. Publishes short shorts. Length: 500 words. Also publishes poetry. Sometimes comments on rejected mss.

How to Contact: Send complete ms with a cover letter. Include 1 page bio. Accepts queries by e-mail. Responds in 1 week to queries; "near deadline—May/November" to mss. Send SASE and #10 SASE for reply only or send a disposable copy of ms. Accepts simultaneous submissions and reprints. Sample copy for $6. Guidelines free for #10 SASE. Reviews novels and short story collections. Send books to Christopher M.

Payment/Terms: Pays 1 contributor's copy; additional copies $5. Pays on publication for one-time rights.

Advice: "Don't bore me with puppy dogs and the morose/sappy feelings you have about death. Belt out a good, short, thought-provoking, graphic, uncommon piece."

FISH DRUM MAGAZINE, Murray Hill Station, P.O. Box 966, New York NY 10156. Fax: (212)947-2305. E-mail: fishdrum@earthlink.net. Website: www.fishdrum.com. **Editor:** Suzi Winson. Magazine: 6×9; 80-odd pages;

glossy cover; illustrations; photos. "Lively, emotional vernacular modern fiction, art and poetry." Annual. Estab. 1988 by Robert Winson (1959-1995). *"Fish Drum* includes lively, vernacular, prose and poetry that follows the working novel. Themes include Zen practice, the South West, et.al." Circ. 2,000.

Needs: Contemporary, erotica, ethnic, experimental, fantasy, literary, prose poem, regional, science fiction and Zen-oriented works. "Most of the fiction we've published is in the form of short, heightened prose-pieces." Recently published work by Tom Ireland, Herbert Genzmer, Judith Barry and Andrew Franck. Receives 6-10 unsolicited mss/month. Accepts 1-2 mss/issue. Also publishes literary essays, literary criticism, poetry.

How to Contact: No simultaneous submissions. Responds in 3 months to mss. SASE. Reviews novels and short story collections.

Payment/Terms: Pays in contributor's copies; charges for extras. Acquires first North American serial rights. Sends galleys to author.

$ ☑ ☒ **FIVE POINTS: A Journal of Literature and Art**, Georgia State University, University Plaza, Atlanta GA 30303-3083. (404)651-0071. Fax: (404)651-3167. E-mail: msexton@gsu.edu. Website: www.webdelsol.com/five-points (includes excerpts from issue, guidelines, announcements and links). **Contact:** Megan Sexton, managing editor. Magazine: 6×9; 200 pages; cotton paper; glossy cover; and photos. *Five Points* is "committed to publishing work that compels the imagination through the use of fresh and convincing language." Triannual. Estab. 1996. Circ. 2,000.
● Fiction first appearing in *Five Points* has been anthologized in *Best American Fiction* and Pushcart anthologies.

Needs: List of upcoming themes available for SASE. Receives more than 250 unsolicited mss/month. Accepts 4 mss/issue; 15-20 mss/year. Does not read mss April 30-September 1. Publishes ms up to 6 months after acceptance. **Publishes 1 new writer/year.** Published work by Frederick Busch, Ursula Hegi and Melanie Rae Thon. Length: 7,500 words average. Publishes short shorts. Also publishes literary essays and poetry. Sometimes comments on or critiques rejected ms.

How to Contact: Send complete ms with a cover letter. Include 3-4 line bio and list of publications. Send SASE for reply to query. No simultaneous submissions. Sample copy $7. Guidelines free on website.

Payment/Terms: Pays $15/page minimum; $250 maximum, free subscription to magazine and 2 contributor's copies; additional copies $4. Acquires first North American serial rights. Sends galleys to author. Sponsors contest: Paul Bowles Prize, annual award for fiction published in *Five Points*.

Advice: "We place no limitations on style or content. Our only criterion is excellence. If your writing has an original voice, substance, and significance, send it to us. We will publish distinctive, intelligent writing that has something to say and says it in a way that captures and maintains our attention."

☑ ◎ **FLINT HILLS REVIEW**, Dept. of English, Box 4019, Emporia State University, Emporia KS 66801-5087. (620)341-6916. Fax: (620)341-5547. E-mail: webbamy@emporia.edu. Website: www.fhr/index.htm (includes guidelines, subscription information, nonfiction contest guidelines and information, links to Bluestem Press, information about each issue, and links to ESU Creative Writing program and faculty). **Contact:** Amy Sage Webb, co-editor. Magazine: 9×6; 115 pages; 60 lb. paper; glossy cover; illustrations; photos. *"FHR* seeks work informed by a strong sense of place or region, especially Kansas and the Great Plains region. We seek to provide a publishing venue for writers of the Great Plains and Kansas while also publishing authors whose work evidences a strong sense of place, writing of literary quality, and accomplished use of language and depth of character development." Annual. Estab. 1996. Circ. 500. Member, CLMP.

Needs: Ethnic/multicultural, gay, historical, regional (Plains), translations. "No religious, inspirational, children's." Wants to see more "writing of literary quality with a strong sense of place, fidelity to region, strong regional voice, strong images of place which contradict stereotypical images of the place." List of upcoming themes available online. Receives 5-15 unsolicited mss/month. Accepts 2-5 mss/issue; 2-5 mss/year. Does not read mss April-December. Publishes ms up to 4 months after acceptance. **Publishes 4 new writers/year.** Recently published work by Walt McDonald, Amy Kolen, Virgil Suarez and Lisa Knopp. Length: 1 page-5,000 words; average length: 3,000 words. Publishes short shorts. Average length: 1,500 words. Also publishes literary essays, literary criticism and poetry.

How to Contact: Send complete ms with a cover letter. Accepts submissions by e-mail, fax and disk. Include brief bio. Responds in 5 weeks to queries; 6 months to mss. Send a disposable copy of ms and #10 SASE for reply only. Accepts simultaneous and multiple submissions. Sample copy for $5.50. Guidelines for SASE, by e-mail, fax or on website. Reviews novels, short story collections and nonfiction books of interest to writers. Send review copies to Amy Sage Webb.

Payment/Terms: Pays 2 contributor's copies; additional copies $5.50. Pays on publication for one-time rights.

Advice: "Strong imagery and voice, writing that is informed by place or region, writing of literary quality with depth of character development. Hone the language down to the most literary depiction that is possible in the shortest space that still provides depth of development without excess length."

☑ **THE FLORIDA REVIEW**, Dept. of English, University of Central Florida, Orlando FL 32816. (407)823-2038. Fax: (407)823-6582. E-mail: rushin@pegasus.cc.ucf.edu. Website: pegasus.cc.ucf.edu/~english/floridareview/home.htm (includes writer's guidelines, contest information, covers and selections from recent issues). **Contact:** Pat Rushin. Magazine: 6×9; 144 pages; semigloss full-color cover; perfect-bound. "We publish fiction of high 'literary' quality—stories that delight, instruct and aren't afraid to take risks. Our audience consists of avid readers of contemporary fiction, poetry and personal essay." Semiannual. Estab. 1972. Circ. 1,000.

Needs: Contemporary, experimental and literary. "We welcome experimental fiction, so long as it doesn't make us feel lost or stupid. We aren't especially interested in genre fiction (science fiction, romance, adventure, etc.), though a good story can transcend any genre." Receives 200 mss/month. Accepts 6-8 mss/issue; 12-16 mss/year. Publishes ms within 3-6 months of acceptance. **Publishes 2-4 new writers/year.** Recently published work by Nicholas Montemarano, John Salter, Susan Magee and Stephen Dixon. Also publishes poetry and essays.

How to Contact: Send complete ms with cover letter. Responds in 4 months. SASE required. Accepts simultaneous submissions. Sample copy for $6. Guidelines for SASE. Reviews novels and short story collections.

Payment/Terms: Pays in contributor's copies. Small honorarium occasionally available. "Copyright held by U.C.F.; reverts to author after publication. (In cases of reprints, we ask that a credit line indicate that the work first appeared in the *F.R.*)"

Advice: "Every page, every paragraph, every sentence must compell us forward. Keep trying, take a fresh approach, and keep sending."

FLYWAY, A Literary Review, Iowa State University, 206 Ross Hall, Ames IA 50011. (515)294-8273. Fax: (515)294-6814. E-mail: flyway@iastate.edu. Website: www.instate.edu/publications/flyway/homepage.html. **Contact:** Stephen Pett, editor. Literary magazine: 8½×11; 64 pages; quality paper; cover stock; some illustrations; photos. "We publish quality fiction. Our stories are accompanied by brief commentaries by their authors, the sort of thing a writer might say introducing a piece at a reading." Triannual. Estab. 1995. Circ. 500.

Needs: Literary. Receives 50 unsolicited mss/month. Accepts 2-5 mss/issue; 10-12 mss/year. Publishes mss 5 months after acceptance. **Publishes 7-10 new writers/year.** Published work by Duane Niatum, Christina D. Allen-Yazzie, Jacob Appel. Length: 5,000 words; average length: 3,500 words. Publishes short shorts; average length: 500 words. Often comments on rejected mss.

How to Contact: Send complete ms with cover letter. Send SASE. Sample copy for $8. Guidelines for SASE.

Payment/Terms: Pays 2 contributor's copies; additional copies $6. Pays on publication for one-time rights.

Advice: "Quality, originality, voice, drama, tension. Make it as strong as you can."

$ FREEFALL MAGAZINE, The Alexandra Writers' Centre Society, 922 Ninth Ave. SE, Calgary, Alberta T2G 0S4 Canada. Phone/fax: (403)264-4730. E-mail: awcs@telusplanet.net. Website: www.alexandrawriters.org (includes editors, guidelines, contest information and entry form, subscription form). **Contact:** Barbara Howard, editor. Magazine: 8½×11; 40 pages; bond paper; bond stock; illustrations; photos. "*FreeFall* features the best of new, emerging writers and gives them the chance to get into print along with established writers. Now in its thirteenth year, *FreeFall* seeks to attract readers looking for well-crafted stories, poetry, and artwork." Semiannual. Estab. 1990. Circ. under 500. Member, Alberta Magazine Publishers Association (AMPA).

Needs: Literary. "No science fiction, horror." Wants to see more well-crafted literary fiction. Accepts 3-5 mss/issue; 6-10 mss/year. Does not read mss January-February, June-August. Publishes ms 6 months after acceptance. **Publishes 40% new writers/year.** Recently published work by Lowell Blood, Jan Houston, Wayne Arthurson, Karen Horeth, J. Anne Saul, Beth Raugust, Ellen Kelly, Nick Carding, Allan Girling, Kari Strutt, Cyndy Butler, Myriam Dostert and Dianne Wex. Length: 500-3,000 words; average length: 2,500 words. Publishes short shorts. Average length: 500 words. Also publishes poetry. Sometimes comments on rejected mss.

How to Contact: Send complete ms with a cover letter. Include estimated word count, brief bio, e-mail address. Responds in 3 months to mss. Send SASE (or IRC) for return of ms or send a disposable copy of ms with #10 SASE for reply only, or e-mail address for reply. Accepts previously published submissions. Sample copy for $6.50 (US). Guidelines for SASE, e-mail or on website.

Payment/Terms: Pays $5 (Canadian)/printed page and 1 contributor's copy; additional copies $8.50 (US). Pays on publication for first North American serial rights.

Advice: "We look for thoughtful word usage that conveys clear images and encourages further exploration of the story's ideas and neat, clean presentation of work. Carefully read *FreeFall* guidelines before submitting. Do not fold manuscript and submit in 9×11 envelope. Include SASE/IRC for reply and/or return of manuscript. You may contact us by e-mail after initial hardcopy submission. For accepted pieces a request is made for disk or e-mail copy. Web presence attracts submissions from writers all over the world."

FRONT & CENTRE, Black Bile Press, 136-A Billings Ave., Ottawa, Ontario K1H 5K9 Canada. (613)731-6161. E-mail: firth@istar.ca. **Contact:** Matthew Firth. editor. Magazine: letter-size; 50-60 pages; illustration; photos. "We look for new fiction from Canadian and international writers—bold, aggressive work that does not compromise quality." Semiannual. Estab. 1998. Circ. 500.

Needs: Literary, "contemporary realism/gritty urban. No science fiction, horror, mainstream, romance or religious." Receives 30-40 unsolicited mss/month. Accepts 10-12 mss/issue; 20-25 mss/year. Publishes ms 6 months after acceptance. Agented fiction 10%. **Publishes 1-2 new writers/year.** Published work by Kenneth J. Harvey, David Rose, Laura Hird, Gregorio Santo Arena and Lindsey Tipping. Length: 50-4,000 words; average length: 2,500 words. Publishes short shorts. Average length: 200 words. Always comments on rejected mss.

How to Contact: Send complete ms with a cover letter. Include estimated word count, brief bio and list of publications. Responds in 2 weeks to queries; 4 months to mss. Send SASE (or IRC) for return of ms or send a disposable copy of ms and #10 SASE for reply only. Accepts multiple submissions. Sample copy for $5. Guidelines for SASE or by e-mail. Reviews novels, short story collections and nonfiction books of interest to writers. Send review copies to Matthew Firth.

Payment/Terms: Pays 2 contributor's copies; additional copies $5. Pays on publication for first rights. Not copyrighted.
Advice: "We look for attention to detail; unique voice; not overtly derivative; bold writing; not pretentious. We would like to see more realism. Read the magazine first—simple as that!"

FRONTIERS: A Journal of Women Studies, Washington State University, Frontiers, Women's Studies, Box 644007, Pullman WA 99164-4007. E-mail: frontier@wsu.edu. **Contact:** Fiction Editor. Magazine: 6×9; 200 pages; photos. "Women studies; academic articles in all disciplines; criticism; exceptional creative work (art, short fiction, photography, poetry)."
Needs: Feminist, multicultural, lesbian. "We want to see fiction that deals with women's lives and experience from a feminist perspective." Receives 15 unsolicited mss/month. Accepts 7-12 mss/issue. Publishes ms 6-12 months after acceptance. **Publishes 2 new writers/year.** Published work by Elizabeth Bell, Nadine Chapman, Tricia Currans-Sheehan and Alethea Eason.
How to Contact: Send 3 copies of complete ms with cover letter. Responds in 1 month to queries; up to 6 months to mss. SASE. Writer's guidelines for #10 SASE. Sample copy for $20.
Payment/Terms: Pays 2 contributor's copies. Acquires first North American serial rights.
Advice: "We are a *feminist* journal. *Frontiers* aims to make scholarship in women studies, and *exceptional* creative work, accessible to a cross-disciplinary audience inside and outside academia. Read short fiction in *Frontiers* before submitting."

$ ☑ ☑ FUTURES MYSTERIOUS ANTHOLOGY MAGAZINE, (formerly *Futures Magazine*), 3039 38th Ave. S, Minneapolis MN 55406-2140. (612)724-4023. E-mail: babs@suspenseunlimited.net. Website: www.futuresforst orylovers.com (includes excerpts, writer's guidelines, names of editors, interviews with authors, fiction not included in print version, contests, cover art, color posters, greeting cards for writers for sale and single copy and subscription information). **Contact:** Earl Staggs, senior fiction editor. Magazine: 8½×11; 120 pages; illustrations; cartoons. "We are primarily mystery and its subgenres but include multi-genre as well as literary—we offer inspiration and guidance and we're fun! We help writers—entering and nominating for Edgars, Derringer Award, Pushcart Prize, New Century Award and more." Quarterly. Estab. 1998. Circ. 2,000.
● Publisher Babs Lakey received a Derringer Award from the Short Mystery Fiction Society.
Needs: Cartoons, ethnic/multicultural, experimental, feminist, gay, glitz, horror, humor/satire, lesbian, literary, mainstream, mystery/suspense (amateur sleuth, cozy, police procedural, private eye/hardboiled), psychic/supernatural/occult, romance, science fiction, thriller/espionage, western, young adult/teen. "We would like to see more thrillers, more mystery and suspense, also family mainstream. No erotica or pornography." List of upcoming themes available for SASE. Receives 200 unsolicited mss/month. Accepts 45-60 mss/issue; 250 mss/year. Publishes ms 3-8 months after acceptance. **Publishes at least 15 new writers/year.** Published work by Henry Slesar, David Harford, Ashok Banker and Elizabeth Serini. Length: up to 12,000 words maximum; average length: 2,500 words. Publishes short shorts. Average length: 300-1,000 words. Also publishes literary essays, literary criticism and poetry. Sometimes comments on rejected mss.
How to Contact: Refer to online guidelines; guidelines also inside every issue. Accepts submissions by e-mail only. "Send e-mail; paste inside the e-mail with name, address, word count, genre, bio. No snail mail." Responds in 2 months to mss. Accepts simultaneous and multiple submissions, but put each in a separate e-mail. Sample copy for $8. Guidelines for SASE or by e-mail.
Payment/Terms: Pays $10-25 and many awards (2 publishers choices in each issue receive additional fee and award); additional copies $7.50. Acquires first rights. Sponsors contests. Visit website for details.
Advice: "The Internet makes us want, and used to getting, instant gratification. People are getting published without editing their works. We are attempting to keep up with today while still hanging on to the values of solid good creative works. Please make the effort to read a copy before you submit."

GARGOYLE, P.O. Box 6216, Arlington VA 22206-0216. (877)327-2141 (toll free). E-mail: gargoyle@atticsbook s.com. Website: www.atticusbooks.com. **Contact:** Richard Peabody and Lucinda Ebersole, editors. Literary magazine: 6×9; 200 pages; illustrations; photos. "*Gargoyle* began in 1976 with twin goals: to discover new voices and to rediscover overlooked talent. These days we publish a lot of fictional efforts written by poets. We have always been more interested in how a writer tells a story than in plot or story per se." Annual. Estab. 1976. Circ. 2,000.
Needs: Erotica, ethnic/multicultural, experimental, gay, lesbian, literary, mainstream/contemporary, translations, "good short stories with sports and music backgrounds." Wants to see more Canadian, British, Australian and third world fiction. "No romance, horror, science fiction." Receives 50-200 unsolicited mss/month. Accepts 10-15 mss/issue. Reads only in summer (June, July, August). Publishes ms 6-12 months after acceptance. Agented fiction 5%. **Publishes 2-3 new writers/year.** Recently published work by Rebecca Brown, Kenneth Carroll, Wanda Coleman and Doug Rice. Length: 30 pages maximum; average length: 5-10 pages. Publishes short shorts. Length: 2-3 pages. Also publishes literary essays, criticism and poetry. Sometimes comments on rejected ms.
How to Contact: Send complete ms. Responds in 2 weeks to queries; 3 months to mss. Send SASE for reply, return of ms or send a disposable copy of ms. Accepts simultaneous submissions. Sample copy for $12.95.
Payment/Terms: Pays 1 contributor's copy; additional copies for ½ price. Acquires first rights, first North American rights or first British rights. Sends prepublication galleys to author.
Advice: "We have to fall in love with a particular fiction."

$ ☑ ☒ THE GEORGIA REVIEW, The University of Georgia, Athens GA 30602-9009. (706)542-3481. Fax: (706)542-0047. E-mail: garev@arches.uga.edu. Website: www.uga.edu/~garev (includes writer's guidelines, names of editors, order/subscription info, guestbook, current issue contents and more). **Contact:** T.R. Hummer, editor. Associate Editor: Stephen Corey. Journal: 7×10; 208 pages (average); 50 lb. woven old-style paper; 80 lb. cover stock; illustrations; photos. "*The Georgia Review* is a journal of arts and letters, featuring a blend of the best in contemporary thought and literature—essays, fiction, poetry, visual art and book reviews for the intelligent nonspecialist as well as the specialist reader. We seek material that appeals across disciplinary lines by drawing from a wide range of interests." Quarterly. Estab. 1947. Circ. 5,000.

● Stories first published in *The Georgia Review* have been anthologized in *Best American Short Stories, Best American Mystery Stories, Best Stories from the South* and the *Pushcart Prize Collection. The Georgia Review* was a finalist for the National Magazine Award in Fiction in 2000.

Needs: Experimental and literary. "We're looking for the highest quality fiction—work that is capable of sustaining subsequent readings, not throw-away pulp magazine entertainment. Nothing that fits too easily into a 'category.' " Receives about 300 unsolicited fiction mss/month. Accepts 3-4 mss/issue; 12-15 mss/year. Does not read unsolicited mss May 15-August 15. Would prefer *not* to see novel excerpts. **Published new writers within the last year.** Published work by Mary Hood, Barry Lopez, James Tate and Kent Nelson. Length: Open. Also publishes literary essays, literary criticism, poetry. Occasionally critiques rejected mss.

How to Contact: Send complete ms (one story) with SASE. No multiple submissions. Usually responds in 3 months. Sample copy for $7; guidelines for #10 SASE. Reviews short story collections.

Payment/Terms: Pays $40/printed page, 1 year complimentary subscription and 1 contributor's copy; reduced charge for additional copies. Pays on publication for first North American serial rights. Sends galleys to author.

☑ GERTRUDE: A Journal of Voice & Vision. E-mail: editor@gertrudejournal.com. Website: www.gertrudejournal .com (includes writer's guidelines, excerpts, subscription info, events, links). **Contact:** Eric Delehoy, editor. Magazine: 5×8½, 36-48 pages; 60 lb. paper; glossy card cover; illustrations; photos. *Gertrude* is a "biannual publication featuring the voices and visions of the gay, lesbian, bisexual, transgender and supportive community." Estab. 1999. Circ. 550.

● At press time, *Gertrude* was relocating from Colorado to Portland, Oregon. Please see the website for their new address.

Needs: Ethnic/multicultural, feminist, gay, humor/satire, lesbian, literary, mainstream. "No romance, pornography or mystery." Wants more humorous and multicultural fiction. "We'd like to publish more humor and positive portrayals of gays—steer away from victim roles, pity." Receives 3-5 unsolicited mss/month. Accepts 2-3 mss/issue; 4-6 mss/ year. Publishes ms 1-2 months after acceptance. **Publishes 2-3 new writers/year.** Recently published work by Carol Guess, Demrie Alonzo, Henry Alley and Scott Pomfret. Length: 200-2,000 words; average length: 1,500 words. Publishes short shorts. Length: 200-500 words. Also publishes poetry. Often comments on or critiques rejected ms.

How to Contact: Send complete ms with a cover letter. Include estimated word count, 1 paragraph bio and list of publications. Responds in 4 months to mss. Send SASE for reply to query and a disposable copy of ms. No simultaneous submissions. Accepts multiple submissions (no more than two). Sample copy for $5, 6×9 SAE and 3 1st class stamps. Guidelines for #10 SASE.

Payment/Terms: Pays 1-2 contributor's copies; additional copies $4. Payment on publication. Author retains rights upon publication. Not copyrighted.

Advice: "We look for strong characterization, imagery and new, unique ways of writing about universal experiences. Follow the construction of your work until the ending. Many stories start out with zest, then flipper and die. Show us, don't tell us."

$ ☑ ☒ THE GETTYSBURG REVIEW, Gettysburg College, Gettysburg PA 17325. (717)337-6770. Fax: (717)337-6775. Website: www.gettysburgreview.com (includes writer's guidelines, staff biographies and excerpts from the most recent issues). Editor: Peter Stitt. **Contact:** Mark Drew, assistant editor. Magazine: 6¾×10; 170 pages; acid free paper; full color illustrations. "Quality of writing is our only criterion; we publish fiction, poetry, and essays." Quarterly. Estab. 1988. Circ. 4,500.

● Work appearing in *The Gettysburg Review* has also been included in *Prize Stories: The O. Henry Awards*, the *Pushcart Prize* anthology, *Best American Fiction, Best American Poetry, New Stories from the South, Harper's* and elsewhere. It is also the recipient of a Lila Wallace-Reader's Digest grant and NEA grants.

Needs: Contemporary, experimental, historical, humor/satire, literary, mainstream, regional and serialized novel. "We require that fiction be intelligent, and aesthetically written." Receives 350 mss/month. Accepts 15-20 mss/issue; 60-80 mss/year. Publishes ms within 1 year of acceptance. **Publishes 1-5 new writers/year.** Published work by Robert Olen Butler, Joyce Carol Oates, Naeem Murr, Tom Perrotta, Alison Baker and Peter Baida. Length: 1,000-20,000 words; average length: 3,000 words. Occasionally publishes short shorts. Also publishes literary essays, some literary criticism, poetry. Sometimes critiques rejected mss.

How to Contact: Send complete ms with cover letter September through May. Responds in up to 6 months. SASE. Accepts simultaneous submissions. Sample copy for $7 (postage paid). Does not review books per se. "We do essay-reviews, treating several books around a central theme." Send review copies to editor.

Payment/Terms: Pays $25/printed page, subscription to magazine and contributor's copy; charge for extra copies. Pays on publication for first North American serial rights.

Advice: "Reporting time can take more than three months. It is helpful to look at a sample copy of *The Gettysburg Review* to see what kinds of fiction we publish before submitting."

GINOSKO, between literary vision and spiritual realities, P.O. Box 246, Fairfax CA 94978-0246. (415)785-2802. E-mail: RobertPaulCesaretti@hotmail.com. **Contact:** Robert Cesaretti, editor. Magazine: 4×6; 50-60 pages; standard paper; card cover; illustrations; photos. "We look for literature that contains a spiritual content, for mercy, faith, in a very human context." Published "when material permits."

Needs: Experimental, literary, stylized; "consider 'Pagan Night' by Kate Braverman, 'Driving the Heart' by Jason Brown, 'Customs of the Country' by Madison Smartt Bell." Wants to see more prose poems. "Do not want conventional work." **Publishes 4 new writers/year.** Recently published work by Ritchie Swanson and D.L. Olsen. Receives 15-20 unsolicited mss/month. Length: 500-15,000 words.

How to Contact: Send complete ms with a cover letter. Accepts submissions by e-mail. Responds in 1-3 months to mss. SASE for return of ms. Accepts simultaneous and reprint submissions.

Payment/Terms: Pays 1 contributor's copy. Acquires one-time rights.

Advice: "I am looking for a style that conveys spiritual hunger and yearning, yet avoids religiosity and convention— *between literary vision and spiritual realities.*"

GLASS TESSERACT, Glass Tesseract, P.O. Box 702, Agoura Hills CA 91376. E-mail: editor@glasstesseract.com or glasstesseract@earthlink.net. Website: www.glasstesseract.com (includes excerpts, guidelines, names of editors, price). **Contact:** Michael Chester, editor. Magazine: 5½×8½; 48-96 pages; trade edition saddle-stapled with cardstock cover; premium edition comb-bound with color frontispiece and linen paper. "Addressed to a literary readership, *Glass Tesseract* is versatile, publishing stories that range in style and treatment from traditional to wide-open experimental. The purpose of the magazine is to help bring works of art into the world. Rotating selections from the print magazine appear and reappear on the website in a continual fiction and poetry kaleidoscope. The print magazine is published once or twice per year." The hard-copy magazine is published once or twice/year. Estab. 2001.

Needs: Experimental, literary, mainstream. "No sentimental, moralizing, devotional, cute, coy, or happy-face stories." Publishes ms 6-12 months after acceptance. Recently published work by Bonnie J. Glover, Jordan Jones, Ann Lewinson and Helen E. Wright. Length: 200-2,000 words; average length: 1,000 words. Publishes short shorts. Average length: 500 words. Also publishes poetry. Sometimes comments on rejected mss.

How to Contact: E-mail complete ms with or without a cover note. Accepts submissions by e-mail only. Include estimated word count and list of publications. Responds in up to 4 months to mss. Accepts simultaneous, previously published and multiple submissions (up to 3 stories). Sample copy of trade edition for $5. Guidelines by e-mail or on website.

Payment/Terms: Pays 3 contributor's copies (1 premium and 2 trade); additional trade copies $5. Back copies of trade edition $4, any 2 consecutive copies $9. Premium edition a flat $12 each. Pays on publication for one-time rights. Sometimes sends galleys to author.

Advice: "We look for a style of language that, whether lean or rich, is artfully constructed without being pretentious, strained, or laden with clichés. We want characters who have dimensionality, not fitting into standard all-good, all-bad, all-wise, or all-innocent molds. We want story lines that emerge naturally (if not inevitably) from the nature of the characters and the language. Read the stories we have published. Send e-mail to the editor with any questions."

$ GLIMMER TRAIN STORIES, Glimmer Train Press, 710 SW Madison St., Suite 504, Portland OR 97205. (503)221-0836. Fax: (503)221-0837. E-mail: info@glimmertrain.com. Website: www.glimmertrain.com (includes writer's guidelines, story excerpts and a Q&A section for writers). **Editors:** Susan Burmeister-Brown and Linda Swanson-Davies. Magazine: 6¾×9¼; 160 pages; recycled, acid-free paper; 20 illustrations; 12 photographs. Quarterly. Estab. 1990. Circ. 13,000.

● *Glimmer Train* ranked on *Writer's Digest*'s "Top 30" list of best markets for fiction writers. The magazine also sponsors an annual short story contest for new writers and a very short fiction contest.

Needs: Literary. Receives 4,000 unsolicited mss/month. Accepts 10 mss/issue; 40 mss/year. Reads in January, April, July, October. Publishes ms up to 2 years after acceptance. Agented fiction 20%. **Publishes 12 new writers/year.** Published work by Judy Budnitz, Brian Champeau, Ellen Cooney, Andre Dubus III, Thomas Kennedy, Chris Offutt, Alberto Rios and Monica Wood. Length: up to 12,000 words. Sometimes comments on rejected mss.

How to Contact: Submit work online at www.glimmertrain.com. Accepted work published in *Glimmer Train Stories*. Sample copy for $10. Guidelines provided online.

Payment/Terms: Pays $500 and 10 contributor's copies. Pays on acceptance for first rights. Sends galleys to author when requested.

Advice: "When a story stays with us after the first reading, it gets another reading. Those stories that simply don't let us set them aside, get published. Read good fiction. It will often improve the quality of your own writing."

GLOBAL CITY REVIEW, City College of New York, 138th St. and Convent Ave., New York NY 10031. (212)650-7382. E-mail: globalcityreview@ccny.cuny.edu. Website: www.webdelsol.com/globalcityreview (includes excerpts, guidelines, back issue info). **Contact:** Linsey Abrams. Magazine: 4.125×6.75; 172 pages; stock paper; cardstock cover. "The perspective of *GCR* is feminist—women are an important focus, as are writers who write from a gay and lesbian or minority position, culturally decentralized voices because of age or culture, international perspectives, the silenced, the poor, etc. The point is an opening of literary space." Semiannual. Estab. 1993. Circ. 500. Member, CLMP.

Needs: Ethnic/multicultural (general), experimental, feminist, gay, lesbian, literary, translations. "No genre fiction." Upcoming themes: "Our Bodies, Ourselves" (spring), deadline December 1; "Insanity" (fall), deadline May 1. Receives 25-30 unsolicited mss/month. Accepts 4-6 mss/issue; 8-12 mss/year. Does not read mss December 2-February 28 and

May 2-September 30. Publishes ms 6-12 months after acceptance. Recently published work by Cornelius Eady, Carolyn Ferrell and Frederic Tuten. Length: 10 pages (maximum). Publishes short shorts. Also publishes literary essays, literary criticism and poetry.

How to Contact: Send complete ms with a cover letter. Include brief bio and list of publications. Responds in 6-10 months to mss. Send a disposable copy of ms and #10 SASE for reply only. Accepts simultaneous submissions. Sample copy for $7. Guidelines for SASE or on website. Reviews novels, short story collections and nonfiction books of interest to writers. Send review copies to Linsey Abrams.

Payment/Terms: Pays 2 contributors copies; additional copies $7. Pays on publication for one-time rights.

$⊘ GRAIN, Saskatchewan Writers' Guild, P.O. Box 67, Saskatoon, Saskatchewan S7K 3K1 Canada. (306)244-2828. Fax: (306)244-0255. E-mail: grainmag@sasktel.net. Website: www.grainmagazine.ca (includes history, news, subscription and contest information). Editor: Elizabeth Philips. **Contact:** Marlis Wesseler, fiction editor. Literary magazine: 6×9; 128 pages; Chinook offset printing; chrome-coated stock; some photos. Quarterly. Estab. 1973. Circ. 1,700.

Needs: Contemporary, experimental, literary, mainstream and prose poem. Want to see more magic realism. "No propaganda—only artistic/literary writing. No genre fiction. No mss "that stay *within* the limits of conventions such as women's magazine type stories, science fiction; none that push a message." Receives 80 unsolicited fiction mss/month. Accepts 8-12 mss/issue; 32-48 mss/year. Recently published work by Catherine Hunter, David W. Henderson, Karen Munro and Joel S. Ballantyne. Length: "No more than 30 pages." Also publishes poetry and creative nonfiction. Occasionally critiques rejected mss.

How to Contact: Send complete ms with SASE (or IRC) and brief letter. Accepts queries by e-mail or fax. No simultaneous submissions. Responds within 4 months to mss. Publishes ms an average of 4 months after acceptance. Sample copy for $7.95 plus postage. No e-mail submissions.

Payment/Terms: Pays $40/page up to $175 and 2 contributor's copies. Pays on publication for first Canadian serial rights. "We expect acknowledgment if the piece is republished elsewhere."

Advice: "Submit a story to us that will deepen the imaginative experience of our readers. *Grain* has established itself as a first-class magazine of serious fiction. We receive submissions from around the world. If Canada is a foreign country to you, we ask that you *do not* use U.S. postage stamps on your return envelope. If you live outside Canada and neglect the International Reply Coupons, we *will not* read or reply to your submission. We look for attention to detail, credibility, lucid use of language and metaphor and a confident, convincing voice. Sweat the small stuff. Make sure you have researched your piece, that the literal and metaphorical support one another."

$⊘ ⌥ GRAND STREET, 214 Sullivan St., Suite 6C, New York NY 10012. (212)533-2944. Fax (212)228-9260. Website: www.grandstreet.com. Editor: Jean Stein. **Contact:** Radhika Jones, associate editor. Magazine: 7¾×9½; 240-270 pages; illustrations; art portfolios. "We publish new fiction and nonfiction of all types." Biannual. Estab. 1981. Circ. 7,000.

● Work published in *Grand Street* has been included in the *Best American Short Stories*.

Needs: Poetry, essays, translations. Agented fiction 90%. Published work by Durs Grunbëin, José Saramago, Ozren Kebo, Jorge Luis Borges and Mike Davis. Length: 9,000 words maximum; average length: 4,000 words.

How to Contact: *Not accepting unsolicited fiction mss.* Sample copy for $15; $18 overseas and Canada.

Payment/Terms: Pays $250-1,000 and 2 contributor's copies. Pays on publication for first North American serial rights. Sends galleys to author.

⊕ $ GRANTA, The Magazine of New Writing, 2-3 Hanover Yard, Noel Rd., London N1 8BE England. Phone: 020 7704 9776. Fax: 020 7704 0474. E-mail: editorial@granta.com. Website: www.granta.com. Editor: Ian Jack. **Contact:** Fatema Ahmed, editorial assistant. Magazine: paperback, 256 pages approx.; photos. "*Granta* magazine publishes fiction, reportage, biography and autobiography, history, travel and documentary photography. It rarely publishes 'writing about writing.' The realistic narrative—the story—is its primary form." Quarterly. Estab. 1979. Circ. 80,000.

Needs: Literary. "No fantasy, science fiction, romance, historical, occult or other 'genre' fiction." Themes decided as deadline approaches. Receives 100 unsolicited mss/month. Accepts 0-1 ms/issue; 1-2 mss/year. Percentage of agented fiction varies. **Publishes 1-2 new writers/year.** Length: open.

How to Contact: Responds in 3 months to mss. Send SAE and IRCs for reply, return of ms or send a disposable copy of ms. Accepts simultaneous submissions. Sample copy £12.95.

Payment/Terms: Pays £75-5,000 and 3 contributor's copies. Acquires variable rights. Sends galleys to author.

Advice: "We are looking for the best in realistic stories; originality of voice; without jargon, connivance or self-conscious 'performance'—writing that endures."

⊘ GRASSLANDS REVIEW, P.O. Box 626, Berea OH 44017-0626. E-mail: grasslandsreview@aol.com. Website: hometown.aol.com/glreview/prof/index.htm (includes guidelines, contest information, sample text, table of contents for

---

CHECK THE CATEGORY INDEXES, located at the back of the book, for publishers interested in specific fiction subjects.

latest issue). **Contact:** Laura B. Kennelly, editor. Magazine: 6×9; 80 pages. *Grasslands Review* prints creative writing of all types; poetry, fiction, essays for a general audience. "Designed as a place for new writers to publish." Semiannual. Estab. 1989. Circ. 300.

Needs: Contemporary, ethnic, experimental, fantasy, horror, humor/satire, literary, prose poem, regional, science fiction and western. "Nothing pornographic or overtly political or religious." Accepts 1-3 mss/issue. Reads only in October and March. Publishes ms 6 months after acceptance. **Publishes 5 new writers/year.** Published work by Catherine Ferguson and Charles Edward Brooks. Length: 100-3,500 words; average length: 1,500 words. Publishes short shorts (100-150 words). Also publishes poetry. Sometimes critiques rejected mss and recommends other markets.

How to Contact: Send complete ms in October or March *only* with cover letter. No simultaneous submissions. Responds in 3 months to mss. SASE. Sample copy for $4.

Payment/Terms: Pays in contributor's copies. Acquires one-time rights. Publication not copyrighted.

Advice: "A fresh approach, imagined by a reader for other readers, pleases our audience. We are looking for fiction which leaves a strong feeling or impression—or a new perspective on life. The *Review* began as an in-class exercise to allow experienced creative writing students to learn how a little magazine is produced. It now serves as an independent publication, attracting authors from as far away as the Ivory Coast, but its primary mission is to give unknown writers a start."

THE GREEN HILLS LITERARY LANTERN, Published by Truman State University, Division of Language & Literature, Kirksville MO 63501. (660)785-4513. E-mail: JackGHLL@earthlink.net. Website: http://ll.truman.edu/ghllweb. Co-Editors: Joe Benevento (poetry) and Jack Smith (fiction). Send fiction to P.O. Box 375, Trenton MO 64683. **Contact:** Sara King, fiction editor. Magazine: 6×9; 200-300 pages; good quality paper with glossy 4-color cover. "The mission of *GHLL* is to provide a literary market for quality fiction writers, both established and beginners, and to provide quality literature for readers from diverse backgrounds. We also see ourselves as a cultural resource for North Missouri. Our publication works to publish the highest quality fiction—dense, layered, subtle, and, at the same time, fiction which grabs the ordinary reader. We tend to publish traditional short stories, but we are open to experimental forms." Annual. Estab. 1990. Circ. 500.

Needs: Ethnic/multicultural, experimental, feminist, humor/satire, literary, mainstream/contemporary and regional. "Fairly traditional short stories but we are open to experimental. Our main requirement is literary merit. Wants more quality fiction about rural culture. No adventure, crime, erotica, horror, inspirational, mystery/suspense, romance." Receives 40 unsolicited mss/month. Accepts 7-10 mss/issue. Publishes ms 6-12 months after acceptance. Recently published work by Ian MacMillan, Mark Wisniewski, Karl Harshbarger, and Robert Garner McBrearty. **Publishes 0-1 new writer/year.** Length: 7,000 words maximum; average length: 3,000 words. Publishes short shorts. Also publishes poetry. Sometimes comments on rejected mss.

How to Contact: Send complete ms with a cover letter. Include bio (50-100 words) with list of publications. Accepts queries (only) by e-mail. Responds in 4 months to mss. SASE for return of ms. Accepts simultaneous submissions and multiple submissions (2-3). Sample copy for $7 (includes envelope and postage).

Payment/Terms: Pays 2 contributor's copies. Acquires one-time rights. Sends galleys to author.

Advice: "We look for strong character development, substantive plot and theme, visual and forceful language within a multilayered story. Make sure your work has the flavor of life, a sense of reality. A good story, well-crafted, will eventually get published. Find the right market for it, and above all, don't give up."

$ GREEN MOUNTAINS REVIEW, Johnson State College, Box A-58, Johnson VT 05656. (802)635-1350. Editor-in-Chief: Neil Shepard. **Contact:** Tony Whedon, fiction editor. Magazine: digest-sized; 160-200 pages. Semiannual. Estab. 1975 (new series, 1987). Circ. 1,700.

● *Green Mountain Review* has received a Pushcart Prize and Editors Choice Award.

Needs: Adventure, contemporary, experimental, humor/satire, literary, mainstream, serialized/excerpted novel, translations. Receives 80 unsolicited mss/month. Accepts 6 mss/issue; 12 mss/year. Publishes ms 6-12 months after acceptance. Reads mss September 1 through March 1. **Publishes 0-4 new writers/year.** Published work by Howard Norman, Debra Spark, Valerie Miner and Peter LaSalle. Length: 25 pages maximum. Publishes short shorts. Also publishes literary criticism, poetry. Sometimes critiques rejected mss.

How to Contact: Send complete ms with cover letter. "Manuscripts will not be read and will be returned between March 1 and September 1." Responds in 1 month to queries; 6 months to mss. SASE. Accepts simultaneous submissions (if advised). Sample copy for $5.

Payment/Terms: Pays contributor's copies, 1-year subscription and small honorarium, depending on grants. Acquires first North American serial rights. Rights revert to author upon request. Sends galleys to author upon request.

Advice: "We're looking for more rich, textured, original fiction with cross-cultural themes. The editors are open to a wide spectrum of styles and subject matter as is apparent from a look at the list of fiction writers who have published in its pages. One issue was devoted to Vermont fiction, and another issue filled with new writing from the People's Republic of China, and a recent issue devoted to literary ethnography."

GREEN'S MAGAZINE, Fiction for the Family, Green's Educational Publications, Box 3236, Regina, Saskatchewan S4P 3H1 Canada. **Contact:** David Green, editor. Magazine: 5¼×8½; 96 pages; 20 lb. bond paper; matte cover stock; line illustrations. Publishes "solid short fiction suitable for family reading." Quarterly. Estab. 1972.

Needs: Adventure, fantasy, humor/satire, literary, mainstream, mystery/suspense and science fiction. "No erotic or sexually explicit fiction." Receives 20-30 mss/month. Accepts 10-12 mss/issue; 40-50 mss/year. Publishes ms usually within 3-6 months of acceptance. Agented fiction 1%. **Publishes 6 new writers/year.** Recently published work by Stella Barnes, Randall Garrison and Marc Igler. Length: 1,500-4,000 words; 2,500 words preferred. Also publishes poetry. Sometimes critiques rejected mss.

How to Contact: Send complete ms. "Cover letters welcome but not necessary." Responds in 2 months. SASE (in Canada), SAE and IRC (for US and overseas). Accepts multiple submissions. Sample copy for $5. Guidelines for #10 SASE (IRC). Reviews short story and poetry collections.

Payment/Terms: Pays in contributor's copies. Acquires first North American serial rights.

Advice: "No topic is taboo, but we avoid sexuality for its own sake, and dislike material that is needlessly explicit or obscene. We look for strongly written stories that explore their characters through a subtle blending of conflicts. Plots should be appropriate, rather than overly ingenious or reliant on some *deus ex machina*. It must be a compression of experience or thoughts, in a form that is both challenging and rewarding to the reader. We have no form rejection slip. If we cannot use a submission, we try to offer constructive criticism in our personal reply. Often, such effort is rewarded with reports from our writers that following our suggestions has led to placement of the story or poem elsewhere."

THE GREENSBORO REVIEW, English Dept., 134 McIver Bldg., UNC Greensboro, P.O. Box 26170, Greensboro NC 27402-6170. (336)334-5459. E-mail: jlclark@uncg.edu. Website: www.uncg.edu/eng/mfa (includes writer's guidelines, literary awards guidelines, address, deadlines, subscription information, sample work). **Contact:** Jim Clark, editor. Fiction editor changes each year. Send mss to the editor. Magazine: 6×9; approximately 128 pages; 60 lb. paper; 65 lb. cover. Literary magazine featuring fiction and poetry for readers interested in contemporary literature. Semiannual. Circ. 800.

• Stories from *The Greensboro Review* have been included in *The Best American Short Stories*, *Prize Stories: The O. Henry Awards*, *New Stories from the South*, and *Pushcart Prize*.

Needs: Contemporary and experimental. Accepts 6-8 mss/issue, 12-16 mss/year. **10% of all work published is by previously unpublished authors.** Published work by Robert Morgan, George Singleton, Robert Olmstead, Jean Ross Justice, Dale Ray Phillips and Kelly Cherry. Length: 7,500 words maximum.

How to Contact: Send complete ms with SASE. Accepts multiple submissions. No simultaneous submissions or previously published works. Unsolicited manuscripts must arrive by September 15 to be considered for the spring issue and by February 15 to be considered for the fall issue. Manuscripts arriving after those dates may be held for the next consideration. Responds in 4 months. Sample copy for $5.

Payment/Terms: Pays in contributor's copies. Acquires first North American serial rights.

Advice: "We want to see the best being written regardless of theme, subject or style."

THE GRIFFIN, Gwynedd-Mercy College, P.O. Box 901, 1325 Sumneytown Pike, Gwynedd Valley PA 19437-0901. (215)646-7300. Fax: (215)923-3060. E-mail: z31w@aol.com or kaleraol.gmc.edu. **Contact:** Anne K. Kaler, Ph.D., editor. Editor: Susan E. Wagner. Literary magazine: 8½×5½; 112 pages. "*The Griffin* is a literary journal sponsored by Gwynedd-Mercy College. Its mission is to enrich society by nurturing and promoting creative writing that demonstrates a unique and intelligent voice. We seek writing which accurately reflects the human condition with all its intellectual, emotional, and ethical challenges." Semiannual. Estab. 1999. Circ. 500.

Needs: Adventure, ethnic/multicultural (general), family saga, fantasy, feminist, historical, horror, humor/satire, literary, mainstream, mystery/suspense, religious (general), romance, science fiction, thriller/espionage, western. "No slasher, graphic violence or sex." Receives 2-3 unsolicited mss/month. Accepts mss depending on the quality of work submitted. Publishes ms 3-6 months after acceptance. **Publishes 10-15 new writers/year.** Published work by Pat Carr, Linda Wisniewski and Michael McGregor. Length: 2,500 words; average length: 2,000 words. Publishes short shorts; average length: 1,000 words. Also publishes literary essays and poetry.

How to Contact: Send complete ms with cover letter. Accepts submissions by e-mail, fax and disk. Include estimated word count and brief bio. Responds in 1 month to queries; 6 months to mss. Send SASE for return of ms or send disposable copy of ms and #10 SASE for reply only. Accepts simultaneous submissions "if notified." Sample copy for $6. Guidelines for SASE or e-mail.

Payment/Terms: Pays in 2 contributor's copies; additional copies for $6. Pays on publication for one-time rights.

Advice: "Looking for well-constructed works that explore universal qualities, respect for the individual and community, justice and integrity. Check our description and criteria. Rewrite until you're sure every word counts. We publish the best work we find regardless of industry trends."

THE GSU REVIEW, Georgia State University, P.O. Box 1894, Atlanta GA 30303. (404)651-4804. Fax: (404)651-1710. E-mail: kchaple@emory.edu. Website: www.gsu.edu/wwwrev/. Editor: Katie Chaple. **Contact:** Gregg Johnson, fiction editor. Magazine. "*The GSU Review* is a biannual literary magazine published poetry, fiction, creative nonfiction and artwork. We want original voices searching to rise above the ordinary. No subject or form biases." Semiannual.

Needs: Literary, novel excerpts. "No pornography." Accepts 40 unsolicited mss/year. Length: 1,000-7,500 words. Publishes short shorts.

How to Contact: Send complete ms. Include 3-4 line bio; name, address, phone and e-mail address. SASE for notification. Accepts queries by mail and e-mail. Responds in 1 month to queries; 1-2 months to mss. Sample copy for $5. Guidelines for SASE or on website.

Payment/Terms: Pays 1 contributor's copy. Acquires one-time rights.

$ ⬛ ⬛ **GULF COAST, A Journal of Literature & Fine Arts**, Dept. of English, University of Houston, Houston TX 77204-3012. (713)743-3223. Fax: (713)743-3215. Website: www.gulfcoast.uh.edu. **Contact:** Viet Dinh, fiction editor. Editors change each year. Magazine: 6×9; 144 pages; stock paper; gloss cover; illustrations; photos. "Innovative fiction for the literary-minded." Estab. 1987. Circ. 1,000.

● Work published in *Gulf Coast* has been selected for inclusion in the *Pushcart Prize* anthology and *Best American Short Stories*.

Needs: Contemporary, ethnic, experimental, literary, regional, translations. Wants more "cutting-edge, experimental" fiction. "No children's, genre, religious/inspirational." Receives 150 unsolicited mss/month. Accepts 6-8 mss/issue; 12-16 mss/year. Publishes ms 6 months-1 year after acceptance. Agented fiction 5%. Published work by Amy Storrow, Beverly Lowry, Diana Joseph, Karen Mary Penn and J. David Stevens. Length: no limit. Publishes short shorts. Sometimes critiques rejected mss.

How to Contact: Send complete ms with brief cover letter. "List previous publications; please notify us if the submission is being considered elsewhere." Responds in 6 months. Accepts simultaneous submissions. Back issue for $6, 7×10 SAE and 4 first-class stamps. Guidelines on website or for #10 SASE.

Payment/Terms: Pays contributor's copies and *small* honorariam for one-time rights.

Advice: "Rotating editorship, so please be patient with replies. As always, please send one story at a time."

$ ⬛ **HAPPY**, The Happy Organization, 240 E. 35th St., 11A, New York NY 10016. (212)689-3142. E-mail: bayardx @aol.com. Editor: Bayard. **Contact:** Fiction Editor. Magazine: 5½×8; 150-200 pages; 60 lb. text paper; 150 lb. cover; perfect-bound; illustrations; photos. Quarterly. Estab. 1995. Circ. 500.

Needs: Erotica, ethnic/multicultural, experimental, fantasy, feminist, gay, horror, humor/satire, lesbian, literary, psychic/ supernatural/occult, science fiction. No "television rehash or religious nonsense." Want more work that is "strong, angry, empowering, intelligent, God-like, expressive." Receives 300-500 unsolicited mss/month. Accepts 30-40 mss/ issue; 100-150 mss/year. **30-50% of work published is by new writers.** Publishes ms 6-12 months after acceptance. Length: 6,000 words maximum; average length: 1,000-3,500 words. Publishes short shorts. Often comments on rejected mss.

How to Contact: Send complete ms with a cover letter. Include estimated word count. Accepts queries by e-mail. Responds in 1 week to mss. Send SASE for reply, return of ms or send a disposable copy of ms. Accepts simultaneous submissions. Sample copy for $15.

Payment/Terms: Pays average of 1¢/word, minimum $10 and 1 contributor's copy. Pays on publication for one-time rights.

Advice: "Excite me!"

⬛ ⬛ **HARD ROW TO HOE**, Potato Eyes Foundation, P.O. Box 541-I, Healdsburg CA 95448. (707)433-9786. **Contact:** Joe E. Armstrong, editor. Magazine: 8½×11; 12 pages; 60 lb. white paper; illustrations; photos. "We look for literature of rural life, including environmental, Native American and foreign (English only) subjects. Book reviews, short story, poetry and a regular column. So far as we know, we are the only literary newsletter that features rural subjects." Triannual. Estab. 1982. Circ. 200.

Needs: Rural, environmental, Native American, foreign (English only). "No urban subjects. We would like to see more fiction on current rural lifestyles." Receives 5-10 unsolicited mss/month. Accepts 2-3 mss/issue; 6-8 mss/year. Publishes ms 10 months after acceptance. **Publishes 2 new writers/year.** Recently published work by Gary Every and Jane Bradury. Length: 2,000 words maximum; average length: 1,200 words. Publishes short shorts. Average length: 600 words. Also publishes literary essays and poetry. Often comments on rejected mss.

How to Contact: Send complete ms with a cover letter. Include brief bio. Accepts submissions on disk (Mac). Responds in 2 weeks to queries; 6 weeks to mss. Send SASE for return of ms or send a disposable copy of ms and #10 SASE for reply only. Accepts multiple submissions. Sample copy for $3. Guidelines for SASE. Reviews novels, short story collections and nonfiction books (of rural subjects). Send review copies to editor.

Payment/Terms: Pays 2 contributor's copies; additional copies $3. Pays on publication for one-time rights.

Advice: "Work must exhibit authentic setting and dialogue."

$ ⬛ **HARPUR PALATE at Binghamton University**, Dept. of English, Binghamton University, P.O. Box 6000, Binghamton NY 13902-6000. (607)355-4761. Website: http://harpurpalate.binghamton.edu (includes guidelines and contest information, editors' contact information, subscription information, and sample fiction and poetry content from current and past issues). **Contact:** Toiya Kristen Finley, fiction editor. Magazine: 5½×8; 80-120 pages; coated or uncoated paper; 80 lb. coated or uncoated cover; illustrations; photos. "We believe writers should explore different genres to tell their stories. *Harpur Palate* accepts pieces regardless of genre, as long as the works pay attention to craft, structure, language, and the story is well told." Semiannual. Estab. 2001. Circ. 500.

Needs: Adventure, ethnic/multicultural, experimental, fantasy, historical, horror, humor/satire, literary, mainstream, mystery/suspense, science fiction. "Also magical realism, metafiction, slipstream, fiction blurring genre boundaries that might have trouble finding a home somewhere else. No solipsistic or self-centered/pretentious fiction, erotica, pornography, excessive profanity, or shock value for shock value's sake. No fiction that doesn't have a strong sense of plot. No fiction that reads like autobiography." Receives 50 unsolicited mss/month. Accepts 5-10 mss/issue; 10-20 mss/year. Does not read mss March 16-July 31 and October 16-December 31. Publishes ms 2 months after acceptance. **Publishes**

5 new writers/year. Recently published work by Hugh Cook, Ward Parker, Paul Michel, M. Eveliha Galang and Bruce Halland Rogers. Length: 250-8,000 words; average length: 2,000-4,000 words. Publishes short shorts. Average length: 500-750 words. Also publishes poetry. Sometimes comments on rejected mss.

How to Contact: Send complete ms with a cover letter. "Include e-mail address on cover if have one. Submitters should check our guideline information on the website for e-mail submissions." Include estimated word count, brief bio, list of publications (OK if don't have any). Responds in 2 weeks to queries; 3 months (hopefully sooner) to mss. Send SASE for return of ms or send a disposable copy of ms and #10 SASE for reply only. Accepts simultaneous submissions (please note this in cover letter). Sample copy for $7.50. Guidelines for SASE, by e-mail or on website.

Payment/Terms: Pays $5-20 (when funding is available) and 2 contributor's copies; additional copies $5. Pays on publication for first North American serial and electronic rights. Sponsors contest: John Gardner Memorial Prize for Fiction. $500 prize and publication in summer issue of *Harpur Palate*.

Advice: "There's nothing new under the sun, but we're looking for stories that do inventive things with fiction. We don't try to define what 'art' is or put limitations on what 'art' can be, and we try to have an eclectic mix of genre, mainstream, and experimental works in every issue. We are always interested in seeing literary speculative fiction and literary mystery/suspense as well as more mainstream stories. We would like to see more literary speculative fiction in the vein of Orwell, Huxley, Borges, García Márquez and Calvino; literary mystery in the vein of Whitehead. The editorial board chooses manuscripts during final selection meetings after the reading period deadlines. Most of us are writers and know what it's like to wait for editorial responses to arrive in the mailbox. If we would like to hold your fiction manuscript for final selection, we will inform you."

$ **THE HARPWEAVER**, Harpweaver, Brock University, St. Catherines, Ontario L2S 3A1 Canada. Phone: (905)688-5550, ext. 3472. Fax: (905)688-4461. E-mail: harpweav@spartan.or.brocku.ca. **Contact:** Co-editor. Magazine: 5½×8½; 100-128 pages; illustrations; photos. Publishes short fiction, reviews, poetry and visual arts for a general, literate audience. Semiannual. Estab. 1996. Circ. 700.

Needs: Welcomes all categories and styles of fiction. Receives 10-15 mss/month. Accepts 2-3 mss/issue; 4-6 mss/year. Publishes ms 3 months after acceptance. **Publishes 5-6 new writers/year.** Recently published work by Nonalesia Earle, Joy Howit Nann, Richard Scarsbrook. Length: 5,000 words maximum. Publishes short shorts. Also publishes poetry.

How to Contact: Send complete ms with a cover letter. Accepts submissions by e-mail or on disk. Include estimated word count, brief bio and list of publications. Responds in 2 months to mss. Send SASE. Accepts multiple submissions. Sample copy for $4. Guidelines by e-mail. Reviews novels, short story collections and nonfiction books of interest to writers.

Payment/Terms: Pays $10 minimum. Pays on publication for one-time rights. Not copyrighted.

HARVARD REVIEW, Harvard University, Lamont Library, Level 5, Cambridge MA 02138. (617)495-9775. E-mail: harvrev@fas.harvard.edu (inquiries only). Website: http://hcl.harvard.edu/Houghton/departments/harvardrev iew/Hrhome.html. Magazine: 6×9; 192-240 pages; illustrations; photographs. Semiannual. Estab. 1992. Circ. 2,000.

Needs: Literary. Receives 80-100 unsolicited mss/month. Accepts 2 mss/issue; 4 mss/year. Publishes ms 3-6 months after acceptance. **Publishes 3-4 new writers/year.** Recently published work by John Updike, David Mamet, Paul Harding and Helen Vendler. Length: 1,000-7,000 words; average length 3,000-5,000 words. Publishes short shorts. Also publishes literary essays, literary criticism and poetry. Sometimes comments on rejected mss.

How to Contact: Send complete ms with cover letter. Include brief bio. Responds to queries in 2 months; mss in 3-6 months. Send SASE for return of ms or disposable copy of ms and SASE for reply only. Accepts simultaneous submissions. Sample for $5. Guidelines on website.

Payment/Terms: Pays 2 contributor's copies; additional copies $6. Pays on publication for first North American serial rights. Sends prepublication galleys to author.

HAWAI'I PACIFIC REVIEW, Hawai'i Pacific University, 1060 Bishop St., Honolulu HI 96813. (808)544-1108. Fax: (808)544-0862. E-mail: pwilson@hpu.edu. Website: www.hpu.edu. **Contact:** Patrice M. Wilson, editor. Magazine: 6×9; 100 pages; glossy coated cover. "*Hawai'i Pacific Review* is looking for poetry, short fiction, and personal essays that speak with a powerful and unique voice. We encourage experimental narrative techniques and poetic styles, and we welcome works in translation." Annual.

Needs: Ethnic/multicultural (general), experimental, fantasy, feminist, historical (general), humor/satire, literary, mainstream, regional (Pacific), translations. "Open to all types as long as they're well done. Our audience is adults, so nothing for children/teens." Receives 25-40 unsolicited mss/month. Accepts 5-10 mss/year. Does not read mss January-August each year. Publishes ms 10 months after acceptance. **Publishes 1-2 new writers/year.** Published work by Rosemary Edghill, D. Prinzo and Stephen Dixon. Length: 250-5,000 words. Publishes short shorts. Also publishes literary essays and poetry. Sometimes comments on rejected mss.

How to Contact: Send complete ms with a cover letter. Include estimated word count, brief bio and list of publications. Responds in 2 weeks to queries; up to 15 weeks to mss. Send SASE for return of ms or send a disposable copy of ms and #10 SASE for reply only. Accepts simultaneous submissions (must be cited in the cover letter). Sample copy for $5.

Payment/Terms: Pays 2 contributor's copies; additional copies $5. Pays on publication for first North American serial rights.

Advice: "We look for the unusual or original plot; prose with the texture and nuance of poetry. Character development or portrayal must be unusual/original; humanity shown in an original insightful way (or characters); sense of humor where applicable. Be sure it's a draft that has gone through substantial changes, with supervision from a more experienced writer if you're a beginner."

$ ▨ ▧ HAYDEN'S FERRY REVIEW, NSSWM Box 871502, Arizona State University, Tempe AZ 85287-1502. (480)965-1243. Fax: (480)965-2229. E-mail: hfr@asu.edu. Website: www.haydensferryreview.org. **Contact:** Fiction Editor. Editors change every 1-2 years. Magazine: 6×9; 128 pages; fine paper; illustrations; photos. "Contemporary material by new and established writers for a varied audience." Semiannual. Estab. 1986. Circ. 1,300.

• Work from *Hayden's Ferry Review* has been selected for inclusion in *Pushcart Prize* anthologies.

Needs: Contemporary, experimental, literary, prose poem, regional. Possible special fiction issue. Receives 250 unsolicited mss/month. Accepts 5 mss/issue; 10 mss/year. Publishes mss 3-4 months after acceptance. Published work by T.C. Boyle, Raymond Carver, Ken Kesey, Rita Dove, Chuck Rosenthal and Rick Bass. Length: No preference. Publishes short shorts. Also publishes literary essays.

How to Contact: Send complete ms with cover letter. Responds in up to 5 months from deadline to mss. SASE. Sample copy for $6. Guidelines for SAE. "Please, no electronic submissions."

Payment/Terms: Pays $25/page with a maximum of $100 and 2 contributor's copies. Acquires first North American serial rights. Sends page proofs to author.

▨ $ ▧ THE HEARTLANDS TODAY, The Firelands Writing Center, Firelands College of BGSU, Huron OH 44839. (419)433-5560. E-mail: lsmithdog@aol.com. Website: www.theheartlandstoday.org (includes writer's guidelines, names of editors, interviews with authors, excerpts from publication). Managing Editor: Larry Smith. Editors: Nancy Dunham, Connie W. Everett, David Shevin and Zita Sodeika. **Contact:** Fiction Editor. Magazine: 6×9; 160 pages; b&w illustrations; 15 photos. *Material must be set in the Midwest.* "We prefer material that reveals life in the Midwest today for a general, literate audience." Annual. Estab. 1991.

Needs: Ethnic, humor, literary, mainstream, regional (Midwest). Receives 15 unsolicited mss/month. Accepts 6 mss/issue. Does not read mss August-December. "We edit between January 1 and June 5. Submit then." 2002 theme is "A Life's Work"; 2003 theme is "Our Natural World." Publishes ms 6 months after acceptance. Published work by Wendell Mayo, Tony Tomassi, Gloria Bowman. Length: 4,500 words maximum. Also publishes literary essays, poetry. Sometimes critiques rejected mss.

How to Contact: Send complete ms with cover letter. Responds in 2 months to mss. Send SASE for ms, not needed for query. Accepts simultaneous submissions, if noted. Sample copy for $5. "We edit January to June. June 5th deadline."

Payment/Terms: Pays $10-20 and 2 contributor's copies. Pays on publication for first rights.

Advice: "We look for writing that connects on a human level, that moves us with its truth and opens our vision of the world. If writing is a great escape for you, don't bother with us. We're in it for the joy, beauty or truth of the art. We look for a straight, honest voice dealing with human experiences. We do not define the Midwest, we hope to be a document of the Midwest. If you feel you are writing from the Midwest, send your work to us. We look first at the quality of the writing."

▨ ▧ HEAVEN BONE, Heaven Bone Press, Box 486, Chester NY 10918. (845)469-2326. E-mail: heavenbone@aol.com. **Contact:** Steven Hirsch and Kirpal Gordon, editors. Magazine: 8½×11; 96-116 pages; 60 lb. recycled offset paper; full color cover; computer clip art, graphics, line art, cartoons, halftones and photos scanned in tiff format. "Expansive, fine surrealist and experimental literary, earth and nature, spiritual path. We use current reviews, essays on spiritual and esoteric topics, creative stories. Also: reviews of current poetry releases and expansive literature." Readers are "scholars, surrealists, poets, artists, musicians, students." Annual. Estab. 1987. Circ. 2,500.

Needs: Esoteric/scholarly, experimental, fantasy, psychic/supernatural/occult, regional, spiritual. "No violent, thoughtless, exploitive or religious fiction." Receives 45-110 unsolicited mss/month. Accepts 5-15 mss/issue; 12-30 mss/year. Publishes ms 2 weeks-10 months after acceptance. **Publishes 3-4 new writers/year.** Published work by Keith Abbott and Stephen-Paul Martin. Length: 1,200-5,000 words; average length: 3,500 words. Publishes short shorts. Also publishes literary essays, literary criticism, poetry. Sometimes critiques rejected mss.

How to Contact: Query first; send complete ms with cover letter. Include short bio of recent activities. Responds in 3 weeks to queries; up to 10 months to mss. Send SASE for reply or return of ms. Accepts reprint submissions. Accepts electronic submissions via "Apple Mac versions of Macwrite, Microsoft Word or Writenow 3.0." Sample copy for $10. Guidelines for SASE. Reviews novels and short story collections.

Payment/Terms: Pays in contributor's copies; charges for extras. Acquires first North American serial rights. Sends galleys to author, if requested.

Advice: "Read a sample issue first. Our fiction needs are temperamental, so please query first before submitting. We prefer shorter fiction. Do not send first drafts to test them on us. Please refine and polish your work before sending. Always include SASE. We are looking for the unique, unusual and excellent."

Ⓝ ▨ HIGHWAY 14, P.O. Box 1130, Fort Collins CO 80522-1130. E-mail: editors@highway14.net. Website: www.highway14.net (includes writer's guidelines, names of editors, literary events). **Contact:** Alex Paozols, editor. Magazine: 5¼×8⅜; 150 pages; 60 lb. white paper; card c1s stock cover; illustrations; photos. "*Highway 14* is a prose literary magazine with an obsession for fiction, semantic antics, and gourmet Thai cuisine. We reveal the consequences of environmental destruction and pollution, frivolous culture, religious bigotry and capitalist ruin. Sometimes our pages offer a solution. Our audience ranges from people who can't get enough to read to those who have forgotten what a pleasure it is to pick up a book and leave the world." Triannual. Estab. 2002. Circ. 750.

Needs: Literary, translations. "No poetry." Receives 90 unsolicited mss/month. Accepts 18 mss/issue; 54 mss/year. Publishes ms 6 months after acceptance. **Publishes 20 new writers/year.** Recently published work by George Singleton, Kristin Prevallet, J. Robert Lennon, Jason Ockert and Christine Hume. Also publishes literary essays and literary criticism. Sometimes comments on rejected mss.

How to Contact: Send complete ms with a cover letter. Include estimated word count. Responds in 3 weeks to queries; 6 weeks to mss. Send SASE for return of ms or send a disposable copy of ms and #10 SASE for reply only. Accepts simultaneous and multiple submissions. Sample copy for $10. Guidelines for SASE or on website.

Payment/Terms: Pays 3 contributors copies; additional copies $7. Acquires first rights. Sends galleys to author. Not copyrighted.

Advice: "Originality is the key for us. Narcissism, sensationalism, and sentimentality can often ruin a story. We admire stories that deconstruct plot and predictability with the innovative use of language—found in Raymond Roussel, Nathalie Sarraute and Ben Marcus. We are drawn to literature that is subtle with strong narrative, that is unassuming yet intelligent. We are eager to read stories that explore racial, ethnic, religious and culture identity with regard and disregard for landscape. D'Agata's lyric essay is breaking some new ground and it is territory we are willing to explore. We also think the nineteenth-century European novel still has something to say."

$ ⊘ ⊻ HINDSIGHT, A journal of short stories and essays, Maple Leaf Press, P.O. Box 313, Piscataway NJ 08855-0313. E-mail: mapleleafpress@aol.com. **Contact:** Lawrence J. Imboden, editor. Magazine: 8½×11; 96 pages; 20 lb. paper; cardstock cover. "*Hindsight* publishes short stories and essays, preferably by new, unpublished/underpublished writers of all ages—college students, senior citizens who have written for years but have never attempted to be published. It publishes unknown writers of talent trying to establish their writing careers. It gives new talents a chance to be heard, a chance the large, well-established fiction magazines seldom offer. And it distributes the magazine to bookstores free." Annual. Estab. 2002.

Needs: Literary, mainstream, young adult/teen (easy-to-read, problem novels, sports, coming of age). "No action/adventure, children's stories, erotica, gothic, romance, science fiction, vampire stories." Accepts 6-12 mss/issue. Publishes ms up to 1 year after acceptance. **Publishes 6-10 new writers/year.** Length: 1,500-7,000 words; average length: 4,000 words. Also publishes literary essays. Often comments on rejected mss.

How to Contact: Send complete ms with a cover letter. Include estimated word count and brief bio. Responds in 1 month to queries; 4 months to mss. SASE. Guidelines for SASE. Reviews short story collections. Send review copies to Lawrence Imboden, editor.

Payment/Terms: Pays up to $50 and 1-3 contributor's copies. Pays on publication for first North American serial rights.

Advice: "There must be a clear conflict/goal, a major decision to be made by the protagonist, or a significant change in attitude/behavior. Strong, sympathetic, active protagonist a must—realistic dialogue. Write the kind of stories that you enjoy reading. Submit stories that mean something to you. The readers will feel your passion. Go to bookstores and read the other fiction anthologies/magazines. Learn the value of patience, of resting your story for a month and rereading it. Too many publications reject quality stories because of a restrictive word count policy. *Hindsight* will publish any short story of quality regardless of its size, never rejecting a powerful work because it won't fit, nor will we ask a writer to make major cuts to make it fit. New writers with talent but no publications to their credit are not published enough. *Hindsight* will help correct this for the new writers."

N ⊘ HUDSON VALLEY LITERARY MAGAZINE, J-Mac Publishing, P.O. Box 386, Vails Gate NY 12584. Phone/fax: (845)534-8640. E-mail: author45@aol.com. Website: www.hvlm.com. **Contact:** Julia A. McGuire, editor/publisher. Magazine: 8½×11; 48 pages; glossy paper and cover stock; illustrations; photos. "We adhere to a general audience, encourage use in classrooms and promote writing by all ages. We are unique in that we serve all writers outside the Hudson Valley and also promote special programs within our Hudson Valley." Quarterly; Spring/Summer issue is combined. Estab. 1999. Circ. 2,000. Member, Council of Literary Magazines and Presses.

Needs: Children's/juvenile (adventure, fantasy, mystery, preschool), family saga, humor/satire, literary, mystery/suspense (amateur sleuth), science fiction (soft/sociological), young adult/teen (adventure, fantasy/science fiction, mystery/suspense). Receives 20 unsolicited mss/month. Accepts 2-3 mss/issue; 12-15 mss/year. Publishes ms 2-3 months after acceptance. Recently published work by Frank Kieck and Carol A. DiGiovanni. Length: 3,000 words maximum. Publishes short shorts. Average length: 1,200 words. Also publishes poetry. Sometimes comments on rejected mss.

How to Contact: Send complete ms with a cover letter. Accepts submissions by e-mail. Include estimated word count and brief bio. Responds in 1 month to queries; 5-6 weeks to mss. Send a disposable copy of ms and #10 SASE for reply only. Accepts simultaneous and previously published submissions. Sample copy for $8. Guidelines for SASE, e-mail or on website.

Payment/Terms: Pays 3 contributors copies; additional copies $5. Acquires one-time rights. Sends galleys to author. Check website for contest, awards information.

Advice: "We suggest beginning writers share their work with credible writing support groups in their areas to make sure they get some critique and feedback."

$ ● **THE ICONOCLAST**, 1675 Amazon Rd., Mohegan Lake NY 10547-1804. **Contact:** Phil Wagner, editor. Journal. 8½ × 5½; 40-64 pages; 20 lb. white paper; 50 lb. cover stock; illustrations. "*The Iconoclast* is a self-supporting, independent, unaffiliated general interest magazine with an appreciation of the profound, absurd and joyful in life. Material is limited only by *its* quality and *our* space. We want readers and writers who are open-minded, unafraid to think, and actively engaged with the world." Published 6 times/year. Estab. 1992. Circ. 1,000-3,000 (special issues).

Needs: Adventure, ethnic/multicultural, humor/satire, literary, mainstream/contemporary, science fiction. Wants to see more "literary fiction with plots. Nothing militant, solipsistic, or silly. No slice of life, character studies." Receives 150 unsolicited mss/month. Accepts 3-6 mss/issue; 25-30 mss/year. Publishes ms 9-12 months after acceptance. **Publishes 8-10 new writers/year.** Recently published work by Stephen Graham Jones, Laura Albritton and E.G. Silverman. Length: 100 words minimum; 2,000-2,500 words preferred (occasionally longer). Publishes short shorts. Also publishes essays, poetry. Sometimes comments on rejected mss.

How to Contact: Send complete ms. Responds in 1 month. Send SASE for reply, return of ms or send a disposable copy of the ms labeled as such. Sample copy for $2.50. Reviews novels and short story collections.

Payment/Terms: Pays 1¢/word and 2-5 contributor's copies; additional copies $1.50 (40% discount). Pays on acceptance for first time rights.

Advice: "We like fiction that has something to say (and not about its author). We hope for work that is observant, intense and multi-leveled. Follow Pound's advice—'make it new.' Write what you want in whatever style you want without being gross, sensational, or needlessly explicit—then pray there's someone who can appreciate your sensibility. Read good fiction. It's as fundamental as learning how to hit, throw and catch is to baseball. With the increasing American disinclination towards literature, stories must insist on being heard. Read what is being published—then write something better—and different. Do all rewrites before sending a story out. Few editors have time to work with writers on promising stories; only polished."

● **THE IDAHO REVIEW**, Boise State University, English Dept., 1910 University Dr., Boise ID 83725. (208)426-1002. Fax: (208)426-5426. E-mail: mwieland@boisestate.edu. **Contact:** Mitch Wieland, editor. Magazine: 6 × 9; 180-200 pages; acid-free accent opaque paper; coated cover stock; photos. "A literary journal for anyone who enjoys good fiction." Annual. Estab. 1998. Circ. 1,000. Member, C.L.M.P.

Needs: Experimental, literary. "No genre fiction of any type." Receives 150 unsolicited mss/month. Accepts 5-7 mss/issue; 5-7 mss/year. "We do not read from December 16-August 31." Publishes ms 1 year after acceptance. Agented fiction 5%. **Publishes 1 new writer/year.** Recently published work by Rick Bass, Carol Bly, William Kittredge and Doris Betts. Length: open; average length: 7,000 words. Publishes short shorts. Average length: 750 words. Also publishes literary essays and poetry. Sometimes comments on rejected mss.

How to Contact: Send complete ms with a cover letter. Include estimated word count, brief bio and list of publications. Responds in 5 months to mss. Send SASE for return of ms or send a disposable copy of ms and #10 SASE for reply only. Accepts simultaneous and multiple submissions. Sample copy for $8.95. Guidelines for SASE. Reviews novels, short story collections and nonfiction books of interest to writers.

Payment/Terms: Pays free subscription to the magazine and 5 contributor's copies; additional copies $5. Pays on publication for first North American serial rights. Sends galleys to author.

Advice: "We look for strongly crafted work that tells a story that needs to be told. We demand vision and intelligence and mystery in the fiction we publish."

N ● **THE IDIOT**, Anarchaos Press, P.O. Box 69163, Los Angeles CA 90069. E-mail: idiotsubmissions@yahoo.com. Website: www.theidiotmagazine.com. Dictator-for-Life: Sam Hayes. **Contacts:** Brian Campbell and Toni Plummer, lackeys. Magazine: 5½ × 8½; 48 pages; 20 lb. white paper; cardboard glossy cover; illustrations. "For people who enjoy Dennis Miller, Woody Allen, S.J. Perelman, James Thurber, and Camus. We're looking for black comedy. Death, disease, God, religion, micronauts are all subjects of comedy. Nothing is sacred, but it needs to be funny. I don't want whimsical, I don't want amusing, I don't want some fanciful anecdote about a trip you took with your uncle when you were eight. I want laugh-out-loud-fall-on-the-floor-funny. If it's cute, give it to your mom, your sweetheart, or your puppy dog. Length doesn't matter, but most comedy is like soup. It's an appetizer, not a meal. Short is often better. Bizarre, obscure, referential, and literary are all appreciated. My audience is mostly comprised of bitter misanthropes who play Russian Roulette between airings of 'The Simpsons' each day. I want dark." Annual. Estab. 1993. Circ. 250-300.

Needs: Humor/satire. Wants more short, dark humor. Publishes ms 6-12 months after acceptance. **Publishes 1-3 new writers/year.** Recently published work by Joe Deasy, Dan Medeiros, Mike Buckley and Mark Romyn. Length: 2,000 words maximum; average length: 500 words. Mostly looking for short shorts. Also publishes poetry. Sometimes comments on rejected mss.

How to Contact: Send or e-mail complete ms with a cover letter. Include estimated word count and bio (30-50 words). Accepts queries/mss by e-mail. Responds in 1 month to queries; 3 months to mss. Send SASE for reply, return of ms or send a disposable copy of ms. Accepts simultaneous, reprint and electronic submissions. Sample copy for $5.

Payment/Terms: Pays 1 contributor copy. Acquires one-time rights. Sends galleys to author if time permits.

VISIT THE WRITER'S MARKET WEBSITE at www.writersmarket.com for hot new markets, daily market updates, writers' guidelines and much more.

Advice: "Nothing over 2,000 words unless it's the funniest damned thing on the face of this or any other Earth. If you're too cheap to buy a copy of our magazine, then check out our website—though not nearly as funny, it will give you an idea of what we're looking for. And we have our first writing contest! See website for rules and conditions."

ILLUMINATIONS: An International Magazine of Contemporary Writing, c/o Dept. of English, College of Charleston, 66 George St., Charleston SC 29424-0001. (843)953-1993. Fax: (843)953-3180. E-mail: lewiss@cofc.edu. Website: www.cofc.edu/Illuminations (includes writer's guidelines and information on back issues). **Contact:** Simon Lewis, editor. Magazine: 5×8; 80 pages; illustrations. "*Illuminations* is one of the most challengingly eclectic little literary magazines around, having featured writers from the United States, Britain and Romania as well as Southern Africa." Annual. Estab. 1982. Circ. 400.
Needs: Literary. Receives 4 unsolicited mss/month. Accepts 2 mss/year. **Publishes 1 new writer/year.** Published work by Klaus de Albuquerque. Length: 400-1,500. Mainly publishes poetry. Sometimes comments on or critiques rejected ms.
How to Contact: Send complete ms with a cover letter. Accepts inquiries by e-mail, fax and on disk. Include estimated word count and 50 word bio. Responds in 2 weeks to queries; 2 months to mss. Send SASE for reply, return of ms or send a disposable copy of ms. No simultaneous submissions. Sample copy for $10 and a 6×9 envelope. Guidelines free.
Payment/Terms: Pays 2 contributor's copies of current issue; 1 of subsequent issue. Acquires one-time rights.

IMAGE, A Journal of the Arts & Religion, The Center for Religious Humanism, 3307 Third Ave. W, Seattle WA 98119. (206)281-2988. E-mail: image@imagejournal.org. Website: www.imagejournal.org. **Editor:** Greg Wolfe. Magazine: 7×10; 136 pages; glossy cover stock; illustrations; photos. "*Image* is a showcase for the encounter between religious faith and world-class contemporary art. Each issue features fiction, poetry, essays, memoirs, an in-depth interview and articles about visual artists, film, music, etc. and glossy 4-color plates of contemporary visual art." Quarterly. Estab. 1989. Circ. 4,000. Member, CLMP.
Needs: Literary, humor/satire, regional, religious, translations. Receives 60 unsolicited mss/month. Accepts 2 mss/issue; 8 mss/year. Publishes ms within 1 year after acceptance. Agented fiction 5%. Recently published work by Annie Dillard, Bret Lott and Melanie Rae Thon. Length: 2,000-8,000 words; average length: 5,000 words. Also publishes literary essays and poetry.
How to Contact: Send complete ms with a cover letter. Include bio. Responds in 1 month to queries; 3 months to mss. Send SASE for reply, return of ms or send a disposable copy of ms. No electronic submissions. Sample copy for $12. Reviews novels and short story collections.
Payment/Terms: Pays $10/page ($100 minimum) and 4 contributor's copies; additional copies for $5. Pays on publication. Sends galleys to author.
Advice: "Fiction must grapple with religious faith, though the settings and subjects need not be overtly religious."

INDIANA REVIEW, Ballantine Hall 465, 1020 E. Kirkwood Ave., Bloomington IN 47405-7103. (812)855-3439. Fax: (812)855-4253. E-mail: inreview@indiana.edu. Website: www.indiana.edu/~inreview/ir.html (includes writer's guidelines, excerpts from publication, back issues, subscription/back issue order form, current news, staff, supporters). **Contact:** Danit Brown, fiction editor. Editors change yearly. Magazine: 6×9; 160 pages; 50 lb. paper; Glatfelter cover stock. *Indiana Review* is a nonprofit literary magazine dedicated to showcasing the talents of emerging and established writers. "Our mission is to offer the highest quality writing within a wide aesthetic." Semiannual. Estab. 1976. Circ. 2,000.
   ● Work published in *Indiana Review* received a Pushcart Prize (2001) and was included in *Best New American Voices* (2001). *IR* also received an Indiana Arts Council Grant and a National Endowment In the Arts grant.
Needs: Ethnic, literary, regional, translations. Also considers novel excerpts. "No genre fiction. We look for stories which integrate theme, language, character and form. We like mature, sophisticated fiction which has consequence beyond the world of its narrator." Receives 200 unsolicited mss each month. Accepts 7-9 prose mss/issue. **Publishes 6-8 new writers/year.** Recently published work by Tim Westmoreland, Charles Johnson, Ray Gonzalez and Crystal Wilkinson. Length: 1-35 magazine pages. Upcoming theme: Borders (May 2004), deadline December 2003. Also publishes literary essays, poetry and reviews.
How to Contact: Send complete ms with cover letter. Cover letters should be *brief* and demonstrate specific familiarity with the content of a recent issue of *Indiana Review*. SASE. Accepts simultaneous submissions (if notified *immediately* of other publication) and multiple submissions. Responds in 3 months. Publishes ms an average of 3-6 months after acceptance. Does not read mss mid-December-mid-January. Sample copy for $8. Sponsors annual $1,000 fiction and poetry contests. SASE for guidelines.
Payment/Terms: Pays $5/page and 2 contributor's copies. Acquires first North American serial rights.
Advice: "Because our editors change each year, so do our literary preferences. It's important that potential contributors are familiar with the most recent issue of *Indiana Review* via library, sample copy or subscription. Beyond that, we look for prose that is well crafted and socially relevant. Dig deep. Don't accept your first choice descriptions when you are revising. Cliché and easy images sink 90% of the stories we reject. Understand the magazines you send to—investigate!"

INKWELL MAGAZINE, Manhattanville College, 2900 Purchase St., Purchase NY 10577. (914)323-5300. Fax: (914)694-0348. Website: www.manhattanville.edu/inkwellmag/index.htm. **Contact:** Jeremy Church, editor. Magazine: 7×10; 120-170 pages; 60 lb. paper; 10 pt C1S, 4/c cover; illustrations; photos. "*Inkwell Magazine* is committed to presenting top quality poetry, prose and artwork in a high quality publication. *Inkwell* is dedicated to discovering new talent, and to encouraging and bringing the talents of working writers and artists' to a wider audience. We encourage diverse voices and have an open submission policy for both art and literature." Annual. Estab. 1995. Circ. 1,000. Member, CLMP.

Needs: Experimental, humor/satire, literary. "No erotica, children's literature, romance, religious." List of upcoming themes available for SASE. Receives 1,500 unsolicited mss/year. Accepts 45 mss/issue. Does not read mss February-September. Publishes ms 2 months after acceptance. **Publishes 3-5 new writers/year.** Recently published work by Maureen Howard, Denise Shekerjian, Robert Ryser, Phyllis Carito and Susan Kelly-DeWitt. Length: 5,000 words maximum; average length: 3,000 words. Publishes short shorts. Also publishes poetry. Sometimes comments on rejected mss.

How to Contact: Send complete ms with a cover letter. Include estimated word count, list of publications and cover letter with name, address, telephone and e-mail. Responds in 2 months to queries; 4-6 months to mss. Send a disposable copy of ms and #10 SASE for reply only. Sample copy for $6. Guidelines for SASE.

Payment/Terms: Pays 1 contributor's copy; additional copies $10.50. Acquires first rights. Sponsors annual poetry and short fiction contests. Send SASE for guidelines.

Advice: "We look for well-crafted original stories with a strong voice."

INTERBANG: Dedicated to perfection in the art of writing, P.O. Box 1574, Venice CA 90294. (310)450-6372. E-mail: heather@interbang.net. Website: www.interbang.net (includes back issues and writer's guide). **Contact:** Heather Hoffman, editor. Magazine: 8½×7, 30 pages; 60 lb. paper; card cover stock; illustrations; photos. Quarterly. Estab. 1995. Circ. 2,000.

Needs: Adventure, ethnic/multicultural, experimental, family saga, fantasy (space fantasy, sword and sorcery), feminist, gay, glitz, historical (general), horror (dark fantasy, futuristic, psychological, supernatural), humor/satire, lesbian, literary, mainstream, military/war, mystery/suspense (amateur sleuth, cozy, police procedural, private eye/hardboiled), New Age, psychic/supernatural/occult, regional, science fiction (hard science/technological, soft/sociological), thriller/espionage, translations. "No travel or children's." Wants to see more historical fiction, science fiction/fantasy. Receives 50 unsolicited mss/month. Accepts 5 mss/issue; 25 mss/year. Publishes ms 1 month after acceptance. Agented fiction 5%. **Publishes 50 new writers/year.** Published work by Sharon Mesmer, Ron Bloom, L. Fitzgerald Sjöberg. Length: 2,500 words average. Publishes short shorts. Also publishes literary essays. Sometimes comments on or critiques rejected ms.

How to Contact: Send complete ms with a cover letter. Accepts inquiries by e-mail. Include estimated word count and bio. Responds in 2 weeks to queries; 3 months to mss. Send SASE for reply, return of ms or send a disposable copy of ms. Accepts simultaneous submissions. Sample copy free. Reviews novels, short story collections and nonfiction books. Send books to editor.

Payment/Terms: Pays free subscription to the magazine, an *Interbang* T-shirt and 5 contributor's copies. Pays on publication for one-time rights.

Advice: "We're looking for well-written stories with strong, vivid descriptions, well-developed characters and complex themes. Focus on a consistent narrative style. We do not publish stories that read like a TV show. We want stories with style and depth."

$ ⊘ THE IOWA REVIEW, University of Iowa, 308 EPB, Iowa City IA 52242. (319)335-0462. E-mail: iowa-review@uiowa.edu. Website: www.uiowa.edu/~iareview. Editor: David Hamilton. **Contact:** Fiction Editor. Magazine: 5½×8½; 200 pages; first-grade offset paper; Carolina CS1 10-pt. cover stock. "Stories, essays, poems for a general readership interested in contemporary literature." Triannual. Estab. 1970. Circ. 2,000.

Needs: "We are open to a range of styles and voices and always hope to be surprised by work we then feel we need." Receives 600 unsolicited fiction mss/month. Agented fiction less than 2%. Accepts 4-6 mss/issue, 12-18 mss/year. Does not read mss April-August. "We discourage simultaneous submissions." **Published new writers within the last year.** Published work by Joshua Harmon, Katherine Vaz, Mary Helen Stefaniak and Steve Tomasula. Also publishes literary essays, literary criticism, poetry.

How to Contact: Send complete ms with cover letter. "Don't bother with queries." SASE for return of ms. Responds in 4 months to mss. Publishes ms an average of 12-18 months after acceptance. Sample copy for $7. Guidelines for SASE. Reviews novels and short story collections (3-6 books/year).

Payment/Terms: Pays $10/page and 2 contributor's copies; additional copies 30% off cover price. Pays on publication for first North American serial rights.

Advice: "We have no set guidelines as to content or length; we look for what we consider to be the best writing available to us and are pleased when writers we believe we have discovered catch on with a wider range of readers. It is never a bad idea to look through an issue or two of the magazine prior to a submission."

⊘ ◎ IRIS: A Journal About Women, P.O. Box 800588, University of Virginia, Charlottesville VA 22908. (434)924-4500. E-mail: iris@virginia.edu. Coordinating Editor: Kim Roberts. **Contact:** Fiction Editor. Magazine: 8½×11; 80 pages; glossy paper; heavy cover; illustrations; artwork; photos. "Material of particular interest to women. For a feminist audience, college educated and above." Semiannual. Estab. 1980. Circ. 3,500.

Needs: Experimental, feminist, lesbian, literary, mainstream. "I don't think what we're looking for particularly falls into the 'mainstream' category—we're just looking for well-written stories of interest to women (particularly feminist women)." Receives 300 unsolicited mss/year. Accepts 5 mss/year. Publishes ms within 1 year after acceptance. **Publishes 1-2 new writers/year.** Published work by Sheila Thorne, Marsha Recknagel and Denise Laughlin. Length: 2,500-4,000 words average. Sometimes critiques rejected mss.

How to Contact: Send complete ms with cover letter. Include "previous publications, vocation, other points that pertain. Make it brief!" Accepts queries by e-mail. Responds in 3 months to mss. SASE. Accepts simultaneous submissions. Accepts electronic submissions sent as Word attachment via e-mail. Sample copy for $5. Guidelines with SASE. Label: Fiction Editor.

Payment/Terms: Pays in contributor's copies and 1 year subscription. Acquires one-time rights.

Advice: "I select mss which are lively imagistically as well as in the here-and-now; I select for writing which challenges the reader. My major complaint is with stories that don't elevate the language above the bland sameness we hear on the television and everyday. Read the work of the outstanding women writers, such as Alice Munro and Louise Erdrich."

$ ☑ ◎ **IRREANTUM, Exploring Mormon Literature**, The Association for Mormon Letters, P.O. Box 51364, Provo UT 84605. (801)714-1326. E-mail: irreantum2@cs.com. Website: www.aml-online.org (includes basic information, names of editors). **Contact:** Tory Anderson. Magazine or Zine: 8½×5½; 68-100 pages; 20 lb. paper; 20 lb. color cover; illustrations; photos. "While focused on Mormonism, *Irreantum* is a cultural, humanities-oriented magazine, not a religious magazine. Our guiding principle is that Mormonism is grounded in a sufficiently unusual, cohesive and extended historical and cultural experience that it has become like a nation, an ethnic culture. We can speak of a Mormon literature at least as surely as we can of a Jewish or Southern literature. *Irreantum* publishes stories, one-act dramas, stand-alone novel and drama excerpts, and poetry by, for or about Mormons (as well as author interviews, essays and reviews). The magazine's audience includes readers of any or no religious faith who are interested in literary exploration of the Mormon culture, mindset and worldview through Mormon themes and characters. *Irreantum* is currently the only magazine devoted to Mormon literature." Quarterly. Estab. 1999. Circ. 400.

Needs: Adventure, ethnic/multicultural (Mormon), experimental, family saga, fantasy, feminist, historical, horror, humor/satire, literary, mainstream, mystery/suspense, New Age, psychic/supernatural/occult, regional (Western USA/Mormon), religious, romance, science fiction, thriller/espionage, translations, young adult/teen. Receives 5 unsolicited mss/month. Accepts 3 mss/issue; 12 mss/year. Publishes ms 3-12 months after acceptance. **Publishes 6 new writers/year.** Recently published work by Anne Perry, Brady Udall, Brian Evenson and Robert Kirby. Length: 1,000-7,000 words; average length: 5,000 words. Publishes short shorts. Also publishes literary essays, literary criticism and poetry. Sometimes comments on rejected mss.

How to Contact: Send complete ms with a cover letter. Accepts submissions by e-mail and disk. "Note: Submissions by other than e-mail or floppy are strongly discouraged." Include brief bio and list of publications. Responds in 2 weeks to queries; 2 months to mss. Send a disposable copy of ms and #10 SASE for reply only. Accepts simultaneous submissions, previously published work and multiple submissions. Sample copy for $5. Guidelines for e-mail. Reviews novels, short story collections and nonfiction books of interest to writers. Send review copies to AML, P.O. Box 51364, Provo UT 84605.

Payment/Terms: Pays $0-100 and 2 contributor's copies; additional copies $3. Pays on publication for one-time and electronic rights.

Advice: "*Irreantum* is not interested in didactic or polemnical fiction that primarily attempts to prove or disprove Mormon doctrine, history or corporate policy. We encourage beginning writers to focus on human elements first, with Mormon elements introduced only as natural and organic to the story. Readers can tell if you are honestly trying to explore the human experience or if you are writing with a propagandistic agenda either for or against Mormonism. For conservative, orthodox Mormon writers, beware of sentimentalism, simplistic resolutions, and foregone conclusions."

N ☑ **THE JABBERWOCK REVIEW**, Mississippi State University, Drawer E, Dept. of English, Mississippi State MS 39762. (662)325-3644. E-mail: jabberwock@org.msstate.edu. Website: www.msstate.edu/org/jabberwock/ (includes writer's guidelines, interviews with authors, community-related events). **Contact:** Fiction Editor (revolving editorship). Magazine: 8½×5½; 120 pages; glossy cover; illustrations; photos. "We are located in the South—love the South—but we publish good writing from anywhere and everywhere. And from anyone. We respect writers of reputation—and print their work—but we take great delight in publishing new and emerging writers as well." Semiannual. Estab. 1979. Circ. 500.

Needs: Ethnic/multicultural, experimental, feminist, gay, lesbian, literary, mainstream, regional, translations. "No science fiction, romance." Receives 150 unsolicited mss/month. Accepts 7-8 mss/issue; 15 mss/year. "We do not read during the summer (May 1 to September 1). Manuscripts sent during that time will be held until fall, when we start reading again." Publishes ms 4-6 months after acceptance. Agented fiction 5%. **Publishes 1-5 new writers/year.** Recently published work by James Wilcox, Margo Rabb, Cris Mazza and Richard Lyons. Length: 250-5,000 words; average length: 4,000 words. Publishes short shorts. Average length: 1,000 words. Also publishes literary essays and poetry. Sometimes comments on rejected mss.

How to Contact: Send complete ms with a cover letter. Responds in 5 months to mss. Send SASE (or IRC) for return of ms. Accepts simultaneous submissions "with notification of such." Sample copy for $5. Guidelines for SASE or by e-mail.

Payment/Terms: Pays 2 contributor's copies. Sponsors contests. Visit website or write for guidelines.

Advice: "It might take a few months to get a response from us, but your manuscript will be read with care. Our editors enjoy reading submissions (really!) and will remember writers who are persistent and commited to getting a story 'right' through revision."

$ ⬜ ◎ JAPANOPHILE, Box 7977, Ann Arbor MI 48107. (734)930-1553. Fax: (734)930-9968. E-mail: japanoph ile@aol.com. Website: www.japanophile.com (includes writer's guidelines, sample fiction). **Contact:** Susan Lapp and Madeleine Vala, editors. Magazine: 5¼×8½; 58 pages; illustrations; photos. Magazine of "articles, photos, poetry, humor, short stories about Japanese culture, not necessarily set in Japan, for an adult audience, most with a college background and who like to travel." Semiannual. Estab. 1974. Circ. 800.

Needs: Adventure, historical, humor/satire, literary, mainstream, and mystery/suspense. "No erotica, science fiction or horror. Published special fiction issue last year; plans another." Receives 40-100 unsolicited fiction mss/month. Accepts 12 ms/issue, 15-20 mss/year. Published work by Suzanne Kamata, Amy Chavez and Matt Malcomson. **Publishes 12 new writers/year.** Length: 2,000-6,000 words; average length: 3,200 words. Also publishes essays, book reviews, literary criticism and poetry.

How to Contact: Send complete ms with SASE, cover letter, bio and information about story. Accepts queries/mss by e-mail and fax. Accepts simultaneous and reprint submissions. Responds in 2 months to mss. Sample copy for $4; guidelines for #10 SASE.

Payment/Terms: Pays $20. Pays on publication for all rights, first North American serial rights or one-time rights (depends on situation). Stories submitted to the magazine may be entered in the annual contest. *A $5 entry fee must accompany each submission* to enter contest. Prizes include $100 plus publication for the best short story. Deadline: December 31.

Advice: "Most of the work included in *Japanophile* is set in recent times, but the magazine will accept material set back as far as pre-WWII. We look for originality and sensitivity to cultural detail. Clarity and directness of expression make manuscripts stand out. Short stories usually involve Japanese and 'foreign' (non-Japanese) characters in a way that contributes to understanding of Japanese culture and the Japanese people. However, a *good* story dealing with Japan or Japanese cultural aspects anywhere in the world will be considered, even if it does not involve this encounter or meeting of Japanese and foreign characters. Some stories may also be published in an anthology with approval of the author and additional payment."

⬤ JEOPARDY, Literary Arts Magazine, Mail Stop #9100, Western Washington University, Bellingham WA 98225. (360)650-3118. E-mail: jeopardy@cc.wwu.edu. Website: jeopardy.wwu.edu (includes writer's guidelines, names of editors, short fiction, artwork, poetry, links to other online mags). **Contact:** Carter Hasegawa. Editors change every year. Magazine: 5×7; 192 pages; 70 lb. paper; glossy cover stock; illustrations; photos. "*Jeopardy Magazine*'s intended audience is an intelligent readership that enjoys risks, surprises and subtlety. Our philosophy is that reputation is nothing and words/images are everything. We focus on the best work published by local student writers coupled with the best work by established national writers." Annual. Estab. 1965. Circ. 1,500.

Needs: Contemporary, ethnic, gay, historical, lesbian, literary. "No long stories. We are not interested in conventional narratives, plot-driven fiction or formulaic genre fiction." Receives 250 unsolicited mss/month. Accepts 8-10 mss/year. Reading period: September 15-April 15. Publishes ms 3 months after acceptance. **Publishes 30 new writers/year.** Published work by Brenda Miller, Sheila Fox and J.C. Schmidt. Length: 250-5,000 words; average length: 1,500 words. Also publishes literary essays, poetry.

How to Contact: Send complete ms with cover letter and 50-word bio. SASE and disposable copy of the ms. Does not return mss. Accepts simultaneous and multiple submissions. Responds in 6 months. Sample copy for $5. Guidelines for #10 SASE.

Payment/Terms: Pays 2 contributor's copies. Acquires one-time rights.

Advice: "A clear, insightful voice and style are major considerations. Things that will get your manuscript recycled: tired representations of sex and/or death and/or angst. We like writers who take risks! Know your characters thoroughly—know why someone else would want to read about what they think or do. Then, submit your work and don't give up at initial failures. Don't send us stories about being a writer/artist and/or a college student/professor. We would like to see more fiction pieces which involve unique or unexpected situations and characters. We look for a strong voice, a willingness to take risks, and writers who are willing to push the boundaries of what's been done. Have something to say and say it well. Proofreading helps."

$ ⬤ THE JOURNAL, Dept of English, The Ohio State University, 164 W. 17th Ave., Columbus OH 43210. (614)292-4076. Website: www.cohums.ohio-state.edu/english/journals/the_journal. **Contact:** Kathy Fagan (poetry); Michelle Herman (fiction), editors. Magazine: 6×9; 150 pages. "We are open to all forms of quality fiction and poetry." For an educated, general adult audience. Semiannual. Estab. 1973. Circ. 1,500.

Needs: No romance, science fiction or religious/devotional. Accepts 2 mss/issue. Receives approximately 100 unsolicited fiction mss/month. Usually publishes ms within 1 year of acceptance. Agented fiction 10%. **Published new writers within the last year.** Published work by Stephen Dixon, Norma Rosen, Mark Jacobs and Liza Wieland. Length: Open. Critiques rejected mss when there is time.

How to Contact: Send complete ms with cover letter. Responds within 3 months. SASE. Sample copy for $7; guidelines for SASE.

Payment/Terms: Pays $30 stipend when funds are available and contributor's copies; $5 charge for extras.

Terms: Acquires first North American serial rights. Sends galleys to author.

Advice: Mss are rejected because of "lack of understanding of the short story form, shallow plots, undeveloped characters. Cure: read as much well-written fiction as possible. Our readers prefer 'psychological' fiction rather than stories with intricate plots. Take care to present a clean, well-typed submission."

$ ⬜ ◎ ⬛ **KALEIDOSCOPE: Exploring the Experience of Disability through Literature and the Fine Arts**, 701 S. Main St., Akron OH 44311-1019. (330)762-9755. Fax: (330)762-0912. E-mail: mshiplett@udsakron.o rg. Website: www.udsakron.org (includes guidelines, upcoming themes and names of editors). Editor-in-Chief: Darshan Perusek, Ph.D. Senior Editor: Gail Willmott. **Contact:** Fiction Editor. Magazine: 8½×11; 56-64 pages; non-coated paper; coated cover stock; illustrations (all media); photos. "*Kaleidoscope* Magazine explores the experiences of disability through literature and the fine arts. Unique in the field of disability studies, it is not an advocacy, rehabilitation, or independent living journal but expresses the experiences of disability from the perspective of individuals, families, healthcare professionals, and society as a whole. Each issue explores a specific theme which deals with disability. Readers include people with and without disabilities." Semiannual. Estab. 1979. Circ. 1,000.

- *Kaleidoscope* has received awards from the American Heart Association, the Great Lakes Awards Competition and Ohio Public Images.

Needs: "We look for well-developed plots, engaging characters and realistic dialogue. We lean toward fiction that emphasizes character and emotions rather than action-oriented narratives." Upcoming theme: "Multicultural Perspectives on Disability" (deadline March 2003). "No fiction that is stereotypical, patronizing, sentimental, erotic, or maudlin. No romance, religious or dogmatic fiction; no children's literature." Receives 20-25 unsolicited fiction mss/month. Accepts 10 mss/year. Approximately 1% of fiction is agented. **Publishes 1 new writer/year.** Recently published work by James M. Bellarosa, Gerald R. Wheeler, Nate Haken and Robert Schuler. Length: 5,000 words maximum. Also publishes poetry.

How to Contact: Query first or send complete ms and cover letter. Accepts queries by fax and e-mail. Include author's educational and writing background and if author has a disability, how it has influenced the writing. SASE. Accepts simultaneous, previously published and multiple submissions. Responds in 1 month to queries; 6 months to mss. Sample copy for $5. Guidelines for #10 SASE.

Payment/Terms: Pays $10-125 and 2 contributor's copies; additional copies $6. Pays on publication for first rights. Reprints permitted with credit given to original publication.

Advice: "Read the magazine and get submission guidelines. We prefer that writers with a disability offer original perspectives about their experiences; writers without disabilities should limit themselves to our focus in order to solidify a connection to our magazine's purpose. Do not use stereotypical, patronizing and sentimental attitudes about disability."

◎ **KALLIOPE, A Journal of Women's Literature & Art**, Florida Community College at Jacksonville, 3939 Roosevelt Blvd., Jacksonville FL 32205. (904)381-3511. Website: www.fccj.org/kalliope (includes guidelines, subscription information, contents of current issue, covers, contest information, cassette information, back issues, events, history and post address). Editor: Mary Sue Koeppel. **Contact:** Fiction Editor. Magazine: 7¼×8¼; 120 pages; 70 lb. coated matte paper; Bristol cover; 16-18 halftones per issue. "A literary and visual arts journal for women, *Kalliope* celebrates women in the arts by publishing their work and by providing a forum for their ideas and opinions." Short stories, short shorts, poems, plays, reviews and visual art. Biannual. Estab. 1978. Circ. 1,550.

Needs: "Quality short fiction by women writers. No science fiction or fantasy. Would like to see more experimental fiction." Accepts up to 10 mss/issue depending on length. Receives approximately 100 unsolicited fiction mss each month. **Publishes 3 new writers/year.** Recently published work by Edith Pearlman, Bette Howland, Susan Hubbard and Mary Gardner. Preferred length: 750-2,000 words, but occasionally publishes longer (and shorter) pieces. Also publishes poetry and short shorts. "We dedicated an entire issue to short shorts and it was very successful." Critiques rejected mss "when there is time and if requested."

How to Contact: Send complete ms with SASE and short contributor's note. No simultaneous submissions. Responds in 3 months on ms. Does not read mss May-August. Publishes ms an average of 1-3 months after acceptance. Sample copy: $9 for current issue; $7 for issues from '89-2001; $4 for issues from '78-'88. Reviews short story collections and novels.

Payment/Terms: Pays 2 contributor's copies or 1-years subscription. Acquires first rights. Discount for extras. "We accept only unpublished work. Copyright returned to author upon request."

Advice: "Read our magazine. The work we consider for publication will be well written and the characters and dialogue will be convincing. We like a fresh approach and are interested in new or unusual forms. Make us believe your characters; give readers an insight which they might not have had if they had not read you. We would like to publish more work by minority writers." Manuscripts are rejected because "1) nothing *happens*!, 2) it is thinly disguised autobiography (richly disguised autobiography is OK), 3) ending is either too pat or else just trails off, 4) characterization is not developed, and 5) point of view falters."

◎ ⬛ **KARAMU**, English Department, Eastern Illinois University, 600 Lincoln Ave., Charleston IL 61920. (217)581-6297. Editor: Olga Abella. **Contact:** Fiction Editor. Literary magazine: 5×8; 132-136 pages; illustrations; photos. "*Karamu* is a literary magazine of ideas and artistic expression independently produced by the faculty members and associates of Eastern Illinois University. We publish writing that captures something essential about life, which goes beyond the superficial, and which develops voice genuinely. Contributions of essays, fiction, poetry and artwork of interest to a broadly educated audience are welcome." Annual. Estab. 1969. Circ. 500.

- *Karamu* has received two Illinois Arts Council Awards.

Needs: Adventure, ethnic/multicultural, experimental, feminist, gay, historical, humor/satire, lesbian, literary, mainstream/contemporary, regional. "No pornographic, religious, political or didactic stories—no dogma or proselytizing." List of upcoming editorial themes available for SASE. Receives 60-70 unsolicited mss/month. Accepts 10-15 fiction mss/issue. Does not read mss March 1-September 1. Publishes ms 1 year after acceptance. **Publishes 3-6 new writers/ year.** Recently published work by Joyce Goldenstern, Ron McFarland, Rolaine Hochstein and J. Weintraub. Length: 3,500 words maximum. Publishes short shorts, poetry and creative nonfiction. Sometimes comments on rejected ms.

How to Contact: Query first. Include estimated word count, 1-paragraph bio and list of publications. Responds in 1 week to queries. Send SASE for reply. Accepts simultaneous and multiple submissions. Sample copy for $7.50 or $6 for back issues. Guidelines for SASE.

Payment/Terms: Pays 1 contributor's copy; additional copies at discount. Acquires one-time rights.

Advice: Looks for "convincing, well-developed characters and plots expressing aspects of human nature or relationships in a perceptive, believable and carefully considered and written way."

KELSEY REVIEW, Mercer County College, P.O. Box B, Trenton NJ 08690. (609)586-4800, ext. 3326. Fax: (609)586-2318. E-mail: kelsey.review@mccc.edu. Website: www.mccc.edu (includes deadlines and writer's guidelines). **Contact:** Robin Schore, editor-in-chief. Magazine: 7×14; 98 pages; glossy paper; soft cover. "Must live or work in Mercer County, NJ." Annual. Estab. 1988. Circ. 1,750.

Needs: Open. Regional (Mercer County only). Receives 120 unsolicited mss/year. Accepts 24 mss/issue. Reads mss only in May. Publishes ms 1-2 months after acceptance. **Publishes 8 new writers/year.** Recently published work by Janet Kirk, Teresa Malley and Michael White. Length: 2,000 words maximum. Publishes short shorts. Also publishes essays, poetry and line art. Always comments on rejected mss.

How to Contact: Send complete ms with cover letter. SASE for return of ms. Accepts queries/mss by e-mail. Accepts multiple submissions. Responds in 2 months. Sample copy free.

Payment/Terms: Pays 5 contributor's copies. Rights revert to author on publication.

Advice: Looks for "quality, intellect, grace and guts. Avoid sentimentality, overwriting and self-indulgence. Work on clarity, depth and originality."

THE KENYON REVIEW, Kenyon College, Gambier OH 43022. (740)427-5208. Fax: (740)427-5417. E-mail: kenyonreview@kenyon.edu. Website: www.kenyonreview.org (includes excerpts, advertising information, issue highlights, writer's guidelines, summer programs and author bios and photos). Editor: David H. Lynn. **Contact:** Fiction Editor. "Our mission is to publish best contemporary writing by established and emerging writers alike. Our audience is anyone who appreciates fine writing and literature." Triannual. Estab. 1939. Circ. 5,000.

● Work published in the *Kenyon Review* has been selected for inclusion in *Pushcart Prize* anthologies and Best American Short Stories.

Needs: Condensed/excerpted novel, contemporary, ethnic, experimental, feminist, gay, historical, humor/satire, lesbian, literary, mainstream, translations. Receives 400 unsolicited mss/month. Unsolicited mss typically read only from September 1 through March 31. Publishes ms 12-18 months after acceptance. Recently published work by Patrick White, Anesa Miller, Yvonne Jackson and Michael Dahlie. Length: 3-15 typeset pages preferred.

How to Contact: Send complete ms with cover letter. Responds to mss in 4 months. SASE. No simultaneous or electronic submissions. Sample copy for $9.

Payment/Terms: Pays $10-15/page. Pays on publication for first-time rights. Sends copyedited version to author for approval.

Advice: "We look for strong voice, unusual perspective, and power in the writing."

KEREM, Creative Explorations in Judaism, Jewish Study Center Press, Inc., 3035 Porter St. NW, Washington DC 20008. (202)364-3006. Website: www.kerem.org. **Contact:** Sara R. Horowitz and Gilah Langner, editors. Magazine: 6×9; 128 pages; 60 lb. offset paper; glossy cover; illustrations; photos. "*Kerem* publishes Jewish religious, creative, literary material—short stories, poetry, personal reflections, text study, prayers, rituals, etc." Occasional. Estab. 1992. Circ. 2,000

Needs: Jewish: feminist, humor/satire, literary, religious/inspirational. Receives 10-12 unsolicited mss/month. Accepts 1-2 mss/issue. Publishes ms 2-10 months after acceptance. Recently published work by Marge Piercy, William Novak and Anita Diamant. Length: 6,000 words maximum. Also publishes literary essays, poetry.

How to Contact: Send complete ms with a cover letter. Should include 1-2 line bio. Accepts ms by e-mail and on disk. Responds in 2 months to queries; 5 months to mss. Send SASE for reply, return of ms or send a disposable copy of ms. Accepts simultaneous and multiple submissions. Sample copy for $8.50. For writer's guidelines, please check website.

Payment/Terms: Pays free subscription and 2-10 contributor's copies. Acquires one-time rights.

Advice: "Should have a strong Jewish content. We want to be moved by reading the manuscript!"

KIMERA: A JOURNAL OF FINE WRITING, N. 1316 Hollis, Spokane WA 99201. E-mail: kimera@js.spokane. wa.us. Website: www.js.spokane.wa.us/kimera. **Contact:** Jan Strever, editor. Electronic and print magazine. "*Kimera* attempts to meet John Locke's challenge: Where is the head with no chimeras? We seek fiction that pushes the edge in terms of language use and craft." Semiannual online; annual print version. Estab. 1995. Circ. 2,000 (online), 300 (print).

Needs: Eclectic, energetic fiction. "Nothing badly conceived; attention to the muscularity of language." No erotica. Receives 50 mss/month. Accepts 5 mss/issue. Publishes mss up to 1 year after acceptance. **Publishes new writers.** Published work by L. Lynch and G. Thomas. Publishes short shorts. Also publishes literary essays and poetry. Sometimes comments on rejected mss.

insider report

Discovering new writers is top priority for Nancy Zafris of *The Kenyon Review*

As the old saying goes, "Those who can't, teach"—or, when it comes to publishing—they edit. But the old saying doesn't apply to Nancy Zafris, a critically acclaimed writer who is also fiction editor of *The Kenyon Review*.

In addition to writing and editing, Zafris teaches, too. In the summer of 1996, when she was on the faculty of the Kenyon Review Writers Workshop, *Kenyon Review* editor David Lynn asked her to become an advisory editor. In this capacity, Zafris solicited work for the magazine and helped with the slush pile. She and Lynn also began exchanging their own work (Lynn is a fiction writer, too), and it became clear that they were like-minded readers. In 1998, Lynn asked Zafris to become the magazine's fiction editor.

Nancy Zafris

Zafris's own fiction has been published in more than two dozen literary magazines, including *New England Review, Antioch Review, Glimmer Train*, and *Missouri Review*. She has taught fiction writing at the University of Pittsburgh, the Ohio State University and Centre College, and each summer she teaches at the Kenyon Review Writers Workshop. Her first collection of stories, *The People I Know*, won the Flannery O'Connor Award for Short Fiction, as well as the Ohioana Library Association Book Award for best work of fiction. Her new novel, *The Metal Shredders*, has just been published by BlueHen Books, the new literary imprint of Penguin Putnam.

Here Zafris talks about wearing both a writer's and editor's hat, the excitement of finding new voices, and what *Kenyon Review* editors look for in fiction.

How does the magazine's editorial selection process work?

A group of select Kenyon undergraduates goes through the slush pile and makes up the review routing slips. Manuscripts solicited by me go directly to me, as do manuscripts with cover letters that indicate an impressive body of fiction work or a personal recommendation. (The same is true for poetry going to our poetry editor, David Baker.) Students read the remaining slush pile. If two or more students, many of them creative writers and senior English majors, think a piece is not worthy of publication, it is returned as rejected. If even one student sees merit in the work, it is sent on to David Lynn for further consideration. David may decide himself to accept or reject, or he may choose to send it to me for further review. (I work at home; the manuscripts are sent to me through the mail. Several times a year I drive up to Gambier, Ohio, from my home in Columbus 50 miles away, usually just to touch base, have lunch, socialize a little.)

David does the final selecting. We don't work by committee. I send David work that I think should either be accepted or seriously considered, or looked at for another reason. David lets me know what he's thinking about work that I've sent him. He'll say, "What do you think?" "I'm thinking of asking for a revision." "I don't like this as well as you do." "Let's talk about this." "Not this story, but you're right, this is a writer we should encourage." Or any variety of the preceding, but in the end the decision is his. If David finds work on his own that he's interested in, he usually lets me see it as well, unless I'm not available.

Has the fiction in *The Kenyon Review* changed since you arrived?

I hope I've had some influence, if only for the fact that I feel I'm a qualified sounding board for David Lynn. We're both fiction writers, and we both have similar visions of what the short story can and should do, and, on a personal level, though we tease each other mercilessly, we are very close friends. So I think our serious discussions about *The Kenyon Review* have been fruitful. As someone who wears only one hat, I'm also able to concentrate on fiction more than David is. Part of my job is to find ways to search beyond the slush pile and the MFA pipeline.

What's the most rewarding aspect of your job?

David and I both agree that finding new writers, encouraging them, working on revisions with them, and then bringing them into print, is the most rewarding thing we do. On these occasions, both writer and editor feel great. It's especially wonderful as an editor if you find them—if you go up after a reading, for example, and introduce yourself. Hearing a fresh literary voice, spotting potential, and helping to bring that writer before new readers—that's very exciting for me as an editor, writer, and reader alike.

But finding new writers is also hard. One, because of the volume of work we receive. Two, because our staff is so small (and so underpaid, I might add). Three, because the work often isn't yet of high enough quality. That being said, we've succeeded in finding new writers and new work. I've found work that was eventually published by going to readings and plays. I've found new talent through an airport conversation, in the senior-citizen writing group I teach, through friends who are always on the lookout for me. And we've published several stories by participants in our summer writing program.

Do you typically accept stories "as is," or do you end up doing a lot of editing?

I haven't kept track, but I think about half the stories have undergone revision. Sometimes a story grabs David and me so much we don't want to let go. Usually these stories work great two-thirds of the way through, and then we find the ending too flat, too reliant on pure description, too—I hate to say this, but I will—too MFA The revision usually involves some e-mails back and forth, maybe even some phone calls. Most often, however, the revision comes about because of a fairly general suggestion one of us has made in a rejection letter. It's up to the writer at that point to decide whether he or she wants to take on a major reworking, with no assurance that the revised version will be accepted. Most good writers answer the challenge because good writers always want their story to be better, whether or not *The Kenyon Review* is the final publisher of it.

You spent six months in the Czech Republic as a Fulbright Fellow. Did the experience influence your taste in short fiction?

To a degree that surprised me. My Czech students had negative reactions to the contemporary American short stories I had them read. They found them too focused on a narrow personal journey with not enough intellectual curiosity and political involvement. Sometimes I agreed with them, sometimes I really disagreed, but I've certainly taken home their dismissiveness and turned it over in my mind—more for my own work than my work as an editor.

You once praised a short-story collection for its "refusal to offer contemporary narrative product, pumped-up service stops along the writer's own road." What did you mean?

That's a blurb way of saying that fiction these days has moved toward an autobiographical accounting. Some fiction reads more like creative nonfiction (and some creative nonfiction reads more like fiction).

How do your lives as writer and editor inform one another?

I tend to keep them pretty separate. In some ways I think I'm honing my skills as a hypocrite, following that old parental dictate to children: "Do as I say, not as I do." I know I'm breaking rules with my own stories. I will say, however, that in doing so I'm quite willing to accept the rejections that are bound to follow until I find an accommodating place. This is surely an oversimplification, but as an editor I've found that good writers sometimes enjoy their own writing a bit too much and forget to tell the story, while poorer writers tell a good story but with an unenchanting writing style. I do bear that in mind when I write my own stuff.

Have you ever rejected a story that you later wished you'd accepted?

Yes. Not because I later saw it in a magazine since I know many stories we reject will find good homes, and I'm always pleased—and relieved—when I see the story published. But there are stories I'll find myself thinking about several months, even years, after I've rejected them. Until I see them published somewhere, I'll continue to feel a little regret.

Do you think it's harder or easier to get published by a good literary magazine these days?

I think it's harder. There are more writers (and many more young writers), more manuscripts, more ambition, more MFA students being introduced by their professors, which means you have to take time with them. The result, I think, is that there is far less opportunity to help a writer shape, rethink, and revise his or her piece. It's a shame because I believe a truly superior story probably needs quite a bit of work to get all its layers both mined and then synchronized into a seamless dramatization. In the meantime, a less ambitious work, perfectly coiffed, can sneak in.

Anything else?

Check out our new website at www.kenyonreview.org.

   —*Will Allison*

(See the essay on online literary magazines by *The Kenyon Review*'s David Lynn on page 67.)

How to Contact: Send complete ms with a cover letter. Accepts mss by e-mail. Include bio. Responds in 3 weeks to queries; 3 months to mss. Send SASE for return of ms, SASE for reply only, or disposable copy of ms. Accepts simultaneous submissions. Sample copy: $5. Guidelines free.

Payment/Terms: Pays 1 contributor's copy. Pays on publication for first rights. Sponsors contest: visit website for details.

Advice: "We look for clarity of language. Read other writers and previous issues."

KIOSK, English Department, S.U.N.Y. at Buffalo, 306 Clemens Hall, Buffalo NY 14260. (716)645-2575. E-mail: ed-kiosk@acsu.buffalo.edu. Website: wings.buffalo.edu/kiosk (includes writer's guidelines, names of editors, representative fiction and poetry from issues). **Contact:** Gordon Hadfield, editor-in-chief. Magazine: 5½×8½; 150 pages; 80 lb. cover; illustrations. "We seek innovative, non-formula fiction and poetry." Annual. Estab. 1986. Circ. 500.
Needs: Literary. "While we subscribe to no particular orthodoxy, we are most hospitable to stories with a strong sense of voice, narrative direction and craftsmanship." No genre fiction. Wants more experimental fiction. Receives 50 mss/month. Accepts 10-20 mss/issue. Publishes ms within 6 months of acceptance. **Published new writers within the last year.** Recently published work by Mark Jacobs, Jay Atkinson and Richard Russo. Length: 7,500 words maximum; 3,000 words preferred. Publishes short shorts, "the shorter the better." Also publishes poetry. Sometimes critiques rejected mss.
How to Contact: Send complete mss with cover letter. Accepts queries/mss by e-mail. Does not read mss June-August. Responds in 4 months to mss. SASE. Accepts simultaneous and reprint submissions. Sample copy for $5. Guidelines for SASE.
Payment/Terms: Pays in contributor's copies. Acquires one-time rights.
Advice: "First and foremost, *Kiosk* is interested in sharp writing. Make it new, but also make it worth the reader's effort. Demand our attention with the first paragraph and maintain it to the end. Read as many different journals as possible. See what people are writing and publishing."

N. LAKE EFFECT, A Journal of the Literary Arts, Penn State Erie, Humanities and Social Sciences, Station Rd., Erie PA 16563-1501. (814)898-6281. Fax: (814)898-6032. E-mail: gol1@psu.edu. **Contact:** George Looney, editor-in-chief. Magazine: 5½×8½; 136-150 pages; 55 lb. natural paper; 12 pt. C1S cover. "In addition to seeking strong, traditional stories, *Lake Effect* is open to more experimental, language-centered fiction as well." Annual. Estab. as *Lake Effect*, 2001; as *Tempus*, 1978. Circ. 500. Member, CLMP.
Needs: Experimental, literary, mainstream. "No children's/juvenile, fantasy, science fiction, romance or young adult/teen." Receives 30 unsolicited mss/month. Accepts 5-6 mss/issue. Publishes ms 1 year after acceptance. **Publishes 2-3 new writers/year.** Recently published work by Joanna Howard, Steve Cushman, Michael Smith and Karen McKim. Length: 4,500 words maximum; average length: 2,600 words. Publishes short shorts. Also publishes literary essays and poetry.
How to Contact: Send complete ms with a cover letter. Include a brief bio and list of publications. Responds in 3 weeks to queries; 4-6 months to mss. Send SASE for return of ms or send a disposable copy of ms and #10 SASE for reply only. Accepts simultaneous submissions. Sample copy for $6. Guidelines for SASE.
Payment/Terms: Pays 2 contributor's copies; additional copies $2. Acquires first and one-time rights. Not copyrighted.
Advice: "We're looking for strong, well-crafted stories that emerge from character and language more than plot. The language is what makes a story stand out (and a strong sense of voice). Be sure to let us know immediately should a submitted story be accepted elsewhere."

THE LAMP-POST, of the Southern California C.S. Lewis Society, 1106 W. 16th St., Santa Ana CA 92706. (949)347-1255. E-mail: dgclark@adelphia.net. **Contact:** David G. Clark, editor. Magazine: 5½×8½; 34 pages; 7 lb. paper; 8 lb. cover; illustrations. "We are a literary review focused on C.S. Lewis and like writers." Quarterly. Estab. 1977. Circ. 200.
Needs: "Literary fantasy and science fiction for children to adults." Publishes ms 9 months after acceptance. **Publishes 3-5 new writers/year.** Published work by Rita Quinton and DJ Kolacki. Length: 1,000-5,000 words; average length: 2,500 words. Also publishes literary essays, literary criticism and poetry. Sometimes comments on rejected mss.
How to Contact: Query first or send complete ms with a cover letter. Accepts queries/mss by e-mail. Include 50-word bio. Responds in 2 months. Send SASE for reply, return of ms or send a disposable copy of ms. No simultaneous submissions. Accepts reprints and electronic (disk) submissions. Sample copy for $3. Guidelines for #10 SASE. Reviews fiction or criticism having to do with Lewis or in his vein. Send books to: Dr. David W. Landrum, book review editor, Cornerstone College, 1001 E. Beltline, NE, Grand Rapids MI 49525.
Payment/Terms: Pays 3 contributor's copies; additional copies $3. Acquires first North American serial rights or one-time rights.
Advice: "We look for fiction with the supernatural, mythic feel of the fiction of C.S. Lewis and Charles Williams. Our slant is Christian but we want work of literary quality. No inspirational. Is it the sort of thing Lewis, Tolkien and Williams would like—subtle, crafted fiction? If so, send it. Don't be too obvious or facile. Our readers aren't stupid."

N. LANDFALL/UNIVERSITY OF OTAGO PRESS, University of Otago Press, P.O. Box 56, Dunedin, New Zealand. Fax: (64)3 479-8385. E-mail: landfall@otago.ac.nz. Editor: Justin Paton. **Contact:** Fiction Editor.
Needs: Publishes fiction, poetry, commentary and reviews of New Zealand books. Length: maximum 10,000 words but shorter work is preferred. "We concentrate on publishing work by New Zealand writers, but occasionally accept work from elsewhere."

 A BULLET INTRODUCES COMMENTS by the editor of *Novel & Short Story Writer's Market* indicating special information about the listing.

$ 🌓 ◎ LARCOM REVIEW, The Arts and Literature of New England, The Larcom Press, P.O. Box 161, Prides Crossing MA 01965. (978)927-8707. Fax: (978)927-8904. E-mail: amp@larcompress.com. Website: www.larcom press.com. **Contact:** Ann Perrott, publisher. Magazine: 8½×11; 160-200 pages; acid free paper; 10 pt. CIS cover; illustrations; photos. *"The Larcom Review* is interested in all aspects of the New England landscape and its people. Our journal showcases contemporary works by writers and artists of New England. Works range from traditional to contemporary themes." Semiannual. Estab. 1999. Circ. 300. Member, American Booksellers Association.

Needs: Family saga, literary, mainstream, inspirational. "No science fiction, violence, sexual themes." Would like to see more short mysteries. Receives 200-300 unsolicited mss/month. Accepts 6-10 mss/issue; 15-30 mss/year. Publishes ms 2-3 months after acceptance. **Publishes 1-2 new writers/year.** Recently published work by Ann Struthers, Jebba M. Handley and Rachel Hyde. Length: 3,000 words maximum; average length: 1,500-2,500 words. Publishes short shorts. Also publishes literary essays, literary criticism and poetry. Often comments on rejected mss.

How to Contact: Send complete ms with a cover letter or query first with article. Accepts submissions by fax and disk. Include an estimated word count, brief bio and telephone number. Must send SASE (or IRC) for return of ms. Sample copy for $7. Guidelines for SASE. Reviews novels, short story collections and nonfiction books of interest to writers.

Payment/Terms: Pays $25-300 and 1 contributor's copy; additional copies discounted 50%. Pays on publication for first North American serial rights. Sends galleys to author.

Advice: "Within the story, there should be something underlying—something more than just characters and dialogue, a deeper meaning for people to walk away with. Follow guidelines carefully with any press. Read those authors that do get published. Ask for feedback—keep trying."

◖ THE LAUREL REVIEW, Northwest Missouri State University, Dept. of English, Maryville MO 64468. (660)562-1739. E-mail: abenson@mail.nwmissouri.edu. **Contact:** Amy Benson, Nancy Mayer, William Trowbridge, David Slater and Beth Richards, co-editors. Associate Editors: Leigh Allison Wilson, Ann Cummins, Jeff Mock, Randall R. Freisinger and Catie Rosemurgy. Reviewer: Peter Makuck. Magazine: 6×9; 124-128 pages; good quality paper. "We publish poetry and fiction of high quality, from the traditional to the avant-garde. We are eclectic, open and flexible. Good writing is all we seek." Biannual. Estab. 1960. Circ. 900.

Needs: Literary and contemporary. "No genre or politically polemical fiction." Accepts 3-5 mss/issue, 6-10 mss/year. Receives approximately 120 unsolicited fiction mss each month. Approximately 1% of fiction is agented. **Publishes 1-2 new writers/year.** Published work by Christine Sneed, Judith Kitchen and James Doyle. Length: 1,000-10,000 words. Sometimes publishes literary essays; also publishes poetry.

How to Contact: Send complete ms with SASE. No simultaneous submissions. Reading period: September 1-May 1. Responds in 4 months to mss. Publishes ms an average of 1-12 months after acceptance. Sample copy for $5.

Payment/Terms: Pays 2 contributor's copies and 1 year subscription. Acquires first rights. Copyright reverts to author upon request.

Advice: "Nothing really matters to us except our perception that the story presents something powerfully felt by the writer and communicated intensely to a serious reader. (We believe, incidentally, that comedy is just as serious a matter as tragedy, and we don't mind a bit if something makes us laugh out loud; we get too little that makes us laugh, in fact). We try to reply promptly, though we don't always manage that. In short, we want good poems and good stories. We hope to be able to recognize them, and we print what we believe to be the best work submitted."

Ⓝ $ 🌓 ◎ LE FORUM, Supplement Littéraire, Franco-American Research Opportunity Group, University of Maine, Franco American Center, Orono ME 04469-5719. (207)581-3764. Fax: (207)581-1455. E-mail: lisa_michaud @umit.maine.edu. Website: www.francomaine.org. **Contact:** Lisa Michaud, managing editor. Tabloid size, magazine format: 36 pages; illustrations; photos. Publication was founded to stimulate and recognize creative expression among Franco-Americans, all types of readers, including literary and working class. This publication is used in classrooms. Circulated internationally. Quarterly. Estab. 1986. Circ. 5,000.

Needs: "We will consider any type of short fiction, poetry and critical essays having to do with Franco-American experience. They must be of good quality in French or English. We are also looking for Canadian writers with French-North American experiences." Receives about 10 unsolicited mss/month. Accepts 2-4 mss/issue. **Published new writers within the last year.** Length: 750-2,500 words; average length: 1,000 words. Occasionally critiques rejected mss.

How to Contact: Send complete ms with cover letter. Accepts mss by fax, e-mail and on disk. Include a short bio and list of previous publications. Responds in 3 weeks to queries; 1 month to mss. SASE. Accepts simultaneous and reprint submissions.

Payment/Terms: Pays $10 and 3 copies for one-time rights.

Advice: "Write honestly. Start with a strongly felt personal Franco-American experience. If you make us feel what you have felt, we will publish it. We stress that this publication deals specifically with the Franco-American experience."

◖ LEAPINGS LITERARY MAGAZINE, 2455 Pinercrest Dr., Santa Rosa CA 95403-8946. (707)544-4861. Fax: (707)568-7531. E-mail: editserv@compuserve.com. Website: home.inreach.com/editserv/leapings.html (includes writer's guidelines). Editor: S.A. Warner. **Contact:** Fiction Editor. Magazine: 5×8; 40 pages; 20 lb. paper; glossy cover; illustrations; photos. "Eclectic magazine emphasizing diversity." Semiannual. Estab. 1998. Circ. 200.

Needs: Adventure, ethnic/multicultural, experimental, fantasy, feminist, humor satire, literary, mainstream, mystery/ suspense, science fiction. "No romance." Receives 30 unsolicited mss/month. Accepts 2 mss/issue; 4 mss/year. Publishes ms 6 months after acceptance. Less than 10% of fiction accepted is agented. **Publishes 5 new writers/year.** Publishes short shorts. Also publishes literary essays, literary criticism, poetry. Sometimes comments on rejected mss.

How to Contact: Send complete ms with a cover letter. Include estimated word count. Responds in 6 weeks. Send SASE for reply, return of ms or send a disposable copy of ms. No simultaneous submissions. Sample copy for $5. Guidelines free for #10 SASE. Reviews novels and short story collections. Send books to S.A. Warner.

Payment/Terms: Pays 2 contributor's copies; additional copies $5. Pays on publication for first rights.

Advice: Looks for "good presentation and sound writing showing the writer has worked at his/her craft. Write and rewrite and only submit it when you've made the work as crisp and clear as possible."

THE LICKING RIVER REVIEW, University Center, Northern Kentucky University, Highland Heights KY 41099. (859)572-5812. E-mail: lrr@nku.edu. **Contact:** Andrew Miller, faculty advisor. Magazine: 7×11; 96 pages; photos. Annual. Estab. 1991. Circ. 1,500.

Needs: Experimental, literary, mainstream/contemporary. "No erotica." Wants more experimental. Receives 40 unsolicited mss/month. Accepts 7-9 mss/year. Does not read mss January-August. Publishes ms 6 months after acceptance. **Publishes 2-3 new writers/year.** Recently published work by William Rushton, Michael Schafner, Mary Winters, Ronna Wineberg and Ryan Van Cleave. Length: 5,000 words maximum. Publishes short shorts. Also publishes poetry.

How to Contact: Send complete ms with a cover letter. Accepts queries by e-mail. Include list of publications. Responds in 6 months to mss. SASE for return of manuscript or send disposable copy of ms. No simultaneous submissions. Sample copy for $5.

Payment/Terms: Pays 2 contributor's copies. Pays on publication.

Advice: "We look for good writing and an interesting, well-told story. Read a sample copy first. Don't do what everyone else is doing. Be fresh, original. Write what you like—it will show. Tell a story you care about and work on it every day until you love it before sending it out."

LIGHT QUARTERLY, P.O. Box 7500, Chicago IL 60680. Website: www.lightquarterly.com. Editor: John Mella. **Contact:** Fiction Editor. Magazine: 6×9; 64 pages; Finch opaque (60 lb.) paper; 65 lb. color cover; illustrations. "Light and satiric verse and prose, witty but not sentimental. Audience: intelligent, educated, usually 'professional.'" Quarterly. Estab. 1992. Circ. 1,000.

Needs: Humor/satire, literary. Receives 10-40 unsolicited fiction mss/month. Accepts 2-4 mss/issue. Publishes ms 6-24 months after acceptance. Published work by X.J. Kennedy, J.F. Nims and John Updike. Length: 600-2,000 words; 1,200 words preferred. Publishes short shorts. Also publishes literary essays, literary criticism and poetry. Sometimes comments on rejected mss.

How to Contact: Query first. Include estimated word count and list of publications. Responds in 1 month to queries; 4 months to mss. Send SASE for reply, return of ms or send a disposable copy of ms. No simultaneous submissions. Accepts electronic submissions (disk only). Sample copy for $6 (plus $2 for 1st class). Guidelines for #10 SASE. Reviews novels and short story collections. Send review copies to review editor.

Payment/Terms: Pays contributor's copies (2 for domestic; 1 for foreign). Acquires first North American serial rights. Sends galleys to author.

Advice: Looks for "high literary quality; wit, allusiveness, a distinct (and distinctive) style. Read guidelines or issue first."

THE LISTENING EYE, Kent State University Geauga Campus, 14111 Claridon-Troy Rd., Burton OH 44021. (440)286-3840. E-mail: grace_butcher@msn.com. **Contact:** Grace Butcher, editor. Magazine: 5½×8½; 60 pages; photographs. "We publish the occasional very short story, in any subject and any style, but the language must be strong, unusual, free from cliché and vagueness. We are a shoestring operation from a small campus but we publish high-quality work." Annual. Estab. 1970. Circ. 250.

Needs: Literary. "Pretty much anything will be considered except porn." Accepts 1-2 mss/issue. Does not read mss April 15 through January 1. Publishes ms 3-4 months after acceptance. Recently published work by Lyn Lifshin. Maximum length: 750 words. Publishes short shorts. Also publishes poetry. Sometimes comments on rejected ms.

How to Contact: Send complete ms with brief cover letter. Include brief bio and list of publications. Responds to queries in 4 weeks; mss in 4 months. Send SASE for return of ms or disposable copy of ms with SASE for reply only. Accepts previously published submissions. Sample copy for $3 and $1 postage. Guidelines for SASE.

Payment/Terms: Pays 2 contributor's copies; additional copies $3 with $1 postage. Pays on publication for one-time rights.

Advice: "We look for powerful, unusual imagery, content and plot. Short, short."

$ **LITERAL LATTÉ, Mind Stimulating Stories, Poems & Essays**, Word Sci, Inc., 61 E. Eighth St., Suite 240, New York NY 10003. (212)260-5532. E-mail: litlatte@aol.com. Website: www.literal-latte.com (includes excerpts, writer's guidelines, names of editors, interviews with authors, fiction not included in print version). **Contact:** Jeff Bockman, editor. Magazine: 11×17; 24 pages; newsprint paper; 50 lb. cover; illustrations; photos. "Publishes great writing in many flavors and styles. *Literal Latté* expands the readership for literary magazines by offering free copies in New York coffeehouses and bookstores." Bimonthly. Estab. 1994. Circ. 25,000. Member, CLMP.

Needs: Experimental, fantasy, literary, science fiction. Receives 4,000 mss/month. Accepts 5-8 mss/issue; 40 mss/year. Publishes ms 6 months after acceptance. Agented fiction 5%. **Publishes 6 new writers/year.** Length: 500-6,000 words; average length: 4,000 words. Publishes short shorts. Often comments on rejected mss.

How to Contact: Send complete ms with a cover letter. Include estimated word count and brief bio. Responds in 6 months to mss. Send SASE for return of mss or send a disposable copy of ms and #10 SASE for reply only or e-mail for reply only. Accepts simultaneous and multiple submissions. Sample copy for $3. Guidelines for SASE, e-mail or check website. Reviews novels, short story collections and nonfiction books of interest to writers.

Payment/Terms: Pays 10 contributor's copies, a free subscription to the magazine and 2 gift certificates; additional copies $1. Pays on publication for first and one-time rights. Sponsors contest; guidelines for SASE, e-mail or on website.

Advice: "Keeping free thought free and challenging entertainment are not mutually exclusive. Words make a manuscript stand out, words beautifully woven together in striking and memorable patterns."

THE LITERARY REVIEW, An International Journal of Contemporary Writing, Fairleigh Dickinson University, 285 Madison Ave., Madison NJ 07940. (973)443-8564. Fax: (973)443-8364. E-mail: tlr@fdu.edu. Website: www.webdelsol.com/tlr/ (includes subscription information, writer's guidelines, names of editors, chapbooks and selections from printed issues). **Contact:** Walter Cummins, editor-in-chief. Magazine: 6×9; 140 pages; professionally printed on textpaper; semigloss card cover; perfect-bound. "Literary magazine specializing in fiction, poetry, and essays with an international focus. Our audience is general with a leaning toward scholars, libraries and schools." Quarterly. Estab. 1957. Circ. 2,300.

   • Work published in *The Literary Review* has been included in *Editor's Choice*, *Best American Short Stories* and *Pushcart Prize* anthologies.

Needs: Works of high literary quality only. Does not want to see "overused subject matter or pat resolutions to conflicts." Receives 50-60 unsolicited fiction mss/month. Approximately 1-2% of fiction is agented. **Publishes 80% new writers/year.** Published work by Irvin Faust, Todd James Pierce, Joshua Shapiro and Susan Schwartz Senstadt. Length: 5,000 words maximum. Acquires 15-20 mss/year. Does not read submissions during June, July and August. Also publishes literary essays, literary criticism, poetry. Occasionally critiques rejected mss.

How to Contact: Send 1 complete ms with SASE. "Cover letter should include publication credits." Responds in 3 months to mss. Publishes ms an average of 1½-2 years after acceptance. Considers multiple submissions. Sample copy for $5; guidelines for SASE. Reviews novels and short story collections.

Payment/Terms: Pays 2 contributor's copies; 25% discount for extras. Acquires first rights.

Advice: "We want original dramatic situations with complex moral and intellectual resonance and vivid prose. We don't want versions of familiar plots and relationships. Too much of what we are seeing today is openly derivative in subject, plot and prose style. We pride ourselves on spotting new writers with fresh insight and approach."

THE LONG STORY, 18 Eaton St., Lawrence MA 01843. (978)686-7638. E-mail: rpburnham@mac.com. Website: www.longstorymagazine.com. **Contact:** R.P. Burnham, editor. Magazine: 5½×8½; 150-200 pages; 60 lb. paper; 65 lb. cover stock; illustrations (b&w graphics). For serious, educated, literary people. "No science fiction, adventure, romance, etc. We publish high literary quality of any kind, but especially look for stories that have difficulty getting published elsewhere—committed fiction, working class settings, left-wing themes, etc." Annual. Estab. 1983. Circ. 1,200.

Needs: Contemporary, ethnic, feminist and literary. Receives 30-40 unsolicited mss/month. Accepts 6-7 mss/issue. **50% of writers published are new.** Length: 8,000-20,000 words. Best length: 8,000-12,000 words.

How to Contact: Send complete ms with a brief cover letter. Responds in 2 months. Publishes ms an average of 3 months to 1 year after acceptance. SASE. May accept simultaneous submissions ("but not wild about it"). Sample copy for $6.

Payment/Terms: Pays 2 contributor's copies; $5 charge for extras. Acquires first rights.

Advice: "Read us first and make sure submitted material is the kind we're interested in. Send clear, legible manuscripts. We're not interested in commercial success; rather we want to provide a place for long stories, the most difficult literary form to publish in our country."

LOST AND FOUND TIMES, Luna Bisonte Prods, 137 Leland Ave., Columbus OH 43214. (614)846-4126. **Contact:** John M. Bennett, editor. Magazine: 5½×8½; 56 pages; good quality paper; good cover stock; illustrations; photos. Theme: experimental, avant-garde and folk literature, art. Published irregularly (twice yearly). Estab. 1975. Circ. 300.

Needs: Contemporary, experimental, literary, prose poem. Prefers short pieces. The editor would like to see more short, extremely experimental pieces. "No 'creative writing' workshop stories." Also publishes poetry. Accepts approximately 2 mss/issue. **Published new writers within the last year.** Published work by Spryszak, Steve McComas, Willie Smith, Rupert Wondolowski, Al Ackerman.

How to Contact: Query with clips of published work. SASE. No simultaneous submissions. Responds in 1 week to queries, 2 weeks to mss. Sample copy for $7.

Payment/Terms: Pays 1 contributor's copy. Rights revert to authors.

LOUISIANA LITERATURE, A Review of Literature and Humanities, Southeastern Louisiana University, SLU 792, Hammond LA 70402. (504)549-5783. Fax: (504)549-5021. E-mail: ngerman@selu.edu. Website: www.selu.edu. Editor: Jack Bedell. **Contact:** Norman German, fiction editor. Magazine: 6¾×9¾; 150 pages; 70 lb. paper; card cover; illustrations. "Essays should be about Louisiana material; preference is given to fiction and poetry with Louisiana and Southern themes, but creative work can be set anywhere." Semiannual. Estab. 1984. Circ. 400 paid; 500-700 printed.

Needs: Literary, mainstream, regional. "No sloppy, ungrammatical manuscripts." Receives 100 unsolicited fiction mss/month. Accepts mss related to special topics issues. May not read mss June through July. Publishes mss 6-12 months maximum after acceptance. **Publishes 4 new writers/year.** Published work by Anthony Bukowski, Tim Parrish, Robert Phillips and Andrew Otis Haschemeyer. Length: 1,000-6,000 words; 3,500 words preferred. Also publishes literary essays (Louisiana themes), literary criticism, poetry. Sometimes comments on rejected mss.

How to Contact: Send complete ms. Responds in 3 months to mss. SASE. Sample copy for $8. Reviews novels and short story collections (mainly those by Louisiana authors).

Payment/Terms: Pays usually in contributor's copies. Acquires one-time rights.

Advice: "Cut out everything that is not a functioning part of the story. Make sure your manuscript is professionally presented. Use relevant specific detail in every scene. We love detail, local color, voice and craft. Any professional manuscript stands out."

THE LOUISIANA REVIEW, % Division of Liberal Arts, Louisiana State University at Eunice, P.O. Box 1129, Eunice LA 70535. (337)550-1328. E-mail: mgage@lsue.edu. **Contact:** Dr. Maura Gage, editor. Magazine: 7½×11; 124 pages; glossy cover; illustrations; photos. "While we will accept some of the better works submitted by our own students, we prefer excellent work by Louisiana writers as well as those outside the state who tell us their connection to it." Annual. Estab. 1999. Circ. 500-700.

Needs: Ethnic/multicultural (Cajun or Louisiana culture), historical (Louisiana-related or setting), regional (Louisiana), romance (gothic). Receives 25 unsolicited mss/month. Accepts 5-7 mss/issue. Does not read mss April-December. Publishes ms up to 11 months after acceptance. Recently published work by Tom Bonner, Laura Cario and Sheryl St. Germaine. Length: 1,000-3,000 words; average length: 2,000 words. Publishes short shorts. Also publishes poetry. Sometimes comments on rejected mss.

How to Contact: Send complete ms with a cover letter. Accepts submissions by disk (with a hard copy attached, Microsoft Word only). Include letter stating connection to Louisiana. Responds in 5 weeks to queries; 10 weeks to mss. Send SASE (or IRC) for return of ms. Accepts previously published work and multiple submissions. Sample copy for $3. Reviews novels, short story collections and nonfiction books of interest to writers.

Payment/Terms: Pays 1-2 contributor's copies; additional copies $3. Pays on publication for one-time rights. Not copyrighted (but has an ISSN #).

Advice: "We do like to have fiction play out visually as a film would rather than static and undramatred."

THE LOUISVILLE REVIEW, College of Arts and Sciences, Spalding University, 851 S. Fourth St., Louisville KY 40203. (502)585-9911, ext. 2777. E-mail: louisvillereview@spalding.edu. Website: www.louisvillereview.org. **Contact:** Sena Jeter Naslund, editor. Literary magazine. "We are a literary journal seeking original stories with fresh imagery and vivid language." Semiannual. Estab. 1976.

Needs: Literary. Receives 25-30 unsolicited mss/month. Accepts 4-6 mss/issue; 8-12 mss/year. Publishes ms 6 months after acceptance. **Publishes 2-4 new writers/year.** Recently published work by Maura Stanton, Ursula Hegi, Robin Lippincott, Jhumpa Lahiri. Publishes short shorts. Also publishes literary essays and poetry. Sometimes comments on rejected mss.

How to Contact: Send complete ms with cover letter. Include estimated word count, brief bio and list of publications. Accepts multiple submissions. Responds in 6 months to queries and mss. Send SASE for return of ms or send disposable copy of ms and #10 SASE for reply only.

Payment/Terms: Pays 2 contributor's copies.

$ LYNX EYE, ScribbleFest Literary Group, 542 Mitchell Dr., Los Osos CA 93402. (805)528-8146. Fax: (805)528-7676. E-mail: pamcully@aol.com. **Contact:** Pam McCully, co-editor. Magazine: 5½×8½; 120 pages; 60 lb. book paper; varied cover stock. "*Lynx Eye* is dedicated to showcasing visionary writers and artists, particularly new voices." Quarterly. Estab. 1994. Circ. 500.

Needs: Adventure, condensed/excerpted novel, erotica, ethnic/multicultural, experimental, fantasy (science), feminist, gay, historical, horror, humor/satire, lesbian, literary, mainstream/contemporary, mystery/suspense, romance, science fiction, serialized novel, translations, westerns. "No horror with gratuitous violence or YA stories." Receives 500 unsolicited mss/month. Accepts 30 mss/issue; 120 mss/year. Publishes ms approximately 3 months after acceptance (contract guarantees publication within 12 months or rights revert and payment is kept by author). **Publishes 30 new writers/year.** Published work by Anjali Banerjee, Jean Ryan, Karen Wendy Gilbert, Jack Random and Robert R. Gass. Length: 500-5,000 words; average length: 2,500 words. Also publishes artwork, literary essays, poetry.

How to Contact: Send complete ms with a cover letter. Include name and address on page one; name on *all* other pages. Responds in 3 months. Send SASE for reply, return of ms or send a disposable copy of ms. Accepts multiple submissions. Sample copy for $7.95. Guidelines for #10 SASE.

Payment/Terms: Pays $10 and 3 contributor's copies; additional copies $3.95. Pays on acceptance for first North American serial rights.

Advice: "We consider any well-written manuscript. Characters who speak naturally and who act or are acted upon are greatly appreciated. Your high school English teacher was correct. Basics matter. Imaginative, interesting ideas are sabotaged by lack of good grammar, spelling and punctuation skills. Most submissions are contemporary/mainstream. We could use some variety. Please do not confuse confessional autobiographies with fiction."

THE MACGUFFIN, Schoolcraft College, Department of English, 18600 Haggerty Rd., Livonia MI 48152-2696. (734)462-4400, ext. 5292 or 5327. Fax: (734)462-4679. E-mail: macguffin@schoolcraft.cc.mi.us. Website: www.macguf

fin.org (includes guidelines, contests and special issues). Editor: Arthur J. Lindenberg. Managing Editor: Michael Steinberg. **Contact:** Elizabeth Kircos, fiction editor. Poetry Editor: Carol Was. Magazine: 6×9; 164 pages; 60 lb. paper; 110 lb. cover; b&w illustrations; photos. "*The MacGuffin* is a literary magazine which publishes a range of material including poetry, nonfiction and fiction. Material ranges from traditional to experimental. We hope our periodical attracts a variety of people with many different interests." Triannual. Quality fiction a special need. Estab. 1984. Circ. 600.

Needs: Adventure, contemporary, ethnic, experimental, fantasy, historical (general), humor/satire, literary, mainstream, prose poem, psychic/supernatural/occult, science fiction, translations. "No religious, inspirational, juvenile, romance, horror, pornography." Upcoming themes: "Writing in Translation." The issue focuses on all translations of freedom. This will be published in June, 2003. We will consider works until March 15, 2003. Receives 25-40 unsolicited mss/month. Accepts 5-10 mss/issue; 10-30 mss/year. Does not read mss between July 1-August 15. Publishes ms 6 months to 2 years after acceptance. Agented fiction: 10-15%. **Published 30 new writers within the last year.** Recently published work by Michael Steinberg, Tommy Zurhellen and Priscilla Donovan. Length: 100-5,000 words; average length: 2,000-2,500 words. Publishes short shorts. Also publishes literary essays. Occasionally critiques rejected mss and recommends other markets.

How to Contact: Send complete ms with cover letter, which should include: "1. *brief*, 50-word biographical information; 2. note that this *is not* a simultaneous submission." Responds in 3 months. SASE. Accepts electronic submissions. Sample copy for $6; current issue for $7. Guidelines free.

Payment/Terms: Pays 2 contributor's copies. Acquires one-time rights.

Advice: "We want to give promising new fiction writers the opportunity to publish alongside recognized writers. Be persistent. If a story is rejected, try to send it somewhere else. When we reject a story, we may accept the next one you send us. When we make suggestions for a rewrite, we may accept the revision. There seems to be a great number of good authors of fiction, but there are far too few places for publication. However, this is changing. Make your characters come to life. Even the most ordinary people become fascinating if they live for your readers."

⬤ THE MADISON REVIEW, Department of English, Helen C. White Hall, 600 N. Park St., University of Wisconsin, Madison WI 53706. (608)263-0566. E-mail: madreview@mail.student.wisc.edu. Website: http://mendota.english.wisc.edu/~madrev (includes contact information, magazine's history, publishing and prize guidelines, fiction [short story, poetry]). **Contact:** Drew Miller and Elizabeth Staudt, fiction editors. Magazine: 6×9; 180 pages. "Magazine of fiction and poetry with special emphasis on literary stories and some emphasis on Midwestern writers." Semiannual. Estab. 1978. Circ. 1,000.

Needs: Experimental and literary stories, prose poems, novel excerpts and stories in translation. "We would like to see more contemporary fiction; however, we accept fiction of any creative form and content. No historical fiction." Receives 10-50 unsolicited fiction mss/month. Acquires approximately 6 mss/issue. Does not read mss May-September. Publishes ms an average of 4 months after acceptance. **Publishes 4 new writers/year.** Recently published work by Maurice Glenn Taylor and John McNally. Length: 4,000 words average. Also publishes poetry.

How to Contact: Send complete ms with cover letter and SASE. Accepts submissions on disk. Include estimated word count, 1-page bio and list of publications. "The letter should give one or two sentences of relevant information about the writer—just enough to provide a context for the work." Responds in 4 months to mss. Accepts multiple submissions. Sample copy for $3 via postal service or e-mail.

Payment/Terms: Pays 2 contributor's copies; $2.50 charge for extras. Acquires first North American serial rights.

⬚ $ ⬤ ⬛ MALAHAT REVIEW, University of Victoria, P.O. Box 1700, STN CSC, Victoria, British Columbia V8W 2Y2 Canada. (250)721-8524. Website: www.malahatreview.com (includes guidelines, contest info, names of editors and recent contributors). E-mail: malahat@uvic.ca (for queries only). **Contact:** Marlene Cookshaw, editor. Quarterly. Circ. 1,200.

● *The Malahat Review* has received the National Magazine Award for poetry and fiction.

Needs: "General fiction and poetry." Publishes 3-4 stories/issue. **Publishes 4-5 new writers/year.** Published work by Niki Singh, Mark Anthony Jarman, Elizabeth Moret Ross, Andrew Pyper and Chris Fink. Length: 10,000 words maximum.

How to Contact: "Enclose proper postage on the SASE (or send IRC)." Responds in 3 months. No simultaneous submissions. Sample copy: $11 available through the mail; guidelines available upon request or on the web.

Payment/Terms: Pays $30/printed page and contributor's copies.

Advice: "We do encourage new writers to submit. Read the magazines you want to be published in, ask for their guidelines and follow them. Write for information on *Malahat*'s novella competitions."

⬚ ⬤ MANGROVE, University of Miami's Literary Magazine, Americonsult, 5700 NW 72nd St., Miami FL 33136. (305)717-3300. Fax: (305)717-3500. E-mail: aaaprinter@aol.com. **Contact:** Zachary Hickman. Magazine: 120 pages. "Our goal at *Mangrove* is to publish the best work without discriminating with regard to theme, style or form. We publish a wide range of material." Annual. Estab. 1992. Circ. 250.

Needs: Literary, ethnic/multicultural, mainstream/contemporary, regional, translations. Receives 10-20 unsolicited mss/month. Accepts 3-4 mss/issue. Publishes in May. Notifies writers of acceptance in May. Reads ms August-December. Recently published work by William Jackson and Orlando Ricardo Menes. Length: 20,000 words maximum. Publishes short shorts. Also publishes poetry. Sometimes comments on rejected ms.

How to Contact: Send complete ms. Include estimated word count, one-paragraph bio and list of publications with submission. SASE for reply. Accepts simultaneous, previously published and multiple submissions. Sample copy for $6, SAE. Guidelines for SASE.

Payment/Terms: Pays 3 contributor's copies. Acquires one-time rights.

Advice: "We look for stories with a distinct voice that make us look at the world in a different way. Send only one story at a time and send us your best."

$ ◙ ⅄ MANOA, A Pacific Journal of International Writing, English Dept., University of Hawaii, Honolulu HI 96822. (808)956-3070. Fax: (808)956-7808. E-mail: mjournal-l@hawaii.edu. Website: www.hawaii.edu/mjournal (includes writer's guidelines, names of editors, short fiction and poetry). Editor: Frank Stewart. **Contact:** Ian MacMillan, fiction editor. Magazine: 7×10; 240 pages. "An American literary magazine, emphasis on top US fiction and poetry, but each issue has a major guest-edited translated feature of recent writings from an Asian/Pacific country." Semiannual. Estab. 1989.

- *Manoa* has received numerous awards, and work published in the magazine has been selected for prize anthologies.

Needs: Contemporary, excerpted novel, literary, mainstream and translation (from US and nations in or bordering on the Pacific). "Part of our purpose is to present top U.S. fiction from throughout the U.S., not only to U.S. readers, but to readers in Asian and Pacific countries. We are not limited to stories related to or set in the Pacific." Accepts 1-2 mss/issue; 2-4/year. Publishes ms 6-24 months after acceptance. Agented fiction 10%. **Publishes 1-2 new writers/year.** Recently published work by Ha Jin, Catherine Ryan Hyde, Samrat Upadhyay and Josip Novakovich. Publishes short fiction. Also publishes essays, book reviews, poetry.

How to Contact: Send complete ms with cover letter or through agent. Responds in 6 months. SASE. Accepts simultaneous submissions; query before sending e-mail. Sample copy for $10. Reviews novels and short story collections. Send books or reviews to Reviews Editor.

Payment/Terms: Pays "competitive rates," and contributor's copies. Acquires first North American serial rights and one-time reprint rights. Sends copyedited galleys to author.

◙ ⅄ MANY MOUNTAINS MOVING, a literary journal of diverse contemporary voices, 420 22nd St., Boulder CO 80302-7909. (303)545-9942. Fax: (303)444-6510. E-mail: mmm@mmminc.org. Website: www.mmminc. org (includes guidelines for submission, contest guidelines). **Contact:** Naomi Horii, editor. Magazine: 6×8¾; 300 pages; recycled paper; color/heavy cover; illustrations; photos. "We publish fiction, poetry, general-interest essays and art. We try to seek contributors from all cultures." Semiannual. Estab. 1994. Circ. 2,500.

- Work from *Many Mountains Moving* has been reprinted in *Pushcart* anthology and *Best American Poetry.*

Needs: Ethnic/multicultural, experimental, feminist, gay, historical, humor/satire, lesbian, literary, mainstream/contemporary, translations. "No genre fiction. Plans special fiction issue or anthology." Receives 400 unsolicited mss/month. Accepts 4-6 mss/issue; 12-18 mss/year. Publishes ms 2-8 months after acceptance. Agented fiction 1%. Published work by Stephen Dobyns, Steven Huff, Rahna Reiko Rizzuto and Mathew Chacko. **"We try to publish at least one new writer per issue; more when possible."** Length: 3,000-10,000 words average. Publishes short shorts. Also publishes literary essays, poetry. Sometimes comments on rejected mss.

How to Contact: Send complete ms with a cover letter. Include estimated word count, list of publications. Responds in 2 weeks to queries; 3 months to mss. Send SASE for reply, return of ms or send a disposable copy of ms. Accepts simultaneous submissions. Sample copy for $6.50 and enough IRCs for 1 pound of airmail/printed matter. Guidelines for #10 SASE.

Payment/Terms: Pays 3 contributor's copies; additional copies for $3. Acquires first North American serial rights. Sends galleys to author "if requested." Sponsors a contest, $200 prize. Send SASE for guidelines. Deadline: December 31.

Advice: "We look for top-quality fiction with fresh voices and verve. We would like to see more humorous literary stories. Read at least one issue of our journal to get a feel for what kind of fiction we generally publish."

◙ ⅄ THE MARLBORO REVIEW, The Marlboro Review Inc., P.O. Box 243, Marlboro VT 05344-0243. (802)254-4938. E-mail: marlboro@marlbororeview.com. Website: www.marlbororeview.com (includes excerpts, guidelines, subscription forms, short reviews, more). **Contact:** Helen Fremont, fiction editor. Magazine: 6×9; 80-120 pages; 60 lb. paper; photos. "We are interested in cultural, philosophical, scientific and literary issues. Approached from a writer's sensibility. Our only criterion for publication is strength of work." Semiannual. Estab. 1996. Circ. 300. Member, CLMP, AWP

- Works published in *The Marlboro Review* have received Pushcart Prizes.

Needs: Literary, translations. Receives 150 unsolicited mss/month. Accepts 2-3 mss/issue; 4-6 mss/year. "Accepts manuscripts June through September." Publishes ms 1 year after acceptance. Published work by Jenny Browne, Kathleen Lester, Nancy Eimers and Alberto Rios. Length: 500-12,000 words; average length: 7,000 words. Publishes short shorts. Average length: 1,000 words. Also publishes literary essays, literary criticism and poetry.

How to Contact: Send complete ms with a brief cover letter (short bio, publication history if appropriate). Responds in 3 months to queries; 4 months to mss. Send SASE for return of ms or send a disposable copy of ms and #10 SASE for reply only. Accepts simultaneous and multiple submissions. Sample copy for $8.75. Guidelines for SASE or on website. Reviews novels, short story collections and nonfiction books of interest to writers. Send review copies to Ellen Dudley, editor.

Payment/Terms: Pays 2 contributor's copies; additional copies $5. Pays on publication. All rights revert to author on publication. Sometimes sends galleys to author.

Advice: "We're looking for work with a strong voice and sense of control. Do your apprenticeship first. The minimalist impulse seems to be passing and for that we are grateful. We love to see great, sprawling, musical, chance-taking fiction. *The God of Small Things* is the favorite of more than one editor here."

$ 🖉 📰 THE MASSACHUSETTS REVIEW, South College, University of Massachusetts, Amherst MA 01003. (413)545-2689. Fax: (413)577-0740. E-mail: massrev@external.umass.edu. Website: www.massreview.org (includes general overview, information on editors, excerpts, guidelines). Editors: Mary Heath, Paul Jenkins, David Lenson. **Contact:** Fiction Editor. Magazine: 6×9; 172 pages; 52 lb. paper; 65 lb. vellum cover; illustrations; photos. Quarterly. Estab. 1959. Circ. 1,200.

• Stories from the *Massachusetts Review* have been anthologized in the *100 Best American Short Stories of the Century* and the *Pushcart Prize* anthology.

Needs: Short stories. Wants more prose less than 30 pages. "No mystery or science fiction." Does not read fiction mss June 1-October 1. **Publishes 3-5 new writers/year.** Recently published work by Ahdaf Soueif, Elizabeth Denton and Nicholas Montemarano. Approximately 5% of fiction is agented. Also accepts poetry. Critiques rejected mss when time permits.

How to Contact: Send complete ms. No ms returned without SASE. Accepts multiple and simultaneous submissions, if noted. Responds in 2 months. Publishes ms an average of 9-12 months after acceptance. Sample copy for $8. Guidelines available for SASE or on website.

Payment/Terms: Pays $50 maximum. Pays on publication for first North American serial rights.

Advice: "Shorter rather than longer stories preferred (up to 28-30 pages)." Looks for works that "stop us in our tracks." Manuscripts that stand out use "unexpected language, idiosyncrasy of outlook and are the opposite or ordinary."

🖉 MATRIARCH'S WAY: JOURNAL OF FEMALE SUPREMACY, Artemis Creations, 3395 Nostrand Ave., 2J, Brooklyn NY 11229-4053. Phone/fax: (718)648-8215. E-mail: artemispub@sysmatrix.net. Website: www.artemiscreations.com (includes contest news, subscription info, purpose). Editor: Shirley Oliveira. **Contact:** Fiction Editor. Magazine: 5½×8½; illustrations; photos. *Matriarch's Way* is a "matriarchal feminist" publication. Biannual. Estab. 1996.

Needs: Condensed/excerpted novel, erotica (quality), ethnic/multicultural, experimental, fantasy (science, sword and sorcery), feminist (radical), horror, humor/satire, literary, psychic/supernatural/occult, religious/inspirational, romance (futuristic/time travel, gothic, historical), science fiction (soft/sociological), serialized novel. "No Christian anything." Want more "femme dominant erotica and sci-fi." Upcoming themes: "Science of Matriarchy" and "What it Means to be a Female 'Other.' " Receives 10 unsolicited mss/week. Often comments on rejected mss. **50% of work published is by new writers.**

How to Contact: Query first, query with clips of published work or query with synopsis plus 1-3 chapters of novel. Accepts queries/mss by e-mail and disk. Include estimated word count, bio and list of publications with submission. Responds in 1 week to queries; 6 weeks to mss. SASE for reply or send a disposable copy of ms. Sample copy for $10. Reviews novels and short story collections and excerpts "We need book reviewers, original or reprints. We supply books."

Payment/Terms: Acquires one-time rights.

Advice: Looks for "a knowledge of subject, originality and good writing style. If you can best Camille Paglia, you're on your way!" Looks for "professional writing—equates with our purpose/vision—brave and outspoken."

🖉 MEDICINAL PURPOSES, Literary Review, Poet to Poet Inc., 86-37 120 St., #2D, % Catterson, Richmond Hill NY 11418. (718)847-2150, (718)847-2150. **Contact:** Thomas M. Catterson, managing editor; Anthony Scarpantonio, prose editor. Magazine: 8½×11; 40 pages; illustrations. "*Medicinal Purposes* publishes quality work that will benefit the world, though not necessarily through obvious means." Semiannual. Estab. 1995. Circ. 1,000.

Needs: Adventure, erotica, ethnic/multicultural, experimental, fantasy, feminist, gay, historical, horror, humor/satire, lesbian, literary, mainstream/contemporary, mystery/suspense, psychic/supernatural/occult, regional, romance, science fiction, senior citizen/retirement, sports, westerns, young adult/teen. "Please no pornography, or hatemongering." Receives 15 unsolicited mss/month. Accepts 2-3 mss/issue; 8 mss/year. Publishes ms up to four issues after acceptance. **Publishes 24 new writers/year.** Recently published work by Charles E. Brooks and Bernadette Miller. Length: 50-3,000 words; average length: 2,000 words. "We prefer maximum of 10 double-spaced pages." Publishes short shorts. Also publishes literary essays, poetry. Sometimes comments on rejected mss.

How to Contact: Send complete ms with a cover letter. Include estimated word count, brief bio, Social Security number. Responds in 6 weeks to queries; 8 weeks to mss. SASE. Sample copy for $9, 6×9 SAE and 4 first-class stamps. Guidelines free for #10 SASE.

Payment/Terms: Pays 2 contributor's copies. Acquires first rights.

Advice: "Writers should know how to write. This occurs less often than you expect. Try to be entertaining, and write a story that was worth the effort in the first place."

$ 🖉 📰 MERIDIAN, The Semiannual from the University of Virginia, University of Virginia, P.O. Box 400145, Charlottesville VA 22904-4121. (804)924-3354. Fax: (804)924-1478. E-mail: meridian@virginia.edu. Website: www.engl.virginia.edu/meridian (includes excerpts, cover, guidelines, contact info). **Contact:** Fiction Editor. Literary magazine: 6×9; 160 pages; some illustrations. "Produced in affiliation with the University of Virginia's M.F.A. Program in Creative Writing, *Meridian* seeks to publish the best fiction, poetry, and other writing from established and emerging writers." Semiannual. Estab. 1998. Circ. 800.

● Three stories from *Meridian* were included in *New Stories From the South 2001*, one story was included among the *100 Best Stories of 2002* by the O. Henry Award Anthology and work appearing in Meridian has also been included in the Pushcart Prize anthology.

Needs: "We are open to all literary short fiction, of any reasonable theme or length." Receives 200-400 unsolicited mss/month. Accepts 8 mss/issue; 16 mss/year. Publishes ms 3-6 months after acceptance. Agented fiction 15%. **Publishes 10 new writers/year.** Recently published work by Christopher Tilghman, Percival Everett, Christie Hodgen and Karl Iagnemma. Length: any; average length: 6,000 words. Publishes short shorts. Also publishes literary essays, literary criticism and poetry. Rarely comments on rejected mss.

How to Contact: Send complete ms with cover letter. Include estimated word count, brief bio, list of publications and e-mail address. Responds in up to 4 months to mss. Send SASE for return of ms or send disposable copy of ms and #10 SASE for reply only. Accepts simultaneous and multiple submissions. Sample copy for $7. Guidelines for SASE or on website.

Payment/Terms: Pays $15/printed page, $250 maximum and 2 contributor's copies; additional copies $3.50. Acquires first North American serial rights. Sends galleys to author.

Advice: "Strong action, vivid characters, dynamic language. Keep cover letters brief and factual."

$ ⬛ **MICHIGAN QUARTERLY REVIEW**, University of Michigan, 3032 Rackham, Ann Arbor MI 48109-1070. (734)764-9265. E-mail: mqr@umich.edu. Website: www.umich.edu/~mqr (includes history and description of magazine; information on current and forthcoming issues, subscription information). Editor: Laurence Goldstein. **Contact:** Fiction Editor. "An interdisciplinary journal which publishes mainly essays and reviews, with some high-quality fiction and poetry, for an intellectual, widely read audience." Quarterly. Estab. 1962. Circ. 1,800.

● Stories from *Michigan Quarterly Review* have been selected for inclusion in *The Best American Short Stories*, *O. Henry* and *Pushcart Prize* volumes.

Needs: Literary. "No genre fiction written for a market. Would like to see more fiction about social, political, cultural matters, not just centered on a love relationship or dysfunctional family." Receives 200 unsolicited fiction mss/month. Accepts 2 mss/issue; 8 mss/year. **Publishes 1-2 new writers/year.** Published work by Nicholas Delbanco, Elizabeth Searle, Marian Thurm and Lucy Ferriss. Length: 1,500-7,000 words; average length: 5,000 words. Also publishes poetry, literary essays.

How to Contact: Send complete ms with cover letter. "I like to know if a writer is at the beginning, or further along, in his or her career. Don't offer plot summaries of the story, though a background comment is welcome." Responds in 2 months. SASE. No simultaneous submissions. Sample copy for $2.50 and 2 first-class stamps.

Payment/Terms: Pays $8-10/printed page. Pays on publication for first rights. Awards the Lawrence Foundation Prize of $1,000 for best story in *MQR* previous year.

Advice: "There's no beating a good plot and interesting characters, and a fresh use of the English language. (Most stories fail because they're written in such a bland manner, or in TV-speak.) Be ambitious, try to involve the social world in the personal one, be aware of what the best writing of today is doing, don't be satisfied with a small slice of life narrative but think how to go beyond the ordinary."

$ ◐ ⬛ **MID-AMERICAN REVIEW**, Department of English, Bowling Green State University, Bowling Green OH 43403. (419)372-2725. Website: www.bgsu.edu/midamericanreview (includes submission guidelines, sample work and contest info). **Contact:** Michael Czyzniejewski, fiction editor. Magazine: 6×9; 176 pages; 60 lb. bond paper; coated cover stock. "We try to put the best possible work in front of the biggest possible audience. We publish serious fiction and poetry, as well as critical studies in contemporary literature, translations and book reviews." Biannual. Estab. 1981.

● Work published in *Mid-American Review* has received the Pushcart Prize.

Needs: Experimental, literary, memoir, prose poem, traditional and translations. "No genre fiction. Would like to see more short shorts." Receives about 150 unsolicited fiction mss/month. Accepts 6-8 mss/issue. Approximately 5% of fiction is agented. **Publishes 4-8 new writers/year.** Recently published work by Aimee Bender, Steve Almond, Alvin Greenberg and Melanie Rae Thon. Length: 25 pages maximum. Also publishes essays and poetry. Occasionally critiques rejected mss. Sponsors the Sherwood Anderson Short Fiction Award.

How to Contact: Send complete ms with SASE. Responds in about 4 months. Publishes ms an average of 6 months after acceptance. Sample copy for $5. Reviews novels and short story collections. Send books to editor-in-chief.

Payment/Terms: Pays $10/page, up to $50 and 2 contributor's copies; charges for additional copies. Acquires first North American serial rights.

Advice: "We look for well-written stories that make the reader want to read on past the first line and page. Clichéd themes and sloppy writing turn us off immediately. Read literary journals to see what's being published in today's market. We tend to publish work that is more non-traditional in style and form, but are open to all literary non-genre submissions."

◎ **MINAS TIRITH EVENING-STAR**, W.W. Publications, Box 7871, Flint MI 48507. **Contact:** Philip Helms, editor. Magazine: 5½×8½; 24 pages; typewriter paper; black ink illustrations; photos. Magazine of J.R.R. Tolkien and fantasy—fiction, poetry, reviews, etc. for general audience. Quarterly. Published special fiction issue; plans another. Estab. 1967. Circ. 500.

Needs: "Fantasy and Tolkien." Receives 5 unsolicited mss/month. Accepts 1 ms/issue; 5 mss/year. **Publishes 5-10 new writers/year.** Length: 5,000 words maximum; 1,000-1,200 words preferred. Publishes short shorts. Also publishes literary essays, literary criticism, poetry. Occasionally critiques rejected mss.
How to Contact: Send complete ms and bio. Accepts mss by fax and on disk. Responds in 2 months. SASE. No simultaneous submissions. Accepts reprint and multiple submissions. Sample copy for $2. Reviews novels and short story collections.
Terms: Acquires first rights.
Advice: Goal is "to expand knowledge and enjoyment of J.R.R. Tolkien's and his son Christopher Tolkien's works and their worlds."

MINDPRINTS, A Literary Journal, Disabled Student Programs and Services, Allan Hancock College, 800 S. College Dr., Santa Maria CA 93454-6399. (805)922-6966, ext. 3274. Fax: (805)922-3556. E-mail: pfahey@hancock.cc.ca.us. Website: www.hancock.cc.ca.us/studentservices/learning_assistance/mindprints/index.html. **Contact:** Paul Fahey, editor. Magazine: 6×9; 125-150 pages; 50 lb. white offset paper; glossy cover; illustrations; photos. "*Mindprints, A Literary Journal* is one of a very few college publications created as a forum for writers and artists with disabilities or for those with an interest in the field. The emphasis on flash fiction and the fact that we are a national journal as well puts us on the cutting edge of today's market." Annual. Estab. 2000. Circ. 500.
• *Mindprints* ranked on *Writer's Digest*'s "Top 30" list of best fiction markets.
Needs: Literary, mainstream. Receives 20-30 unsolicited mss/month. Accepts 60 mss/year. Does not read mss June-August. Publishes ms 6 months after acceptance. **Publishes 25-30 new writers/year.** Published work by Catherine Ryan Hyde, Ingrid Reti, Wendy Whitaker and Denize Lavoie Cain. Length: 250-750 words; average length: 500 words. Publishes short shorts. Average length: 400-500 words. Also publishes poetry. Often comments on rejected mss.
How to Contact: Send complete ms with a cover letter. No e-mail submissions unless writer resides outside US. Include estimated word count, brief bio, list of publications and "reasons why you are submitting to *Mindprints*; your interest in the disability field, etc." Responds in 1 week to queries; 4 months to mss. Send a disposable copy of ms and #10 SASE for reply only. Accepts simultaneous, previously published and multiple (2 shorts/memoirs) submissions. Sample copy for $5 and $2 postage or IRCs. Guidelines for SASE, by e-mail or fax.
Payment/Terms: Pays 1 contributor's copy; additional copies $5. Pays on publication for one-time rights. Not copyrighted.
Advice: "We look for a great hook; a story that grabs us from the beginning; fiction and memoir with a strong voice and unusual themes; stories with a narrowness of focus yet broad in their appeal. We would like to see more flash or very short fiction. Read and study the flash fiction genre. *Flash Fiction* by Thomas, Thomas and Hazuka is highly recommended. Revise, revise, revise. Do not send manuscripts that have not been proofed. Our mission is to showcase as many voices and world views as possible. We want our readers to sample creative talent from a national and international group of published and unpublished writers and artists."

THE MINNESOTA REVIEW, A Journal of Committed Writing, Dept. of English, University of Missouri, Columbia MO 65211. (573)882-3059. Fax: (573)882-5785. E-mail: WilliamsJeff@missouri.edu. Website: http://theminnesotareview.org (includes writer's guidelines, names of editors, excerpts from publication). **Contact:** Jeffrey Williams, editor. Magazine: 5¼×7½; approximately 200 pages; some illustrations; occasional photos. "We emphasize socially and politically engaged work." Semiannual. Estab. 1960. Circ. 1,500.
Needs: Experimental, feminist, gay, historical, lesbian, literary. Receives 50-75 mss/month. Accepts 3-4 mss/issue; 6-8 mss/year. Publishes ms within 6-12 months after acceptance. **Publishes 3-5 new writers/year.** Recently published work by E. Shaskan Bumas, Carlos Fuentes, Maggie Jaffe and James Hughes. Length: 1,500-6,000 words preferred. Publishes short shorts. Also publishes literary essays, literary criticism, poetry. Occasionally critiques rejected mss and recommends other markets.
How to Contact: Send complete ms with optional cover letter. Responds in 3 weeks to queries; 3 months to mss. SASE. Accepts simultaneous and multiple submissions. Reviews novels and short story collections. Send books to book review editor.
Payment/Terms: Pays in contributor's copies. Charge for additional copies. Acquires first rights.
Advice: "We look for socially and politically engaged work, particularly short, striking work that stretches boundaries."

$ THE MISSING FEZ, A Biannual Publication of Unconventional and Otherwise Abnormal Literature, Red Felt Publishing, P.O. Box 57310, Tucson AZ 85711. (520)747-2348. E-mail: missingfez@hotmail.com. Website: www.missingfez.com. **Contact:** Eleanor Horner, fiction editor. Magazine: 8½×7; 18-20 pages; semigloss paper; glossy cover. "We strive to publish fiction of high quality which for some reason falls outside the traditional literary spectrum." Biannual. Estab. 2000. Circ. 1,000.
Needs: Erotica, experimental, fantasy (space fantasy), feminist, gay, horror, humor/satire, literary, mainstream, mystery/suspense (private eye/hardboiled), psychic/supernatural/occult, science fiction, thriller/espionage. Would like to see more humor, satire, experimentation. "Please do not send anecdotes or lessons of morality." Receives 30 unsolicited mss/month. Accepts 10-15 mss/issue; 20-30 mss/year. Publishes ms 6-12 months after acceptance. Agented fiction 20%. **Publishes 10-15 new writers/year.** Published work by Joanna Kosowsky, Peter Hoffman and Alice Whittenburg. Length: 10-8,000 words; average length: 5,000 words. Publishes short shorts. Average length: 1,000 words. Also publishes poetry. Always comments on rejected mss.

How to Contact: Send complete ms with a cover letter and $3 reading fee payable to: Red Felt Publishing. Include estimated word count and list of publications. Responds in 6-12 weeks to mss. Send a disposable copy of ms and #10 SASE for reply only. Accepts simultaneous submissions. Sample copy for $3. Guidelines for SASE or by e-mail.
Payment/Terms: Pays $25 and 2 contributor's copies; additional copies $3. Pays on acceptance for first rights. Sponsors contest. Send SASE for guidelines. Visit website for sample pieces and upcoming contest info.
Advice: "We get a lot of stories about morality and doing the right thing—we would like to see less of this."

■ ■ MISSISSIPPI REVIEW, University of Southern Mississippi, Box 5144, Hattiesburg MS 39406-5144. (601)266-4321. Fax: (601)266-5757. E-mail: fb@netdoor.com. Website: http://sushi.st.usm.edu/mrw/. (The website publishes new work, independent of the print edition. It is open for electronic submissions. Check the site for current reading editors.) **Contact:** Rie Fortenberry, managing editor. "Literary publication for those interested in contemporary literature—writers, editors who read to be in touch with current modes." Semiannual. Estab. 1972. Circ. 1,500.
Needs: Literary, contemporary, fantasy, humor, translations, experimental, avant-garde and "art" fiction. Quality writing. "No juvenile or genre fiction." Theme issues for the print edition are solicited; theme issues for the web version are listed on the site and are open to unsolicited submissions. Buys varied amount of mss/issue. Does not read mss in summer. **Publishes 10-20 new writers/year.** Published work by Jason Brown, Terese Svoboda and Barry Hannah. Length: 30 pages maximum.
How to Contact: Not currently reading unsolicited work. Submit work via e-mail to our World Wide Web publication, which is a monthly (except August) and publishes more new work than we are able to in the print version. Send submissions to fb@netdoor.com as ASCII files in the text of your e-mail message, or as Microsoft Word or WordPerfect attachments to your message. Sample copy for $8.
Payment/Terms: Pays in contributor's copies. Acquires first North American serial rights.

$ ■ ▼ THE MISSOURI REVIEW, 1507 Hillcrest Hall, University of Missouri—Columbia, Columbia MO 65211. (573)882-4474. Fax: (573)884-4671. Website: www.missourireview.org (includes guidelines, contest information, staff photos, editorial column, short fiction, poetry, essays, interviews, features and book reviews). **Contact:** Speer Morgan, editor. Magazine: 6×9; 212 pages. Theme: fiction, poetry, essays, reviews, interviews, cartoons, "all with a distinctly contemporary orientation. For writers, and the general reader with broad literary interests. We present nonestablished as well as established writers of excellence. The *Review* often runs feature sections or special issues dedicated to particular topics frequently related to fiction." Published 3 times/academic year. Estab. 1977. Circ. 6,800.
● This magazine had stories anthologized in the *Pushcart Prize Anthology, Best American Short Stories, Best American Erotica* and *New Stories From the South.*
Needs: Condensed/excerpted novel, ethnic/multicultural, humor/satire, literary, contemporary. "No genre or children's." Receives approximately 400 unsolicited fiction mss each month. Accepts 5-7 mss/issue; 16-20 mss/year. **Publishes 6-10 new writers/year.** Recently published work by Judy Troy, Willa Rabinowitz, Jesse Lee Kercheval and Michael Byers. No preferred length. Also publishes personal essays, poetry. Often critiques rejected mss.
How to Contact: Send complete ms with SASE. May include brief bio and list of publications. Responds in 10 weeks. Send SASE for reply, return of ms or send disposable copy of ms. Sample copy for $8.
Payment/Terms: Pays $30/printed page minimum on signed contract for all rights. Awards William Peden Prize in fiction; $1,000 to best story published in *Missouri Review* in a given year. Also sponsors Editors' Prize Contest with a prize of $2,000 for fiction, $2,000 for essays and the Larry Levis Editors' Prize for poetry, with a prize of $2,000; and the Tom McAfee Discovery Prize in poetry for poets who have not yet published a book.

Ⓝ ■ MM REVIEW, Finishing Line Press, P.O. Box 1016, Cincinnati OH 45201-1016. E-mail: finishingl@aol.com. Website: members.aol.com/finishingl (includes writer's guidelines, contests and books sales information). Editor: C.J. Morrison. **Fiction editor:** Elle Larkin. Magazine: 6×9; 35 pages; cotton paper; linen or cotton cover. "We are a literary magazine interested in publishing serious verse and excellent fiction, drama and essays." Semiannual. Estab. 1998. Circ. 500.
Needs: Literary. "No children's/juvenile or young adult/teen. No erotica." Receives 50 unsolicited mss/month. Accepts 1-4 mss/issue; 2-8 mss/year. Publishes ms 6 months after acceptance. **Publishes 20% new writers/year.** Published work by Alexandra Grilikhes, Rane Arroyo, Leah Maines, Tanya Preminger and Irene Sedeora. Word length: 500-700 words average. Publishes short shorts. Length: 500 words. Also publishes literary essays, poetry and drama. Often comments on or critiques rejected ms.
How to Contact: Send complete ms with a cover letter. "We want a cover letter and bio listing past publication credits, if any. Please no long bios, 50-75 words." Responds in 1 month to queries; 6 months to mss. Reviews novels, short story collections and nonfiction of interest to writers. Send books to *MM Review.*
Payment/Terms: Pays 1 contributor's copy; additional copies $4. Pays on publication for one-time rights. "Rights revert back to authors after publication." Sends galleys to the author.
Advice: "Excellence is our only criteria. We enjoy 'pushing the envelope' and are interested in experimental and cutting edge writing. We do not want 'grandma stories.' Send a clean manuscript free of typos, spelling/grammar errors and/or coffee stains! Please do not send long bios listing every place you have been published since high school plus your cat's name! No 'cute' cover letters. Writing is a business."

Ⓝ ■ MOBIUS, The Journal of Social Change, 505 Christianson, Madison WI 53714. (608)242-1009. E-mail: fmschep@charter.net. Website: www.mobiusmagazine.com. **Contact:** Fred Schepartz, editor. Magazine: 8½×11; 16-

24 pages; 60 lb. paper; 60 lb. cover. "Looking for fiction which uses social change as either a primary or secondary theme. This is broader than most people think. Need social relevance in one way or another. For an artistically and politically aware and curious audience." Quarterly. Estab. 1989. Circ. 1,500.

Needs: Contemporary, ethnic, experimental, fantasy, feminist, gay, historical, horror, humor/satire, lesbian, literary, mainstream, prose poem, science fiction. "No porn, no racist, sexist or any other kind of ist. No Christian or spiritually proselytizing fiction." Wants to see more science fiction, erotica "assuming it relates to social change." Receives 15 unsolicited mss/month. Accepts 3-5 mss/issue. Publishes ms 3-9 months after acceptance. **Publishes 10 new writers/ year.** Recently published work by Margaret Karmazin and Ken Byrnes. Length: 500-5,000 words; 3,500 words preferred. Publishes short shorts. Length: 500 words. Always critiques rejected mss.

How to Contact: Send complete ms with cover letter. Accepts submissions by e-mail. Responds in 4 months. SASE. Accepts simultaneous, multiple and reprint submissions. Sample copy for $2, 9×12 SAE and 3 first-class stamps. Guidelines for SASE. "Please include return postage, not IRCs, in overseas submissions."

Payment/Terms: Pays contributor's copies. Acquires one-time rights and electronic rights for www version.

Advice: "Note that fiction and poetry may be simultaneously published in e-version of *Mobius*. Due to space constraints of print version, some works may be accepted in e-version, but not print version. We like high impact, we like plot and character-driven stories that function like theater of the mind." Looks for "first and foremost, good writing. Prose must be crisp and polished; the story must pique my interest and make me care due to a certain intellectual, emotional aspect. Second, *Mobius* is about social change. We want stories that make some statement about the society we live in, either on a macro or micro level. Not that your story needs to preach from a soapbox (actually, we prefer that it doesn't), but your story needs to have *something* to say."

THE MOCHILA REVIEW, International Literary Journal, Dept. of English, Foreign Languages & Journalism, Missouri Western State College, 4525 Downs Dr., St. Joseph MO 64507. Website: www.mwsc.edu/~mochila. **Contact:** Faculty Advisor. Magazine: 9×6; 112-160 pages; b&w paper; perfect binding; illustrations; photos. "In the material we publish we want to express the emotions and spirit, to claim the deep resonance of shared time." Annual. Estab. 2000. Circ. 750. Member, CLMP.

Needs: Adventure, ethnic/multicultural, excerpted novel, experimental, fantasy, feminist, gay, historical, horror, humor/ satire, lesbian, literary, mainstream, military/war, mystery/suspense, New Age, psychic/supernatural/occult, regional (Midwest especially), religious, science fiction, thriller/espionage, translations, western, young adult/teen. "No poorly done work of any kind—no pornography, no graphic/sexual violence." Receives 25 unsolicited mss/month. Accepts 4-6 mss/issue. Does not read mss December 2-July 30. Publishes ms 3 months after acceptance. **Publishes 2 new writers/ year.** Recently published work by Alice Brooks-Smith, Mary Cantrell, Rick Christman and Paulo da Costa. Length: 2,500-4,500 words; average length: 3,500 words. Publishes short shorts. Average length: 1,000 words. Also publishes literary essays and poetry.

How to Contact: Send complete ms with a cover letter. Send hard copy only, then on disk if accepted. Include estimated word count. Responds in 4-6 weeks to queries; 2-3 months to mss. Send SASE for return of ms or send a disposable copy of ms and #10 SASE for reply only. Accepts multiple submissions. Sample copy for $6. Guidelines for SASE or on website. Reviews short story collections and nonfiction books of interest to writers. Send review copies to Faculty Editor.

Payment/Terms: Pays 2 contributor's copies; additional copies $6; back issues $3. Acquires first North American serial rights. Sends galleys to author. Each submission published is considered for the John Gilgun Award for Fiction— there is no fee. See online guidelines or send SASE.

MOTA, An Annual Anthology of Fine Fiction, Triple Tree Publishing, P.O. Box 5684, Eugene OR 97405. (541)338-3184. Fax: (541)484-5358. E-mail: submit@tripletreepub.com. Website: www.tripletreepub.com (includes submission guidelines, contest information for emerging writers contest). **Contact:** Editor. Magazine: 5½×8½; 300 pages; 60 lb. paper. "It is our intention to publish an extraordinary annual anthology of fiction, devoted to the challenging issues of our times as played out in fictional scenarios." Annual. Estab. 2002.

Needs: Adventure, erotica, ethnic/multicultural, experimental, family saga, fantasy, feminist, gay, historical, horror, humor/satire, lesbian, literary, mainstream, military/war, mystery/suspense, New Age, psychic/supernatural/occult, religious, romance, science fiction, thriller/espionage, translations, western. Upcoming themes: Courage (2003); Integrity (2004). Receives 30 unsolicited mss/month. Accepts 20 mss/year. Publishes ms 6 months after acceptance. **Publishes 10 percent new writers/year.** Maximum length: 8,000 words; average length: 3,000 words. Publishes short shorts.

How to Contact: Send complete ms with cover letter. Include estimated word count and list of publications. Responds to queries/mss in December (after deadline). Send disposable copy of ms and SASE for reply only. Accepts simultaneous, previously published and multiple submissions. Sample copy for $16.95 and postage. Guidelines for SASE and on website.

Payment/Terms: Pays $100 and 1 contributor's copy. Pays on publication for one time rights. Sends prepublication galleys to author.

Advice: "Be original—remember, your strength is your strangeness. Submit only your absolute best. Competition is stiff."

NASSAU REVIEW, Nassau Community College, State University of New York, 1 Education Dr., Garden City NY 11530-6793. (516)572-7792. **Contact:** Editorial Board. Magazine: 6½×9½; 200 pages; heavy stock paper and cover; illustrations; photos. "Looking for high-level, professionally talented fiction on any subject matter except science fiction. Intended for a college and university faculty-level audience. Not geared to college students or others of that age who have not yet reached professional competency." Annual. Estab. 1964. Circ. 1,200. Member, Council of Literary Magazines & Presses.

Needs: Historical (general), humor/satire, literary, mainstream, mystery/suspense (amateur sleuth, cozy). "No science fiction." Receives 40-50 unsolicited mss/month. Accepts 7-10 mss/year. Does not read mss April-October. Publishes ms 6 months after acceptance. **Publishes 2 new writers/year.** Published work by Louis Phillips, Dick Wimmer, Norbert Petsch and Mike Lipstock. Length: 2,000-6,000 words; average length: 3,000-4,000 words. Publishes short shorts. Average length: 1,200 words. Also publishes literary essays, literary criticism and poetry.

How to Contact: Send 3 copies of complete ms with a cover letter. Include brief bio and list of publications. No simultaneous submissions. Responds in 2 weeks to queries; up to 6 months to mss. Send a disposable copy of ms and #10 SASE for reply only. Sample copy free.

Payment/Terms: Pays contributor's copies. Acquires one-time rights. Sponsors contest for best short story each year. $150 prize.

Advice: "We look for narrative drive, perceptive characterization and professional competence."

N. ○ NATURAL BRIDGE, English Department, University of Missouri–St. Louis, 8001 Natural Bridge Rd., St. Louis MO 63121-4499. (314)516-7327. Fax: (314)516-5781. E-mail: natural@jinx.umsl.edu. Website: www.umsl.edu/~natural (includes writer's guidelines, excerpts, calls for submissions to future special issues, editors' bios, background and philosophy. **Contact:** David Carkeet, editor. Magazine: 6×9; 250 pages; 60 lb. opaque recycled paper; 12 pt. coated matte cover. "*Natural Bridge* is published by the UM-St. Louis MFA Program. Faculty and graduate students work together in selecting manuscripts, with a strong emphasis on originality, freshness, honesty, vitality, energy, and linguistic skill. We work closely with writers when a piece merits it." Semiannual. Estab. 1999. Circ. 400. Member, CLMP.

Needs: Literary. List of upcoming themes available for SASE or online. Receives 750 unsolicited mss/year. Accepts 35 mss/issue; 70 mss/year. Submit only July 1-August 31 and November 1-December 31. Publishes ms 9 months after acceptance. **Publishes 5 new writers/year.** Recently published work by A.E. Hotchner, Brian Doyle, Jennifer Haigh and Jim Ray Daniels. Publishes short shorts. Also publishes personal essays and poetry. Sometimes comments on rejected mss.

How to Contact: Send complete ms with a cover letter. Include brief bio. Responds in 5 months to mss. Send SASE for return of ms or send a disposable copy of ms and #10 SASE for reply only. Accepts simultaneous submissions. Sample copy for $8. Guidelines for SASE, e-mail or on website.

Payment/Terms: Pays 2 contributor's copies; additional copies $5. Acquires first North American serial rights.

Advice: "We look for fresh stories, extremely well written, on any subject. We publish mainstream literary fiction. We want stories that work on first and subsequent readings—stories, in other words, that both entertain and resonate. Study the journal. Read all of the fiction in it, especially in a fiction-heavy issue like no. 4 or no. 6."

○ NEBO, A Literary Journal, Arkansas Tech University, Dept. of English, Russellville AR 72801. (501)968-0256. Editors change each year. **Contact:** Dr. Michael Karl Ritchie, editor. Literary, fiction and poetry magazine: 5×8; 50-60 pages. For a general, academic audience. Annual. Estab. 1983. Circ. 500.

Needs: Literary, mainstream, reviews. Upcoming theme: pop icon fiction and poetry (fiction and poetry that plays with the roles of pop icons). Receives 20-30 unsolicited fiction mss/month. Accepts 2 mss/issue; 6-10 mss/year. Does not read mss May 1-September 1. **Published new writers within the last year.** Published work by Steven Sherrill, J.B. Bernstein, Jameson Currier, Tricia Lande and Joseph Nicholson. Length: 3,000 words maximum. Also publishes literary essays, literary criticism, poetry. Occasionally critiques rejected mss.

How to Contact: Send complete ms with SASE and cover letter with bio. No simultaneous submissions. Responds in 3 months to mss. Publishes ms an average of 6 months after acceptance. Sample copy for $6. "Submission deadlines for all work are November 15 and January 15 of each year." Reviews novels and short story collections.

Payment/Terms: Pays 1 contributor's copy. Acquires one-time rights.

Advice: "A writer should carefully edit his short story before submitting it. Write from the heart and put everything on the line. Don't write from a phony or fake perspective. Frankly, many of the manuscripts we receive should be publishable with a little polishing. Manuscripts should *never* be submitted with misspelled words or on 'onion skin' or colored paper."

○ ☒ THE NEBRASKA REVIEW, University of Nebraska at Omaha, Omaha NE 68182-0324. (402)554-3159. E-mail: jreed@unomaha.edu. **Contact:** James Reed, fiction editor. Magazine: 5½×8½; 108 pages; 60 lb. text paper; chrome coat cover stock. "*TNR* attempts to publish the finest available contemporary fiction, poetry and creative nonfiction for college and literary audiences." Publishes 2 issues/year. Estab. 1973. Circ. 1,000.

● Work published in *The Nebraska Review* was reprinted in *New Stories From the South* and the *Pushcart Prize Anthology.*

Needs: Contemporary, humor/satire, literary and mainstream. "No genre fiction." Receives 40 unsolicited fiction mss/month. Accepts 4-5 mss/issue, 8-10 mss/year. Reads for the *Nebraska Review* Awards in Fiction and Poetry and Creative Nonfiction September 1 through November 30. Open to submissions January 1-April 30; does not read May 1-August 31. **Publishes 2-3 new writers/year.** Published work by Cris Mazza, Mark Wisniewski, Stewart O'Nan, Elaine Ford and Tom Franklin. Length: 5,000-6,000 words average. Also publishes poetry and creative nonfiction.

How to Contact: Send complete ms with SASE. Responds in 6 months. Publishes ms an average of 6-12 months after acceptance. Sample copy for $4.50.

Payment/Terms: Pays 2 contributor's copies and 1 year subscription; additional copies $4. Acquires first North American serial rights.

Advice: "Write stories in which the lives of your characters are the primary reason for writing and techniques of craft serve to illuminate, not overshadow, the textures of those lives. Sponsors a $500 award/year—write for rules."

NEOTROPE, Broken Boulder Press, P.O. Box 6305, Santa Barbara CA 93160. E-mail: apowell10@hotmail.com. Website: www.brokenboulder.com (includes submission guidelines, ordering information and addresses, samples of published work, and general information about press). Editors: Adam Powell, Paul Silvia. **Contact:** Adam Powell. Magazine: 5½×8½; 160 pages; perfect-bound; illustrations; photos. "We view *Neotrope* as a deprogramming tool for refugees from MPW programs and fiction workshops. We are seeking aggressively experimental fiction. We publish new and progressive forms of fiction writing, stories that are experimental in structure, style, subject matter and execution. We don't target any specific groups, but trust our audience to define itself." Published annually in January. Estab. 1998. Circ. 1,100.

Needs: Experimental fiction and drama. "No genre fiction, erotica, gothic, inspirational, nothing traditional." Receives 60-100 unsolicited mss/month. Accepts 12-15 mss/issue. Publishes ms up to 1 year after acceptance. **Publishes 1-5 new writers/year.** Recently published works by Joy Kaplan, Matvei Yankelevich, John Wurth and William Jackson. Length: open. Publishes short shorts. Always comments on rejected ms.

How to Contact: Send complete ms with a cover letter and SASE. Responds in 1 month. Accepts multiple submissions. Sample copy for $5 postpaid. Guidelines free.

Payment/Terms: Pays 5 contributor's copies; additional copies at cost. Acquires one-time rights. Usually sends galleys to author.

Advice: "If it reminds me of something I've seen before, it's not ready for *Neotrope*. You can never take too much time to develop your art. I despise this unwritten code of honor among editors which prohibits all but the most general and impersonal replies with returned manuscripts. Most editors don't even bother to sign their names to a xeroxed rejection slip. Those people who are confident enough to set themselves up as the caretakers of contemporary literature have an obligation to prove their worth by helping other writers along."

NERVE COWBOY, Liquid Paper Press, P.O. Box 4973, Austin TX 78765. Website: www.onr.com/user/junagins/nervecowboy.com.html. **Contact:** Joseph Shields or Jerry Hagins, editors. Magazine: 7×8½; 60-64 pages; 20 lb. paper; card stock cover; illustrations. "*Nerve Cowboy* publishes adventurous, comical, disturbing, thought-provoking, accessible poetry and fiction. We like to see work sensitive enough to make the hardest hard-ass cry, funny enough to make the most hopeless brooder laugh and disturbing enough to make us all glad we're not the author of the piece." Semiannual. Estab. 1996. Circ. 300.

● Sponsors an annual chapbook contest for fiction or poetry. Deadline January 30. Send SASE for details.

Needs: Literary. No "racist, sexist or overly offensive" work. Wants more "unusual stories with rich description and enough twists and turns that leaves the reader thinking." Receives 40 unsolicited mss/month. Accepts 2-3 mss/issue; 4-6 mss/year. Publishes ms 6-12 months after acceptance. **Publishes 5-10 new writers/year.** Recently published work by Albert Huffstickler, Celeste Bowman, Dave Newman, Marie Goyette, Charlene Logan and Mark Safrank. Length: 1,500 words maximum; average length: 750-1,000 words. Publishes short shorts. Also publishes poetry.

How to Contact: Send complete ms with a cover letter. Include bio and list of publications. Responds in 2 weeks to queries; 2 months to mss. Send SASE for reply, return of ms or send disposable copy of ms. No simultaneous submissions. Accepts reprints. Sample copy for $5. Guidelines for #10 SASE.

Payment/Terms: Pays 1 contributor's copy. Acquires one-time rights.

Advice: "We look for writing which is very direct and elicits a visceral reaction in the reader. Read magazines you submit to in order to get a feel for what the editors are looking for. Write simply and from the gut."

NEW DELTA REVIEW, Creative Writing Programs, English Dept./Louisiana State University, Baton Rouge LA 70803-5001. (225)578-4079. E-mail: new-delta@lsu.edu. Website: www.english.lsu.edu/journals/ndr (includes submission guidelines, current issue, writing samples, archives, contest information, MFA program information, staff list). Editor-in-Chief: Andrew Spear. **Contact:** Sean Cavenaugh, fiction editor. Editors change every year. Magazine: 6×9; 75-125 pages; high quality paper; glossy card cover; b&w illustrations and artwork. "We seek vivid and exciting work from new and established writers. We have published fiction from writers such as Stacy Richter, Mark Poirier and George Singleton." Semiannual. Estab. 1984. Circ. 500.

● *New Delta Review* also sponsors the Matt Clark Prizes for fiction and poetry. Work from the magazine has been included in the *Pushcart Prize* anthology.

Needs: Contemporary, humor/satire, literary, mainstream, prose poem, translations. "No Elvis stories, overwrought 'Southern' fiction seemingly inspired by Tennessee Williams, or cancer stories. And no metafiction, either." Receives 200 unsolicited mss/ month. Accepts 3-4 mss/issue, 6-8 mss/year. **Publishes 1-3 new writers/year.** Recently published work by George Berridge, Jr., Ted Graf, Hayley R. Mitchell and Rebecah Edwards. Length: 250 words minimum; average length: 15 ms pages. Publishes short shorts. Also publishes poetry. Rarely critiques rejected mss.

How to Contact: Send complete ms with cover letter. Cover letter should include estimated word count, bio "credits, if any; no synopses, please." Accepts queries/mss by fax. No simultaneous submissions. Responds to queries in 3 weeks; 3 months to mss. SASE (or IRC). Reads from August 15-May 15. Sample copy for $6. Reviews novels and short story collections.

Payment/Terms: Pays in contributor's copies. Charge for extras. Acquires first North American serial rights and electronic rights. Sponsors award for fiction writers in each issue. Matt Clark Prize winner published in Spring. Mss selected for publication are automatically considered.

Advice: "Our staff is open-minded and youthful. We base decisions on merit, not reputation. The manuscript that's most enjoyable to read gets the nod."

$ ◐ NEW ENGLAND REVIEW, Middlebury College, Middlebury VT 05753. (802)443-5075. E-mail: nereview @mail.middlebury.edu. Website: www.middlebury.edu/~nereview (includes guidelines, staff, ordering information, sample works from current and back issues). **Contact:** Stephen Donadio, editor. Magazine: 7×10; 180 pages; 50 lb paper; coated cover stock. A literary quarterly publishing fiction, poetry and essays with special emphasis on contemporary cultural issues, both in the US and abroad. For general readers and professional writers. Quarterly. Estab. 1977. Circ. 2,000.

Needs: Literary. Receives 250 unsolicited fiction mss/month. Accepts 5 mss/issue; 20 mss/year. Does not read mss June-August. **Publishes 1-2 new writers/year.** Recently published work by Steve Almond, Padgett Powell, Peter Cameron and Joann Kobin. Publishes ms 3-9 months after acceptance. Agented fiction: less than 5%. Prose length: 10,000 words maximum, double spaced. Novellas: 30,000 words maximum. Publishes short shorts occasionally. Sometimes critiques rejected mss.

How to Contact: Send complete ms with cover letter. "Cover letters that demonstrate that the writer knows the magazine are the ones we want to read. We don't want hype, or hard-sell, or summaries of the author's intentions. Will consider simultaneous submissions, but must be stated as such." Responds in 15 weeks to mss. SASE.

Payment/Terms: Pays $10/page, $20 minimum and 2 contributor's copies; charge for extras. Pays on publication for first rights and reprint rights. Sends galleys to author.

Advice: "It's best to send one story at a time, and wait until you hear back from us to try again."

◐ NEW LAUREL REVIEW, New Orleans Poetry Forum/New Laurel Review, 828 Lesseps St., New Orleans LA 70117. Phone/fax: (504)947-6001. **Editor:** Lee Meitzen Grue. Poetry Editor: Lenny Emmanuel. Magazine: 6½×8; 125 pages; 60 lb. white paper; illustrations; photos. Journal of poetry, fiction, critical articles and reviews. "We have published such internationally known writers as James Nolan, Tomris Uyar and Yevgeny Yevtushenko." Readership: "Literate, adult audiences as well as anyone interested in writing with significance, human interest, vitality, subtlety, etc." Published irregularly. Estab. 1970. Circ. 500. Member, Council of Editors of Learned Journals.

Needs: Literary, ethnic/multicultural, excerpted novel, translations, "cutting edge." No "dogmatic, excessively inspirational or political" material. No science fiction. Want more classic short story and experimental short story. Acquires 1-2 fiction mss/issue. Receives approximately 25 unsolicited fiction mss each month. Does not read mss during summer months and December. Agented fiction 10%. **Publishes 2-3 new writers/year.** Recently published work by Frank Durham. Length: about 10 printed pages. Publishes short shorts. Also publishes literary essays and poetry. Critiques rejected mss when there is time.

How to Contact: Send complete ms with a cover letter. Include bio and list of publications. Responds in 3 months. Send SASE for reply or return of ms. No simultaneous submissions. Sample copy for $10. "Authors need to look at sample copy before submitting."

Payment/Terms: Pays 1 contributor's copy; additional copies $10, discounted. Acquires first rights.

Advice: "Patience: magazines have little or no money and are staffed by working writers."

$ ◐ ⛉ NEW LETTERS MAGAZINE, University of Missouri-Kansas City, University House, 5101 Rockhill Rd., Kansas City MO 64110. (816)235-2610. Fax: (816)235-2611. E-mail: stewartr@umkc.edu. Website: www.umkc. edu/newletters (includes writer's and awards guidelines, back issue availability, samples from magazine, staff information). **Contact:** Robert Stewart, editor. Magazine: 14 lb. cream paper; illustrations. "We publish good literary contemporary writing, interviews, translations, photography, and art. The writing features a mix of poetry, fiction, and essay. It is distributed internationally and targets college-educated readers." Quarterly. Estab. 1971 (continuation of *University Review*, founded 1935). Circ. 2,500.

● *New Letters Magazine* received a Pushcart prize for fiction.

Needs: Contemporary, ethnic, experimental, humor/satire, literary, mainstream, translations. "Generally don't publish straight genre fiction." **Publishes 20% new writers/year.** Recently published work by Thomas E. Kennedy, Sheila Kohler, Rosellen Brown and Janet Burroway. Agented fiction: 10%. Also publishes short shorts. Rarely critiques rejected mss.

How to Contact: Send complete ms with cover letter. Does not read mss May 15-October 15. Responds in 3 weeks to queries; up to 18 weeks to mss. SASE for ms. No simultaneous or multiple submissions. Sample copy $5.50 or on website.

Payment/Terms: Pays honorarium—depends on grant/award money; 2 contributor's copies. Sends galleys to author.

Advice: "Seek publication of representative chapters in high-quality magazines as a way to the book contract. Try literary magazines first."

◐ NEW MIRAGE QUARTERLY, Good Samaritan Press, P.O. Box 803282, Santa Clarita CA 91380. (661)799-0694. E-mail: adorxyz@aol.com. **Contact:** Jorita Lee, senior editor. Magazine: 5×8; 16 pages; illustrations. "We are issued by the Mirage Group of Southern California, a writers association. Much of the material we publish is the work of our members." Quarterly. Estab. 1997. Circ. 100.

Needs: Fantasy, literary, mainstream, religious, romance, science fiction. "We would like to see more Christian literature, science fiction, romance." Receives 1 unsolicited ms/month. Publishes ms 6 months after acceptance. **Publishes 7 new writers/year.** Published work by Eugenia Hairston. Publishes short shorts. Also publishes literary criticism and poetry. Sometimes comments on rejected mss.

How to Contact: Send complete ms with a cover letter. Accepts submissions by e-mail. Responds in 6 weeks to queries. Send SASE for return of ms. Accepts simultaneous, previously published and multiple submissions. Sample copy for $7. Reviews novels, short story collections and nonfiction books of interest to writers.

Payment/Terms: Pays 1 contributor's copy; additional copies $26. Pays on publication. Sends galleys to author. Not copyrighted. Sponsors contest. "Send SASE for standards."

Advice: "The basics are important—organization, clarity, spelling, plot, etc. We recommend working with a writers association."

$ ◑ ▼ NEW ORLEANS REVIEW, Box 195, Loyola University, New Orleans LA 70118. (504)865-2295. Fax: (504)865-2294. E-mail: noreview@loyno.edu. Website: www.loyno.edu/~noreview/ (includes current issue, table of contents, cover, subscription form, submission guidelines, links, masthead, back issues (covers/table of contents). **Contact:** Christopher Chambers, editor. Journal: 6×9; perfect bound; 200 pages; photos. "Publishes poetry, fiction, translations, photographs, nonfiction on literature, art and film. Readership: those interested in contemporary literature and culture." Biannually. Estab. 1968. Circ. 1,300.

● Work from the *New Orleans Review* has been anthologized in *Best American Short Stories* the *Pushcart Prize Anthology.*

Needs: "Quality fiction from traditional to experimental. No romance. Want more experimental fiction." **Publishes 12 new writers/year.** Recently published work by Gordon Lish, Michael Martone, Carolyn Sanchez and Josh Russell.

How to Contact: Send complete ms with SASE. Accepts queries/mss by fax. Accepts simultaneous submissions (if we are notified immediately upon acceptance elsewhere). No fax or e-mail submissions. Responds in 4 months. Sample copy for $7.

Payment/Terms: Pays $25-50 and 2 copies. Pays on publication for first North American serial rights.

Advice: "We're looking for dynamic writing that demonstrates attention to the language, and a sense of the medium, writing that engages, surprises, moves us. We're not looking for genre fiction, or academic articles. We subscribe to the belief that in order to truly write well, one must first master the rudiments: grammar and syntax, punctuation, the sentence, the paragraph, the line, the stanza. We receive about 3,000 manuscripts a year, and publish about 5% of them. Check out a recent issue, send us your best, proofread your work, be patient, be persistent."

▧ ◑ ▼ THE NEW ORPHIC REVIEW, New Orphic Publishers, 706 Mill St., Nelson, British Columbia V1L 4S5 Canada. (250)354-0494. Fax: (250)352-0743. **Contact:** Ernest Hekkanen, editor-in-chief. Magazine: 5½×8½; 120 pages; common paper; 100 lb. color cover. "In the traditional *Orphic* fashion, our magazine accepts a wide range of styles and approaches—from naturalism to the surreal, but, please, get to the essence of the narrative, emotion, conflict, state of being, whatever." Semiannual. Estab. 1998. Circ. 300.

● Margrith Schaner's story, "Dream Dig" was included in *The Journey Prize Anthology*, 2001.

Needs: Ethnic/multicultural, experimental, fantasy, historical (general), literary, mainstream. "No detective or sword and sorcery stories." List of upcoming themes available for SASE. Receives 20 unsolicited mss/month. Accepts 10 mss/issue; 22 mss/year. Publishes ms up to 1 year after acceptance. **Publishes 6-8 new writers/year.** Recently published work by Eveline Hasler (Swiss), Leena Krohn (Finnish), Pekka Salmi and Heinrich Müller. Length: 2,000-10,000 words; average length: 3,500 words. Publishes short shorts. Average length: 3,500 words. Also publishes literary essays, literary criticism and poetry. Sometimes comments on rejected mss.

How to Contact: Send complete ms with a cover letter. Include estimated word count, brief bio and list of publications. Responds in 1 month to queries; 4 months to mss. Send SASE (or IRC) for return of ms or send a disposable copy of ms and #10 SASE for reply only. Accepts simultaneous and multiple submissions. Sample copy for $15. Guidelines for SASE. Reviews novels, short story collections and nonfiction books of interest to writers. Send review copies to Margrith Schraner.

Payment/Terms: Pays 1 contributor's copy; additional copies $12. Pays on publication for first North American serial rights.

Advice: "I like fiction that deals with issues, accounts for every motive, has conflict, is well-written and tackles something that is substantive. Don't be mundane; try for more, not less."

the new renaissance, An international magazine of ideas & opinions, emphasizing literature and the arts, The Friends of "the new renaissance", 26 Heath Rd., #11, Arlington MA 02474-3645. E-mail: wmichaud@gwi.net. **Contact:** Michal Anne Kucharski, co-editor. Magazine: 6×9; 144-182 pages; 70 lb. matte white paper; 4-color cover; illustrations; photos; artwork: 80 lb. dull glossy. "*tnr* is dedicated to publishing a diverse magazine, with a variety of styles, statements and tones for a sophisticated general audience. We publish assorted long & short fiction, including bilingual (Italian, German, French, Danish, Russian [Cyrillic], etc . . .), and Indian fiction in translation." Semiannual. Estab. 1968. Circ. 1,300.

Needs: Ethnic (general), experimental, psychological, supernatural, humor, satire, literary, regional (general), translations. "We do not want to see a heavy amount of commercial or popular fiction. Within the last two years we have been receiving quasi-naturalistic fiction and we like to see less." Receives 40-70 unsolicited mss/month (January-June); 20-35 mss/month (September 1-October 31). Accepts 3-5 mss/issue; 6-10 mss/year. Does not read mss in July-August or November-December. Publishes ms 10-18 months after acceptance. Agented fiction 4-5%. **Publishes 1-2 new writers/ year.** Recently published work by B. Wongar, Emil Draitser, Valery Krupnik and Cari Scribner. Length: 250-10,500 words. Also publishes literary essays, literary criticism and poetry. Often comments on rejected mss.

How to Contact: All fiction and poetry submissions are tied to our awards programs and require a $16.50 entry fee (U.S.) for nonsubscribers; $11.50 for subscribers; add $3 foreign. Send complete ms with cover letter. Include estimated word count with submission. Responds in 1 month to queries; 6-7 months to mss. Send SASE (or IRC) for return of ms or send disposable copy of ms and #10 SASE for reply. Accepts two stories if the mss are 4 pages or less. Guidelines for SASE or e-mail. Reviews novels, short story collections and nonfiction books. Send to fiction, poetry, or nonfiction editors.

Payment/Terms: Pays $48-80 and 1 contributor's copy (under 30 pages), 2 copies 31-36 pages. Offers discount for additional copies. Acquires all rights; after publication, rights returned to writer. "After the third issue of each volume is published, we have independent judges (one for fiction, one for poetry) decide the best work in a volume."

Advice: "We're looking for the individual voice, in both style and vision. We prefer density in characterization and/ or dialogue, atmosphere, etc. We're not as interested in the 'Who Cares?' fiction. We like a story to be memorable; we leave the particulars of what to the individual writers. We feel that the first-person narration is becoming an all too predictable commonplace. We too often hear from writers who are not familiar with the litmag but who should be aware of, at least, what some independents are doing."

NEW STONE CIRCLE, New Stone Circle, 1185 E. 1900 North Rd., White Heath IL 61884. (217)762-5801. Fax: (217)388-4096. E-mail: m-hays@uiuc.edu. **Contact:** Mary Hays, fiction editor. Magazine: 8½×5½; 40-58 pages; illustrations; photos. "Our intention is to create a forum for a conversation between artists of our time." Annual. Estab. 1994. Circ. 100.

● *New Stone Circle* has won Pipistrelle Award for Best Literary Magazine.

Needs: "No racist or misogynist work." Receives 30 unsolicited mss/month. Accepts 4-5 mss/issue; 4-10 mss/year. Publishes ms 1 year after acceptance. Agented fiction 1%. **Publishes 1-2 new writers/year.** Recently published work by Christine Chiu, Cris Mazza, Elizabeth Weiser and Jessica Inclan. Publishes short shorts.

How to Contact: Send complete ms with a cover letter. Accepts submissions by disk (Mac compatible). Include brief bio and list of publications. Responds in 2 months to queries; 6 months to mss. Send SASE for return of ms or send a disposable copy of ms and #10 SASE for reply only. Accepts simultaneous submissions, previously published work and multiple submissions. Sample copy for $4.50. Guidelines for SASE. Reviews novels and short story collections.

Payment/Terms: Pays 1 contributor's copy; additional copies $3.50. Pays on publication for one-time rights. Sends galleys to author. Sponsors contest. Send SASE for guidelines.

Advice: "Show fresh imagery. As a reader, I want to be transported to the fictional world. Keep reading, keep writing, keep sending your work out."

THE NEW WRITER, P.O. Box 60, Cranbrook TN17 2ZR United Kingdom. 01580 212626. Fax: 01580 212041. E-mail: editor@thenewwriter.com. Website: www.thenewwriter.com (includes editorials, guidelines, extracts, links, etc.) **Contact:** Suzanne Ruthven, editor. Magazine: A4; 56 pages; illustrations; photos. Contemporary writing magazine which publishes "the best in fact, fiction and poetry." Publishes 6 issues per annum. Estab. 1996. Circ. 1,500. "We consider short stories from subscribers only but we may also commission guest writers."

Needs: "We will consider most categories apart from stories written for children. No horror, erotic or cosy fiction." Accepts 4 mss/issue; 40 mss/year. Publishes ms up to 1 year after acceptance. Agented fiction 5%. **Majority of work is by previously unpublished writers.** Published work by Alan Dunn, Annabel Lamb, Laureen Vonnegut and Stephen Finucan. Length: 2,000-5,000 words; average length: 3,500 words. Publishes short shorts. Average length: 1,500 words. Also publishes literary essays, literary criticism and poetry. Often comments on rejected mss.

How to Contact: Query with clips of published work. Accepts queries but not mss by e-mail and fax. Include estimated word count, brief bio and list of publications. Responds in 2 months to queries; 4 months to mss. Send SASE (or IRC) for return of ms or send a disposable copy of ms and #10 SASE for reply only. Accepts simultaneous submissions. Sample copy for SASE and A4 SAE with IRCs only. Guidelines for SASE. Reviews novels, short story collections and nonfiction books of interest to writers.

Payment/Terms: Pays £10 per story by credit voucher; additional copies £1.50. Pays on publication for first rights. Sponsors contest, prose and poetry prizes (entry via website).

Advice: "Hone it—always be prepared to improve the story. It's a competitive market."

$ **NEW YORK STORIES**, English Dept., LaGuardia Community College, E-103, 31-10 Thomson Ave., Long Island City NY 11101. (718)482-5673. **Contact:** Daniel Caplice Lynch, editor. Magazine: 9×11; 48 pages; photos. "Stories should have strong characters, fresh voices and distinctive angles of vision. We are open to the best work we can find from around the world. The stories do not need to be set in New York, but we do welcome stories that explore the city's diversity. Stories above 5,000 words have less chance due to space constraints. We publish six to eight an issue." Triannual. Estab. 1998.

Needs: Ethnic/multicultural, experimental, feminist, gay, humor/satire, lesbian, literary, mainstream/contemporary, regional. Receives 300 unsolicited mss/month. Accepts 6-8 mss/issue; up to 24 mss/year. Does not read mss June-August. Publishes ms 6 months after acceptance. Agented fiction 5%. **Publishes 2 new writers/year.** Length: 100 words minimum; average length: 2,500-3,000 words. Publishes short shorts. Also publishes literary essays, especially about New York. Sometimes comments on rejected mss.

How to Contact: Send complete ms with a cover letter. Include 1-paragraph bio and e-mail address. Responds in 2 months to queries; 3 months to mss. Send SASE for return of ms or send disposable copy of ms. Accepts simultaneous submissions and reprints. Guidelines for #10 SASE or by e-mail. Sample copy for $5.95.

Payment/Terms: Pays $100-$1,000. Pays on publication.

Advice: "Fresh angles of vision, dark humor and psychological complexity are hallmarks of our short stories. Present characters who are 'alive.' Let them breathe. To achieve this, revise, revise, revise. Lately, the industry of publishing fiction seems to be playing it safe. We want your best—no matter what."

N $ ◑ NIGHT TRAIN, People, Action, Consequence, Night Train Publications, Inc., 85 Orchard St., Somerville MA 02144. (617)953-3831. E-mail: submission@nighttrainmagazine.com. Website: www.nighttrainmagazine.com (includes guidelines, statement of aesthetics, recent news, editorial and masthead information, contest information, excerpts from forthcoming issues as well as current issue content and fiction not included in the print version). **Contact:** Rusty Barnes, fiction editor. Magazine: 6×9; 200 page; 60 lb. Glatfelter Natural paper; 12 pt. glossy laminated cover; illustrations; photos. "We publish *Night Train* for anyone interested in the best available contemporary literature. We welcome all kinds of stories, but we strongly prefer those with an edge: fiction that leaves us gasping for breath, stories with people—real people—who are actors in their own lives and accept consequences for what they do. We honor the traditions of the short story, but realize that to live, those traditions need new interpretations, new vision—a thrust forward. We provide a venue for writers to show us where the art will go, and trust them to take us there." Semiannual. Estab. 2002. Circ. 1,000.

Needs: Experimental, literary, mainstream. "A first-person, present-tense story would have to be remarkable for us to consider publishing it, but we rule out nothing. We also have a bias against stories about the pained and tortured life of writers; we're writers too, but we don't find that interesting; again, it would have to be beyond excellent for us to consider." Receives 350 unsolicited mss/month. Accepts 20-25 mss/issue; 40-50 mss/year. Publishes ms 6 months after acceptance. **Publishes 5-10 new writers/year.** Recently published work by Maryanne Stahl, Thomas Cobb and Edward Falco. Length: 250-10,000 words; average length: 3,000 words. Publishes short shorts. Average length: 750 words. Often comments on rejected mss.

How to Contact: Accepts submissions by e-mail and disk. Include estimated word count and brief bio. Responds in 2 months to queries; 3 months to mss. Send a disposable copy of ms and #10 SASE for reply only. Accepts simultaneous and multiple submissions. Sample copy for $9.95. Guidelines for SASE or on website. Reviews novels and short story collections. Send review copies to Rusty Barnes, fiction editor.

Payment/Terms: Pays 2¢/word minimum to $100 maximum, 2 contributor's copies, a lifetime subscription and 2 gift subscriptions; additional copies $6.95. Pays on publication for first North American serial, one-time anthology and electronic rights. Sends galleys to author. See website for details of the Richard Yates Fiction Award Competition.

Advice: "We want to see characters who are active participants in their own lives, who recognize the impact they have on others, who think about the things they do and suffer (or not) as a result of those actions. *Night Train* is a place where blood, bone and nerve—the basic elements of stories—matter. Careless language, ethereal subject matter or lack of grounding in the 'whys' of human behavior will make us unhappy. Please read the guidelines and aesthetic statement on our website; and look at our editor's favorites pages. They're there for one reason: to help you understand what we like."

$ ◑ NIMROD, International Journal of Prose and Poetry, University of Tulsa, 600 S. College Ave., Tulsa OK 74104-3126. (918)631-3080. Fax: (918)631-3033. E-mail: nimrod@utulsa.edu. Website: www.utulsa.edu/nimrod/ (includes writer's guidelines, excerpts from published work, contest rules, theme issue announcements, ed-in-chief name and subscription/sample issue order form). **Contact:** Gerry McLoud, fiction editor. Magazine: 6×9; 192 pages; 60 lb. white paper; illustrations; photos. "We publish one thematic issue and one awards issue each year. A recent theme was "The Celtic Fringe," a compilation of poetry and prose from all over the world. We seek vigorous, imaginative, quality writing. Our mission is to discover new writers and publish experimental writers who have not yet found a 'home' for their work." Semiannual. Estab. 1956. Circ. 3,000.

Needs: "We accept contemporary poetry and/or prose. May submit adventure, ethnic, experimental, prose poem or translations. No science fiction or romance." Receives 120 unsolicited fiction mss/month. **Published 5-10 new writers within the last year.** Recently published work by Felicia Ward, Ellen Bass, Jeanette Turner Hospital and Kate Small. Length: 7,500 words maximum. Also publishes poetry.

How to Contact: SASE for return of ms. Accepts queries by e-mail. No mss by e-mail except for writers living overseas. Accepts simultaneous and multiple submissions. Responds in 5 months. Sample copy: "to see what *Nimrod* is all about, send $10 for a back issue."

Payment/Terms: Pays 2 contributor's copies.

Advice: "We have not changed our fiction needs: quality, vigor, distinctive voice. We have, however, increased the number of stories we print. See current issues. We look for fiction that is fresh, vigorous, distinctive, serious and humorous, seriously-humorous, unflinchingly serious, ironic—whatever. Just so it is quality. Strongly encourage writers to send #10 SASE for brochure for annual literary contest with prizes of $1,000 and $2,000."

◑ 96 Inc., P.O. Box 15559, Boston MA 02215-0011. (617)267-0543. Fax: (617)262-3568. E-mail: to96inc@ici.net. Website: www.96inc.com. **Contact:** Vera Gold or Nancy Mehegan, editors. Magazine: 8½×11; 64 pages; 20 lb. paper; matte cover; illustrations; photos. "*96 Inc.* promotes the process; integrates beginning/young with established writers; reaches out to audiences of all ages and backgrounds." Annual. Estab. 1992. Circ. 3,000.

Needs: All types, styles and subjects. Receives 200 unsolicited mss/month. Accepts 12-15 mss/issue; 30 mss/year. Agented fiction 10%. **Publishes 2-10 new writers/year.** Published work by Rose Moss, Alene Bricken, Harlyn Aizley, Sharon Stratis and Judith Stitzel. Length: 1,000-7,000 words. Publishes short shorts. Also publishes literary essays, literary criticism and poetry. Sometimes comments on rejected mss.

How to Contact: Query first. Accepts mss on disk. Include estimated word count, bio (100 words) and list of publications. Responds in 3 weeks to queries; up to 1 year to mss. Send SASE for reply, return of ms or send a disposable copy of ms. Accepts simultaneous and multiple submissions. Sample copy for $7.50. Guidelines for #10 SASE. Reviews novels and short story collections on occasion.

Payment/Terms: Pays 4 contributor's copies. Pays on publication for one-time rights.

Advice: Looks for "good writing in any style. Pays attention to the process. Read at least one issue. Be patient—it takes a very long time for readers to go through the thousands of manuscripts."

NITE-WRITER'S INTERNATIONAL LITERARY ARTS JOURNAL, Nite Owl Press, 137 Pointview Rd., Suite 300, Pittsburgh PA 15227. (412)885-3798. E-mail: cexpression@msn.com. Editor: John A. Thompson, Sr. Associate Editor: Bree A. Orner. **Contact:** Fiction Editor. Magazine: 8½×11; 30-50 pages; bond paper; illustrations. *"Nite-Writer's International Literary Arts Journal* is dedicated to the emotional intellectual with a creative perception of life." Quarterly. Estab. 1993. Circ. 250.

Needs: Adventure, erotica, historical, humor/satire, literary, mainstream/contemporary, religious/inspirational, romance, senior citizen/retirement, sports, young adult/teen (adventure). Plans special fiction issue or anthology. Receives 3-5 unsolicited mss/month. Accepts 1-2 mss/issue; 5-8 mss/year. Publishes ms within 1 year after acceptance. Published work by Julia Klatt Singer, Jean Oscarson Schoell, Lawrence Keough and S. Anthony Smith. Length: 1,500 words average. Publishes flash fiction of 1,000 words. Also publishes literary essays, literary criticism, poetry. Often comments on rejected mss.

How to Contact: Send complete ms with a cover letter. Include estimated word count, 1-page bio, list of publications. Responds in 6 months. SASE for return of ms. Accepts simultaneous submissions. Sample copy for $6, 9×13 SAE and 6 first-class stamps. Guidelines for legal size SASE.

Payment/Terms: Does not pay. Copyright reverts to author upon publication.

Advice: "Read a lot of what you write, study the market; don't fear rejection, but use it as a learning tool to strengthen your work before resubmitting. Express what the heart feels."

$ THE NORTH AMERICAN REVIEW, University of Northern Iowa, Cedar Falls IA 50614-0516. (319)273-6455. Fax: (319)273-4326. E-mail: nar@uni.edu. Website: http://webdelsol.com/NorthAmReview/NAR. Editor: Vince Gotera. **Contact:** Grant Tracey, fiction editor. "The *NAR* is the oldest literary magazine in America and one of the most respected; though we have no prejudices about the subject matter of material sent to us, our first concern is quality." Bimonthly. Estab. 1815. Circ. 4,000.

● Works published in *The North American Review* have won the Pushcart Prize.

Needs: Open (literary). "No flat narrative stories where the interiority of the character is the paramount concern." Wants to see more "well-crafted literary stories that emphasize family concerns. We'd also like to see more stories engaged with environmental concerns." **Publishes 2 new writers/year.** Recently published work by Gary Gildner, Maryanne O'Hara and G.W. Clift. Reads fiction mss from January 1 to April 1 only.

How to Contact: Send complete ms with SASE. No simultaneous submissions. Sample copy for $5.

Payment/Terms: Pays $5 per 350 words of prose, $20 minimum and 2 contributor's copies; additional copies $4.50. Pays on publication for first North American serial rights.

Advice: "Stories that do not condescend to the reader or their character are always appealing to us. We also like stories that have characters doing things (acting upon the world instead of being acted upon). We also like a strong narrative arc. Stories that are mainly about language need not apply. Your first should be your second best line. Your last sentence should be your best. Everything in the middle should approach the two."

NORTH DAKOTA QUARTERLY, University of North Dakota, Box 7209, University Station, Grand Forks ND 58202. (701)777-3322. Fax: (701)777-3650. E-mail: ndq@sage.und.nodak.edu. Website: www.und.nodak.edu/org/ndq (includes editors, subscription and submission information, excerpts, sample table of contents). Editor: Robert W. Lewis. **Contact:** James Robison, fiction editor. Poetry Editor: Jay Meek. Magazine: 6×9; 200 pages; bond paper; illustrations; photos. *"North Dakota Quarterly* is a quarterly literary journal publishing essays in the humanities; some short stories, some poetry." University audience. Quarterly. Estab. 1911. Circ. 700.

● Work published in *North Dakota Quarterly* was selected for inclusion in *The O. Henry Awards* anthology. The editors are especially interested in work by Native American writers.

Needs: Contemporary, ethnic, experimental, feminist, historical, humor/satire, literary. Receives 100-120 unsolicited mss/month. Accepts 4 mss/issue; 16 mss/year. **Publishes 4-5 new writers/year.** Recently published work by Debra Marquart, Derek Wolcott, Sherry Fairchok, Peter Nabokov and Catharine Ryan Hyde. Length: 3,000-4,000 words average. Also publishes literary essays, literary criticism, poetry. Sometimes comments on or critiques rejected ms.

How to Contact: Send complete ms with cover letter. Include one-paragraph bio. "But it need not be much more than hello; please read this story; I've published (if so, best examples) . . ." SASE. Accepts multiple submissions. Responds in 3 months. Publishes ms an average of 1 year after acceptance. Sample copy for $8. Reviews novels and short story collections.

Payment/Terms: Pays 2-4 contributor's copies; 30% discount for extras. Acquires one-time rights. Sends galleys to author.

⬤ NORTHEAST ARTS MAGAZINE, P.O. Box 4363, Portland ME 04101. **Contact:** Mr. Leigh Donaldson, publisher. Magazine: 6½×9½; 32-40 pages; matte finish paper; card stock cover; illustrations; photos. Bimonthly. Estab. 1990. Circ. 750.
Needs: Ethnic, gay, historical, literary, mystery/suspense (private eye), prose poem (under 2,000 words). "No obscenity, racism, sexism, etc." Receives 50 unsolicited mss/month. Accepts 1-2 mss/issue; 5-7 mss/year. Publishes ms 2-4 months after acceptance. Agented fiction 20%. Length: 750 words preferred. Publishes short shorts. Sometimes critiques rejected mss.
How to Contact: Send complete ms with cover letter. Include short bio. Responds in 1 month to queries; 4-6 months to mss. SASE. Accepts simultaneous submissions. Sample copy for $4.50, SAE and 75¢ postage. Guidelines free.
Payment/Terms: Pays 2 contributor's copies. Acquires first North American serial rights.
Advice: Looks for "creative/innovative use of language and style. Unusual themes and topics."

⬤ NORTHWEST REVIEW, 369 PLC, University of Oregon, Eugene OR 97403. (541)346-3957. Website: darkwing .uoregon.edu/~engl/deptinfo/NWR.html. Editor: John Witte. **Contact:** Janice MacCrae, fiction editor. Magazine: 6×9; 140-160 pages; high quality cover stock; illustrations; photos. "A general literary review featuring poems, stories, essays and reviews, circulated nationally and internationally. For a literate audience in avant-garde as well as traditional literary forms; interested in the important writers who have not yet achieved their readership." Triannual. Estab. 1957. Circ. 1,200.
Needs: Contemporary, experimental, feminist, literary and translations. Accepts 4-5 mss/issue, 12-15 mss/year. Receives approximately 100 unsolicited fiction mss each month. **Published new writers within the last year.** Published work by Diana Abu-Jaber, Madison Smartt Bell, Maria Flook and Charles Marvin. Length: "Mss longer than 40 pages are at a disadvantage." Also publishes literary essays, literary criticism, poetry. Critiques rejected mss when there is time. Sometimes recommends other markets.
How to Contact: Send complete ms with SASE. "No simultaneous submissions are considered." Responds in 4 months. Sample copy for $4. Reviews novels and short story collections. Send books to John Witte.
Payment/Terms: Pays 3 contributor's copies and one-year subscription; 40% discount on extras. Acquires first rights.

$ ⬤ NORTHWOODS JOURNAL, A Magazine for Writers, Conservatory of American Letters, P.O. Box 298, Thomaston ME 04861. (207)354-0998. Fax: (207)354-8953. E-mail: cal@americanletters.org. Website: www.ameri canletters.org (includes guidelines and catalogue). Editor: R.W. Olmsted. **Contact:** Ken Sieben, fiction editor (submit fiction to Ken Sieben, 253 Ocean Ave., Sea Bright NJ 07760). Magazine: 5½×8½; 32-64 pages; white paper; 70 lb. text cover; offset printing; some illustrations; photos. "No theme, no philosophy—for writers and for people who read for entertainment." Quarterly. Estab. 1993. Circ. 200.
Needs: Adventure, experimental, fantasy (science fantasy, sword and sorcery), literary, mainstream/contemporary, mystery/suspense (amateur sleuth, police procedural, private eye/hard-boiled, romantic suspense), psychic/supernatural/ occult, regional, romance (gothic, historical), science fiction (hard science, soft/sociological), sports, westerns (frontier, traditional). Publishes special fiction issue or anthology. "Would like to see more first-person adventure. No porn or evangelical." Receives 20 unsolicited mss/month. Accepts 12-15 mss/year. **Publishes 15 new writers/year.** Recently published work by Richard Vaughn and Lorraine Elizabeth Hemingway. Length: 2,500 words maximum. Also publishes literary essays, literary criticism and poetry.
How to Contact: *Charges $3 reading fee per 2,500 words.* Read guidelines *before* submitting. Send complete ms with a cover letter. Include word count and list of publications. There is a $3 fee per story ($2 for CAL members; make checks payable to Ken Sieben. The magazine gets none of the reading fee). Responds in 2 days to queries; by next deadline plus 5 days to mss. Send SASE for reply, return of ms or send a disposable copy of ms. No simultaneous submissions. No electronic submissions. Sample copies: $5.50 next issue, $8.75 current issue, $13.25 back issue (if available), all postage paid or send 6×9 SASE with first-class postage affixed and $5.50). Guidelines for #10 SASE. Reviews novels, short story collections and poetry.
Payment/Terms: Varies, "minimum $3/published page." Pays on acceptance for first North American serial rights.
Advice: "Read guidelines, read the things we've published. Know your market."

$ ⬤ NOTRE DAME REVIEW, University of Notre Dame, English Department, Creative Writing, Notre Dame IN 46556. (219)631-6952. Fax: (219)631-8209. E-mail: english.ndreview.1@nd.edu. Website: www.nd.edu/~ndr/review. htm (includes guidelines, editors, additional poetry, fiction, book reviews, art, audio clips of authors and photos). Senior Editor: Steve Tomasula. Poetry Editor: John Matthias. Fiction Editor: William O'Rourke. **Contact:** Managing Editor. Literary magazine: 6×9; 115 pages; 50 lb. smooth paper; illustrations; photos. "The *Notre Dame Review* is an independent, non-commercial magazine of contemporary American and international fiction, poetry, criticism and art. We are

SENDING TO A COUNTRY other than your own? Be sure to send International Reply Coupons (IRC) instead of stamps for replies or return of your manuscript.

especially interested in work that takes on big issues by making the invisible seen, that gives voice to the voiceless. In addition to showcasing celebrated authors like Seamus Heaney and Czelaw Milosz, the *Notre Dame Review* introduces readers to authors they may have never encountered before, but who are doing innovative and important work. In conjunction with the *Notre Dame Review*, the on-line companion to the printed magazine, the *Notre Dame Re-view* engages readers as a community centered in literary rather than commercial concerns, a community we reach out to through critique and commentary as well as aesthetic experience." Semiannual. Estab. 1995. Circ. 2,000.

Needs: "We're eclectic. No genre fiction." Upcoming theme issues planned. List of upcoming themes or editorial calendar available for SASE. Receives 75 unsolicited fiction mss/month. Accepts 4-5 mss/issue; 10 mss/year. Does not read mss November-January or May-August. Publishes ms 6 months after acceptance. **Publishes 1 new writer/year.** Published work by Ed Falco, Jarda Cerverka and David Green. Length: 3,000 words maximum. Publishes short shorts. Also publishes literary criticism and poetry.

How to Contact: Send complete ms with cover letter. Include 4-sentence bio. Responds in 4 months. Send SASE for response, return of ms, or send a disposable copy of ms. Accepts simultaneous submissions. Sample copy for $6.

Payment/Terms: Pays $5-25 and contributor's copies. Pays on publication for first North American serial rights.

Advice: "We're looking for high quality work that takes on big issues in a literary way. Please read our back issues before submitting."

OASIS, Oasis Books, 12 Stevenage Rd., London SW6 6ES United Kingdom. **Contact:** Ian Robinson, editor. Published 3 times/year. Circ. 400. Publishes usually 1 story/issue.

Needs: "Innovative, experimental fiction. No science fiction, fantasy, surreal. Wants non-standard, 'experimental' short stories." Published work by Sheila E. Murphy (USA), Henrikas Radauskas (Lithuania), D.F. Lewis (UK), Neil Leadbeater (Scotland) and Michael Wilding (Australia). Length: 1,800 words maximum.

Payment/Terms: Pays in copies. Sample copy available for $5 check (made payable to Robert Vas Dias) and 4 IRCs.

Advice: "Have a look at a copy of the magazine before submitting. We look for originality of thought and expression, and a willingness to take risks, both in prose and poetry."

$ ⬤ OASIS, A Literary Magazine, P.O. Box 626, Largo FL 33779-0626. (727)345-8505. E-mail: oasislit@aol.com. **Contact:** Neal Storrs, editor. Magazine: 70 pages. "Literary magazine first, last and always—looking for styles that delight and amaze, that are polished and poised. Next to that, content considerations relatively unimportant—open to all." Quarterly. Estab. 1992. Circ. 500.

Needs: High-quality writing. Also publishes translations. Receives 150 unsolicited mss/month. Accepts 6 mss/issue; 24 mss/year. Publishes ms 4-6 months after acceptance. **Publishes 2 new writers/year.** Published work by Wendell Mayo, Al Masarik and Mark Wisniewski. Length: no minimum or maximum. Also publishes literary essays and poetry. Occasionally comments on rejected mss.

How to Contact: Send complete ms with or without a cover letter. Accepts queries/mss by e-mail. Usually reports same day. Send SASE for reply, return of ms or send a disposable copy of ms. Accepts simultaneous, multiple, reprint and electronic (e-mail) submissions. Sample copy for $7.50. Guidelines for #10 SASE.

Payment/Terms: Pays $15-30 and 1 contributor's copy. Pays on publication for first rights.

Advice: "If you want to write good stories, read good stories. Cultivate the critical ability to recognize what makes a story original and true to itself."

N: OBSIDIAN III: LITERATURE IN THE AFRICAN DIASPORA, Dept. of English, North Carolina State University, Raleigh NC 27695-8105. (919)515-4153. Fax: (919)515-1836. E-mail: obsidian@social.chass.ncsu.edu. Website: www.ncsu.edu/chass/obsidian/index.html (includes contact information, indexes of recent issues). **Contact:** Joyce Pettis, editor. Fiction Editor: Opal Moore. Magazine: 6×9; 130 pages. "Creative works in English by black writers, scholarly critical studies by all writers on black literature in English." Published 2 times/year (spring/summer, fall/winter). Estab. 1975. Circ. 500.

Needs: Ethnic (pan-African), feminist, literary. All writers on black topics. Accepts 7-9 mss/year. **Publishes 20 new writers/year.** Recently published work by Sean Henry, R. Flowers Rivera, Terrance Hayes, Eugene Kraft and Kwane Dawes. Length: 1,500-10,000 words.

How to Contact: Send complete ms in duplicate and on disc with SASE. Accepts queries/mss by fax, e-mail and disk. Responds in 3 months. Publishes ms an average of 4-6 months after acceptance. Sample copy for $6.

Payment/Terms: Pays in contributor's copies. Acquires one-time rights. Sponsors contests occasionally; guidelines published in magazine.

Advice: "Following proper format is essential. Your title must be intriguing and text clean. Never give up. Some of the writers we publish were rejected many times before we published them."

N: ⬤ ◎ OHIO TEACHERS WRITE, Ohio Council of Teachers of English Language Arts, 644 Overlook Dr., Columbus OH 43214. E-mail: rmcclain@bright.net. **Contact:** Tom McCracken, editor. Editors change every 2 years. Magazine: 8½×11; 50 pages; 60 lb. white offset paper; 65 lb. blue cover stock; illustrations; photos. "The purpose of the magazine is threefold: (1) to provide a collection of fine literature for the reading pleasure of teachers and other adult readers; (2) to encourage teachers to compose literary works along with their students; (3) to provide the literate citizens of Ohio a window into the world of educators not often seen by those outside the teaching profession." Annual. Estab. 1995. Circ. 1,000.

• Submissions are limited to Ohio educators.

One Story offers single author showcase

Great short stories are like a great meal. First the reader's appetite is whetted, then sated. After reading a great story, there's no room for seconds—the only thing left to do is savor the experience. In *One Story*, a new magazine published by Maribeth Batcha and edited by Hannah Tinti, readers hungry for such an experience might find just what they're looking for.

Maribeth Batcha and Hannah Tinti

In each issue, *One Story* offers exactly that: a single story, mailed every three weeks to subscribers in a compact format. Why just one story? As the website (www.one-story.com) explains, "We believe that short stories are best read alone. They should not be sandwiched in between a review and an exposé on liposuction, or placed after another work of fiction that is so sad or funny or long that the reader is worn out by the time they turn to another."

The idea for the format of *One Story* came to Batcha while she was working for *Lingua Franca* magazine. "I was developing a newsletter budget, and I saw how inexpensive it was to send out smaller things," says Batcha, who holds an MFA from Columbia University. With the relatively low cost, she wondered why there hadn't been a fiction magazine with a smaller format—especially since short stories seemed ideally suited for such an experiment. "I thought it would be sort of fun to send a short story out in the mail," she says. "I've been in writing groups where we would send each other a story in the mail, and it's really exciting when you get one and it's really good and you finish it, and that's all you have. There's nothing else. You don't feel pressure to read another one, you just get to enjoy one story."

The idea of a subscription-based magazine that gave readers the chance to read short stories one at a time took shape quickly. "After I thought of it, it seemed so obvious," Batcha says. "I called a bunch of people—friends who knew more about journals—to see if there was anybody else doing it, or why I *shouldn't* do it, but their response was pretty much, 'Hey, I wonder why nobody thought of this before!' People are really excited about it—it's an easy concept to get your mind around."

One Story is intended to be more reader-friendly than other literary journals. "It's hard to reach readers in a journal format," says Batcha. "I think this is much friendlier." The website touts *One Story* as "artfully designed, lightweight, easy to carry, and ready to entertain on buses, in bed, in subways, in cars, in the park, in the bath, in the waiting rooms of doctors, on the couch in the afternoon or in line at the supermarket." In short, *One Story* is meant to appeal to readers with busy schedules and many demands on their attention.

But readers aren't the only ones who benefit from the *One Story* approach. Writers, too, like the fact that their stories don't have to share space. "The authors we've approached love the idea," Batcha says. "It really showcases their story and allows it to stand on its own."

The editor of *One Story* agrees. "It's much more appealing to writers, because it allows them to be the star," Tinti says. "Each writer we publish, their name is right there, front and center on the cover. If you want to get out there and get published, what better way to get your name and face out there than to have a little magazine that's entirely about you? That makes it appealing not only to beginning writers, but also to more established ones."

Before she came to *One Story*, Tinti, who holds an MA from New York University's Creative Writing program, developed her editorial skills at magazines including *The Atlantic Monthly* and *Boston Review*. As editor of *One Story*, she takes a collaborative approach with authors. "The author has a say in the appearance of the magazine—how they'd like the font to be, the formatting, the overall layout," she says. "Because we're only publishing one story, we can alter the magazine and do different things, which is not typically the case at larger literary magazines. We want to give authors more say, because they are going to be carrying the issue themselves."

In fact, the *One Story* concept proved so appealing that Batcha and Tinti were able to garner submissions from some noted writers as well as from newcomers. The first issue of *One Story*, published in March of 2002, featured the story "Villanova" by John Hodgman, whose work has appeared in the online version of *McSweeney's*, as well as *This American Life*. Subsequent issues will feature stories by Robin J. Lauzon (*Quarterly West, Eratica*) and Gregory Maguire, whose novels include *Lost* and *Confessions of an Ugly Stepsister*, which was adapted for ABC's *Wonderful World of Disney*.

So what kind of stories interest *One Story*? "We've selected stories that are a little different than those you'll read elsewhere," says Tinti. "Not necessarily experimental but definitely brave. Each one contains a whole world." She cites George Saunders' short story "Pastoralia" as the type of story she'd like to see—"doing something a little more original, interesting, something you might not see somewhere else."

Due to its unique format, however, *One Story* has looser editorial guidelines than many magazines. "I don't want to have a specific kind of form," says Tinti. "People always say there's a certain kind of *New Yorker* story, or a certain kind of *Harper's* story. We are going to be open to different kinds of work. Because we're doing an individual format, it makes it easier for us to do that. We don't have to worry about it fitting in with other stories or other articles."

With so many competing journals, *One Story* seeks to stand out by doing something a little different. It offers both short story writers and readers a new format to enjoy the genre they love—"because," as the magazine proclaims, "there is always time for one story!"

—*Travis Adkins*

Needs: Adventure, ethnic/multicultural, experimental, fantasy (science fantasy), feminist, gay, historical, humor/satire, lesbian, literary, mainstream/contemporary, regional, religious/inspirational, romance (contemporary), science fiction (hard science, soft/sociological), senior citizen/retirement, sports, westerns (frontier, traditional), teaching. Receives 2 unsolicited mss/month. Accepts 7 mss/issue. "We read only in May when editorial board meets." Publishes ms 3-4 months after acceptance. Published work by Lois Spencer, Harry R. Noden, Linda J. Rice and June Langford Berkley. Length: 2,000 words maximum. Publishes short shorts. Also publishes poetry. Often comments on rejected ms.
How to Contact: Send 6 copies of complete ms with a cover letter. Include 30-word bio. Responds by July 30th. Send SASE with postage clipped for return of ms or send a disposable copy of ms. Sample copy $6.
Payment/Terms: Pays 2 contributor's copies; additional copies $6. Acquires first rights.

N **$** **○** **ONE STORY**, P.O. Box 1326, New York NY 10156. E-mail: submissions@one-story.com. Website: www.one-story.com (includes writer's guidelines, staff information, subscription information). Publisher: Maribeth Batcha. **Contact:** Hannah Tinti, editor. "We believe that short stories are best read alone. They should not be sandwiched in between a review and an exposé on liposuction, or placed after another work of fiction that is so sad or funny or long that the reader is worn out by the time they turn to it. The experience of reading a story by itself is usually found only in MFA programs or writing workshops. This is a shame. Besides, there is always time to read one story." Estab. 2002.

Needs: Literary. "We are looking for stories that leave readers feeling satisfied and are strong enough to stand alone. They can be any style and on any subject as long as they are good. We are looking for previously unpublished material, however if a story has been published outside North America, it will be considered." Recently published work by John Hodgman, Arlaina Tibensky and Michael Backus. Length: 3,000-10,000 words.

How to Contact: Submit complete ms with cover letter. Accepts submissions by e-mail. Include full mailing address and phone number. Send SASE for return of ms, or disposable copy of ms and SASE for reply only.

Payment/Terms: Pays $100 and 5 contributor's copies. Pays on publication for first North American serial rights.

OPEN SPACES QUARTERLY, PMB 134, 6327 C SW Capitol Hwy., Portland OR 97201-1937. (503)227-5764. Fax: (503)227-3401. E-mail: info@open-spaces.com. Website: www.open-spaces.com (includes overview, contents of current and back issues, sample articles and creative writing, submission guidelines, contact information). Editor: Penny Harrison. **Contact:** A. Bradley, fiction editor. Magazine: 64 pages; illustrations; photos. "We are a high-quality, general-interest publication with an intelligent, well-educated readership appreciative of well-written, insightful work." Quarterly. Estab. 1997.

Needs: "Excellence is the issue—not subject matter." Accepts 2 mss/issue; 8 mss/year. Published work by William Kittredge, Terence O'Donnell, Pattiann Rogers and David James Duncan. Publishes short shorts. Also publishes literary essays and poetry. Sometimes comments on rejected mss.

How to Contact: Send complete ms with a cover letter. Accepts queries/mss by fax. Include short bio, social security number and list of publications. SASE for return of ms or send a disposable copy of ms. Sample copy for $10. Guidelines free for SASE.

Payment/Terms: Pays on publication.

Advice: "The surest way for a writer to determine whether his or her material is right for us is to read the magazine."

ORCHID, Celebrating Stories and the Art of Storytelling, 3096 Williamsburg, Ann Arbor MI 48108. E-mail: editors@orchidlit.com. Website: www.orchidlit.org (includes writer's guidelines, staff information, subscription information). Executive Editors: Maureen Aitken, Cathy Mellet, Keith Hood. **Contact:** Editorial Board. "*Orchid* celebrates stories and the art of storytelling. We publish fiction, interviews on the craft of fiction and articles examining the role of short stories as literature. Our mission includes championing new and emerging writers. Each issue is compiled with this mission in mind." Estab. 2002.

Needs: Literary. "We consider fiction of all lengths: short shorts, short stories, novellas and novel excerpts." Recently published work Jonis Agee, E.J. Levy and Guo Liang.

How to Contact: Submit complete ms with cover letter. No e-mail submissions. Send SASE for return of ms or disposable copy of ms with SASE for reply only. No previously published work.

Payment/Terms: Pays 3 contributor's copies. Pays on publication for first rights.

OTHER VOICES, The University of Illinois at Chicago, Dept. of English (M/C 162), 601 S. Morgan St., Chicago IL 60607. (312)413-2209. Fax: (312)413-1005. E-mail: othervoices@listserv.uic.edu. Website: www.othervoicesmagazine.org (includes writer's guidelines, names of editors, e-mail address and subscription information). Editors: Lois Hauselman and Gina Frangello. **Contact:** Lois Hauselman or Gina Frangello. Magazine: 5⅞×9; 168-205 pages; 60 lb. paper; coated cover stock; occasional photos. "Original, fresh, diverse stories and novel excerpts" for literate adults. Semiannual. Estab. 1985. Circ. 1,500.

Needs: Fiction only. Contemporary, excerpted novel, experimental, humor/satire and literary. "No taboos, except ineptitude and murkiness. No science fiction, romance, horror, 'chick-lit or futuristic.' Would like to see more one-act plays and experimental literary stories." Receives 300 unsolicited fiction mss/month. Accepts 17-20 mss/issue. **Publishes 6 new writers/year.** Published work by Aimee Bender, Wanda Coleman, Cris Mazza and Dan Chaon. Length: 5,000 words maximum; average length: 4,000 words.

How to Contact: Send ms with SASE October 1 to April 1 only. No e-mail submissions. Mss received during non-reading period are returned unread. Cover letters "should be brief and list previous publications. Also, list title of submission. Most beginners' letters try to 'explain' the story—a big mistake." Accepts simultaneous submissions. Responds in 3 months to mss. Sample copy for $7 (includes postage). Guidelines for #10 SASE.

Payment/Terms: Pays in contributor's copies and modest cash gratuity. Acquires one-time rights.

Advice: "There are so *few* markets for *quality* fiction! By publishing up to 40 stories a year, we provide new and established writers a forum for their work. Send us your best voice, your best work, your best best."

OUTERBRIDGE, English 2S-218, The College of Staten Island (CUNY), 2800 Victory Blvd., Staten Island NY 10314. (718)982-3651. **Editor:** Charlotte Alexander. Magazine: 5½×8½; approximately 110 pages; 60 lb. white offset paper; 65 lb. cover stock. "We are a national literary magazine publishing mostly fiction and poetry. To date, we have had several special focus issues (the 'urban' and the 'rural' experience, 'Southern,' 'childhood,' 'nature and the environment,' 'animals,' 'love and friendship'). For anyone with enough interest in literature to look for writing of quality and writers on the contemporary scene who deserve attention. There probably is a growing circuit of writers, some academics, reading us by recommendations." Annual. Estab. 1975. Circ. 500-700.

New magazine *Orchid* focuses on emerging writers

The story of the literary magazine *Orchid* is one of three writers who decided to take matters into their own hands.

Keith Hood, Maureen Aitken, and Cathy Mellett are members of Critical Connection, a monthly writers workshop started by Hood in 1999 in Ann Arbor, Michigan. One day, the three found themselves lamenting the difficulties of getting their work published.

"All three of us have seen our work in print, but our stories are rejected more often than not," says Hood. "Maureen came up with the idea of starting a journal. We agreed from the beginning that it would be inappropriate to publish our own work, but we knew that many talented writers share our frustration with the difficulties of getting published, and we felt the need to provide a forum for such writers."

Today, Hood is managing editor and Aitken and Mellett are executive editors of *Orchid*, a biannual literary magazine that debuted in spring 2002 and champions the work of new and emerging writers.

"We know firsthand that the saturated market keeps many good writers from being introduced to the public," says Aitken. "We hope that Orchid will encourage other people to start journals or small presses. But that means extra effort from all of us to make contributions and take risks. So that's really what *Orchid* is about: three people wanting to make a contribution."

In addition to interviews with Janet Burroway and Alyce Miller, the first issue of *Orchid* contains an impressive fiction lineup of new and established writers including Garnett Kilberg Cohen, Stephen Dixon, E.J. Levy, Daniel Mueller, Tanja Pajevic, Alison Umminger, plus the first published story by Viet Nguyen. The second issue of the magazine features the work of at least two previously unpublished writers.

In the following interview, Hood, who also serves as *Orchid*'s art director, discusses the magazine's mission, its selection process, and the challenges facing a new literary journal.

What distinguishes *Orchid* from other literary journals?

We're not a one-of-a-kind journal, but our focus on fiction and our not being connected to a university or college (aka academia) puts us in the minority of serious literary journals.

How does your selection process work?

I'm the first reader for all unsolicited manuscripts. Stories that are poorly written and stories that do not meet our guidelines (i.e., they must be typed on one side of the page only and double-spaced) receive automatic rejections. I read the remaining stories and assign them a score before passing them on to Maureen and Cathy. Then they read each story and assign it a score. The combined scores and intense discussions determine whether we will continue to consider the story for publication. As you can see, the final decision on which manuscripts are published is reached by consensus.

How extensively do you edit the stories you accept?

It depends. For example, our first issue contained 18 stories. We made no changes to nine of the stories, suggested minor edits for six stories, and asked for rewrites of three stories. We're currently working with a writer whose work we like a lot, and it's actually been through two rewrites so far.

Do you have any editorial dislikes or pet peeves?

I don't know that I'd call them editorial dislikes, but there are common flaws among the submissions we receive. We receive far too many submissions that are anecdotes, instead of stories. Another common problem is writers attempting to be clever or gimmicky. Beginnings are a problem. Most stories don't get into the central conflict early enough. Endings are a bigger problem. It's very disappointing to read a story that is fairly good and then find that the ending is flat. Many writers have a tendency to wrap things up too neatly. There are far too many endings that don't spring from the events in the story. And far too many writers seem to be fond of surprise endings.

I do have one pet peeve—and I know it's petty—but stories submitted in envelopes smaller than 9 × 12 drive me crazy. I'll read a story submitted that way, and if the story is good we'd accept it, but I prefer a flat manuscript to one that has been stuffed into a #10 envelope.

Orchid's mission includes "championing new and emerging writers." What does this mean, in practical terms?

We think that the best journals provide a good blend of established, new, and emerging writers. Those terms (established, new, emerging) are bandied about a lot and not easily defined. An "emerging" writer strikes us as one with a number of publication credits in major journals (maybe they've also published a novel or collection of stories). A "new" writer may have no publication credits or very few publication credits in major journals. Our main goal is to provide a forum for talented writers.

How do you choose the nonfiction (interviews and articles) that appear in *Orchid*?

So far, the nonfiction portions of *Orchid* have been interviews, and these interviews have been conducted by the editors. We are interested in reading unsolicited interviews and articles. We look for articles, interviews, and creative nonfiction pieces that either tell a story or shed light on the art of storytelling.

What are the challenges of launching a literary magazine?

The main challenges are financing and distribution. No one connected with this project is receiving a salary, and many expenses are paid out of pocket. I'd like to sneak a positive thought in here. The community of writers has been very supportive. When we started the journal, we put a call out to fellow writers for subscriptions and contributions and were gratified by the response. We also received a very generous gift from one benefactor which helped cover the printing costs of our premier issue.

Distribution is a catch-22 in many ways. A national presence is important, but to get the journal into the big chains and other bookstores around the country requires a distributor, and you can't get a distributor until you have an actual journal to show them. That made getting a first issue onto bookshelves difficult to say the least. We have arrangements with some local independent bookstores, and a creative-writing teacher at a local college has made the journal a required textbook. We're still working on solving the distribution problem.

What's your best advice for a writer who wants to submit work to *Orchid*?
Read! Read! Read! And read some more. Read and/or subscribe to several literary journals. Of course, we'd love you to read and subscribe to *Orchid*. Other journals with heavy fiction content that I recommend are *Alaska Quarterly Review*, *Other Voices*, and *Witness*. Read short-story collections and anthologies such as the *Best American Short Stories* and *The O. Henry Awards* series. Read books on the craft of writing. Understand the essentials of craft. Know the meaning and practical application of "in medias res" and "Freytag's Triangle."
   —*Will Allison*

(For more information on *Orchid*, please see the listing on page 217. For more information on Critical Connection, visit their Web site at www.criticalconnection.org.)

Needs: Literary. "No *Reader's Digest* style; that is, very popularly oriented. We like to do interdisciplinary features, e.g., literature and music, literature and science and literature and the natural world." Accepts 8-10 mss/year. Does not read mss July-August. **Published new writers within the last year.** Recently published work by Henry Alley, Gary Fricke, Max Ludwigton, Kyoko Yoshida and Cara Chamberlein. Length: 10-25 pages. Also publishes poetry. Sometimes recommends other markets.
How to Contact: Query. Send complete ms with cover letter. "Don't talk too much, 'explain' the work, or act apologetic or arrogant. If published, tell where, with a brief bio." SASE (or IRC). Responds in 10 weeks to queries and mss. No multiple submissions. Sample copy for $6 for annual issue.
Payment/Terms: Pays 2 contributor's copies; charges ½ price of current issue for extras to its authors. Acquires one-time rights. Requests credits for further publication of material used by *OB*.
Advice: "Read our publication first. Don't send out blindly; get some idea of what the magazine might want. A *short* personal note with biography is appreciated. Competition is keen. Read an eclectic mix of classic and contemporary literature. Beware of untransformed autobiography, but *everything* in one's experience contributes."

N ⬤ ◎ **Y** **OWEN WISTER REVIEW**, Student Publications Board, P.O. Box 3625, University of Wyoming, Laramie WY 82071. (307)766-3819. Fax: (307)766-4027. E-mail: bi@uwyo.edu attn. OWR editor. **Contact:** Fiction Selection Committee. Editors change each year, contact selection committee. Magazine: 6×9; 92 pages; 60 lb. matte paper; 80 lb. glossy cover; illustrations; photos. "Though we are a university publication, our audience is wider than just an academic community. We're looking for fiction, poetry and artwork that captures some portion of the spirit of the American West: of yesterday and today." Semiannual. Estab. 1978. Circ. 600.
   ● *Owen Wister Review* has won numerous awards and honors far surpassing many student-run publications. The magazine received Best of Show award from the Associated Collegiate Press/College Media Advisors and six individual Gold Circle Awards from the Columbia Scholastic Press Association.
Needs: Ethnic/multicultural, experimental, humor/satire, literary, translations. Receives 12-15 unsolicited mss. Acquires 3 mss/issue; 6-8 mss/year. "Summer months are generally down time for *OWR*." Publishes ms 2-3 months after acceptance. **Publishes many new writers/year.** Published work by Jon Billman, Amy Epstein, Pete Fromm, Jill Patterson, Val Pexton and Gary Wallace. Length: 7,500 words maximum; average length: 1,300 words. Publishes short shorts. Also publishes literary essays, literary criticism and poetry.

How to Contact: Send complete ms with cover letter. Accepts queries/submissions by e-mail. Should include bio, list of publications. "*OWR* is published once a year in the spring semester. Deadline is December 1 prior to the publication in the spring." Responds in 3 weeks to queries; 3 months to mss. Send SASE for reply, return of ms or send disposable copy of the ms. Sample copy for $5. Guidelines free.
Payment/Terms: Pays 1 contributor's copy; 10% off additional copies. Acquires one-time rights.
Advice: "We seek well-written pieces that break barriers and take readers to new vantage points. Dream, write, revise and share. Fiction only gains life through its readers. We currently are including a distinct, separate Spoken Word CD version of the Owen Wister Review. This allows us to increase our submissions and our audience."

$ ☑ ◎ THE OXFORD AMERICAN, The Southern Magazine of Good Writing, P.O. Box 1156, Oxford MS 38655. (662)236-1836. Website: www.oxfordamericanmag.com. **Contact:** Marc Smirnoff, editor. Magazine: 8½×11; 100 pages; glossy paper; glossy cover; illustrations; photos. Quarterly. Estab. 1992. Circ. 40,000.
Needs: Regional (Southern); stories set in the South. Published work by Lewis Nordan, Donna Tartt, Florence King and Tony Earley. Also publishes literary essays and poetry. Sometimes comments on rejected mss.
How to Contact: Send complete ms. Send SASE for reply, return of ms or send a disposable copy of ms. No simultaneous submissions without indicating as such. No e-mail or faxed submissions. "No further guidelines available than those stated here." Sample copy for $10. "We review novels, nonfiction or short story collections only."
Payment/Terms: Pays $100 minimum. Pays on publication for first rights; prices vary.
Advice: "I know you've heard it before—but we appreciate those writers who try to get into the spirit of the magazine which they can best accomplish by being familiar with it."

Ⓝ ☑ ▼ OXFORD MAGAZINE, Bachelor Hall, Miami University, Oxford OH 45056. (513)529-1279. Editor: Brian Seidman. Editors change every year. **Send submissions to:** "Fiction Editor." Magazine: 6×9; 120 pages; illustrations. Annual. Estab. 1985. Circ. 1,000.
• *Oxford* has been awarded two Pushcart Prizes.
Needs: Literary, ethnic, experimental, humor/satire, feminist, gay/lesbian, translations. Receives 150 unsolicited mss/month. Reads mss September through December. **Published new writers within the last year.** Published work by Stephen Dixon, Andre Dubus and Stuart Dybek. Length: 2,000-4,000 words average. "We will accept long fiction (over 6,000 words) only in cases of exceptional quality." Publishes short shorts. Also publishes poetry.
How to Contact: Send complete ms with cover letter, which should include a short bio or interesting information. Accepts simultaneous submissions, if notified. Responds in 2 months, depending upon time of submissions; mss received after December 31 will be returned. SASE. Sample copy for $5.
Payment/Terms: Pays in contributor's copies. Acquires one-time rights.
Advice: "*Oxford Magazine* is looking for humbly vivid fiction; that is to say, fiction that illuminates, which creates and inhabits an honest, carefully rendered reality populated by believable, three-dimensional characters. We want more stories—from undiscovered writers—that melt hair and offer the heat of a character at an emotional crossroads. Send us stories that are unique; we want fiction no one else but you could possibly have written."

☑ OYSTER BOY REVIEW, P.O. Box 77842, San Francisco CA 94107-0842. E-mail: fiction@oysterboyreview.com. Website: www.oysterboyreview.com (includes full text of print issues, all back issues, submission and subscription information, staff, author index, related links). **Contact:** Damon Sauve, publisher, fiction editor. Electronic and print magazine. "We publish kick-ass, teeth-cracking stories."
• At presstime, *Oyster Boy Review* was closed to submissions due to a backlog of manuscripts. Please check the website for updates.

☑ PACIFIC COAST JOURNAL, French Bread Publications, P.O. Box 56, Carlsbad CA 92018. E-mail: paccoastj@f renchbreadpublications.com. Website: www.frenchbreadpublications.com/pcj (includes guidelines, contest information, past published work). Editor: Stillson Graham. **Contact:** Stephanie Kylkis, fiction editor. Magazine: 5½×8½; 40 pages; 20 lb. paper; 67 lb. cover; illustrations; b&w photos. "Slight focus toward Western North America/Pacific Rim." Quarterly (or "whenever we have enough money"). Estab. 1992. Circ. 200.
Needs: Ethnic/multicultural, experimental, feminist, historical, humor/satire, literary, science fiction (soft/sociological, magical realism). "No children's." Receives 30-40 unsolicited mss/month. Accepts 3-4 mss/issue; 10-12 mss/year. Publishes ms 6-18 months after acceptance. **Publishes 3-5 new writers/year.** Published work by Tamara Jane, Lisa Garrigues and Charles Ordine. Length: 4,000 words maximum; 2,500 words preferred. Publishes short shorts. Also publishes literary essays and poetry. Sometimes comments on rejected mss.
How to Contact: Send complete ms with a cover letter. Include 3 other publication titles that are recommended as good for writers. Responds in 6-9 months. Send SASE for reply, return of ms or send a disposable copy of ms. Accepts simultaneous, reprint and electronic submissions (Mac or IBM disks). Sample copy for $2.50, 6×9 SASE. Reviews novels and short story collections.
Payment/Terms: Pays 1 contributor's copy. Acquires one-time rights.
Advice: "We tend to comment more on a story not accepted for publication when an e-mail address is provided as the SASE. There are very few quality literary magazines that are not backed by big institutions. We don't have those kinds of resources so publishing anything is a struggle. We have to make each issue count."

Ⓝ ☑ pacific REVIEW, Dept. of English and Comparative Lit., San Diego State University, 5500 Campanile Dr., San Diego CA 92182-8140. E-mail: pacificREVIEW_sdsu@yahoo.com. Website: http://pacificREVIEW.sdsu.edu

(includes guidelines, subscription services, e-boutique, excerpts, masthead, links to literary community, photographs from readings). **Contact:** Gwendolyn Spring Kurtz, editor-in-chief. Magazine: 6×9; 200 pages; book stock paper; paper back, extra heavy cover stock; b&w illustrations, b&w photos. "*pacific REVIEW* publishes the work of emergent literati, pairing their efforts with those of established artists. It is available at West Coast independent booksellers, university and college libraries, and is taught as text in numerous University Literature and Creative Writing classes." Circ. 2,000.
Needs: "We seek high-quality fiction and give preference to pieces that interrogate identity, in particular those works that explore identity in the context of West Coast/California and border culture." For information on theme issues see website. **Publishes 15 new writers/year.** Recently published work by Ai, Alurista, Susan Daitch, Lawrence Ferlinghetti and William T. Vollmann. Length: 4,000 words maximum.
How to Contact: Send original ms with SASE. Responds in 3 months to mss. Sample copy for $10.
Payment/Terms: Pays 2 contributor's copies. Acquires first serial rights. All other rights revert to author."
Advice: "We welcome all submissions, especially those created in or in the context of the West Coast/California and the space of our borders."

PALO ALTO REVIEW, A Journal of Ideas, Palo Alto College, 1400 W. Villaret, San Antonio TX 78224. (210)921-5021. Fax: (210)921-5008. E-mail: eshull@accd.edu. **Contact:** Bob Richmond and Ellen Shull, editors. Magazine: 8½×11; 60 pages; 60 lb. natural white paper (50% recycled); illustrations; photos. "Not too experimental nor excessively avant-garde, just good stories (for fiction). Ideas are what we are after. We are interested in connecting the college and the community. We would hope that those who attempt these connections will choose startling topics and interesting angles with which to investigate the length and breadth of the teaching/learning spectrum, life itself." Semiannual (spring and fall). Estab. 1992. Circ. 500-600.
● *Palo Alto Review* was awarded the Pushcart Prize for 2001.
Needs: Adventure, ethnic/multicultural, experimental, fantasy, feminist, historical, humor/satire, literary, mainstream/contemporary, mystery/suspense, regional, romance, science fiction, translations, westerns. Upcoming themes available for SASE. Receives 100-150 unsolicited mss/month. Accepts 2-4 mss/issue; 4-8 mss/year. Does not read mss March-April and October-November when putting out each issue. Publishes ms 2-15 months after acceptance. **Publishes 30 new writers/year.** Published work by Layle Silbert, Naomi Chase, Kenneth Emberly, C.J. Hannah, Tom Juvik, Kassie Fleisher and Paul Perry. Length: 5,000 words maximum. Publishes short shorts. Also publishes articles, interviews, literary essays, literary criticism, poetry. Always comments on rejected mss.
How to Contact: Send complete ms with a cover letter. "Request sample copy and guidelines." Accepts queries by e-mail. Include brief bio and brief list of publications. Responds in 4 months. Send SASE for reply, return of ms or send a disposable copy of ms. Accepts simultaneous and electronic (Macintosh disk) submissions. Sample copy for $5. Guidelines for #10 SASE.
Payment/Terms: Pays 2 contributor's copies; additional copies for $5. Acquires first North American serial rights.
Advice: "Good short stories have interesting characters confronted by a dilemma working toward a solution. So often what we get is 'a moment in time,' not a story. Generally, characters are interesting because readers can identify with them. Edit judiciously. Cut out extraneous verbiage. Set up a choice that has to be made. Then create tension—who wants what and why they can't have it."

PANGOLIN PAPERS, Turtle Press, P.O. Box 241, Nordland WA 98358. (360)385-3626. E-mail: trtlbluf@olympus.net. Website: www.olympus.net/community/trtlbluf/trtlbluf.htm. **Contact:** Pat Britt, managing editor. Magazine: 5½×8½; 120 pages; 24 lb. paper; 80 lb. cover. "Best quality literary fiction for an informed audience." Triannual. Estab. 1994. Circ. 500.
Needs: Experimental, humor/satire, literary, translations. "We would like to see more funny but literate stories. No genre such as romance or science fiction." Plans to publish special fiction issues or anthologies in the future. Receives 60 unsolicited mss/month. Accepts 7-10 mss/issue; 20-30 mss/year. Publishes ms 4-12 months after acceptance. Agented fiction 10%. **Publishes 3-4 new writers/year.** Published work by Jack Nisbet and Barry Gifford. Length: 100-7,000 words; average length: 3,500 words. Publishes short shorts. Length: 400 words. Also publishes literary essays. Sometimes comments on rejected mss.
How to Contact: Send complete ms with a cover letter. Include estimated word count and short bio. Accepts mss on disk. Responds in 2 months to mss. Send SASE for reply, return of ms or send a disposable copy of ms. No simultaneous submissions. Sample copy for $6 and $1.50 postage. Guidelines for #10 SASE.
Payment/Terms: Pays 2 contributor's copies. Offers annual $200 prize for best story. Acquires first North American serial rights. Sends galleys to author.
Advice: "We are looking for original voices; good story, tight writing. Edit your material and cut mercilessly. Follow the rules and be honest in your work."

$ THE PARIS REVIEW, 541 E. 72nd St., New York NY 10021. (212)861-0016. Fax: (212)861-4504. Website: www.parisreview.com (includes history, excerpts from the magazine, masthead, audio clips). **Contact:** George A. Plimpton, editor. Magazine: 5¼×8½; about 260 pages; illustrations; photos (unsolicited artwork not accepted). "Fiction and poetry of superlative quality, whatever the genre, style or mode. Our contributors include prominent, as well as less well-known and previously unpublished writers. Writers at Work interview series includes important contemporary writers discussing their own work and the craft of writing." Quarterly.
● Work published in *The Paris Review* received five Pushcart awards. It ranked on *Writer's Digest*'s "Top 30" list of best markets for writers.

Needs: Literary. Receives about 1,000 unsolicited fiction mss each month. **Publishes 5 new writers/year.** Recently published work by Thomas Wolfe, Denis Johnson, Melissa Pritchard, Jim Shepard and Jonathan Safran Foer. No preferred length. Also publishes literary essays, poetry.

How to Contact: *Send complete ms with SASE to Fiction Editor, 541 E. 72nd St., New York NY 10021.* Responds in 4 months. Accepts simultaneous and multiple submissions. Sample copy for $12. Writer's guidelines for #10 SASE. Sponsors annual Aga Khan Fiction Contest award of $1,000, and The Paris Review Discovery Prize of $1,000.

Payment/Terms: Pays up to $1,000. Pays on publication for all rights. Sends galleys to author.

⭕ PARTING GIFTS, 3413 Wilshire, Greensboro NC 27408-2923. E-mail: rbixby@aol.com. Website: users.aol.com/marchst (includes guidelines and samples). **Contact:** Robert Bixby, editor. Magazine: 5×7; 72 pages. "*Parting Gifts* seeks good, powerful and short fiction that stands on its own and takes no prisoners." Semiannual. Estab. 1988.

Needs: "Brevity is the second most important criterion behind literary quality." Publishes ms within one year of acceptance. Published work by Ray Miller, Katherine Taylor, Curtis Smith and William Snyder, Jr. Length: 250-1,000 words. Also publishes poetry. Sometimes critiques rejected mss.

How to Contact: Send complete ms with cover letter. Accepts submissions by e-mail. Responds in 1 day to queries; 1 week to mss. Accepts simultaneous and multiple submissions. SASE.

Payment/Terms: Pays in contributor's copies. Acquires one-time rights.

Advice: "Read the works of Amy Hempel, Jim Harrison, Kelly Cherry, C.K. Williams and Janet Kauffman, all excellent writers who epitomize the writing *Parting Gifts* strives to promote. I look for original voice, original ideas, original setting and characters, language that makes one weep without knowing why, a deep understanding or keen observation of real people in real situations. The magazine is online, along with guidelines and feedback to authors; reading any one or all three will save a lot of postage."

$⭕ PARTISAN REVIEW, 236 Bay State Rd., Boston MA 02215. (617)353-4260. Fax: (617)353-7444. E-mail: partisan@bu.edu. Website: www.partisanreview.com (includes excerpts, writer's guidelines and subscription information). Editor-in-Chief: William Phillips. Editor: Edith Kurzweil. **Contact:** Fiction Editor. Magazine: 6×9; 160 pages; 40 lb. paper; 60 lb. cover stock. "Theme is of world literature and contemporary culture: fiction, essays and poetry with emphasis on the arts and political and social commentary, for the general intellectual public and scholars." Quarterly. Estab. 1934. Circ. 8,000.

Needs: Contemporary, experimental, literary, prose poem, regional and translations. Receives 100 unsolicited fiction mss/month. Buys 1-2 mss/issue; 4-8 mss/year. Published work by Leonard Michaels, Muriel Spark and Doris Lessing. Length: open.

How to Contact: Send complete ms with SASE and cover letter listing past credits. No simultaneous submissions. Responds in 4 months to mss. Sample copy for $6 and $1.50 postage.

Payment/Terms: Pays $25-200 and 2 contributor's copies. Pays on publication for first rights.

Advice: "Please research the type of fiction we publish. Often we receive manuscripts which are entirely inappropriate for our journal. Sample copies are available for sale and this is a good way to determine audience."

⭕ 💡 THE PATERSON LITERARY REVIEW, Passaic County Community College, One College Blvd., Paterson NJ 07505. (973)684-6555. Fax: (973)523-6085. E-mail: mgillan@pccc.cc.nj.us. **Contact:** Maria Mazziotti Gillan, editor. Magazine: 6×9; 336 pages; 60 lb. paper; 70 lb. cover; illustrations; photos. Annual.

● Work from *PLR* has been included in the *Pushcart Prize* anthology and *Best American Poetry*.

Needs: Contemporary, ethnic, literary. "We are interested in quality short stories, with no taboos on subject matter." Receives about 60 unsolicited mss/month. Publishes ms about 6 months to 1 year after acceptance. **5% of work published is by new writers.** Published work by Robert Mooney and Abigail Stone. Length: 1,500 words maximum. Also publishes literary essays, literary criticism, poetry.

How to Contact: Submit no more than 1 story at a time. Submission deadline: March 1. Send SASE for reply or return of ms. "Indicate whether you want story returned." Accepts simultaneous submissions. Sample copy for $13. Reviews novels and short story collections.

Payment/Terms: Pays in contributor's copies. Acquires first North American rights.

Advice: Looks for "clear, moving and specific work."

⭕ 🎯 PEARL, A Literary Magazine, Pearl, 3030 E. Second St., Long Beach CA 90803-5163. Phone/Fax: (562)434-4523. E-mail: mjohn5150@aol.com. Website: www.pearlmag.com (includes writer's guidelines, contest guidelines, subscription information, books, current issue, about the editors). **Contact:** Marilyn Johnson, editor. Magazine: 5½×8½; 96 pages; 60 lb. recycled, acid-free paper; perfect-bound; coated cover; b&w drawings and graphics. "We are primarily a poetry magazine, but we do publish some *very short* fiction and nonfiction. We are interested in lively, readable prose that speaks to *real* people in direct, living language; for a general literary audience." Biannual. Estab. 1974. Circ. 600.

Needs: Contemporary, humor/satire, literary, mainstream, prose poem. "We will only consider short-short stories up to 1,200 words. Longer stories (up to 4,000 words) may only be submitted to our short story contest. All contest entries are considered for publication. Although we have no taboos stylistically or subject-wise, obscure, predictable, sentimental, or cliché-ridden stories are a turn-off." Publishes an all fiction issue each year. Receives 10-20 unsolicited mss/month. Accepts 1-10 mss/issue; 12-15 mss/year. Submissions accepted September-May *only*. Publishes ms 6 months to 1 year after acceptance. **Publishes 1-5 new writers/year.** Published work by John Brantingham, Suzanne Greenberg,

Gina Ochsner, Helena Maria Viramontes, Lisa Glatt and Gerald Locklin. Length: 500-1,200 words; average length: 1,000 words. Accepts multiple submissions. Also publishes poetry. Sponsors an annual short story contest. Send SASE for complete guidelines.

How to Contact: Send complete ms with cover letter including publishing credits and brief bio. Accepts simultaneous submissions. Responds in 2 months to mss. SASE. Sample copy for $7 (postpaid). Guidelines for #10 SASE.

Payment/Terms: Pays 1 contributor's copy. Acquires first North American serial rights. Sends galleys to author.

Advice: "We look for vivid, *dramatized* situations and characters, stories written in an original 'voice,' that make sense and follow a clear narrative line. What makes a manuscript stand out is more elusive, though—more to do with feeling and imagination than anything else . . ."

PEMBROKE MAGAZINE, Box 1510, University of North Carolina at Pembroke, Pembroke NC 28372. (910)521-6358. Website: www.uncp/pembrokemagazine.edu. Editor: Shelby Stephenson. **Contact:** Tina Emanuel, managing editor. Magazine: 6×9; approximately 200 pages; illustrations; photos. Magazine of poems and stories plus literary essays. Annual. Estab. 1969. Circ. 500.

Needs: Open. Receives 120 unsolicited mss/month. Publishes short shorts. **Published new writers within the last year.** Published work by Fred Chappell, Robert Morgan. Length: open. Occasionally critiques rejected mss and recommends other markets.

How to Contact: Send complete ms. No simultaneous submissions. Responds in up to 3 months. SASE. Sample copy for $8 and 9×10 SAE.

Payment/Terms: Pays 1 contributor's copy.

Advice: "Write with an end for *writing*, not publication."

PENINSULAR, Literary Magazine, Cherrybite Publications, Linden Cottage, 45 Burton Rd., Little Neston, Cheshire CH64 4AE England. Phone: 0151 353 0967. Fax: 0870 165 6282. E-mail: helicon@globalnet.co.uk. Website: www.cherrybite.co.uk (includes guidelines, brief magazine description, competition rules). **Contact:** Shelagh Nugent, editor. Magazine: 90 pages; card cover. "We're looking for brilliant short fiction to make the reader think/laugh/cry. A lively, up and coming quality magazine." Quarterly. Estab. 1985. Circ. 400. "We ask only that a potential writer buy at least one copy. Subscribing is not essential."

Needs: Adventure, ethnic/multicultural (general), fantasy (space fantasy), gay, historical (general), horror (futuristic, psychological, supernatural), humor/satire, lesbian, literary, New Age, psychic/supernatural/occult, science fiction (soft/sociological). Wants to see more science fiction, historical, adventure. "I'll read anything but avoid animals telling the story and clichés. No pornography or children's fiction. Also avoid purple prose." Receives 50 unsolicited mss/month. Accepts 10 mss/issue; 40 mss/year. Publishes ms 3-6 months after acceptance. **Publishes 4-5 new writers/year.** Published work by Alex Keegan, Sarah Klerbart, PDR Lindsay and Leigh Eduardo. Length: 1,000-4,000 words; average length: 3,000 words. Publishes short shorts. Average length: 1,000 words. Often comments on rejected mss.

How to Contact: Send for guidelines. Prefers hard copy for submissions. Include estimated word count. Responds in 1 week to queries; 2 weeks to mss. "I often write comments on the manuscript." Accepts simultaneous submissions and previously published work. Sample copy for $5. Guidelines for SASE with 2 IRCs or by e-mail.

Payment/Terms: Pays £5 sterling per 1,000 words or can pay in copies and subscriptions; additional copies £5 sterling or equivalent in dollars cash. Pays on publication for one-time rights. Sponsors contest. "Send IRCs for current competition details."

Advice: "We look for impeccable presentation and grammar, outstanding prose, original story line and the element of difference that forbids me to put the story down. A good opening paragraph usually grabs me. Read one or two copies and study the guidelines. A beginning writer should read as much as possible. The trend seems to be for stories written in first person/present tense and for stories without end leaving the reader thinking 'so what?' Stories not following this trend stand more chance of being published by me!"

PENNSYLVANIA ENGLISH, Penn State DuBois, College Place, DuBois PA 15801. (814)375-4814. Fax: (814)375-4784. E-mail: ajv2@psu.edu. "Mention Pennsylvania English in the subject line or at the beginning of the message." **Contact:** Antonio Vallone, editor. Magazine: 5½×8½; up to 180 pages; perfect bound; full color cover featuring the artwork of a Pennsylvania artist. "Our philosophy is quality. We publish literary fiction (and poetry and nonfiction). Our intended audience is literate, college-educated people." Annual. Estab. 1985. Circ. 500.

Needs: Short shorts, literary, contemporary mainstream. "No genre fiction or romance." Publishes ms within 12 months after acceptance. **Publishes 4-6 new writers/year.** Published work by Dave Kress, Dan Leone and Paul West. Length: "no maximum or minimum." Publishes short shorts. Also publishes literary essays, literary criticism, poetry. Sometimes critiques rejected mss.

How to Contact: Send complete ms with cover letter. No e-mail submissions. Responds in 6 months. SASE. Accepts simultaneous submissions.

Payment/Terms: Pays in 3 contributor's copies. Acquires first North American serial rights.

Advice: "Quality of the writing is our only measure. We're not impressed by long-winded cover letters detailing awards and publications we've never heard of. Beginners and professionals have the same chance with us. We receive stacks of competently written but boring fiction. For a story to rise out of the rejection pile, it takes more than basic competence."

THE PERALTA PRESS, College of Alameda, 555 Atlantic Ave., Alameda CA 94501. (510)748-2340. E-mail: zenmanme@aol.com. Website: www.peraltapress.org (includes guidelines, names of editors and excerpts). **Contact:** Jay Rubin, editor. Literary magazine: 6×9; 150 pages. "*The Peralta Press* provides a podium for a diverse blend of established and emerging 21st century voices cutting across race, gender, ethnic, age, religious, political and sexually oriented boundaries. We publish short fiction, short creative nonfiction and poetry without predetermined editorial themes. Goal is to include approximately 16 prose pieces and 50 poems." Annual. Estab. 2000. Circ. 1,500. "It's a good idea to submit through our annual writing contest (entry fee $10/story). Contest entries considered before general submissions."

Needs: Adventure, erotica, ethnic/multicultural, feminist, gay, glitz, historical, horror, humor/satire, lesbian, mainstream, military/war, mystery/suspense, psychic/supernatural/occult. Receives 12 unsolicited mss/month. Accepts 16 mss/issue; 16 mss/year. Publishes ms 4 months after acceptance. **Publishes 12 new writers/year.** Recently published work by Shawna Chandler, Susan Lester, Richard May and Carla S. Schick. Length: 300-2,000 words; average length: 1,800. Publishes short shorts; average length: 700 words. Also publishes literary essays, literary criticism and poetry. Sometimes comments on rejected mss.

How to Contact: Send complete ms with cover letter. Include estimated word count and brief bio in 50 words. Send SASE for return of ms or send disposable copy of ms and #10 SASE for reply only. Sample copy for $10. Guidelines for SASE.

Payment/Terms: Pays 1 contributor's copy; additional copies $10. Acquires one-time rights and electronic rights.

Advice: "Most accepted manuscripts are submitted to our annual writing contest. Visit our website for details or write to request guidelines."

PEREGRINE, published by Amherst Writers & Artists Press, P.O. Box 1076, Amherst MA 01004-1076. (413)253-3307. Fax: (413)253-7764. E-mail: awapress@aol.com. Website: www.amherstwriters.com (includes writer's guidelines, names of editors, excerpts from publication and interviews with authors). **Contact:** Nancy Rose, co-editor. Magazine: 6×9; 120 pages; 60 lb. white offset paper; glossy cover. "*Peregrine* has provided a forum for national and international writers for over 21 years, and is committed to finding excellent work by new writers as well as established authors. We publish what we love, knowing that all editorial decisions are subjective, and that all work has a home somewhere." Annual.

Needs: Poetry and prose—short stories, short short. "No previously published work. No children's stories. We welcome work reflecting diversity of voice." Accepts 6-12 fiction mss/issue. Publishes ms an average of 4 months after acceptance. **Published 6-8 new writers/year.** Recently published work by Stephanie Dickinson, William Gagnon, Jaclyn Honig and Brenda Seidman. "We like to be surprised. We look for writing that is honest, unpretentious, and memorable." Length: 3,000 words maximum. Short pieces have a better chance of publication.

How to Contact: Send #10 SASE to "Peregrine Guidelines" or visit website for writer's guidelines. "No electronic submissions." Send ms with cover letter; include 40-word (maximum) biographical note, prior publications and word count. Accepts simultaneous and multiple submissions. Enclose sufficiently stamped SASE for return of ms; if disposable copy, enclose #10 SASE for response. Deadline for submission: April 1, 2003. Read October-April. Sample copy $10.

Payment/Terms: Pays contributor's copies. All rights return to writer upon publication.

Advice: "We look for heart and soul as well as technical expertise. Trust your own voice. Familiarize yourself with *Peregrine*." Every ms is read by several readers; all decisions are made by editors.

[N!] **PERIMETER, A Journal of International Poetry and Art**, 301 W. Orion, Santa Ana CA 92707. (714)979-5597. E-mail: perimeter@worldnet.att.net. Website: www.perimeter.home.att.net. **Contact:** Jared Millar, editor. Magazine: 5½×8½; 26 pages; 24 lb. paper. "We are a 'little magazine' featuring mostly poetry but quite fond of great short fiction. The spirit is avante-garde but with no allegiance to any particular movement or school." Annual. Estab. 1997. Circ. 50.

Needs: Literary. "No juvenile, science fiction, genre." Receives 2 unsolicited mss/month. Accepts 1-2 mss/year. Publishes mss 6-12 months after acceptance. **Publishes 1 new writer/year.** Recently published work by Ronald MacKinnon Thompson, John Sweet and Virgil Suarez. Length: 100-2,500 words; average length: 1,500 words. Publishes short shorts. Sometimes comments on rejected mss.

How to Contact: Send complete ms with cover letter. Accepts submissions by e-mail. Include estimated word count and brief bio. Responds in 4 months. Send SASE for return of ms or disposable copy of ms and SASE for reply only. Accepts previously published submissions. Sample copy for $2. Guidelines for SASE or by e-mail.

Payment/Terms: Pays 1 contributor's copy; additional copies $2. Pays on publication for one time rights.

Advice: "We look for excellent writing, imagery and word play. Rewrite, edit, read!"

[N!] **PHANTASMAGORIA**, Century College English Dept., 3300 Century Ave. N, White Bear Lake MN 55110. (651)779-3410. E-mail: allenabigail@hotmail.com. **Contact:** Abigail Allen, editor. Magazine: 5½×8½; 140-200 pages. "We publish literary fiction, poetry and essays (no scholarly essays)." Semiannual. Estab. 2001. Circ. 1,000. Member, CLMP.

Needs: Experimental, literary, mainstream. "No children's stories or young adult/teen material." Receives 60 unsolicited mss/month. Accepts 20-30 mss/issue; 40-60 mss/year. Publishes ms 6 months after acceptance. **Publishes 5-10 new writers/year.** Recently published work by Greg Mulcahy, Alvin Greenberg, Thaddeus Rutkowski and Elaine Ford. Length: 4,000 words maximum; average length: 2,500 words. Publishes short shorts. Also publishes literary essays and poetry.

How to Contact: Send complete ms with a cover letter. Include brief bio. Responds in 2 weeks to queries; 2-4 months to mss. Send SASE (or IRC) for return of ms or send a disposable copy of ms and #10 SASE for reply only. Sample copy for $7. Guidelines for SASE. Reviews novels, short story collections and nonfiction books of interest to writers. Send review copies to editor.

Payment/Terms: Pays 2 contributor's copies. Acquires first North American serial rights.

PHOEBE, A Journal of Literary Arts, George Mason University, MSN 2D6, 4400 University Dr., Fairfax VA 22030. (703)993-2915. E-mail: phoebe@gmu.edu. Website: www.gmu.edu/pubs/phoebe/index.htm (includes writer's guidelines, fiction and poetry contest guidelines, subscription information, past issue descriptions, etc.). **Contact:** Matt Ellsworth, fiction editor. Editors change each year. Magazine: 8½×8½; 116 pages; 80 lb. paper; 0-5 illustrations; 0-10 photos. "We publish mainly fiction and poetry with occasional visual art." Published 2 times/year. Estab. 1972. Circ. 3,000.

Needs: "Looking for a broad range of fiction and poetry. We encourage writers and poets to experiment, to stretch the boundaries of genre. No romance, western, juvenile, erotica." Receives 30 mss/month. Accepts 3-5 mss/issue. Does not read mss in summer. Publishes ms 3-6 months after acceptance. **Publishes 9 new writers/year.** Published work by Gina Ochsner, W.P. Osborn and Ralph Tyler. Length: no more than 35 pages of fiction, no more than 15 pages of poetry.

How to Contact: Send complete ms with cover letter. Include "name, address, phone, brief bio." SASE. Accepts simultaneous submissions. Sample copy for $6.

Payment/Terms: Pays 2 contributor's copies. Acquires one-time rights. All rights revert to author.

Advice: "We are interested in a variety of fiction and poetry. We encourage writers and poets to experiment and stretch boundaries of genre. We suggest potential contributors study previous issues. Each year *Phoebe* sponsors fiction and poetry contests, with $1,000 awarded to the winning short story and poem. The deadline for both the Greg Grummer Award in Poetry and the Phoebe Fiction Prize is December 1. E-mail or send SASE for complete contest guidelines."

$ PIG IRON PRESS, Box 237, 27 N. Phelps, Youngstown OH 44501. (330)747-6932. Fax: (330)747-0599. E-mail: pig_iron_press@cboss.com. **Editor:** Jim Villani. Annual series: 8½×11; 144 pages; 60 lb. offset paper; 85 pt. coated cover stock; b&w illustrations; b&w 120 line photos. "Contemporary literature by new and experimental writers." Annually. Estab. 1975. Circ. 1,000.

● At press time, Pig Iron Press was not accepting unsolicited submissions; resumption date to be announced.

Needs: Literary and thematic. "No mainstream." Accepts 60-70 mss/issue. Receives approximately 75-100 unsolicited mss/month. Published work by Charles Darling, Jim Sanderson and J.D. Winans. Length: 8,000 words maximum. Also publishes literary nonfiction, poetry. Sponsors contest. Send SASE for details.

How to Contact: Send complete ms with SASE. No simultaneous submissions. Responds in 4 months. Sample copy for $5.

Payment/Terms: Pays $5/printed page and 2 contributor's copies on publication for first North American serial rights; $5 charge for extras.

Advice: "Looking for work that is polished, compelling and magical."

PIKEVILLE REVIEW, Pikeville College, Sycamore St., Pikeville KY 41501. (606)218-5002. Fax: (606)218-5225. E-mail: eward@pc.edu. Website: www.pc.edu (includes writer's guidelines, names of editors, short fiction). **Editor:** Elgin M. Ward. **Contact:** Fiction Editor. Magazine: 8½×6; 120 pages; illustrations; photos. "Literate audience interested in well-crafted poetry, fiction, essays and reviews." Annual. Estab. 1987. Circ. 500.

Needs: Ethnic/multicultural, experimental, feminist, humor/satire, literary, mainstream/contemporary, regional, translations. Receives 60-80 unsolicited mss/month. Accepts 3-4 mss/issue. Does not read mss in the summer. Publishes ms 6-8 months after acceptance. **Publishes 20 new writers/year.** Published work by Jim Wayne Miller and Robert Morgan. Length: 15,000 words maximum; average length: 5,000 words. Publishes short shorts. Also publishes literary essays and poetry. Often critiques rejected mss. Sponsors occasional fiction award: $50.

How to Contact: Send complete ms with cover letter. Include estimated word count. Send SASE for reply, return of ms or send a disposable copy of ms. Accepts simultaneous submissions. Sample copy for $4. Reviews novels and short story collections.

Payment/Terms: Pays 5 contributor's copies; additional copies for $3. Acquires first rights.

Advice: "Send a clean manuscript with well-developed characters."

$ PLANET-THE WELSH INTERNATIONALIST, P.O. Box 44, Aberystwyth, Ceredigion, SY23 3ZZ Cymru/ Wales UK. Phone: 01970-611255. Fax: 01970-611197. E-mail: planet.enquiries@planetmagazine.org.uk. Website: www.planetmagazine.org.uk (includes details of staff; excepts from current and past issues; details of *Planet's* aims and interests). **Contact:** John Barnie, fiction editor. Bimonthly. Circ. 1,400. Publishes 1-2 stories/issue.

Needs: "A literary/cultural/political journal centered on Welsh affairs but with a strong interest in minority cultures in Europe and elsewhere. No magical realism, horror, science fiction." Would like to see more "inventive, imaginative fiction that pays attention to language and experiments with form." Published work by Harriet Richards, Katie O'Reilly and Guy Vanderhaeghe. Length: 1,500-4,000 words maximum.

How to Contact: No submissions returned unless accompanied by an SAE. Writers submitting from abroad should send at least 3 IRCs for return of typescript; 1 IRC for reply only.

Payment/Terms: Writers receive 1 contributor's copy. Payment is at the rate of £40 per 1,000 words for prose; a minimum of £25 per poem (in the currency of the relevant country if the author lives outside the UK). Sample copy: cost (to USA & Canada) £2.87. Writers' guidelines for SAE.

Advice: "We do not look for fiction which necessarily has a 'Welsh' connection, which some writers assume from our title. We try to publish a broad range of fiction and our main criterion is quality. Try to read copies of any magazine you submit to. Don't write out of the blue to a magazine which might be completely inappropriate to your work. Recognize that you are likely to have a high rejection rate, as magazines tend to favor writers from their own countries."

$ 🖉 📺 **PLEIADES**, Department of English & Philosophy, Central Missouri State University, Martin 336, Warrensburg MO 64093-5046. (660)543-4425. Fax: (660)543-8544. E-mail: kdp8106@cmsu2.cmsu.edu. Website: www. cmsu.edu/englphil/pleiades.htm (includes guidelines, editors, sample poetry or prose). Editor: R.M. Kinder. **Contact:** Susan Steinberg, fiction editor. Poetry: Kevin Prufer. Magazine: 5½×8½; 150 pages; 60 lb. paper; perfect-bound; 8 pt. color cover. Sponsored in part by Missouri Arts Council. "*Pleiades* publishes poetry, fiction, essays, occasional drama, interviews and reviews for a general educated audience." Semiannual. Estab. 1939. Circ. 3,000.

● Work from *Pleiades* appears in recent volumes of *The Best American Poetry, Pushcart Prizes,* and *Best American Fantasy and Horror.*

Needs: Ethnic/multicultural, experimental, especially cross-genre, feminist, gay, humor/satire, literary, mainstream/contemporary, regional, translations. "No westerns, romance, mystery, etc. Nothing pretentious, didactic or overly sentimental." Receives 100 unsolicited fiction mss/month. Accepts 8 mss/issue; 16 mss/year. "We're slower at reading manuscripts in the summer." Publishes ms 6-12 months after acceptance. **Publishes 3-4 new writers/year.** Recently published work by Sherman Alexie, Joyce Carol Oates and James Tate. Length: 800-8,000 words; average length: 3,000-6,000 words. Also publishes literary essays, literary criticism and poetry. Sometimes comments on rejected mss.

How to Contact: Send complete ms with a cover letter. Accepts queries by e-mail but not submissions. Include 75-100 bio, Social Security number and list of publications. Responds in 3 weeks to queries; 4 months to mss. Send SASE for reply, return of ms or send a disposable copy of ms. Accepts simultaneous submissions. Sample copy (including guidelines) for $6.

Payment/Terms: Pays $10 or subscription and 1 contributor's copy. Pays on publication for first North American serial rights.

Advice: Looks for "a blend of language and subject matter that entices from beginning to end. Send us your best work. Don't send us formula stories. While we appreciate and publish well-crafted traditional pieces, we constantly seek the story that risks, that breaks form and expectations and wins us over anyhow."

$ 🖉 📺 **PLOUGHSHARES**, Emerson College, 120 Boylston St., Boston MA 02116. (617)824-8753. Website: www.pshares.org. Editor: Don Lee. **Contact:** Fiction Editor. "Our mission is to present dynamic, contrasting views on what is valid and important in contemporary literature, and to discover and advance significant literary talent. Each issue is guest-edited by a different writer. We no longer structure issues around preconceived themes." Triquarterly. Estab. 1971. Circ. 6,000.

● Work published in *Ploughshares* has been selected regularly for inclusion in the *Best American Short Stories* and *O. Henry Prize* anthologies. In fact the magazine has the honor of having the most stories selected from a single issue (three) to be included in *Best American Short Stories*. Guest editors have included Richard Ford, Tim O'Brien and Ann Beattie. *Ploughshares* ranked on *Writer's Digest*'s "Top 30" list of best markets for fiction writers.

Needs: Literary. "No genre (science fiction, detective, gothic, adventure, etc.), popular formula or commercial fiction whose purpose is to entertain rather than to illuminate." Buys 30 mss/year. Receives 1,000 unsolicited fiction mss each month. **Published new writers within the last year.** Published work by Rick Bass, Joy Williams and Andre Dubus. Length: 300-6,000 words.

How to Contact: Reading period: postmarked August 1 to March 31. Cover letter should include "previous pubs." SASE. Responds in 5 months to mss. Sample copy for $8. (Please specify fiction issue sample.) Current issue for $9.95. Guidelines for #10 SASE.

Payment/Terms: Pays $25/page, $50 minimum; $250 maximum, copies and a subscription. Pays on publication for first North American serial rights. Offers 50% kill fee for assigned ms not published.

Advice: "Be familiar with our fiction issues, fiction by our writers and by our various editors (e.g., Sue Miller, Tobias Wolff, Rosellen Brown, Richard Ford, Jayne Anne Phillips, James Alan McPherson) and more generally acquaint yourself with the best short fiction currently appearing in the literary quarterlies, and the annual prize anthologies (*Pushcart Prize, O. Henry Awards, Best American Short Stories*). Also realistically consider whether the work you are submitting is as good as or better than—in your own opinion—the work appearing in the magazine you're sending to. What is the level of competition? And what is its volume? Never send 'blindly' to a magazine, or without carefully weighing your prospect there against those elsewhere. Always keep a log and a copy of the work you submit."

🖉 **POETRY & PROSE ANNUAL**, Golden Mean, P.O. Box 541, Manzanita OR 97130. (503)717-0112. E-mail: poetry@poetryproseannual.com. Website: www.poetryproseannual.com (includes writer's guidelines, names of editors, extracts, photographs, prose not necessarily included in print version). **Contact:** Sandra Foushée, editor. Magazine: 7×8½; 104 pages; semi-gloss paper; glossy cover; illustrations; photos. "*Poetry & Prose Annual* is organized and edited to be read as a whole, as a book, the prose (both fiction and nonfiction) and poetry directed to an enlightened intelligence with a positive perspective on the world." Annual. Estab. 1997. Circ. 1,000.

● There is a $20 entry fee for the contest for the Gold Pen Award. The entry fee includes a subscription.

Needs: Adventure, ethnic/multicultural, experimental, family saga, feminist, historical, humor/satire, literary, mainstream, mystery/suspense (amateur sleuth, cozy), New Age, psychic/supernatural, regional, romance. Accepts 20-30 mss/issue; 20-30 mss/year. **Publishes 40% new writers/year.** Published work by Mark Christopher Eades, June Stromberg, Robin Reid and Kay Kinnear. Length: 2,500 words maximum; average length: 1,200 words. Publishes short shorts. Average length: 500 words. Also publishes literary essays and poetry. Sometimes comments on rejected mss.

How to Contact: Send complete ms with a cover letter. Include estimated word count, brief bio and list of publications. Responds in 5 months to mss. Send a disposable copy of ms and #10 SASE for reply only. Accepts simultaneous (with notification if the piece is accepted elsewhere), previously published (if author has retained copyright) and multiple submissions. Sample copy for $10. Guidelines for SASE or on website.

Payment/Terms: Pays 2 contributor's copies and subscription to magazine; additional copies $8. Pays on publication for one-time and electronic rights. Sponsors contest: Gold Pen Award. With the submission, writer is automatically a participant.

Advice: "We look for substantive and enlightening ideas, a writing style with clarity and ingenuity, an awareness of emotional, intellectual, and physical consciousness. Follow the submission guidelines completely and enclose all the required elements. Familiarize yourself with the editorial intent of the *Annual*. The trend toward short short stories fits our format well, but we are open to longer prose, both fiction and nonfiction."

THE POINTED CIRCLE, Portland Community College-Cascade, 705 N. Killingsworth St., Portland OR 97217. (503)978-5087. Fax: (503)978-5050. E-mail: ckimball@pcc.edu. Student editorial staff, editors. **Contact:** Cynthia Kimball, English instructor, faculty advisor. Magazine: 80 pages; b&w illustrations; photos. "Anything of interest to educationally/culturally mixed audience." Annual. Estab. 1980.

Needs: Contemporary, ethnic, literary, prose poem, regional. "We will read whatever is sent, but encourage writers to remember we are a quality literary/arts magazine intended to promote the arts in the community. No pornography." Acquires 3-7 mss/year. Accepts submissions only December 1-February 15, for July 1 issue. **Publishes 10 new writers/ year.** Published work by Dan Raphael, Stephanie Dickinson and Vera Schwarcz. Length: 3,000 words maximum.

How to Contact: Send complete ms with cover letter and brief bio, #10 SASE. Accepts submissions by e-mail, fax and disk. "We encourage submissions on IBM disks in MS Word. The editors consider all submissions without knowing the identities of the contributors, so please do not put your name on the works themselves." Accepts multiple submissions. Sample copy for $4.50 payable to English Department. Entry guidelines, send #10 SASE. Submitted materials will not be returned; SASE for notification only.

Payment/Terms: Pays 1 copy. Acquires one-time rights.

Advice: "Looks for quality—topicality—nothing trite. The author cares about language and acts responsibly toward the reader, honors the reader's investment of time and piques the reader's interest."

PORCUPINE LITERARY ARTS MAGAZINE, P.O. Box 259, Cedarburg WI 53012-0259. (262)375-3128. E-mail: ppine259@aol.com. Website: members.aol.com/ppine259 (includes writer's guidelines, cover art, interviews, excerpts, subscription information, table of contents). Editor: W.A. Reed. **Contact:** Chris Skoczynski, fiction editor. Magazine: 5×8½; 125 pages; glossy color cover stock; art work and photos. Publishes "primarily poetry and short fiction. Novel excerpts are acceptable if self-contained. No restrictions as to theme or style." Semiannual. Estab. 1996. Circ. 1,500.

Needs: Condensed/excerpted novel, ethnic/multicultural, literary, mainstream/contemporary. "No pornographic or religious." Receives 30 unsolicited mss/month. Accepts 3 mss/issue; 6 mss/year. Publishes ms within 1 year of acceptance. **Publishes 4-6 new writers/year.** Published work by Judith Ford, Holly Day, Yang Huang and Jeffrey Perso. Length: 2,000-7,500 words; average length: 3,500 words. Publishes literary essays and poetry. Sometimes comments on rejected mss.

How to Contact: Send complete ms with a cover letter. Accepts queries/mss by e-mail. Include estimated word count, 5-line bio and list of publications. Responds in 2 weeks to queries; 2 months to mss. Send SASE for reply, return of ms or send a disposable copy of ms. No simultaneous submissions. Sample copy for $5. Guidelines for #10 SASE.

Payment/Terms: Pays 1 contributor's copy; additional copies for $8.95. Pays on publication for one-time rights.

Advice: Looks for "believable dialogue and a narrator I can see and hear and smell. Form or join a writers' group. Read aloud. Rewrite extensively."

POTOMAC REVIEW, The Journal of Arts & Humanities, Montgomery College, Paul Peck Humanities Institute, 51 Mannakee St., Rockville MD 20850. (301)251-7417. Fax: (301)738-1745. E-mail: wattrsedge@aol.com. Website: www.montgomerycollege.edu/potomacreview (includes editor's note, contents page, contact information, submission guidelines, some sampling of stories, poems). Editor: Eli Flam. **Contact:** Christa Watters. Magazine: 5½×8½; 248 pages; 50 lb. paper; 65 lb. cover; illustrations; photos. *Potomac Review* "explores the inner and outer terrain of the Mid-Atlantic and beyond via a challenging diversity of prose, poetry and b&w artwork." Biannual. Estab. 1994. Circ. 2,000.

Needs: "Stories with a vivid, individual quality that get at 'the concealed side' of life." Special section opens each issue, e.g., upcoming "On Nation Ground for Fall/Winter 2002-03," "On Stage" for Spring/Summer 2003. Receives about 75 unsolicited mss/month. Accepts 40-50 mss/issue. Publishes ms within 1 year after acceptance. Agented fiction under 5%. **Publishes up to 20 new writers/year.** Recently published work by Jeffrey Hammond, Ann Knox, Kenneth Carroll, Hilary Tham and Ori Z. Soltes. Length: up to 5,000 words; average length: 2,000 words. Publishes short shorts from 250 words. Humor (plus essays, cogent nonfiction of all sorts) welcome.

How to Contact: Send complete ms with a cover letter. Include estimated word count, 2-3 sentence bio. Responds in 3 weeks to queries; 3 months to mss. Send SASE for reply, return of ms or send a disposable copy of ms. Accepts simultaneous and occasional reprint submissions. Sample copy for $10. Submission guidelines for #10 SASE or see website. Reviews novels, short story collections, other books.
Payment/Terms: Pays 1 or more contributor's copy; additional copies for a 40% discount.
Advice: "Have something to say in an original voice; check the magazine first; rewriting often trumps the original."

POTPOURRI, P.O. Box 8278, Prairie Village KS 66208. (913)642-1503. Fax: (913)642-3128. E-mail: editor@pot pourri.org. Website: www.potpourri.com (includes guidelines; contents; reprints of fiction, poetry, creative nonfiction; author profiles; contests; subscription information and e-newsletter). Senior Editor: Polly W. Swafford. **Contact:** John Weber, fiction editor. Magazine: 8×11; 76 pages; glossy cover. "Literary magazine: short stories, poetry, haiku, creative nonfiction, travel and original illustrations for a general adult audience." Quarterly. Estab. 1989. Circ. 3,000.
Needs: Adventure, contemporary, ethnic, experimental, fantasy, historical (general), humor/satire, literary, mainstream, suspense, romance (contemporary, historical, romantic suspense), science fiction (soft/sociological), western (frontier stories). "*Potpourri* accepts a broad genre; hence its name. No material that promotes or degrades religious, political or sexual points of view will be accepted." Receives 75 unsolicited fiction mss/month. Accepts 10-12 fiction mss/issue; 60-80 prose mss/year. Publishes ms 10-12 months after acceptance. Agented fiction 1%. **Publishes 3-4 new writers/ year.** Published work by Thomas E. Kennedy, Richard Moore, David Ray and Deborah Shouse. Length: 3,500 words maximum. Also publishes poetry and literary essays. Sometimes critiques rejected mss. *Potpourri* offers annual awards (of $100 each) for best of volume in fiction and poetry, more depending on grants received, and sponsors the Annual Council on National Literatures Award. "Manuscripts must celebrate our multicultural and/or historic background." Reading fee: $5 per story. Send SASE for guidelines.
How to Contact: Send complete ms with cover letter. Accepts queries by e-mail and fax. Include "complete name, address, phone number, e-mail address, brief summary statement about submission, short author bio." Responds in 4 months. SASE. Accepts simultaneous submissions when advised at time of submission. Sample copy for $4.95 with 9×12 envelope. Guidelines for #10 SASE.
Payment/Terms: Pays contributor's copies. Acquires first rights.
Advice: "We look for well-crafted stories of literary value and stories with reader appeal. First, does the manuscript spark immediate interest and the introduction create the effect that will dominate? Second, does the action in dialogue or narration tell the story? Third, does the conclusion leave something with the reader to be long remembered? We look for the story with an original idea and an unusual twist. We are weary of excessive violence and depressing themes in fiction and are looking for originality in plots and some humorous pieces."

$ **POTTERSFIELD PORTFOLIO**, P.O. Box 40, Station A, Sydney, Nova Scotia B1P 6G9 Canada. **Contact:** Douglas Arthur Brown, editor. Magazine: 8×11; 96 pages. "Literary magazine interested in well-written fiction and poetry. No specific thematic interests or biases." Biannual. Estab. 1979. Circ. 2,000.
Needs: "Canadian submissions only. Foreign submissions by invitation only." Receives 40-50 fiction mss/month. Buys 4-5 fiction mss/issue. Published work by David Adams Richards, Vivette Kady and M.J. Hull. Length: 4,000 words maximum. Sometimes comments on rejected mss.
How to Contact: Send complete ms with cover letter. Include estimated word count and 50-word bio. No simultaneous submissions. No fax or e-mail submissions. Responds in 3 months. "*Always* include a SASE with sufficient *Canadian* postage, or IRCs, for return of the manuscript or a reply from the editors." Sample copy for $9 (US).
Payment/Terms: Pays contributor's copy and $10 Canadian/printed page to a maximum of $50. Pays on publication for first Canadian serial rights.
Advice: "Provide us with a clean, proofread copy of your story. Include a brief cover letter with biographical note, but don't try to sell the story to us."

THE PRAIRIE JOURNAL OF CANADIAN LITERATURE, Prairie Journal Press, Box 61203, Brent-wood Postal Services, Calgary, Alberta T2L 2K6 Canada. E-mail: prairiejournal@yahoo.com. Website: www.geocities. com/prairiejournal/ (includes guidelines, poems of the month, news and reviews). **Contact:** A.E. Burke, editor. Journal: 7×8½; 50-60 pages; white bond paper; Cadillac cover stock; cover illustrations. Journal of creative writing and scholarly essays, reviews for literary audience. Semiannual. Published special fiction issue last year. Estab. 1983.
Needs: Contemporary, literary, prose poem, regional, excerpted novel, novella, double-spaced. Canadian authors given preference. Publishes "a variety of types of fiction—fantasy, psychological, character-driven, feminist, etc. We publish authors at all stages of their careers from well-known to first publication. No romance, erotica, pulp, westerns." Publishes anthology series open to submissions: *Prairie Journal Poetry II* and *Prairie Journal Fiction III*. Receives 50 unsolicited mss each month. Accepts 10-15 mss/issue; 20-30 mss/year. Suggests sample issue before submitting ms. **Publishes 10 new writers/year.** Published work by Robert Clark and Christopher Blais. Length: 100-3,000 words; average length: 2,500 words. Suggested deadlines: April 1 for spring/summer issue; October 1 for fall/winter. Also publishes literary essays, literary criticism, poetry. Sometimes critiques rejected mss and recommends other markets.
How to Contact: Send complete ms. Responds in 1 month. SASE (IRC). Sample copy for $8 (Canadian) and SAE with $1.10 for postage or IRC. Include cover letter of past credits, if any. Reply to queries for SAE with 55¢ for postage or IRC. No American stamps. Reviews excerpts from novels and short story collections. Send only 1 story.
Payment/Terms: Pays contributor's copies and modest honoraria. Acquires first North American serial rights. In Canada author retains copyright with acknowledgement appreciated.

Advice: "We like character-driven rather than plot-centered fiction." Interested in "innovational work of quality. Beginning writers welcome! There is no point in simply republishing known authors or conventional, predictable plots. Of the genres we receive fiction is most often of the highest calibre. It is a very competitive field. Be proud of what you send. You're worth it."

PRAIRIE SCHOONER, University of Nebraska, English Department, P.O. Box 880334, Lincoln NE 68588-0334. (402)472-0911. Fax: (402)472-9771. E-mail: eflanaga@unlnotes.unl.edu. Website: www.unl.edu/schooner/psmain .htm (includes guidelines, editors, table of contents and excerpts of current issue). **Contact:** Hilda Raz, editor. Magazine: 6×9; 200 pages; good stock paper; heavy cover stock. "A fine literary quarterly of stories, poems, essays and reviews for a general audience that reads for pleasure." Quarterly. Estab. 1926. Circ. 3,200.

• *Prairie Schooner*, one of the oldest publications in this book, has garnered several awards and honors over the years. Work appearing in the magazine has been selected for anthologies including *Pushcart Prizes* and *Best American Short Stories*. *Prairie Schooner* ranked on *Writer's Digest*'s "Top 30" list of best markets for fiction writers.

Needs: Good fiction (literary). Accepts 4-5 mss/issue. Receives approximately 500 unsolicited fiction and poetry mss each month. Mss are read September through May only. **Published new writers within the last year.** Published work by Joyce Carol Oates, Judith Ortiz Coter, Chitra Divakaruni, Daniel Stern and Janet Burroway. Length: varies. Also publishes poetry. Offers annual prize of $1,000 for best fiction, two $1,000 prizes for excellence in writing, $500 for best new writer (poetry or fiction), two $250 prizes for prose or poetry, one $500 and two $1,000 awards for best poetry, and four to six $250 Reader's Choice awards (for work published in the magazine in the previous year).

How to Contact: Send complete ms with SASE and cover letter listing previous publications—where, when. Does not accept mss by e-mail or fax. Responds in 4 months. Sample copy for $5. Reviews novels, poetry, short story and essay collections.

Payment/Terms: Pays in contributor's copies and prize money awarded. Acquires all rights. Will reassign rights upon request after publication.

Advice: "*Prairie Schooner* is eager to see fiction from beginning and established writers. Be tenacious. Accept rejection as a temporary setback and send out rejected stories to other magazines. *Prairie Schooner* is not a magazine with a program. We look for good fiction in traditional narrative modes as well as experimental, meta-fiction or any other form or fashion a writer might try. Create striking detail, well-developed characters, fresh dialogue; let the images and the situations evoke the stories' themes. Too much explication kills a lot of otherwise good stories. Be persistent. Keep writing and sending out new work. Be familiar with the tastes of the magazines where you're sending. We are receiving record numbers of submissions. Prospective contributors must sometimes wait longer to receive our reply."

prechelonian, a literary & fine art magazine, blue night press, 1003 Lakeway, Kalamazoo MI 49001. (616)552-9349. E-mail: Jadhbat@aol.com. **Contact:** Derek Pollard, fiction editor. Magazine: 5½×8½; 25-30 pages; archival, acid-free paper; 80 lb. card cover. "We publish quality experimental fiction and poetry from emerging and established writers. The editors at blue night press place a great deal of emphasis on structural experimentation and formal exploration—work that successfully moves beyond the mere craft of writing and seeks to enter into dialogue with theory." Annual. Estab. 1991. Circ. 250-300.

Needs: Erotica, ethnic/multicultural (general), experimental, feminist, gay, historical (general), humor/satire, lesbian, literary, western (frontier saga, traditional). "No adventure, fantasy, horror, New Age, romance, mystery/suspense." Receives 25-40 unsolicited mss/month. Publishes ms 6-12 months after acceptance. Agented fiction 1%. Published work by Brandon LaBelle, William Lee, Chad Allen and Matt Dube. Length: 100-2,500 words. Publishes short shorts. Also publishes literary essays, literary criticism and poetry. Often comments on rejected mss.

How to Contact: Send complete ms with a cover letter. Responds in 2 weeks to queries; 1 month to mss. Send SASE (or IRC) for return of ms or send a disposable copy of ms and #10 SASE for reply only. Accepts simultaneous, previously published and multiple submissions. Sample copy for $5. Guidelines for SASE. Reviews novels, short story collections and nonfiction books of interest to writers. Send review copies to Derek Pollard, editor.

Payment/Terms: Pays 2 contributor's copies. Pays on publication.

Advice: "We look for work with a focal combination on both the parts and the whole. The writing must be done in earnest. Manuscripts must be well-written and intuitively sound. Have conviction in your work; be able to go toe-to-toe over it, otherwise we're not interested."

PRISM INTERNATIONAL, Buch E462-1866 Main Mall, University of British Columbia, Vancouver, British Columbia V6T 1Z1 Canada. (604)822-2514. Fax: (604)822-3616. E-mail: prism@interchange.ubc.ca. Website: www.prism.arts.ubc.ca (includes entire year of issues, writer's guidelines, contest information, PRISM news and e-mail address). Executive Editor: Mark Mallet. **Contact:** Billeh Nickerson, editor. Magazine: 6×9; 72-80 pages; Zephyr book paper; Cornwall, coated one side cover; artwork on cover. "An international journal of contemporary writing—fiction, poetry, drama, creative nonfiction and translation." Readership: "public and university libraries, individual subscriptions, bookstores—a world-wide audience concerned with the contemporary in literature." Quarterly. Estab. 1959. Circ. 1,200.

• *PRISM international* has won numerous magazine awards and stories first published in *PRISM* have been included in the *Journey Prize Anthology* every year since 1991.

Needs: New writing that is contemporary and literary. Short stories and self-contained novel excerpts. Works of translation are eagerly sought and should be accompanied by a copy of the original. Would like to see more translations.

"No gothic, confession, religious, romance, pornography, or sci-fi." Also looking for creative nonfiction that is literary, not journalistic, in scope and tone. Buys approximately 70 mss/year. Receives over 100 fiction unsolicited mss each month. "*PRISM* publishes both new and established writers; our contributors have included Franz Kafka, Gabriel Garcia Marquez, Michael Ondaatje, Margaret Laurence, Mark Anthony Jarman, Gail Anderson-Dargatz and Eden Robinson." **Publishes 7 new writers/year.** Published works by Mark Anthony Jarman, Matt Cohen and Cynthia Flood. Submissions should not exceed 5,000 words "though flexible for outstanding work" (only one long story per submission, please). Publishes short shorts. Also publishes poetry and drama. Sponsors annual short fiction contest with $2,000 (Canadian) grand prize: send SASE (IRC) for details.

How to Contact: Send complete ms with SASE or SAE, IRC and cover letter with bio, information and publications list. "Keep it simple. U.S. contributors take note: Do not send U.S. stamps, they are not valid in Canada. Send International Reply Coupons instead." Responds in 6 months. Sample copy for $5 (U.S./Canadian).

Payment/Terms: Pays $20 (Canadian)/printed page and 1 year's subscription. Pays on publication for first North American serial rights. Selected authors are paid an additional $10/page for digital rights.

Advice: "Read several issues of our magazine before submitting. We are committed to publishing outstanding literary work. We look for strong, believeable characters; real voices; attention to language; interesting ideas and plots. Send us fresh, innovative work which also shows a mastery of the basics of good prose writing. Poorly constructed or sloppy pieces will not receive serious consideration. We welcome e-mail submissions and are proud to be one of few print literary journals who offer additional payment to select writers for digital publication. Too many e-mail submissions, however, come to us unpolished and unprepared to be published. Writers should craft their work for e-mail submission as carefully as they would for submissions through traditional methods. They should send one piece at a time and wait for our reply before they send another."

$ ☑ **PROVINCETOWN ARTS**, Provincetown Arts, Inc., 650 Commercial St., P.O. Box 35, Provincetown MA 02657. (508)487-3167. Fax: (508)487-8634. E-mail: www.capecodaccess.com. **Contact:** Christopher Busa, editor. Magazine: 9×12; 184 pages; 60 lb. coated paper; 12 pcs. cover; illustrations; photos. "*PA* focuses broadly on the artists, writers and theater of America's oldest continuous art colony." Annual. Estab. 1985. Circ. 8,000.

Needs: Plans special fiction issue. Receives 300 unsolicited mss/year. Buys 5 mss/issue. Publishes ms 3 months after acceptance. Published work by Carole Maso and Hilary Masters. Length: 1,500-8,000 words; average length: 3,000 words. Publishes short shorts. Also publishes literary essays, literary criticism, poetry. Sometimes critiques rejected mss and recommends other markets.

How to Contact: Send complete ms with cover letter including previous publications. No simultaneous submissions. Responds in 2 weeks to queries; 3 months to mss. SASE. Sample copy for $7.50. Reviews novels and short story collections.

Payment/Terms: Pays $75-300. Pays on publication for first rights. Sends galleys to author.

☑ **PUCKERBRUSH REVIEW**, Puckerbrush Press, 76 Main St., Orono ME 04473. (207)866-4868/581-3832. **Contact:** Constance Hunting, editor/publisher. Magazine: 9×12; 80-100 pages; illustrations. "We publish mostly new Maine writers; interviews, fiction, reviews, poetry for a literary audience." Semiannual. Estab. 1979. Circ. approx. 500.

Needs: Belles-lettres, experimental, gay (occasionally), literary. "Wants to see more original, quirky and well-written fiction. No genre fiction. Nothing cliché, nothing overly sensational except in its human interest." Receives 30 unsolicited mss/month. Accepts 6 mss/issue; 12 mss/year. Publishes ms 1 year after acceptance. **Publishes 6 new writers/year.** Recently published work by Mary Gray Hughes, Michael Alpert and Carolyn Cooke. Sometimes publishes short shorts. Also publishes literary essays, literary criticism, poetry. Sometimes critiques rejected mss.

How to Contact: Send complete ms with cover letter. "No disks please!" Responds in 2 months. SASE. Accepts simultaneous and multiple submissions. Sample copy for $2. Guidelines for SASE. Sometimes reviews novels and short story collections.

Payment/Terms: Pays in contributor's copies.

Advice: "I don't want to see tired plots or treatments. I want to see respect for language—the right words, true views of human nature. Don't follow clichés, but don't be too outré either."

☑ ◎ **QUARTER AFTER EIGHT, A Journal of Prose and Commentary**, QAE, Ellis Hall, Ohio University, Athens OH 45701. (740)593-2827. E-mail: quarteraftereight@hotmail.com. Website: www.quarteraftereight.com (includes guidelines, sample submissions, table of contents and links). **Contact:** Tony Viola, editor-in-chief. Magazine: 6×9; 310 pages; 20 lb. glossy cover stock; photos. "We look to publish work which challenges boundaries of genre, style, idea, and voice." Annual.

Needs: Condensed/excerpted novel, erotica, ethnic/multicultural, experimental, gay, humor/satire, lesbian, literary, mainstream/contemporary, translations. "No traditional, conventional fiction." Send SASE for list of upcoming themes. Receives 150-200 unsolicited mss/month. Accepts 40-50 mss/issue. Does not read mss mid-March-mid-September. Publishes ms 6-12 months after acceptance. Agented fiction 15%. **Publishes 10-15 new writers/year.** Recently published work by Virgil Suárez, Maureen Sexton, John Gallaher and Amy England. Length: 10,000 words maximum; average length: 3,000 words. Publishes short shorts. Also publishes literary essays, literary criticism, prose poetry. Also sponsors an annual prose contest: $300 award. Sometimes comments on rejected ms.

How to Contact: Send complete ms with a cover letter. Include short bio and list of publications. Responds in 3 months. Send SASE for return of ms or send a disposable copy of ms. Accepts simultaneous submissions and multiple submissions (up to 5 short works and 2 longer works). Sample copy for $10, 8×11 SAE and $1.60 postage. Guidelines for #10 SASE. Reviews novels and short story collections. Send books to Book Review Editor, Patrick Madden.

Payment/Terms: Pays 2 contributor's copies; additional copies $10. Acquires first North American serial rights. Rights revert to author upon publication. Sponsors contest. Send SASE for guidelines.

Advice: "We look for fiction that is experimental, exploratory, devoted to and driven by language—that which succeeds in achieving the *QAE* aesthetic. Please subscribe to our journal and read what is published. We do not publish traditional lined poetry or straightforward conventional stories. We encourage writers to submit after they have gotten acquainted with the *QAE* aesthetic."

$ ◨ ▼ QUARTERLY WEST, University of Utah, 200 S. Central Campus Dr., Room 317, Salt Lake City UT 84112-9109. (801)581-3938. Fax: (801)585-5167. Website: www.utah.edu/quarterlywest (includes novella guidelines, submission guidelines, recent issues with samples of contributors' work). Editor: David Hawkins. **Contact:** Steve Tuttle, fiction editor. Magazine: 6×9; 224 pages; 60 lb. paper; 5-color cover stock; illustrations; photos rarely. "We try to publish a variety of fiction and poetry from all over the country based not so much on the submitting author's reputation but on the merit of each piece. Our publication is aimed primarily at an educated audience interested in contemporary literature and criticism." Semiannual. "We sponsor a biennial novella competition." (Next competition held in 2000). Estab. 1976. Circ. 1,800.

• *Quarterly West* was awarded First Place for Editorial Content from the American Literary Magazine Awards. Work published in the magazine has been selected for inclusion in the *Pushcart Prize* anthology and *The Best American Short Stories* anthology.

Needs: Literary, contemporary, experimental, translations. No detective, science fiction or romance. Accepts 6-10 mss/issue, 12-20 mss/year. Reads mss between September 1 and May 1 only. "Submissions received between May 2 and August 31 will be returned unread." Receives 300 unsolicited fiction mss each month. **Publishes 3 new writers/year.** Recently published work by Catherine Ryan Hyde, David Shields, James Tate and David Roderick. No preferred length; interested in longer, "fuller" short stories, as well as short shorts.

How to Contact: Send complete ms. Brief cover letters welcome. Send SASE for reply or return of ms. No fax or e-mail submissions. Accepts simultaneous submissions with notification. Responds in up to 8 months; "sooner, if possible." Sample copy for $7.50.

Payment/Terms: Pays $15-50 and 2 contributor's copies. Pays on publication for all rights (negotiable).

Advice: "We publish a special section of short shorts every issue, and we also sponsor a biennial novella contest. We are open to experimental work—potential contributors should read the magazine! We solicit occasionally, but tend more toward the surprises—unsolicited. Don't send more than one story per submission, and wait until you've heard about the first before submitting another."

🌐 ◨ $ QWF (QUALITY WOMEN'S FICTION), Breaking the Boundaries of Women's Fiction, P.O. Box 1768, Rugby, Warks CVZ1 4ZA United Kingdom. Phone: 01788 334302. Fax: 01788 334702. E-mail: jo@qwfmagazine.co.uk. **Contact:** Jo Good, editor. Send submissions to Sally Zigmond, assistant editor QWF, 18 Warwick Crescent, Harrogate, N. Yorks HG2 8JA. Magazine: A5; 80-90 pages; glossy paper. "*QWF* gets under the skin of the female experience and exposes emotional truth." Bimonthly. Estab. 1994. Circ. 2,000.

Needs: Erotica, ethnic/multicultural, experimental, fantasy, feminist, gay, horror (psychological, supernatural), humor/satire, lesbian, literary, New Age, psychic/supernatural/occult, science fiction (soft/sociological), translations. Receives 30-50 unsolicited mss/month. Accepts 12 mss/issue; 72 mss/year. Does not read mss June-August. Publishes ms up to 18 months after acceptance. **Publishes 20 new writers/year.** Published work by Julia Darling, Sally Zigmond and Diana Forrester. Length: 1,000-4,500 words; average length: 2,500 words. Publishes short shorts. Average length: 900 words. Also publishes literary criticism. Always comments on rejected mss.

How to Contact: Send complete ms, cover letter. Accepts submissions by disk. Include estimated word count, brief bio, list of publications and IRCs or stamps. Responds in 2 weeks to queries; 3 months to mss. Send SASE (or IRC) for return of ms or send a disposable copy of ms and #10 SASE (or IRC) for reply only. Accepts previously published work. Guidelines for SASE (or IRC), by e-mail or fax. Reviews novels, short story collections and nonfiction books of interest to writers.

Payment/Terms: Pays £10 sterling maximum. Pays on publication for first British serial rights. Sponsors contest. SASE or IRC for details.

Advice: "Take risks with subject matter. Study at least one copy of *QWF*. Ensure story is technically sound."

$ ◨ RAIN CROW, P.O. Box 11013, Chicago IL 60611-0013. E-mail: submissions@rain-crow.com. Website: http://rain-crow.com/ (includes writer's guidelines, sample issue, back issue sales, contest news, author news, advertising rates). **Contact:** Michael S. Manley, editor. Magazine/journal: 8½×5½; 144-160 pages; white bond paper; glossy cover; illustrations; photos. "*Rain Crow* publishes new and experienced writers in many styles and genres. I look for eclectic, well-crafted, entertaining fiction aimed at those who enjoy literature for its pleasures." Triannual. Estab. 1997. Circ. 300. Member, CLMP.

Needs: Erotica, experimental, literary, mainstream, speculative fiction, translations. "No propaganda, pornographic, juvenile, or formulaic fiction. No poetry." Receives 120-150 unsolicited mss/month. Accepts 10-12 mss/issue; 30 mss/year. Publishes ms within 6 months after acceptance. **Publishes several new writers/year.** Published work by Susan

Neville, Peter Johnson, Paul Maliszewski, Peter Hynes, Carolyn Allesio and Laura Denham. Length: 250-8,000 words; average length: 3,500 words. Also publishes novellas, creative nonfiction, short shorts. No poetry. Sometimes comments on rejected mss.

How to Contact: Send complete ms with a cover letter. May also e-mail submissions. Include list of publications. Responds in 5 months. Send SASE for reply, return of ms or send a disposable copy of ms. Accepts simultaneous submissions, reprints and electronic submissions. Sample copy for $7. Guidelines for #10 SASE (1 IRC) or on website.

Payment/Terms: Pays $5 per page, free subscription to magazine and 2 contributor's copies; additional copies for 20% discount. Pays on publication for one-time rights. Sends galleys to author.

Advice: "I look for attention to craft: voice, language, character and plot working together to maximum effect. I look for stories that deserve rereading and that I would gladly recommend others read. Send your best work. Present your work professionally. Unique, credible settings and situations that entertain get the most attention."

N **RAINBOW CURVE**, P.O. Box 93206, Las Vegas NV 89193-3206. Website: www.rainbowcurve.net (includes information on magazine and editors, submission guidelines). **Contact:** Daphne Young and Julianne Bonnet, editors. Magazine: 5½×8½; 100 pages; 60 lb. paper; coated cover. "*Rainbow Curve* publishes fiction and poetry that dabble at the edge; contemporary work that evokes emotion. Our audience is those interested in exploring new worlds of experience and emotion; raw, visceral work is what we look for." Semiannual. Estab. 2002. Circ. 500.

Needs: Ethnic/multicultural, experimental, feminist, gay, lesbian, literary. "No genre fiction (romance, western, fantasy, sci-fi)." Receives 30 unsolicited mss/month. Accepts 8-10 mss/issue; 16-20 mss/year. Publishes ms 6 months after acceptance. Agented fiction 1%. **Publishes 80% new writers/year.** Recently published work by Catherine Ryan Hyde, Terry Ehret, Tamara Guirado and Barry Ballard. Length: 500-10,000 words; average length: 7,500 words. Publishes short shorts. Average length: 1,000 words. Sometimes comments on rejected mss.

How to Contact: Send complete ms with a cover letter. Include brief bio. Responds in 3 months to mss. Send SASE for return of ms or send a disposable copy of ms and #10 SASE for reply only. Accepts simultaneous submissions. Sample copy for $6. Guidelines for SASE or on website.

Payment/Terms: Pays 2 contributor's copies; additional copies $5. Acquires one-time rights. Sends galleys to author.

Advice: "Unusual rendering of usual subjects and strong narrative voice make a story stand out. Unique glimpses into the lives of others—make it new."

RATTAPALLAX, Rattapallax Press, 532 La Guardia Place, Suite 353, New York NY 10012. (212)560-7459. E-mail: info@rattapallax.com. Website: www.rattapallax.com. **Contact:** Alan Cheuse, fiction editor. Literary magazine: 6×9; 128 pages; bound; some illustrations; photos. "General readership. Our stories must be character driven with strong conflict. All accepted stories are edited by our staff and the writer before publication to ensure a well-crafted and written work." Semiannual. Estab. 1999. Circ. 2,000.

Needs: Literary. Receives 15 unsolicited mss/month. Accepts 3 mss/issue; 6 mss/year. Publishes ms 3-6 months after acceptance. Agented fiction 15%. **Publishes 2 new writers/year.** Published work by Stuart Dybek, Dana Gioia and William P.H. Root. Length: 1,000-10,000 words; average length: 5,000 words. Publishes short shorts; average length: 1,000 words. Also publishes poetry. Often comments on rejected mss.

How to Contact: Send complete ms with cover letter. Reports in 3 months to queries and mss. Send SASE for return of ms. Sample copy for $7.95. Guidelines for SASE or on website.

Payment/Terms: Pays 2 contributor's copies; additional copies $7.95. Pays on publication for first North American serial rights. Sends galleys to author.

Advice: "Character driven, well-crafted, strong conflict."

N **THE RAVEN CHRONICLES, A Magazine of Transcultural Art, Literature and the Spoken Word**, The Raven Chronicles, 1634 11th Ave., Seattle WA 98122-2419. (206)323-4316. Fax: (206)323-4316. E-mail: editors@ravenchronicles.org. Website: www.ravenchronicles.org (includes guidelines, editors, short fiction, prose, poetry, separate monthly topics for online publication, art gallery, reviews of live spoken word events). Managing Editor: Phoebe Bosché. **Contact:** Matt Briggs, fiction editor. Poetry Editor: Jody Aliesan. Webmaster: Scott Martin. Magazine: 8½×11; 48-64 pages; 50 lb. book paper; glossy cover; b&w illustrations; photos. "*The Raven Chronicles* is designed to promote transcultural art, literature and the spoken word." Triannual. Estab. 1991. Circ. 2,500-5,000.

Needs: Political, cultural essays, ethnic/multicultural, literary, regional. "No romance, fantasy, mystery or detective." Receives 300-400 mss/month. Buys 35-50 mss/issue; 105-150 mss/year. Publishes 3-6 months after acceptance. **Publishes 50-100 new writers/year.** Published work by David Romtvedt, Sherman Alexie, D.L. Birchfield, Nancy Redwine, Diane Glancy, Greg Hischak and Sharon Hashimoto. Length: 2,500 words maximum (but negotiable); average length: 2,000 words. Publishes short shorts. Length: 300-500 words. Also publishes literary essays, reviews, literary criticism, poetry. Sometimes critiques rejected mss.

MARKET CONDITIONS are constantly changing! If you're still using this book and it is 2004 or later, buy the newest edition of *Novel & Short Story Writer's Market* at your favorite bookstore or order from Writer's Digest Books by calling 1-800-448-0915.

How to Contact: Send complete ms with a cover letter. Include estimated word count. Accepts queries but no submissions by e-mail. Responds in 3 months to mss. Send SASE for return of ms. Accepts simultaneous submissions. Sample copy for $5.50. Guidelines for #10 SASE.

Payment/Terms: Pays $10-40 and 2 contributor's copies; additional copies at half cover cost. Pays on publication for first North American serial rights. Sends galleys to author.

Advice: Looks for "clean, direct language, written from the heart and experimental writing. Read sample copy, or look at *Before Columbus* anthologies and *Greywolf Annual* anthologies."

⬤ RE:AL, The Journal of Liberal Arts, Stephen F. Austin State University, P.O. Box 13007, Nacogdoches TX 75962-3007. (409)468-2059. Fax: (409)468-2614. E-mail: f_real@titan.sfasu.edu. Website: http://libweb.sfasu.edu/real/default.htm. (includes complete interactive-version of printed journal). **Contact:** W. Dale Hearell, editor. Academic journal: 6×10; perfect-bound; 175-225 pages; "top" stock. Editorial content: 30% fiction, 30% poetry, 30% scholarly essays and criticism; book reviews (assigned after query) and interviews. "Work is reviewed based on the intrinsic merit of the scholarship and creative work and its appeal to a sophisticated international readership (U.S., Canada, Great Britain, Ireland, Brazil, Puerto Rico, Italy)." Semiannual. Estab. 1968. Circ. 400.

Needs: Adventure, contemporary, genre, science fiction, historical, experimental, regional. Receives 1,400-1,600 unsolicited mss/2 issues. Accepts 5-10 fiction mss/issue. Publishes ms 1-12 months after acceptance. **Publishes 20 new writers/year.** Published work by Holly Kulak, Cyd Adams, John Dublin and Salem Pflueger. Length: 1,000-5,000 words. Occasionally critiques rejected mss and conditionally accepts on basis of critiques and changes.

How to Contact: Send 2 copies of ms with cover letter. No simultaneous submissions. Accepts multiple submissions (up to 2). Responds in 2 weeks to queries; 1 month to mss. SASE. Sample copy and writer's guidelines for $20. Guidelines for SASE.

Payment/Terms: Pays 2 contributor's copies; charges for extras. Rights revert to author.

Advice: "Please study an issue. *RE:AL* seeks finely crafted stories that include individualistic ideas and approaches, allowing and encouraging deeper repeated readings. Have your work checked by a well-published writer—who is not a good friend. Also proofread for grammatical and typographical errors. A manuscript must show that the writer is conscious of what he or she is attempting to accomplish in plot, character and theme. A short story isn't written but constructed; the ability to manipulate certain aspects of a story is the sign of a conscious storyteller."

N ⬤ RED CEDAR REVIEW, Dept. of English, 17C Morrill Hall, Michigan State University, East Lansing MI 48824. (517)655-6307. E-mail: rcreview@msu.edu. Website: www.msu.edu/~rcreview (includes writer's guidelines, editors' names, subscription information). Editors change yearly. **Contact:** Dan Roosien, fiction editor. Magazine: 5½×8½; 100 pages. Theme: "literary—poetry and short fiction." Biannual. Estab. 1963. Circ. 400.

Needs: Literary. "Good stories with character, plot and style, any genre, but with a real tilt toward literary fiction." Accepts 3-4 mss/issue, 6-10 mss/year. **Publishes 4 new writers/year.** Length: 5,000 words maximum.

How to Contact: Query with unpublished ms with SASE. No simultaneous submissions. Responds in 4 months to mss. Publishes ms up to 4 months after acceptance. Sample copy for $4.

Payment/Terms: Pays 2 contributor's copies. $6 charge for extras. Acquires first rights.

⬤ RED ROCK REVIEW, Community College of Southern Nevada, 3200 E. Cheyenne Ave., N. Las Vegas NV 89030. (702)651-4094. Fax: (702)876-6773. E-mail: richard_logsdon@ccsn.nevada.edu. Website: www.ccsn.nevada.edu/english/redrockreview/index.html. **Contact:** Dr. Richard Logsdon, senior editor. Magazine: 5×8; 125 pages. "We're looking for the very best literature. Stories need to be tightly crafted, strong in character development, built around conflict. Poems need to be tightly crafted, characterized by expert use of language." Semiannual. Estab. 1995. Circ. 250. Member, CLMP.

Needs: Experimental, literary, mainstream. Receives 350 unsolicited mss/month. Accepts 40-60 mss/issue; 80-120 mss/year. Does not read mss during summer. Publishes ms 3-5 months after acceptance. **Publishes 5-10 new writers/year.** Recently published work by Willis Barnstone, Dorianne Laux, Kim Addonizio and David Benia. Length: 1,500-5,000 words; average length: 3,500 words. Publishes short shorts. Average length: 3,500 words. Also publishes literary essays, literary criticism and poetry. Sometimes comments on rejected mss.

How to Contact: Send complete ms with a cover letter. Accepts submissions by disk. Include brief bio and list of publications. Responds in 2 weeks to queries; 3 months to mss. Send SASE (or IRC) for return of ms. Accepts simultaneous submissions and multiple submissions. Sample copy for $5.50. Guidelines for SASE, by e-mail or on website.

Payment/Terms: Pays 2 contributor's copies. Pays on acceptance for first rights.

⬤ RED WHEELBARROW, De Anza College, 21250 Stevens Creek Blvd., Cupertino CA 95014-5702. (408)864-8600. E-mail: splitterrandolph@fhda.edu. **Contact:** Randolph Splitter, editor-in-chief. Magazine: 6×9; 100-216 pages; photos. "Contemporary poetry, fiction, creative nonfiction, b&w graphics, comics and photos." Annual. Estab. 1976 as *Bottomfish*; 2000 as *Red Wheelbarrow*. Circ. 250-500.

Needs: "Thoughtful, personal writing. We welcome submissions of all kinds, and we seek to publish a diverse range of styles and voices from around the country and the world." Receives 50-100 unsolicited fiction mss/month. Accepts 8-10 mss/issue. Agented fiction 1%. Publishes mss an average of 6 months after acceptance. **Publishes 0-2 new writers/year.** Recently published work by George Keithly, Bill Teitelbaum and K.P. Bath. Length: 4,000 words maximum; average length: 2,500 words. Publishes short shorts; average length: 400 words. Also publishes poetry.

How to Contact: Reads mss September through January. Submission deadline: January 31; publication date: July. Accepts queries by e-mail. Submit 1 short story or up to 3 short shorts with cover letter, brief bio, list of publications and SASE. "Sorry, we cannot return manuscripts." Writer's guidelines for SASE or by e-mail. Responds in 6 months. No reprints. Accepts simultaneous submissions. Sample copy for $5.

Payment/Terms: Pays 2 contributor's copies. Acquires first North American serial rights.

Advice: "Write freely and intensely. Then rewrite. Resist clichés and stereotypes."

REFLECT, 1317-D Eagles Trace Path, Chesapeake VA 23320-3033. (757)547-4464. **Contact:** W.S. Kennedy, editor. Magazine: 5½×8½; 48 pages; pen & ink illustrations. "Spiral Mode fiction and poetry for writers and poets—professional and amateur." Quarterly. Estab. 1979.

Needs: Spiral fiction. "The four rules to the Spiral Mode fiction form are: (1) The story a situation or condition. (2) The outlining of the situation in the opening paragraphs. The story being told at once, the author is not overly-involved with dialogue and plot development, may concentrate on *sound*, *style*, *color*—the superior elements in art. (3) The use of a concise style with euphonic wording. Good poets may have the advantage here. (4) The involvement of Spiral Fiction themes—as opposed to Spiral Poetry themes—with love, and presented with the mystical overtones of the Mode." Would like to see more mystical fiction. "No smut, bad taste, socialist." Theme issues during 2003: Seasons—spring, summer, autumn, winter; March 12, June 12, September 12, December 12 deadlines for submissions; issued approximately 30 days later. Accepts 2-6 mss/issue; 8-24 mss/year. Publishes ms 3 months after acceptance. **Publishes 4 new writers/year.** Published work by David D. Bell, BZ Niditch, Ruth Wildes Schuler and Dr. Elaine Hatfield. Length: 2,000 words maximum; average length: 1,500 words. Publishes short shorts. Sometimes critiques rejected mss.

How to Contact: Send complete ms with cover letter. Responds in 2 months to mss. SASE. Accepts multiple submissions. Sample copy for $2. (Make checks payable to W.S. Kennedy.) Guidelines in each issue of *Reflect*.

Payment/Terms: Pays contributor's copies. Acquires one-time rights. Publication not copyrighted.

Advice: "Subject matter usually is not relevant to the successful writing of Spiral Fiction, as long as there is some element or type of *love* in the story, and provided that there are mystical references. (Though a dream-like style may qualify as 'mystical.')"

REFLECTIONS LITERARY JOURNAL, Piedmont Community College, P.O. Box 1197, Roxboro NC 27573. (336)599-1181. E-mail: thrasht@piedmont.cc.nc.us. **Contact:** Tami Sloane Thrasher, editor. Magazine: 128 pages. "We publish work which addresses and transcends humanity and cultures." Annual. Estab. 1999. Circ. 500.

Needs: Literary, translations. Receives 30 unsolicited mss/month. Accepts 5 mss/issue. Publishes ms 4 months after acceptance. **Publishes 2 new writers/year.** Recently published work by Tim McLaurin, Lynn Veach Sadler and Emily A. Kern. Length: 5,000 words maximum; average length: 2,500 words. Publishes short shorts. Also publishes poetry.

How to Contact: Send complete ms with a cover letter. Include estimated word count and brief bio. Send SASE (or IRC) for return of ms or send a disposable copy of ms and #10 SASE for reply only. Sample copy for $6. Guidelines for SASE or by e-mail. "Note that our annual deadline is December 31. Submissions accepted only July 1-December 31."

Payment/Terms: Pays 1 contributor's copy; additional copies $6 pre-publication; $7 post-publication. Pays on publication for first North American serial rights. Sponsors annual poetry and fiction awards. Guidelines available for SASE or by e-mail.

Advice: "We look for good writing with a flair, which captivates an educated lay audience. Don't take rejection letters personally. We turn away a lot of work we'd like to use simply because we don't have room for everything we like. For that reason, we're more likely to accept shorter well-written stories than longer stories of the same quality. Also, stories that contain unnecessary profanity, which is profanity that doesn't contribute to the story's plot, structure, or intended tone, are rejected immediately."

$ **THE REJECTED QUARTERLY, A Journal of Quality Literature Rejected at Least Five Times**, Black Plankton Press, P.O. Box 1351, Cobb CA 95426. E-mail: bplankton@juno.com. Editor: Daniel Weiss. **Contact:** Daniel Weiss, Jeff Ludecke, fiction editors. Magazine: 8½×11; 40 pages; 60 lb. paper; 10 pt. coated cover stock; illustrations. "We want the best literature possible, regardless of genre. We do, however, have a bias toward the unusual and toward speculative fiction. We aim for a literate, educated audience. *The Rejected Quarterly* believes in publishing the highest quality rejected fiction and other writing that doesn't fit anywhere else. We strive to be different, but will go for quality every time, whether conventional or not." Published at least twice/year. Estab. 1998.

Needs: Experimental, fantasy, historical, humor/satire, literary, mainstream/contemporary, mystery/suspense, romance (futuristic/time travel only), science fiction (soft/sociological), sports. Receives 30 unsolicited mss/month. Accepts 4-6 mss/issue; 8-24 mss/year. Publishes ms 1-12 months after acceptance. **Publishes 1-2 new writers/year.** Recently published work by Vera Searles, RC Cooper and Stephen Jones. Length: 8,000 words maximum; average length: 5,000 words. Publishes short shorts. Also publishes literary essays, literary criticism, poetry. Often comments on rejected ms.

How to Contact: Send complete ms with a cover letter and 5 rejection slips. Include estimated word count, 1-paragraph bio and list of publications. Accepts queries by e-mail. Responds in 2 weeks to queries; up to 9 months to mss. Send SASE for reply, return of ms or send a disposable copy of ms. Accepts reprint submissions. Sample copy $6 (IRCs for foreign requests). Reviews novels, short story collections and nonfiction.

Payment/Terms: Pays $5 and 1 contributor's copy; additional copies, one at cost, others $5. Pays on acceptance for first rights. Sends galleys to author if possible.

Advice: "We are looking for high-quality writing that tells a story or expresses a coherent idea. We want unique stories, original viewpoints and unusual slants. We are getting far too many inappropriate submissions. Please be familiar with the magazine. Be sure to include your rejection slips! Send out quality rather than quantity. Work on one piece until it is as close to a masterpiece in your own eyes as you can get it. Find the right place for it. Be selective in ordering samples, but do be familiar with where you're sending your work."

$ 🌙 💙 RIVER STYX, Big River Association, 634 N. Grand Blvd., 12th Floor, St. Louis MO 63103-1218. (314)533-4541. Fax: (314)533-3345. E-mail: r-t-newman@hotmail.com. Website: www.riverstyx.org (includes writer's guidelines, names of editors, contest and theme issue information, excerpts and art from publication). **Contact:** Richard Newman, editor. Magazine: 6×9; 100 pages; color card cover; perfect-bound; b&w visual art. "No theme restrictions; only high quality, intelligent work." Triannual. Estab. 1975.

● *River Styx* has twice received the Stanley Hanks Award, and has had stories appear in *New Stories from the South*.

Needs: Excerpted novel chapter, contemporary, ethnic, experimental, feminist, gay, satire, lesbian, literary, mainstream, prose poem, translations. "No genre fiction, less thinly veiled autobiography." Receives 350 unsolicited mss/month. Accepts 2-6 mss/issue; 6-12 mss/year. Reads only May through November. **Publishes 20 new writers/year.** Published work by Julianna Baggott, Naomi Shihab Nye, Molly Peacock and Eric Shade. Length: no more than 20-30 manuscript pages. Publishes short shorts. Also publishes poetry. Sometimes critiques rejected mss and recommends other markets.

How to Contact: Send complete ms with name and address on every page. SASE required. Responds in 3-5 months to mss. Accepts simultaneous submissions, "if a note is enclosed with your work and if we are notified immediately upon acceptance elsewhere." Sample copy for $7.

Payment/Terms: Pays 2 contributor's copies, 1-year subscription and $8/page "if funds available." Acquires first North American serial rights.

Advice: "We want high-powered stories with well-developed characters. We like strong plots, usually with at least three memorable scenes, and a subplot often helps. No thin, flimsy fiction with merely serviceable language. Short stories shouldn't be any different than poetry–every single word should count. One could argue every word counts more since we're being asked to read 10 to 30 pages."

🌙 ROANOKE REVIEW, Roanoke College, 221 College Lane, Salem VA 24153-3794. (540)375-2380. **Contact:** Paul Hanstedt, editor. Magazine: 6×9; 200 pages; 60 lb. paper; 70 lb. cover. "We're looking for fresh, thoughtful material that will appeal to a broader as well as literary audience. Humor encouraged." Annual. Estab. 1964. Circ. 500.

Needs: Erotica, feminist, gay, humor/satire, lesbian, literary, mainstream, regional. No pornography, science fiction or horror. Receives 50 unsolicited mss/month. Accepts 5-10 mss/year. Does not read mss March 1-September 1. Publishes ms 6 months after acceptance. Agented fiction 5%. **Publishes 4-5 new writers/year.** Recently published work by June Spence, Valerie Cummings and Bill Roorbach. Length: 1,000-6,000 words; average length: 1,500 words. Publishes short shorts. Also publishes poetry. Sometimes comments on rejected mss.

How to Contact: Send complete ms with a cover letter. Include brief bio. Responds in 1 month to queries; 6 months to mss. Send SASE for return of ms or send a disposable copy of ms and #10 SASE for reply only. Accepts simultaneous submissions. Sample copy for 8×11 SAE with $2 postage. Guidelines for SASE.

Payment/Terms: Pays 2 contributor's copies; additional copies $5. Pays on publication for one-time rights.

Advice: "Pay attention to sentence-level writing—verbs, metaphors, concrete images. Don't forget, though, that plot and character keep us reading. We're looking for stuff that breaks the MFA story style."

[N] 🌙 THE ROCKFORD REVIEW, The Rockford Writers Guild, 7721 Venus St., Loves Park IL 61111. Website: http://writersguild1.tripod.com. Editor: Cindy Guentherman. **Contact:** Max Dodson, prose editor. Magazine: 5⅜×8½; 50 pages; b&w illustrations; b&w photos. "We look for prose and poetry with a fresh approach to old themes or new insights into the human condition." Triquarterly. Estab. 1971. Circ. 750.

Needs: Ethnic, experimental, fantasy, humor/satire, literary, regional, science fiction (hard science, soft/sociological). Recently published work by James Bellarosa, Sean Michael Rice, John P. Kristofco and L.S. Sekishiro. Length: Up to 1,300 words. Also publishes one-acts and essays.

How to Contact: Send complete ms. "Include a short biographical note—no more than four sentences." Accepts simultaneous and multiple submissions (no more than 3). Responds in 2 months to mss. SASE. Sample copy for $6. Guidelines for SASE.

Payment/Terms: Pays contributor's copies. "Two $25 editor's choice cash prizes per issue." Acquires first North American serial rights.

Advice: "We must understand it, and when we read it we must say 'wow.' If it makes us also either laugh or cry, that is good. Read what is being published lately, and try a few samples. Like shoes, it must fit."

🌐 🌙 📷 $ ROOM OF ONE'S OWN, P.O. Box 46160, Station D, Vancouver, British Columbia V6J 5G5 Canada. E-mail: contactroom@hotmail.com. Website: www.islandnet.com/Room/enter (includes selected works from current issue). **Contact:** Growing Room Collective. Magazine: 112 pages; illustrations; photos. "*Room of One's Own* is Canada's oldest feminist literary journal. Since 1975, *Room* has been a forum in which women can share their unique perspectives on the world, each other and themselves." Quarterly. Estab. 1975.

Needs: Feminist, literary. "No humor, science fiction, romance." Receives 60-100 unsolicited mss/month. Accepts 18-20 mss/issue; 75-80 mss/year. Publishes ms 1 year after acceptance. **Publishes 15-20 new writers/year.** Length: 5,000 words maximum. Also publishes poetry.

How to Contact: Send complete ms with a cover letter. Include estimated word count and brief bio. Send a disposable copy of ms and #10 SASE or IRC for reply only. Reviews novels, short story collections and nonfiction books of interest to writers. Send review copies to Virginia Aulin.
Payment/Terms: Pays $35 Canadian, free subscription to the magazine and 2 contributor's copies. Pays on publication for first North American serial rights.

THE ROUND TABLE, A Journal of Poetry and Fiction, P.O. Box 18673, Rochester NY 14618. Editors: Alan and Barbara Lupack. Magazine: 6×9; 64 pages. "We publish serious poetry and fiction based on or alluding to the Arthurian legends." Annual. Estab. 1984. Circ. 150.
Needs: "Any approach with a link to Arthurian legends. The quality of the fiction is the most important criterion." **Published new writers within the last year.** Publishes ms about 9 months after acceptance. Publishes short shorts. Publishes chapbooks.
How to Contact: Send complete ms with cover letter. Responds usually in 4 months, but stories under consideration may be held longer. SASE for ms. Accepts simultaneous submissions—if notified immediately upon acceptance elsewhere. Sample copy for $4 (specify fiction issue). Guidelines for SASE.
Payment/Terms: Pays 3 contributor's copy, reduced charge for extras.

$ SAN DIEGO WRITERS' MONTHLY, 3910 Chapman St., San Diego CA 92101. (619)266-0896. E-mail: mcarthy@sandiego-online.com. Website: www.sandiego-online.com (includes names of editors, agent's corner, calendar of local events, writers' workshops). **Contact:** Mark Clements, fiction editor. Literary magazine: 8×10; 32 pages; 60 lb. paper; illustrations; photos. "*San Diego Writers' Monthly* publishes excellent fiction from around the country with an emphasis on the writing community of San Diego county." Monthly. Estab. 1991. Circ. 500.
Needs: Adventure, ethnic/multicultural (general), family saga, fantasy (space fantasy), historical (general), horror (psychological), humor/satire, literary, mainstream/contemporary, mystery/suspense (police procedural, private eye/hard-boiled), New Age/mystic/spiritual, regional (southwest US), religious (inspirational), romance (contemporary, futuristic/time travel, gothic, historical, romantic suspense), science fiction (soft/sociological), thriller/espionage, western (traditional), young adult/teen (adventure, fantasy/science fiction, historical, horror, mystery/suspense, western). "No children's/juvenile, erotica, occult, translations. Wants to see more general ethnic/multicultural." Receives 25-100 unsolicited mss/month. Accepts 2 mss/issue; 24 mss/year. Recently published work by Susan Vreeland and J.T. O'Hara. **Publishes 12-15 new writers/year.** Length: 2,500-4,000 words. Also publishes literary essays, criticism and poetry. Sometimes comments on rejected ms.
How to Contact: Send complete ms with a cover letter. Accepts mss by mail and disk. Include estimated word count, 25-50 word bio, list of publications. Send SASE for reply and a disposable copy of ms. Accepts reprint and multiple submissions. Sample copy for $4. Guidelines for SASE. Reviews novels, short story collections or nonfiction books of interest to writers. Send books to editor.
Payment/Terms: Pays $15-25 and 1 contributor's copy. Pays on publication for one-time rights.
Advice: We look for good bones (structure), a strong plot and/or character development, good command of the written word; entertaining fiction with depth. Follow the guidelines, revise, make it tight and concise, send it out."

SANSKRIT, Literary Arts Magazine of UNC Charlotte, University of North Carolina at Charlotte, Highway 49, Charlotte NC 28223-0001. (704)687-2326. Fax: (704)687-3394. E-mail: sanskrit@email.uncc.edu. Website: www.uncc.edu/life/sanskrit. **Contact:** Jenice Bastien, editor-in-chief. Magazine: 9×12, 64 pages. "*Sanskrit* is an award-winning magazine produced with two goals in mind: service to the student staff and student body, and the promotion of unpublished and beginning artists. Our intended audience is the literary/arts community of UNCC, Charlotte, other schools and contributors and specifically individuals who might never have read a literary magazine before." Annual. Estab. 1968.
 • *Sanskrit* has received the Pacemaker Award, Associated College Press, Gold Crown Award and Columbia Scholastic Press Award.
Needs: "Not looking for any specific category—just good writing." Receives 50 unsolicited mss/month. Acquires 2-3 mss/issue. Publishes in late March. Deadline: first Friday in November. Published work by Bayard. Length: 250-3,500 words. Publishes short shorts. Also publishes poetry. Seldom critiques rejected mss.
How to Contact: Send complete manuscript with cover letter. Accepts queries/mss by e-mail and fax. SASE. Accepts simultaneous and multiple submissions (no more than 5 short stories at a time). Sample copy for $10. Guidelines for #10 SAE.
Payment/Terms: Pays contributor's copy. Acquires one-time rights. Publication not previously copyrighted.
Advice: "Remember that you are entering a market often saturated with mediocrity—an abundance of cute words and phrases held together by clichés simply will not do."

SANTA MONICA REVIEW, Santa Monica College, 1900 Pico Blvd., Santa Monica CA 90405. (310)434-4242. **Contact:** Andrew Tonkovich, editor. Magazine: 250 pages. "The editors are committed to fostering new talent as well as presenting new work by established writers. There is also a special emphasis on presenting and promoting writers who make their home in Southern California." Estab. 1989. Circ. 4,000.
Needs: Literary, experimental. "No crime and detective, mysogyny, footnotes, TV, dog stories. Want more self-conscious, smart, political, humorous, digressive, meta-fiction." Publishes special fiction issues or anthologies. Receives

250 unsolicited mss/month. Accepts 10 mss/issue; 20 mss/year. Agented fiction 10%. **Publishes 5 new writers/year.** Recently published work by Gary Amdahl, Michael Cadnum and Dylan Landis. Also publishes literary essays, memoirs and novel chapters.

How to Contact: Send complete ms with a cover letter. Responds in 3 months. Send a disposable copy of ms. Accepts simultaneous and multiple submissions. Sample copy for $7.

Payment/Terms: Pays 2 contributor's copies. Acquires first North American serial rights. Sends galleys to author.

SCRIVENER CREATIVE REVIEW, 853 Sherbrooke St. W., Montreal, Quebec H3A 2T6 Canada. (514)398-6588. E-mail: scrivenermag@hotmail.com. **Contacts:** Leemor Valin and Matt Frassica, fiction editors. Coordinating Editors: Farah Baig and Meredith Needham. Magazine: 8×9; 100 pages; matte paper; illustrations; b&w photos. "*Scrivener* is a creative journal publishing fiction, poetry, graphics, photography, reviews, interviews and scholarly articles. We encourage new and emerging talent; our audience comprises primarily university-aged students." Annual. Estab. 1980. Circ. 500.

Needs: Open, "good writing." Would like to see "fewer relationship stories; no hate stories; wants more experimental submissions." Receives 10 unsolicited mss/month. Accepts 20 mss/year. Does not read mss May 1-Sept 1. Publishes ms 2 months after acceptance. **Publishes 2-3 new writers/year.** Published work by Lisa Propst and Martine Fournier. Length: 20 pages maximum. Occasionally publishes short shorts. Also publishes literary essays, literary criticism, poetry. Often critiques rejected mss.

How to Contact: Send complete ms with a cover letter and SASE (or IRC). Include "critical statements; where we can reach you; 50-100 word bio; education; previous publications." Accepts queries/mss by e-mail and on disk. Accepts multiple submissions. Responds in 4 months to queries and mss. Sample copy for $7 (US in USA; Canadian in Canada). Guidelines for SAE/IRC. Reviews novels and short story collections. Send books to Nonfiction Editor.

Payment/Terms: Pays contributor's copies; charges for extras. Rights retained by the author.

Advice: "Fiction we accept must stand out from the others in terms of interesting content and style. We look for writing that is innovative, vibrant, image-laden, crafted and compelling. It must not be more than 20 pages double-spaced."

$ ● THE SEATTLE REVIEW, Padelford Hall Box 354330, University of Washington, Seattle WA 98195. (206)543-9865. E-mail: seaview@english.washington.edu. Website: http://depts.washington.edu/engl/seaview1.html (includes short fiction, guidelines, list of back issues, mission statement and visuals of covers). **Contact:** Colleen J. McElroy, editor. Magazine: 6×9. "Includes general fiction, poetry, craft essays on writing, and one interview per issue with a Northwest writer." Semiannual. Published special fiction issue. Estab. 1978. Circ. 1,000.

Needs: Contemporary, ethnic, experimental, fantasy, feminist, gay, historical, horror, humor/satire, lesbian, literary, mainstream, prose poem, psychic/supernatural/occult, regional, science fiction, excerpted novel, mystery/suspense, translations, western. Wants more creative nonfiction. "We also publish a series called Writers and their Craft, which deals with aspects of writing fiction (also poetry)—point of view, characterization, etc., rather than literary criticism, each issue." Does not want to see "anything in bad taste (porn, racist, etc.)." Receives about 100 unsolicited mss/week. Does not read mss June-September. Agented fiction 25%. **Published new writers within the last year.** Recently published work by Ivan Doig, Daniel Orozco, Frederick Busch, Peter Bacho, Jewell Parker Rhodes and David Guterson. Length: 500-5,500 words; average length: 3,500 words. Publishes short shorts.

How to Contact: Send complete ms. Responds in 8 months. Accepts multiple submissions. SASE. Sample copy "half-price if older than one year." Current issue for $6; some special issues $8.

Payment/Terms: Pays 2 contributor's copies; charge for extras. Copyright reverts to writer on publication; "please request release of rights and cite *SR* in reprint publications."

Advice: "Beginners do well in our magazine if they send clean, well-written manuscripts. We've published a lot of 'first stories' from all over the country and take pleasure in discovery."

● SEEMS, Lakeland College, Box 359, Sheboygan WI 53082-0359. (920)565-1276. Fax: (920)565-1206. E-mail: kelder@excel.net. **Contact:** Karl Elder, editor. Magazine: 7×8½; 40 pages. "We publish fiction and poetry for an audience which tends to be highly literate. People read the publication, I suspect, for the sake of reading it." Published irregularly (35 issues in 31 years). Estab. 1971. Circ. 500.

Needs: Literary. "We would like to see more quickfiction—that which straddles the boundaries between prose and poetry." Accepts 4 mss/issue. Receives 12 unsolicited fiction mss each month. **Publishes 1-2 new writers/year.** Recently published work by Rick Henry, Norman Lock and Natalia Nebel. Length: 5,000 words maximum. Publishes short shorts. Also publishes poetry. Critiques rejected mss when there is time.

How to Contact: Send complete ms with SASE. Responds in 3-4 months to mss. Accepts multiple submissions. Does not accept simultaneous or e-mail submissions. Publishes ms an average of 1-2 years after acceptance. Sample copy for $4.

Payment/Terms: Pays 1 contributor's copy; $4 charge for extras. Rights revert to author.

Advice: "Send clear, clean copies. Read the magazine in order to help determine the taste of the editor. The story must invoke the imagination, the setting must become visible, the piece needs to be original or at least unusual in some manner, and the prose must be economical. Above all else, it must be economical. Good fiction contains all of the essential elements of poetry; study poetry and apply those elements to fiction. Our interest is shifting to story poems, the grey area between genres."

$ ● THE SEWANEE REVIEW, University of the South, 735 University Ave., Sewanee TN 37383-1000. (931)598-1246. E-mail: rjones@sewanee.edu. Website: www.sewanee.edu/sreview/home.html (includes extracts from recent and back issues, magazine's history, writers' guidelines, links to other literary sites). Editor: George Core. **Contact:** Fiction Editor. Magazine: 6×9; 192 pages. "A literary quarterly, publishing original fiction, poetry, essays on literary and related subjects, book reviews and book notices for well-educated readers who appreciate good American and English literature." Quarterly. Estab. 1892. Circ. 3,500.

Needs: Literary, contemporary. No erotica, science fiction, fantasy or excessively violent or profane material. Editor prefers stories that have a plot. Buys 10-15 mss/year. Receives 100 unsolicited fiction mss each month. Does not read mss June 1-August 31. **Publishes 2-3 new writers/year.** Length: 6,000-7,500 words. Critiques rejected mss "when there is time." Sometimes recommends other markets.

How to Contact: Send complete ms with SASE and cover letter stating previous publications, if any. Responds in 6 weeks to mss. Sample copy for $8.25. Writer's guidelines for SASE.

Payment/Terms: Pays $10-12/printed page; 2 contributor's copies; $4.25 charge for extras. Pays on publication for first North American serial rights and second serial rights by agreement.

Advice: "Send only one story at a time, with a serious and sensible cover letter. We think fiction is of greater general interest than any other literary mode."

$☺ SHENANDOAH, The Washington and Lee Review, 2nd Floor, Troubadour Theater, Lexington VA 24450-0303. (540)463-8908. Fax: (540)463-8461. E-mail: rodsmith@wlu.edu. Website: http://shenandoah.wlu.edu (includes samples, contents of current issue, guidelines, information on prizes, subscription, classroom text, FAQ's, links to other sites, staff bios). **Contact:** R.T. Smith, editor. Magazine: 6×9; 124 pages. "We are a literary journal devoted to excellence." Quarterly. Estab. 1950. Circ. 2,000.

Needs: Literary. Receives 400-500 unsolicited fiction mss/month. Accepts 5 mss/issue; 20 mss/year. Does not read mss during summer. Publishes ms 6-12 months after acceptance. **"In 2001, we published 59 writers new to our pages."** Recently published work by Mary Oliver, Rodney Jones and Reynolds Price. Publishes short shorts. Also publishes literary essays, literary criticism and poetry.

How to Contact: Send complete ms with cover letter. Include a 3-sentence bio and list of publications (see website). Responds in 10 weeks to mss. Send a disposable copy of ms. Sample copy for $8. Guidelines for #10 SASE or on website.

Payment/Terms: Pays $25/page, $2.50/line (poetry) and free subscription to the magazine on publication. Acquires first North American serial rights. Sends galleys to author. Sponsors contest.

Advice: Looks for "thrift, precision, originality. As Frank O'Connor said, 'Get black on white.' "

$☺ SIDE SHOW, Short Story Anthology, Somersault Press, 404 Vista Height Rd., Richmond CA 94805. E-mail: jisom@atdial.net. **Contact:** Shelley Anderson, editor. Book (paperback): 5½×8½; 300 pages; 50 lb. paper; semi-gloss card cover with color illustration; perfect-bound. "Quality short stories for a general, literary audience." Estab. 1991. Circ. 3,000.

● Previously published as an annual anthology, *Side Show* will now publish a book once they have the requisite number of publishable stories (approximately 20-30). There is no longer a yearly deadline. Stories are accepted year round.

Needs: Contemporary, ethnic, feminist, gay, humor/satire, literary, mainstream. "Nothing genre, religious, pornographic; no essays, novels, memoirs." Receives 50-60 unsolicited mss/month. Accepts 25-30 mss/issue. Publishes ms up to 9 months after acceptance. **Publishes 5-10 new writers/per book.** Recently published work by Dorothy Bryant and George Rabasa. 25% of fiction by previously unpublished writers. Length: Open. Critiques rejected mss, if requested.

How to Contact: Accepts queries by e-mail. All submissions entered in contest. *$10 entry fee* (includes copy of recent *Side Show*). No guidelines. Send complete ms with cover letter and entry fee. Responds in 6 weeks to mss with SASE. Accepts simultaneous submissions. Multiple submissions encouraged (entry fee covers all submissions mailed in same envelope). Sample copy for $10 and $2 postage and handling ($.83 sales tax CA residents).

Payment/Terms: Pays $5/printed page. Pays on publication for first North American serial rights. Sends galleys to author. All submissions entered in our contest for cash prizes of $100 (1st), $75 (2nd) and $50 (3rd).

Advice: Looks for "readability, vividness of characterization, coherence, inspiration, unusual or compelling subject matter, imagination, point of view, originality, plausibility. If your fiction isn't inspired, you probably won't be published by us (i.e., style and craft alone won't do it)."

[N] ☺ SIERRA NEVADA COLLEGE REVIEW, Sierra Nevada College, 999 Tahoe Blvd., Incline Village NV 89451. (775)831-1314. Fax: (775)831-1347. E-mail: jsaraceno@sierranevada.edu. **Editor:** June Sylvester Saraceno. Magazine: 5½×8½; 50-100 pages; coated paper; card cover; saddle-stitched. "We are open to many kinds of work but avoid what we consider trite, sentimental, contrived. . . ." Annual. Estab. 1990. Circ. 200-250 (mostly college libraries).

● The majority of work published in this review is poetry.

Needs: Experimental, literary, mainstream/contemporary, regional. Would like to see more flash fiction (sudden fiction or short, short stories). "No science fiction or children's stories." Receives about 50 unsolicited mss/month. Accepts 2-3 mss/year. Does not read mss April 1-September 1. Work is published by next issue (published in May, annually). Recently published work by Marisella Veiga and Margot Meyers. Length: 1,000 words maximum; average length: 500 words. Publishes short shorts. Also publishes literary essays, literary criticism and poetry. Sometimes comments on rejected mss.

How to Contact: Send complete ms with a cover letter. Include estimated word count and bio. Send SASE for reply, return of ms or send a disposable copy of ms. Accepts simultaneous and multiple submissions. Sample copy for $2.50.

Payment/Terms: Pays 2 contributor's copies. Acquires one-time rights.
Advice: Looks for "memorable characters, close attention to detail which makes the story vivid. We are interested in flash fiction. Also regional work that catches the flavor of place and time—like strong characters. No moralizing, inspirational work. Tired of trite love stories—cynicism bores us."

SLIPSTREAM, Box 2071, New Market Station, Niagara Falls NY 14301. (716)282-2616. E-mail: editors@slipstreampress.org. Website: www.slipstreampress.org (includes guidelines, editors, current needs, info on current and past releases, sample poems, contest info). **Contact:** Dan Sicoli, editor. Magazine: 7×8½; 80-100 pages; high quality paper; card cover; illustrations; photos. "We use poetry and short fiction with a contemporary urban feel." Estab. 1981. Circ. 500.
Needs: Contemporary, erotica, ethnic, experimental, humor/satire, literary, mainstream and prose poem. "No religious or romance." Wants to see more experimental. Occasionally publishes theme issues; query for information. Receives over 25 unsolicited mss/month. Accepts 2-4 mss/issue; 6 mss/year. Recently published work by E.R. Baxter III and Greg Ames. Length: under 15 pages. Publishes short shorts. Rarely critiques rejected mss. Sometimes recommends other markets.
How to Contact: "Query before submitting." Responds within 2 months. Accepts multiple submissions. Send SASE for reply or return of ms. Sample copy for $7. Guidelines for #10 SASE. No electronic submissions.
Payment/Terms: Pays 2 contributor's copies. Acquires one-time rights.
Advice: "Writing should be honest, fresh; develop your own style. Check out a sample issue first. Don't write for the sake of writing, write from the gut as if it were a biological need. Write from experience and mean what you say, but say it in the fewest number of words."

THE SMALL POND MAGAZINE, Box 664, Stratford CT 06615. (203)378-4066. Editor: Napoleon St. Cyr. **Contact:** Fiction Editor. Magazine: 5½×8½; 42 pages; 60 lb. offset paper; 65 lb. cover stock; illustrations (art). "Features contemporary poetry, the salt of the earth, peppered with short prose pieces of various kinds. The college educated and erudite read it for good poetry, prose and pleasure." Triannual. Estab. 1964. Circ. 300.
Needs: "Rarely use the formula stories you'd find in *Cosmo*, *Redbook*, *Ladies Home Journal*, etc. Philosophy: Highest criteria, originality, even a bit quirky is OK. Don't mind O. Henry endings but better be exceptional. Readership: College grads, and college staff, ⅓ of subscribers are college and university libraries." No science fiction, children's. Accepts 10-12 mss/year. Longer response time in July and August. Receives approximately 40 unsolicited fiction mss each month. **Publishes 1-2 new writers/year.** Recently published work by Judah Jacobowitz, Charles Rammelcamp, Joshua R. Pahigian and Ruth Innes. Length: 200-2,500 words. Critiques rejected mss when there is time. Sometimes recommends other markets.
How to Contact: Send complete ms with SASE and short vita. Responds in up to 3 months. Publishes ms an average of 2-18 months after acceptance. Sample copy for $4; $3 for back issues.
Payment/Terms: Pays 2 contributor's copies; $3/copy charge for extras, postage paid. Acquires all rights.
Advice: "Send for a sample copy first. All mss must be typed. Name and address and story title on front page, name of story on succeeding pages and paginated. I look for polished, smooth progression—no clumsy paragraphs or structures where you know the author didn't edit closely. Also, no poor grammar. Beginning and even established poets read and learn from reading lots of other's verse. Not a bad idea for fiction writers, in their genre, short or long fiction."

SNAKE NATION REVIEW, Snake Nation Press, Inc., #2 West Force St., 110, Valdosta GA 31601. (912)244-0752. Fax: (912)253-9125 (call first). E-mail: jeana@snakenationpress.org. Website: www.snakenationpress.org. **Contact:** Jean Arambula, editor. 6×9; 110 pages; acid free 70 lb. paper; 90 lb. cover; illustrations; photos. "We are interested in all types of stories for an educated, discerning, sophisticated audience." Quarterly. Estab. 1989. Circ. 2,000.
Needs: "Short stories of 5,000 words or less, poems (any length), art work that will be returned after use." Condensed/excerpted novel, contemporary, erotica, ethnic, experimental, fantasy, feminist, gay, horror, humor/satire, lesbian, literary, mainstream, mystery/suspense, prose poem, psychic/supernatural/occult, regional, science fiction, senior citizen/retirement. "We want our writers to have a voice, a story to tell, not a flat rendition of a slice of life." Plans annual anthology. Receives 200 unsolicited mss/month. Buys 8-10 mss/issue; 40 mss/year. Publishes ms 6 months after acceptance. Agented fiction 1%. Published work by Robert Earl Price and O. Victor Miller. Length: 300-5,500 words; average length: 3,500 words. Publishes short shorts. Length: 500 words. Also publishes literary essays, poetry. Reviews novels and short story collections. Sometimes critiques rejected mss and recommends other markets.
How to Contact: Send complete ms with cover letter. Responds to queries in 3 months. SASE. Sample copy for $6, 8×10 SAE and 90¢ postage. Guidelines for SASE.
Payment/Terms: Pays 2 contributor's copies. Acquires one-time rights. Sends galleys to author.

$ SNOWY EGRET, P.O. Box 9, Bowling Green IN 47833. Publisher: Karl Barnebey. Editor: Philip Repp. **Contact:** Fiction Editor. Magazine: 8½×11; 50 pages; text paper; heavier cover; illustrations. "*Snowy Egret* explores the range of human involvement, particularly psychological, with the natural world. Its fiction depicts characters who identify strongly with nature, either positively or negatively, and who grow in their understanding of themselves and the world of plants, animals and landscape." Semiannual. Estab. 1922. Circ. 500.
Needs: Nature writing, including 'true' stories, eye-witness accounts, descriptive sketches and traditional fiction. "We are interested in penetrating psychological and spiritual journeys of characters who have strong ties to or identifications with the natural world. No works written for popular genres: horror, science fiction, romance, detective, western, etc." Would like to see more "honest, inciteful observation and depiction of nature." Receives 25 unsolicited mss/month.

Accepts up to 6 mss/issue; up to 12 mss/year. Publishes ms 6-12 months after acceptance. **Publishes 4-6 new writers/ year.** Recently published work by James Hinton, Ron Gielgun, Alice Cross and Maeve Mullin Ellis. Length: 500-10,000 words; 1,000-3,000 words preferred. Publishes short shorts. Length: 400-500 words. Sometimes critiques rejected mss.
How to Contact: Send complete ms with cover letter. "Cover letter optional: do not query." Responds in 2 months. SASE. Accepts simultaneous (if noted) submissions. Sample back issues for $8 and 9×12 SAE. Send #10 SASE for writer's guidelines.
Payment/Terms: Pays $2/page and 2 contributor's copies; charge for extras. Pays on publication for first North American serial rights and reprint rights. Sends galleys to author.
Advice: Looks for "honest, freshly detailed pieces with plenty of description and/or dialogue which will allow the reader to identify with the characters and step into the setting; fiction in which nature affects character development and the outcome of the story."

SO TO SPEAK, A Feminist Journal of Language and Art, George Mason University, 4400 University Dr., MS 2D6, Fairfax VA 22030-4444. (703)993-3625. E-mail: sts@gmu.edu. Website: www.gmu.edu/org/sts. **Contact:** Anne William Davis, fiction editor. Editors change every year. Magazine: 7×10; approximately 70 pages. "We are a feminist journal of language and art." Semiannual. Estab. 1988. Circ. 1,300.
Needs: Ethnic/multicultural, experimental, feminist, lesbian, literary, mainstream/contemporary, regional, translations. "No science fiction, mystery, genre romance, porn (lesbian or straight)." Receives 100 unsolicited mss/month. Accepts 2-3 mss/issue; 6 mss/year. Publishes ms 6 months after acceptance. **Publishes 2 new writers/year.** Length: 6,000 words maximum; average length: 4,000 words. Publishes short shorts. Also publishes literary essays, literary criticism, book reviews, poetry and artwork. Sometimes comments on rejected mss.
How to Contact: Send complete ms with a cover letter. Include bio (50 words maximum) and SASE. Responds in 6 months to mss. SASE for return of ms or send a disposable copy of ms. Accepts simultaneous submissions. Sample copy for $6. Guidelines for #10 SASE. We do not read between March 15 and August 15.
Payment/Terms: Pays contributor's copies. Acquires first North American serial rights.
Advice: "Every writer has something they do exceptionally well; do that and it will shine through in the work. We look for quality prose with a definite appeal to a feminist audience. We are trying to move away from strict genre lines."

SONGS OF INNOCENCE, Pengradonian Publications, P.O. Box 719, New York NY 10101-0719. E-mail: mmpendragon@aol.com. Editor: Michael Pendragon. **Contact:** Fiction Editor. Literary magazine/journal: 9×6; 175 pages; perfect bound; illustrations. "A literary publication which celebrates the nobler aspects of humankind and the human experience. Along with sister-publication, *Penny Dreadful*, *Songs* seeks to provide a forum for poetry and fiction in the 19th century/Romantic/Victorian tradition." Triannual. Circ. estimated 200.
Needs: Fantasy, historical (19th century or earlier), literary, New Age, psychic/supernatural/occult. "No children's/ young adult; modern tales; Christian (or anything dogmatic)." Receives 100 unsolicited mss/month. Accepts 15 mss/ issue; 30 mss/year. Publishes ms up to 2 years after acceptance. Length: 500-5,000 words. Publishes short shorts. Also publishes literary essays, literary criticism, poetry. Often comments on rejected mss. Published works by John Berbrich, John B. Ford, Ann Kucera and Jason E. Schlismann.
How to Contact: Send complete ms with a cover letter. Include estimated word count, 1 page or less bio and list of publications. Accepts mss by e-mail or disk. Responds in 3 weeks to queries; 6-12 months to mss. SASE for reply and send a disposable copy of ms. Accepts simultaneous submissions and reprints. Sample copy for $10, 9×6 SAE. Guidelines for SASE.
Payment/Terms: Pays 1 contributor's copy; additional copies $10 each. Pays on publication for one-time rights. Sends galleys to author.
Advice: "We prefer tales set in 1910 or earlier (preferably earlier). We prefer prose in the 19th century/Victorian style. We do not like the terse, modern, post-Hemingway 'see Dick run' style. Tales should transcend genres and include a spiritual supernatural element (without becoming fantasy). Avoid strong language, sex, etc. Include name and address on the title page. Include word count on title page. Double space, 12-pt. Times/Courier font, etc. (usual professional format). We select stories/poems that appeal to us and do not base selection on whether one has been published elsewhere."

SOUTH CAROLINA REVIEW, Strode Tower, Clemson University, Clemson SC 29634-1503. (864)656-3543. Fax: (864)656-1345. E-mail: cwayne@clemson.edu. Website: www.clemson.edu/caah/cedp (includes introduction page/ background, editorial and publication policy, tables of contents for all issues, subscription page). **Contact:** Wayne Chapman, editor. Magazine: 6×9; 200 pages; 60 lb. cream white vellum paper; 65 lb. cream white vellum cover stock. Semiannual. Estab. 1967. Circ. 500.
Needs: Literary and contemporary fiction, poetry, essays, reviews. Receives 50-60 unsolicited fiction mss each month. Does not read mss June-August or December. **Published new writers within the last year.** Published work by Joyce Carol Oates, Rosanne Coggeshall and Stephen Dixon. Rarely critiques rejected mss.
How to Contact: Send complete ms with SASE. Requires text on disk upon acceptance in WordPerfect or Microsoft Word format. Responds in 4 months to mss. "No unsolicited reviews." Sample copy for $10.
Payment/Terms: Pays in contributor's copies.

SOUTH DAKOTA REVIEW, University of South Dakota, Box 111, University Exchange, Vermillion SD 57069. (605)677-5184. Fax: (605)677-5298. E-mail: sdreview@usd.edu. Website: www.usd.edu/engl/SDR/index.html (includes masthead page with editors' names and submission/subscription guidelines, sample covers, sample story and essay excerpts and poems). Editor: Brian Bedard. **Contact:** Fiction Editor. Magazine: 6×9; 140-170 pages; book paper; glossy cover stock; illustrations sometimes; photos on cover. "Literary magazine for university and college audiences and their equivalent. Emphasis is often on the American West and its writers, but will accept mss from anywhere. Issues are generally personal essay, fiction, and poetry with some literary essays." Quarterly. Estab. 1963. Circ. 500.

Needs: Literary, contemporary, ethnic, regional. "We like very well-written, thematically ambitious, character-centered short fiction. Contemporary Western American setting appeals, but not necessary. No formula stories, horror, or adolescent 'I' narrator." Receives 40 unsolicited fiction mss/month. Accepts about 40 mss/year. Summer editor accepts mss in April through June. Agented fiction 5%. Publishes short shorts of 5 pages double-spaced typescript. **Publishes 3-5 new writers/year.** Published work by Jon Hassler, Stephanie Dickinson and Marie Argeris. Length: 1,000-6,000 words. (Has made exceptions, up to novella length.) Sometimes recommends other markets.

How to Contact: Send complete ms with SASE. "We like cover letters that are not boastful and do not attempt to sell the stories but rather provide some personal information about the writer which can be used for a contributor's note." Responds in 10 weeks. Publishes ms an average of 1-6 months after acceptance. Sample copy for $5.

Payment/Terms: Pays 1-year subscription and 2 contributor's copies. Acquires first and reprint rights.

Advice: Rejects mss because of "careless writing; often careless typing; stories too personal ('I' confessional); aimlessness of plot, unclear or unresolved conflicts; subject matter that editor finds clichéd, sensationalized, pretentious or trivial. We are trying to use more fiction and more variety."

THE SOUTHEAST REVIEW, (formerly *Sundog: The Southeast Review*), English Department, Florida State University, Tallahassee FL 32306-1036. (850)644-2773. E-mail: southeastreview@english.fsu.edu. Website: www.englis h.fsu.edu/southeastreview (includes names of editors and writer's guidelines). "*The Southeast Review* is published for a literary audience with a sophisticated, intelligent knowledge of the fiction genre." **Contact:** Ed Tarkington, fiction editor. Magazine: 6×9; 60-100 pages; 70 lb. paper; 10 pt. Krome Kote cover; illustrations; photos. Biannual. Estab. 1979. Circ. 2,000.

Needs: "We want stories (under 3,000 words) with striking images, fresh language, and a consistent voice." Would like to see more literary fiction. "No genre or formula fiction. We receive approximately 180 submissions per month; we accept less than 5%. We will comment briefly on rejected mss when time permits." **Publishes 4-6 new writers/ year.** Recently published work by Ann Pancake, Ron Rash and Richard Newman.

How to Contact: Send complete ms with SASE and a brief cover letter. Accepts submissions on disk. Responds in 2 months. Publishes ms an average of 2-6 months after acceptance. Sample copy for $5. Subscriptions for $9.

Payment/Terms: Pays 2 contributor's copies. Acquires first North American serial rights which then revert to author.

Advice: "Avoid trendy experimentation for its own sake (present-tense narration, observation that isn't also revelation). Fresh stories, moving, interesting characters and a sensitivity to language are still fiction mainstays. Also publishes winner and runners-up of the World's Best Short Short Story Contest sponsored by the Florida State University English Department."

SOUTHERN CALIFORNIA ANTHOLOGY, University of Southern California, Waite Phillips Hall, Room 404, Los Angeles CA 90089-4034. (213)740-3252. Fax: (213)740-5775. E-mail: courtmack@hotmail.com. Website: www.usc.edu/dept/LAS/mpw. **Contact:** Editor. Magazine: 5½×8½; 142 pages; semigloss cover stock. "The *Southern California Anthology* is a literary review that contains an eclectic collection of previously unpublished quality contemporary fiction, poetry and interviews with established literary people, published for adults of all professions; of particular interest to those interested in serious contemporary literature." Annual. Estab. 1983. Circ. 1,500.

Needs: Contemporary, ethnic, experimental, feminist, historical, humor/satire, literary, mainstream, regional, serialized/ excerpted novel. "No juvenile, religious, confession, romance, science fiction or pornography." Receives 40 unsolicited fiction mss each month. Accepts 1-2 mss/issue. Does not read February-September. Publishes ms 4 months after acceptance. **Publishes 1-2 new writers/year.** Recently published work by James Tate, Susan Hubbard, Alice Fulton, Carmelia Leonte and Philip Appleman. Length: 10-15 pages average; 2 pages minimum; 25 pages maximum. Publishes short shorts.

How to Contact: Send complete ms with cover letter or submit through agent. Cover letter should include list of previous publications. Accepts multiple submissions. Responds in 1 month to queries; 4 months to mss. Send SASE for reply or return of ms. Sample copy for $4. Guidelines for #10 SASE.

Payment/Terms: Pays in contributor's copies. Acquires first rights.

Advice: "The *Anthology* pays particular attention to craft and style in its selection of narrative writing."

SOUTHERN HUMANITIES REVIEW, Auburn University, 9088 Haley Center, Auburn University AL 36849. Website: www.auburn.edu/english/shr/home.htm. Co-editors: Dan R. Latimer and Virginia M. Kouidis. **Contact:** Fiction Editor. Magazine: 6×9; 100 pages; 60 lb. neutral pH, natural paper; 65 lb. neutral pH med. coated cover stock; occasional illustrations; photos. "We publish essays, poetry, fiction and reviews. Our fiction has ranged from very traditional in form and content to very experimental. Literate, college-educated audience. We hope they read our journal for both enlightenment and pleasure." Quarterly. Estab. 1967. Circ. 800.

Needs: Serious fiction, fantasy, feminist, humor and regional. Receives approximately 25 unsolicited fiction mss each month. Accepts 1-2 mss/issue, 4-6 mss/year. Slower reading time in summer. **Published new writers within the last year.** Recently published work by William Cobb, Heimito von Doderer, Greg Johnson and Dieter Kühn. Length: 3,500-15,000 words. Also publishes literary essays, literary criticism, poetry. Critiques rejected mss when there is time. Sometimes recommends other markets.

How to Contact: Send complete ms (one at a time) with SASE and cover letter with an explanation of topic chosen—"special, certain book, etc., a little about author if he/she has never submitted." Responds in 3 months. Sample copy for $5; $7 outside US. Reviews novel and short story collections.

Payment/Terms: Pays 2 contributor's copies; $5 charge for extras. Rights revert to author upon publication. Sends galleys to author.

Advice: "Send us the ms with SASE. If we like it, we'll take it or we'll recommend changes. If we don't like it, we'll send it back as promptly as possible. Read the journal. Send typewritten, clean copy carefully proofread. We also award annually the Hoepfner Prize of $100 for the best published essay or short story of the year. Let someone whose opinion you respect read your story and give you an honest appraisal. Rewrite, if necessary, to get the most from your story."

$ 🖉 🖤 THE SOUTHERN REVIEW, Louisiana State University, 43 Allen Hall, Baton Rouge LA 70803-5005. (225)578-5108. Fax: (225)578-5098. E-mail: jeaster@lsu.edu. Website: www.lsu.edu/thesouthernreview (includes subscription information, staff, guidelines, table of contents, current issue). **Contact:** John Easterly, associate editor. Magazine: 6¾×10; 240 pages; 50 lb. Glatfelter paper; 65 lb. #1 grade cover stock. "A literary quarterly publishing critical essays, poetry and fiction for a highly intellectual audience." Quarterly. Estab. 1935. Circ. 3,100.

● Several stories published in *The Southern Review* were Pushcart Prize selections.

Needs: Literary. "We emphasize style and substantial content. No mystery, fantasy or religious mss." Accepts 4-5 mss/issue. Receives approximately 300 unsolicited fiction mss each month. Does not read mss June-August. Publishes ms 6-9 months after acceptance. Agented fiction 1%. **Publishes 4-6 new writers/year.** Published work by William Gay, Romulus Linney, Richard Bausch and Ingrid Hill. Length: 2,000-10,000 words. Also publishes literary essays, literary criticism, poetry. Sponsors annual contest for best first collection of short stories published during the calendar year.

How to Contact: Send complete ms with cover letter and SASE. "Prefer brief letters giving information on author concerning where he/she has been published before, biographical info and what he/she is doing now." Responds in 2 months to mss. Sample copy for $8. Guidelines free for SAE. Reviews novels and short story collections.

Payment/Terms: Pays $12/printed page and 2 contributor's copies. Pays on publication for first North American serial rights. Sends galleys to author.

Advice: "Develop a careful, clear style. Although willing to publish experimental writing that appears to have a valid artistic purpose, *The Southern Review* avoids extremism and sensationalism."

🖉 SOUTHWEST REVIEW, P.O. Box 750374, 307 Fondren Library West, Southern Methodist University, Dallas TX 75275-0374. (214)768-1037. Fax: (214)768-1408. E-mail: swr@mail.smu.edu. Website: www.southwestreview.org. Editor: Willard Spiegelman. **Contact:** Elizabeth Mills, senior editor. Magazine: 6×9; 144 pages. "The majority of our readers are college-educated adults who wish to stay abreast of the latest and best in contemporary fiction, poetry, literary criticism and books in all but the most specialized disciplines." Quarterly. Estab. 1915. Circ. 1,600.

Needs: "High literary quality; no specific requirements as to subject matter, but cannot use sentimental, religious, western, poor science fiction, pornographic, true confession, mystery, juvenile or serialized or condensed novels." Receives approximately 200 unsolicited fiction mss each month. Recently published work by Tracy Daugherty, Millicent Dillon and Mark Jacobs. Length: prefers 3,000-5,000 words. Also publishes literary essays and poetry. Occasionally critiques rejected mss.

How to Contact: Send complete ms with SASE. Responds in 6 months to mss. Publishes ms 6-12 months after acceptance. Accepts multiple submissions. Sample copy for $6. Guidelines for SASE.

Payment/Terms: Payment varies; writers receive 3 contributor's copies. Pays on publication for first North American serial rights. Sends galleys to author.

Advice: "We have become less regional. A lot of time would be saved for us and for the writer if he or she looked at a copy of the *Southwest Review* before submitting. We like to receive a cover letter because it is some reassurance that the author has taken the time to check a current directory for the editor's name. When there isn't a cover letter, we wonder whether the same story is on 20 other desks around the country."

🖉 ◎ SOUTHWESTERN AMERICAN LITERATURE, Center for the Study of the Southwest, Southwest Texas State University, 601 University Dr., San Marcos TX 78666. (512)245-2232. Fax: (512)245-7462. E-mail: mb13@swt.edu. Website: http://wp29.english.swt.edu/css/cssindex.htm. Editors: Mark Busby, D.M. Heaberlin. **Contact:** Twister Marquiss, fiction editor. Magazine: 6×9; 125 pages; 80 lb. cover stock. "We publish fiction, nonfiction, poetry, literary criticism and book reviews. Generally speaking, we want material concerning the Greater Southwest, or material written by southwestern writers." Semiannual. Estab. 1971. Circ. 300.

Needs: Ethnic/multicultural, literary, mainstream/contemporary, regional. No science fiction or romance. Receives 10-15 unsolicited mss/month. Accepts 1-2 mss/issue; 4-5 mss/year. Publishes ms up to 6 months after acceptance. **Publishes 1-2 new writers/year.** Published work by Jerry Craven, Paul Ruffin, Robert Flynn and Philip Heldrich. Length: 6,250 words maximum; average length: 6,000 words. Publishes short shorts. Also publishes literary essays, literary criticism, poetry. Sometimes comments on rejected ms.

How to Contact: Send complete ms with a cover letter. Include estimated word count, 20-word bio and list of publications. Accepts queries by e-mail. Responds in 2 months. SASE for return of ms. Accepts simultaneous submissions. Sample copy $7. Guidelines free. Reviews novels and short story collections. Send books to Mark Busby.

Payment/Terms: Pays 2 contributor's copies; additional copies $7. Acquires first rights.

Advice: "We look for crisp language, interesting approach to material; regional emphasis is desired but not required. Read widely, write often, revise carefully. We are looking for stories that probe the relationship between the tradition of Southwestern American literature and the writer's own imagination in creative ways. We seek stories that move beyond stereotype and approach the larger defining elements of regional literature with three qualities: originality, supple language, and humanity. We want stories with regional elements and also ones that, as William Faulkner noted in his Nobel Prize acceptance speech, treat subjects central to good literature—the old verities of the human heart such as honor and courage and pity and suffering, fear and humor, love and sorrow."

🄾 **SPEAK UP**, Speak Up Press, P.O. Box 100506, Denver CO 80250. (303)715-0837. Fax: (303)715-0793. E-mail: SpeakUPres@aol.com. Website: www.speakuppress.org. **Contact:** Gretchen Bryant, senior editor. Magazine: 5½×8½; 128 pages; 55 lb. Glat. Supple Opaque Recycled Natural paper; 12 pt. CIS cover; illustrations; photos. "*Speak Up* features the original fiction, nonfiction, poetry, plays, photography and artwork of young people 13-19 years old. *Speak Up* provides a place for teens to be creative, honest and expressive in an uncensored environment." Annual. Estab. 1999. Circ. 2,900.

Needs: Teen writers. Receives 30 unsolicited mss/month. Accepts 30 mss/issue; 30 mss/year. Publishes ms 3-12 months after acceptance. **Publishes 20 new writers/year.** Length: 5,000 words maximum; average length: 500 words. Publishes short shorts. Also publishes literary essays and poetry.

How to Contact: Send complete ms with a cover letter. Accepts submissions by e-mail and fax. Responds in 3 months to queries. Send SASE for return of ms. Accepts simultaneous submissions, previously published work and multiple submissions. Sample copy free. Guidelines for SASE, by e-mail, fax or on website.

Payment/Terms: Pays 2 contributor's copies. Pays on publication for all, first North American serial or one-time rights.

🄾 ♛ **SPINDRIFT**, Shoreline Community College, 16101 Greenwood Ave. North, Seattle WA 98155. (206)546-5864. E-mail: spindrift@short.cfc.edu. Website: http://elmo.shore.cfc.edu/spindrift (includes guidelines, editorial staff, excerpts, general information). **Contact:** Literary Editor. Magazine: 140 pages; quality paper; photographs; b&w artwork. "We published a variety of fiction, most of which would be considered literary. Authors are from all over the map, but we give priority to writers from our community." Annual. Estab. around 1967. Circ. 500.

● *Spindrift* has received awards for "Best Literary Magazine" from the Community College Humanities Association both locally and nationally and awards from the Pacific Printing Industries.

Needs: Contemporary, ethnic, experimental, historical (general), prose poem, regional, serialized/excerpted novel, translations. "No detective, science fiction, romance, religious/inspirational. We look for fresh, original works that is not forced or 'straining' to be literary." Receives up to 300 mss/year. Accepts up to 20 mss/issue. Does not read during spring/summer. Publishes ms 3-4 months after acceptance. **Publishes 5-6 new writers/year.** Recently published work by Ed Harkness and Virgil Suarez. Length: 250-4,500 words. "Would like to see well-written short shorts."

How to Contact: Send complete ms and cover letter with bio, name, address, phone. Do not place name on ms. Accepts multiple submissions; "please indicate in cover letter." Submit by February 1. Responds by March 15 if SASE is included. Sample copy for $8, 8×10 SAE and $1 postage; sample back issue for $2.

Payment/Terms: Pays in contributor's copies; charge for extras. Acquires first rights. Publication not copyrighted.

Advice: "Let the story tell itself; don't force or overdo the language. Show the reader something new about people, situations, life itself."

🄼 **SPINNING JENNY**, Black Dress Press, P.O. Box 1373, New York NY 10276. E-mail: submissions@blackdresspress.com. Website: www.blackdresspress.com (includes guidelines, subscription information, catalog). **Contact:** C.E. Harrison. Magazine: 112 pages; 60 lb. paper; offset printed; perfect bound; illustrations. Literary magazine publishing short stories and novel excerpts. Estab. 1994. Member, CLMP.

Needs: Experimental, literary. Publishes ms less than 1 year after acceptance. **Publishes 3 new writers/year.**

How to Contact: Send up to 20 pages with a cover letter. Accepts submissions by e-mail; check guidelines first. Responds in 2 months. Send SASE for return of ms or send a disposable copy of ms and #10 SASE for reply only. Accepts electronic submissions (check guidelines first). Guidelines for SASE or on website.

Payment/Terms: Pays 5 contributor's copies.

🄾 🄶 **SPITBALL**, 5560 Fox Rd., Cincinnati OH 45239. (513)385-2268. Website: www.angelfire.com/oh5/spitball (includes guidelines, information on CASEY Award). **Editor:** Mike Shannon. Magazine: 5½×8½; 96 pages; 55 lb. Glatfelter Natural, neutral pH paper; 10 pt. CS1 cover stock; illustrations; photos. Magazine publishing "fiction and poetry about *baseball* exclusively for an educated, literary segment of the baseball fan population." Biannually. Estab. 1981. Circ. 2,000.

Needs: Confession, contemporary, experimental, historical, literary, mainstream and suspense. "We're looking for literary fiction about baseball *exclusively*! If it ain't about baseball, don't send it!" Receives 100 unsolicited fiction mss/year. Accepts 16-20 mss/year. **Published new writers within the last year.** Published work by Dallas Wiebe, Michael Gilmartin and W.P. Kinsella. Length: 20 typed double-spaced pages. "The longer it is, the better it has to be."

How to Contact: Send complete ms with cover letter and SASE. Include brief bio about author. Accepts multiple submissions. Reporting time varies. Publishes ms an average of 3 months after acceptance. *First-time submitters are required to purchase a sample copy for $6.*

Payment/Terms: "No monetary payment at present. We may offer nominal payment in the near future." Pays 2 free contributor's copies per issue in which work appears. Acquires first North American serial rights.

Advice: "Our audience is mostly college educated and knowledgeable about baseball. The stories we have published so far have been very well written and displayed a firm grasp of the baseball world and its people. In short, audience response has been great because the stories are simply good as stories. Thus, mere use of baseball as subject is no guarantee of acceptance. We are always seeking submissions. Unlike many literary magazines, we have no backlog of accepted material. Also, don't forget to *tell a story*. Devise a plot, make something *happen*!"

N $ ✎ SPRING HILL REVIEW, A Journal of Northwest Culture, P.O. Box 621, Brush Prairie WA 98606. (360)892-1178. E-mail: springhillreview@aol.com. **Contact:** Carolyn Schultz-Rathbun, editor. Magazine: 11½×15; 12-16 pages; newsprint; illustrations; photos. "*SHR* is a journal of contemporary Northwest U.S. culture, commenting on and challenging Northwest politics, arts and social and spiritual issues. It is an eclectic blend of nonfiction, fiction, poetry and artwork, aimed at baby-boomers and edited from a Christian worldview. This means that we rest on the fact that human beings can live lives of dignity and meaning, first because we are created in the image of God, and then because we have been invited to live in a covenant relationship with God and with each other through Jesus Christ." Monthly. Estab. 2001. Circ. 5,000.

Needs: Adventure, ethnic/multicultural, experimental, family saga, historical, humor/satire, literary, mainstream, mystery/suspense, regional (Pacific Northwest), science fiction, translations, western, novel excerpts. "No children's, no religious, no romance. *SHR* is a general market publication—no overtly evangelistic material, please, and no material written for a specifically Christian audience. We welcome submissions from writers of a variety of belief systems." Receives 0-3 unsolicited mss/month, "would like more." Accepts 4-6 mss/year, "would like to use more." Publishes ms 1-2 months after acceptance. Recently published work by Larry Tritten, James R. Daniels, Ella Higginson and Jane Kirkpatrick. Length: 600-1,500 words; average length: 800 words. Publishes short shorts. Average length: 800 words. Also publishes literary essays and poetry. Sometimes comments on rejected mss.

How to Contact: Send complete ms with a cover letter. Prefers submissions by e-mail. Include estimated word count, brief bio and list of publications. Responds in 2 months to queries; 3 months to mss. Send SASE for return of ms or send a disposable copy of ms and #10 SASE for reply only. Accepts simultaneous submissions and previously published work. Sample copy for $2. Guidelines for SASE or e-mail. Reviews novels and short story collections. Send review copies to Carolyn Schultz-Rathbun, editor.

Payment/Terms: Pays $10-15 and 1 contributor's copy; additional copies $1. Pays on publication for first North American serial, one-time and second serial rights.

Advice: "We look for strong characterization (show, don't tell); strong plot (although action may be interior)—even if it is initially a surprise, the denouément must be inevitable; strong sense of place. No propaganda disguised as fiction. If you're a beginning writer, say so, and be open to the possibility of feedback from an editor. If at first you don't succeed, submit your work to us again."

$ ☐ ◎ ▼ STONE SOUP, The Magazine By Young Writers and Artists, Children's Art Foundation, Box 83, Santa Cruz CA 95063. (831)426-5557. E-mail: gmandel@stonesoup.com. Website: www.stonesoup.com (includes writer's guidelines, sample copy, links, projects, international children's art). **Contact:** Ms. Gerry Mandel, editor. Magazine: 7×10; 48 pages; high quality paper; photos. Stories, poems, book reviews and art by children through age 13. Readership: children, librarians, educators. Published 6 times/year. Estab. 1973. Circ. 20,000.

- This is known as "the literary journal for children." *Stone Soup* has previously won the Ed Press Golden Lamp Honor Award and the Parent's Choice Award.

Needs: Fiction by children on themes based on their own experiences, observations or special interests. Also, some fantasy, mystery, adventure. "No clichés, no formulas, no writing exercises; original work only." Receives approximately 1,000 unsolicited fiction mss each month. Accepts approximately 15 mss/issue. **Published new writers within the last year.** Length: 150-2,500 words. Also publishes literary essays and poetry. Critiques rejected mss upon request.

How to Contact: Send complete ms with cover letter. "We like to learn a little about our young writers, why they like to write, and how they came to write the story they are submitting." SASE. No simultaneous submissions. Responds in 1 month to mss. Does not respond to mss that are not accompanied by an SASE. Publishes ms an average of 3-6 months after acceptance. Sample copy for $4. Guidelines for SASE. Reviews children's books.

Payment/Terms: Pays $35 and 2 contributor's copies; $2.75 charge for extras. Buys all rights. Subscription: $33/ year.

Advice: Mss are rejected because they are "derivatives of movies, TV, comic books; or classroom assignments or other formulas. Go to our website, where you can see many examples of the kind of work we publish."

N ⊕ $ ✎ STORIE, all write, Leconte, Via Suor Celestina Donati 13/E, Rome Italy 00167. Phone/fax: (+39)06 614 8777. E-mail: storie@tiscali.it. Website: www.storie.it (includes description of magazine, past issues in Italian and English, excerpts, subscription information, writer's guidelines). **Contact:** Gianluca Bassi, editor; Barbara Pezzopane, assistant editor; Sophie Schlondorff, foreign editor. Magazine; 186 pages; illustrations; photographs. "*Storie* is one of Italy's leading literary magazines. Committed to a truly crossover vision of writing, the bilingual (Italian/English) review publishes high-quality fiction and poetry, interspersed with the work of alternative wordsmiths such as filmmakers and musicians. Through writings bordering on narratives and interviews with important contemporary writers, it explores the culture and craft of writing." Bimonthly. Estab. 1989. Circ. 20,000.

Needs: Literary. Receives 150 unsolicited mss/month. Accepts 6-10 mss/issue; 30-50 mss/year. Does not read mss in August. Publishes ms about 2 months after acceptance. **Publishes 20 new writers/year.** Recently published work by Robert Coover, T.C. Boyle, Ariel Dorfman and Tess Gallagher. Length: 2,000-6,000 words; average length: 3,000 words.

Publishes short shorts. Also publishes literary essays, literary criticism and poetry. Sometimes comments on rejected mss. "*Storie* reserves the right to include a brief review of interesting submissions not selected for publication in a special column in the magazine."

How to Contact: Send complete ms with cover letter. "Ms may be submitted directly by regular post without querying first; however, we do not accept unsolicited mss via e-mail. Please query via e-mail first." Accepts submissions on disk. Include brief bio. Responsed to queries in 1 month; mss in 6 months. ("We only contact writers if their work has been accepted."). Accepts multiple submissions. Sample copy for $8. Guidelines on website.

Payment/Terms: Pays $30-600 and 2 contributor's copies ("we also arrange for and oversee a high-quality, professional translation of the piece"). Pays on publication for first rights (in English and Italian).

Advice: "More than erudite references or a virtuoso performance, what we're interested in is the recording of a human experience in a genuine, original voice."

STORYQUARTERLY, 431 Sheridan Rd., Kenilworth IL 60043-1220. (847)256-6998. Fax: (847)256-6997. E-mail: storyquarterly@yahoo.com. Website: www.storyquarterly.com (includes contents of each issue, links to individual stories from former issues, submission guidelines, subscription information, coming events). Editor: M.M.M. Hayes. **Contact:** Fiction Editors. Magazine: 6×9; 500 pages; good quality paper; an all-story magazine, committed to a full range of styles and forms. "We publish contemporary American and international fiction of high quality, in a full range of styles and forms, outstanding writing and fresh insights; we need great humor and serious literary stories of any type or style (nothing gimmicky), of no preferred length, stories that break your heart and make you laugh, that explore others and deepen understanding. Short-shorts as well as fully rendered work, memoir and novel excerpts with a sense of closure." Annual. Estab. 1975. Circ. 4,500.

• *StoryQuarterly* ranked on *Writer's Digest*'s "Top 30" list of best markets for fiction writers. *StoryQuarterly* received honorable mentions in *O. Henry Prize Stories*, *Best American Stories*. *O'Leary Prize Essays* and *Pushcart Prize Collection* in the last 3 years. The publication also won Illinois Arts Council Awards, two apiece in the last 3 years, as well as the Dan Curley Award from the Illinois Arts Council in 2000, for the best story submitted to the Arts Council that year.

Needs: "Great humor, serious and well-written stories that get up and run from the first page. "No genre stories." Receives 1,500 unsolicited fiction mss/month. Accepts 40-50 mss/issue. **Publishes new writers in every issue.** Recently published work by J.M. Coetzee, Robin Butler, Stuart Dybek, Reginald Gibbons, Gail Godwin, Alice Hoffman, Charles Johnson, Romulus Linney, Jim McManus and Askold Melnyczuk.

How to Contact: Send complete ms. E-mail preferred or regular mail with SASE only. Responds in 3-4 months to mss. Sample copy for $7. Guidelines on website.

Payment/Terms: Pays 10 contributor's copies and a life subscription (value $200). Acquires first North American serial rights. Copyright reverts to author after publication. Electronic publishing agreement available.

Advice: "Send one manuscript at a time, subscribe to the magazine, send SASE with hard copy submissions. Fiction selected based on command and use of the language, originality of material, sense of a larger world outside the hermitage of the story. A sense of humor goes a very long way, as long as it's not simply ridicule. Literary magazines (even the independents) deal with reality in ways the industry trends do not. Smashing openings, middles that build and create tension, and well-earned and surprising endings all figure in the composition of an outstanding story."

STRUGGLE, A Magazine of Proletarian Revolutionary Literature, Box 13261, Detroit MI 48213-0261. (213)273-9039. E-mail: timhall11@yahoo.com. **Contact:** Tim Hall, editor. Magazine: 5½×8½; 36-72 pages; 20 lb. white bond paper; colored cover; illustrations; occasional photos. Publishes material related to "the struggle of the working class and all progressive people against the rule of the rich—including their war policies, racism, exploitation of the workers, oppression of women and general culture, etc." Quarterly. Estab. 1985.

Needs: Contemporary, ethnic, experimental, feminist, historical (general), humor/satire, literary, prose poem, regional, science fiction, senior citizen/retirement, translations, young adult/teen (10-18). "The theme can be approached in many ways, including plenty of categories not listed here. Readers would like fiction about the anti-globalization movement, the fight against racism, prison conditions. Would also like to see more fiction that depicts the life, work and struggle of the working class of every background; also the struggles of the 1930s and 60s illustrated and brought to life. No romance, psychic, mystery, western, erotica, religious." Receives 10-12 unsolicited fiction mss/month. Publishes ms 6 months or less after acceptance. **Published new writers within the last year.** Recently published work by Gillian Lynn Katz, Ulysses McClendon and Evan Lowry. Length: 4,000 words maximum; average length: 1,000-3,000 words. Publishes short shorts. Normally critiques rejected mss.

How to Contact: Send complete ms; cover letter optional. "Tries to" report in 3-4 months. SASE. Accepts e-mail, simultaneous, multiple and reprint submissions. Sample copy for $2.50. Make checks payable to Tim Hall-Special Account.

Payment/Terms: Pays 2 contributor's copies. No rights acquired. Publication not copyrighted.

Advice: "Write about the oppression of the working people, the poor, the minorities, women, and if possible, their rebellion against it—we are not interested in anything which accepts the status quo. We are not too worried about plot and advanced technique (fine if we get them!)—we would probably accept things others would call sketches, provided they have life and struggle. For new writers: just describe for us a situation in which some real people confront some problem of oppression, however seemingly minor. Observe and put down the real facts. Experienced writers: try your 'committed'/experimental fiction on us. We get poetry all the time. We have increased our fiction portion of our content in the last few years. The quality of fiction that we have published has continued to improve. If your work raises an interesting issue of literature and politics, it may get discussed in letters and in my editorial. I suggest ordering a sample."

THE STYLES, P.O. Box 7171, Madison WI 53707. E-mail: timothy@thestyles.org. Website: www.thestyles.org (includes writer's guidelines, names of staff, about our publication, contributors, subscription information). **Contact:** Sophia Estante or Amara Dante Verona, editors. Magazine: 8×8; 128 pages; 60 lb. white perfect-bound matte lamination; 10 point cover. "*The Styles* is a publication of eclectic content with emphasis on artistic excellence in experimental fiction and nonfiction. We publish short stories, short plays, and poetry. We encourage literary essays, prose poetry and short-shorts." Quarterly. Estab. 2000. Circ. 1,000.

Needs: Experimental, literary, humor. "No genre fiction." Publishes ms 3-9 months after acceptance. Length: 6,000 words maximum. Publishes short shorts. Also publishes literary essays and poetry. Often comments on rejected mss.

How to Contact: Send complete ms with a cover letter or query. Include brief bio. Responds in 2 weeks to queries; 2 months to mss. Send SASE for return of ms or send a disposable copy of ms and #10 SASE for reply only. Accepts simultaneous and multiple submissions. Sample copy for $10. Guidelines for SASE or on website.

Payment/Terms: Pays 1 contributor's copy. Acquires first North American serial rights. "Sometimes sends prepublication galleys to author."

Advice: "Our readers want to be challenged, they want something new, but also really want to enjoy what they read. Think: good stories, funny shorts, innovative poetry. Stuff people remember because they really loved reading it."

SULPHUR RIVER LITERARY REVIEW, P.O. Box 19228, Austin TX 78760-9228. (512)292-9456. **Contact:** James Michael Robbins, editor. Magazine: 5½×8½; 145 pages; illustrations; photos. "*SRLR* publishes literature of quality—poetry and short fiction with appeal that transcends time. Audience includes a broad spectrum of readers, mostly educated, many of whom are writers, artists and educators." Semiannual. Estab. 1978. Circ. 400.

Needs: Ethnic/multicultural, experimental, feminist, humor/satire, literary, mainstream/contemporary and translations. Would like to see more experimental, surreal and imaginative fiction. "No religious, juvenile, teen, sports, romance or mystery." Receives 30-40 unsolicited mss/month. Accepts 4-5 mss/issue; 8-10 mss/year. Publishes ms 1-2 years after acceptance. **Publishes few new writers/year.** Recently published work by Russell Thorburn, William Drem, Cara Chamberlain and Ken Holland. Publishes short shorts. Also publishes literary essays, literary criticism and poetry. Critiques or comments on rejected mss when requested.

How to Contact: Send complete ms with a cover letter. Include short bio and list of publications. Responds in 1 week to queries; 1 month to mss. Send SASE for reply, return of ms or send a disposable copy of ms. No simultaneous submissions. Sample copy for $7.

Payment/Terms: Pays 2 contributor's copies; additional copies for $7. Acquires first North American serial rights.

Advice: Looks for "Quality. Imagination served perfectly by masterful control of language."

A SUMMER'S READING, 409 Lakeview Dr., Sherman IL 62684-9432. (217)496-3012. E-mail: t_morrissey@hot mail.com. **Contact:** Ted Morrissey, publisher/editor. Magazine: 8½×5½; 75 pages; 20 lb paper; card cover; full color cover, b&w inside; illustrations; photos. "Unlike the majority of literary magazines, our primary reading time is the summer. We want to provide one more attractive, well-edited outlet for new, emerging and established writers and artists." Annual. Estab. 1997. Circ. 200.

Needs: Experimental, literary, translations, narrative essays, prose poetry. "No genre." Receives 60 unsolicited mss/month. Accepts 3-6 mss/issue; 3-6 mss/year. "Reading is slow during 'academic' year." Publishes ms up to 1 year after acceptance. **Publishes 1 new writer/year.** Recently published work by William Jackson, Barbara Peck, Christine Zilius and Mark Wisniewski. Length: 500-8,000 words; average length: 3,000-5,000 words. Publishes short shorts. Also publishes poetry. Often comments on rejected mss.

How to Contact: Send complete ms with a cover letter. Include estimated word count, brief bio, list of publications and e-mail address. Responds in up to 1 year to mss. Send SASE (or IRC) for return of ms or send a disposable copy of ms and #10 SASE for reply only. Accepts simultaneous, previously published "if noted" and multiple submissions "if very short." Sample copy for $5. Guidelines for SASE or by e-mail. Reviews novels, short story collections "if space allows." Send review copies to publisher.

Payment/Terms: Pays 2 contributor's copies; additional copies $4.50. Pays on publication for one-time rights. Sends galleys to author.

Advice: "We look for a combination of a plot which keeps us turning the pages and a practiced writing style. We will be fair. Your work has a better chance of getting published if it's on our desk instead of yours. Not being university affiliated, it is difficult to find reliable readers—thus reporting time is slower than we prefer."

SYCAMORE REVIEW, Department of English, Purdue University, West Lafayette IN 47907. (765)494-3783. Fax: (765)494-3780. E-mail: sycamore@purdue.edu. Website: www.sla.purdue.edu/sycamore (includes back and current issues, index, submission guidelines, subscription information, journal library). Editor-in-Chief: Paul D. Reich. Editors change every two years. **Contact:** Fiction Editor. Magazine: 5½×8½; 150-200 pages; heavy, textured, uncoated paper; heavy laminated cover. "Journal devoted to contemporary literature. We publish both traditional and experimental fiction, personal essay, poetry, interviews, drama and graphic art. Novel excerpts welcome if they stand alone as a story." Semiannual. Estab. 1989. Circ. 1,000.

Needs: Contemporary, experimental, humor/satire, literary, mainstream, regional, translations. "We generally avoid genre literature, but maintain no formal restrictions on style or subject matter. No science fiction, romance, children's."

Would like to see more experimental fiction. Publishes ms 3 months to 1 year after acceptance. **10% of material published is by new writers.** Published work by Lucia Perillo, June Armstrong, W.P. Osborn and William Giraldi. Length: 250 words minimum; 3,750 words preferred. Also publishes poetry, "this has included Billy Collins, Thomas Lux, Kathleen Peirce and Vandana Khanna." Sometimes critiques rejected mss and recommends other markets.

How to Contact: Send complete ms with cover letter. Cover letter should include previous publications and address changes. Only reads mss August 1 through March 1. Responds in 4 months. SASE. Accepts simultaneous submissions. Sample copy for $7. Guidelines for #10 SASE.

Payment/Terms: Pays in contributor's copies; charge for extras. Acquires one-time rights.

Advice: "We publish both new and experienced authors but we're always looking for stories with strong emotional appeal, vivid characterization and a distinctive narrative voice; fiction that breaks new ground while still telling an interesting and significant story. Avoid gimmicks and trite, predictable outcomes. Write stories that have a ring of truth, the impact of felt emotion. Don't be afraid to submit, send your best."

⊕ $ TAKAHE, P.O. Box 13-335, Christchurch, 8001, New Zealand. (03)359-8133. E-mail: mark.johnstone@paradi se.net.nz. Website: www.nzwriters.co.nz (includes writer's guidelines and the names of editors). **Contact:** Mark Johnstone, administrator. "A literary magazine which appears three or four times a year, and publishes short stories and poetry by both established and emerging writers. The publisher is the Takahe Collective Trust, a charitable trust formed by established writers to help new writers and get them into print."

How to Contact: Send complete ms with brief bio and SASE (IRC for overseas submissions). No e-mail submissions. Single spacing, indented paragraphs and double quotation marks for direct speech. Any use of foreign languages must be accompanied by an English translation.

Payment/Terms: Pays $NZ30 ($US12) to each writer/poet appearing in a particular issue regardless of number/length of items. Amount is subject to change according to circumstances. Editorials and literary commentaries are by invitation only and, not being covered by our grant, are not paid for. All contributors receive two copies of the issue in which their work appears. Copyright reverts to the author on publication."

$ ◯ TAMEME, New Writing from North America/Nueva literatura de Norteamérica, Tameme, Inc., 199 First St., Los Altos CA 94022. (650)941-2037. Fax: (650)941-5338. E-mail: editor@tameme.org. Website: www.tam eme.org (includes editor, contributors, writer's guidelines, staff, index of magazine). Editor: C.M. Mayo. **Contact:** Fiction Editor. Magazine: 6×9; 220 pages; good quality paper; heavy cover stock; illustrations; photos. "*Tameme* is an annual bilingual magazine dedicated to publishing new writing from North America in side-by-side English-Spanish format. *Tameme*'s goals are to play an instrumental role in introducing important new writing from Canada and the United States to Mexico, and vice versa, and to provide a forum for the art of literary translation." Estab. 1996. Circ. 1,000. Member, Council of Literary Magazines and Presses (CLMP).

Needs: Ethnic/multicultural, literary, translations. "No genre fiction." Plans special fiction issue or anthology. Receives 50-150 unsolicited mss/month. "No romance, mystery or western." Accepts 3-4 mss/issue; 6-8 mss/year. Publishes ms 1 year after acceptance. Agented fiction 5%. **Publishes 1-3 new writers/year.** Published work by Fabio Morábito, Margaret Atwood, Juan Villoro, Jaime Sabines, Edwidge Danticat, A. Manette Ansay, Douglas Glover and Marianne Toussaint. Publishes short shorts. Also publishes literary essays and poetry.

How to Contact: First check guidelines on website or send for guidelines with SASE. Accepts simultaneous submissions. Sample copy for $14.95.

Payment/Terms: Pays 3 contributor's copies to writers; $20 per double-spaced WordPerfect page to translators. Pays on publication for one-time rights. Sends galleys to author.

Advice: "We're looking for whatever makes us want to stand up and shout YES! Read the magazine, send for guidelines (with SASE) or check guidelines on website, then send only your best, with SASE. No electronic submissions please."

$ ◯ TAMPA REVIEW, 401 W. Kennedy Blvd., Box 19F, University of Tampa, Tampa FL 33606-1490. (813)253-6266. Fax: (813)258-7593. E-mail: utpress@ut.edu. Website: www.tampareview.ut.edu. Editor: Richard Mathews. **Contact:** Lisa Birnbaum, Kathleen Ochshorn, fiction editors. Magazine: 7½×10½; hardback; approximately 100 pages; acid-free paper; visual art; photos. "Interested in fiction of distinctive literary quality." Semiannual. Estab. 1988.

Needs: Contemporary, ethnic, experimental, fantasy, historical, literary, mainstream, prose poem, translations. "We are far more interested in quality than in genre. Nothing sentimental as opposed to genuinely moving, nor self-conscious style at the expense of human truth." Buys 4-5 mss/issue. Publishes ms within 7 months-1 year of acceptance. Agented fiction 20%. Published work by Elizabeth Spencer, Lee K. Abbott, Lorrie Moore, Gordon Weaver and Tim O'Brien. Length: 250-6,000 words. Publishes short shorts "if the story is good enough." Also publishes literary essays (must be labeled nonfiction), poetry.

How to Contact: Send complete ms with cover letter and SASE. Include brief bio. No simultaneous submissions. Does not accept fax, e-mail or disk submissions. Reads September through December; reports January through May. Sample copy for $7 (includes postage) and 9×12 SAE. Guidelines on website or for #10 SASE.

Payment/Terms: Pays $10/printed page. Pays on publication for first North American serial rights. Sends galleys to author upon request.

Advice: "There are more good writers publishing in magazines today than there have been in many decades. Unfortunately, there are even more bad ones. In T. Gertler's *Elbowing the Seducer*, an editor advises a young writer that he wants to hear her voice completely, to tell (he means 'show') him in a story the truest thing she knows. We concur. Rather than a trendy workshop story or a minimalism that actually stems from not having much to say, we would like to see stories that make us believe they mattered to the writer and, more importantly, will matter to a reader. Trim until only the essential is left, and don't give up belief in yourself. And it might help to attend a good writers' conference, e.g. Wesleyan or Bennington."

TAPROOT LITERARY REVIEW, Taproot Writer's Workshop, Inc., Box 204, Ambridge PA 15003. (724)266-8476. E-mail: taproot10@aol.com. **Contact:** Tikvah Feinstein, editor. Magazine: 5½×8½; 93 pages; #20 paper; hard cover; attractively printed; saddle-stitched. "We select on quality, not topic. Variety and quality are our appealing features." Annual. Estab. 1987. Circ. 500.

Needs: Literary. "No pornography, religious, popular, romance fiction. Want more multicultural-displaced people living among others in new places." The majority of mss published are received through their annual contest. Receives 20 unsolicited mss/month. Accepts 6 fiction mss/issue. **Publishes 2-4 new writers/year.** Published work by Laura Hogan, Kathleen Downey and Susan Williams. Length: 250-3,000 words maximum (no longer than 10 pages, double-spaced maximum); 2,000 words preferred. Publishes short shorts. Length: 300 words preferred. Sometimes comments on rejected mss. Also publishes poetry. Sponsors annual contest. Entry fee: $15/story. Deadline: December 31. Send SASE for details.

How to Contact: Send for guidelines first. Send complete ms with a cover letter. Accepts queries by e-mail, mss by e-mail and disk. Include estimated word count and bio. Responds in 6 months. Send SASE for return of ms or send a disposable copy of ms. No simultaneous submissions. Sample copy for $5, 6×12 SAE and 5 first-class stamps. Guidelines for #10 SASE.

Payment/Terms: Awards $25 in prize money for first place fiction and poetry winners each issue; certificate for 2nd and 3rd place; 1 contributor's copy. Acquires first rights.

Advice: "*Taproot* is getting more fiction submissions and every one is read entirely. This takes time, so response can be delayed at busy times of year. Our contest is a good way to start publishing. Send for a sample copy and read it through. Ask for a critique and follow suggestions. Don't be offended by any suggestions—just take them or leave them and keep writing. Looks for a story that speaks in its unique voice, told in a well-crafted and complete, memorable style, a style of signature to the author. Follow writer's guidelines. Research markets. Send cover letter. Don't give up."

TEARS IN THE FENCE, 38 Hod View, Stourpaine, Nr. Blandford Forum, Dorset DT11 8TN England. Phone: 01258-456803. Fax: 01258-454026. E-mail: poets@wanderingdog.co.uk. Website: www.wanderingdog.co.uk. Editor: David Caddy. **Contact:** Sarah Hopkins, fiction editor. Three issues per annum.

Needs: A magazine of poetry, fiction, drama, criticism and reviews, open to a variety of contemporary voices from around the world. It has contributing editors in France, Australia and the US. **Publishes 1-2 new writers/year.** Recently published work by Brian Marley, Dave Newman, Jay Merill, Alan Wakeley and Rob Mimpriss. Publishes short and long fiction. Publishes 3-4 stories/issue.

Payment/Terms: Pays complimentary copies. Sample copy for $7 (US).

Advice: "Look for firm narrative control with an economical style that takes the reader far beyond the obvious and inconsequential. Explore the market by buying sample copies."

TERMINUS: A JOURNAL OF LITERATURE AND ART, Terminus, Inc., 3963 Wolcott Circle, Atlanta GA 30340. E-mail: terminus@altavista.com. **Contact:** Fiction Editors. Magazine/journal: 6¾×9¾; 100 pages; heavy weight paper; card stock cover; illustrations; photos. "*Terminus* is a twice-yearly journal with the primary mission of publishing the finest writing and art across a broad range of readers. Each issue features some combination of essays, stories, poetry, art, and book reviews. We seek to publish the most thought-provocative, socially and/or culturally aware writing available. While we want to push the boundaries of general aesthetics and standards, we also want to produce writing that is accessible to a wide audience. We seek to live up to the highest standards in publishing, always growing and reaching new levels of understanding and awareness both within our immediate community and within the greater community of our country and world. We produce a CD with each issue featuring authors reading their work." Semiannual. Estab. 2002. Circ. 1,000.

Needs: Literary, translations. Receives 50 unsolicited mss/month. Accepts 2-6 mss/issue; 4-12 mss/year. Publishes ms up to 1 year after acceptance. Recently published work by Virgil Suarez, Askold Skalsky, Miller Williams and R.S. Gwynn. Length: 250-3,500 words; average length: 2,500 words. Publishes short shorts. Also publishes literary essays, literary criticism and poetry. Sometimes comments on rejected mss.

How to Contact: Send complete ms with a cover letter. Accepts submissions by e-mail and disk. Include estimated word count, brief bio and list of publications. Responds in 1 month to queries; 4 months to mss. Send SASE for return of ms or send a disposable copy of ms and #10 SASE for reply only. Accepts simultaneous and multiple submissions. Guidelines by e-mail.

Payment/Terms: Pays 2 contributor's copies; additional copies $8. Acquires first North American serial rights.

$ ⬛ THEMA, Box 8747, Metairie LA 70011-8747. (504)887-1263. E-mail: thema@cox.net. **Contact:** Virginia Howard, editor. Magazine: 5½×8½; 200 pages; Grandee Strathmore cover stock; b&w illustrations. "*Thema* is a theme-related literary journal, each issue with a different, unusual theme. The journal is designed to provide a stimulating forum for established and emerging literary artists, to serve as source material and inspiration for teachers of creative writing, and to provide readers with a unique collection of well-plotted, nonscatalogic stories and sensitively-constructed poetry." Triannual. Estab. 1988.

Needs: Adventure, contemporary, experimental, humor/satire, literary, mainstream, mystery/suspense, prose poem, psychic/supernatural/occult, regional, science fiction, sports, western. "Nothing pornographic, scatalogical or erotic. Each issue is based on a specified premise—a different unique theme for each issue. Many types of fiction acceptable, but must fit the premise." Upcoming themes (deadlines for submission in 2003): "Off on a Tangent" (March 1); "The Middle Path" (July 1); and "Stone, Paper, Scissors" (November 1). Publishes ms within 6 months of acceptance. **Publishes 8 new writers/year.** Recently published work by Ayse Papatya Bucak, Sid Gustafson, Penny Perry and Merilyn Wakefield. Length: fewer than 6,000 words preferred. Publishes short shorts. Also publishes poetry. Sometimes critiques rejected mss and recommends other markets.

How to Contact: Send complete ms with cover letter, include "name and address, brief introduction, specifying the intended target issue for the mss." Accepts queries by e-mail. Responds in 1 week to queries; 5 months after deadline for specified issue. Accepts simultaneous and multiple submissions. SASE. Sample copy for $8. Guidelines available on website or for SASE.

Payment/Terms: Pays $25; $10 for short shorts. Pays on acceptance for one-time rights.

Advice: "Do not submit a manuscript unless you have written it for a specified premise. If you don't know the upcoming themes, send for guidelines first, before sending a story. We need more stories told in the Mark Twain/O. Henry tradition in magazine fiction."

⬛ THIN AIR, Graduate Creative Writing Association of Northern Arizona University, P.O. Box 23549, Flagstaff AZ 86002. (520)523-6743. Website: www.nau.edu/~english/thinair (includes guidelines and list of editors). **Contact:** Fiction Editor. Editors change each year. Magazine: 8½×11; 50-60 pages; illustrations; photos. Publishes "contemporary voices for a literary-minded audience." Semiannual. Estab. 1995. Circ. 500.

Needs: Condensed/excerpted novel, ethnic/multicultural, experimental, literary, mainstream/contemporary. "No children's/juvenile, horror, romance, erotica. We would like to see more intelligent comedy." Editorial calendar available for SASE. Receives 75 unsolicited mss/month. Accepts 5-8 mss/issue; 10-15 mss/year. Does not read mss May-September. Publishes ms 6-9 months after acceptance. Solicited fiction 35%. **Publishes 3-8 new writers/year.** Recently published work by Orman Dacy. Length: 6,000 words maximum. Publishes short shorts. Also publishes literary essays, literary criticism, creative nonfiction, poetry and interviews. Interviews have included Thom Jones, Alan Lightman and Rick Bass

How to Contact: Send complete ms with a cover letter. Include estimated word count and list of publications. Accepts ms on disk. Responds in 1 month to queries; 5 months to mss. Send SASE for reply, return of ms or send a disposable copy of ms. Accepts simultaneous submissions. Sample copy for $5. Guidelines free. Reviews novels and short story collections.

Payment/Terms: Pays 2 contributor's copies; additional copies for $4. Pays on publication for first North American serial rights. Sponsors contest; send SASE for guidelines.

Advice: Looks for "writers who know how to create tension and successfully resolve it."

🌐 THE THIRD HALF MAGAZINE, "Amikeco," 16, Fane Close, Stamford, Lincolnshire PE9 1HG England. Phone: (01780)754193. **Contact:** Kevin Troop, fiction editor.

Needs: "*The Third Half* literary magazine publishes mostly poetry, but editorial policy is to publish as much *short* short story writing as possible in separate books." **Publishes new writers.** Recently published work by Michael Bangerter, Sam Smith, Michael Newman and Hannah Welfare. Length: 2,000 words maximum.

Payment/Terms: Pays in contributor's copies. Sample copy £4.95; £5.50 by post in England; £10 overseas.

⬛ THORNY LOCUST, TL Press, P.O. Box 32631, Kansas City MO 64171-5631. (816)501-4178. E-mail: editors@t hornylocust.com. **Contact:** Silvia Kofler. Magazine: 32 pages; illustrations; photos. "*Thorny Locust* is a literary quarterly produced in a dusty corner of the publisher's hermitage. We are interested in poetry, fiction, and artwork with some 'bite'—e.g., satire, epigrams, well-structured tirades, black humor, and bleeding-heart cynicism. Absolutely no natural or artificial sweeteners, unless they're the sugar-coating on a strychnine tablet. We are not interested in polemics, gratuitous grotesques, somber surrealism, weeping melancholy, or hate-mongering. To rewrite Jack Conroy, 'We prefer polished vigor to crude banality.'" Estab. 1993. Circ. 200.

Needs: Ethnic/multicultural (general), experimental, humor/satire, literary. Receives 4-5 unsolicited mss/month. Accepts 1 ms/issue; 2-3 mss/year. Publishes ms up to 2 months after acceptance. Length: 250-2,000 words; average length: 1,500 words. Publishes short shorts. Average length: 500 words. Also publishes poetry. Rarely comments on rejected mss.

How to Contact: Send complete ms with a cover letter. Include brief bio. Responds in 3 months to queries. Send SASE (or IRC) for return of ms or send a disposable copy of ms and #10 SASE for reply only. Accepts simultaneous submissions. Sample copy for $3. Guidelines for SASE or by e-mail.

Payment/Terms: Pays 1 contributor's copy. Acquires one-time rights.

insider report

For Daniel Orozco, slow isn't necessarily bad

Daniel Orozco

Some writers are able to finish a novel in a year's time. Others take that long just to write a single short story. Count Daniel Orozco among the slow-pokes. It's not unusual for the San Francisco-born writer to spend more than a year on a story (one, he confesses, took 22 years). Though he used to wish he could write faster, he's come to see that he produces his best work by taking his time.

Readers have found his stories worth the wait. Orozco's work has appeared in *The Best American Short Stories* and *The Pushcart Prize* anthologies, as well as in top literary magazines such as *Story*, *Zoetrope: All-Story*, and *Mid-American Review*.

After earning his MFA from the University of Washington in 1994, Orozco became a Scowcroft and L'Heureux Fellow (1997-99) and then a Jones Lecturer in Fiction (1999-2002) in the creative writing program at Stanford University. He's currently at work on a novella and a collection of stories.

In the following interview, Orozco discusses the difficulties of being a slow writer and explains how he came to terms with his glacial but successful composition process.

How long does it typically take you to write a short story?
"Typically" is a tough concept for me to grasp, because my experience with each story is so different. I finished a story called "Orientation" in about 11 months, from first draft to final draft and publication. That story was only ten manuscript pages, and that's the fastest I'd ever written anything. ("Orientation" first appeared in *The Seattle Review* and was selected for *The Best American Short Stories 1995*.) The slowest is about 22 years—a story I first wrote in 1978 for a beginning fiction writing class, then set aside for a couple of decades, then picked up again and revised over spring and summer of 2000. "I Run Every Day" appeared in *Zoetrope: All-Story* the following year.

How much time do you spend writing a first draft, compared to revising it?
I'd say it breaks down to about one-quarter of the time actually writing the first draft, and three-quarters revising. I don't enjoy banging out that first draft because it's always awful and embarrassing to read, but it would be hard to revise a story without a first draft. Drafting and revising do overlap, though. I often begin revising before the first draft is finished—elaborating on the details of a setting to establish mood, or reworking the opening paragraph until the voice sounds right. Sometimes when I nail the story's physical atmo-

sphere by working one setting description, or when I nail the voice of the story, this helps me to finish the first draft.

What's your chief impetus for revision—your own sense that the story isn't finished? Feedback from editors or other readers? The response you get at readings?
My *first* impetus for revision is my own vague sense of story closure. If the ending isn't working—if it doesn't ring like a bell—then the story doesn't feel done to me. After that, trusted readers and editors help a lot; they reveal story problems that I would never catch because I've been inside the story for so long.

When a story takes a long time to finish, is it usually a matter of writer's block, a deliberate composition process, the amount of time you spend at the keyboard, or something else?
My slowness as a writer seems to be part of a deliberate composition process. Before I actually begin writing a story, it goes through what I call Gestation and Frustration. Gestation: A story for me begins as an image or situation knocking around in my head, followed by months of notes jotted on scraps of paper, or entered into a file on my PC. This is followed finally by attempts at writing a first draft. Then, Frustration: I can set an unfinished draft aside for anywhere from days to months, during which time I do some reading or research on the story—a great way to avoid actually writing it—or I research or write another story. Eventually, I get back to finishing the first draft, and then I get to revising.

As you've become more experienced, do you find that you write slower, or faster?
There's nothing to be done about the process of Gestation and Frustration. But when I am actually at the keyboard, I do find the writing to go a bit faster. With experience I've become more adept at craft—more familiar with the mechanics of, say, moving a character across a room; more adept at finding the right word or phrase, at zeroing in on the most telling descriptive detail.

Is slow writing a virtue or a curse?
I used to bitch and moan about how slowly and inefficiently I wrote, about how long it would take me to squeeze out a story. I've only recently come to terms with my composition process, and now I embrace it as simply the way I write stories, stories that I am happy with. I used to wish I wrote faster, but I don't anymore. It's like wishing I were taller—it just ain't gonna happen.

Do you discuss writing speed with your students?
I teach a writing course that is ten weeks long. I tell my students that the deadlines for submitting stories (two or three during the quarter) in so brief a course are arbitrary but necessary constraints on the composition process. Arbitrary because deadlines inhibit the room a writer often needs to move toward even a first draft; necessary because deadlines compel at least a first draft to get done, no matter how bad it may be; necessary also because working under time pressure can train a writer to focus, to be more productive. I tell my students that I am a slow writer and that I understand their frustration in being forced to finish something quickly.

Have you found ways to finish stories more quickly without sacrificing quality?
Nope. To quote Popeye: I yam what I yam.
　　—*Will Allison*

Advice: "We look for work that is witty and original. Edit your work carefully."

⬛ ◯ THOUGHT MAGAZINE, P.O. Box 117098, Burlingame CA 94011-7098. E-mail: thoughtmagazine@yahoo
.com. Website: www.ThoughtMagazine.org (includes excerpts, guidelines, names of editors, interviews with authors,
speaker series, community service program, online supplement to print journal). **Contact:** Kevin Feeney, publisher.
Magazine: 8½×11; 50 pages; 60 lb. paper; 80 lb. cover stock; illustrations. "We publish both emerging writers as well
as emerging talent in our literary journal focused on the art of writing, rather than the business of publishing. We publish
stories that have truth to them, ones that force the reader to contemplate his own life. *Thought Magazine* is interested
in a personal and collaborative relationship with its authors." Semiannual. Estab. 2000. Circ. 2,000.
Needs: Adventure, family saga, literary, mainstream. "No graphic sex/violence or heavy religious themes." Receives
30-50 unsolicited mss/month. Accepts 10 mss/issue; 20 mss/year. Publishes ms 1-3 months after acceptance. **Publishes
10 new writers/year.** Recently published work by Susan Parker, Gerald Nicosia, Norman Zelaya and Shawna Chandler.
Length: 1,500-3,000 words; average length: 2,000 words. Publishes short shorts. Average length: 600 words. Also
publishes literary essays, literary criticism and poetry. Often comments on rejected mss.
How to Contact: Send complete ms with a cover letter. Accepts submissions by e-mail and disk. Include estimated
word count and brief bio. Responds in 1 week to queries; 1 month to mss. Send SASE for return of ms or send a disposable
copy of ms and #10 SASE for reply only. Accepts simultaneous, multiple and previously published submissions. Sample
copy for $6. Guidelines for SASE, e-mail or on website.
Payment/Terms: Pays 1 contributor's copy; additional copies $6. Acquires one-time rights. Sends galleys to author
upon request. Sponsors writer's contest; guidelines on website, by e-mail or for SASE.
Advice: "We look for stories that make the reader feel strong emotions—anger, frustration, ecstasy, excitement. Be
original, be yourself, be truthful."

$ ◯ ⬛ THE THREEPENNY REVIEW, P.O. Box 9131, Berkeley CA 94709. (510)849-4545. Website: www.thre
epennyreview.com. **Contact:** Wendy Lesser, editor. Tabloid: 10×17; 40 pages; Electrobrite paper; white book cover;
illustrations. "Serious fiction." Quarterly. Estab. 1980. Circ. 9,000.
 • *The Threepenny Review* has received GE Writers Awards, CLMP Editor's Awards, NEA grants, Lila Wallace
 grants and inclusion of work in the *Pushcart Prize Anthology*.
Needs: Literary. "Nothing 'experimental' (ungrammatical)." Receives 300-400 mss/month. Accepts 3 mss/issue; 12
mss/year. Does *not* read mss June through August. Publishes 6-12 months after acceptance. Agented fiction 5%. Published Sigrid Nunez, Dagoberto Gilb, Gina Berriault and Leonard Michaels. Length: 5,000 words maximum. Publishes
short shorts. Also publishes literary essays, literary criticism, poetry.
How to Contact: Send complete ms with a cover letter. *Does not accept e-mail or faxed submissions.* Responds in 1
month to queries; 2 months to mss. Send SASE for reply, return of ms or send a disposable copy of the ms. No
simultaneous submissions. Sample copy for $10. Guidelines for #10 SASE or on website. Reviews novels and short
story collections.
Payment/Terms: Pays $200 and free subscription to the magazine; additional copies at half price. Pays on acceptance
for first North American serial rights. Sends galleys to author.

⬛ ◯ TICKLED BY THUNDER, Helping Writers Get Published Since 1990, Tickled By Thunder Publishing
Co., 14076 86A Ave, Surrey British Columbia V3W 0V9 Canada. (604)591-6095. E-mail: thunder@istar.ca. Website:
www.home.istar.ca/~thunder. **Contact:** Larry Lindner, publisher. Magazine: digest-sized; 24 pages; bond pages; bond
cover stock; illustrations; photos. "*Tickled By Thunder* is designed to encourage beginning writers of fiction, poetry
and nonfiction." Quarterly. Estab. 1990. Circ. 1,000.
Needs: Fantasy, humor/satire, literary, mainstream, mystery/suspense, science fiction, western. "No overly indulgent
horror, sex, profanity or religious material." Receives 25 unsolicited ms/month. Accepts 3 mss/issue; 12 mss/year.
Publishes ms 3-9 months after acceptance. **Publishes 10 new writers/year.** Published work by Rick Cook and Jerry
Shane. Length: 2,000 words maximum; 1,500 words average. Publishes short shorts: average length 300 words. Also
publishes literary essays, literary criticism and poetry.
How to Contact: Send complete ms with cover letter. Include estimated word count and brief bio. Responds in 3
months to queries; 6 months to mss. Send SASE (or IRC) for return of ms; or send disposable copy of ms and #10
return SASE for reply only. Accepts simultaneous, multiple and previously published submissions. Sample copy for
$2.50. Guidelines for SASE, via e-mail, or on website. Reviews novels, short story collections and nonfiction books of
interest to writers. Send material to Larry Lindner.
Payment/Terms: Pays on publication for first and reprint rights.
Advice: "Make your characters breathe on their own. Use description mixed with action."

$ ◯ TIMBER CREEK REVIEW, 8969 UNCG Station, Greensboro NC 27413. (336)334-2952. E-mail: timber_cree
k_Review@hoopsmail.com. **Contact:** John M. Freiermuth, editor. Assistant Editor: Roslyn Willett. Newsletter:
5½×8½; 80-88 pages; computer generated on copy paper; saddle-stapled with 40 lb. colored paper cover; some illustrations. "Fiction, satire/humor, poetry and travel for a general audience." Quarterly. Estab. 1992. Circ. 140-160.
Needs: Adventure, contemporary, ethnic, feminist, historical, humor/satire, literary, mainstream, mystery/suspense
(cozy, private eye), regional, western. "No religion, children's, gay, romance." Receives 500-600 unsolicited mss/year.
Accepts 30-40 mss/year. Publishes ms 2-6 months after acceptance. **Publishes 0-3 new writers/year.** Recently published
work by Patricia Abbott, Jim Meirose, Brian Ames and Marcia L. Herlow. Length: 2,500-7,000 words; average length:
3,500 words.

How to Contact: Cover letter required. "There are no automatons here, so don't treat us like machines. We may not recognize your name at the top of the manuscript. A few lines about yourself breaks the ice, the names of three or four magazines that have published you in the last year or two would show your reality, and a bio blurb of 37 +/- words including the names of two or three of the magazines you send the occasional subscription check (where you aspire to be?) could help. If you are not sending a check to some little magazine that is supported by subscriptions and the blood, sweat and tears of the editors, why would you send your manuscript to any of them and expect to receive a warm welcome? No requirement to subscribe or buy a sample, but they are available at $15 and $4.25 and are encouraged. There are no phony contests and never a reading fee. We read all year long, but may take one to six months to respond." Accepts simultaneous submissions but no reprints.

Payment/Terms: Pays $10-35 and 1-year subscription to magazine for first story published. Acquires one-time rights. Publication not copyrighted.

Advice: "Stop watching TV and read that literary magazine where your last manuscript appeared."

$ ○ TIN HOUSE, P.O. Box 10500, Portland OR 97296-0500. (503)274-4393. Fax: (503)222-1154. E-mail: tinhouse@aol.com. Website: www.tinhouse.com. Editor-in-Chief: Win McCormack. **Contact:** Rob Spillman and Elissa Schappell, fiction editors. Literary magazine: 7×9; 200 pages, 50 lb. paper; glossy cover stock; illustrations and photos. Quarterly.

Needs: Experimental, literary. Accepts 3-4 mss/issue. Publishes ms up to one year after acceptance. Length: 2,000-5,000 words; average length: 3,500 words. Publishes short shorts. Also publishes literary essays, literary criticism and poetry.

How to Contact: Send complete ms with a cover letter or submit through an agent. Include estimated word count. Responds in 6 weeks to mss. Send SASE for return of ms. Accepts simultaneous submissions. Sample copy for $16. Guidelines for $2.

Payment/Terms: Pays $100-800 and 2 contributor's copies; additional copies $16. Acquires first North American serial and Anthology rights.

Advice: "Our criteria are boldness of concept, intense level of emotion and energy, precision of observation, deployment of imagination, grace of style. Any sentence read at random is impeccable and as good as any other in the work. Do not send anything that does not make you feel like laughing or crying, or both, when you read it yourself."

○ TOUCHSTONE LITERARY JOURNAL, P.O. Box 130233, Spring TX 7739s-0233. E-mail: panthercreek3@hotmail.com. Website: www.panthercreekpress.com. Editor/Publisher: Guida Jackson. **Contact:** Julia Gomez-Rivas, fiction editor. Magazine: 5½×8½; 56 pages; linen paper; coated stock cover; perfect bound; b&w illustrations; occasional photos. "Literary and mainstream fiction, but enjoy experimental work and multicultural. Audience middle-class, heavily academic. We are eclectic and given to whims—i.e., two years ago we devoted a 104-page issue to West African women writers." Annual (with occasional special supplements). Estab. 1976. Circ. 1,000.

Needs: Humor/satire, literary, translations. "No erotica, religious, juvenile, stories written in creative writing programs that all sound alike." List of upcoming themes available for SASE. Publishes special fiction issue or anthology. Receives 20-30 mss/month. Accepts 3-4 mss/issue. Does not read mss in December. Publishes ms within the year after acceptance. Published work by Ann Alejandro, Lynn Bradley, Roy Fish and Julia Mercedes Castilla. Length: 250-5,000 words; 2,500 words preferred. Publishes short shorts. Length: 300 words. Also publishes literary essays, literary criticism and poetry. Sometimes comments on rejected mss.

How to Contact: Send complete ms with a cover letter. Include estimated word count and 3-sentence bio. Responds in 6 weeks. Send SASE for return of ms. Accepts multiple submissions. Guidelines for #10 SASE.

Payment/Terms: Pays 2 contributor's copies; additional copies $7. Acquires one-time rights. Sends galleys to author (unless submitted on disk).

Advice: "We like to see fiction that doesn't read as if it had been composed in a creative writing class. If you can entertain, edify, or touch the reader, polish your story and send it in. Don't worry if it doesn't read like our other fiction."

○ ◎ TRADESMAN MAGAZINE, Tradesman magazine, P.O. Box 3462, Ann Arbor MI 48106-3462. **Contact:** K. Walker, editor. Magazine: digest-sized; about 40 pages; card stock cover; 24 lb. bond inside pages. "There aren't many magazines that specialize in publishing gay erotic fiction, especially ones that are open to gay 'humanistic' fiction, as well as genre types such as science fiction and fantasy (which have gay characters)." Triannual. Estab. 2001. Circ. 250.

Needs: Erotica, gay, lesbian. "We do not want anything that does not have a gay angle, or a gay character. We're interested in seeing what writers can do with categories or genres such as sci-fi, fantasy and others." Accepts 3 mss/issue; 12 mss/year. Publishes ms 2 months after acceptance. Length: 1,500-3,000 words; average length: 2,500 words. Publishes short shorts. Also publishes poetry. Sometimes comments on rejected mss.

How to Contact: "Send a complete manuscript; query if unsure." Accepts submissions on disk. Include estimated word count and brief bio. Responds in 1 month to queries; 3 months to mss. Send SASE for return of ms. Accepts simultaneous and multiple submissions. "Response time would be a little longer for multiple submissions." Sample copy for $5.

Payment/Terms: Pays 2 contributor's copies; additional copies $2.50. Pays on publication for first North American serial rights.

Advice: "Out intended audience is people who read thoughtful gay fiction. You can tell if someone is writing gay fiction who really doesn't have any knowledge of gay subcultures. We look for good writing, and work that is professionally submitted. Anything you send in should either be gay-themed or have a major character who the reader knows is gay. We're open to lesbian characters too. Also, it's sort of nice if, when writers send in manuscripts, they would indicate that they don't want manuscripts returned (assuming they've included no SASE, or SASE without sufficient postage). This may seem obvious, but I don't enjoy throwing manuscripts out unless a writer actually says that he or she wants me to."

TRANSITION, An International Review, Duke University Press, 69 Dunster St., Cambridge MA 02138. (617)496-2845. Fax: (617)496-2877. E-mail: transition@fas.harvard.edu. Website: http://web-dubois.fas.harvard.edu/transition (includes contents of all issues, abstracts, editorial history and current info, purchasing and subscription info). **Contact:** Michael Vazquez, executive editor. Magazine: 9½×6½; 150-175 pages; 70 lb. Finch Opaque paper; 100 lb. white Warren Lustro dull cover; illustrations; photos. "*Transition* magazine is a quarterly, international review known for compelling and controversial writing on race, ethnicity, culture and politics. This prestigious magazine is edited at Harvard University, and editorial board members include heavy-hitters such as Toni Morrison, Jamaica Kincaid and bell hooks. The magazine also attracts famous contributors such as Spike Lee, Philip Gourevitch and Carlos Fuentes." Quarterly. Estab. 1961. Circ. 3,500.
 • Winner of Alternative Press Award for international reporting 2000; finalist in the 2000 National Magazine Award in General Excellence category.
Needs: Ethnic/multicultural (general), historical, humor satire, literary, regional (Africa diaspora, India, Third World, etc.) Receives 10 unsolicited mss/month. Accepts 4-6 mss/year. Publishes ms 3-4 months after acceptance. Agented fiction 30-40%. **Publishes 1 new writer/year.** Published work by George Makana Clark, Paul Beatty and Victor D. LaValle. Length: 4,000-8,000 words; average length: 7,000 words. Also publishes literary essays and literary criticism. Sometimes comments on rejected mss.
How to Contact: Send complete ms with a cover letter or query with clips of published work. Include brief bio and list of publications. Responds in 2 months to queries; 4 months to mss. Send disposable copy of ms and #10 SASE for reply only. Accepts simultaneous submissions. Sample copy for $8.99 through website. Guidelines for SASE. Reviews novels, short story collections and nonfiction books of interest to writers.
Payment/Terms: Pays 3 contributor's copies. Rights negotiable. Sends galleys to author.
Advice: "We look for a non-white, alternative perspective, dealing with issues of race, ethnicity in an unpredictable, provocative way, but not exclusively."

TRIQUARTERLY, Northwestern University, 2020 Ridge Ave., Evanston IL 60208-4302. (847)491-3490. **Contact:** Susan Firestone Hahn, editor. Magazine: 6×9¼; 240-272 pages; 60 lb. paper; heavy cover stock; illustration; photos. "A general literary quarterly. We publish short stories, novellas or excerpts from novels, by American and foreign writers. Genre or style is not a primary consideration. We aim for the general but serious and sophisticated reader. Many of our readers are also writers." Triannual. Estab. 1964. Circ. 5,000.
 • Stories from *Triquarterly* have been reprinted in *The Best American Short Stories*, *Pushcart Prizes* and *O. Henry Prize* Anthologies.
Needs: Literary, contemporary and translations. "No prejudices or preconceptions against anything *except* genre fiction (romance, science fiction, etc.)." Accepts 10 mss/issue, 30 mss/year. Receives approximately 500 unsolicited fiction mss each month. Does not read or accept mss between April 1 and September 30. Agented fiction 10%. **Publishes 1-5 new writers/year.** Published work by John Barth, Chaim Potok, Joyce Carol Oates and Robert Girardi. Length: no requirement. Publishes short shorts.
How to Contact: Send complete ms with SASE. No simultaneous submissions. Responds in 4 months to mss. Publishes ms an average of 6-12 months after acceptance. Sample copy for $5.
Payment/Terms: Pays 2 contributor's copies; cover price less 40% discount for extras. Pays on publication for first North American serial rights. Sends galleys to author. Honoraria vary, depending on grant support.

UNBOUND, Suny Potsdam, Dept. of English and Communication, Morey Hall, SUNY Potsdam, Potsdam NY 13676. (315)267-2043. E-mail: unbound@potsdam.edu. Website: www2.potsdam.edu/henryrm/unbound.html. **Contact:** Rick Henry, editor. Magazine. "*Unbound* seeks fiction that exceeds the page. We are interested in collage, avant-garde, experimental, new media, multimedia fiction that maintains a strong narrative thread." Annual. Estab. 2002.
Needs: Experimental. "No genre fiction." Does not read mss March-August. Publishes short shorts.
How to Contact: Send complete ms with a cover letter. Include brief bio. Responds in 2 months to queries; 10 weeks to mss (or by February). Send SASE for return of ms or send a disposable copy of ms and #10 SASE for reply only. Accepts multiple submissions. Guidelines for SASE or by e-mail.
Payment/Terms: Pays 1 contributor's copy; additional copies $5. Pays on publication for first North American serial rights.
Advice: "We look for an intelligent relationship between a fiction's form and content. Fiction need not be limited by the borders of 8½×11 sheets of paper."

THE UNDERWOOD REVIEW, Hanover Press, Ltd., P.O. Box 596, Newtown CT 06470-0596. (203)426-3388. Fax: (203)426-3398. E-mail: hanoverpress@earthlink.net. **Contact:** Faith Vicinanza, editor. Magazine: 6×9; 144-288 pages; cream paper and cover; illustrations; photos. "*The Underwood Review*, a literary/art journal, publishes poetry, short stories, interviews, essays, photography (b&w), and pen and ink artwork." Annual. Estab. 1998. Member, CLMP.

Needs: Erotica, ethnic/multicultural, experimental, family saga, fantasy, feminist, gay, humor/satire, lesbian, literary, mainstream, psychic/supernatural/occult. Receives 20 unsolicited mss/month. Accepts 10 mss/year. Reads mss twice a quarter in order of receipt. Publishes ms 6-8 months after acceptance. Length: 500-5,000 words; average length: 3,500 words. Publishes short shorts. Also publishes literary essays and poetry.

How to Contact: Send complete ms with a cover letter. Accepts submissions on disk. Include brief bio and list of publications. Responds in 3-6 months. Send SASE for return of ms or send a disposable copy of ms and #10 SASE for reply only. Accepts simultaneous and multiple submissions. Sample copy for $10. Guidelines for SASE.

Payment/Terms: Pays 2 contributor's copies; additional copies $10. Acquires first, first North American serial and one-time rights.

Advice: Looks for fiction that is "original, edgy, risky, engaging. Open to new voices."

THE UNKNOWN WRITER, P.O. Box 698, Ramsey NJ 07446. E-mail: unknown_writer_2000@yahoo.com. Website: www.munno.net/unknownwriter (includes guidelines, selections from previous issues and current issue, staff bios). **Contact:** Rick Maffei, fiction editor. Magazine: 6×9; 40 pages; saddle-stitched; cardstock cover; illustrations; photos. "We exist to give newer writers a place to publish their quality writing. We want authors with limited publishing credits who have a strong, detailed, compelling story to tell. We publish work that strives to make a direct connection with the reader in a fresh, intelligent way. Our goals are to entertain our audience and to provide a literary, professional product with a small-press edge that beginning writers will be proud to list as a credit. Our intended audience is readers of all ages who prefer original, smart fiction and poetry and wish to escape the mediocrity of mainstream publications and authors." Quarterly. Estab. 1995.

Needs: Adventure, ethnic/multicultural, experimental, fantasy, gay, horror, lesbian, literary, mystery/suspense, science fiction. "No erotic, religious or graphic violence." **Publishes many new writers/year.** Accepts 4-5 mss/issue; 16-20 mss/year. Publishes ms up to 1 year after acceptance. Length: 50-5,000 words. Average length: 2,500 words. Publishes short shorts and poetry. Sometimes comments on rejected mss.

How to Contact: Send complete ms with a cover letter and short bio. Accepts submissions by e-mail. Include estimated word count. Responds in 3 weeks to queries; 4 months to mss. Send SASE for return of ms or send a disposable copy of ms and #10 SASE for reply only. Accepts simultaneous and multiple submissions. Guidelines for SASE, by e-mail or on website.

Payment/Terms: Pays 2 contributor's copies. Pays on publication for first rights.

Advice: "We look for strong characters, rich detail, and a clear conflict with a reasonable but not predictable resolution. Please use proper spelling and grammar, consistent point of view, and a good pace. We like a quirky, imaginative bend to almost any subject. We encourage future submissions when we like the style."

UNMUZZLED OX, Unmuzzled Ox Foundation Ltd., 105 Hudson St., New York NY 10013. (212)226-7170. E-mail: mandreox@aol.com. **Contact:** Michael Andre, editor. Magazine: 5½×8½. "Magazine about life for an intelligent audience." Published irregularly. Estab. 1971. Circ. 7,000.

● Recent issues of this magazine have included poetry, essays and art only. Check before sending submissions.

Needs: Contemporary, literary, prose poem and translations. No commercial material. Receives 20-25 unsolicited mss/month. Also publishes poetry. Occasionally critiques rejected mss.

How to Contact: "Please no phone calls and no e-mail submissions. Correspondence by mail *only*. Cover letter is significant." Responds in 1 month. SASE. Sample copy for $10.

Payment/Terms: Pays in contributor's copies.

Advice: "You may want to check out a copy of the magazine before you submit."

UNWOUND, A Journal with Delusions of Grandeur, P.O. Box 835, Laramie WY 82073. E-mail: unwound@partlycloudy.com. Website: www.fyuocuk.com/unwound (includes sample poems, interviews, art, guidelines and e-mail). **Contact:** Lindsay Wilson, editor. Magazine: digest size; 52 pages; heavy cover stock; illustrations; photos. "*Unwound* is a journal about contemporary life that seeks to recreate the world through writing and the mind that comes into contact with it. No traditional forms—I want to break from tradition. I want the work in *Unwound* to be new and to challenge old ideas." Semiannual. Estab. 1998. Circ. 200.

Needs: Erotica, ethnic/multicultural, humor/satire, literary, mainstream, regional (all), surrealism. Especially interested in flash fiction. Receives 5 unsolicited mss/month. Accepts 1-2 mss/issue; 2-5 mss/year. Publishes ms 1-6 months after acceptance. Agented fiction 10%. Recently published work by Daniel Crocker, Mark Wisniewski, Tim Scannel and Nathan Graziano. Length: 3,000 words maximum; average length: 2,000 words. Publishes short shorts. Average length: 200 words. Also publishes literary essays, literary criticism and poetry. Sometimes comments on rejected mss.

How to Contact: Send complete ms on disk. Include estimated word count and brief bio. SASE is a must. Responds in 2 months to queries; 4 months to mss. Send SASE for return of ms. Accepts multiple submissions. Sample copy for $3. Guidelines for SASE, e-mail or on website. Reviews novels, short story collections and nonfiction books of interest to writers. Send review copies to Lindsay Wilson.

Payment/Terms: Pays 1 contributor's copy; additional copies $2. Acquires one-time rights. Sends galleys to author through e-mail only. Not copyrighted.

Advice: "I'm looking for work that is surreal and has concerns for the image, but is still able to maintain an informal and identifiable voice. I'm looking for words and works that are trying to do something new and fresh."

VESTAL REVIEW, A flash fiction magazine, Vestal Review, 2609 Dartmouth Dr., Vestal NY 13850. E-mail: editor@stny.rr.com. Website: www.vestalreview.net (includes full content, including fiction, writer's guidelines, masthead, etc.). **Contact:** Mark Budman, publisher/editor. Magazine: 8½×5½; 22 pages; heavy cover stock; illustrations. "*Vestal Review* is the magazine specializing in flash fiction (stories under 500 words). In our ten quarterly issues up to date, we had an honor of publishing many good writers, including Aimee Bender and Mike Resnick. We accept only e-mail submissions." Quarterly. Circ. 1,500.

• Vestal Review received a Golden Web Award in 2002-2003.

Needs: Mainstream, literary, ethnic/multicultural, speculative fiction, horror. Receives 60-100 unsolicited mss/month. Accepts 7-8 mss/issue; 28-32 mss/year. Does not read mss March, June, September and December. Publishes ms 2-3 months after acceptance. **Publishes 2-3 new writers/year.** Recently published work by Aimee Bender, Mike Resnick, Leslie What and Liz Rosenberg. Length: 50-500 words; average length: 400 words. Publishes short shorts. Sometimes comments on rejected mss.

How to Contact: Send complete ms with a cover letter. "E-mail submissions only." Include estimated word count, brief bio and list of publications. Responds in 1 week to queries; 2 months to mss. Accepts simultaneous and multiple submissions. Sample copy for $5. Guidelines on website.

Payment/Terms: Pays $0.03-0.1/word and 1 contributor's copy; additional copies $5. Pays on publication for first North American serial and electronic rights. Sends galleys to author.

Advice: "We like literary fiction, with a plot, that doesn't waste words. Don't send jokes masked as stories."

$ THE VINCENT BROTHERS REVIEW, The Vincent Brothers Company, 4566 Northern Circle, Riverside OH 45424-5733. (937)367-3702. E-mail: vincentbrothersrev@earthlink.net. **Editor:** Kimberly Willardson. Magazine: 5½×8¼; 88-175 perfect-bound pages; 60 lb. white coated paper; 60 lb. Oxford (matte) cover; b&w illustrations; photos. "*The Vincent Brothers Review*'s mission is to broaden the appreciation for creative writing and contemporary graphic arts. *TVBR*'s goal is also to serve as a bridge between the academic literary journals and the commercial slicks, between the 'zines and the established small presses. We publish at least one theme issue per year. Writers must send SASE for information about upcoming theme issues. Each issue of *TVBR* contains poetry, b&w art, at least six short stories and usually one nonfiction piece. For a mainstream audience looking for an alternative to the slicks." Biannual. Estab. 1988. Circ. 450.

Needs: Adventure, condensed/excerpted novel, contemporary, ethnic, experimental, feminist, historical, humor/satire, literary, mainstream, mystery/suspense (amateur sleuth, cozy, private eye), prose poem, regional, science fiction (soft/sociological), senior citizen/retirement, serialized novel, translations, western (adult, frontier, traditional). "We love to read funny stories. Humorous fiction is quite difficult to writer—it usually appears as amusing anecdotes. We look for stories we want to pass on to other readers; stories we ourselves want to read again and again." Upcoming themes: "Taking Flight/Flight and Flying," deadline February 28; "Ohio's Ethnic Neighborhoods," deadline November 30. Receives 200-250 unsolicited mss/month. Buys 6-15 mss/issue; 30 mss/year. Publishes ms 2-4 months after acceptance. **Publishes 4-6 new writers/year.** Recently published work by Paul Headrick, Gerald Wheeler, Stephen Graham Jones and Jerry Gabriel. Length: 250-7,000 words; average length: 3,500 words. Maximum 10,000 words for novel condensations. Publishes short shorts. Length: 250-1,000 words. Also publishes literary essays, literary criticism, poetry. Often critiques rejected mss and sometimes recommends other markets.

How to Contact: "Send query letter *before* sending novel excerpts or condensations! *Send only one short story at a time*—unless sending short shorts." Send complete ms. Accepts simultaneous submissions (but not preferred) and multiple submissions (only if the pieces are short, 2-3 pages). Responds in 1 month to queries; 3 months to mss with SASE. Recent sample copies are $11.50. Perfect-bound back issues are $6.50; saddle-stitched (stapled) back issues are $5. Guidelines for #10 SASE. Reviews novels and short story collections.

Payment/Terms: Pays $25-350. (Pays $25 minimum on short stories, usually more, up to $350). Pays on acceptance for first North American serial rights. $200 first place; $100 second; $50 third for annual short story contest. Charge (discounted) for extras.

Advice: "We look for stories that pull us into their world immediately. Most writers mistakenly believe the first sentence is what's important. For us, it's the second sentence. It's the second sentence that lets us know the writer has command of the story and is taking us on a road we'll want to follow until we've read the last word of the story. Read, read, read some more of what the magazines are publishing. Read everything from Xeroxed 'zines to *The New Yorker*. Subscribe to at least three of the magazines/journals you like reading. Read the work of your peers."

WAR, LITERATURE & THE ARTS: An International Journal of the Humanities, Dept. of English & Fine Arts, United States Air Force Academy, 2354 Fairchild Dr., Suite 6D45, USAF Academy CO 80840-6242. (719)333-3930. Fax: (719)333-3932. E-mail: donald.anderson@usafa.af.mil. Website: www.usafa.edu/dfeng/wla. **Contact:** Donald Anderson, editor. Magazine: 6×9; 200 pages; illustrations; photos. "*WLA* seeks artistic depictions of war from all periods and cultures. From time immemorial, war and art have reflected one another. It is the intersection of war and art that *WLA* seeks to illuminate." Semiannual. Estab. 1989. Circ. 500. Member, Council of Editors of Learned Journals, CLMP.

Needs: No fantasy, science fiction. Accepts 2 mss/issue; 4 mss/year. Publishes ms 1 year after acceptance. Agented fiction 50%. **Publishes 2 new writers/year.** Published work by Paul West, Philip Caputo, Robert Morgan and Philip Appleman. Publishes short shorts. Also publishes literary essays, literary criticism and poetry. Sometimes comments on rejected mss.

How to Contact: Send complete ms with a cover letter. Include brief bio and list of publications. Responds in 6 weeks to queries; 6 months to mss. Send a disposable copy of ms and #10 SASE for reply only. Accepts simultaneous submissions "if told." Sample copy for $5. Guidelines on website. Reviews novels, short story collections and nonfiction books of interest to writers. Send review copies to the editor.

Payment/Terms: Pays 2 contributor's copies; additional copies $5. Pays on publication for first North American serial and electronic rights. Sends galleys to author.

Advice: "Our only criterion is literary excellence and fresh language. Our current writer's guidelines are 'Make the world new.' "

N **⊕** **$** **☉** **WASAFIRI**, Dept. of English, Queen Mary & Westfield College, University of London, Mile End Road, London EI4NS UK. E-mail: wasafiri@qmw.ac.uk. Website: www.qmw.ac.uk/wasafiri (includes writer's guidelines, editors, content/backlist). **Contact:** Ms. Susheila Nasta, editor. Triannual. Circ. 5,000. "Publishes critical articles, interviews, reviews, fiction and poetry by and about African, Asian, Caribbean, Pacific and Black British writers. We welcome any writing for consideration which falls into our areas of interest. Work from writers outside Britain is a major part of our interest. Articles should be double-spaced and follow MLA guidelines." Publishes 2-3 short stories/issue. Length: 500-2,000 words.

Needs: Literary. "No romance, science fiction, fantasy. Would like to see more contemporary, adventurous fiction." Published work by Jamal Mahoub, Leila Aboulela and Meera V. Pilay. **Publishes 20% new writers/year.** Upcoming themes: "Poetry in the USA" (spring 2003); "Film" (winter 2003); "20 Years of Wasafiri" (summer 2004); "Focus on Africa" (spring); "Travel" (autumn).

Payment/Terms: Pays contributor's copies and a small fee.

Advice: "We're looking for clarity of style and nonflowery language. Read extensively, and read and reread your own writing."

✿ **◑** **$** **WASCANA REVIEW OF CONTEMPORARY POETRY AND SHORT FICTION**, University of Regina, Regina, Saskatchewan S4S 0A2 Canada. (306)585-4302. Fax: (306)585-4827. E-mail: michael.trussler@uregina .ca. Website: www.uregina.ca/english/wrhome.htm (includes excerpts from publication, description of journal and its mandate). **Contact:** Dr. Michael Trussler, editor. "Literary criticism, fiction and poetry for readers of serious fiction." Semiannual. Estab. 1966. Circ. 500.

Needs: Literary and critical essays. "No fiction that's predictable, that lacks an original voice. Frankly, we're also tired of coming-of-age stories, particularly macho ones." Check website for upcoming themes. Buys 8-10 mss/year. Receives approximately 20 unsolicited fiction mss/month. Agented fiction 5%. **Publishes 2-3 new writers/year.** Length: 2,000-6,000 words. Occasionally recommends other markets.

How to Contact: Accepts queries by e-mail. Send complete ms with SASE. Responds in 2 months to mss. Publishes ms an average of 6 months after acceptance. Sample copy for $5. Guidelines with SASE.

Payment/Terms: Pays $3/page for prose; $10/page for poetry; 2 contributor's copies. Pays on publication for first North American rights.

Advice: "Stories we receive are often technically incompetent or deal with trite subjects. Usually stories are longer than necessary by about one-third. Be more ruthless in cutting back on unnecessary verbiage. All approaches to fiction are welcomed by the *Review* editors—but we continue to seek the best in terms of style and technical expertise. As our calls for submission state, the *Wascana Review* continues to seek "short fiction that combines craft with risk, pressure with grace."

◑ **WASHINGTON SQUARE, Literary Review of New York University's Creative Writing Program**, NYU Creative Writing Program, 19 University Place, 2nd Floor, New York NY 10003-4556. (212)992-9685. Fax: (212)427-7285. E-mail: wsmgr@hotmail.com. Website: www.nyu.edu/gsas/program/cwp/wsr.htm (includes writer's guidelines, excerpts from recent issues, editor's names). **Contact:** James Pritchard, fiction editor. Editors change each year. Magazine: 5½×8½; 144 pages; photographs. "*Washington Square* is the literary review produced by New York University's Graduate Creative Writing Program. We publish outstanding works of fiction and poetry by the students and faculty of NYU as well as the work of writers across the country." Semiannual. Estab. 1996. Circ. 2,000. Member, CLMP.

Needs: Condensed/excerpted novel, ethnic/multicultural, experimental, humor, literary, mainstream/contemporary. No adventure, children's, erotica, horror, fantasy. Would like to see more contemporary, experimental, humor, short-shorts. Receives 75 unsolicited mss/month. Accepts 5 mss/issue; 10 mss/year. Publishes ms 3-5 months after acceptance. Agented fiction 20%. **Publishes 2 new writers/year.** Recently published work by Arthur Japin, Ron Carlson, Elizabeth Stuckey-French and Mark Jarman. Length: 7,000 words maximum; average length: 5,000 words. Publishes short shorts. Also publishes poetry. Sometimes comments on rejected mss.

How to Contact: Send complete ms with a cover letter. Include estimated word count (only put name on first page). Responds in 2 weeks to queries; up to 5 months to mss. Send SASE for reply, return of ms or send a disposable copy of ms. Accepts simultaneous submissions. Sample copy for $6.

Payment/Terms: Pays 2 contributor's copies and 1-year subscription; additional copies for $6. Acquires first North American serial rights.

Advice: "We look for work that is polished and challenging; stories that, for whatever reason, stand out from other stories. We welcome and seek work that takes risks in both form and content, but the risk needs to be balanced with a careful attention to craft. Above all, send us stories that you're excited about."

WEST WIND REVIEW, 1250 Siskiyou Blvd., Ashland OR 97520. (503)552-6518. E-mail: westwind@tao.sou.e du. **Contact:** Dottie Lou Taylor, editor. Editors change each year. Magazine: 5¾×8½; 150-250 pages; illustrations; photos. "Literary journal publishing prose/poetry/art. Encourages new writers, accepts established writers as well, with an audience of people who like to read challenging fiction." Annual. Estab. 1980. Circ. 500.
Needs: Adventure, ethnic/multicultural, experimental, historical (general), humor/satire, literary, mainstream/contemporary, mystery/suspense, regional, romance, senior citizen/retirement, sports, translations—"just about anything." No pornography. "Would like to see more fiction that flows from character rather than plot. Would like to see more fiction that takes stylistic risks." Receives 6-60 unsolicited mss/month. Accepts 15-20 mss/issue. Publishes ms almost immediately after acceptance. **Publishes 5-10 new writers/year.** Published work by Virgil Suarez. Length: 3,000 words maximum. Publishes short shorts. Also publishes poetry. Sometimes comments on rejected ms.
How to Contact: Send complete ms with a cover letter. Include estimated word count and short bio. Responds by March 1 to mss. Send SASE for reply, return of ms or send a disposable copy of ms. No simultaneous submissions. For guidelines send SASE.
Payment/Terms: Accepted authors receive 1 free copy. Authors retain all rights.
Advice: "Good writing stands out. Content is important but style is essential. Clearly finished pieces with subtle action, reaction and transformation are what we like."

$ WESTERLY, Arts Bldg., University of Western Australia, Crawley, Western Australia 6009. 08 9380 2101. Fax: 08 9380 1030. E-mail: westerly@cyllene.uwa.edu.au. Website: www.arts.uwa.edu.au/westerly (includes details of current issue, past issues, forthcoming issues and information about subscribing and contributing). "*Westerly* publishes lively fiction and poetry as well as intelligent articles. *Westerly* is not a specialist academic journal but aims to generate interest in the literature and culture of Australia and its neighboring regions. We differ from other journals in that our focus is more towards the West Coast of Australia and the Indian Ocean region (Asia, India, etc.)." **Contact:** Monica Anderson, administrator. Annual (November). Circ. 1,000.
Needs: "An annual of poetry, prose and articles of a literary and cultural kind, giving special attention to Australia and Southeast Asia. No romance, children's, science fiction." Publishes ms 3-6 months after acceptance.
How to Contact: SASE (IRC). Accepts queries by e-mail. Material under consideration for publication may be held until August 31 each year; submission deadline is June 30.
Payment/Terms: Pays $40 (AUS) minimum and 1 contributor's copy. Sample copy for $10 (AUS) plus $2 postage.

WESTVIEW, A Journal of Western Oklahoma, Southwestern Oklahoma State University, 100 Campus Dr., Weatherford OK 73096-3098. (580)774-3168. Editor: Fred Alsberg. **Contact:** Fiction Editor. Magazine: 8½×11; 64 pages; 24 lb. paper; slick color cover; illustrations; photos. Semiannual. Estab. 1981. Circ. 400.
Needs: Contemporary, ethnic (especially Native American), humor, literary, prose poem. "No pornography, violence, or gore. No overly sentimental. We are particularly interested in writers of the Southwest; however, we accept work of quality from elsewhere." Receives 20 unsolicited mss/month. Accepts 5 mss/issue; 10 mss/year. Publishes ms 3-12 months after acceptance. Published work by Diane Glancy, Wendell Mayo, Jack Matthews and Mark Spencer. Length: 2,000 words average. Also publishes literary essays, literary criticism, poetry. Occasionally critiques rejected mss.
How to Contact: Accepts simultaneous submissions. Send complete ms with SASE. Responds in 2 months. "We welcome submissions on a 3.5 disk formatted for WordPerfect 5.0, IBM or Macintosh. Please include a hard copy printout of your submission."
Payment/Terms: Pays contributor's copy. Acquires first rights.

Ⓝ WHISKEY ISLAND MAGAZINE, Dept. of English, Cleveland State University, Cleveland OH 44115-2440. (216)687-2056. Fax: (216)687-6943. E-mail: whiskeyisland@csuohio.edu. Website: www.csuohio.edu/whiskey_is land (includes writer's guidelines, contest guidelines, staff information, history, short fiction, poetry, subscription information). Editors change each year. Magazine of fiction and poetry, including experimental works, with no specific theme. "We provide a forum for new writers and new work, for themes and points of view that are both meaningful and experimental, accessible and extreme." Biannual. Estab. 1978. Circ. 2,500.
Needs: "Would like to see more short shorts, flash fiction." Receives 100 unsolicited fiction mss/month. Accepts 46 mss/issue. Reads submissions September through April only. **Publishes 5-10 new writers/year.** Published Vickie A. Carr and John Fulmer. Length: 5,000 words maximum. Also publishes poetry (poetry submissions should contain no more than 10 pages).
How to Contact: Send complete ms with SASE. Accepts queries/mss by fax. No simultaneous or previously published submissions. Responds in 4 months to mss. Sample copy for $5.
Payment/Terms: Pays 2 contributor's copies. Acquires one-time rights.
Advice: "We seek a different voice, controlled language and strong opening. Childhood memoirs are discouraged."

WIND MAGAZINE, P.O. Box 24548, Lexington KY 40524. (859)227-6849. E-mail: wind@wind.org. **Contact:** Chris Green, editor. Magazine: 6×9; 100 pages. "Eclectic literary journal with stories, poems, book reviews from small presses, essays. Readership is students, professors, farmers, cafe-dwellers." Semiannually. Estab. 1971. Circ. 450.
Needs: Literary, experimental, mainstream/contemporary, translations. Accepts 2 fiction mss/issue; 6 mss/year. Publishes ms less than 1 year after acceptance. Published work by Normandi Ellis, Graham Shelby and B.Z. Niditch. Length: 4,500 words maximum. Publishes short shorts, length: 300-400 words. Also publishes literary essays and literary criticism. Sometimes comments on rejected mss.

How to Contact: Send complete ms with a cover letter. Include estimated word count and 50-word bio. No e-mail submissions accepted. Responds in 2 weeks to queries; 4 months to mss. Send SASE for reply, return of ms or send a disposable copy of ms. Accepts simultaneous submissions. Sample copy for $6. Reviews novels and short story collections from small presses.

Payment/Terms: Pays 1 contributor's copy; additional copies for $3.50. Acquires first North American serial rights and anthology reprint rights.

○ **WINDHOVER: A Journal of Christian Literature**, University of Mary Hardin-Baylor, P.O. Box 8008, Belton TX 76513. (254)295-4564. E-mail: dwnixon@umhb.edu. Website: www.literarytexas.com (includes excerpts, writer's guidelines, names of editors). **Contact:** Donna Walker-Nixon, editor. Magazine: 6×9; white bond paper. "We want to publish literary fiction by writers of faith." Annual. Estab. 1997. Circ. 500.

Needs: Ethnic/multicultural (general), experimental, family saga, fantasy, historical (general), humor/satire, literary. "No erotica." Receives 30 unsolicited mss/month. Accepts 5 mss/issue; 5 mss/year. Publishes ms 1 year after acceptance. **Publishes 5 new writers/year.** Published work by Walt McDonald, James Schaap, Jeanne Murray Walker and David Hopes. Length: 1,500-4,000 words; average length: 3,000 words. Publishes short shorts. Average length: 150 words. Also publishes literary essays and poetry. Sometimes comments on rejected mss.

How to Contact: Send all submissions by e-mail to windhover@umhb.edu. Include estimated word count, brief bio and list of publications. Responds in 3 weeks to queries; 4 months to mss. "Do not send submissions by snail mail since we forward submissions via e-mail to our board of editors and do not accept snail mail submissions." Accepts simultaneous submissions. Sample copy for $6. Guidelines by e-mail.

Payment/Terms: Pays 2 contributor's copies; additional copies $8. Pays on publication for first rights.

Advice: "Be patient. We have an editorial board and sometimes replies take longer than I like. We particularly look for convincing plot and character development."

◨ **THE WORCESTER REVIEW**, Worcester Country Poetry Association, Inc., 6 Chatham St., Worcester MA 01609. (508)797-4770. Website: www.geocities.com/Paris/LeftBank/6433. Editor: Rodger Martin. **Contact:** Fiction Editor. Magazine: 6×9; 100 pages; 60 lb. white offset paper; 10 pt. CS1 cover stock; illustrations; photos. "We like high quality, creative poetry, artwork and fiction. Critical articles should be connected to New England." Annual. Estab. 1972. Circ. 1,000.

Needs: Literary, prose poem. "We encourage New England writers in the hopes we will publish at least 30% New England but want the other 70% to show the best of writing from across the US." Receives 20-30 unsolicited fiction mss/month. Accepts 2-4 mss/issue. Publishes ms an average of 6 months to 1 year after acceptance. Agented fiction less than 10%. Recently published work by Robert Pinsky, Marge Piercy, Wes McNair and Ervon Boland. Length: 1,000-4,000 words; average length: 2,000 words. Publishes short shorts. Also publishes literary essays, literary criticism, poetry. Sometimes critiques rejected mss and recommends other markets.

How to Contact: Send complete ms with cover letter. Responds in 9 months to mss. SASE. Accepts simultaneous submissions if other markets are clearly identified. Sample copy for $6; guidelines free.

Payment/Terms: Pays 2 contributor's copies and honorarium if possible. Acquires one-time rights.

Advice: "Send only one short story—reading editors do not like to read two by the same author at the same time. We will use only one. We generally look for creative work with a blend of craftsmanship, insight and empathy. This does not exclude humor. We won't print work that is shoddy in any of these areas."

◨ **WORDS OF WISDOM**, 8969 UNCG Station, Greensboro NC 27413. (336)334-2952. E-mail: wowmail@hoops mail.com. **Contact:** Mikhammad Abdel-Ishara, editor. Assistant Editor: Roslyn Willett. Newsletter: 5½×8½; 76-88 pages; computer generated on copy paper; saddle-stapled with 40 lb. colored paper cover; some illustrations. "Fiction, satire/humor, poetry and travel for a general audience." Estab. 1981. Circ. 150-160.

Needs: Adventure, contemporary, ethnic, feminist, historical, humor/satire, literary, mainstream, mystery/suspense (cozy, private eye), regional, western. "No religion, children's, gay or romance." Receives 450-500 unsolicited mss/year. Accepts 67-75 mss/year. Publishes ms 2-6 months after acceptance. **Publishes 0-5 new writers/year.** Recently published work by Tim McCoy, Robert Steiner, Susan Carrithers, David Sapp and Margene Whitler Hucek. Length: 1,200-6,000 words; average length: 3,000 words.

How to Contact: Cover letter required. "There are no automatons here, so don't treat us like machines. We may not recognize your name at the top of the manuscript. A few lines about yourself breaks the ice, the names of three or four magazines that have published you in the last year or two would show your reality, and a bio blurb of 37 +/- words including the names of two or three of the magazines you send the occasional subscription check (where you aspire to be?) could help. If you are not sending a check to some little magazine that is supported by subscriptions and the blood, sweat and tears of the editors, why would you send your manuscript to any of them and expect to receive a warm welcome? No requirement to subscribe or buy a sample, but they are available at $14 and $4 and are encouraged. There are no phony contests and never a reading fee. We read all year long, but may take one to six months to respond." Seldom comments on rejections. Accepts simultaneous submissions but no reprints.

Payment/Terms: Pays subscription to magazine for first story published. Acquires one-time rights. Publication not copyrighted.

Advice: "Stop watching TV and read that magazine of stories where your last manuscript appeared."

○ ◎ **WRITING FOR OUR LIVES**, Running Deer Press, 647 N. Santa Cruz Ave., Annex, Los Gatos CA 95030-4350. (408)354-8604. **Contact:** Janet M. McEwan, editor. Magazine: 5¼×8¼; 80 pages; 70 lb. recycled white paper;

80 lb. recycled cover. "*Writing For Our Lives* is a periodical which serves as a vessel for poems, short fiction, stories, letters, autobiographies, and journal excerpts from the life stories, experiences and spiritual journeys of women. Audience is women and friends of women." Annual. Estab. 1992. Circ. 500.

Needs: Ethnic/multicultural, experimental, feminist, humor/satire, lesbian, literary, translations, "autobiographical, breaking personal or historical silence on any concerns of women's lives. No genre fiction. *Women writers only, please.* We have no preannounced themes." Receives 15-20 unsolicited mss/month. Accepts 10 mss/issue; 20 mss/year. Publishes ms 2-24 months after acceptance. **Publishes 3-5 new writers/year.** Published work by Sabah Akbar, Anjali Banerjee, Debra Kay Vest, Lisa M. Ortiz and Luci Yamamoto. Length: 2,100 words maximum. Publishes short shorts. Also publishes poetry. Rarely comments on rejected mss.

How to Contact: Send complete ms and bio with a cover letter. "Publication date is October. Closing date for mss is August 15. Initial report immediate; next report, if any, in 1-18 months." Send 2 SASE's for reply, and one of them must be sufficient for return of ms if desired. Accepts simultaneous, multiple and reprint submissions. Sample copy for $6-8 (in California add 8.25% sales tax), $9-11 overseas. Guidelines for #10 SASE.

Payment/Terms: Pays 2 contributor's copies; additional copies for 50% discount and 2 issue subscription at 50% discount. Acquires one-time rights in case of reprints and first worldwide English language serial rights.

Advice: "It is in our own personal stories that the real herstory of our time is told. This periodical is a place for exploring the boundaries of our empowerment to break long historical and personal silences. While honoring the writing which still needs to be held close to our hearts, we can begin to send some of our heartfelt words out into a wider circle."

$ **THE YALE REVIEW**, Yale University/Blackwell Publishers Inc., P.O. Box 208243, New Haven CT 06520-8243. (203)432-0499. Fax: (203)432-0510. Editor: J.D. McClatchy. **Contact:** Susan Bianconi, fiction editor. Magazine: 9¼×6; 180-190 pages; book stock paper; glossy cover; illustrations; photos. "*The Yale Review* is meant for the well-read general reader interested in a variety of topics in the arts and letters, in history, and in current affairs." Quarterly. Estab. 1911. Circ. 7,000.

Needs: Mainstream/contemporary. Receives 80-100 unsolicited mss/month. Accepts 1-3 mss/issue; 7-12 mss/year. Publishes ms 3 months after acceptance. Agented fiction 25%. Published work by Steven Millhauser, Deborah Eisenberg, Jeffrey Eugenides, Sheila Kohler, Joe Ashby Porter, Julie Orringer, John Barth and James McCourt. Publishes short shorts (but not frequently). Also publishes literary essays, poetry.

How to Contact: Send complete ms with a cover letter. Include estimated word count and list of publications. Responds in 1 month to queries; 2 months to mss. Send SASE for reply, return of ms or send a disposable copy of ms. Always include SASE. No simultaneous submissions. Reviews novels and short story collections. Send books to the editors.

Payment/Terms: Pays $300-400 and 2 contributor's copies; additional copies for $8.50. Pays on publication. Sends galleys to author. "Awards by the editors; cannot be applied for."

Advice: "We find that the most accomplished young writers seem to be people who keep their ears open to other voices; who read widely."

N **THE YALOBUSHA REVIEW, The Literary Journal of the University of Mississippi**, University Publishing, University of Mississippi, Rebel Dr. West, Sam Hall, University MS 38677. (662)915-7066. Fax: (662)915-7419. E-mail: jmaples@olemiss.edu. Editors change each year. Magazine: 6×9; 126 pages; illustrations; photos. "With the new M.F.A. program at the University, the *Yalobusha Review* gives M.F.A. and M.A. students a chance to produce a quality journal. This year we ar doubling the size to 126 pages, enlarging the review and including artwork." Annual. Estab. 1995. Circ. 500.

Needs: Experimental, family saga, historical, humor/satire, literary, mainstream. "No genre or formula fiction." List of upcoming themes available for SASE. Receives 35 unsolicited mss/month. Accepts 4-5 mss/issue. Does not read mss May 15 through August 15. Publishes ms 6 months after acceptance. Recently published work by David Galef, Paul Bowers and Kiki R. Nusbaumer. Length: 1,000-5,000 words; average length: 5,000 words. Publishes short shorts; average length: 1,500 words. Also publishes poetry.

How to Contact: Send complete ms with a cover letter. Accepts submissions on disk (Mac only). Include brief bio. Responds in 6 weeks to queries; 6 months to mss. Send disposable copy of ms and #10 SASE for reply only. Accepts multiple submissions. Sample copy for $10. Guidelines for SASE.

Payment/Terms: Pays 2 contributor's copies; additional copies $10. Acquires all rights.

Advice: "We look for writers with a strong, distinct voice and good stories to tell."

YEMASSEE, The literary journal of the University of South Carolina, Department of English, University of South Carolina, Columbia SC 29208. (803)777-2085. Fax: (803)777-9064. E-mail: yemassee@gwm.sc.edu. Website: www.cla.sc.edu/ENGL/yemassee/index.htm (includes cover of latest issue, origin of name and subscription info). **Contact:** Corinna McLeod, editor. Magazine: 5½×8½; 70-90 pages; 60 lb. natural paper; 65 lb. cover; cover illustration. "We are open to a variety of subjects and writing styles. *Yemassee* publishes primarily fiction and poetry, but we are also interested in one-act plays, brief excerpts of novels, essays, reviews and interviews with literary figures. Our essential consideration for acceptance is the quality of the work." Semiannual. Estab. 1993. Circ. 375.

• Stories from *Yemassee* have been selected for publication in *Best New Stories of the South*.

Needs: Condensed/excerpted novel, ethnic/multicultural, experimental, feminist, gay, historical, humor/satire, lesbian, literary, regional. "No romance, religious/inspirational, young adult/teen, children's/juvenile, erotica. Wants more experimental." Receives 30 unsolicited mss/month. Accepts 1-3 mss/issue; 2-6 mss/year. "We hold manuscripts until our reading periods—October 1 to November 15 and March 15 to April 30." Publishes ms 2-4 months after acceptance. **Publishes 6 new writers/year.** Published work by Robert Coover, Chris Railey, Virgil Suarez, Susan Ludvigson and Kwame Dawes. Length: 4,000 words or less. Publishes short shorts. Also publishes literary essays and poetry.

How to Contact: Send complete ms with a cover letter. Include estimated word count, brief bio, Social Security number and list of publications. Responds in 2 weeks to queries, 4 months after deadlines to mss. Send SASE for reply, return of ms or send disposable copy of ms. Accepts simultaneous submissions. Sample copy for $5. Guidelines for #10 SASE.

Payment/Terms: Pays 2 contributor's copies; additional copies $3. All submissions are considered for the *Yemassee* awards—$200 each for the best poetry and fiction in each issue when funding permits. Acquires first rights

Advice: "Our criteria are based on what we perceive as quality. Generally that is work that is literary. We are interested in subtlety and originality, interesting or beautiful language; craft and precision. Read more, write more and revise more. Read our journal and any other journal before you submit to see if your work seems appropriate. Send for guidelines and make sure you follow them."

N **⊕** **◎** **YORKSHIRE JOURNAL**, Smith Settle Ltd., Ilkley Road, Otley, W. Yorkshire LS21 3JP England. 01943-467958. Fax: 01943-850057. Editor: Mark Whitley. Magazine: 245mm × 175mm; 120 pages; matte art paper; art board cover stock; illustrations; photos. "We publish historical/factual articles, poetry and short stories by and about the county of Yorkshire in England." Quarterly. Estab. 1993. Circ. 3,000.

Needs: Regional, "anything about Yorkshire." Receives 2-4 unsolicited mss/month. Accepts 2-3 mss/year. Published work by Denis Yeadon, Neville Slack, Mary Walsh and Alex Marwood. Length: 1,500 words average. Often comments on rejected mss.

How to Contact: Query first. Include estimated word count and 50-word bio with submission. Responds in 6 weeks to queries; 10 weeks to mss. Send SASE (or IRCs) for reply, return of ms or send a disposable copy of ms. Accepts reprints and electronic submissions (disk or modem). Sample copy for $10. Guidelines for SASE (or IRC).

Payment/Terms: Pay varies; includes 1 contributor's copy; additional copies $10. Pays on publication for first rights.

Advice: "Fiction must be about Yorkshire in some way. Send in an outline first, not the completed manuscript."

$ **◙** **☑** **ZOETROPE: All-Story**, AZX Publications, 916 Kearny St., San Francisco CA 94133. (415)788-7500. Fax: (415)989-7910. E-mail: info@all-story.com. Website: www.all-story.com (includes information on short story contests, online writer's workshop, upcoming events, etc.) **Contact:** Tamara Straus, editor-in-chief. Magazine: 10½ × 14; 60 pages; illustrations; photos. Quarterly. *Zoetrope: All-Story* presents a new generation of classic stories. Inspired by the Coppola heritage of independence and creativity, the magazine is at once innovative and deeply traditional. It explores the intersection of fiction and film and anticipates some of its stories becoming memorable films." Estab. 1997. Circ. 30,000.

● This journal won the 2002 National Magazine Award for fiction. Stories from *Zoetrope* have received the O. Henry Prize, the Pushcart Prize and have been reprinted in *New Stories from the South* and received honorable mentions in *Best American Short Stories*. *Zoetrope: All-Story* ranked on *Writer's Digest*'s "Top 30" list of best markets for fiction writers.

Needs: Literary, mainstream/contemporary, one act plays. "No genre fiction or excerpts from larger works." Receives 600 unsolicited mss/month. Accepts 5-7 mss/issue; 32-40 mss/year. Publishes ms approximately 6 months after acceptance. Agented fiction 15%. **Publishes 4-6 new writers/year.** Recently published work by Arthur Bradford, A.M. Homes, Jane Smiley and Susan Straight.

How to Contact: Send complete manuscript (no more than 1) with a cover letter. Accepts queries by mail. Include estimated word count and list of publications. SASE. Accepts simultaneous submissions. Sample copy for $5.95 and 9 × 12 SAE and $1.70 postage. Guidelines for #10 SASE.

Payment/Terms: Pays $1,500 for first serial rights and 2 year option on movie rights for unsolicited submissions; $6,000 for commissioned works. Sponsors contest.

Advice: "We like fiction that really tells a full story. Voices that we haven't heard before and solid prose help a story stand out."

$ **◙** **◎** **ZYZZYVA, the last word: west coast writers & artists**, POB 590069, San Francisco CA 94159-0069. (415)752-4393. Fax: (415)752-4391. E-mail: editor@zyzzyva.org. Website: www.zyzzyva.org (includes guidelines, names of editors, selections from current issues, editor's note). **Contact:** Howard Junker, editor. Magazine: 6×9; 192 pages; graphics; photos. "Literate" magazine featuring West Coast writers and artists. Triquarterly. Estab. 1985. Circ. 4,000.

Needs: Contemporary, experimental, literary, prose poem. West Coast US writers only. Receives 400 unsolicited mss/month. Accepts 8 fiction mss/issue; 24 mss/year. Agented fiction: 10%. **Publishes 20 new writers/year.** Recently published work by Wanda Coleman, Jill Soloway and F.X. Toole. Length: varies. Also publishes literary essays.

How to Contact: Send complete ms. "Cover letters are of minimal importance." Accepts submissions by e-mail and disk. Responds in 2 weeks to mss. SASE. No simultaneous or reprint submissions. Sample copy for $6. Guidelines on masthead page.

Payment/Terms: Pays $50. Pays on acceptance for first North American serial rights.

Advice: "Keep the faith."

Small Circulation Magazines

This section of *Novel & Short Story Writer's Market* contains general interest, special interest, regional and genre magazines with circulations of under 10,000. Although these magazines vary greatly in size, theme, format and management, the editors are all looking for short stories. Their specific fiction needs present writers of all degrees of expertise and interests with an abundance of publishing opportunities.

Although not as high-paying as the large-circulation consumer magazines, you'll find some of the publications listed here do pay writers 1-5¢/word or more. Also, unlike the big consumer magazines, these markets are very open to new writers and relatively easy to break into. Their only criteria is that your story be well written, well presented, and suitable for their particular readership.

DIVERSITY IN OPPORTUNITY

Among the diverse publications in this section are magazines devoted to almost every topic, every level of writing and every type of writer. Some of the markets listed here publish fiction about a particular geographic area or by authors who live in that locale.

SELECTING THE RIGHT MARKET

First, zero in on those markets most likely to be interested in your work. If you write genre fiction, check out specific sections for lists of magazines publishing in that genre (mystery, page 83; romance, page 97; science fiction/fantasy & horror, page 109). For other types of fiction, begin by looking at the Category Index starting on page 606. If your work is more general—or conversely, very specialized—you may wish to browse through the listings, perhaps looking up those magazines published in your state or region. Also check the Zine and Online Markets sections for other specialized and genre publications.

In addition to browsing through the listings and using the Category Index, check the ranking codes at the beginning of listings to find those most likely to be receptive to your work. This is especially true for beginning writers, who should look for magazines that say they are especially open to new writers (□) and for those giving equal weight to both new and established writers (◖). For more explanation about these codes, see the inside front and back covers of this book.

Once you have a list of magazines you might like to try, read their listings carefully. Much of the material within each listing carries clues that tell you more about the magazine. The "Quick Start" Guide to Publishing Your Fiction starting on page 2 describes in detail the listing information common to all the markets in our book.

The physical description appearing near the beginning of the listings can give you clues about the size and financial commitment to the publication. This is not always an indication of quality, but chances are a publication with expensive paper and four-color artwork on the cover has more prestige than a photocopied publication featuring a clip art self-cover. For more information on some of the paper, binding and printing terms used in these descriptions, see Printing and Production Terms Defined on page 594.

FURTHERING YOUR SEARCH

It cannot be stressed enough that reading the listing is only the first part of developing your marketing plan. The second part, equally important, is to obtain fiction guidelines and read the actual magazine. Reading copies of a magazine helps you determine the fine points of the magazine's publishing style and philosophy. There is no substitute for this type of hands-on research.

Unlike commercial magazines available at most newsstands and bookstores, it requires a little more effort to obtain some of the magazines listed here. You may need to send for a sample copy. We include sample copy prices in the listings whenever possible. See The Business of Fiction Writing on page 58 for the specific mechanics of manuscript submission. Above all, editors appreciate a professional presentation. Include a brief cover letter and send a self-addressed envelope for a reply or a self-addressed envelope in a size large enough to accommodate your manuscript, if you would like it returned. Be sure to include enough stamps or International Reply Coupons (for replies from countries other than your own) to cover your manuscript's return. Many publishers today appreciate receiving a disposable manuscript, eliminating the cost to writers of return postage and saving editors the effort of repackaging manuscripts for return.

Most of the magazines listed here are published in the US. You will also find some English-speaking markets from around the world. These foreign publications are denoted with a ⊕ symbol at the beginning of listings. To make it easier to find Canadian markets, we include a ⬥ symbol at the start of those listings.

⊕ ◪ ▢ ALBEDO ONE, The Irish Magazine of Science Fiction, Fantasy and Horror, Albedo One, 2 Post Rd., Lusk, Co Dublin Ireland. Phone: (+353)1-8730177. E-mail: bobn@eircom.net. Website: www.yellowbrickroad.ie/albedo. **Contact:** Editor, *Albedo One*. Magazine: A4; 44 pages. "We hope to publish interesting and unusual fiction by new and established writers. We will consider anything, as long as it is well-written and entertaining, though our definitions of both may not be exactly mainstream. We like stories with plot and characters that live on the page. Most of our audience are probably committed genre fans, but we try to appeal to a broad spectrum of readers—the narrow focus of our readership is due to the public-at-large's unwillingness to experiment with their reading/magazine purchasing rather than any desire on our part to be exclusive." Triannual. Estab. 1993. Circ. 900.
Needs: Comics/graphic novels, experimental, fantasy, horror, literary, science fiction. Receives more than 20 unsolicited mss/month. Accepts 15-18 mss/year. Publishes ms 1 year after acceptance. **Publishes 4 new writers/year.** Length: 2,000-5,000 words; average length: 4,000 words. Also publishes literary criticism. Sometimes comments on rejected mss.
How to Contact: Send complete ms with a cover letter. Accepts submissions by fax and disk. Responds in 4 months to mss. Send a disposable copy of ms and #10 SASE for reply only. Sample copy for $9. Guidelines available by e-mail or on website. Reviews novels, short story collections and nonfiction books of interest to writers.
Payment/Terms: Pays 1 contributor's copy; additional copies £5 plus p&p. Pays on publication for first rights.
Advice: "We look for good writing, good plot, good characters. Read the magazine, and don't give up."

◪ ALEMBIC, Singularity Rising Press, P.O. Box 28416, Philadelphia PA 19149. (215)743-4927. E-mail: alembic33@aol.com. **Contact:** Larry Farrell, editor. Magazine: 8½×11; 64 pages; bond paper; illustrations. "*Alembic* is a literary endeavor magically bordering intersecting continua." The magazine publishes poems, stories and art. Quarterly. Estab. 1999. Circ. 100.
Needs: Fantasy (space fantasy, sword and sorcery), horror (dark fantasy, futuristic, psychological, supernatural), literary, mystery/suspense (amateur sleuth, cozy, police procedural, private eye/hardboiled), science fiction (hard science/technological, soft/sociological), thriller/espionage. No children's, religious, romance. Would like to see more mystery. Receives 15 unsolicited mss/month. Accepts 6 mss/issue; 24 mss/year. Publishes ms 9-18 months after acceptance. **Publishes 15 new writers/year.** Recently published work by William S. Frankl and Bill Glose. Length: 1,000-5,000 words; average length: 3,000 words. Publishes short shorts. Average length: 1,000 words. Also publishes poetry. Often comments on rejected mss if requested.
How to Contact: Send complete ms with a cover letter. Include estimated word count, brief bio and list of publications. Responds in up to 6 months to mss. Accepts multiple submissions. Sample copy for $5. Guidelines for SASE or by e-mail. Reviews novels, short story collections and nonfiction books of interest to writers.
Payment/Terms: Pays 1 contributor's copy; additional copies $3.50. Pays on publication for first North American serial rights. Sends galleys to author. Not copyrighted. Sponsors contest. Send for guidelines.
Advice: "Fiction we publish has to grab me and make me care what will or won't happen to the characters. Write, rewrite and rewrite again. After all that, keep on submitting. A rejection never killed anyone."

◪ ANTHOLOGY, P.O. Box 4411, Mesa AZ 85211-4411. (480)461-8200. E-mail: lisa@anthology.org. Website: www.anthologymagazine.com (includes guidelines and links to literary sites). **Contact:** Elissa Harris, prose editor. Magazine: 8½×11; 20-28 pages; 20 lb. paper; 60-100 lb. cover stock; illustrations; photos. "Our intended audience is anyone who likes to read good fiction." Bimonthly. Estab. 1994. Circ. 500-1,000.
Needs: Adventure, children's/juvenile (5-9 and 10-12 years); fantasy (science fantasy, sword and sorcery), humor/satire, literary, mystery/suspense (amateur sleuth, police procedural, private eye/hardboiled), science fiction (hard science, soft/sociological). No erotica or graphic horror. Receives 20-30 unsolicited mss/month. Accepts 2-3 mss/issue; 12-18 mss/

year. Publishes ms 6-12 months after acceptance. **Publishes 8-10 new writers/year.** Recently published work by Elisha Porat, Kent Robinson and Sarah Mlynowski. Length: 3,000-6,000 words average. Publishes short shorts. Also publishes poetry.

How to Contact: Send complete ms with a cover letter. Include estimated word count. Responds in 1 month to queries; 2 months to mss. Send SASE for reply, return of ms or send disposable copy of ms. Accepts simultaneous submissions. Sample copy for $3.95. Guidelines for SASE. Reviews chapbooks and audio books.

Payment/Terms: Pays 1 contributor's copy; additional copies $2. Acquires one-time rights.

Advice: "Is there passion in the writing? Is there forethought? Will the story make an emotional connection to the reader? Send for guidelines and a sample issue. If you see that your work would not only fit into, but add something to *Anthology*, then send it."

$ ◑ ◎ **ARCHAEOLOGY**, P.O. Box 1264, Huntington WV 25714. **Contact:** fiction editor. Magazine: 8½×11; 24 pages; illustrations; photos. Authors are "archaeology writers who have a message for children and young adults." Quarterly. Estab. 1993. Circ. 10,000.

Needs: Children's/juvenile (adventure, historical, mystery, preschool, series), historical, mystery/suspense (procedural), young adult/teen (adventure, historical, mystery/suspense, series, western), archaeology. No science fiction. Receives 50 unsolicited mss/month. Accepts 4 mss/issue; 16-20 mss/year. Publishes ms 1-3 months after acceptance. Published work by Linda Lyons and Rocky Nivison. Length: 500 words minimum. Also publishes poetry. Always comments on rejected ms.

How to Contact: Send complete ms with a cover letter. Include estimated word count, bio and list of publications. Responds in 1 month to queries; 2 months to mss. Send SASE for reply, return of ms or send disposable copy of ms. Accepts simultaneous, multiple and reprint submissions. Sample copy for $10. Guidelines free.

Payment/Terms: Pays 2-5¢/word maximum and 2 contributor's copies. Pays on acceptance for first rights. Sends prepublication galleys to author.

Advice: "Guidelines are the best reference to knowing if a manuscript or filler is acceptable for a magazine. Writers' time and resources can be saved by submitting their work to publications that need their style of writing. Guidelines for *Archaeology* are sent for a SASE."

$ ◑ ◎ ▼ **ARTEMIS MAGAZINE, Science and Fiction for a Space-Faring Age**, 1380 East 17th St., Suite 201, Brooklyn NY 11230-6011. E-mail: magazine@lrcpubs.com. Website: www.lrcpublications.com (includes writer's guidelines, names of editors, reviews, author information, letters, news, etc.). **Contact:** Ian Randal Strock, editor. Magazine: 8½×11; 64 pages; glossy; illustrations. "The magazine is an even mix of science and fiction. We are a proud sponsor of the Artemis Project, which is constructing a commercial, manned moon base. We publish science articles for the intelligent layman, and near-term, near-Earth hard science fiction stories." Quarterly. Estab. 1999.

● Short stories published in *Artemis* have been nominated for Hugo and Nebula awards, and have been named to the Year's Best Science Fiction 6.

Needs: Adventure, science fiction, thriller/espionage. No fantasy, inspirational. Receives 200 unsolicited mss/month. Accepts 4-7 mss/issue. Publishes ms 3-12 months after acceptance. **Publishes 4 new writers/year.** Recently published work by Joseph J. Lazzaro, Fred Lerner, Ron Collins, Linda Dunn, Stanley Schmidt and Jack Williamson. Length: 1-15,000 words; average length: 2,000-8,000 words. Publishes short shorts. Also publishes poetry. Often comments on rejected ms.

How to Contact: Send complete ms with a cover letter. Include estimated word count, 1-3-paragraph bio, Social Security number, list of publications. Responds in 1 month to mss. Send a disposable copy of ms with SASE for reply. *Submissions sent without SASE will not be read.* Sample copy for $5 and a 9×12 SAE with 4 first-class stamps. Guidelines for SASE. Reviews novels, short story collections and nonfiction books of interest to writers and readers. Send books to editor.

Payment/Terms: Pays 3-5¢/word and 3 contributor's copies. Pays on acceptance for first rights. Sends prepublication galleys to author.

Advice: "Write the best possible story you can. Read a lot of fiction that you like, and reread it a few times. (If it doesn't hold up to rereading, it might not be so great. And don't give me any rip-offs of current television shows, video or role-playing games, or movies.) Then go over your story again, and make it even better. Remember that neatness counts when you prepare your manuscript (also, knowledge of the English language and grammar, and the concepts of fiction). Then send it to the magazine that publishes fiction most like the story you've written. Remember that you're up against many hundreds of manuscripts for a very few slots in the magazine. Make your story absolutely fantastic. In my case, a science fiction story must contain both science and fiction. Remember that, to be interesting to the reader, your story will probably be about the most important moment or event in the character's life."

🌐 **$** ◎ **AUREALIS**, Australian Fantasy and Science Fiction, P.O. Box 2164, Mt. Waverley, Victoria 3149 Australia. Website: www.sf.org.au/aurealis (includes writer's guidelines, names of editors, interviews with authors, forum,

---

INTERESTED IN A PARTICULAR GENRE? Check our sections for: **Mystery/ Suspense**, page 74; **Romance**, page 86; **Science Fiction/Fantasy & Horror**, page 100.

competitions, market news, online bookshop). **Contact:** Keith Stevenson, fiction editor. "*Aurealis* promotes the best in science fiction, fantasy and horror to an ever-widening audience in Australia and worldwide." Semiannually. Circ. 2,500.

Needs: Publishes 7 stories/issue: science fiction, fantasy and horror short stories. **Publishes 4 new writers/year.** Recently published work by Robert Hood, Richard Harland, Cory Daniells and Robert N. Stephenson. Length: 2,000-8,000 words.

How to Contact: "No reprints; no stories accepted elsewhere. Send one story at a time." Accepts submissions on disk. Guidelines for SAE with IRC or visit our website. Sample copy for $10 (Aus).

Payment/Terms: Pays 2-6¢ (Aus)/word and contributor's copy.

Advice: "We want original concepts, strong/believable characters, satisfying denouements, tightly written fiction. Look for new perspectives, write economically, and show real people in fantastic situations."

$ ⬛ ◎ ⬛ THE BARK, The Modern Dog Culture Magazine, The Bark, Inc., 2810 Eighth, Berkeley CA 94710. (510)704-0827. Fax: (510)704-0933. E-mail: editor@thebark.com. Website: www.thebark.com. **Contact:** Claudia Kawczynska, editor-in-chief. Magazine: 8½×11; 96 pages; matte gloss paper; illustrations; photos. "We are the only cultural/literary arts publication for the modern dog lover. We explore the unique bond between ourselves and our dogs." Quarterly. Estab. 1997. Circ. 75,000. Member, IPA.

● *The Bark* has received an *Utne Reader* Alternative Press award in lifestyle coverage.

Needs: Adventure, children's/juvenile (adventure, animal), comics/graphic novels, feminist, gay, humor/satire, literary, short story collections. Would like to see more fiction which deals with "dogs as an archetype—not breed-specific." Receives 15 unsolicited mss/month. Publishes ms 6 months after acceptance. **Publishes 10 new writers/year.** Recently published work by Ann Patchett, Rick Bass and Maeve Brennan. Length: 500-2,000 words; average length: 1,200 words. Publishes short shorts. Also publishes literary essays and poetry.

How to Contact: Query with clips of published work. Include estimated word count, brief bio, Social Security number and list of publications. Responds in 6 months to queries and mss. Send a disposable copy of ms and #10 SASE for reply only. Accepts simultaneous submissions, previously published work and multiple submissions. Sample copy for $5. Guidelines for SASE or by e-mail. Reviews novels, short story collections and nonfiction books of interest to writers.

Payment/Terms: Compensation varies by word count. Also pays free subscription to the magazine and contributor's copies. Pays on publication for first rights.

$ ⬛ BASEBALL, P.O. Box 1264, Huntington WV 25714. Magazine: 8½×11; illustrations; photos. Quarterly. Estab. 1998. Circ. 10,000.

Needs: Children's/juvenile (sports), young adult/teen (sports), baseball. Would like to see more history. Length: 500 words minimum. Also publishes poetry. Often comments on rejected ms.

How to Contact: Send complete ms with a cover letter. Include estimated word count, bio and list of publications. Responds in 1 month to queries; 2 months to mss. Send SASE for reply, return of ms or send disposable copy of ms. Accepts simultaneous and reprint submissions. Sample copy for $10. Guidelines free.

Payment/Terms: Pays 2-5¢/word maximum and contributor's copies. Pays on acceptance for first rights. Sends prepublication galleys to author.

$ ⬛ BRIDAL GUIDES, P.O. Box 1264, Huntington WV 25714. **Contact:** fiction editor. Magazine: 8½×11; illustrations; photos. "*Bridal Guides* emphasis is on wedding planning, primarily for Christians of any denomination. We provide free material for Christian writers' groups on request." Quarterly. Estab. 1993. Circ. 10,000.

Needs: Children's/juvenile, romance, young adult/teen (romance); the emphasis is on weddings. Would like to see more romance for Christians and children's Christian stories. Receives 25 unsolicited mss/month. Accepts 1-4 mss/issue; 24-30 mss/year. Publishes ms 1-3 months after acceptance. **Publishes 12 new writers/year.** Length: 500 words minimum. Also publishes poetry. Always comments on rejected ms.

How to Contact: Send complete ms with a cover letter. Include estimated word count, bio and list of publications. Responds in 1 month to queries; 2 months to mss. Send SASE for reply, return of ms or send disposable copy of ms. Accepts simultaneous and reprint submissions. Sample copy for $10. Guidelines free.

Payment/Terms: Pays 2-5¢/word and 2 contributor's copies. Pays on acceptance for first rights. Sends prepublication galleys to author.

⬛ $ ⬛ CHALLENGING DESTINY, New Fantasy & Science Fiction, Crystalline Sphere Publishing, R.R. #6, St. Marys Ontario N4X 1C8 Canada. E-mail: csp@golden.net. Website: home.golden.net/~csp/ (includes previews of published and upcoming magazines, writer's guidelines, interviews with authors, reviews of books, movies, soundtracks and games, links to other websites). **Contact:** David M. Switzer, editor. Magazine: 8×5¼; 120 pages; Kallima 10 pt cover; illustrations. "We publish all kinds of science fiction and fantasy short stories." Quarterly. Estab. 1997. Circ. 300.

Needs: Fantasy, science fiction. No horror, short short stories. Receives 40 unsolicited mss/month. Accepts 6 mss/issue, 24 mss/year. Publishes ms 1-3 months after acceptance. **Publishes 6 new writers/year.** Recently published work by Hugh Cook, Rudy Kremberg and D.K. Latta. Length: 2,000-10,000 words; average length: 6,000 words. Often comments on rejected mss.

How to Contact: Send complete ms with a cover letter. Include estimated word count. Responds in 1 month to queries; 2 months to mss. Send SAE and IRC for reply, return of ms or send disposable copy of ms. Accepts simultaneous submissions. Sample copy for $6.50. Guidelines for 1 IRC. Reviews novels and short story collections. Send books to James Schellenberg.

Payment/Terms: Pays 1¢/word plus 2 contributor's copies. Acquires first North American serial rights. Sends galleys to author.

Advice: "Manuscripts with a good story and interesting characters stand out. We look for fiction that entertains and makes you think. If you're going to write short fiction, you need to read lots of it. Don't reinvent the wheel. Use your own voice."

○ **THE CIRCLE MAGAZINE**, Circle Publications, 173 Grandview Rd., Wernersville PA 19565. Phone/fax: (610)670-7017. E-mail: circlemag@aol.com. Website: www.circlemagazine.com (includes guidelines, poetry and fiction not in print issue, links, etc.) **Contact:** Penny Talbert, editor. Magazine: 8½×5½; 48-52 pages; white offset paper; illustrations; photos. "*The Circle* is an eclectic mix of culture and subculture. Our goal is to provide the reader with thought-provoking reading that they remember." Quarterly.

Needs: Adventure, experimental, humor/satire, literary, mainstream, mystery/suspense, New Age, psychic/supernatural/occult, romance, science fiction, thriller/espionage. No religious fiction. Receives 100 unsolicited mss/month. Accepts 3-5 mss/issue; 12-20 mss/year. Publishes ms 1-4 months after acceptance. Recently published work by David McDaniel, Bart Stewart, Ace Boggess and Stephen Forney. Length: 2,000-6,000 words; average length: 3,500 words. Publishes short shorts. Average length: 1,200 words. Also publishes literary essays, literary criticism and poetry. Sometimes comments on rejected mss.

How to Contact: Send complete ms with a cover letter. Accepts submissions by e-mail, fax and disk. E-mail submissions should be in body of text or attached as a text file. Include estimated word count, brief bio and list of publications. Responds in 1 month to queries; 4 months to mss. Send SASE (or IRC) for return of ms or send a disposable copy of ms and #10 SASE for reply only. Accepts simultaneous submissions, previously published work and multiple submissions. Sample copy for $4. Guidelines on website.

Payment/Terms: Pays 1 contributor's copy; additional copies $4. Pays on publication for one-time and electronic rights.

Advice: "The most important thing is that submitted fiction keeps our attention and interest. The most typical reason for rejection: bad endings! Proofread your work and send it in compliance with our guidelines."

○ **COCHRAN'S CORNER**, 1003 Tyler Court, Waldorf MD 20602-2964. Phone/fax: (301)870-1664. President: Ada Cochran. **Contact:** Jeanie Saunders, editor. Magazine: 5½×8; 52 pages. "We publish fiction, nonfiction and poetry. Our only requirement is no strong language." For a "family" audience. Quarterly magazine. Estab. 1986. Circ. 500.

Needs: Adventure, children's/juvenile, historical, horror, humor/satire, mystery/suspense, religious/inspirational, romance, science fiction, young adult/teen (10-18 years). Would like to see more mystery and romance fiction. "Mss must be free from language you wouldn't want your/our children to read." Plans a special fiction issue. Receives 50 mss/month. Accepts 4 mss/issue; 8 mss/year. Publishes ms by the next issue after acceptance. **Publishes approximately 30 new writers/year.** Published work by James Hughes, Ellen Sandry, James Bennet, Susan Lee and Judy Demers. Length: 300-1,000 words; 500 words preferred. Also publishes literary essays, literary criticism, poetry.

How to Contact: "Right now we are forced to limit acceptance to *subscribers only.*" Send complete ms with cover letter. Responds in 3 weeks to queries; 6-8 weeks to mss. SASE for manuscript. Accepts simultaneous and reprint submissions. Sample copy for $5, 9×12 SAE and 90¢ postage. Guidelines for #10 SASE.

Payment/Terms: Pays in contributor's copies. Acquires one-time rights.

Advice: "I feel the quality of fiction is getting better. The public is demanding a good read, instead of having sex or violence carry the story. I predict that fiction has a good future. We like to print the story as the writer submits it if possible. This way writers can compare their work with their peers and take the necessary steps to improve and go on to sell to bigger magazines. Stories from the heart desire a place to be published. We try to fill that need. Be willing to edit yourself. Polish your manuscript before submitting to editors."

🄽 ◎ **COLD-DRILL MAGAZINE**, English Dept., Boise State University, 1910 University Dr., Boise ID 83725. (208)426-3862. **Editor:** Malia Collins. Faculty Advisor: Mitchell Wieland. Magazine: perfect-bound; illustrations; photos. For adult audiences. Annual. Estab. 1970. Circ. 300.

Needs: "The 2003 issue will not have a theme; it will be open to all forms of writing and artwork." Length: determined by submissions.

How to Contact: Send ms with SASE.

Payment/Terms: Pays in contributor's copies. Acquires first rights.

🄽 **COMMUNITIES MAGAZINE**, 52 Willow St., Marion NC 28752. Phone/fax: (828)652-8517. E-mail: communities@ic.org. Website: www.ic.org/ (includes samples of articles, ads, from current and back issues). **Contact:** Diana Christian, editor. Guest editors change with each issue. "Articles on intentional communities—cohousing, ecovillages, urban group houses, student co-ops, rural communes, land-trust communities, and other forms of community (including non-residential)—as well as worker co-ops and workplace democracy. Written for people generally interested in intentional community and cooperative ventures, current and former community members, and people seeking to form or join an intentional community or co-op venture." Quarterly magazine. Estab. 1973. Circ. 4,000.

Needs: "Utopian" stories, science fiction (soft/sociological). "Stories set in intentional communities or cooperatively run organizations." Each issue focused around a theme. Accepts "1-2 mss/year (more if we got them)." **Publishes 25-30 new writers/year.** Length: 750-3,000 words.

How to Contact: "To submit an article, please first send for writer's guidelines." Accepts queries/mss by e-mail and fax. Responds in 1 month to queries; 6-8 weeks to mss. Accepts simultaneous and previously published submissions. Sample copy for $6. *Communities Magazine*, 138 Twin Oaks Rd., Louisa VA 23093.

Payment/Terms: Pays 1 year subscription (4 issues) or 4 contributor's copies. Acquires first North American rights.

Advice: "We receive too many articles and stories which are completely off topic (in which the writer assumes we are about community in the generic sense, i.e., "community spirit," a neighborhood or town), by people who have no idea what an intentional community is, and/or who have never seen the magazine. We ask that writers read a sample issue first. We like the personal touch; concrete, visual, tightly written, upbeat, or offbeat message; short. No abstract, negative or loosely written, long fiction."

CREATIVE WITH WORDS PUBLICATIONS, Creative With Words Publications, P.O. Box 223226, Carmel CA 93922. Fax: (831)655-8627. E-mail: cwwpub@usa.net. Website: http://members.tripod.com/CreativeWithWords. **Contact:** Brigitta Geltrich, publisher/editor. Magazine: 8½×5½; 50-70 pages; illustrations; photos. "We want writers to look at the world from a different perspective, research topics thoroughly, be creative, apply brevity, tell the story from a character's point of view, tighten dialogue, be less descriptive, proofread before submitting and be patient." Monthly. Estab. 1975.

Needs: Children's/juvenile (animal, historical), historical (general), humor/satire, young adult/teen (adventure, historical). "We are a family publication—no violence, horror or overly-religious work." Upcoming themes: Animals, School, Nature/Season, Folklore. Receives 100 unsolicited mss/month. Accepts 12 mss/year. "We accept when deadline is due; notification is within 30 days after deadline." Recently published work by Najwa Salam Brax, June K. Silconas, Steven Dotterem and David Napolin. Length: 800 words maximum; average length: 500 words "shorter ones have greater chance." Also publishes short shorts. Also publishes poetry. Sometimes comments on rejected mss.

How to Contact: Send complete ms with a cover letter with SASE. Include estimated word count. Responds in 2 months after deadline. Sample copy for $6. Guidelines for SASE or on website.

Payment/Terms: 20% reduction of cost of issue (1-9 copies), 30% reduction (10-19 copies), 40% reduction (20+ copies). Acquires first rights. Sponsors contest: The Best of the Month and Online contests.

Advice: "Read the guidelines. Write for the reader, what the reader wants to read, don't write what you want the reader to read."

DANCE, P.O. Box 1264, Huntington WV 25714. **Contact:** fiction editor. "*Dance* features stories with a multicultural or ethnic flavor that deliver a positive message." Magazine: 8½×11; illustrations; photos. Quarterly. Estab. 1993. Circ. 10,000.

Needs: Children's/juvenile, young adult/teen, dance. Receives 25 unsolicited mss/month. Accepts 4 mss/issue; 16-20 mss/year. Publishes ms 1-3 months after acceptance. **Publishes 12 new writers/year.** Length: 500 words minimum. Also publishes literary essays, criticism and poetry. Always comments on rejected ms.

How to Contact: Send complete ms with a cover letter. Include estimated word count, bio and list of publications. Responds in 1 month to queries; 2 months to mss. Send SASE for reply, return of ms or send disposable copy of ms. Accepts simultaneous and reprint submissions. Sample copy for $10. Guidelines free.

Payment/Terms: Pays 2-5¢/word and contributor's copies. Pays on acceptance for first rights. Sends prepublication galleys to author.

DARK HORIZONS, Beech House, Chapel Lane, Moulton, Cheshire CW9 8PQ England. **Contact:** Debbie Bennett, editor. Published 2 times/year. Circ. 500. Publishes 10-15 stories/issue. "We are a small press fantasy magazine. Our definition of fantasy knows no bounds, covering science, heroic, dark and light fantasy and horror fiction. We also use occasional poetry."

Needs: Fantasy, dark fantasy. No space opera, hard SF, horror. Length: 6,000-8,000 words maximum.

How to Contact: Send ms with brief cover letter and IRCs or e-mail address for return of ms. Accepts mss by e-mail and on disk. Sample copy available via website.

Payment/Terms: Pays contributor's copies.

Advice: "We look for a good story with a beginning, middle, end, and point to it."

DESCANT, Ft. Worth's Journal of Fiction and Poetry, Texas Christian University, TCU Box 297270, Ft. Worth TX 76129. (817)257-6537. Fax: (817)257-6239. E-mail: descant@tcu.edu. Website: http://eng.tcu.edu.usefulsites/descant.htm. **Contact:** Dave Kuhne, editor. Magazine: 6×9; 150 pages; acid free paper; paper cover. "*descant* seeks high quality poems and stories in both traditional and innovative form. Offers $500 poetry award and $500 fiction award for best poem and story in an issue." Annual. Estab. 1956. Circ. 750. Member, CLMP.

● Work first published in *descant* has been anthologized in *Best American Short Stories*. *descant* also sponsors the Frank O'Connor Prize for fiction ($500) and the Sandra Brown Award for best short story in an issue ($250). Write for details.

Needs: Literary. "No horror, romance, fantasy, erotica." Receives 20-30 unsolicited mss/month. Accepts 15-20 mss/year. Does not read mss May, June, July, August. Publishes ms up to 1 year after acceptance. **Publishes 50% new writers/year.** Recently published work by William Harrison, Annette Sanford, Miller Williams and John Perryman. Length: 1,000-5,000 words; average length: 2,500 words. Publishes short shorts. Also publishes poetry.

How to Contact: Send complete ms with a cover letter. Include estimated word count and brief bio. Responds in 2 months to mss. Send a disposable copy of ms and #10 SASE for reply only. Accepts simultaneous submissions. Sample copy for $6. Guidelines for SASE. by e-mail or fax.

Payment/Terms: Pays 2 contributors copies; additional copies $6. Pays on publication for one-time rights.

Advice: "We look for character and quality of prose. Send your best short work."

DREAM INTERNATIONAL/QUARTERLY, U.S. Address: Charles I. Jones, #H-1, 411 14th St., Ramona CA 92065-2769. **Contact:** Charles I. Jones, editor-in-chief. Magazine: 8½×11; 143 pages; Xerox paper; parchment cover stock; some illustrations; photos. "Although we accept material from professional writers, we encourage 'new' (unpublished) writers, as well. Our hope is to attract writers interested in dreams and the dream state. We hope to extend this interest to fantasy which is dream-related or inspired. We hope to attract readers (writers) with like interests." Quarterly. Estab. 1981. Circ. 65-100.

Needs: Confession, erotica (soft), fantasy (dream), historical, horror, humor/satire, literary, prose poem, psychic/supernatural/occult, science fiction, young adult/teen (10-18). "No material that is not dream related or dream-related fantasy. Often we receive 'dream' or 'dreams' used in the title that we find is not a dream-related piece. We would like to see submissions that deal with dreams that have an influence on the person's daily waking life. Suggestions for making dreams beneficial to the dreamer in his/her waking life. We would also like to see more submissions dealing with lucid dreaming." Receives 35-40 unsolicited mss/month. Accepts 20 mss/issue; 50-55 mss/year. Publishes ms 8 months to 3 years after acceptance. Agented fiction 1%. **Publishes 20-30 new writers/year.** Recently published work by Timothy Scott, Carmen M. Pursifull, Richard W. Sullivan and Robert Michael O'Hearn. Length: 1,000-1,500 words. Publishes short shorts. Also publishes literary essays, poetry (poetry submissions to Carmen M. Pursifull, 809 W. Maple St., Champaign IL 61820-2810. Hard copy only for poetry. No electronic submissions please! Send SASE for poetry guidelines).

How to Contact: Submit ms. Responds in 6 weeks to queries; 3 months to mss. SASE. Accepts simultaneous and reprint submissions. Sample copy for $14. Guidelines $2 with SAE and 2 first-class stamps. Subscription: $56 (1-year); $112 (2-year). "Accepted mss will not be returned unless requested at time of submission."

Payment/Terms: Pays in contributor's copy (contributors must pay $4.50 for postage and handling). Acquires first North American serial rights. Sends prepublication galleys to author on request.

Advice: "Both poetry and prose submissions must be concise and free of ramblings and typographical errors. The material should be interesting and appealing and something that our readers can relate to. New and 'unique' material always grabs our attention. Write about what you know. Make the reader stand up and take notice. Avoid rambling and stay away from clichés in your writing unless, of course, it is of a humorous nature and is purposefully done to make a point."

ELEMENTS MAGAZINE, 3534 Chimera Lane, Houston TX 77051-4240. (713)614-8389. E-mail: washington-bernard@hotmail.com. **Contact:** Bernard Washington, editor. Magazine: 8½×11; 50 pages; bonded paper; illustrations; photos. "Our audience comprises all who want a new perspective about current events, literature and the arts. We publish items from new and unpublished authors in every issue." Bimonthly. Circ. 500. Member, The Small Press Review.

Needs: Children's/juvenile (adventure, animal, easy-to-read, historical, sports), ethnic/multicultural, family saga, feminist, gay, historical (general), horror (futuristic), humor/satire, lesbian, literary, mainstream, mystery/suspense, religious (general, inspirational, religious romance), romance (contemporary, futuristic/time travel, historical, romantic suspense), science fiction (soft/sociological), western (frontier saga, traditional), young adult/teen (adventure, easy-to-read, historical, problem novels, sports, western). No child pornography. Wants to see more humorous fiction. Receives 3 unsolicited mss/month. Accepts 3 mss/issue; 36 mss/year. Publishes ms 2 months after acceptance. **Publishes 5 new writers/year.** Recently published work by Richard Robbins, Glen Laundry and Paul Truttman. Length: 500-1,000 words; average length: 800 words. Publishes short shorts. Average length: 1,500 words. Also publishes literary essays, literary criticism and poetry. Sometimes comments on rejected mss.

How to Contact: Send complete ms with a cover letter. Include estimated word count, brief bio and list of publications. Responds in 3 weeks to queries; 1 month to mss. Send SASE (or IRC) for return of ms or send a disposable copy of ms and #10 SASE for reply only. Accepts simultaneous, previously published and multiple submissions. Sample copy for 9×12 SAE with $2 postage. Guidelines for SASE. Reviews novels, short story collections and nonfiction books of interest to writers. Send review copies to Bernard Washington.

Payment/Terms: Copies for $8. Pays on publication for one-time rights.

READ 'THE BUSINESS OF FICTION WRITING' section for information on manuscript preparation, mailing tips, rights and more.

Advice: "Fiction must be written well and entertaining. A manuscript stands out for its clarity and style. Be original and write well—write something everyday and keep a positive attitude."

⬤ ◎ **THE ELOQUENT UMBRELLA,** Linn-Benton Community College, 6500 SW Pacific Blvd., Albany OR 97321-3779. (541)753-3335. E-mail: terrance.millet@linnbenton.edu. **Contact:** Terrance Millet. Magazine: illustrations; photos. "*The Eloquent Umbrella's* purpose is to showcase art, photography, poetry and prose of Linn and Benton Counties in Oregon." Annually. Estab. 1990. Circ. 500.

Needs: Regional. "No slander, pornography or other material unsuitable for community reading." Accepts 50-100 mss/issue. Deadline January 15 each year. Reads mss during winter term only; publishes in spring. Length: 2,000 words maximum. Publishes short shorts. Also publishes literary essays, literary criticism and poetry.

How to Contact: Send complete ms with cover letter. Include 1- to 5-line bio. Responds in 6 weeks to mss. SASE for return of ms or send a disposable copy of ms. Accepts simultaneous and multiple submissions. Sample copy for $2 and 8½×11 SAE.

Payment/Terms: Rights remain with author.

Advice: "The magazine is created by a collective editorial board and production team in a literary publication class."

⬤ **ENIGMA,** Audacious/Bottle Press, 402 South 25 St., Philadelphia PA 19146. (215)545-8694. E-mail: sydx@att.net. **Contact:** Syd Bradford, publisher. Magazine: 8½×11; 100 pages; 24 lb. white paper; illustrations; photos. "Everything is done—except printing—by me, the publisher. No editors, etc. Eclectic—I publish articles, fiction, poetry." Quarterly. Estab. 1989. Circ. 90.

Needs: Adventure, experimental, fantasy, historical, horror, humor/satire. "No sentimental or religious fiction." Accepts 30 mss/issue. Publishes ms 3 months after acceptance. **Publishes 20 new writers/year.** Recently published work by Richard A. Robbins, Eleanor Leslie and Diana K. Rubin. Length: 1,000-3,000 words; average length: 1,500 words. Publishes short shorts. Also publishes literary essays, literary criticism and poetry.

How to Contact: Send complete ms with a cover letter. Accepts submissions by e-mail. Include brief bio. Send SASE (or IRC) for return of ms. Sample copy for $6. Guidelines for SASE. Reviews novels, short story collections and nonfiction books of interest to writers.

Payment/Terms: Pays 1 contributor's copy; additional copies $6, plus $1.30 postage. Sends galleys to author.

Advice: "I look for imaginative writing, excellent movement, fine imagery, stunning characters."

⬤ **EYES,** 3610 North Doncaster Ct., Apt. X7, Saginaw MI 48603-1862. (517)498-4112. E-mail: fjm3eyes@aol.com. Website: http://members.aol.com/eyeonweb/index.html (includes guidelines, contact information, stories and reviews). **Contact:** Frank J. Mueller, III, editor. Magazine: 8½×11; 40+ pages. "No specific theme. Speculative fiction and surrealism most welcome. For a general, educated, not necessarily literary audience." Estab. 1991.

Needs: Contemporary, horror (psychological), mainstream, ghost story. "Especially looking for speculative fiction and surrealism. Would like to see more ghost stories, student writing. Dark fantasy OK, but not preferred." No sword/sorcery, overt science fiction, pornography, preachiness or children's fiction. Accepts 5-9 mss/issue. Publishes ms up to 1 year or longer after acceptance. **Publishes 15-20 writers/year.** Length: 6,000 words maximum. Sometimes comments on rejected mss.

How to Contact: Query first or send complete ms. A short bio is optional. Responds in 1 month to queries; 3 months or longer to mss. SASE. No simultaneous submissions. Sample copy for $6; extras $4. Subscriptions $20/4 issues. (Checks to Frank J. Mueller III.) Guidelines for #10 SASE.

Payment/Terms: Pays 1 contributor's copy. Acquires one-time rights.

Advice: "Pay attention to character. A strong plot, while important, may not be enough alone to get you in *Eyes*. Atmosphere and mood are also important. Please proofread. If you have a manuscript you like enough to see in *Eyes*, send it to me. Above all, don't let rejections discourage you. I would encourage the purchase of a sample to get an idea of what I'm looking for. Read stories by authors such as Algernon Blackwood, Nathaniel Hawthorne, Shirley Jackson, Henry James and Poe. Also, please write for information concerning chapbooks."

▣ **$FANTASTIC STORIES OF THE IMAGINATION,** DNA Publications, Inc., P.O. Box 329, Brightwaters NY 11781. (631)666-5276. E-mail: fantasticstories@dnapublications.com. Website: www.dnapublications.com. **Contact:** Edward J. McFadden III, editor. Magazine: 50-72 pages; glossy paper; four color glossy cover; illustrations. "We feature science fiction in all its forms. While elements in the story must be science fiction/fantasy oriented, mixing genres is permissible." Estab. 1992. Circ. 6,000.

Needs: Fantasy (space fantasy, sword and sorcery, dark), horror (dark fantasy, futuristic), science fiction (hard science/technological, soft/sociological). Receives 400-500 unsolicited mss/month. Accepts 8-10 mss/issue; 32-40/year. Publishes ms 1-2 years after acceptance. Agented fiction 20%. **Publishes 5-10 new writers/year.** Length: 2,000-15,000 words; average length: 6,000 words. Also publishes poetry. Sometimes comments on rejected ms.

How to Contact: Send complete ms with cover letter. Include estimated word count, brief bio, Social Security number, list of publications. Send SASE for return of ms or disposable copy of ms and SASE for reply only. Sample copy for $6. Guidelines for SASE or on website.

Payment/Terms: Pays .01-.05¢/word and 1 contributor's copy. Pays 60 days after publication for first North American serial rights and one-time non-exclusive reprint rights for Best Of anthology.

N $ ◨ ◎ THE FIVE STONES, Newsletter for Small Churches, ABCUSA, P.O. Box 851, Valley Forge PA 19482-0851. (800)ABC3USA. E-mail: ruthann.glover@abc-usa.org. **Contact:** Tont Pappas, editor. Magazine specializing in small church issues: 8½×11; 16 pages; illustrations; photos. "*The Five Stones* features an exclusive focus on issues related to small congregations." Quarterly. Estab. 1980. Circ. 500.

Needs: Ethnic/multicultural (general), historical (religion), religious (inspirational). Receives 1 unsolicited ms/month. Accepts 4 mss/year. Publishes ms 1 year after acceptance. **Publishes 5 new writers/year.** Length: 300-3,000 words; average length: 1,000 words. Publishes short shorts. Sometimes comments on rejected mss.

How to Contact: Send complete ms with a cover letter or query first. Accepts submissions by e-mail, fax and disk. Include estimated word count and brief bio. Responds in 4 months to queries; 8 months to mss. Send SASE for return of ms or send a disposable copy of ms and #10 SASE for reply only. Accepts simultaneous, previously published and multiple submissions. Sample copy free with SASE. Guidelines for SASE or by fax. Reviews novels, short story collections and nonfiction books of interest to writers. Send review copies to the editor.

Payment/Terms: Pays $5 (maximum) and 2 contributors copies; additional copies $3. Pays on publication. Not copyrighted.

Advice: "Fiction must apply to life in small congregations/towns/neigborhoods."

N $ FUN FOR KIDZ, Bluffton News Publishing and Printing Company, P.O. Box 227, 103 N. Main St., Bluffton OH 45817-0227. (419)358-4610. Fax: (419)358-5027. Website: www.funforkidz.com (includes excerpts, contact information, subscription information). **Contact:** Virginia Edwards, associate editor. Magazine: 7×8; 49 pages; illustrations; photographs. "*Fun for Kidz* focuses on activity. The children are encouraged to solve problems, explore, and develop character. Target age: 6-13 years." Bimonthly. Estab. 2002. Circ. 1,000.

Needs: Children's juvenile (adventure, animal, easy-to-read, fantasy, historical, mystery, preschool, series, sports). Upcoming themes include: Bugs; Oceans; Animals; Camping; Fun with Stars; Healthy Fun; Summer Splash; In the Mountains; Fun with Words. List of upcoming themes for SASE. Accepts 10 mss/issue; 60 mss/year. Length: 3 pages for fiction. Publishes short shorts. Also publishes poetry. Always comments on rejected mss.

How to Contact: Send complete ms with cover letter. Include estimated word count and brief bio. Responds to queries in 6 weeks; mss in 6 months. Send SASE for return of ms or disposable copy of ms with SASE for reply only. Accepts simultaneous and multiple submissions. Sample copy for $4. Guidelines for SASE.

Payment/Terms: Pays 5¢/word and 1 contributor's copy. Pays on publication for first rights.

Advice: "Work needs to be appropriate for a children's publication ages 6-13 years. Request a theme list so story submitted will work into an upcoming issue."

N $ ◨ ◎ GATEWAY S-F MAGAZINE, Stories of Science & Faith, GateWay Publishing House, 1833 S. Westmoorland Ave., Los Angeles CA 90006-4621. (213)749-1044. E-mail: gateway59@hotmail.com. Website: www.geocities.com/scifieditor/index.html (includes editorial, guidelines, guestpage, comics page, book reviews, serials and longer fiction works). **Contact:** John A.M. Darnell, assistant editor. Christian SF magazine: 5½×8½; 72 pages; white bond paper; glossy cover; illustrations. "We are a print publication with a web edition, specializing in hard science fiction plots with Christian themes." Quarterly. Estab. 2000. Circ. 250.

Needs: Fantasy (space fantasy), horror (futuristic), religious (religious fantasy, religious mystery/suspense, religious thriller), romance (futuristic/time travel), science fiction (hard science/technological, soft/sociological, Christian), young adult/teen (fantasy/science fiction). Receives 20-30 unsolicited mss/month. Accepts 20 mss/issue; 80 mss/year. Publishes ms 6 months after acceptance. **Publishes 40 new writers/year.** Length: 500-7,500 words; average length: 2,500 words. Publishes short shorts. Average length: 1,200 words. Always comments on rejected mss.

How to Contact: "We prefer e-mail submission with MS Word.doc files as attachments." Include estimated word count, brief bio, postal address, e-mail address phone number. Accepts previously published submissions. Sample copy for $7.50. Guidelines for SASE. by e-mail or on website.

Payment/Terms: Pays $5-10 and 1 contributors copy; additional copies $5. Pays on publication for first North American serial and electronic rights. Not copyrighted.

Advice: "We look for good, solid writing, no typos or weak grammar, hard sf plots, Christian themes, good book, rapid advance of plot, no experimental forms. Visit us online for a sense of what we publish."

$ ◨ GHOST TOWN, P.O. Box 1264, Huntington WV 25714. **Contact:** fiction editor. Magazine: 8½×11; illustrations; photos. Quarterly. Estab. 1999.

Needs: Children's/juvenile (historical), historical (ghost towns), western, young adult/teen (historical). No science fiction. Wants to see more "westerns set in true-to-life ghost towns." Receives 50 unsolicited mss/month. Accepts 4 mss/issue; 16-20 mss/year. Publishes ms 1-3 months after acceptance. **Publishes 12 new writers/year.** Length: 500 words minimum. Also publishes poetry. Always comments on rejected ms.

How to Contact: Send complete ms with a cover letter. Include estimated word count, bio and list of publications. Responds in 1 month to queries; 2 months to mss. Send SASE for reply, return of ms or send disposable copy of ms. Accepts simultaneous and reprint submissions. Sample copy for $10. Guidelines free.

Payment/Terms: Pays 2-5¢/word and contributor's copies. Pays on acceptance for first rights. Sends prepublication galleys to author.

Advice: "Photographs with ms are a plus."

GLOBAL TAPESTRY JOURNAL, BB Books, 1 Spring Bank, Longsight Rd., Copster Green, Blackburn, Lancashire BB1 9EU England. **Contact:** Dave Cunliffe, editor. Alexander Shaw, fiction editor. Global Tapestry Journal is a manifestation of exciting creativity." Magazine. Limited press run: 1,000-1,500/issue.

Needs: "Post-underground with avant-garde, experimental, alternative, counterculture, psychedelic, mystical, anarchist etc. fiction for a bohemian and counterculture audience." No genre. **Publishes 20-50 new writers/year.** Published fiction by Lain Sinclair, Chris Challis, John Power and Jeff Cloves.

How to Contact: Accepts unsolicited mss. SAE, IRCs. Responds in 2-6 weeks.

Payment/Terms: Pays contributor's copy. Sample copy for $4 (Sterling Cheque, British Money Order or dollar currency).

$ HARDBOILED, Gryphon Books, P.O. Box 209, Brooklyn NY 11228-0209. Website: www.gryphonbooks.c om. **Contact:** Gary Lovisi, editor. Magazine: Digest-sized; 100 pages; offset paper; color cover; illustrations. Publishes "cutting edge, hard, noir fiction with impact! Query on nonfiction and reviews." Quarterly. Estab. 1988.

Needs: Mystery/suspense (private eye, police procedural, noir). No "pastches, violence for the sake of violence." Wants to see more nonprivate eye hard-boiled. Receives 40-60 mss/month. Accepts 10-20 mss/year. Publishes ms within 6 months-2 years of acceptance. **Published 5-10 new writers/year.** Published work by Andrew Vachss, Stephen Solomita, Joe Hensley, Mike Black. Length: 2,000-3,000 words. Sometimes comments on rejected mss and recommends other markets.

How to Contact: Query first or send complete ms with cover letter. Accepts submissions by fax and on disk. Query with SASE only on anything over 3,000 words. No full-length novels. Responds in 1 month to queries; 2 months to mss. SASE. Accepts simultaneous submissions, but query first. Sample copy for $8. Subscriptions are 5 issues for $35.

Payment/Terms: Pays $5-50 and 2 contributor's copies. Pays on publication for first North American serial rights. Copyright reverts to author.

Advice: By "hardboiled" the editor does not mean rehashing of pulp detective fiction from the 1940s and 1950s but, rather, realistic, gritty material. We look for good writing, memorable characters, intense situations. Lovisi could be called a pulp fiction "afficionado," however. He also publishes *Paperback Parade* and holds an annual vintage paperback fiction convention each year.

HEIST MAGAZINE, P.O. Box 2, Newcastle University Union, Callaghan NSW 2308 Australia. 0419-31-MOCK. E-mail: heist@mockfrog.com. Website: www.mockfrog.com/heist (includes writer's guidelines). **Contact:** Matthew Ward, editor. Magazine: 32 pages; bond 80 gsm paper; 150 gsm cover; illustrations; photos. "*Heist Magazine* aims to capture the essense of male-dom through writing and art." Quarterly. Estab. 1998. Circ. 1,000.

• *Heist* has received the Jethro Californian Memorial Prize for Short Stories, 2000. Considers work by men only.

Needs: Adventure, erotica, experimental, family saga, fantasy (space fantasy, sword and sorcery), historical (general), horror (dark fantasy, futuristic, psychological, supernatural), humor satire, literary, mainstream, military/war, mystery/suspense (amateur sleuth, police procedural, private eye/hardboiled, Bindaburra), short story collections, thriller/espionage (amateur sleuth, police procedural, private eye/hardboiled, Bindaburra), western (frontier saga, traditional), men. "We do not want chapters from unpublished novels. We want short stories in their entirety. Anything that captures the essence of what it is like to be a man. And that does not have to mean tales of guys going into the woods, standing around a roaring fire and rubbing bear fat into their stomachs." Receives 50 unsolicited mss/month. Accepts 15 mss/issue; 60 mss/year. Publishes ms 3 months after acceptance. **50% of works published are by new writers.** Recently published work by Rick Mager, Dick Robin and Daniel S. Irwin. Length: 500-2,000 words. Also publishes poetry. Sometimes comments on rejected mss.

How to Contact: Send complete ms with a cover letter. Accepts queries/mss by e-mail. Include estimated word count, 50 word bio, list of publications, SASE. Responds in 2 weeks to queries; 2 months to mss. Send SASE for reply, return of ms or send a disposable copy of ms. Accepts simultaneous submissions. Sample copy for $5, A4 envelope and IRCs. Guidelines available on website.

Payment/Terms: Pays 1 contributor's copy; additional copies $5. Pays on publication for first rights. Sometimes sends galleys to author.

Advice: Looks for work "accessible to most readers, not too obscure. Enjoyable. *Heist* is a fiction mag. We usually get too much poetry, so send fiction. Don't send a chapter from that (as yet) unpublished novel. Try to send a slice of life! Read as many of other people's short stories as you can (try Chandler, Carver et al)."

HURRICANE ALICE, A Feminist Quarterly, Hurricane Alice Fn., Inc., Dept. of English, Rhode Island College, Providence RI 02908. (401)456-8377. E-mail: mreddy@ric.edu. **Contact:** Maureen Reddy, executive editor. Fiction is collectively edited. Tabloid: 11 × 17; 12-16 pages; newsprint stock; illustrations; photos. "We look for feminist fictions with a certain analytic snap, for serious readers, seriously interested in emerging forms of feminist art/artists." Quarterly. Estab. 1983. Circ. 600-700.

Needs: Experimental, feminist, gay, humor/satire, lesbian, science fiction, translations, work by young women. "No coming-out stories, defloration stories, abortion stories, dreary realism. Would like to see more speculative and experimental fiction." Receives 30 unsolicited mss/month. Publishes 8-10 stories annually. Publishes mss up to 1 year after acceptance. **Publishes 4-5 new writers/year.** Published work by Vickie Nelson, Mary Sharratt and Kathryn Duhamel. Length: up to 3,500 words maximum. Publishes short shorts. Occasionally comments on rejected mss.

How to Contact: Send complete ms with cover letter. "A brief biographical statement is never amiss. Writers should be sure to tell us if a piece was commissioned by one of the editors." Responds in 9 months. SASE for response. Accepts simultaneous submissions, but must be identified as such. Sample copy for $2.50, 11×14 SAE and 2 first-class stamps.
Payment/Terms: Pays 6 contributor's copies. Acquires one-time rights.
Advice: "Fiction is a craft. Just because something happened, it isn't a story; it becomes a story when you transform it through your art, your craft."

HYBOLICS, Da Literature and Culture of Hawaii, Hybolics, Inc., P.O. Box 3016, Aiea HI 96701. (808)366-1272. E-mail: hybolics@lava.net. Website: www.hybolics.com (includes writer's guidelines and back issue ordering information). **Contact:** Lee Tonouchi, co-editor. Magazine: 8½×11; 80 pages; 80 lb. coated paper; cardstock cover; illustrations; photos. "We publish da kine creative and critical work dat get some kine connection to Hawaii." Annual. Estab. 1999. Circ. 1,000.
Needs: Comics/graphic novels, ethnic/multicultural, experimental, humor/satire, literary. "No genre fiction. Wants to see more sudden fiction." Receives 5 unsolicited mss/month. Accepts 10 mss/year. Publishes ms 1 year after acceptance. **Publishes 3 new writers/year.** Recently published work by Darrell Lum, Rodney Morales, Lee Cataluna and Lisa Kanae. Length: 1,000-8,000 words; average length: 4,000 words. Publishes short shorts. Also publishes literary essays, literary criticism and poetry.
How to Contact: Send complete ms with a cover letter. Include estimated word count, brief bio and list of publications. Responds in 5 weeks to queries; 5 months to mss. Send SASE (or IRC) for return of ms or send a disposable copy of ms and #10 SASE for reply only. Sample copy for $13.35. Guidelines for SASE.
Payment/Terms: Pays 2 contributor's copies; additional copies $7.25. Pays on publication for first rights.

$ ◙ ◎ IN THE FAMILY, The Magazine for Queer People and Their Loved Ones, 7850 N. Silverbell, Suite 114-188, Tucson AZ 85743. (520)579-8043. E-mail: lmarkowitz@aol.com. Website: www.inthefamily.com (includes writer's guidelines, bulletin board, overview of magazine content and back issue themes). Editor: Laura Markowitz. **Contact:** Helena Lipstadt, fiction editor. Magazine: 8½×11, 32 pages; coated paper; coated cover; illustrations; photos. "We use a therapy lens to explore the diverse relationships and families of lesbians, gays, bisexuals and their straight relations." Quarterly. Estab. 1995. Circ. 2,000.
Needs: Ethnic/multicultural, feminist, gay, humor/satire, lesbian. No erotica or science fiction. Would like to see more short stories. List of upcoming themes available for SASE. Receives 25 unsolicited mss/month. Accepts 1 ms/issue; 4 mss/year. Publishes ms 3-6 months after acceptance. **Publishes 6 new writers/year.** Recently published work by Lori Soderlind and Irene Marshall. Length: 2,500 words maximum; average length: 2,000 words. Publishes short shorts. Also publishes literary essays and poetry. Sometimes comments on rejected mss.
How to Contact: Send complete ms with a cover letter. Include estimated word count and 40-word bio. Responds in 6 weeks to queries and mss. Send SASE for reply, return of ms or send disposable copy of ms. Accepts multiple submissions. Sample copy for $6. Guidelines free. Reviews published novels and short story collections. Send books to Book Review Editor.
Payment/Terms: Pays $35, free subscription to magazine and 5 contributor's copies. Acquires first rights.
Advice: "We're looking for beautiful writing relevant to our magazine's theme. Story must relate to our theme of gay/lesbian/bi relationships and family in some way. Read a few issues and get a sense for what we publish. Shorter is better."

INKY TRAIL NEWS, Inky Trail News, 55 N. Walnut, #226, Mt. Clemens MI 48043. E-mail: wendy@inkytrails.com. Website: www.inkytrails.com. **Contact:** Wendy Fisher, editor. Tabloid newspaper: 24-28 pages; newsprint; some illustrations; photos. "Friendship newsletter for women/seniors, penpals, journaling, memories, crafts and more." Bimonthly. Estab. 1993. Circ. 500.
Needs: Historical (general memories), mainstream, women penpals, new writers, homelife, personal journals, gardening, seniors, crafts. Receives 2-3 unsolicited mss/month. Accepts 2-3 mss/issue. Publishes 3-4 months after acceptance. **Publishes 60-100 new writers/year.** Recently published work by Martha Green, Janice Caldwell and Bonnie Patterson. Length: 600 words; average length: 600-800 words. Publishes short shorts.
How to Contact: Send complete ms with cover letter. Accepts submissions by e-mail or on disk. Responds to queries and ms within days (if submitted by e-mail). Send SASE for return of ms or send a disposable copy of ms and #10 SASE for reply only. Accepts simultaneous submissions, previously published work and multiple submissions. Sample copy for $3. Guidelines for SASE, e-mail or on website.
Payment/Terms: Pays 6 contributor's copies or free subscription to magazine; additional copies $1. Pays on for publication for one-time and electronic rights.
Advice: "Use our topics."

◙ ◎ ITALIAN AMERICANA, URI/CCE 80 Washington St., Providence RI 02903-1803. (401)277-5306. Fax: (401)277-5100. E-mail: bonomo@etal.ui.edu. Website: www.uri.edu/prov/italian/italian.html (includes writer's guidelines, names of editors). **Contact:** C.B. Albright, editor. Poetry Editor: Dana Gioia. Magazine: 6×9; 240 pages; varnished cover; perfect-bound; photos. "*Italian Americana* contains historical articles, fiction, poetry and memoirs, all concerning the Italian experience in the Americas." Semiannual. Estab. 1974. Circ. 1,200.
Needs: Italian American: literary. No nostalgia. Wants to see more fiction featuring "individualized characters." Receives 10 mss/month. Accepts 3 mss/issue; 6-7 mss/year. Publishes up to 1 year after acceptance. Agented fiction

5%. **Publishes 2-4 new writers/year.** Recently published work by Mary Caponegro and Sal LaPuma. Length: 20 double-spaced pages. Publishes short stories. Also publishes literary essays, literary criticism, poetry. Sometimes comments on rejected mss. Sponsors $500-1,000 literature prize annually.

How to Contact: Send complete ms (in triplicate) with a cover letter. Accepts queries by fax. Include 3-5 line bio, list of publications. Responds in 1 month to queries; 2 months to mss. Send SASE for reply, return of ms or send a disposable copy of ms. No simultaneous submissions. Sample copy for $7. Guidelines for SASE. Reviews novels and short story collections. Send books to Professor John Paul Russo, English Dept., Univ. of Miami, Coral Gables, FL 33124.

Payment/Terms: Awards one $250 prize to best fiction of year and 1 contributor's copy; additional copies $7. Acquires first North American serial rights.

Advice: "Please individualize characters, instead of presenting types (i.e., lovable uncle, etc.). No nostalgia."

JEWISH CURRENTS MAGAZINE, 22 E. 17th St., New York NY 10003-1919. (212)924-5740. Fax: (212)414-2227. Magazine: 8½×11; 40 pages. "We are a secular, progressive, independent Jewish bimonthly, pro-Israel though not Zionist, printing fiction, poetry articles and reviews on Jewish politics and history, Holocaust/Resistance; mideast peace process, Black-Jewish relations, labor struggles, women's issues. Audience is secular, left/progressive, Jewish, mostly urban." Bimonthly. Estab. 1946. Circ. 2,000.

Needs: Contemporary, ethnic, feminist, historical, humor/satire, literary, senior citizen/retirement, translations. "Must be well written! We are interested in *authentic* experience and readable prose; humanistic orientation. Must have Jewish theme. Could use more humor; short, smart, emotional and intellectual impact. No religious, sectarian; no porn or hard sex, no escapist stuff. Go easy on experimentation, but we're interested." Upcoming themes (submit at least 6 months in advance): "Black-Jewish Relations" (January/February); "International Women's Day, Holocaust/Resistance, Passover" (March/April); "Israel" (May/June); "Jews in the USSR & Ex-USSR" (July-August); Jewish Book Month," "Hanuka" (November/December). Receives 6-10 unsolicited fiction mss/month. Accepts 0-1 ms/issue; 8-10 mss/year. Recently published work by Lanny Lefkowitz, Galena Vromen, Alex B. Stone. Length: 1,000-3,000 words; average length: 1,800 words. Also publishes literary essays, literary criticism, poetry.

How to Contact: Send complete ms with cover letter. "Writers should include brief biographical information, especially their publishing histories." SASE. Responds in 2 months to mss. Publishes ms 2-24 months after acceptance. No mss by fax, e-mail or disk. Sample copy for $3 with SAE and 3 first-class stamps. Reviews novels and short story collections.

Payment/Terms: Pays complimentary one-year subscription and 6 contributor's copies. "We readily give reprint permission at no charge." Sends galleys to author.

Advice: Noted for "stories with Jewish content and personal Jewish experience—e.g., immigrant or Holocaust memories, assimilation dilemmas, dealing with Jewish conflicts OK. Space is increasingly a problem. Be intelligent, imaginative, intuitive and absolutely honest. Have a musical ear, and an ear for people: how they sound when they talk, and also hear what they don't say."

JOURNAL OF POLYMORPHOUS PERVERSITY Wry-Bred Press, Inc., 630 First Ave., Suite 32-P, New York NY 10016. (212)689-5473. Fax: (212)689-6859. E-mail: info@psychhumor.com. Website: www.psychhumor.com (includes excerpts). **Contact:** Glenn Ellenbogen, editor. Magazine: 6¾×10; 24 pages; 60 lb. paper; antique india cover stock; illustrations with some articles. "*JPP* is a humorous and satirical journal of psychology, psychiatry, and the closely allied mental health disciplines." For "psychologists, psychiatrists, social workers, psychiatric nurses, *and* the psychologically sophisticated layman." Semiannual. Estab. 1984.

Needs: Humor/satire. "We only consider materials that are funny or that relate to psychology *or* behavior." Receives 50 unsolicited mss/month. Accepts 8 mss/issue; 16 mss/year. Most writers published last year were previously unpublished writers. Length: 4,000 words maximum; average length: 1,500 words. Comments on rejected mss.

How to Contact: Send complete ms *in triplicate.* Include cover letter and SASE. Responds in 3 months to mss. SASE. Accepts multiple submissions. Sample copy for $7. Guidelines for #10 SASE.

Payment/Terms: Pays 2 contributor's copies; additional copies $7.

Advice: "We will *not* look at poetry. We only want to see intelligent spoofs of scholarly psychology and psychiatry articles written in scholarly scientific language. Take a look at *real* journals of psychology and try to lampoon their *style* as much as their content. There are few places to showcase satire of the social sciences, thus we provide one vehicle for injecting a dose of humor into this often too serious area. Occasionally, we will accept a piece of creative writing written in the first person, e.g. 'A Subjective Assessment of the Oral Doctoral Defense Process: I Don't Want to Talk About It, If You Want to Know the Truth' (the latter being a piece in which Holden Caulfield shares his experiences relating to obtaining his Ph.D. in Psychology). Other creative pieces have involved a psychodiagnostic evaluation of The Little Prince (as a psychiatric patient) and God being refused tenure (after having created the world) because of insufficient publications and teaching experience."

SENDING TO A COUNTRY other than your own? Be sure to send International Reply Coupons (IRC) instead of stamps for replies or return of your manuscript.

KRAX MAGAZINE, 63 Dixon Lane, Leeds LS12 4RR, Yorkshire, Britain, U.K. **Contact:** A. Robson, co-editor. "*Krax* publishes lighthearted, humorous and whimsical writing. It is for anyone seeking light relief at a gentle pace. Our audience has grown middle-aged along with us, especially now we're annual and not able to provide the instant fix demanded by the teens and twenties." Appears 1-2 times/year.

Needs: "We publish mostly poetry of a lighthearted nature but use comic or spoof fiction, witty and humorous essays. No war stories, horror, space bandits, boy-girl soap opera. Would like to see more whimsical items, trivia ramblings or anything 'daft.' " Accepts 1 ms/issue. **Publishes 1 new writer/year.** Recently published work by Rachel Kendall. Recently published work by Jim Sullivan. Length: 2,000 words maximum.

How to Contact: No specific guidelines but cover note appreciated.

Payment/Terms: Pays contributor's copies. Sample copy for $2 direct from editor.

Advice: "Don't spend too long on scene-setting or character construction as this inevitably produces an anti-climax in a short piece. We look for original settings, distinctive pacing, description related to plot, i.e. only dress a character in bow tie and gumboots if you're have a candlelight supper in The Everglades. Look at what you enjoy in all forms of fiction from strip cartoons to novels, movies to music lyrics then try to put some of this into your own writing. Send IRCs or currency notes for return postal costs."

LEFT CURVE, P.O. Box 472, Oakland CA 94604-0472. (510)763-7193. E-mail: editor@leftcurve.com. Website: www.ncal.verio.com/~leftcurv. **Contact:** Csaba Polony, editor. Magazine: 8½×11; 144 pages; 60 lb. paper; 100 pt. C1S gloss layflat lamination cover; illustrations; photos. "*Left Curve* is an artist-produced journal addressing the problem(s) of cultural forms emerging from the crises of modernity that strive to be independent from the control of dominant institutions, based on the recognition of the destructiveness of commodity (capitalist) systems to all life." Published irregularly. Estab. 1974. Circ. 2,000.

Needs: Contemporary, ethnic, experimental, historical, literary, prose poem, regional, science fiction, translations, political. "No topical satire, religion-based pieces, melodrama. We publish critical, open, social/political-conscious writing." Receives approximately 12 unsolicited fiction mss/month. Accepts approximately 1 ms/issue. Publishes ms a maximum of 12 months after acceptance. Published work by Pëter Lengyel and Michael Filas. Length: 500-2,500 words; average length: 1,200 words. Publishes short shorts. Sometimes comments on rejected mss.

How to Contact: Send complete ms with cover letter. Include "statement of writer's intent, brief bio and reason for submitting to *Left Curve*." Accepts electronic submissions; "prefer 3½ disk and hard copy, though we do accept e-mail submissions." Responds in 6 months. SASE. Sample copy for $10, 9×12 SAE and $1.24 postage. Guidelines for 1 first-class stamp.

Payment/Terms: Pays in contributor's copies. Rights revert to author.

Advice: "We look for continuity, adequate descriptive passages, endings that are not simply abandoned (in both meanings). Dig deep; no superficial personalisms, no corny satire. Be honest, realistic and gouge out the truth you wish to say. Understand yourself and the world. Have writing be a means to achieve or realize what is real."

LONG SHOT, Long Shot Productions, P.O. Box 6238, Hoboken NJ 07030. E-mail: dshot@mindspring.com. Website: www.longshot.org (includes excerpts, writer's guidelines, names of editors, interview w/ authors, poetry, fiction, books to order). **Contact:** Danny Shot, editor. Literary magazine: 5×8; 192 pages; white paper; 10pt c1s cover stock; some illustrations; photos. "Writing for the real world. Dark, gritty, humorous, light, fantastic, surreal, imaginative." Semiannual. Estab. 1982.

Needs: Comics/graphic novels, erotica, ethnic (general and specific culture), fantasy, feminist, gay, humor/satire, lesbian, literary, science fiction. "No romance, Nazi-fetish." Receives 50 unsolicited mss/month. Accepts 2-3 mss/issue; 4-6 mss/year. Publishes ms 4-6 months after acceptance. Publishes 5 new writers/year. Recently published work by Wanda Coleman, Barbara Peck, Bara Swain. Length: 1-12 pages; average length: 5 pages. Publishes short shorts. Also publishes poetry. Rarely comments on rejected mss.

How to Contact: Send complete ms with cover letter or submit through an agent. Accepts submissions on disk, definitely no e-mail submissions. Responds in 4 months to queries; 2 months to mss. Accepts simultaneous submissions. Sample copy for $8. Guidelines by e-mail or on website.

Payment/Terms: Pays 3 contributor's copies; additional copies 50% of the cover price. Pays on publication for first North American serial and electronic rights.

Advice: "We look for passsion. If it seems like the writer gives a shit about what he/she is writing about we'll consider it. Write like you give a damn about what you're writing about. Passion is irrestable to editors."

$ ◯ ◎ MAJESTIC BOOKS P.O. Box 19097A, Johnston RI 02919-0097. E-mail: majesticbk@aol.com. **Contact:** Cindy MacDonald, fiction editor. Bound softcover short story anthologies; 5½×8½; 224 pages; 50 lb. paper; C1S cover stock. "Majestic Books is a small press which was formed to give children an outlet for their work. We publish softcover bound anthologies of fictional stories by children, for children and adults who enjoy the work of children." Triannual. Estab. 1993. Circ. 250.

Needs: Stories written on any subject by children (under 18) only. Children's/juvenile (10-12 years), young adult (13-18 years). Receives 50 unsolicited mss/month. Accepts 100 mss/year. Publishes ms 1 year maximum after acceptance. **Publishes 95 new writers/year.** Published work by Ellen Green and Emily Breyfogle. Length: 2,000 words maximum. Publishes short shorts. Also publishes literary essays.

How to Contact: Send complete ms with a cover letter. Include estimated word count and author's age. Accepts submissions by e-mail and disk. Responds in 3 weeks. Send SASE for reply. Accepts simultaneous and multiple submissions. Sample copy for $5. Guidelines for #10 SASE.

Payment/Terms: Pays 10% royalty for all books sold due to the author's inclusion.

Advice: "We love stories that will keep a reader thinking long after they have read the last word. Be original. We have received some manuscripts of shows we have seen on television or books we have read. Write from inside you and you'll be surprised at how much better your writing will be. Use *your* imagination."

⬤ MEDUSA'S HAIRDO MAGAZINE, Byrd White Press, 2631 Seminole Ave., Ashland KY 41102. E-mail: medusashairdo@yahoo.com. Website: http://victorian.fortunecity.com/brambles/4/mh/ (includes guidelines, news, cover art). **Contact:** Beverly Moore, editor. Magazine: 8½×11; 24 pages; glossy cover; illustrations. "We are the magazine of modern mythology—not a rehash of classical myth, but the stories that define or describe our times." Semiannual. Estab. 1995. Circ. 50.

Needs: Humor/satire, literary, mainstream, science fiction (soft/sociological). "No erotica or extreme violence. I'm also not likely to accept politically slanted stories in categories like ethnic, feminist, religious, etc." Receives 30 unsolicited mss/month. Accepts 4-6 mss/issue; 8-12 mss/year. Publishes ms 1 year after acceptance. Length: 4,000 words maximum; average length: 2,000 words. Publishes short shorts. Average length: 1,000 words. Also publishes poetry. Often comments on rejected mss.

How to Contact: Send complete ms with a cover letter. Accepts submissions by e-mail as text only. Include estimated word count and cover letter with name, address, e-mail, subtitles. Responds in 2 weeks to queries; 2 months to mss. Send a disposable copy of ms and #10 SASE for reply only. Accepts simultaneous submissions, previously published work and multiple submissions (3 stories maximum). Sample copy for $4.50. Guidelines for SASE or by e-mail.

Payment/Terms: Pays 1 contributor's copy; additional copies $4.50. Acquires first North American serial rights.

Advice: "Let me know in your cover letter that you are a beginner. I'll try to help."

$ ◎ THE MIRACULOUS MEDAL, The Central Association of the Miraculous Medal, 475 E. Chelten Ave., Philadelphia PA 19144-5785. (215)848-1010. Website: www.cmphila.org/camm/. Editor: Rev. William J. O'Brien, C.M. **Contact:** Charles Kelly, general manager. Magazine. Quarterly.

Needs: Religious/inspirational. Receives 25 unsolicited fiction mss/month. Accepts 2 mss/issue; 8 mss/year. Publishes ms up to 2 years or more after acceptance.

How to Contact: Query first with SASE. Sample copy and fiction guidelines free.

Payment/Terms: Pays 2¢/word minimum. Pays on acceptance for first rights.

◻ MOUNTAIN LUMINARY, P.O. Box 1187, Mountain View AR 72560-1187. (870)585-2260. Fax: (870)269-4110. E-mail: ecomtn@mvtel.net. **Contact:** Anne Thiel, editor. Magazine; photos. "*Mountain Luminary* is dedicated to bringing information to people about the Aquarian Age; how to grow with its new and evolutionary energies and how to work with the resultant changes in spirituality, relationships, environment and the planet. *Mountain Luminary* provides a vehicle for people to share ideas, philosophies and experiences that deepen understanding of this evolutionary process and humankind's journey on Earth." International quarterly. Estab. 1985.

Needs: Humor/satire, metaphor/inspirational/Aquarian-Age topics. Accepts 8-10 mss/year. Publishes ms 6 months after acceptance. **Publishes 2 new writers/year.** Published work by Alex Bledson and Sakie Brown.

How to Contact: Query with clips of published work. SASE for return of ms. Accepts queries/mss by fax and e-mail. Accepts simultaneous submissions. Sample copy and writer's guidelines free.

Payment/Terms: Pays 1 contributor's copy. "We may offer advertising space as payment." Acquires first rights.

Advice: "We look for stories with a moral—those with insight to problems on the path which raise the reader's awareness. Topical interests include: New Age/Aquarian Age, astrology, crystals, cultural and ethnic concerns, dreams, ecosystems, the environment, extraterrestrials, feminism, folklore, healing and health, holistic and natural health, inspiration, juvenile and teen issues, lifestyle, meditation, men's issues, metaphysics, mysticism, nutrition, parallel dimensions, prayer, psychic phenomenon, self-help, spirituality and women's issues."

🌐 MSLEXIA, For Women Who Write, Mslexia Publications Ltd., P.O. Box 656, Newcastle Upon Tyne NE99-2RP United Kingdom. Phone: (00)44-191-2616656. Fax: (00)44-191-2616636. E-mail: postbag@mslexia.demon.co.uk. Website: www.mslexia.co.uk. **Contact:** Debbie Taylor, marketing manager. Magazine: A4; 60 pages; some illustrations; photos. "*Mslexia* is for women who write, who want to write, who have a specialist interest in women's writing of who teach creative writing. *Mslexia* is a blend of features, articles, advice, listings, and original prose & poetry. Many parts of the magazine are open to submission from any women. Please request contributors guidelines prior to sending in work." Quarterly. Estab. 1999. Circ. 8,000.

Needs: Each issue is to a specific theme. Themes for SAE. Some themes included erotica, death writing from a male perspective & body image. No work from men accepted. Publishes ms 3-4 months after acceptance. **Publishes 40-50 new writers/year.** Length: 2,000 words; average length: 1,000-2,000 words. Publishes short shorts. Average length: 1,000-2,000 words. Also publishes poetry.

How to Contact: Query first. Accepts submissions by e-mail. Responds in 2 weeks to queries; 3 months to mss. Sample copy for £4.95 (sterling). Guidelines for SAE, e-mail, fax or on website.

Payment/Terms: Pays in contributors copies.

Advice: "We look for an unusual slant on the theme. Well structured, short pieces. Also intelligent, humorous, or with a strong sense of voice. Consider the theme and all obvious interpretations of it. Try to think of a new angle/slant. Dare to be different. Make sure the piece is strong on craft as well as content."

$ ⬤ NEW ENGLAND WRITERS' NETWORK, P.O. Box 483, Hudson MA 01749-0483. (978)562-2946. E-mail: NEWNmag@aol.com. Editor: Glenda Baker. **Contact:** Liz Aleshire, fiction editor. Poetry Editor: Judy Adourian. Magazine: 8½×11; 24 pages; coated cover. "We are devoted to helping new writers get published and to teaching through example and content. We are looking for well-written stories that grab us from the opening paragraph." Quarterly. Estab. 1994. Circ. 200.

- *New England Writers' Network* has a new feature called New Voices. A story by a previously unpublished fiction writer is spotlighted under the heading New Voices.

Needs: Adventure, condensed/excerpted novel, ethnic/multicultural, humor/satire, literary, mainstream/contemporary, mystery/suspense, religious/inspirational, romance. "We will consider anything except pornography or extreme violence." Accepts 5 mss/issue; 20 mss/year. Reads mss only from June 1 through September 1. Publishes ms 4-12 months after acceptance. **Publishes 10-12 new writers/year.** Recently published work by Laura Pedersen, Esther Holt and Pat Car. Length: 2,000 words maximum. Publishes short shorts. Also publishes poetry and 3-4 personal essays per issue. Always comments on rejected mss.

How to Contact: Send complete ms with a cover letter. Include estimated word count. Bio on acceptance. Responds in 4 months. SASE for return of ms. No simultaneous submissions. Sample copy for $5.50. Guidelines free. "We do not review story collections or novels. We do publish 2,000-word (maximum) novel excerpts. Writer picks the excerpt—do not send novel."

Payment/Terms: Pays $10 for fiction, $5 for personal essays, $3 per poem and 1 contributor's copy. Pays on publication for first North American serial rights.

Advice: "We are devoted to helping new writers get published and to teaching through example and content. Give us a try! Please send for guidelines and a sample."

ℕ ◎ NEW METHODS, The Journal of Animal Health Technology, P.O. Box 22605, San Francisco CA 94122-0605. (707)459-4535. E-mail: norwal13@yahoo.com. Website: www.geocities.com/norwal13photos.yahoo.com/norwal13. **Contact:** Ronald S. Lippert, AHT, publisher. Newsletter ("could become magazine again"): 8½×11; 2-4 pages; 20 lb. paper; illustrations; "rarely" photos. Network service in the animal field educating services for mostly professionals in the animal field; e.g., animal health technicians. Monthly. Estab. 1976. Circ. 5,608.

Needs: Animals: contemporary, experimental, historical, mainstream, regional. No stories unrelated to animals. Receives 12 unsolicited fiction mss/month. Accepts one ms/issue; 12 mss/year. Length: Open. "Rarely" publishes short shorts. Occasionally critiques rejected mss.

How to Contact: Query first with theme, length, expected time of completion, photos/illustrations, if any, biographical sketch of author, all necessary credits or send complete ms. Response time varies (up to 4 months). SASE for query and ms. Accepts simultaneous and multiple submissions. Sample copy and guidelines for $2.90.

Payment/Terms: No payment. Acquires one-time rights. Back issue and guidelines only with SASE for $2, must mention Writer's Digest Books.

Advice: Sponsors contests: theme changes but generally concerns the biggest topics of the year in the animal field. "Emotion, personal experience—make the person feel it. We are growing."

$ ⬤ ▼ NIGHT TERRORS, 1202 W. Market St., Orrville OH 44667-1710. (330)683-0338. E-mail: dedavidson@night-terrors-publications.com. Website: www.night-terrors-publications.com (includes updated guidelines, bios of the editor and writers, short fiction, order info, links to other sites of interest to writers and readers of horror). **Contact:** D.E. Davidson, editor/publisher. Magazine: 8½×11; 52 pages; 80 lb. glossy cover; illustrations; photos. "*Night Terrors* publishes quality, thought-provoking horror fiction for literate adults." Quarterly. Estab. 1996. Circ. 1,000.

- *Night Terrors* has had 22 stories listed in the Honorable Mention section of *The Year's Best Fantasy and Horror, Annual Collections.*

Needs: Horror, psychic/supernatural/occult. "Night Terrors does not accept stories involving abuse, sexual mutilation or stories with children as main characters. We publish traditional supernatural/psychological horror for a mature audience. Our emphasis is on literate work with a chill." Wants to see more psychological horror. Receives 50 unsolicited mss/month. Accepts 12 mss/issue; 46 mss/year. Does not read mss June-August. Publishes ms 6-12 months after acceptance. **Publishes 16 new writers/year.** Published work by John M. Clay, Ken Goldman, and Barbara Rosen. Length: 2,000-5,000 words; average length: 3,000 words. Often comments on rejected mss.

How to Contact: Send complete ms with a cover letter. Include estimated word count, 50-word bio and list of publications. Responds in 1 week to queries; 3 months to mss. Send SASE for reply, return of ms or send a disposable copy of ms. Accepts simultaneous submissions. Sample copy for $6 (make checks to Night Terrors Publications). Guidelines free for #10 SASE.

Payment/Terms: "Pays 2 contributor's copies for nonprofessional writers; additional copies for $4.50. Pays by arrangement with professional writers." Pays on publication for first North American serial rights. Sends galleys to author.

Advice: "I publish what I like. I like stories which involve me with the viewpoint character and leave me with the feeling that his/her fate could have or might be mine. Act professionally. Check your work for typos, spelling, grammar, punctuation, format. Send your work flat. And if you must, paper clip it, don't staple. Include a brief, to-the-point cover letter."

◯ THE NOCTURNAL LYRIC, Journal of the Bizarre, The Nocturnal Lyric, P.O. Box 542, Astoria OR 97103. E-mail: nocturnallyric@melodymail.com. Website: www.angelfire.com/ca/nocturnallyric (includes guidelines, poetry, names of upcoming writers, specials on back issues. **Contact:** Susan Moon, editor. Magazine: 8½×5½; 40 pages; illustrations. "Fiction and poetry submitted should have a bizarre horror theme. Our audience encompasses people who stand proudly outside of the mainstream of society." Published 3 times/year. Estab. 1987. Circ. 400.

Needs: Horror (dark fantasy, futuristic, psychological, supernatural, satirical). "No sexually graphic material—it's too overdone in the horror genre lately." Receives 25-30 unsolicited mss/month. Accepts 8-9 mss/issue; 30 mss/year. Publishes ms 1 year after acceptance. **Publishes 20 new writers/year.** Recently published work by Rene Dumas, Kevin Christinat and Kent Robinson. Length: 2,000 words maximum; average length: 1,500 words. Publishes short shorts. Average length: 500 words. Also publishes literary essays and poetry. Rarely comments on rejected mss.

How to Contact: Send complete ms with a cover letter. Include estimated word count. Responds in 1 month to queries; 8 months to mss. Send SASE (or IRC) for return of ms. Accepts simultaneous, previously published and multiple submissions. Sample copy for $2 (back issue); $3 (current issue). Guidelines for SASE or on website. Reviews novels, short story collections and nonfiction books of interest to writers. Send review copies to the editor.

Payment/Terms: Pays with discounts on subscription and copies of issue. Pays on acceptance for one-time rights. Not copyrighted.

Advice: "A manuscript stands out when the story has a very original theme and the ending is not predictable. Don't be afraid to be adventurous with your story. Mainstream horror can be boring. Surreal, satirical horror is what true nightmares are all about."

◐ THE OAK, 1530 Seventh St., Rock Island IL 61201. (309)788-3980. **Contact:** Betty Mowery, editor. Magazine: 8½×11; 8-10 pages. "To provide a showcase for new authors while showing the work of established authors as well; to publish wholesome work, something with a message." Bimonthly. Estab. 1991. Circ. 300.

Needs: Adventure, contemporary, experimental, fantasy, humor, mainstream, prose poem. No erotica or love poetry. Receives 25 mss/month. Accepts up to 12 mss/issue. Publishes ms within 3 months of acceptance. **Publishes 25 new writers/year.** Length: 500 words maximum.

How to Contact: Send complete ms. Responds in 1 week. SASE. Accepts simultaneous, multiple and reprint submissions. Sample copy for $3. Subscription $10 for 4 issues. SASE for contest guidelines.

Payment/Terms: None, but not necessary to buy a copy in order to be published. Acquires first rights.

Advice: "I do not want erotica, extreme violence or killing of humans or animals for the sake of killing. Just be yourself when you write. Also, write *tight*. Please include SASE or manuscripts will be destroyed. Be sure name and address are on the manuscript. Study the markets for length of manuscript and what type of material is wanted."

◪ $◐ ON SPEC, Box 4727, Edmonton, Alberta T6E 5G6 Canada. (780)413-0215. Fax: (780)413-0215. E-mail: onspec@canada.com. Website: www.icomm.ca/onspec (includes writer's guidelines, past editorials, excerpts from published fiction, links to writer's Internet resources). **Contact:** Diane L. Walton, editor. Magazine: 5¼×8; 112 pages; illustrations. "We publish speculative fiction by new and established writers, with a strong preference for Canadian-authored works." Quarterly. Estab. 1989. Circ. 2,000.

Needs: Fantasy and science fiction. No condensed or excerpted novels, religious/inspirational stories, fairy tales. "We would like to see more horror, fantasy, science fiction—well-developed stories with complex characters and strong plots." Receives 100 mss/month. Accepts 10 mss/issue; 40 mss/year. "We read manuscripts during the month after each deadline: February 28/May 31/August 31/November 30." Publishes ms 6-18 months after acceptance. **Publishes 10-15 new writers/year.** Recently published work by James Van Pelt, David Kirtle, Allen Weiss and Steve Mohn. Length: 1,000-6,000 words; average length: 4,000 words. Also publishes poetry. Often comments on rejected mss.

How to Contact: Send complete ms with a cover letter. No submissions by e-mail or fax. Include estimated word count, 2-sentence bio and phone number. Responds in 5 months to mss. SASE for return of ms or send a disposable copy of ms plus #10 SASE for response. Include Canadian postage or IRCs. Accepts simultaneous submissions. Sample copy for $7. Guidelines for #10 SASE.

Payment/Terms: Pays $40-180 and 2 contributor's copies; additional copies for $7. Pays on acceptance for first North American serial rights.

Advice: "We're looking for original ideas with a strong SF element, excellent dialogue, and characters who are so believable, our readers will really care about them."

◎ PARADOXISM, Anti-literary Journal, University of New Mexico, Gallup NM 87301. Fax: (505)863-7532 (Attn. Dr. Smarandache). E-mail: smarand@unm.edu. Website: www.gallup.unm.edu/~smarandache/lit.htm. **Contact:** Florentin Smarandache, editor. Magazine: 8½×11; 100 pages; illustrations. "The paradoxism is an avant-garde movement set up by the editor in the 1980s in Romania as an antitotalitarian protest, based on excessive use of antithesis, antimonies, contradictions, paradoxes in the creation. It tries to generalize the art, to make the unliterary become literary." Annually. Estab. 1993. Circ. 500.

Needs: "Crazy, uncommon, experimental, avant-garde"; also ethnic/multicultural. Plans specific themes in the next year. Publishes annual special fiction issue or anthology. Receives 3-4 unsolicited mss/month. Accepts 10 mss/issue.

Published work by Dan Topa and Anatol Ciocanu. Length: 500-1,000 words. Publishes short shorts. Also publishes literary essays, literary criticism and poetry. Focus on new literary terms such as paradoxist distich, tautological distich, dual distich.

How to Contact: Query with clips of unpublished work. Responds in 2 months to mss. Send a disposable copy of ms. Sample copy for $19.95 and 8½×11 SASE.

Payment/Terms: Pays 1 contributor's copy. Not copyrighted.

Advice: "The Basic Thesis of the paradoxism: everything has a meaning and a non-meaning in a harmony each other. The Essence of the paradoxism: a) the sense has a non-sense, and reciprocally b) the non-sense has a sense. The Motto of the paradoxism: 'All is possible, the impossible too!' The Symbol of the paradoxism: (a spiral—optic illusion, or vicious circle)."

N $ PENNY-A-LINER, P.O. Box 2163, Wenatchee WA 98807-2163. (509)662-7858. E-mail: ptl2163@aol.com. Website: maxpages.com/redrosebushpre (includes writer's guidelines, names of editors, short fiction, letters). **Editor:** Ella M. Dillon. Magazine: 8½×11; 44 pages; book stock paper; coated cover; illustrations; photos. "*Penny-a-Liner* features family reading—positive, entertaining." Triannual.

Needs: Adventure, children's/juvenile (adventure, animal, easy-to-read, fantasy, historical, mystery, preschool, series, sports, all ages), comics/graphic novels, ethnic/multicultural (general), experimental, family saga, fantasy (space fantasy, sword and sorcery), feminist, historical (general), horror (dark fantasy, futuristic, psychological, supernatural), humor satire, literary, mainstream, military/war, mystery/suspense (amateur sleuth, cozy, police procedural, private eye/hard-boiled), regional, religious (children's religious, general religious, inspirational, religious fantasy, religious mystery/suspense, religious thriller, religious romance), romance (contemporary, futuristic/time travel, gothic, historical, regency period, romantic suspense), science fiction (hard science/technological, soft/sociological), short story collections, thriller/espionage, translations, western (frontier saga, traditional), young adult/teen (adventure, easy-to-read, fantasy/science fiction, historical, horror, mystery/suspense, problem novels, romance, series, sports, western). "No pornography or explicit sexual content." Publishes "as many new writers as possible." Length: 10-3,500 words; average length: 500-2,000 words. Publishes short shorts. Also publishes literary essays, literary criticism and poetry.

How to Contact: Send complete ms with cover letter. Accepts queries/mss by e-mail. Include name and address on each page. Responds in 1 month to queries and mss. SASE for reply or send a disposable copy of ms. Accepts simultaneous submissions and reprints. Sample copy and guidelines free.

Payment/Terms: Pays 1¢/word, 1 contributor's copy; additional copies $4 each. Pays on publication for one-time rights.

Advice: "We encourage submissions from previously unpublished authors. Please type and double space your manuscript, and include year, name and address on each page. Neatness counts. Be friendly and courteous—do not make demands."

THE PIPE SMOKER'S EPHEMERIS, The Universal Coterie of Pipe Smokers, 20-37 120 St., College Point NY 11356-2128. **Contact:** Tom Dunn, editor. Magazine: 8½×11; 84-116 pages; offset paper and cover; illustrations; photos. Pipe smoking and tobacco theme for general and professional audience. Irregular quarterly. Estab. 1964.

Needs: Pipe smoking related: historical, humor/satire, literary. Publishes ms up to 1 year after acceptance. Length: 5,000 words maximum; average length: 2,500 words. Also publishes short shorts. Occasionally critiques rejected mss.

How to Contact: Send complete ms with cover letter. Responds in 2 weeks to mss. Accepts simultaneous submissions and reprints. Sample copy for 8½×11 SAE and 6 first-class stamps.

Payment/Terms: Acquires one-time rights.

$ THE POST, Publishers Syndication International, P.O. Box 6218, Charlottesville VA 22906-6218. Fax: (434)242-0488. E-mail: asam@firstra.com. Website: www.publisherssyndication.com/. **Contact:** A.P. Samuels, editor. Magazine: 8½×11; 32 pages. Monthly. Estab. 1988.

Needs: Adventure, mystery/suspense (private eye), romance (romantic suspense, historical, contemporary), western (traditional). "No explicit sex, gore, weird themes, extreme violence or bad language." Receives 35 unsolicited mss/month. Accepts 1 ms/issue; 12 mss/year. Time between acceptance and publication varies. Agented fiction 10%. **Publishes 1-3 new writers/year.** Length: 10,000 words average.

How to Contact: Send complete ms with cover letter. Responds to mss in 5 weeks. Guidelines for #10 SASE.

Payment/Terms: Pays ½-4¢/word. Pays on acceptance for all rights.

Advice: "Manuscripts must be for a general audience."

◐ ◎ **PRAYERWORKS, Encouraging, God's people to do the real work of ministry—intercessory prayer**, The Master's Work, P.O. Box 301363, Portland OR 97294-9363. (503)761-2072. E-mail: vannm1@aol.com. **Contact:** V. Ann Mandeville, editor. Newsletter: 5½×8; 4 pages; bond paper. "Our intended audience is 70% retired Christians and 30% families. We publish 350-500 word devotional material—fiction, nonfiction, biographical poetry, clean quips and quotes. Our philosophy is evangelical Christian serving the body of Christ in the area of prayer." Estab. 1988. Circ. 1,000.

Needs: Religious/inspirational. "Subject matter may include anything which will build relationship with the Lord—prayer, ways to pray, stories of answered prayer, teaching on a Scripture portion, articles that will build faith, or poems will all work. We even use a series occasionally. No nonevangelical Christian fiction." Publishes 2-6 months after acceptance. **Publishes 30 new writers/year.** Recently published work by Allen Audrey and Petey Prater. Length: 350-500 words; average length: 350-500 words. Publishes short shorts. Also publishes poetry. Often comments on rejected mss.

How to Contact: Send complete ms with a cover letter. Include estimated word count and a very short bio. Responds in 1 month. Send SASE for reply, return of ms or send a disposable copy of ms. Accepts simultaneous and multiple submissions and reprints. Sample copy and guidelines for #10 SASE.

Payment/Terms: Pays free subscription to the magazine and contributor's copies. Pays on publication. Writer retains all rights. Not copyrighted.

Advice: Stories "must have a great take-away—no preaching; teach through action. Be thrifty with words—make them count."

$ ◪ **PSI**, P.O. Box 6218, Charlottesville VA 22906-6218. Fax: (804)964-0096. E-mail: asam@publisherssyndication .com. Website: www.publisherssyndication.com. **Contact:** A.P. Samuels, editor. Magazine: 8½×11; 32 pages; bond paper; self cover. "Mystery and romance." Bimonthly. Estab. 1987.

Needs: Adventure, romance (contemporary, historical, young adult), mystery/suspense (private eye), western (traditional). No ghoulish, sex, violence. Wants to see more believable stories. Receives 35 unsolicited mss/month. Accepts 1-2 mss/issue. **Publishes 1-3 new writers/year.** Length: 10,000 (stories) and 30,000 (novelettes) words average. Comments on rejected mss "only on a rare occasion."

How to Contact: Send complete ms with cover letter. Responds in 2 weeks to queries; 6 weeks to mss. SASE. Accepts electronic submissions via disk.

Payment/Terms: Pays 1-4¢/word plus royalty. Pays on acceptance for all rights.

Advice: "Manuscripts must be for a general audience. Just good plain story telling (make it compelling). No explicit sex or ghoulish violence."

$ **THE PSYCHIC RADIO**, 1111 Elmwood Ave., Rochester NY 14620-3005. (716)241-1200, ext. 1288. **Contact:** Lester Billips Jr., editor. Magazine: full size; 32-64 pages; 70 lb. text gloss; 100 lb. text gloss card cover. "My magazine uses stories, poems or essays which are either religious or are slanted toward the growing psychic/occult problem in America today." Quarterly. Estab. 2001.

Needs: Fantasy (sword and sorcery), horror (futuristic, psychological, supernatural), new age, psychic/supernatural/ occult, religious (general, inspirational, religious fantasy), science fiction (soft/sociological). "No plain horror." Accepts 5-10 mss/issue; 20-25 mss/year. Publishes in 3-4 months after acceptance. Recently published work by Jean Reed. Publishes short shorts. Also publishes literary essays and poetry. Sometimes comments on rejected mss.

How to Contact: Send complete ms with cover letter. Include estimated word count and brief bio. Responds in 1 month to queries and mss. Send SASE for return of ms or send a disposable copy of ms and #10 SASE for reply only. Accepts simultaneous submissions, previously published work and multiple submissions. Sample copy for $2.50. Guidelines for SASE.

Payment/Terms: Pays $20-50 and contributor's copies; additional copies $2.50. Pays on acceptance for one-time rights.

Advice: "I look for work with relevance to the growing psychic/occult problem in America today. Be honest and be urgent."

◐ ◎ **QUEEN OF ALL HEARTS**, Queen Magazine, Montfort Missionaries, 26 S. Saxon Ave., Bay Shore NY 11706-8993. (631)665-0726. Fax: (631)665-4349. E-mail: montfortpub@optonline.net. **Contact:** Roger M. Charest, S.M.M., managing editor. Magazine: 7¾×10¾; 48 pages; self cover stock; illustrations; photos. Magazine of "stories, articles and features on the Mother of God by explaining the Scriptural basis and traditional teaching of the Catholic Church concerning the Mother of Jesus, her influence in fields of history, literature, art, music, poetry, etc." Bimonthly. Estab. 1950. Circ. 2,500.

Needs: Religious/inspirational. "No mss not about Our Lady, the Mother of God, the Mother of Jesus." **Publishes 6 new writers/year.** Published work by Richard O'Donnell and Jackie Clements-Marenda. Length: 1,500-2,000 words. Sometimes recommends other markets.

How to Contact: Send complete ms with SASE. Accepts queries/mss by e-mail and fax (mss by permission only). Responds in 1 month to mss. Publishes ms 6-12 months after acceptance. Sample copy for $2.50 with 9×12 SAE.

Payment/Terms: Varies. Pays 6 contributor's copies.

Advice: "We are publishing stories with a Marian theme."

◪ $ ◯ ◎ **QUEEN'S QUARTERLY, A Canadian Review**, Queen's University, Kingston, Ontario K7L 3N6 Canada. Phone/fax: (613)533-2667. Fax: (613)533-6822. E-mail: qquarter@post.queensu.ca. Website: info.queensu.ca./

quarterly. **Contact:** Boris Castel, editor. Magazine: 6×9; 800 pages/year; illustrations. "A general interest intellectual review, featuring articles on science, politics, humanities, arts and letters. Book reviews, poetry and fiction." Quarterly. Estab. 1893. Circ. 3,000.

Needs: Contemporary, historical, literary, mainstream, women's. "*Special emphasis on work by Canadian writers.*" Accepts 2 mss/issue; 8 mss/year. **Published new writers within the last year.** Published work by Gail Anderson-Dargatz, Mark Jarman, Rick Bowers and Dennis Bock. Length: 2,000-3,000 words. Also publishes literary essays, literary criticism, poetry.

How to Contact: "Send complete ms with SASE and/or IRC. No reply with insufficient postage." Accepts submissions by e-mail. Responds within 3 months. Sample copy for $6.50. Reviews novels and short story collections.

Payment/Terms: Pays $100-300 for fiction, 2 contributor's copies and 1-year subscription; additional copies $5. Pays on publication for first North American serial rights. Sends galleys to author.

N **$ ROMANCE AND BEYOND**, Briada Press, Inc., 3527 Ambassador Caffery, PMB 9, Lafayette LA 70503. (337)991-9095. E-mail: rbeyond@aol.com. Website: www.romanceandbeyond.com (includes excerpts, writer's guidelines, contest information, ordering information). **Contact:** Mary Tarver, senior editor. Anthology: 4¼×7; 340 pages; 20 lb. paper; glossy cover. "We publish speculative romance stories and poems-combining science fiction, fantasy or the paranormal with happily ever after." Annual. Estab. 1998.

Needs: Romance: fantasy, space fantasy, sword and sorcery, psychic/supernatural, gothic. "No pornography." Receives 100 unsolicited mss during reading period. Accepts 15 mss/year. Does not read mss from April to October. Publishes ms 9 months after acceptance. **Publishes 12 new writers/year.** Recently published work by Sharon Hartley, Linnea Sinclair, Denise Agnew and Ralan Conley. Length: 5,000-10,000 words. Publishes short shorts.

How to Contact: Send complete ms with cover letter. Non-US writers may query by e-mail first. "No unsolicited submissions by e-mail, fax or on disk. If an non-US writer has queried us, we will accept their submission by e-mail." Include estimated word count, brief bio and list of publications. Responds to queries in 1 month; mss in 6 months. Send disposable copy of ms with SASE for reply only. IRC's welcome. Accepts simultaneous, previously published and multiple submissions. Sample copy for $14.95, $16.95 outside US. Guidelines for SASE and on website.

Payment/Terms: Pays 5¢/word and 1 contributor's copy. Writers receive 25% discount on all future purchases. Pays on acceptance for one-time rights. Sends prepublication galleys to author.

Advice: Read a copy of our magazine before submitting. Visit our website for excerpts and guidelines before submitting. Stories range from dark to humorous, from beauty and beast science fiction romance to contemporary paranormal romance. We look for well-written short stories with complex characters and plots. All stories must have romantic conflict between the male and female protagonists resolved in a satisfactory manner; i.e. all stories must have a happy ending.

Payment/Terms: Pays 1-2 contributor's copies. Not copyrighted.

SKIPPING STONES: A Multicultural Children's Magazine, P.O. Box 3939, Eugene OR 97403-0939. (541)342-4956. E-mail: skipping@efn.org. Website: www.efn.org/~skipping (includes writer's guidelines). **Contact:** Arun N. Toké, executive editor. Magazine: 8½×11; 36 pages; recycled 50 lb. halopaque paper; 100 lb. text cover; illustrations; photos. "*Skipping Stones* is a multicultural, international, nature awareness magazine for children 8-16, and their parents and teachers." Published 5 times a year. Estab. 1988. Circ. 2,500.

• *Skipping Stones* has received EdPress and NAME awards.

Needs: Children's/juvenile (8-16 years): ethnic/multicultural, feminist, religious/inspirational, young adult/teen, international, nature. No simplistic, fiction for the sake of fiction, mystery, violent/abusive language or science fiction. "We want more authentic pieces based on truly multicultural/intercultural/international living experiences of authors. We welcome works by people of color." Upcoming themes: "Living Abroad," "Crosscultural Communications," "Living With Disability," "Challenging Disability," "Celebrations," "Folktales," "Turning Points in Life . . ." List of upcoming themes available for SASE. Receives 50 mss/month. Accepts 5-8 mss/issue; 20-25 mss/year "from adult contributors." Publishes ms 3-12 months after acceptance. **Publishes up to 15 new writers/year.** Published work by Jon Bush, Kathleen Ahrens and Linda Raczek. Length: 250-1,000 words; average length: 750 words. Publishes short shorts. Also publishes literary essays and poetry (by youth under 18). Often comments on rejected mss. Sponsors contests and awards for writers under 17 years of age.

How to Contact: Send complete ms with a cover letter. Accepts queries/mss by e-mail. Include 50- to 100-word bio with background, international or intercultural experiences. Responds in 1 month to queries; 4 months to mss. Send SASE for reply, return of ms or send a disposable copy of ms. Accepts simultaneous submissions. Sample copy for $5, and 4 first-class stamps. Guidelines for #10 SASE.

Payment/Terms: Pays 1 or more contributor's copies; additional copies for $3. Acquires first North American serial rights and nonexclusive reprint rights.

Advice: Looking for stories with "multicultural/multiethnic theme. Realistic and suitable for 8- to 16-year-olds (with use of other languages when appropriate). Promoting social and nature awareness. In addition to encouraging children's creativity, we also invite adults to submit their own writing and artwork for publication in *Skipping Stones*. Writings and artwork by adults should challenge readers to think and learn, cooperate and create."

N **SLATE AND STYLE, Magazine of the National Federation of the Blind Writers Division,** NFB Writer's Division, 2704 Beach Dr., Merrick NY 11566. (516)868-8718. Fax: (516)868-9076. E-mail: loristay@aol.com. **Contact:** Tom Stevens, fiction editor. Newsletter: 8×10; 32 print/40 Braille pages; cassette and large print. "Articles of interest to writers, and resources for blind writers." Quarterly. Estab. 1982. Circ. 200.

Needs: Adventure, contemporary, fantasy, humor/satire, blindness. No erotica. "Avoid theme of death." Does not read mss in June or July. **Publishes 8-10 new writers/year.** Recently published work by Alma Hinkle, Marie Anna Pape and Lois Wencil. Length: 3,000 words maximum. Publishes short shorts. Also publishes literary criticism and poetry. Critiques rejected mss only if requested.

How to Contact: Responds in 3-6 weeks. Accepts queries by e-mail. Large print sample copy for $2.50.

Payment/Terms: Pays in contributor's copies. Acquires one-time rights. Publication not copyrighted. Sponsors contests for fiction writers.

Advice: "Keep a copy. Editors can lose your work. Consider each first draft as just that and review your work before you send it. SASE a must. Although we circulate to blind writers, I do not wish to see articles on blindness by sighted writers unless they are married to, or the son/daughter/parent of a blind person. In general, we do not even print articles on blindness, preferring to publish articles on alternate techniques a blind writer can use when writing."

○ **STEPPING OUT OF THE DARKNESS**, Puritan/Jewish Newsletter, P.O. Box 712, Hingham MA 02043. (781)878-5531. E-mail: ThePuritanLight@aol.com. Website: www.members.tripod.com/puritan55 (includes excerpts, writers' guidelines). **Contact:** Editor. Newsletter/magazine: 9-12 pages. "Our main focus is on New England in earlier centuries. We uncover lost spiritual truths in Holy living (with the help of such great figures as Richard Baxter, Gov. John Winthrop, Cotton Mather and many more.) We also print current concerns, poetry and inspirational fiction. We like to see work from children and teens as well as adults. Our publication is read by Christians and also those who are unsure about God. We also print Jewish stories." Monthly (8 issues). Estab. 1998. Circ. 50.

Needs: Children's/juvenile, family saga, historical (general), religious (children's, general, inspirational), young adult/teen (adventure, historical), general family, Jewish stories. No fantasy. Accepts 1 ms/issue; 8 mss/year. Publishes ms 1-6 months after acceptance. Length: 500-1,400 words; average length: 900. Publishes short shorts; average length: 500 words. Also publishes poetry. Always comments on rejected mss.

How to Contact: Send complete ms with cover letter. Include estimated word count and brief bio. Responds in 2 months to queries; 2 months to mss. Send disposable copy of ms and #10 SASE for reply only. Accepts multiple submissions. Sample package for $3. Guidelines for SASE.

Payment/Terms: Pays 2 contributor's copies. Acquires one-time rights.

Advice: "Fiction must be biblically accurate, well-written, and have a great message. We are always willing to work with new writers."

○ **THE STORYTELLER, A Writers Magazine,** 2441 Washington Rd., Maynard AR 72444. (870)647-2137. Fax: (870)647-2137. E-mail: storyteller1@cox-internet.com. Website: http://freewebz.com/fossilcreek. **Contact:** Regina Cook Williams, editor. Tabloid: 8½×11; 64 pages; typing paper; glossy cover; illustrations. "This magazine is open to all new writers regardless of age. I will accept short stories in any genre and poetry in any type. Please keep in mind, this is a family publication." Quarterly. Estab. 1996.

● *Note:* nonsubscribers must pay reading fee: $1/poem, $2/short story.

Needs: Adventure, historical, humor/satire, literary, mainstream/contemporary, mystery/suspense, regional, religious/inspirational, romance, senior citizen/retirement, sports, westerns, young adult/teen. "I will not accept pornography, erotica, science fiction, new age, foul language, horror or graphic violence." Wants more well-plotted mysteries. Publishes ms 3-9 months after acceptance. **Publishes 30-40 new writers/year.** Published work by Mellie Justad, Rick Jankowski, Dusty Richards, and Tony Hillerman. Length: 200-1,500 words. Publishes short shorts. Also publishes literary essays and poetry. Sometimes comments on rejected mss.

How to Contact: Send complete ms with a cover letter. Include estimated word count and 5-line bio. Responds in 1 month to queries; 2 months to mss. Send SASE for reply, return of ms or send a disposable copy of ms. Accepts simultaneous and reprint submissions. "*Must* tell where and when it was first published." Sample copy for $6. Guidelines for #10 SASE.

Payment/Terms: "Readers vote quarterly for their favorites in all categories. Winning authors receive certificate of merit and free copy of issue in which their story or poem appeared. We now nominate for the Pushcard Prize."

Advice: "Follow the guidelines. No matter how many times this has been said, writers still ignore this basic and most important rule." Looks for "professionalism, good plots and unique characters. Purchase a sample copy so you know the kind of material we look for. Even though this is for unpublished writers, don't send us something you would not send to paying markets." Would like more "well-plotted mysteries and suspense and a few traditional westerns. Avoid sending anything that children or young adults would not (or could not) read, such as really bad language."

$ ◎ **THE STRAND MAGAZINE**, Box 1418, Birmingham, MI 48012-1418. (800)300-6657. Fax: (248)874-1046. E-mail: strandmag@worldnet.att.net. **Contact:** A. F. Gulli, editor. Quarterly mystery magazine. Estab. 1998. "After an absence of nearly half a century, the magazine known to millions for bringing Sir Arthur Conan Doyle's ingenious detective, Sherlock Holmes, to the world has once again appeared on the literary scene. First launched in 1891, *The Strand* included in its pages the works of some of the greatest writers of the 20th century: Agatha Christie, Dorothy Sayers, Margery Allingham, W. Somerset Maugham, Graham Greene, P.G. Wodehouse, H.G. Wells, Aldous Huxley and many others. In 1950, economic difficulties in England caused a drop in circulation which forced the magazine to cease publication."

Needs: Mysteries, detective stories, tales of terror and the supernatural "written in the classic tradition of this century's great authors. Stories can be set in any time or place, provided they are well written and the plots interesting and well thought out. We are NOT interested in submissions with any sexual content." Length: 2,000-6,000 words, "however, we may occasionally publish short shorts of 1,000 words or sometimes go as long as a short novella."

How to Contact: Send complete ms, typed, double-spaced on one side of each page. SASE (IRCs if outside the US). Responds in 4 months.

Payment/Terms: Pays $50-175. Pays on acceptance for first North American serial rights.

🌐 💿 **STUDIO: A JOURNAL OF CHRISTIANS WRITING,** 727 Peel St., Albury 2640 Australia. Phone/fax: (+61)26021-1135. E-mail: pgrover@bigpond.com. **Contact:** Paul Grover, managing editor. Quarterly. Circ. 300.

Needs: "*Studio* publishes prose and poetry of literary merit, offers a venue for new and aspiring writers, and seeks to create a sense of community among Christians writing." Accepts 30-40 mss/year. **Publishes 40 new writers/year.** Recently published work by Andrew Lansdown and Benjamin Gilmour. Length: 500-5,000 words.

How to Contact: Send SASE. "Overseas contributors must use International postal coupons in place of stamped envelope." Responds in 1 month to ms. Sample copy for $8 (Aus).

Payment/Terms: Pays in copies; additional copies are discounted. "Copyright of individual published pieces remains with the author, while each edition as a whole is copyright to studio." Subscription $48 (Australian) for 4 issues (1 year). International draft in Australian dollars and IRC required, or Visa or MasterCard facilities available.

💲 💿 **TALEBONES, Fiction on the Dark Edge,** Fairwood Press, 5203 Quincy Ave. SE, Auburn WA 98092-8723. (253)735-6552. E-mail: talebones@nventure.com. Website: www.fairwoodpress.com (includes guidelines, submission requirements, excerpts, news about the magazine, bios). **Contact:** Patrick and Honna Swenson, editors. Magazine: digest size; 84 pages; standard paper; glossy cover stock; illustrations; photos. "We like stories that have punch, but still entertain. We like dark science fiction and dark fantasy, humor, psychological and experimental works." "Mostly" quarterly. Estab. 1995. Circ. 700.

Needs: Fantasy (dark), humor/satire, science fiction (hard science, soft/sociological, dark). "No straight slash and hack horror. No cat stories or stories told by young adults. Would like to see more science fiction." Receives 200 mss/month. Accepts 6-7 mss/issue; 24-28 mss/year. Publishes ms 3-4 months after acceptance. **Publishes 2-3 new writers/year.** Recently published work by Leslie What, Tony Daniel, William Barton, Nina Kiriki Hoffman. Length: 1,000-6,000 words; average length: 3,000-4,000 words. Publishes short shorts. Length: 1,000 words. Also publishes poetry.

How to Contact: Send complete ms with a cover letter. "We no longer accept e-mail submissions. Queries by e-mail OK." Include estimated word count and 1-paragraph bio. Responds in 1 week to queries; 1 month to mss. Send SASE for reply, return of ms or send a disposable copy of ms. Sample copy for $6. Guidelines for SASE. Reviews novels and short story collections.

Payment/Terms: Pays 1-2¢/word and 1 contributor's copy; additional copies $3.50. Pays before publication for first North American serial rights. Sends galleys to author.

Advice: "The story must be entertaining, but should blur the boundary between science fiction and horror. Most of our stories have a dark edge to them, but often are humorous or psychological. Be polite and know how to properly present a manuscript. Include a cover letter, but keep it short and to the point."

💿 💿 **UP DARE?,** la Pierna Tierna Press, 13304 Rachel Rd. SE, Albuquerque NM 87123-5631. (505)296-9919. **Contact:** Mary M. Towne, editor. "The only requirement is that all submitted material must pertain to folks with physical or psychological handicaps." Magazine: digest-sized; 48 pages; illustrations. Bimonthly. Estab. 1997.

Needs: Fiction and poetry. Looks for "honesty, plain language and message." No smut. **Publishes 10 new writers/year.** Recently published work by Denyce Hering, Kenneth Austin, Jane Lonnquist, Gordon Graves and Robert Deluty. Length: 2,000 words maximum; poetry to 36 lines.

How to Contact: "We will take single-spaced and even double-sided submissions so long as they are legible. We prefer to optically scan all material to avoid typos. We will not insist on an SASE if you truly have financial limitations. We're trying to make it as easy as possible. We will take short (250 words or less) pieces in Braille." Accepts submissions on disk. Accepts multiple submissions. Sample copy for $2.50. Guidelines for #10 SASE.

Advice: "Perfect structure and grammar are not as important as verisimilitude. We will not use euphemisms—a chair with a leg missing is a 'three-legged chair,' not a 'challenged seat.' We would like to hear from folks who are handicapped, but we aren't closing the door to others who understand and help or just have opinions to share. We will take reprints if the original appearance is identified."

💲 💿 **VIRGINIA QUARTERLY REVIEW,** One West Range, P.O. Box 400223, Charlottesville VA 22904-4223. (434)924-3124. Fax: (434)924-1397. **Contact:** Staige Blackford, editor. "A national magazine of literature and discussion. A lay, intellectual audience; people who are not out-and-out scholars but who are interested in ideas and literature." Quarterly. Estab. 1925. Circ. 4,000.

MARKET CONDITIONS are constantly changing! If you're still using this book and it is 2004 or later, buy the newest edition of *Novel & Short Story Writer's Market* at your favorite bookstore or order from Writer's Digest Books by calling 1-800-448-0915.

Needs: Adventure, contemporary, ethnic, feminist, humor, literary, romance, serialized novels (excerpts) and translations. "No pornography." Buys 3 mss/issue, 20 mss/year. Length: 3,000-7,000 words.

How to Contact: Query or send complete ms. SASE. Responds in 2 weeks to queries, 2 months to mss. Sample copy for $5.

Payment/Terms: Pays $10/printed page. Pays on publication for all rights. "Will transfer upon request." Offers Emily Clark Balch Award for best published short story of the year.

Advice: Looks for "stories with a somewhat Southern dialect and/or setting. Humor is welcome; stories involving cancer and geriatrics are not."

$ ⬛ ◎ WEBER STUDIES: Vices and Viewpoints of the Contemporary West, 1214 University Circle, Ogden UT 84408-1214. (801)626-6473. E-mail: blroghaar@weber.edu. Website: http://weberstudies.weber.edu (includes full web edition of journal). **Contact:** Brad L. Roghaar, editor. Magazine: 7½×10; 120-140 pages; coated paper; 4-color cover; illustrations; photos. "We seek the following themes: preservation of and access to wilderness, environmental cooperation, insight derived from living in the West, cultural diversity, changing federal involvement in the region, women and the West, implications of population growth, a sense of place, etc. We love good writing that reveals human nature as well as the natural environment." Triannual "with occasional 4th issues." Estab. 1984. Circ. 1,000.

Needs: Adventure, comics/graphic novels, ethnic/multicultural, experimental, fantasy (space fantasy), feminist, gay, historical, humor satire, literary, mainstream, military/war, mystery/suspense, New Age, psychic/supernatural/occult, regional (contemporary western US), science fiction, short story collections, translations, western (frontier saga, traditional, contemporary). No children's/juvenile, erotica, religious or young adult/teen. Receives 50 unsolicited mss/month. Accepts 3-6 mss/issue; 9-18 mss/year. Publishes ms up to 18 months after acceptance. **Publishes "few" new writers/ year**. Recently published work by Rex Burns, Steven Beeber and Gerald Vizenor. Length: 5,000 words maximum. Publishes short shorts. Also publishes critical essays, poetry and personal narrative. Sometimes comments on rejected ms.

How to Contact: Send complete ms with a cover letter. Include estimated word count, bio (not necessary), and list of publications (not necessary). Responds to mss in 3 months. Send SASE for return of ms or disposable copy of ms. Accepts multiple submissions. Sample copy for $10.

Payment/Terms: Pays $70-150, free subscription to the magazine and 1 contributor's copy. Pays on publication for first serial rights, electronic edition rights and requests electronic archive permission. Sends galleys to author.

Advice: "Is it true? Is it new? Is it interesting? Will the story appeal to educated readers who are concerned with the contemporary western United States? Declining public interest in reading generally is of concern. We publish both in print media and electronic media because we believe the future will expect both options."

⬛ THE WHITE CROW, Osric Publishing, P.O. Box 4501, Ann Arbor MI 48106-4501. E-mail: chris@osric.com. Website: www.wcrow.com (includes writer's guidelines, staff contact list, excerpts from publication). **Contact:** Christopher Herdt, editor. Zine: 5½×8; 32 pages; 20 lb. white paper; 60 lb. cover stock; illustrations; photos. "We seek solid literary works which will appeal to an intelligent but not necessarily literary audience." Quarterly. Estab. 1994. Circ. 200.

Needs: Experimental, humor/satire, literary, translations. No erotica, horror. "Wants to see more satire, and more decent character fiction." Receives 6 mss/month. Accepts 1-2 mss/issue; 6 mss/year. Publishes ms up to 4 months after acceptance. **Publishes 1 new writer/year.** Recently published work by Karen Loeb, Scott Sciortino and May Spangler. Length: 300-3,000 words; average length: 2,500 words. Publishes short shorts. Also publishes literary essays and poetry.

How to Contact: Send complete ms with cover letter. Include estimated word count and a 30-word bio. Responds in 6 months. Send SASE for return of ms. Accepts simultaneous submissions and reprints. Sample copy for $2.

Payment/Terms: Pays 2 contributor's copies; additional copies for $1. Acquires one-time rights. Not copyrighted.

Advice: "Is the story focused? Is it driven by a coherent, meaningful idea that can be grasped by an intelligent (but not literary) reader? We're here to edit a publication, not your writing, so please proofread your ms. Running spell check is a fabulous idea too."

⬛ ◎ YARNS AND SUCH, Creative With Words Publications, Box 223226, Carmel CA 93922. Fax: (831)655-8627. E-mail: cwwpub@usa.net. Website: members.tripod.com/CreativeWithWords (includes themes, guidelines, submittal form, cost of back issues, advertising rates, editorial statement; editing tips of current issue; best of the month salute and winning writing). **Contact:** Brigitta Geltrich (general editor) and Bert Hower (nature editor). Booklet: 5½×8½; more than 50 pages; bond paper; illustrations. Folklore. 12-14 issues annually. Estab. 1975. Circ. varies.

Needs: Ethnic, humor/satire, mystery/suspense (amateur sleuth, private eye), regional, folklore. "Poems have a better chance to be accepted. Do not submit essays. Four times a year we publish an anthology of the writings of young writers, titled: *We are Writers Too!*" No violence or erotica, overly religious fiction or sensationalism. List of themes available for SASE. Receives 500 unsolicited fiction mss/month. Publishes ms 1-2 months after deadline. **Published new writers within the last year.** Length: 800 words average; limits poetry to 20 lines or less, 46 characters per line or less. Critiques rejected mss "when requested, *then we charge $20/prose, up to 1,000 words.*"

How to Contact: Query first or send complete ms with cover letter and SASE. Accepts queries/mss by e-mail with writer's e-mail address given. "Reference has to be made to which project the manuscript is being submitted. Unsolicited mss without SASE will be destroyed after holding them 1 month." Responds in 2 weeks to queries; 2 months to mss; longer on specific thematic anthologies. Accepts electronic (disk) submissions via Macintosh and IBM/PC. Sample copy for $6. Guidelines for #10 SASE.

Payment/Terms: No payment; 20% reduction on each copy ordered; 30% reduction on each copy on orders of 10 or more. Acquires one-time rights. Offers "Best of the Month" one free copy.

Advice: "We have increased the number of anthologies we are publishing to 12-14 per year and offer a greater variety of themes. We look for clean family-type fiction. Also, we ask the writer to look at the world from a different perspective, research topic thoroughly, be creative, apply brevity, tell the story from a character's viewpoint, tighten dialogue, be less descriptive, proofread before submitting and be patient. We will not publish every manuscript we receive. It has to be in standard English, well-written, proofread. We do not appreciate receiving manuscripts where we have to do the proofreading and the correcting of grammar."

ZOPILOTE, Oldie Publications, 824 S. Mill Ave., Suite 219, Tempe AZ 85281. (480)557-7195. E-mail: zopilote1 @mindspring.com. Website: www.zopilote.com. **Contact:** Marco Albarrán, publisher. Magazine: 8½×11; 26 pages; illustrations; photos. "*Zopilote* magazine is one of the few cultural magazines that promotes indigenous and Latino cultures in the U.S. We publish material pertinent to the history, ways of life, philosophies, traditions and changes taking place right now." Bimonthly. Estab. 1993. Circ. 5,000. Member, Council of Literary Magazines and Presses.

Needs: Comics/graphic novels, ethnic/multicultural (indigenous Latino), historical (indigenous Latino), literary, science fiction (ancient science of the Americas), western (indigenous Latino). "No religious, romance, erotica." Receives 5-10 unsolicited mss/month. Accepts 3 mss/issue; 18-20 mss/year. Publishes ms 3-5 months after acceptance. **Publishes 60-70% new writers/year.** Recently published work by Roberto Rodriquez, Cristina Gonzalez and Carmen Vaxones Martinez. Length: 150-500 words; average length: 300 words. Publishes short shorts. Also publishes literary essays, literary criticism and poetry. Sometimes comments on rejected mss.

How to Contact: Send complete ms with a cover letter. Accepts submissions by e-mail. Include estimated word count, brief bio and list of publications. Responds in 6 weeks. Send a disposable copy of ms and #10 SASE for reply only. Accepts simultaneous submissions, previously published work and multiple submissions. Sample copy free for 8½×11 SAE and $3 postage. Guidelines by e-mail. Reviews novels, short story collections and nonfiction books of interest to writers.

Payment/Terms: Pays 5 contributor's copies; additional copies $3.50.

Zines

Zines differ vastly from one another in appearance and content, but their common source seems to be a need to voice opinions. Although they've always been around, it was not until the '70s, and possibly beginning with the social upheaval of the '60s, that the availability of photocopiers and computers provided an easy, cheap way to produce the self-published and usually self-written zines. And now, with the cyberspace explosion, an overwhelming number of e-zines are springing up in an electronic format every day (See the Online Markets section, page 301, for Internet-only zines).

SELF-EXPRESSION AND ARTISTIC FREEDOM

The editorial content of zines runs the gamut from traditional and genre fiction to personal rants and highly experimental work. Artistic freedom, however, is a characteristic of all zines. Although zine editors are open to a wide range of fiction that more conventional editors might not consider, don't make the mistake of thinking they expect any less from writers than the editors of other types of publications. Zine editors look for work that is creative and well presented and that shows the writer has taken time to become familiar with the market. And since most zines are highly specialized, familiarity with the niche markets they offer is extremely important.

Some of the zines listed here have been published since the early '80s, but many are relatively new and some were just starting publication as they filled out the questionnaire to be included in this edition of *Novel & Short Story Writer's Market*. Unfortunately, due to the waning energy and shrinking funds of their publishers (and often a lack of material), few last for more than several issues. Fortunately, though, some have been around since the late '70s and early '80s, and hundreds of new ones are launched every day.

While zines represent one of the most volatile groups of publications in *Novel & Short Story Writer's Market*, they are also the most open to submissions by beginning writers. As mentioned above, the editors of zines are often writers themselves and welcome the opportunity to give others a chance at publication.

SELECTING THE RIGHT MARKET

Zero in on the zines most likely to be interested in your work by browsing through the listings. This is especially important since zines are the most diverse and specialized markets listed in this book. If you write genre fiction, check out the specific sections for lists of magazines publishing in that genre (mystery, page 83; romance, page 97; science fiction/fantasy & horror, page 109). For other types of fiction, check the Category Index (starting on page 606) for the appropriate subject heading.

In addition to browsing through the listings and using the Category Index, check the ranking codes at the beginning of listings to find those most likely to be receptive to your work. Most all zines are open to new writers (▢) or to both new and established writers (◪). For more explanation about these codes, see the inside front and back covers of this book.

Once you have a list of zines you might like to try, read their listings carefully. Zines vary greatly in appearance as well as content. Some paper zines are photocopies published whenever the editor has material and money, while others feature offset printing and regular distribution schedules. And a few have evolved into four-color, commercial-looking, very slick publications. The physical description appearing near the beginning of the listings gives you clues about the size and financial commitment to the publication. This is not always an indication of quality, but chances are a publication with expensive paper and four-color artwork on the cover has more prestige than a photocopied publication featuring a clip art self-cover. If you're a new writer or your work is considered avant garde, however, you may be more interested in the photocopied zine or one of the electronic zines. For more information on some of the paper, binding and printing terms used in these descriptions, see Printing and Production Terms Defined on page 594. Also, The "Quick Start" Guide to Publishing Your Fiction, starting on page 2, describes in detail the listing information common to all markets in our book.

FURTHERING YOUR SEARCH

Reading the listings is only the first part of developing your marketing plan. The second part, equally important, is to obtain fiction guidelines and a copy of the actual zine. Reading copies of the publication helps you determine the fine points of the zine's publishing style and philosophy. Especially since zines tend to be highly specialized, there is no substitute for this hands-on, eyes-on research.

Unlike commercial periodicals available at most newsstands and bookstores, it requires a little more effort to obtain most of the paper zines listed here. You will probably need to send for a sample copy. We include sample copy prices in the listings whenever possible.

N $ ABSOLUTE MAGNITUDE, Science Fiction Adventures, DNA Publications, P.O. Box 2988, Radford VA 24143-2988. E-mail: dnapublications@dnapublications.com. **Editor:** Warren Lapine. Zine: 8½ × 11; 64 pages; newsprint; color cover; illustrations. "We publish technical science fiction that is adventurous and character driven." Quarterly. Estab. 1993. Circ. 9,000.
- *Absolute Magnitude* ranked on *Writer's Digest*'s "Top 30" list of best markets for fiction writers.

Needs: Science fiction: adventure, hard science. No fantasy, horror, funny science fiction. Receives 300-500 unsolicited mss/month. Accepts 7-10 mss/issue; 28-40 mss/year. Publishes ms 3-6 months after acceptance. Agented fiction 5%. Published work by Hal Clement, Chris Bunch, C.J. Cherryh, Barry B. Longyear and Harlan Ellison. Length: 1,000-25,000 words; average length: 5,000-12,000 words. Publishes very little poetry. Often comments on rejected ms.

How to Contact: Do NOT query. Send complete ms with a cover letter. Should include estimated word count and list of publications. Send SASE for reply or return of ms. Sample copy for $5. Reviews novels and short story collections.

Payment/Terms: Pays 7-10¢/word. Pays on acceptance for first North American serial rights. Sometimes sends galleys to author.

Advice: "We want good writing with solid characterization, also character growth, story development, and plot resolution. We would like to see more character-driven stories."

N ⊘ ◎ ALIEN WORLDS, Fading Shadows, Inc., 504 E. Morris St., Seymour TX 76380. (940)889-4292. E-mail: fadingshadows@juno.com. **Contact:** Ginger Johnson. Zine specializing in sci-fi: 8½ × 5½; 80-84 pages; 20 lb. bond paper; b&w stock cover; illustrations. "*Alien Worlds* is designed to entertain, not shock, and features genre fiction, no articles or poetry. We do encourage letters of comment." Monthly. Estab. 1997. Circ. 75.

Needs: Fantasy (space fantasy, sword and sorcery), science fiction (hard science/technological, soft/sociological, space opera), young adult/teen (adventure, easy-to-read, fantasy/science fiction, mystery/suspense, series, western). "No horror, weird, or pornography." Receives 20 unsolicited mss/month. Accepts 10-20 mss/issue; "hundreds" of mss/year. Publishes ms within 6 months after acceptance. Agented fiction 90%. **Publishes 20 new writers/year.** Recently published work by Mike Black and Len Jellema. Length: 1,000-80,000 words; average length: 10,000 words. Publishes short shorts. Average length: 1,000 words. Always comments on rejected mss.

How to Contact: Send complete ms with a cover letter. Accepts submissions by e-mail and disk. Include estimated word count and brief bio. Responds in 1 month. Send SASE (or IRC) for return of ms or send a disposable copy of ms and #10 SASE for reply only. Accepts simultaneous, previously published and multiple submissions. Sample copy for $6.30. Guidelines for SASE or by e-mail.

Payment/Terms: Pays 2 contributors copies; additional copies $3. Pays on publication for one-time rights. Not copyrighted.

Advice: "We want fiction that is well written, well plotted, with good characterization, and enough action to keep the readers' interest. Don't write sloppy stories, relying on shock scenes. We expect clean works to give to our readers. It's highly suggested that anyone interested in submitting stories to one of our genre magazines, they at least buy a sample copy of that title to see what the magazine is like."

N ◯ ◎ ANY DREAM WILL DO, Stories Written By, For, and About Persons Diagnosed With Mental Illness, Any Dream Will Do, Inc., 1830 Kirman Ave., #C1, Reno NV 89502-3381. (775)786-0345. E-mail: cassjmb@ igemail.com. Website: www.willigocrazy.org (includes writer's guidelines, names of editors, fiction not included in print version and tips on how to write a story for the *Any Dream Will Do Review*). **Contact:** Jean M. Bradt, Ph.D., editor. Magazine: 5½ × 8½; 50-70 pages. "The *Any Dream Will Do Review* publishes short stories and essays which depict people diagnosed or diagnosible with mental illness, their feelings, and their experiences, and/or are written by someone who has been diagnosed with mental illness." Semiannual. Estab. 2001.

Needs: Adventure, ethnic/multicultural, experimental, fantasy, feminist, historical (general), horror (futuristic, psychological, supernatural), humor/satire, literary, mainstream, mystery/suspense (amateur sleuth), psychic/supernatural/occult, romance, science fiction (soft/sociological), thriller/espionage, western, special interests: mental illness. "No erotica, testimonials, poetry, political themes, true-life stories, confessions." Accepts 8 mss/issue; 16 mss/year. Publishes ms 3 months after acceptance. **Mostly publishes stories from new writers.** Length: 400-4,000 words. Publishes short shorts. Often comments on rejected mss.

How to Contact: Send complete ms by e-mail or snail mail. Include name, land address, e-mail address. Responds in 2 months. Accepts multiple submissions. Sample copy for $2. Guidelines for SASE, by e-mail or on website.

Payment/Terms: Pays 1 contributors copy. Acquires all rights. Not copyrighted.

Advice: "Please make sure that your work is clean, well-written and proofread many times. No poems, testimonials, or true life stories, please. Just fiction, intimate personal (not political) essays, or humor you wrote yourself. We admit that we are choosy. We seek realistic stories about the mentally ill, yet we do not accept stories which might leave mentally ill readers with the feeling that they have been denigrated in any way. What's more, our definition of 'mental illness' is strict: brain disorders normally treated by psychiatrists or psychologists. For example, we do not accept stories or essays about developmental disabilities, epilepsy, or Alzheimer's. We do accept stories or essays about depression, hypochondria, SAD, PTSD and, of course, bipolar disorder and schizophrenia. Base the story on your actual experiences. Base at least one character in the story, preferably the hero or narrator, on yourself. Include your own feelings—all of them. And proofread for errors over and over. For more tips, click on www.willigocrazy.org/Ch08.htm."

ART:MAG, P.O. Box 70896, Las Vegas NV 89170-0896. (702)734-8121. E-mail: magman@iopener.net. **Contact:** Peter Magliocco, editor. Zine: 70-90 pages; 20 lb. bond paper; b&w pen and ink illustrations; photos. Publishes "irreverent, literary-minded work by committed writers," for "small press, 'quasi-art-oriented' " audience. Annual. Estab. 1984. Circ. under 500.

Needs: Condensed/excerpted novel, confession, contemporary, erotica, ethnic, experimental, fantasy, feminist, gay, historical (general), horror, humor/satire, lesbian, literary, mainstream, mystery/suspense, prose poem, psychic/supernatural/occult, regional, science fiction, translations and arts. Wants to see more "daring and thought-provoking" fiction. No "slick-oriented stuff published by major magazines." Receives 1 ms/month. Accepts 1-2 mss/year. Does not read mss July-October. Publishes ms within 3-6 months of acceptance. **Publishes 1-2 new writers/year.** Recently published work by Jeff Weddle. Length: 250-3,000 words; 2,000 words preferred. Also publishes literary essays "if relevant to aesthetic preferences," literary criticism "occasionally," poetry. Sometimes comments on rejected mss.

How to Contact: Send complete ms with cover letter. Responds in 3 months. SASE. Accepts simultaneous submissions. Sample copy for $5, 6×9 SAE and 79¢ postage. Two-year subscription for $10. Guidelines for #10 SASE.

Payment/Terms: Pays contributor's copies. Acquires one-time rights.

Advice: "Seeking more novel and quality-oriented work, usually from solicited authors. Magazine fiction today needs to be concerned with the issues of fiction writing itself—not just with a desire to publish or please the largest audience. Think about things in the fine art world as well as the literary one and keep the hard core of life in between."

babysue, P.O. Box 33369, Decatur GA 30033. (404)320-1178. Websites: www.babysue.com and www.LMNOP.com (includes comics, poetry, fiction and a wealth of music reviews). **Contact:** Don W. Seven, editor. Zine: 8½×11; 32 pages; illustrations; photos. "*babysue* is a collection of music reviews, poetry, short fiction and cartoons for anyone who can think and is not easily offended." Biannual. Estab. 1983. Circ. 5,000.

- Sometimes funny, very often perverse, this 'zine featuring mostly cartoons and "comix" definitely is not for the easily offended.

Needs: Erotica, experimental and humor/satire. Receives 5-10 mss/month. Accepts 3-4 mss/year. Publishes ms within 3 months of acceptance. Published work by Daniel Lanette, Massy Baw, Andrew Taylor and Barbara Rimshaw. Publishes short shorts. Length: 1-2 single-spaced pages.

How to Contact: Query with clips of published work. SASE. Accepts simultaneous submissions. No submissions via e-mail.

Payment/Terms: Pays 1 contributor's copy.

Advice: "Create out of the love of creating, not to see your work in print!"

THE BLACK LILY, Fantasy and Medieval Review, Southern Goblin Productions, 8444 Cypress Circle, Sarasota FL 34243-2006. (941)351-4386. E-mail: gkuklews@ix.netcom.com. Editor: Vincent Kuklewski. **Contact:** Elena Kuklewski, stories editor. Review Editor: Karen Snow. Zine specializing in high fantasy, work set in a Pre-1600 A.D. level of technology, and history articles: 64 pages; 24 lb. paper; card cover; illustrations; photos. Quarterly. Estab. 1996. Circ. 150+ (subscribers in six countries).

Needs: Fantasy (sword and sorcery), medieval, Renaissance, humor/satire, literary, mystery/suspense, world folklore. No science fiction or gratuitous gore. Upcoming themes: "Dragons" (June); "Norsemen" (November). Receives 10-

20 unsolicited mss/month. Accepts 2-4 mss/issue; 25-30 mss/year. Publishes ms 4-10 months after acceptance. Recently published work by Scott Urban, Mary Choo, Natasha Bennett and Stepan Chapman. Length: 1,500-60,000 words; average length: 3,000-4,000 words. Also publishes literary essays, literary criticism and poetry. Sponsors 2 short story contests/year: details for SASE. Often comments on rejected manuscripts.

How to Contact: Send complete manuscript with a cover letter or e-mail submission with cover letter. Include estimated word count and 2-line bio. Responds in 1 month to queries; 3 months to mss. Send SASE for reply and send a disposable copy of ms. Accepts reprints and electronic submissions. Reviews novels and short story collections. Send books to Karen Snow.

Payment/Terms: Pays $3 minimum; $25 maximum and 1 contributor's copy. Pays on acceptance for first international serial rights "for 3 years or until publication, whichever comes first."

Advice: "Never, ever send stories with a post-1600 AD level of technology. We generally prefer to publish work with a high fantasy or medieval setting but have published stories ranging from the Bronze Age to Elizabethan England. We also publish in each issue a folktale from any of the world's cultures. We love knights, castles, Vikings, Ancient Egypt, 1001 Arabian Nights, dragons, goblins, dryads, dark forests, ruins, wizardry, Beowulf, Cynewulf, and the Icelandic Sagas. Sex in stories is okay. We strive to publish one history article per issue. Because we send *The Black Lily* overseas, we are seeking stories written in Russian and Swedish."

BLACK PETALS, Fossil Publications, 11627 Taft, Wichita KS 67209-1036. E-mail: blkptls@sctelcom.net. Website: www.blackpetals.com (includes writer's guidelines, subscription information, addresses, editors' names, sample story). **Contact:** Kenneth James Crist, editor. Zine specializing in horror/science fiction: digest size; perfect-bound; over 88 pages; photocopied; illustrations. "A little something special for those special readers of oddity and terror. *Black Petals* is about the dark side of science fiction and the bizarre and unusual in horror—mature audience *only*." Quarterly. Estab. 1997. Circ. 200.

Needs: Experimental, horror, psychic/supernatural; science fiction (soft/sociological). Wants more speculative science fiction. No children's or romance, "Star Trek," vampires, werewolves, stories from "beyond the grave. We don't get nearly enough science fiction that is based on current scientific fact—or even scientific speculation. We look for original ideas, strong characters, emotional involvement, good, vivid background." Receives over 15-20 unsolicited mss/month. Accepts 14-20 mss/issue. **Publishes 6-8 new writers/year.** Recently published work by Eric S. Brown, Vic Fortezza, Raymond A. Valent and Christina Sng. Length: 3,500 words maximum; average length: 1,500 words. Publishes short shorts. Also publishes poetry. Always comments on rejected mss.

How to Contact: Send complete ms. Include estimated word count and list of publications. Responds in 2-4 weeks to queries and mss. "Disposable copies please. No e-mail submissions except from overseas." Accepts simultaneous and multiple submissions and reprints. Sample copy for $4. Guidelines for #10 SASE.

Payment/Terms: Pays contributor's copies; additional copies $4.

Advice: "My best advice—submit! How do you know if you'll get published unless you submit! Also, obtain a sample copy, follow guidelines and don't watch the mailbox. New unpublished writers are high on my list. If I have time I'll even help edit a manuscript. If I reject a manuscript, I encourage writers to send something else. Don't ever be discouraged, and don't wallpaper your office with rejection notes—toss them! If an editor gives advice, pay attention. Do research. Learn to spell and use a dictionary and thesaurus."

THE BROBDINGNAGIAN TIMES, 96 Albert Rd., Cork, Ireland. Phone: (21)4311227. **Contact:** Giovanni Malito, editor. Zine specializing in short international work: $6 \times 8\frac{1}{2}$; 8 pages; 80 gramme paper; illustrations. "*TBT* believes that there are no boundaries in literature, geographical or otherwise. There are no obvious editorial slants. We are interested in any prose from anyone anywhere provided it is short (600 words maximum)." Quarterly. Estab. 1996. Circ. 250.

Needs: Ethnic/multicultural, experimental, humor/satire, literary, science fiction (hard science/technological, soft/sociological). "No stories with an Irish slant." Wants to see more minimalist work, "akin to prose poetry." Receives 4-6 unsolicited mss/month. Accepts 2 mss/issue; 8 mss/year. Publishes ms in next issue after acceptance. **Publishes 1 new writer/year.** Recently published work by Robert Cole, Christopher Woods and A. Migliore. Length: 50-1,000 words; average length: 600 words. Publishes short shorts. Average length: 500 words. Also publishes literary essays, poetry. Always comments on rejected ms.

How to Contact: Send complete ms with a cover letter. Include estimated word count. Responds in 1 week to queries; 3 weeks to mss. Send SASE (IRCs) for reply, return of ms or send a disposable copy of ms. Accepts simultaneous, multiple and reprint submissions. Sample copy for #10 SAE and 2 IRCs. Guidelines for #10 SAE and 1 IRC.

Payment/Terms: Pays 1 contributor's copy; additional copies for postage. Acquires one-time rights for Ireland/U.K. Sends galleys to author if required. Copyrighted Ireland/U.K.

Advice: "Crisp language. Economy of language. These are important, otherwise almost anything goes."

BURNING SKY: Adventures in Science Fiction Terror, Thievin' Kitty Publications, P.O. Box 341, Marion MA 02738. E-mail: theedge@capecod.net. Website: http://beam.to/thievinkitty (includes guidelines, current and back issue information, cover art, ordering information, information on editors). **Contact:** Greg F. Gifune, editor. Associate editors: Carla Gifune and Chuck Deude. Zine specializing in science fiction horror: digest; 30-40 pages; white bond; glossy card cover. *Burning Sky* publishes "sci/fi horror blends ONLY." Triannual. Estab. 1998. Circ. 500.

Needs: Horror and science fiction blends. Receives more than 100 unsolicited mss/month. Accepts 5-6 mss/issue; 15-18 mss/year. Does not read January, May and September. Publishes ms 1-4 months after acceptance. Agented fiction

1-2%. **Publishes 1-3 new writers/year.** Published work by D. F. Lewis, Michael Laimo, Suzanne Donahue, Christopher Stires, Denis Kirk and Stephen van Maanen. Length: 500-3,500 words; average length: 2,000-3,000 words. Also publishes literary criticism. Often comments on rejected ms.

How to Contact: Send complete ms with a cover letter. Accepts queries by e-mail, but no mss. Include estimated word count, bio, list of publications and cover letter. Responds in 1 week to queries; 2 months to mss. Send SASE for reply, return of ms or send a disposable copy of ms. Sample copy for $4 in US, $5 elsewhere. Reviews novels, short story collections and nonfiction books of interest to writers. Send books to editor.

Payment/Terms: Pays 1 contributor's copy; additional copies $4. Pays on publication. Sends galleys to author on request.

Advice: "We like strong, concise, lean writing, stories that follow our very specific guidelines of blending sci-fi and horror, stories with an 'edge of your seat' quality. Thought-provoking, tension filled and genuinely frightening stories with realistic dialogue and a gritty style. Do not send straight sci-fi or horror stories. We need elements of both. Read a copy. *Burning Sky* is a very particular market, but we are proud to have published three first stories in our first three issues, along with more established writers. Send us a well written story in proper manuscript format that fits our guidelines. We don't want highly technical or introverted ramblings—we want exciting, highly entertaining and frightening stories."

CHILDREN, CHURCHES AND DADDIES LITERARY MAGAZINE, the un-religious, non-family oriented publication, Scars Publications and Design, 829 Brian Court, Gurnee IL 60031-3155. E-mail: ccandd96@aol.com. Website: http://scars.tv (includes all issues, writings, guidelines). **Contact:** Janet Kuypers, editor-in-chief. E-zine and literary magazine: laser paper; cmyk color cover stock; some illustrations; photos. "We look for detail-oriented writing that makes a gripping sense of action." Estab. 1993.

Needs: Ethnic/multicutural, feminist, gay, horror (futuristic, psychological, supernatural), lesbian, literary, mainstream, mystery/suspense, psychic/supernatural/occult. No religious, romantic or children's writings. Accepts 25-45 mss/issue; 25-45 mss/year. Publishes ms 1 year after acceptance. Agented fiction 60-80%. **Publishes 75% new writers/year.** Recently published work by Gabriel Athens, Marina Arturo, Alexandria Rand, MacKenzie Silver, Helena Wolfe and Sydney Anderson. Publishes short shorts. Also publishes poetry.

How to Contact: Send complete ms with cover letter by e-mail. Include e-mail address. Responds in 1 month to queries; 2 months to mss. Send SASE for return of ms or send a disposable copy of the ms and #10 SASE for reply only. Sample copy free on website; e-mail query for cost of purchasing back issues in book form. Guidelines for SASE, e-mail, or on website.

Payment/Terms: Acquires one-time and electronic rights.

Advice: "Use descriptive detail, gripping logic and reason. We want to feel like we are living in a scene we are reading about. View our issues and guidelines online and enter our contest."

CLARK STREET REVIEW, P.O. Box 1377, Berthoud CO 80513-2377. (970)669-5175. E-mail: clarkreview@earthlink.net. Website: http://home.earthlink.net/~clarkreview/ (includes guidelines only). **Contact:** Ray Foreman, editor. Zine specializing in poetry and short fiction: 5½×8½; 20 pages; 20 lb. paper; 20 lb. cover stock. "We publish only interesting narrative poetry and short shorts with insights about people, places and life lived—our readers are mainly writers who have been around." Publishes 6-8 issues/year. Estab. 1998. Circ. 100.

Needs: Mainstream. No children's and "dull, my-vacation stories." Receives 10 unsolicited mss/month. Accepts 20-40 mss/year. Publishes ms 6 months after acceptance. Recently published work by Ray Dickson, Lamar Thomas, Laurel Speer and Ron Baatz. Length: 800 words maximum; average length: 400-700 words. Also publishes literary essays, literary criticism and poetry.

How to Contact: Send complete ms with a cover letter. Include estimated word count. Responds in 1 month. Send a disposable copy of ms and #10 SASE for reply only. Accepts simultaneous submissions, previously published work and multiple submissions. Sample copy for $2. Guidelines for SASE or by e-mail.

Payment/Terms: Pays 1 contributor's copy.

Advice: "Read a lot of good short stories and some poor ones from beginners and discover the difference."

CLASSIC PULP FICTION STORIES, An All Genre Magazine, Fading Shadows, Inc., 504 E. Morris St., Seymour TX 76380. (940)889-4292. E-mail: fadingshadows@juno.com. Website: http://home.att./fadingshadows/index.html. **Contact:** Ginger Johnson. Zine: 8½×5½; 80-84 pages; 20 lb. bond paper; b&w cover stock; illustrations. "*Classic Pulp Fiction Stories* is designed to entertain, not shock, and features genre fiction, no articles or poetry. We do encourage letters of comment." Monthly. Estab. 1995. Circ. 75.

Needs: Adventure (adventure, animal, easy-to-read, fantasy, mystery, series, ages 12-90), fantasy (space fantasy, sword and sorcery), military/war, mystery/suspense (amateur sleuth, police procedural, private eye/hardboiled), science fiction (hard science/technological, soft/sociological, space opera), thriller/espionage, western (frontier saga, traditional), young adult/teen (adventure, easy-to-read, fantasy/science fiction, mystery/suspense, series, western). "No horror, weird, or pornography." Receives 20 unsolicited mss/month. Accepts 10-20 mss/issue; "hundreds" of mss/year. Publishes ms within 6 months after acceptance. Agented fiction 90%. **Publishes 20 new writers/year.** Recently published work by Mike Black and Len Jellema. Length: 1,000-80,000 words; average length: 10,000 words. Publishes short shorts. Average length: 1,000 words. Always comments on rejected mss.

How to Contact: Send complete ms with a cover letter. Accepts submissions by e-mail and disk. Include estimated word count and brief bio. Responds in 1 month. Send SASE (or IRC) for return of ms or send a disposable copy of ms and #10 SASE for reply only. Accepts simultaneous, previously published and multiple submissions. Sample copy for $6.30. Guidelines for SASE or by e-mail.

Payment/Terms: Pays 2 contributors copies; additional copies $3. Pays on publication for one-time rights. Not copyrighted.

Advice: "We look for fiction that is well written, well plotted, with good characterization, and enough action to keep the readers' interest. Don't write sloppy stories, relying on shock scenes. We expect clean works to give to our readers. It's highly suggested that anyone interested in submitting stories to one of our genre magazines, they at least buy a sample copy of that title to see what the magazine is like."

A COMPANION IN ZEOR, 1622B Swallow Crest Dr., Edgewood MD 21040-1751. Fax: (410)676-0164. E-mail: klitman323@aol.com or karenlitman@juno.com. Website: www.simegen.com/sgfandom/rimonslibrary/cz. (includes guidelines, back issue flyers, etc.). **Contact:** Karen MacLeod, editor. Fanzine: 8½ × 11; 60 pages; "letter" paper; heavy blue cover; b&w line illustrations; occasional b&w photos. Publishes science fiction based on the various Universe creations of Jacqueline Lichtenberg. Occasional features on Star Trek, and other interests, convention reports, reviews of movies and books, recordings, etc. Published irregularly. Estab. 1978. Circ. 300.

- *Companion in Zeor* is one fanzine devoted to the work and characters of Jacqueline Lichtenberg. Lichtenberg's work includes several future world, alien and group culture novels and series including the Sime/Gen Series and The Dushau trilogy. She's also penned two books on her own vampire character and she co-authored *Star Trek Lives*.

Needs: Fantasy, humor/satire, prose poem, science fiction. "No vicious satire. Nothing X-rated. Homosexuality prohibited unless *essential* in story. Occasionally receives one manuscript a month." Publication of an accepted ms "goes to website posting. " Occasionally comments on rejected mss and recommends other markets.

How to Contact: Query first or send complete ms with cover letter. "Prefer cover letters about any writing experience prior, or related interests toward writing aims." Responds in 1 month. SASE. Accepts simultaneous submissions. Sample copy price depends on individual circumstances. Guidelines for #10 SASE. "I write individual letters to all queries. No form letter at present." SASE for guidelines or can be sent by e-mail. Reviews science fiction/fantasy collections or titles. "We can accept e-mail queries and manuscripts through AOL providers."

Payment/Terms: Pays in contributor's copies. Acquires first and electronic rights.

Advice: "Send concise cover letter asking what the author would like me to do for them if the manuscript cannot be used by my publication. They should follow guidelines of the type of material I use, which is often not done. I have had many submissions I cannot use as they are general fiction. Ask for guidelines before submitting to a publication. Write to the best of your ability and work with your editor to develop your work to a higher point than your present skill level. Take constructive criticism and learn from it. Electronic publishing seems the way the industry is heading. Receipt of manuscripts can only be through klitman323@aol.com. Juno cannot handle attachments. People can learn more through the domain—www.simegen.com/index.html."

DETECTIVE MYSTERY STORIES, Fading Shadows, Inc., 504 E. Morris St., Seymour TX 76380. (940)889-4292. E-mail: fadingshadows@juno.com. Website: http://home.att./fadingshadows/index.html. **Contact:** Ginger Johnson. Zine specializing in detective and mystery: 8½ × 5½; 80-84 pages; 20 lb. bond paper; b&w cover stock; illustrations. "*Detective Mystery Stories* is designed to entertain, not shock, and features genre fiction, no articles or poetry. We do encourage letters of comment." Monthly. Estab. 1998. Circ. 75.

Needs: Mystery/suspense (amateur sleuth, police procedural, private eye/hardboiled), thriller/espionage, young adult/teen (adventure, easy-to-read, fantasy/science fiction, mystery/suspense, series, western). "No horror, weird, or pornography." Receives 20 unsolicited mss/month. Accepts 10-20 mss/issue; "hundreds" of mss/year. Publishes ms within 6 months after acceptance. Agented fiction 90%. **Publishes 20 new writers/year.** Recently published work by Mike Black and Len Jellema. Length: 1,000-80,000 words; average length: 10,000 words. Publishes short shorts. Average length: 1,000 words. Always comments on rejected mss.

How to Contact: Send complete ms with a cover letter. Accepts submissions by e-mail and disk. Include estimated word count and brief bio. Responds in 1 month. Send SASE (or IRC) for return of ms or send a disposable copy of ms and #10 SASE for reply only. Accepts simultaneous, previously published and multiple submissions. Sample copy for $6.30. Guidelines for SASE or by e-mail.

Payment/Terms: Pays 2 contributors copies; additional copies $3. Pays on publication for one-time rights. Not copyrighted.

Advice: "We look for fiction that is well written, well plotted, with good characterization, and enough action to keep the readers' interest. Don't write sloppy stories, relying on shock scenes. We expect clean works to give to our readers. It's highly suggested that anyone interested in submitting stories to one of our genre magazines, they at least buy a sample copy of that title to see what the magazine is like."

DEVIL BLOSSOMS, Asterius Press, P.O. Box 5122, Seabrook NJ 08302-3511. E-mail: theeditor@asteriuspress.com. Website: www.asteriuspress.com (includes guidelines, online bookstore, interviews, articles, etc.). **Contact:** John C. Erianne, publisher/editor. Zine specializing in fiction and poetry: 7 × 10; 24 pages; 20-30 lb. paper; card stock cover. "This is a publication for radical free-thinking geniuses—Twain, De Sade, Swift, Dostoyevsky, etc. would have found a home here. If you are in this tradition, you too may find a home." Semiannual. Estab. 1998. Circ. 750-1,000.

Needs: Erotica, experimental, horror (psychological), humor/satire, literary, science fiction (soft/sociological). "No romance, inspirational, New Age, supernatural horror." Receives 200 unsolicited mss/month. Accepts 3-4 mss/issue; 6-8 mss/year. Publishes ms 6 months after acceptance. **Publishes 1-2 new writers/year.** Recently published work by Stephanie Savage, Jim Sullivan and Brendan Connell. Length: 300-2,500 words; average length: 1,500 words. Publishes short shorts. Average length: 750 words. Also publishes poetry. Sometimes comments on rejected mss.

How to Contact: Send complete ms with a cover letter. Accepts submissions by e-mail as text in message body. No file attachments. Include estimated word count and name and address in the upper left-hand corner. Responds in 1 week to queries; 3 weeks to mss. Send SASE (or IRC) for return of ms or send a disposable copy of ms and #10 SASE for reply only. Accepts simultaneous submissions. Sample copy for $5 payable by checks or money order to John C. Erianne. CC orders available on the website. Guidelines for SASE or on website.

Payment/Terms: Pays 1 contributor's copy; additional copies $5. Pays on publication for first and non-exclusive one-time reprint (anthology) rights.

Advice: "I look for originality, interesting characters and tales that take risks. Safe, boring, middle-of-the-road crap has no place here. Present yourself in a professional manner, follow the guidelines, leave your ego at home, have talent, but most of all remember that it is not my job to impress you."

N ○ ◑ **DOUBLE DANGER TALES**, Fading Shadows, Inc., 504 E. Morris St., Seymour TX 76380. (940)889-4292. E-mail: fadingshadows@juno.com. Website: http://home.att./fadingshadows/index.html. **Contact:** Ginger Johnson. Zine specializing in super heroes: 8½ × 5½; 80-84 pages; 20 lb. bond paper; b&w cover stock; illustrations. "*Double Danger Tales* is designed to entertain, not shock, and features genre fiction, no articles or poetry. We do encourage letters of comment." Monthly. Estab. 1997. Circ. 75.

Needs: Adventure, children's/juvenile (adventure, animal, easy-to-read, fantasy, mystery, series, ages 12-90), fantasy (space fantasy, sword and sorcery), mystery/suspense, science fiction (hard science/technological, soft/sociological, space opera), thriller/espionage, young adult/teen (adventure, easy-to-read, fantasy/science fiction, mystery/suspense, series). "No horror, weird, or pornography." Receives 20 unsolicited mss/month. Accepts 10-20 mss/issue; "hundreds" of mss/year. Publishes ms within 6 months after acceptance. Agented fiction 90%. **Publishes 20 new writers/year.** Recently published work by Mike Black and Len Jellema. Length: 1,000-80,000 words; average length: 10,000 words. Publishes short shorts. Average length: 1,000 words. Always comments on rejected mss.

How to Contact: Send complete ms with a cover letter. Accepts submissions by e-mail and disk. Include estimated word count and brief bio. Responds in 1 month. Send SASE (or IRC) for return of ms or send a disposable copy of ms and #10 SASE for reply only. Accepts simultaneous, previously published and multiple submissions. Sample copy for $6.30. Guidelines for SASE or by e-mail.

Payment/Terms: Pays 2 contributors copies; additional copies $3. Pays on publication for one-time rights. Not copyrighted.

Advice: "We look for fiction that is well written, well plotted, with good characterization, and enough action to keep the readers' interest. Don't write sloppy stories, relying on shock scenes. We expect clean works to give to our readers. It's highly suggested that anyone interested in submitting stories to one of our genre magazines, they at least buy a sample copy of that title to see what the magazine is like."

N $ ◎ **DREAMS & NIGHTMARES, The Magazine of Fantastic Poetry**, 1300 Kicker Rd., Tuscaloosa AL 35404. (205)553-2284. E-mail: dragontea@earthlink.net. Website: home.earthlink.net/~dragontea/index.html. ourworld-.compuserve.com/homepages/Anamnesis/dn.htm (includes guidelines, poetry, bibliographic archive of magazine). **Contact:** David C. Kopaska-Merkel, editor. Zine: 5½ × 8½; 24 pages; ink drawing illustrations. "*DN* is mainly a poetry magazine, but I *am* looking for short-short stories. They should be either fantasy or science fiction." Estab. 1986. Circ. 250.

Needs: Experimental, fantasy, humor/satire, science fiction. "Try me with anything *except*: senseless violence, misogyny or hatred (unreasoning) of any kind of people, sappiness." Receives 5-10 unsolicited fiction mss/month. Accepts 1-2 mss/issue; 3-6 mss/year. Publishes ms 1-9 months after acceptance. Recently published work by Nancy Bennett, D.F. Lewis, William John Watkins. Length: 1,000 words maximum; average length: 500 words. Publishes short shorts. Length: 500 or fewer words. Sometimes comments on rejected mss. Also publishes poetry.

How to Contact: Send complete ms. Responds in 1-3 weeks to queries; 1-6 weeks to mss. SASE. No simultaneous submissions. Accepts electronic submissions (ASCII or RTF). Sample copy for $3. Guidelines for #10 SASE.

Payment/Terms: Pays $5 and 2 contributor's copies. Pays on acceptance for one-time rights.

Advice: "I don't want pointless violence or meandering vignettes. I do want extremely short science fiction or fantasy fiction that engages the reader's interest from word one. I want to be *involved*. Start with a good first line, lead the reader where you want him/her to go and end with something that causes a reaction or provokes thought."

N $ ◑ ◎ **DREAMS OF DECADENCE, Vampire Poetry and Fiction**, DNA Publications, Inc., P.O. Box 2988, Radford VA 24143-2988. E-mail: dnapublications@iname.com. **Editor:** Angela G. Kessler. Zine: 50 pages; illustrations. Specializes in "vampire fiction and poetry for vampire fans." Quarterly. Estab. 1995. Circ. 7,500.

Needs: Vampires. "I am not interested in seeing the clichés redone." Receives 300 unsolicited mss/month. Accepts 4 mss/issue; 12 mss/year. Publishes ms 1-6 months after acceptance. Length: 1,000-7,000 words; average length: 4,000 words. Also publishes poetry. Always comments on rejected mss.

How to Contact: Send complete ms with cover letter. Include estimated word count, 1-paragraph bio and list of publications. Responds in 2 months to mss. Send SASE for reply, return of ms or send a disposable copy of ms. Accepts simultaneous submissions. Sample copy for $5. Guidelines for #10 SASE. Reviews novels and short story collections.

Payment/Terms: Pays 1-5¢/word and 2 contributor's copies; additional copies for $2.50. Pays on publication for first North American serial rights.

Advice: "I like stories that take the traditional concept of the vampire into new territory, or look at it (from within or without) with a fresh perspective. Don't forget to include a SASE for reply or return of manuscript. Also, to see what an editor wants, *read an issue.*"

◐ THE EDGE, TALES OF SUSPENSE, Thievin' Kitty Publications, P.O. Box 341, Marion MA 02738. E-mail: theedge@capecod.net. Website: http://beam.to/thievinkitty (includes guidelines, samples, and updates). **Contact:** Greg F. Gifune, editor. Associate Editors: Carla S. Gifune, Chuck A. Deude. Zine specializing in varied genre suspense: digest-sized; 80-88 pages; heavy stock paper; heavy card cover. "We publish a broad range of genres, subjects and styles. While not an easy magazine to break into, we offer thrilling, 'edge of your seat' fiction from both seasoned and newer writers. We focus on the writing, not illustrations or distracting bells and whistles. Our goal is to present a quality, entertaining publication." Triannual. Estab. 1998. Circ. 1,000.

Needs: Adventure, erotica, gay, horror, lesbian, mystery/suspense (police procedural, private eye/hardboiled, noir), psychic/supernatural/occult, westerns with supernatural or horror element only. "Emphasis is on horror, crime and blends." No children's, young adult, romance, humor. Receives over 100 unsolicited mss/month. Accepts 10-12 mss/issue; 30-36 mss/year. Publishes ms 1-4 months after acceptance. Agented fiction 1-2%. **Publishes 1-6 new writers/year.** Published work by Ken Goldman, John Roux, Scott Urban, Stefano Donati, Suzanne Donahue, Robert Dunbar and Michael Laimo. Length: 700-8,000 words; average length: 2,500-4,500 words. Also publishes poetry. Always comments on rejected ms.

How to Contact: Send complete ms with a cover letter. Include estimated word count, brief bio and list of publications. Responds in 8 weeks. Send SASE for reply, return of ms or send a disposable copy of ms. Accepts simultaneous submissions but not preferred. Sample copy for $6 U.S., $7 elsewhere (includes postage). Guidelines for #10 SASE. No e-mail submissions.

Payment/Terms: Pays 1 contributor's copy; additional copies $5. Acquires one-time rights.

Advice: "We look for taut, tense thrillers with realistic dialogue, engaging characters, strong plots and endings that are both powerful and memorable. Graphic violence, sex and profanity all have their place but do not have to be gratuitous. We will not accept anything racist, sexist, sacrilegious, or stories that depict children or animals in violent or sexual situations!"

$◻ ENCOUNTER, meeting God Face-to-Face, Standard Publishing, 8121 Hamilton Ave., Cincinnati OH 45231. (513)931-4050. Fax: (513)931-0950. E-mail: kcarr@standardpub.com. Website: www.standardpub.com, look for *Encounter* in the curriculum section; (includes lists of Standard Publishing's products and how to order them). **Contact:** Kelly Carr, editor. Zine specializing in Christian teens: 8½×11; 8 pages; glossy paper; illustrations; photos. "We seek to cause teens to look at their relationship with God in a new light and encourage them to live out their faith." Weekly. Estab. 1951. Circ. 35,000.

Needs: Religious, young adult/teen. Short stories that have Christian principles. "No non-religious fiction." List of upcoming themes available for SASE. Receives 35 unsolicited mss/month. Accepts 2 mss/issue; 45 mss/year. Publishes ms 1 year after acceptance. Length: 500-1,100 words. Always comments on rejected mss.

How to Contact: Send complete ms with a cover letter. Include estimated word count and Social Security number. Responds in 3 months. Send SASE (or IRC) for return of ms or send a disposable copy of ms and #10 SASE for reply only. Accepts simultaneous submissions, previously published work and multiple submissions. Sample copy free for 11×13 SASE. Guidelines for SASE.

Payment/Terms: Pays 6-8¢/word and 5 contributor's copies. Pays on acceptance.

Advice: "We look for realistic teenagers with up-to-date dialogue who cope with modern-day problems."

$◨ ◉ ▦ FLESH & BLOOD, Quiet Tales of Horror & Dark Fantasy, Flesh & Blood Press, 121 Joseph St., Bayville NJ 08721. E-mail: HorrorJack@aol.com. Website: http://zombie. horrorseek.com/horror/fleshnblood. (includes news, updates, guidelines, sales, releases). **Contact:** Jack Fisher, senior editor/publisher. Magazine: digest sized; 44-52 pages; 60 lb. paper; thick/glossy, 2-color cover; "fully and lavishly illustrated." "We publish fiction with heavy emphasis on the supernatural, fantastic and bizarre." Triannual. Estab. 1997. Circ. 500.

● *Flesh & Blood* won the 2002 *Writer's Digest* Zine competition and the Jobs in Hell Best Magazine Award in 2001. Work published in *Flesh & Blood* has been anthologized in the *Year's Best Fantasy & Horror.*

Needs: Fantasy (light), horror (dark fantasy, supernatural). "Do not let our title deceive you; we want stories that mix the fantastical and whimsical with horror." Receives 250-400 unsolicited mss/month. Accepts 7-9 mss/issue; 21-36 mss/year. Publishes ms 6-10 months after acceptance. Agented fiction 1%. **Publishes 4-6 new writers/year.** Recently

VISIT THE WRITER'S MARKET WEBSITE at www.writersmarket.com for hot new markets, daily market updates, writers' guidelines and much more.

published work by Wendy Rathbone, Jay Bonansinga and Jack Ketchum. Length: 500-4,000 words; average length: 2,000 words. Publishes short shorts. Average length: 100-500 words. Also publishes poetry. Often comments on rejected mss.

How to Contact: Send complete ms with a cover letter. Accepts submissions by e-mail. Include brief bio and list of publications. Responds in 2 weeks. Send SASE (or IRC) for return of ms. Accepts previously published work. Sample copy for $5; $13 for 3-issue subscription. Guidelines free for SASE or by e-mail.

Payment/Terms: Pays $5-80 plus 1 contributor's copy. Pays within 3 months after acceptance for first North American serial rights.

Advice: "Stories that mix one or more of the following elements with a horrific/weird idea/plot have a good chance: the fantastical, whimsical, supernatural, bizarre; stories should have unique ideas and be strongly written; the weirder and more offbeat, the better."

$ THE FUNNY PAPER, F/J Writers Service, P.O. Box 22557, Kansas City MO 64113-0557. E-mail: felix22557@aol .com. Website: www.angelfire.com/biz/funnypaper. **Contact:** F.H. Fellhauer, editor. Zine specializing in humor, contest and poetry: 8½×11; 10 pages. Published 4 times/year. No summer or Christmas. Estab. 1985.

Needs: Children/juvenile, humor satire, literary. "No controversial fiction." Length: 1,000 words. Publishes short shorts. Maximum length: 1,000 words. Also publishes poetry. Sometimes comments on rejected mss.

How to Contact: Send for guidelines. Accepts mss by e-mail. Include estimated word count with submission. Send disposable copy of ms and #10 SASE for reply only. Accepts simultaneous submissions. Sample copy for $2. Guidelines for SASE, e-mail or on website.

Payment/Terms: Prizes for stories, jokes and poems for $5-100 (humor, inspirational, fillers). No fee. Additional copies $2. Pays on publication for one-time rights.

Advice: "Do your best work, no trash. We try to keep abreast of online publishing and provide information."

$ □ THE FUNNY TIMES, 2176 Lee Rd., Cleveland Heights OH 44118. (216)371-8600. E-mail: ft@funnytimes.c om. Website: www.funnytimes.com (includes information about *The Funny Times*, cartoon of the week and laugh links). **Contact:** Ray Lesser and Susan Wolpert, editors. Zine specializing in humor: tabloid; 24 pages; newsprint; illustrations. *The Funny Times* is a "liberal-left monthly humor review." Estab. 1985. Circ. 60,000.

Needs: "Anything funny." Receives hundreds of unsolicited mss/month. Accepts 5 mss/issue; 60 mss/year. Publishes ms 1-6 months after acceptance. Agented fiction 10%. **Publishes 10 new writers/year.** Length: 500-700 words average. Publishes short shorts.

How to Contact: Send complete ms with a cover letter. Include list of publications. Responds in 3 months. Send SASE for return of ms or disposable copy of ms. Accepts simultaneous and reprint submissions. Sample copy for $3, 11×14 SAE and 80¢ 1st class postage. Guidelines on website.

Payment/Terms: Pays $50, free subscription to the zine and 5 contributor's copies. Pays on publication for one-time rights.

Advice: "It must be funny."

$ ○ ◎ HADROSAUR TALES, Hadrosaur Productions, P.O. Box 8468, Las Cruces NM 88006-8468. (505)527-4163. E-mail: hadrosaur.productions@verizon.net. Website: www.hadrosaur.com (includes news, ordering information, publication updates, guidelines, links to author websites). **Contact:** David L. Summers, editor. Zine specializing in science fiction: 5½×8½; 100-125 pages; 50 lb. white stock; 80 lb. cover. "Based in Las Cruces, New Mexico, Hadrosaur Productions provides entertaining, high quality, and thought provoking literary science fiction and fantasy stories to avid book readers throughout the United States and the world. We are committed to focusing on the needs of our customers, ever-changing technology, and the industry. The formats of products offered include the magazine *Hadrosaur Tales*, books, audio cassettes and CDs." Triannual. Estab. 1995. Circ. 100.

Needs: Fantasy (space fantasy, sword and sorcery), science fiction (hard science/technological, soft/sociological). "No graphic violence. No graphic/explicit sex. I do not want to see fiction with no science fiction/fantasy/mythic elements." Receives 15 unsolicited mss/month. Accepts 7-10 mss/issue; 21-30 mss/year. Does not read mss January 1-April 30 and June 15-October 31. Publishes ms 1 year after acceptance. **Publishes 8 new writers/year.** Recently published work by Justin Stanchfield, Mark Fewell, Christina Sng and Bonnie McDaniel. Length: 1,000-6,000 words; average length: 4,000 words. Also publishes poetry. Always comments on rejected mss.

How to Contact: Send complete ms with a cover letter. Accepts submissions by e-mail. Include estimated word count, brief bio and list of publications. Responds in 1 month to queries; 4 months to mss. Send SASE (or IRC) for return of ms or send a disposable copy of ms and #10 SASE for reply only. Sample copy for $6.95. Guidelines for SASE or on website.

Payment/Terms: Pays $6 and 2 contributor's copies; additional copies $4.76. Pays on acceptance for one-time rights.

Advice: "First and foremost, I look for engaging drama and believable characters. With those characters and situations, I want you to take me someplace I've never been before. The story I'll buy is the one set in a new world or where the unexpected happens, but yet I cannot help but believe in the situation because it feels real. Read absolutely everything you can get your hands on, especially stories and articles outside your genre of choice. This is a great source for original ideas."

◙ **JACK MACKEREL MAGAZINE**, Rowhouse Press, P.O. Box 23134, Seattle WA 98102-0434. **Contact:** Greg Bachar, editor. Zine: 5½×8½; 40-60 pages; Xerox bond paper; glossy card cover stock; b&w illustrations; photos. "We enjoy simple literary fiction that explores big ideas. We publish unconventional art, poetry and fiction." Quarterly. Estab. 1993. Circ. 1,000.

Needs: Condensed/excerpted novel, literary, surreal. No genre fiction. Publishes occasional chapbooks and anthologies. Receives 20-100 unsolicited mss/month. Accepts 10-20 mss/issue; 40-75 mss/year. Published work by William Waltz, Brett Astor and Jenny Sheppard. Length: 250-5,000 words. Publishes short shorts. Also publishes literary essays, literary criticism and poetry.

How to Contact: Send complete ms with a cover letter. Include bio with submission. Accepts submissions on disk and multiple submissions. Send SASE for reply, return of ms or send a disposable copy of ms.

Payment/Terms: Pays 2 contributor's copies.

$◙ LADY CHURCHILL'S ROSEBUD WRISTLET, An Occasional Outburst, Small Beer Press, 360 Atlantic Ave., PMB 132, Brooklyn NY 11217. E-mail: info@lcrw.net. Website: www.lcrw.net/lcrw (includes guidelines, contents and occasional extras not in the zine). **Contact:** Gavin Grant, editor. Zine: half legal size; 40 pages; 60 lb. paper; cardstock cover; illustrations; photos. Semiannual. Estab. 1996. Circ. 200.

Needs: Comics/graphic novels, experimental, fantasy, feminist, literary, science fiction, short story collections, translations. Receives 25 unsolicited mss/month. Accepts 4-6 mss/issue; 8-12 mss/year. Publishes ms 6 months after acceptance. **Publishes 2-4 new writers/year.** Recently published work by Amy Beth Forbes, Jeffrey Ford, Carol Emshwiller and Theodora Goss. Length: 200-7,000 words; average length: 3,500 words. Publishes short shorts. Average length: 500 words. Also publishes literary essays and poetry. Sometimes comments on rejected mss.

How to Contact: Send complete ms with a cover letter. Include estimated word count. Responds in 2 weeks to queries; 1 month to mss. Send SASE (or IRC) for return of ms or send a disposable copy of ms and #10 SASE for reply only. Sample copy for $4. Guidelines on website. Reviews novels, short story collections and nonfiction books of interest to writers.

Payment/Terms: Pays $10-20 and 2 contributor's copies; additional copies $4. Pays on publication for first or one-time rights.

Advice: "I like fiction that tends toward the speculative."

$◎ LEADING EDGE, Magazine of Science Fiction and Fantasy, TLE Press, 3163 JKHB, Provo UT 84602. (801)378-4455. E-mail: ltle@byu.edu. Website: http://leadingedge.byu.edu (includes excerpts, writer's, artist's, advertising guidelines, previews, subscription information). **Contact:** Ellen Lund, fiction director. Zine specializing in science fiction; 5½×8½; 120 pages; card stock; some illustrations. "*The Leading Edge* is dedicated to helping new writers make their way into publishing. We send critiques back with every story. We don't print anything with heavy swearing, violence that is too graphic, or explicit sex. We have an audience that is about 50% Latter Day Saints." Semiannual. Estab. 1981. Circ. 400.

Needs: Fantasy (space fantasy, sword/sorcery), science fiction (hard science/technological, soft/sociological). Receives 60 unsolicited mss/month. Accepts 6 mss/issue; 12 mss/year. Publishes ms 1-6 months after acceptance. **Publishes 9-10 new writers/year.** Recently published work by Orson Scott Card, Dan Wells and Dave Wolverton. Length: 12,000 words; average length 7,000 words. Publishes short shorts. Average length: 1,200 words. Also publishes poetry. Always comments on rejected mss.

How to Contact: Send complete ms with cover letter. Include estimated word count, brief bio and list of publications. Responds in 5 months on mss. Send disposable copy of ms and #10 SASE for reply only. Accepts multiple submissions. Sample copy for $4.50. Guidelines for SASE. Review novels, short story collections and nonfiction books of interest.

Payment/Terms: Pays 1¢/word; $100 maximum and 2 contributor's copies; additional copies $3.95. Pays on publication for first North American serial rights. Sends galleys to author.

Advice: "Don't base your story on your favorite TV show, book or game. Be original, creative and current. Base science fiction on recent science, not '50s horror flicks."

▢ ◎ **LITERALLY HORSES (REMUDA), Western Fiction, Cowboy Poetry, Horse Themed Poetry & Fiction, Western Book & Music Reviews**, Equestrienne Ltd., 208 Cherry Hill St., Kalamazoo MI 49006. (616)345-5915. E-mail: literallyhorses@aol.com. **Contact:** Laurie A. Cerny, publisher/editor. Zine specializing in horse/cowboy-related fiction/poetry: 5¼×8½; 80 pages; 40 lb. paper; 20 lb. cover stock; illustrations; photos. "We showcase poetry/fiction that has a horse/cowboy, western lifestyle theme. Most of the mainstream horse publications, as well as ones that publish western history, ignore these genres. I'm very interested in subject material geared toward the English riding discipline of the horse industry, as well as horse racing, driving. etc." Biannual. Estab. 1999. Circ. 1,000. Member, American Horse Publications, Western Writers of America.

Needs: Children's/juvenile (horse; ages 7-13), comics/graphic novels, western (frontier saga, traditional, cowboy/rodeo related). "No horror, gay, erotica." Receives 25 unsolicited mss/month. Accepts 25 mss/year. Publishes ms 6 months after acceptance. **Publishes 50 new writers/year.** Recently published work by Lora Butcher, Rod Miller, Emery Mehok and Chris Buethe. Length: 1,500-2,500 words; average length: 1,500 words. Publishes short shorts. Average length: 500 words. Also publishes literary criticism and poetry. Sometimes comments on rejected mss.

How to Contact: Send complete ms with a cover letter. Include brief bio. Responds in 6 weeks to mss. Send a disposable copy of ms and #10 SASE for reply only. Accepts simultaneous submissions, previously published work and multiple submissions. Sample copy for $4.95. Guidelines for SASE. Reviews novels, short story collections and nonfiction books of interest to writers.

Payment/Terms: Pays complimentary subscription; additional copies $3.95. Pays on publication for one-time rights. Sponsors annual contest. Deadline is July 31 of each year. SASE for rules.

Advice: "Right now many other mainstream literary publications seem to be interested in very dark, disturbed fiction. I'm focusing on fiction that is positive (it still may deal with hard issues) and spiritual. A reader should come away feeling good and not depressed after reading the fiction in *Literally Horses (Remuda)*."

LOW BUDGET SCIENCE FICTION, Cynic Press, P.O. Box 40691, Philadelphia PA 19107. **Contact:** Joseph Farley, editor. Magazine specializing in science fiction: 8½×11; 24-40 pages; 20 lb. paper; 70 lb. cover; illustrations; photographs. "Quirky science fiction, horror and fantasy have a home here." Biannual. Estab. 2002. Circ. 100.

Needs: Science fiction: erotica, experimental, hard science/technological, cross-genre; fantasy: space fantasy, sword and sorcery, cross-over. Receives 5 unsolicited mss/month. Accepts 4-10 mss/issue. Does not read mss "in my sleep." Recently published work by Ernest Swallow and Brad Wells. Length: 300-5,000 words; average length 4,000 words. Publishes short shorts. Sometimes comments on rejected mss.

How to Contact: Send complete ms with cover letter. Include brief bio and list of publications. Responds in 4 months. Send SASE for return of ms or send disposable copy of ms with SASE for reply only. Accepts simultaneous and previously published submissions. Sample copy for $7. Reviews novels, short story collections and nonfiction of interest to writers. Send copies to Joseph Farley.

Payment/Terms: Pays 1 contributor's copy; additional copies $7. Pays on publication for one-time rights.

Advice: "Finding a good manuscript is like falling in love: you may know it when you first see it, or you may need to get familiar with it for awhile."

$ MUSHROOM DREAMS, 14537 Longworth Ave., Norwalk CA 90650-4724. **Contact:** Jim Reagan, editor. Magazine: 8½×5½; 32 pages; 20 lb. paper; heavy cover stock; illustrations. "Eclectic content with emphasis on literary quality." Semiannually. Estab. 1997. Circ. 100.

Needs: Realistic or naturalistic fiction. No gay, lesbian, fantasy. Receives 10-15 unsolicited mss/month. Accepts 3 mss/issue; 6 mss/year. Publishes ms 6-12 months after acceptance. **Publishes 1 new writer/year.** Recently published work by William E. Meyer, Jr., Joanna Fried, Leslie Woolf Hedley and Michael Fowler. Length: 250-1,800 words; average length: 800 words. Publishes short shorts. Length: 250 words. Also publishes poetry. Often comments on rejected ms.

How to Contact: Send complete ms with a cover letter. Include estimated word count, short paragraph bio. Responds in 1 week to queries; 6 weeks to mss. Send SASE for reply or return of ms. Accepts simultaneous and reprint submissions. Sample copy $1. Guidelines free.

Payment/Terms: Pays $5-10 and 2 contributor's copies; additional copies $1. Pays on publication for first rights.

Advice: "We look for writers who read, period."

NUTHOUSE, Your Place for Humor Therapy, Twin Rivers Press, P.O. Box 119, Ellenton FL 34222. E-mail: nuthouse449@aol.com. Website: http://hometown.aol.com/Nuthous499/index2.html (includes writer's guidelines, readers' letters, excerpts). **Contact:** Dr. Ludwig "Needles" Von Quirk, chief of staff. Zine: digest-sized; 12-16 pages; bond paper; illustrations; photos. "Humor of all genres for an adult readership that is not easily offended." Published every 6 weeks. Estab. 1993. Circ. 100.

Needs: Humor/satire: erotica, experimental, fantasy, feminist, historical (general), horror, literary, main-stream/contemporary, mystery/suspense, psychic/supernatural/occult, romance, science fiction and westerns. Plans annual "Halloween Party" issue featuring humorous verse and fiction with a horror theme. Deadline: July 31. Receives 30-50 unsolicited mss/month. Accepts 5-10 mss/issue; 50-60 mss/year. Publishes ms 6-12 months after acceptance. **Publishes 10-15 new writers/year.** Recently published work by Norris D. Hertzog and Jim Sullivan. Length: 100-1,000 words; average length: 500 words. Publishes short shorts. Length: 100-250 words. Also publishes literary essays, literary criticism and poetry. Often comments on rejected mss.

How to Contact: Send complete ms with a cover letter. Include estimated word count, bio (paragraph) and list of publications. Responds in 1 month to mss. SASE for return of ms or send disposable copy of ms. Accepts simultaneous and reprint submissions. Sample copy for $1.25 (payable to Twin Rivers Press). Guidelines for #10 SASE.

Payment/Terms: Pays 1 contributor's copy. Acquires one-time rights. Not copyrighted.

Advice: Looks for "laugh-out-loud prose. Strive for original ideas; read the great humorists—Saki, Woody Allen, Robert Benchley, Garrison Keillor, John Irving—and learn from them. We are turned off by sophomoric attempts at humor built on a single, tired, overworked gag or pun; give us a story with a beginning, middle and end."

OFFICE NUMBER ONE, 2111 Quarry Rd., Austin TX 78703. E-mail: onocdingus@aol.com. **Contact:** Carlos B. Dingus, editor. Zine: 8½×11; 12 pages; 60 lb. standard paper; b&w illustrations; photos. "I look for short stories, imaginary news stories or essays (under 400 words) that can put a reader on edge—avoid profanity or obscenity, make a point that frees the reader to see several worlds." Biannual zine specializing in satire, humor and views from alternate realities. Estab. 1989. Circ. 1,000.

Needs: Fictional news articles, experimental, fantasy, horror, humor/satire, literary, psychic/supernatural/occult, also fictional reviews, limericks. Receives 16 unsolicited mss/month. Buys 1-3 mss/issue; 16 mss/year. Publishes ms 6-12 months after acceptance. **Publishes 10-15 new writers/year.** Length: 400 words maximum, 150 best. Also publishes literary essays and poetry. Sometimes comments on rejected mss if requested.

How to Contact: Send complete ms with optional cover letter. Include estimated word count. Responds in 6-8 weeks. Send SASE for reply, return of ms or send disposable copy of ms. Will consider simultaneous submissions, reprints. Sample copy for $2 with SAE and 3 first-class stamps. Guidelines for SASE.

Payment/Terms: Pays 1 contributor's copy. Additional copies for $1 plus $1.50 postage and 9×12 SASE. Acquires rights for "any and all office Number One publications."

Advice: "Clean writing, no unnecessary words, clear presentation. Express *one* good idea. Write for an audience that you can identify. I'm planning to publish more *shorter* fiction. I plan to be more up-beat and to focus on a journalistic style—and broaden what can be accomplished within this style. It seems like the Internet is taking away from print media. However, I also think the Internet cannot replace print media for fiction writing."

◎ ONCE UPON A WORLD, PMB 111, 1631 W. Craig Rd. #9, North Las Vegas NV 89032. E-mail: ejalward@yaho o.com. **Contact:** Emily Alward, editor. Zine: $8\frac{1}{2} \times 11$; 80-100 pages; white paper; card stock cover; pen & ink illustrations. "Our goal is to publish unique science fiction and fantasy stories which may not fit the parameters of much commercial fiction because of its emphasis on world-building and character interaction." Annually. Estab. 1988. Circ. 150.

Needs: Fantasy, science fiction. No realistic "stories in contemporary settings"; horror; stories using Star Trek or other media characters; stories with completely negative endings. Wants to see more "stories set in worlds with alternate political, economic or family arrangements." Upcoming theme: Effective Non-lethal Counters to Violence/Terrorism (in a SF setting—deadline July 2003). Receives 20 unsolicited mss/month. Accepts 8-12 mss/issue; per year "varies, depending on backlog." Publishes ms from 2 months to 1½ years after acceptance. **Publishes 5 new writers/year.** Recently published work by Jeff Kozzi, B.J. Nold and Don Stockard. Length: 400-10,000 words; average length: 3,000 words. Publishes short shorts. Also publishes poetry. Sometimes comments on rejected mss and recommends other markets.

How to Contact: Send complete manuscript. Responds in 2-4 weeks to queries; 2-16 weeks to mss. SASE. "Reluctantly" accepts simultaneous submissions. Sample copy for $9. Make checks payable to Emily Alward. Guidelines for #10 SASE. Reviews novels and short story collections.

Payment/Terms: Pays contributor's copies. Acquires first rights. "Stories copyrighted in author's name; copyrights not registered."

Advice: "Create your own unique universe, and then show its texture and how it 'works' in the story. This is a good way to try out a world that you're building for a novel. But, don't forget to also give us interesting characters with believable problems. Submit widely, but pay attention to editors' needs and guidelines—don't scattershot. Take on new challenges—i.e., never say 'I only write science fiction, romance, or even fiction in general—you never know where your 'sideline' work is going to impress an editor. We aim to fill some niches not necessarily well-covered by larger publishers currently: science fantasy; cross-genre; SF love stories; and non-cyber centered futures. Also, we see too many stories with generic, medieval-type world settings and premises."

◐ ▼ OUTER DARKNESS, Where Nightmares Roam Unleashed, Outer Darkness Press, 1312 N. Delaware Place, Tulsa OK 74110. **Contact:** Dennis Kirk, editor. Zine: $8\frac{1}{2} \times 5\frac{1}{2}$; 60-80 pages; 20 lb. paper; 90 lb. matte cover; illustrations. Specializes in imaginative literature. "Variety is something I strive for in *Outer Darkness*. In each issue we present readers with great tales of science fiction and horror along with poetry, cartoons and interviews/essays. I seek to provide readers with a magazine which, overall, is fun to read. My readers range in age from 16 to 70." Quarterly. Estab. 1994. Circ. 500.

● Fiction published in *Outer Darkness* has received honorable mention in *The Year's Best Fantasy and Horror*.

Needs: Fantasy (science), horror, mystery/suspense (with horror slant), psychic/supernatural/occult, romance (gothic), science fiction (hard science, soft/sociological). No straight mystery, pure fantasy—works which do not incorporate elements of science fiction and/or horror. Also, no slasher horror with violence, gore, sex instead of plot. Wants more "character driven tales—especially in the genre of science fiction and well-developed psychological horror. I do not publish works with children in sexual situations and graphic language should be kept to a minimum." Receives 75-100 unsolicited mss/month. Accepts 7-9 mss/issue; 20-50 mss/year. **Publishes 2-5 new writers/year.** Recently published work by Ray Naylor, Jon Picciuolo, Suzanne Donahue and David Summers. Length: 1,000-5,000 words; average length: 3,000 words. Also publishes interviews and poetry. Always comments on rejected mss.

How to Contact: Send complete ms with a cover letter. Include estimated word count, 50- to 75-word bio, list of publications and "any awards, honors you have received." Responds in 2 weeks to queries; 3 months to mss. Send SASE for reply, return of ms or send a disposable copy of ms. Accepts simultaneous and multiple submissions. Sample copy for $3.95. Guidelines for #10 SASE.

INTERESTED IN A PARTICULAR GENRE? Check our sections for: **Mystery/Suspense**, page 74; **Romance**, page 86; **Science Fiction/Fantasy & Horror**, page 100.

Payment/Terms: Pays 3 contributor's copies for fiction, 2 for poetry and 3 for art. Pays on publication for one-time rights.

Advice: "I look for strong characters and well developed plot. And I definitely look for suspense. I want stories which move—and carry the reader along with them. Be patient and persistent. Often it's simply a matter of linking the right story with the right editor. I've received many stories which were good, but not what I wanted at the time. However, these stories worked well in another horror-sci-fi zine."

PENNY DREADFUL, Tales & Poems of Fantastic Terror, Pendragonian Publications, P.O. Box 719, New York NY 10101-0719. E-mail: mmpendragon@aol.com. Website: www.pennydreadful.org. **Contact:** Michael Pendragon, editor. Zine specializing in horror: 9×6; 175 pages; illustrations; photos. Publication to "celebrate the darker aspects of man, the world and their creator. We seek to address a highly literate audience who appreciate horror as a literary art form." Biannual. Estab. 1996. Circ. 200.
  ● *Penny Dreadful* won several Honorable Mentions in St. Martin's Press's *The Year's Best Fantasy and Horror* competition.

Needs: Fantasy (dark symbolist), horror, psychic/supernatural/occult. Wants more "tales set in and in the style of the 19th century." No modern settings "constantly referring to 20th century persons, events, products, etc." List of upcoming themes available for SASE. Receives 100 unsolicited mss/month. Accepts 10 mss/issue; 30 mss/year. "*Penny Dreadful* reads all year until we have accepted enough submissions to fill more than one year's worth of issues." **Publishes 1-3 new writers/year.** Recently published work by James S. Dorr, Scott Thomas, John B. Ford, Susan E. Abramski, Paul Bradshaw and John Light. Length: 500-5,000 words. Publishes short shorts. Also publishes poetry. Always comments on rejected mss.

How to Contact: Send complete ms with a cover letter. Include estimated word count, bio and list of publications. Responds in up to 1 year to queries and mss. Send SASE for reply, return of ms or send disposable copy of ms. Accepts simultaneous submissions and reprints. Sample copy for $10. Subscription for $25. Guidelines for #10 SASE.

Payment/Terms: Pays 1 contributor copy. Acquires one-time rights. Sends galleys to author. Not copyrighted.

Advice: "Whenever possible, try to submit to independent zines specializing in your genre. Be prepared to spend significant amounts of time and money. Expect only one copy as payment. Over time—if you're exceptionally talented and/or lucky—you may begin to build a small following."

PINDELDYBOZ, Pindeldyboz, 21-17 25th Rd., Astoria NY 11102. Website: www.pindeldyboz.com or www.pboz.net. **Contact:** Whitney Pastorek, senior editor. Literary magazine: 8½×11; 272 pages; matte cover; illustrations. "Fiction by the contemporary authors you love to read and those you'd love if you only knew them. We have an unique philosophy and will not create something you will not absolutely love." Semiannual. Estab. 2001.

Needs: Comics/graphic novels, experimental, humor/satire, literary, translation. Upcoming themes available online. Receives 25 unsolicited mss/month. Accepts 16 print mss/issue; 32 print mss/year; 5 web mss/year; 110 web mss/year. Publishes ms 3 months after acceptance. **Publishes 25-30 new writers/year.** Recently published work by Neal Pollock, Dan Kennedy, Bryce Newhart, Corey Mesler, Rob Maitra, Ben Greenman, Jason Wilson and Mike Magnuson. Length: 250+ words; average length: 2,000. Publishes short shorts. Average length: 500 words. Also publishes literary essays and poetry. Sometimes comments on rejected mss.

How to Contact: Send complete copy of ms with cover letter. Accepts mss by e-mail and disk. Include brief bio, list of publications and phone number with submission. Responds in 2 weeks to queries; 3 months to mss. Send SASE (or IRC) for return of the ms and disposable copy of ms and #10 SASE for reply only. Accepts simultaneous and multiple submissions. Sample copy for $12. Guidelines on website.

Payment/Terms: Pays 2 contributor's copies; additional copies $10. Pays on publication for one-time rights.

Advice: "We look for good grammar. Bad grammar stands out but in a bad way. Make us laugh. Make us smile. Make us peanut butter and jelly sandwiches."

BERN PORTER INTERNATIONAL, (formerly *Bern Porter Cosmographic*), 50 Salmond St., Belfast ME 04915. (207)338-4303. E-mail: bernporterinternational@yahoo.com. **Contact:** Natasha Bernstein and Sheila Holtz, editors. Magazine: 8½×11; 8 pages; illustrations; photos. "Experimental prose and poetry at the edge of established literary forms." Monthly. Estab. 1997.

Needs: Experimental, literary, prose poem, translations, international. "No long conventional narratives. Want more short vignettes and surreal prose-poems." Receives 30-50 unsolicited mss/month. Publishes ms immediately after acceptance. **Publishes 12 new writers/year.** Published work by Stephen Jama, Natasha Bernstein, C.A. Conrad, T. Anders Carson and Anne Welsh. Length: 2 pages maximum. Publishes short shorts.

How to Contact: Query first. Accepts queries by e-mail. Responds in 1 week. Accepts simultaneous and reprint submissions. Sample copy $2. Guidelines free.

Payment/Terms: Pays in copies.

Advice: "Do not compromise your style and vision for the sake of the market. Megamarketing of authors by big mega publishers sucks. We seek to counter this trend by giving voice to authors who would not be heard in that world."

PROSE AX, doses of prose, poetry, visual and audio art, P.O. Box 22643, Honolulu HI 96823-2643. E-mail: prose_ax@att.net. Website: www.proseax.com. **Contact:** J. Calma, editor. Zine and online magazine specializing in prose, poetry and art: 8½×7; 24-30 pages; 20 lb. paper; illustrations; photos. "We are a literary journal that publishes stimulating, fresh prose and poetry. We are committed to publishing new or ethnic writers or ethnic themes. The style of our website and print version is very visual, very stylish, and I think this makes our publication different. We present fresh voices in a fresh way." Quarterly. Estab. 2000. Circ. 450-500 print; 50 unique visitors average per day to website.

• *Prose Ax* ranked on *Writer's Digest*'s "Top 30" list of best markets for fiction writers.

Needs: Ethnic/multicultural (general), experimental, literary fantasy (fantastic realism), literary, novel excerpts that work well alone, flash fiction. "No genre, especially romance and mystery." Receives 30-50 unsolicited mss/month. Accepts 3-7 mss/issue. Publishes ms 1-3 months after acceptance. **Publishes 30 new writers/year.** Length: 50-5,000 words; average length: 1,000. Publishes short shorts. Average length: 500 words. Recently published work by Eric Paul Shafer, Ken Goldman, Suzanne Frischkorn, Jasmine Orr, Jason D. Smith, K.J. Stevens and Kenneth Champeon. Also publishes literary essays and poetry. Often comments on rejected mss.

How to Contact: Send complete copy of ms with cover letter. Accepts mss by e-mail. Include estimated word count with submission. Responds in 1-2 months. Send disposable copy of ms and #10 SASE for reply only. Accepts simultaneous, multiple and previously published submissions. Sample copy free with SASE (8×12 SAE and $1.50 postage or IRC) if available. Guidelines send SASE, e-mail or on website. Reviews novels, short story collections and nonfiction books.

Payment/Terms: Pays 2 contributor's copies; additional copies send SASE. Pays on publication for one-time and electronic rights. Sends galleys to author. Sponsors contest: All accepted pieces eligible to win Potent Prose Ax Award. Pays $10 for most potent fiction; $5 for most potent poetry.

Advice: "A good story has good details and descriptions. Read our zine first to see if what you write will fit in with the tone and style of *Prose Ax*. Write a little hello to us instead of sending only your mss."

N ○ RALPH'S REVIEW, RC Publications, 129A Wellington Ave., Albany NY 12203-2637. (518)459-0883. E-mail: rcpub@juno.com. **Contact:** Ralph Cornell, editor. Zine: $8\frac{1}{2} \times 11$; 20-35 pages; 20 lb. bond paper and cover. "To let as many writers as possible get a chance to publish their works, fantasy, sci-fi, horror, poetry. We are adding home remedies and gardening tips. Audience: adult, young adult, responsible, self-contained, conscious human beings." Quarterly. Estab. 1988. Circ. 200.

Needs: Adventure, fantasy (science fantasy), horror, humor/satire, literary, psychic/supernatural/occult, science fiction, stamp and coin collecting, dinosaurs, environmental, fishing. No extreme violence, racial, gay/lesbian/x-rated. Publishes annual special fiction issue or anthology. Receives 10-15 unsolicited mss/month. Accepts 1-2 mss/issue; 12-15 mss/year. Publishes ms 2-4 months after acceptance. Published work by Ralph Cornell, Celeste Plowden, Bob Holmes and Renese Carlisle. **Publishes 10-20 new writers/year.** Length: 50-2,000 words; average length: 500-1,000 words. *$2 reading fee for all stories over 500 words.* Publishes short shorts. Also publishes poetry. Sometimes comments on rejected mss.

How to Contact: Send complete ms with a cover letter. Include 1-paragraph bio and list of publications. Responds in 3 weeks to queries; 3 months to mss. Send SASE for reply, return of ms or send a disposable copy of ms. Accepts simultaneous and reprint submissions. Sample copy for $2, 9×12 SAE and 5 first-class stamps. Guidelines for #10 SASE. Reviews novels or short story collections.

Payment/Terms: Pays 1 contributor's copy; additional copies for $2. Acquires first North American serial rights.

Advice: Looks for manuscripts "that start out active and continue to grow until you go 'Ahh!' at the end. Something I've never read before. Make sure spelling is correct, content is crisp and active, characters are believable. Must be horrific, your worst nightmare, makes you want to look in the corner while sitting in your own living room."

$ SPELLBOUND MAGAZINE, A fantasy magazine for young readers, Eggplant Productions, 135 Shady Lane, Bolingbroke IL 60440. (847)928-9925. Fax: (801)720-0706. E-mail: spellbound@eggplant-productions.com. Website: www.eggplant-productions.com/spellbound/ (includes writer's guidelines, upcoming themes and previews of issues). **Contact:** Raechel Henderson Moon, fiction editor. Zine: A5; 48 pages; 20lb paper; 80lb cover stock; some illustrations. "*Spellbound* is a quarterly fantasy magazine for children ages 9-13. Our goal is to introduce children to the wonderful world of fantasy in all its forms. We publish poetry and fiction that is fun, positive and doesn't talk down to our readers." Quarterly. Estab. 1999. Circ. Less than 100.

Needs: Children's/juvenile (fantasy). No after school special types of fiction. Receives 15 unsolicited mss/month. Accepts 5 mss/issue; 20 mss/year. Publishes ms 6-12 months after acceptance. **Publishes 50% new writers/year.** Length: 500-2,500 words; average length: 1,800 words. Publishes short shorts. Average length: 1,000 words. Also publishes poetry. Always comments on rejected mss.

How to Contact: Send complete ms with cover letter. We only accepts e-mail submissions. Include estimated word count, brief bio and postal mailing address. Responds in 6 weeks to queries and mss. Accepts simultaneous and multiple submissions. Sample copy for $5. Guidelines for free on website.

Payment/Terms: Pays $5 and 2 contributor's copies; additional copies $2. Pays on acceptance for first World English-language rights.

Advice: "Looking for fiction that makes me feel something. I am looking for stories that use bold images and memorable characters. Ultimately, I choose the types of stories I would like to read as a child. Read the guidelines carefully. Keep in mind the age of our audience and have fun with the story."

$ ◐ ◎ STARSHIP EARTH, Black Moon Publishing, P.O. Box 484, Bellaire OH 43906. (740)676-5659. E-mail: shadowhorse@earthlink.net. Editor: Kirin Lee. **Contact:** Ms. Silver Shadowhorse, fiction editor. Zine specializing in the sci-fi universe: $8\frac{1}{2} \times 11$; 60 pages; glossy paper and cover; illustrations; photos. "We are mostly non-fiction with one piece of fiction per month." Monthly. Estab. 1995. Circ. 30,000.

Needs: Fantasy (science fantasy), science fiction (hard science, soft/sociological, historical). Wants more hard science fiction. No "sword and sorcery, religious, mystery, erotica or comedy." Would like to see more "hard science fiction." Publishes special fiction issues or anthologies. Receives 100-200 unsolicited mss/month. Accepts 1 ms/issue; 12 mss/year. Publishes ms 16-18 months after acceptance. **Publishes 10 new writers/year.** Published work by Jackson Frazier and Sean Kennedy. Length: 3,000 words maximum; average length: 2,000-3,000 words. Publishes short shorts. Sometimes comments on rejected mss.

How to Contact: Query or send complete ms with a cover letter. Include estimated word count, short bio and list of publications. Responds in 3 weeks to queries; 3-4 months to mss. Send SASE for reply, return of ms or send disposable copy of ms. Guidelines for #10 SASE. Reviews novels and short story collections. Send books to Jenna Dawson.

Payment/Terms: Pays 1¢/word minimum; 3¢/word maximum and 1 contributor's copy. Acquires first rights.

Advice: "Get our guidelines. Submit in the correct format. Send typed or computer printed manuscripts only. Avoid bad language, explicit sex and violence. Do not include any religious content. Manuscripts stand out when they are professionally presented."

TRANSCENDENT VISIONS, Toxic Evolution Press, 251 S. Olds Blvd., 84-E, Fairless Hills PA 19030-3426. (215)547-7159. **Contact:** David Kime, editor. Zine: letter size; 24 pages; xerox paper; illustrations. "*Transcendent Visions* is a literary zine by and for people who have been labeled mentally ill. Our purpose is to illustrate how creative and articulate mental patients are." Annual. Estab. 1992. Circ. 200.

• *Transcendent Visions* has received excellent reviews in many underground publications.

Needs: Experimental, feminist, gay, humor/satire, lesbian. Especially interested in material dealing with mental illness. "I do not like stuff one would find in a mainstream publication. No porn." Would like to see more "quirky, nonmainstream fiction." Receives 5 unsolicited mss/month. Accepts 5-7 mss/issue; 7 mss/year. Publishes ms 3-4 months after acceptance. Recently published work by Brian McCarvill, Roger D. Coleman and Emil Vachas. Length: under 10 pages typed, double-spaced. Publishes short shorts. Also publishes poetry.

How to Contact: Send complete ms with cover letter. Include half-page bio. Responds in 1 month. Send disposable copy of ms. Accepts simultaneous submissions and reprints. Sample copy for $2.

Payment/Terms: Pays 1 contributor's copy. Pays on publication for one-time rights.

Advice: "We like unusual stories that are quirky. We like shorter pieces. Please do not go on and on about what zines you have been published in or awards you have won, etc. We just want to read your material, not know your life story. Please don't swamp me with tons of submissions. Send up to five stories. Please print or type your name and address."

N ✂ URBAN GRAFFITI, Greensleeve Editions, P.O. Box 41164, Edmonton, Alberta T6J-6M7 Canada. E-mail: cogwheels@worldgate.com. **Contact:** Mark McCawley, editor. Zine specializing in fiction; 7×11; 28 pages; Xerox paper; some illustrations; photos. "Litzine of transgressive, discursive, post-realist writing (primarily fiction) concerned with the struggles of hard-edged urban living, alternative lifestyles, deviant culture, and presented in their most raw and unpretentious form. Adult audience/adult themes. Anti-literary. No-holds-barred exploration of the underside of contemporary urban existance (using sex, violence, shock value, parody, cynicism, irony, and black humour to do so)." Semiannual. Estab. 1993. Circ. 250.

Needs: Comics/graphic novels, erotica, gay, humor/satire, lesbian. Receives 200 unsolicited mss/month. Accepts 10-15 mss/issue; 20-30 mss/year. Publishes ms 3-12 months after acceptance. **Publishes 2-3 new writers/year.** Recently published work by Matthew Firth, Glenn Gustafson and Sonja Saikaley. Length: 500-7,000 words; average length: 3,000 words. Publishes short shorts. Average length: 1,000 words. Also publishes poetry.

How to Contact: Send complete ms with cover letter. Accepts submissions by e-mail or disk. Include estimated word count and creative bio. Responds in 2 weeks to queries; 3 months to mss. Send disposable copy of ms and #10 SASE for reply only. Accepts multiple submissions. Sample copy for $3. Guidelines for SASE or by e-mail. Reviews novels, short story collections and nonfiction books.

Payment/Terms: Pays in 5 contributor's copies; additional copies for $4. Pays on publication for first anthology rights.

Advice: "How well manuscripts adheres to the mandate of the litzine. Be honest and trust your instincts. If it's raunchy, realistic and puts forth the author's own viewpoint (or world view), the better chance the author has of being accepted by my publication."

Online Markets

As production and distribution costs go up and subscribers numbers fall, more and more magazines are giving up print publication and moving online. Relatively inexpensive to maintain and quicker to accept and post submissions, online fiction sites are growing fast in numbers and legitimacy. Says the editor of *EWGPresents*: "We have the means to reach a universal audience by the click of a mouse. Writers are gifted with a new medium of exposure and the future demands taking advantage of this format."

Writers exploring online opportunities for publication will find a rich and diverse community of voices. Genre sites are strong, in particular those for science fiction/fantasy and horror (see the award-winning *Alternate Realities Webzine, Scifi.com* and *Deep Outside SFFH*). Mainstream short fiction markets are also growing exponentially (see *American Feed Magazine, Cenotaph* and *Intertext*, among many others). Online literary journals range from the traditional (*The Barcelona Review, Paumonok Review*) to those with a decidedly more quirky, regional bent (*The Dead Mule School of Southern Literature, Big Country Peacock Chronicle*). Writers will also find here more highly experimental work that could exist no where else than in cyberspace, such as the hypertext fiction found on *Drunken Boat*.

Online journals are gaining respect for the writers who appear on their sites. As Jill Adams, publisher and editor of *The Barcelona Review*, says: "We see our Internet review, like the small independent publishing houses, as a means of counterbalancing the big-business mentality of the multi-national publishing houses. At the same time, we want to see our writers 'make it big.' Last year we heard from more and more big houses asking about some of our new writers, wanting contact information, etc. So I see a healthy trend in that big houses are, finally—after being skeptical and confused—looking at it seriously and scouting online."

While the medium of online publication is different, the traditional rules of publishing apply to submissions. Writers should research the site and archives carefully, looking for a match in sensibility for their work among the varied sites publishing. They should then follow submission guidelines exactly, and submit courteously. True, these sites aren't bound by traditional print schedules, so your work theoretically may be published more quickly. But that doesn't mean a larger staff, so do exercise patience with editors considering your manuscript.

Also, while reviewing the listings in this market section, notice they are grouped differently from other market listings. In our literary magazines section, for example, you'll find primarily only publications searching for literary short fiction. But Online Markets are grouped by medium, so you'll find publishers of mystery short stories listed next to those looking for horror next to those specializing in flash fiction, so review with care. In addition, those online markets with print counterparts, such as *North American Review*, you will find listed in the print markets sections.

A final note about online publication: like literary journals, the majority of these markets are either nonpaying or very low paying. In addition, writers will not receive print copies of the publications because of the medium. So in most cases, do not expect to be paid for your exposure.

$ ◩ THE ABSINTHE LITERARY REVIEW, P.O. Box 328, Spring Green WI 53588. E-mail: staff@absinthe-literary-review.com. Website: www.absinthe-literary-review.com. **Contact:** Charles Allen Wyman, editor. Electronic literary magazine (print issue planned for late 2003-early 2004 launch). "*ALR* publishes short stories, novel excerpts, poems and literary essays. Our target audience is the literate individual who enjoys creative language use, character-driven fiction and the clashing of worlds—real and surreal, poetic and prosaic, sacred and transgressive."

Needs: "Transgressive works dealing with sex, death, disease, madness, and the like; the clash of archaic with modern day; archetype, symbolism; surrealism, philosophy, physics, existential, postmodern, and post-postmodern flavoring; experimental or flagrantly textured (but not sloppy or casual) fiction; intense crafting of language from the writer's writer. See website for information on annual Eros and Thanatos issue and Absinthe Editors' Prize. Anathemas: mainstream storytellers; "Oprah" fiction, high school or beginner fiction, poetry or fiction that contains no capital letters or punctuation, "hot" trends, genre and utterly normal prose or poetry, first, second or third drafts, pieces that exceed our stated word count by thousands of words, writers who do not read and follow our online guidelines." **Publishes 5-10 new writers/year.** Recently published work by Virgil Suarez, James Reidel and Dan Pope. Length: 5,000 words maximum. Reviews novels, short story collections and literary nonfiction works of interest to writers.

How to Contact: "Read online submission guidelines, then send fiction submissions to fiction@absinthe-literary-review.com. Though we now accept snail mail submissions, *we prefer e-mail.*"

Payment/Terms: "Effective January 1, 2003: $2-10 for fiction and essay; $1-10 for poetry. Absinthe Editors' Prize: $25."

Advice: "Be erudite but daring in your writing. Draw from the past to drag meaning from the present. Kill cliché. Invest your work with layers of meaning that subtly reveal multiple realities. Do not submit pieces that are riddled with spelling errors and grammatical snafus. Above all, be professional. For those of you who don't understand what this means, please send your manuscripts elsewhere until you have experienced the necessary epiphany."

N $ ⚠ ☣ ALTERNATE REALITIES WEBZINE, Alternate Realities, 5026 N.E. 57th Ave., Portland OR 97218. (503)249-7125. Fax: (503)249-2758. E-mail: fanwrite@aol.com. Website: www.alternaterealitieszine.com. **Contacts:** Joan M. McCarty (fanwrite@aol.com); Carole Muir, sci-fi, mystery/thriller (crlmuir@aol.com); Geof Lucier, horror (horrorman1@aol.com); Eric Brown, fantasy (incubusvane@aol.com). Online magazine: illustrations. "*Alternate Realities Webzine* is an online publication specializing in all things sci-fi, fantasy, horror and mystery/thrillers. We publish 2 stories (minimum) per issue of the listed genres. In addition, we have sections for the aspiring author with market listings, and resource links, as well as sections for the established author, such as website hosting, press release section, and book reviews. *Alternative Realities* also has sections on genre artwork, poetry, and movie reviews. In addition to our regular story sections, we also print (limited) longer works of fiction (no novel length, please)." Bimonthly. Estab. 1997.

● *Alternate Realities Webzine* received the Crypt Crawl Reader's Choice Award, the Readers List Readers Choice Award and the Preditors and Editors Readers Choice/Writer's Resource Award.

Needs: Fantasy (space fantasy, sword and sorcery), horror (dark fantasy, futuristic, psychological, supernatural), humor/satire, mystery/suspense (police procedural, private eye/hardboiled), psychic/supernatural/occult, science fiction (hard science/technological), thriller/espionage. "No romance, religion." "We do a Halloween double issue every year where all stories accepted in all the genres we represent must have a dark theme to them. This issue is the September/October issue and all submissions should be in no later than August 1. To have a story considered solely for this issue, make sure you put 'Halloween Submission' on it." Receives 100 unsolicited mss/month. Accepts between 8-12 mss/issue; 56-100 mss/year. Publishes ms 1-3 months after acceptance. **Publishes 75% new writers/year.** Recently published work by W.R. Rieser, Simon Wood, Jason Brannon, Eric S. Brown and Robert Sagirs. Length: 1,500-5,000 words; average length: 2,600-4,000 words. "We do have a section for Serials and long fiction over the 5,000 word count, however, it is difficult to get into this section." Publishes short shorts. Average length: 500-1,000 words. Also publishes literary essays and literary criticism. Often comments on rejected mss.

How to Contact: Send complete ms with a cover letter. Accepts submissions by e-mail and disk. Include estimated word count, list of publications, mailing address and e-mail address, even with file attachments. Responds in 1 month to queries; 2-3 months to mss. Accepts previously published and multiple submissions. Guidelines for SASE. Reviews novels, short story collections and nonfiction books of interest to writers. Send review copies to Joan M. McCarty, senior editor.

Payment/Terms: Pays $5-15. Pays on publication for electronic rights. Sends galleys to author.

Advice: "We look for originality, making the old new, and the new outstanding! If you want to sell a vampire story, or a story with a dragon, do it with special flare. Otherwise, if you use the same out plotlines that have been done to death, we will be passing on it. Also, we are not editors in the sense of correcting every submission's work, so if you submit something make sure it is the very best you can send, otherwise it is in the slush pile."

▲ AMERICAN FEED MAGAZINE, American Feed Magazine, 35 Hinsdale Ave., Winsted CT 06098. (860)738-4897. E-mail: editor@americanfeedmagazine.com. Website: www.Americanfeedmagazine.com. **Contact:** Shaw Izikson, editor. Online magazine: illustrations; photos. "We like to give a place for new voices to be heard, as well as established voices a place to get a wider audience for their work." Estab. 1994.

Needs: Adventure, comics/graphic novels, ethnic/multicultural, experimental, family saga, fantasy, feminist, glitz, historical, horror, humor/satire, literary, mainstream, mystery/suspense, New Age, psychic/supernatural/occult, science fiction, thriller/espionage. Receives 100 unsolicited mss/month. Accepts 15 mss/issue. Publishes ms 2 months after acceptance. **Publishes 15 new writers/year.** Published work by Joshua Farber and Daniel LaFavbre. Average length: 1,500. Publishes short shorts. Also publishes literary essays, literary criticism and poetry. Always comments on rejected mss.

How to Contact: Send complete ms with a cover letter. Accepts submissions on disk. Include estimated word count and brief bio. Responds in 2 months to queries and mss. Send SASE (or IRC) for return of ms or send a disposable copy of ms and #10 SASE for reply only. Accepts simultaneous, previously published and multiple submissions. Guidelines by e-mail or on website. Reviews novels, short story collections and nonfiction books of interest to writers. Send review copies to Shaw Izikson.

Payment/Terms: Acquires one-time rights.

Advice: "Make sure the story flows naturally, not in a forced way. You don't need a vivid imagination to write fiction, poetry or anything. Just look around you, because life is usually the best inspiration."

$ 🖸 **ANOTHEREALM**, 33537 N. Evergreen Dr., Gages Lake IL 60030. (847)543-4126. E-mail: gmarkette@aol.c om. Website: www.anotherealm.com. **Contact:** Gary A. Markette, senior editor. "*Anotherrealm* publishes short stories dealing with science fiction, fantasy, and horror themes. We strive for excellence. Our audience is anyone who enjoys good stories that are well written." New stories 2 times/month. Weekly. Estab. 1998. Member, Zine Guild.
Needs: Fantasy (space fantasy, sword and sorcery), horror (dark fantasy, futuristic, psychological, supernatural), science fiction (hard science/technological, soft/sociological). No gratuitous pornography (that is, no material—pornographic or not—that does not advance the story), no westerns (unless science fiction, fantasy or horror-themed), no romances (unless ditto), no historical fiction (unless . . . you get the idea). Receives 100 unsolicited mss/month. Accepts 24-30 mss/year. Reads October through November, "although submissions are accepted year-round." Publishes ms 3-10 months after acceptance. **Publishes 80% new writers/year.** Length: 5,000 words maximum. Often comments on rejected ms.
How to Contact: Send complete ms with a cover letter pasted as part of e-mail. Include estimated word count. Acknowledges submissions within days. Responds to mss after reading period. Accepts previously published work and multiple submissions. "No hard copy submissions; no attachments downloaded." Sample copy and guidelines free on website.
Payment/Terms: Pays $10. Pays on publication for electronic rights.
Advice: "We look for stories that are well written, well plotted, well told, or all of the above."

▓ 🖸 **ASCENT, Aspirations For Artists**, Ascent, 1560 Arbutus Dr., Nanoose Bay, British Columbia C9P 9C8 Canada. E-mail: ascent@bcsupernet.com. Website: www.bcsupernet.com/users/ascent. **Contact:** David Fraser, editor. E-zine specializing in short fiction (all genres) and poetry, essays, visual art: 40 electronic pages; illustrations; photos. "*Ascent* is a quality electronic publication dedicated to promotions and encouraging aspiring writers of any genre. The focus however is toward interesting experimental writing in dark mainstream, literary, science fiction, fantasy and horror. Poetry can be on any theme. Essays need to be unique, current and have social, philosophical commentary." Quarterly. Estab. 1997.
Needs: Erotica, experimental, fantasy (space fantasy, sword and sorcery), feminist, horror (dark fantasy, futuristic, psychological, supernatural), literary, mainstream, mystery/suspense, New Age, psychic/supernatural/occult, science fiction (hard science/technological, soft/sociological). List of upcoming themes available online. Receives 20-30 unsolicited mss/month. Accepts 5 mss/issue; 20 mss/year. Publishes ms 3 months after acceptance. **Publishes 5-10 new writers/ year.** Recently published work by Taylor Graham, Janet Buck, Jim Manton, Steve Cartwright, Don Stockard, Margaret Karmazin, Bill Hughes. Length: 500-4,000 words; average length: 2,000 words. Publishes short shorts. Average length: 2,000 words. Also publishes literary essays, literary criticism and poetry. Sometimes comments on rejected mss.
How to Contact: "Query by e-mail with word attachment." Accepts submissions by e-mail. Include estimated word count, brief bio and list of publications. Responds in 1 week to queries; 3 months to mss. Accepts simultaneous, previously published and multiple submissions. Guidelines by e-mail or on website. Reviews novels, short story collections and nonfiction books of interest to writers.
Payment/Terms: "No payment at this time. Rights remain with author."
Advice: "Short fiction should first of all tell a good story, take the reader to new and interesting imaginary or real places. Short fiction should use language lyrically and effectively, be experimental in either form or content and take the reader into realms where they can analyze and think about the human condition. Write with passion for your material, be concise and economical and let the reader work to unravel your story. In terms of editing, always proofread to the point where what you submit is the best it possibly can be. Never be discouraged if your work is not accepted; it may be just not the right fit for a current publication."

BABEL, the Multilingual, Multicultural Online Journal of Arts and Ideas, E-mail: malcolm@towerofbabel.com. Website: www.towerofbabel.com. **Contact:** Malcolm Lawrence, editor-in-chief. Electronic zine. Publishes "regional reports from international stringers all over the planet, as well as features round table discussions, fiction, columns, poetry, erotica, travelogues, reviews of all the arts and editorials. We are an online community involving an extensive group of over 50 artists, writers and programmers, and over 150 translators representing (so far) 35 of the world's languages."
Needs: "There are no specific categories of fiction that we are not interested in. Possible exceptions: lawyers/vampires, different genders hailing from different planets, cold war military scenarios and things that go bump in the suburban night." Recently published work by Nicholas P. Snoek, Yves Jaques, Doug Williamson, A.L. Fern, Laura Feister, Denzel J. Hankinson, Pete Hanson and Malcolm Lawrence.
How to Contact: Send queries/mss by e-mail. "Please send submissions with a résumé/cv or biography, as Microsoft Word attached to e-mail." Reviews novels and short story collections.

● **A BULLET INTRODUCES COMMENTS** by the editor of *Novel & Short Story Writer's Market* indicating special information about the listing.

Advice: "We would like to see more fiction with first-person male characters written by female authors as well as more fiction with first-person female characters written by male authors. The best advice we could give to writers wanting to be published in our publication is simply to know what you're writing about and to write passionately about it. We should also mention that the phrase 'dead white men' will only hurt your chances. The Internet is the most important invention since the printing press and will change the world in the same way. One look at *Babel* and you'll see our predictions for the future of electronic publishing."

THE BARCELONA REVIEW, Correu Vell 12 - 2, 08002 Barcelona, Spain. Phone/fax: (00) 34 93 319 15 96. E-mail: editor@barcelonareview.com. Website: www.barcelonareview.com. **Contact:** Jill Adams, editor. "*TBR* is an international review of contemporary, cutting-edge fiction published in English, Spanish and Catalan. Our aim is to bring both new and established writers to the attention of a larger audience. Well-known writers such as Alicia Erian in the U.S., Michael Faber in the U.K., Carlos Gardini in Argentina, and Andrés Ibàñez in Spain, for example, were not known outside their countries until appearing in *TBR*. Our multilingual format increases the audience all the more. Internationally-known writers, such as Irvine Welsh and Douglas Coupland, have contributed stories that ran in small press anthologies available in only one country. We try to keep abreast of what's happening internationally and to present the best finds every two months. Our intended audience is anyone interested in contemporary, cutting-edge fiction; we assume that our readers are well read and familiar with contemporary fiction in general."

• *The Barcelona Review* ranked on *Writer's Digest*'s "Top 30" list of best markets for fiction writers and in the top 5 of *WD*'s best online fiction publications.

Needs: Short fiction. Length: 4,000 words maximum. Also publishes articles and essays, book reviews and author interviews. "Most, but not all of our fiction lies somewhere out of the mainstream. Our bias is towards potent and powerful cutting-edge material; given that general criteria we are open to all styles and techniques and all genres. No slice-of-life stories, vignettes or sentimental writing, and nothing that does not measure up, in your opinion, to the quality of work in our review, which we expect submitters to be familiar with." **Published 20 new writers in 2001.** "That number will increase as the quality of writing presents itself." Recently published work by Pinckney Benedict, A.M. Home, George Saunders, Alicia Grian and Dennis Cooper. Length: 4,000 words maximum.

How to Contact: Send submissions by e-mail as an attached file. Hard copies accepted but cannot be returned. No simultaneous submissions.

Payment/Terms: "In lieu of pay we offer a highly professional Spanish translation to English language writers and vice versa to Spanish writers."

Advice: "Send top drawer material that has been drafted two, three, four times—whatever it takes. Then sit on it for a while and look at it afresh. Keep the text tight (rewrite until every unnecessary word is eliminated). Grab the reader in the first paragraph and don't let go. Keep in mind that a perfectly crafted story that lacks a punch of some sort won't cut it. Make it new, make it different. Surprise the reader in some way. Read the best of the short fiction available in your area of writing to see how yours measures up. Don't send anything off until you feel it's ready and then familiarize yourself with the content of the review/magazine to which you are submitting."

BIG COUNTRY PEACOCK CHRONICLE, Online Magazine, RR1, Box 89K-112, Aspermont TX 79502. (806)254-2322. E-mail: publisher@peacockchronicle.com. Website: www.peacockchronicle.com. **Contact:** Audrey Yoeckel, owner/publisher. Online magazine. "We publish articles, commentaries, reviews, interviews, short stories, serialized novels and novellas, poetry, essays, humor and anecdotes. Due to the nature of Internet publication, guidelines for lengths of written works are flexible and acceptance is based more on content. Content must be family friendly. Writings that promote hatred or violence will not be accepted. *The Big Country Peacock Chronicle* is dedicated to the preservation of community values and traditional folk cultures. In today's society, we are too often deprived of a solid feeling of community which is so vital to our security and well-being. It is our attempt to keep the best parts of our culture intact. Our goal is to build a place for individuals, no matter the skill level, to test their talents and get feedback from others in a non-threatening, friendly environment. The original concept for the magazine was to open the door to talented writers by providing not only a publishing medium for their work but support and feedback as well. It was created along the lines of a smalltown publication in order to remove some of the anxiety about submitting works for first time publication." Monthly. Estab. 2000.

• *Big Country Peacock Chronicle* was named the Heartland Heartbeat Featured Site for February, 2001.

Needs: Adventure, children's/juvenile (adventure, animal, easy-to-read, fantasy, historical, mystery, preschool, series, sports), ethnic/multicultural (general), family saga, fantasy (space fantasy, sword and sorcery), gay, historical (general), horror (futuristic, psychological, supernatural), humor/satire, literary, military/war, mystery/suspense (amateur sleuth, police procedural, private eye/hardboiled), psychic/supernatural/occult, regional, religious (children's religious), romance (gothic, historical, romantic suspense), science fiction (soft/sociological), thriller/espionage, translations, western (frontier saga, traditional). "While the genre of the writing or the style does not matter, excessive or gratuitous violence, foul language, and sexually explicit material is not acceptable." Accepts 2-3 mss/issue (depending on length). Publishes ms 3 months after acceptance. Recently published work by Meredith Weber and Julie Alexander. Length: 3,500 words maximum; average length: 2,500 words. Publishes short shorts. Average length: fewer than 1,500 words. Also publishes literary essays, literary criticism and poetry. Always comments on rejected mss.

How to Contact: Send cover letter and entire item for submission if under 1,500 words or 1,500 word clip of longer pieces. Accepts submissions by e-mail. Include estimated word count, brief bio, list of publications and Internet contact information, i.e., e-mail, website address. Responds in 3 weeks to queries; 6 weeks to mss. Send SASE (or IRC) for return of ms or send a disposable copy of ms and #10 SASE for reply only. Accepts simultaneous, previously published and multiple submissions. Guidelines by e-mail or on website. Reviews novels, short story collections and nonfiction books of interest to writers. Send review copies to Audrey Yoeckel, publisher@peacockchronicle.com.

Payment/Terms: Acquires electronic rights. Sends galleys to author. "While the authors and artists retain sole copyright to the material they submit to the *Peacock Chronicle*, the submission of that material constitutes permission for nonexclusive, perpetual rights for the free electronic distribution of archived material unless otherwise negotiated."

Advice: "We look for writing that promotes community and traditional values regardless of genre. If the story takes place on Mars or in the Old West, or is about relationships, history, adventure, etc., it must contain an identifiable positive attitude toward social structures and individual differences. We look for continuity and coherence. The work should be clean with a minimum of typographical errors. The advantage to submitting works to us is the feedback and support. We work closely with our writers, offering promotion, resource information, moral support and general help to achieve success as writers. While we recommend doing business with us via the Internet, we have also published writers who do not have access. For those new to the Internet, we also provide assistance with the best ways to use it as a medium for achieving success in the field."

BLACKBIRD, (formerly *New Virginia Review*), Virginia Commonwealth University Department of Fiction, P.O. Box 843082, Richmond VA 23284. (804)225-4729. E-mail: blackbird@vcu.edu. Website: www.blackbird.vcu.edu. **Contact:** Fiction Editor. Online journal. "Blackbird strives to maintain the highest quality of writing and design, bringing the best things about a print magazine to the outside world. We publish fiction that is carefully crafted, thoughtful and surprising." Biannual. Estab. 1978. Circ. 2,000.

Needs: Contemporary, experimental, literary, mainstream, serialized/excerpted novel. No blue, science fiction, romance, children's. Receives 50-100 unsolicited fiction mss/month. Accepts an average of 15 mss/issue. Does not read mss May 15-August 15. Publishes ms an average of 6-9 months after acceptance. Length: no minimum; 8,000 words maximum; average length: 5,000-6,500 words. Also publishes poetry. Sometimes critiques rejected mss.

How to Contact: Send complete ms with cover letter, name, address, telephone number, brief biographical comment. Responds in 3-5 months. SASE (or IRC). Sample copy online.

Payment/Terms: Pays on publication for first North American serial rights.

Advice: "We like a story that invites us into its world, that engages our senses, soul and mind."

THE BLUE MOON REVIEW, 14313 Winter Ridge Lane, Midlothian VA 23113. E-mail: fiction@thebluemoon.com. Website: www.TheBlueMoon.com. **Contact:** Theron Montgomery, fiction editor. Electronic magazine: Illustrations and photos. Quarterly. Estab. 1994. Circ. 25,000.

● *The Blue Moon Review* ranked on *Writer's Digest*'s "Top 30" list of best markets for fiction writers.

Needs: Experimental, feminist, gay, lesbian, literary, mainstream/contemporary, regional, translations. No genre fiction or condensed novels. Wants to see more "brilliant, insightful, experimental work." Receives 40-70 unsolicited mss/month. Accepts 7-10 mss/issue; 51-60 mss/year. Publishes ms up to 9 months after acceptance. Published work by Edward Falco, Deborah Eisenberg, Robert Sward and Aldo Alvarez. Length: 3,000 words maximum. Publishes short shorts. Also publishes literary essays, literary criticism, poetry. Sometimes comments on rejected mss.

How to Contact: Send complete ms with a cover letter via e-mail. Only accepts electronic submissions. Include a brief bio, list of publications and e-mail address if available. Responds in 2 months to mss. Accepts simultaneous and electronic submissions. Sample copy and guidelines available at above website.

Payment/Terms: Acquires first North American serial and one-time anthology rights. Rights revert to author upon request.

Advice: "We look for strong use of language or strong characterization. Manuscripts stand out by their ability to engage a reader on an intellectual or emotional level. Present characters with depth regardless of age and introduce intelligent concepts that have resonance and relevance."

BOVINE FREE WYOMING. E-mail: submissions@bovinefreewyoming.com. Website: www.bovinefreewyoming.com (includes entire publication, guidelines and contact information). **Contact:** Vickie L. Knestaut, editor. Online magazine. "*Bovine Free Wyoming* is a quarterly electronic publication of literature and art for a general reading audience. We aim to raise the standards for electronic publications by offering quality literature and art to our readers, and an attractive rights and payment package to our writers and artists." Quarterly. Estab. 2000. Circ. 13,000 hits/month.

Needs: Adventure, ethnic/multicultural, experimental, family saga, fantasy, feminist, gay, historical, horror, humor/satire, lesbian, literary, mainstream, military/war, mystery/suspense, New Age, psychic/supernatural/occult, regional, religious, science fiction, thriller/espionage, translations, western. Receives 20 unsolicited mss/month. Accepts 5 mss/issue; 20 mss/year. Publishes ms 3 months after acceptance. **Publishes 2 new writers/year.** Recently published work by Eric Melbye, Lynn Bey, Allen M. Heller, Jolie Braun and L.B. Sedlacek. Length: 5,000 words (maximum); average length: 2,000 words. Publishes short shorts. Average length: 500 words. Also publishes literary essays and poetry. Sometimes comments on rejected mss.

How to Contact: Send complete ms with a cover letter. Accepts submissions by e-mail. Include estimated word count, brief bio and e-mail address. Responds in 2 weeks to queries; 1 month to mss. Accepts simultaneous, previously published and multiple submissions. Sample copy free. Guidelines on website.

Payment/Terms: Pays $10. Pays on acceptance for electronic rights. Sends galleys to author.

Advice: "We aim to appeal to a general reading audience, so genre fiction doesn't go over well with us unless it has qualities that exceed the requirements of genre. What really stands out to us is fiction that tells a story and generally contains conflict, plotting, and character development. Read at least one issue to gauge our interests, and then read and adhere to the submission guidelines. Also, make sure the story has conflict, and the characters are more interesting than the writer."

BULK HEAD, Laxative of the Literary Mind, Bridge Burner's Publishing, P.O. Box 5255, Mankato MN 56002-5255. (507)385-0635. E-mail: editor@bulkhead.org. Website: www.bulkhead.org. **Contact:** Curtis Meyer, publisher. Online magazine: illustrations; photos. "We are an online literary magazine specializing in short fiction. Most of the work we publish is humorous, angry, sarcastic, experimental and energetic." Quarterly. Estab. 2000.
Needs: "We like shorter stories—slice of life type short shorts." Comics/graphic novels, erotica, ethnic/multicultural (general), experimental, feminist, gay, humor/satire, lesbian, literary, mainstream, New Age, psychic/supernatural/occult, regional. "We do not publish hardcore genre stories. We do not publish religious material." Receives 15 unsolicited mss/month. Accepts 2-3 mss/issue; 6-12 mss/year. Publishes ms 3 months after acceptance. **Publishes 10 new writers/year.** Recently published work by Neil Harrison, Bruce Nelson, Charles Frank Roethel, Jay Marvin, Tessa Derksen, John Lee Clark, Neil Stanoff and Paul Dilsaver. Length: 50-3,500 words; average length: 2,000 words. Publishes short shorts. Average length: 900 words. Also publishes literary essays and poetry. Rarely comments on rejected mss.
How to Contact: Send complete ms with a cover letter. Accepts submissions by e-mail and disk. "Write 'Bulk Head Submissions' in the subject line." Include estimated word count, brief bio and list of publications. Responds in 3 months to queries; 6 months to mss. Send SASE (or IRC) for return of ms or send a disposable copy of ms and #10 SASE for reply only. Sample copy free. Guidelines on website.
Payment/Terms: Acquires first rights. Sponsors contest.
Advice: "We like energetic, angry, slice-of-life short fiction. We like action and dialogue. We want short fiction; not stories. There is a difference. Action and dialogue are good. Formulas are bad."

$ THE CAFE IRREAL, International Imagination. E-mail: editors@cafeirreal.com. Website: www.cafe irreal.com. **Contact:** Alice Whittenburg, G.S. Evans, editors. E-zine; illustrations. "*The Cafe Irreal* is a webzine focusing on short stories and short shorts of an irreal nature." Semiannually.
• *The Cafe Irreal* ranked on *Writer's Digest*'s "Top 30" list of best markets for fiction writers, and was listed as one of the top 25 Internet Markets by *Writer's Digest.*
Needs: Experimental, fantasy (literary), science fiction (literary), translations. "No horror or 'slice-of-life' stories; no genre or mainstream science fiction or fantasy." Accepts 10-15 mss/issue; 20-30 mss/year. Publishes mss 6 months after acceptance. Recently published translations of works by Anna Maria Shua, Cristovam Buarque and Jana Moravcova. Length: no minimum; 2,000 words maximum (excerpts from longer works accepted). Publishes short shorts. Also publishes literary essays, literary criticism. Often comments on rejected ms.
How to Contact: Electronic submissions only. No attachments; include submission in body of e-mail. Include estimated word count. Responds in 2 months to mss. Accepts reprint submissions from print sources only. "Please indicate where and when it was published." See website for sample copy and guidelines.
Payment/Terms: Pays 1¢/word, $2 minimum. Pays on publication for first rights, one-time rights. Sends galleys (the html document via e-mail) to author.
Advice: "Forget formulas. Write about what you *don't* know, take me places I couldn't *possibly* go, don't try to make me care about the characters. Read short fiction by writers such as Kafka, Kobo Abe, Julio Cortazar, Leonora Carrington and Stanislaw Lem. Also read our website and guidelines."

CARVE MAGAZINE, Mild Horse Press, P.O. Box 72231, Davis CA 95617. E-mail: editor@carvezine.com. Website: www.carvezine.com. **Contact:** Melvin Sterne, senior editor. Bimonthly online journal with annual printed "best of" anthology. Estab. 2000. Online circ. 4,000/month. *Carve Magazine* nominates for the Pushcart, O. Henry, Best American and Best of Beacon anthologies. Member, Council of Literary Magazines and Presses.
Needs: Short stories only. Literary fiction. No genre, poetry or nonfiction. Publishes 70+ stories/year. We are read in more than 40 countries worldwide and publish a mix of US and foreign authors. **Publishes 10-20 new writers/year.** Recently published work by Nan Leslie, Tanya Egan Gibson, XuXi, Robin Parks, Richard Messer and Gina Ochsner. Hosts the Raymond Carver Short Story Award at *Carve Magazine* ($1,500 first prize).
How to Contact: Electronic submissions only. Visit our website at www.carvezine.com for guidelines and to submit. Length: 10,000 words maximum. Accepts simultaneous submissions if identified (except for contest). Responds in 2-3 months. Occasionally critiques mss.
Advice: "We look for stories with strong characterization, conflict, and tightly written prose. Do you know what a fictive moment is? We generally dislike gimmicky and experimental fiction. If you tell a good story, we'll read it."

CENOTAPH, Fiction for the New Millennium, Cayuse Press, P.O. Box 66003, Burien WA 98166-0003. E-mail: editor@cenotaph.net. Website: www.cenotaph.net (includes submission guidelines, features, writer's resources and two writers forums). **Contact:** Paul Tylor, editor. Electronic literary journal ("electronic submissions *only*, please."). "Published quarterly, *Cenotaph* is fiction for the new millennium, and seeks innovative fiction, shimmering with vision and originality for a literate audience." Estab. 1999.
Needs: Adventure, ethnic/multicultural (general), fantasy, historical, literary, mainstream, mystery/suspense, thriller/espionage, translations, cross-genre, science fiction, surrealism, magic realism, speculative. Romance (of any orientation) is acceptable if not sexually graphic. No children's, young adult, excessive violence, pro-drug or erotica. Wants to see more mystery, cross-genre, historical, surrealism. Receives 30 unsolicited mss/month. Publishes 10-12 mss/issue; 40-

48 mss/year. Publishes ms 2-6 months after acceptance. **Willing to publish new writers.** Recently published work by Paul Tylor, Mary Chandler, Teresa White. Length: 800-2,500 words; average length: 1,500 words; prefers 2,000 words. Sometimes comments on rejected mss.

How to Contact: Send complete ms with a cover letter by e-mail only. No attachments will be accepted. Include estimated word count, 100-200 word bio and list of publications. Responds in 2 months after deadline to mss. Accepts multiple submissions. Prefers unpublished work, but will consider previously published, with proper documentation. Writer retains copyright. Guidelines and deadlines available on website. We will also no longer accept postal submissions. No postal mss will be returned.

Payment/Terms: Acquires one-time rights.

Advice: "Read and study the guidelines, then follow them when submitting. We are always looking for new voices and original stories. Short works best on the Internet—we are interested in good writing, period. Your work won't make the short list if it exhibits sloppy mechanics. We're more attracted to stories under 1,000 words. We look forward to working with you."

$ **C/OASIS, New Writing for a New World**, Sun Oasis Publishing, 491 Moraga Way, Orinda CA 94563. (925)258-9026. Fax: (603)971-5013. E-mail: eide491@earthlink.net. Website: www.sunoasis.com/oasis.html. **Contact:** David Eide, editor. Online magazine. "We look for excellent fiction by experienced writers who have some publication under their belt. Writers from India, Australia, England as well as the USA have been published." Monthly. Estab. 1998. Circ. 3,000 unique visitors/month.

Needs: Literary, experimental. "No romance, religious, young adult." Receives 10-20 unsolicited mss/month. Accepts 1-3 mss/issue; 9-10 mss/year. Publishes ms 1-2 months after acceptance. Recently published work by Robert Marazas and Andrew McIntyre. Length: 1,000-4,000 words; average length: 2,000 words. Publishes short shorts. Average length: 1,000 words. Also publishes literary essays and poetry. Sometimes comments on rejected mss.

How to Contact: Accepts submissions by e-mail. Responds in 1 month to queries; 3 months to mss. Accepts previously published submissions. Guidelines by e-mail ("in the subject line write submission/Oasis") or on website. Reviews novels, short story collections and nonfiction books of interest to writers. Send review copies to David Eide.

Payment/Terms: Pays $15-20. Pays on publication for one-time and reprint rights.

Advice: "Tell your own story in your own way."

collectedstories.com, spin a yarn, weave a story, collectedstories.com, Columbia U. Station, P.O. Box 250626, New York NY 10025. (718)609-9454. E-mail: info@collectedstories.com. Website: www.collectedstories.com (includes short fiction, offering original stories, books, author interviews, excerpts and reports on upcoming releases, deals, contests and other news related to the form). **Contact:** Dara Albanese and Wendy Ball, co-publishers. Online magazine: photos. "An online magazine devoted exclusively to short fiction, *collectedstories.com* considers itself unique in that it not only publishes original short stories but also reports on various aspects related to the short form, featuring upcoming releases, author interviews, news on short story book deals, etc. The founders strive to provide the short form with a quality venue of its own." Bimonthly. Estab. 2000.

Needs: Literary. "No young adult or children's fiction." Receives 40 unsolicited mss/month. Accepts 4 mss/issue; 24 mss/year. Publishes ms 1 month after acceptance. **Publishes 7 new writers/year.** Recently published work by David Fickett, Amy Halloran, James Iredell and Rawn M. James, Jr. Length: 500-5,000 words; average length: 1,800 words. Publishes short shorts. Average length: 900 words.

How to Contact: Submit mss via online form. Accepts submissions by e-mail. Include information from contact form. Responds in 1 week to queries; 3 months to mss. Accepts previously published and multiple submissions. Sample copy online. Guidelines by e-mail or on website. Reviews novels, short story collections and nonfiction books of interest to writers. Send review copies to Dara Albanese.

Payment/Terms: Writer retains copyright. Sends galleys to author.

Advice: "Since stories are accepted on a revolving basis at *collectedstories.com,* criteria may vary in that a story is up against the best of only that particular batch under consideration for the next issue at that particular time. We select the most readable stories, that is, stories that are original, compelling or with a sense of character, and evidence of talent (or promise of talent) with prose. Writers should become familiar with a publication before submission, develop a strong hold on grammar and thereby submit only clean, finished works for consideration."

CONSPIRE, a journal of literary art, CanAm, 201 Astor Ave., Lansing MI 48910. E-mail: thealu@adelphia.net. Website: www.conspire.org. **Contact:** Fanoula Sevastos, prose editor. Online magazine specializing in poetry and prose. Quarterly. Estab. 1996. Circ. 500-1,000 visitors/month average. Member, ILEF—Internet Literary Editor's Fellowship.

Needs: Adventure, children's/juvenile (adventure, animal, fantasy), ethnic/multicultural, experimental, family saga, fantasy, feminist, gay, glitz, historical, horror (dark fantasy, futuristic, psychological, supernatural), humor/satire, lesbian, literary, mainstream, military/war, mystery/suspense, New Age, regional, science fiction (soft/sociological), thriller/espionage, translations, young adult/teen. "No pornography, religious or erotic." Upcoming themes: Every spring we publish a women's issue. List of upcoming themes available online. Receives 10-15 unsolicited mss/month. Accepts 5-12 mss/issue; 25-40 mss/year. "Generally, we don't read manuscripts 2-3 weeks prior to the release of a new issue." Publishes ms within 3 months after acceptance. **Publishes 10-15 new writers/year.** Recently published work by Daniela Gioseffi, Elish Porat, Walter Cummins and Jason Gurley. Length: 500-2,000 words. Publishes short shorts. Also publishes literary essays, literary criticism, flash fiction, creative nonfiction and poetry.
How to Contact: Send complete ms with a cover letter. Accepts submissions by e-mail. Include estimated word count and brief bio. Responds in 3 month to queries and mss. Accepts previously published and multiple submissions. Guidelines on website. Reviews novels, short story collections and nonfiction books of interest to writers. Send review copies to thealu@adelphia.net.
Payment/Terms: Payment is publication.
Advice: "We look for fiction that is well-crafted and innovative, and shows diversity, creative language, imagistic power and continuity."

$ CONVERSELY, Conversely, Inc., PMB #121, 3053 Fillmore St., San Francisco CA 94123-4009. E-mail: writers@conversely.com. Website: www.conversely.com. "We are a webszine, all our content is online." **Contact:** Alejandro Gutierrez, editor. Online magazine specializing in relationships between men and women. Illustrations; photos. "*Conversely* is dedicated to exploring relationships between women and men, every stage, every aspect, through different forms of writing, essays, memoirs, and fiction. Our audience is both female and male, mostly between 18-35 age range. We look for writing that is intelligent, provocative, and witty; we look for topics that are original and appealing to our readers." Quarterly, some sections are published biweekly. Estab. 2000.
Needs: Literary, "must be about romantic relationships between women and men." No erotica, gothic, science fiction. Receives 300 unsolicited mss/month. Accepts 1-3 mss/issue; 8-12 mss/year. Publishes ms 3 months after acceptance. **Publishes 2-4 new writers/year.** Published work by Tod Goldberg, Stephanie Aulenback and Jim Nichols. Length: 500-3,000 words; average length: 2,500 words.
How to Contact: Send complete ms with cover letter. Accepts submissions by e-mail. "We much prefer e-mail over regular mail." Include telephone numbers, estimated word count, brief bio, list of publications and notice if ms is simultaneous. Responds in 2 weeks to queries; 2 months to mss. Send disposable copy of ms and #10 SASE for reply only (include e-mail and phone number if sending by regular mail). Accepts simultaneous submissions. Complete guidelines on website.
Payment/Terms: Pays $50-100. Pays on publication for electronic rights (90 days exclusive, non-exclusive there after). Sends galleys to author.
Advice: "We look for stories that hold attention from start to finish, that cover original topics or use a fresh approach, that have a compelling narrative voice. We prefer stories that deal with relationships in an insightful, honest way, and that surprise by revealing more about a character than was expected. Keep in mind our target audience. Know when to start and know where to end, what to leave out and what to keep in."

THE COPPERFIELD REVIEW, A Journal for Readers and Writers of Historical Fiction, Meredith Allard, Publisher, P.O. Box 11091, Canoga Park CA 91309. E-mail: info@copperfieldreview.com. Website: www.copperfieldreview.com (includes the journal: historical fiction and essays, reviews and interviews related to historical fiction). **Contact:** Meredith Allard, editor-in-chief. "*The Copperfield Review* is an online literary journal that publishes historical fiction and articles, reviews and interviews related to historical fiction. We believe that by understanding the lessons from our past through historical fiction we can gain better insight into the nature of our society today, as well as a better understanding of ourselves." Quarterly. Estab. 2000.
  • *The Copperfield Review* ranked on *Writer's Digest*'s "Top 30" list of best markets for fiction writers.
Needs: Historical (general), romance (historical), western (frontier saga, traditional). "We will consider submissions in most fiction categories, but the setting must be historical in nature." Does not want to see "anything not related to historical fiction." Receives 30 unsolicited mss/month. Accepts 7-10 mss/issue; 28-40 mss/year. Publishes ms 3 months after acceptance. **"Between 30-50% of our authors are first time."** Published work by RD Larson, Aidan Baker, Anthony Arthur, Lad Moore and Anu Kumar. Length: 500-3,000 words; average length: 1,500 words. Publishes short shorts. Average length: 500 words. Also publishes literary essays, literary criticism and poetry. Often comments on rejected mss.
How to Contact: Send complete ms with a cover letter. Accepts submissions by e-mail, fax and disk. Include estimated word count and brief bio. Name and e-mail address should appear on the first page of the submission. Send e-mail submissions to info@copperfieldreview.com. Responds in 6 weeks to queries and mss. Send SASE (or IRC) for return of ms or send a disposable copy of ms and #10 SASE for reply only. Accepts simultaneous, previously published and multiple submissions. Sample copy available online. Guidelines on website. Reviews novels, short story collections and nonfiction books of interest to writers. Send review copies to Meredith Allard, editor-in-chief.
Payment/Terms: Acquires one-time rights. Sponsors contest. Guidelines will be posted on *Copperfield*.
Advice: "*The Copperfield Review* wishes to showcase the very best in literary historical fiction. Stories that use historical periods and details to illuminate universal truths will immediately stand out. We are thrilled to receive thoughtful work that is polished, poised, and written from the heart. Be professional, and only submit your very best work. Be certain

to adhere to a publication's submission guidelines, and always treat your e-mail submissions with the same care you would use with traditional publishers. Above all, be strong and be true to your calling as a writer. It is a difficult, frustrating, but wonderful journey."

COTWORLD CREATIVE MAGAZINE, Cotworld Independent, 2008-66 Isabella St., Toronto, Ontario M4Y-1N3 Canada. (416)964-1241. E-mail: webmaster@cotworld.com. Website: www.cotworld.com. **Contact:** Mark O'Sullivan, editor-in-chief. "*Cotworld* is not a print publication. *Cotworld* is an online community where writers can publish and discuss their work." Online magazine: some illustrations; photos. Monthly. Estab. 1999. Circ. approximately 30,000 hits/month.

Needs: Anything. Accepts 4-5 mss/issue; 48-68 mss/year. Publishes "immediately." **Publishes 20 new writers/year.** Length: 2,000-3,500 words; average length: 2,500 words. Publishes short shorts. Average length: 2,500 words.

How to Contact: "Go to www.cotworld.com and register online in order to submit your work." Guidelines on website.

Payment/Terms: "The writer retains all ownership. We're just a showcase."

CRIMSON, Night Terrors Publications, 1202 W. Market St., Orrville OH 44667-1710. (330)683-0338. E-mail: dedavidson@night-terrors-publications.com. Website: www.night-terrors-publications.com (includes excerpts, writer's guidelines, editor bio, free reading, articles, links of interest to readers and writers, writer bios, NT screen saver, etc.). **Contact:** D. E. Davidson, editor/publisher. E-zine specializing in dark works: equivalent to 8½×5½; equivalent to 35-60 pages. "*Crimson* publishes stories submitted to *Night Terrors Magazine* which the editor finds to have merit but which do not fit the concept for *Night Terrors Magazine*. Genre doesn't matter and the magazine is free." Estab. 1999. Circ. 700.

Needs: "*Crimson* publishes any story of sufficient quality which was submitted to *Night Terrors Magazine* but for various reasons was not appropriate for that publications. This could include science fiction, horror, religious, literary, erotica, fantasy or most other adult categories of fiction. "No graphic sex or violence toward children and women. No stories written specifically for *Crimson*. Please read the *Night Terrors* guidelines and write with the goal of publication there." Receives 100 unsolicited mss/month. Accepts 4 mss/issue; 24 mss/year. Publishes ms 4 months after acceptance. **Publishes 10 new writers/year.** Published work by A. R. Morlan, Ezra Claverie, Vera Searles and Craig Maull. Length: 2,000-5,000 words; average length: 3,000 words. Sometimes comments on rejected mss.

How to Contact: Send complete ms with cover letter. Include estimated word count, brief bio and list of publications with submission. Responds in 3 months. Send disposable copy of ms and #10 SASE for reply only. Accepts simultaneous submissions. Sample copy and guidelines free on website.

Payment/Terms: Pays 1 (printed) contributor's copy; or all back issues on CD. Pays on publication for one-time electronic and one-time print rights. Sends galleys to author. Not copyrighted.

Advice: "Please read our guidelines before submitting. These are available on our website. Be professional. Do not submit stories which are less than 2,000 words or longer than 5,000 words. Do not submit stories folded. Send stories only in a 9×12 envelope. Do not use small type. Please use 12pt New Roman or Courier or equivalent. Proof your work. Use appropriate ms format and always include SASE. Send only one story at a time."

$ DANA LITERARY SOCIETY ONLINE JOURNAL, Dana Literary Society, P.O. Box 3362, Dana Point CA 92629-8362. E-mail: ward@danaliterary.org. Website: www.danaliterary.org (includes fiction, nonfiction and poetry. Also included: editorial commentary and writer's guidelines. All details can be viewed on website). **Contact:** Robert L. Ward, director. Online journal. "Fiction we publish must be well-crafted and thought-provoking. We prefer works that have a message or moral." Monthly. Estab. 2000. Approximately 8,000 visitors to website monthly.

Needs: Humor/satire. Also stories with a message or moral. "Most categories are acceptable if work is mindful of a thinking audience. No romance, children/juvenile, religion/inspirational, pornographic, excessively violent or profane work. Would like to see more humor/satire." Receives 30 unsolicited mss/month. Accepts 3 mss/issue; 36 mss/year. Publishes ms 3 months after acceptance. **Publishes 15 new writers/year.** Recently published work by A.B. Jacobs, James Hall, Jerry McCarty. Length: 800-2,500 words; average length: 2,000 words. Also publishes literary essays and poetry. Often comments on rejected mss.

How to Contact: "Submissions should be clearly legible, preferably typed, either single or double-spaced, and include your name, mailing address, and e-mail address on the first page. They should be snail-mailed to Dana Literary Society, P.O. Box 3362, Dana Point CA 92629-8362, along with a self-addressed stamped #10 envelope. No cover letter is required. Each work must be the original creation of the submitter. Both unpublished and previously published works are welcome." Responds in 2 weeks to mss. Send a disposable copy of ms and #10 SASE for reply only. Accepts simultaneous and previously published submissions. Guidelines on website.

Payment/Terms: Pays $50 for each short story accepted. Pays on online publication for right to display in online journal for 1 month. Not copyrighted.

Advice: "Success requires two qualities: ability and tenacity. Perfect your technique through educational resources, expansion of your scope of interests and regular reevaluation and as required, revision of your works. Profit by a wide exposure to the writings of others. Submit works systematically and persistently, keeping accurate records so you know what went where and when. Take to heart responses and suggestions and plan your follow-up accordingly."

DARGONZINE. E-mail: dargon@shore.net. Website: www.dargonzine.org. **Contact:** Ornoth D.A. Liscomb, editor. Electronic zine specializing in fantasy. "*DargonZine* is an electronic magazine that prints original fantasy fiction by aspiring Internet writers. The Dargon Project is a collaborative anthology whose goal is to provide a way for aspiring fantasy writers on the Internet to meet and become better writers through mutual contact and collaboration as well as contact with a live readership via the Internet."

Needs: Fantasy. "Our goal is to write fantasy fiction that is mature, emotionally compelling, and professional. Membership in the Dargon Project is a requirement for publication." **Publishes 4-12 new writers/year.**

How to Contact: Guidelines available on website.

Payment/Terms: "As a strictly noncommercial magazine, our writers' only compensation is their growth and membership in a lively writing community. Authors retain all rights to their stories."

Advice: "The Readers' and Writers' FAQs on our website provide much more detailed information about our mission, writing philosophy, and value of writing for DargonZine."

N **⊘** **DARK MOON RISING,** c/o Angela Silliman, P.O. Box 42844, Cincinnati, OH 45242. E-mail: editor@darkm oonrising.com or submit@darkmoonrising.com. Website: www.darkmoonrising.com. **Senior Editor:** Angela Silliman. "*Dark Moon Rising* is an intelligent and creative venue for science fiction, fantasy, horror and related genres. We publish well-crafted stories, imaginative poetry and vivid artwork. *Dark Moon Rising* is deeply committed to showcasing the work of both new and established artists." Published 6 times/year.

Needs: "We publish short (less than 5,000 words) science fiction, fantasy, horror and related genre fiction, as well as poetry and artwork fitting these genres. Our readership ranges in age and both genders, and come from around the world. The attitude of the e-zine is to maintain something around the level of PG-13 for all published materials. We are not interested in anything with excessive strong language, intensive gore or pornography. We are also not looking for anything in the mystery or romance genres." Would like to see more "character driven fantasy." Publishes 5-10 mss/ issue. **Publishes 10 or more new writers/year.** Recently published work by Donna Marie Robb, L. Joseph Shosty, Mark Allen, T.G. Browning, J. Alan Erwin.

How to Contact: "Please read submission guidelines posted on website before submitting." Query by e-mail. E-mail short stories (less than 5,000 words) and poetry without query. Guidelines on website. "If e-mail is not available to a writer, he or she may submit work to our land mail address. However, reply times will take longer, and writers should check out our submission guidelines before sending anything via land mail."

Payment/Terms: "We currently offer no compensation, but we do not ask for any rights, other than 60 day publication rights. After 60 days, the author may request that the story be removed if rights are sold elsewhere."

Advice: "Read what we have online already to get a feel for what we generally publish, what we like, etc. If we like a story we'll work with you to get it just right. Have someone else read over your story for typos and missing words. As a writer, I know that when you've worked on a piece for a while, and you know what it's supposed to say, you may overlook errors. Reading out loud also helps in the revision process. Don't be afraid to submit your work! Electronic publishing is a great place for new and beginning authors to have a chance to get their work published. Though I don't think that electronic publishing will ever replace print publishing, it's a great place to get off to a good start. Also, it's a great way to see what works, and what doesn't—usually for free. I think that the online world is a booming market for short fiction and most magazines, zines, and other short story markets will be moving into the arena in the future."

◎ **THE DEAD MULE,** P.O. Box 835, Winterville NC 28590. E-mail: contact@deadmule.com. Submissions e-mail: deadmulesubmission@hotmail.com. Website: www.deadmule.com. **Contacts:** Valerie MacEwan, editor (editor@deadm ule.com) or Phoebe Kate Foster, associate editor (phoebe_kate_foster@hotmail.com). "*The Dead Mule* is an online literary magazine featuring Southern fiction, articles, poetry and essays, and is proud to claim a long heritage of Southern literary excellence. We consider any writing with a Southern slant. By that we mean the author needs either Southern roots or the writing must be Southern in subject matter. Estab. 1996 as "the first online Southern Literary Journal, we've published almost 200 writers and are damn proud of it."

Needs: Literary. Also nonfiction articles about the South including festival critiques, Nascar worshipping diatribes, and championship wrestling tributes. Always, always, stories about mules. "Special poetry issue in September; special fiction issue published in the December/January *Dead Mule*."

How to Contact: See website for complete details. Send complete ms by e-mail. Do not send attachments—copy and paste your submission into the body of the e-mail. Length: 2,500 words maximum.

Payment/Terms: Acquires first electronic rights. All rights revert to the author on publication. "Works distributed by *The Dead Mule* may not be republished for profit in any form without the express consent of the author. Any specific works published in *The Dead Mule* may not be entered into any database without the express permission of the author and notification of *The Dead Mule*."

Advice: "What we want are writers. Pure and simple. Folks who write about the South. While long lists of previously published works are impressive, they don't matter much around here. That's why we don't include that type of information. We don't think anyone is less of a writer because their list is short. You're a writer because you say you are. Also, you've worked hard on whatever it is you wrote. Don't blow it all by not submitting correctly. If you're thinking about submitting, remember to tell us why, if it's not obvious from the content, you should be admitted to The Dead Mule School of Southern Literature. Before we read the submission, we need to know why you think you're 'Southern.' Remember, no good Southern fiction is complete without a dead mule."

$ **⊘** **DEEP OUTSIDE SFFH,** 6549 Mission Gorge Rd., PMB 260, San Diego CA 92120. E-mail: editors@clockto werfiction.com. Website: www.outsideclocktowerbooks.com. **Contact:** John Cullen or Brian Callahan, editors. Web-only magazine. "*Outside* is a paying professional magazine of SF and dark imaginative fiction, aimed at people who love to read sharply-plotted, character-driven genre fiction. At the same time, we are interested in fiction that transcends the limitations, and ventures outside the stereotypes, of genre fiction." Monthly. Estab. 1998. Circ. 5,000+.

Needs: Horror (dark fantasy, futuristic, psychological), science fiction (hard science/technological, soft/sociological). No pornography, excessive gore, "or vulgarity unless it directly furthers the story (sparingly, at that)." No sword and sorcery, elves, high fantasy, cookie-cutter space opera. Receives 100-150 unsolicited mss/month. Accepts 1 ms/issue; 12 mss/year. Publishes ms 1-3 months after acceptance. **Publishes 1-3 new writers/year.** Recently published work by Pat York, Melanie Tem, Paul Martens and Joel Best. Length: 2,000-4,000 words. Sometimes comments on rejected ms.

How to Contact: Send complete ms with a cover letter. "Manuscripts must be sent by postal mail only." Include estimated word count; list of publications. Responds in 3 months. Send disposable copy of ms and SASE for reply.

Payment/Terms: Pays 3¢/word. Pays on acceptance for first rights. Sends prepublication galleys to author.

Advice: "We look for the best quality story. Genre comes second. We look for polished, first-rate, professional fiction. It is most important to grab us from the first three paragraphs—not only as a common standard but because that's how we lead with both the monthly newsletter and the main page of the magazine. Please read the tips and guidelines at the magazine's website for up-to-the-moment details. Do not send envelopes asking for guidelines, please—all the info is online at our website."

$DRUNKEN BOAT, An Online Journal of Arts & Literature, Drunken Boat, 233 Park Place #27, Brooklyn NY 11238. (718)398-5822. E-mail: editors@drunkenboat.com. Website: www.drunkenboat.com. **Contact:** Ravi Shankar, editor. Online magazine. "Drunkenboat.com is dedicated to creating an arena where works of art endemic to the medium of the web (hypertext, digital animation, music) can coexist with works of more traditional print forms of representation (poetry, critical and fictive prose, photography). It is our conviction that while digital technology will not, in the near future, supplant the print publishing industry, opportunities exist on the web to create new communities of artists and readers that are more egalitarian in terms of accessibility and less narrow in the scope of potential genre than those offered by the conventional print journal. We believe in the kind of creative cross-pollination that includes on the same site, for example, a poem and the oral recording of a thespian's monologue or a collection of short films alongside a collaboratively evolving work of fiction. *Drunken Boat* was intended from the outset to be a non-profit venture that exists exclusively online and includes a diverse group of newly emerging and well-established artists." Semiannual. Estab. 1999. Circ. 10,000.

Needs: "We don't want to see inarticulate stories with poorly developed plots and/or characters." Accepts 5 mss/year. Publishes ms 6 months after acceptance. Length: 10-10,000 words. Also publishes literary essays, literary criticism and poetry.

How to Contact: Send complete ms with a cover letter.

Payment/Terms: Pays $100.

Advice: "At *Drunken Boat* we are especially interested in work that utilizes the web in a dynamic way. Think of the medium of representation as an integral park of aesthetic expression. We are also looking for the highest quality work: thoughtful, provocative, musical work that evinces a knowledge of literary tradition alongside a recognition of the modern moment."

ANTONIN DVORAK'S NOCTURNE HORIZONS, ADVORAK.COM, P.O. Box 251, Painted Post NY 14870. E-mail: visitingwriters@advorak.com. Website: www.ADVORAK.com. E-zine: www.advorak.com/Horizons/Flaindex.html. **Contact:** Ms. Rebecca Dvorak. E-zine specializing in fantasy, science fiction and horror. Photos. "Our publication is hosted by a writer for his audience. If you want to share Dvorak's readership, and you write similar work, submit!" Quarterly. Estab. 2001. Circ. 1,000.

Needs: Adventure, fantasy (supernatural), horror (dark fantasy, futuristic, psychological, supernatural), psychic/supernatural/occult, romance (supernatural), science fiction (hard science/technological, soft/sociological), thriller/espionage. "No religious, erotica, children's juvenile, gay or feminist." Receives 20 unsolicited mss/month. Accepts 3-5 mss/issue; 12-20 mss/year. Publishes ms 2 months after acceptance. **Publishes 7 new writers/year.** Length: 1,000-10,000 words; average length: 6,000. Publishes short shorts. Average length: 1,000 words. Also publishes poetry. Sometimes comments on rejected mss. "We now have our annual short story contest 'Paradise' underway, with more than $500 in cash and prizes. See the website for details."

How to Contact: Send complete ms with cover letter by e-mail. Accepts mss by e-mail or on disk. Include estimated word count, brief bio and list of publications with submission. Responds in 4-6 weeks. Send SASE (or IRC) for return of ms or disposable copy of ms and #10 SASE for reply only. Accepts simultaneous and multiple submissions. Guidelines on website.

Payment/Terms: Acquires first electronic rights. Sends galleys to author. Not copyrighted.

TO RECEIVE REGULAR TIPS AND UPDATES about writing and Writer's Digest publications via e-mail, send an e-mail with "SUBSCRIBE NEWSLETTER" in the body of the message to newsletter-request@writersdigest.com

Advice: "We love to read a good story. Grammar and writing style can always be polished. Without a compelling story, there is nothing to polish. Write, write, and write some more. Writing is a talent, but also a skill. E-zines are popping up all over the Internet. We pride ourselves on standing out. We provide a cutting-edge design and fill it with cutting-edge work."

EWGPRESENTS, 406 Shady Lane, Cayce SC 29033. (803)794-8869. E-mail: EWGBet@aol.com. Website: www.ewgpresents.com. **Contact:** EWGBet@aol.com, fiction editor. Electronic zine. "A contemporary journal of literary quality by new and established writers. *EWGPresents* continues to provide an online forum for writers to present their works internationally, and to usher literature into the digital age."

Needs: Literary. "No pornography or excessive violence and gore beyond the legitimate needs of a story. When in doubt, leave it out." **Publishes 50-60 new writers/year.** Published work by Tessa Nardi, L.C. Mohr, Mary Gordon, Jeffrey L. Jackson and Vasilis Afxentiou.

How to Contact: Send queries/mss by e-mail only. No attachments. Submissions should be directed to specific departments with work on the body of the e-mail. Read and adhere to guidelines provided at the zine.

Advice: "We seek well-written, professionally executed fiction, with attention to basics—grammar, punctuation, usage. Be professional. Be creative. And above all, be yourself. We have the means to reach a universal audience by the click of a mouse. Writers are gifted with a new medium of exposure and the future demands taking advantage of this format."

FAILBETTER.COM, Failbetter, 63 Eighth Ave., #3A, Brooklyn NY 11217. E-mail: editor@failbetter.com. Website: www.failbetter.com (includes access to current and all past issues, contact and submission information). **Contact:** Thom Didato or David Mclendon, editors. Online journal specializing in literary fiction, poetry and art. "*failbetter.com* is a quarterly online magazine in the spirit of a traditional literary journal—dedicated to publishing quality fiction, poetry and artwork. While the web plays host to hundreds, if not thousands, of genre-related literary sights (i.e., sci fi and horror—many of which have merit) *failbetter.com* is not one of them." Quarterly. Estab. 2000. Circ. 20,000.

Needs: Literary. "No genre fiction—romance, fantasy or science fiction." Always would like to see "more character driven literary fiction where something happens!" Receives 25-50 unsolicited mss/month. Accepts 3-5 mss/issue; 12-20 mss/year. Publishes ms 4 months after acceptance. **Publishes 4-6 new writers/year; at least 1/issue.** Recently published work by Amanda Davis, Myla Goldberg, Heidi Julavits, Sam Lipsyte, David Ohle. Nominates select works for Pushcart consideration. Publishes short shorts. Average length: 1,500 words. Often comments on rejected mss.

How to Contact: Send complete ms with a cover letter or send e-mail to submissions@failbetter.com. Accepts submissions by e-mail and disk. "Please send all submissions in the body of the e-mail—do not send attachments. If you wish to send a Word attachment, please query first." Responds in 2 weeks to queries; 1 month to mss. Send a disposable copy of ms and #10 SASE for reply only. Accepts simultaneous submissions. Guidelines on website.

Payment/Terms: Acquires one-time rights, all other rights revert to author.

Advice: "Read an issue. Read our guidelines! *failbetter.com* places a high degree of importance on originality, believing that even in this age of trends it is still possible. *failbetter.com* is not looking for what is current or momentary. We are not concerned with length: one good sentence may find a home here; as the bulk of mediocrity will not. Most importantly, know that what you are saying could only come from you. When you are sure of this, please feel free to submit."

THE FAIRFIELD REVIEW, 544 Silver Spring Rd., Westport CT 06880. (203)256-1970. Fax: (203)256-1970. E-mail: FairfieldReview@hpmd.com. Website: www.fairfieldreview.org. **Contact:** Edward and Janet Granger-Happ, Pamela Pollak, editors. Electronic magazine. "Our mission is to provide an outlet for poetry, short stories and essays, from both new and established writers and students, which are accessible to the general public."

Needs: Short stories, poetry, essays. Would like to see more stories "rich in lyrical imagery and those that are more humorous." **Publishes over 20 new writers/year.** Recently published work by Nan Leslie (Pushcart nominee), Josh Karp and Tom Brennan. "We encourage students and first-time writers to submit their work."

How to Contact: Electronic submissions strongly encouraged. Replies to submissions by e-mail only—author must include e-mail address. Fax submissions accepted.

Advice: "In addition to the submission guidelines found in each issue on our website, we recommend reading the essay *Writing Qualities to Keep in Mind* from our Editors and Authors page on the website. Keep to small, directly experienced themes; write crisply using creative, poetic images; avoid the trite expression."

FICTION INFERNO, The Literary Magazine that Burns You Up, S.O.L. Enterprises, 147 Treehill Loop, Eugene OR 97405-3553. E-mail: editor@fictioninferno.com. Website: www.fictioninferno.com. **Contact:** Max E. Keele, publisher. E-zine specializing in literary speculative fiction. "*Fiction Inferno* is a free literary journal publishing the most exciting short speculative, fantasy, and strange fiction available. *Fiction Inferno* prefers to publish literate, high-quality speculative and imaginative fiction that doesn't fit elsewhere. Dangerous fiction. Experimental fiction. Subversive fiction. Outrageous fiction. We hope to help reinvigorate the field of speculative fiction with an evolved iteration of the New Wave speculative vision of Phillip K. Dick, Harlan Ellison, Norman Spinrad, et al." Quarterly. Estab. 2001. Circ. 4,000/issue.

Needs: Erotica, experimental, fantasy (space fantasy, sword and sorcery), horror (dark fantasy, futuristic, psychological, supernatural), psychic/supernatural/occult, science fiction (hard science/technological, soft/sociological), literary excellence with limited market potential. "No psycho-killer, religious, TV or movie-inspired, dull." Receives 50 unsolicited mss/month. Accepts 3-4 mss/issue; 12 mss/year. Publishes ms 3-6 months after acceptance. **Publishes 5 new writers/**

year. Recently published work by Richard D. Slay, Jane Gwaltney, Max E. Keele and Jay Arr Henderson. Length: 1-50,000 words; average length: 7,000 words. Publishes short shorts. Average length: 500 words. Sometimes comments on rejected mss.

How to Contact: Send complete ms with a cover letter. Accepts submissions by e-mail only. Include estimated word count and brief bio. Responds in 3 weeks to queries; 4 months to mss. Accepts simultaneous, previously published and multiple submissions. Reviews novels, short story collections and nonfiction books of interest to writers. Send review copies to Max E. Keele, publisher.

Payment/Terms: Pays $25. Pays on publication for one-time and electronic rights. Sends galleys to author. Sponsors contest. "Check website for announcements, rules, requirements."

Advice: "*Fiction Inferno* is an Internet magazine devoted to publishing speculative fiction of literary quality, including, but not strictly limited to the genres more commonly referred to as science fiction, fantasy, horror, and experimental. Our goal at *FI* is to find and publish the best fiction available from authors of any and all backgrounds, whether well-established in their writing careers or just starting out. The only objective criteria for making the pages of *FI* is well-crafted, innovative fiction. Of course, the subjective criteria is, we have to like it. What do we like? Inventiveness, daring, uniqueness of voice, unusual subject matter, fiction that *does something*. Read everything. Know what's been done before and try something else. Practice. Talk to others who are at your same level of writing, and talk to others who are better than you, and talk to others who are just starting. Join workshops and groups. Take classes. Read everything. Write a lot. I mean a whole lot. Don't get discouraged if nobody seems to want your story. Write another one."

5-TROPE. E-mail: 5trope@webdelsol.com. Website: www.webdelsol.com/5-trope. **Contact:** Chad Johnson, senior fiction editor. Online literary journal. "*5-Trope* aims to publish the new and original in fiction, poetry and new media. We hope to appeal to writers and readers with a seriousness about playing with language and form." Bimonthly. Estab. 1999. Circ. 5,000.

Needs: Comics/graphic novels, experimental, literary. "No religious, horror, fantasy, espionage." Receives 50 unsolicited fiction mss/month. Publishes 6 mss/issue, 30 mss/year. Publishes mss one month after acceptance. **Publishes 5 previously unpublished writers/year.** Recently published work by Gary Lutz, Maile Chapman and Sarah Levine. Length: 250-5,000 words; average length 2,500 words. Publishes short shorts. Average length: 100 words. Also publishes poetry. Sometimes comments on rejected mss.

How to Contact: Send submission within the body of an e-mail to cxjohnson98@hotmail.com. Accepts submissions by e-mail. Include brief bio. "Copyright symbols, statements regarding reservation of rights and photos attached to submissions not required." Sample copy free on website. Guidelines on website.

Payment/Terms: Acquires first rights. Sends prepublication galleys to author.

Advice: "We look for originality in language and form, coupled with a strong authorial presence. The first thing a writer should do before submitting is to read several issues of *5-Trope* to get a feel for what we're looking for."

$ ⬛ **flashquake, An Online Journal of Flash Literature**, River Road Studios, P.O. Box 2154, Albany NY 12220-0154. E-mail: dorton@flashquake.org. Website: www.flashquake.org. "Our website is our publication. We do create a CD version of the site as a contributor's copy. Included on the website are fiction, nonfiction, plays, poetry, artwork and submission guidelines." **Contact:** Debi Orton, publisher. E-zine specializing in flash literature. "*flashquake* is a new quarterly online literary journal specifically centered around flash literature—flash fiction, flash memoir, flash plays and poetry. Our goal is to create a literary venue for all things flash. Send us your best flash, works that leave your readers thinking. We define flash as works less than 1,000 words. Shorter pieces will impress us; poetry can be up to 35 lines. Plays should be no more than 10 minutes in length when performed. We want the best story you can tell us in the fewest words you need to do it! Move us, engage us, give us a complete story that only you could have written."

Needs: Ethnic/multicultural (general), experimental, literary, flash literature of all types: fiction, memoir, plays, poetry and artwork. "Not interested in romance, graphic sex, graphic violence, or work of a religious nature." Accepts 25-30 mss/issue; 100-120 mss/year. Publishes ms 1-3 months after acceptance. Length: 1,000 maximum words. Publishes short shorts. Average length: 500-750 words. Also publishes literary essays and literary criticism. Sometimes comments on rejected mss.

How to Contact: Accepts submissions by postal mail and e-mail. Submit to flashquake.org. Include estimated word count, brief bio, mailing address and e-mail address. Guidelines and submission instructions on website.

Payment/Terms: Pays $5-25. Pays on acceptance for electronic rights. Sponsors occasional contests. Contributors of fiction, nonfiction, poetry and plays are eligible for payment.

Advice: "Read our submission guidelines before submitting. Proofread your work thoroughly! We will instantly reject your work for spelling and grammar errors. Save your document as plain text and paste it into an e-mail message. We will not open attachments. We want work that the reader will think about long after reading it, stories that compel the reader to continue reading them. We do like experimental work, but that should not be construed as a license to forget narrative clarity, plot, character development or reader satisfaction."

⬛ ◎ **THE GREEN TRICYCLE: "The fun-to-read lit mag!"** Cayuse Press, P.O. Box 66003, Burien WA 98166-0003. E-mail: editor@greentricycle.com. Website: http://greentricycle.com ("The website offers everything writers need for publication in the *Green Tricycle*. You'll find guidelines, themes, deadlines, current and archived issues, tools and tips for writers, freebies, and access to forums open to all writers.") **Contact:** B. Benepe, publisher. "*The Green Tricycle* is an online thematic literary journal, with three themes per issue. Each piece is limited to 200 words. We accept poetry, micro-fiction, mini-essays, letters, and drama, as long as it addresses the theme in an original manner." Quarterly. Estab. 1999.

Needs: Literary. Wants more mystery, literary and cross-genre. "No erotica, horror, or occult—too much of that is on the Internet already." List of upcoming themes available on website. Receives 100-300 unsolicited mss/month. Accepts 30 mss/issue; 120 mss/year. Publishes ms 1-3 months after acceptance. Agented fiction 10%. **Publishes 25 new writers/ year.** Recently published work by Paul Tylor and Diane Schuller. Word length: 175 words average; 100 words minimum; 200 words maximum. Also publishes literary essays and poetry. Sometimes comments on or critiques rejected ms.

How to Contact: Send complete ms with a cover letter. "Online submissions only. No attachments." Include estimated word count, 25-30 word bio and list of publications. Responds in 2 months. Sample copy and guidelines free online. Reviews novels, short story collections and nonfiction books of interest to writers. Contact the publisher.

Payment/Terms: Acquires one-time rights. Sponsors contest: information on website.

Advice: "I look for originality. A creative approach to the theme catches my attention. Be original. Read the magazine. Sloppy mechanics are sickening. Write the best you can without using four-letter words."

$ ⊙ GUIDEPOSTS FOR KIDS (On the Web), 1050 Broadway, Suite 6, Chesterton IN 46304. (219)929-4429. E-mail: rtolin@guideposts.org. Website:www.gp4k.com (for children, includes sample stories, games, interactives). **Contact:** Rosanne Tolin, managing editor. Editor-in-Chief: Mary Lou Carney. "Value-centered website for kids 6-13 years old. Not preachy, concerned with contemporary issues." E-zine. Estab. 2001. Circ. 60,000 unique visitors/month.

● The magazine publishes many new writers but is primarily a market for writers who have already been published.

Needs: Children's/juvenile: fantasy, historical (general), humor, mystery/suspense, holidays. "No 'adult as hero' or 'I-prayed-I-got' stories." Receives 200 unsolicited mss/month. Accepts 1-2 mss/issue; 6-10 mss/year. **Publishes 1-2 new writers/year.** Published work by Beverly Patt and Lisa Harkrader. Length: 600-1,400 words; 900 words preferred. Also publishes small amount of poetry. Sometimes comments on rejected mss; "only what shows promise."

How to Contact: Send complete ms with cover letter. Include estimated word count, Social Security number, phone number and SASE. Responds in 2 months. Send SASE for reply, return of ms or send disposable copy of ms. Accepts ms by e-mail and fax. Accepts simultaneous submissions. Guidelines for #10 SASE.

Payment/Terms: Pays $150-300. Pays on acceptance for electronic and non-exclusive print rights.

Advice: "We're looking for the good stuff. Fast-paced, well-crafted stories aimed at kids 8-12 years of age. Stories should reflect strong traditional values. Don't preach. This is not a Sunday School handout, but a good solid piece of fiction that reflects traditional values and morality. Build your story around a solid principle and let the reader gain insight by inference. Don't let adults solve problems. While adults can appear in stories, they can't give the characters life's answers. Don't make your kid protagonist grateful and awed by sage, adult advice. Be original. We want a good mix of fiction—contemporary, historical, fantasy, sci-fi, mystery—centered around things that interest and concern kids. A kid reader should be able to identify with the characters strongly enough to think. '*I know just how he feels!*' Create a plot with believable characters. Here's how it works: the story must tell what happens when someone the reader likes (character) reaches an important goal (climax) by overcoming obstacles (conflict). Let kids be kids. Your dialogue (and use plenty of it!) should reflect how the kids sound, think and feel. Avoid slang, but listen to how real kids talk before you try and write for them. Give your characters feelings and actions suitable for the 4th to 6th grader."

⊙ THE HORSETHIEF'S JOURNAL, Celebrating the Literature of the New West, Cayuse Press, P.O. Box 66003, Burien WA 98166-0003. E-mail: cayuse-press@usa.com. Website: www.cayuse-press.com (includes submission guidelines, deadlines, current and archived issues, tools and tips for writers and a poetry forum). **Contact:** Barbara Benepe, editor-in-chief. Electronic literary journal. "*The Horsethief's Journal* is a triannual online literary journal showcasing the best in contemporary poetry, short fiction and memoir for the general reader. We prefer fiction that illuminates the human condition and complements the memoir and poetry we publish. Our audience spans all ages." Triannual. Estab. 1998.

Needs: Adventure, ethnic/multicultural (general), historical, literary, mainstream, mystery/suspense, regional (western US), thriller/espionage, translations, cross-genre fiction. "No erotica, horror, occult, children's, young adult, sappy romance." Receives 30 unsolicited mss/month. Accepts 2-5 mss/issue; 6-15/year. Publishes ms 1-3 months after acceptance. **Publishes 3 new writers/year.** Recently published work by Paul Tylor and Mary Chandler. Length: 200-3,000 words; average length: 1,500 words. Publishes short shorts. Length: 300 words. Also publishes literary essays and poetry. Sometimes comments on rejected ms.

How to Contact: Send complete ms with a cover letter by e-mail only; no attachments. Include estimated word count, 100-200 word bio and list of publications. Responds in 2 months to mss. Inquire about simultaneous and reprint submissions. Accepts multiple submissions. Guidelines available on website. Reviews novels, short story collections and nonfiction books of interest to writers. Send books to editor.

Payment/Terms: Acquires one-time rights.

Advice: "We're looking for stories with an original slant. No clichéd plots, characters or themes. Polish. Polish. Polish. Poor diction, grammar errors—bad mechanics in general—will get you a rejection. Read the magazine. Be original."

⊙ IN POSSE REVIEW ON WEB DEL SOL. E-mail: submissions@webdelsol.com. Website: www.webdelsol.c om. **Contact:** Rachel Callaghan, editor. Poetry Editor: Ilya Kaminsky. E-zine specializing in literary fiction, poetry, and creative nonfiction. "The best of literary fiction, creative nonfiction and poetry from, well, whoever writes it—we welcome all serious writers; especially those who can demonstrate fresh new style and a slightly skewed point of view. *IPR* is interested in looking for non-PC work concerning ethnic issues. See website for details." Quarterly or Triannual.

Needs: Adventure, erotica, ethnic/multicultural, experimental, family saga, fantasy, feminist, gay, historical, horror (literary), humor/satire, lesbian, literary, mystery/suspense, science fiction, western (literary). Accepts 10 mss/issue; 90 mss/year. Publishes 3 months after acceptance. **Publishes 10 new writers/year.** Length: 3,500 words; average length: 1,500 words. Publishes short shorts. Average length: 500 words. Also publishes literary essays, poetry and book reviews. Sometimes comments on rejected mss.

How to Contact: Cut and paste ms into e-mail. Include estimated word count, brief bio and list of publications. Responds in 3 months to mss. Accepts multiple submissions but limit is 2 short stories. Guidelines on website.

Payment/Terms: Acquires electronic rights for 120 days. Sends galleys to author by e-mail.

Advice: "We have very eclectic tastes. Whatever turns us on at that moment. Different, surprising, cutting edge, intriguing, but well-written is best. A manuscript that stands out is one we would consider printing out. Make sure you have a complete story, not slice of life or good start. Wait after writing and re-read. Use spelling and grammar checkers."

INTERTEXT. E-mail: editors@intertext.com. Submissions to: submissions@intertext.com. Website: www.intertext.com. **Contact:** Jason Snell, editor. Electronic zine. "Our readers are computer literate (because we're online only) and appreciate entertaining fiction. They're usually accepting of different styles and genres—from mainstream to historical to science fiction to fantasy to horror to mystery—because we don't limit ourselves to one genre. They just want to read a story that makes them think or transports them to an interesting new place."

Needs: "Well-written fiction from any genre or setting." Especially looking for intelligent science fiction. No "exploitative sex or violence. We will print stories with explicit sex or violence, but not if it serves no purpose other than titillation." No pornography, fan fiction, novels or by-the-book swords and sorcery. **Publishes 16 new writers/year.** Published work by Jim Cowon, Richard Kadrey, Levi Asher, Marcus Eubanks and Ellen Brenner.

How to Contact: Electronic submissions only. Stories should be in ASCII, HTML, or Microsoft Word formats. Full guidelines available on website.

Advice: "Have a clear writing style—the most clever story we've seen in months still won't make it if it's written badly. Try to make our readers think in a way they haven't before, or take them to a place they've never thought about before. And don't be afraid to mix genres—our readers have come to appreciate stories that aren't easily labeled as being part of one genre or another."

THE JOLLY ROGER, P.O. Box 1087, Chapel Hill NC 27514. (919)960-0933. E-mail: drake@jollyroger.com. Website: www.jollyroger.com. **Editor:** Drake Raft. Electronic magazine. "Literature composed in the context of the Western Canon."

Needs: "Conservative and traditional fiction, epic poetry, prose and short stories. Looking for rhyme, meter, words that mean things, plot and character. Publishes an occasional novel or collection of poetry." **Publishes 10-20 new writers/year.** Recently published work by Drake Raft, Becket Knottingham, Elliot McGucken and Bootsy McClusky.

How to Contact: Electronic and traditional submissions accepted.

KENNESAW REVIEW, Kennesaw State University, Dept of English, Building 27, 1000 Chastain Rd., Kennesaw GA 30144-5591. (770)423-6346. Website: www.kennesaw.edu/kr. **Contact:** Robert W. Hill, editor. Managing Editors: Amy Whitney and Maren Blake. Online literary journal. "Just good fiction, all themes, for a general audience." Semiannual. Estab. 1987.

Needs: Excerpted novel, contemporary, ethnic, experimental, feminist, gay, humor/satire, literary, mainstream, regional. No romance. Receives 25-60 mss/month. Accepts 2-4 mss/issue. Publishes ms 12-18 months after acceptance. Published work by Julie Brown, Stephen Dixon, Robert Morgan, Carolyn Thorman. Length: 9-30 pages. Also publishes reviews of collections of short stories. Length: 500 words.

How to Contact: Send complete ms with cover letter. Include previous publications. Responds 2 months to mss. SASE. Accepts simultaneous and multiple submissions. Guidelines on website.

Payment/Terms: Acquires first publication rights only. Acknowledgment required for subsequent publication.

Advice: "Use the language well and tell an interesting story. Send it on. Be open to suggestions."

LITERARY WITCHES, 2610 Broadway St., Ft. Wayne IN 46807. (260)744-9197. E-mail: novaqueer@aol.com. Website: members.aol.com/MeierAvila/index.html. **Contact:** Sabrina Counts, fiction editor. Electronic zine. "A postmodern journal exploring diverse literary art, rooted in feminist and literary theory. *Literary Witches* publishes work that reflects and explores post-modernism, reconstruction, hypertext, transgendered experimentation, multiculturalism, queer theory, feminism, postfeminism. *Literary Witches* is a journal of the mind and body, a cyber-gathering of academic theory and experimental fiction."

Needs: Ethnic/multicultural, experimental, feminist, gay, lesbian, literary. "Please do not send fantasy, vampire stories. Wants postmodern literature and fiction. We are especially interested in work exploring queer discourse, the body and postmodern piracy." **Publishes "a few" new writers/year.** Published works by Kathy Acker, Doug Rice, Cheryl Meier and Marita Avila.

How to Contact: Accepts queries/mss by e-mail. "Please submit your work in the body of e-mail along with your address and phone number or send in hardcopy."

Advice: "We feature literary art by the best American authors as well as diverse or new writers. Published work has been in the form of poetry, essays, short shorts, novel excerpts, hypertext, interviews, plays, listserve or e-mail excerpts.

Our journal has a diverse audience of feminists, queers, scholars, artists, activists and is suggested reading for numerous university courses. We have had over 10,000 hits during the two years our publication has been in cyberspace. Read *Literary Witches* before sending your work for consideration. Electronic publishing is very important right now. For example, *Literary Witches* is becoming involved with an electronic journal that was just awarded the first Guggenheim grant for a cyber publication. And because of continuing accessibility to cyberspace, electronic journals can be reached by diverse groups of people. Work previously available only in hardcopy can be remade in cyberspace and remain in publication for long periods. Artists and audiences find one another.''

MARGIN: Exploring Modern Magical Realism, E-mail: msellma@attglobal.net or smike10@qwest.net. Website: www.magical-realism.com (includes novel excerpts, short stories, poetry, links, reading lists, special features, reviews, essays, creation nonfiction, articles). **Contact:** Tamara Kaye Sellman, editor. Electronic anthology specializing in magical realism. "*Margin* seeks, in a variety of ways, to answer the question, 'what is magical realism?' " Perpetual, always accessible. Estab. 2000. Circ. 1,500 unique visitors a month, 500 subscribers.

● *Margin* has received the Arete "Wave of a Site" award. The editor of *Margin* is on hiatus at publication time. The opening of the next reading period will be announced on the website. Subscribe to be automatically notified.

Needs: Ethnic/multicultural, fantasy (magical realism), feminist, gay, historical, horror (supernatural), lesbian, mainstream, psychic/supernatural/occult, regional, science fiction (only if it bridges with magical realism), translations (query first). "No magical realist knockoffs, no stock fantasy with elves or angels. Nothing gratuitous—if you are unsure what magical realism is, visit the website and look at our discussion of criteria before submitting." Receives 100 mss/month. Publishes ms within 6 months after acceptance. **Publishes new writers.** Recently published work by George Harrar, Michael Valdez Moses, Franz Wright. Length: 3,500 words. Publishes short shorts. Also publishes literary essays and literary criticism. Sometimes comments on rejected mss.

How to Contact: Send complete ms with cover letter. Margin accepts electronic submissions only—no attachments. See website for guidelines. Send complete ms with cover message, bio, top ten list of fave works of magical realisim and a 100-word personal definition of magical realism. Query first on translated work. Reviews novels, short story collections, and nonfiction books.

Payment/Terms: Funds distributed to contributors as they are acquired. Rights negotiable.

Advice: "Technical strength, unique, engaging style, well-developed and inventive story. Manuscript must be magical realism. Do not send more than one submission at a time. You will not get a fair reading if you do. Always enclose SASE. Do not inquire before 3 months. Send us your 'A' list, no works-in-progress."

TIMOTHY McSWEENEY'S INTERNET TENDENCY, 429 7th St., Brooklyn NY 11215 (land mail east of the Mississippi); 826 Valencia St., San Francisco CA 94110 (land mail west of the Mississippi). E-mail: printsubmissions@m csweeneys.net or websubmissions@mcsweeneys.net. Website: www.mcsweeneys.net. **Contact:** Dave Eggers, Sean Wilsey, Todd Pruzen, Lawrence Weschler, Diane Vadino and Kevin Shay, editors. "*Timothy McSweeney's Internet Tendency* is an offshoot of *Timothy McSweeney's Quarterly Concern*, a journal created by nervous people in relative obscurity, and published four times a year." Visit the website for guidelines for submission to the print edition.

Needs: Literary.

How to Contact: Submit the first 300 words of ms via e-mail, to the "print submissions" or "web submissions" address. If the piece is under 1,000 words, paste the entire submission in the e-mail. Include a "brief and sober" bio and cover letter. Attach the entire ms to the e-mail submission, if possible as an Microsoft Word file. Attachments in BinHex form cannot be read. If your piece is under 1,000 words, paste the entire submission into the e-mail. "Stories submitted without the author's phone number cannot be considered." Responds in up to 4 months to mss. "Please be patient." Sometimes comments on rejected ms. SASE for editor comments.

Payment/Terms: Pays contributor copies for stories published in the print edition.

Advice: "Do not submit your written work to both the print submissions address and the web submissions address, as seemingly hundreds of writers have been doing lately. If you submit a piece of writing intended for the magazine to the web submissions address, you will confuse us, and if you confuse us, we will accidently delete your work without reading it, and then we will laugh and never give it another moment's thought, and sleep the carefree sleep of young children. This is very, very serious."

MERCURY BOOKS, Where Words Have Wings!, Cayuse Press, P.O. Box 66003, Burien WA 98166-0003. E-mail: publisher@mercurybooks.com. Website: www.mercurybooks.com/ (includes guidelines, deadlines and all previous issues, as well as an author chat room and other features). **Contact:** Barbara Benepe, publisher. Online magazine. "Each issue is devoted entirely to the works of one author." Currently publish two collections/year. Estab. 2001.

Needs: Literary. "We seek to publish author's collection of short fiction or poetry, or a mix of fiction and poetry. We will consider new or unpublished authors. The work must be outstanding and the author must be willing to work with our editorial staff."

CHECK THE CATEGORY INDEXES, located at the back of the book, for publishers interested in specific fiction subjects.

How to Contact: "Please visit website for our detailed checklist for submissions and please follow them carefully. Collections chosen for publication will be announced in January and will be published later in the year. You must include your address, phone number and e-mail address so we can contact you. We will consider previously published material if you own the copyright and provide complete publication documentation. Ideally, we prefer a mix of new material with previously published work. We seek to become the first publisher of a writer's collected works and provide an attractive format for presentation." Guidelines on website.

Payment/Terms: Receives continuous promotion of author's work. Acquire one-time or first-electronic rights.

Advice: "Be original. Read and follow the guidelines. Please include complete documentation with any previously published work."

N ◐ THE MID-SOUTH REVIEW, A Journey into the Heart of the South. Website: www.geocities.com/midsouthreview (includes guidelines, fiction, poetry, essays, subscription information). **Contact:** Jeff Martindale, editor. Online magazine. "We are an online literary journal featuring fiction, essays, and poetry with special interest in Southern culture and history. Our mission is to publish the best stories written by and about Mid-Southerners." Monthly. Estab. 2002.

Needs: Humor/satire, literary, mainstream, "anything about the South." "No gore, violence, hate, erotica, and science fiction." List of upcoming themes available online. Accepts 3-5 mss/issue. Publishes ms 2-4 months after acceptance. Recently published work by Jeff S. Martindale and Scottie H. Freeman. Length: 2,500 words (maximum); average length: 1,500 words. Publishes short shorts. Average length: 750 words. Also publishes literary essays and poetry. Sometimes comments on rejected mss.

How to Contact: Send complete ms with a cover letter. Accepts submissions by e-mail only. Include estimated word count and brief bio "always paste submission in body of e-mail. No attachments." Responds in 1-2 months to queries; 2-3 months to mss. Accepts simultaneous and previously published submissions. Guidelines on website.

Payment/Terms: Pays free subscription to the magazine.

Advice: "Rewrite! Rewrite! Rewrite! Spend as much or more time rewriting your work than on your first draft. Follow submission guidelines to the letter. Incorrect submissions reduce your chances of getting published. Don't take rejection personally."

◐ MILLENNIUM SCIENCE FICTION & FANTASY, P.O. Box 8118, Roswell NM 88202-8118. E-mail: jopoppub@jopoppub.com. Website: www.jopoppub.com (includes guidelines, short fiction, writers' pages, news, chatroom, sagas, poetry, flash fiction, art). Editor: S. Joan Popek. **Fiction Editor:** Diana R. Moreland. E-zine with print "Best Of" quarterly. Monthly e-zine publishes science fiction, fantasy and psychological horror, "offering the best of short speculative fiction we can find." Estab. 1993. Circ. 2,000. Member of the Horror Zine Association.

Needs: Fantasy (space fantasy), horror (dark fantasy, futuristic, psychological, supernatural, humor satire, science fiction (hard science/technological, soft/sociological), young adult (fantasy/science fiction, horror). "No explicit language, sex or violence. No graphic blood, guts or exploitation pieces." List of upcoming themes available for SASE. Receives 100 unsolicited mss/month. Accepts 4-5 mss/issue; 48-60 mss/year. Does not read mss October 31-January 1. Publishes ms 2-8 months after acceptance. **Publishes 1-3 new writers/year.** Recently published Greg F. Giyune and Patricia L. White. Length: 50-2,500 words; average length: 2,000 words. Publishes short shorts. Length: 100 words. Also publishes literary criticism and poetry. Often comments on rejected ms.

How to Contact: Send complete ms with a cover letter through website. Write "story submission" in your subject line. Accepts queries/mss by e-mail. Include estimated word count, 50-100 word bio and list of publications. Responds in 2 weeks to 4 months to queries; 2 weeks to 3 months to mss. Send SASE for reply, return of ms or send a disposable copy of ms. Accepts reprint submissions. Sample copy for $6.50. Guidelines on website. Reviews novels, short story collections and nonfiction books of interest to writers. Send books to Editor.

Payment/Terms: Pays $5-20 and 1 contributor's copy; additional copies $3. Pays on acceptance for one-time rights. Sponsors contest: see website for details.

Advice: "We have a standard rule-three grammar errors in the first paragraph is an automatic reject. We are leaning more towards e-mail submissions and welcome electronic copies of accepted manuscripts."

N ◐ MONKEYPLANET, Monkeyplanet.com, 150 E. 27th St., Suite 1F, New York NY 10016. (732)548-8700. Fax: (732)548-7888. E-mail: editor@monkeyplanet.com. Website: www.monkeyplanet.com (includes stories, editors, authors, guidelines and art gallery). **Contact:** Perry Waddell, editor-in-chief. Magazine: 100 pages. "*Monkeyplanet* is an online magazine for those too young to be Baby Boomers and too old for Gen X. *Monkeyplanet* has fiction, travel, poetry, reviews and short stories." Quarterly. Estab. 1998. Circ. "thousands of website hits."

Needs: Adventure, ethnic/multicultural, experimental, fantasy, feminist, gay, glitz, historical, horror, hummor/satire, lesbian, literary, mainstream, mystery/suspense, regional, science fiction, thriller/espionage. List of upcoming themes available online. Receives 5 unsolicited mss/month. Accepts 12 mss/issue; 48 mss/year. Publishes ms 1-2 weeks after acceptance. Agented fiction 1%. **Publishes 10 new writers/year.** Recently published work by Rick Overton, Mark Salon and Anya Krugoudy Silver. Length: 300-1,500 words; average length: 300 words. Publishes short shorts. Average length: 300 words. Also publishes literary essays, literary criticism and poetry.

How to Contact: Query with clips of published work. Accepts submissions by e-mail and disk. Include estimated word count, brief bio and list of publications. Responds in 2 months to queries. Send SASE (or IRC) for return of ms or send a disposable copy of ms and #10 SASE for reply only. Accepts simultaneous submissions, previously published work and multiple submissions. Guidelines on website. Reviews novels, short story collections and nonfiction books of interest to writers. Send review copies to editor.

Payment/Terms: Acquires one-time electronic rights.

moonbomb press. E-mail: paul@moonbomb.com. Website: www.moonbomb.com. **Contact:** Paul C. Choi, editor. Electronic zine. "We are contemporary, urban, irreverent, ethnic, random."

Needs: Short stories, poetry, short plays, any fictional format, autobiographical non-fiction, fictional journalism. No children's fiction. Wants more fictional realism and essays. "The main thing we seek in any piece of writing is a clear, identifiable voice. If this voice is also unique, we are even more pleased." **Publishes 2 new writers/year.** Published work by Eve Pearlman and Sheryl Ridenour.

How to Contact: Electronic submissions only.

Advice: "Be bold. Do not try to be what you are not. Anything so contrived is obviously so. Content and structure are important, but the voice—the heart behind the writing—is even more essential."

THE MOONWORT REVIEW, Moonwort Publications, 422 S. Greensboro St., Carrboro NC 27510. (919)929-8786. E-mail: moonwort@nc.rr.com. Website: www.themoonwortreview.com. **Contact:** RC Rutherford. E-zine specializing in fiction and poetry. Quarterly. Estab. 2001. Circ. 200. Member, HTML Writers Guild.

Needs: Experimental, literary, mainstream, mystery/suspense (amateur sleuth, cozy, police procedural, private eye/hardboiled), New Age. "No horror or romance." Receives 20 unsolicited mss/month. Accepts 10-12 mss/issue; 60-80 mss/year. Publishes ms 2 months after acceptance. Agented fiction 10%. **Publishes 40-50 new writers/year.** Recently published work by Al Maginnes, Lee Upton, Janet Buck, Sara Claytor and Ed Lynsky. Length: 500-5,000 words; average length: 2,000 words. Publishes short shorts. Average length: 500 words. Also publishes literary essays, literary criticism and poetry. Sometimes comments on rejected mss.

How to Contact: Send complete ms with a cover letter. Accepts submissions by e-mail. Include estimated word count, brief bio and list of publications. Responds in 1 month. Guidelines on website.

Payment/Terms: Acquires one-time and electronic rights.

Advice: "I look for strong characters and setting; original imagery; original voice."

NUVEIN ONLINE, (626)401-3466. Fax: (626)401-3460. E-mail: editor@nuvein.com. Website: www.nuvein.com. **Editor:** Enrique Diaz. Electronic zine. "We are open to short works of fiction which explore topics divergent from the mainstream. Especially welcome are stories with a point of view opposite traditional and stereotypical views of minorities, including women and gays. Of course we are not averse to stories dealing with such changes. Our philosophy is to provide a forum for voices rarely heard in other publications."

• Nuvein Online has been awarded the Visionary Media Award.

Needs: Short fiction, serials, graphic e-novels and poetry. Wants more "experimental, cyberfiction, serialized fiction, ethnic, as well as pieces dealing with the exploration of sexuality." **Publishes 20 new writers/year.** Recently published work by Ronald L. Boerem, Enrique Diaz, Mia Lawrence and Scott Essman.

How to Contact: Send queries/mss by e-mail, post or fax.

Advice: "Read over each submission before sending it, and if you, as the writer, find the piece irresistible, e-mail it to us immediately!"

THE ORACULAR TREE, A Transformational E-zine, The Oracular Tree, 208-167 Morgan Ave., Kitchener, Ontario N2A 2M4 Canada. (519)895-1947. E-mail: editor@oraculartree.com. Website: www.oraculartree.com (includes archive of essays, articles, stories, poems which serve to offer alternatives to the endings of our current cultural stories and myths). **Contact:** Jeff Beardwood, editor. E-zine specializing in transformation. "We believe the stories we tell ourselves and each other predict the outcome of our lives. We can affect gradual societal transformation by changing the endings to some of our most deeply rooted cultural stories. The genre is not as important as the message and the high quality of the writing. We accept stories, poems, articles and essays which will reach well-educated open minded readers around the world. *The Oracular Tree* offers a forum for those who see a need for change; who want to add their voices to a growing search for alternatives." Weekly postings each Friday to the website. Estab. 1997. Circ. 25,000 hits/month.

Needs: Feminist, literary, New Age. "We'll look at any genre that is well-written and can examine a new cultural paradigm. No tired dogma, no greeting card poetry, please." Receives 10-12 unsolicited mss/month. Accepts 25-50 mss/year. Publishes ms 3 weeks after acceptance. **Publishes 20-30 new writers/year.** Recently published work by Dr. Richard Taylor, Dr. David Peat, Margaret Karmazin, and Dr. Elaine Hatfield. Publishes short shorts. Average length: 800 words. Also publishes literary essays and poetry. Often comments on rejected mss.

How to Contact: Send complete ms with a cover letter. Accepts submissions by e-mail (submit in plain text or rich text format). Responds in 2 weeks to queries; 2 months to mss. Accepts simultaneous, previously published and multiple submissions. Sample copy and guidelines on website.

Payment/Terms: Author retains copyright; one-time archived posting. Not copyrighted.

Advice: "The underlying idea must be clearly expressed. The language should be appropriate to the tale, using creative license and an awareness of rhythm. We look for a juxtaposition of ideas that creates resonance in the mind and heart of the reader. Write from your honest voice. Trust your writing to unfold."

N ⭕ **OUTSIDER INK**, Outsider Media, 201 W. 11th St., New York NY 10014. (212)691-4345. E-mail: editor@out sidermedia.com. Website: www.outsiderink.com. **Contact:** Sean Meriwether, editor. E-zine specializing in alternative fiction, poetry and artwork. "*Outsider Ink* is an online quarterly only. Each issue contains five fiction pieces, two poetry sections, and one visual artist. A monthly feature spotlights an individual, normally an underpublished poet or writer. *Outsider Ink* has established a core international readership by publishing new material with a diverse range of adult themes. We are all outsiders, artist and non-artist alike, but there are those brave enough to share their experiences with the world. Rattle my cage and demand my attention, tell me your story the way you want it to be told. I am looking for the harsh and sometimes ugly truths. Dark humor is especially appreciated." Quarterly. Estab. 1999. Circ. 30,000 hits/issue.

Needs: Literary. "No mainstream, genre fiction, children's or religious." Receives 200 unsolicited mss/month. Accepts 5 mss/issue; 20 mss/year. Publishes ms 3 months after acceptance. **Publishes 15 new writers/year.** Recently published work by Daniel A. Olivas, Greg Wharton, Maryanne Stahl and Ray Van Horn, Jr. Length: 8,000 words (maximum); average length: 2,000 words. Publishes short shorts. Average length: 800 words. Also publishes poetry. Often comments on rejected mss.

How to Contact: Send complete ms with a cover letter. Accepts submissions by e-mail. Include estimated word count and brief bio. Responds in 1 week to queries; 3 months to mss. Send SASE (or IRC) for return of ms or send a disposable copy of ms and #10 SASE for reply only. Accepts simultaneous, previously published and multiple submissions. Guidelines by e-mail or on website.

Payment/Terms: Acquires electronic rights. Sends galleys to author (preview of site prior to launch). Not copyrighted.

Advice: "*Outsider Ink* publishes work that isn't afraid to cover unexplored territory, both emotionally and physically. Though we want work that pushes the envelope, it should maintain a literary foundation. We aren't looking for fiction or poetry that is weird for the sake of being weird, we want prose with a point and a mind of its own. Take the time to familiarize yourself with the e-zine before submitting. The bulk of submissions are not accepted because they are inappropriate to the venue. *Outsider Ink* encourages new writers, and has acted as a launching pad to other venues. Trust your own voice when editing your own material. If you think it isn't ready yet, don't submit it, finish it first."

$ ⭕ **PAINTED BRIDE QUARTERLY**, Painted Bride Art Center, Rutgers University, 311 N. Fifth St., Camden NJ 08102-1519. (856)225-6129. Fax: (856)225-6607. E-mail: volk@camden.rutgers.edu. Website: www.pbq.rutgers.edu (includes entire quarterly issue, writer's guidelines, news on upcoming events). **Contact:** Kathleen Volk-Miller, managing editor. Literary magazine: 6×9; 96-100 pages; illustrations; photos. "*PBQ* seeks literary fiction, experimental and traditional." Quarterly. Estab. 1973. Circ. 1,000.

Needs: Contemporary, ethnic, experimental, feminist, gay, lesbian, literary, prose poem and translations. "No genre fiction." **Publishes 24 new writers/year.** Recently published work by Jennifer Swender, Jo-Anne M. Watts and Rita Welty Bourke. Length: 5,000 words maximum; average length: 3,000 words. Publishes short shorts. Also publishes literary essays, literary criticism, poetry. Occasionally critiques rejected mss. "Every spring we publish a film-related issue."

How to Contact: Send complete ms. Responds in 6 months. SASE. Sample copy for $6. Reviews novels and short story collections. Send books to editor.

Payment/Terms: Pays $5/accepted piece and 1 contributor's copy, 1 year free subscription; 50% off additional copies. Acquires first North American serial rights.

Advice: Looks for "freshness of idea incorporated with high-quality writing. We receive an awful lot of nicely written work with worn-out plots. We want quality in whatever—we hold experimental work to as strict standards as anything else. Many of our readers write fiction; most of them enjoy a good reading. We hope to be an outlet for quality. A good story gives, first, enjoyment to the reader. We've seen a good many of them lately, and we've published the best of them."

🌸 ⭕ **PAPERPLATES, a magazine for fifty readers**, Perkolator Kommunikation, 19 Kenwood Ave., Toronto, Ontario M6C 2R8 Canada. (416)651-2551. Fax: (416)651-2910. E-mail: magazine@paperplates.org. Website: www.pap erplates.org. **Contact:** Bethany Gibson, fiction editor. Electronic magazine. Published 2-3 times/year. Estab. 1990.

Needs: Condensed/excerpted novel, ethnic/multicultural, feminist, gay, lesbian, literary, mainstream/contemporary, translations. "No science fiction, fantasy or horror." Receives 2-3 unsolicited mss/week. Accepts 2-3 mss/issue; 6-9 mss/year. Publishes ms 6-8 months after acceptance. Published work by Celia Lottridge, C.J. Lockett, Deirdre Kessler and Marvyne Jenoff. Length: 1,500-3,500 words; average length: 3,000 words. Publishes short shorts. Also publishes literary essays, literary criticism and poetry.

How to Contact: Send complete ms with a cover letter. Responds in 6 weeks to queries; 3 months to mss. Send SASE for reply, return of ms or send a disposable copy of ms. Accepts simultaneous submissions and electronic submissions. Guidelines for #10 SASE.

Payment/Terms: Pays 1 contributor's copy. Pays on publication for first North American serial rights.

◎ **PARADOXISM**, University of New Mexico, 200 College Rd., Gallup NM 87301. Fax: (505)863-7532. E-mail: smarand@unm.edu. Website: www.gallup.unm.edu/~smarandache/lit.htm. Online magazine. **Contact:** Dr. Florentin Smarandache. "*Paradoxism* is an avant-garde movement based on excessive use of antinomies, antitheses, contradictions, paradoxes in the literary creations set up by the editor in the 1980s as an anti-totalitarian protest." Annual. Estab. 1990.

Needs: Experimental, literary. "No traditional fiction." Receives 5 unsolicited mss/month. Publishes short shorts. Also publishes literary essays, literary criticism and poetry. Sometimes comments on rejected mss.

How to Contact: Accepts simultaneous submissions. Guidelines on website.
Payment/Terms: Pays subscription. Pays on publication. Not copyrighted.
Advice: "We look for work that refers to the paradoxism or is written in this paradoxist style."

THE PAUMANOK REVIEW. E-mail: submissions@paumanokreview.com. Website: www.paumanokreview.c om. (includes full text of magazine, guidelines, archives and publishing information). **Contact:** Katherine Arline, editor. Online literary magazine. "*TPR* is dedicated to publishing and promoting the best in world art and literature. The audience is international, well-educated and looking for insight and entertainment from talented new and established voices." Quarterly. Estab. 2000. Circ. "thousands of unique visitors/issue; more than 50 countries."
Needs: Experimental, historical, humor/satire, literary, mainstream. Receives 100 unsolicited mss/month. Accepts 6-8 mss/issue; 24-32 mss/year. Publishes ms 6 weeks after acceptance. Agented fiction 1%. **Publishes 4 new writers/year.** Recently published work by Elisha Porat, Barry Spacks, Walter McDonald. Length: 1,500-6,000 words; average length: 3,000 words. Publishes short shorts. Average length: 800 words. Also publishes literary essays, art, music and poetry. Always comments on rejected mss.
How to Contact: Send complete ms with a cover letter. Accepts submissions by e-mail. Include estimated word count, brief bio, list of publications and where you discovered *The Paumanok Review*. Responds in 1 week to queries; 1 month to mss. Accepts simultaneous submissions and previously published work. Sample copy and guidelines online.
Payment/Terms: Free classified ads for the life of the magazine. Acquires one-time and anthology rights. Sends galleys to author.
Advice: "*TPR* was created to bridge the gap between highly specialized e-zines and affluent mega-zines closed to new writers. *TPR* is the ideal place for a writer's first electronic submission since the process closely follows print publishing's methods. Though this is an English-language publication, it is not U.S. or U.K.-centric. Please submit accordingly. TPR is a publication of Wind River Press, which also publishes *Critique Magazine* and select electronic and traditional books."

PBW, 513 N. Central Ave., Fairborn OH 45324. (937)878-5184. E-mail: rianca@aol.com. **Contact:** Richard Freeman, editor. Electronic disk zine: 700 pages; illustrations. "*PBW* is an experimental floppy disk that 'prints' strange and 'unpublishable' in an above-ground-sense writing." Quarterly electronic zine. Featuring avant-garde fiction and poetry. Estab. 1988.
Needs: Erotica, experimental, gay, lesbian, literary. No "conventional fiction of any kind." Receives 3 unsolicited mss/ month. Accepts 40 mss/issue; 160 mss/year. Publishes ms within 3 months after acceptance. **Publishes 10-15 new writers/year.** Published work by Dave Castleman, Marie Markoe and Henry Hardee. Length: open. Publishes short shorts and novels in chapters. Publishes literary essays, literary criticisms and poetry. Always comments on rejected mss.
How to Contact: Send complete ms with a cover letter. Accepts queries by e-mail. "Manuscripts are only taken if sent on disk." Responds in 2 weeks. Send SASE for reply, return of ms or send a disposable copy of ms. Accepts simultaneous, multiple, reprint and electronic (Mac or modem) submissions. Sample copy for $2. Reviews novels and short story collections.
Payment/Terms: Pays 1 contributor's copy. All rights revert back to author. Not copyrighted.

PEGASUS ONLINE, the Fantasy and Science Fiction E-zine. E-mail: editors@pegasusonline.com. Website: www.pegasusonline.com. **Contact:** Scott F. Marlowe, editor. Electronic zine. "*Pegasus Online* focuses on the genres of science and fantasy fiction. We look for original work which inspires and moves the reader, writing which may cause him or her to think, and maybe even allow them to pause for a moment to consider the how's and why's of those things around us."
Needs: Fantasy, science fiction. "More specifically, fantasy is to be of the pure fantastic type: dragons, goblins, magic and everything else you can expect from something not of this world. Science fiction can or cannot be of the 'hard' variety." No "excessive profanity or needless gore." **Publishes 16 new writers/year.**
How to Contact: Electronic submissions only. Send mss by e-mail to submissions@pegasusonline.com.
Advice: "Tell a complete tale with strong characters and a plot which draws the reader in from the very first sentence to the very last. The key to good fiction writing is presenting readers with characters they can identify with at some level. Your characters certainly can be larger than life, but they should not be all-powerful. Also, be careful with grammar and sentence structure. We get too many submissions which have good plot lines, but are rejected because of poor English skills. The end-all is this: we as humans read because we want to escape from reality for a short time. Make us feel like we've entered your world and make us want to see your characters succeed (or not, depending on your plot's angle), and you've done your job and made us happy at the same time."

$ ◻ ◎ ▼ PERIDOT BOOKS, Tri-Annual Online Magazine of SF, Fantasy & Horror, Peridot Consulting, Inc., 1225 Liberty Bell Dr., Cherry Hill NJ 08003. (856)354-0786. E-mail: editor@peridotbooks.com. Website: www.peridotbooks.com. **Contact:** Ty Drago, editor. Online magazine specializing in science fiction fantasy and horror. "We are an e-zine by writers for writers. Our articles focus on the art, craft and business of writing. Our links and editorial policy all focus on the needs of fiction authors." Triannual. Estab. 1998.
• Peridot Books won the Page One Award for Literary Contribution.
Needs: Fantasy (space fantasy, sword and sorcery, sociological), horror (dark fantasy, futuristic, supernatural), science fiction (hard science/technological, soft/sociological). "No media tie-ins (Star Trek, Star Wars, etc., or space opera, vampires)." Receives 150 unsolicited mss/month. Accepts 8 mss/issue; 24 mss/year. Publishes ms 2 months after

acceptance. Agented fiction 5%. **Publishes 10 new writers/year.** Published work by Brenden Connell, E.K. Rivera, Katherine Irving and David Oven. Length: 1,500-7,500 words; average length: 4,500 words. Also publishes literary essays and literary criticism. Often comments on rejected mss.

How to Contact: Send complete ms with a cover letter, electronic only. Accepts submissions by e-mail. Include estimated word count, brief bio, list of publications and name and e-mail address in the body of the story. Responds in 6 weeks to mss. Accepts simultaneous, previously published and multiple submissions. Guidelines on website.

Payment/Terms: Pays 5¢/word. Pays on publication for one-time and electronic rights.

Advice: "Give us something original, preferably with a twist. Avoid gratuitous sex or violence. Funny always scores points. Be clever, imaginative, but be able to tell a story with proper mood and characterization. Put your name and e-mail address in the body of the story. Read the site and get a feel for it before submitting."

$ ◯ 🖾 PIF. 1426 Harvard Ave., #451, Seattle WA 98122-3813. (360)493-0596. E-mail: editor@pifmagazine.com. Website: http://pifmagazine.com. **Contact:** Rachel Sage, editor. Electronic magazine (pifmagazine.com): circ. 100,000. Monthly. Estab. 1995.

• *Pif* ranked on *Writer's Digest's* "Top 30" list of best markets for fiction writers.

Needs: Literary, experimental, very short ("micro") fiction. No genre fiction. Receives 200-300 mss/month. Accepts 1-2 mss/electronic issue. Publishes 1-4 months after acceptance. Length: 4,000 words maximum. Recently published work by Julia Slavin, Brad Bryant, Richard Madelin. **Publishes several new writers/year.** Also publishes poetry, book reviews, essays and interviews.

How to Contact: Electronic submissions only. Online submissions form and guidelines at http://pifmagazine.com/submit/. Responds in 8-10 weeks. Accepts simultaneous submissions. Sometimes comments on rejected mss.

Payment/Terms: Pays $50-200. Pays on publication.

THE PINK CHAMELEON, The Pink Chameleon. E-mail: dpfreda@juno.com. Website: www.geocities.com/thepinkchameleon/index.html. **Contact:** Mrs. Dorothy Paula Freda, editor/publisher. Family-oriented electronic magazine. Illustrations. Annual. Estab. Online 2000; print 1985-1999.

Needs: Fantasy, historical, mystery, adventure, sports, all ages, experimental, family saga, fantasy (space fantasy, sword and sorcery), humor/satire, literary, mainstream, mystery (amateur sleuth, cozy, police procedural, private eye/hardboiled), psychic/supernatural/occult, religious (children's religious, general, inspirational, religious fantasy, religious mystery/suspense, religious thriller, religious romance), romance (contemporary, futuristic/time travel, gothic, historical, regency period, romantic suspense), science fiction (hard science/technological, soft/sociological), thriller/espionage, western (frontier saga, traditional), young adult/teen (adventure, easy-to-read, fantasy/science fiction, historical). "No violence for the sake of violence." Receives 50 unsolicited mss/month. Publishes ms within the year after acceptance. **Publishes 50% new writers/year.** Recently published work by Deanne F. Purcell, James W. Collins and Darlene Palenik. Length: 500-2,500 words; average length: 2,000. Publishes short shorts. Average length: 500 words. Also publishes literary essays and poetry. Always comments on rejected mss.

How to Contact: E-mail submissions with short biography. Accepts mss only by e-mail. No attachments, send work in the body of the e-mail. Include estimated word count and brief bio with submission. Responds in 1 month. Accepts multiple and previously published submissions. Guidelines send e-mail or on website.

Payment/Terms: Acquires one-time rights for 1 year but will return rights earlier upon request.

Advice: "Simple, honest, evocative emotion; upbeat submissions that give hope for the future; well-paced plots; stories, poetry, articles, essays that speak from the heart. Read guidelines carefully. Use a good, but not ostentatious opening hook. Stories should have a beginning, middle and end that make the reader feel the story was worth his or her time. This also applies to articles and essays. In the latter two, wrap your comments and conclusions in a neatly packaged paragraph. Turnoffs include violence, bad language used as padding and to sensationalize. Simple, genuine and sensitive work does not need to shock with vulgarity to be interesting and enjoyable."

⊕ THE PLAZA, A Space for Global Human Relations, U-Kan Inc., Yoyogi 2-32-1, Shibuya-ku, Tokyo 151-0053, Japan. Tel: +81-(3)-3379-3881. Fax: +81-(3)-3379-3882. E-mail: plaza@u-kan.co.jp. Website: u-kan.co.jp (includes contribution guide, contents of the current and back issues, representative works by *The Plaza* writers). **Contact:** Leo Shunji Nishida, publisher/fiction editor. "*The Plaza* is an intercultural and bilingual magazine (English and Japanese). Our focus is the 'essence of being human.' Some works are published in both Japanese and English (translations by our staff if necessary). The most important criteria is artistic level. We look for works that reflect simply 'being human.' Stories on intercultural (not international) relations are desired. *The Plaza* is devoted to offering a spiritual *Plaza* where people around the world can share their creative work. We introduce contemporary writers and artists as our generation's contribution to the continuing human heritage." Quarterly. Online publication which is freely available to all readers on the Internet.

Needs: Length: less than 2,500 words (longer stories may be recommended for serial publication). Wants to see more fiction "of not human beings, but being human. Of not international, but intercultural. Of not social, but human relationships." No political themes: religious evangelism; social commentary. Publishes about 2 stories/issue. **Publishes 3 new writers/year.** Recently published work by Joe Kernac, Eleanor Lohse and Kikuzou Hidari.

How to Contact: Send complete ms with cover letter. Accepts queries/mss by e-mail and fax. Accepts multiple submissions.

Advice: "The most important consideration is that which makes the writer motivated to write. If it is not moral but human, or if it is neither a wide knowledge nor a large computer-like memory, but rather a deep thinking like the quietness in the forest, it is acceptable. While the traditional culture of reading of some thousands of years may be destined to be extinct under the marvellous progress of civilization, *The Plaza* intends to present contemporary works as our global human heritage to readers of forthcoming generations."

🌐 **$**⚪ **PREMONITIONS** (formerly *The Zone*), Pigasus Press, 13 Hazely Combe, Arreton, Isle of Wight, PO30 3AJ England. E-mail: pigasus.press@virgin.net. Website: http://website.lineone.net/~pigasus.press/index.html. **Contact:** Tony Lee, editor. Magazine. "A magazine of quality science fiction plus articles and reviews." Publishes up to 6 stories/issue. Biannually.
Needs: Science fiction (hard, contemporary science fiction/fantasy). No sword and sorcery, supernatural horror. Length: 1,000-5,000 words.
How to Contact: "Potential contributors are advised to study recent issues of *Premonitions*. Unsolicited submissions are always welcome but writers must enclose SAE/IRC for reply, plus adequate postage to return ms if unsuitable."
Payment/Terms: Pays 1 contributor copy plus flat rate of £5 or $10/story. Sample copies available: £1.50 each (UK only), £3.50 (Europe), £4.10 (USA/Canada), £4.25 (rest of world). All checks and postal orders must be made payable to Tony Lee. Orders from overseas—please pay via International Postal Order in UK currency, no foreign checks accepted.

THE PROSE MENAGERIE. E-mail: caras@reporters.net. Website: www.geocities.com/Soho/Studios/5116/index.ht ml. **Contact:** Cara Swann, editor. E-zine. "*The Prose Menagerie* is a mixture of interesting prose, essays, and articles as well as fiction (short stories/novellas/poetry)."
Needs: Literary. No erotica, science fiction, children's, horror. Wants more "meaningful themes." **Publishes 15-20 new writers/year.** Recently published work by Allen Woodman, John K. Trammell and Zalman Velvel.
How to Contact: Send queries/mss by e-mail. Send in body of e-mail and/or attached as plain ASCII text file only. No MS Word files accepted. Accepts multiple submissions.
Payment/Terms: "Since *The Prose Menagerie* is only available online, the writer maintains copyright; and while there is no payment, there is wide exposure for new and unknown writers, eagerly promoted along with those who do have name recognition."
Advice: "Submit a piece of writing that has meaning, whether it is poetry, fiction or articles. Also open to those who wish to present ideas for regular columns and book reviews."

◔ **PULSE**, Heartsounds Press, 17100 Bear Valley Rd. PMB 308, Victorville CA 92392. (760)243-8043. E-mail: lpinto3402@aol.com or mim47@aol.com. Website: www.heartsoundspress.com. **Fiction and Nonfiction Editor:** Liz Pinto. Poetry Editor: Carol Bockofner. E-zine specializing in literary short stories, essays and poetry. Quarterly. Estab. 1999.
Needs: Literary, mainstream. No "porn, romance, horror." Receives 25-30 unsolicited mss/month. Publishes ms 2-3 months after acceptance. **Publishes 5 new writers/year.** Recently published work by Frank Criscenti, Geraldine Tyler, Karen Wallace, Marcy Sheiner, David Steinberg and Lyn Lifshin. Word length: 3,000 words average; 5,000 words maximum. Also publishes literary essays, literary criticism and poetry. Sometimes comments on or critiques rejected ms.
How to Contact: Send complete ms with a cover letter. Accepts inquiries by e-mail. Include estimated word count, 50-100 word bio and list of publications. Responds in 6 weeks to ms. Send SASE for reply, return on ms or send a disposable copy of ms. Accepts simultaneous submissions. Guidelines free for #10 SAE.
Payment/Terms: Pays "in gobs of gratitude." Rights revert to writer.
Advice: " 'Does it work?' is the only criteria I use. Ask yourself: 'Is this story the best it can be?' The print market continues to narrow. We work to give more writers a forum for their work."

$◕ **RADIANCE, Your Online Source for Body Acceptance**, Box 30246, Oakland CA 94604. (510)482-0680. E-mail: alice@radiancemagazine.com. Website: www.radiancemagazine.com. **Contact:** Alice Ansfield, editor. "From their 16 years in print, articles, interviews and resources have been put on their website for all to read. Also, you'll find a *Radiance* kids project. Our theme is to encourage women to live fully now, whatever their body size. To stop waiting to live or feel good about themselves until they lose weight." Quarterly. Estab. 1984.
  • As of this printing, *Radiance* is not accepting any submissions. Check website for any updates.

◔ **REALPOETIK: A Little Magazine of the Internet**, 840 W. Nickerson St. #11, Seattle WA 98119. (206)282-3776. E-mail: salasin@scn.org. Website: www.scn.org/realpoetik. "This is an archive/website for the mailing list/e-mail aspect of *RealPoetik*." Editor: Sal Salasin. **Contact:** Fiction Editor. E-zine. "We publish the new, lively, exciting and unexpected in vernacular English. Any vernacular will do." Weekly. Estab. 1993.
Needs: "We do not want to see anything that fits neatly into categories. We subvert categories." Publishes ms 2-4 months after acceptance. **Publishes 20-30 new writers/year.** Word length: 250-500 average. Publishes short shorts. Also publishes literary essays, literary criticism and poetry. Sometimes comments on or critiques rejected ms.

VISIT THE WRITER'S MARKET WEBSITE at www.writersmarket.com for hot new markets, daily market updates, writers' guidelines and much more.

How to Contact: "E-mail to salacin@scn.org." Responds to queries in 1 month. Send SASE for reply, return of ms or send a disposable copy of ms. No simultaneous submissions. Reviews novels, short story collections and poetry.
Payment/Terms: Acquires one-time rights. Sponsors contest.
 Advice: "Be different, but interesting. Humor and consciousness are always helpful. Write short. We're a postmodern e-zine."

N: ⊘ RENAISSANCE ONLINE MAGAZINE, P.O. Box 3246, Pawtucket RI 02861-2331. E-mail: kridolfi@renaissancemag.com. Website: www.renaissancemag.com (includes archives and guidelines). **Contact:** Kevin Ridolfi, editor. Electronic zine. "*Renaissance* provides an open forum and exchange for an online community seeking for diversity on the jumbled and stagnant Internet. Works should be well-written and should deal with the effective resolution of a problem."
Needs: Short fiction, serial fiction, poetry, essays, humor, young adult. "No lewd, adult fiction." **Publishes 6 new writers/year.** Recently published work by Sharon Suendsen, Rob Kerr, and Steve Mueske. Length: 800-2,000 words.
How to Contact: Electronic and traditional submissions accepted, electronic (e-mail) submissions preferred.
Advice: "Browse through *Renaissance*'s past issues for content tendencies and submission requirements. Don't be afraid to go out on a short limb, but please limit yourself to our already existing categories."

⊘ ⚑ THE ROSE & THORN LITERARY E-ZINE, Showcasing Emerging and Established Writers and A Writer's Resource. E-mail: raven763@aol.com or baquinn@aol.com. Website: members.aol/Raven763 (includes writer's resources, current issue, submissions guidelines and staff information). Managing Editor: Jasmin Randick.
Contact: Barbara Quinn, fiction editor. E-zine specializing in literary works of fiction, poetry and essays: 35-40 pages; illustrations; photos. "We created *The Rose & Thorn Literary E-zine* for readers and writers alike. We offer inspiration from eclectic works of distinction and provide a forum for emerging and established voices. We blend contemporary writing with traditional prose and poetry in an effort to promote the literary arts and expand the venue of standard publishing." Quarterly. Estab. 1998. Circ. 12,000.
 • At press time *Rose & Thorn* was closed to submissions. See the website for updates. *The Rose & Thorn Literary E-zine* ranked on *Writer's Digest*'s "Top 30" list of best markets for fiction writers.
Needs: Adventure, ethnic/multicultural (general), experimental, fantasy, historical, horror (dark fantasy, futuristic, psychological, supernatural), humor satire, literary, mainstream, mystery/suspense, New Age, regional, religious (inspirational, religious fantasy), romance (contemporary, futuristic/time travel, gothic, historical, regency period, romantic suspense), science fiction (hard science/technological, soft/sociological), thriller/espionage, western. Receives "several hundred" unsolicited mss/month. Accepts 8-10 mss/issue; 40-50 mss/year. "We are very open to unpublished writers and encourage submissions by both emerging and established writers. About 50% of accepted manuscripts are by unpublished writers." Recently published work by Elisha Poret and Vasilis Afxentiou, who was awarded the 2001 Silver Rose Award for Excellence in the Art of the Short Story. Length: 250-2,000 words. Publishes short shorts. Length: 250-750 words. Also publishes literary essays and poetry. Sometimes comments on rejected mss.
How to Contact: Send queries/mss by e-mail to Jasmin Randick, managing editor at raven763@aol.com or Barbara Quinn, co-managing editor at baquinn@aol.com. Include estimated word count, 150 word bio, list of publications and authors byline. Responds in 1 week to queries; 1 month to mss. Accepts simultaneous submissions and reprints. Sample copy and guidelines free.
Payment/Terms: "No payment except feedback from visitors and subscribers to the site. Writer retains all rights—our goal is to showcase exceptional writers." Sends galleys to author.
Advice: "Clarity, control of the language, evocative stories that tug at the heart and make their mark on the reader long after it's been read. We look for uniqueness in voice, style and characterization. New twists on old themes are always welcome. Use all aspects of good writing in your stories, including dynamic characters, strong, narrative voice and a riveting and original plot. We have eclectic tastes so go ahead and give us a shot. Read the publication and other quality literary journals to see if your work would fit with our style. Always check your spelling and grammar before submitting. Reread your submission with a critical eye and ask yourself, does it evoke an emotional response? Have I completely captured my reader? Check your submission for 'it' and 'was' and see if you can come up with a better way to express yourself. Be unique."

⊘ RPPS/FULLOSIA PRESS, (formerly *Fullosia Press*), Rockaway Park Philosophical Society, 299-9 Hawkins Ave., Suite 865, Ronkonkoma NY 11779. Fax: (631)588-9428. E-mail: deanofrpps@aol.com. Website: http://rpps_fullosia_press.tripod.com. **Contact:** J.D. Collins, editor. E-zine. "One-person, part-time. Publishes fiction and nonfiction. Our publication is right wing and conservative but amenable to the opposition's point of view. We promote an independent America. We are anti-global, anti-UN. Collects unusual news from former British or American provinces. Fiction interests include military, police, private detective, courthouse stories." Monthly. Estab. 1999. Circ. 100.
Needs: Historical (American), military/war, mystery/suspense, thriller/espionage. Upcoming themes: Christmas, St. Patrick's Day, Fourth of July. Publishes ms 1 week after acceptance. Recently published work by Glen Cunningham, Peter Layton, Dr. Kelly White MD and James Davies. Length: 500-2,000 words; average length: 750 words. Publishes short shorts. Also publishes literary essays. Always comments on rejected mss.
How to Contact: Query first. Accepts submissions by e-mail, fax and disk. Include brief bio and list of publications. Responds in 1 week to queries; 1 month to mss. Send SASE (or IRC) for return of ms. Accepts simultaneous, previously published work and multiple submissions. Guidelines for SASE. Reviews novels, short story collections and nonfiction.
Payment/Terms: No payment. Acquires electronic rights.
Advice: "Make your point quickly. If you haven't done so, after five pages, everybody hates you and your characters."

$ ◎ ▼ SCIFI.COM, PMB 391, 511 Avenue of the Americas, New York NY 10011-8436. (212)989-3742. E-mail: datlow@www.scifi.com. Website: www.scifi.com (includes all fiction, guidelines, edit info). **Contact:** Ellen Datlow, fiction editor. E-zine specializing in science fiction. "Largest and widest-ranging science fiction site on the web. Affiliated with the Sci Fi Channel, *Science Fiction Weekly*, news, reviews, comics, movies, and interviews." Weekly. Estab. 2000. Circ. 50,000/day.

   • *Scifi.com* ranked on *Writer's Digest*'s "Top 30" list of best markets for fiction writers. Linda Nagata's novella *Goddess*, first published on *Scifi.com*, was the first exclusively net-published piece of fiction to ever win the Nebula Award from the Science Fiction & Fantasy Writers of America. Andy Duncan's story "Pottawatamic Giant" won the World Fantasy Award.

Needs: Fantasy (urban fantasy), science fiction (hard science/technological, soft/sociological). "No space opera, sword and sorcery, poetry or high fantasy." Receives 100 unsolicited mss/month. Accepts 1 mss/issue; 35 mss/year. Publishes ms within 6 months after acceptance. Agented fiction 2%. Recently published work by Carol Emshwiller, Robert Reed, Nancy Kress and James P. Blaylock. Length: 1,500-20,000 words; average length: 7,500 words. Sometimes comments on rejected mss.

How to Contact: Send complete ms with cover letter. Include estimated word count and list of publications. Responds in 2 months to mss. Send SASE for return of ms or send a disposable copy of ms and #10 SASE for reply only. Guidelines for SASE or on website.

Payment/Terms: Pays 20¢/word up to $3,500. Pays on acceptance for first, electronic and anthology rights.

Advice: "We look for crisp, evocative writing, interesting characters, good storytelling. Check out the kinds of fiction we publish if you can. If you read one, then you know what I want."

⦿ SHADES OF DECEMBER, Box 244, Selden NY 11784. (631)736-4155. E-mail: fiction@shadesofdecember.com. Website: www.shadesofdecember.com (includes guidelines, reviews, sample work, upcoming themes). **Contact:** Brandy Danner, editor. Electronic magazine. "Good writing comes in all forms and should not be limited to overly specific or standard genres. Our intended audience is one that is varied in taste and open to the unorthodox." Quarterly. Estab. 1998. Circ. 200-300.

Needs: Experimental, humor/satire, literary, mainstream/contemporary. "We are not limited in the categories of writing that we will consider for publication." Accepts 1-4 mss/issue; 8-16 mss/year. Publishes ms 1-6 months after acceptance. **Publishes 2-6 new writers/year.** Recently published work by Katherine Arline, Marzena Adriana Czarnecka and Angela Lam. Length: 4,000 words maximum. Prefers 2,800. Publishes short shorts. Also publishes scripts. Sometimes comments on rejected ms.

How to Contact: Send complete ms with a cover letter. Include bio (75 words or less). Responds in 1-3 months. Send SASE for reply, return of ms or send a disposable copy of ms. Accepts simultaneous submissions. Electronic submissions preferred. Make checks payable to Alexander Danner. Sample (print) copy $7. Guidelines for #10 SASE or by e-mail.

Payment/Terms: Pays 2 contributor's copies. Acquires first serial rights.

Advice: "We like to see work that strays from the conventional. While we print good writing in any form, we prefer to see work that takes risks."

▼ SHADOW VOICES. E-mail: phantomlady@geocities.com. Website: www.geocities.com/Athens/Styx/1713/index.html. **Contact:** Vida Janulaitis, editor. Electronic zine. "If you speak of the unknown and reach into the darkness of your soul, share your deepest thoughts. Send me your poetry and short stories."

Needs: "Well written fiction or poetry that reveals your inner thoughts. No pornography, or racist material that may inspire someone to do harm to any form of life or property." Wants more fiction that "allows the writer to reveal a different side of life and put those feelings into words." The best writing grabs your attention from the beginnings and surprises you in the end. Recently published work by Taylor Graham, Rich Logsdon and Vida Janulaitis. Publishes new and established writers.

How to Contact: Accepts queries/mss by e-mail. "Each and every submission should be sent on a separate e-mail, no file attachments please. At the top of each page place 'the title of the work,' your real name, complete e-mail address and a short bio. Please indicate submission in the e-mail subject line."

Advice: "Please edit your work carefully. I will assume poetic license. Most of all, write what's inside of you and be sincere about it. Everyone has a unique style, make yours stand out."

◖ SNREVIEW: Starry Night Review—A Literary E-Zine, 197 Fairchild Ave, Fairfield CT 06432-4856. (203)366-5991. Fax: (203)336-4793. E-mail: SNReviewezine@aol.com. Website: members.aol.com/jconln1221/snreview.htm. **Contact:** Joseph Conlin, editor. E-zine specializing in literary short stories, essays and poetry. "The *SNReview* searches for material that not only has strong characters and plot but also a devotion to imagery." Quarterly. Estab. 1999.

Needs: "We only want literary and mainstream." Receives 10 mss/month. Accepts 5 mss/issue; 20 mss/year. Publishes ms up to 6 months after acceptance. **Publishes 20 new writers/year.** Published work by E. Lindsey Balkan, Marie Griffin and Jonathan Lerner. Word length: 4,000 words average; 1,500 words minimum; 7,000 words maximum. Also publishes literary essays, literary criticism and poetry.

How to Contact: Send complete ms with a cover letter via e-mail only. Include 100 word bio and a list of publications. Responds in 1 month. Accepts simultaneous and reprint submissions. Sample copy and guidelines free on website.

Payment/Terms: Acquires first rights. Sends prepublication webpages to the author.

STARK RAVING SANITY. E-mail: info@starkravingsanity.com. Website: www.starkravingsanity.com. **Contact:** Mike S. Dubose and H. Roger Baker II, editors. Electronic zine. "We have published short stories, poems, novel excerpts, prose poems, poetic prose, micro-fiction and everything in between. Our intended audience is anyone looking for an entertaining work of substance."

Needs: "Anything goes, as long as it fits our eclectic, ever changing tastes. We want works that illustrate a variant view of reality—but then again all works do just that. So anything of quality is what we like. No hate prose or porn." **Publishes 2-3 new writers/year.** Recently published work by Joe Flowers, R.N. Friedland, Jonathan Lowe and Len Kruger.

How to Contact: Electronic submissions accepted only. "Send 2-20 pages in the body of an e-mail message or as a text-only attachment (DOS or MS Word). Please read the guidelines (available online)."

Advice: "In taking fiction, I like (and look for) characters who act as if they are real, situations that are interesting, and writing that sings. I will accept first-time writers if the writing does not look like it came from a first-timer. In other words, I want quality. Please be professional. Read the journal. Read and follow the guidelines. And keep in mind also that we too are real people on schedules. Mutual respect, please."

$ STICKMAN REVIEW, Stickman Review, 2890 N. Fairview Dr., Flagstaff AZ 86004. (928)913-0869. E-mail: editors@stickmanreview.com. Website: www.stickmanreview.com. **Contact:** Anthony Brown, Darrin English, editors. Online journal specializing in literary fiction. "Stickman Review considers previously unpublished fiction of literary quality. We welcome all stories whose first purpose is literary. We consider all mainstream and experimental literary fiction. We are very unlikely to publish genre fiction unless the story transcends the typical requirements of the genre. Semiannual. Estab. 2001.

Needs: Erotica, ethnic/multicultural, experimental, feminist, gay, humor/satire, lesbian, literary. "Preferably no romance, religious or inspirational fiction." Accepts 5-10 mss/issue, 10-20/year. Publishes ms 3 months after acceptance. Length: 250-10,000 words; average length 3,000 words. Publishes short shorts. Average length 750 words. Also publishes literary essays and poetry. Sometimes critiques rejected mss.

How to Contact: Submit electronically to fiction@stickmanreview.com. Responds in 1 month to queries; 2 months to mss. Accepts simultaneous and multiple submissions. Guidelines on website.

Payment/Terms: Pays $20. Pays on acceptance for all rights. Publication is not copyrighted.

Advice: "To see the kinds of stories we publish, read what the best literary magazines are publishing today. We seek literary fiction, first and foremost. Avoid sending us stories that fall under a specific genre."

$ STILLWATERS JOURNAL, An Online Journal of Dark Fiction, Marietta Publishing, 677 Valleywide Dr., Dallas GA 30157-9394. Phone/fax: (678)363-9351. E-mail: submissions@stillwatersjournal.com. Website: http://stillwatersjournal.com. **Contact:** James Shimkus, associate editor. E-zine specializing in dark fiction. "We publish high quality humor and dark fantasy. The story must have an element of the supernatural or weird. We prefer dark fiction with a literary sensibility. We publish for an adult audience." Bimonthly. Estab. 2000.

Needs: Fantasy (slipstream), horror (dark fantasy, futuristic, supernatural), cross-genre. "We'd prefer not to receive serial killer/spree killer/family annihilator stories, but we will consider anything, as long as it is weird." Upcoming themes: Halloween issue, deadline August 31; Christmas/Holidays issue, deadline October 31. Receives 50 unsolicited mss/month. Accepts 2 mss/issue; 12 mss/year. "Reads manuscripts during February and September." Publishes ms 2-4 months after acceptance. **Publishes 2-4 new writers/year.** Recently published work by Charlee Jacob, Richard Dansky and James Moore. Length: 7,500 words (maximum); average length: 5,000 words. Publishes short shorts. Average length: 1,000 words. Also publishes literary essays and literary criticism.

How to Contact: Send complete ms with a cover letter (e-mail ms as embedded text or word file). Accepts submissions by e-mail. Include estimated word count and brief bio. Responds in 1-2 weeks to queries; 3-6 months to mss. Send SASE (or IRC) for return of ms or send a disposable copy of ms and #10 SASE for reply only. Accepts simultaneous and multiple submissions. Guidelines for SASE, by e-mail or on website.

Payment/Terms: Pays $50. Pays on acceptance for first rights.

Advice: "We look for a unique voice. Good prose. Good atmosphere. Although we do read every submission, we usually know whether we like a story or not by the end of the first page. Read. Read inside and outside the genre."

STORY BYTES—Very Short Stories, E-mail: editor@storybytes.com. Website: www.storybytes.com (includes issues, mailing lists, subscription info, submission guidelines). **Contact:** M. Stanley Bubien, editor. Electronic zine. "*Story Bytes-Very Short Stories* is strictly an electronic publication, appearing on the Internet in three forms. First, the stories are sent to an electronic mailing list of readers. They also get placed on the *Story Bytes* website, in both HTML and PDF format."

Needs: "Stories must be very short—having a length that is the power of 2 specifically: 2, 4, 8, 16, 32, 64, 128, 256, 512, 1,024 and 2,048 words long." No sexually explicit material. "Would like to see more material dealing with religion. Not necessarily 'inspirational' stories, but those that show the struggles of living a life of faith in a realistic manner." **33% of works published are by new writers.** Recently published work by Richard K. Weems, Joseph Lerner, Lisa Cote, Thomas Sennet, Mark Hansen and Wendy Williams. Preferred length: 256-512 words. Publishes short shorts.

How to Contact: Accepts queries/mss by e-mail. "I prefer plain text with story title, authorship and word count. Only accepts electronic submissions." See website for complete guidelines.

Advice: "In *Story Bytes*, the very short stories themselves range in topic. Many explore a brief event—a vignette of something unusual, unique and, at times, something even commonplace. Some stories can be bizarre, while others quite lucid. Some are based an actual events, while others are entirely fictional. Try to develop conflict early on (in the first sentence if possible!), and illustrate or resolve this conflict through action rather than description. I believe we'll find an audience for electronic published works primarily in the short story realm. Very few people want to sit in front of their computer to read *War and Peace!* But, most people gladly read e-mail, and messages in this form can easily range from 2 to 1,000 words."

THE 13TH WARRIOR REVIEW, Asterius Press, P.O. Box 5122, Seabrook NJ 08302-3511. E-mail: theeditor@a steriuspress.com. Website: www.asteriuspress.com (includes guidelines, interviews, articles, etc.). **Contact:** John C. Erianne, publisher/editor. Online magazine. Triannual. Estab. 2000.
Needs: Erotica, experimental, humor/satire, literary, mainstream. "Some genre fiction if of literary quality." Receives 200 unsolicited mss/month. Accepts 4-5 mss/issue; 10-15 mss/year. Publishes ms 6 months after acceptance. **Publishes 1-2 new writers/year.** Recently published work by George Lynn, Ehren Biving and D. Olsen. Length: 300-3,000 words; average length: 1,500 words. Publishes short shorts. Average length: 250 words. Also publishes literary essays, literary criticism and poetry. Sometimes comments on rejected mss.
How to Contact: Send complete ms with a cover letter. Accepts submissions by e-mail "as text in message body—no attachments." Include estimated word count, brief bio and address/e-mail. Responds in 1 week to queries; 3 weeks to mss. Send SASE (or IRC) for return of ms or send a disposable copy of ms and #10 SASE for reply only. Accepts simultaneous submissions "if so noted." Guidelines on website. Reviews novels, short story collections and nonfiction books of interest to writers. Send review copies to Asterius Press.
Payment/Terms: Acquires first and electronic rights.

THRESHOLDS QUARTERLY, School of Metaphysics Associates Journal, SOM Publishing, School of Metaphysics World Headquarters, 163 Moon Valley Rd., Windyville MO 65783. (417)345-8411. Fax: (417)345-6668 (call first, computerized). E-mail: som@som.org. Website: www.som.org (includes interviews, fiction, bios, articles, essays). **Contact:** Dr. Barbara Condron, editor. Senior Editor: Dr. Laurel Clark. Electronic magazine. "The School of Metaphysics is a nonprofit educational and service organization invested in education and research in the expansion of human consciousness and spiritual evolution of humanity. For all ages and backgrounds. Themes: dreams, healing, science fiction, personal insight, morality tales, fables, humor, spiritual insight, mystic experiences, religious articles, creative writing with universal themes." Quarterly. Estab. 1975. Circ. 5,000.
Needs: Adventure, fantasy, humor, psychic/supernatural, religious/inspirational, science fiction. "No dark, sexual, drug-oriented fiction." Wants to see more "innovative, inspiring, uplifting" work. Upcoming themes: "Dreams, Visions, and Creative Imagination" (February); "Health and Wholeness" (May); "Intuitive Arts" (August); "Man's Spiritual Consciousness" (November). Receives 5 unsolicited mss/month. Length: 4-6 double-spaced typed pages. Publishes short shorts. Also publishes literary essays and poetry. Often comments on rejected mss.
How to Contact: Query with outline; will accept unsolicited ms with cover letter; no guarantee on time length to respond. Include bio (1-2 paragraphs). Send SASE for reply, return of ms or send a disposable copy of ms. Sample copy for 9×12 SAE and $1.50 postage. Guidelines for #10 SASE.
Advice: "We encourage works that have one or more of the following attributes: uplifting, educational, inspirational, entertaining, informative and innovative."

TOASTED CHEESE, Toasted Cheese. Website: www.toasted-cheese.com. **Contact:** submit@toasted-cheese .com. E-zine specializing in fiction, poetry and flash fiction. "*Toasted Cheese* accepts submissions of previously unpublished fiction, flash fiction and poetry. Our focus is on quality of work, not quantity. Some issues of *Toasted Cheese* will therefore contain fewer/more pieces than previous issues. We don't restrict publication based on subject matter. *Toasted Cheese* encourages submissions from innovative writers in all genres." Bimonthly. Estab. 2001. Approximately 1,000 hits/month, or 2,000/e-zine issue.
Needs: Adventure, children's/juvenile, ethnic/multicultural, experimental, fantasy, feminist, gay, historical, horror, humor/satire, lesbian, literary, mainstream, mystery/suspense, New Age, psychic/supernatural/occult, romance, science fiction (soft/sociological), thriller/espionage, western, young adult/teen. "No fan fiction. No chapters or excerpts unless they read as a stand-alone story. No first drafts. See submission guidelines." Receives 5 (not including "Best of Boards") unsolicited mss/month. Accepts 3-5 mss/issue; 18-30 mss/year. Publishes ms 2 months after acceptance. **Publishes 9 new writers/year.** Recently published work by Mona Wanlass, Janet Mullany, Lori F. Dehn, Trina L. Talma and Linda Easley. Length: 500-5,000 words; average length: 1,500 words. Publishes short shorts. Average length: 500 words (less than 500 for flash fiction). Also publishes poetry. Often comments on rejected mss.
How to Contact: Send complete ms with a cover letter. Accepts submissions by e-mail. Include estimated word count, brief bio and list of publications. Responds in 2 months. Accepts simultaneous print submissions only; no simultaneous electronic submissions. Sample copy online. Guidelines by e-mail or on website.
Payment/Terms: Acquires electronic rights. Sponsors contest.

MARKET CONDITIONS are constantly changing! If you're still using this book and it is 2004 or later, buy the newest edition of *Novel & Short Story Writer's Market* at your favorite bookstore or order from Writer's Digest Books by calling 1-800-448-0915.

Advice: "We are looking for clean, professional writing from writers of any level. Accepted stories will be concise and compelling. We are looking for writers who are serious about the craft: tomorrow's literary stars before they're famous. Take your submission seriously, yet remember that humor and levity are appreciated. You are submitting not to traditional 'editors' but to fellow writers who appreciate the efforts of those in the trenches."

TROUT. E-mail: editor@troutmag.org. Website: www.troutmag.org. **Editor:** Robin Parkinson. E-zine. *Trout* is "slightly fishy, but never coarse."
Needs: "We publish humorous fiction, with a strong British slant. Our material ranges from themed collections of one-liners to a novel-length multi-threaded serial. The intended audience is composed of intelligent, articulate, literate people with a sense of humor and enough understanding of British culture to follow the jokes. No non-humorous fiction." Would like to see more "humorous short stories." **Publishes 3-4 new writers/year.** Recently published work by Joann L. Dominik, Ric Craig, Andy Gittins, Elly Kelly, Steve Lewin, Sue McCoan and Alexander MacDonald.
How to Contact: "*Trout* does not accept unsolicited manuscripts, manuscript fragments or synopses. Writers who might wish to contribute to *Trout* should contact the editor by e-mail and be prepared to show a sample of their work."
Payment/Terms: "*Trout* is entirely noncommercial. We receive no payment so we have none to pass on."
Advice: "Read us. If you find what you read amusing and feel that you are capable of writing material in a similar vein then talk to us. However, if you don't understand what we're getting at, we would not recommend that you attempt to 'slant' your material to fit what you perceive *Trout* 's philosophy to be. We are interested in writers whose natural 'voice' matches what we are doing."

12-GAUGE.COM, (formerly *12-Gauge Review*), InGauge Media LLC, 192 Washington Park, 3rd Floor, Brooklyn NY 11205. (718)852-4816. Fax: (718)222-3737. E-mail: info@ingaugemedia.com. Website: www.12gauge.com. Fiction Editor: Gowan Campbell. Online magazine. Monthly. Estab. 1995.
● At press time, *12-gauge.com*'s website submission engine was temporarily down. This publication prefers to receive submissions via the website. Visit www.12gauge.com for updates.
Needs: Comics/graphic novels, erotica, ethnic/multicultural, experimental, gay, glitz, humor/satire, lesbian, literary, mainstream, military/war, regional, science fiction (hard science, soft/sociological). Receives 100 unsolicited mss/month. Accepts 2 mss/issue; 24/year. Publishes ms 3-4 weeks after acceptance. Agented fiction: 5%. Publishes 10-12 previously unpublished writers/year. Length: 4,000 words maximum; average length: 3,000. Publishes short shorts. Also publishes essays, criticism, poetry. Sometimes comments on rejected mss.
How to Contact: Send complete ms with cover letter. Accepts submissions by e-mail or on disk. Include estimated word count, brief bio, list of publications and contact information. Simultaneous and previously published submissions okay. Guidelines available via e-mail or on website.
Payment/Terms: Negotiable. Acquires one-time rights.
Advice: "Work must be original but shouldn't try too hard."

○ **VOIDING THE VOID**®, 8 Henderson Place, New York NY 10028. E-mail: mail@vvoid.com. or EELIPP@aol.com. Website: www.voidingthevoid.com. **Contact:** E.E. Lippincott, editor-in-chief. Electronic zine and hard copy specializing in personal world views: 8½ × 11; 8 pages; mock newsprint hard copy. "A small reader specializing in individuals' fictional and nonfictional views of the world around them." Monthly. Estab. 1997. Circ. 2,000 both in US and UK.
Needs: All categories. "We will consider anything the potential contributor feels is appropriate to the theme 'tangibility.' All fiction genres OK." Publishes holiday issues; submit at least 3 months prior to holiday. Receives 100 unsolicited mss/month. Accepts 5-10 mss/issue; 120 mss/year. Publishes ms immediately to 1 year after acceptance. Published work by Erik Seims, Craig Coleman, R. Ambardar, T. Liam Vederman and Jenny Wu. Length: no length restrictions. Publishes short shorts. Also publishes literary essays, literary criticism, poetry. Always comments on rejected ms.
How to Contact: Send complete ms with a cover letter; send electronic submissions via website or direct e-mail. Include estimated word count. Responds in 2 weeks to queries; 3 months to mss. Send SASE for reply or return of ms. Accepts simultaneous and reprint (with date and place indicated) submissions. Guidelines for #10 SASE. Reviews novels and short story collections.
Payment/Terms: Pays 4 contributor's copies. Acquires one-time rights. Individual issues not copyrighted.
Advice: "*Voiding the Void* is not about the 'writing' or the 'art' so much as it is about the human being behind it all."

▣ ◎ **VQ ONLINE,** 8009 18th Lane SE, Lacey WA 98053. (360)455-4607. E-mail: jmtanaka@webtv.net. Website: http://community.webtv.net/JM/TANAKA/VQ. **Contact:** Janet Tanaka, editor. "VQ Online readers are professional and amateur volcanologists and other volcanophiles. It is not a journal, but an interesting e-zine that features fiction, poetry, nonfiction articles, book and movie reviews, and announcements of interest to volcano scientists." Updated 4 times/year.
Needs: Short stories or serialized novellas. Nothing pornographic. "Must have volcanoes as a central subject, not just window dressing." **Publishes 15-20 new writers/year.** Recently published work by Susan Mauer, Bill West and Wendall Duffield.
How to Contact: Accepts queries by e-mail and disk (if convertible to ASCII).
Payment/Terms: Pays in contributor's copies.
Advice: "Material must be scientifically accurate."

▣ ◑ **WILD VIOLET,** Wild Violet, P.O. Box 39706, Philadelphia PA 19106-9706. E-mail: wildvioletmagazine@yahoo.com. Website: www.wildviolet.net. **Contact:** Alyce Wilson, editor. Online magazine: illustrations; photos. "Our goal is to democratize the arts: to make the arts more accessible and to serve as a creative forum for writers and artists. Our audience includes English-speaking readers from all over the world, who are interested in both 'high art' and pop culture." Quarterly. Estab. 2001.

Needs: Comics/graphic novels, ethnic/multicultural, experimental, fantasy (space fantasy, sword and sorcery), feminist, gay, horror (dark fantasy, futuristic, psychological, supernatural), humor/satire, lesbian, literary, New Age, psychic/supernatural/occult, science fiction (hard science/technological, soft/sociological). "No stories where sexual or violent content is just used to shock the reader. No racist writings." Receives 15 unsolicited mss/month. Accepts 5 mss/issue; 20 mss/year. Publishes ms 3 months after acceptance. **Publishes 7 new writers/year.** Recently published work by Sadie O'Deay, Chris Martinez, C.C. Parker, Linda Oatman High and Jeff Brendle. Length: 500-6,000 words; average length: 3,000 words. Publishes short shorts. Average length: 600 words. Also publishes literary essays, literary criticism and poetry. Sometimes comments on rejected mss "when requested."

How to Contact: Send complete ms with a cover letter. Prefers submissions by e-mail, with story in the body of the e-mail or as a .txt attachment. Include estimated word count and brief bio. Responds in 1 week to queries; 3-6 weeks to mss. Send SASE for return of ms or send a disposable copy of ms and #10 SASE for reply only. Accepts simultaneous and multiple submissions. Guidelines by e-mail. Reviews novels, short story collections and nonfiction books of interest to writers. Send review copies to Alyce Wilson.

Payment/Terms: Writers receive bio and links on contributor's page on publication. Rights retained by author. Sponsors contest.

Advice: "We look for stories that are well-paced and show character and plot development. Even short shorts should do more than simply paint a picture. Manuscripts stand out when the author's voice is fresh and engaging. Avoid muddying your story with too many characters and don't attempt to shock the reader with an ending you have not earned. Experiment with styles and structures, but don't resort to experimentation for its own sake."

◐ WILMINGTON BLUES. E-mail: editor@wilmingtonblues.com. Website: www.wilmingtonblues.com. **Editor:** Trace Ramsey. Electronic zine.

Needs: Humor/satire, literary. Receives 60-80 unsolicited mss/month. Publishes ms 1 month after acceptance. **Publishes as many new writers as possible.** Published work by Alex Stolis and Steve Gibbs. Length: 250-10,000 words; average length: 2,500 words. Publishes short shorts. Length: 250 words. Also publishes essays, poetry. Often comments on rejected mss.

How to Contact: Electronic submissions only. "Please submit work as a text attachment to an e-mail." Include estimated word count, bio, e-mail address. Responds in 2 weeks to queries; 1 month to mss. Accepts simultaneous submissions.

Payment/Terms: Acquires one-time rights.

Advice: "If your work has something to offer, it will be published. We offer comments on work that isn't accepted, and we encourage resubmissions!"

◑ ZUZU'S PETALS QUARTERLY, P.O. Box 4853, Ithaca NY 14852. (607)539-1141. E-mail: info@zuzu.com. Website: zuzu.come. **Contact:** T. Dunn, editor. Electronic magazine. "Arouse the senses; stimulate the mind." Estab. 1992.

Needs: Ethnic/multicultural, feminist, gay, humor/satire, lesbian, literary, regional. No "romance, sci-fi, the banal, TV style plotting." Receives 300 unsolicited mss/month. Accepts 1-5 mss/issue; 4-15 mss/year. Publishes ms 4-6 months after acceptance. Agented fiction 10%. Published work by Norah Labiner, Vincent Zandri and LuAnn Jacobs. Length: 1,000-6,000 words. Publishes short shorts. Also publishes hypertext fiction (flexible length). Length: 350 words. Also publishes literary essays, literary criticism and poetry. Sometimes comments on rejected mss.

How to Contact: Send complete ms with a cover letter. Include estimated word count and list of publications. Responds in 2 weeks to queries; 2 weeks to 2 months to mss. Send SASE (or IRC) for reply, return of ms or send a disposable copy of ms. Accepts simultaneous and electronic submissions. Back issue for $5. Guidelines free. Reviews novels and short story collections. Send to Doug DuCap, Reviewer.

Advice: Looks for "strong plotting and a sense of vision. Original situations and true to life reactions."

Consumer Magazines

In this section of *Novel & Short Story Writer's Market* are consumer magazines with circulations of more than 10,000. Many have circulations in the hundreds of thousands or millions. While much has been made over the shrinking consumer magazine market for fiction, new markets are opening. *Seventeen* magazine, for example, has placed new emphasis on publishing fiction. And among the oldest magazines listed here are ones not only familiar to us, but also to our parents, grandparents and even great-grandparents: *The Atlantic Monthly* (1857); *The New Yorker* (1925); *Capper's* (1879); *Esquire* (1933); and *Ellery Queen's Mystery Magazine* (1941).

Consumer periodicals make excellent markets for fiction in terms of exposure, prestige and payment. Because these magazines are well-known, however, competition is great. Even the largest consumer publications buy only one or two stories an issue, yet thousands of writers submit to these popular magazines.

Despite the odds, it is possible for talented new writers to break into print in the magazines listed here. Your keys to breaking into these markets are careful research, professional presentation and, of course, top-quality fiction.

TYPES OF CONSUMER MAGAZINES

In this section you will find a number of popular publications, some for a broad-based, general-interest readership and others for large but select groups of readers—children, teenagers, women, men and seniors. There are also religious and church-affiliated magazines, publications devoted to the interests of particular cultures and outlooks, and top markets for genre fiction.

SELECTING THE RIGHT MARKET

Unlike smaller journals and publications, most of the magazines listed here are available at newsstands and bookstores. Many can also be found in the library, and guidelines and sample copies are almost always available by mail or online. Start your search by reviewing the listings, then familiarize yourself with the fiction included in the magazines that interest you.

Don't make the mistake of thinking that just because you are familiar with a magazine, their fiction is the same today as when you first saw it. Nothing could be further from the truth—consumer magazines, no matter how well established, are constantly revising their fiction needs as they strive to expand their audience base.

In a magazine that uses only one or two stories an issue, take a look at the nonfiction articles and features as well. These can give you a better idea of the audience for the publication and clues to the type of fiction that might appeal to them.

If you write genre fiction, check out the specific sections for lists of magazines publishing in that genre (mystery, page 83; romance, page 97; science fiction/fantasy & horror, page 109). For other types of fiction look in the Category Index beginning on page 606. There you will find a list of markets that say they are looking for a particular subject.

FURTHERING YOUR SEARCH

See The "Quick Start" Guide to Publishing Your Fiction (page 2) for information about the material common to all listings in this book. In this section in particular, pay close attention to the number of submissions a magazine receives in a given period and how many they publish in the same period. This will give you a clear picture of how stiff your competition can be.

While many of the magazines listed here publish one or two pieces of fiction in each issue, some also publish special fiction issues once or twice a year. We have indicated this in the listing information. We also note if the magazine is open to novel excerpts as well as short fiction and we advise novelists to query first before submitting long work.

The Business of Fiction Writing, beginning on page 58, covers the basics of submitting your work. Professional presentation is a must for all markets listed. Editors at consumer magazines are especially busy, and anything you can do to make your manuscript easy to read and accessible will help your chances of being published. Most magazines want to see complete manuscripts, but watch for publications in this section that require a query first.

As in the previous section, we've included our own comments in many of the listings, set off by a bullet (●). Whenever possible, we list the publication's recent awards and honors. We've also included any special information we feel will help you in determining whether a particular publication interests you.

The maple leaf symbol ( ) identifies our Canadian listings. You will also find some English-speaking markets from around the world. These foreign magazines are denoted with ⊕ at the beginning of the listings. Remember to use International Reply Coupons rather than stamps when you want a reply from a country other than your own.

For More Information

For more on consumer magazines, see issues of *Writer's Digest* (by F&W Publications) and other industry trade publications available in larger libraries.

For news about some of the genre publications listed here and information about a particular field, there are a number of magazines devoted to genre topics, including *The Mystery Review*, *Locus* (for science fiction); *Science Fiction Chronicle*; and *Romance Writers' Report* (available to members of Romance Writers of America).

ADVENTURES, (formerly *Wonder Time*), WordAction Publications, 6401 The Paseo, Kansas City MO 64131-1213. (816)333-7000. **Contact:** Pamela Smits, editor. Magazine: 8¼×11; 4 pages; self cover; color illustrations. Hand-out story paper published through WordAction Publications; stories follow outline of Sunday School lessons for 6-8 year-olds. Weekly. Circ. 45,000.

Needs: Religious/inspirational. Wants "family time activities and ideas." Stories must have first- to second-grade readability. Receives 50-75 unsolicited fiction mss/month. Accepts 1 ms/issue. **Publishes 20 new writers/year.** Length: 100 words.

How to Contact: Send complete ms with SASE. Responds in 6 weeks. Sample copy and curriculum guide with SASE.

Payment/Terms: Pays on acceptance for all rights.

Advice: "Basic themes reappear regularly. Please write for a theme list. Ask for guidelines, sample copies, theme list before submitting."

$ AFRICAN VOICES, A Soulful Collection of Art and Literature, African Voices Communications, Inc., 270 W. 96th St., New York NY 10025. (212)865-2982. Fax: (212)316-3335. E-mail: africanvoices@aol.com. Website: www.africanvoices.com. **Contact:** Carolyn A. Butts, publisher/editor. Managing Editor: Layding Kaliba. Fiction Editor: Kim Horne. Book Review Editor: Debbie Officer. Magazine: 52 pages; illustrations; photos. "*AV* publishes enlightening and entertaining literature on the varied lifestyles of people of color." Quarterly. Estab. 1993. Circ. 20,000.

Needs: African-American: children's/juvenile (10-12 years), condensed/excerpted novel, erotica, ethnic/multicultural, gay, historical (general), horror, humor/satire, literary, mystery/suspense, psychic/supernatural/occult, religious/inspirational, science fiction, young adult/teen (adventure, romance). List of upcoming themes available for SASE. Publishes special fiction issue. Receives 20-50 unsolicited mss/month. Accepts 20 mss/issue. Publishes ms 3-6 months after acceptance. Agented fiction 5%. **Publishes 30 new writers/year.** Published work by Junot Díaz, Michel Marriott and Carol Dixon. Length: 500-3,000 words; average length: 2,000 words. Occasionally publishes short shorts. Also publishes literary essays and poetry.

How to Contact: Query with clips of published work. Include short bio. Accepts submissions by e-mail and on disk. Responds in 3 months to queries and mss. Send SASE for return of ms. Accepts simultaneous, reprint and electronic submissions. Sample copy for $5 and 9×12 SASE. Guidelines free. Subscriptions are $12 for 1 year. Reviews novels and short story collections. Send books to Book Editor.

Payment/Terms: Pays $25 maximum and 5 contributor's copies. Pays on publication for first North American serial rights.

Advice: "A manuscript stands out if it is neatly typed with a well-written and interesting story line or plot. Originality encouraged. We are interested in more horror, erotic and drama pieces. *AV* wants to highlight the diversity in our culture. Stories must touch the humanity in us all."

$ **AIM MAGAZINE,** P.O. Box 1174, Maywood IL 60153. (708)343-4414. Website: www.aimmagazine.org. Editor: Myron Apilado, EdD. **Contact:** Ruth Apilado, associate editor. Magazine: 8½×11; 48 pages; slick paper; photos and illustrations. Publishes material "to purge racism from the human bloodstream through the written word—that is the purpose of *Aim Magazine*." Quarterly. Estab. 1973. Circ. 10,000.

Needs: Open. No "religious" mss. Published special fiction issue last year; plans another. Receives 25 unsolicited mss/month. Buys 15 mss/issue; 60 mss/year. **Publishes 40 new writers/year.** Published work by Christina Touregny, Thomas Lee Harris, Michael Williams and Jake Halpern. Length: 800-1,000 words average. Publishes short shorts. Sometimes comments on rejected mss.

How to Contact: Send complete ms. Include SASE with cover letter and author's photograph. Accepts simultaneous submissions. Responds in 1 month. Sample copy for $4 with SAE (9×12) and $1.80 postage. Guidelines for #10 SASE.

Payment/Terms: Pays $15-25. Pays on publication for first rights.

Advice: "Search for those who are making unselfish contributions to their community and write about them. Write about your own experiences. Be familiar with the background of your characters." Known for "stories with social significance, proving that people from different ethnic, racial backgrounds are more alike than they are different."

$ **AMERICAN GIRL,** Pleasant Company Publications, 8400 Fairway Place, Box 620986, Middleton WI 53562-0986. (608)836-4848. E-mail: im_agmag_editor@pleasantco.com. Website: www.americangirl.com. Editor: Kristi Thom. **Contact:** Magazine Department Assistant. Magazine: 8½×11; 52 pages; illustrations; photos. "Four-color bimonthly magazine for girls age 8-12. Our mission is to celebrate girls, yesterday and today. We publish fiction up to 2,300 words and the protagonist is a girl between 8-12. We want thoughtfully developed children's literature with good characters and plots." Estab. 1992. Circ. 750,000.

Needs: Children's/juvenile (girls 8-12 years): "contemporary, realistic fiction, adventure, historical, problem stories." No romance, science fiction, fantasy. Receives 100 unsolicited mss/month. Accepts 6 mss/year. Length: 2,300 words maximum. Publishes short shorts. Also publishes literary essays and poetry (if age appropriate). **Publishes 2-3 new writers year.** Recently published work by Kay Thompson, Mavis Jukes and Susan Shreve.

How to Contact: Send complete ms. Include bio (1 paragraph). Send SASE for reply, return of ms or send a disposable copy of ms. Accepts simultaneous submissions. Send SASE for guidelines. Sample copy for $3.95 plus $1.93 postage.

Payment/Terms: Pays in cash; amount negotiable. Pays on acceptance for first North American serial rights. Sends galleys to author.

Advice: "We're looking for excellent character development within an interesting plot."

N **$** **ANALOG SCIENCE FICTION AND FACT,** Dell Magazines, 475 Park Ave. S., New York NY 10016. (212)686-7188. Fax: (212)686-7414. E-mail: analog@dellmagazines.com. Website: http://analogsf.com (includes current contents, excerpts, guidelines, contact information, cululative story index, reader forum, etc.). **Contact:** Stanley Schmidt, editor. Magazine: 144 pages; illustrations; photos. "*Analog* features science fiction solidly extrapolated from real science, aimed at an intelligent audience with a serious interest in the future." Publishes 11 times/year, including one "double" issue. Estab. 1930. Circ. 50,000.

● Fiction published in *Analog* has won numerous Nebula and Huga Awards.

Needs: Science fiction (hard science/technological, soft/sociological). "No fantasy or stories in which the scientific background is implausible or plays no essential role." Receives 500 unsolicited mss/month. Accepts 6 mss/issue; 70 mss/year. Publishes ms 5-12 months after acceptance. Agented fiction 5%. **Publishes 3-4 new writers/year.** Length: 200-20,000 words (40,000-80,000 for serials); average length: 10,000 words. Publishes short shorts. Average length: 800 words. Sometimes comments on rejected mss.

How to Contact: Send complete ms with a cover letter. Query first for serials only. Include estimated word count. Responds in 1 month. Send SASE for return of ms or send a disposable copy of ms and #10 SASE for reply only. Accepts multiple submissions (though this is usually not to the author's advantage). Sample copy for $5. Guidelines for SASE or on website. Reviews novels, short story collections and nonfiction books of interest to writers. Send review copies to Tom Easton.

INTERESTED IN A PARTICULAR GENRE? Check our sections for: **Mystery/Suspense**, page 74; **Romance**, page 86; **Science Fiction/Fantasy & Horror**, page 100.

Payment/Terms: Pays $.04-.08/word and 2 contributors copies; additional copies $2.25 (graduated scale depending on number ordered). Pays on acceptance for first North American serial and nonexclusive foreign serial rights. Sends galleys to author. Not copyrighted.

Advice: "I'm looking for irresistibly entertaining stories that make me think about things in ways I've never done before. Read several issues to get a broad feel for our tastes, but don't try to imitate what you read."

$⊘ THE ANNALS OF ST. ANNE DE BEAUPRÉ, Redemptorist Fathers, P.O. Box 1000, St. Anne de Beaupré, Quebec G0A 3C0 Canada. (418)827-4538. Fax: (418)827-4530. **Contact:** Father Roch Achard, C.Ss.R., editor. Magazine: 8×11; 32 pages; glossy paper; photos. "Our aim is to promote devotion to St. Anne and Catholic family values." Monthly. Estab. 1878. Circ. 50,000.

Needs: Religious/inspirational. "We only wish to see something inspirational, educational, objective, uplifting. Reporting rather than analysis is simply not remarkable." Receives 50-60 unsolicited mss/month. Published work by Beverly Sheresh and Eugene Miller. Publishes short stories. Length: 1,500 maximum. Always comments on rejected ms.

How to Contact: Send complete, typed, double spaced ms with a cover letter. Include estimated word count. Responds in 1 month. Send SASE for reply or return of ms. No simultaneous submissions. Free sample copy and guidelines. Please state "rights" for sale.

Payment/Terms: Pays 3-4¢/word on acceptance and 3 contributor's copies on publication for first North American rights. "No reprints."

N ⊘ ◎ APPALACHIA JOURNAL, Appalachian Mountain Club, 5 Joy St., Boston MA 02108. (617)523-0636. **Contact:** Lucille Daniel, editor. Magazine: 6×9; 160 pages; 60 lb. recycled paper; 10 pt. CS1 cover; 5-10 illustrations; 20-30 photos. "*Appalachia* is the oldest mountaineering and conservation journal in the country. It specializes in backcountry recreation and conservation topics (hiking, canoeing, cross-country skiing, etc.) for outdoor (including armchair) enthusiasts." Semiannually (June and December). Estab. 1876. Circ. 15,000.

Needs: Prose, poem, sports. Receives 5-10 unsolicited mss/month. Accepts 1-2 mss/issue; 2-4 mss/year. Publishes ms 6-12 months after acceptance. Length: 500-4,000 words average. Publishes short shorts.

How to Contact: Send complete ms with cover letter. Accepts submissions on disk. No simultaneous submissions. Accepts multiple submissions. Responds in 1 month to queries; 3 months to mss. SASE (or IRC) for query. Sample copy for $5. Guidelines for #10 SAE.

Payment/Terms: Pays contributor's copies. Occasionally pays $100-300 for a feature—usually assigned.

Advice: "All submissions should be related to conservation, mountaineering, and/or backcountry recreation both in the Northeast and throughout the world. Most of our journal is nonfiction. The fiction we publish is mountain-related and often off-beat. Send us material that says, I went to the wilderness and *thought* this; not I went there and did this."

$⊘ ART TIMES, Commentary and Resources for the Fine and Performing Arts, P.O. Box 730, Mt. Marion NY 12456. Phone/fax: (845)246-6944. Website: www.arttimesjournal.com. **Contact:** Raymond J. Steiner, editor. Magazine: 12×15; 24 pages; Jet paper and cover; illustrations; photos. "Arts magazine covering the disciplines for an over-40, affluent, arts-conscious and literate audience." Monthly. Estab. 1984. Circ. 23,000.

Needs: Adventure, contemporary, ethnic, fantasy, feminist, gay, historical, humor/satire, lesbian, literary, mainstream and science fiction. "We seek quality literary pieces. Nothing violent, sexist, erotic, juvenile, racist, romantic, political, etc." Receives 30-50 mss/month. Accepts 1 ms/issue; 11 mss/year. Publishes ms within 48-60 months of acceptance. **Publishes 6 new writers/year.** Length: 1,500 words maximum. Publishes short shorts.

How to Contact: Send complete ms with cover letter. No electronic submissions. Accepts multiple and simultaneous submissions. Responds in 6 months. SASE. Sample copy for $1.75, 9×12 SAE and 3 first-class stamps. Guidelines for #10 SASE.

Payment/Terms: Pays $25, free one-year subscription to magazine and 6 contributor's copies. Pays on publication for first North American serial rights.

Advice: "Competition is greater (more submissions received), but keep trying. We print new as well as published writers."

$⊘ ◎ ▼ ASIMOV'S SCIENCE FICTION, 475 Park Ave. S., Floor 11, New York NY 10016-6901. (212)686-7188. Fax: (212)686-7414. E-mail: asimovs@dellmagazines.com. Website: www.asimovs.com (includes guidelines, names of editors, short fiction, interviews with authors, editorials, and more). **Contact:** Gardner Dozois, editor. Executive Editor: Sheila Williams. Magazine: 5¼×8¼ (trim size); 144 pages; 30 lb. newspaper; 70 lb. to 8 pt. C1S cover stock; illustrations; rarely photos. Magazine consists of science fiction and fantasy stories for adults and young adults. Publishes "the best short science fiction available." Estab. 1977. Circ. 50,000. 11 issues/year (one double issue).

 • Named for a science fiction "legend," *Asimov's* regularly receives Hugo and Nebula Awards. Editor Gardner Dozois has received several awards for editing including Hugos and those from *Locus* and *Science Fiction Chronicle* magazines.

Needs: Science fiction (hard science, soft sociological), fantasy. No horror or psychic/supernatural. Would like to see more hard science fiction. Receives approximately 800 unsolicited fiction mss each month. Accepts 10 mss/issue. Publishes ms 6-12 months after acceptance. Agented fiction 10%. **Publishes 6 new writers/year.** Recently published work by Ursula LeGuin and Larry Niven. Length: up to 20,000 words. Publishes short shorts. Comments on rejected mss "when there is time."

How to Contact: Send complete ms with SASE. Responds in 3 months. Guidelines for #10 SASE. Sample copy for $5 and 9×12 SASE. Reviews novels and short story collections. Send books to Book Reviewer.

Payment/Terms: Pays 6-8¢/word for stories up to 7,500 words; 5¢/word for stories over 12,500; $450 for stories between those limits. Pays on acceptance for first World English serial rights plus specified foreign rights, as explained in contract. Very rarely buys reprints. Sends galleys to author.

Advice: "We are looking for character stories rather than those emphasizing technology or science. New writers will do best with a story under 10,000 words. Every new science fiction or fantasy film seems to 'inspire' writers—and this is not a desirable trend. Be sure to be familiar with our magazine and the type of story we like; workshops and lots of practice help. Try to stay away from trite, cliched themes. Start in the middle of the action, starting as close to the end of the story as you possibly can. We like stories that extrapolate from up-to-date scientific research, but don't forget that we've been publishing clone stories for decades. Ideas must be fresh."

N: $ ⬛ ◎ THE ASSOCIATE REFORMED PRESBYTERIAN, The Associate Reformed Presbyterian, Inc., 1 Cleveland St., Greenville SC 29601. (864)232-8297. **Contact:** Ben Johnston, editor. Magazine: 8½×11; 32-48 pages; 50 lb. offset paper; illustrations; photos. "We are the official magazine of our denomination. Articles generally relate to activities within the denomination—conferences, department work, etc., with a few special articles that would be of general interest to readers." Monthly. Estab. 1976. Circ. 6,000.

Needs: Contemporary, juvenile, religious/inspirational, spiritual, young adult/teen. "Stories should portray Christian values. No retelling of Bible stories or 'talking animal' stories. Stories for youth should deal with resolving real issues for young people." Receives 30-40 unsolicited fiction mss/month. Accepts 10-12 mss/year. Publishes ms within 1 year after acceptance. Recently published work by Tommy Kirkland, George Dreackslin and Genie Dickerson. Length: 300-750 words (children); 1,250 words maximum (youth). Sometimes comments on rejected mss.

How to Contact: Include cover letter. Responds in 6 weeks to queries and mss. Accepts simultaneous submissions. Sample copy for $1.50; Guidelines for #10 SASE.

Payment/Terms: Pays $20-75 for first rights and contributor's copies.

Advice: "Currently we are seeking stories aimed at the 10 to 15 age group. We have an oversupply of stories for younger children."

$ THE ATLANTIC MONTHLY, 77 N. Washington St., Boston MA 02114. (617)854-7749. Fax: (617)854-7877. E-mail: mcurtis@theatlantic.com. Editor: Michael Kelly. **Contact:** C. Michael Curtis, senior editor. Managing Editor: Cullen Murphy. General magazine for an educated readership with broad cultural interests. Monthly. Estab. 1857. Circ. 500,000.

• *The Atlantic Monthly* ranked on *Writer's Digest's* "Top 30" list of best markets for fiction writers.

Needs: Literary and contemporary. "Seeks fiction that is clear, tightly written with strong sense of 'story' and well-defined characters." Accepts 15-18 stories/year. Receives 1,000 unsolicited fiction mss each month. **Publishes 11-12 new writers/year.** Recently published work by Mary Gordon, Donald Hall and Roxana Robinson. Preferred length: 2,000-6,000 words.

How to Contact: Send cover letter and complete ms with SASE. Accepts multiple submissions. Responds in 2 months or less to mss.

Payment/Terms: Pays $3,000/story. Pays on acceptance for first North American serial rights.

Advice: When making first contact, "cover letters are sometimes helpful, particularly if they cite prior publications or involvement in writing programs. Common mistakes: melodrama, inconclusiveness, lack of development, unpersuasive characters and/or dialogue."

N: $ ⬛ ◎ BALLOON LIFE, The Magazine for Hot Air Ballooning, 2336 47th Ave., SW, Seattle WA 98116. (206)935-3649. Fax: (206)935-3326. E-mail: tom@balloonlife.com. Website: www.balloonlife.com/ (includes guidelines, sample issues). **Contact:** Tom Hamilton, editor. Magazine: 8½×11; 48 pages; color, b&w photos. Publishes material "about the sport of hot air ballooning. Readers participate in hot air ballooning as pilots, crew, official observers at events and spectators."

Needs: Humor/satire, related to hot air ballooning. "Manuscripts should involve the sport of hot air ballooning in any aspect. Prefer humor based on actual events; fiction seldom published." Accepts 4-6 mss/year. Publishes ms within 3-4 months after acceptance. Length: 800-1,500 words; average length: 1,200 words. Publishes short shorts. Length: 400-500 words. Sometimes comments on rejected mss and recommends other markets.

How to Contact: Send complete ms with cover letter that includes Social Security number. Accepts queries/mss by e-mail and fax (ms by permission only). Responds in 3 weeks to queries; 2 weeks to mss. SASE. Accepts simultaneous and reprint submissions. Sample copy for 9×12 SAE and $1.94 postage. Guidelines for #10 SASE.

Payment/Terms: Pays $25-75 and contributor's copies. Pays on publication for first North American serial, one-time or other rights.

Advice: "Generally the magazine looks for humor pieces that can provide a light-hearted change of pace from the technical and current event articles. An example of a work we used was titled 'Balloon Astrology' and dealt with the character of a hot air balloon based on what sign it was born (made) under."

$ ⬛ THE BEAR DELUXE MAGAZINE, Orlo, 2516 NW 29th, P.O. Box 10342, Portland OR 97296. (503)242-1047. Fax: (503)243-2645. E-mail: bear@orlo.org. Website: www.orlo.org (includes writing guidelines). **Contact:** Tom Webb, editor. Magazine: 11×14; 68 pages; newsprint paper; Kraft paper cover; illustrations; photos. "*The Bear Deluxe* has an environmental focus, combining all forms and styles. Fiction should have environmental thread to it and should be engaging to a cross-section of audiences. The more street-level, the better." Triannual. Estab. 1993. Circ. 19,000.

• *The Bear Deluxe* has received a publishing grant from the Oregon Council for the Humanities.

Needs: Environmentally focused: humor/satire, literary, science fiction. "We would like to see more nontraditional forms. No detective, children's or horror." List of upcoming themes available for SASE. Receives 20-30 unsolicited mss/month. Accepts 2-3 mss/issue; 8-12 mss/year. Publishes ms 6 months after acceptance. **Publishes 5-6 new writers/year.** Recently published work by Peter Houlahan, John Reed and Karen Hueler. Length: 900-4,000 words; average length: 2,500 words. Publishes short shorts. Also publishes literary essays, literary criticism, poetry, reviews, opinion, investigative journalism, interviews and creative nonfiction. Sometimes comments on rejected mss.

How to Contact: Send complete ms with a cover letter and clips. Include estimated word count, 10 to 15-word bio, list of publications. Accepts queries/mss by e-mail and disk. Responds in 6 months. Send a disposable copy of mss. Accepts simultaneous and electronic (disk is best, then e-mail) submissions. Sample copy for $3. Guidelines for #10 SASE. Reviews novels and short story collections.

Payment/Terms: Pays free subscription to the magazine, contributor's copies and 5¢ per published word; additional copies for postage. Acquires first or one-time rights. Not copyrighted.

Advice: "Keep sending work. Write actively and focus on the connections of man, nature, etc., not just flowery descriptions. Urban and suburban environments are grist for the mill as well. Have not seen enough quality humorous and ironic writing. Interview and artist profile ideas needed. Juxtaposition of place welcome. Action and hands-on great. Not all that interested in environmental ranting and simple 'walks through the park.' Make it powerful, yet accessible to a wide audience."

$ ⊘ BOMB MAGAZINE, New Art Publications, 594 Broadway, Suite 905, New York NY 10012. (212)431-3943. Fax: (212)431-5880. E-mail: info@bomb.com. Website: www.bombsite.com. Editor-in-Chief: Betsy Sussler. **Contact:** Lucy Raven, associate editor. Magazine: 11×14; 104 pages; 70 lb. glossy cover; illustrations; photos. Publishes "work which is unconventional and contains an edge, whether it be in style or subject matter." Quarterly. Estab. 1981.

Needs: Contemporary, experimental, novel excerpts. No genre: romance, science fiction, horror, western. Upcoming theme: "The Americas," featuring work by artists and writers from Central and South America (no unsolicited mss for theme issue, please). Receives 50 unsolicited mss/week. Accepts 6 mss/issue; 24 mss/year. Publishes ms 3-6 months after acceptance. Agented fiction 70%. **Publishes 2-3 new writers/year.** Recently published work by Melanie Rae Thon, Carole Maso, Molly McQuade and Mary Jo Bang. Length: 10-12 pages average. Publishes interviews.

How to Contact: Send complete ms up to 25 pages in length with cover letter. Responds in 4 months to mss. SASE. Accepts multiple submissions. Sample copy for $7 with $1.67 postage.

Payment/Terms: Pays $100 and contributor's copies. Pays on publication for first or one-time rights. Sends galleys to author.

Advice: "We are committed to publishing new work that commercial publishers often deem too dangerous or difficult. The problem is, a lot of young writers confuse difficult with dreadful. Read the magazine before you even think of submitting something."

$ ⊘ ▨ BOSTON REVIEW, A political and literary forum, 30 Wadsworth St., E53-407, MIT, Cambridge MA 02139. (617)253-3642. Fax: (617)252-1549. E-mail: bostonreview@mit.edu. Website: http://bostonreview.mit.edu bostonreview/ (includes full issue 1 month after publication, poetry and fiction links page, guidelines and contests guidelines, bookstore listing and subscription info). Managing Editor: Jeff Decker. **Contact:** Jodi Daynard, fiction editor. A bimonthly magazine "providing a forum of ideas in politics, literature and culture. Essays, reviews, poetry and fiction are published in every issue. Audience is well educated and interested in under recognized writers." Magazine: 10¾×14¼; 60 pages; newsprint. Estab. 1975. Circ. 30,000.

● *Boston Review* is the recipient of a Pushcart Prize in poetry.

Needs: Contemporary, ethnic, experimental, literary, prose poem, regional, translations. "No romance, erotica, genre fiction." Receives 150 unsolicited fiction mss/month. Buys 4-6 mss/year. Publishes ms an average of 4 months after acceptance. Published work by David Mamet, Rhoda Stamell, Jacob Appel, Elisha Porat and Diane Williams. Length: 4,000 words maximum; average length: 2,000 words. Occasionally comments on rejected ms.

How to Contact: Send complete ms with cover letter and SASE. "You can almost always tell professional writers by the very thought-out way they present themselves in cover letters. But even a beginning writer should find some link between the work (its style, subject, etc.) and the publication—some reason why the editor should consider publishing it." No queries or manuscripts by e-mail. Responds in 4 months. Accepts simultaneous submissions (if noted). Sample copy for $5. Reviews novels and short story collections. Send books to Ian Lague, managing editor.

Payment/Terms: Pays $50-100 and 5 contributor's copies. Pays after publication for first rights.

Advice: "I'm looking for stories that are emotionally and intellectually substantive and also interesting on the level of language. Things that are shocking, dark, lewd, comic, or even insane are fine so long as the fiction is *controlled* and purposeful in a masterly way. Subtlety, delicacy and lyricism are attractive too. Work tirelessly to make the work truly polished before you send it out. Make sure you know the publication you're submitting—don't send blind."

$ ◎ BOWHUNTER MAGAZINE, The Number One Bowhunting Magazine, Primedia Special Interest Publications, 6405 Flank Dr., Harrisburg PA 17112. (717)657-9555. Fax: (717)657-9552. E-mail: bowhunter_magazine @primediamags.com. Website: www.bowhunter.com (includes writer's guidelines). Founder/Editor Emeritus: M.R. James. Associate Publisher/Managing Editor: Jeffrey S. Waring. **Contact:** Dwight Schuh, editor. Magazine: 8×10½; 150 pages; 75 lb. glossy paper; 150 lb. glossy cover stock; illustrations; photos. "Written by and for bowhunters dedicated to offering readers updated conservation news, game forecasts, details of the latest in equipment choices; a reference manual of the sport's history and serving as a forum for experts and readers to exchange ideas and success stories." Bimonthly. Circ. 180,000.

Needs: Bowhunting, outdoor adventure. "Writers must expect a very limited market. We buy only one or two fiction pieces a year. Writers must know the market—bowhunting—and let that be the theme of their work. No 'me and my dog' types of stories; no stories by people who have obviously never held a bow in their hands." Receives 25 unsolicited fiction mss/month. Accepts 30 mss/year. Publishes ms 3 months to 2 years after acceptance. **Publishes 3-4 new writers/ year.** Recently published work by John "Maggie" McGee. Length: 500-2,000 words; average length: 1,500 words. Publishes short shorts. Length: 500 words. Sometimes comments on rejected mss and recommends other markets.

How to Contact: Query first or send complete ms with cover letter. Accepts mss by e-mail, fax and disk. Responds in 2 weeks to queries; 1 month to mss. Sample copy for $2 and 8½×11 SAE with appropriate postage. Guidelines for #10 SASE.

Payment/Terms: Pays $100-350. Pays on acceptance for first worldwide serial rights.

Advice: "We have a resident humorist who supplies us with most of the 'fiction' we need. But if a story comes through the door which captures the essence of bowhunting and we feel it will reach out to our readers, we will buy it. Despite our macho outdoor magazine status, we are a bunch of English majors who love to read. You can't bull your way around real outdoor people—they can spot a phony at 20 paces. If you've never camped out under the stars and listened to an elk bugle and try to relate that experience without really experiencing it, someone's going to know. We are very specialized; we don't want stories about shooting apples off people's heads or of Cupid's arrow finding its mark. James Dickey's *Deliverance* used bowhunting metaphorically, very effectively . . . while we don't expect that type of writing from everyone, that's the kind of feeling that characterizes a good piece of outdoor fiction."

$ ⊘ BOYS' LIFE, For All Boys, Boy Scouts of America, Magazine Division, Box 152079, 1325 W. Walnut Hill Lane, Irving TX 75015-2079. (972)580-2355. Website: www.boyslife.org. **Contact:** Rich Haddaway, associate editor. Magazine: 8×11; 68 pages; slick cover stock; illustrations; photos. "*Boys' Life* covers Boy Scout activities and general interest subjects for ages 8 to 18, Boy Scouts, Cub Scouts and others of that age group." Monthly. Estab. 1911. Circ. 1,300,000.

Needs: Adventure, humor/satire, mystery/suspense (young adult), science fiction, sports, western (young adult), young adult. "We publish short stories aimed at a young adult audience and frequently written from the viewpoint of a 10- to 16-year-old boy protagonist." Receives approximately 150 unsolicited mss/month. Accepts 12-18 mss/year. **Publishes 1 new writer/year.** Recently published work by Gary Paulsen, G. Clifton Wisler, Iain Lawrence and Ben Bova. Length: 500-1,500 words; average length: 1,200 words. "Very rarely" comments on rejected ms.

How to Contact: Send complete ms with SASE. "We'd much rather see manuscripts than queries." Responds in 2 months. For sample copy "check your local library." Guidelines for SASE.

Payment/Terms: Pays $750 and up ("depending on length and writer's experience with us"). Pays on acceptance for one-time rights.

Advice: "*Boys' Life* writers understand the readers. They treat them as intelligent human beings with a thirst for knowledge and entertainment. We tend to use some of the same authors repeatedly because their characters, themes, etc., develop a following among our readers. Read at least a year's worth of the magazine. You will get a feeling for what our readers are interested in and what kind of fiction we buy."

$ ⊘ Ⓨ BOYS' QUEST, The Bluffton News Publishing & Printing Co., P.O. Box 227, Bluffton OH 45817-0227. (419)358-4610. Fax: (419)358-5027. Website: www.boysquest.com (includes samples of magazine content, order form). **Contact:** Marilyn Edwards, editor. Magazine: 7×9; 50 pages; enamel paper; illustrations; photos. "Our target audience is the 8-10 year old boy (our wider audience is ages 5-13). We feature stories, articles of a wholesome nature. Traditional childhood themes are stressed, our thinking being that innocent childhood interests should be cultivated, not skipped over." Bimonthly. Estab. 1994. Circ. 10,000

● *Boy's Quest* received an EDPRESS Distinguished Achievement Award for Excellence in Educational Journalism, and a Silver Award-Gallery of Superb Printing.

Needs: Children's/juvenile (5-9 years, 10-13 years) adventure, ethnic/multicultural, historical, sports. "No violence, romance, science fiction, fantasy, fads. We would like to see more wholesome adventure and humorous stories." Upcoming themes: It's a Mystery, cats, water, inventions, bugs, horses, space and turtles. List of upcoming themes available for SASE. Receives 300-400 unsolicited mss/month. Accepts 20-40 mss/year. Agented fiction 2%. **Publishes 40 new writers/year.** Recently published work by Eve Marar, John Hillman, Marcie Tichenor, John Thomas Waite, Carolyn Mott Ford and Robert Redding. Length: 500 words maximum; average length: 300-500 words. Publishes short shorts. Length: 250-300 words. Also publishes poetry. Always comments on rejected mss.

How to Contact: Send complete ms with a cover letter. Include estimated word count, 1 page bio, Social Security number, list of publications. Responds in 1 month to queries; 6-10 weeks to mss. Accepts simultaneous, multiple and reprint submissions. Sample copy for $4 and 9×12 SASE. Themes and guidelines for #10 SASE. Reviews novels and short story collections.

Payment/Terms: Pays 5¢/word and 1 contributor's copy; additional copies $4, $2.50 for 10 or more. Pays on publication for first North American serial rights.

Advice: "Must be written with a boy's perspective in mind. No need to have 'tough guy' dialogue when writing about boy-ish adventures, experiences."

$ 🌐 ◎ BUGLE, Elk Country and the Hunt, Rocky Mountain Elk Foundation, P.O. Box 8249, Missoula MT 59807-8249. (406)523-3481. Fax: (406)523-4550. E-mail: dburgess@rmef.org. Website: www.rmef.org/ (includes writer's guidelines, names of editors and excerpts). Editor: Dan Crockett. **Contact:** Don Burgess, hunting/human interest editor. Assistant Editor: Lee Cromrich. Magazine: 8½×11; 114-172 pages; 55 lb. Escanaba paper; 80 lb. sterling cover; b&w, 4-color illustrations; photos. "The Rocky Mountain Elk Foundation is a nonprofit conservation organization established in 1984 to help conserve critical habitat for elk and other wildlife. *BUGLE* specializes in research, stories (fiction and nonfiction), art and photography pertaining to the world of elk and elk hunting." Bimonthly. Estab. 1984.
Needs: Elk-related adventure, children's/juvenile, historical, human interest, natural history, conservation. "We would like to see more humor. No formula outdoor or how-to writing. No stories of disrespect to wildlife." Upcoming themes: "Bowhunting"; "Odd Elk Behavior/Weird, Scary, Paranormal Doings in Elk Country"; "The Pilgrimage Phenomenon of Hunters Journeying From the East to the Rockies and Southwest Each Fall to Hunt Elk." Receives 20-30 unsolicited mss/month. Accepts 3-4 mss/issue; 18-24 mss/year. Publishes ms up to 4 years after acceptance. **Publishes 12 new writers/year.** Recently published work by Rick Bass and Susan Ewing. Length: 1,500-5,000 words; 2,500 words preferred. Publishes short shorts. Also publishes literary essays and poetry.
How to Contact: Query first or send complete ms with a cover letter. Accepts queries/mss by e-mail, fax and disk (ms by permission only). Accepts multiple submissions. Include estimated word count and bio (100 words). Responds in 1 month to queries; 3 months to ms. Send SASE for reply, return of ms or send a disposable copy of ms. Sample copy for $5. Guidelines free.
Payment/Terms: Base freelance rates: pays 20¢/word maximum. Pays on acceptance for one-time rights.
Advice: "We accept fiction and nonfiction stories pertaining in some way to elk, other wildlife, hunting, habitat conservation, and related issues."

$ 🎖 CALLIOPE, Exploring World History, Cobblestone Publishing, Co., 30 Grove St., Suite C, Peterborough NH 03458. Fax: (603)924-7380. Website: www.cobblestonepub.com. Managing Editor: Lou Waryncia. **Contact:** Rosalie Baker, editor. Magazine. "*Calliope* covers world history (east/west) and lively, original approaches to the subject are the primary concerns of the editors in choosing material. For 8-14 year olds." Monthly except June, July, August. Estab. 1990. Circ. 11,000.
● Cobblestone Publishing also publishes the children's magazines *Appleseeds, Footsteps, Odyssey, Cobblestone* and *Faces*, some listed in this section. *Calliope* has received the Ed Press Golden Lamp and One-Theme Issue awards.
Needs: Material must fit upcoming theme; write for themes and deadlines. Childrens/juvenile (8-14 years). "Authentic historical and biographical fiction, adventure, retold legends, folktales, etc. relating to the theme." Send SASE for guidelines and theme list. Published after theme deadline. Published work by Duane Damon and Amita V. Sarin. Publishes 5-10 new writers/year. Length: 800 words maximum. Publishes short shorts.
How to Contact: Query first or query with clips of published work (if new to *Calliope*). Include a brief cover letter stating estimated word count and 1-page outline explaining information to be presented, extensive bibliography of materials used. Responds in several months (if interested, response 5 months before publication date). Send SASE (or IRC) for reply (writers may send a stamped reply postcard to find out if query has been received). Sample copy for $4.95, 7½×10½ SAE and $2 postage. Guidelines for #10 SAE and 1 first-class stamp or on website.
Payment/Terms: Pays 20-25¢/word. Pays on publication for all rights.
Tips: "We primarily publish historical nonfiction. Fiction should be retold legends or folktales related to appropriate themes."

$ 🌐 🎖 CAMPUS LIFE MAGAZINE, Christianity Today, Int'l., 465 Gundersen Dr., Carol Stream IL 60188. (630)260-6200. Fax: (630)260-0114. E-mail: CLmag@campuslife.net. Website: www.campuslife.net (includes writer's guidelines, names of editors, excerpts, and fiction not included in print edition). **Contact:** Chris Lutes, assistant editor. Managing Editor: Christopher Lutes. Magazine: 8¼×11¼; 100 pages; 4-color and b&w illustrations; 4-color and b&w photos. "Teen magazine with a Christian point of view." Articles "vary from serious to humorous to current trends and issues, for teen readers." Bimonthly. Estab. 1942. Circ. 100,000.
● *Campus Life* regularly receives awards from the Evangelical Press Association.
Needs: "All fiction submissions must be contemporary, reflecting the teen experience in the new millennium. We are a Christian magazine but are *not* interested in sappy, formulaic, sentimentally religious stories. We *are* interested in well-crafted stories that portray life realistically, stories high school and college youth relate to. Writing must reflect a Christian world view. If you don't understand our market and style, don't submit." Accepts 5 mss/year. Reading and response time slower in summer. **Publishes 3-4 new writers/year.** Length: 1,000-2,000 words average, "possibly longer."
How to Contact: Query with short synopsis of work, published samples and SASE. Accepts queries by e-mail and fax. Responds in 6 weeks to queries. Sample copy for $3 and 9½×11 envelope.
Payment/Terms: Pays "generally" 15-20¢/word and 2 contributor's copies. Pays on acceptance for one-time rights.
Advice: "We print finely-crafted fiction that carries a contemporary teen (older teen) theme. First person fiction often works best. Ask us for sample copy with fiction story. We want experienced fiction writers who have something to say to young people without getting propagandistic."

$ 🌐 CAPPER'S, Ogden Publications, Inc. 1503 S.W. 42nd St., Topeka KS 66609-1265. (785)274-4346. Fax: (785)274-4305. E-mail: cappers@ogdenpubs.com. Website: www.cappers.com (includes sample items from publication and subscription information). **Contact:** Ann Crahan, editor. Magazine: 36-56 pages; newsprint paper and cover stock; photos. A "clean, uplifting and nonsensational newspaper for families, from children to grandparents." Biweekly. Estab. 1879. Circ. 250,000.

• *Capper's* is interested in longer works of fiction, 7,000 words or more. They would like to see more stories with older characters.

Needs: Serialized novels suitable for family reading. "We accept novel-length stories for serialization. No fiction containing violence, sexual references or obscenity. We would like to see more western romance, pioneer stories." Receives 2-3 unsolicited fiction mss each month. Accepts 4-6 stories/year. Recently published work by C.J. Sargent and Mona Exinger. Published new writers within the last year. Length: 7,000-40,000 words.

How to Contact: Send complete ms with SASE. Cover letter and/or synopsis helpful. Responds in 8 months on ms. Sample copy for $2.

Payment/Terms: Pays $75-300 for one-time serialization and contributor's copies (1-2 copies as needed for copyright). Pays on acceptance for second serial (reprint) rights and one-time rights.

Advice: "Since we publish in serialization, be sure your manuscript is suitable for that format. Each segment needs to be compelling enough so the reader remembers it and is anxious to read the next installment. Please proofread and edit carefully. We've seen major characters change names partway through the manuscript."

CELESTIAL PRODUCTS, Box 3636, Ft. Pierce FL 34948. (772)460-1874. E-mail: ray@celestialpro.net. Website: www.celestialpro.net (includes short fiction club information). **Contact:** Editor. Magazines and newspapers "specializing in alternative lifestyles." Publications vary in size, 56-80 pages. "Group of 26 erotica, soft core publications for swingers, single males, married males, gay males, transgendered and bisexual persons." Bimonthly, quarterly and monthly. Estab. 1975. Circ. combined is 2,000,000.

• This is a group of regional publications with explicit sexual content, graphic personal ads, etc. Not for the easily offended.

Needs: Erotica, fantasy, swinger, fetish, gay, lesbian. Receives 8-10 unsolicited mss/month. Accepts 1-2 mss/issue; 40-50 mss/year. Publishes ms 1-3 months after acceptance. **Publishes 3-6 new writers/year.** Length: 2,000-3,500 words. Sometimes comments on rejected mss.

How to Contact: Query first, query with clips of published work or send complete ms with cover letter. SASE. Accepts submissions by e-mail and on disk. Accepts simultaneous, multiple and reprint submissions. Sample copy for $7. Guidelines with SASE.

Payment/Terms: First submission, free subscription to magazine; subsequent submissions $25 on publication for all rights or first rights; all receive 3 contributor's copies.

Advice: "Know your grammar! Content must be of an adult nature but well within guidelines of the law. Fantasy, unusual sexual encounters, swinging stories or editorials of a sexual bent are acceptable. Read Henry Miller!"

CHICKADEE, Owl Communications, 49 Front St. E, 2nd Floor, Toronto, Ontario M5E 1B3 Canada. (416)340-2700. Fax: (416)340-9769. E-mail: owl@owlkids.com. Website: www.owlkids.com. **Contact:** Angela Keenlyside, managing editor. Magazine: 8½×11¾; 36 pages; glossy paper and cover stock; illustrations; photos. "*Chickadee* is created to give children aged 6-9 a lively, fun-filled look at the world around them. Each issue has a mix of activities, puzzles, games and stories." Published 10 times/year. Estab. 1979. Circ. 110,000.

• *Chickadee* has won several awards including the Ed Press Golden Lamp Honor award and the Parents' Choice Golden Seal and Silver Seal awards.

Needs: Juvenile, new readers: animal, humorous, nature/environment. "No religious, anthropomorphic animal, romance, material that talks down to kids." Accepts 1 ms/issue; 10 mss/year. **Published new writers within the last year.** Length: 600-700 words.

How to Contact: Send complete ms and cover letter with $1 or IRC to cover postage and handling (must be international postal coupon). Accepts simultaneous submissions. Responds in 3 months. Sample copy for $4. Guidelines for SAE and IRC.

Payment/Terms: Pays $25-350 (Canadian) and 3 contributor's copies. Pays on publication for all rights. Occasionally buys reprints.

Advice: "Read back issues to see what types of fiction we publish. Common mistakes include loose, rambling, and boring prose; stories that lack a clear beginning, middle and end; unbelievable characters; and overwriting."

**FOR EXPLANATIONS OF THESE SYMBOLS,
SEE THE INSIDE FRONT AND BACK COVERS OF THIS BOOK.**

$ ◎ CICADA, Carus Publishing Company, 315 Fifth St., Peru IL 61354. (815)224-6656. Fax: (815)224-6615. E-mail: mmiklavcic@caruspub.com. Website: www.cricketmag.com or www.cicadamag.com. **Contact:** Deborah Vetter, executive editor. Associate Editor: Tracy Schoenle. Literary magazine: 128 pages; some illustrations. Bimonthly. Estab. 1998. Circ. 15,000.

Needs: Young adult/teen (adventure, fantasy/science fiction, historical, mystery/suspense, romance, sports, western, humor). "Our readership is age 14-21. Submissions should be tailored for high-school and college-age audience, not junior high or younger." Accepts 10 mss/issue; 60 mss/year. Publishes 1 year after acceptance. Length: 3,000-15,000 words; average length: 5,000 words. Also publishes poetry. Sometimes comments on rejected mss.

How to Contact: Send complete ms with cover letter. Include estimated word count and brief bio. Responds in 3 months to mss. Send SASE for return of ms or send disposable copy of ms and #10 SASE for reply only. Accepts simultaneous submissions (if ms is tagged as simultaneous submission). Sample copy for $8.50. Guidelines for SASE or on website. Reviews novels "geared toward our teen readership."

Payment/Terms: Fiction and articles pay 25¢/word and 2 contributor's copies. Poems: up to $3/line and 2 contributor's copies; additional copies $4. Pays on publication. Sends edited ms for author approval. "For stories and poems previously unpublished, *CICADA* purchases all rights. For stories and poems previously published, *CICADA* purchases second North American publication rights. Fees vary, but are generally less than fees for first publication rights. For recurring features, *CICADA* purchases the material outright. The work becomes the property of *CICADA,* and is copyrighted in the name of Carus Publishing Company. A flat fee per feature is usually negotiated.

Advice: "Quality writing, good literary style, genuine teen sensibility, depth, humor, good character development, avoidance of stereotypes. Read several issues to familiarize yourself with our style."

$ ○ ◎ CITYCYCLE MOTORCYCLE NEWS, Motormag Corp., P.O. Box 808, Nyack NY 10960-0808. (845)353-MOTO. Fax: (845)353-5240. E-mail: bigcheese@motorcyclenews.cc. Website: www.motorcyclenews.cc (includes short fiction, interviews with authors). **Contact:** Mark Kalan, editor. Magazine: tabloid; 64 pages; newsprint; illustrations; photos. Monthly magazine about motorcyling. Estab. 1990. Circ. 50,000.

Needs: "Anything about motorcycles." No "sexual fantasy." Accepts 10 mss/year. Publishes ms 2-6 months after acceptance. Length: 750-2,000 words average. Publishes short shorts. Also publishes literary essays, literary criticism and poetry. Sometimes comments on rejected mss.

How to Contact: Query with clips of published work. Responds in 1 month to queries. Send SASE for reply. Accepts reprints. Sample copy for $3 and 9×12 SAE. Guidelines for #10 SASE. Reviews novels and short story collections. Send books to editor.

Payment/Terms: Pays up to $150. Pays on publication for one-time rights.

Advice: "Articles, stories and poetry can be about any subject, fiction or non-fiction, as long as the subject pertains to motorcycles or the world of motorcycling. Examples would include fiction or non-fiction stories about traveling cross-country on a motorcycle, biker lifestyle or perspective, motorcycling/biker humor, etc. Stories should reflect the love of riding motorcycles and the experience of what riding is like. Romance is fine. Science fiction is fine as long as it will interest our mostly male audience."

$ ☑ CLUBHOUSE, Focus on the Family, 8605 Explorer Dr., Colorado Springs CO 80920. (719)531-3400. **Contact:** Suzanne Hadley, assistant editor. Editor: Jesse Florea. Magazine: 8×11; 24 pages; illustrations; photos. Publishes literature for kids aged 8-12. "Stories must have moral lesson included. *Clubhouse* readers are 8- to 12-year-old boys and girls who desire to know more about God and the Bible. Their parents (who typically pay for the membership) want wholesome, educational material with Scriptual or moral insight. The kids want excitement, adventure, action, humor or mystery. Your job as a writer is to please both the parent and child with each article." Monthly. Estab. 1987. Circ. 115,000.

Needs: Children's/juvenile (8-12 years), religious/inspirational. "No science fiction." Receives 150 unsolicited ms/month. Accepts 1 ms/issue. Agented fiction 15%. **Publishes 8 new writers/year.** Published work by Sigmund Brower and Nancy Rue. Length: 500-1,200 words average.

How to Contact: Send complete ms with cover letter. Include estimated word count, bio and list of publications. Responds in 6 weeks. Send SASE for reply, return of ms or send a disposable copy of ms. Sample copy for $1.50. Guidelines free.

Payment/Terms: Pays $250 maximum for first-time contributor and 5 contributor's copies; additional copies available. Pays on acceptance for first North American serial rights.

Advice: Looks for "humor with a point, historical fiction featuring great Christians or Christians who lived during great times; contemporary, exotic settings; holiday material (Christmas, Thanksgiving, Easter, President's Day); parables; fantasy (avoid graphic descriptions of evil creatures and sorcery); mystery stories; choose-your-own adventure stories and westerns. No contemporary, middle-class family settings (we already have authors who can meet these needs) or stories dealing with boy-girl relationships."

$ ◐ ◎ ☒ COBBLESTONE, Discover American History, 30 Grove St., Suite C, Peterborough NH 03458. (603)924-7209. Fax: (603)924-7380. Website: www.cobblestonepub.com. **Contact:** Meg Chorlian, editor. Magazine. "Historical accuracy and lively, original approaches to the subject are primary concerns of the editors in choosing material. For 8-14 year olds." Monthly (except June, July and August). Estab. 1979. Circ. 30,000.

• Cobblestone Press also publishes *Calliope* and *Faces* as well as *Odyssey* (science magazine), *Footsteps* (African American magazine) and *Appleseeds* (for 7-9 year olds). *Cobblestone* has received Ed Press and Parent's Choice awards.

Needs: "American history is our primary need." Material must fit upcoming theme; write for theme list and deadlines. Childrens/juvenile (8-14 years). "Authentic historical and biographical fiction, adventure, retold legends, etc., relating to the theme." Upcoming themes available for SASE. Published after theme deadline. Length: 800 words maximum. Publishes short shorts. Also publishes poetry.

How to Contact: Query first or query with clips of published work (if new to *Cobblestone*). Include estimated word count. "Include detailed outline explaining the information to be presented in the article and bibliography of material used." Responds in several months. If interested, responds to queries 5 months before publication date. Send SASE (or IRC) for reply or send self-addressed postcard to find out if query was received. Accepts electronic submissions (disk, Microsoft Word or MS-DOS). Sample copy for $4.95, 7½ × 10½ SAE and $2 postage. Guidelines for #10 SAE and 1 first-class stamp or on website.

Payment/Terms: Pays 20-25¢/word. Pays on publication for all rights.

Advice: Writers may send for *Cobblestone*'s free catalog for a listing of subjects covered in back issues.

$ ◎ COUNTRY WOMAN, Reiman Publications, 5400 South 60th St., Greendale WI 53129. (414)423-0100. Website: www.countrywomanmagazine.com (includes articles, photos, recipes from current issue). Editor: Ann Kaiser. **Contact:** Kathleen Anderson, managing editor. Magazine: 8½ × 11; 68 pages; excellent quality paper; excellent cover stock; illustrations and photographs. "Stories should have a rural theme and be of specific interest to women who live on a farm or ranch, or in a small town or country home, and/or are simply interested in country-oriented topics." Bimonthly. Estab. 1971.

Needs: Fiction must be upbeat, heartwarming and focus on a country woman as central character. "Many of our stories and articles are written by our readers! No contemporary, urban pieces that deal with divorce, drugs, etc." Recently published work by Patricia Frederick, Monique Haen and Lorrie Ann Jackson. **Publishes 4-6 new writers/year.** Publishes 1 fiction story/issue. Length: 1,000 words.

How to Contact: Send $2 and SASE for sample copy and writer's guidelines. All manuscripts should be sent to Kathy Pohl, Executive Editor. Responds in 3 months. Include cover letter and SASE. Accepts simultaneous and reprint submissions.

Payment/Terms: Pays $90-125 for fiction. Pays on acceptance for one-time rights.

Advice: "Read the magazine to get to know our audience. Send us country-to-the-core fiction, not yuppie-country stories—our readers know the difference! Very traditional fiction—with a definite beginning, middle and end, some kind of conflict/resolution, etc. We do not want to see contemporary avant-garde fiction—nothing dealing with divorce, drugs, etc., or general societal malaise."

◻ ◎ ▼ CREATIVE KIDS, Prufrock Press, P.O. Box 8813, Waco TX 76714-8813. (254)756-3337. Fax: (254)756-3339. E-mail: creative_kids@prufrock.com. Website: www.prufrock.com (includes catalog, submission guidelines and information about our staff). **Contact:** Libby Lindsey, editor. Magazine: 7 × 10½; 36 pages; illustrations; photos. Material by children for children. Published 4 times/year. Estab. 1980. Circ: 45,000.

• *Creative Kids* featuring work by children has won Ed Press and Parents' Choice Gold and Silver Awards.

Needs: "We publish work by children ages 8-14." Publishes short stories, essays, games, puzzles, poems, opinion pieces and letters. Accepts 3-4 mss/issue; 12-16 mss/year. Publishes ms up to 2 years after acceptance. **Published new writers within the last year.** No novels.

How to Contact: Send complete ms with cover letter; include name, age, birthday, home address, school name and address, grade, statement of originality signed by teacher or parent. Must include SASE for response. Do not query. Responds in 1 month to mss. SASE. Sample copy for $3. Guidelines for SASE.

Payment/Terms: Pays 1 contributor's copy. Acquires all rights.

Advice: "*Creative Kids* is designed to entertain, stimulate and challenge the creativity of children ages 8 to 14, encouraging their abilities and helping them to explore their ideas, opinions and world. Your work reflects you. Make it neat, have it proofread and follow ALL guidelines."

$ ◻ ◎ ▼ CRICKET MAGAZINE, Carus Publishing Company, P.O. Box 300, Peru IL 61354. (815)224-6656. **Contact:** Marianne Carus, editor-in-chief. Magazine: 8 × 10; 64 pages; illustrations; photos. Magazine for children, ages 9-14. Monthly. Estab. 1973. Circ. 75,000.

• *Cricket* has received a Parents Choice Award, and awards from Ed Press. Carus Corporation also publishes *Spider, the Magazine for Children, Ladybug, the Magazine for Young Children, Babybug,* and *Cicada.*

Needs: Adventure, contemporary, ethnic, fantasy, historic fiction, folk and fairytales, humorous, juvenile, mystery, science fiction and translations. No adult articles. All issues have different "mini-themes." Receives approximately 1,100 unsolicited fiction mss each month. Publishes ms 6-24 months or longer after acceptance. Accepts 180 mss/year. Agented fiction 1-2%. **Published new writers within the last year.** Published work by Peter Dickinson, Mary Stolz and Jane Yolen. Length: 500-2,000 words.

How to Contact: Do not query first. Send complete ms with SASE. List previous publications. Responds in 3 months to mss. Sample copy for $5. Guidelines for SASE.

Payment/Terms: Pays up to 25¢/word and 2 contributor's copies; $2 charge for extras. Pays on publication for all rights. Sends edited mss for approval. Buys reprints.

Advice: "Do not write *down* to children. Write about well-researched subjects you are familiar with and interested in, or about something that concerns you deeply. Children *need* fiction and fantasy. Carefully study several issues of *Cricket* before you submit your manuscript." Sponsors contests for readers of all ages.

$ ◨ ◎ CRUSADER MAGAZINE, Calvinist Cadet Corps, Box 7259, Grand Rapids MI 49510-7259. (616)241-5616. Fax: (616)241-5558. Website: www.calvinistcadets.org (includes writers guidelines and themes). **Contact:** G. Richard Broene, editor. Magazine: 8½×11; 24 pages; illustrations; photos. Magazine "for boys (ages 9-14) who are members of the Calvinist Cadet Corps. *Crusader* publishes stories and articles that have to do with the interests and concerns of boys, teaching Christian values subtly." 7 issues/year. Estab. 1958. Circ. 10,000.

Needs: Adventure, comics, juvenile, religious/inspirational, spiritual and sports. No fantasy, science fiction, fashion, horror or erotica. List of upcoming themes available for SASE or on website. Receives 60 unsolicited fiction mss/month. Buys 3 mss/issue; 18 mss/year. Publishes ms 4-11 months after acceptance. Published work by Douglas DeVries and Betty Lou Mell. **Publishes 0-3 new writers/year.** Length: 800-1,500 words; average length: 1,200 words. Publishes short shorts.

How to Contact: Send complete ms and SASE with cover letter including theme of story. Responds in 1-3 months. Accepts simultaneous, multiple and previously published submissions. Sample copy with a 9×12 SAE and 4 first-class stamps. Guidelines for #10 SASE.

Payment/Terms: Pays 4-6¢/word and 1 contributor's copy. Pays on acceptance for one-time rights. Buys reprints.

Advice: "On a cover sheet, list the point your story is trying to make. Our magazine has a theme for each issue, and we try to fit the fiction to the theme. All fiction should be about a young boy's interests—sports, outdoor activities, problems—with an emphasis on a Christian perspective. No simple moralisms. Avoid simplistic answers to complicated problems."

$ ◨ ◎ DISCOVERIES, WordAction Publishing Company, 6401 The Paseo, Kansas City MO 64131-1213. (816)333-7000 ext. 2728. Fax: (816)333-4439. E-mail: khendrixson@nazarene.org. **Contact:** Kathy Hendrixson, editorial assistant. Story paper: 8½×11; 4 pages; illustrations. "Committed to reinforce the Bible concept taught in Sunday School curriculum, for ages 8-10 (grades 3-4)." Weekly.

Needs: Religious stories, puzzles, Bible trivia (miscellaneous areas of interest to children 5-10 years old), 100-200 words. "Avoid fantasy, science fiction, personification of animals and cultural references that are distinctly American. Nothing preachy. No unrealistic dialogue." List of upcoming themes available for SASE. Accepts 1 story, 1 Bible trivia, and 1 puzzle/issue. Publishes ms 1-2 years after acceptance. **Publishes 5-7 new writers/year.** Story length: 500 words.

How to Contact: Send complete ms with cover letter and SASE. Accepts ms by e-mail, fax and disk. Accepts multiple submissions. Send SASE for sample copy and guidelines.

Payment/Terms: Pays 5¢/word. Pays on acceptance or on publication for multiple rights.

Advice: "Stories should vividly portray definite Christian emphasis or character building values, without being preachy."

$ ◨ ◎ DISCOVERY TRAILS, Gospel Publishing House, 1445 N. Boonville Ave., Springfield MO 65802-1894. (417)862-2781. Fax: (417)862-6059. E-mail: discoverytrails@gph.org. Website: www.radiantlife.org. **Contact:** Sinda S. Zinn, editor. Magazine: 8×10; 4 pages; coated offset paper; art illustrations; photos. "A Sunday school take-home paper of articles and fictional stories that apply Christian principles to everyday living for 10- to 12-year-old children." Weekly. Estab. 1954. Circ. 20,000.

Needs: Contemporary, juvenile, religious/inspirational, spiritual, sports. Adventure and mystery stories and serials are welcome. No Biblical fiction, Halloween, Easter "bunny," Santa Claus or science fiction. Accepts 2 mss/issue. **Published new writers within the last year.** Published work by Ellen Javernick, Carolyn Short and Theresa Bubulka. Length: 800-1,000 words. Publishes short shorts.

How to Contact: Send complete ms with SASE. Accepts submissions by e-mail. Responds in 6 weeks. Free sample copy and guidelines with SASE.

Payment/Terms: Pays 7-10¢/word and 3 contributor's copies. Pays on acceptance.

Advice: "Know the age level and direct stories or articles relevant to that age group. Since junior-age children (grades 5 and 6) enjoy action, fiction provides a vehicle for communicating moral/spiritual principles in a dramatic framework. Fiction, if well done, can be a powerful tool for relating Christian principles. It must, however, be realistic and believable in its development. Make your children be children, not overly mature for their age. We would like more serial stories. Write for contemporary children, using setting and background that includes various ethnic groups."

$ ◍ ♟ ESQUIRE, The Magazine for Men, Hearst Corp., 250 W. 55th St., New York NY 10019. (212)649-4020. Fax: (212)977-3158. Website: www.esquire.com. Editor: David Granger. **Contact:** Adrienne Miller, literary editor. Magazine. Monthly. Estab. 1933. Circ. 750,000. General readership is college educated and sophisticated, between ages 30 and 45.

 • *Esquire* is well-respected for its fiction and has received several National Magazine Awards. Work published in *Esquire* has been selected for inclusion in the *Best American Short Stories* and *O. Henry* anthologies.

Needs: No "pornography, science fiction or 'true romance' stories." Publishes special fiction issue in July. Receives over 10,000 unsolicited mss/year. Rarely accepts unsolicited fiction. Recently published work by Russell Banks, Tim O'Brien, Richard Russo and David Means.

How to Contact: Send complete ms with cover letter or submit through an agent. Accepts simultaneous and multiple submissions. Guidelines for SASE.

Payment/Terms: Pays in cash on acceptance, amount undisclosed. Publishes ms an average of 2-6 months after acceptance.

Advice: "Submit one story at a time. We receive over 10,000 stories a year, so worry a little less about publication, a little more about the work itself."

$ ⬛ ◎ EVANGEL, Light & Life Communications, P.O. Box 535002, Indianapolis IN 46253-5002. (317)244-3660. **Contact:** Julie Innes, editor. Sunday school take-home paper for distribution to adults who attend church. Fiction involves people coping with everyday crises, making decisions that show spiritual growth. Magazine: 5½×8½; 8 pages; 2- and 4-color illustrations; color and b&w photos. Weekly. Estab. 1897. Circ. 18,000.

Needs: Religious/inspirational. "No fiction without any semblance of Christian message or where the message clobbers the reader." Receives approximately 300 unsolicited fiction mss/month. Accepts 3-4 mss/issue, 156-200 mss/year. **Publishes 10 new writers/year.** Published work by Karen Leet and Dennis Hensley. Length: 250-1,200 words.

How to Contact: Send complete ms with SASE. Responds in 2 months. Accepts multiple submissions. Sample copy and writer's guidelines with #10 SASE.

Payment/Terms: Pays 4¢/word and 2 contributor's copies. Pays on publication.

Advice: "Choose a contemporary situation or conflict and create a good mix for the characters (not all-good or all-bad heroes and villains). Don't spell out everything in detail; let the reader fill in some blanks in the story. Keep him guessing." Rejects mss because of "unbelievable characters and predictable events in the story."

$ ◎ FACES, People, Places and Cultures, A Cobblestone Publication, Cobblestone Publishing, Co., 30 Grove St., Suite C, Peterborough NH 03458. (603)924-7209. Fax: (603)924-7380. E-mail: faces@cobblestonepub.com. Website: www.cobblestonepub.com. Editor: Elizabeth Crooker. **Contact:** Lou Waryncia, managing editor. Magazine. "*Faces* is a magazine about people and places in the world for 8 to 14-year-olds." Estab. 1984. Circ. 15,000. Monthly, except June, July and August.

● Cobblestone also publishes *Cobblestone* and *Calliope*, listed in this section.

Needs: All material must relate to theme; send for theme list. Children's/juvenile (8-14 years), "retold legends, folk tales, stories from around the world, etc., relating to the theme." Length: 800 words preferred. Publishes short shorts.

How to Contact: Query first or query with clips of published work. Themes posted on website. Send query 6-9 months prior to theme issue publication date. Include estimated word count and bio (2-3 lines). Responds 4 months before publication date. Send SASE for reply. Sample copy for $4.95, 7½×10½ SAE and $2 postage. Guidelines for SASE.

Payment/Terms: Pays 20-25¢/word. Pays on publication for all rights.

Advice: "Study past issues of the magazine to become familiar with our style and content. Writers with anthropological and/or travel experience are particularly encouraged; *Faces* is about world culture."

Ⓝ $ ⬛ THE GEM, Churches of God, General Conference, Box 926, Findlay OH 45839. (419)424-1961. E-mail: communications@cggc.org. Website: www.cggc.org. **Contact:** Rachel Foreman, editor. Magazine: 6×9; 8 pages; 50 lb. uncoated paper; illustrations (clip art). "True-to-life stories of healed relationships and growing maturity in the Christian faith for senior high students through senior citizens who attend Churches of God, General Conference Sunday Schools." Weekly. Estab. 1865. Circ. 7,000.

Needs: Adventure, humor, mainstream, religious/inspirational, senior citizen/retirement. Nothing that denies or ridicules standard Christian values. "No science fiction or Y2K stories." Prefers personal testimony or nonfiction short stories. Receives 45 unsolicited fiction mss/month. Accepts 1 ms every 2-3 issues; 20-25 mss/year. Publishes ms 4-12 months after submission. Length: 500-1,700 words; average length: 1,500 words.

How to Contact: Send complete ms with cover letter ("letter not essential, unless there is information about author's background which enhances story's credibility or verifies details as being authentic"). Responds in 6 months. SASE. Accepts simultaneous and reprint submissions. Sample copy and guidelines for #10 SASE. "If more than one sample copy is desired along with the guidelines, will need 2 oz. postage."

Payment/Terms: Pays $10-15 and contributor's copies on publication for one-time rights. Charge for extras (postage for mailing more than one).

Advice: "There is not shortcut. The key to writing well is to read everything you can and then to write and write and write."

$ ⬛ GOLF JOURNAL, United States Golf Assoc., Golf House, P.O. Box 708, Far Hills NJ 07931-0708. (908)470-5016. Fax: (908)781-1112. E-mail: golfjournal@usga.org. Website: www.usga.org (includes excerpts from publication). Editor: Brett Avery. **Contact:** Catherine Wolf, managing editor. Magazine: 48-56 pages; self cover stock; illustrations; photos. "The magazine's subject is golf—its history, lore, rules, equipment and general information. The focus is on amateur golf and those things applying to the millions of American golfers. Our audience is generally professional, highly literate and knowledgeable; they read *Golf Journal* because of an interest in the game, its traditions, and its noncommercial aspects." Published 9 times/year. Estab. 1948. Circ. 750,000.

Needs: Poignant or humorous essays and short stories. "Golf jokes will not be used." Accepts 6 mss/year. Recently published work by Don Marquis and J.G. Nursall. Length: 500-2,000 words.

How to Contact: Send complete ms with SASE. Responds in 2 months to mss. Sample copy for SASE.

Payment/Terms: Pays $500-1,500 and 5 contributor's copies. Pays on acceptance.

Advice: "Know your subject (golf); familiarize yourself first with the publication." Rejects mss because "fiction usually does not often serve the function of *Golf Journal*, which, as the official magazine of the United States Golf Association, deals chiefly with the history, lore and rules of golf."

$ ⊘ GOOD HOUSEKEEPING, 959 Eighth Ave., New York NY 10019.
● Because of the heavy volume of fiction submissions, *Good Housekeeping* is not accepting unsolicited submissions at this time.

$ ⦿ GRIT, American Life & Traditions, Ogden Publications, Inc., 1503 S.W. 42nd St., Topeka KS 66609-1265. (785)274-4300. Fax: (785)274-4305. E-mail: grit@cjnetworks.com. Website: www.grit.com (includes cover story from current issue plus titles of other features and book and products store). Note on envelope: Attn: Fiction Department. Tabloid: 50 pages; 30 lb. newsprint; illustrations; photos. "*Grit* is a 'good news' publication and has been since 1882. Fiction should be 1,200 words or more and wholesome, inspiring, perhaps compelling in nature. Audience is *conservative*; readers tend to be 40+ from smaller towns, rural people who love to read." Biweekly. Estab. 1882. Circ. 200,000.
● *Grit* is considered one of the leading family-oriented publications.
Needs: Adventure, nostalgia, condensed novelette, mainstream/contemporary (conservative), mystery/suspense, light religious/inspirational, romance (contemporary, historical), science fiction, westerns (frontier, traditional). "No sex, violence, drugs, obscene words, abuse, alcohol, or negative diatribes." Send SASE for editorial calendar. "Special Storytellers issue; 5-6 manuscripts needed; submit in June." Buys 1 mss/issue; 30 mss/year. **Publishes 20-25 new writers/year.** Recently published work by John Floyd, Dede Hammond, Genevieve White and Don White. Length: 1,200 words minimum; 4,000-6,000 words maximum for serials; average length: 1,500 words. Also publishes poetry.
How To Contact: Send complete ms with cover letter. Include estimated word count, brief bio, Social Security number, list of publications with submission. Send SASE for return of ms. No simultaneous submissions. Sample copy for $4 postage/appropriate SASE. No e-mail or fax submissions. Accepts fax submissions.
Payment/Terms: Purchases first North American serial or one-time rights.

$ ⦿ HARPER'S MAGAZINE, 666 Broadway, 11th Floor, New York NY 10012. (212)420-5720. Website: www.harpers.org (includes submission guidelines). **Editor:** Lewis H. Lapham. Magazine: 8×10¾; 80 pages; illustrations. Magazine for well-educated, widely read and socially concerned readers, college-aged and older, those active in political and community affairs. Monthly. Circ. 218,000.
Needs: Contemporary and humor. Stories on contemporary life and its problems. Receives 600 unsolicited fiction mss/year. Accepts 12 mss/year. Published work by David Guterson, David Foster Wallace, Johnathan Franzen, Steven Millhauser, Lisa Roney, Rick Moody and Steven Dixon. **Published new writers within the last year.** First published David Foster Wallace. Length: 3,000-5,000 words.
How to Contact: Query to managing editor, or through agent. Responds in 6 weeks to queries.
Payment/Terms: Pays $1,000-2,000. Pays on acceptance for rights, which vary on each author materials and length. Sends galleys to author.

$ HEMISPHERES, The Magazine of United Airlines, Pace Communications, 1301 Carolina St., Greensboro NC 27401. (336)378-6065. Website: www.hemispheresmagazine.com (includes mastheads, archived travel articles, information about Faux Faulkner and Imitation Hemingway contests). **Contact:** Lisa Fann, fiction editor and Shelby Bateman, senior editor. Magazine: 8×10; 190 pages; 45 lb. paper; 120 lb. West Vaco cover; illustrations; photos. "*Hemispheres* is an inflight magazine that interprets 'inflight' to be a mode of delivery rather than an editorial genre. As such, Hemispheres' task is to engage, intrigue and entertain its primary readers—an international, culturally diverse group of affluent, educated professionals and executives who frequently travel for business and pleasure on United Airlines. The magazine offers a global perspective and a focus on topics that cross borders as often as the people reading the magazine. That places our emphasis on ideas, concepts, and culture rather than products. We present that perspective in a fresh, artful and sophisticated graphic environment." Monthly. Estab. 1992. Circ. 500,000.
● The editors at *Hemispheres* are hoping to increase the amount of fiction they publish in 2003.
Needs: Ethnic/multicultural, historical, humor/satire, literary, mainstream, mystery/suspense, regional. Receives 30-40 unsolicited ms/month. Publishes 4 mss/year. Publishes ms 4-6 months after acceptance. **Publishes 1 new writer/year.** Published work by Ray Bradbury, Caroline Koeppel, Robert Olen Butler, Frederick Waterman. Length: 1,000-3,500 words.
How to Contact: Send complete ms with cover letter. Include estimated word count, brief bio and list of publications. Responds in 2 months to queries and mss. Send disposable copy of ms and SASE for reply. Accepts multiple submissions. Sample copy for $7.50. Guidelines for SASE.

READ 'THE BUSINESS OF FICTION WRITING' section for information on manuscript preparation, mailing tips, rights and more.

Payment/Terms: Varies by author. Pays by the word and in contributor's copies; additional copies $7.50. Buys first world rights. Sometimes sends galleys to author. Sponsors the Faux Faulkner and Imitation Hemingway competitions. Details on website.

Advice: "In our information-saturated, hyperlinked age, fiction is often viewed as a bit superfluous. It doesn't solve whatever problem we have this second, and so is often relegated to a position of entertainment—something enjoyable to be fit in around the more important aspects of life. But good fiction has much longer lasting value—it should entertain, certainly, but it should also cause us to reconsider, to look at things from another perspective, to mull over what's really important. It should encourage us to explore with new eyes the mysteries of life."

N $ ◯ HIGH ADVENTURE/HIGH ADVENTURE LEADER, Assemblies of God—Royal Rangers, 1445 N. Boonville Ave., Springfield MO 65802-1894. (417)862-2781. Fax: (417)831-8230. E-mail: rangers@ag.org. Website: www.royalrangers.ag.org. **Contact:** Rev. Jerry Parks, editor. Magazine: 8 × 10¾; 16-32 pages; 50 lb. gloss paper; illustrations; photos. "*High Adventure/High Adventure Leader* is a ministry publication to boys age 5-17 and to adult leaders over age 18, and is designed to encourage readers in their faith and guide them in their spiritual growth. Fictional accounts and nonfiction articles are used to minister to our readers." Quarterly. Estab. 1971. Circ. 125,000.

Needs: Children's/juvenile (adventure, historical, sports, ages 5-17), historical (general), religious (children's religious), young adult/teen (adventure, historical, sports), camping. List of upcoming themes available for SASE. Receives 50-60 unsolicited mss/month. Accepts 8-10 mss/issue; 32-40 mss/year. Publishes ms 3-6 months after acceptance. **Publishes 10-20 new writers/year.** Length: 300-900 words; average length: 500 words. Publishes short shorts. Comments on rejected mss "by request."

How to Contact: Send complete ms with a cover letter. Accepts submissions by e-mail, fax and disk. Include brief bio and list of publications. Responds in 1 month to queries; 3 months to mss. Send a disposable copy of ms and #10 SASE for reply only. Accepts simultaneous, previously published and multiple submissions. Sample copy free. Guidelines for SASE, by e-mail or fax.

Payment/Terms: Pays $.06/word and 3 contributors copies. Pays on publication for one-time and electronic rights.

Advice: "Stories must capture the interest of boys age 5-17 with a positive and encouraging message."

$ ◯ ◎ ▼ HIGHLIGHTS FOR CHILDREN, 803 Church St., Honesdale PA 18431-1895. (570)253-1080. Fax: (570)251-7847. E-mail: eds@highlights-corp.com. Website: www.highlights.com (includes editorial guidelines, contact information and excerpts). Editor: Christine French Clark. **Contact:** Marileta Robinson, senior editor. Magazine: 8½ × 11; 42 pages; uncoated paper; coated cover stock; illustrations; photos. "This book of wholesome fun is dedicated to helping children grow in basic skills and knowledge, in creativeness, in ability to think and reason, in sensitivity to others, in high ideals, and worthy ways of living—for children are the world's most important people. We publish stories for beginning and advanced readers. Up to 400 words for beginners (ages 3-7), up to 800 words for advanced (ages 8-12)." Monthly. Circ. 2.5 million.

● *Highlights* has won the Paul A. Witty Short Story Award from the International Reading Association, Parent's Choice Award, Parent's Guide to Children's Media Award, Awards for Editorial Excellence from the Association of Educational Publishers.

Needs: Juvenile (ages 2-12); adventure, animal, contemporary, fantasy, folktales, history, humorous, multicultural, problem-solving, sports. Unusual stories appealing to both girls and boys; stories with good characterization, strong emotional appeal, vivid, full of action. "Need stories that begin with action rather than description, have strong plot, believable setting, suspense from start to finish." Length: 400-800 words for older readers; 100-400 for younger readers. "No war, crime or violence." Receives 600-800 unsolicited fiction mss/month. Accepts 6-7 mss/issue. Also publishes rebus (picture) stories of 120 words or under for the 3- to 7-year-old child. **Publishes 30 new writers/year.** Recently published work by Eileen Spinelli, Toby Speed, Marilyn Kratz and Ruskin Bond. Comments on rejected mss occasionally, "especially when editors see possibilities in story."

How to Contact: Send complete ms with SASE and include a rough word count and cover letter "with any previous acceptances by our magazine; any other published work anywhere." Accepts multiple submissions. Responds in 2 months. Guidelines with SASE.

Payment/Terms: Pays $100 and up. Pays on acceptance for all rights. Sends galleys to author.

Advice: "We accept a story on its merit whether written by an unpublished or an experienced writer. Mss are rejected because of poor writing, lack of plot, trite or worn-out plot, or poor characterization. Children *like* stories and learn about life from stories. Children learn to become lifelong fiction readers by enjoying stories. Feel passion for your subject. Create vivid images. Write a child-centered story; leave adults in the background."

$ ◯ ◎ ▼ ALFRED HITCHCOCK'S MYSTERY MAGAZINE, Dell Magazines, 475 Park Ave. S., New York NY 10016. (212)686-7188. Website: www.themysteryplace.com (includes guidelines, stories, subscription forms and logic puzzles). **Contact:** Linda Landrigan, editor. Mystery fiction magazine: 5¼ × 8⅜; 144 pages; 28 lb. newsprint paper; 60 lb. machine-/coated cover stock; illustrations; photos. Published 11 times/year, including 1 double issue. Estab. 1956.

● Stories published in *Alfred Hitchcock's Mystery Magazine* have won Edgar Awards for "Best Mystery Story of the Year," Shamus Awards for "Best Private Eye Story of the Year" and Robert L. Fish Awards for "Best First Mystery Short Story of the Year."

Needs: Mystery and detection (amateur sleuth, private eye, police procedural, suspense, etc.). No sensationalism. Number of mss/issue varies with length of mss. Length: up to 14,000 words. Recently published work by Joyce Carol Oates, Jeremiah Healy, Kathy Lynn Emerson and Jan Burke.
How to Contact: Send complete ms and SASE. Responds in 2-3 months. Guidelines for SASE. Sample issue for $5.
Payment/Terms: Pays 8¢/word. Pays on publication.

$ ⊘ ◎ ⛊ HOPSCOTCH: THE MAGAZINE FOR GIRLS, The Bluffton News Publishing & Printing Co., P.O. Box 164, Bluffton OH 45817-0164. (419)358-4610. Fax: (419)358-5027. Website: www.hopscotchmagazine.com (includes samples of articles and order info). **Contact:** Marilyn Edwards, editor. Magazine: 7×9; 50 pages; enamel paper; pen & ink illustrations; photos. Publishes stories for and about girls ages 5-13. "We are trying to produce a wholesome magazine for girls 5-13, encouraging childhood. We publish stories, articles, poetry, word games, etc. of a wholesome nature. We celebrate and encourage innocent and traditional childhood interests, believing young girls need to experience a nurturing childhood rather than being thrust into an early young adulthood." Bimonthly. Estab. 1989. Circ. 9,000.

● *Hopscotch* is indexed in the *Children's Magazine Guide* and *EdPress* and has received a Parents' Choice Gold Medal Award and EdPress Awards.

Needs: Children's/juvenile (5-9, 10-13 years): adventure, ethnic/multicultural, historical (general), sports. "No fantasy, science fiction, romance, monsters, parent-child dilemmas. We would like to see more stories that rhyme and stories that have a subtle moral." Upcoming themes: Zoo Animals; Hats; Women of Courage; Ballet; That's Entertainment; Weather; Astronomy; Water Creatures; It's a Mystery. "All writers should consult the theme list before sending in articles." Current theme list available for SASE. Receives 300-400 unsolicited mss/month. Accepts 20-40 mss/year. Agented fiction 2%. Published work by Lois Grambling, Betty Killion, John Thomas Waite, Kelly Musselman, Marilyn Helmer and Joyce Styron Madsen. Length: 300-750 words; 500-750 words preferred. Publishes short shorts. Length: 250-400 words. Also publishes poetry, puzzles, hidden pictures and crafts. Always comments on rejected mss.
How to Contact: Send complete ms with cover letter. Include estimated word count, 1-page bio, Social Security number and list of publications. Responds in 1 month to queries; 10 weeks to mss. Send SASE for reply, return of ms or send disposable copy of the ms. Accepts simultaneous, multiple and reprint submissions. Sample copy for $4 and 9×12 SASE. Themes and guidelines for #10 SASE. Reviews novels and short story collections.
Payment/Terms: Pays 5¢/word (extra for usable photos or illustrations) and 1 contributor's copy; additional copies $4; $2.50 for 10 or more. Pays before publication for first North American serial rights.
Advice: "Make sure you have studied copies of our magazine to see what we like. Follow our theme list. We are looking for wholesome stories. This is what our publication is all about."

$ ⊘ ◎ HORIZONS, The Magazine of Presbyterian Women, 100 Witherspoon St., Louisville KY 40202-1396. (502)569-5688. Fax: (502)569-8085. E-mail: sdunne@ctr.pcusa.org. Website: www.pcusa.org/horizons/ (includes writer's guidelines, themes and deadlines, excerpts and staff contacts). **Contact:** Sharon Dunne, assistant editor. Magazine: 8×11; 40 pages; illustrations; photos. Magazine owned and operated by Presbyterian Women offering "information and inspiration for Presbyterian women by addressing current issues facing the church and the world." Bimonthly. Estab. 1988. Circ. 21,000.
Needs: Ethnic/multicultural, feminist, historical, humor/satire, literary, mainstream/contemporary, religious/inspirational, senior citizen/retirement, translations. "No sex/violence or romance." List of upcoming themes available for SASE. Receives 50 unsolicited mss/month. Accepts 1 ms/issue. Publishes ms 4 months after acceptance. **Publishes 10 new writers/year.** Published work by Charlotte Johnstone. Length: 800-1,200 words. Publishes short shorts. Length: 500 words. Also publishes literary essays, fiction and poetry. Sometimes comments on rejected mss.
How to Contact: Send complete ms with cover letter. Include estimated word count and Social Security number. Responds in 2 weeks to queries; 3 weeks to mss. SASE or send a disposable copy of ms. Accepts mss by e-mail, fax and disk. Accepts simultaneous and multiple submissions. Sample copy for 9×12 SAE. Guidelines for #10 SASE. Reviews novels and short story collections. Send books to Sharon Dunne.
Payment/Terms: Pays $50/page and 2 contributor's copies on publication for all rights; additional copies for $2.50.
Advice: "We are most interested in stories or articles that focus on current issues—family life, the mission of the church, and the challenges of culture and society—from the perspective of women committed to Christ."

$ ⊘ HUMPTY DUMPTY'S MAGAZINE, Children's Better Health Institute, Box 567, 1100 Waterway Blvd., Indianapolis IN 46206. (317)636-8881. Fax: (317)684-8094. Website: www.humptydumptymag.org. **Contact:** Nancy S. Axelrad, editor. Magazine: 7⅜×10⅛; 36 pages; 35 lb. paper; coated cover; illustrations; some photos. Children's magazine "seeking to encourage children, ages 4-6, in healthy lifestyle habits, especially good nutrition and fitness." Publishes 8 issues/year.

● *Humpty Dumpty's Magazine* is not currently considering new fiction. The Children's Better Health Institute also publishes *Children's Digest, Children's Playmate, Jack and Jill* and *Turtle,* some of which are listed in this section.

Needs: Juvenile health-related material. "No inanimate talking objects, animal stories and science fiction." Wants more "health and fitness stories with a positive slant." Rhyming stories should flow easily with no contrived rhymes. Receives 100-200 unsolicited mss/month. Accepts 2-3 mss/issue. **Publishes 1-2 unpublished writers/year.** Recently published work by Marilyn Kratz, Joyce LaMer and Jill Peplinski. Length: 300 words maximum.

How to Contact: Send complete ms with SASE. No queries. Responds in 3 months. Sample copy for $1.75. Editorial guidelines for SASE. Accepts multiple submissions.

Payment/Terms: Pays up to 22¢/word for stories plus 10 contributor's copies. Pays on publication for all rights. (One-time book rights returned when requested for specific publication.)

Advice: "In contemporary stories, characters should be up-to-date, with realistic dialogue. We're looking for health-related stories with unusual twists or surprise endings. We want to avoid stories and poems that 'preach.' We try to present the health material in a positive way, utilizing a light humorous approach wherever possible." Most rejected mss "are too wordy or not age appropriate."

N **$** **⬚** **◎** **INDIA CURRENTS, The Complete Indian American Magazine**, Box 21285, San Jose CA 95151. (408)274-6966. Fax: (408)274-2733. **Contact:** Vandana Kumar, managing editor. E-mail: editor@indiacurrents.com. Magazine: 8½×11; 104 pages; newsprint paper; illustrations; photos. "The arts and culture of India as seen in America for Indians and non-Indians with a common interest in India." Monthly. Estab. 1987. Circ. 25,000.

Needs: All Indian content: contemporary, ethnic, feminist, historical (general), humor/satire, literary, mainstream, regional, religious/inspirational, romance, translations (from Indian languages). "We seek material with insight into Indian culture, American culture and the crossing from one to another." Receives 12 unsolicited mss/month. Accepts 1 ms/issue; 12 mss/year. Publishes ms 2-6 months after acceptance. **Published new writers within the last year.** Published work by Chitra Divakaruni, Jyotsna Sreenivasan and Rajini Srikanth. Length: 2,000 words.

How to Contact: Send complete ms with cover letter and clips of published work. Responds in 3 months to mss. SASE. Accepts simultaneous and reprint submissions. Accepts electronic submissions. Sample copy for $3.

Payment/Terms: Pays $50/1,000 words. Pays on publication for one-time rights (print and website).

Advice: "Story must be related to India and subcontinent in some meaningful way. The best stories are those which document some deep transformation as a result of an Indian experience, or those which show the humanity of Indians."

⬚ **◎** **▼** **INDIAN LIFE**, Indian Life Ministries, P.O. Box 3765, RPO, Redwood Post Office, Winnipeg, Manitoba R2W 3R6 Canada. (204)661-9333 or (800)665-9275 in Canada only. Fax: (204)661-3982. E-mail: jim.editor@indianlife.org. Website: www.indianlife.org. **Contact:** Jim Uttley, editor. Newspaper: 11×17 Tabloid; 24 pages; newsprint paper and cover stock; illustrations; full cover; photos. A nondenominational Christian newspaper written and read mostly by Native Americans. Bimonthly. Estab. 1979. Circ. 32,000.

• *Indian Life* has won several awards for "Higher Goals in Christian Journalism" and "Excellence" from the Evangelical Press Association. The newspaper also won awards from the Native American Press Association.

Needs: Contemporary stories of Native Americans in everyday life. Ethnic (Indian), historical (general), juvenile, religious/inspirational, young adult/teen, native testimonies, Bible teaching articles. No erotic or stories of Native American spirituality. **Publishes 4 new writers/year.** Recently published work by Crying Wind and Dorene Meyer. Length: 1,000-1,200 words average.

How to Contact: Query letter preferred. Accepts submissions by e-mail, fax and disk. Accepts simultaneous submissions. Responds in 1 month to queries. Sample copy and guidelines for $2.50 and 8½×11 SAE.

Advice: "Keep it simple with an Indian viewpoint at about a ninth grade reading level."

A **▼** **LADIES' HOME JOURNAL**, Published by Meredith Corporation, 125 Park Ave., 20th Floor, New York NY 10017. (212)557-6600. Editor-in-Chief: Diane Salvatore. **Contact:** Shana Aborn, books/fiction editor. Magazine: 190 pages; 34-38 lb. coated paper; 65 lb. coated cover; illustrations; photos.

• *Ladies' Home Journal* has won several awards for journalism.

Needs: Book mss and short stories, *accepted only through an agent*. Return of unsolicited material cannot be guaranteed. Published work by Fay Weldon, Anita Shreve, Jane Shapiro and Anne Rivers Siddons. Length: approximately 2,000-2,500 words.

How to Contact: Send complete ms with cover letter (credits). Accepts simultaneous submissions. Publishes ms 4-12 months after acceptance.

Payment/Terms: Acquires First North American rights.

Advice: "Our readers like stories, especially those that have emotional impact. Stories about relationships between people—husband/wife—mother/son—seem to be subjects that can be explored effectively in short stories. Our readers' mail and surveys attest to this fact: Readers enjoy our fiction and are most keenly tuned to stories dealing with children. Fiction today is stronger than ever. Beginners can be optimistic; if they have talent, I do believe that talent will be discovered. It is best to read the magazine before submitting."

$ **⬚** **◎** **▼** **LADYBUG**, Cricket Magazine Group, P.O. Box 300, Peru IL 61354. (815)224-6656. **Contact:** Marianne Carus, editor-in-chief. Editor: Paula Morrow. Magazine: 8×10; 36 pages plus 4-page pullout section; illustrations. "*Ladybug* publishes original stories and poems by the world's best children's authors. For young children, ages 2-6." Monthly. Estab. 1990. Circ. 125,000.

• *Ladybug* has received the Parents Choice Award; the Golden Lamp Honor Award and the Golden Lamp Award from Ed Press, and Magazine Merit awards from the Society of Children's Book Writers and Illustrators.

Needs: Fantasy (children's), folk tales, humor, juvenile, picture stories, preschool, read-out-loud stories and realistic fiction. Length: 300-750 words preferred.

How to Contact: Send complete ms with cover letter. Include word count on ms (do not count title). Responds in 3 months. SASE. Accepts reprints. Guidelines for #10 SASE or on website. Sample copy for $5. For guidelines *and* sample send 9×12 SAE (no stamps required) and $5.

Payment/Terms: Pays 25¢/word (less for reprints). Pays on publication for all rights or second serial (reprint) rights. For recurring features, pays flat fee and copyright becomes property of Cricket Magazine Group.

Advice: Looks for "well-written stories for preschoolers: age-appropriate, not condescending. We look for rich, evocative language and sense of joy or wonder."

$ ◻ ◎ ⛉ LIGUORIAN, "A Leading Catholic Magazine," Liguori Publications, 1 Liguori Dr., Liguori MO 63057-9999. (800)464-2555. Fax: (800)325-9526. E-mail: aweinert@liguori.org. Website: www.ligourian.org (includes condensed articles from present issue, writer's guidelines and subscription information). **Contact:** Fr. Allan Weinert, CSSR, editor-in-chief. Magazine: 5 × 8½; 64 pages; b&w illustrations; photos. "*Liguorian* is a general interest magazine firmly committed to orthodox Catholic Christianity. Our effort is to inform and inspire, making spirituality accessible to our readers and assisting them in those matters most important to them—their families, their work, their own personal growth—as they live out their life in an ever-changing world." Publishes 10 issues/year. Estab. 1913. Circ. 230,000.

• *Liguorian* received Catholic Press Association awards for 2001 including Third Place: Best Short Story ("Spinoza's Socks," by Mary Beth Leymaster).

Needs: Religious/inspirational, young adult and senior citizen/retirement (with moral Christian thrust), spiritual. "Stories submitted to *Liguorian* must have as their goal the lifting up of the reader to a higher Christian view of values and goals. We are not interested in contemporary works that lack purpose or are of questionable moral value." Receives approximately 25 unsolicited fiction mss/month. Accepts 12 mss/year. **Publishes 8-10 new writers/year.** Published work by Darlene Takarsh, Mary Beth Teymaster and Maeve Mullen Ellis. Length: 1,500-2,000 words preferred. Also publishes short shorts. Occasionally comments on rejected mss "if we feel the author is capable of giving us something we need even though this story did not suit us."

How to Contact: Send complete ms with SASE. Accepts disk submissions compatible with IBM, using a WordPerfect 5.1 program; prefers hard copy with disk submission. Accepts submissions by e-mail and fax. Responds in 3 months to mss. Sample copy and guidelines for #10 SASE.

Payment/Terms: Pays 10-12¢/word and 5 contributor's copies. Pays on acceptance for all rights. Offers 50% kill fee for assigned mss not published.

Advice: "First read several issues containing short stories. We look for originality and creative input in each story we read. Since most editors must wade through mounds of manuscripts each month, consideration for the editor requires that the market be studied, the manuscript be carefully presented and polished before submitting. Our publication uses only one story a month. Compare this with the 25 or more we receive over the transom each month. Also, many fiction mss are written without a specific goal or thrust, i.e., an interesting incident that goes nowhere is *not a story*. We believe fiction is a highly effective mode for transmitting the Christian message and also provides a good balance in an unusually heavy issue."

🅽 ◎ LILITH MAGAZINE, The Independent Jewish Women's Magazine, 250 W. 57th St., Suite 2432, New York NY 10107. (212)757-0818. E-mail: lilithmag@aol.com. Editor: Susan Weidman Schneider. **Contact:** Yona Zeldis McDonough, fiction editor. Magazine: 48 pages; 80 lb. cover; b&w illustrations; b&w and color photos. Publishes work relating to Jewish feminism, for Jewish feminists, feminists and Jewish households. Quarterly. Estab. 1976. Circ. 25,000.

Needs: Ethnic, feminist, lesbian, literary, prose poem, religious/inspirational, spiritual, translation, young adult. "Nothing that does not in any way relate to Jews, women or Jewish women." Receives 15 unsolicited mss/month. Accepts 1 ms/issue; 4 mss/year. Publishes ms up to 1 year after acceptance. Published work by Lesléa Newman, Marge Piercy and Gloria Goldreich. Publishes short shorts.

How to Contact: Send complete ms with cover letter, which should include a 2-line bio. Responds in 2 months to queries; 6 months to mss. SASE. Accepts simultaneous and reprint submissions but must be indicated in cover letter. Sample copy for $6. Writer's guidelines for #10 SASE. Reviews novels and short story collections. Send books to Susan Weidman Schneider.

Payment/Terms: Varies. Acquires first rights.

Advice: "Read the magazine to be familiar with the kinds of material we publish."

🅽 $ ◻ LISTEN, Celebrating Positive Choices, Review & Herald Publishing Association, 55 W. Oak Ridge Dr., Hagerstown MD 21740. (301)393-4010. Fax: (301)393-4055. E-mail: ajacobs@rhpa.org. Website: www.listenmagazine.org. **Contact:** Anita Jacobs, editor. Magazine: 32 pages; glossy paper; illustrations; photos. "*Listen* publishes fiction about giving teens choices about real-life situations and moral issues in a secular way." Monthly (September-May). Circ. 40,000.

Needs: Young adult/teen (easy-to-read, sports), anti-drug, alcohol, tobacco, positive role models. Upcoming themes: Tobacco (May), deadline December 2002. Length: 1,000-1,200 words; average length: 1,200 words.

How to Contact: Send complete ms with a cover letter. Query first. Accepts submissions by e-mail, fax and disk. Include Social Security Number and address. Responds in 6 weeks. Send SASE. Accepts simultaneous, previously published and multiple submissions. Sample copy for $2; 2 stamps 9 × 12 envelope. Guidelines for SASE, by e-mail, fax or on website.

Payment/Terms: Pays $50-250 and 3 contributors copies; additional copies $2. Pays on acceptance for first rights.

$ ◻ ◎ LIVE, Assemblies of God, 1445 N. Boonville, Springfield MO 65802-1894. (417)831-8000. Fax: (417)862-6059. E-mail: rl-live@gph.org. Website: www.radiantlife.org (includes writer's guidelines, names of editors, short fiction and non-fiction and devotionals). **Contact:** Paul W. Smith, editor. "A take-home story paper distributed weekly in young adult/adult Sunday school classes. *Live* is a story paper primarily. Stories in both fiction and narrative style are welcome. Poems, first-person anecdotes and humor are used as fillers. The purpose of *Live* is to present in short story form realistic characters who utilize biblical principles. We hope to challenge readers to take risks for God and to resolve their problems scripturally." Weekly. Circ. 90,000.

Needs: Religious/inspirational prose, poem and spiritual. "Inner city, ethnic, racial settings." No controversial stories about such subjects as feminism, war or capital punishment. Accepts 2 mss/issue. **Publishes 75-100 new writers/year.** Recently published work by Carrie Darlington, Chris Williams, Melodie Wright and Dorothy B. Kidney. Length: 500-1,700 words.

How to Contact: Send complete ms. Accepts disk submissions. Accepts queries and submissions by e-mail and fax. Social Security number and word count must be included. Accepts simultaneous submissions. Responds in 6 weeks. Sample copy and guidelines for SASE.

Payment/Terms: Pays 10¢/word (first rights); 7¢/word (second rights). Pays on acceptance.

Advice: "Study our publication and write good, inspirational stories that will encourage people to become all they can be as Christians. Stories should go somewhere! Action, not just thought—life; interaction, not just insights. Heroes and heroines, suspense and conflict. Avoid simplistic, pietistic conclusions, preachy, critical or moralizing. We don't accept science or Bible fiction. Stories should be encouraging, challenging, humorous. Even problem-centered stories should be upbeat." Reserves the right to change titles, abbreviate length and clarify flashbacks for publication.

LIVING LIGHT NEWS, Living Light Ministries, #200, 5306-89 St., Edmonton, Alberta T6E 5P9 Canada. (780)468-6397. Fax: (780)468-6872. E-mail: shine@livinglightnews.org. Website: www.livinglightnews.org (includes sample articles from current issues, archives of past articles, writer's guidelines and mission statement). **Contact:** Jeff Caporale. Newspaper: 11×17; 40 pages; newsprint; electrobrite cover; illustrations; photos. "Our publication is an evangelical Christian newspaper sharing the good news of Jesus Christ in a fresh and contemporary way for non-Christians. We only publish Christmas-related fiction in our special Christmas issue." Bimonthly. Estab. 1995. Circ. 28,000. Member, Evangelical Press Association.

Needs: Religious (inspirational), Christmas fiction focusing on the true meaning of Christmas, humorous Christmas pieces. Christmas deadline is November 1st. Receives 3-4 unsolicited mss/month. Accepts 5 mss/year. Published 2-6 months after acceptance. **Publishes 2-6 new writers/year.** Length: 400-1,200 words; average length: 700 words. Publishes short shorts. Average length: 700 words. Always comments on rejected mss.

How to Contact: Send complete ms with cover letter. Accepts mss by e-mail and disk. Include estimated word count, brief bio and list of publications with submissions. Responds in 1 month to queries; 2 months to mss. Send SASE (or IRC) in Canadian postage for return of ms or disposable copy of ms and #10 SASE for reply only. Accepts simultaneous, multiple and previously published submissions. Sample copy free with SASE (9×13; $2.50 in Canadian postage). Guidelines for SASE, e-mail or on website.

Payment/Terms: Pays 8¢ (US)/word and 2 contributor's copies; additional copies: $2.50. Pays on publication for first, first North American serial, one-time, electronic, second and reprint rights.

Advice: "We are looking for lively, humorous, inviting or heart-warming Christmas-related fiction that focuses on the non-materialistic side of Christmas or shares God's love and grace with others. Try to write with pizzazz. We get many bland submissions. Do not be afraid to use humor and have fun."

LONDON REVIEW OF BOOKS, 28 Little Russell St., London WC1A 2HN England. Phone: (020)7209 1101. Fax: (020)7209 1102. E-mail: edit@lrb.co.uk. Website: www.lrb.co.uk (includes excerpts, some archived articles). **Contact:** Mary Kay Wilmers, editor. "The London Review of Books is dedicated to carrying on the tradition of the English essay. We publish 2-3 pieces of fiction each year." Circ. 38,000.

Needs: Literary. Recently published work by James Wood and Alan Bennett.

How to Contact: Accepts mss by e-mail, fax and disk.

Payment/Terms: Pays variable rate and 6 contributor's copies.

Advice: "We look for quality."

MAGAZINE OF FANTASY & SCIENCE FICTION, Spilogale, Inc., P.O. Box 3447, Hoboken NJ 07030. Phone/fax: (201)876-2551. E-mail: sandsf@aol.com. Website: www.sfsmag.com or www.sfsite.com/fsf (includes writer's guidelines, letter column, subscription information, nonfiction features, current issue, information on back issues and links). **Contact:** Gordon Van Gelder, editor. Magazine: illustrations on cover only. Publishes science fiction and fantasy. "We publish speculative fiction of all sorts—fantasy, horror, science fiction, or anything inbetween. Our readers are age 13 and up." Monthly. Estab. 1949. Circ. 50,000.

● The *Magazine of Fantasy and Science Fiction* won a 2001 Hugo Award for "Different Kinds of Darkness" by David Langford and a 2000 World Fantasy Award for Gordon Van Gelder for "Special Award-Professional."

Needs: Adventure, fantasy (space fantasy, sword and sorcery), horror (dark fantasy, futuristic, psychological, supernatural), science fiction (hard science/technological, soft/sociological), young adult/teen (fantasy/science fiction, horror). "We're always looking for more science fiction." Receives 500-700 unsolicited fiction submissions/month. Buys 5-8 fiction mss/issue ("on average"); 75-100 mss/year. **Publishes 2-8 new writers/year.** Published work by Ray Bradbury, Ursula K. Le Guin, Joyce Carol Oates and Robert Sheckley. Length: 25,000 words maximum; average length: 7,000 words. Publishes short shorts. Comments on rejected ms, "if quality warrants it." Sometimes recommends other markets.

How to Contact: Send complete ms with cover letter. Responds in 2 months. SASE (or IRC). Accepts previously published submissions (but please indicate where it was published). Sample copy for $5. Guidelines for SASE, by e-mail or on website.

Payment/Terms: Pays 5-8¢/word; additional copies $2.10. Pays on acceptance for first North American serial rights; foreign, option on anthology if requested.

Advice: "A well-prepared manuscript stands out better than one with fancy doo-dads. Fiction that stands out tends to have well-developed characters and thinks through the implications of its fantasy elements. It has been said 100 times before, but read an issue of the magazine before submitting. In the wake of the recent films, we are seeing more fantasy stories about sorcerers than we can possibly publish."

$ 🖊 **MATURE LIVING,** Lifeway Christian Resources of the Southern Baptist Convention, MSN 175, 1 Lifeway Plaza North, Nashville TN 37234-0175. (615)251-2485. Fax: (615)277-8272. **Contact:** David Seay, editor-in-chief. Magazine: 8½×11; 52 pages; non-glare paper; slick cover stock; full color illustrations; photos. "Our magazine is Christian in content and the material required is what would appeal to 55 and over age group: inspirational, informational, nostalgic, humorous. Our magazine is distributed mainly through churches (especially Southern Baptist churches) that buy the magazine in bulk and distribute it to members in this age group." Monthly. Estab. 1977. Circ. 330,000.

Needs: Humor, religious/inspirational and senior citizen/retirement. Avoid all types of pornography, drugs, liquor, horror, science fiction and stories demeaning to the elderly. Receives 10 mss/month. Buys 1-2 mss/issue. Publishes ms an average of 1 year after acceptance. Length: 800-1,200 words; prefers 1,000.

How to Contact: Send complete ms with SASE. "No queries please." Include estimated word count and Social Security number. Responds in 2 months. Guidelines for SASE.

Payment/Terms: Pays $75 on acceptance; 3 contributor's copies. Acquires all rights or will consider first rights.

Advice: Mss are rejected because they are too long or subject matter unsuitable. "Our readers seem to enjoy an occasional short piece of fiction. It must be believable, however, and present senior adults in a favorable light."

$ 🖊 ◎ **MATURE YEARS,** United Methodist Publishing House, 201 Eighth Ave. S., Nashville TN 37202. (615)749-6292. Fax: (615)749-6512. E-mail: matureyears@umpublishing.org. **Contact:** Marvin W. Cropsey, editor. Magazine: 8½×11; 112 pages; illustrations; photos. Magazine "helps persons in and nearing retirement to appropriate the resources of the Christian faith as they seek to face the problems and opportunities related to aging." Quarterly. Estab. 1953.

Needs: Humor, intergenerational relationships, nostalgia, older adult issues, religious/inspirational, spiritual (for older adults). "We don't want anything poking fun at old age, saccharine stories or anything not for older adults. Must show older adults (age 55 plus) in a positive manner." Accepts 1 ms/issue, 4 mss/year. Publishes ms 1 year after acceptance. Published work by Ann S. Gray, Betty Z. Walker and Vickie Elaine Legg. **Published new writers within the last year.** Length: 1,000-1,800 words.

How to Contact: Send complete ms with SASE and Social Security number. Accepts mss by e-mail (preferred). No simultaneous submissions. Responds in 2 months. Sample copy for 10½×11 SAE and $5.

Payment/Terms: Pays 6¢/word. Pays on acceptance.

Advice: "Practice writing dialogue! Listen to people talk; take notes; master dialogue writing! Not easy, but well worth it! Most inquiry letters are far too long. If you can't sell me an idea in a brief paragraph, you're not going to sell the reader on reading your finished article or story."

🍁 **$** 🖊 **MESSENGER OF THE SACRED HEART,** Apostleship of Prayer, 661 Greenwood Ave., Toronto, Ontario M4J 4B3 Canada. (416)466-1195. **Contact:** Rev. F.J. Power, S.J. and Alfred DeManche, editors. Magazine: 7×10; 32 pages; coated paper; self-cover; illustrations; photos. Magazine for "Canadian and U.S. Catholics interested in developing a life of prayer and spirituality; stresses the great value of our ordinary actions and lives." Monthly. Estab. 1891. Circ. 14,000.

Needs: Religious/inspirational. Stories about people, adventure, heroism, humor, drama. No poetry. Accepts 1 ms/issue. Length: 750-1,500 words. Recommends other markets.

How to Contact: Send complete ms with SAE. Rarely buys reprints. Responds in 1 month. Sample copy for $1.50 (Canadian).

Payment/Terms: Pays 6¢/word and 3 contributor's copies. Pays on acceptance for first North American serial rights.

Advice: "Develop a story that sustains interest to the end. Do not preach, but use plot and characters to convey the message or theme. Aim to move the heart as well as the mind. If you can, add a light touch or a sense of humor to the story. Your ending should have impact, leaving a moral or faith message for the reader."

$ 🖊 ◎ **MONTANA SENIOR NEWS,** Barrett-Whitman Co., Box 3363, Great Falls MT 59403. (406)761-0305. Fax: (406)761-8358. E-mail: montsrnews@imt.net. **Contact:** Jack Love, editor. Tabloid: 11×17; 60-80 pages; newsprint paper and cover; illustrations; photos. Publishes "everything of interest to seniors, except most day-to-day political items like Social Security and topics covered in the daily news. Personal profiles of seniors, their lives, times and reminiscences." Bimonthly. Estab. 1984. Circ. 30,000.

Needs: Historical, senior citizen/retirement, western (historical or contemporary). No fiction "unrelated to experiences to which seniors can relate." Buys 1 or fewer mss/issue; 4-5 mss/year. Length: 500-800 words preferred. Publishes short shorts. Length: 500-800 words.

How to Contact: Send complete ms with cover letter and phone number. Only responds to selected mss. Accepts simultaneous and reprint submissions. Accepts queries by e-mail. Sample copy for 9×12 SAE and $3 postage and handling.

Payment/Terms: Pays 5¢/word. Pays on publication for first rights or one-time rights.

N $ ☑ MY FRIEND, The Catholic Magazine for Kids, Pauline Books & Media, 50 St. Paul's Ave., Boston MA 02130. (617)522-8911. E-mail: myfriend@pauline.org. **Contact:** Sister Kathryn James Hermes, editor. Magazine: 8½×11; 32 pages; smooth, glossy paper and cover stock; illustrations; photos. Magazine of "religious truths and positive values for children in a format which is enjoyable and attractive. Each issue contains lives of saints, short stories, science corner, contests, projects, etc." Monthly during school year (September-June). Estab. 1979. Circ. 11,000.

Needs: Juvenile, religious/inspirational, spiritual (children), sports (children). Receives 60 unsolicited fiction mss/month. Accepts 3-4 mss/issue; 30-40 mss/year. Published work by Diana Jenkins and Sandra Humphrey. Recently published new writers within the past year. Length: 600-1,200 words; average length: 850 words.

How to Contact: Send complete ms with SASE. Responds in 2 months to mss. "Manuscripts are often put on long-term hold for a specific issue. They can be requested back at any time during this hold period. Notification of acceptance or nonacceptance about 6 months before the issue the manuscript is being held for." Publishes ms an average of 1 year after acceptance. Sample copy for $2 and 9×12 SAE ($1.24 postage). Guidelines and upcoming themes for SASE.

Payment/Terms: Pays $70-150 (stories, articles). Pays on acceptance.

Advice: "We are particularly interested in fun and amusing stories with backbone. Good dialogue, realistic character development, current lingo are necessary. We have a need for each of these types at different times. We prefer child-centered stories in a real-world setting."

$ ☺ NA'AMAT WOMAN, Magazine of NA'AMAT USA, The Women's Labor Zionist Organization of America, 350 Fifth Ave., Suite 4700, New York NY 10118-3903. (212)563-5222. **Contact:** Judith A. Sokoloff, editor. "Magazine covering a wide variety of subjects of interest to the Jewish community—including political and social issues, arts, profiles; many articles about Israel; and women's issues. Fiction must have a Jewish theme. Readers are the American Jewish community." Published 4 times/year. Estab. 1926. Circ. 20,000.

Needs: Contemporary, ethnic, literary. Receives 10 unsolicited fiction mss/month. Accepts 3-5 fiction mss/year. Length: 1,500-3,000 words. Also buys nonfiction.

How to Contact: Query first or send complete ms with SASE. Responds in 3 months to mss. Free sample copy for 9×11½ SAE and $1.20 postage.

Payment/Terms: Pays 10¢/word and 2 contributor's copies. Pays on publication for first North American serial rights; assignments on work-for-hire basis.

Advice: "No maudlin nostalgia or romance; no hackneyed Jewish humor and no poetry."

🌐 $ ☺ NEW IMPACT, AnSer House of Marlow UK, Courtyard Offices, 140 Oxford Rd., Marlow, Buckinghamshire SL7 2NT England. (44)01628 481581. Fax: (44)01628 475570. E-mail: info@anserhouse.co.uk. Website: www.anserhouse.co.uk (a leading forum for diversity issues from a minority perspective). **Contact:** Zulf Ali. Magazine: 60 pages; photos. "*AnSer House of Marlow UK* is the leading establishment in the United Kingdom for encouraging and developing good diversity practice. It publicly enhances diversity as opposed to the pejorative 'equal opportunity' because it assumes everyone is equal as a base. Our main mission is to raise the profile, value and achievements of visible culturally diverse communities in the UK; to advance the cause and practice of true diversity in British society; to encourage those with influence to value personal difference, and to work in partnership with the White majority to increase cultural understanding and mutual respect." Bimonthly. Estab. 1993. Circ. 10,000.

Needs: Ethnic/multicultural, fantasy. "No romance, mono-cultural, horror, science fiction or religious." Receives 15-30 unsolicited mss/month. Accepts 1 ms/issue; 6 mss/year. Publishes ms 4 months after acceptance. **Publishes 3 new writers/year.** Recently published work by Jesse Quinones, R.A. Bolden and Jeannete Dean. Length: 1,200-1,600 words; average length: 1,400 words. Publishes short shorts. Average length: 1,400 words. Also publishes poetry.

How to Contact: Send complete ms with a cover letter. Accepts submissions by e-mail. Include brief bio. Responds in 1 month to mss. Send SASE. Accepts simultaneous and multiple submissions. Sample copy free with SASE (A4 and $5 postage). Guidelines for SASE.

Payment/Terms: Pays $40-60 "only after second submission is published." Pays on publication for first rights.

Advice: "We select short stories according to individual appeal. Keep submissions between 1,200 and 1,400 words; possibly reflect personal or life experience; be appealing to diverse audience; not relating to romance, religious or horror themes."

$ ☺ ☺ NEW MYSTERY, The Best New Mystery Stories, 101 W. 23rd St., PH-1, New York NY 10011-7703. (212)353-1582. E-mail: editorial@newmystery.com. Website: www.NewMystery.com (includes book and film reviews, short shorts and investigative journalism). **Contact:** editor. Magazine: 8½×11; 96 pages; illustrations; photos. "Mystery, suspense and crime." Quarterly. Estab. 1990. Circ. 90,000.

Needs: Mystery/suspense (cozy to hardboiled). "No horror or romance." Wants more suspense and espionage. Plans special annual anthology. Receives 350 unsolicited mss/month. Buys 6-10 ms/issue. Agented fiction 50%. **Publishes 1 new writer/issue.** Published work by Stuart Kaminsky and Andrew Greeley. Length: 3,000-5,000 words preferred. Also buys short book reviews 500-3,000 words. Sometimes comments on rejected mss.

How to Contact: *New Mystery charges a $7 fee for purchase of a contributor's packet, which includes guidelines and 2 sample copies.* Send complete ms with cover letter. "We cannot be responsible for unsolicited manuscripts." Responds in 1 month to ms. SASE. Sample copy for $5, 9×12 SAE and 4 first-class stamps.
Payment/Terms: Pays $25-1,000. Pays on publication for negotiated rights.
Advice: Stories should have "believable characters in trouble; sympathetic lead; visual language." Sponsors "Annual First Story Contest."

$  **THE NEW YORKER,** The New Yorker, Inc., 4 Times Square, New York NY 10036. **Contact:** Fiction Department. A quality magazine of interesting, well-written stories, articles, essays and poems for a literate audience. Weekly. Estab. 1925. Circ. 750,000.
How to Contact: Send complete ms with SASE. Responds in 3 months to mss. Publishes 1 ms/issue.
Payment/Terms: Varies. Pays on acceptance.
Advice: "Be lively, original, not overly literary. Write what you want to write, not what you think the editor would like. Send poetry to Poetry Department."

$ **ON THE LINE,** Mennonite Publishing House, 616 Walnut Ave., Scottdale PA 15683-1999. (724)887-8500. Website: www.mph.org (includes guidelines and general information). **Editor:** Mary Clemens Meyer. Magazine: 7×10; 28 pages; illustrations; some photos. "A Christian magazine with the goal of helping children grow in their understanding and appreciation of God, the created world, themselves and other people." For children ages 9-14. Weekly. Estab. 1970. Circ. 5,500.
Needs: Problem-solving stories with Christian values for older children and young teens (9-14 years). No fantasy or fictionalized Bible stories. Wants more mystery and humorous. Receives 50-100 unsolicited mss/month. Accepts 52 mss/year. Recently published work by Judy Stoner, Karen L. Rempel-Arthur, Sandra Smith and Danielle Hammelef. **Publishes 10-20 new writers/year.** Length: 800-1,500 words.
How to Contact: Send complete ms noting whether author is offering first-time or reprint rights. Responds in 1 month. SASE. Accepts simultaneous and previously published work. Free sample copy and guidelines.
Payment/Terms: Pays on acceptance for one-time rights.
Advice: "We believe in the power of story to entertain, inspire and challenge the reader to new growth. Know children and their thoughts, feelings and interests. Be realistic with characters and events in the fiction. Stories do not need to be true, but need to *feel* true. We look for easy readibility, realistic kids and grownups, humor, fun characters and plot movement without excessive description. Watch kids, interact with kids, listen to kids. It will show up in your writing."

$ **OPTIONS, The *Bi*-Monthly,** AJA Publishing, Box 170, Irvington NY 10533. (914)591-2011. E-mail: dianaed@bellsouth.net. Website: www.youngandtight.com/men (includes short fiction). **Contact:** Diana Sheridan, associate editor. Magazine: digest-sized; 114 pages; newsprint paper; glossy cover stock; illustrations; photos. Sexually explicit magazine for and about bisexuals. "Please read our Advice subhead." 10 issues/year. Estab. 1982. Circ. 100,000.
Needs: Erotica, bisexual, gay, lesbian. "First person as-if-true experiences." Accepts 8 unsolicited fiction mss/issue. "Very little" of fiction is agented. **Published new writers within the last year.** Length: 2,000-3,000 words. Sometimes comments on rejected mss.
How to Contact: "We prefer you send submissions via e-mail as an attachment. We can read most major word processing programs for MAC or PC, and e-mail submissions get fastest answer. If unable to send via e-mail, send complete ms by snail mail with disk enclosed if at all possible. Cover letter okay but not needed. Responds usually within 24 hours to e-mail submissions, 3 weeks to snail mail. Enclose SASE for all snail mail submissions—if manuscript is disposable enclose business-size SASE for reply only." Sample copy for $2.95 and 6×9 SAE with 5 first-class stamps. Guidelines for SASE.
Payment/Terms: Pays $100 for mss that arrive in readable electronic format; $80 for hardcopy only mss. Pays on publication for all rights. Will reassign book rights on request.
Advice: "Read a copy of *Options* carefully and look at our spec sheet before writing anything for us. That's not new advice, but to judge from some of what we get in the mail, it's necessary to repeat. We only buy two bi/lesbian pieces per issue; need is greater for bi/gay male mss. Though we're a bi rather than gay magazine, the emphasis is on same-sex relationships. If the readers want to read about a male/female couple, they'll buy another magazine. Gay male stories sent to *Options* will also be considered for publication in *Beau,* or one of our other gay male magazines. Must get into the hot action by 1,000 words into the story. (Sooner is fine too!) *Most important:* We *only* publish male/male stories that feature 'safe sex' practices unless the story is clearly something that took place pre-AIDS."

N $ **PAKN TREGER, Culture, History, Art, Life,** National Yiddish Book Center, 1021 West St., Amherst MA 01002. (413)256-4900. Fax: (413)256-4700. E-mail: yiddish@bikher.org. Website: www.yiddishbookcenter.org. **Contact:** Nancy Sherman, editor. Magazine: 52 pages; illustrations; photos. "*Pakn Treger* is a journal of contemporary Jewish culture with emphasis on literature and Yiddish culture." Triannual. Estab. 1983. Circ. 22,000.

● **A BULLET INTRODUCES COMMENTS** by the editor of *Novel & Short Story Writer's Market* indicating special information about the listing.

Needs: Ethnic/multicultural (specific culture: Jewish), Jewish culture, Yiddish literature. "No sentimental or nostalgic styles; no fables, myths or allegories." Receives 20 unsolicited mss/month. Accepts 1 ms/issue; 3 mss/year. Publishes ms 3 months after acceptance. **Publishes 1 new writer/year.** Recently published work by Rachel Kadish, Curt Leviant and Jonathan Rosen. Length: 2,000-6,000 words; average length: 4,000 words. Publishes short shorts. Average length: 2,000 words. Also publishes literary essays and literary criticism.

How to Contact: Send complete ms with a cover letter. "No phone calls." Include estimated word count, brief bio and list of publications. Responds in 1 month to queries; 3 months to mss. Send SASE for return of ms. Accepts simultaneous submissions. Sample copy for $6. Guidelines by e-mail or on website.

Payment/Terms: Pays $400-1,200 and 2-4 contributors copies; additional copies $6. Pays on publication for all rights. Sends galleys to author. Not copyrighted.

Advice: "We look for quality of writing, originality of ideas, thoughtful consideration of Jewish issues."

N ⊕ $ ◑ PEOPLE'S FRIEND, D.C. Thomson & Co., Ltd., 80 Kingsway East, Dundee DD4 8SL Scotland. 01382 223131. Fax: 01382 452491. **Contact:** Fiction Editor. Weekly. Estab. 1869. Circ. 400,000.

Needs: Specializes in women's fiction. Would like to see more young romances. "British backgrounds preferred (but not essential) by our readership. Quite simply, we aim to entertain. Stories should have believable, well-developed characters in situations our readers can relate to. Our readers tend to be traditionalists." No stories of the supernatural, or extreme sex or violence. Published work by Betty McInnes, Shirley Worral and Christina Jones. "We actively encourage new authors and do our best to help and advise." Publishes 5 stories/issue. Length: 1,000-3,000 words.

How to Contact: Accepts multiple submissions. Sample copy and guidelines available on application.

Payment/Terms: Pays $75-85 and contributor's copies.

Advice: Looks for manuscript with "emotional content and characterization. It must make enjoyable reading; it mustn't shock."

N ⚘ ◑ THE PEOPLE'S MAGAZINE, The Peoples Church, 374 Sheppard Ave. E., Willowdale, Ontario L4G 6M1 Canada. (416)222-3341, ext. 142. Fax: (905)727-6228. **Contact:** Dr. Timothy Starr. Magazine: 8×11; 24 pages; 28 lb. paper; illustrations; photos. "*The People's Magazine* has a family emphasis." Quarterly. Estab. 1930.

Needs: Children's/juvenile (adventure), family saga, religious (children's religious, general religious, inspirational). Receives several unsolicited mss/month. Accepts 2 mss/year. Publishes ms 3-6 months after acceptance. Agented fiction 15%. **Publishes several new writers/year.** Length: 350-500 words; average length: 500 words. Publishes short shorts. Sometimes comments on rejected mss.

How to Contact: Query with clips of published work. Accepts submissions by e-mail, fax and disk. Include estimated word count, brief bio and list of publications. Responds in 2 weeks to queries. Send a disposable copy of ms and #10 SASE for reply only. Accepts simultaneous, previously published and multiple submissions. Guidelines by e-mail or fax.

Payment/Terms: Sends galleys to author. Not copyrighted.

Advice: "Submit but exercise patience if not accepted."

$ ◑ PLAYBOY MAGAZINE, 680 N. Lake Shore Dr., Chicago IL 60611. (312)751-8000. **Contact:** Fiction Editor. Monthly magazine. "As the world's largest general-interest lifestyle magazine for men, *Playboy* spans the spectrum of contemporary men's passions. From hard-hitting investigative journalism to light-hearted humor, the latest in fashion and personal technology to the cutting edge of the popular culture, *Playboy* is and always has been both guidebook and dream book for generations of American men . . . the definitive source of information and ideas for over 10 million readers each month. In addition, *Playboy*'s 'Interview' and '20 Questions' present profiles of politicians, athletes and today's hottest personalities." Estab. 1953, Circ. 3,283,000.

How to Contact: Query first. "Fiction manuscripts must be no longer than 7,500 words for acceptance." Send SASE for guidelines.

Advice: "*Playboy* does not consider poetry, plays, story outlines or novel-length manuscripts."

$ ◑ ◎ ⛊ POCKETS, Devotional Magazine for Children, The Upper Room, 1908 Grand Ave., Box 340004, Nashville TN 37203-0004. (615)340-7333. Fax: (615)340-7267. E-mail: pockets@upperroom.org. Website: www.upperroom.org/pockets (includes themes, guidelines and contest guidelines). Editor: Janet R. Knight. **Contact:** Lynn W. Gilliam, associate editor. Assistant Editor: Amy Bremers. Editorial Assistant: Patricia P. McIntyre. Magazine: 7×11; 48 pages; color and 2-color illustrations; some photos. Magazine for children ages 6-11. "The magazine offers stories, activities, prayers, poems—geared to giving children a better understanding of themselves as children of God. The magazine's fiction tends to feature children dealing with real-life situations from a faith perspective." Published monthly except for January. Estab. 1981. Estimated circ. 99,000.

• *Pockets* has received honors from the Educational Press Association of America.

Needs: Adventure, contemporary, ethnic, historical (general), juvenile, religious/inspirational. No fantasy, science fiction, talking animals. "All submissions should address the broad theme of the magazine. Each issue is built around one theme with material which can be used by children in a variety of ways. Scripture stories, fiction, poetry, prayers, art, graphics, puzzles and activities are included. Submissions do not need to be overtly religious. They should help children experience a Christian lifestyle that is not always a neatly-wrapped moral package, but is open to the continuing revelation of God's will. Seasonal material, both secular and liturgical, is desired. No violence, horror, sexual and racial stereotyping or fiction containing heavy moralizing. No dying grandparents (or those with Alzheimer's). Grandparents of today are a vibrant group." Receives approximately 200 unsolicited fiction mss/month. Accepts 4-5 mss/issue; 44-60 mss/year. **Publishes 15 new writers/year.** Length: 600-1,400 words; average length: 1,200 words.

How to Contact: Send complete ms with SASE. Accepts previously published submissions. Accepts multiple submissions. Responds in 6 weeks. Publishes ms 1 year to 18 months after acceptance. Sample copy free with SASE (4 first-class stamps). Send SASE with request for guidelines and themes. "Strongly advise sending for themes or checking website before submitting."

Payment/Terms: Pays 14¢/word and 2-5 contributor's copies. Pays on acceptance for first North American serial rights.

Advice: "Listen to children as they talk with each other. Send for a sample copy, guidelines and themes before submitting. Many manuscripts we receive are simply inappropriate. Each issue is theme-related. Please send for list of themes. New themes published in December of each year. Include SASE." Sponsors annual fiction writing contest. Send for guidelines or check website. $1,000 award and publication.

◖ PORTLAND MAGAZINE, Maine's City Magazine,, 578 Congress St., Portland ME 04101. (207)775-4339. Fax: (207)775-2334. E-mail: editor@portlandmonthly.com. Website: www.portlandmagazine.com. **Contact:** Colin Sargent, editor. Magazine: 56 pages; 60 lb. paper; 100 lb. cover stock; illustrations; photos. "City lifestyle magazine—fiction style, business, real estate, controversy, fashion, cuisine, interviews and art relating to the Maine area." Monthly. Estab. 1986. Circ. 100,000.

Needs: Contemporary, historical, literary. Receives 20 unsolicited fiction mss/month. Accepts 1 mss/issue; 10 mss/year. Publishes short shorts. **Publishes 50 new writers/year.** Recently published work by C.D.B Bryan and Sebastian Junger. Length: 3 double-spaced typed pages.

How to Contact: Query first. "Fiction below 700 words, please." Send complete ms with cover letter. Responds in 6 months. SASE. Accepts submissions by e-mail.

Payment/Terms: Pays on publication for first North American serial rights.

Advice: "We publish ambitious short fiction featuring everyone from Frederick Barthelme to newly discovered fiction by Edna St. Vincent Millay."

$ ◖ PURPOSE, Mennonite Publishing House, 616 Walnut Ave., Scottdale PA 15683-1999. (724)887-8500. Fax: (724)887-3111. E-mail: horsch@mph.org. Website: www.mph.org (includes information about products, editors' names, writer's guidelines). **Contact:** James E. Horsch, editor. Magazine: 5⅜×8⅜; 8 pages; illustrations; photos. "Magazine focuses on Christian discipleship—how to be a faithful Christian in the midst of everyday life situations. Uses personal story form to present models and examples to encourage Christians in living a life of faithful discipleship." Weekly. Estab. 1968. Circ. 11,500.

Needs: Historical, religious/inspirational. No militaristic/narrow patriotism or racism. Receives 100 unsolicited mss/month. Accepts 3 mss/issue; 140 mss/year. **Publishes 15-25 new writers/year.** Recently published work by Eleanor Behman, Robert W. Browne, Joyce G. Bradslaw, Mary Guckian and Nancy Tester. Length: 750 words maximum; average length: 500 words. Occasionally comments on rejected mss.

How to Contact: Send complete ms only. Responds in 2 months. Accepts simultaneous and multiple submissions as well as previously published work. Sample copy for 6×9 SAE and 2 first-class stamps. Guidelines free with sample copy only.

Payment/Terms: Pays up to 5¢/word for stories and 2 contributor's copies. Pays on acceptance for one-time rights.

Advice: Many stories are "situational—how to respond to dilemmas. Looking for first-person storylines. Write crisp, action moving, personal style, focused upon an individual, a group of people, or an organization. The story form is an excellent literary device to use in exploring discipleship issues. There are many issues to explore. Each writer brings a unique solution. The first two paragraphs are crucial in establishing the mood/issue to be resolved in the story. Work hard on developing these."

$ ◖ ◎ ▼ ELLERY QUEEN'S MYSTERY MAGAZINE, Dell Magazines, 475 Park Ave. S., New York NY 10016. (212)686-7188. Fax: (212)686-7414. E-mail: elleryqueen@dellmagazines.com. Website: www.themysteryplace. com (includes writer's guidelines, short fiction, book reviews and magazine's history and awards). **Contact:** Janet Hutchings, editor. Magazine: 5⅜×8½; 144 pages with special 240-page combined September/October issue. "*Ellery Queen's Mystery Magazine* welcomes submissions from both new and established writers. We publish every kind of mystery short story: the psychological suspense tale, the deductive puzzle, the private eye case—the gamut of crime and detection from the realistic (including the policeman's lot and stories of police procedure) to the more imaginative (including "locked rooms" and "impossible crimes"). *EQMM* has been in continuous publication since 1941. From the beginning three general criteria have been employed in evaluating submissions: We look for strong writing, an original and exciting plot, and professional craftsmanship. We encourage writers whose work meets these general criteria to read an issue of *EQMM* before making a submission." Magazine for lovers of mystery fiction. Published 11 times/year. Estab. 1941. Circ. 300,000.

● *Ellery Queen's Mystery Magazine* ranked on *Writer's Digest's* "Top 30" list of best markets for fiction writers. *EQMM* has won numerous awards and sponsors its own award for best stories of the year, nominated by its readership.

Needs: "We accept only mystery, crime, suspense and detective fiction." No explicit sex or violence. Wants more classical whodunits. Receives approximately 200 unsolicited fiction mss each month. Accepts 10-15 mss/issue. Publishes ms 6-12 months after acceptance. Agented fiction 50%. **Publishes 10 new writers/year.** Recently published work by Jeffery Deaver, Joyce Carol Oates and Ruth Rendell. Length: 2,500-10,000 words. Publishes minute mysteries of 250 words; novellas of 20,000 words from established authors. Critiques rejected mss "only when a story might be a possibility for us if revised." Sometimes recommends other markets.

How to Contact: Send complete ms with SASE. Cover letter should include publishing credits and brief biographical sketch. Accepts simultaneous and multiple submissions. Responds in 3 months to mss. Guidelines with SASE. Sample copy for $5.

Payment/Terms: Pays 5¢/word and up. Pays on acceptance for first North American serial rights. Occasionally buys reprints.

Advice: "We have a Department of First Stories and usually publish at least one first story an issue, i.e., the author's first published fiction. We select stories that are fresh and of the kind our readers have expressed a liking for. In writing a detective story, you must play fair with the reader, providing clues and necessary information. Otherwise you have a better chance of publishing if you avoid writing to formula."

$⊘✠ RANGER RICK MAGAZINE, National Wildlife Federation, 8925 Leesburg Pike, Vienna VA 22184. (703)790-4000. Editor: Gerald Bishop. **Contact:** Deborah Churchman, fiction editor. Magazine: 8×10; 40 pages; glossy paper; 60 lb. cover stock; illustrations; photos. "*Ranger Rick* emphasizes conservation and the enjoyment of nature through full-color photos and art, fiction and nonfiction articles, games and puzzles, and special columns. Our audience ranges in ages from 7-12, with the greatest number in the 7 and up. We aim for a fourth grade reading level. They read for fun and information." Monthly. Estab. 1967. Circ. 650,000.

• *Ranger Rick* has won several Ed Press awards. The editors say the magazine has had a backlog of stories recently, yet they would like to see more *good* mystery and science fiction stories (with nature themes).

Needs: Adventure, fantasy, humor, mystery (amateur sleuth), science fiction and sports. "Interesting stories for kids focusing directly on nature or related subjects. Fiction that carries a conservation message is always needed, as are adventure stories involving kids with nature or the outdoors. Moralistic 'lessons' taught children by parents or teachers are not accepted. Human qualities are attributed to animals only in our regular feature, 'Adventures of Ranger Rick.' " Receives about 150-200 unsolicited fiction mss each month. Accepts about 6 mss/year. Published fiction by Leslie Dendy. Length: 900 words maximum. Comments on rejected mss "when there is time."

How to Contact: Query with sample lead and any clips of published work with SASE. May consider simultaneous submissions. Very rarely buys reprints. Responds in 3 months to queries and mss. Publishes ms 8 months to 1 year after acceptance, but sometimes longer. Sample copy for $2. Guidelines for legal-sized SASE.

Payment/Terms: Pays $600 maximum/full-length ms. Pays on acceptance for all rights. Sends galleys to author.

Advice: "For our magazine, the writer needs to understand kids and that aspect of nature he or she is writing about—a difficult combination! Manuscripts are rejected because they are contrived and/or condescending—often overwritten. Some manuscripts are anthropomorphic, others are above our readers' level. We find that fiction stories help children understand the natural world and the environmental problems it faces. Beginning writers have a chance equal to that of established authors *provided* the quality is there. Would love to see more science fiction and fantasy, as well as mysteries."

⊘ REDBOOK, The Hearst Corporation, 224 W. 57th St., New York NY 10019. (212)649-2000. **Contact:** Fiction Editor. Magazine: 8×10¾; 150-250 pages; 34 lb. paper; 70 lb. cover; illustrations; photos. "*Redbook's* readership consists of American women, ages 25-44. Most are well-educated, married, have children and also work outside the home." Monthly. Estab. 1903. Circ. 3,200,000.

Needs: Query. *Redbook* was not accepting unsolicited mss at the time of publication.

$⊘✠ ST. ANTHONY MESSENGER, 28 W. Liberty St., Cincinnati OH 45202. (513)241-5615. Fax: (513)241-0399. E-mail: stanthony@americancatholic.org. Website: www.AmericanCatholic.org (includes Saint of the day, selected articles, product information). **Contact:** Father Pat McCloskey, O.F.M., editor. Magazine: 8×10¾; 60 pages; illustrations; photos. "*St. Anthony Messenger* is a Catholic family magazine which aims to help its readers lead more fully human and Christian lives. We publish articles which report on a changing church and world, opinion pieces written from the perspective of Christian faith and values, personality profiles, and fiction which entertains and informs." Monthly. Estab. 1893. Circ. 340,000.

• This is a leading Catholic magazine, but has won awards for both religious and secular journalism and writing from the Catholic Press Association, the International Association of Business Communicators, the Society of Professional Journalists and the Cincinnati Editors Association.

Needs: Contemporary, religious/inspirational, senior citizen/retirement and spiritual. "We do not want mawkishly sentimental or preachy fiction. Stories are most often rejected for poor plotting and characterization; bad dialogue—listen to how people talk; inadequate motivation. Many stories say nothing, are 'happenings' rather than stories." No fetal journals, no rewritten Bible stories. Receives 60-70 unsolicited fiction mss/month. Accepts 1 ms/issue; 12 mss/year. Publishes ms up to 1 year after acceptance. **Publishes 3 new writers/year.** Recently published work by Geraldine Marshall Gutfreund, John Salustri, Beth Dotson, Miriam Pollikatsikis and Joseph Pici. Length: 2,000-3,000 words. Comments on rejected mss "when there is time." Sometimes recommends other markets.

How to Contact: Send complete ms with SASE. Queries should usually come by regular mail, but will also accept them by e-mail and fax. Responds in 2 months. Sample copy and guidelines available. Reviews novels and short story collections. Send books to Barbara Beckwith, book review editor.

Payment/Terms: Pays 16¢/word maximum and 2 contributor's copies; $1 charge for extras. Pays on acceptance for first serial rights.

Advice: "We publish one story a month and we get up to 1,000 a year. Too many offer simplistic 'solutions' or answers. Pay attention to endings. Easy, simplistic, deus ex machina endings don't work. People have to feel characters in the stories are real and have a reason to care about them and what happens to them. Fiction entertains but can also convey a point and sound values."

$ 🖉 ◎ SEEK®, Standard Publishing, 8121 Hamilton Ave., Cincinnati OH 45231-2396. (513)931-4050. Fax: (513)931-4050. E-mail: ewilmoth@standardpub.com. Website: www.standardpub.com. **Contact:** Eileen H. Wilmoth, senior editor. Magazine: 5½×8½; 8 pages; newsprint paper; art and photos in each issue. "Inspirational stories of faith-in-action for Christian young adults; a Sunday School take-home paper." Weekly. Estab. 1970. Circ. 40,000.

Needs: Religious/inspirational. Accepts 150 mss/year. Publishes ms an average of 1 year after acceptance. **Publishes 20-30 new writers/year.** Length: 500-1,200 words.

How to Contact: Send complete ms with SASE. Accepts queries by mail, fax or e-mail. Accepts multiple submissions. Buys reprints. Responds in 3 months. Free sample copy and guidelines.

Payment/Terms: Pays 5¢/word on acceptance.

Advice: "Write a credible story with Christian slant—no preachments; avoid overworked themes such as joy in suffering, generation gaps, etc. Most manuscripts are rejected by us because of irrelevant topic or message, unrealistic story, or poor character and/or plot development. We use fiction stories that are believable."

$ 🖉 SEVENTEEN, Primedia Consumer Magazines, 1440 Broadway, New York NY 10018. Website: www.seventeen.com. **Contact:** Fiction Editor. Magazine: 8½×11; 125-400 pages; 40 lb. coated paper; 80 lb. coated cover stock; illustrations; photos. A general interest magazine with fashion; beauty care; pertinent topics such as current issues, attitudes, experiences and concerns of teenagers. Monthly. Estab. 1944. Circ. 2.5 million.

Needs: High-quality literary fiction. No science fiction, action/adventure or pornography. Receives 200 unsolicited fiction mss/month. Accepts 6-9 mss/year. Agented fiction 50%. **Publishes 3 new writers/year.** Recently published work by Thisbe Nissen, Meg Cabot, David Schickler and Alice Sebold. Length: approximately 750-3,000 words.

How to Contact: Send complete ms with SASE and cover letter with relevant credits. Responds in 3 months to mss. Guidelines for submissions with SASE.

Payment/Terms: Pays $500-2,500 on acceptance for one-time rights.

Advice: "Respect the intelligence and sophistication of teenagers. *Seventeen* remains open to the surprise of new voices. Our commitment to publishing the work of new writers remains strong; we continue to read every submission we receive. We believe that good fiction can move the reader toward thoughtful examination of her own life as well as the lives of others—providing her ultimately with a fuller appreciation of what it means to be human. While stories that focus on female teenage experience continue to be of interest, the less obvious possibilities are equally welcome. We encourage writers to submit literary short stories concerning subjects that may not be immediately identifiable as 'teenage,' with narrative styles that are experimental and challenging. Too often, unsolicited submissions possess voices and themes condescending and unsophisticated. Also, writers hesitate to send stories to *Seventeen* that they think too risqué or sophisticated. Good writing holds the imaginable and then some, and if it doesn't find its home here, we're always grateful for the introduction to a writer's work. We're more inclined to publish cutting edge fiction than simple, young adult fiction."

$ 🖉 ◎ 🛡 SHINE BRIGHTLY, GEMS (Girls Everywhere Meeting the Savior) Girls' Clubs, Box 7259, Grand Rapids MI 49510. (616)241-5616. Fax: (616)241-5558. E-mail: sara@gemsgc.org. Website: www.gospelcom.net/gems. Editor: Jan Boone. **Contact:** Sara Lynne Hilton, managing editor. Magazine: 8½×11; 24 pages; 50 lb. paper; 50 lb. cover stock; illustrations; photos. "Our purpose is to lead girls into a living relationship with Jesus Christ and to help them see how God is at work in their lives and the world around them. Puzzles, crafts, stories, articles, and club input for girls ages 9-14." Monthly. Circ. 16,000.

● *Shine Brightly* has received awards for fiction and illustration from the Evangelical Press Association.

Needs: Adventure, ethnic, juvenile and religious/inspirational. Write for upcoming themes. Each year has an overall theme and each month has a theme to fit with yearly themes. Receives 50 unsolicited fiction mss/month. Buys 3 mss/issue; 30 mss/year. **Published new writers within the last year.** Published work by A.J. Schut. Length: 400-1,000 words; average length: 800 words.

How to Contact: Send complete ms with 8×10 SASE. Cover letter with short description of the manuscript. Responds in 2 months. Accepts simultaneous and previously published submissions. Sample copy for 8×10 SASE. Free guidelines.

Payment/Terms: Pays 3-5¢/word. Pays on publication for simultaneous, first or second serial rights.

Advice: "Try new and refreshing approaches. No fluffy fiction with Polyanna endings. We want stories dealing with real issues facing girls today. The one-parent, new girl at school is a bit overdone in our market. We have been dealing with issues like AIDS, abuse, drugs, and family relationships in our stories—more awareness-type articles."

CHECK THE CATEGORY INDEXES, located at the back of the book, for publishers interested in specific fiction subjects.

◻ **$** ◎ **SOJOURNER, The Women's Forum,** 42 Seaverns Ave., Jamaica Plain MA 02130. (617)524-0415. E-mail: info@sojourner.org. Website: www.sojourner.org. **Contact:** Amy Pett, editor. Magazine: 11×17; 48 pages; newsprint; illustrations; photos. "Feminist journal publishing interviews, nonfiction features, news, viewpoints, poetry, reviews (music, cinema, books) and fiction for women." Published monthly. Estab. 1975. Circ. 45,000.

Needs: "Writing on race, sex, class and queerness." Experimental, fantasy, feminist, lesbian, humor/satire, literary, prose poem and women's. Query for upcoming themes. Receives 20 unsolicited fiction mss/month. Accepts 10 mss/ year. Agented fiction 10%. Published work by Ruth Ann Lonardelli and Janie Adams. Published new writers within the last year. Length: 1,000-4,000 words; average length: 2,500 words.

How to Contact: Send complete ms with SASE and cover letter with description of previous publications; current works. Accepts simultaneous submissions. Responds in 8 months. Publishes ms an average of 6 months after acceptance. Sample copy for $3 with 10×13 SASE. Guidelines for SASE.

Payment/Terms: Pays subscription to magazine and 2 contributor's copies, $15 for first rights. No extra charge up to 5 contributor's copies; $1 charge each thereafter.

Advice: "Pay attention to appearance of manuscript! Very difficult to wade through sloppily presented fiction, however good. Do write a cover letter. If not cute, it can't hurt and may help. Mention previous publication(s)."

$ ◪ ◎ **SPIDER, The Magazine for Children,** Carus Publishing Co./Cricket Magazine Group, P.O. Box 300, Peru IL 61354. (800)588-8585. Website: www.spidermag.com. **Contact:** Marianne Carus, editor-in-chief. Assistant Editor: Heather Delabre. Magazine: 8×10; 33 pages; illustrations; photos. "*Spider* publishes high-quality literature for beginning readers, mostly children ages 6 to 9." Monthly. Estab. 1994. Circ. 76,000.

 • Carus Publishing also publishes *Cricket, Ladybug, Babybug* and *Cicada.*

Needs: Children's/juvenile (6-9 years), fantasy (children's fantasy), humor and folk tales. "No religious, didactic, or violent stories, or anything that talks down to children." Accepts 4 mss/issue. Publishes ms 2-3 years after acceptance. Agented fiction 2%. Published work by Lissa Rovetch, Ursula K. LeGuin and Eric Kimmel. Length: 300-1,000 words; average length: 775 words. Also publishes poetry. Often comments on rejected ms.

How to Contact: Send complete ms with a cover letter. Include exact word count. Responds in 3 months. Send SASE for return of ms. Accepts simultaneous and reprint submissions. Sample copy for $5. Guidelines for #10 SASE.

Payment/Terms: Pays 25¢/word and 2 contributor's copies; additional copies $2. Pays on publication for first rights or one-time rights.

Advice: "Read back issues of *Spider.*" Looks for "quality writing, good characterization, lively style, humor."

$ ◪ ◎ **STANDARD,** Nazarene International Headquarters, 6401 The Paseo, Kansas City MO 64131. (816)333-7000. Fax: (816)333-4439. E-mail: ssm@nazarene.org. Website: www.nazarene.org. **Contact:** Everett Leadingham, editor. Magazine: 8½×11; 8 pages; illustrations; photos. Inspirational reading for adults. "In *Standard* we want to show Christianity in action, and we prefer to do that through stories that hold the reader's attention." Weekly. Estab. 1936. Circ. 165,000.

Needs: "Looking for stories that show Christianity in action." Accepts 200 mss/year. Publishes ms 14-18 months after acceptance. **Published new writers within the last year.** Length: 500-1,200 words.

How to Contact: Send complete ms with name, address and phone number. Responds in 3 months to mss. SASE. Accepts simultaneous submissions but will pay only reprint rates. Sample copy and guidelines for SAE and 2 first-class stamps.

Payment/Terms: Pays 3½¢/word; 2¢/word (reprint). Pays on acceptance. Pays contributor's copies on publication.

Advice: "Be conscientious in your use of Scripture; don't overload your story with quotations. When you quote the Bible, quote it exactly and cite chapter, verse, and version used. (We prefer the NIV). *Standard* will handle copyright matters for Scripture. Except for quotations from the Bible, written permission for the use of any other copyrighted material (especially song lyrics) is the responsibility of the writer. Keep in mind the international audience of *Standard* with regard to geographic references and holidays. We cannot use stories about cultural, national, or secular holidays. Do not mention specific church affiliations. *Standard* is read in a variety of denominations. Do not submit any manuscript which has been submitted to or published in any of the following: *Vista, Wesleyan Advocate, Holiness Today, Preacher's Magazine, World Mission, Women Alive,* or various teen and children's publications produced by WordAction Publishing Company. These are overlapping markets."

$ ◪ **THE SUN,** The Sun Publishing Company, Inc., 107 N. Roberson St., Chapel Hill NC 27516. (919)942-5282. Fax: (919)932-3101. Website: www.thesunmagazine.org (includes guidelines, staff list and order forms). **Contact:** Sy Safransky, editor. Magazine: 8½×11; 48 pages; offset paper; glossy cover stock; photos. "While we tend to favor personal writing, we're open to just about anything—even experimental writing, if it doesn't make us feel stupid. Surprise us; we often don't know what we'll like until we read it." Monthly. Estab. 1974. Circ. 60,000.

Needs: Open to all fiction. Receives approximately 500 unsolicited fiction mss each month. Accepts 2 ms/issue. **Publishes 4-6 new writers/year.** Recently published work by Katherine Vaz, Alicia Erian and Steve Almond. Length: 7,000 words maximum. Also publishes poetry.

How to Contact: Send complete ms with SASE. Responds in 3 months. Publishes ms an average of 6-12 months after acceptance. Sample copy for $5

Payment/Terms: Pays up to $500, 2 contributor's copies, and a complimentary one-year subscription. Pays on publication for one-time rights. Publishes reprints.

Tips: "We favor honest, personal writing with an intimate point of view."

TEEN VOICES, Because you're more than just a pretty face, Women Express, Inc., 515 Washington St., Floor 6, Boston MA 02111-1759. (617)426-5505. Fax: (617)426-5577. E-mail: ellyn@teenvoices.com. Website: www.teenvoices.com. **Contact:** Ellyn Ruthstrom, managing editor. Magazine: 8⅜×10⅞; 48-68 pages; 50 lb. gloss; cover 70 lb. gloss with UV coat; illustrations; photos. "*Teen Voices* is an interactive, educational forum that challenges media images of women and serves as a vehicle of change, improving young women's social and economic status. *Teen Voices* is written by, for and about young women. Also provides a vehicle for mutual support between teens and adult women." Quarterly. Estab. 1990. Circ. 60,000. Member, Independent Press Association.

Needs: Adventure, children's/juvenile, comic/graphic novels, ethnic (general), experimental, family saga, fantasy, feminist, gay, humor/satire, lesbian, literary, mainstream, military/war, mystery/suspense, regional, religious, young adult/teen (easy-to-read). "*Teen Voices* only publishes submissions written by and for teen girls, ages 12-19. We will not publish anything written by a boy or an adult." Upcoming themes available online. Receives 250 unsolicited mss/month. Accepts 40 mss/issue; 160 mss/year. Published 4-5 months after acceptance. **Publishes 160 new writers/year.** Average length: 500 words. Publishes short shorts. Average length: 500 words. Also publishes literary essays and poetry. Sometimes comments on rejected mss.

How to Contact: Send complete ms with cover letter. Accepts mss by e-mail and fax. Include brief bio with submissions. Responds in 3 weeks. Send disposable copy of ms and #10 SASE for reply only. Accepts simultaneous, multiple and previously published submissions. Sample copy for $5. Guidelines for SASE, e-mail, fax, or on website.

Payment/Terms: Pays 5 contributor's copies; additional copies: $5. Acquires all rights.

Advice: "We try to publish as many teen girls as possible, especially those who don't normally have the opportunities and encouragement to write and be published. We also focus on issues that are not usually addressed in typical teen magazines, such as activism, teen pregnancy, cultural harmony, social justice, feminism, and empowerment. Write about what makes you think, what makes you angry, what makes you cry and what makes you laugh. Issues that are important to you, as a teen girl, are important to us at *Teen Voices*."

$ **TRUE CONFESSIONS**, Sterling/MacFadden Partnership, 333 Seventh Ave., New York NY 10001-5004. (212)979-4800. Fax: (212)979-4825. E-mail: trueconfessionstales@yahoo.com. **Contact:** Pat Byrdsong, editorial director. Magazine: 8×10½; 112 pages; photos. "*True Confessions* is a women's magazine featuring true-to-life stories about working class women and their families." Monthly.

Needs: "Family problems, crime, modern social problems, ie., abuse, sexual discrimination, addiction, etc. Also stories about multicultural experience—Latino, African, Asian, Native American stories encouraged. Must be written in first-person. No science fiction or third person stories. Wants to see more first-person inspirationals, thrillers, mysteries, romances with an edge." **Publishes 48 new writers/year.** Length: 3,000-7,500 words. "Also publishes two- and three-part stories which should not exceed 16,000 words." Also publishes "mini-stories" of 1,200-2,000 words.

How to Contact: Query first. "E-mail queries only." Responds in 3 months to queries. Sample copy for $2.99.

Payment/Terms: Pays 3¢/word or a flat $100 rate for mini-stories and 1 contributors copy. Pays after publication.

Advice: "Emotionally charged stories with a strong emphasis on characterization and well-defined plots are preferred. Stories should be intriguing, suspenseful, humorous, romantic, or tragic. The plots and characters should reflect American life. I want stories that cover the wide spectrum of America. I want to feel as though I intimately know the narrator and her/her motivation. If your story is dramatically gripping and/or humorous, features three-dimensional characters, and a realistic conflict, you have an excellent chance of making a sale at *True Confessions*. I suggest writers read three to four issues of *True Confessions* before sending submission. Do not talk down to our readers. Contemporary problems should be handled with insight and a fresh angle. Timely, first-person stories told by a sympathetic narrator are always needed as well as good romantic stories."

$ **TURTLE MAGAZINE FOR PRESCHOOL KIDS**, Children's Better Health Institute, 1100 Waterway Blvd., Indianapolis IN 46206-0567. (317)636-8881. Fax: (317)684-8094. Website: www.turtlemag.com. **Contact:** Terry Harshman, editor. Magazine of picture stories and articles for preschool children 2-5 years old.

● The Children's Better Health Institute also publishes *Children's Digest, Children's Playmate, Jack and Jill* and *Humpty Dumpty*, also listed in this section.

Needs: Juvenile (preschool). Special emphasis on health, nutrition, exercise and safety. Also has need for "very simple science experiments, and simple food activities." Receives approximately 100 unsolicited fiction mss/month. **Publishes 16-20 new writers/year.** Recently published work by Eileen Spinelli, Valeri Gorbachev and Timothy LaBelle. Length: 100-300 words.

How to Contact: Send complete ms with SASE. No queries. Responds in 10 weeks. Send SASE for Editorial Guidelines. Accepts multiple submissions. Sample copy for $1.75.

Payment/Terms: Pays up to 22¢/word (approximate); varies for poetry and activities; includes 10 complimentary copies of issue in which work appears. Pays on publication for all rights.

Advice: "Become familiar with recent issues of the magazine and have a thorough understanding of the preschool child. You'll find we are catering more to our youngest readers, so think simply. Also, avoid being too heavy-handed with health-related material. First and foremost, health features should be fun! Because we have developed our own turtle character ('PokeyToes'), we are not interested in fiction stories featuring other turtles."

U.S. CATHOLIC MAGAZINE, Claretian Publications, 205 W. Monroe St., Chicago IL 60606. (312)236-7782. Fax: (312)236-8207. Website: www.uscatholic.org. **Contact:** Maureen Abood. Magazine: 8½×11; 50 pages; photos. Monthly. Estab. 1927. Circ. 35,000. Member, Associated Church Press, Religious Communicators Council, Catholic Press Association.

Needs: Ethnic/multicultural (general), family saga, religious. Receives 100 unsolicited mss/month. Accepts 1 ms/issue; 12 mss/year. Publishes ms 2-3 months after acceptance. **Publishes 20% new writers/year.** Length: 800-1,500 words; average length: 1,200 words. Publishes short shorts. Also publishes poetry.
How to Contact: Send complete ms with a cover letter. Include estimated word count. Send a disposable copy of ms and #10 SASE for reply only. Guidelines by e-mail or on website. Reviews novels, short story collections and nonfiction books of interest to writers. Send review copies to Maureen Abood.
Payment/Terms: Pays on publication for first and electronic rights.

N $ ◖ THE WAR CRY, 615 Slaters Lane, Alexandria VA 22313. (703)684-5500. Fax: (703)684-5539. E-mail: war_cry@usn.salvationarmy.org. Website: www.thewarcry.com (includes forum, selected articles from *War Cry* and *Young Salvationist*, devotional page, guidelines, letters to the editor form, information on journals and books). **Contact:** Lt. Colonel Marlene Chase, editor-in-chief. Magazine: 8½×11; 24 pages; glossy; illustrations; photos. Biweekly. Estab. 1883. Circ. 300,000. Member, Evangelical Press Association.
Needs: Family saga, religious (general religious, inspirational), for college-age youth. "No fantasy, science fiction or New Age." Upcoming themes available for #10 SASE. Receives 30 unsolicited mss/month. Accepts 1 ms/issue; 10 mss/year. Publishes ms 6 weeks-1 year after acceptance. **Publishes 5 new writers/year.** Recently published work by Philip Yancey and Bob Robeson. Word length: 800 words average; 300 words minimum; 1,200 words maximum. Publishes short shorts. Also publishes poetry. Sometimes comments on rejected ms.
How to Contact: Send complete ms with a cover letter. Inquiries by fax and e-mail OK. Include estimated word count and social security number. Responds in 3 weeks to queries; 2 months to mss. Send SASE for return of ms or disposable copy of ms. Accepts simultaneous, multiple and reprint submissions. Sample copy and guidelines for #10 SAE.
Payment/Terms: Pays 10-20¢/word; 12¢ for reprints and 2 contributor's copies. Payment on acceptance. Acquires first rights and one-time rights.
Advice: "We publish limited amounts of fiction, so it must be outstanding. No 'flights of fancy.' Make sure fiction is realistic and involving with good characterization. Get a sample copy."

N ◖ ◎ WINNER, Saying No to Drugs and Yes to Life, Review & Herald Publishing Association, 55 W. Oak Ridge Dr., Hagerstown MD 21740. (301)393-4010. Fax: (301)393-4055. E-mail: ajacobs@rhpa.org. Website: www.winnermagazine.org (includes stories, answers to questions, names of staff, items for kids, teachers, and parents, order info and contact info). **Contact:** Anita Jacobs, editor. Magazine: 8⅛×10⅝; 16 pages; illustrations; photos. "*Winner* emphasizes positive lifestyles for grades 4-6. It is anti-drug, alcohol, smoking. We want positive moral values presented in a secular way." Monthly (September-May).
Needs: Children's/juvenile (adventure, easy-to-read, sports, ages 8-12). Upcoming themes: Tobacco (May), deadline December 2002. List of upcoming themes available by SASE or online. Length: 1,000-1,200 words; average length: 1,200 words. Also publishes poetry.
How to Contact: Send complete ms with a cover letter. Accepts submissions by e-mail, fax and disk. Include Social Security number and address. Responds in 2 months. Send SASE for return of ms. Accepts simultaneous, previously published and multiple submissions. Sample copy for $2. Guidelines for SASE, by e-mail, fax or on website.
Payment/Terms: Pays 3 contributors copies; additional copies $2. Pays on acceptance.

$ ◖ ◎ WITH: The Magazine for Radical Christian Youth, Faith & Life Resources, Box 347, Newton KS 67114-0347. (316)283-5100. Fax: (316)283-0454. E-mail: deliag@gcmc.org. Website: www.withonline.org/ (includes excerpts). **Contact:** Carol Duerksen, editor. Editorial Assistant: Delia Graber. Magazine: 8½×11; 32 pages; 60 lb. coated paper and cover; illustrations; photos. "Our purpose is to help teenagers understand the issues that impact them and to help them make choices that reflect Mennonite-Anabaptist understandings of living by the Spirit of Christ. We publish all types of material—fiction, nonfiction, teen personal experience, etc." Published 6 times/year. Estab. 1968. Circ. 6,100.
Needs: Contemporary, ethnic, humor/satire, mainstream, religious, young adult/teen (15-18 years). "We accept issue-oriented pieces as well as religious pieces. No religious fiction that gives 'pat' answers to serious situations." Would like to see more humor. List of upcoming themes available for SASE. Receives about 50 unsolicited mss/month. Accepts 1-2 mss/issue; 10-12 mss/year. Publishes ms up to 1 year after acceptance. **Publishes 1-3 new writers/year.** Recently published work by Steven James. Length: 400-2,000 words; 1,500 words preferred.
How to Contact: Send complete ms with cover letter, include short summary of author's credits and what rights they are selling. Responds in 2 months to mss. SASE. Accepts mss by e-mail and fax. Accepts simultaneous, multiple and reprint submissions. Sample copy for 9×12 SAE and $1.21 postage. Guidelines for #10 SASE.
Payment/Terms: Pays 4¢/word for reprints; 6¢/word for simultaneous rights (one-time rights to an unpublished story); 6-10¢/word for assigned stories (first rights). Supplies contributor's copies; charge for extras.
Advice: "Each story should make a single point that our readers will find helpful through applying it in their own lives. Request our theme list and detailed guidelines (enclose SASE). All our stories are theme-related, so writing to our themes greatly improves your odds."

$ ◻ WOMAN'S WORLD MAGAZINE, The Woman's Weekly, 270 Sylvan Ave., Englewood Cliffs NJ 07632. E-mail: dearww@aol.com. **Contact:** Johnene Granger, fiction editor. Magazine; 9½×11; 54 pages. "We publish short romances and mini-mysteries for all women, ages 18-68." Weekly. Estab. 1980. Circ. 1.5 million.

Needs: Romance (contemporary), mystery. "We buy contemporary romances of 1,500 words. Stories must revolve around a compelling, true-to-life relationship dilemma; may feature a male or female protagonist, and may be written in either the first or third person. We are *not* interested in stories of life-or-death, or fluffy, fly-away style romances. No explicit sex or historic, foreign or science fiction settings. When we say romance, what we really mean is relationship, whether it's just beginning or is about to celebrate its 50th anniversary." Receives 2,500 unsolicited mss/month. Accepts 2 mss/issue; 104 mss/year. Publishes mss 2-3 months after acceptance. Published work by Linda S. Reilly, Linda Yellin and Tim Myers. Length: romances—1,400 words; mysteries—1,000 words.

How to Contact: Send complete ms, "double spaced and typed in number 12 font." Cover letter not necessary. Include name, address, phone number and fax on first page of mss. *No queries.* Responds in 8 months. SASE. Guidelines for SASE.

Payment/Terms: Romances—$1,000, mysteries—$500. Pays on acceptance for first North American serial rights only.

Advice: "Familiarize yourself totally with our format and style. Read at least a year's worth of *Woman's World* fiction. Analyze and dissect it. Regarding romances, scrutinize them not only for content but tone, mood and sensibility."

THE WORLD OF ENGLISH, P.O. Box 1504, Beijing China. **Contact:** Yu-Lun Chen, chief editor. Monthly. Circ. 300,000.

● *The World of English* was named among the 100 Key National Social Periodicals for 2002-2003.

Needs: "We welcome contributions of short and pithy articles that would cater to the interest of our reading public, new and knowledgeable writings on technological finds, especially interesting stories and novels, etc."

How to Contact: Accepts mss by e-mail or fax.

Payment/Terms: "As our currency is regrettably inconvertible, we send copies of our magazines as the compensation for contributions."

Advice: "Aside from literary works, we put our emphasis on the provision of articles that cover various fields in order to help readers expand their vocabulary rapidly and enhance their reading level effectively, and concurrently to raise their level in writing. Another motive is to render assistance to those who, while learning English, are able also to enrich their knowledge and enlarge their field of vision."

WY'EAST HISTORICAL JOURNAL, Crumb Elbow Publishing, P.O. Box 294, Rhododendron OR 97049. (503)622-4798. **Contact:** Michael P. Jones, editor. Journal: 5½×8½; 60 pages; top-notch paper; hardcover and soft-bound; illustrations; photos. "The journal is published for Cascade Geographic Society, a nonprofit educational organization. Publishes historical or contemporary articles on subjects like the history of Oregon's Mt. Hood, the Columbia River, the Pacific NW, the Old Oregon Country, Indian myths and legends, westward trails, the Pony Express and mining. For young adults to elderly." Quarterly. Estab. 1992. Circ. 2,500.

Needs: Open. Special interests include wildlife and fisheries, history of fur trade in Pacific Northwest, the Oregon Trail and Indians. "All materials should relate—somehow—to the region the publication is interested in." Publishes annual special fiction issue in winter. Receives 10 unsolicited mss/month. Accepts 1-2 mss/issue; 22-24 mss/year. Publishes ms up to one year after acceptance. Published work by Joel Palmer. Publishes 5-10 new writers/year. Publishes short shorts. Recommends other markets. "We have several other publications through Crumb Elbow Publishing where we can redirect the material."

How to Contact: Query with clips of published work or send complete ms with cover letter. Responds in 2 months "depending upon work load." SASE (required or material will *not* be returned). Accepts simultaneous and reprint submissions. Guidelines for #10 SASE.

Payment/Terms: Pays contributor's copies on publication. Acquires one-time rights.

Advice: "A ms has to have a historical or contemporary tie to the Old Oregon Country, which was the lands that lay west of the Rocky Mountains to the Pacific Ocean, south to and including Northern California, and north to and including Alaska. It has to be about such things as nature, fish and wildlife, the Oregon Trail, pioneer settlement and homesteading, the Indian wars, gold mining, wild horses, Native American way of life and culture—which are only a few ideas. It has to be written in a non-offensive style, meaning please remove all four-letter words or passages dealing with loose sex and racist comments. Do not be afraid to try something a little different. If you write for the marketplace you might get published, but you loose something in the creative presentation. Write to please yourself and others will recognize your refreshing approach. We have a special need for ghost stories of the old and new west."

SENDING TO A COUNTRY other than your own? Be sure to send International Reply Coupons (IRC) instead of stamps for replies or return of your manuscript.

Book Publishers

In this section, you will find many of the "big-name" book publishers. Many of these publishers remain tough markets for new writers or for those whose work might be considered literary or experimental. Indeed, some only accept work from established authors, and then often only through an author's agent. Although having your novel published by one of the big commercial publishers listed in this section is difficult, it is not impossible. The trade magazine *Publishers Weekly* regularly features interviews with writers whose first novels are being released by top publishers. Many editors at large publishing houses find great satisfaction in publishing a writer's first novel.

On page 589 of this year's edition, you'll find the publishing industry's "family tree", which maps out each of the large book publishing conglomerates' divisions, subsidiaries, and imprints. Each parent company and most subsidiaries and divisions should also have listings in this section—distinguished by the ◪ icon—detailing its imprints and the address of its headquarters. Remember, most manuscripts are acquired by imprints, not their parent company, so avoid submitting to any listing with the ◪ icon.

Also listed here are "small presses" publishing four or more titles annually. Included among them are small and mid-size independent presses, university presses, and other nonprofit publishers. Introducing new writers to the reading public has become an increasingly more important role of these smaller presses at a time when the large conglomerates are taking less chances on unknown writers. Many of the successful small presses listed in this section have built their reputations and their businesses in this way and have become known for publishing prize-winning fiction.

These smaller presses also tend to keep books in print longer than larger houses. And, since small presses publish a smaller number of books, each title is equally important to the publisher, and each is promoted in much the same way and with the same commitment. Editors also stay at small presses longer because they have more of a stake in the business—often they own the business. Many smaller book publishers are writers themselves and know first-hand the importance of a close editor-author or publisher-author relationship.

TYPES OF BOOK PUBLISHERS

Large or small, the publishers in this section publish books "for the trade." That is, unlike textbook, technical or scholarly publishers, trade publishers publish books to be sold to the general consumer through bookstores, chain stores or other retail outlets. Within the trade book field, however, there are a number of different types of books.

The easiest way to categorize books is by their physical appearance and the way they are marketed. Hardcover books are the more expensive editions of a book, sold through bookstores and carrying a price tag of around $20 and up. Trade paperbacks are soft-bound books, also sold mostly in bookstores, but they carry a more modest price tag of usually around $10 to $20. Today a lot of fiction is published in this form because it means a lower financial risk than hardcover.

Mass market paperbacks are another animal altogether. These are the smaller "pocket-size" books available at bookstores, grocery stores, drug stores, chain retail outlets, etc. Much genre or category fiction is published in this format. This area of the publishing industry is very open to the work of talented new writers who write in specific genres such as science fiction, romance, and mystery.

At one time publishers could be easily identified and grouped by the type of books they do. Today, however, the lines between hardcover and paperback books are blurred. Many publishers known for publishing hardcover books also publish trade paperbacks and have paperback imprints. This enables them to offer established authors (and a very few lucky newcomers) hard-soft deals in which their book comes out in both versions. Thanks to the mergers of the past decade, too, the same company may own several hardcover and paperback subsidiaries and imprints, even though their editorial focuses may remain separate.

CHOOSING A BOOK PUBLISHER

In addition to checking the bookstores and libraries for books by publishers that interest you, you may want to refer to the Category Index at the back of this book to find publishers divided by specific subject categories. If you write genre fiction, check our new genre sections for lists of book publishers: (mystery, page 83; romance, page 97; science fiction/fantasy & horror, page 109). The subjects listed in the Indexes are general. Read individual listings to find which subcategories interest a publisher. For example, you will find several romance publishers listed in the For Romance Writers Section, but read the listings to find which type of romance is considered—gothic, contemporary, Regency or futuristic. See How to Use This Book to Publish Your Fiction for more on how to refine your list of potential markets.

The icons appearing before the names of the publishers will also help you in selecting a publisher. These codes are especially important in this section, because many of the publishing houses listed here require writers to submit through an agent. A ☑ icon identifies those that mostly publish established and agented authors, while a ○ points to publishers most open to new writers. See the inside front and back covers of this book for a complete list and explanations of symbols used in this book.

IN THE LISTINGS

As with other sections in this book, we identify new listings with a ▣ symbol. In this section, most with this symbol are not new publishers, but instead are established publishers who were unable or decided not to list last year and are therefore new to this edition.

In addition to the ▣ symbol indicating new listings, we include other symbols to help you in narrowing your search. English-speaking foreign markets are denoted by a ⊕ . The maple leaf symbol ❖ identifies Canadian presses. If you are not a Canadian writer, but are interested in a Canadian press, check the listing carefully. Many small presses in Canada receive grants and other funds from their provincial or national government and are, therefore, restricted to publishing Canadian authors.

We continue to include editorial comments set off by a bullet (●) within listings. This is where we include information about any special requirements or circumstances that will help you know even more about the publisher's needs and policies. The ▨ symbol identifies publishers who have recently received honors or awards for their books. And the ▣ symbol indicates that a publisher accepts agented submissions only.

Each listing includes a summary of the editorial mission of the house, an overarching principle that ties together what they publish. Under the heading **Contact:** we list one or more editors, often with their specific area of expertise.

Book editors asked us again this year to emphasize the importance of paying close attention to the Needs and How to Contact subheads of listings for book publishers. Unlike magazine editors who want to see complete manuscripts of short stories, most of the book publishers listed here ask that writers send a query letter with an outline and/or synopsis and several chapters of their novel. The Business of Fiction Writing, beginning on page 58 of this book, outlines how to prepare work to submit directly to a publisher.

There are no subsidy book publishers listed in *Novel & Short Story Writer's Market*. By subsidy, we mean any arrangement in which the writer is expected to pay all or part of the cost of producing, distributing, and marketing his book. We feel a writer should not be asked to share in any cost of turning his manuscript into a book. All the book publishers listed here told us that they *do not charge writers* for publishing their work. *If any of the publishers listed here ask you to pay any part of publishing or marketing your manuscript, please let us know.*

A NOTE ABOUT AGENTS

Some publishers are willing to look at unsolicited submissions, but most feel having an agent is to the writer's best advantage. In this section more than any other, you'll find a number of publishers who prefer submissions from agents. That's why we've included a section of agents open to submissions from fiction writers (page 117).

For listings of more agents and additional information on how to approach and deal with them, see the 2003 *Guide to Literary Agents*, published by Writer's Digest Books. Be wary of those who charge large sums of money for reading a manuscript. Reading fees do not guarantee representation. Think of an agent as a potential business partner and feel free to ask tough questions about his or her credentials, experience and business practices.

ⓘ *For More Information*

Check out issues of *Publishers Weekly* for publishing industry trade news in the U.S. and around the world or *Quill & Quire* for book publishing news in the Canadian book industry.

For more small presses see the *International Directory of Little Magazines and Small Presses* published by Dustbooks (P.O. Box 100, Paradise CA 95967). To keep up with changes in the industry throughout the year, check issues of two small press trade publications: *Small Press Review* (also published by Dustbooks) and *Independent Publisher* (Jenkins Group, Inc., 400 W. Front St., Traverse City MI 49684).

 A&B PUBLISHERS GROUP, 1000 Atlantic Ave., Brooklyn NY 11238. (718)783-7808. Fax: (718)783-7267. E-mail: maxtay@webspan.net. **Contact:** Maxwell Taylor, production manager (children's, adult nonfiction); Wendy Gift, editor (fiction). Estab. 1992. Publishes hardcover originals, trade paperback originals and reprints. **Publishes 30% of books from first-time authors; 30% from unagented writers.** Averages 12 titles/year.
Needs: Query with SASE. Recently published *Baggage Check* (fiction).
How to Contact: Accepts simultaneous submissions. Responds in 2 months to queries; 5 months to mss.
Terms: Pays 5-12% royalty on net receipts. Offers $500-2,500 advance. Publishes book 18 months after acceptance of ms. Book catalog free.
Advice: "Read, read, read. The best writers are developed from good reading. There is not enough attention to quality. Read, write and revise until you get it almost right."

◖ ABSEY & CO., INC., 23011 Northcrest Dr., Spring TX 77389. (281)257-2340. Fax: (281)251-4676. E-mail: abseyandco@aol.com. Website: www.absey.com (includes authors, titles and descriptions, contact information). **Contact:** Edward E. Wilson, publisher. "We are interested in book-length fiction of literary merit with a firm intended audience." Publishes hardcover and paperback originals. Averages 6-10 titles/year. **Published 3-5 new writers within the last year.**
Needs: Juvenile, mainstream/contemporary, short story collections. Also publishes poetry. Published *Where I'm From*, by George Ella Lyon; and *Dragonfly*, by Alice McLerran.
How to Contact: Accepts unsolicited mss. Send query letter. Send SASE or IRC for return of ms. Does not accept e-mail submissions. Responds in 3 months to queries; 9 months to mss.
Terms: Pays royalties of 8-15% on net price. Publishes ms 1 year after acceptance. Guidelines available for #10 SASE.
Advice: "Since we are a small, new press looking for good manuscripts with a firm intended audience, we tend to work closely and attentively with our authors. Many established authors who have been with the large New York houses have come to us to publish their work because we work closely with them."

ACADEMY CHICAGO PUBLISHERS, 363 W. Erie St., Chicago IL 60610. (312)751-7300. Website: www.acad emychicago.com (submission guidelines, catalog, press history). **Contact**: Anita Miller, senior editor. Estab. 1975. Midsize independent publisher. "In addition to publishing reprints of neglected classics, Academy Chicago publishes original trade fiction and nonfiction" in paperback and hardback.

• *Cutter's Island*, by Vincent Panella placed in both the Foreward Magazine's Book of the Year contest and the 2000 Independent Publishers Awards.

Needs: Biography, history, academic and anthologies. Only the most unusual mysteries, no private-eyes or thrillers. No explicit sex or violence. Serious fiction, no romance/adventure. "We will consider historical fiction that is well researched. No science fiction/fantasy, no religious/inspirational, no how-to, no cookbooks. In general, we are very conscious of women's roles. We publish very few children's books." Recently published *Clean Start*, by Patricia Margaret Page (first fiction); *Cutter's Island: Caesar in Captivity*, by Vincent Panella (first fiction, historical); and *Murder at the Panionic Games*, by Michael B. Edward.

How to Contact: Does not accept unsolicited mss. Query with first three consecutive chapters, triple spaced. Include cover letter briefly describing the content of your work. Send SASE or IRC for return of ms. "Manuscripts without envelopes will be discarded. *Mailers* are a *must*, even from agents."

Terms: Pays royalties of 5-10% on net; no advance. Publishes ms 18 months after acceptance. Sends galleys to author.

Advice: "At the moment we are swamped with manuscripts and anything under consideration can be under consideration for months."

ACE SCIENCE FICTION, Berkley Publishing Group, Imprint of Penguin Putnam Inc., 375 Hudson St., New York NY 10014. (212)366-2000. **Contact**: Susan Allison, editor-in-chief; Anne Sowards, associate editor. Estab. 1948. Publishes paperback originals and reprints and 6-10 hardcovers per year. Number of titles: 6/month. Buys 85-95% agented fiction.

Needs: Science fiction and fantasy. No other genre accepted. No short stories. Published *Forever Peace*, by Joe Haldeman; *Neuromancer*, by William Gibson; *King Kelson's Bride*, by Katherine Kurtz.

How to Contact: Accepts unsolicited mss. Query with outline/synopsis and 3 sample chapters. Send SASE. No simultaneous submissions. Responds in 2 months minimum to mss. "Queries answered immediately if SASE enclosed." Publishes ms an average of 18 months after acceptance.

Terms: Standard for the field. Sends galleys to author.

Advice: "Good science fiction and fantasy are almost always written by people who have read and loved a lot of it. We are looking for knowledgeable science or magic, as well as sympathetic characters with recognizable motivation. We are looking for solid, well-plotted science fiction: good action adventure, well-researched hard science with good characterization and books that emphasize characterization without sacrificing plot. In fantasy we are looking for all types of work, from high fantasy to sword and sorcery." Submit fantasy and science fiction to Anne Sowards.

ACEN PRESS, DNA Press, 730 Daniel Dr., Collegeville PA 19426. (610)489-8404. Fax: (208)692-2855. E-mail: dnapress@yahoo.com. **Contact**: Alexander Kuklin, Ph.D., managing editor (children scientific books); Xela Schenk, operations manager (New Age). Estab. 1998. Publishes trade paperback originals. **Publishes 90% of books from first-time authors; 100% from unagented writers.** Averages 10 titles/year; imprint publishes 5 titles/year.

Needs: Juvenile, science fiction, young adult. "All books should be oriented to explaining science even if they do not fall 100% under the category of science fiction." Recently published *How Do Witches Fly?*, by Alexander Kuklin.

How to Contact: Submit complete ms. Accepts simultaneous submissions. Responds in 2 weeks to queries; 6 weeks to mss.

Terms: Pays 10-20% royalty. Publishes book 4 months after acceptance of ms. Book catalog free; ms guidelines free.

Advice: "Quick response, great relationships, high commission/royalty."

ACME PRESS, P.O. Box 1702, Westminster MD 21158. (410)848-7577. **Contact**: Ms. E.G. Johnston, managing editor. Estab. 1991. "We operate on a part-time basis and publish 1-2 novels/year." Publishes hardcover and paperback originals. **Published new writers within the last year.** Averages 1-2 fiction titles/year.

Needs: Humor/satire. "We publish only humor novels, so we don't want to see anything that's not funny." Published *She-Crab Soup*, by Dawn Langley Simmons (fictional memoir/humor); *Biting the Wall*, by J. M. Johnston (humor/mystery); *Hearts of Gold*, by James Magorian (humor/mystery); and *Super Fan*, by Lyn A. Sherwood (comic/sports).

How to Contact: Accepts unsolicited mss. Query with outline/synopsis and first 50 pages or submit complete ms with cover letter. Include estimated word count. Send SASE for reply, return of ms or send a disposable copy of ms. Agented fiction 25%. Responds in 2 weeks to queries; 6 weeks to mss. Accepts simultaneous submissions. Always comments on rejected mss.

Terms: Pays 25 author's copies and 50% of profits. Sends galleys to author. Publishes ms 1 year after acceptance. Guidelines and book catalog available for #10 SASE.

ADAEX EDUCATIONAL PUBLICATIONS, P.O. Box AK188, Kumasi, Ghana. Fax: 233-51-30282. **Contact**: Asare Konadu Yamoah, publisher; George Apraku Dentu, fiction editor. Distributes titles through bookstores. Promotes titles through advertising, direct mail.

Needs: Looks for cultural development, romance, literary translators and copyright brokers. "Publication development organization for Ghanaian, African and world literature: novels, workbooks, language development, etc." Published *Strange Happenings* and *Creatures of Circumstance*, by Asare Konadu. Average 5-10 fiction titles/year. Length: 8-250 typed pages.

How to Contact: Send brief summary and first and last chapter.

Terms: Pays advance and royalties.

Advice: "Manuscripts should be very clear in terms of language, the message it conveys should be universal."

ADVENTURE BOOK PUBLISHERS, Durksen Enterprises Ltd., 3545-32 Ave. NE, #712, Calgary, Alberta T1Y 6M6 Canada. Phone/fax: (403)285-6844. E-mail: adventure@puzzlesbyshar.com. Website: www.puzzlesbyshar. com/adventurebooks/ (includes e-book sales with secure ordering, basic instructions for queries, FAQs, who and where we are, how we publish and all about e-books, including browsing samples). **Contact:** S. Durksen, editor. Estab. 1998. "Small, independent. e-books and some print versions (trade edition style). We are unique in that we are beginning to supply 'physical' e-books to bookstores." Publishes e-books (download and disk versions). **Published 20 new writers within the last year.** Plans 40 first novels this year. Averages 50 total titles, 45 fiction titles/year.

Needs: Adventure, children's/juvenile, fantasy (space fantasy, sword and sorcery), historical (general), humor/satire, military/war, mystery/suspense (amateur sleuth, cozy, police procedural, private eye/hardboiled), romance (contemporary, historical, romantic suspense), science fiction (hard science/technological, soft/sociological), thriller/espionage, western (frontier saga, traditional), young adult/teen (adventure, fantasy/science fiction, mystery/suspense, problem novels, romance, series, sports, western). Recently published *Wolfe's Pack*, by Robert M. Blacketer (adventure/military); *The Triumph Mine*, by AJ Lee (fiction); and *Blood Drops Through Time*, by Christine Westendorp (historical fiction/fantasy).

How to Contact: Does not accept unsolicited mss; returns mss "if adequate international postage and envelopes are provided." Query via e-mail with 1-2 page synopsis. Include estimated word count and brief bio. Responds in 3 weeks to queries; up to 6 months to mss. Accepts ms submissions "only by invitation and in accordance with guidelines given to those invited." Always comments on rejected mss.

Terms: Pays royalties of 20%. Does not send galleys to author. Publishes ms 7-10 months after acceptance. Guidelines available on website.

Advice: "Good stories can be told without excessive sex and violence graphically detailed for shock value only. We do not consider works of a pornographic, illegal or harmful nature. Preference is given to mainstream manuscripts as opposed to topics with time or issue limitations. Please take the time to proofread with a critical eye before submitting."

AGELESS PRESS, P.O. Box 5915, Sarasota FL 34277-5915. Phone/fax: (941)952-0576. E-mail: irishope@comcast.net. Website: http://mywebpages.comcast.net/irishope/index.html (includes contest winners, articles, book excerpts). **Contact:** Iris Forrest, editor. Estab. 1992. Independent publisher. Publishes paperback originals. Books: acid-free paper; notched perfect binding; no illustrations. Average print order: 5,000. First novel print order: 5,000. **Published new writers within the last year.** Averages 1 title/year.

Needs: Experimental, fantasy, humor/satire, literary, mainstream/contemporary, mystery/suspense, New Age/mystic/spiritual, science fiction, short story collections, thriller/espionage. Looking for material "based on personal computer experiences." Stories selected by editor. Published *Computer Legends, Lies & Lore*, by various (anthology); and *Computer Tales of Fact & Fantasy*, by various (anthology).

How to Contact: Does not accept unsolicited mss. Send query letter. Accepts queries by e-mail and fax. Send SASE or IRC for return of ms or send a disposable copy of ms and SASE for reply only. Responds in 1 week. Accepts simultaneous submissions, electronic (5¼ or 3.5 IBM disk or on CD) submissions in ASCII format. Sometimes comments on rejected mss.

Terms: Average advance: negotiable. Publishes ms 6-12 months after acceptance.

Advice: "Query! Don't send work without a query!"

ALEF DESIGN GROUP, 4423 Fruitland Ave., Los Angeles CA 90058. (213)585-7312. Website: www.alefdesign.com. **Contact:** Jane Golub. Estab. 1990. Publishes hardcover and trade paperback originals. **Publishes 80% of books from first-time authors; 100% from unagented writers.** Averages 25 titles/year; imprint publishes 10 titles/year.

Needs: Juvenile, religious, young adult. "We publish books of Judaic interest only." Recently published *The Road to Exile*, by Didier Nebot (fiction).

How to Contact: Query with SASE. Accepts simultaneous submissions. Responds in 6 months to mss.

Terms: Pays 10% royalty. Offers advance. Publishes book 3 years after acceptance of ms. Ms guidelines for 9×12 SAE with 10 first-class stamps.

ALGONQUIN BOOKS OF CHAPEL HILL, Subsidiary of Workman Publishing, P.O. Box 2225, Chapel Hill NC 27515-2225. (919)967-0108. Website: www.algonquin.com. Publishes hardcover and trade paperback originals and trade paperback reprints of in-house titles. Averages 24 total titles/year.

Imprint(s): Front Porch Paperbacks.

Needs: Literary.

How to Contact: Query by mail prior to submitting ms. No queries/submissions by phone, fax, e-mail. "Visit our website for full submission policy."

AMBASSADOR BOOKS, INC., 71 Elm St., Worcester MA 01609. (508)756-2893. Fax: (508)757-7055. Website: www.ambassadorbooks.com. **Contact:** Kathryn Conlan, acquisitions editor. Publishes hardcover and trade paperback originals. **Publishes 50% of books from first-time authors; 90% from unagented writers.** Averages 7 titles/year.

Needs: Books with a spiritual/religious theme. Juvenile, literary, picture books, religious, spiritual, sports, young adult. Recently published *Emmanuel McClue and the Mystery of the Shroud*, by Tony McCaffrey; *The Lion Who Couldn't Roar*, by John Powers.

How to Contact: Query with SASE or submit complete ms. Accepts simultaneous submissions. Responds in 3 months to queries.

Terms: Pays 8-10% royalty on retail price. Publishes book 1 year after acceptance of ms. Book catalog free or online at website.

N: ◎ AMERICAN ATHEIST PRESS, P.O. Box 5733, Parsippany NJ 07054-6733. (908)276-7300. Fax: (908)276-7402. E-mail: editor@atheists.org. Website: www.atheists.org. **Contact:** Frank Zindler, editor. Estab. 1959. Publishes trade paperback originals and reprints. Publishes quarterly journal, *American Atheist*, for which are needed articles of interest to atheists. **Publishes 40-50% of books from first-time authors; 100% from unagented writers.** Averages 12 titles/year.

Imprints: Gustav Broukal Press.

Needs: Humor (satire of religion or of current religious leaders), anything of particular interest to atheists. "We rarely publish any fiction. But we have occasionally released a humorous book. No mainstream. For our press to consider fiction, it would have to tie in with the general focus of our press, which is the promotion of atheism and free thought."

How to Contact: Submit outline, sample chapter(s). Accepts simultaneous submissions. Responds in 4 months to queries.

Terms: Pays 5-10% royalty on retail price. Offers advance. Publishes book within 2 years after acceptance of ms. Book catalog for 6½×9 ½ SAE; ms guidelines for 9×12 SAE.

Advice: "We will need more how-to types of material—how to argue with creationists, how to fight for state/church separation, etc. We have an urgent need for literature for young atheists."

N: ○ ♥ AMERICANA PUBLISHING, INC., 303 San Mateo N.E., Suite 104A, Albuquerque NM 87108. (505)265-6121. Fax: (505)255-6189. E-mail: editor@americanabooks.com. Website: www.americanabooks.com (includes audio books and print books of various genres, including mystery, thriller, adventure, sci-fi, religious). **Contact:** Lisa Savard, managing editor (mystery, thriller, adventure, sci-fi, religious). Estab. 1997. "Small, independent publisher of audio books and print books." Publishes paperback originals. Books: offset printing; perfect-bound. Average print order: 1,000; first novel print order: 1,000. **Published 2 new writers within the last year.** Plans 6 first novels this year. Averages 9 total titles, 8 fiction titles/year.

● Americana Publishing received the Audie Award for "Best New Audio Book Publisher 2001."

Needs: Adventure, fantasy (space fantasy), historical, literary, mystery/suspense (amateur sleuth, cozy, police procedural, private eye/hardboiled), religious (general religious, inspirational), romance (contemporary, historical, romantic suspense), science fiction (soft/sociological), thriller/espionage, western, young adult/teen (fantasy/science fiction, mystery/suspense). Recently published *Last Chance Out*, by Staci Rizner (YA science fiction, debut author); *The Killings Cards*, by Lon Campanozzi (mystery); and *Beloved Leah*, by Cindy Davis (religious). Publishes the Mike Amato Detective series.

How to Contact: Accepts unsolicited mss. Query with outline/synopsis and first 2 chapters. Include estimated word count, brief bio and list of publishing credits. Send disposable copy of ms and SASE for reply only. Agented fiction 20% print books; 80% audio books. Responds in 2 months to queries; 6 months to mss. Accepts simultaneous submissions. No electronic or disk submissions. Sometimes comments on rejected mss.

Terms: Pays royalties of 10%. Sends galleys to author. Publishes ms 1-2 years after acceptance. Guidelines available for SASE; book catalog free.

♣ ◐ ◎ ANVIL PRESS, P.O. Box 3008, MPO, Vancouver, British Columbia V6B 3X5 Canada; or Lee Building, #204-A, 175 E. Broadway, Vancouver, British Columbia V5T 1W2 Canada. (604)876-8710. Fax: (604)879-2667. E-mail: subter@portal.ca. Website: www.anvilpress.com (includes writer's guidelines, names of editors, book catalog, sample of magazine, contest info). **Contact:** Brian Kaufman, managing editor. Estab. 1988. "2-person operation with volunteer editorial board. Anvil Press publishes contemporary fiction, poetry and drama, giving voice to up-and-coming Canadian writers, exploring all literary genres, discovering, nurturing and promoting new Canadian literary talent." Publishes paperback originals. Books: offset or web printing; perfect-bound. Average print order: 1,000-1,500. First novel print order: 1,000. **Published new writers within the last year.** Averages 8 total titles/year.

Needs: Experimental, contemporary modern, literary, short story collections. Recently published *The Beautiful Dead End*, by Clint Hutzulak; *Bogman's Music*, by Tammy Armstrong (poetry); *Shylock*, by Mark Leiren-Young (drama); and *Socket*, by David Zimmerman (winner of the 3-Day Novel-Writing Contest).

How to Contact: Canadian writers only (with the exception of 3-Day Novel-Writing Contest). Accepts unsolicited mss. Send query letter or query with outline/synopsis and 1-2 sample chapters. Include estimated word count and bio.

READ 'THE BUSINESS OF FICTION WRITING' section for information on manuscript preparation, mailing tips, rights and more.

Send SASE or SAE and IRC for return of ms or send a disposable copy of ms and SASE or SAE and IRC for reply only. Responds in 4 months to queries; up to 6 months to mss. Accepts simultaneous submissions (please note in query letter that manuscript is a simultaneous submission).

Terms: Pays royalties of 15% (of final sales). Average advance: $400. Sends galleys to author. Publishes ms within contract year. Book catalog available for 9 × 12 SASE and 2 first-class stamps.

Advice: "We are only interested in writing that is progressive in some way—form, content. We want contemporary fiction from serious writers who intend to be around for awhile and be a name people will know in years to come. Read back titles, look through our catalog before submitting."

ARCADE PUBLISHING, 141 Fifth Ave., New York NY 10010. (212)475-2633. Fax: (212)353-8148. President, Editor-in-Chief: Richard Seaver. **Contact:** Richard Seaver, Jeannette Seaver, Cal Barksdale, Greg Camer and Darcy Falkenhagen. Estab. 1988. Independent publisher. Publishes hardcover originals and paperback reprints. Books: 50-55 lb. paper; notch, perfect-bound; illustrations. Average print order: 10,000. First novel print order: 3,500-7,500. **Published new writers within the last year.** Averages 45 total titles, 12-15 fiction titles/year. Distributes titles through AOL Time Warner Book Grove.

Needs: Literary, mainstream/contemporary, mystery/suspense, translations. No romance, science fiction, young adult. Published *Trying to Save Piggy Sneed*, by John Irving; *Destiny*, by Tim Parks; *Requiem for a Lost Empire*, by Andrei Makine; *The Chalon Heads*, by Barry Maitland; and *Virgin*, by Robin Maxwell.

How to Contact: Does not accept unsolicited mss. Submit through an agent only. Agented fiction 100%. Responds in 2 weeks to queries; 4 months to mss.

Terms: Pays negotiable advances and royalties and 10 author's copies. Guidelines and book catalog available for SASE.

ARSENAL PULP PRESS, 103-1014 Homer St., Vancouver, British Columbia V6B 2W9 Canada. (604)687-4233. Fax: (604)669-8250. E-mail: contact@arsenalpulp.com. Website: www.arsenalpulp.com (includes guidelines, ordering information, book catalog and publicity information). **Contact:** Linda Field, editor. Literary press. Publishes paperback originals. Average print order: 1,500-3,500. First novel print order: 1,500. **Published new writers within the last year.** Averages 12-15 total writers, 2 fiction writers/year. Distributes titles through Whitecap Books (Canada) and Consortium (U.S.). Promotes titles through reviews, excerpts and print advertising.

Needs: Ethnic/multicultural (general), feminist, gay, lesbian, literary, short story collections. No genre fiction, i.e. westerns, romance, horror, mystery, etc. Recently published *One Man's Trash*, by Ivan Coyote (short fiction/lesbian); *The Uncanny*, by Bruce Grenville (visual art/cultural studies); and *How It All Began*, by Bommi Baumann (current affairs).

How to Contact: Accepts unsolicited mss. Query with cover letter, outline/synopsis and 2 sample chapters. Include list of publishing credits. Send SASE for return of ms or send disposable copy of ms and SASE for reply only. Agented fiction 10%. Responds in 1 month to queries; 4 months to mss. Accepts simultaneous submissions. Sometimes comments on rejected mss.

Terms: Pays royalties of 10%. Negotiable advance. Sends galleys to author. Publishes ms 1 year after acceptance. Guidelines and book catalog available free for 9 × 11 SASE.

Advice: "We very rarely publish American writers."

ARTE PUBLICO PRESS, University of Houston, 452 Cullen Performance Hall, Houston TX 77204-2004. (713)743-2841. Fax: (713)743-2847. Website: www.arte.uh.edu. **Contact:** Dr. Nicolás Kanellos, publisher. Estab. 1979. "Small press devoted to the publication of contemporary U.S.-Hispanic literature. Mostly trade paper; publishes 30 books/year. Publishes fiction and belles lettres." Average print order 2,000-5,000. First novel print order 2,500-5,000.

Imprint(s): Piñata Books featuring children's and young adult literature by U.S.-Hispanic authors.

• Arte Publico Press is the oldest and largest publisher of Hispanic literature for children and adults in the United States.

Needs: Mainstream, contemporary, ethnic, literary, written by US-Hispanic authors. Published *Project Death*, by Richard Bertematti (novel/mystery); *A Perfect Silence*, by Alba Ambert; *Song of the Hummingbird*, by Graciela Limón; and *Little Havana Blues: A Cuban-American Literature Anthology*.

How to Contact: Accepts unsolicited mss. Query with outline/synopsis and sample chapters or complete ms with cover letter. Agented fiction 1%. Responds in 1 month to queries; 4 months to mss. Sometimes comments on rejected mss.

Terms: Pays royalties of 10% on wholesale price. Average advance: $1,000-3,000. Provides 20 author's copies; 40% discount on subsequent copies. Sends galleys to author. Publishes ms minimum 2 years after acceptance. Guidelines for SASE; book catalog free on request.

Advice: "Include cover letter in which you 'sell' your book—why should we publish the book, who will want to read it, why does it matter, etc."

ARTEMIS PRESS, SRS Internet Publishing, 236 W. Portal Ave. #525, San Francisco CA 94127. Phone/fax: (866)216-7333. E-mail: info@artemispress.com. Website: www.artemispress.com. **Contact:** Susan R. Skolnick, publisher and editor-in-chief; Hedda James, editor. Estab. 2000. "Small electronic publisher of fiction and nonfiction titles of interest to the worldwide women's community. We specialize in lesbian-related works. We are open to working with new authors and provide extremely personalized services." Publishes electronic originals. **Published 3 new writers within the last year.** Plans 6 first novels this year. Averages 6-10 total titles; 4-6 fiction titles/year. Titles distributed and promoted online.

Needs: Adventure, historical, humor/satire, psychic/supernatural, romance, short story collections, thriller/espionage, romance, ethnic/multicultural, experimental, family saga, fantasy, feminist, lesbian, literary, mainstream, mystery/suspense, New Age/mystic, science fiction. Recently published *Observers and Other Stories*, by Eleanor Lehrman (short story collection); *Down the Rabbit Hole*, by Lynne Jamneck (mystery/suspense); *Minding Therapy*, by Ros Johnson (humor/satire). Publishes two mystery series, the Delicate Fears series and Samantha Skellar mysteries.

How to Contact: Accepts unsolicited mss. Query with synopsis and 3 sample chapters. Accepts queries by e-mail. Include estimated word count, brief bio and Social Security number with submission. Send disposable copy of ms and SASE for reply only. Agented fiction: 10%. Responds in 1 month to queries; 3 months to mss. Considers simultaneous submissions, electronic submissions and submissions on disk. Often comments on rejected mss.

Terms: Pays royalties of 40%. Sends prepublication galleys to author. Publishes ms 6 months after acceptance. Guidelines and catalog available on website.

Advice: "We like to see clean manuscripts and an indication that the author has proofed and self-edited before submitting. We work collaboratively with our authors in all phases of publication and expect the same efforts of our authors in return."

⊘ ◎ ☒ ATHENEUM BOOKS FOR YOUNG READERS, Imprint of Simon & Schuster, 1230 Avenue of the Americas, New York NY 10022. (212)698-2715. Website: www.simonsays.com. **Contact:** Caitlyn Dlouhy, executive editor (picture book, middle grade, YA fiction); Richard Jackson, editorial director, Richard Jackson Books (picture book, middle grade, YA fiction); Anne Schwartz, editorial director, Anne Schwartz Books (picture book, YA fiction). Second largest imprint of large publisher/corporation. Publishes hardcover originals. Books: illustrations for picture books, some illustrated short novels. Average print order: 7,500-10,000. First novel print order: 6,500. Averages 100 total titles, 25 middle grade and YA fiction titles/year.

● In the past year, four books by Atheneum have received awards: *Olivia*, by Ian Falconer, Caldecott Honor; *Clever Beatrice*, by Margaret Willey, Charlotte Zolotow Award; *Goin' Someplace Special*, by Pat McKissock, Coretta Scott King Award; and *Silent Night*, by Sandy Turner, Ragazzi Award.

Needs: Juvenile (adventure, animal, contemporary, fantasy, historical, sports, preschool/picture book), young adult/teen (fantasy/science fiction, historical, mystery, problem novels, sports, spy/adventure). No "paperback romance type" fiction. Recently published *Horace and Morris But Mostly Dolores*, by James Howe; *Kate and the Beanstalk*, by Mary Pope Osborne; *America*, by E.R. Frank (YA novel); and *Audrey and Barbara*, by Janet Lawson (picture book fiction; debut author).

How to Contact: Does not accept unsolicited mss. Send query letter. Send SASE or IRC for return of the ms. Agented fiction 40%. Responds in 6 weeks to queries. Accepts simultaneous submissions "if we are so informed."

Terms: Pays royalties of 10%. Average advance: $6,000. "Along with advance and royalties, authors receive ten free copies of their book and can purchase more at a special discount." Sends galleys to author. Guidelines available for #10 SASE.

Advice: "We have few specific needs except for books that are fresh, interesting, and well written. Again, fad topics are dangerous, as are works you haven't polished to the best of your ability. (The competition is fierce.) Other things we don't need at this time are safety pamphlets, ABC books, coloring books and board books. In writing picture books texts, avoid the copy and 'cutesy', such as stories about characters with alliterative names. Query letter for all submissions. We do not accept unsolicited manuscripts."

Ⓝ ◖ AUTHORLINK PRESS, 3720 Millswood Dr., Irving TX 75062. (972)650-1986. Fax: (972)650-6222. E-mail: admin@authorlink.com. Website: www.authorlink.com. **Contact:** Doris Booth, editor-in-chief (mainstream, women's fiction); Elaine Lanmon, associate editor (mainstream, science fiction, fantasy, horror). Estab. 1996. "Small or midsize independent publisher. Our press is best noted for true crime and criminal profiling, though our focus is broadening." Publishes paperback originals and reprints. Books: text, 60 lb. cream paper; traditionally printed; perfect-bound. Average print order: less than 10,000. First novel print order: varies. Plans 0 first novels this year. Averages 12 total titles, 3-6 fiction titles/year. Distributes titles through Ingram, Baker & Taylor. Promotes titles through direct mailings to media, booksellers and libraries, also online promotion.

Needs: Fantasy, historical, horror, mainstream, military/war, mystery/suspense, religious, romantic suspense, thriller/espionage. "No children's, young adult or poetry please!" Recently published *Harps on the Willow*, by P.T. Sherman (mainstream, debut author). Publishes *New American Review*.

How to Contact: Query by e-mail with outline/synopsis. Include estimated word count, brief bio and list of publishing credits. Agented fiction 10%. Responds in 1 month to queries; 2-3 months to mss. Accepts simultaneous and electronic submissions (no attachments). Sometimes comments on rejected mss.

Terms: Pays royalties of 8-12% retail or 40% of net, depending on contract. Publishes ms 8-12 months after acceptance.

Advice: "We are publishing fewer titles through June 2003 due to the sluggish economy, but should increase our releases in late 2003 and into 2004."

Ⓝ AUTONOMEDIA, P.O. Box 568, Williamsburgh Station, Brooklyn NY 11211. (718)963-2603. Fax: (718)963-2603. E-mail: info@autonomedia.org. Website: www.autonomedia.org. **Contact:** Jim Fleming, acquisitions editor. Estab. 1984. Publishes trade paperback originals and reprints. **Publishes 30% of books from first-time authors; 90% from unagented writers.** Averages 25 titles/year.

Needs: Erotica, experimental, feminist, gay/lesbian, literary, mainstream/contemporary, occult, science fiction, short story collections. Recently published *The Anarchists*, by John Henry MacKay.

How to Contact: Submit synopsis, SASE. Accepts simultaneous submissions. Responds in 2 months to queries.
Terms: Pays variable royalty. Offers $100 advance. Publishes book 6 months after acceptance of ms. Book catalog for $1; ms guidelines online.

AVALON BOOKS, Imprint of Thomas Bouregy Company, Inc., 160 Madison Ave., New York NY 10016. (212)598-0222. E-mail: editorial@avalonbooks.com. Website: www.avalonbooks.com. **Contact:** Erin Cartwright, senior editor; Mira Son, assistant editor. Publishes hardcover originals. **Published new writers within the last year.** Averages 60 titles/year. Distributes titles through Baker & Taylor, libraries, Barnes&Noble.com and Amazon.com. Promotes titles through *Library Journal*, Booklist and local papers.
Needs: "Avalon Books publishes wholesome romances, mysteries, westerns. Intended for family reading, our books are read by adults as well as teenagers and their characters are all adults. There is no graphic sex in any of our novels. Currently, we publish 10 books bimonthly: two contemporary romances, two historical romances, two career romances, two mysteries and two westerns. All westerns are historical." Published *A Golden Trail of Murder*, by John Paxson (mystery); *Renovating Love*, by Mary Leask (romance); *Shannon US Marshall*, by Charles Friend (western); and *Brooklyn Ballerina*, by Zelda Benjamin (career romance).
How to Contact: Does not accept unsolicited mss. Query with the first 3 chapters and a brief synopsis (2-3 pages). "We'll contact you if we're interested." Send SASE (ms size) or IRC for return of ms. Responds in about 4 months. "Send SASE for a copy of our writer's guidelines or visit our website www.avalonbooks.com."
Terms: The first half of the advance is paid upon signing of the contract; the second within 30 days after publication. Usually publishes ms within 6-8 months.

BAEN BOOKS, P.O. Box 1403, Riverdale NY 10471-0671. (718)548-3100. Website: www.baen.com (includes writer's guidelines, chat line, annotated catalog, author bios, tour information). Publisher and Editor: Jim Baen. **Contact:** Toni Weisskopf, executive editor. Estab. 1983. "We publish books at the heart of science fiction and fantasy." Independent publisher. Publishes hardcover and paperback originals and paperback reprints. **Published new writers within the last year.** Plans 2-3 first novels this year. Averages 120 fiction titles/year. Distributes titles through Simon & Schuster.
Imprint(s): Baen Science Fiction and Baen Fantasy.
Needs: Fantasy and science fiction. Interested in science fiction novels (based on real science) and fantasy novels "that at least strive for originality." Published *A Civil Campaign*, by Lois McMaster Bujold; *Ashes of Victory*, by David Weber; *Sentry Peak*, by Harry Turtledove.
How to Contact: Accepts unsolicited mss. Submit ms or outline/synopsis and 3 consecutive sample chapters with SASE (or IRC). Responds in 9 months. Does not accept simultaneous submissions. Responds in 8 months to queries; 1 year to mss. Occasionally comments on rejected mss.
Terms: Pays in royalties on retail price; offers advance. Sends galleys to author. Guidelines available for SASE.
Advice: "Keep an eye and a firm hand on the overall story you are telling. Style is important but less important than plot. Good style, like good breeding, never calls attention to itself. Read *Writing to the Point*, by Algis Budrys. We like to maintain long-term relationships with authors."

BAKER BOOKS, a division of Baker Book House, P.O. Box 6287, Grand Rapids MI 49516-6213. (616)676-9185. Fax: (616)676-2315. Website: www.bakerbooks.com (includes catalog, submission policy, book excerpts and features, company history, advance info. on future releases). **Contact:** Jeanette Thomason, special projects editor (mystery, literary, women's fiction); Lonnie Hall DuPont, editorial director (all genres); Vicki Crumpton, acquisitions editor (all genres). Estab. 1939. "Midsize publisher of work that interests Christians." Publishes hardcover and paperback originals. Books: web offset print; average print order: 5,000-10,000; first novel print order: 5,000. Averages 130 total titles. Distributes titles through Ingram and Spring Arbor into both CBA and ABA markets worldwide.
Needs: "We are mainly seeking fiction of two genres: contemporary women's fiction and mystery." No fiction that is not written from a Christian world view or of a genre not specified. Published *Praise Jerusalem!* and *Resting in the Bosom of the Lamb*, by Augusta Trobaugh (contemporary women's fiction); *Things Hoped For, Things Not Seen*, by James Schaap (western, literary); and *Face to Face*, by Linda Dorrell (mystery).
How to Contact: Does not accept unsolicited mss. Submit through "literary agents or First Edition, the ECPA manuscript service on the ECPA website (www.ECPA.org). Book proposals posted on this website are available for review by all member publishers of the Evangelical Christian Publishers Association." No simultaneous submissions. Sometimes comments on rejected ms.
Terms: Pays royalties of 14% (of net). Offers advance. Sends galleys to author. Publishes ms 1 year after acceptance. Guidelines available for #10 SASE; book catalog for 9½ × 12½ SAE and 3 first-class stamps.
Advice: "We are not interested in historical fiction, romances, science fiction, Biblical narratives or spiritual warfare novels. Do not call to 'pass by' your idea."

BALLANTINE BOOKS, (Division of Random House, Inc.), 1540 Broadway, 11th Floor, New York NY 10036. (800)200-3552. Fax: (800)200-3552. E-mail: bfi@randomhouse.com. Website: www.randomhouse.com/BB. Estab. 1952. "Ballantine's list encompasses a large, diverse offering in a variety of formats." Publishes hardcover, trade paperback, and mass market paperback books.
Imprint(s): Ballantine Books; Del Ray; Fawcett (mystery line); Ivy (romance); Library of Contemporary Thought; Lucas Books; One World; Wellspring.

◑ Ⓐ BANCROFT PRESS, P.O. Box 65360, Baltimore MD 21209. (410)358-0658. Fax: (410)764-1967. E-mail: bruceb@bancroftpress.com. Website: www.bancroftpress.com (includes booklist, guidelines and mission statement). **Contact:** Bruce Bortz, editor. Estab. 1991. "Small independent press publishing literary and commercial fiction, often by journalists." Publishes hardcover and paperback originals. First novel print order: 5,000-7,500. **Published 2 new writers within the last year.** Averages 4-6 total titles, 2-4 fiction titles/year.
   • *The Re-Appearance of Sam Webber*, by Scott Fuqua is an ALEX Award winner.
Needs: Ethnic/multicultural (general), family saga, feminist, gay, glitz, historical, humor/satire, lesbian, literary, mainstream, military/war, mystery/suspense (amateur sleuth, cozy, police procedural, private eye/hardboiled), New Age/mystic, regional, science fiction (hard science/technological, soft/sociological), thriller/espionage, translations, western (frontier saga, traditional), young adult/teen (historical, problem novels, series). Published *Those Who Trespass*, by Bill O'Reilly (thriller); *The Re-Appearance of Sam Webber*, by Scott Fuqua (literary); and *Malicious Intent*, by Mike Walker (Hollywood).
How to Contact: Accepts unsolicited mss. Query with outline/synopsis and 3 sample chapters. Accepts queries by e-mail and fax. Include bio and list of publishing credits. Send SASE for reply, return of ms or send a disposable copy of ms. Agented fiction 100%. Responds in 6 months. Accepts simultaneous submissions. Sometimes comments on rejected mss.
Terms: Pays royalties of 6-8%. Average advance: $750. Sends galleys to author. Publishes ms 18 months after acceptance.
Advice: "Be patient, send a sample, know your book's audience."

✪ BANTAM DELL PUBLISHING GROUP, (Division of Random House, Inc.), 1540 Broadway, New York NY 10036. (212)782-9000. Fax: (212)302-7985. Estab. 1945. "In addition to being the nation's largest mass market paperback publisher, Bantam publishes a select yet diverse hardcover list." Publishes hardcover, trade paperback and mass market paperback originals; mass market paperback reprints.
Imprint(s): Bantam Hardcover; Bantam Trade Paperback; Bantam Mass Market; Crimeline; Domain; Fanfare; Spectra; Delacorte Press; The Dial Press; Delta; DTP; Dell; Island.

Ⓐ ✿ BANTAM DOUBLEDAY DELL BOOKS FOR YOUNG READERS, Random House Children's Publishing, A Division of Random House, Inc., 1540 Broadway, New York NY 10036. (212)782-9000. Fax: (212)782-9452. Website: www.randomhouse.com/kids. Vice President/Publisher: Beverly Horowitz. **Contact:** Michelle Poplof, editorial director. Publishes 300 titles/year.
   • *Bud, Not Buddy*, by Christopher Paul Curtis won the Newbery Medal and the Coretta Scott King Award.
Imprint(s): Delacorte Books for Young Readers, Doubleday Books for Young Readers; Laurel Leaf; Skylark; Starfire; Yearling Books.
Needs: Humor, mystery, fantasy, adventure, historical, picture books, chapter books, middle-grade, young adult. Recently published *Bud, Not Buddy*, by Christopher Paul Curtis; *My Friend John*, by Charlotte Zolotow; and *Ties That Bind, Ties That Break*, by Lensey Namiska.
How to Contact: Agented fiction only. Unsolicited submissions accepted for/through Delacorte Contest for a First Young Adult Novel or Marguerite de Angeli Contest for contemporary or historical fiction set in North America for readers age 7-10. Send SASE for contest guidelines. Responds in up to 4 months. Accepts simultaneous submissions but must be indicated as such.

Ⓝ BARBOUR PUBLISHING, INC., P.O. Box 719, Uhrichsville OH 44683. (740)922-6045. Website: www.barbourbooks.com. **Contact:** Paul Muckley, senior editor (all areas); Rebecca Germany, managing editor (fiction). Estab. 1981. Publishes hardcover, trade paperback and mass market paperback originals and reprints. **Publishes 40% of books from first-time authors; 95% from unagented writers.** Averages 200 titles/year.
Imprints: Heartsong Presents (contact Rebecca Germany, managing editor), Barbour Books and Promise Press (contact Paul Muckley, senior editor).
Needs: Historical, mainstream/contemporary, religious, romance, short story collections, western. "All of our fiction is 'sweet' romance. No sex, no bad language, etc. Audience is evangelical/Christian, and we're looking for wholesome material for young as well as old. Common writer's mistakes are a sketchy proposal, an unbelievable story and a story that doesn't fit our guidelines for inspirational romances." Recently published *Betrayed*, by Rosey Dow and Andrew Snaden (fiction).
How to Contact: Submit 3 sample chapter(s), synopsis, SASE. Accepts simultaneous submissions. Responds in 1 month to queries; 3 months to proposals; 3 months to mss.
Terms: Pays 0-12% royalty on net price or makes outright purchase of $500-5,000. Offers $500-2,500 advance. Publishes book 2 years after acceptance of ms. Book catalog online or for 9×12 SAE with 2 first-class stamps; ms guidelines for #10 SASE or online.
Advice: "Audience is evangelical/Christian conservative, non-denominational, young and old. We're looking for *great concepts*, not necessarily a big name author or agent. We want to publish books that will sell millions, not just 'flash in the pan' releases. Send us your ideas!"

◎ BARDSONG PRESS, P.O. Box 775396, Steamboat Springs CO 80477. (970)870-1401. Fax: (970)879-2657. E-mail: celts@bardsongpress.com. Website: www.bardsongpress.com (includes book catalog, writers guidelines, contest guidelines information and articles promoting our subjects of interest). **Contact:** Ann Gilpin, editor (Celtic history/

historical fiction). Estab. 1997. "Small independent press which specializes in historical novels and poetry with Celtic themes." Publishes hardcover originals and paperback reprints. Averages 1-2 total titles/year. Member, PMA, SPAN, CIPA.

Needs: Historical fiction (Celtic). Recently published *In the Shadow of Dragons*, by Kathleen Cunningham Guler (historical fiction). Publishes the Macsen's Treasure Series.

How to Contact: Does not accept unsolicited mss; will return if SASE provided. Query with outline/synopsis. Accepts e-mail queries. Include a brief bio and a list of publishing credits with submission. Writers should send SASE or IRC for return of the ms. Agented fiction: 50%. Responds in 2 months to queries; 4 months to mss. Considers simultaneous and disk submissions. No e-mail submissions. Sometimes comments on rejected mss.

Terms: Payment varies. Sends galleys to author. Time between acceptance and publication is 18 months. Guidelines available for SASE or on website; book catalogs on website or by mail.

Advice: "We are looking for work that reflects the ageless culture, history, symbolism, mythology and spirituality that belongs to Celtic heritage. Settings can range from ancient times to early twentieth century and include the earliest European territories, the current nations of Wales, Scotland, Ireland, Cornwall, Isle of Man, Brittany and Galicia, as well as lands involved in the Celtic Diaspora."

N **◎** **BAREFOOT BOOKS**, 3 Bow St., 3rd Floor, Cambridge MA 02138. (617)576-0660. Fax: (617)576-0049. E-mail: alisonkeehn@barefootbooks.com. Website: www.barefootbooks.com. **Contact:** Alison Keehn, associate editor (picture books and anthologies of folktales). Publishes hardcover and trade paperback originals. **Publishes 35% of books from first-time authors; 60% from unagented writers.** Averages 30 titles/year.

Needs: Juvenile. Barefoot Books only publishes children's picture books and anthologies of folktales and poetry. "We do not publish novels. We are no longer accepting unsolicited manuscripts as we were before because the response has been overwhelming. We do accept query letters, and we encourage authors to send the first page of their manuscript with the query letter." Recently published *Daddy Island*, by Philip Wells (picture book); *Fiesta Femenina: Celebrating Women in Mexican Folktale*, by Mary-Joan Gerson (illustrated anthology).

How to Contact: Query with SASE or submit First page of ms. Accepts simultaneous submissions. Responds in 2 months to queries; 2 months to proposals; 3 months to mss.

Terms: Pays 2.5-5% royalty on retail price or makes outright purchase of $5.99-19.99. Offers advance. Publishes book 2 years after acceptance of ms. Book catalog for #10 SASE.

Advice: "Our audience is made up of children and parents, teachers and students, of many different ages and cultures." "Since we are a small publisher, and we definitely publish for a 'niche' market, it is helpful to look at our books and our website before submitting, to see if your book would fit into our list."

N **◎** **BARRON'S EDUCATIONAL SERIES, INC.**, 250 Wireless Blvd., Hauppauge NY 11788. (631)434-3311. Fax: (631)434-3217. Website: barronseduc.com. **Contact:** Wayne Barr, managing editor/director of acquisitions. Estab. 1941. Publishes hardcover, paperback and mass market originals and software. **Publishes 40% of books from first-time authors; 75% from unagented writers.** Averages 400 titles/year.

Needs: Juvenile.

How to Contact: Submit sample chapter(s), synopsis. Accepts simultaneous submissions. Responds in 3 months to queries; 8 months to mss.

Terms: Pays 12-14% royalty on net receipts. Offers $3-4,000 advance. Publishes book 18 months after acceptance of ms. Book catalog free.

Advice: "Audience is mostly educated self-learners and hobbyists. The writer has the best chance of selling us a book that will fit into one of our series. Children's books have less chance for acceptance because of the glut of submissions. SASE must be included for the return of all materials. Please be patient for replies."

◙ **◢** **◎** **BEACH HOLME PUBLISHERS LTD.**, 226-2040 W. 12th Ave., Vancouver, British Columbia V6J 2G2 Canada. (604)733-4868. Fax: (604)733-4860. E-mail: bhp@beachholme.bc.ca. Website: www.beachholme.bc.ca (includes guidelines, reviews, authors, excerpts, titles, ordering information). **Contact:** Michael Carroll, publisher; Sarah Warren, publishing coordinator. Estab. 1971. Publishes trade paperback originals. Averages 14 titles/year. "Accepting only Canadian submissions." **Published 6 new writers within the last year.** Titles distributed through Stewart House Distribution (Canada) and Insomniac Group (US).

Imprints: Sandcastle Books (YA novels), Porcepic Books (literary fiction/poetry), Prospect Books (literary nonfiction).

Needs: Adult literary fiction from authors published in Canadian literary magazines. Young adult (Canada historical/regional). "Interested in excellent quality, imaginative writing." Recently published *North of the Equator*, by Cyril Dabydeen (short fiction); *Hail Mary Corner*, by Brian Payton (novel); *Cold Clear Morning*, by Lesley Choyce (novel).

How to Contact: Query with outline and two chapters. Responds in 4 months.

Terms: Pays royalties of 10% on retail price. Average advance: $500. Publishes ms 1 year after acceptance. Guidelines available free.

Advice: "Make sure the manuscript is well written. We see so many that only the unique and excellent can't be put down. Prior publication is a must. This doesn't necessarily mean book-length manuscripts, but a writer should try to publish his or her short fiction."

◢ **FREDERIC C. BEIL, PUBLISHER, INC.**, 609 Whitaker St., Savannah GA 31401. E-mail: beilbook@beil.com. Website: www.beil.com. **Contact:** Frederic C. Beil III, president; Mary Ann Bowman, editor. Estab. 1983. "Our objectives are (1) to offer to the reading public carefully selected texts of lasting value; (2) to adhere to high standards in the

choice of materials and in bookmarking craftsmanship; (3) to produce books that exemplify good taste in format and design; and (4) to maintain the lowest cost consistent with quality." General trade publisher. Publishes hardcover originals and reprints. Books: acid-free paper; letterpress and offset printing; Smyth-sewn, hardcover binding; illustrations. Average print order: 3,000. First novel print order: 3,000. Averages 14 total titles, 4 fiction titles/year.
Imprint(s): The Sandstone Press, Hypermedia, Inc.
Needs: Historical, biography, literary, regional, short story collections, translations. Published *The Dry Well*, by Marlin Barton (fiction); *Joseph Jefferson*, by Arthur Bloom (biography); and *Goya, Are You With Me Now?*, by H.E. Francis (fiction).
How to Contact: Does not accept unsolicited mss. Send query letter. Responds in 1 week to queries.
Terms: Payment "all negotiable." Sends galleys to author. Book catalog available free.
Advice: "Write about what you love."

BERKLEY PUBLISHING GROUP, (Division of Penguin Putnam Inc.), 375 Hudson St., New York NY 10014. (212)366-2000. E-mail: online@penguinputnam.com. Website: www.penguinputnam.com. Estab.1955. "Berkley is proud to publish in paperback some of the country's most significant best-selling authors." Publishes paperback and mass market originals and reprints.
Imprint(s): Ace Books; Berkley Books; Boulevard; Diamond Books; HP Books; Jam; Jove; Perigee; Prime Crime; Riverhead Books (paperback).

BETHANY HOUSE PUBLISHERS, 11400 Hampshire Ave. S., Bloomington MN 55438. (612)829-2500. Fax: (952)829-1304. Website: www.bethanyhouse.com. Estab. 1956. "The purpose of Bethany House Publisher's publishing program is to relate biblical truth to all areas of life—whether in the framework of a well-told story, of a challenging book for spiritual growth, or of a Bible reference work." Publishes hardcover and trade paperback originals and mass market paperback reprints. Averages 120-150 total titles/year.
Needs: Adult historical fiction, teen/young adult, children's fiction series (age 8-12) and Bethany Backyard (age 6-12). New interest in contemporary fiction. Recently published *The Covenant*, by Beverly Lewis (fiction).
How to Contact: Does not accept unsolicited fiction. Send 1-page query by fax *only*.
Terms: Pays negotiable royalty on wholesale price. Offers negotiable advance. Guidelines available on website; book catalog for 9×12 SAE with 5 first-class stamps.

BILINGUAL PRESS, Hispanic Research Center, Arizona State University, P.O. Box 872702, Tempe AZ 85287-2702. (480)965-3867. Fax: (480)965-8309. E-mail: brp@asu.edu. Website: www.asu.edu/brp. **Contact:** Gary Keller, editor. Estab. 1973. "University affiliated." Publishes hardcover and paperback originals and reprints. Books: 60 lb. acid-free paper; single sheet or web press printing; perfect-bound. Average print order: 4,000 copies (1,000 casebound, 3,000 soft cover). **Published 4 new writers within the last year.** Averages 8 total titles, 5 fiction titles/year.
Needs: Ethnic, literary, short story collections. "We are always on the lookout for Chicano, Puerto Rican, Cuban-American or other U.S.-Hispanic themes with strong and serious literary qualities and distinctive and intellectually important themes. We have been receiving a lot of fiction set in Latin America (usually Mexico or Central America) where the main character is either an ingenue to the culture or a spy, adventurer or mercenary. We don't publish this sort of 'Look, I'm in an exotic land' type of thing. Also, novels about the Aztecs or other pre-Columbians are very iffy." Recently published *Fantasmas: Supernatural Stories by Mexican American Writers; Stars Always Shine*, by Rick Riverra (debut author); and *Valedictorian and Other Stories*, by S.D. Navarro (debut author).
How to Contact: Accepts unsolicited mss. Send query letter and 2-3 sample chapters with SASE or IRC for reply. Include brief bio and list of publishing credits with submission. Accepts queries by e-mail. Responds in 6 weeks to queries; 2-6 months to mss.
Terms: Pays royalties of 10%. Average advance: $500. Provides 10 author's copies. Sends galleys to author. Publishes ms 2 years after acceptance. Guidelines available for e-mail; book catalog free.
Advice: "Writers should take the utmost care in assuring that their manuscripts are clean, grammatically impeccable, and have perfect spelling. This is true not only of the English but the Spanish as well. All accent marks need to be in place as well as other diacritical marks. When these are missing it's an immediate first indication that the author does not really know Hispanic culture and is not equipped to write about it. We are interested in publishing creative literature that treats the U.S.-Hispanic experience in a distinctive, creative, revealing way. The kinds of books that we publish we keep in print for a very long time irrespective of sales. We are busy establishing and preserving a U.S.-Hispanic canon of creative literature."

BIRCH BROOK PRESS, P.O. Box 81, Delhi NY 13753. Fax: (607)746-7453. E-mail: birchbrk@yahoo.com or catskill.net. Website: www.birchbrookpress.info. **Contact:** Tom Tolnay, publisher. Estab. 1982. Small publisher of popular culture and literary titles in handcrafted letterpress editions. Specializes in fiction anthologies with specific theme, and an occasional novella. "Not a good market for full-length novels." Books: 80 lb. vellum paper; letterpress printing; wood engraving illustrations. Average print order: 500-1,000. Averages 4-6 total titles, 2-3 fiction titles/year. Member, Small Press Center, Academy of American Poets. Distributes titles through Ingram, Baker and Taylor, Barnes&Noble.com, Amazon.com. Promotes titles through website, catalogs, direct mail and group ads.
Imprint(s): Birch Brook Press, Persephone Press and Birch Brook Impressions.
Needs: Literary, regional (Adirondacks), special interest (fly-fishing, baseball, books about books, outdoors), translations (literary). "We make specific calls for fiction when we are doing an anthology." Plans to publish literary-quality anthology of short fiction relating to fly fishing. Published *Magic & Madness in the Library*, edited by Eric Graeber

(fiction collection); *Kilimanjaro Burning*, by John Robinson (novella); *Fateful Choices*, edited by Marshall Brooks and Stephanie Greene; *A Punk in Gallows, America*, by P.W. Fox; *White Buffalo*, by Peter Skinner; *Cooperstown Chronicles*, by Peter Rutkoff.

How to Contact: Prefers samples with query letter. Must include SASE. Responds in up to 6 weeks to queries; up to 3 months to mss. Accepts simultaneous submissions. Sometimes comments on rejected mss.

Terms: Pays modest flat fee on anthologies. Guidelines and catalog available for SASE.

Advice: "Write well on subjects of interest to BBP such as outdoors, fly fishing, baseball, music, literary novellas, books about books, cultural history."

BLACK HERON PRESS, P.O. Box 95676, Seattle WA 98145. Fax: (206)363-5210. Website: www.blackhero npress.com (includes book catalog and interviews with authors). **Contact:** Jerry Gold, publisher. Estab. 1984. Two-person operation; no immediate plans to expand. "We're known for literary fiction. We've done several Vietnam War titles and several surrealistic fictions." Publishes paperback and hardback originals. Average print order: 2,000. First novel print order: 1,500. **Publishes 1-2 new writers/year.** Averages 4 fiction titles/year. Distributes titles nationally through Midpoint Trade Books.

• Five books published by Black Heron Press have won awards from King County Arts Commission.

Needs: Adventure, contemporary, experimental, humor/satire, literary, science fiction. Vietnam war novel—literary. "We don't want to see fiction written for the mass market. If it sells to the mass market, fine, but we don't see ourselves as a commercial press." Published *Somebody*, by Laurie Blauner (literary fiction, debut author); *Rikers*, by Paul Volponi (adult/YA fiction, debut author); and *Moses in Sinai*, by Simone Zelitch (historical fiction).

How to Contact: Query with first 50 pages only. Responds in 3 months to queries. Accepts simultaneous submissions.

Terms: Pays standard royalty rates. No advance.

Advice: "A query letter should tell me: 1) number of words; 2) number of pages; 3) if ms is available on disk; 4) if parts of novel have been published; 5) if so, where? And at least scan some of our books in a bookstore or library. Most submissions we get have come to the wrong press."

BLACK LACE BOOKS, Virgin Publishing, Thames Wharf Studios, Rainville Rd., London W6 9HA United Kingdom. Phone: +44(0207)386 3300. Fax: +44(0207)386 3360. E-mail: ksharp@virgin-books.co.uk. Website: www.blacklace-books.co.uk (includes book catalog, mission statements). **Contact:** Kerri Sharp, senior commissioning editor. Estab. 1993. Publishes paperback originals. Plans 15 first novels this year. Averages 24 fiction titles/year.

Imprint(s): Nexus Fetish Erotic Fiction for Men; Paul Copperwaite, editor; Black Lace Erotic Fiction for Women; Kerri Sharp, editor. "Nexus and Black Lace are the leading imprints of erotic fiction in the UK.

Needs: Erotica. "Female writers only for the Black Lace Series." Especially needs erotic fiction in contemporary settings. Publishes 2 erotic short story anthologies by women per year.

How to Contact: Accepts unsolicited mss. Query with synopsis and 2 sample chapters. Include estimated word count. Send SASE or IRC for return of ms. Agented fiction 25%. Responds in 1 month to queries; 6 months to mss. Accepts simultaneous submissions. Always comments on rejected mss.

Terms: Pays royalties of 7½%. Average advance: $1,000. Sends galleys to author. Publishes ms 7 months after acceptance. Guidelines available for SASE; book catalogs free.

Advice: "Contemporary settings are strongly preferred. Open to female authors only. Read the guidelines first."

JOHN F. BLAIR, PUBLISHER, 1406 Plaza Dr., Winston-Salem NC 27103. (336)768-1374. Fax: (336)768-9194. Website: www.blairpub.com. **Contact:** Carolyn Sakowski, president. Estab. 1954. Small independent publisher. Publishes hardcover and paperback originals. Books: Acid-free paper; offset printing; illustrations. Average print order: 5,000. "Among our 17-20 books, we do one novel a year."

Needs: Prefers regional material dealing with southeastern U.S. No confessions or erotica. "Our editorial focus concentrates mostly on nonfiction." Published *Freedom's Altar*, by Charles Price; *Caveat*, by Laura Kalpakian; and *Something Blue*, by Jean Spaugh.

How to Contact: Accepts unsolicited mss. Send query letter or submit complete ms with cover letter (prefers query). Send SASE or IRC for return of ms. Accepts simultaneous submissions. Responds in 1 month. Complete guidelines available on website.

Terms: Negotiable. Publishes ms 1-2 years after acceptance. Book catalog available free.

Advice: "We are primarily interested in nonfiction titles. Most of our titles have a tie-in with North Carolina or the southeastern United States. Please enclose a cover letter and outline with the manuscript. We prefer to review queries before we are sent complete manuscripts. Queries should include an approximate word count."

THE BLUE SKY PRESS, Imprint of Scholastic Inc., 557 Broadway, New York NY 10012-3999. (212)343-6100. Fax: (212)343-4831. Website: www.scholastic.com. **Contact** The editors. Blue Sky Press publishes primarily juvenile picture books. Publishes hardcover originals. Averages 15 titles/year.

• Because of a long backlog of books, the Blue Sky Press is not accepting unsolicited submissions.

Needs: Juvenile: adventure, fantasy, historical, humor, mainstream/contemporary, picture books, multicultural, folktales. Published *Bluish*, by Virginia Hamilton (novel); *No, David!*, by David Shannon (picture book); and *To Every Thing There is a Season*, by Leo and Diane Dillon (multicultural/historical).

How to Contact: Agented fiction 25%. Responds in 6 months to queries from previously published authors.

Terms: Pays 10% royalty on wholesale price, between authors and illustrators. Publishes ms 2½ years after acceptance.

THE BOOKS COLLECTIVE, 214-21 10405 Jasper Ave., Edmonton, Alberta T5J 3S2 Canada. (780)448-0590. Fax: (780)448-0640. E-mail: admin@bookscollective.com. Website: www.bookscollective.com. **Contact:** Candas J. Dorsey or Timothy J. Anderson. Estab. 1992. "Small independent publisher of Canadian literary fiction, poetry, contemporary memoir and speculative." Publishes hardcover and paperback originals. Averages 4-10 total titles/year.

Needs: Plans to publish an anthology of Speculative Fiction. Recently published *Green Music*, by Ursula Pflug (speculative fiction); *Gypsy Messenger*, by Marijan Megla (poetry); and *Running Through the Devil's Club*, by Deborah Huford (nonfiction, debut author).

How to Contact: Accepts unsolicited mss. Send query letter or query with outline/synopsis and 3 sample chapters. Accepts queries by e-mail. Send SASE or IRC for return of ms. Accepts simultaneous submissions. Sometimes comments on rejected mss.

Terms: Sends galleys to author. Guidelines available for SASE; book catalog on website.

Advice: "Only Canadian writers have their manuscripts read. All non-Canadian writers' manuscripts returned unread. Canadian writers living abroad must use Canadian stamps on SASEs. Most of our books are solicited by the press. Timelines for manuscript consideration are long."

BOOKS FOR ALL TIMES, INC., Box 2, Alexandria VA 22313. Website: www.bfat.com. **Contact:** Joe David, publisher/editor. Estab. 1981. One-man operation. Publishes paperback originals. Has published 3 fiction titles to date.

Needs: Contemporary, literary, short story collections. "No novels at the moment; hopeful, though, of publishing a collection of quality short stories. No popular fiction or material easily published by the major or minor houses specializing in mindless entertainment. Only interested in stories of the Victor Hugo or Sinclair Lewis quality."

How to Contact: Send query letter with SASE. Responds in 1 month to queries. Occasionally comments on rejected mss.

Terms: Pays negotiable advance. "Publishing/payment arrangement will depend on plans for the book." Book catalog available free with SASE.

Advice: Interested in "controversial, honest stories which satisfy the reader's curiosity to know. Read Victor Hugo, Fyodor Dostoyevsky and Sinclair Lewis for an example."

BOOKS IN MOTION, 9922 E. Montgomery, Suite #31, Spokane WA 99206. (509)922-1646. Website: www.booksinmotion.com (includes contact info, author profiles, catalog, company profile, and special promotions). **Contact:** Cameron Beierle, editor. Website: www.booksinmotion.com. Estab. 1980. "Audiobook company, national marketer. Publishes novels in audiobook form *only*." Published new writers within the last year. Averages 100 total titles, 90 fiction titles each year. Distributes titles through Internet, direct mail and various retailers as well as through its own nationwide rental program. Promotes titles through nationwide rental program, catalog, Internet website features and by client newsletters.

Needs: Action/adventure, westerns, mystery, science fiction (non-technical), fantasy, some romance. Recently published *Magic Kingdom for Sale*, by Terry Brooks; and *Partners in Crime*, by J.A. Jance. Have published over 140 new authors in last 3 years.

How to Contact: No unsolicited mss. "Seeking returned audio rights on previously published works. Know who controls subrights—you, your agent, your publisher—prior to contacting Books in Motion." Agented fiction 10%. Responds in up to 3 months. Accepts simultaneous submissions.

Terms: Pays royalties of 10%. "We pay royalties every 6 months. Royalties that are received are based on the gross sales that any given title generates during the 6-month interval. Authors must be patient since it usually takes a minimum of one year before new titles will have significant sales." Publishes ms 6-12 months after acceptance. Book catalog available free.

Advice: "Our audience is 20% women, 80% men. Many of our audience are truck drivers, who want something interesting to listen to. We prefer a minimum of profanity and no gratuitous sex. We want novels with a strong plot. The fewer the characters, the better it will work on tape. Six-tape audiobooks sell and rent better than any other size in the unabridged format. One hour of tape is equal to 40 pages of double-spaced, 12 pitch, normal margin, typed pages."

BOREALIS PRESS, 110 Bloomingdale St., Ottawa, Ontario K2C 4A4 Canada. Fax: (613)829-7783. E-mail: borealis@istar.ca. Website: www.borealispress.com (includes names of editors, authors, all Borealis Press and Tecumseh Press books currently in print). **Contact:** Frank Tierney, editor; Glenn Clever, editor. Estab. 1970. "Publishes Canadiana, especially early works that have gone out of print, but also novels of today and shorter fiction for young readers." Publishes hardcover and paperback originals and reprints. Books: standard book-quality paper; offset printing; perfect and cloth binding. Average print order: 1,000. Buys juvenile mss with b&w illustrations. **Published new writers within in the last year.** Averages 20 total titles/year. Promotes titles through website, catalogue distribution, fliers for titles, ads in media.

CHECK THE CATEGORY INDEXES, located at the back of the book, for publishers interested in specific fiction subjects.

● Borealis Press has a "New Canadian Drama," with 7 books in print. The series won Ontario Arts Council and Canada Council grants.

Imprint(s): *Journal of Canadian Poetry*, Tecumseh Press Ltd., Canadian Critical Editions Series.

Needs: Contemporary, literary, juvenile, young adult. "Must have a Canadian content or author; query first." Recently published *Blue: Little Cat Come Home to Stay*, by Donna Richards (young adult); *Biography of a Beagle*, by Gail MacMillan (novel); *The Love of Women*, Jennifer McVaugh (comic novel).

How to Contact: Send query letter. Send SASE (Canadian postage) or IRC. Accepts queries by e-mail, fax. No simultaneous submissions. Responds in 2 weeks to queries; 4 months to mss. Publishes ms 1-2 years after acceptance.

Terms: Pays royalties of 10% and 3 free author's copies. No advance. Sends galleys to author.

Advice: "Have your work professionally edited. Our greatest challenge is finding good authors, i.e., those who submit innovative and original material."

BOSON BOOKS, C&M Online Media, Inc., 3905 Meadow Field Lane, Raleigh NC 27606. (919)233-8164. Fax: (919)233-8578. E-mail: cm@cmonline.com. Website: www.cmonline.com. (All books may be purchased through the website). **Contact:** Acquisitions Editor. Estab. 1994. "We are an online book company with distribution at our website and through ten separate distributors such as CyberRead.com, powells.com, ebooks.com, mobipocket.com and barnesandnoble.com. Publishes online originals and reprints. **Published 6 new writers within the last year.** Averages 12 total titles, 9 fiction titles/year. Member, Association of Online Publishers.

Needs: "The quality of the writing is our only consideration." Publishes ongoing series of Holocaust narratives by eyewitnesses.

How to Contact: Does not accept or return unsolicited mss. Query with synopsis and 2 sample chapters. Accepts queries by e-mail. Electronic submissions only.

Terms: Pays royalties of 25%. Sends galleys to author. Guidelines and book catalog available on website.

Advice: "We want to see only excellence in writing."

BOYDS MILLS PRESS, Subsidiary of *Highlights for Children*, 815 Church St., Honesdale PA 18431. (570)253-1164. Website: www.boydsmillspress.com (includes names of editors, author information, book information and reviews). **Contact**: Larry Rosler, editorial director. Estab. 1990. "Independent publisher of quality books for children of all ages." Publishes hardcover originals and trade paperback reprints. Books: Coated paper; offset printing; case binding; 4-color illustrations. Average print order: varies. **Published 2 new writers within the last year.** Plans 4 fiction titles/year. Distributes titles through independent sales reps and via order line directly from Boyds Mills Press. Promotes titles through sales and professional conferences, sales reps, reviews.

Needs: Juvenile, young adult (adventure, animal, contemporary, ethnic, historical, humor, mystery, sports). No fantasy, romance, horror. Recently published *Sharks! Strange and Wonderful*, by Laurence Pringle; *Groover's Heart*, by Carole Crowe; and *Storm Coming!*, by Audrey B. Baird.

How to Contact: Accepts unsolicited mss. Query with first 3 chapters and synopsis; submit complete ms for picture books. Responds in 1 month to mss. Accepts simultaneous submissions. Agented fiction 80%.

Terms: Pays standard rates. Sends pre-publication galleys to author. Time between acceptance and publication depends on "what season it is scheduled for." Guidelines available for #10 SASE.

Advice: "Read through our recently-published titles and review our catalogue. If your book is too different from what we publish, then it may not fit our list. Feel free to query us if you're not sure."

BRANDEN BOOKS, Subsidiary of Branden Press, P.O. Box 812 094, Wellesley MA 02482. (781)235-3634. Fax: (781)790-1056. E-mail: branden@branden.com. Website: www.branden.com. **Contact**: Adolph Caso, editor. Estab. 1967. Publishes hardcover and paperback originals and reprints. Books: 55-60 lb. acid-free paper; case- or perfect-bound; illustrations. Average print order: 5,000. Averages 15 total titles, 5 fiction titles/year.

Imprint(s): I.P.L., Dante University Press, Four Seas, Branden Publishing Co.

Needs: Ethnic, historical, literary, military/war, short story collections and translations. Looking for "contemporary, fast pace, modern society." No porno, experimental or horror. Published *I, Morgain*, by Harry Robin; *The Bell Keeper*, by Marilyn Seguin; and *The Straw Obelisk*, by Adolph Caso.

How to Contact: Does not accept unsolicited mss. Query *only* with SASE. Responds in 1 week to queries, with either "we cannot use" or "send entire manuscript."

Terms: Pays royalties of 5-10% minimum. Advance negotiable. Provides 10 author's copies. Sends galleys to author. Publishes ms "several months" after acceptance.

Advice: "Publishing more fiction because of demand. *Do not make phone, fax or e-mail inquiries.* Do not oversubmit; single submissions only; do not procrastinate if contract is offered. Our audience is a well-read general public, professionals, college students, and some high school students. We like books by or about women."

GEORGE BRAZILLER, INC., 171 Madison Ave., Suite 1105, New York NY 10016. (212)889-0909. **Acquisitions:** Mary Taveros, production editor. Publishes hardcover and trade paperback originals and reprints. Publishes 25 titles/year.

Needs: Ethnic, gay, lesbian, literary. "We rarely do fiction but when we have published novels, they have mostly been literary novels." Published *Blindsight*, by Herve Guibert; and *Papa's Suitcase*, by Gerhard Kopf (literary fiction).

How to Contact: Submit 4-6 sample chapters with SASE. Agented fiction 20%. Responds in 3 months to proposals.

Terms: Pays standard royalty: 8% paperback; 10-15% hardback. Publishes ms 10 months after acceptance. Guidelines and book catalog available free.

N ⬤ ◎ BREAKAWAY BOOKS, P.O. Box 24, Halcottsville NY 12438. Phone/fax: (212)898-0408. E-mail: editorial@breakawaybooks.com. Website: www.breakawaybooks.com. **Contact**: Garth Battista, fiction editor (sports fiction). Estab. 1994. "Small press specializing in fine literary books on sports." Publishes hardcover originals and paperback reprints. **Published 3 new writers within the last year.** Averages 9 total titles, 8 fiction titles/year. Sometimes comments on rejected mss.
Needs: Sports.
How to Contact: Accepts unsolicited mss. Query with outline/synopsis and sample chapters. Submit complete ms with cover letter. Unsolicited queries/correspondence by e-mail OK. Include bio and list of publishing credits. Send SASE for reply, return of ms or send disposable copy of ms. Agented fiction 50%. Accepts simultaneous and electronic submissions.
Terms: Pays royalties of 7.5% minimum; 10% maximum. Sends galleys to author. Publishes ms 9-18 months.

N ⬤ BRIDGE WORKS PUBLISHING CO., 221 Bridge Lane, Box 1798, Bridgehampton NY 11932. (516)537-3418. Fax: (516)537-5092. E-mail: bap@hamptons.com. **Contact:** Barbara Phillips, editorial director. Estab. 1992. "We are very small, doing only 9-12 books a year. We publish quality fiction and nonfiction. Our books are routinely reviewed in major publications." Publishes hardcover originals. Average print order: 5,000. Published new writers within the last year. Plans 6 novels this year and 80% fiction next year. Distributes titles through National Book Network.
Needs Humor/satire, literary, translations. Recently published *Aria*, by Susan Segal and *The Angel Cohen*, by Claude Campbell.
How to Contact: Accepts unsolicited mss, but "must send query letter first. If you are a first-time writer, do not query or send manuscripts unless work has been edited by a freelance editor." Include estimated word count and list of publishing credits. Send SASE for reply or return of ms. Agented fiction 50%. Responds in 2 weeks to queries; 2 months to mss. Sometimes comments on rejected mss.
Terms: Pays royalties of 10% maximum "based on cover price with a reserve against returns." Average advance: $1,000. Sends galleys to author. Publishes ms 1 year after acceptance.
Advice: "We are interested in discovering new writers and we work closely with our authors in both the editorial and marketing processes."

N ⬤ ◎ BROADMAN & HOLMAN PUBLISHERS, LifeWay Christian Resources, 127 Ninth Ave. N., Nashville TN 37234. (615)251-2438. Fax: (615)251-3752. **Contact:** Leonard G. Goss, editorial director (historical, romance, contemporary, suspense, western, thrillers, etc.). Estab. 1934. "Large, commercial evangelical Christian publishing firm. We publish Christian fiction in all genres." Publishes hardcover and paperback originals. **Published 10 new writers within the last year.** Plans 5 first novels this year. Averages 150 total titles, 25 fiction titles/year. Member, ECPA. Distributes and promotes titles "on a national and international scale through a large sales organization."
Needs: Adventure, mystery/suspense, religious (general religious, inspirational, religious fantasy, religious mystery/suspense, religious thriller, religious romance), western. Recently published *Sea of Glory*, by Ken Wales and David Poling (historical, debut author); *The Third Dragon*, by Frank Simon (mystery/intrigue); and *Friends and Enemies*, by Steve Bly (western).
How to Contact: Does not accept unsolicited fiction mss. Query with outline/synopsis and 2 sample chapters. Accepts queries by e-mail. Include estimated word count, brief bio and list of publishing credits. Send disposable copy of ms and SASE for reply only. Agented fiction 50%. Responds in 1 month to queries; 2 months to mss. Considers simultaneous submissions. No electronic or disk submissions. Sometimes comments on rejected mss.
Terms: Pays royalties of 14-18%. Pays negotiable advance. Sends galleys to author. Publishes ms up to 10 months after acceptance. Guidelines available for SASE; book catalog free.

A BROADWAY BOOKS, The Doubleday Broadway Publishing Group, A Division of Random House, Inc. 1540 Broadway, New York NY 10036. (212)782-9000. Fax: (212)782-8338. Website: www.broadwaybooks.com. **Contact:** Gerald Howard, publisher/editor-in-chief; Luke Dempsey, senior editor (sports, media, fiction). Estab. 1995. Broadway publishes general interest nonfiction and fiction for adults. Publishes hardcover and trade paperback originals and reprints.
Needs: Commercial literary fiction. Published *Freedomland*, by Richard Price.
How to Contact: Accepts agented fiction only.

N ⬤ A CADMUS EDITIONS, Box 126, Tiburon CA 94920-0126. (707)762-1050. E-mail: cebiz@cadmus-editions.com. Website: www.cadmus-editions.com. **Contact:** Jeffrey Miller, editor. Estab. 1979. Emphasis on quality literature. Publishes hardcover and paperback originals. Books: approximately 25% letterpress; 75% offset printing; perfect and case binding. Average print order: 2,000. First novel print order: 2,000. Averages 1-3 total titles/year. Distributes titles through Small Press Distribution, Berkeley CA.
Needs: Literary. Published *The Wandering Fool*, by Yunus Emre, translated by Edouard Roditi and Guzin Dino; *The Hungry Girls*, by Patricia Eakins; and *Zig-Zag*, by Richard Thornley.
How to Contact: No unsolicited mss. Agented material only. No e-mailed queries.
Terms: Pays negotiated royalty.

⬛ ◎ CAITLIN PRESS, INC., P.O. Box 2387 Station B, Prince George, British Columbia V2N 2S6 Canada. (250)964-4953. Fax: (250)964-4970. E-mail: caitlin_press@telus.net. Website: www.caitlin-press.com (includes writer's guidelines, catalogue, what's new, author tours, interviews, author bios, about US order info). **Contact:** Cynthia Wilson.

Estab. 1977. "We publish books about the British Columbia interior or by people from the interior." Publishes trade paperback and soft cover originals. Averages 6-7 titles/year. Distributes titles directly from publisher and through general distribution and Harbour Publishing. Promotes titles through *BC Book World*, *Candian Books in Print* and website.

Needs: Adventure, historical, humor, mainstream/contemporary, short story collections, young adult.

How to Contact: Accepts unsolicited mss. Send query letter with SASE. Responds in 3 months to queries. Accepts simultaneous submissions.

Terms: Pays royalties of 15% on wholesale price. Publishes ms 18 months after acceptance.

Advice: "Our area of interest is British Columbia and Northern Canada. Submitted manuscripts should reflect our interest area."

CALYX BOOKS, P.O. Box B, Corvallis OR 97339-0539. (503)753-9384. Fax: (541)753-0515. E-mail: calyx@proaxis.com. **Contact**: M. Donnelly, director; Micki Reaman, managing editor. Estab. 1986. "Calyx exists to publish women's literary and artistic work and is committed to publishing the works of all women, including women of color, older women, lesbians, working-class women, and other voices that need to be heard." Publishes hardcover and paperback originals. Books: offset printing; paper and cloth binding. Average print order: 4,000-10,000 copies. First novel print order: 4,000-5,000. **Published 1 new writer within the last year.** Averages 3 total titles/year. Distributes titles through Consortium Book Sales and Distribution. Promotes titles through author reading tours, print advertising (trade and individuals), galley and review copy mailings, presence at trade shows, etc.

• "We are closed for book submissions until further notice."

Needs: Contemporary, ethnic, experimental, feminist, lesbian, literary, short story collections, translations. Published *Into the Forest*, by Jean Hegland (women's literature); *Undertow*, by Amy Schutzer (lesbian literature); and *The End of the Class Wars*, by Catherine Brady (short stories). Past anthologies include *Forbidden Stitch: An Asian American Women's Anthology*; *Women and Aging*; *Present Tense: Writing and Art by Young Women*; and *A Line of Cutting Women*.

How to Contact: Send SASE for submission guidelines. Accepts requests by e-mail.

Terms: Pays royalties of 10% minimum, author's copies (depends on grant/award money). Average advance: $200-500. Sends galleys to author. Publishes ms 2 years after acceptance. Guidelines available for #10 SASE; book catalog free.

CANADIAN INSTITUTE OF UKRAINIAN STUDIES PRESS, CIUS Toronto Publications Office, University of Toronto, 1 Spadina Crescent, Room 109, Toronto, Ontario M5S 2J5 Canada. (416)978-6934. Fax: (416)978-2672. E-mail: cius@chass.utoronto.ca. Website: www.utoronto.ca/cius. **Contact**: Roman Senkus, director or publications; Marko Stech, managing director. Estab. 1976. "We publish scholarship about Ukraine and Ukrainians in Canada." Publishes hardcover and trade paperback originals and reprints. Publishes 5-10 titles/year.

Needs: Ukrainian literary works. "We do not publish fiction except for use as college textbooks." Recently published *History of Ukraine-Rus'* Volume VIII, by Mykhailo Hrushevsky; *From Nationalism to Universalism*, by Vladimir Jabotinsky; *On Sunday Morning She Gathered Herbs*, by Olha Kobylianska; and *A Concordance to the Poetic Works of Taras Shevchenko*, by Oleh Ilnytzkyj and George Hawrysch.

How to Contact: Query or submit complete ms. Accepts queries by fax or e-mail. Responds in 1 month to queries; 3 months to mss.

Terms: Nonauthor-subsidy publishes 20-30% of books. Pays 0-2% royalty on retail price. Publishes ms 2 years after acceptance. Guidelines and book catalog available free.

Advice: "We are a scholarly press and do not normally pay our authors. Our audience consists of university students and teachers and the general public interested in Ukrainian and Ukrainian-Canadian affairs."

CANDLEWICK PRESS, Subsidiary of Walker Books Ltd. (London), 2067 Massachusetts Ave., Cambridge MA 02140. (617)661-3330. Fax: (617)661-0565. E-mail: bigbear@candlewick.com. Website: www.candlewick.com (catalog, guidelines, author interviews). **Contact:**Karen Lotz, president and publisher; Liz Bicknell, editorial director/associate publisher; Joan Powers, editorial director (novelty); Mary Lee Donovan, executive editor (nonfiction/fiction); Amy Ehrlich, editor at large (picture books); Kara LaReau, editor (fiction/poetry); Sarah Ketchersid, editor; Deborah Wayshak, senior editor (fiction); Jamie Michalak, associate editor (fiction/picture book); Cynthia Platt, editor (fiction/nonfiction). Candlewick Press publishes high-quality illustrated children's books for ages infant through young adult. "We are a truly child-centered publisher." Estab. 1991. Publishes hardcover originals, trade paperback originals and reprints. Publishes 200 titles/year.

Needs: Juvenile. Recently published *Because of Winn-Dixie*, by Kate DiCamillo; *Handel, Who Knew What He Liked*, by M.T. Anderson, illustrated by Kevin Hawkes; and *A Poke in the 'I'*, edited by Paul Janeczko, illustrated by Chris Raschka.

How to Contact: Currently not accepting unsolicited ms.

Terms: Pays royalties of 10% on retail price. Advance varies. Publishes ms 3 years after acceptance for illustrated books, 1 year for others.

CAROLINA WREN PRESS, INC./LOLLIPOP POWER BOOKS, 120 Morris St., Durham NC 27701. (919)560-2738. Fax: (919)560-2759. E-mail: carolina@carolinawrenpress.org. Website: www.carolinawrenpress.org. **Contact:** Andrea Selch or David Kellogg. Estab. 1976. "Small, one person, part-time, nonprofit. We depend on grants to operate. We cater to new writers who have been historically under-represented, especially women, people of color, minorities, etc." Publishes paperback originals. Books: 6×9 paper; typeset; various bindings; illustrations. Average print order: 1,500. First novel print order: 1,500. **Published 1 new writer within the last year.** Averages 2 total titles, 1 fiction title/year. Member, SPD. Distributes titles through Amazon.com, Barnes & Noble, Borders, Ingram and Baker & Taylor.

Needs: Children's/juvenile (non-stereotypical), ethnic/multicultural, experimental (poetry), feminist, gay, lesbian, literary, short story collections. "We are especially interested in children's literature on the subjects of health, illness, mental illness, healing, etc." Recently published *Piece Logic*, by Erica Hunt; *Gorgon Goddess*, by Evie Shockley; *Churchboys and Other Sinners*, by Preston Allen; *Succory*, by Andrea Selch; and *Gold Indigoes*, by George Elliott Clarke.

How to Contact: Accepts unsolicited mss. Send query letter. Accepts queries by e-mail or mail. Include brief bio. Send SASE or IRC for return of ms. Agented fiction "only one of 40" submissions. Responds in 3 months to queries; 6 months to mss.

Terms: Pays in author's copies (10% of print run) and 50% off list price for additional copies. Sends galleys to author. Publishes ms 1 year after acceptance.

Advice: "Please do not submit unless in response to advertised call on specific topic. Workshop your manuscript before submitting." Offers the Sonja H. Stone fiction contest every few years; see website for details.

CAROLRHODA BOOKS, INC., Division of the Lerner Publishing Group, 241 First Ave. N., Minneapolis MN 55401. (612)332-3344. Fax: (612)332-7615. Website: www.lernerbooks.com. **Contact:** Rebecca Poole, submissions editor. Estab. 1969. Carolrhoda Books seeks creative picture books, middle-grade fiction, historical fiction and K-6 children's nonfiction. Publishes hardcover originals. Averages 50-60 titles/year.

Needs: Juvenile, historical, picture books, multicultural, fiction for beginning readers. "We continue to add fiction for middle grades and 8-10 picture books per year. Not looking for folktales or anthropomorphic animal stories." Published *The War*, by Anais Vaugelade; *Little Wolf's Haunted Hill for Small Horrors*, by Ian Whybrow. Carolrhoda does not publish alphabet books, puzzle books, song books, textbooks, workbooks, religious subject matter or plays.

How to Contact: "Submissions are accepted in the months of March and October only. Submissions received in any other month will be returned unopened." Query with SASE or send complete ms for picture books or 3 sample chapters. Send SASE or IRC for return of ms. Responds in 6 months. Accepts simultaneous submissions.

Terms: Pays royalty on wholesale price, makes outright purchase or negotiates payments of advance against royalty. Advance varies. Guidelines for SASE; book catalog available for 9×12 SASE with $3.50 in postage. No phone calls.

CARTWHEEL BOOKS, Imprint of Scholastic, Inc., 557 Broadway, New York NY 10012. (212)343-6100. Fax: (212)343-4444. Website: www.scholastic.com. Vice President/Editorial Director: Ken Geist. **Contact:** Grace Maccarone, executive editor; Sonia Black, senior editor; Jane Gerver, executive editor. Estab. 1991. "Cartwheel Books publishes innovative books for children, ages 3-9. We are looking for 'novelties' that are books first, play objects second. Even without its gimmick, a Cartwheel Book should stand alone as a valid piece of children's literature." Publishes hardcover originals. Averages 85-100 titles/year.

Needs: Children's/juvenile (fantasy, humor, juvenile, mystery, picture books, science fiction, holiday/seasonal). "The subject should have mass market appeal for very young children. Humor can be helpful, but not necessary. Mistakes writers make are a reading level that is too difficult, a topic of no interest or too narrow, or manuscripts that are too long." Published *Little Bill* (series), by Bill Cosby (picture book); *Dinofours* (series), by Steve Metzger (picture book); and *The Haunted House*, by Fiona Conboy (3-D puzzle storybook).

How to Contact: *Agented submissions or previously published authors only.* Responds in 2 months to queries; 6 months to mss. Accepts simultaneous submissions.

Terms: Pays royalty on retail price. Offers advance. Publishes ms 2 years after acceptance. Guidelines available free; book catalog for 9×12 SASE.

Advice: Audience is young children, ages 3-9. "Know what types of books the publisher does. Some manuscripts that don't work for one house may be perfect for another. Check out bookstores or catalogs to see where your writing would 'fit' best."

CATBIRD PRESS, 16 Windsor Rd., North Haven CT 06473-3015. E-mail: catbird@pipeline.com. Website: www.catbirdpress.com (includes writer's guidelines, full book catalog, reviews and excerpts). **Contact:** Robert Wechsler. Estab. 1987. "Catbird is only looking for writers who are deeply interested in prose style and have a great deal of knowledge of stylistic alternatives. We are not interested in plot-and-character-oriented naturalistic fiction, or any sort of genre fiction, but in more creative and imaginative approaches to reality. Most of our fiction has a comic (although often darkly comic)vision, but is not comic in the sense of wacky characters, plots, and writing, or satirical attacks on contemporary society as a whole." Publishes hardcover and paperback originals. Books: acid-free paper; offset printing; some illustrations. Average print order, 2,000. Average first novel print order 1,500.

Needs: Literary translations, especially from Czech and German. Recently published *Aspects of the Novel: A Novel*, by David R. Slavitt (American Literary Novel); *Cross Roads*, by Karel Capek (Czech literary short stories); and *Living Parallel*, by Alexander Kliment (Czech literary novel).

How to Contact: Accepts unsolicited mss. Query with outline/synopsis and 1 sample chapter. Include estimated word count, brief bio, and list of publishing credits. Agented fiction: 20%. Responds within 1 month. Considers simultaneous submissions; no electronic or disk submissions. Rarely comments on rejected mss.

Terms: Pays royalties of 7-10%. Average advance is $2,000. Provides author's copies. Sends galleys to author. Time between acceptance and publication varies widely, from 6-24 months. Guidelines available for SASE, on website; book catalogs free.

Advice: "Because more first-rate writers are being dropped by big houses, the quality of what we see has gone up and we look for more quality in the work of new authors."

CAVE BOOKS, 756 Harvard Ave., St. Louis MO 63130. (314)862-7646. E-mail: rawatson@artsci.wustl.edu. Website: www.cavebooks.com. **Contact:** Richard Watson, editor. Estab. 1985. Small press devoted to books on caves, karst and speleology. Fiction: novels about cave exploration only. Publishes hardcover and paperback originals and reprints. Books: acid free paper; offset printing. Average print order: 1,500. **Published 2 new writers within the last year.** Averages 4 total titles, 0.2 fiction titles/year.
Needs: Adventure, caves, karst, speleology. Recently published *Emergence*, by Marian McConnell (novel).
How to Contact: Accepts unsolicited mss. Send query letter. Accepts queries by e-mail. Send SASE or IRC for return of ms or send disposable copy of ms and SASE for reply only. Responds in 2 weeks to queries; 2 months to mss. Accepts simultaneous submissions. Sometimes comments on rejected mss.
Terms: Pays royalties of 10%. Sends galleys to author. Publishes ms 18 months after acceptance.
Advice: "In the last three years we have received only three novels about caves, and we have published one of them. We get dozens of inappropriate submissions."

CHRISTCHURCH PUBLISHERS LTD., 2 Caversham St., London SW3 4AH United Kingdom. Fax: 0044 171 351 4995. **Contact:** James Hughes, fiction editor. Averages 25 fiction titles/year. Length: 30,000 words minimum.
Needs: "Miscellaneous fiction, also poetry. More 'literary' style of fiction, but also thrillers, crime fiction etc."
How to Contact: Query with synopsis (*"brief* synopsis favored"), or letter.
Terms: Pays royalties and advance. "We have contacts and agents worldwide."

N **CHRONICLE BOOKS FOR CHILDREN**, 85 Second St., 6th Floor, San Francisco CA 94105. (415)537-3730. Fax: (415)537-4420. E-mail: frontdesk@chroniclebooks.com. Website: www.chroniclekids.com. **Contact:** Victoria Rock, director of Children's Books; Beth Weber, managing editor; Jennifer Vetter, editor; Susan Pearson, editor-at-large; Samantha McFerrin, editorial assistant. Publishes hardcover and trade paperback originals. **Publishes 5% of books from first-time authors; 25% from unagented writers.** Averages 40-50 titles/year.
Needs: Mainstream/contemporary, multicultural, young adult, picture books; middle grade fiction; young adult projects. Recently published *Ghost Wings*; *Dream Carver*; *Star in the Darkness*.
How to Contact: "We do not accept proposals by fax, via e-mail, or on disk. Please be sure to include an SASE large enough to hold your materials. Projects submitted without an appropriate SASE will be recycled." Query with synopsis and SASE. Send complete ms for picture books. Accepts simultaneous submissions. Responds in 2-18 weeks to queries; 5 months to mss.
Terms: Pays 8% royalty. Offers variable advance. Publishes book 18 months after acceptance of ms. Book catalog for 9×12 SAE with 3 first-class stamps; ms guidelines for #10 SASE.
Advice: "We are interested in projects that have a unique bent to them—be it in subject matter, writing style, or illustrative technique. As a small list, we are looking for books that will lend our list a distinctive flavor. Primarily we are interested in fiction and nonfiction picture books for children ages up to eight years, and nonfiction books for children ages up to twelve years. We publish board, pop-up, and other novelty formats as well as picture books. We are also interested in early chapter books, middle grade fiction, and young adult projects."

CLARION BOOKS, Imprint of Houghton Mifflin Company, 215 Park Ave. S., New York NY 10003. Website: www.houghtonmifflinbook.com. **Contact:** Dinah Stevenson, editorial director; Michele Coppola, editor (YA, middle-grade, chapter book); Jennifer B. Greene, editor (YA, middle-grade, chapter book); Lynne Polvino, associate editor (YA, middle-grade, chapter book). Estab. 1965. "Clarion is a strong presence in the fiction market for young readers. We are highly selective in the areas of historical and contemporary fiction. We publish chapter books for children ages 7-10 and middle grade novels for ages 9-14, as well as picture books and nonfiction." Publishes hardcover originals. Averages 50 titles/year.
● Clarion author Linda Sue Park received the 2002 Newbery Award for her book *A Single Shard*. David Wiesner received the 2002 Caldecott Award for *The Three Pigs*.
Needs: Recently published *The Great Blue Yonder*, by Alex Shearer (contemporary, middle-grade); *When My Name Was Keoko*, by Linda Sue Park (historical fiction); and *Dunk*, by David Cubar (contemporary YA).
How to Contact: "Please submit entire manuscript for novels (no queries, please). Send to only *one* Clarion editor."

N **CLEIS PRESS**, P.O. Box 14684, San Francisco CA 94114-0684. (415)575-4700. Fax: (415)575-4700. Website: www.cleispress.com. **Contact:** Frederique Delacoste, editor. Estab. 1980. Midsize independent publisher. Publishes paperback originals and reprints. **Published new writers within the last year.** Plans 1 first novel every other year. Averages 20 total titles, 5 (3 are anthologies) fiction titles/year.
● Cleis Press has received the Best Fiction Firecracker for *The Leather Daddy and the Femme*, by Carol Queen Award, the Fab Award, and the Firecracker for Outstanding Press for 1999.
Needs: Feminist, gay/lesbian, literary. Published *Black Like Us* (fiction); *Sexually Speaking: Collected Sex Writings*, by Gore Vidal (essays); and *A Fragile Union*, by Joan Nestle (essays), which won a Lambda Literary Award.
How to Contact: Accepts unsolicited mss. Accepts queries by e-mail. Send complete ms with cover letter. Include 1- or 2-page bio, list of publishing credits. Send SASE or IRC for return of ms or send disposable copy of ms and SASE for reply only. Agented fiction 10%. Responds in 1 month to queries.

Terms: Pays variable royalty on retail price. Advance is negotiable. Sends galleys to author. Publishes ms up to 2 years after acceptance. Catalog for SAE and 2 first-class stamps.

N CLOUD PEAK, 730 W. 51st St., Casper WY 82601. E-mail: pharwitz@wyoming.com. **Contact:** Paul Harwitz. Publishes hardcover, trade paperback and mass market paperback originals and reprints. **Publishes 10% of books from first-time authors; 50% from unagented writers.** Averages 36 titles/year.
Needs: Adventure, fantasy, historical, horror, humor, juvenile, military/war, multicultural, multimedia, mystery, poetry, science fiction, suspense, western, Native American. "Do everything you can to make the book a real 'page-turner,' Plots and sub-plots must be plausible and suited to the locale(s). Main and secondary characters must speak dialog which matches their respective personality traits. Blacks, Spanish-speaking people and other 'minorities' must *not* be portrayed stereotypically. Historical accuracy is important." Recently published *The Watcher*, by Robert Kammen (Western/supernatural/ecological).
How to Contact: Query with SASE. All unsolicited mss returned unopened. Accepts simultaneous submissions. Responds in 2 months.
Terms: Pays 10% royalty for nonfiction; percentage for fiction varies. Publishes book 1-2 years after acceptance of ms. Book catalog and ms guidelines for #10 SASE or on website.
Advice: "Buy, read and study the *Novel & Short Story Writer's Market* each year. Writing must flow. Imagine you are a reader visiting a bookstore. Write the first page of the book in such a way that the reader feels *compelled* to buy it. It helps a writer to work from an outline. When we solicit a manuscript for consideration, we like to receive a floppy disk, in order to conserve trees."

N COASTAL CAROLINA PRESS, 2231 Wrightsville Ave., Wilmington NC 28403. Website: www.coastalcarolina press.org. Hardcover, trade paperback and mass market paperback originals and trade paperback reprints. **Publishes 70% of books from first-time authors; 100% from unagented writers.** Publishes 6-8 titles/year.
Needs: Adventure, ethnic, historical, humor, juvenile, literary, mainstream/contemporary, military/war, multicultural, mystery, regional, short story collections, suspense, young adult. Publishes books with regional niche. Recently published *Island Murders*, by Wanda Campbell (fiction).
How to Contact: Query with SASE.
Terms: Pays royalty. Publishes book 1 year after acceptance of ms. Book catalog and submission guidelines on website.

N ◐ ♥ COFFEE HOUSE PRESS, 27 N. Fourth St., Minneapolis MN 55401. (612)338-0125. **Contact:** Chris Fischbach, senior editor. Estab. 1984. "Nonprofit publisher with a small staff. We publish literary titles: fiction and poetry." Publishes hardcover and paperback originals. Books: acid-free paper; cover illustrations. Average print order: 3,000. First novel print order: 3,000-4,000. **Published new writers within the last year.** Averages 12 total titles, 6 fiction titles/year.
● This successful nonprofit small press has received numerous grants from various organizations including the NEA, the Mellon Foundation and Lila Wallace/Readers Digest.
Needs: Contemporary, ethnic, experimental, literary. Publishes anthologies, but they are closed to unsolicited submissions. Published *Ex Utero*, by Laurie Foos (first novel); *Gunga Din Highway*, by Frank Chin (novel); and *A .38 Special & a Broken Heart*, by Jonis Agee (short stories).
How to Contact: Accepts unsolicited mss. Query with samples and SASE. Agented fiction 10%. Responds in 2 months to queries; 6 months to mss.
Terms: Pays royalties of 8%. Average advance: $3,000. Provides 15 author's copies. Guidelines available for #10 SASE with 55¢ postage.

◐ ♥ COMMUTERS LIBRARY, Sound Room Publishers, P.O. Box 3168, Falls Church VA 22043. (703)790-8250. Fax: (703)790-8234. E-mail: commlib@bellatlantic.com. Website: www.commuterslibrary.com. **Contact:** Joe Langenfeld, editor. Estab. 1991. "Small publisher of audiobooks (many classics) with plans to publish new works of fiction and nonfiction, primarily novellas." Publishes audiobooks. Plans 5-10 first novellas this year. Averages 80 total titles, 70 fiction titles/year.
● Audio Best of the Year for six years.
Imprint(s): Commuters Library, Joe Langenfeld (fiction and nonfiction).
Needs: Adventure, children's/juvenile, family saga, fantasy, historical, horror, humor/satire, literary, mainstream, military/war, mystery/suspense, New Age/mystic, western, young adult/teen. "Novellas—popular genres."
How to Contact: Accepts unsolicited mss. Query with outline/synopsis and 1 sample chapter. Accepts e-mail and fax queries. Include estimated word count with submission. Agented fiction: 0%. Responds in 1 month to queries; 3 months to mss. Considers simultaneous submissions and disk submissions (word Perfect); no electronic submissions.
Terms: Pays royalties of 5-10%. Average advance: $200-1,000. Does not send galleys to author. Guidelines available for SASE. Time between acceptance and publication is up to 1 year.
Advice: "Audio books are growing in popularity. Authors should consider going directly to audio for special works. Give us good writing 10,000 to 20,000 words in length."

N ◎ COMPANION PRESS, P.O. Box 2575, Laguna Hills CA 92654. Fax: (949)362-4489. E-mail: sstewart@com panionpress.com. Website: www.companionpress.com. **Contact:** Steve Stewart, publisher. Publishes trade paperback originals. **Publishes 50% of books from first-time authors; 100% from unagented writers.** Averages 6 titles/year.

Needs: Gay/lesbian (bisexual, transgender), novels. Recently published *Rent Boys, Hustlers & Escorts* (erotic anthology).

How to Contact: Query with SASE. Responds in 1 month.

Terms: Pays 6-8% royalty on retail price. Publishes book 9 months after acceptance of ms. Book catalog and ms guidelines online.

COMPASS POINT MYSTERIES/TORY CORNER EDITIONS, The Quincannon Publishing Group, P.O. Box 8100, Glen Ridge NJ 07028. Phone/fax: (973)669-8367. E-mail: editors@QuincannonGroup.com. Website: www.QuincannonGroup.com (includes everything necessary—contacts, writers' etiquette and guidelines, catalogue, sales channels. **Contact:** Holly Benedict, editor (mystery fiction); Alan Quincannon, editor (miscellaneous fiction). Estab. 1990. "Compass Point Mysteries specializes in regional mystery novels made unique by involving some element of a region's history (the setting and time-frame or the mystery's origin). If at all possible, we like to tie each of these novels to a regional museum where they can be sold with some degree of exclusivity. From time to time Tory Corner Editions considers fiction which is set at a particular historic site but whose subject matter may fall outside the parameters of the mystery genre." Publishes paperback originals and reprints (on very rare occasions if they meet the specified criteria). Books: trade paperbacks; perfect binding. Average print order: 500; first novel print order: 500. Averages 3 total titles, 1-2 fiction titles/year. "We seek to place our novels almost exclusively in the gift shops of the regional museums they feature and schedule periodic booksignings at those locales. Our novels are also offered through Internet booksellers and local independent bookstores."

Needs: Mystery/suspense (amateur sleuth, cozy, psychic/supernatural), regional (mysteries). Recently published *Wind of Time* (romantic mystery) and *Wicked is the Wind* (cozy mystery), both by John Dandola; and *Echoes from the Castle Walls*, by John Hays Hammond, Jr. (collection of mystery/horror stories).

How to Contact: Does not accept unsolicited mss. Send query letter (not by e-mail); no agented submissions. Include estimated word count and brief bio; also "a letter of intent from the museum director and/or museum board of directors of the featured historic site stating that the manuscript has been read and approved and that, if published, the title will be stocked by the museum gift shop." Responds in 6 weeks to queries; up to 9 months to mss. Always comments on rejected mss.

Terms: "Books are published in runs of 500 and reprinted as supplies necessitate. Authors are paid a flat fee per run. Fees vary as to the cover price of each book." Sends galleys to author. Publishes ms 1 year after acceptance. Guidelines and book catalog available on website.

Advice: "Unfortunately, we are finding that many would-be authors consider that once they have created a plot and a premise and their computers have made their submissions look pretty, editors can be relied upon to anonymously rewrite their manuscripts. Editors are only a part of the guiding process and storytelling requires an awareness of succinctness and pacing, a mastery of language and grammar, and a willingness to polish and restructure. Our mystery novels should first tell a good interesting story which just happens to be a mystery, and they should usually not run more than 224 typeset pages. Besides using an historic site as a locale, our fiction must be well-written; it will be judged first and foremost on that merit. Please also bear in mind that an affiliation with a specific museum does not guarantee acceptance of any manuscript."

CONFLUENCE PRESS INC., 500 Eighth Ave., Lewis-Clark State College, Lewiston ID 83501-2698. (208)792-2336. Fax: (208)792-2850. E-mail: conpress@lcsc.edu. Website: www.confluencepress.com (includes guidelines, ordering information, featured titles, catalog). **Contact:** James R. Hepworth, fiction editor. Estab. 1976. Small trade publisher. Publishes hardcover and paperback originals and reprints. Books: 60 lb. paper; photo offset printing; Smyth-sewn binding. Average print order: 1,500-5,000 copies. Published new writers within the last year. Averages 3-5 total titles each year. Distributes titles through Midpoint Trade Books, Internet, Partners West Distributing, Northwest Interpretive Assoc.

Imprint(s): James R. Hepworth Books and Blue Moon Press.

• Books published by Confluence Press have received The Idaho Book Award, Western States Book Awards and awards from the Pacific Northwest Booksellers Association.

Needs: Contemporary, literary, mainstream, short story collections, translations. "Our needs favor serious fiction, 1 fiction collection a year, with preference going to work set in the contemporary western United States." Published *Cheerleaders From Gomorrah*, by John Rember (literary fiction); and *Gifts and Other Stories*, by Charlotte Holmes (literary fiction, debut author).

How to Contact: Query first. SASE with both query and ms. Agented fiction 50%. Responds in 2 months. Accepts simultaneous submissions. Accepts queries by e-mail and fax. *Critiques rejected mss for $25/hour.*

Terms: Pays royalties of 10%. Advance is negotiable. Provides 10 author's copies; payment depends on grant/award money. Sends galleys to author. Book catalog available for 6×9 SASE.

Advice: "We are very interested in seeing first novels from promising writers who wish to break into serious print. We are also particularly keen to publish the best short story writers we can find. We are also interested in finding volume editors for our American authors series. Prospective editors should send proposals."

CONTEXT BOOKS, 368 Broadway, Suite 314, New York NY 10013. (212)233-4880. Fax: (212)964-1810. E-mail: info@contextbooks.com. Website: www.contextbooks.com. **Contact:** Beau Friedlander. Estab. 1999. Books:

offset printing; cloth/paper binding; illustrations. Average print order 20,000. Average first novel print order: 10,000. Plans 1 first novel this year. Averages 8 total titles, 6 fiction titles/year. Member, ABA. Titles distributed through Publisher's Group West. Promotes titles on a "book by book basis."

● Context Books has received an Independent Publishers Prize, NBCC nomination, QPBC New Vision and *L.A. Times* Book Prize.

Needs: Comics/graphic ethnic/multicultural, experimental, feminist, historical, horror (supernatural, futuristic), literary, mainstream, military/war, short story collections. Publishes the *Esquire's Big Book of Fiction*. Recently published *After Dachau*, by Daniel Quinn (fiction); *Assorted Fire Events*, by David Means (short stories); *Mind the Doors*, by Zinovy Zinik (Russian literature).

How to Contact: Sometimes accepts unsolicited mss. Does not return unsolicited mss. Submit complete ms with cover letter. No queries by e-mail, fax or phone. Agented fiction: 99.9%. Responds in 4 months. Considers simultaneous submissions; no electronic submissions.

Terms: Pays royalties of 7½-15%. Pays advance and author's copies. Time between acceptance and publication is 1 year. Guidelines available for SASE; book catalogs for 9×12 SASE.

Advice: "Tell me who you are in three sentences; tell me what the work accomplishes in the same."

COTEAU BOOKS, Thunder Creek Publishing Co-operative Ltd., 401-2206 Dewdney Ave., Regina, Saskatchewan S4R 1H3 Canada. (306)777-0170. Fax: (306)522-5152. E-mail: coteau@coteaubooks.com. Website: www.coteaubooks.com. **Contact:** Nik L. Burton, managing editor. Estab. 1975. "Coteau Books publishes the finest Canadian fiction, poetry drama and children's literature, with an emphasis on western writers." Independent publisher. Publishes paperback originals. Books: #2 offset or 60 lb. hi-bulk paper; offset printing; perfect-bound; 4-color illustrations. Average print order: 1,500-3,000; first novel print order: approx. 1,500. **Published new writers within the last year.** Averages 18 total titles, 6-8 fiction titles/year. Distributes titles through General Distribution Services.

Needs: Novels, short fiction, middle years and young adult fiction. No science fiction. No children's picture books. Publishes Canadian authors only. Recently published *The Phantom Queen*, by Ven Begamudre; *Silence of the Country*, by Kristjana Gunnars; and *A Promise of Salt*, by Lorie Miseck.

How to Contact: *Canadian writers only.* Accepts unsolicited mss. Submit complete ms with cover letter and résumé to Acquisitions Editor. Accepts queries by e-mail. Send SASE or IRC for return of ms. Responds in 3 months. Sometimes comments on rejected mss.

Terms: "We're a co-operative and receive subsidies from the Canadian, provincial and local governments. We do not accept payments from authors to publish their works." Sends galleys to author. Publishes ms 1-2 years after acceptance. Book catalog available for 8½×11 SASE.

Advice: "We publish short-story collections, novels, drama, nonfiction and poetry collections, as well as literary interviews and children's books. This is part of our mandate. The work speaks for itself! Be bold. Be creative. Be persistent!"

COVENANT COMMUNICATIONS, INC., Box 416, American Fork UT 84003-0416. (801)756-1041. Website: www.covenant-lds.com. **Publishes 35% of books from first-time authors; 100% from unagented writers.** Publishes 50+ titles/year.

Needs: "We publish exclusively to the 'Mormon' (The Church of Jesus Christ of Latter-Day Saints) market. All work must appeal to that audience." Adventure, fantasy, historical, humor, juvenile, literary, mainstream/contemporary, mystery, picture books, regional, religious, romance, science fiction, spiritual, suspense, young adult.

How to Contact: Submit completed manuscript with synopsis and one-page cover letter. Responds in 4 months to mss. Ms guidelines online.

Terms: Pays 6½-15% royalty on retail price. Publishes book 6-12 months after acceptance of ms.

Advice: Our audience is exclusively LDS (Latter-Day Saints, "Mormon").

CREATIVITY UNLIMITED PRESS, 30819 Casilina, Rancho Palos Verdes CA 90274. (310)377-7908. **Contact:** Rochelle Stockwell. Estab. 1980. One-person operation with plans to expand. Publishes paperback originals and self-hypnosis cassette tapes. Books: perfect binding; illustrations. Average print order: 2,500. First novel print order 1,000. Averages 2 total titles/year.

Needs: Published *Insides Out*, by Shelley Stockwell (plain talk poetry); *Sex and Other Touchy Subjects* (poetry and short stories); *Time Travel: Do-It Yourself Past Life Regression Handbook*; *Denial is Not a River in Egypt*; and *Hypnosis: How to Put a Smile on Your Face and Money in Your Wallet*.

How to Contact: Write for more information.

CRESCENT MOON, Box 393, Maidstone, Kent ME14 5XU United Kingdom. E-mail: jr@crescentmoon.org.uk. Website: www.crescentmoon.org.uk. Subsidiaries: Joe's Press, *Passion Magazine, Pagan America*. **Contact:** J. Robinson, director. Estab. 1988. Small independent publisher. Publishes hardcover and paperback originals. Published new writers within the last year. Plans 1-2 first novels this year. Averages 25 total titles, 1-2 fiction titles/year. Sometimes comments on rejected ms.

Needs: Erotica, experimental, feminist, gay, lesbian, literary, New Age/mystic/spiritual, short story collections, translations. Plans anthology. Send short stories to editor.

How to Contact: Accepts unsolicited mss. Query with outline/synopsis and 2 sample chapters. Include estimated word count, list of publishing credits. Send SASE (IRCs) for reply, return of ms or send a disposable copy of ms. Agented fiction 10%. Responds in 1 month to queries; 4 months to mss. Accepts simultaneous submissions.

Terms: Negotiable. Sends galleys to author. Publishes ms 12-18 months after acceptance. Guidelines available for SASE (2 IRCs); book catalog for SASE (2 IRCs).

Advice: "We publish a small amount of fiction, and mainly in *Pagan Magazine* and *Passion Magazine*."

CRICKET BOOKS, Carus Publishing, 332 S. Michigan Ave., Suite 1100, Chicago IL 60604. (312)939-1500. Fax: (312)939-8150. Website: www.cricketbooks.net (includes backlist, new books, ordering instructions). **Contact:** Submissions Editor. Estab. 1999. "Small, independent publisher able to integrate publishing with related *Cricket* and *Cobblestone* magazine groups. We publish children's fiction and nonfiction, from picture books to high young adult." Publishes hardcover and paperback originals. **Published 2 new writers within the last year.** Plans 2 first novels this year. Averages 20 total titles, 10 fiction titles/year. Distributes titles through PGW. Promotes titles through in-house marketing.

● Received the 2002 Batchelder Award, the 2000 Bram Stoker and the 2000 Scott O'Dell.

Imprint(s): Cricket Books, picture books to young adults; Marcato Books, fiction and nonfiction for teens.

Needs: Children's/juvenile (adventure, animal, easy-to-read, fantasy, historical, mystery, preschool/picture book, sports), young adult/teen (adventure, easy-to-read, fantasy/science fiction, historical, horror, mystery/suspense, problem novels, romance, sports, western). Also early chapter books and middle-grade fiction. Plans anthologies for Christmas, dragons, poetry and Cricket Magazine's anniversary editor selects stories. Recently published *Seek*, by Paul Fleischman (YA fiction); *Robert and the Weird and Wacky Facts*, by Barbara Seuling (chapter book); and *Scorpio's Child*, by Kezi Matthews (fiction, ages 11-14).

How to Contact: Accepts unsolicited mss. Submit complete ms with cover letter. Include estimated word count and list of publishing credits. Send SASE or IRC for return of ms or send disposable copy of ms and SASE for reply only. Agented fiction 20%. Responds in 2 months to queries; 4 months to mss. Accepts simultaneous submissions. No electronic or disk submissions. Sometimes comments on rejected mss.

Terms: Pays royalties of 2-10%. Offers negotiable advance. Sends galleys to author. Publishes 18 months after acceptance. Guidelines available for SASE or on website.

CROSS-CULTURAL COMMUNICATIONS, 239 Wynsum Ave., Merrick NY 11566-4725. (516)868-5635. Fax: (516)379-1901. E-mail: cccpoetry@aol.com. Website: www.cross-culturalcommunications.com. **Contact:** Stanley H. Barkan, editorial director. Estab. 1971. "Small/alternative literary arts publisher focusing on the traditionally neglected languages and cultures in bilingual and multimedia format." Publishes chapbooks, magazines, anthologies, novels, audio cassettes (talking books) and video cassettes (video books, video mags); hardcover and paperback originals. Publishes new women writers series, Holocaust series, Israeli writers series, Dutch writers series, Asian-, African- and Italian-American heritage writers series, Polish writers series, Armenian writers series, Native American writers series, Latin American writers series.

● Authors published by this press have received international awards including Nat Scammacca, who won the National Poetry Prize of Italy and Gabriel Preil, who won the Bialik Prize of Israel.

Needs: Contemporary, literary, experimental, ethnic, humor/satire, juvenile and young adult folktales, and translations. "Main interests: bilingual short stories and children's folktales, parts of novels of authors of other cultures, translations; some American fiction. No fiction that is not directed toward other cultures. For an annual anthology of authors writing in other languages (primarily), we will be seeking very short stories with original-language copy (other than Latin, script should be print quality 10/12) on good paper. Title: *Cross-Cultural Review Anthology: International Fiction 1*. We expect to extend our *CCR* series to include 10 fiction issues: *Five Contemporary* (Dutch, Swedish, Yiddish, Norwegian, Danish, Sicilian, Greek, Israeli, etc.) *Fiction Writers*." Published *Sicilian Origin of the Odyssey*, by L.G. Pocock (bilingual English-Italian translation by Nat Scammacca); *Sikano L'Americano!* and *Bye Bye America*, by Nat Scammacca; and *Milkrun*, by Robert J. Gress.

How to Contact: Accepts unsolicited mss. Query with SAE with $1 postage to include book catalog. "Note: Original language ms should accompany translations." Accepts simultaneous submissions. Responds in 1 month.

Terms: Pays "sometimes" 10-25% in royalties and "occasionally" by outright purchase, in author's copies—"10% of run for chapbook series," and "by arrangement for other publications." No advance.

Advice: "Write because you want to or you must; satisfy yourself. If you've done the best you can, then you've succeeded. You will find a publisher and an audience eventually. Generally, we have a greater interest in nonfiction, novels and translations. Short stories and excerpts from novels written in one of the traditional neglected languages are preferred—with the original version (i.e., bilingual). Our kinderbook series will soon be in production with a similar bilingual emphasis, especially for folktales, fairy tales, and fables."

CROSSQUARTER PUBLISHING GROUP, P.O. Box 8756, Santa Fe NM 87504. (505)438-9846. Website: www.crossquarter.com. **Contact:** Anthony Ravenscroft. Publishes case and trade paperback originals and reprints. **Publishes 90% of books from first-time authors.** Averages 5-10 titles/year.

Needs: Science fiction, visionary fiction.

How to Contact: Query with SASE. Accepts simultaneous submissions. Responds in 3 months to queries.

Terms: Pays 8-10% royalty on wholesale or retail price. Publishes book 1 year after acceptance of ms. Book catalog for $1.75; ms guidelines online.

Advice: "Audience is earth-conscious people looking to grow into balance of body, mind, heart and spirit."

CROSSTIME, Crossquarter Publishing Group, P.O. Box 8756, Santa Fe NM 87505. Phone/fax: (505)438-9846. E-mail: info@crossquarter.com. Website: www.crossquarter.com (includes guidelines, contact information, catalog). **Contact:** Anthony Ravenscroft (visionary, speculative science). Estab. 1985. Small publisher. Publishes paperback originals. Books: recycled paper; docutech or offset printing; perfect-bound. First novel print order: 1,000. **Published 2 new writers within the last year.** Plans 2 first novels this year. Averages 6-8 total titles, 4 fiction titles/year. Member, SPAN, PMA.

Needs: Mystery/suspense (occult), New Age/mystic, psychic/supernatural, romance (occult), science fiction, young adult/teen (fantasy/science fiction). Plans an anthology of Paul B. Duquette Memorial Short Science Fiction contest winners. Guidelines on website. Recently published *The Shamrock and the Feather*, by Dori Dalton (debut author); *Shyla's Initiative*, by Barbara Casey (occult romance); and *CrossTIME SF Anthology* (science fiction).

How to Contact: Does not accept unsolicited mss. Returns unsolicited mss if SASE provided. Send query letter. Accepts queries by e-mail. Include estimated word count, brief bio, Social Security number and list of publishing credits. Send SASE or IRC for return of ms or send disposable copy of ms and SASE for reply only. Responds in 3 months to queries; 6 months to mss. Accepts simultaneous submissions. Encourages electronic and disk submissions.

Terms: Pays royalties of 6-10%. Provides 5-10 author's copies. Sends galleys to author. Publishes ms 6-9 months after acceptance. Guidelines available for SASE and on website; book catalog for $1 or on website.

CROSSWAY BOOKS, Division of Good News Publishers, 1300 Crescent, Wheaton IL 60187-5800. (630)682-4300. Fax: (630)682-4785. Website: www.Crosswaybooks.org (includes catalog and guidelines). **Contact:** Jill Carter. Estab. 1938. " 'Making a difference in people's lives for Christ' as its maxim, Crossway Books lists titles written from an evangelical Christian perspective." Midsize evangelical Christian publisher. Publishes hardcover and paperback originals. Average print order 5,000-10,000 copies. Averages 80 total titles, 5 fiction titles/year. Member, ECPA. Distributes titles through Christian bookstores and catalogs. Promotes titles through magazine ads, catalogues.

Needs: Christian—historical, literary, western. "All fiction published by Crossway Books must be written from the perspective of evangelical Christianity. It must understand and view the world through a Christian worldview." Recently published *Freedom's Shadow*, by Marlo Schalesky (historical); *The Outlaw's Twin Sister*, by Stephen Bly (western/historical); *Picture Rock*, by Stephen Bly (western/historical). Publishes The Belles of Lordsburg series (western) and The Winds of Freedom series (historical).

How to Contact: Accepts unsolicited mss. Send query with estimated word count, brief bio and list of publishing credits. Send SASE for return of ms or send disposable copy with SASE for reply only. Agented fiction: 5%. Does not accept queries by fax or e-mail. Responds in 6 weeks to queries; 3 months to mss. Accepts simultaneous submissions. No e-mail or disk submissions.

Terms: Pays royalties. Negotiates advance. Publishes ms 18 months or more after acceptance. Guidelines available for SASE and on website; book catalog for 9×14 SAE and $2.38 in postage.

Advice: "With so much Christian fiction on the market, we are carefully looking at our program to see the direction we wish to proceed. Be sure your project fits into our guidelines and is written from an evangelical Christian worldview. 'Religious' or 'Spiritual' viewpoints will not fit."

CROWN PUBLISHING GROUP, (Division of Random House, Inc.), 299 Park Ave., New York NY 10171. (212)572-2600. Fax: (212)940-7408. E-mail: crownbiz@randomhouse.com. Website: www.randomhouse.com/crown. Estab. 1933. "The group publishes a selection of popular fiction and nonfiction by both established and rising authors."

Imprint(s): Bell Tower; Clarkson Potter; Crown Business; Crown Publishers, Inc.; Harmony Books; Shaye Areheart Books; Three Rivers Press.

CUMBERLAND HOUSE PUBLISHING, 431 Harding Industrial Dr., Nashville TN 37211. (615)832-1171. Fax: (615)832-0633. E-mail: info@cumberlandhouse.com. **Contact:** Ron Pitkin, president. "We look for unique titles with clearly defined audiences." Publishes hardcover and trade paperback originals and reprints. Averages 35 titles/year. Imprint averages 3 titles/year.

Imprint(s): Cumberland House Hearthside; Julia M. Pitkin, editor-in-chief.

Needs: Mystery, historical. Recently published *Roseflower Creek*, by H.L. Miles; and *Chickamauga*, by James Reasoner.

How to Contact: Does not accept unsolicited mss. Send query letter. Writers should know "the odds are really stacked against them." Agented fiction 20%. Responds in 3 months to queries; 5 months to mss. Accepts simultaneous submissions.

Terms: Pays royalties of 10-20% on wholesale price. Average advance: $1,000-10,000. Publishes ms an average of 8 months after acceptance. Book catalog available for 8×10 SAE and 4 first-class stamps. Guidelines available free.

Advice: Audience is "adventuresome people who like a fresh approach to things. Writers should tell what their idea is, why it's unique and why somebody would want to buy it—but don't pester us."

DAN RIVER PRESS, Conservatory of American Letters, P.O. Box 298, Thomaston ME 04861-0298. (207)354-0998. Fax: (207)354-8953. E-mail: cal@americanletters.org. Website: www.americanletters.org (includes guidelines, editors, book catalog). **Contact:** Richard S. Danbury, fiction editor. Estab. 1977. "Small press publisher of fiction and

---

● **A BULLET INTRODUCES COMMENTS** by the editor of *Novel & Short Story Writer's Market* indicating special information about the listing.

biographies owned by a non-profit foundation." Publishes hardcover and paperback originals. Books: paperback; offset printing; perfect and cloth binding; illustrations. Average print order: 500; first novel print order: 500-1,000. Averages 2-3 total titles, 2-3 fiction titles/year. Promotes titles through the author's sphere of influence. Distributes titles by mail order to libraries and bookstores.

Needs: Family saga, fantasy (space fantasy, sword and sorcery), historical (general), horror (dark fantasy, futuristic, psychological, supernatural), humor/satire, literary, mainstream, mystery/suspense (amateur sleuth, police procedural, private eye/hardboiled), New Age/mystic, psychic/supernatural, regional, religious (general religious, inspirational, religious mystery/suspense, religious thriller, religious romance), romance (contemporary, futuristic/time travel, gothic, historical, romantic suspense), science fiction (hard science/technological, soft/sociological), short story collections, thriller/espionage, western (frontier saga, traditional), outdoors/fishing. Publishes poetry and fiction anthology (submission guidelines to *Dan River Anthology* on the Web). Recently published *Dan River Anthology 2002*, by R.S. Danbury III, editor (poetry and short stories); and *Wytopitloc: Tales of a Deer Hunter*, by Ed Rau Jr. (hunting stories).

How to Contact: Accepts unsolicited mss. Submit synopsis with cover letter. Include estimated word count, brief bio and list of publishing credits. Send SASE or IRC for return of ms or send disposable copy and SASE for reply only. Responds in 1 month to queries; 2 months to mss. Accepts simultaneous submissions.

Terms: Pays royalties of 10-15% of amount received. Average advance: $250. Pays 1 author's copy. Sends galleys to author. Publishes ms 8-12 months after acceptance. Guidelines available on website; book catalog available for 6×9 SAE and 2 oz. postage or on website.

Advice: "Spend some time developing a following."

JOHN DANIEL AND COMPANY, PUBLISHERS, P.O. Box 21922, Santa Barbara CA 93121. (805)962-1780. Fax: (805)962-8835. E-mail: dand@danielpublishing.com. Website: www.danielpublishing.com. **Contact:** John Daniel, publisher. Estab. 1980. "We publish small books, usually in small editions, but we do so with pride." Publishes hardbound and paperback originals. Publishes poetry, fiction, nonfiction. Average print order: 2,000. Averages 4 total titles/year. Distributes through SCB Distributors. Promotes through direct mail, reviews.

Needs: Publishes poetry, fiction and nonfiction; specializes in belles lettres, literary memoir. Recently published *Between Man & Woman Keys*, by Rosalind Brackenburg (short stories); *A Hole in the Water*, by Mae Briskin (novel); and *The House on Q Street*, by Ann L. McLaughlin (novel).

How to Contact: Accepts unsolicited mss. Responds in 2 months. Accepts simultaneous submissions.

Terms: Pays royalties of 10% of net receipts. No advance.

Advice: "Write for the joy of writing. That's as good as it gets."

DANTE UNIVERSITY OF AMERICA PRESS, INC., P.O. Box 812158, Wellesley MA 02482. (781)790-1056. E-mail: danteu@danteuniversity.org. Website: www.danteuniversity.org. **Contact:** Adolph Caso, president. "The Dante University Press exists to bring quality, educational books pertaining to our Italian heritage as well as the historical and political studies of America. Profits from the sale of these publications benefit the Foundation, bringing Dante University closer to a reality." Estab. 1975. Publishes hardcover and trade paperback originals and reprints. Publishes 5 titles/year. Average print order for a first book is 3,000.

Needs: Translations from Italian and Latin. Recently published *Marconi My Beloved*, by C. Marconi; *Unpaid Ballads*, by A. Mirini; and *Italian Poetry*, by Ridinger/Renello.

How to Contact: Query first with SASE. Agented fiction 50%. Responds in 2 months.

Terms: Pays royalty. Negotiable advance. Publishes ms 10 months after acceptance.

MAY DAVENPORT, PUBLISHERS, 26313 Purissima Rd., Los Altos Hills CA 94022. (650)947-1275. Fax: (650)947-1373. E-mail: mdbooks@earthlink.net. Website: www.maydavenportpublishers.com (includes catalog, author information). **Contact:** May Davenport, editor/publisher. Estab. 1976. "We prefer books which can be *used* in high schools as supplementary readings in English or creative writing courses. Reading skills have to be taught, and novels by humorous authors can be more pleasant to read than Hawthorne's or Melville's novels, war novels, or novels about past generations. Humor has a place in literature." Publishes hardcover and trade paperback originals. Averages 4 titles/year. Distributes titles through direct mail order.

Imprint(s): md Books (nonfiction and fiction).

Needs: Humor, literary. "We want to focus on novels junior and senior high school teachers can share with their reluctant readers in their classrooms." Recently published *A Life on the Line*, by Michael Horton (novel); *Surviving Sarah*, by Dinah Leigh (novel); *Significant Footsteps*, by Ashley E. Grange (novel).

How to Contact: Query with SASE. Responds in 1 month.

Terms: Pays royalties of 15% on retail price. No advance. Publishes ms 1 year after acceptance. Guidelines and book catalog available for #10 SASE.

Advice: "Just write humorous fictional novels about today's generation with youthful, admirable, believable characters to make young readers laugh. TV-oriented youth need role models in literature, and how a writer uses descriptive adjectives and similes enlightens youngsters who are so used to music, animation, special effects with stories."

DAW BOOKS, INC., Distributed by Penguin Putnam Inc., 375 Hudson St., 3rd Floor, New York NY 10014-3658. (212)366-2096. Fax: (212)366-2090. E-mail: daw@penguinputnam.com. Website: www.dawbooks.com. Publishers: Elizabeth Wollheim and Sheila Gilbert. **Contact:** Peter Stampfel, submissions editor. Estab. 1971. Publishes hardcover and paperback originals and reprints. Averages 60-80 titles/year.

Needs: "We are interested in science fiction and fantasy novels. We need science fiction more than fantasy right now, but we're still looking for both. We like character-driven books with attractive characters. We're not looking for horror novels, but we are looking for mainstream suspense thrillers. We accept both agented and unagented manuscripts. Long books are absolutely not a problem. We are not seeking collections of short stories or ideas for anthologies." Recently published *Otherland: Sea of Silver Light*, by Tad Williams (science fiction).

How to Contact: First send query letter with SASE or IRC for reply. Simultaneous submissions "returned unread at once unless prior arrangements are made by agent." Responds in 6 weeks "or longer if a second reading is required."

Terms: Pays in royalties with an advance negotiable on a book-by-book basis. Sends galleys to author. Book catalog available free.

Advice: "We strongly encourage new writers. Research your publishers and submit only appropriate work."

DEL REY BOOKS, The Ballantine Publishing Group, A Division of Random House, Inc., 1540 Broadway, New York NY 10036. (212)782-8449. E-mail: Delray@randomhouse.com. Website: www.randomhouse.com/delrey/ (includes writers guidelines, names of editors, an online newsletter with updates, author interviews and contests). **Contact:** Betsy Mitchell, editor-in-chief; Shelly Shapiro, senior editor; Steve Saffel, senior editor; Chris Schluep, editor; Kathleen O'Shea David, assistant editor. Estab. 1977. "In terms of mass market, we basically created the field of fantasy bestsellers. Not that it didn't exist before, but we put the mass into mass market." Publishes hardcover originals and paperback originals and reprints. Plans 6-7 first novels this year. Averages 70 fiction titles/year.

Needs: Fantasy ("should have the practice of magic as an essential element of the plot"), alternate history ("novels that take major historical events, such as the Civil War, and bend history in a new direction sometimes through science fiction and fantasy devices"), science fiction ("well-plotted novels with good characterization, exotic locales, and detailed alien cultures"). Recently published *Vitals*, by Greg Bear; *Demons*, by John Shirley; *Morgawr*, by Terry Brooks; *The Fifth Sorceress*, by Robert Newcomb; and *The Scar*, by China Mieville.

How to Contact: Does not accept unsolicited mss. Sometimes comments on rejected mss.

Terms: Pays royalty on retail price. "Advance is competitive." Publishes ms 1 year after acceptance. Sends galleys to author.

Advice: Has been publishing "more fiction and hardcovers, because the market is there for them. Read a lot of science fiction and fantasy, such as works by Anne McCaffrey, David Eddings, Larry Niven, Arthur C. Clarke, Terry Brooks, Frederik Pohl, Barbara Hambly. When writing, pay particular attention to plotting (and a satisfactory conclusion) and characters (sympathetic and well-rounded) because those are what readers look for."

DELACORTE PRESS, The Bantam Dell Publishing Group, A Division of Random House, Inc., 1540 Broadway, New York NY 10036. (212)782-9000. Fax: (212)782-9523. Website: www.randomhouse.com. **Contact:** Jackie Cantor (women's fiction and general fiction). Publishes hardcover and trade paperback originals. Averages 36 total titles/year.

Needs: Recently published *The Cottage*, by Danielle Steele; *Tell No One*, by Harlan Coben.

How to Contact: *Agented submissions only.* No simultaneous submissions.

Terms: Offers advance.

DELIRIUM BOOKS, P.O. Box 338, N. Webster UB 46555. (574)594-1607. E-mail: srstaley@deliriumbo oks.com. Website: www.deliriumbooks.com (includes author pages, online ordering, catalog, message boards, chat room and general info on Delirium's staff and author guidelines). **Contact:** Shane R. Staley, editor-in-chief (horror); Bob Strauss, associate editor (horror). Estab. 1999. "Delirium is one of the upcoming independent publishers in the horror genre. Noted for publishing edgy horror fiction and not afraid to push the envelope." Publishes hardcover originals and reprints. Books: 60 lb. natural/white paper; digitally printed; stitched binding. Average print order: 300. First novel print order: 300. Plans 2 first novels this year. Averages 8 total titles, 8 fiction titles/year. Distributes and promotes titles through website, Amazon, B&N.com and specialty bookstores.

Needs: Horror (psychological, supernatural). Wants "edgy novels within the horror genre." Plans anthology titled *Corrosion*; check website for guidelines and reading times. Recently published *Heretics*, by Greg F. Gifune (horror); *Cobwebs & Whispers*, by Scott Thomas (horror); and *Maternal Instinct*, by J.F. Gonzalez (horror).

How to Contact: Accepts unsolicited mss. Query with outline/synopsis and 3 sample chapters. Accepts queries by e-mail. Include estimated word count. Send disposable copy of ms and SASE for reply only. Responds in 2 weeks to queries; 3-6 months to mss. No simultaneous, electronic or disk submissions.

Terms: Pays royalties of 10-20%. Sends galleys to author. Guidelines and book catalog available on website.

Advice: "Since the horror genre has been in a recent growth period, we are increasing the number of titles we publish per year. Delirium specializes in limited edition hardcovers. Delirium has been known to publish edgy fiction, extreme and the hardcore. Please don't write specifically for the mainstream horror markets and submit your manuscripts to Delirium."

DESCANT PUBLISHING, P.O. Box 12973, Mill Creek WA 98082. (206)235-3357. Fax: (646)365-7513. E-mail: bret@descantpub.com. Website: www.descantpub.com. **Contact:** Bret Sable, senior editor (nonfiction); Alex Royal, editor (fiction). Estab. 2001. Publishes hardcover, trade paperback, mass market paperback, and electronic originals. **Publishes 50% of books from first-time authors; 50% from unagented writers.** Averages 10-12 titles/year.

Needs: Fantasy, horror, mainstream/contemporary, mystery, religious, science fiction, suspense. "Fresh storylines are critical." Recently published *The Stories of Those Who Were There*, by Peter Orullian (historical fiction).

How to Contact: Query with SASE. Accepts simultaneous submissions. Responds in 3 months.

Terms: Pays 6-15% royalty. Publishes book 18 months after acceptance of ms. Ms guidelines for #10 SASE.

THE DESIGN IMAGE GROUP INC., 231 S. Frontage Rd., Suite 17, Burr Ridge IL 60527. (630)789-8991. Fax: (630)789-9013. E-mail: dig@designimagegroup.com. Website: www.designimagegroup.com (includes book catalog and links). **Contact:** Editorial Committee. Estab. 1998. "Horror and mystery fiction micropublisher distributing exclusively through normal trade channels." Publishes paperback originals. Books: offset paper; offset printing; perfect binding. Average print order: 3,000. First novel print order: 3,000. **Published 1 new writer within the last year.** Averages 3-6 total titles, 3-6 fiction titles/year. Member, HWA, MWA, PMA. Distributes titles through Ingram, Baker & Taylor and Brodart.

Needs: Horror, supernatural. Looking for "traditional supernatural horror fiction." Publishes horror anthology. Guidelines announced in writers' and genre publications in advance. Recently published *The Big Switch*, by Jack Bludis (first fiction, novel); *Martyrs*, by Edo van Belkom (horror); and *Doomed to Repeat It*, by D.G.K. Goldberg (first fiction, horror).

How to Contact: Accepts unsolicited mss. Send query letter or query with synopsis and 3 sample chapters. Send SASE or IRC for return of ms or send a disposable copy of the ms and SASE for reply only. Agented fiction 15%. Responds in 4 months. Accepts simultaneous submissions. Often comments on rejected mss.

Terms: Pays royalties of 10-15% against advance or 30% royalty without advance on wholesale price, not cover. Sends galleys to author. Publishes ms 3-6 months after acceptance. Guidelines available for SASE; book catalog for 9 × 12 SASE or see website.

Advice: "We publish traditional supernatural horror (vampires, ghosts, werewolves, witches, etc.) and neo-noir dark mysteries. Please send for writers guidelines, they're quite specific and helpful."

DIAL BOOKS FOR YOUNG READERS, Penguin Putnam Inc., 345 Hudson St., 3rd Floor, New York NY 10014-3657. (212)366-2800. Website: www.penguinputnam.com. President/Publisher: Nancy Paulsen. Editorial Director: Lauri Hornik. **Contact:** Submissions Editor. Estab. 1961. Trade children's book publisher. Publishes hardcover originals. Averages 50 titles/year, mainly fiction.

Imprint(s): Easy-to-Read Books.

Needs: Adventure, fantasy, juvenile, picture books, young adult. Especially looking for "lively and well-written novels for middle grade and young adult children involving a convincing plot and believable characters. The subject or theme should not already be overworked in previously published books. The approach must not be demeaning to any minority group, nor should the roles of female characters (or others) be stereotyped, though we don't think books should be didactic. No topics inappropriate for juvenile, young adults and middle grade audiences. No plays." Recently published *Asteroid Impact*, by Doug Henderson; *A Year Down Yonder*, by Richard Parl; and *The Missing Mitten Mystery*, by Steven Kellog.

How to Contact: Does not accept unsolicited mss; agented submissions only. Send query letter with SASE. Occasionally comments on rejected ms. Responds in 3 months to queries.

Terms: Pays royalties. Offers varied advance. No simultaneous submissions. "We will send a catalog to anyone who sends 4 first-class stamps with a self-addressed, 9 × 12 envelope."

THE DIAL PRESS, The Bantam Dell Publishing Group, A Division of Random House, Inc., 1540 Broadway, New York NY 10036. (212)782-9000. Website: www.bbd.com. **Contact:** Susan Kamil, vice president, editorial director. Estab. 1924. Averages 6-12 titles/year.

Needs: Literary. Recently published *Mary and O'Neil* (short story collection); and *Niagara Falls All Over Again* (fiction).

How to Contact: *Agented submissions only.* Accepts simultaneous submissions.

Terms: Pays royalty on retail price. Offers advance. Publishes ms 18 months after acceptance.

DISKUS PUBLISHING, P.O. Box 43, Albany IN 47320. E-mail: books@diskuspublishing.com. Website: www.diskuspublishing.com (includes writer's guidelines, names of editors, book catalog, interviews with authors, About Us, submission status log, About Our Authors). **Contact:** Marilyn Nesbitt, editor-in-chief; Joyce McLaughlin, inspirational and children's editor; Holly Janey, submissions editor. Estab. 1997. Publishes paperback originals and e-books. **Published 10 new writers within the last year.** Averages 60 total titles, 50 fiction titles/year. Member, AEP, PMA.

- *The Best Laid Plans*, by Leta Nolan Childers was the #1 bestselling e-book of 1999. *Paper Roses* was a winner of The Rising Star Contest for Historical Fiction. *Eye of the Beholder* was a finalist (inspirational genre) in the Eppie Awards.

Needs: Adventure, children's/juvenile, ethnic/multicultural (general), family saga, fantasy (space fantasy), historical, horror, humor/satire, literary, mainstream, military/war, mystery/suspense, psychic/supernatural, religious, romance, science fiction, short story collections, thriller/espionage, western, young adult/teen. Recently published *The Best Laid Plans*, by Leta Nolan Childers (romance); *Brazen*, by Lori Foster (adventure/romance); and *A Change of Destiny*, by Marilynn Mansfield (science fiction/futuristic).

How to Contact: Accepts unsolicited mss. No queries; complete ms only. Include estimated word count, brief bio, list of publishing credits and genre. Send SASE or IRC for return of ms or send disposable copy of ms and SASE for reply only. Agented fiction 5%. Accepts simultaneous submissions and submissions on disk plus print out of synopsis and first chapter. Sometimes comments on rejected mss.

Terms: Pays royalties of 40%. Sends galleys to author. Publishes ms 6-8 months after acceptance. Guidelines available free for #10 SASE; book catalog for #10 SASE or online.

N: ◎ DIVERSITY INCORPORATED, 953 E. Johnson St., Madison WI 53703. (608)259-8370. Fax: (608)259-8371. E-mail: info@diversityincorporated.com. Website: www.diversityincorporated.com (includes writer's guidelines, title information). **Contact:** Blake Stewart (sci-fi, mystery, mainstream); Benjamin LeRoy (horror, experimental, literary). Estab. 1995. "We are a small press run by people in their 20s. We'll look at a longshot project." Publishes hardcover and paperback originals. Books: 60 lb. offset paper; offset or digitally printed; perfect-bound. Average print order: 1,000. First novel print order: 1,000. **Published 3 new writers within the last year.** Plans 0-2 first novels this year. Averages 3-5 total titles, 2 fiction titles/year. Member, PMA. Distributes titles through Baker & Taylor.

Needs: Adventure, comics/graphic novels, ethnic/multicultural, experimental, horror (dark fantasy, psychological, supernatural), literary, mainstream, mystery/suspense (amateur sleuth, cozy, police procedural, private eye/hardboiled), science fiction (hard science/technological, soft/sociological), short story collections, thriller/espionage. Needs "good psychological or suspense horror. Not formulaic, but well thought out plots and characters that get inside the reader's head." Plans anthology of short stories. Editors select stories. Recently published *Red Sky, Red Dragonfly*, by John Galligan (literary/mystery, debut author); and *Unfortunate Incidents*, by Anthony Gancarski (short stories).

How to Contact: Accepts unsolicited mss. Send query letter. Accepts queries by e-mail. Include estimated word count, brief bio and list of publishing credits. Send disposable copy of ms and SASE for reply only. Agented fiction 35%. Responds in 2 weeks to queries; 2 months to mss. Accepts simultaneous, electronic and disk submissions.

Terms: Pays royalties of 6-10%. Offers negotiable advance. Sends galleys to author. Publishes ms up to 1 year after acceptance. Guidelines available for SASE and on website; book catalog free.

Advice: "We're publishing more fiction, and we're trying to go more mainstream. We'll still consider underdog/experimental projects, though. Unless the book is a guaranteed seller, it'll probably be done as a paperback due to financial considerations. Please make sure the book is polished. Be objective. Can it be better? Don't send it yet."

A DOUBLEDAY ADULT TRADE, The Doubleday Broadway Publishing Group, A Division of Random House, Inc., 1540 Broadway., New York NY 10036. (212)782-9000. Fax: (212)782-9700. Website: www.doubleday.com. **Contact**: William Thomas, vice president/editor-in-chief. Estab. 1897. Publishes hardcover and paperback originals and paperback reprints. Averages 200 titles/year.

Imprint(s): Currency; Nan A. Talese; Religious Division; Image; Anchor Books.

Needs: Adventure, confession, ethnic, experimental, feminist, gay/lesbian, historical, humor, literary, mainstream/contemporary, religious, short story collections, suspense. Recently published *The Street Lawyer*, by John Grisham.

Terms: "Doubleday is not able to consider unsolicited queries, proposals or manuscripts unless submitted through a bona fide literary agent." Pays in royalties; offers advance. Publishes ms 1 year after acceptance.

■ DOUBLEDAY BROADWAY PUBLISHING GROUP, (Division of Random House, Inc.), 1540 Broadway, New York NY 10036. (212)782-9000. Fax: (212)302-7985. Website: www.randomhouse.com/doubleday. Estab. 1897. Publishes hardcover and paperback, fiction and nonfiction.

Imprint(s): The Anchor Bible; Anchor Books; Currency; DD Equestrian Library; Dolphin Books; Double D Western; Doubleday Activity Books; Foundation Books; Galilee Books; Image Books; Jerusalem Bible; Loveswept; Made Simple Books; Main Street / Back List; New Jerusalem Bible; Nan A. Talese Books; Outdoor Bible Series; Perfect Crime; Spy Books.

🍁 A DOUBLEDAY CANADA, Random House of Canada, A Division of Random House, Inc., 1 Toronto St., Suite 300, Toronto, Ontario M5C 2V6 Canada. Website: www.randomhouse.ca. Publishes hardcover and paperback originals. Averages 50 total titles/year.

Imprint(s): Seal Books (mass market publisher); Anchor Canada (trade paperback publisher).

How to Contact: Does not accept unsolicited mss. Agented fiction only.

N A ◎ DOUBLEDAY RELIGIOUS PUBLISHING, Doubleday Broadway Publishing Group, Random House, Inc., 1540 Broadway, New York NY 10036. (212)354-6500. Fax: (212)782-3735. Website: www.randomhouse.com. **Contact:** Eric Major, vice president, religious division; Trace Murphy, executive editor; Andrew Corbin, editor. Estab. 1897. Publishes hardcover and trade paperback originals and reprints. **Publishes 3% from unagented writers.** Averages 45-50 titles/year; imprint publishes 12 titles/year.

Imprints: Image Books, Anchor Bible Commentary, Anchor Bible Reference, Galilee, New Jerusalem Bible.

Needs: Religious.

How to Contact: *Agented submissions only.* Accepts simultaneous submissions. Responds in 3 months to proposals.

Terms: Pays 7½-15% royalty. Offers advance. Publishes book 1 year after acceptance of ms. Book catalog for SAE with 3 first-class stamps.

N ◐ ◎ DOWN EAST BOOKS, Division of Down East Enterprise, Inc., P.O. Box 679, Camden ME 04843-0679. Fax: (207)594-7215. **Contact:** Chris Cornell, editor (Countrysport); Michael Steere, associate editor (general). Estab. 1954. "We are primarily a regional publisher concentrating on Maine or New England." Publishes hardcover and trade paperback originals and trade paperback reprints. Averages 20-24 titles/year. First novel print order: 3,000.

Imprint(s): Countrysport Press, edited by Chris Cornell (fly fishing and wing-shooting nonfiction).

Needs: Juvenile, regional. "We publish 1-2 juvenile titles/year (fiction and nonfiction), and 1-2 adult fiction titles/year." Published *Tides of the Heart*, by Thomas M. Sheehan (novel); *Day Before Winter*, by Elisabeth Ogilvie (novel); and *My Brothers' Keeper*, by Nancy Johnson (young adult novel).

How to Contact: Query first with SASE. Responds in 3 months to queries.

Terms: Pays royalties of 10-15% on net receipts. Publishes ms 1 year after acceptance. Guidelines available for 9×12 SAE with 3 first-class stamps.

DOWN THERE PRESS, Subsidiary of Open Enterprises Cooperative, Inc., 938 Howard St., #101, San Francisco CA 94103-4100. Fax: (415)974-8989. E-mail: downtherepress@excite.com. Website: www.goodvibes.com/dtp/dtp.html (includes titles, author bios, excerpts, guidelines, calls for submissions). **Contact:** Leigh Davidson, managing editor. Estab. 1975. Small independent press with part-time staff; part of a large worker-owned cooperative. "Devoted exclusively to the publication of sexual health books for children and adults. We publish books that are innovative, lively and practical, providing realistic physiological information with nonjudgmental techniques for strengthening sexual communication." Publishes paperback originals. Books: Web offset printing; perfect binding; some illustrations. Average print order: 5,000. First novel print order: 3,000-5,000. **Published new writers within the last year.** Averages 1-2 total titles, 1 fiction title each year. Member, Publishers Marketing Association and Northern California Book Publicity and Marketing Association.

Imprint(s): Yes Press, Red Alder Books and Passion Press (audio division).

Needs: Erotica, feminist; sex education topics/sex-positive nonfiction. "So far, our only fiction titles are anthologies of short erotic fiction by women." Published *Herotica 6*, edited by Marcy Sheiner (anthology); *Sex Spoken Here: Erotic Reading Circle Stories*, edited by Carol Queen and Jack Davis (anthology); and *Sex Toy Tales*, edited by A. Semans and Cathy Winks. *Still Doing It: Women and Men Over 60 Write About Their Sexuality*, edited by Joani Blank (nonfiction) won the 2001 *Independent Publishers* Award 2001.

How to Contact: Accepts unsolicited mss. Prefers book proposals rather than entire ms. Include cover letter, table of contents (description of each chapter), sample chapters, estimated word count. Send by postal mail only; no e-mail. Send SASE or IRC for return of ms or send disposable copy of ms and SASE for reply only. Responds in up to 9 months to mss. Accepts simultaneous submissions. Sometimes comments on rejected mss.

Terms: Pays royalties and author's copies. Sends galleys to author. Publishes ms 18 months after acceptance. Guidelines and book catalog available for #10 SASE.

DRAGON MOON PRESS, 64312, 5512 Fourth St. N.W., Calgary, Alberta T2K 6J0 Canada. E-mail: publisher@dragonmoonpress.com. Website: www.dragonmoonpress.com (includes writer's guidelines, links to helpful resources for writers, book descriptions and chapter samples, author information). **Contact:** Gwen Gades, publisher; Christine Mains, submissions editor. Estab. 1992. "Dragon Moon Press is a leading Canadian publishing house dedicated to new and exciting voices in science fiction and fantasy. At Dragon Moon Press, we continue to improve how we do business and continue to seek out quality manuscripts and authors. Show us a great story with well developed characters and plot lines, show us that you are interested in the industry, and show us your desire to create a great book and you may just find yourself published by Dragon Moon Press." Publishes hardcover and paperback originals. Books: 60 lb. offset paper; offset and POD printing; perfect-bound. Average print order: 250-1,000. First novel print order: 250-1,000. **Published 1 new writer within the last year.** Plans 2 first novels this year. Averages 2 total titles, 2 fiction titles/year. "Distributed through Ingram Distribution Services. Promoted locally, through authors, and promoted online at leading retail bookstores like Amazon, Barnes & Noble, Chapters, etc."

Imprint(s): Dragon Moon Press; Gwen Gades, Christine Mains, editors; fantasy and science fiction.

Needs: Fantasy (space fantasy, sword and sorcery, epic, historical), horror (dark fantasy, futuristic, supernatural—no vampires), science fiction (hard science/technological, soft/sociological). Wants "strong, traditional fantasy featuring dragons, high adventure and great magic!" Recently published *Legends of the Serai*, by J.C. Hall (fantasy). Publishes *MOREVI: The Chronicles of Rafe & Askana*, epic fantasy series by Lisa Lee & Tee Morris.

How to Contact: Accepts unsolicited mss. Send query letter or query with outline/synopsis and 3 sample chapters. Include estimated word count, brief bio, list of publishing credits and synopsis. Send SASE or IRC for return of ms. Responds in 2-3 months to queries; 6-8 months to mss. "We officially read full manuscripts twice a year in December and August. You are welcome to drop us an e-mail at publisher@dragonmoonpress.com to get an update." Accepts simultaneous, electronic and disk submissions (but query before sending).

Terms: Pays royalties of 8-15%. Sends galleys to author. Guidelines and book catalog available on website.

Advice: "First, be patient. Read our guidelines at dragonmoonpress.com. Not following our submission guidelines can be grounds for automatic rejection. Second, we view publishing as a family affair. Be ready to participate in the process, and show some enthusiasm and understanding in what we do. Remember also, this is a business and not about egos, so keep yours on a leash! Finally, educate yourself about the industry and the truths surrounding it. The first book will not make you rich. Neither will your second. The reward with Dragon Moon Press is not so much in money as it is in the experience and the satisfaction in the final work. Show us a great story with well developed characters and plot lines, show us that you are interested in the industry, and show us your desire to create a great book and you may just find yourself published by Dragon Moon Press."

DREAMCATCHER PUBLISHING INC., One Market Square, Suite 306 Dockside, Saint John, New Brunswick E2L 4Z6 Canada. (506)632-4008. Fax: (506)632-4009. E-mail: dcpub@fundy.net. Website: www.dreamcatcher.nb.ca. **Contact:** Yvonne Wilson, editor-in-chief (trade books: novels, occasional collections of short stories); Joan Allison (children's). Estab. 1998. "Dreamcatcher Publishing Inc. is small, independent and literary. We look for, but are not limited to, the work of writers from eastern Canada." Publishes paperback originals. Books: comutell coated paper; web printing; perfect binding; illustrations by artists with BFA. Average print order: 2-3,000; first novel print order: 1,000. **Published 2 new writers within the last year.** Plans 1-2 first novels this year. Averages 4 total titles, 3 fiction titles/year. Distributes titles through CanBook (Toronto).

Needs: Children's/juvenile, humor/satire, literary, mainstream, regional (Atlantic Canada), romance (contemporary), short story collections, young adult/teen (adventure, fantasy/science fiction, mystery/suspense, problem novels). Recently published *A Light Above the Sun*, by Yvonne Wilson (children's) and *Dancing With the Dead*, by Vernon Oickle (literary).

How to Contact: Send query letter. Accepts queries by e-mail, fax and phone. Include estimated word count, brief bio and list of publishing credits. Send SASE or IRC for return of ms; or disposable copy of ms and SASE for reply only. Responds in 2 weeks to queries; 2 months to mss. Often critiques or comments on rejected mss.

Terms: Pays royalties of 7-12%. Sends galleys to author. Publishes ms 1-2 years after acceptance. Guidelines available on website; book catalogs on website.

Advice: "Be businesslike. Phone first, but not till you have a well prepared manuscript ready to show us. Our interests in fiction are eclectic, but we may say no. Never ask if we will look at an unfinished manuscript to see if it is worth finishing. Spelling and punctuation count."

DUFOUR EDITIONS, P.O. Box 7, Chester Springs PA 19425-0007. (610)458-5005. Fax: (610)458-7103. E-mail: tlavoie@dufoureditions.com. Website: www.dufoureditions.com. **Contact:** Thomas Lavoie, associate publisher. Estab. 1940s. Small independent publisher, tending toward literary fiction. Publishes hardcover and paperback originals and reprints. Averages 6-7 total titles, 1-2 fiction titles/year. Promotes titles through catalogs, reviews, direct mail, sales reps, Book Expo and wholesalers.

Needs: Literary, short story collections, translations. "We like books that are slightly off-beat, different and well written." Recently published *Tideland*, by Mitch Cullin; *The Case of the Pederast's Wife*, by Clare Elfman; *Lost Love in Constantinople*, by Milorad Pavic; *Night Sounds and Other Stories*, by Karen Shoemaker; *From the Place in the Valley Deep in the Forest*, by Mitch Cullen (short stories); and *Beyond Faith and Other Stories*, by Tom Noyes.

How to Contact: Send query letter only. Accepts queries by fax or e-mail. Include estimated word count, bio and list of publishing credits. Include SASE for reply. Responds in 3 weeks to queries; 3 months to mss.

DUNDURN PRESS LTD., 8 Market St., Suite 200, Toronto, Ontario M5E 1M6 Canada. (416)214-5544. Website: www.dundurn.com. **Contact:** Acquisitions Editor. Estab. 1972. Publishes hardcover and trade paperback originals and reprints. **Publishes 50% of books from first-time authors; 85% from unagented writers.** Averages 50-60 titles/year.

• Dundurn publishes books by Canadian authors.

Needs: Literary, mystery, young adult. Recently published *Ten Good Seconds of Silence*, by Elizabeth Ruth.

How to Contact: Query with SASE or submit sample chapter(s), synopsis, author bio. Accepts simultaneous submissions. Responds in 3-4 months to queries.

Terms: Pays 10% royalty on net receipts. Publishes book an average of 1 year after acceptance of ms. Ms guidelines free.

THOMAS DUNNE BOOKS, Imprint of St. Martin's Press, 175 Fifth Ave., New York NY 10010. (212)674-5151. Website: www.stmartins.com. **Contact:** Tom Dunne. Publishes wide range of fiction and nonfiction. Publishes hardcover originals, trade paperback originals and reprints. Averages 210 titles/year.

Needs: Mainstream/contemporary, mystery/suspense, "women's" fiction, thrillers. Recently published *Winter Solstice*, by Rosamunde Pilcher; and *Marines of Autumn*, by James Brady.

How to Contact: "Thomas Dunne Books does not accept any manuscripts, proposals or queries unless solicited by a legitimate literary agent first."

Terms: Pays royalties of 10-15% on retail price for hardcover, 7½% for paperback. Advance varies with project. Publishes ms 1 year after acceptance. Guidelines and book catalog available free.

DUTTON, Imprint of Penguin Putnam Inc., 375 Hudson St., New York NY 10014. (212)366-2000. Website: www.penguinputnam.com. Editor-in-Chief: Brian Tart. Estab. 1852. Publishes hardcover originals.

Needs: Adventure, historical, literary, mainstream/contemporary, mystery, short story collections, suspense. Recently published *The Darwin Awards II*, by Wendy Northcutt (humor); *Falling Angels*, by Tracy Chevalier (fiction); and *The Oath*, by John Lescroart (fiction).

How to Contact: Agented mss only. Accepts simultaneous submissions. Responds in 6 months.

Terms: Pays royalties and author's copies; offers negotiable advance. Sends galleys to author. Publishes ms 12-18 months after acceptance. Book catalog available for SASE.

Advice: "Write the complete manuscript and submit it to an agent or agents. They will know exactly which editor will be interested in a project."

DUTTON CHILDREN'S BOOKS, Penguin Putnam Inc., 345 Hudson St., New York NY 10014. (212)414-3700. (212)414-3397. Website: www.penguinputnam.com. **Contact:** Lucia Monfried (picture books, easy-to-read, fiction); Stephanie Owens Lurie, president and publisher (picture books and fiction); Donna Brooks, editorial director (books for all ages with distinctive narrative style); Susan Van Metre, senior editor (character-oriented picture books and middle grade fiction); Alissa Heyman, associate editor (fiction, poetry, picture books); Jennifer Mattson (fiction, fantasy, picture books); Meredith Mundy Wasinger, editor (picture books, fiction, nonfiction). Estab. 1852. Dutton Children's Books publishes fiction and nonfiction for readers ranging from preschoolers to young adults on a variety of subjects. Publishes hardcover originals. Averages 100 titles/year.

Needs: Dutton Children's Books has a complete publishing program that includes picture books; easy-to-read books; and fiction for all ages, from "first-chapter" books to young adult readers. Recently published *Miss Bindergarter Takes a Field Trip With Kindergarten*, by Joseph Slate, illustrated by Ashley Wolff (picture book); *Horace Splatty, the Cupcaked Crusader*, by Lawrence David, illustrated by Barry Gott (chapter book); and *12 Again*, by Sue Corbett (novel).

How to Contact: Does not accept unsolicited mss. Send query with SASE.

Terms: Offers advance. Pays royalty on retail price.

○ ◎ **E.M. PRESS, INC.,** P.O. Box 336, Warrenton VA 20188. Phone/fax: (540)349-9958 (call first for fax). E-mail: empress2@erols.com. Website: www.empressinc.com. President: Beth A. Miller. **Contact**: Montana Umbel, assistant publisher. Estab. 1991. "A small press devoted to publishing quality work that might otherwise go unpublished." Publishes paperback and hardcover originals. Books: 50 lb. text paper; offset printing; perfect binding; illustrations. Average print order: 1,200-5,000. Averages 4 total titles, fiction, poetry and nonfiction, each year. Distributes titles through wholesalers and direct sales. Promotes titles through radio and TV, Interview Report, direct mailings and Ingram's catalogs.

Needs: "We're emphasizing nonfiction and a children's line, though we still consider 'marketable' fiction." Recently published *Looking for Pa*, by Geraldine Lee Susi (young reader) and *Moving the Nest, A Mid-Life Guide to Relocating*, by Bernard and Rhoda Faller.

How to Contact: Accepts unsolicited mss. Submit outline/synopsis and sample chapters or complete ms with cover letter. Include estimated word count. Send SASE or IRC for return of ms or send disposable copy of the ms and SASE for reply only. Agented fiction 10%. Responds in 3 months to queries; 3 months to mss. Accepts simultaneous submissions.

Terms: Amount of royalties and advances varies. Sends galleys to author. Publishes ms 18 months after acceptance. Guidelines available for SASE.

◐ ◎ **EAKIN PRESS**, P.O. Drawer 90159, Austin TX 78709-0159. (512)288-1771. Fax: (512)288-1813. E-mail: virginia@eakinpress.com. Website: www.eakinpress.com. **Contact:** Virginia Messer, publisher. Estab. 1978. Eakin specializes in Texana and Western Americana for juveniles and adults.

Imprint(s): Nortex; Sunbelt/Eakin; Eakin Press.

Needs: Juvenile. Specifically needs historical fiction for school market, juveniles set in Southwest for Southwest grade schoolers. Nonfiction adult with Texas or Southwest theme. Published *Inside Russia*, by Inez Jeffry.

How to Contact: Prefers queries, but accepts unsolicited mss. Send SASE for guidelines. Agented fiction 5%. Accepts simultaneous submissions. Responds in 3 months to queries.

Terms: Pays royalties; no advance. Sends galleys to author. Publishes ms 18 months years after acceptance. Writers guidelines for #10 SASE. Book catalog available for $1.25.

Advice: "Only fiction with strong Southwest theme. We receive around 1,200 queries or unsolicited mss a year."

◼ ◎ **ECW PRESS**, 2120 Queen St. E., Suite 200, Toronto, Ontario M4E 1E2 Canada. (416)694-3348 Fax: (416)698-9906. E-mail: info@ecwpress.com. Website: www.ecwpress.com. Estab. 1979. **Contact:** Jack David, publisher.

Needs: Literary. Receives 1,000 mss/year; publishes 8-12 books/year.

How to Contact: "Rarely" accepts unsolicited mss. Submit sample chapter, 15-25 pages double-spaced with SASE and IRC with sufficient postage. Include cover letter, brief bio, and publication history. Responds in between 2 weeks and 4 months. "We hope for the former and apologize for the latter."

Advice: "We are idiosyncratically picky about the kind of fiction we can stomach. We dabble almost exclusively in Canadian-authored fiction, unless you're Don DeLillo or Martin Amis . . . well, you get the idea."

◼ ◎ **EDGE SCIENCE FICTION & FANTASY PUBLISHING**, P.O. Box 1714, Calgary, Alberta T2P 2L7 Canada. (403)254-0160. Fax: (403)254-0456. E-mail: editor@edgewebsite.com. Website: www.edgewebsite.com (includes writer's guidelines, author bios, excerpts from forthcoming books, company background, writers' resources, catalog, sales/order pages). **Contact**: Cheyenne Grewe, editorial manager (science fiction/fantasy). Estab. 1996. "We are an independent publisher of science fiction and fantasy novels in hard cover or trade paperback format. We produce high-quality books with lots of attention to detail and lots of marketing effort. We want to encourage, produce and promote thought-provoking and fun-to-read science fiction and fantasy literature by 'Bringing the magic alive: one world at a time' (as our motto says) with each new book released." Publishes hardcover originals and trade paperback originals. Books: natural offset paper; offset/web printing; HC/perfect binding; b&w illustration only. Average print order: 2,000-3,000. First novel print order: 2,000. Plans 4 first novels this year. Averages 3-5 total titles. Member of Books Publishers Association of Alberta (BPAA), Independent Publishers Association of Canada (IPAC), Publisher's Marketing Association (PMA), Small Press Center.

Imprints: Edge, Alien Vistas, Riverbend.

Needs: Fantasy (space fantasy, sword and sorcery), science fiction (hard science/technological, soft/sociological). Recently published *Throne Price*, by Lynda Williams and Alison Sinclair (science fantasy); *Keaen*, by Till Noever (fantasy); and *Lyskarion: The Song of the Wind*, by J.A. Cullum (fantasy). Length: up to 100,000 words.

How to Contact: "We accept unsolicited manuscripts, but first send SAE and IRCs for submission guidelines. Visit our website for guidelines." No submissions by e-mail. Query with outline/synopsis and 3 sample chapters. Include estimated word count. Send #10 SASE and SASE suitable for return of sample chapters with IRCs. Responds in 1 month to queries; 4 months to mss. Rarely comments on rejected mss. Guidelines and writers' resources available on website.

Terms: Pays royalties of 8-10%. Average advance: negotiable. Sends galleys to author. Publishes ms 2-3 years after acceptance. Guidelines available for SASE and on website.

Advice: "Send us your best, polished, completed manuscript. Use proper manuscript format. Take the time before you submit to get a critique from people who can offer you useful advice. When in doubt, visit our website for helpful resources, FAQs and other tips."

LES ÉDITIONS DU VERMILLON, 305 St. Patrick St., Ottawa, Ontario K1N 5K4 Canada. (613)241-4032. Fax: (613)241-3109. E-mail: editver@ca.inter.net. Website: www.citymax.net/vermillon (includes book catalog). **Contact**: Jacques Flamand, editorial director. Publishes trade paperback originals. **Published new writers within the last year.** Averages 15 books/year. Distributes titles through Prologue in Canada. Promotes titles through advertising, book fairs and media.

• *Lithochronos*, poetry by Andrée Christensen and Jacques Flamand was awarded the Prix Trillium 2000, and *Toronto, je t'aime*, novel by Didier Leclair, the Prix Trillium 2001.

Needs: Juvenile, literary, religious, short story collections, young adult. Recently published *Le chien de Shibuya*, by J.-Fr. Somain (adventure, youth); *La Vie L'Écriture*, by Gabrielle Poulin (essay); and *Le dernier vol du Petit Prince/ The Last Flight of the Little Prince*, by Jean-Pierre de Villers (bilingual fiction).

How to Contact: Query with SASE or IRC for reply. Responds in 6 months to mss.

Terms: Pays royalties of 10%. Offers no advance. Publishes ms 18 months after acceptance. Book catalog available free.

EERDMANS BOOKS FOR YOUNG READERS, William B. Eerdmans Publishing Co., 255 Jefferson Ave. SE, Grand Rapids MI 49503. (616)459-4591. Fax: (616)459-6540. **Contact:** Judy Zylstra, editor. Publishes picture books and middle reader and young adult fiction and nonfiction. Averages 12-15 titles/year.

Needs: Juvenile, picture books, young adult, middle reader. Recently published *Secrets in the House of Delgado*, by Gloria Miklowitz.

How to Contact: Submit complete mss for picture books and novels or biographies under 200 pages with SASE. For longer books, send query letter and 3 or 4 sample chapters with SASE. Accepts simultaneous submissions. Responds in 6 weeks to queries.

Terms: Pays 5-7½% royalty on retail price. Publishes middle reader and YA books 1 year after acceptance. Publishes picture books 2-3 years after acceptance. Book catalog for large SASE.

WM. B. EERDMANS PUBLISHING CO., 255 Jefferson Ave. SE, Grand Rapids MI 49503. (616)459-4591. Fax: (616)459-6540. Website: www.eerdmans.com. **Contact**: Jon Pott, editor-in-chief, fiction editor (adult fiction); Judy Zylstra, fiction editor (children). Estab. 1911. "Although Eerdmans publishes some regional books and other nonreligious titles, it is essentially a religious publisher whose titles range from the academic to the semi-popular. We are a midsize independent publisher. We publish the occasional adult novel, and these tend to engage deep spiritual issues from a Christian perspective." Publishes hardcover and paperback originals and reprints. **Published new writers within the last year.** Averages 140 total titles, 6-8 fiction titles (mostly for children)/year.

Imprint(s): Eerdmans Books for Young Readers.

• Wm. B. Eerdmans Publishing Co.'s titles have won awards from the American Library Association and The American Bookseller's Association.

Needs: Religious (children's, general, fantasy). Published *At Break of Day*, by Nikki Grimes (children's); *The Goodbye Boat*, by Mary Joslin (children's); and *A Traitor Among Us*, by Elizabeth Van Steenwyk (middle reader).

How to Contact: Accepts unsolicited mss. Query with outline/synopsis and 2 sample chapters. Include 150- to 200-word bio and list of publishing credits. Send either SASE for return of ms or send disposable copy of ms and SASE for reply only. Agented fiction 5%. Responds in 6 weeks to queries. Accepts simultaneous submissions, "if notified." Sometimes comments on rejected ms.

Terms: Pays royalties of 7% minimum. Average advance: negotiable. Sends galleys to author. Publishes ms 12-18 months after acceptance. Guidelines and book catalog available free.

Advice: "Our readers are educated and fairly sophisticated, and we are looking for novels with literary merit."

ELECTRIC WORKS PUBLISHING, 605 Ave. C.E., Bismarck ND 58501. (701)255-0356. E-mail: editors @electricpublishing.com. Website: www.electricpublishing.com. **Contact:** James R. Bohe, editor-in-chief. Publishes digital books. **Publishes 70% of books from first-time authors; 85% from unagented writers.** Averages 50 titles/year.

Needs: Adventure, ethnic, experimental, fantasy, gothic, historical, horror, humor, juvenile, literary, mainstream/contemporary, military/war, multicultural, multimedia, mystery, occult, plays, poetry in translation, regional, religious, romance, science fiction, short story collections, spiritual, sports, suspense, western, young adult. Recently published *Felling of the Sons*, by Monette Bebow-Reinhard; *Marzipan*, by George Laidlaw.

How to Contact: *Electronic submissions only.* Submit ms in digital format. Accepts simultaneous submissions. Responds in 5 months to queries.

Terms: Pays 36-40% royalty on wholesale price. Publishes book 3 months after acceptance of ms. Book catalog and ms guidelines online.

N◎ EMPIRE PUBLISHING SERVICE, P.O. Box 1344, Studio City CA 91614-0344. (818)789-4980. **Contact:** Joseph Witt. Publishes hardcover reprints and trade paperback originals and reprints. **Publishes 50% of books from first-time authors; 95% from unagented writers.** Averages 40 titles/year; imprint publishes 15 titles/year.
Imprints: Gaslight Publications, Gaslight Books, Empire Publications, Empire Books.
Needs: Sherlock Holmes. Recently published *Elementary My Dear Watson*, by William Alan Landes.
How to Contact: Query with SASE. Responds in 1 month to queries; up to 1 year to mss.
Terms: Pays 6-10% royalty on retail price. Offers variable advance. Publishes book up to 2 years after acceptance of ms. Book catalog for #10 SASE; ms guidelines for $1 or #10 SASE.

⛐ ⊘ EMPYREAL PRESS, P.O. Box 1746, Place Du Parc, Montreal, Quebec H2W 2R7 Canada. Website: www.ska rwood.com. **Contact:** Colleen B. McCool. "Our mission is the publishing of literature which doesn't fit into any standard 'mold'—writing which is experimental yet grounded in discipline, imagination." Publishes trade paperback originals. Publishes 50% previously unpublished writers/year. Publishes 1-4 titles/year.
• Empyreal Press is not currently accepting unsolicited manuscripts "due to extremely limited resources."
How to Contact: No unsolicited mss.
Terms: Book catalog available for #10 SASE.
Advice: "Seriously consider self-publication: for instance, Roddy Doyle's *The Commitments* was published by the author himself. Talk about a success. Small and large presses, Empyreal included, are overloaded, some with waiting lists up to 5 years long. By publishing one's own work, one maintains full control, especially if the work is a commercial success."

⊘ Ⓐ M. EVANS & CO., INC., 216 E. 49th St., New York NY 10017. (212)688-2810. Fax: (212)486-4544. E-mail: editorial@mevans.com. Website: www.mevans.com (includes book catalog). **Contact:** Editor. Estab. 1960. Publishes hardcover and trade paper nonfiction and a small fiction list. Averages 30-40 titles/year.
Needs: "Small general trade publisher specializing in nonfiction titles on health, nutrition, diet, cookbooks, parenting, popular psychology."
How to Contact: Does not accept unsolicited mss. Agented fiction: 100%. Accepts simultaneous submissions.
Terms: Pays in royalties and offers advance; amounts vary. Sends galleys to author. Publishes ms 6-12 months after acceptance.

◉ FAITH KIDS™, Imprint of Cook Communications Ministries, 4050 Lee Vance View, Colorado Springs CO 80918. (719)536-0100. Fax: (719)536-3296. Website: www.faithkids.com. **Contact:** Heather Gemmen, senior editor. "Faith Kids Books publishes works of children's inspirational titles, ages 1-12, with a clear biblical value to influence children's spiritual growth." Publishes hardcover and trade paperback originals. Publishes 40 titles/year.
Needs: "Picture books, devotionals, Bible storybooks, for an age range of 1-12. We're particularly interested in materials for beginning readers."
How to Contact: "Faith Kids is accepting unsolicited manuscripts at this time." Queries from previously published authors preferred. Query with SASE. Responds in 6 months to queries. Accepts simultaneous submissions, if so noted.
Terms: Pays variable royalty on retail price. Offers advance. "Looking for work-for-hire proposals." Publishes ms 2 years after acceptance. Writer's guidelines for #10 SASE.

⛐ FARRAR, STRAUS & GIROUX INC., 19 Union Square W., New York NY 10003. (212)741-6900. Fax: (212)741-6973. E-mail: editorialfsg@fsgee.com. Website: www.fsgbooks.com. Estab.1946. Publishes hardcover and trade paperback originals and reprints.
Imprint(s): MIRASOL Libros Juveniles; North Point Press; Sunburst Books; Hill & Wang; Faber and Faber; FSG Juvenile Program Books for Young Readers.

Ⓐ FARRAR, STRAUS & GIROUX PAPERBACKS, 19 Union Square W., New York NY 10003. (212)741-6900. FSG Paperbacks emphasizes literary nonfiction and fiction, as well as poetry. Publishes hardcover and trade paperback originals and reprints. Averages 170 total titles/year.
Needs: Literary. Recently published *The Corrections*, by Jonathon Franzen; and *The Hunting of L.*, by Howard Norman.
How to Contact: No unsolicited ms.

N◎ FATHOM PUBLISHING COMPANY, P.O. Box 200448, Anchorage AK 99520-0448. (907)272-3305. Fax: (907)272-3305. E-mail: fathompub@aol.com. **Contact:** Constance Taylor, publisher. Averages 0-1 trade paperback originals/year on Alaskana history, legal issues and reference.
Needs: Wants Alaska-related fiction.
How to Contact: Query with SASE or submit outline, 1 sample chapter(s). Does not accept simultaneous submissions. Responds in 2 months to queries.
Terms: Pays 10-15% royalty on retail price.

FC2, Dept. of English, FSU, Tallahassee FL 32306-1580. (850)644-2260. E-mail: fc2@english.fsu.edu. Website: http:// FC2.org (includes guidelines, backlist, press history, reviews and interviews). **Contact:** R.M. Berry, publisher (fiction);

Brenda L. Mills, managing editor. Estab. 1974. Publisher of innovative fiction. Publishes hardcover and paperback originals. Books: perfect/Smyth binding; illustrations. Average print order: 2,200. First novel print order: 2,200. **Published new writers within the last year.** Plans 2 first novels, 4 novels total; 1 first story collection this year. Averages 6 total titles, 6 fiction titles each year. Often comments on rejected mss. Titles distributed through Northwestern U.P.

Needs: Formally innovative, experimental, modernist/postmodern, avant-garde, anarchist, feminist, gay, minority, cyberpunk. Published *Book of Lazarus*, by Richard Grossman; *Is It Sexual Harassment Yet?*, by Cris Mazza; *Liberty's Excess*, by Lidia Yuknavitch; *Aunt Rachel's Fur*, by Raymond Federman.

How to Contact: Accepts unsolicited mss. Query first with outline/synopsis. Include 1-page bio, list of publishing credits. SASE with ms. Agented fiction 5%. Responds in 3 weeks to queries; 4 months to mss. Accepts simultaneous submissions. Send queries to: FC2, Unit for Contemporary Literature, Illinois State University, 109 Fairchild Hall, Normal IL 61790-4241.

Terms: Pays royalties of 7½%. Sends galleys to author. Publishes ms up to 2 years after acceptance.

Advice: "Be familiar with our list."

THE FEMINIST PRESS AT THE CITY UNIVERSITY OF NEW YORK, 365 Fifth Ave., Suite 5406, New York NY 10016. (212)817-7915. Fax: (212)817-1593. Website: www.feministpress.org (includes writer's guidelines, online catalog, teacher's resources). **Contact:** Molly Vaux, publisher. Estab. 1970. Small, nonprofit literary and educational publisher. "The Feminist Press publishes only fiction reprints by classic American women authors and translations of distinguished international women writers." Publishes hardcover and paperback originals and reprints. "We use an acid-free paper, perfect-bind our books, four color covers; and some cloth for library sales if the book has been out of print for some time; we shoot from the original text when possible. We always include a scholarly and literary afterword, since we are introducing a text to a new audience. Average print run: 2,500." Publishes no original fiction; exceptions are anthologies and international works. Averages 10-15 total titles, 4-8 fiction titles/year (reprints of feminist classics only). Member, CLMP, Small Press Association. Distributes titles through Consortium Book Sales and Distribution. Promotes titles through author tours, advertising, exhibits and conferences. Charges "permissions fees (reimbursement)."

Needs: Nonsexist children's/juvenile, short story collections, young adult (nonsexist), ethnic, feminist, lesbian, literary, translations, women's. Needs fiction by "U.S. women of color writers from 1920 to 1970 who have fallen out of print." Published *Apples From the Desert*, by Savyon Liebrecht (short stories, translation); *The Parish and the Hill*, by Mary Doyle Curran (fiction, reprint); *Allegra Maud Goldman*, by Edith Konecky (fiction, reprint); and *Red Sand, Blue Sky*, by Cathy Applegate (fiction, YA).

How to Contact: Does not accept unsolicited mss. Query by e-mail only to jcasella@gc.cuny.edu; limit 200 words with 'submission' as subject line. Include word count, brief bio and list of publishing credits. Send SASE. Responds in 2 months to e-mail queries. Accepts simultaneous submissions.

Terms: Pays royalties of 10% on net sales. Average advance: $250-500. Pays 5-10 author's copies. Sends first proofs to author. Publishes ms 18-24 months after acceptance. Guidelines available on website; catalogs free on website.

FLORIDA ACADEMIC PRESS, P.O. Box 540, Gainesville FL 32602. (352)332-5104. Fax: (352)331-6003. E-mail: fapress@worldnet.att.net. **Contact:** Max Vargas, CEO (nonfiction/self-help); Sam Decalo, managing editor (academic); Florence Dusek, assistant editor (fiction). Publishes hardcover and trade paperback originals. **Publishes 80% of books from first-time authors; 100% from unagented writers.** Publishes 6 titles/year.

Needs: Literary, regional.

How to Contact: Submit complete ms. Responds in 1-6 months to mss.

Terms: Pays 5-8% royalty on retail price. depending if paperback or hardcover. Publishes book 3-5 months after acceptance of ms. Book catalog and ms guidelines free.

Advice: Considers complete mss only. "Manuscripts we decide to publish must be re-submitted in camera-ready form."

FOCUS PUBLISHING, INC., P.O. Box 665, Bemidji MN 56619. (218)759-9817. Fax: (218)751-2183. E-mail: focus@paulbunyan.net. **Contact:** Jan Haley, vice president. Estab. 1994. Publishes hardcover and trade paperback originals and reprints. **Publishes 90% of books from first-time authors; 100% from unagented writers.** Averages 4-6 titles/year.

Needs: Juvenile, picture books, religious, young adult. "We are looking for Christian books for men and young adults. Be sure to list your target audience."

How to Contact: Query and submit synopsis. Responds in 2 months to queries.

Terms: Pays 7-10% royalty on retail price. Publishes book 1 year after acceptance of ms. Book catalog free.

Advice: "I prefer SASE inquiries, synopsis and target markets. Please don't send 5 lbs. of paper with no return postage. Our focus is on Christian living books for adults and children. Only Biblically-sound proposals considered."

FORGE BOOKS, Tom Doherty Associates, LLC, 175 5th Ave., New York NY 10010. (212)388-0100. Fax: (212)388-0191. Website: www.tor.com (includes FAQ, writer's guidelines, info on authors and upcoming books, first

---

SENDING TO A COUNTRY other than your own? Be sure to send International Reply Coupons (IRC) instead of stamps for replies or return of your manuscript.

chapter of selected books, list of award winners). **Contact**: Melissa Ann Singer, senior editor (general fiction, mysteries, thriller); Patrick Nielsen Hayden, senior editor (science fiction, fantasy). Estab. 1980. "Forge imprint specializes in thrillers, historicals, and mysteries. Tor imprint focuses on science fiction, fantasy and horror." Publishes hardcover and paperback originals. **Published new writers within the last year.** Averages 130 total titles, 129 fiction titles/year.
Imprint(s): Forge, Tor, Orb.
Needs: Historical, horror, mainstream/contemporary, mystery/suspense (amateur sleuth, police procedural, private eye/ hardboiled), thriller/espionage, western (frontier saga, traditional), science fiction, fantasy.
How to Contact: Accepts unsolicited mss. Query with outline/synopsis and first 3 sample chapters. Include estimated word count, bio and list of publishing credits. SASE for reply. Agented fiction 95%. Responds in 4 months to proposals. Sometimes comments on rejected mss.
Terms: Pays royalties. Sends galleys to author. Publishes ms 12-18 months after acceptance.
Advice: "The writing mechanics must be outstanding for a new author to break into today's market."

N ◎ FORT ROSS INC., 26 Arthur Place, Yonkers NY 10701-1703. (914)375-6448. Fax: (914)375-6439. E-mail: ftross@ix.netcom.com. Website: www.fortross.net (includes description of Fort Ross Inc., including examples of published books, available rights and catalog of the authors and artists). **Contact:** Dr. Vladimir P. Kartsev. Estab. 1992. "We publish only well-established American/Canadian fantasy, science fiction and romance writers who would like to have their novels translated in Russia and Eastern Europe by our publishing house in cooperation with the local publishers." Publishes hardcover and paperback translations. **Published 3 new writers within the last year.** Averages 10 total titles/year.
Needs: Adventure, fantasy (space fantasy, sword and sorcery), mystery/suspense (amateur sleuth, police procedural, private eye/hardboiled), romance (contemporary, futuristic/time travel), science fiction (hard science/technological, soft/ sociological), thriller/espionage. Recently published *The Harem*, Liza Dulby; *Lolita's Diary*, by Pia Pera (novel); and *Killers Are Storming . . .*, by Aleshkin (mystery).
How to Contact: Does not accept unsolicited mss. Send query letter. Include estimated word count, brief bio and list of publishing credits. Send SASE or IRC for reply. Responds in 1 month. Accepts simultaneous submissions.
Terms: Publishes ms 1 year after acceptance. Pays royalties of 4-9%. Average advance: $500-1,000; negotiable. Does not send galleys of translated novels to author.

N ◎ FOUNTAINHEAD PRODUCTIONS, INC., 145 Broad St., Matawan NJ 07747. (732)566-1800. Fax: (732)566-7336. E-mail: exec@fountainheadpub.com. Website: www.fountainheadpub.com. **Contact:** J.G. Fennessy, editor; Kathleen M. Leo, associate editor; Michael McMahon, associate editor. Estab. 1999. "Small independent publisher. We publish a wide range of titles and are not 'niche' publishers. We also sponsor the national writing contest and publish the contest winners. In 2002, we are only accepting submissions through the national writing contest. Details on website." Publishes hardcover and paperback originals and hardcover and paperback reprints. Books: type of paper, method of printing, binding and illustrations vary. Average print order: varies; first novel print order: varies. **Published 1 new writer within the last year.** Plans 5-10 first novels this year. Averages 10 total titles, 7 fiction titles/year. Distributes titles through Lightning Source, a division of Ingram Books. Promotes titles through pre-press reviews.
Needs: Adventure, ethnic/multicultural, fantasy, historical, horror, humor/satire, literary, mainstream, military/war, mystery/suspense, psychic/supernatural, regional, religious, romance, science fiction, thriller/espionage, western; special interests (Irish/Celtic science fiction). Recently published *Domestics*, by J.G. Fennessy (Irish). Publishes *In the Parishes of Ireland* trilogy.
How to Contact: Does not accept or return unsolicited mss. Query with 2-3-page outline/synopsis. Accepts queries by e-mail and fax. Include estimated word count, brief bio and list of publishing credits. Responds in 2 months to queries; 3 months to mss. Accepts simultaneous submissions, electronic submissions (proposals only) and disk. Often comments on rejected mss.
Terms: Pays royalties of 5-15%. Sends galleys to author. Publishes ms 8-12 months after acceptance. Guidelines available on Internet.
Advice: "The availability of electronic media and publishing are making fiction more desirable than ever. Follow our guidelines and send your best writing when requested."

◐ ▼ FOUR WALLS EIGHT WINDOWS, 39 W. 14th St., #503, New York NY 10011. (212)206-8965. E-mail: edit@4w8w.com. Website: www.4w8w.com (includes complete catalog, featured books and ordering information). **Contact**: Jofie Ferrari-Adler, editor. Estab. 1987. "We are a small independent publisher." Publishes hardcover and paperback originals and paperback reprints. Books: quality paper; paper or cloth binding; illustrations sometimes. Average print order: 3,000-7,000. First novel print order: 3,000-5,000. **Published new writers within the last year.** Averages 30 total titles; approximately 9 fiction titles/year. Distributes titles through Publishers Group West, the largest independent distributor in the country. Promotes titles through author tours, bound galleys, select advertising, postcard mailing, etc.

• Four Walls Eight Windows' books have received mention from the *New York Times* as "Notable Books of the Year" and have been nominated for *L.A. Times* fiction and nonfiction prizes.

Needs: Nonfiction. Published *The Angle Quickest for Flight*, by Steven Kotler (novel); *Extremities*, by Kathe Koja (stories); *Beast of the Heartland*, by Lucius Shepard (stories); and *Lost Pages*, by Paul DiFillipo (science fiction).

How to Contact: Does not accept unsolicited submissions. "Query letter accompanied by sample chapter, outline and SASE is best. Useful to know if writer has published elsewhere, and if so, where." Accepts electronic queries but *not* submissions. Agented fiction 50%. Responds in 2 months. Accepts simultaneous submissions. No electronic submissions.

Terms: Pays standard royalties. Average advance: varies. Sends galleys to author. Publishes ms 1-2 years after acceptance. Book catalog available free.

Advice: "Please read our catalog and/or our website to be sure your work would be compatible with our list."

FRONT STREET, INC., 20 Battery Park Ave., #403, Asheville NC 28801. (828)236-3097. Fax: (828)236-3098. E-mail: contactus@frontstreetbooks.com. Website: www.frontstreetbooks.com (includes writer's guidelines, names of editors, book catalog, interviews with authors, first chapters of some books). **Contact:** Stephen Roxburgh, president and publisher; Joy Neaves, editor. Estab. 1994. "Small independent publisher of high-quality picture books and literature for children and young adults." Publishes hardcover originals. Distributes titles through PGW. Titles promoted on Internet, in catalog, by sales representatives, at library and education conferences.

- *A Step from Heaven*, by An Na won the Michael L. Printz Award for 2002. *Carver: A Life in Poems*, by Marilyn Nelson won a Newbery Honor 2002 and a Coretta Scott King Honor.

Needs: Children's/juvenile (adventure, animal, fantasy, historical, mystery, sports), young adult/teen (adventure, fantasy/science fiction, historical, mystery/suspense, problem novels, sports). "No longer accepting unsolicited picture book manuscripts." Recently published *The Shakeress*, by Kimberly Hueston (YA fiction, debut author); *Little Chicago*, by Adam Rapp (YA fiction); *Wolf on the Fold*, by Judith Clarke (YA fiction).

How to Contact: Accepts unsolicited mss. Query with outline/synopsis and a few sample chapters or submit complete ms with cover letter. Accepts queries by fax and e-mail. Include short bio and list of publishing credits. Send SASE for reply, return of ms or send disposable copy of ms. Agented fiction 10%. Responds in 2 weeks to queries; 4 months to mss. Accepts simultaneous submissions. No electronic submissions.

Terms: Pays royalties. Offers advance.

FYOS ENTERTAINMENT, LLC, P.O. Box 2021, Philadelphia PA 19103. (215)972-8067. Fax: (215)972-8076. E-mail: info@fyos.com. Website: www.fyos.com. **Contact:** Tonya Marie Evans, editor-in-chief (poetry, African-American fiction); Susan Borden Evans, general manager (African-American fiction). Publishes hardcover originals and trade paperback originals. Averages 2-3 titles/year.

Needs: Multicultural, poetry, romance, short story collections. "We concentrate acquisition efforts on poetry and fiction of interest primarily to the African-American reader. We are looking for thought-provoking, well-written work that offers a 'quick and entertaining' read." Recently published *Seasons of Her*, by T. Evans; *SHINE!*, by T. Evans.

How to Contact: Query with SASE. Accepts simultaneous submissions. Responds in 1-3 months to queries; 3-6 months to mss.

Terms: Pays 10-15% royalty on retail price. or a 60 (publisher)/40 (author) split of net receipts. Will also consider outright purchase opportunities. Publishes book 1 year after acceptance of ms. Book catalog for #10 SASE; ms guidelines for #10 SASE.

Advice: "Neatness counts! Present yourself and your work in a highly professional manner."

GASLIGHT PUBLICATIONS, Empire Publishing Services, P.O. Box 1344, Studio City CA 91614-0344. (818)784-8918. **Contact:** Simon Waters, fiction editor (Sherlock Holmes only). Estab. 1960. Publishes hardcover and paperback originals and reprints. Books: paper varies; offset printing; binding varies; illustrations. Average print order: 5,000. First novel print order: 5,000. **Published 1 new writer within the last year.** Averages 4-12 total titles, 2-4 fiction titles/year. Promotes titles through sales reps, trade, library, etc.

Needs: Sherlock Holmes only. Recently published *On the Scent with Sherlock Holmes*, by Walter Shepherd; *Sherlock Holmes, The Complete Bagel Street Saga*, by Robert L. Fish; and *Subcutaneously, My Dear Watson*, by Jack Tracy (all Sherlock Holmes). Publishes the Sherlock Holmes Mysteries series.

How to Contact: Accepts unsolicited mss. Send query letter. Include estimated word count, brief bio and list of publishing credits. Send SASE or IRC for return of ms or send disposable copy of the ms and SASE for reply only. Agented fiction 10%. Responds in 2 weeks to queries; up to 1 year to mss.

Terms: Pays royaltiesof 8-10%. (Royalty and advances dependant on the material.) Sends prepublication galleys to author. Publishes ms 1-6 months after acceptance. Guidelines available for SASE; book catalog for 9×12 SAE and $2 postage.

Advice: "Please send only Sherlock Holmes material. Other stuff just wastes time and money."

GAY SUNSHINE PRESS AND LEYLAND PUBLICATIONS, P.O. Box 410690, San Francisco CA 94141. Fax: (415)626-1802. Website: www.gaysunshine.com. **Contact:** Winston Leyland, editor. Estab. 1970. Midsize independent press. Publishes hardcover and paperback originals. Books: natural paper; perfect-bound; illustrations. Average print order: 5,000-10,000.

- Gay Sunshine Press has received a Lambda Book Award for *Gay Roots* (volume 1), named "Best Book by a Gay or Lesbian Press," and received grants from the National Endowment for the Arts.

Needs: Literary, experimental, translations—all gay male material only. "We desire fiction on gay themes of *high literary quality* and prefer writers who have already had work published in literary magazines. We also publish erotica—short stories and novels." Published *Partings at Dawn: An Anthology of Japanese Gay Literature from the 12th to the 20th Centuries*; and *Out of the Blue: Russia's Hidden Gay Literature—An Anthology*.

How to Contact: "Do not send an unsolicited manuscript." Query with SASE. Responds in 3 weeks to queries; 2 months to mss. Send $1 for catalog.

Terms: Negotiates terms with author. Sends galleys to author. Pays royalties or by outright purchase.

Advice: "We continue to be interested in receiving queries from authors who have book-length manuscripts of high literary quality. We feel it is important that an author know exactly what to expect from our press (promotion, distribution, etc.) before a contract is signed. Before submitting a query or manuscript to a particular press, obtain critical feedback on your manuscript from knowledgeable people. If you alienate a publisher by submitting a manuscript shoddily prepared/ typed, or one needing very extensive rewriting, or one which is not in the area of the publisher's specialty, you will surely not get a second chance with that press."

N. GENESIS PRESS, INC., 315 Third Ave. N, Columbus MS 39701. (662)329-9927. Fax: (662)329-9399. E-mail: books@genesis-press.com. Website: www.genesis-press.com. **Contact:** Sharon Morgan. Publishes hardcover and trade paperback originals and reprints. **Publishes 50% of books from first-time authors; 90% from unagented writers.** Averages 30 titles/year.

Needs: Erotica, ethnic, literary, multicultural, romance, women's. Recently published *Cherish the Flame*, by Beverly Clark; *No Apologies*, by Seressia Glass.

How to Contact: Query with SASE or submit 3 sample chapter(s), synopsis. Responds in 2 months to queries; 4 months to mss.

Terms: Pays 6-12% royalty on invoice price. Offers $750-5,000 advance. Publishes book 1 year after acceptance of ms. Ms guidelines for #10 SASE.

Advice: "Be professional. Always include a cover letter and SASE. Follow the submission guidelines posted on our website or send SASE for a copy."

THE GLENCANNON PRESS, P.O. Box 633, Benicia CA 94510. (707)745-3933. Fax: (707)747-0311. E-mail: captjaff@pacbell.net. Website: www.glencannon.com (includes book catalog). **Contact:** Bill Harris (maritime, maritime children's). Estab. 1993. "We publish quality books about ships and the sea." Publishes hardcover and paperback originals and hardcover reprints. Books: Smyth; perfect binding; illustrations. Average print order: 1,000. First novel print order: 750. **Published 1 new writer within the last year.** Averages 4-5 total titles, 1 fiction title/year. Member, PMA, BAIPA. Distributes titles through Quality Books, Ingram and Baker & Taylor. Promotes titles through direct mail, magazine advertising and word of mouth.

Imprint(s): Palo Alto Books (any except maritime); Glencannon Press (merchant marine and Navy); Bill Harris, editor.

Needs: Adventure, children's/juvenile (adventure, fantasy, historical, mystery, preschool/picture book), ethnic/multicultural (general), historical (maritime), humor/satire, mainstream, military/war, mystery/suspense, thriller/espionage, western (frontier saga, traditional maritime), young adult/teen (adventure, historical, mystery/suspense, western). Currently emphasizing children's maritime, any age. Recently published *White Hats*, by Floyd Beaver (navy short stories); and *The Crafty Glencannon*, by Guy Gilpatric (merchant marine short stories).

How to Contact: Accepts unsolicited mss. Submit complete ms with cover letter. Include brief bio and list of publishing credits. Send SASE or IRC for return of ms OR send disposable copy of ms and SASE for reply only. Responds in 1 month to queries; 2 months to mss. Accepts simultaneous submissions. Often comments on rejected mss.

Terms: Pays royalties of 10-20%. "Usually author receives $1-2 per copy for each book sold." Sends galleys to author. Publishes ms 6-24 months after acceptance. Book catalog available free and on website.

Advice: "Write a good story in a compelling style."

N. A DAVID R. GODINE, PUBLISHER, INC., 9 Hamilton Place, Boston MA 02108. (617)451-9500. Fax: (617)350-0250. E-mail: info@godine.com. Website: www.godine.com. President: David R. Godine. Estab. 1970. Small independent publisher (5-person staff). Publishes hardcover and paperback originals and reprints. Averages 35 total titles/year.

Imprint(s): Nonpareil Books (trade paperbacks), Verba Mundi (translations), Imago Mundi (photography).

Needs: Literary, historical, children's, translations, short story collections. Recently published *The Last Buffalo Hunter*, by Jake Mosher (fiction).

How to Contact: Does not accept unsolicited mss. Query with SASE.

Terms: Pays royalties on retail price. Publishes ms 3 years after acceptance.

Advice: "Have your agent contact us."

GOTHIC CHAPBOOK SERIES, Gothic Press, 1701 Lobdell Ave., No. 32, Baton Rouge LA 70806-8242. (225)925-2917. E-mail: gothicpt12@aol.com. Website: www.gothicpress.com (includes information, history, links, forums and catalog). **Contact:** Gary W. Crawford, editor (horror, fiction, poetry and scholarship). Estab. 1979. "One person operation on a part-time basis. Publishes horror fiction, poetry, and scholarship and criticism." Publishes paperback originals. Books: printing or photocopying. Average print order: 150-200. Averages 1-2 total titles and fiction titles/year. Distributes titles through direct mail and book dealers.

Needs: Horror (dark fantasy, psychological, supernatural). Need novellas and short stories. Gothic Press is not always an open market. Query first before submitting anything.

How to Contact: Accepts unsolicited mss. Send query letter. Accepts queries by e-mail or phone. Include estimated word count, brief bio and list of publishing credits. Send SASE or IRC for return of ms or send disposable copy of ms and SASE for reply only. Responds in 2 weeks to queries; 4 weeks to mss. Sometimes comments on rejected ms. Pays royalties of 10%. Sends galleys to author. Guidelines available for SASE.

Advice: "Know gothic and horror literature well."

● **GRAYWOLF PRESS,** 2402 University Ave., Suite 203, St. Paul MN 55114. (651)641-0077. Fax: (651)641-0036. E-mail: wolves@graywolfpress.com. Website: www.graywolfpress.org. Director: Fiona McCrae. **Contact:** Anne Czarniecki, executive editor; Katie Dublinski, editor (fiction). Estab. 1974. "Graywolf Press is an independent, nonprofit publisher dedicated to the creation and promotion of thoughtful and imaginative contemporary literature essential to a vital and diverse culture." Growing small literary press, nonprofit corporation. Publishes trade cloth and paperback originals. Books: acid-free quality paper; offset printing; hardcover and soft binding; illustrations occasionally. Average print order: 3,000-10,000. First novel print order: 2,000-6,000. Averages 14-16 total titles, 4-6 fiction titles/year. Distributes titles nationally through Consortium Book Sales and Distribution. "We have an in house marketing staff and an advertising budget for all books we publish."
Needs: Literary, short story collections. Literary fiction; no genre books (romance, western, science fiction, suspense). Recently published *Crying at the Movies*, by Madelon Sprengnether; *Loverboy*, by Victoria Redel; *The Ghost of Bridgetown*, by Debra Spark.
How to Contact: Query with SASE. "Please do not fax or e-mail queries or submissions." Agented fiction: 50%. Responds in 3 months. Accepts simultaneous submissions.
Terms: Pays royalties on retail price; negotiates advance and number of author's copies. Sends galleys to author. Publishes ms 18 months after acceptance. Guidelines for #10 SASE; book catalog free.
Advice: "Please review the catalog and submission guidelines before submitting your work. We rarely publish collections or novels by authors who have not published work previously in literary journals or magazines."

● **GREEN BEAN PRESS,** P.O. Box 237, New York NY 10013. Phone/fax: (718)965-2076. E-mail: gbpress@earthlink.net. Website: www.greenbeanpress.com (includes guidelines, catalog, links, excerpts and special offers). **Contact:** Ian Griffin, editor. Estab. 1993. "Small independent press dedicated to publishing gritty, unique, distinctive authors." Publishes paperback originals and hardcovers. Books: acid-free paper; perfect-bound. Average print order: 1,000; first novel print order: 1,000. **Published 3 new writers within the last year.** Averages 15 total titles, 5 fiction titles/year. Titles distributed through Ingram, Baker & Taylor promotion through print ads, author signings and readings, direct mail and e-mail.
Needs: Humor/satire, literary, mystery (private eye/hardboiled), short story collections. Prefers "shorter works, averaging between 80 and 175 pages." Recently published *Frostbite*, by Nathan Graziano (short story); *One Last Chance*, by Brent McKnight (short story); *Do Not Look Directly Into Me*, by Daniel Crocker (short story); *Wing-Ding at Uncle Tug's*, by Jeff Grimshaw (humor/short story).
How to Contact: Does not accept unsolicited mss; any unsolicited mss will be returned. Send query letter or query with outline/synopsis and 2-4 sample chapters. Accepts e-mail queries. Include brief bio with submission. Agented fiction: 10%. Responds in 1 month to queries; 2 months to mss. No simultaneous, electronic or disk submissions.
Terms: Pays royalties of 10-15%. Sends galleys to author. Time between acceptance and publication is 6-12 months. Guidelines available for SASE or on website; book catalogs free on website.
Advice: "As a result of corporate publishers' 'bestseller only' mentality, there are more and more high-quality authors out there looking for presses they can have closer, more personal relationships with. This is a great opportunity for small independent presses. Let your work speak for itself. If you feel the need to send a letter explaining every little thing about your manuscript, then the manuscript's not doing its job."

[N] ● ◎ **GREENE BARK PRESS,** P.O. Box 1108, Bridgeport CT 06601. (203)372-4861. E-mail: greenebark@aol.com. Website: www.greenebarkpress.com. **Contact:** Michele Hofbauer, associate publisher. "We only publish children's fiction—all subjects, but in reading picture book format appealing to ages 3-9 or all ages." Publishes hardcover originals. **Published new writers within the last year.** Averages 5 titles/year. Distributes titles through Baker & Taylor, Partners Book Distributing and Quality Books. Promotes titles through ads, trade shows (national and regional), direct mail campaigns.
Needs: Juvenile. Recently published *A Pumpkin Story*, by Mariko Shinju and *The Magical Trunk*, by GiGi Tegge.
How to Contact: Submit complete ms with SASE. Does not accept queries or ms by e-mail. Responds in 3 months to mss. Accepts simultaneous submissions.
Terms: Pays royalties of 10-15% on wholesale price. Publishes ms 1 year after acceptance. Guidelines available for SASE; book catalog for $2.
Advice: Audience is "children who read to themselves and others. Mothers, fathers, grandparents, godparents who read to their respective children, grandchildren. Include SASE, be prepared to wait, do NOT inquire by telephone, fax or e-mail."

● ◎ **GREENWILLOW BOOKS,** Imprint of HarperCollins Publishers, 1350 Avenue of the Americas, New York NY 10019. (212)261-6627. Website: www.harperchildrens.com. **Contact:** Fiction Editor. Estab. 1974. "Greenwillow Books publishes quality hardcover books for children." Publishes hardcover originals and reprints. Averages 50-60 titles/year.
Needs: Recently published *The Queen of Attolia*, by Megan Whalen Turner; *Bo & Mzzz Mad*, by Sid Fleischman; *Whale Talk*, by Chris Crutcher; *Year of the Griffen*, by Diana Wynne Jones.
How to Contact: "Unfortunately, we are currently not accepting unsolicited submissions or queries in any form. Due to a change in corporate policy, unsolicited mail will not be opened and cannot be returned."

insider report

Novelist Michael Lowenthal resists gay, Jewish labels

Though much of his work deals with gay and Jewish characters and themes, Michael Lowenthal doesn't think of himself as a writer of "gay fiction" or "Jewish fiction."

"On the rare days when I have the gumption to consider myself anything other than a literary gate-crasher," says the 33-year-old author, "I try to think of myself as a writer, plain and simple. 'Jewish writer,' 'gay writer,' and similar terms are, to my mind, mostly marketing labels or shelving categories. Other people can feel free to think of me and my writing in any way they see fit, but that's all external, after the fact, unrelated to the act or the intention of my own writing."

Michael Lowenthal

Lowenthal is the author of two novels, *Avoidance* (Graywolf Press, 2002) and *The Same Embrace* (Dutton, 1998). His essays and short fiction have appeared in *The New York Times Magazine*, *The Kenyon Review*, *The Southern Review*, *Witness*, *Tin House* and *Nerve*, and have been anthologized in more than a dozen books, including *Neurotica* (Norton), *Best American Gay Fiction* (Little, Brown), *Men on Men 5* (Plume), and *Wrestling with the Angel* (Riverhead). Formerly an editor at University Press of New England, Lowenthal now teaches creative writing at Boston College.

Here, Lowenthal discusses the limitations of genre labels, the definition of "gay fiction," and the differences between working with large and small publishing houses.

Do you consider yourself first and foremost a Jewish writer, a gay writer, or a literary writer?

I was raised Jewish; I am what is generally thought of as gay; while I would never hide these personal characteristics, and while I am certain that they, along with many other traits, influence everything I think and do and write, it's not such a simple equation. My first novel was thick with Jewish themes and terms; my second novel has not a Jewish word in it, and instead focuses on the Amish. Likewise, I've published ten or so short stories in the past few years; half of them are about "gayness" (loosely defined) and the others not at all. I recently published a long story in *Southern Review* that is about a Catholic priest who has a crisis of vocation when he runs into an old college girlfriend. Is that story the work of a "Jewish, gay" writer? Well, yes, it's my work.

I also find the term "literary writer" to be problematic. I certainly aspire to be respected by what we think of as the "literary" establishment. And if "literary" is a category separate from what we think of as "genre" fiction, then sure, I'm "literary." But the term seems to presuppose that a writer who takes care with subtleties of language and character can't also be a commercial success or reach a wide audience. Why not? And for that matter, why is there a literary/genre distinction? Why can't there be literary sci-fi writers and literary thriller writers? Well, of course, there are.

Elizabeth Graver, a "literary" novelist whom I greatly respect, read *Avoidance* and was kind enough to write an endorsement of it, which thrilled me. But I was thrilled as much—or more—by the fact that Elizabeth's babysitter, a woman who didn't complete college, found the manuscript on the table and read it in two sittings and said she couldn't put it down.

If certain labels help me connect with readers from a given demographic, I'm all for it. But if they hinder connections with readers—and I think they so often do—then I find them terribly frustrating and counterproductive. After all, writing is about communication, and I want to communicate with the widest possible audience.

How would you define "gay fiction"?

Much time and debate has been spent on this question, but to be honest, it doesn't interest me very much. I don't see gay fiction as a genre in any conventional or useful sense. If I had to provide a philosophical response, I guess I'd say that gay fiction is fiction either about gay characters and their desires, or that displays a "gay sensibility" (whatever that is). But I think the real answer is that "gay fiction" is a marketing category, encompassing any book that any publisher thinks it might be able to convince gay people to buy.

Do you find the conventions of gay fiction frustrating, liberating (in the way, say, that poets sometimes feel liberated by forms as opposed to free verse), or something in between?

There are no conventions of "gay fiction," because gay fiction, like the gay population, is all over the map. Just as there are gay firefighters and gay hairdressers and gay actuaries, there are gay family sagas and gay murder mysteries and gay parenting tales and gay alien abduction accounts.

Do you think it's harder for writers of gay fiction to get published?

Given the existence of a certain number of gay-specific journals and small presses, it may in fact be slightly easier for gay writers to find outlets for their work. But it certainly seems harder for gay writers who write about gay themes to be published well and to be published widely. There are plenty of exceptions; Michael Cunningham is a prime example. But this country's major, prestigious publishers do seem to be guided by a perception, accurate or not, that "the general reader" is not naturally interested in gay characters. He or she can occasionally be convinced, seems to be the thinking, but only occasionally.

Your first novel was published by a big New York house (Dutton, an imprint of Penguin Putnam); your new book is being published by a medium-sized independent press (Graywolf). How has your experience been different this time around?

By the time *The Same Embrace* was published by Dutton, I was on my third editor and my third publicist; in other words, the people who actually published the novel were two generations removed from the people who had liked it enough to commit to it twelve months earlier. That's how volatile the New York houses are these days.

Graywolf has been the far opposite end of the spectrum. The publisher, Fiona McCrae, read and commented on four separate drafts of *Avoidance*. She is a true editor, from the old school, and her advice changed the novel in crucially valuable ways. Even the marketing director read the novel twice: before and after my revision. I have been consulted on everything from text design to catalogue copy to publication schedule.

Granted, smaller presses have limitations. Graywolf's advance was smaller than Dutton's, and it's even further from something an adult could reasonably live on. Graywolf's budget for me to go on a book tour is much smaller than Dutton's. Their initial distribution may not be as wide (although, now that Graywolf titles will be distributed by Farrar Straus Giroux, this may change).

But I feel like my book matters to the people at Graywolf, and to the company's success. I know that my novel, and my opinions about how to publish it, are valued. And that's a feeling that no amount of money can buy.

—*Will Allison*

GREYCORE PRESS, 2646 New Prospect Rd., Pine Bush NY 12566. (845)744-5081. Fax: (845)744-8081. E-mail: joan123@frontiernet.net. Website: www.greycore.com (includes catalog, upcoming titles, author interviews and contact informtion). **Contact:** Joan Schweighandt, publisher. Estab. 1999. Small independent publisher of quality fiction and nonfiction titles. Publishes hardcover originals. Books: cloth binding. Average print order: 3,000. First novel print order: 3,000. **Published 3 new writers within the last year.** Averages 3 total titles, 2 fiction titles/year. Member, Dustbooks. Distributes titles through Seven Hills.
Needs: Literary, mainstream, short story collections. Recently published *The Secret Keepers*, by Julie Mars; *Conjuring Maud*, by Philip Danze; and *Done In by Innocent Things*, by William Eisner.
How to Contact: Does not accept unsolicited mss. Send query letter. Accepts queries by e-mail and fax. Include estimated word count and list of publishing credits. Send SASE or IRC for return of ms. Responds in weeks to queries; in months to mss. Accepts simultaneous submissions. Sometimes comments on rejected mss.
Terms: Pays royalties of 50% after production costs. Sends galleys to author. Publishes ms 18 months after acceptance.
Advice: "We prefer to get cover letters that include author credentials and the ways in which writers are willing to help publicize their work. We are very small and can't keep up with the number of manuscripts we receive. Our preference is to receive a cover letter, synopsis and the author's credentials via snail mail. We will read e-mail queries too of course, but as e-mails tend to get lost in the shuffle, our preference is snail mail, with SASE."

GROLIER PUBLISHING, Grolier Inc., 90 Sherman Turnpike, Danbury CT 06816. (203)797-3500. Fax: (203)797-3197. Website: www.publishing.grolier.com. Estab. 1895. "Grolier Publishing is a leading publisher of reference, educational and children's books. We provide parents, teachers and librarians with the tools they need to enlighten children to the pleasure of learning and prepare them for the road ahead." Publishes hardcover and trade paperback originals.
Imprint(s): Children's Press, Franklin Watts, Orchard Books.

GROVE/ATLANTIC, INC., 841 Broadway, New York NY 10003. (212)614-7850. Fax: (212)614-7886. "Grove/ Atlantic publishes serious nonfiction and literary fiction." Publishes hardcover originals, trade paperback originals and reprints. Averages 60-70 titles/year.
Imprint(s): Grove Press (Estab. 1952), Atlantic Monthly Press (Estab. 1917).
Needs: Experimental, literary, translations. Published *Four Blondes*, by Candace Bushnell (Atlantic Monthly); and *How the Dead Live*, by Will Self (Grove Press).
How to Contact: Does not accept unsolicited mss. Agented submissions only. Accepts simultaneous submissions.
Terms: Pays royalties of 7½-15% on retail price. Advance varies considerably. Publishes ms 1 year after acceptance. Book catalog available free.

GRYPHON BOOKS, P.O. Box 209, Brooklyn NY 11228. (718)646-6126 (after 6 pm EST). Website: www.gryphonbooks.com. **Contact:** Gary Lovisi, owner/editor. Estab. 1983. Publishes paperback originals and trade paperback reprints. Books: bond paper; offset printing; perfect binding. Average print order: 500-1,000. **Published new writers within the last year.** Averages 10-15 total titles, 12 fiction titles/year.
Imprint(s): Gryphon Books, Gryphon Doubles, Gryphon SF Rediscovery Series.
Needs: Mystery/suspense (private eye/hardboiled, crime), science fiction (hard science/technological, soft/sociological). No supernatural, horror, romance or westerns. Published *The Dreaming Detective*, by Ralph Vaughn (mystery-fantasy-horror); *The Woman in the Dugout*, by Gary Lovisi and T. Arnone (baseball novel); and *A Mate for Murder*, by Bruno Fischer (hardboiled pulp). Publishes Gryphon Double novel series.

How to Contact: "I am not looking for novels now; *will only see a 1-page synopsis with SASE.*" Include estimated word count, 50-word bio, short list of publishing credits, "how you heard about us." Do not send ms. Agented fiction 5-10%. Responds in 1 month to queries; 2 months to mss. Accepts simultaneous and electronic submissions (with hard copy—disk in ASCII). Often comments on rejected mss.

Terms: For magazines, $5-45 on publication plus 2 contributor's copies; for novels/collections payment varies and is much more. Sends galleys to author. Publishes ms 1-3 years after acceptance. Writers guidelines and book catalog for SASE.

Advice: "I am looking for better and better writing, more cutting-edge material with *impact*! Keep it lean and focused."

GUERNICA EDITIONS, Box 117, Station P, Toronto, Ontario M5S 2S6 Canada. (416)658-9888. Fax: (416)657-8885. E-mail: guernicaeditions@cs.com. Website: www.guernicaeditions.com. **Contact:** Antonio D'Alfonso, fiction editor (novel and short story). "Guernica Editions is a small press that produces works of fiction and nonfiction on the viability of pluriculturalism." Publishes paperback originals and reprints. Books: various paper; offset printing; perfect binding. Average print order: 1,500; first novel print order: 1,500. **Published 6 new writers within the last year.** Averages 25 total titles, 18-20 fiction titles/year. Distributes titles through professional distributors.

• Two titles by Guernica Editions have won American Book Awards.

Imprint(s): Prose Series, Antonio D'Alfonso, editor, all; Picas Series, Antonio D'Alfonso, editor, reprints.

Needs: Erotica, literary, translations. "We are open to all styles, but especially shorter pieces." Publishes anthology of Arab women writers/Italian women writers. Recently published *The Blue Whale*, by Stanislao Niero; *A Father's Revenge*, by Pan Bouyoucas; and *Moncton Mantra*, by Gérald Leblanc.

How to Contact: Accepts unsolicited mss. Send query letter. Include estimated word count, brief bio and list of publishing credits. Send IRC for return of ms. Responds in weeks to queries; months to mss.

Terms: Pays royalties of 10%. Average advance: $500-1,000. Sends galleys to author. Publishes ms 12 months after acceptance. Book catalogs available for $5 and on website.

Advice: "Know what publishers do, and send your works only to publisher whose writers you've read and enjoyed."

ROBERT HALE LIMITED, Clerkenwell House, 45/47 Clerkenwell Green, London EC1R 0HT England. Fax: 020-7490-4958. **Contact:** Fiction Editor. Publishes hardcover and trade paperback originals and hardcover reprints. **Published approximately 50 new writers within the last year.**

Imprint(s): J.A. Allen; Caroline Burt, editor (horse books nonfiction); NAG Press (Horological and gemmological nonfiction).

Needs: Historical (not U.S. history), mainstream and western. Length: 40,000-150,000 words. Recently published *Greenwich*, by Harold Fast (mainstream); *The Judas Judge*, by Michael McGarrity (crime); and *The Savage Lord Griffin*, by Joan Smith (regency romance).

How to Contact: Query with synopsis and 2 sample chapters. Accepts queries by fax.

Advice: "Write well and have a strong plot!"

HARCOURT INC., 525 B St., Suite 1900, San Diego CA 92101. (619)231-6616. Fax: (619)699-6777. **Contact:** Jeannette Larson, senior editor (general fiction); Allyn Johnston, editorial director of Harcourt Brace Children's Books; Elizabeth Van Doren, editorial director of Gulliver Books; Paula Wiseman, editorial director of Silver Whistle. Publishes hardcover originals and paperback reprints. **Published "very few" new writers within the last year.** Averages 150 titles/year.

Imprint(s): Harcourt Trade Children's Books, Gulliver Books, Red Wagon Books and Silver Whistle.

• Books published by Harcourt Trade Publishers have received numerous awards including the Caldecott and Newbery medals and selections as the American Library Association's "Best Books for Young Adults."

Needs: Nonfiction for all ages, picture books for very young children, historical, mystery. Published *To Market, To Market*, by Ann Miranda; *Antarctic Antics*, by Judy Sierra; *Armageddon Summer*, by Bruce Coville and Jane Yolen; *Count On Me*, by Alice Provensen.

How to Contact: Does not accept unsolicited mss. Submit through agent only.

Terms: Terms vary according to individual books; pays on royalty basis. Book catalog available for 9×12 SASE.

Advice: "Read as much current fiction as you can; familiarize yourself with the type of fiction published by a particular house; interact with young people to obtain a realistic picture of their concerns, interests and speech patterns."

HARCOURT INC. CHILDREN'S BOOK DIVISION, 525 B St., Suite 1900, San Diego CA 92101. (619)281-6616. Fax: (619)699-6777. Website: www.harcourt.com. "Harcourt Inc. owns some of the world's most prestigious publishing imprints—which distinguish quality products for the juvenile, educational, scientific, technical, medical, professional and trade markets worldwide." Publishes hardcover originals and trade paperback reprints.

Imprint(s): Harcourt Children's Books, Gulliver Books, Silver Whistle, Red Wagon, Odyssey Paperbacks, Magic Carpet, Voyager Books/Libros Viajeros and Green Light Readers.

Needs: Childrens/juvenile, young adult. Recently published *In My World*, by Lois Ehlert; *The Magic Hat*, by Mem Fox; *Armageddon Summer*, by Bruce Coville and Jane Yolen (young adult); and *Pictures 1918*, by Jeanette Ingold (young adult).

How to Contact: Does not accept unsolicited mss or queries. No phone calls.

HARLEQUIN AMERICAN ROMANCE, a Harlequin book line, 300 E. 42nd St., 6th Floor, New York NY 10017. (212)682-6080. Fax: (212)682-4539. Website: www.eharlequin.com. **Contact:** Melissa Jeglinski, associate senior editor. "Upbeat and lively, fast-paced and well plotted, American Romance celebrates the pursuit of love in the backyards, big cities and wide-open spaces of America." Publishes paperback originals and reprints. Books: newspaper print paper; web printing; perfect-bound. **Regularly publishes new writers.**

Needs: Romance (contemporary, American). Needs "all-American stories with a range of emotional and sensual content and are supported by a sense of community within the plot's framework. In the confident and caring heroine, the tough but tender hero, and their dynamic relationship that is at the center of this series, real-life love is showcased as the best fantasy of all!" Manuscripts must be 70,000-75,000 words.

How to Contact: Accepts unsolicited mss. Send query letter or submit complete ms with cover letter. Send SASE or IRC for return of ms or send disposable copy of ms and SASE for reply only. No simultaneous, multiple or disk submissions.

Terms: Pays royalties and advance. Guidelines available for SASE and on website.

N ☕ ○ ◎ HARLEQUIN BLAZE, a Harlequin book line, 225 Duncan Mill Rd., Don Mills, Ontario M3B 3K9 Canada. (416)445-5860. Website: www.eharlequin.com. **Contact:** Birgit Davis-Todd, senior editor. "Harlequin Blaze is an exciting new series that has evolved out of the very successful Temptation line. It will showcase the very best writers and stars from the original Blaze program. It is also a vehicle to build and promote new authors who have a strong sexual edge to their stories. Finally, it is *the* place to be for seasoned authors who want to create a sexy, sizzling, longer contemporary story." Publishes paperback originals and reprints. Books: newspaper print; web printing; perfect-bound. **Regularly publishes new writers.**

Needs: Romance (contemporary). "Sensuous, highly romantic, innovative plots that are sexy in premise and execution. The tone of the books can run from fun and flirtatious to dark and sensual. Submissions should have a very contemporary feel—what it's like to be young and single in the new millennium. We are looking for heroes and heroines in their early 20s and up. There should be an emphasis on the physical relationship developing between the couples. Fully described love scenes along with a high level of fantasy and playfulness. The hero and heroine should make a commitment at the end." Manuscripts must be 70,000-75,000 words.

How to Contact: Accepts unsolicited mss. "New authors should send a query letter outlining their story in a couple of pages. Published authors may query and/or submit chapters and a synopsis." No simultaneous, multiple or disk submissions.

Terms: Pays royalties and advance. Guidelines available for SASE and on website.

Advice: "Are you a *Cosmo* girl at heart? A fan of *Sex and the City*, *Ally McBeal*, or *Friends*? Or maybe you just have an adventurous spirit. If so, then Blaze is the series for you!"

N ☕ ○ ◎ HARLEQUIN DUETS, a Harlequin book line, 225 Duncan Mill Rd., Don Mills, Ontario M3B 3K9 Canada. (416)445-5860. Website: www.eharlequin.com. **Contact:** Birgit Davis-Todd, senior editor. "Harlequin Duets are a delightful combination of romance and comedy. Fast-paced and plot driven, these novels depend upon the comedy building from the relationship between the hero and heroine." Publishes paperback originals and reprints. Books: newspaper print; web printing; perfect-bound. **Regularly publishes new writers.**

Needs: Romance (romantic comedy). "We are looking for a comic premise, a strong humorous voice, and a great romance. A high degree of sexual tension is a must, and while we encourage love scenes, they are not a requirement. So whether your story is a screwball comedy, a comedy of errors or simply the lighter side of love, we are looking for entertaining romance that will bring a smile to the face of every reader." Manuscripts must be 50,000-55,000 words.

How to Contact: Accepts unsolicited mss. Send query letter or submit complete ms with cover letter. Send SASE or IRC for return of ms or send disposable copy of ms and SASE for reply only. No simultaneous, multiple or disk submissions.

Terms: Pays royalties and advance. Sends galleys to author. Guidelines available for SASE and on website.

★ ☕ HARLEQUIN ENTERPRISES, LTD., 225 Duncan Mill Rd., Don Mills, Ontario M3B 3K9 Canada. (416)445-5860. Website: www.eHarlequin.com (includes product listings, guidelines, author information, a full range of related information). Chairman and CEO: Brian E. Hickey. President: Donna Hayes. Vice President Editorial: Isabel Swift. **Contact:** Randall Toye, editorial director (Harlequin, Gold Eagle, Worldwide Library); Tara Gavin, editorial director (Silhouette, Steeple Hill, Red Dress Ink); Diane Moggy, editorial director (MIRA). Estab. 1949. Publishes paperback originals and reprints. Books: Newsprint paper; web printing; perfect-bound. **Published new writers within the last year.** Averages 700 total titles/year. Distributes titles through retail market, direct mail market and overseas through operating companies. Promotes titles through trade and consumer advertising: print, radio, TV.

Imprint(s): Harlequin American Romance, Harlequin Blaze, Harlequin Duets, Harlequin Historical, Harlequin Intrigue, Harlequin Presents, Harlequin Romance, Harlequin Superromance, Harlequin Temptation, Silhouette Desire, Silhouette Intimate Moments, Silhouette Romance, Silhouette Special Edition, Mills & Boon Historical Romance, Mills& Boon Medical Romance, MIRA, Gold Eagle, Worldwide Mysteries, Steeple Hill, Red Dress Ink.

N ○ ◎ HARLEQUIN HISTORICALS, a Harlequin book line, 300 E. 42nd St., 6th Floor, New York NY 10017. (212)682-6080. Fax: (212)682-4539. Website: www.eharlequin.com. **Contact:** Tracy Farrell, senior editor. "The primary element of a Harlequin Historicals novel is romance. The story should focus on the heroine and how her love for one man changes her life forever. For this reason it is very important that you have an appealing hero and heroine, and that their relationship is a compelling one. The conflicts they must overcome—and the situations they face—can be as varied as the setting you have chosen, but there must be romantic tensioni, some spark between your hero and heroine that keeps your reader interested." Publishes paperback originals and reprints. Books: newspaper print; perfect-bound. **Regularly publishes new writers.**

Needs: Romance (historical). "We will not accept books set after 1900. We're looking primarily for books set in North America, England, or France between 1100 and 1900 A.D. We do not buy many novels set during the American Civil War. We are, however, flexible, and will consider most periods and settings. We are not looking for gothics or family sagas, nor are we interested in the kind of comedy of manners typified by straight Regencies. Historical romances set during the Regency period, however, will definitely be considered." Manuscripts must be 99,000-105,000 words.

How to Contact: Accepts unsolicited mss. Send query letter or submit complete ms with cover letter. Send SASE or IRC for return of ms or send disposable copy of ms and SASE for reply only. No simultaneous, multiple or disk submissions.

Terms: Pays royalties and advance. Sends galleys to author. Guidelines available for SASE and on website.

N ○ ◎ HARLEQUIN INTRIGUE, a Harlequin book line, 300 E. 42nd St., 6th Floor, New York NY 10017. (212)682-6080. Fax: (212)682-4539. Website: www.eharlequin.com. **Contact:** Denise O'Sullivan, associate senior editor. "These novels are taut, edge-of-the-seat, contemporary romantic suspense tales of intrigue and desire. Kidnappings, stalkings and women in jeopardy coupled with best selling romantic themes are examples of story lines we love most." Publishes paperback originals and reprints. Books: newspaper print; perfect-bound. **Regularly publishes new writers.**

Needs: Romance (romantic suspense). "Murder mystery, psychological suspense, or thriller; the love story must be inextricably bound to the resolution where all loose ends are tied up neatly—and shared dangers lead right to shared passions. As long as they're in jeopardy and falling in love, our heroes and heroines may traverse a landscape as wide as the world itself. Their lives are on the line—and so are their hearts!" Manuscripts must be 70,000-75,000 words.

How to Contact: Accepts unsolicited mss. Send query letter or submit complete ms with cover letter. Send SASE or IRC for return of ms or send disposable copy of ms and SASE for reply only. No simultaneous, multiple or disk submissions.

Terms: Pays royalties and advance. Sends galleys to author. Guidelines available for SASE and on website.

★ ⊕ HARLEQUIN MILLS & BOON LTD., Subsidiary of Harlequin Enterprises Ltd., Eton House, 18-24 Paradise Rd., Richmond, Surrey TW9 1SR United Kingdom. (44)0208-288-2800. Website: www.millsandboon.co.uk (includes forthcoming titles and author profiles). **Contact:** K. Stoecker, editorial director; Tessa Shapcott, senior editor (Harlequin Presents®); Samantha Bell, senior editor (Harlequin Romance®); Linda Fildew, senior editor (Mills & Boon Historicals); Sheila Hodgson, senior editor (Mills & Boon Medicals). Estab. 1908-1909. "World's largest publisher of brand name category romance; books are available for translation into more than 20 languages and distributed in more than 100 international markets." Publishes paperback originals. Published new writers within the last year. Plans 3-4 first novels this year.

Imprint(s): Harlequin Presents (Mills & Boon Presents), Harlequin Romance (Mills & Boon Tender Romance), Mills & Boon Historicals, Mills & Boon Medicals.

N ⊕ ○ ◎ HARLEQUIN PRESENTS (MILLS & BOON PRESENTS), a Harlequin book line, Eton House, 18-24 Paradise Rd., Richmond, Surrey TW9 1SR United Kingdom. Phone: (44)0208 288 2800. Website: www.millsandboon.co.uk. **Contact:** Tessa Shapcott, senior editor. "Pick up a Harlequin Presents novel and you'll enter a world full of spine-tingling passion and provocative, tantalizing, romantic excitement! Although grounded in reality, these stories offer compelling modern fantasies to readers all around the world, and there is scope within this line to develop relevant, contemporary issues which touch the lives of today's women. Harlequin Presents novels capture the drama and intensity of a powerful, sensual love affair." Publishes paperback originals and reprints. Books: newspaper print; perfect-bound. **Regularly publishes new writers.**

Needs: Romance. Needs "novels written in the third person that feature spirited, independent heroines who aren't afraid to take the initiative, and breathtakingly attractive, larger-than-life heroes. The conflict between these characters should be lively and evenly matched, but always balanced by a developing romance that may include explicit lovemaking." Manuscripts must be 50,000-55,000 words.

How to Contact: Accepts unsolicited mss. Send query letter or submit complete ms with cover letter. Send SASE or IRC for return of ms or send disposable copy of ms and SASE for reply only. No simultaneous, multiple or disk submissions.

Terms: Pays royalties and advance. Sends galleys to author. Guidelines available for SASE and on website.

N ⊕ ○ ◎ HARLEQUIN ROMANCE (MILLS & BOON TENDER ROMANCE), a Harlequin book line, Eton House, 18-24 Paradise Rd., Richmond, Surrey TW9 1SR United Kingdom. Phone: (44)0208 288 2800. Website: www.millsandboon.co.uk. **Contact:** Samantha Bell, senior editor. "These heartwarming stories are written with freshness and sincerity, featuring spirited, engaging heroines portrayed with depth and affection—as well as heroes who are charismatic enough to fulfull every woman's dreams!" Publishes paperback originals and reprints. Books: newspaper print; perfect-bound. **Regularly publishes new writers.**

Needs: Romance. Needs "novels written in third person from the heroine's point of view, with focus almost exclusively on the developing relationship between the protagonists. The emphasis should be on warm and tender, emotions, with no sexual explicitness; lovemaking should only take place when the emotional commitment between the characters justifies it. Readers should be thrilled by the tenderness of their developing relationship, and gripped by romantic suspense as the couple strives to overcome the emotional barriers between them and find true happiness in the romance of a lifetime!" Manuscripts must be 50,000-55,000 words.

How to Contact: Accepts unsolicited mss. Send query letter or submit complete ms with cover letter. Send SASE or IRC for return of ms or send disposable copy of ms and SASE for reply only. No simultaneous, multiple or disk submissions.

Terms: Pays royalties and advance. Sends proofs to author. Guidelines available for SASE and on website.

HARLEQUIN SUPERROMANCE, a Harlequin book line, 225 Duncan Mills Rd., Don Mills, Ontario M3B 3K9 Canada. (416)445-5860. Website: www.eharlequin.com. **Contact:** Paula Eykelhof, senior editor. "The aim of Superromance novels is to produce a contemporary, involving read with a mainstream tone in its situations and characters, using romance as the major themes. To achieve this, emphasis should be placed on individual writing styles and unique and topical ideas." Publishes paperback originals and reprints. Books: newspaper print; perfect-bound. **Regularly publishes new writers.**

Needs: Romance (contemporary). "The criteria for Superromance books are flexible. Aside from length, the determining factor for publication will always be quality. Authors should strive to break free of stereotypes, clichés and worn out plot devices to create strong, believable stories with depth and emotional intensity. Superromance novels are intended to appeal to a wide range of romance readers." Manuscripts must be approximately 85,000 words.

How to Contact: Accepts unsolicited mss. Send query letter or submit complete ms with cover letter. Send SASE or IRC for return of ms or send disposable copy of ms and SASE for reply only. No simultaneous, multiple or disk submissions.

Terms: Pays royalties and advance. Sends galleys to author. Guidelines available for SASE and on website.

Advice: "A general familiarity with current Superromance books is advisable to keep abreast of ever-changing trends and overall scope, but we don't want imitations and we are open to innovation. We look for sincere, heartfelt writing based on true-to-life experiences and fantasies the reader can identify with."

HARLEQUIN TEMPTATION, a Harlequin book line, 225 Duncan Mills Rd., Don Mills, Ontario M3B 3K9 Canada. (416)445-5860. Website: www.eharlequin.com. **Contact:** Birgit Davis-Todd, senior editor. "Temptation is sexy, sassy, and seductive! This is Harlequin's boldest, most sensuous series, focusing on men and women living—and loving—today!" Publishes paperback originals and reprints. Books: newspaper print; perfect-bound. **Regularly publishes new writers.**

Needs: Romance. "Almost anything goes in Temptation: The stories may be humorous, topical, adventurous or glitzy, but at heart they are pure romantic fantasy." Manuscripts must be approximately 60,000 words.

How to Contact: Accepts unsolicited mss. Send query letter or submit complete ms with cover letter. Send SASE or IRC for return of ms or send disposable copy of ms and SASE for reply only. No simultaneous, multiple or disk submissions.

Terms: Pays royalties and advance. Sends galleys to author. Guidelines available for SASE and on website.

Advice: "Think fast-paced, use the desires and language of women today, add a high level of sexual tension along with strong conflicts, and then throw in a good dash of 'what if. . . .' The results should sizzle!"

HARPERCOLLINS CHILDREN'S BOOKS, (Division of HarperCollins), 1350 Avenue of the Americas, New York NY 10019. (212)261-2500. Fax: (212)261-6689. Website: www.harperchildrens.com. Publishes hardcover originals.

Imprint(s): Avon; Joanna Cotler; Greenwillow Books; Laura Geringer Books; HarperFestival; HarperTrophy, Avon, & Tempest; Tempest; HarperCollins Children's Books.

HARPERCOLLINS GENERAL BOOKS GROUP, (Division of HarperCollins Publishers), 10 East 53 St., New York NY 10022. (212)207-7000. Fax: (212)207-7633. Website: www.harpercollins.com. "HarperCollins, one of the largest English language publishers in the world, is a broad-based publisher with strengths in academic, business and professional, children's, educational, general interest, and religious and spiritual books, as well as multimedia titles." Publishes hardcover and paperback originals and paperback reprints.

Imprint(s): Access Press; Amistad Press; Avon; Ecco; Eos; Fourth Estate; HarperAudio; HarperBusiness; HarperCollins; HarperEntertainment; HarperLargePrint; HarperResource; HarperSanFrancisco; HarperTorch; Perennial; Perfect-Bound; Quill; Rayo; ReganBooks; William Morrow.

HARPERCOLLINS PUBLISHERS (NEW ZEALAND) LIMITED, P.O. Box 1, Auckland, New Zealand. Website: www.harpercollins.co.nz. **Contact:** Lorain Day, senior editor. Averages 8-10 fiction titles/year (25-30 nonfiction).

Imprint(s): Flamingo, HarperCollins, Voyager.

Needs: Adult fiction: Flamingo and HarperCollins imprints (60,000+ words); Junior fiction: 9-12 years (15-20,000 words). Recently published *The Stove Rake*, by Denise Keay (historical romance, debut author); *Sharing Blood*, by Jennifer Maxwell (fiction); and *Buddy*, by V.M. Jones (children's novel, debut author).

How to Contact: Submit synopsis or outline, with 3 sample chapters.

Terms: Pays royalties.

Advice: "It is preferred that the author and story have New Zealand connections/content."

⊘ HARVEST HOUSE PUBLISHERS, 990 Owen Loop N, Eugene OR 97402-9173. (541)343-0123. Fax: (541)302-0731. E-mail: kimberly.shumate@harvesthousepublishers.com. Editorial Managing Director: LaRae Weikert. Vice President of Editorial: Carolyn McCready. **Contact:** Acquisitions. Estab. 1974. "We publish exclusively Christian fiction. The foundation of our publishing program is to publish books that 'help the hurts of people' and nurture spiritual growth." Midsize independent publisher. Publishes hardcover and paperback originals and reprints. **Publishes 2-3 new writers/year.** Books: 40 lb. ground wood paper; offset printing; perfect binding. Average print order: 10,000. First novel print order: 10,000-15,000. Average 140 total titles, 15 fiction titles/year.
How to Contact: Does not accept unsolicited mss. Does not accept fax or e-mail submissions. Recommends using Evangelical Christian Publishers Association website (www.ecpa.org) or the Writer's Edge, P.O. Box 1266, Wheaton IL 60189.
Advice: "Attend a writer's conference where one of our editors will be teaching. We also look at fiction represented by a reputable agent."

◑ HAWK PUBLISHING GROUP, 7107 S. Yale Ave. #345, Tulsa OK 74136-1619. (918)492-3677. Fax: (918)492-2120. Website: www.hawkpub.com (includes writer's guidelines, book catalog, forthcoming titles, author information). Estab. 1999. Independent publisher of general trade/commercial books, fiction and nonfiction. Publishes hardcover and paperback originals. **Published 4 new writers within the last year.** Plans 2 first novels this year. Averages 12 total titles, 6 fiction titles/year. Member, PMA, SPAN. Distributes titles through Book Network.
Needs: Recently published *Goddess by Mistake*, by P.C. Cast; and *Awash in the Blood*, by John Wooley.
How to Contact: Accepts unsolicited mss. "Send us a short synopsis and bio, including any prior publishing credits or relevant credentials, with 3 chapters of your book." Submissions will not be returned, so send only copies. No SASE. No submissions by e-mail or by "certified mail or any other service that requires a signature." Replies "only if interested. If you have not heard from us within three months after receipt of your submission, you may safely assume that we were not able to find a place for it in our list."
Terms: Terms vary. Sends galleys to author.

⊘ HELICON NINE EDITIONS, Subsidiary of Midwest Center for the Literary Arts, Inc., P.O. Box 22412, Kansas City MO 64111-2820. (816)753-1016. E-mail: helicon9@aol.com. Website: www.heliconnine.com (includes general information about title, book and author, ording information for books). **Contact:** Gloria Vando Hickok. Estab. 1990. Small press publishing poetry, fiction, creative nonfiction and anthologies. Publishes paperback originals. Books: 60 lb. paper; offset printing; perfect-bound; 4-color cover. Average print order: 1,000-5,000. **Published one new writer within the last year.** Averages 4 total titles, 2-4 fiction titles/year. Also publishes one-story chapbooks called *feuillets*, which come with envelope, 250 print run. Distributes titles through Baker & Taylor, Brodart, Ingrams, Follett (library acquisitions), Midwest Library Service, all major distributors and booksellers. Promotes titles through reviews, readings, radio and television interviews.
How to Contact: Currently not accepting unsolicited mss or query letters.
Terms: Pays royalties, advance and author's copies. "Individual arrangement with author." Sends galleys to author. Publishes ms 6-12 months after acceptance.
Advice: "We accept short story collections. We welcome new writers and first books. Submit a clean, readable copy in a folder or box—paginated with title and name on each page. Also, do not pre-design book, i.e., no illustrations. We'd like to see books that will be read 50-100 years from now."

⊕ HEMKUNT PRESS, Hemkunt Publishers (P) Ltd., A-78 Naraina Industrial Area Phase-I, New Delhi India 110028. Phone: +91-11-579-5079. Fax: +91-11-611-3705. E-mail: hemkunt1@vsnl.com. Website: www.hemkuntpublishers.com (includes company profile, book jackets, prices, ISBN, brief summary). **Contact:** Arvinder Singh, director. "We specialize in children's fiction and storybooks as well as novels and short stories." Distributes titles through direct sales, direct mailings and distributors and short stories.
Needs: "We would be interested in novels and short stories, preferably by authors with a published work. Unpublished work can also be considered. Would like to have distribution rights for US, Canada and UK besides India. Charges fee depending on author profile, ms and marketability." Recently published *More Tales of Birbal & Akbar*, by Sanjana Singh.
How to Contact: Send a cover letter, brief summary, 3 sample chapters (first, last and one other chapter). Accepts queries by e-mail and fax.
Terms: Catalog on request.
Advice: "Send interesting short stories and novels pertaining to the global point of view."

Ⓝ ⊚ HENDRICK-LONG PUBLISHING CO., INC., P.O. Box 1247, Friendswood TX 77549. (281)482-6187. Fax: (281)482-6169. E-mail: hendrick-long@worldnet.att.net. Website: hendricklongpublishing.com. **Contact:** Vilma Long. Estab. 1969. Publishes hardcover and trade paperback originals and hardcover reprints. **Publishes 90% from unagented writers. Averages 8 titles/year.**
Needs: Juvenile, young adult. Recently published *Pioneer Children*, by Betsy Warren; *Maggie Houston*, by Jane Cook.
How to Contact: Query or submit outline/synopsis and 2 sample chapters. Does not accept simultaneous submissions. Responds in 1 month to queries, 2 months if more than one query is sent.
Terms: Pays royalty. Pays royalty on selling price. Offers advance. Publishes book 18 months after acceptance of ms. Book catalog for 8½×11 or 9×12 SASE with 4 first-class stamps; ms guidelines for #10 SASE.

HERODIAS, 185 Bridge Plaza N., Suite 308-A, Fort Lee NJ 07024. (201)944-7600. Fax: (201)944-6363. E-mail: greatblue@acninc.net. Website: www.herodias.com. **Contact:** Paul Williams, editor (fiction, biography, arts). Publishes hardcover originals, trade paperback originals and reprints. **Publishes 25% of books from first-time authors; 75% from unagented writers.** Averages 10 titles/year.
Imprints: Herodias Books for Young Readers (young adult); Little Blue Books (kids)
Needs: Erotica, fantasy, historical, juvenile, literary, mainstream/contemporary, poetry, poetry in translation, young adult. Recently published *The Cuttlefish*, by Maryline Desbiolles; *The Bold Saboteurs*, by Chandler Brassard.
How to Contact: Query with SASE or submit proposal package including synopsis. Accepts simultaneous submissions. Responds in 2 weeks to queries; 3 months to mss.
Terms: Pays 7½-17½% royalty. Offers $500-2,000 advance. Publishes book 1 year after acceptance of ms. Book catalog and writer's guidelines free or on website.

HILL STREET PRESS, Hill Street Press LLC, 191 E. Broad St., #209, Athens GA 30601-2848. (706)613-7200. Fax: (706)613-7204. E-mail: info@hillstreetpress.com. Website: www.hillstreetpress.com (includes writer's guidelines, mission statement, book catalog and interviews). **Contact:** Patrick Allen and Judy Long, editors. Estab. 1998. "Small independent press specializing in southern belles lettres especially nonfiction. We concentrate on high-quality first fiction." Publishes hardcover originals, paperback originals and paperback reprints. Books: acid-free paper, conventional printing, photos/drawings. Average print order: 7,500. First print order: 7,500. **Publishes 5 new writers/year.** Publishes 2 first novels/year. Averages 26 total titles; 5 fiction titles/year.
Needs: Gay, African-American, lesbian, literary, mainstream, regional (southern US). "Reasonable length projects (50,000 to 85,000 words) stand a far better chance of review. Do not submit proposals for works in excess of 125,000 words in length." No short stories. "No cornball moonlight-and-magnolia stuff." Recently published *Prime Leaf*, by Eugene Wall (literary, debut author); *The Worst Day of My Life So Far*, by M.A. Harper (literary); and *Truelove and Homegrown Tomatoes*, by Julie Cannon (mainstream, debut author).
How to Contact: Accepts unsolicited mss. Query with outline/synopsis and 3 sample chapters. Include estimated word count, brief bio, list of publishing credits and résumé. Send SASE for return of ms or send disposable copy of ms and SASE for reply only. Agented fiction 5%; "Let us know at the point of submission if you are represented by an agent." Responds in 3 months to queries; 6 months to mss. Accepts simultaneous submissions; "must be acknowledged upon initial presentation."
Payment/Terms: Pays in royalties. Sends galleys to author. Publishes ms up to 2 years after acceptance. Guidelines available free for SASE; book catalogs for 11×8 SASE with $1.24 postage.
Advice: "Do not submit short stories. Your proposal is your advertisement—sell your work with proposal, query letter, résumé and 3 sample chapters."

HODDER & STOUGHTON/HEADLINE, Hodder Headline, 338 Euston Rd., London NW1 3BH England. Phone: (020)7873 6000. Fax: (020)7873 6024. **Contact:** Mrs. Betty Schwartz, submissions editor, Hodder & Stoughton (adult fiction, nonfiction); Caroline Stofer, submissions editor, Headline (adult fiction). "Big commercial, general book publishers of general fiction/nonfiction, thrillers, romance, sagas, contemporary original, literary, crime." Publishes hardcover and paperback originals and paperback reprints.
Imprint(s): Coronet, Sceptre, Flame, Hodder & Stoughton, NEL, LIR (Headline, Review, Feature).
Needs: Family saga, historical (general), literary, mainstream, mystery/suspense (amateur sleuth, cozy, police procedural, private eye/hardboiled), romance (contemporary, romantic suspense), thriller/espionage.
How to Contact: Accepts unsolicited mss. Query with outline/synopsis and first sample chapter. Accepts queries by e-mail. Include estimated word count and brief bio. Send disposable copy of ms and SASE for reply only. Responds in 2 weeks minimum to queries; 1 month to mss. Accepts simultaneous submissions.
Terms: Guidelines available for SASE; book catalogs for flat A4 SASE.
Advice: "Minimum 80,000 words. For popular fiction titles (i.e. thrillers) we require around 120,000 words. Send cover letter, short synopsis (1-2 pages) and first sample chapter, typewritten, double-spaced. Writing should be of good quality, and commercial. No single short stories."

HOLIDAY HOUSE, INC., 425 Madison, New York NY 10017. (212)688-0085. Fax: (212)421-6134. Editor-in-Chief: Regina Griffin. **Contact:** Suzanne Reinoehl, editor. Estab. 1935. "Holiday House has a commitment to publishing first-time authors and illustrators." Independent publisher of children's books, picture books, nonfiction and novels for young readers. Publishes hardcover originals and paperback reprints. **Published new writers within the last year.** Averages approximately 60 hardcovers and 15 paperbacks/year.
● *The Wright Brothers: How They Invented the Airplane* by Russell Freedman and published by Holiday House was a Newbery Honor Book.

MARKET CONDITIONS are constantly changing! If you're still using this book and it is 2004 or later, buy the newest edition of *Novel & Short Story Writer's Market* at your favorite bookstore or order from Writer's Digest Books by calling 1-800-448-0915.

Needs: Children's books only: literary, contemporary, Judaica and holiday, adventure, humor and animal stories for young readers. Recently published *Sense Pass King*, by Katrin Tchana, illustrated by Trina Schart Hyman; *Dear Whiskers*, by Ann Whitehead Nagda, illustrated by Stephanie Roth; and *Helen Keller*, by Laurie Lawlor. "We're not in a position to be too encouraging, as our list is tight, but we're always open to good writing."
How to Contact: "We ask for query letters only with SASE. We do *not* accept simultaneous submissions. No phone calls, please."
Terms: Royalties, advance are flexible, depending upon whether the book is illustrated. Publishes ms 1-3 years after acceptance.
Advice: "Please submit only one project at a time."

HOLLOW EARTH PUBLISHING, P.O. Box 51480, Boston MA 02205-1480. (617)249-0161. E-mail: hep2@ho tmail.com. **Contact:** Helian Grimes, editor/publisher. Estab. 1983. "Small independent publisher." Publishes hardcover and paperback originals and reprints and e-books. Books: acid-free paper; offset printing; Smythe binding.
Needs: Comics/graphic novels, fantasy (sword and sorcery), feminist, gay, lesbian, literary, New Age/mystic/spiritual, translations. Looking for "computers, Internet, Norse mythology, magic." Publishes various computer application series.
How to Contact: Does not accept unsolicited mss. Contact by e-mail only. Include estimated word count, 1-2 page bio and list of publishing credits. Agented fiction 90%. Responds in 2 months. Accepts submissions on disk.
Terms: Pays in royalties. Sends galleys to author. Publishes ms 6 months after acceptance.
Advice: Looking for "less fiction, more computer information."

HENRY HOLT, Imprint of Henry Holt and Company, 115 W. 18th St., 6th Floor, New York NY 10011. (212)886-9200. **Contact:** Sara Bershtel, associate publisher (Metropolitan Books, literary fiction); Jennifer Barth, editor-in-chief (adult literary fiction); Elizabeth Stein, senior editor (adult trade). Publishes hardcover and paperback originals and reprints.
Imprint(s): John Macrae Books; Metropolitan Books; Henry Holt & Company Books for Young Readers.
How to Contact: Accepts queries; no unsolicited mss. Agented fiction 95%.

HENRY HOLT AND COMPANY, (Unit of Holtzbrinck Publishing Holdings), 115 W 18 St., New York NY 10011. (212)886-9200. Fax: (212)633-0748. E-mail: publicity@hholt.com. Website: www.henryholt.com. Estab. 1866.
Imprint(s): Books for Young Readers; Henry Holt; John Macrae Books; Metropolitan Books; Owl Books; Times Books.

HENRY HOLT & COMPANY BOOKS FOR YOUNG READERS, Imprint of Henry Holt & Co., Inc., 115 W. 18th St., New York NY 10011. (212)886-9200. Fax: (212)645-5832. Website: www.henryholt.com/byr/. **Contact:** Laura Godwin, associate publisher (picture books, chapter books); Nina Ignatowicz, senior editor (picture books, chapter books); Christy Ottaviano, executive editor (picture books, chapter books, middle grade and young adult fiction); Reka Simonsen, editor (picture books, chapter books, middle grade and young adult fiction). Estab. 1866 (Holt). Henry Holt Books for Young Readers publishes excellent books of all kinds (fiction, nonfiction, illustrated) for all ages, from the very young to the young adult. Publishes hardcover originals. Averages 70-80 titles/year.
Needs: Juvenile: adventure, animal, contemporary, fantasy, history, humor, multicultural, sports, suspense/mystery. Picture books: animal, concept, history, humor, multicultural, sports. Young adult: contemporary, fantasy, history, multi-cultural, nature/environment, problem novels, sports. Recently published *When Zachary Beaver Came to Town*, by Kimberly Willis Holt (middle grade fiction); *The Gospel According to Larry*, by Janet Tashijian (YA fiction); *Visiting Langston*, by Willie Perdorno, illustrated by Bryan Collier (picture book); and *Alphabet Under Construction*, by Denise Fleming (picture book).
How to Contact: Accepts unsolicited mss. Query with outline/synopsis or submit complete ms with cover letter. Include estimated word count, brief bio and list of publishing credits. Send SASE or IRC for return of ms. Responds in 4 months. No longer accepts multiple or simultaneous submissions.
Terms: Pays royalty and advance. Publishes ms 18 months after acceptance. Guidelines and book catalog available with SASE or visit website.

HOUGHTON MIFFLIN BOOKS FOR CHILDREN, Imprint of Houghton Mifflin Company, 222 Berkeley St., Boston MA 02116-3764. (617)351-5000. Fax: (617)351-1111. E-mail: children's_books@hmco.com. Website: www.houghtonmifflinbooks.com. (includes titles, job postings, etc.) **Contact:** Hannah Rodgers, submissions coordinator; Kate O'Sullivan, assistant editor; Ann Rider, assistant editor; Margaret Raymo, senior editor; Amy Flynn, editor; Dinah Stevenson (New York City); Walter Lorraine (Walter Lorraine Books). "Houghton Mifflin gives shape to ideas that educate, inform, and above all, delight." Publishes hardcover and trade paperback originals and reprints. **Published 12 new writers within the last year.** Averages approximately 60 titles/year. Promotes titles through author visits, advertising, reviews.
Imprint(s): Clarion Books, New York City, Walter Lorraine Books.
Needs: Adventure, ethnic, historical, humor, juvenile (early readers), literary, mystery, picture books, suspense, young adult, board books. Recently published *Gathering Blue*, by Lois Lowry; *The Circuit*, by Francisco Jimenez; and *When I Was Older*, by Garret Freymann-Weyr.
How to Contact: Submit complete ms with appropriate-sized SASE. Responds in 3 months. Accepts simultaneous submissions. No mss or proposals by e-mail, fax or disk.

Terms: Pays royalties of 5-10% on retail price. Average advance: dependent on many factors. Publishes ms 18 months after acceptance. Guidelines available for #10 SASE; book catalog for 9 × 12 SASE with 3 first-class stamps.

🅰 HOUGHTON MIFFLIN COMPANY, 222 Berkeley St., Boston MA 02116. (617)351-5000. Fax: (617)351-1202. Website: www.hmco.com. **Contact**: Submissions Editor. Estab. 1832. Publishes hardcover and paperback originals and paperback reprints. **Published new writers within the last year.** Averages 100 total titles, 50 fiction titles/year.
Needs: Literary. "We are not a mass market publisher. Study the current list." Recently published *Everything Is Illuminated*, by Jonathon Safram Foer; *In The Forest*, by Edna O'Brien; and *The American Heritage College Dictionary*, 4th Edition.
How to Contact: Does not accept unsolicited mss. Accepts agented submissions only.
Terms: Pays royalties of 10-15%. Average advance: varies. Publishes ms 1-2 years after acceptance.

🔳 ◐ ◎ 🏆 HOUSE OF ANANSI PRESS, 895 Don Mills Rd., 400-2 Park Centre, Toronto, Ontario M3C 1W3 Canada. (416)445-3333. Fax: (416)445-5967. E-mail: info@anansi.ca. Website: www.anansi.ca. **Contact:** Martha Sharpe, publisher, editor. Estab. 1967. "House of Anansi Press finds and publishes innovative literary works of fiction, nonfiction and poetry by Canadian writers. Anansi acquired a reputation early on for its editors' ability to spot talented writers who push the boundaries and challenge the expectations of the literary community." Publishes hardcover and paperback originals and paperback reprints. Books: perfect binding. **Published 2 new writers within the last year.** Averages 10-15 total titles, 2-5 fiction titles/year. Member, ACP, LPG, OBPO. Distributes titles through General Distribution Services.
• Anansi Press received the Giller Prize (shortlist) for 1999.
Needs: Ethnic/multicultural (general), experimental, feminist, gay, literary, short story collections, translations. "All books must be by Canadians or Canadian landed immigrants." Recently published *19 Knives*, by Mark Anthony Jarman (short stories); *This All Happened*, by Michael Winter (literary novel); and *Am I Disturbing You?*, by Anne Hébert (novel in translation). Publishes the CBC Massey Lectures Series.
How to Contact: Accepts unsolicited mss. Query with outline/synopsis and 2 sample chapters. Accepts queries by regular mail only. Include brief bio and list of publishing credits. Send SASE or IRC for return of ms OR send disposable copy of ms and SASE for reply only. Agented fiction 60%. Responds in 6 months. Accepts simultaneous submissions. Sometimes comments on rejected mss.
Terms: Pays royalties of 8-12%. Average advance. Sends first proofs only to author. Publishes ms 6-12 months after acceptance. Guidelines available on website; book catalogs free or on website.
Advice: "Read and submit your work to literary journals and magazines. Attend or participate in literary events— readings, festivals, book clubs. Visit our website, see the kinds of books we publish, think about whether we're the right publisher for your work."

🔳 ◎ HUMANITAS, 990 Croissant Picard, Brossard, Quebec J4W 1S5 Canada. Phone/fax: (450)466-9737. E-mail: humanitas@cyberglobe.net. **Contact:** Constantin Stoiciu, director. Publishes hardcover originals. Publishes, on average, 15 new writers/year. Publishes 20 titles/year. Distributes titles through Quebec-Livres.
• Humanitas publishes novels in French only.
Needs: Fantasy, romance, short story collections. Recently published *Le Fuyard*, by Constatin Stoiciu (fiction); *L'avenir de français dans le monde*, by Axel Maugey (nonfiction); *Les yeux de la comtesse*, by Marie Desjardins (biography); and *Sang mêlé*, by Irina Egli (fiction).
How to Contact: Query first. Accepts queries by fax. No e-mail queries. Accepts simultaneous submissions.
Terms: Pays 10-12% royalty on wholesale price. Publishes ms 2 months after acceptance. Guidelines and book catalog available free.

🅽 ◯ ◎ HUNTINGTON PRESS, 3687 S. Procyon Ave., Las Vegas NV 89103. (702)252-0655. Fax: (702)252-0675. E-mail: books@huntingtonpress.com. Website: www.huntingtonpress.com. **Contact:** Deke Castleman, senior editor. Publishes hardcover and paperback originals. Books: offset printing. First novel print order: 3,000-5,000. **Published 2 new writers within the last year.** Averages 12 total titles, 1 fiction title/year. Member, PMA/SPAN.
Needs: "We focus on novels about gambling and Las Vegas."
How to Contact: Accepts unsolicited mss. Send query letter. Accepts queries by e-mail. Responds in 1 month to queries; 2 weeks to mss. Accepts simultaneous and electronic submissions. Often comments on rejected mss.
Terms: Pays royalties. Sends galleys to author. Publishes ms 1 year after acceptance. Guidelines available for SASE; book catalogs free.

◐ ◎ 🏆 ILLUMINATION PUBLISHING CO., P.O. Box 1865, Bellevue WA 98009-1865. (425)644-7185. Fax: (425)644-9274. E-mail: liteinfo@illumin.com. Website: www.illumin.com (includes guidelines, names of editors, book catalog and reviews). **Contact:** Ruth Thompson, editorial director. Estab. 1987. "Illumination Arts is a small publishing company publishing high quality children's picture books that inspire the mind, touch the heart and uplift the spirit." Publishes hardcover originals. Averages 3-4 children's picture books/year. Distributes titles through Ingram, New Leaf, De Vorss, Book People, Quality, Baker & Taylor, Koen Pacific, Follett Library Resources and bookstores. Promotes titles through direct mailings, website, book shows, posters, catalogs. Publisher arranges author and illustrator signings but expects authors/illustrators to actively promote. Enters many book award events. Member, Book Publishers of the Northwest.

● Illumination Publishing's *The Little Wizard* was selected a Best Children's Book 2001 by The Coalition of Visionary Retailers. *The Right Touch* was a winner of the 1999 Ben Franklin Award (parenting).

Needs: Children's/juvenile (adventure, inspirational, preschool/picture books). Recently published *The Tree*, by Dana Lyons (children's picture book) and *The Whoosh of Gadoosh*, by Pat Skene (children's picture book).

How to Contact: Accepts unsolicited mss. Query first or submit complete ms with cover letter. Include estimated word count and list of publishing credits. Send SASE or IRC for return of ms. Responds in 3 weeks to queries; 2 months to mss. Accepts simultaneous submissions. Often comments on rejected mss.

Terms: Pays royalties. Sends galleys to author. Publishes ms 18 months-2 years after acceptance. Guidelines available for SASE and on website.

Advice: "Submit full manuscripts, neatly typed without grammatical or spelling errors. Expect to be edited many times. Be patient. We are very *painstaking*. Read and follow the guidelines posted on our website."

IMAJINN BOOKS, ImaJinn, P.O. Box 162, Hickory Corners MI 49060-0162. (616)671-4633. Fax: (616)671-4535. E-mail: editors@imajinnbooks.com. Website: www.imajinnbooks.com (includes book list, writer's guidelines, author pictures and bios, ImaJinn book news, tips for writers, etc.). **Contact:** Linda J. Kichline, editor. Estab. 1998. "ImaJinn Books is a small independent publishing house that specializes in romances with story lines involving ghosts, psychics or psychic phenomena, witches, vampires, werewolves, angels, space travel, the future, and any other form of 'other worldly' or 'new-age' type story line. We also publish a science fiction young adult series." Publishes paperback originals and reprints. Books: 50 lb. text stock paper; camera ready and disk to film printing; perfect binding; illustrations occasionally but rare. Average print order: 2,500; first novel print order: 1,000. **Published 8 new writers within the last year.** Averages 12-24 total titles, 12-24 fiction titles/year. Member, SPAN and PMA. Distributes titles through Baker & Taylor, Ingram Books, Amazon.com, BN.com and imajinnbooks.com. Promotes titles through advertising review magazines.

Needs: Fantasy (romance), horror (romance), psychic/supernatural, romance (futuristic/time travel), science fiction (romance), young adult/teen (fantasy/science fiction). "We look for specific story lines based on what the readers are asking for and what story lines in which we're short. We post our current needs on our website." Recently published *Circle of Death*, by Keri Arthur (horror romance); and *Afterimage*, by Jeanette Roycraft (vampire romance).

How to Contact: Does not accept or return unsolicited mss. Send query letter. Accepts queries by e-mail. Include estimated word count, brief bio and list of publishing credits. Send disposable copy of ms and SASE for reply only. Agented fiction 20%. Responds in 3 months to queries; 6 months to mss. Often comments on rejected mss.

Terms: Pays royalties of 8-10%. Sends galleys to author. Publishes ms up to 3 years after acceptance. Guidelines available free for #10 SASE and 33¢ postage; book catalogs free.

Advice: "Carefully read the author guidelines, and read books published by ImaJinn Books."

INSOMNIAC PRESS, 192 Spadina Ave., #403, Toronto, Ontario M5T 2C2 Canada. (416)504-6270. Fax: (416)504-9313. E-mail: mike@insomniacpress.com. Website: www.insomniacpress.com (includes writer's guidelines, author tour info, book descriptions). Estab. 1992. "Midsize independent publisher with a mandate to produce edgy experimental fiction." Publishes paperback originals. First novel print order: 3,000. **Published 15 new writers within the last year.** Plans 4 first novels this year. Averages 20 total titles, 5 fiction titles/year.

Needs: Experimental, gay, lesbian, literary, mainstream, mystery/suspense. Recently published *Pray For Us Sinners*, by Patrick Taylor (novel).

How to Contact: Accepts unsolicited mss. Send query by e-mail. Include estimated word count, brief bio and list of publishing credits. Send SASE or IRC for return of ms or send disposable copy of ms and SASE for reply only. Agented fiction 5%. Responds in 2 weeks to queries; 2 months to mss. Accepts simultaneous submissions. Sometimes comments on rejected ms.

Terms: Pays royalties of 10%. Advance is negotiable. Sends galleys to author. Publishes ms 8 months after acceptance. Guidelines available free on website.

Advice: "Visit our website, read our writer's guidelines."

INTERCONTINENTAL PUBLISHING, 11681 Bacon Race Rd., Woodbridge VA 22192. (703)583-4800. Fax: (703)670-7825. E-mail: icpub@worldnet.att.net. **Contact:** H.G. Smittenaar, publisher. Publishes hardcover and trade paperback originals. Averages 3-4 titles/year.

Needs: Mystery, suspense. Recently published *I'm Okay, You're Dead*, by Spizer (mystery); *Dekok and the Begging Death*, by Baantjer (police procedural).

How to Contact: Submit proposal package, including 1-3 sample chapters, estimated word count and SASE. Accepts simultaneous submissions. Responds ASAP.

Terms: Pays 5% minimum royalty.

Advice: "Be original, write proper English, be entertaining."

INTERLINK PUBLISHING GROUP, INC., 46 Crosby St., Northampton MA 01060-1804. Fax: (413)582-7057. E-mail: info@interlinkbooks.com. **Contact:** Michel Moushabeck, publisher; Pam Thompson, fiction editor. Contemporary fiction in translation published under Emerging Voices: New International Fiction. Estab. 1987. "Midsize independent publisher specializing in world travel, world literature, world history and politics." Publishes hardcover and paperback originals. Books: 55 lb. Warren Sebago Cream white paper; web offset printing; perfect binding. Average print order: 5,000. First novel print order: 5,000. **Published new writers within the last year.** Averages 50 total titles,

2-4 fiction titles/year. Distributes titles through distributors such as Baker & Taylor. Promotes titles through book mailings to extensive, specialized lists of editors and reviewers, authors read at bookstores and special events across the country.

Imprint(s): Interlink Books, Olive Branch Press and Crocodile Books USA.

Needs: "Adult translated fiction from around the world." Published *House of the Winds*, by Mia Yun (first novel); *The Gardens of Light*, by Amin Maalouf (novel translated from French); and *War in the Land of Egypt*, by Yusef Al-Qaid (novel translated from Arabic). Publishes the International Folk Tales series.

How to Contact: Does not accept unsolicited mss. Submit query letter and brief sample only. No queries by e-mail or fax. Send SASE. Responds within 6 weeks to queries.

Terms: Pays royalties of 6-7%. Sends galleys to author. Publishes ms 1-1½ years after acceptance.

Advice: "Our Emerging Voices Series is designed to bring to North American readers the once-unheard voices of writers who have achieved wide acclaim at home, but were not recognized beyond the borders of their native lands. We are also looking for folktale collections (for adults) from around the world that fit in our International Folk Tale Series."

N ● **IRONWEED PRESS,** P.O. Box 754208, Parkside Station, Forest Hills NY 11375. (718)544-1120. Fax: (718)268-2394. E-mail: iwpress@aol.com. Estab. 1996. Small independent publisher. Publishes hardcover and paperback originals. Averages 4 total titles, 1 fiction title/year. Distributes titles through national wholesalers.

How to Contact: "Annually we publish only one original title, selected through our Ironweed Press Fiction Prize. The deadline is in June. For guidelines, please send SASE." See listing for Ironweed Press Fiction Prize in the Contests & Awards section.

● ◎ **ITALICA PRESS,** 595 Main St., #605, New York NY 10044. (212)935-4230. Fax: (212)838-7812. E-mail: inquiries@italicapress.com. Website: www.italica.com (includes authors, titles). **Contact:** Eileen Gardiner and Ronald G. Musto, publishers. Estab. 1985. Small independent publisher of Italian fiction in translation. Publishes paperback originals. Books: 50-60 lb. natural paper; offset printing; illustrations. Average print order: 1,500. "First time translators published. We would like to see translations of Italian writers well-known in Italy who are not yet translated for an American audience." Publishes 6 total titles each year; 2 fiction titles. Distributes titles through website. Promotes titles through website.

Needs: Translations of 20th Century Italian fiction. Published *Eruptions*, by Monica Sarsini; *The Great Bear*, by Ginevra Bompiani; and *Sparrow*, by Giovanni Verga.

How to Contact: Accepts unsolicited mss. Query first. Accepts queries by e-mail and fax. Responds in 3 weeks to queries; 2 months to mss. Accepts simultaneous submissions. Electronic submissions via Macintosh disk. Sometimes critiques rejected mss.

Terms: Pays in royalties of 5-15% and 10 author's copies. Sends pre-publication galleys to author. Publishes ms 1 year after acceptance.

Advice: "Remember we publish *only* fiction that has been previously published in Italian. A *brief* call saves a lot of postage. 90% of the proposals we receive are completely off base—but we are very interested in things that are right on target. Please send return postage if you want your manuscript back."

● ◎ **IVY LEAGUE PRESS, INC.,** P.O. Box 3326, San Ramon CA 94583-8326. (925)736-0601 or 800-IVY-PRESS. Fax: (925)736-0602 or (888)IVY-PRESS. E-mail: ivyleaguepress@worldnet.att.net. **Contact:** Maria Thomas, editor. Publishes hardcover and paperback originals. Specializes in medical thrillers. Books: perfect binding. First novel print order: 5,000. Averages 2 total titles, 1-2 fiction titles/year. Distributes titles through Baker & Taylor and Ingram. Promotes titles through TV, radio and print.

Needs: Mystery/suspense(medical). Published *Allergy Shots*, by Litman.

How to Contact: Does not accept unsolicited mss. Query with outline/synopsis. Include estimated word count, bio and list of publishing credits. Send SASE or IRC for return of the ms or send disposable copy of ms and SASE for reply only. Responds in 2 months to queries. Accepts electronic submissions. Always comments on rejected mss.

Terms: Royalties vary. Sends galleys to author.

Advice: "If you tell a terrific story of medical suspense, one which is hard to put down, we may publish it."

N ● ◎ **JAMESON BOOKS**, 722 Columbus St., P.O. Box 738, Ottawa IL 61350. (815)434-7905. Fax: (815)434-7907. **Contact:** Jameson G. Campaigne, publisher/editor. Estab. 1986. "Jameson Books publishes conservative/libertarian politics and economics, history, biography, Chicago-area themes and pre-cowboy frontier novels (1750-1840)." Publishes hardcover originals. Books: free sheet paper; offset printing. Average print order: 10,000. First novel print order: 5,000. Plans 6-8 novels this year. Averages 6 total titles. Distributes titles through LPC Group/Chicago (book trade).

Needs: Very well-researched western (frontier pre-1850). No cowboys, no science fiction, mystery, poetry, et al. Published *Yellowstone Kelly*, by Peter Bowen; *Wister Trace*, by Loren Estelman; and *One-Eyed Dream*, by Terry Johnston.

How to Contact: Does not accepted unsolicited mss. Query or submit outline/synopsis and 1 sample chapter. Send SASE. Agented fiction 70%. Responds in 6 months to queries. Accepts simultaneous submissions. Occasionally comments on rejected mss.

Terms: Pays royalties of 6-15% on retail. Average advance: $1,500. Sends galleys to author. Publishes ms 1 year after acceptance.

☒ ◔ JIREH PUBLISHING COMPANY, P.O. Box 4263, San Leandro CA 94579-0263. (510)276-3322. E-mail: jaholman@yahoo.com. Website: www.jirehpublishing.com (includes writer's guidelines, author interviews, publishing information for writers and authors). **Contact:** Janice Holman, editor. Estab. 1994. Small independent publisher. "We've just begun our fiction line." Publishes paperback originals. Books: paper varies; POD and offset printed; binding varies. Average print order: varies. First novel print order: varies. Plans 2 first novels this year. Averages 2-3 total titles, 1-2 fiction titles/year. Distributes titles through online bookstores and booksellers (retailers).
Needs: Mystery/suspense, religious (general religious, religious mystery/suspense, religious thriller, religious romance).
How to Contact: Accepts unsolicited mss. Send query letter. Accepts queries by e-mail. Include brief bio and list of publishing credits. Send SASE or IRC for return of ms or send disposable copy of ms and SASE for reply only. Responds in 2 months to queries; 5 months to mss. Accepts simultaneous submissions. No electronic or disk submissions. Sometimes comments on rejected mss.
Terms: Pays royalties of 10-15%. Sends galleys to author. Publishes ms up to 18 months after acceptance. Guidelines available for SASE and on website; book catalog not available.

◔ ◎ JOURNEYFORTH BOOKS, BJU Press, 1700 Wade Hampton Blvd., Greenville SC 29614-0001. (864)242-5100, ext. 4350. E-mail: jb@bjup.com. Website: www.bjup.com. **Contact:** Nancy Lohr, manuscript editor (juvenile fiction). Estab. 1974. "Small independent publisher of excellent, trustworthy novels, information books, audio tapes and ancillary materials for readers pre-school through high school. We desire to develop in our children a love for and understanding of the written word, ultimately helping them love and understand God's word." Publishes paperback originals and reprints. Books: 50 lb. white paper; Webb lithography printing; perfect-bound binding. Average print order: 5,000. First novel print order: 5,000. **Published new writers within the last year.** Averages 12 total titles, 10 fiction titles/year. Distributes titles through Spring Arbor and Appalachian. Promotes titles through CBA Marketplace.
Needs: Children's/juvenile (adventure, animal, easy-to-read, historical, mystery, series, sports), young adults (adventure, historical, mystery/suspense, western). "Our fiction is all based on a moral and Christian word-view." Recently published *Susannah and the Secret Coins*, by Elaine Schulte (historical young adult fiction); *Arby Jenkins Meets His Match*, by Sharon Hambrick (contemporary children's fiction); *Over the Divide*, by Catherine Farnes (young adult fiction).
How to Contact: Accepts unsolicited mss. Query with outline and 5 sample chapters or submit complete ms with cover letter. Include estimated word count, short bio, Social Security number and list of publishing credits. Send SASE or IRC for return of ms or send disposable copy of ms and SASE for reply only. Responds in 1 month to queries; 3 months to mss. Accepts simultaneous submissions.
Terms: Pays royalties. Sends final ms to author. Publishes ms 12-18 months after acceptance. Guidelines and book catalog available free. "Check our webpage for guidelines."
Advice: "Study the publisher's guidelines. Make sure your work is suitable or you waste time for you and the publisher."

☒ JUSTICE HOUSE PUBLISHING, INC., P.O. Box 4233, Spanaway WA 98387. (253)262-0203. Fax: (253)475-2158. E-mail: rashidahreed@aol.com. Website: www.justicehouse.com. Publishes trade paperback originals. **Publishes 100% of books from first-time authors; 100% from unagented writers.** Averages 3-10 titles/year.
Needs: Fantasy, feminist, gay/lesbian, mystery, romance, science fiction, short story collections. "We specialize in lesbian fiction." Recently published *Tropical Storm*, by Melissa Good; *The Deal*, by Maggie Ryan.
How to Contact: Submit complete ms. Does not accept simultaneous submissions. Responds in 2-3 months to queries; 3-6 months to mss.
Terms: Pays 10-15% royalty on wholesale price. Publishes book 2 years after acceptance of ms. Book catalog free; ms guidelines online.
Advice: Audience is comprised of 18 and older eductated lesbian females.

◔ ◎ KAEDEN BOOKS, P.O. Box 16190, Rocky River OH 44116-0190. (440)356-0030. Fax: (440)356-5081. E-mail: jbackus@kaeden.com. Website: www.kaeden.com (includes samples of books, reviews and titles). **Contact:** Kathleen Urmston, fiction editor (children's grades 2-6); Karen Evans, fiction editor (children's K-3). Estab. 1990. "We are an educational publisher of supplemental texts for use in the pre-K to 6th grade market. Our materials are used by teachers in reading instruction in the classroom. These are fully illustrated books with kid-catching, interesting themes that are age appropriate." Publishes paperback originals. Books: offset printing; saddle binding; illustrations. Average print order: 5,000. First novel print order: 5,000. **Published 6 new writers within the last year.** Averages 8-16 total titles/year. Distributes titles through school sales representatives. Promotes titles in professional teacher and reading journals, also partnered with Thinkbox.com.
Needs: Fiction: adventure, children's/juvenile (adventure, animal, historical, mystery, series, sports), ethnic/multicultural, fantasy, historical (general), humor/satire, mystery/suspense (amateur sleuth), science fiction (soft/sociological), short story collections, thriller/espionage. Nonfiction: all subjects. Recently published *When I Go to Grandma's House*, by Brian P. Cleary (fiction); *Sammy's Hamburger Caper*, by Kathleen and Craig Urmston (fiction); and *The Fishing Contest*, by Joe Yung Yukisgi.
How to Contact: Accepts unsolicited mss. Query with outline/synopsis. Include 1-page bio and list of publishing credits. Send a disposable copy of ms and SASE for reply only. Responds only "if interested."
Terms: Negotiable, either royalties or flat fee by individual arrangement with author depending on book. No advance. Publishes ms 6-24 months after acceptance.

Advice: "Our line is expanding with particular interest in fiction/nonfiction for grades two to six. Material must be suitable for use in the public school classroom, be multicultural and be high interest with appropriate word usage and a positive tone for the respective grade."

KAYA PRODUCTION, 373 Broadway, Suite F3, New York NY 10013. (212)343-9503. Fax: (212)343-8291. E-mail: kaya@kaya.com. Website: www.kaya.com. **Contact:** Sunyoung Lee, editor. "Kaya is a small independent press dedicated to the publication of innovative literature from the Asian diaspora." Publishes hardcover originals and trade paperback originals and reprints.
Needs: "Kaya publishes Asian, Asian-American and Asian diasporic materials. We are looking for innovative writers with a commitment to quality literature."
How to Contact: Submit synopsis and 2-4 sample chapters with SASE. Responds in 6 months to mss. Accepts simultaneous submissions.
Terms: Guidelines available at website. Book catalog available free.
Advice: Audience is people interested in a high standard of literature and who are interested in breaking down easy approaches to multicultural literature.

KENSINGTON PUBLISHING CORP., 850 Third Ave., 16th Floor, New York NY 10022. (212)407-1500. Fax: (212)935-0699. Editor-in-Chief: Paul Dinas. **Contact:** Kate Duffy, editorial director (historical romance, regency, erotica); John Scognamiglio, editorial director; Ann LaFarge, executive editor; Karen Thomas, executive editor (Arabesque romance, African American fiction, Dafina Books); Amy Garvey, editor (romance, regency, historical romance); Karen Haas, editor (true crime, westerns). Full service trade commercial publisher, all formats. Averages over 500 total titles/year.
Imprint(s): Arabesque and Dafina (Karen Thomas, executive editor); Ballad, Brava and Encanto (Kate Duffy, editorial director); Citadel; Kensington; Pinnacle; Precious Gems; Twin Streams (Elaine Sparber, senior editor); Zebra.
Needs: "Romance (contemporary, historical, regency, erotica), mysteries, true crime, westerns, multicultural women's fiction, mainstream women's commercial fiction, gay and lesbian fiction and nonfiction, thrillers, romantic suspense, biographies, humor, paranormal, self-help, alternative health, pop culture nonfiction. No science fiction/fantasy, experimental fiction, business texts or children's titles." Recently published *Celebration*, by Fern Michaels.
How to Contact: Does not accept unsolicited mss. Agented submissions only.
Terms: Pays 8-15% royalty on retail price. Offers $2,000-2,000,000 advance. Publishes ms 9 months after acceptance.

KIDS CAN PRESS, 29 Birch Ave., Toronto, Ontario M4V 1E2 Canada. (416)925-5437. Fax: (416)960-5437. Website: www.nelvana.com/kidscanpress/KidsCanPress_3/kcp/f_home.htm. **Contact:** Acquisitions editor. "Our company's goal is to offer books that entertain, inform and delight the most important audience in the world—young readers."
● Due to an exponential increase in submissions following the launch of their website, Kids Can Press will only accept submissions from the US "if you have a publisher's referral (usually a book that has been published already, and is seeking rights), if you have a literary agent or if you are a published author."
Needs: Picture books, young adult.
How to Contact: Query by mail with outline and SASE. "Include SAE large enough to hold your material and sufficient IRCs for return. If you do not want your material recycled, please indicate this in the cover letter. Please specify the genre of the work-picture book or novel-in the front of the envelope. No simultaneous submissions. No fax, disk or e-mail submissions. Do not include artwork."

ALLEN A. KNOLL, PUBLISHERS, 200A W. Victoria St., Suite 3, Santa Barbara CA 93101-3627. (805)564-3377. Fax: (804)966-6657. E-mail: bookinfo@knollpublishers.com. Website: www.knollpublishers.com (book catalog, excerpts, interviews with authors, reading guides). **Contact:** Submissions. Estab. 1990. "Small independent publisher, a few titles a year. Specializes in 'books for intelligent people who read for fun.' " Publishes hardcover originals. Books: offset printing; sewn binding. Titles distributed through Ingram, Baker & Taylor.
Needs: Recently published *What Now, King Lear?*, by Alistair Boyle (mystery); *Too Rich and Too Thin*, by David Champion (mystery); *He's Back*, by Theodore Roosevelt Gardner II (fiction/literature). Publishes the Gil Yates private investigator and Bomber Hanson Mystery series.
How to Contact: Does not accept unsolicited or agented mss; will return mss if SASE provided.
Terms: Payment varies. Sends galleys to author. Guidelines not available; book catalogs free or on website.

ALFRED A. KNOPF, Imprint of The Knopf Publishing Group, A Division of Random House, Inc., 299 Park Ave., New York NY 10171. (212)751-2600. Website: www.aaknopf.com. **Contact:** Senior Editor. Estab. 1915. Book-length fiction of literary merit by known and unknown writers. Publishes hardcover originals. Averages 200 titles/year. **Published new writers in the last year.** Also publishes nonfiction.
Needs: Publishes book-length fiction of literary merit by known or unknown writers. Length: 40,000-150,000. Recently published *Gertrude and Claudius*, by John Updike; *The Emperor of Ocean Park*, by Stephen Carter; and *Balzac and the Little Chinese Seamstress*, by Dai Sijie.

How to Contact: Does not accept unsolicited mss. Query with outline or synopsis. Send SASE or IRC for reply. Agented fiction 90%. Responds within 5 months to mss.

Terms: Pays royalties of 10-15%; offers advance. Must return advance if book is not completed or is unacceptable. Publishes ms 1 year after acceptance.

KNOPF PUBLISHING GROUP, (Division of Random House, Inc.), 299 Park Ave., New York NY 10171. (212)551-2600. Fax: (212)940-7307. Website: www.randomhouse.com/knopf. Estab. 1915. "Throughout its history, Knopf has been dedicated to publishing distinguished fiction and nonfiction." Publishes hardcover and paperback originals and reprints.

Imprint(s): Everyman's Library; Alfred A. Knopf; Pantheon Books; Shocken Books; Vintage Anchor Publishing.

KREGEL PUBLICATIONS, Kregel, Inc., P.O. Box 2607, Grand Rapids MI 49501-2607. (616)451-4775. Fax: (616)451-9330. E-mail: kregelbooks@kregel.com. Website: www.kregel.com (includes book catalog and author's guidelines). **Contact:** Acquisitions Editor. Estab. 1949. Midsize independent Christian publisher. Publishes paperback originals and reprints. Plans 5-10 first novels this year. Averages 100 total titles, 10-15 fiction titles/year. Member, ECPA.

Imprint(s): Kregel Academic & Professional, Jim Weaver (academic/pastoral); Kregel Kid Zone, Steve Barclift (children).

Needs: Adventure, children's/juvenile (adventure, historical, mystery, preschool/picture book, series, sports, Christian), historical, mystery/suspense, religious (children's religious, general religious, inspirational, religious fantasy/sci-fi, religious mystery/suspense, religious thriller, relationships), young adult/teen (adventure). Wants "books with fast-paced, contemporary storylines—strong Christian message presented in an engaging, entertaining style as well as books for juvenile and young adults, especially young women." Recently published *Divided Loyalties*, by L.K. Malone (action/thriller); *A Test of Love*, by Kathleen Scott (relationships); and *Jungle Hideout*, by Jeanette Windle (juvenile/adventure). Publishes the Parker Twins series, juvenile fiction.

How to Contact: Accepts unsolicited mss. Send query letter. Accepts queries by e-mail and fax. Include estimated word count and brief bio. Send SASE or IRC for return of ms or send disposable copy of ms and SASE for reply only. Responds in 3 months. Accepts simultaneous, electronic and disk submissions.

Terms: Pays royalties. Offers negotiable advance. Sends galleys to author. Publishes ms up to 16 months after acceptance. Guidelines available for SASE, by e-mail or on website; book catalog on website.

Advice: "Visit our website and review the titles listed under various subject categories. Does your proposed work duplicate existing titles? Does it address areas not covered by existing titles? Does it break new ground?"

LAST KNIGHT PUBLISHING COMPANY, P.O. Box 270006, Fort Collins CO 80527. (970)391-6857. Fax: (970)493-0924. E-mail: ckaine@lastknightpublishing.com. Website: www.Lastknightpublishing.com. **Contact:** Charles Kaine, publisher/owner. "Small independent publisher interested in various fictional forms. We are interested in books that have a niche market. We are interested in making high quality books, both by the words written and how it is printed." Publishes paperback originals. Books: 70 lb. Vellum opaque paper; offset-printed; perfect-bound. Average print order 1,500-4,000. Average first novel print order: 1,500. **Published 1 new author within the last year.** Plans 2-3 first novels next year. Averages 2-3 total titles/year, all fiction.

Needs: Fantasy (space fantasy, sword and sorcery), historical, horror (dark fantasy, futuristic, supernatural), literary, mainstream, mystery/suspense (amateur sleuth, cozy), psychic/supernatural, thriller/espionage. Recently published *The Breach*, by Brain Kaufman (historical fiction).

How to Contact: Accepts unsolicited mss. Send query. Accepts queries by mail only. Include estimated word count, brief bio and an explanation of "why people will want to read the work." Either send SASE for return of ms or send disposable ms with SASE for reply only. Responds in 6 weeks to queries; 2-3 months to mss. Considers simultaneous submissions. Often comments on rejected mss. Editing/critiques available for fee.

Terms: Authors paid in royalties and negotiable advance. Sends galleys to author. Publishes ms up to 9 months after acceptance. Guidelines available on website.

LEAPFROG PRESS, P.O. Box 1495, 95 Commercial St., Wellfleet MA 02667-1495. (508)349-1925. Fax: (508)349-1180. E-mail: leapfrog@c4.net. Website: www.leapfrogpress.com (includes description of press, mission statement, writer's guidelines, e-mail link, description of books, sample chapters, link to distributor, cover designs). **Contact:** David Witkowsky, acquisitions editor. Estab. 1996. "We search for beautifully written literary titles and endeavor to market them aggressively to national trade and library accounts as well as to sell film, translation, foreign and book club rights." Publishes hardcover and paperback originals and paperback reprints. Books: acid-free paper; sewn binding.

**FOR EXPLANATIONS OF THESE SYMBOLS,
SEE THE INSIDE FRONT AND BACK COVERS OF THIS BOOK.**

Average print order: 5,000. First novel print order: 4,000 (average). Averages 4 total titles, 3-4 fiction titles/year. Distributes titles through Consortium Book Sales and Distribution, St. Paul, MN. Promotes titles through all national review media, bookstore readings, author tours, website, radio shows, chain store promotions, advertisements. Member, Publishers Marketing Association, Bookbuilders of Boston and PEN.

Needs: "Genres often blur; we're interested in good writing. We'd love to see memoirs as well as fiction that comments on the world through the lens of personal, political or family experience." Recently published *The War at Home*, by Nora Eisenberg; *Burnt Umber*, by Sheldon Greene; *Shadows and Elephants*, by Edward Hower; *Paradise Dance*, by Michael Lee; and *The Devil and Daniel Silverman*, by Theodore Roszak.

How to Contact: Query with brief description of book and 2-4 sample chapters (40 pages maximum). Accepts queries by e-mail but, due to volume, does not respond unless interested. Send SASE or IRC for return of ms or send disposable copy of ms and SASE for reply only. Responds in 3-6 months to queries; 6 months to mss. No simultaneous submissions. "Please see website for information. Do not call the office." Sometimes comments on rejected mss.

Terms: Pays royalties of 4-8%. Offers negotiable advance. Provides negotiable number of author's copies. Sends galleys to author. Publishes ms 1-2 years after acceptance.

Advice: "Because editors have so little time, you had best send them your very best work. Editors don't have a lot of time to line edit. They love to work with you but they do not want to rewrite your book for you. In fact, if you send good material that is poorly written, they may wonder if you actually can do the revisions necessary. So don't be impatient. Send your work only when you feel it is as good as you can make it . . . and that means knowing what's out there in the market; knowing how to create characters and a dynamite beginning and a plot that doesn't meander all over the place because you don't know where the story is going. Learn your craft."

LEE & LOW BOOKS, 95 Madison Ave., New York NY 10016. (212)779-4400. Fax: (212)683-1894. Website: www.leeandlow.com. **Contact:** Louise May, executive editor. Estab. 1991. "Our goals are to meet a growing need for books that address children of color, and to present literature that all children can identify with. We only consider multicultural children's picture books. Of special interest are stories set in contemporary America." Publishes hardcover originals—picture books only. Averages 12-15 total titles/year.

Needs: Children's/juvenile (historical, multicultural, preschool/picture book for children ages 2-10). "We do not consider folktales, fairy tales or animal stories." Recently published *Rent Party Jazz*, by William Miller; and *Love to Langston*, by Tony Medina.

How to Contact: Accepts unsolicited mss. Send complete ms with cover letter or through an agent. Send SASE for return of ms or send a disposable ms and SASE for reply only. Agented fiction 30%. Responds in 5 months. Accepts simultaneous submissions. Sometimes comments on rejected mss.

Terms: Pays royalties. Offers advance. Sends galleys to author. Guidelines available for #10 SASE or on website; book catalog for SASE with $1.75 postage.

Advice: "Writers should familiarize themselves with the styles and formats of recently published children's books. Lee & Low Books is a multicultural children's book publisher. We would like to see more contemporary stories set in the U.S. Animal stories and folktales are not considered at this time."

N **LEISURE BOOKS**, Division of Dorchester Publishing Co., Inc., 276 Fifth Ave., Suite 1008, New York NY 10001. (212)725-8811. Fax: (212)532-1054. E-mail: dorchedit@aol.com. Website: www.dorchesterpub.com (includes writer's guidelines, names of editors, authors, titles, etc.). **Contact:** Ashley Kuehl or Leah Hultenschmidt, editorial assistants. Mass-market paperback publisher—originals and reprints. Publishes romances, westerns, horrors and techno-thrillers only. Books: Newsprint paper; offset printing; perfect-bound. Average print order: variable. First novel print order: variable. Plans 25 first novels this year. Averages 150 total titles, 145 fiction titles/year. Promotes titles through ads in *Romantic Times*, author readings, promotional items.

Imprint(s): Leisure Books (contact: Alicia Condon), Love Spell Books (contact: Christopher Keeslar).

Needs: Historical romance, horror, technothriller, western. Looking for "historical romance (90,000-100,000 words)." Published *Pure Temptation*, by Connie Mason (historical romance); and *Frankly My Dear*, by Sandra Hill (time-travel romance).

How to Contact: Accepts unsolicited mss. Send query letter. Include SASE. Agented fiction 70%. Responds in 1 month to queries; up to 8 months to mss. "All mss must be typed, double-spaced on one side and left unbound." No electronic submissions. Comments on rejected mss "only if requested ms requires it."

Terms: Offers negotiable advance. Payment depends "on category and track record of author." Sends galleys to author. Publishes ms within 2 years after acceptance. Romance guidelines for #10 SASE.

Advice: Encourages first novelists "if they are talented and willing to take direction, *and* write the kind of genre fiction we publish. Please include a brief synopsis if sample chapters are requested."

ARTHUR A. LEVINE BOOKS, Imprint of Scholastic Inc., 557 Broadway, New York NY 10012. (212)343-6100. Website: www.scholastic.com. **Contact:** Arthur A. Levine, publisher. "Arthur A. Levine Books is looking for distinctive literature, for whatever's extraordinary." Averages 14 titles/year.

Needs: Juvenile fiction: picture books, novels. Recently published *Frida*, by Jonah Winter, illustrated by Ana Juan; *St. Michael's Scales*, by Neil Connelly (YA novel, debut author); *Blister*, by Susan Shreve (middle-grade novel); and *The Seeing Stone*, by Kevin Crossley-Holland (YA fantasy novel).

How to Contact: Query only. Send SASE. "We are willing to work with first-time authors, with or without agent."

Terms: Pays variable royalty on retail price. Advance varies. Book catalog available available for 9 × 13 SASE.

N. **LINTEL**, 24 Blake Lane, Middletown NY 10940. (212)674-1466. **Contact:** Editorial Director. Estab. 1977. Two-person organization on part-time basis. Publishes hardcover and paperback originals. Books: 90% opaque paper; photo offset printing; perfect binding; illustrations. Average print order: 1,000. First novel print order: 1,200.
Needs: Experimental, feminist, gay, lesbian, regional short fiction. Recently published *June*, by Mary Sanders Smith; and *Notes from a Dark Street*, by Edward Adler.
How to Contact: Accepts unsolicited mss in January and July only. Query with SASE. Accepts simultaneous and photocopied submissions. Responds in 2 months to queries; 3 months to mss. Occasionally comments on rejected mss.
Terms: Negotiated. No advance except 100 copies. Sends galleys to author. Publishes ms 6-8 months after acceptance. Book catalog available free.
Advice: "Lintel is devoted to the kinds of literary art that will never make The Literary Guild or even the Book-of-the-Month Club; that is, literature concerned with the advancement of literary art. We still look for the innovative work ignored by the commercial presses. We consider any ms on its merits alone. We encourage first novelists. Be innovative, advance the *art* of fiction, but still keep in mind the need to reach reader's aspirations as well as your own. Originality is the greatest suspense-building factor. Consistent spelling errors, errors in grammar and syntax can mean only rejection."

LIONHEARTED PUBLISHING, INC., P.O. Box 618, Zephyr Cove NV 89448-0618. (775)588-1388. Fax: (775)588-1386. E-mail: admin@LionHearted.com. Website: www.LionHearted.com (includes writer's guidelines, authors, interviews, titles, articles and writing tips for authors). **Contact:** Historical or Contemporary Acquisitions Editor. Estab. 1994. "Multiple award-winning, independent publisher of single title, mass market paperback, romance novels." Publishes paperback originals. Books: mass market paperback; perfect binding. Also expanded romance into e-book formats. Publishes, on average, 10-12 new writers/year. Averages 12 romantic fiction titles/year. Distributes titles through Ingram, Barnes & Noble, Baker & Taylor, Amazon and Internet website. Promotes titles through trade romance reader magazines, website and Internet.
Needs: Romance (contemporary, futuristic/time travel, historical, Regency, romantic suspense, western, contemporary romantic comedy; over 65,000 words only). Recently published *Lord Darver's Match*, by Susanne Marie Knight (Regency time travel); *Heart of the Diamond*, by Carrie Brock (Regency romance); *Suddenly Love*, by Catherine Sellers (contemporary romance); *The Rebel's Bride*, by JoAnn Delazzari; *Family Portrait*, by Sharon Sobel (Regency romance); *Charades*, by Ann Logan (romantic suspense); *Lover's Never Lie*, by Gael Morrison (romantic suspense); and *The Magic Token*, by Susanne Marie Knight (Regency romance).
How to Contact: Accepts unsolicited e-mail submissions. Query by e-mail only; include 1-3 page synopsis and/or first sample chapters. Include estimated word count, list of publishing credits, cover letter and 1 paragraph story summary and indicate which subgenre of romance applies to ms. Do not send ms by regular mail unless invited by editor. Agented fiction: less than 10%. Responds in up to 3 days to queries; up to 4 months to *solicited* mss. No simultaneous submissions. Always comments on rejected mss.
Terms: Pays royalties of 10% on paperbacks; 30% on electronic books. Sends galleys to author. Publishes ms 18-24 months after acceptance.
Advice: "If you are not an avid reader and fan of romance novels, don't attempt to write romance, and don't waste your time or an editor's by submitting to a publisher of romance. Read a few of our novels (they are a bit different from a category romance) to discover what our editors like."

LITTLE, BROWN AND COMPANY, 1271 Avenue of the Americas, New York NY 10020. (212)522-8700. Website: www.twbookmark.com. **Contact:** Editorial Department. Estab. 1837. "The general editorial philosophy for all divisions continues to be broad and flexible, with high quality and the promise of commercial success always the first considerations." Medium-size house. Publishes adult and juvenile hardcover originals and paperback originals and reprints. Averages 100 total adult titles/year. Number of fiction titles varies.
Imprint(s): Little, Brown; Back Bay; Bulfinch Press.
Needs: Literary, mainstream/contemporary. No science fiction. Published *When the Wind Blows*, by James Patterson; *Angels Flight*, by Michael Connelly; *Sea Glass*, by Anita Shreve; and *City of Bones*, by Michael Connelly.
How to Contact: No unsolicited mss. Query with SASE.
Terms: "We publish on a royalty basis, with advance."

LITTLE, BROWN AND COMPANY ADULT TRADE BOOKS, (Division of AOL Time Warner Book Group), 1271 Avenue of the Americas, New York NY 10020. (212)522-8700. Fax: (212)522-2067. Website: www.twbookmark.com. Estab. 1837. "The general editorial philosophy for all divisions continues to be broad and flexible, with high quality and the promise of commercial success as always the first considerations." Publishes hardcover originals and paperback originals and reprints.
Imprint(s): Arcade Books; Back Bay Books; Bulfinch Press.

LITTLE, BROWN AND COMPANY CHILDREN'S BOOKS, Time Life Building, 1271 Avenue of the Americas, New York NY 10020. (212)522-8700. Website: www.littlebrown.com. Editorial Director/Associate Publisher: Maria Modugno. Senior Associate Editor: Amy Hsu. Editor: Cindy Egan. **Contact:** Leila Little. Estab. 1837. Publishes hardcover originals and trade paperback reprints. Averages 60-70 total titles/year. Books: 70 lb. paper; sheet-fed printing; illustrations. Distributes titles through sales representatives. Promotes titles through author tours, book signings, posters, press kits, magazine and newspapers and Beacon Hill Bookbay.
Imprint(s): Megan Tingley Books (Megan S. Tingley, executive editor).

Needs: Children's/juvenile: adventure, ethnic, historical, humor, mystery, picture books, science fiction, suspense. Recently published *What Every Girl (Except Me) Knows*, by Nora Baskin.

How to Contact: *Agented submissions only.*

Terms: Pays on royalty basis. Offers negotiable advance. Sends galleys to author. Publishes ms 1-2 years after acceptance.

Advice: "Writers should avoid looking for the 'issue' they think publishers want to see, choosing instead topics they know best and are most enthusiastic about/inspired by."

LITTLE, BROWN AND COMPANY CHILDREN'S PUBLISHING, (Division of AOL Time Warner Book Group), 3 Center Plaza, Boston MA 02108-2084. (617)227-0730. Fax: (617)263-2864. Estab. 1837. "We are looking for strong writing and presentation, but no predetermined topics." Publishes hardcover originals, trade paperback reprints.

Imprint(s): Megan Tingley Books; Back Bay Books.

LIVINGSTON PRESS, Station 22, University of Alabama, Livingston AL 35470. E-mail: jwt@uwa.edu. Website: www.livingstonpress.uwa.edu. **Contact:** Joe Taylor, literary editor; Tina Jones, literary editor. Estab. 1984. "Small university press specializing in offbeat and/or Southern literature." Publishes hardcover originals and paperback originals. Books: acid free; offset; some illustrations. Average print order: 2,500. First novel print order: 2,500. **Publishes 3 first novels/year.** Averages 6 total titles, 6 fiction titles/year.

Imprints: Swallow's Tale Press

Needs: Literary, short story collections, off-beat or southern. "We are interested in form and, of course, style." Recently published *Widening the Road*, by Fred Bonnie (stories); *The High Traverse*, by Richard Blarclan (novel); *The Drinking of Spirits*, by Tom Abrams (stories).

How to Contact: Accepts unsolicited mss with SASE. Submit query with outline/synopsis and 3 sample chapters. Include estimated word count, brief bio and list of publishing credits. Send SASE or IRC for return of ms or send a disposable copy of ms and SASE for reply only. *Reads mss in December only.* Responds in 2 months to queries; 8 months to mss. Accepts simultaneous submissions.

Terms: Pays in author's copies and royalties after 1,500 copies. Sends galleys to author. Publishes ms up to 2 years after acceptance. Book catalogs available for SASE.

LLEWELLYN PUBLICATIONS, Llewellyn Worldwide, Ltd., P.O. Box 64383, St. Paul MN 55164-0383. (651)291-1970. Fax: (651)291-1908. E-mail: lwlpc@llewellyn.com. Website: www.llewellyn.com. **Contact:** Nancy J. Mostad, acquisitions manager (New Age, metaphysical, occult); Barbara Wright, acquisitions editor (kits and decks). Estab. 1901. Publishes trade and mass market paperback originals. **Publishes 30% of books from first-time authors; 90% from unagented writers.** Averages 100 titles/year.

Needs: "Authentic and educational, yet entertaining." Occult, spiritual (metaphysical).

How to Contact: Accepts simultaneous submissions. Responds in 3 months to queries.

Terms: Pays 10% royalty on wholesale price or retail price. Book catalog for 9×12 SAE with 4 first-class stamps; ms guidelines for #10 SASE.

LOFT PRESS, INC., P.O. Box 126, Fort Valley VA 22652. (540)933-6210. Website: www.loftpress.com. **Contact:** Ann A. Hunter, editor-in-chief. Publishes hardcover and trade paperback originals and reprints. **Publishes 50% of books from first-time authors; 100% from unagented writers.** Averages 12-20 titles/year; imprint publishes 2-4 titles/year.

Imprints: Eschat Press, Far Muse Press (both contact Stephen R. Hunter, publisher)

Needs: Literary, plays, poetry, poetry in translation, regional, short story collections. Recently published *The Paranoia Factor*, by Alan Peters (adventure fiction); *Vaughan*, by Josephine Barrett.

How to Contact: Submit proposal package including 1 sample chapter(s), synopsis.

Terms: Pays royalty on net receipts. Publishes book 6 months after acceptance of ms.

LONGSTREET PRESS, INC., 2974 Hardman Court, Atlanta GA 30305. (404)254-0110. Fax: (404)254-0116. Website: www.longstreetpress.com. **Contact:** Scott Bard, president/editor. Estab. 1988. Publishes hardcover and trade paperback originals. **Publishes 10% of books from first-time authors.** Averages 45 titles/year.

Needs: Literary, mainstream/contemporary (Southern fiction).

How to Contact: *Agented submissions only.* Accepts simultaneous submissions. Responds in 3 months to queries.

Terms: Pays royalty. Offers advance. Publishes book 1 year after acceptance of ms. Book catalog for 9×12 SAE with 4 first-class stamps or online; ms guidelines for #10 SASE or online.

LOST HORSE PRESS, 105 Lost Horse Lane, Sandpoint ID 83864. (208)255-4410. Fax: (208)255-1650. E-mail: losthorsepress@mindspring.com. **Contact:** Christine Holbert, editor of novels, novellas. Estab. 1998. Publishes hardcover and paperback originals and reprints. Books: 60-70 lb. natural paper; offset printing; b&w illustration. Average print order: 1,000-2,500. First novel print order: 1,000. **Published 2 new writers within the last year.** Plans 2 first novels this year. Averages 4 total titles, 2 fiction titles/year.

● *Woman on the Cross*, by Pierre Delattre, won the *ForeWord Magazine*'s 2001 Book of the Year Award for literary fiction.

Needs: Experimental, lesbian, literary, regional (Pacific NW), short story collections, translations. Recently published *Tales of a Dalai Lama*, by Pierre Delattre (literary fiction); *Love*, by Valerie Martin (short stories); *Sailing Away*, by Richard Morgan (short stories); and *Woman on the Cross*, by Pierre Delattre (literary).

How to Contact: Accepts unsolicited mss. Submit complete ms with cover letter. Accepts queries by e-mail. Include brief bio and list of publishing credits. Send SASE or IRC for return of ms or send disposable copy of ms and SASE for reply only. Responds in 6 months.

Terms: Sends galleys to author. Publishes ms 1-2 years after acceptance. Guidelines available for SASE; book catalog free.

LOVE SPELL, Leisure Books, Division of Dorchester Publishing Co., Inc., 276 Fifth Ave., Suite 1008, New York NY 10001-0112. (212)725-8811. Fax: (212)532-1054. Website: www.dorchesterpub.com (includes submission guidelines, author bios and upcoming release info). **Contact:** Don D'Auria, executive editor (horror, western); Kate Seaver, editor (romance); Ashley Kuehl, editorial assistant (horror, romance, western). "Love Spell publishes quirky sub-genres of romance: time-travel, paranormal, futuristic, lighthearted contemporaries and historicals. Despite the exotic settings, we are still interested in character-driven plots." Mass market paperback publisher—originals and reprints. Books: newsprint paper; offset printing; perfect-bound. Average print order: varies. First novel print order: varies. Plans 15 first novels this year. Averages 10-12 original titles/month.

Needs: Romance (futuristic, time travel, paranormal, historical). Looking for romances of 90,000-115,000 words. Recently published *Island*, by Richard Layman (horror); *Dark Legend*, by Christine Feehan (paranormal romance); and *The Dragon Lord*, by Connie Mason (historical romance).

How to Contact: Accepts unsolicited mss. Query first. No queries by fax. "All mss must be typed, double-spaced on one side and left unbound." Send SASE or IRC for return of ms. Agented fiction 70%. Responds in up to 6 months. Comments "only if requested ms requires it."

Terms: Offers negotiable advance. "Payment depends on category and track record of author." Sends galleys to author. Publishes ms within 2 years after acceptance. Guidelines available for #10 SASE.

Advice: "The best way to learn to write a Love Spell Romance is by reading several of our recent releases. The best written stories are usually ones writers feel passionate about—so write from your heart! Also, the market is very tight these days so more than ever we are looking for refreshing, standout original fiction."

LTDBOOKS, 200 N. Service Rd. West, Unit 1, Suite 301, Oakville, Ontario L6M 2Y1 Canada. Phone/fax: (905)847-6060. E-mail: publisher@ltdbooks.com. Website: www.ltdbooks.com. **Contact:** Dee Lloyd, Terry Sheils, editors. Estab. 1999. "LTDBooks, an energetic presence in the rapidly expanding e-book market, is a multi-genre, royalty-paying fiction publisher specializing in high quality stories with strong characters and great ideas." Publishes electronic books on disk or by download. Books: 3½" floppy disk with cover and jewel case, or as a download. **Published 14 new writers within the last year.** Averages 36 total titles, 36 fiction titles/year. Member, Electronic Publishers Association. Distributes titles through the Internet, Barnes&Noble.com and Powells.

Needs: Adventure, fantasy (space fantasy, sword and sorcery), historical (general), horror (dark fantasy, futuristic, psychological, supernatural), literary, mainstream, mystery/suspense (amateur sleuth, cozy, police procedural, private eye/hardboiled), romance (contemporary, futuristic/time travel, gothic, historical, regency period, romantic suspense), science fiction (hard science/technological, soft/sociological), thriller/espionage, western, young adult/teen (adventure, fantasy/science fiction, historical, horror, mystery/suspense, problem novels, romance, series, sports, western). Recently published *Rat*, by Edward Keyes (follow up to *The French Connection*); *Last Flight of the Arrow*, by Daniel Wyatt. "Our new trade paperback program started June 2001."

How to Contact: Accepts unsolicited mss. Query with synopsis and 3 sample chapters. Prefers queries by e-mail. Include estimated word count, brief bio and list of publishing credits. Send disposable copy of ms and SASE for reply only. Responds in 2 weeks to queries; 6 weeks to mss. Accepts simultaneous submissions, electronic submissions and disk. Always comments on rejected mss.

Terms: Pays royalties of 30%. Sends galleys to author. Publishes ms 6-9 months after acceptance. Guidelines available on website.

Advice: "We publish only fiction. Many of our books are electronic (as download or on disk) with ongoing additions to our new trade paperback program."

THE LYONS PRESS, The Globe Pequot Press, Inc., 246 Goose Lane, Guilford CT 06437. (203)458-4500. Fax: (203)458-4668. Website: www.lyonspress.com. Publisher/President: Tony Lyons. **Contact:** Lilly Golden, editor-at-large (fiction, memoirs, narrative nonfiction); Jay Cassell, senior editor (fishing, hunting, survival, military, history, gardening); Jay McCullogh, editor (narrative nonfiction, travelogues, adventure, military, espionage, international current events, fishing); Lisa Purcell, editor-at-large (history, adventure, narrative nonfiction, cooking, gardening); Bill Bowers, managing editor. Estab. 1984 (Lyons & Burford), 1997 (The Lyons Press). Publishes hardcover and trade paperback originals and reprints. **Publishes 50% of books from first-time authors; 30% from unagented writers.** Averages 240 titles/year.

Needs: Historical, military/war, short story collections (fishing, hunting, outdoor, nature), sports. Recently published *The Hunter, the Hammer, and Heaven*, by Robert Young Pelton.

How to Contact: Query with SASE or submit proposal package including outline, 3-5 sample chapter(s). Accepts simultaneous submissions. Responds in 1 month to queries; 2 months to mss.

Terms: Pays 5-10% royalty on wholesale price. Offers $2,000-7,000 advance. Publishes book 1 year after acceptance of ms. Book catalog online.

MACADAM/CAGE PUBLISHING, 155 Sansome St., Suite 550, San Francisco CA 94104. Phone/fax: (415)986-7502. E-mail: info@macadamcage.com. Website: www.macadamcage.com (includes catalog, authors, book excerpts, submission guidelines, purchasing details). **Contact:** Patrick Walsh, fiction editor. Estab. 1999. Midsize independent publisher. Publishes hardcover and trade paperback originals. Books: web offset printing; case binding. Average first novel print order: 5,000-15,000. **Published 10 new writers within the last year.** Averages 25 titles/year. Member, PMA, ABA, NCIBA. Distributes titles through Baker & Taylor, Ingram, Brodart, Koen and American Wholesale. Promotes titles via in-house marketing/publicity department.

Needs: Historical, literary, mainstream. No romance, science fiction, Christian, New Age. Recently published *The God File*, by Frank Turner Hollon (fiction); *Ella Minnow Pea*, by Mark Dunn (fiction); and *Snow Island*, by Katie Towler (fiction).

How to Contact: Accepts unsolicited mss. Submit proposal package including 3 sample chapters, or ms with cover letter including estimated word count and brief author bio. Send SASE or IRC for return of ms. Agented fiction 50%. Responds in 4 months to queries and mss. Accepts simultaneous submissions. No fax queries. Often comments on rejected mss.

Terms: Pays negotiable royalties. Offers negotiable advance. Sends galleys to author. Publishes ms up to 1 year after acceptance. Guidelines available free for SASE.

MAJESTIC BOOKS, P.O. Box 19097, Johnston RI 02919-0097. E-mail: majesticbk@aol.com. **Contact:** Cindy MacDonald, publisher. "Majestic Books is a small press. We publish young writers under the age of 18 in an anthology filled with poems and short stories." Publishes paperback originals. Books: 60 lb. white paper; offset printing; perfect binding. Average print order: 300. **Published new writers within the last year.** Averages 3 total titles, 3 fiction titles/year. Distribution and promotion of titles is conducted through mail orders.

Needs: Adventure, family saga, fantasy, mainstream, mystery/suspense, psychic/supernatural, romance, science fiction (soft/sociological), thriller/espionage, western, young adult/teen. Recently published *Tribute to Talent*; *Mysteries, Monsters, Memories and More VIII* (short story contest anthology); *Dare to Dream* (anthology); *Reach for the Stars* (anthology), all by various authors.

How to Contact: Accepts unsolicited mss. Submit complete ms with cover letter. Include estimated word count and age (under 18). Send SASE or IRC for return of ms or send disposable copy of ms and SASE for reply only. Responds in 2 weeks to mss. Accepts simultaneous and electronic submissions.

Terms: Pays royalties of 10% on sales relating directly to authors inclusion. Publishes ms 1 year after acceptance. Guidelines available for SASE.

Advice: "Our press only publishes talented young writers under the age of 18. Please include age with all submissions and keep stories under 2,000 words. Originality is a must."

MARCH STREET PRESS, 3413 Wilshire, Greensboro NC 27408-2923. Phone/fax: (336)282-9754. E-mail: rbixby@aol.com. Website: http://users.aol.com/marchst (includes writer's guidelines; names of editors, authors, titles, library of books and past issues). **Contact:** Robert Bixby, editor/publisher. Estab. 1988. Publishes paperback originals. Books: vellum paper; photocopy; perfect binding. Averages 4-6 total titles, 1 or fewer fiction titles/year.

Needs: Literary. Short story collections. Published *Road to Alaska*, by Ray Miller; *Placing Ourselves Among the Living*, by Curtis Smith; *The John-Paul Story*, by Eric Torgersen.

How to Contact: *"Accepts unsolicited mss if $20 reading fee enclosed."* Submit complete ms with a cover letter and reading fee. Send SASE for return of ms or send a disposable copy of ms. Responds in 1 week to queries; 6 months to mss. Accepts simultaneous submissions. Sometimes comments on a rejected ms.

Terms: Pays royalty of 15%. Provides 10 author's copies. Sends galleys to author. Publishes ms 6-12 months after acceptance. Guidelines available for #10 SASE or on website. Obtaining guidelines prior to submission is highly recommended.

MARINE TECHNIQUES PUBLISHING, INC., 126 Western Ave., Suite 266, Augusta ME 04330-7252. (207)622-7984. Fax: (207)621-0821. **Contact:** James L. Pelletier, president/CEO (commercial marine or maritime international); Christopher S. Pelletier, vice president operations (national and international maritime related properties). **Publishes 15% of books from first-time authors.** Averages 3-5 titles/year.

Needs: Must be commercial maritime/marine related.

How to Contact: Submit complete ms. Accepts simultaneous submissions. Responds in 2 months to queries; 6 months to mss.

Terms: Pays 25-43% royalty on wholesale or retail price. Publishes book 6-12 months after acceptance of ms. Book catalog free.

Advice: "Audience consists of commercial marine/maritime firms, persons employed in all aspects of the marine/maritime commercial and recreational fields, persons interested in seeking employment in the commercial marine industry; firms seeking to sell their products and services to vessel owners, operators, and managers in the commercial marine industry worldwide, etc."

MARINER BOOKS, Imprint of Houghton Mifflin, 222 Berkeley St., Boston MA 02116. (617)351-5000. Fax: (617)351-1202. Website: www.hmco.com (includes catalog, interviews, reading guides). **Contact:** Paperback Division. Estab. 1997. Publishes trade paperback originals and reprints.

● Mariner Books' *Interpreter of Maladies*, by debut author Jhumpa Lahiri, won the 2000 Pulitzer Prize for fiction.

Needs: Literary, mainstream/contemporary. Recently published J.K. Galbraith, Anita Desai, Perri Klass, Julia Whitty and Samrat Upadhyay.

How to Contact: Agented submissions only.

Terms: Pays royalty on retail price or makes outright purchase. Advance varies. Book catalog available free.

McBOOKS PRESS, 120 W. State St., Ithaca NY 14850. (607)272-2114. Fax: (607)273-6068. E-mail: mcbook s@mcbooks.com. Website: www.McBooks.com (includes some guidelines, staff names, book catalog). **Contact:** Editorial Director. Estab. 1980. "Small independent publisher; specializes in historical nautical fiction, American publisher of Alexander Kent's Richard Bolitho series, Dudley Pope's Ramage novels." Publishes paperback reprints "mostly." Averages 19 total titles, 17 fiction titles/year. Distributes titles through National Book Network.

Needs: Historical (nautical). Recently published *Ramage and the Rebels*, by Dudley Pope (nautical fiction); *The Wicked Trade*, by Jan Needle (nautical fiction); and *Second to None*, by Alexander Kent (Douglas Reeman) (nautical fiction). Publishes the continuing Bolitho and Ramage series.

How to Contact: Accepts unsolicited queries. Query with outline/synopsis and 1-2 sample chapters. Accepts queries by e-mail. Include list of publishing credits. Send SASE or IRC for return of ms. Mostly agented fiction. Responds in 3 months to queries. Accepts simultaneous submissions.

Advice: "We are small and do not take on many unpublished writers."

MARGARET K. McELDERRY BOOKS, Imprint of the Simon & Schuster Children's Publishing Division, 1230 Sixth Ave., New York NY 10020. (212)698-2761. **Contact:** Emma D. Dryden, vice president and editorial director. Estab. 1971. Publishes hardcover originals. Books: high quality paper; offset printing; three-piece and POB bindings; illustrations. Average print order: 10,000. First novel print order: 6,000. **Published new writers within the last year.** Averages 30 total titles/year.

 • Books published by Margaret K. McElderry Books have received numerous awards including the Newbery and the Caldecott Awards.

Needs: All categories (fiction and nonfiction) for juvenile and young adult: adventure, contemporary, early chapter books, fantasy, poetry, literary and picture books. "We will consider any category. Results depend on the quality of the imagination, the artwork and the writing." Recently published *Bear Snores On*, by Karma Wilson and illustrated by Jane Chapman (picture book); *Green Boy*, by Susan Cooper (middle grade fiction); *Saffy's Angel*, by Hilary McKay (middle grade fiction); and *If the Shoe Fits*, by Laura Whipple and illustrated by Laura Beingessner.

How to Contact: Send query letter.

Terms: Pays in royalties; offers advance. Publishes ms 18-36 months after acceptance.

Advice: "Imaginative writing of high quality is always in demand; also picture books that are original and unusual. Keep in mind that McElderry Books is a very small imprint, so we are very selective about the books we will undertake for publication. We try not to publish any 'trend' books. Be familiar with our list and with what is being published this year by all publishing houses."

MERIWETHER PUBLISHING LTD., 885 Elkton Dr., Colorado Springs CO 80933-7710. (888)594-4436. Website: www.contemporarydrama.com (includes products sold and catalog information). **Contact:** Rhonda Wray, associate editor (church plays); Ted Zapel, editor (school plays, comedies, books). Estab. 1970. "Midsize, independent publisher of plays. We publish plays for teens, mostly one-act comedies, holiday plays for churches and musical comedies. Our books are on the theatrical arts." Publishes paperback originals. Books: quality paper; printing house specialist; paperback binding. Average print order: 5,000-10,000. **Published 25-35 new writers within the last year.** Averages 10 total book titles, 30 plays/musicals/year.

Needs: Religious (children's religious plays and religious Christmas and Easter plays), theatrical arts. Recently published *Jitterbug Juliet*, by Francouer and Dissette (musical); and *Murder in the Manor*, by Bill Hand (comic mystery play).

How to Contact: Accepts unsolicited mss with SASE. Send query letter. Accepts queries by e-mail. Include list of publishing credits. Send SASE or IRC for return of ms or send disposable copy of ms and SASE for reply only. Responds in 3 weeks to queries; 2 months to mss. Accepts simultaneous submissions. Sometimes comments on rejected mss.

Terms: Pays in royalties. Varies to buy-out. Sends galleys to author. Publishes ms 6-12 months after acceptance. Guidelines available for SASE; book catalog for $1.50.

Advice: "If you're interested in writing comedy/farce plays, we're your best publisher."

MICAH PUBLICATIONS, INC., 255 Humphrey St., Marblehead MA 01945. (781)631-7601. Fax: (781)639-0772. E-mail: micah@micahbooks.com. Website: www.micahbooks.com (includes lists of our publications; "writers can survey the website to see what we are interested in"). **Contact:** Roberta Kalechofsky, editor. Estab. 1975. "One-person operation on part-time basis. We only publish about 3 titles a year." Publishes paperback originals and reprints. Books: 60 lb. paper; perfect-bound; some illustrations. Average print order: 800. First novel print order: 800. Averages 3 total titles, 1 fiction title/year.

Needs: Children's/juvenile (animal), family saga, literary, short story collections, translation, animal stories.

How to Contact: Accepts unsolicited mss. Query with outline/synopsis and 2 sample chapters. Include estimated word count, brief bio and list of publishing credits. Send SASE or IRC for return of ms or send disposable copy of ms and SASE for reply only. Responds in 3 months. Accepts simultaneous submissions. Sometimes comments on rejected mss.

Terms: Pays in 12 author's copies. Additional copies at 50% discount. Will divide spin-off benefits if there are any. "We have to insist that the author take responsibility for promoting his/her work." Sends galleys to author. Publishes ms 6-8 months after acceptance. Guidelines available for SASE; book catalogs free.

Advice: "Be honest. Make sure your work is of high literary quality. We don't have time and money to waste on anything but writing excellence."

MID-LIST PRESS, 4324-12th Ave. S., Minneapolis MN 55407-3218. (612)822-3733. Fax: (612)823-8387. E-mail: guide@midlist.org. Website: www.midlist.org (includes writer's guidelines, history and mission, book catalog, ordering information and news). Executive Director: Marianne Nora. **Contact:** Lane Stiles, publisher. Estab. 1989. "We are a nonprofit literary press dedicated to the survival of the mid-list, those quality titles that are being neglected by the larger commercial houses. Our focus is on first-time writers, and we are probably best known for the Mid-List Press First Series Awards." Publishes hardcover and paperback originals and reprints. Books: acid-free paper; offset printing; perfect or Smyth-sewn binding. Average print order: 2,000. **Published 2 new writers within the last year.** Plans 1 first novel this year. Averages 2 fiction titles/year. Distributes titles through Small Press Distribution, Ingram, Baker & Taylor, Midwest Library Service, Brodart, Follett and Emery Pratt. Promotes titles through publicity, direct mail, catalogs, author's events and reviews and awards.

Needs: General fiction. No children's/juvenile, romance, young adult. Recently published *Plan Z, by Leslie Kove*, by Betsy Robinson (first fiction, novel); *Leaving the Neighborhood*, by Lucy Ferriss (first fiction, short fiction); and *Quick Bright Thing*, by Ron Wallace (first fiction, short fiction). Publishes First Series Award for the Novel and First Series Award for Short Fiction. *There is a $20 reading fee for a First Series Award but no charge for publication.*

How to Contact: Accepts unsolicited mss. Send query letter first. Send disposable copy of the ms and SASE for reply only. Agented fiction less than 10%. Responds in 3 weeks to queries; 3 months to mss. Accepts simultaneous submissions.

Terms: Pays royalty of 40-50% of profits. Average advance: $1,000. Sends galleys to author. Publishes ms 12-18 months after acceptance. Guidelines available for #10 SASE or visit website.

Advice: "Write first for guidelines or visit our website before submitting a query, proposal or manuscript. And take the time to read some of the titles we've published."

MIGHTYBOOK, INC., 10924 Grant Rd., #225, Houston TX 77070. (281)955-9855. Fax: (281)890-4818. E-mail: reaves@houston.rr.com. Website: www.mightybook.com. **Contact:** Richard Eaves, acquisitions director. Estab. 1991. "Small independent publisher of electronic, flash-animated, read-aloud picture books on CD-ROM. Much of our marketing and sales are done on the Internet." **Published 10 new writers within the last year.** Averages 15 total titles.

Needs: Children's/juvenile, young adult/teen. Very short children's picture books (100-200 words). Recently published *Oliver's High Five*, by Beverly S. Brown; *How I Feel Happy*, by Marcia Leonard; and *Icky, Sticky and Gooey*, by Kimberly Constant (debut fiction).

How to Contact: Accepts unsolicited mss. Submit complete ms with cover letter. Accepts queries by e-mail, fax and phone. Include estimated word count and brief bio. Send disposable ms and SASE for reply only. Agented fiction 5%. Responds in 6 weeks. Accepts simultaneous submissions, electronic submissions and submissions by disk.

Terms: Pays royalties of 20% gross. No advance. Publishes ms 3-6 months after acceptance. Guidelines and book catalog available on website.

Advice: "Write short picture books with a good moral, but avoid references to violence and avoid controversial topics."

MILKWEED EDITIONS, 1011 Washington Ave. S., Suite 300, Minneapolis MN 55415. (612)332-3192. Fax: (612)215-2550. E-mail: editor@milkweed.org. Website: www.milkweed.org (includes writer's guidelines, mission statement, catalog, poem of day, excerpts from titles). **Contact:** Emilie Buchwald, publisher; Elisabeth Fitz, first reader. Estab. 1980. Nonprofit publisher. Publishes hardcover and paperback originals and paperback reprints. Books: book text quality—acid-free paper; offset printing; perfect or hardcover binding. Average print order: 4,000. First novel print order depends on book. **Published new writers within the last year.** Averages 15 total titles/year. Number of fiction titles "depends on manuscripts." Distributes titles through Publisher's Group West. Each book has its own marketing plan involving print ads, tours, conferences, etc.

● Pattiann Rogers's *Song of the World Becoming* was a finalist for the 2001 *Los Angeles Times* Book Prize.

Needs: For adult readers: literary fiction, nonfiction, poetry, essays; for children (ages 8-12): literary novels. Translations welcome for both audiences. No legends or folktales for children. No romance, mysteries, science fiction. Recently published *The Tree of Red Stars*, by Tessa Bridal (novel); *Hell's Bottom, Colorado*, by Laura Pritchett (first fiction, short stories); and *What a Woman Must Do*, by Faith Sullivan (novel).

How to Contact: Send for guidelines first, then submit complete ms. Responds in 6 months. Accepts simultaneous submissions.

Terms: Pays royalties of 7½% on list price. Advance varies. Sends galleys to author. Publishes ms 1-2 years after acceptance. Book catalog available for $1.50 postage. "Send for guidelines. Must enclose SASE."

Advice: "Read good contemporary literary fiction, find your own voice, and persist. Familiarize yourself with our list before submitting."

MILKWEEDS FOR YOUNG READERS, Imprint of Milkweed Editions, 1011 Washington Ave. S., Suite 300, Minneapolis MN 55415-1246. (612)332-3192. Fax: (612)215-2550. **Contact:** Emilie Buchwald, publisher; Elisabeth Fitz, first reader. Estab. 1984. "Milkweeds for Young Readers are works that embody humane values and contribute to cultural understanding." Publishes hardcover and trade paperback originals. Averages 4 total titles/year. Distributes titles through Publishers Group West. Promotes titles individually through print advertising, website and author tours.

● *Parents Wanted*, by George Harrar, was named "Best Children's Book of the Year" in 2002 by Bank Street.

Needs: For ages 8-12: adventure, animal, fantasy, historical, juvenile and mainstream/contemporary. Recently published *Parents Wanted*, by George Harrar; *Emma and the Ruby Ring*, by Yvonne MacGrory; *Tides*, by V.M. Caldwell (middle-grade novel); and *The $66 Summer*, by John Armistead.

How to Contact: Submit complete ms with cover letter. Agented fiction 30%. Responds in up to 6 months to mss. Accepts simultaneous submissions.

Terms: Pays royalty of 7½% on retail price. Advance varies. Publishes ms 1 year after acceptance. Guidelines available for #10 SASE; book catalog for $1.50.

Advice: "Familiarize yourself with our books before submitting. You need not have a long list of credentials—excellent work speaks for itself."

[N] [⊕] [◻] [◎] MILLS & BOON HISTORICAL ROMANCE, a Harlequin book line, Eton House, 18-24 Paradise Rd., Richmond, Surrey TW9 1SR United Kingdom. Phone: (44)0208 288 2800. Website: www.millsandboon.co.uk. **Contact:** Linda Fildew, senior editor. "This series covers a wide range of British and European historical periods from 1066 to approximately 1920." Publishes paperback originals and reprints. Books: newspaper print; web printing; perfect-bound. **Regularly publishes new writers.**

Needs: Romance. "The romance should take priority, with all the emotional impact of a growing love and should be developed over a relatively short span of time; the historical detail should be accurate, without sounding like a textbook, and should help to create a true sense of the chosen, so the reader becomes immersed in that time." Manuscripts must be 75,000-85,000 words.

How to Contact: Accepts unsolicited mss. "A query letter and brief synopsis is advised." Send SASE or IRC for return of ms or send disposable copy of ms and SASE for reply only. No simultaneous, multiple or disk submissions.

Terms: Pays royalties and advance. Guidelines available for SASE and on website.

[N] [⊕] [◻] [◎] MILLS & BOON MEDICAL ROMANCE, a Harlequin book line, Eton House, 18-24 Paradise Rd., Richmond, Surrey TW9 1SR United Kingdom. Phone: (44)0208 288 2800. Website: www.millsandboon.co.uk. **Contact:** Sheila Hodgson, senior editor. "These are present-day romances in a medical setting." Publishes paperback originals and reprints. Books: newspaper print; web printing; perfect-bound. **Regularly publishes new writers.**

Needs: Romance (medical). Looking for writing with "a good balance between the romance, the medicine, and the underlying story. At least one of the main characters should be a medical professional, and developing the romance is easier if the hero and heroine work together. Medical detail should be accurate but preferably without using technical language. An exploration of patients and their illnesses is permitted, but not in such numbers as to overwhelm the growing love story. Settings can be anywhere in the world." Manuscripts must be 50,000-55,000 words.

How to Contact: Accepts unsolicited mss. Send query letter or submit complete ms with cover letter. Send SASE or IRC for return of ms or send disposable copy of ms and SASE for reply only. No simultaneous, multiple or disk submissions.

Terms: Pays royalties and advance. Sends galleys to authors. Guidelines available for SASE and on website.

Advice: "More detailed guidelines are available on request with a stamped, addressed envelope."

[N] [▼] [A] MIRA BOOKS, an imprint of Harlequin, 225 Duncan Mill Rd., Don Mills, Ontario M3B 3K9 Canada. (416)445-5860. Website: www.eharlequin.com. **Contact:** Dianne Moggy, editorial director. "MIRA Books is proud to publish outstanding mainstream women's fiction for readers around the world." Publishes paperback originals.

Needs: Mainstream contemporary and historical romance, romantic suspense, thrillers, family sagas, relationship novels. Recently published work by Penny Jordan, Debbie Macomber, Diana Palmer, Nan Ryan and Susan Wiggs.

How to Contact: Does not accept unsolicited mss. "At this time, MIRA Books is only accepting agented submissions. Harlequin and Silhouette published authors should contact their editor if interested in submitting to MIRA."

Terms: Pays royalties and advance. Sends galleys to author. Guidelines not available.

[N] [◐] [◎] MOODY PRESS, Moody Bible Institute, 820 N. LaSalle Blvd., Chicago IL 60610. Fax: (312)329-2019. E-mail: acquisitions@moody.edu. Website: www.moodypress.com (includes online catalog, writer's guidelines). **Contact:** Michele Straubel, acquisitions editor (all fiction). Estab. 1894. Small, evangelical Christian publisher. "We publish only fiction that reflects and supports our evangelical worldview and mission." Publishes paperback originals. Plans 1-2 first novels this year. Averages 70-80 total titles, 5-10 fiction titles/year. Member, CBA. Distributes and promotes titles through area sales reps, print advertising, promotional events, Internet, etc.

Needs: Children's/juvenile (series), fantasy, historical, mystery/suspense, religious (children's religious, inspirational, religious fantasy, religious mystery/suspense), science fiction, young adult/teen (adventure, fantasy/science fiction, historical, mystery/suspense, series). Recently published *Courage to Run*, by Wendy Lawton (YA, debut author); *Vinegar Boy*, by Alberta Hause (YA); and *Purity Reigns*, by Stephanie Perry Moore (YA). Publishes ongoing YA series, Daughters of the Faith.

How to Contact: Accepts unsolicited mss. Query with outline/synopsis and 3-5 sample chapters. Accepts queries by e-mail and fax. Include estimated word count, brief bio and list of publishing credits. Send SASE or IRC for return of ms or send disposable copy of ms and SASE for reply only. Agented fiction 50-60%. Responds in 2-3 months. Accepts simultaneous and e-mail submissions. No disk submissions.

Terms: Sends galleys to author. Publishes ms 1 year after acceptance. Guidelines available for SASE and on website; book catalogs free.

Advice: "Get to know Moody Press and understand what kinds of books we publish. We will decline all submissions that do not support our evangelical Christian beliefs and mission."

MOUNTAIN STATE PRESS, 2300 MacCorkle Ave. SE, Charleston WV 25304-1099. (304)357-4767. Fax: (304)357-4715. E-mail: msp1@newwave.net. Website: www.mountainstatepress.com. **Contact**: Lisa Contreras, fiction editor. Estab. 1978. "A small nonprofit press run by a board of 13 members who volunteer their time. We specialize in books about West Virginia or by authors from West Virginia. We strive to give a voice to Appalachia." Publishes paperback originals and reprints. **Published new writers within the last year.** Plans 2-3 first novels this year. Averages 3 total titles, 1-2 fiction titles/year. Distributes titles through bookstores, distributors, gift shops and individual sales (Amazon.com and Barnes & Noble online carry our titles). Promotes titles through newspapers, radio, TV (local author series), mailings and book signings.

Needs: Family saga, historical (West Virginia), military/war, New Age/mystic/spiritual, religious. Currently compiling an anthology of West Virginia authors. Recently published *Homesick for the Hills*, by Alyce Faye Bragg (memoirs, humor); *The Well Ain't Dry Yet*, by Belinda Anderson (short story collection); and *Under the Shade of the Trees: Thomas (Stonewall) Jackson's Life at Jackson's Mill*, by Dennis Norman (historical).

How to Contact: Accepts unsolicited mss. Query with outline/synopsis and 3 sample chapters or submit complete ms with cover letter. Accepts queries by e-mail and fax. Include estimated word count and bio. Send SASE or IRC for return of ms or send disposable copy of ms with SASE for reply only. Responds in up to 6 months to mss. Accepts electronic submissions. Often comments on rejected mss.

Terms: Pays royalties.

Advice: "Topic of West Virginia is the best choice for our press. Send your manuscript in and it will be read and reviewed by the members of the Board of Mountain State Press. We give helpful suggestions and critique the writing."

MOYER BELL LIMITED, 54 Phillips St., Wickford RI 02852-5126. (401)294-0106. Fax: (401)294-1076. E-mail: info@moyerbell.com. Website: www.moyerbell.com. Averages 20 titles/year; imprint publishes 5 titles/year.

Imprints: Asphodel Press.

Needs: Literary.

How to Contact: Query with SASE.

Terms: Pays 5% royalty on retail price. Book catalog online.

MULTNOMAH PUBLISHERS, INC., P.O. Box 1720, Sisters OR 97759. (541)549-1144. Fax: (541)549-8048. E-mail: editorial@multnomahbooks.com. Website: www.multnomahbooks.com. **Contact**: Editorial Dept. Estab. 1987. Midsize independent publisher of evangelical fiction and nonfiction. Publishes paperback originals. Books: perfect binding. Average print order: 15,000. Averages 100 total titles.

  • Multnomah Books has received several Gold Medallion Book Awards from the Evangelical Christian Publishers Association.

Imprint(s): Multnomah Books ("Christian living and popular theology books"); Multnomah Fiction ("Changing lives through the power of story"); Multnomah Gift ("Substantive topics with beautiful, lyrical writing").

Needs: Literary, mystery/suspense, religious/inspirational issue. Recently published *The Protector*, by Dee Henderson (romance/suspense); *Who I Am*, by Melody Carlson (YA); and *The Ishbane Conspiracy*, by Randy Alcorn (contemporary).

How to Contact: Multnomah is currently not accepting unsolicited mss, proposals or queries. Queries accepted through agents and at writers' conferences in which a Multnomah representative is present.

Terms: Pays royalties. Provides 100 author's copies. Sends galleys to author. Publishes ms 1-2 years after acceptance. Guidelines available for SASE or on website.

Advice: "Looking for clean, moral, uplifting fiction. We're particularly interested in contemporary women's fiction, historical fiction, superior romance and mystery/suspense."

MY WEEKLY STORY COLLECTION, D.C. Thomson and Co., Ltd., 22 Meadowside, Dundee DD19QJ, Scotland. **Contact:** Mrs. D. Hunter, fiction editor. "Cheap paperback story library with full-colour cover. Material should not be violent, controversial or sexually explicit." Averages 48 romantic novels/year. Distributes titles through national retail outlets. Promotes titles through display cards in retail outlets and in-house magazine adverts.

Needs: Contemporary and historical novels. Length: approximately 30,000 words.

How to Contact: Query with outline/synopsis and 3 opening chapters.

Terms: Writers are paid on acceptance. Writers guidelines available on request.

Advice: "Avoid too many colloquialisms/Americanisms. Stories can be set anywhere but local colour not too 'local' as to be alien."

THE MYSTERIOUS PRESS, Crime and mystery fiction imprint for Warner Books, 1271 Avenue of the Americas, New York NY 10020. (212)522-7200. Fax: (212)522-7990. Website: www.twbookmark.com. (includes authors, titles, guidelines, bulletin board, tour info, contests). **Contact**: Sara Ann Freed, editor-in-chief. Estab. 1976. Publishes hardcover and paperback originals, trade and paperback reprints. Books: hardcover (some Smythe-sewn) and paperback binding; illustrations rarely. First novel print order: 10,000 copies minimum. **Published new writers within the last year.** Averages 36-45 total titles/year.

Needs: Mystery/suspense. Recently published *Put a Lid on It*, by Donald Westlake; and *Dead Midknight*, by Marcia Muller.

How to Contact: Submit through an agent only.

Terms: Pays royalties of 10% minimum. Average advance: negotiable. Sends galleys to author. Buys hard and softcover rights. Publishes ms 1 year after acceptance.

Advice: "Write a strong and memorable novel, and with the help of a good literary agent, you'll find the right publishing house. Don't despair if your manuscript is rejected by several houses. All publishing houses are looking for new and exciting crime novels, but it may not be at the time your novel is submitted. Hang in there, keep the faith—and good luck."

○ ◎ **THE NAIAD PRESS, INC.**, P.O. Box 10543, Tallahassee FL 32302. (850)539-5965. Fax: (850)539-9731. E-mail: naiadpress@aol.com. Website: www.naiadpress.com (includes complete and detailed catalog, order capacity). **Contact:** Barbara Grier, editorial director. Estab. 1973. "Oldest and largest lesbian publishing company. We are scrupulously honest and we keep our books in print for the most part." Books: 50 lb. offset paper; sheet-fed offset; perfect-bound. Average print order: 12,000. First novel print order: 12,000. Averages 34 total titles/year. Distributes titles through distributors, direct sales to stores and individuals and over the Web. Promotes titles through a first class mailing to over 26,000 lesbians monthly; 2,300 bookstores on mailing list.
 • The Naiad Press is one of the most successful and well-known lesbian publishers. They have also produced eight of their books on audio cassette.
Needs: Lesbian fiction, all genres. Published *She Walks in Beauty*, by Nicole Conn (romance); *Substitute for Love*, by Karin Kallmaker (romance); *Out of Sight*, by Claire McNab (mystery).
How to Contact: Does not accept unsolicited mss. Query with outline/synopsis. Include estimated word count and 2-sentence bio. Send SASE or IRC for reply. Responds in 3 weeks to queries; 3 months to mss.
Terms: Pays royalties of 15% using a standard recovery contract. Occasionally pays royalties of 7½% against cover price. "Seldom gives advances and has never seen a first novel worthy of one. Believes authors are investments in their own and the company's future—that the best author is the author who produces a book every 12-18 months forever and knows that there is a *home* for that book." Publishes ms 1-2 years after acceptance. Book catalog available for legal-sized SASE and $1.50 postage and handling.
Advice: "We publish lesbian fiction primarily and prefer honest work (i.e., positive, upbeat lesbian characters). Lesbian content must be accurate . . . a lot of earlier lesbian novels were less than honest. No breast beating or complaining. Our fiction titles are becoming increasingly *genre* fiction, which we encourage. Original fiction in paperback is our main field, and its popularity increases. We publish books BY, FOR AND ABOUT lesbians. We are not interested in books that are unrealistic. You know and we know what the real world of lesbian interest is like. Don't even try to fool us. Short, well-written books do best. Authors who want to succeed and will work to do so have the best shot."

Ⓝ ◐ **NARWHAL PRESS INC.**, 1436 Meeting St., Charleston SC 29405. (843)853-0510. Fax: (843)853-2528. Website: www.shipwrecks.com. **Contact:** E. Lee Spance, chief editor (sea, military, pirates); Robert P. Stockton, associate editor (sea, military, historical). Estab. 1994. Publishes hardcover and paperback originals. Books and print orders vary. Averages 5 total titles, 3 fiction titles/year. Distributes titles through Ingram, B&T, Sandlapper, Parnassas. Promotes titles through inhouse efforts.
Needs: Adventure, historical (general), literary, mainstream, military/war, mystery/suspense (amateur sleuth, police procedural, private eye/hardboiled), regional (Southeast), special interests: sea, pirates, military, mystery, action/adventure. Recently published *The Collector*, by William B. Kerr (action/adventure); *Judgment Call*, by William Kerr (action/adventure); and *Death's Bright Angel*, by William Kerr (action/adventure).
How to Contact: Accepts unsolicited mss. Send query letter or query with outline/synopsis and 1-2 sample chapters. Accepts queries by fax and phone. Include estimated word count, brief bio and list of publishing credits. Send SASE or IRC for return of ms or send disposable copy of ms and SASE for reply only. Responds in 2 months to queries; 6 months to mss. Accepts simultaneous submissions. No e-mail or disk submissions. Sometimes comments on rejected mss.
Terms: Pays royalties; offers negotiable advance and copies. Payment by individual arrangement with author depending on book. Sends galleys to author. Publishes ms 1 year after acceptance. Guidelines not available; book catalog free or on website.

Ⓝ ☪ **NATURAL HERITAGE/NATURAL HISTORY, INC.**, P.O. Box 95, Station O, Toronto, Ontario M4A 2M8 Canada. (416)694-7907. Fax: (416)690-0819. E-mail: natherbooks@idirect.com. **Contact:** Jane Gibson, editor-in-chief. Publishes hardcover and trade paperback originals. **Publishes 50% of books from first-time authors; 85% from unagented writers.** Averages 12-15 titles/year.
Imprints: Natural Heritage.
Needs: Historical, short story collections. Recently published *Just a Little Later with Eevo and Slim*, by Henry Shykoff.
How to Contact: Query with SASE. Does not accept simultaneous submissions. Responds in 4 months to queries; 6 months to mss.
Terms: Pays 8-10% royalty on retail price. Offers advance. Publishes book 2 years after acceptance of ms. Book catalog free; ms guidelines for #10 SASE.
Advice: "We are a Canadian publisher in the natural heritage and history fields."

◎ **THE NAUTICAL & AVIATION PUBLISHING CO. OF AMERICA INC.**, 1250 Fairmont Ave., Mt. Pleasant SC 29464. (843)856-0561. Fax: (843)856-3164. President: Jan Snouck-Hurgronje. **Contact:** Melissa Pluta, editor. Estab. 1979. Small publisher interested in quality military and naval history and literature. Publishes hardcover originals and reprints. Averages 10 total titles, 1-4 fiction titles/year.

Needs: Revolutionary War, War of 1812, Civil War, WWI and II, Persian Gulf and Marine Corps history. Looks for "novels with a strong military history orientation." Recently published *The Black Flower*, by Howard Bahr; *Lieutenant Christopher and the Quasi-War with France*, by VADM William P. Mack; and *Rifleman Dodd*, by C.S. Forester (all military fiction).

How to Contact: Accepts unsolicited mss. Send ms with cover letter and brief synopsis. SASE necessary for return of mss. Agented fiction "miniscule." Responds in 3 weeks. Accepts simultaneous submissions. Sometimes comments on rejected mss.

Terms: Pays royalties of 10-12% on selling price. After acceptance publishes ms "as quickly as possible—next season." Book catalog available free.

Advice: Encourages first novelists.

NAVAL INSTITUTE PRESS Imprint of U.S. Naval Institute, 291 Wood Rd., Annapolis MD 21402-5034. Fax: (410)295-1084. E-mail: ssprinkle@usni.org. Website: www.nip.org (includes book catalog, author guidelines, staff list, and occasional chat room event with authors). Press Director: Ronald Chambers. **Contact:** Paul Wilderson, executive editor; Tom Cutler, senior acquisitions editor; Eric Mills, acquisitions editor. Estab. 1873. "Best known for introducing Tom Clancy's and Stephen Coonts' first novels. We've been publishing books for 125 years (but do very little fiction) to advance knowledge of the naval and maritime services." First novel print order: 2,500. Averages 80 titles/year. Distributes titles through wholesalers such as Ingram and Baker & Taylor.

Needs: Limited fiction on military and naval themes. Recently published *Dog Company Six*, by Edwin P. Simmons (Korean War novel); and *Punk's War*, by Ward Carroll (first novel).

How to Contact: Send plot outline with sample chapters and sufficient return postage.

Terms: Pays royalties of 5-10% on net sales. Publishes ms 1 year after acceptance. Guidelines available for #10 SASE; book catalog free for 9×12 SASE.

THOMAS NELSON PUBLISHERS, Nelson Publishing Group, Box 141000, Nashville TN 37214-1000. (615)889-9000. Website: www.thomasnelson.com. Estab. 1798. **Contact:** Acquisitions Editor. "Largest Christian book publishers." Publishes hardcover and paperback originals. Averages 150-200 total titles/year.

Needs: Seeking successfully published commercial fiction authors who write for adults from a Christian perspective. Published *Kingdom Come*, by Larry Burkett and T. Davis Bunn; *Dakota Moon* series, by Stephanie Grace Whitson (romance); and *Empty Coffin*, by Robert Wise (mystery/suspense).

How to Contact: Corporate office does not accept unsolicited mss. "No phone queries."

Terms: Pays royalties on net receipts. Publishes ms 1-2 years after acceptance.

Advice: "We are a conservative publishing house and want material which is conservative in morals and in nature."

TOMMY NELSON, Thomas Nelson, Inc., 404 BNA Dr., Bldg. 200, Suite 508, Nashville TN 37217. Fax: (615)902-2415. Website: www.tommynelson.com. Publisher of children's Christian fiction and nonfiction for boys and girls up to age 14. "We honor God and serve people through books, videos, software and Bibles for children that improve the lives of our customers." Publishes hardcover and trade paperback originals. Averages 50-75 total titles/year.

Imprint(s): Word Kids.

Needs: Adventure, juvenile, mystery, picture books, religious. "No stereotypical characters." Recently published *Prayer of Jabez for Kids*, by Bruce Wilkinson.

How to Contact: Does not accept unsolicited mss or simultaneous submissions.

Advice: "Know the CBA market. Check out the Christian bookstores to see what sells and what is needed."

NEW AMERICAN LIBRARY (NAL), Division of Penguin Putnam Inc., 375 Hudson St., New York NY 10014. (212)366-2000. Fax: (212)366-2889. **Contact:** Claire Zion, editorial director, NAL editorial (fiction, nonfiction); Ellen Edwards, executive editor (commercial women's fiction); Laura Anne Gilman, executive editor (science fiction/fantasy/horror); Audrey LeFehr, executive editor (contemporary and historical romance, multicultural fiction); Hilary Ross, associate executive editor (Regency, romance); Tracy Bernstein, executive editor; Laura Ciselli, senior editor (contemporary romance, romantic suspense); Doug Grad, senior editor (thrillers, historical and military fiction/nonfiction); Dan Slater, senior editor (westerns, thrillers, commercial fiction, media tie-ins); Marie Timell, senior editor (New Age, inspirational); Genny Ostertag, editor (mystery, women's fiction). Estab. 1948. Publishes hardcover and paperback originals and paperback reprints. **Published new writers within the last year.**

Imprint(s): Signet, Onyx, Signet Classic, ROC, NAL Accent.

Needs: "All kinds of commercial fiction, including mainstream, historical, Regency, New Age, western, thriller, science fiction, fantasy. Full length novels and collections." Recently published *The Hearing*, by John Lescroart; *Scarlet Feather*, by Maeve Binchy; *Orchid Blues*, by Stuart Woods; and *Always in My Heart*, by Catherine Anderson.

How to Contact: Agented mss only. Queries accepted with SASE. "State type of book and past publishing projects." Simultaneous submissions OK. Responds in 3 months.

INTERESTED IN A PARTICULAR GENRE? Check our sections for: **Mystery/Suspense**, page 74; **Romance**, page 86; **Science Fiction/Fantasy & Horror**, page 100.

Terms: Pays in royalties and author's copies; offers advance. Send galleys to authors. Publishes ms 18 months after acceptance. Book catalog available for SASE.

Advice: "Write the complete manuscript and submit it to an agent or agents."

N ◎ THE NEW ENGLAND PRESS, INC., P.O. Box 575, Shelburne VT 05482. (802)863-2520. Fax: (802)863-1510. E-mail: nep@together.net. Website: www.nepress.com. **Contact:** Christopher A. Bray, managing editor. Estab. 1978. Publishes hardcover and trade paperback originals. **Publishes 50% of books from first-time authors; 90% from unagented writers.** Averages 6-8 titles/year.

Needs: Historical (Vermont, New Hampshire, Maine). "We look for very specific subject matters based on Vermont history and heritage. We are also interested in historical novels for young adults based in New Hampshire and Maine. We do not publish contemporary adult fiction of any kind."

How to Contact: Query with SASE or submit 2 sample chapter(s), synopsis. Accepts simultaneous submissions. Responds in 3 months to queries.

Terms: Pays royalty on wholesale price. Publishes book 15 months after acceptance of ms. Book catalog free.

Advice: "Our readers are interested in all aspects of Vermont and northern New England, including hobbyists (railroad books) and students (young adult fiction and biography). No agent is needed, but our market is extremely specific and our volume is low, so send a query or outline and writing samples first. Sending the whole manuscript is discouraged. We will not accept projects that are still under development or give advances."

◑ NEW HOPE BOOKS, INC., P.O. Box 38, New Hope PA 18938. (888)741-BOOK. Fax: (215)244-0935. E-mail: NewHopeBks@aol.com. Website: www.NewHopeBooks.net (includes book catalog, featured authors, submission guidelines, contact information). **Contact:** Barbara Taylor, publisher; Tamara Hayes, assistant editor. Estab. 1999. "We are a small but quickly growing press that savors zippy, mainstream page turners, which readily adapt to feature film." Publishes hardcover and paperback originals and reprints. **Published 1 new writer within the last year.** Averages 6 total titles, 6 fiction titles/year.

Needs: Adventure, literary, mainstream, mystery/suspense, thriller/espionage. Looks for "plot-driven fiction only that tugs on the heartstrings." Recently published *The Boardwalkers* (murder mystery); and *A Run to Hell* (crime/espionage), both by Frederick Schofield.

How to Contact: Does not accept unsolicited mss. Query with outline/synopsis, word count, first 3 chapters and final chapter. Include e-mail address and/or SASE for reply only. If ms is requested, send disposable copy of ms and e-mail address/SASE for reply only. "Almost all of our fiction is agented." Responds in 2 months to queries; 3 months to mss. Accepts simultaneous submissions.

Terms: Pays royalty. Offers negotiable advance. Sends galleys to author. Publishes ms 1 year after acceptance. Guidelines available free for #10 SASE; book catalog on website.

Advice: "Current industry trends heavily favor our approach. Submissions must perfectly fit our guidelines for consideration."

◑ ◎ NEW VICTORIA PUBLISHERS, P.O. Box 27, Norwich VT 05055-0027. Phone/fax: (802)649-5297. E-mail: newvic@aol.com. Website: www.NewVictoria.com (includes list of titles). **Contact:** Claudia Lamperti, editor; ReBecca Béguin, editor. Estab. 1976. "Publish mostly lesbian fiction—strong female protagonists. Most well known for Stoner McTavish mystery series." Small, three-person operation. Publishes trade paperback originals. Averages 4-6 titles/year. Distributes titles through LPC Group (Chicago), Airlift (London) and Bulldog Books (Sydney, Australia). Promotes titles "mostly through lesbian feminist media."

● *Mommy Deadest*, by Jean Marcy, won the Lambda Literary Award for Mystery.

Needs: Lesbian/feminist: adventure, fantasy, historical, humor, mystery (amateur sleuth), romance. Looking for "strong feminist characters, also strong plot and action. We will consider most anything if it is well written and appeals to a lesbian/feminist audience; mostly mysteries." Publishes anthologies or special editions. Published *Killing at the Cat*, by Carlene Miller (mystery); *Queer Japan*, by Barbara Summerhawk (anthology); *Skin to Skin*, by Martha Miller (erotic short fiction); *Talk Show*, by Melissa Hartman (novel); *Flight From Chador*, by Sigrid Brunel (adventure); and *Do Drums Beat There*, by Doe Tabor (novel),

How to Contact: Accepts unsolicited mss. Query with outline/synopsis and sample chapters. Accepts queries by e-mail, fax. Send SASE or IRC for reply. Responds in 2 weeks to queries; 1 month to mss.

Terms: Pays royalties of 10%. Publishes ms 1 year after acceptance. Guidelines available for SASE; book catalog free.

Advice: "We are especially interested in lesbian or feminist mysteries, ideally with a character or characters who can evolve through a series of books. Mysteries should involve a complex plot, accurate legal and police procedural detail, and protagonists with full emotional lives. Pay attention to plot and character development. Read guidelines carefully."

◆ ◎ NEWEST PUBLISHERS LTD., 201, 8540-109 St., Edmonton, Alberta T6G 1E6 Canada. (780)432-9427. Fax: (780)433-3179. E-mail: info@newestpress.com. Website: www.newestpress.com (includes guidelines and catalog). **Contact:** Ruth Linka, general manager. Estab. 1977. Publishes trade paperback originals. **Published new writers within the last year.** Averages 12 total titles/year, fiction and nonfiction. Promotes titles through book launches, media interviews, review copy mailings and touring.

Imprints: Prairie Play Series (drama), Writer as Critic (literary criticisim).

Needs: Literary. "Our press is interested in western Canadian writing." Published *Man Who Beat the Man*, by F.B. Andre (short stories, debut author); *I'm Frankie Sterne*, by Dave Margoshes (novel); *Tips of the Halo*, by R.F. Darian (mystery, debut author). Publishes the Nunatak New Fiction Series.

How to Contact: Accepts unsolicited mss. SASE necessary for return of ms. Responds in 6 months.
Terms: Pays royalties of 10%. Sends galleys to author. Publishes ms within 18 months after acceptance. Book catalog available for 9×12 SASE.
Advice: *"We publish western Canadian writers only or books about western Canada.* We are looking for excellent quality and originality."

NORTH-SOUTH BOOKS, affiliate of Nord-Sud Verlag AG, 11 E. 26th St., New York NY 10010. (212)706-4545. Website: www.northsouth.com. **Contact:** Julie Amper. Estab. 1985. "The aim of North-South is to build bridges—bridges between authors and artists from different countries and between readers of all ages. We believe children should be exposed to as wide a range of artistic styles as possible with universal themes." **Published new writers within the last year.** Averages 100 titles/year.
• North-South Books is the publisher of the international bestseller, *The Rainbow Fish.*
Needs: Picture books. "We are currently accepting only picture books; all other books are selected by our German office."
How to Contact: Agented fiction only. Query. All unsolicited mss returned unopened.
Terms: Pays royalty on retail price. Publishes ms 2 years after acceptance.

W.W. NORTON & COMPANY, INC., 500 Fifth Ave., New York NY 10110. Fax: (212)869-0856. E-mail: manuscripts@wwnorton.com. Website: www.wwnorton.com. Estab. 1923. Midsize independent publisher of trade books and college textbooks. Publishes literary fiction. Publishes hardcover and paperback originals and reprints. Averages 300 titles/year.
Needs: High-quality literary fiction. No occult, science fiction, religious, gothic, romances, psychic/supernatural, fantasy, horror, juvenile or young adult. Published *Ship Fever*, by Andrea Barrett; *Oyster*, by Jannette Turner Hospital; and *Power*, by Linda Hogan.
How to Contact: Does not accept unsolicited mail; "manuscripts/proposals sent by mail will not be opened. If you would like to submit your proposal by e-mail, paste the text of your query letter and/or sample chapter into the body of the e-mail message. Do not send attachments. We cannot accept complete manuscripts via e-mail. Keep your proposal under six pages." No phone calls.

NW WRITERS' CORPORATION, NSpirit Cultural Newsmagazine, Ogun Books, 30620 Pacific Highway S., Suite 110, Federal Way WA 98003. (253)839-3177. Fax: (253)839-3207. E-mail: nwwriterscorp@aol.com. Website: www.nwwriterscorp.com. **Contact:** Amontaine Woods, executive editor (fiction, inspirational, women); Orisade Awodola, editor (nonfiction, genealogy, history, spiritual, empowerment, black, cultural studies). Estab. 1998. Publishes hardcover and trade paperback originals and reprints. **Publishes 100% of books from first-time authors; 100% from unagented writers.** Averages 6-8 titles/year; imprint publishes 2-3 titles/year.
Needs: Ethnic, historical, multicultural, multimedia, religious, spiritual. "We accept fiction mss based on marketability and review for filming potential." Recently published *Still My Tremblin' Soul*, by Carolyn Y. Parnell (suspense).
How to Contact: Query with SASE. Accepts simultaneous submissions. Responds in 1 month to queries; 3 months to mss.
Terms: Pays 20-25% royalty or makes outright purchase of $1,000-2,000. Publishes book 1 year after acceptance of ms. Book catalog online; ms guidelines online.
Advice: Audience consists of educators, business leaders, college students.

OAK TREE PRESS, Barker Thomas Group Inc., 915 W. Foothill Blvd., #411, Claremont CA 91711. (909)615-8400. Fax: (909)620-7242. E-mail: oaktreepub@aol.com. Website: www.oaktreebooks.com. **Contact:** Billie Johnson, publisher (mysteries, romance, nonfiction); Sarah Wasson, acquisitions editor (all); Barbara Hoffman, senior editor (children's, young adult, educational). Estab. 1998. "Small independent publisher with a philosophy of author advocacy. Welcomes first-time authors and sponsors annual mystery contest which publishes the winning entry." Publishes hardcover and paperback originals and paperback reprints. Books: perfect binding. **Published 4 new writers within the last year.** Averages 10 total titles, 8 fiction titles/year. Member, SPAN, SPAWN. "We do our own distribution." Promotes through website, conferences, PR, author tours.
Imprint(s): Oak Tree Press, Dark Oak Mysteries (mysteries); Timeless Love (romance); Acorn Books for Children (children's, YA).
Needs: Humor/satire, mystery/suspense (amateur sleuth, cozy, police procedural, private eye/hardboiled), romance (contemporary, futuristic/time travel, romantic suspense). Recently published *Hearts Across Forever*, by Mary Montague Sikes (romance); *Deadfall*, by Lynda Douglas (mystery); *Number Please*, by Sheree Petree (mystery); *An Affinity for Murder*, by Anne White (mystery); and *Callie & the Dealer & a Dog Named Jake*, by Wendy Howell Mills (mystery).
How to Contact: Does not accept or return unsolicited mss. Send query letter. Accepts queries by e-mail and fax. Include estimated word count and brief bio with submission. Agented fiction: 1%. Responds in 2-3 weeks to queries; 1-2 months to mss. Accepts simultaneous submissions, electronic submissions. Sometimes comments on rejected mss.
Terms: Pays royalties of 10-20%. Advance is negotiable. Sends galleys to author. Publishes ms 9-18 months after acceptance. Guidelines available for SASE; book catalogs for SASE.
Advice: "Understand the business and be eager and enthusiastic about participating in the marketing and promotion of the title."

insider report

Geoffrey Clark: Mining locale for rich material

Author Geoffrey Clark has turned consistently to his native soil, Michigan, for much of his fiction. "I recall a popular psych film in college classes years ago which demonstrated that young ducks took whatever they saw upon hatching as their mother—a cat, a person or the actual mother duck," he says. "I sometimes feel I was similarly imprinted by the state of Michigan, its topography, landscape, seasonal changes, flora and fauna, etc., all of it later becoming fused with my townspeople, variations which people my fiction."

Geoffrey Clark

Though Clark has lived much of his adult life in New England, he remains an alien of sorts in his adopted Rhode Island—an exile. But this only produces more grist for the mill: "I think to feel yourself something of an exile sharpens the intensity of the need to write and sharpens your perspective."

In five short story collections and two novels, the work that's closest to Clark's heart is *Schooling the Spirit* (Asylum Arts, 1993). *Schooling* centers on Miller Springstead—one of Clark's key male protagonists—a young man with an identity crisis, caught between his Michigan redneck rural roots and his college-educated self, his democratic sensibilities and his occasional elitist sympathies. This was the work Clark "suffered the most over" and "learned the most from" since Miller was, as a character, the farthest from his own personal experience—yet a good character to start with, Clark believes, to gain the proper artistic distance for his subject. The publication of this collection and novella—actually, more of a novel-in-stories—gave Clark a "real impetus" to move on to other projects, namely a novel, *Jackdog Summer* (Indian Chief, 1996), two collections, *All the Way Home* (Avisson, 1997) and *Rabbit Fever* (Avisson, 2000), and his second novel, *Wedding in October* (2002).

In *Jackdog Summer*, Clay "Doc" Knowles comes up against the raw horror of Michigan's redneck, good old boy culture—represented as cruel, intolerant of basic goodness, and bordering on madness. Doc, says Clark, "seeks a place where you can't be reached by the general chaos and evil of the world," but like Axel Heyst of Conrad's *Victory*, he discovers "that the forces of evil and negation will seek him out unerringly nonetheless." The collisions of class and culture are a pervasive feature of Clark's work. His central characters feel the need to affirm their identity in the Michigan soil they sprang from; they feel antagonism, sometimes real hatred, for the uppity Eastern intruders—as well as urban types—with their arrogance born of privilege. Clark's major characters are educated but not urbane. They are drawn to Michigan, but they are not rednecks—though they sometimes hover on being so. Like Clark himself, they are in limbo, unable to get Michigan out of their blood—and not really wanting to.

The form that suits Clark the most is the novel—though he has an impressive list of publications in literary magazines. But with the novel, Clark says, "there's plenty of maneuvering room," and the form itself "can sometimes transcend flaws through its cumulative power—with a story, a single mishandled line can ruin the thing." Also, a novel, being a "big project," allows for a day-to-day kind of engagement, "and at night it sort of sleeps on your scalp, as they say." When Clark finishes a short story, he feels temporarily "lost," but when he's at work on a novel, he has his work before him: "trying to push the imagination forward, but in such a way that the imagination rather than the will is engaged and does the heavy lifting." A story Clark may intend to keep short sometimes "will expand even though I don't want it to." *Wedding in October* began as a story he "desperately" tried to keep to 20 pages, but as he wrote, line breaks became numbered parts, numbered parts chapters, with a series of vignettes and quasi-stories interspersed between the chapters. While short stories threaten to turn into novels, longer narratives often present short story possibilities, with Clark "looking for endings," then backtracking to "where the narrative unit seems to begin."

Clark is a veteran keeper of notebooks, a daily recorder of the life around him. Henry James's notion of being one on whom nothing is lost greatly appeals to him, though Clark doesn't see his own mind so much as a "register"; he likens it more to a "lint brush—it picks up all sorts of junk and sinks it into my consciousness for no good reason I can discern." For years he has jotted down "ideas, bits of dialogue, description, etc.," and Clark says, "I'm sometimes astonished at how much of the stuff I put down without much thought ends up in my fiction."

Writing is the part that Clark likes best—the whole process of getting published the least. Clark recalls what his teacher at Iowa, Richard Yates, once said—that "writing the work was the best of the whole process, and as for the rest, you could have it . . . and he suggested the very best kind of publication was that which came about by accident." On this one, Clark has to laugh: "Try and tell that to an eager-beaver creative writing student!"

For the aspiring writer, Clark cautions that the literary magazine world is "generally a pig-in-a-poke world, so all the more reason to nurture relationships among editors and staff and other writers with whom you share an affinity." For book manuscripts, Clark, with plenty of experience in small press publishing himself, recommends that young authors "practice a kind of 'networking,' and keep in touch with any friends and acquaintances they make in the small press world—about half of my own works have found a home through chance or running into the right person." For instance, editor Greg Boyd at Asylum Arts, publisher of *Schooling*, later moved to another publishing house and solicited *Jackdog Summer*.

Clark believes his most valuable asset as a writer is not talent or intelligence. "I knew people at the workshop whom I felt were vastly superior to me in those respects." It's been his "perseverance, even doggedness." And his patience. "If you don't have a lot of innate patience, now's the time to start developing it. Writing is not an enterprise for people who want things to happen right away."

As to his future literary endeavors, Clark is now working steadily away at another novel on Michigan, *Upstart Clay*. He says, "I see this novel as a kind of multi-level work of fiction that encompasses story, novella and novel: each of the various pieces can exist as a discrete entity, yet can as well correlate with other parts." The novel will be narrated, except for the epilogue, by another of Clark's major characters: Larry Carstairs of *All the Way Home*. "A number of my previous denizens of Ermine Falls [Michigan] will be re-visited in middle-age." *Upstart Clay*

will include all of Clark's "Larry" stories, plus *All the Way Home* (the novella part of the collection by this title), then "a four-part sequence picking up after *All the Way Home*." As Clark says, "Once I get comfortable with my characters, as with the Springstead and Knowles brothers, I like to revisit them in later fiction." The result is that readers get to know Clark's Michigan fictional landscape—his denizens as well as exiles—as this world evolves from work to work, much as one gets to know Hemingway's Michigan or Faulkner's Mississippi.
—Jack Smith

N: THE OAKLEA PRESS, 6912-B Three Chopt Road, Richmond VA 23226. (804)281-5872. Fax: (804)281-5686. E-mail: jgots@oakleapress.com. Website: www.oakleapress.com. **Contact:** John Gotschalk, editor (visionary fiction). Publishes hardcover and trade paperback originals. **Publishes 25% of books from first-time authors; 100% from unagented writers.**
Needs: Mystery, occult, suspense, visionary fiction. "We like fast-paced adventure, suspense, and mystery stories that have an underpinning of metaphysics/spirituality." Recently published *Under a Lemon Moon*, by David Martin (fiction).
How to Contact: Submit proposal package including 1 sample chapter(s), synopsis. Accepts simultaneous submissions. Responds in 1 month to queries; 3 months to mss.
Terms: Pays 10-20% royalty on wholesale price. Publishes book 6 months after acceptance of ms. Book catalog online.

N: OCEAN VIEW BOOKS, P.O. Box 9249, Denver CO 80209. **Contact:** Lee Ballentine, editor. Publishes hardcover originals and trade paperback originals. **Publishes 100% from unagented writers.** Averages 2 titles/year.
Needs: Literary, science fiction. "Ocean View Books is an award-winning publisher of new speculative and slipstream fiction, poetry, criticism, surrealism." Recently published *Missing Pieces*, by Kathryn Ramtan.
How to Contact: Does not accept simultaneous submissions. Responds to queries in 2 months, if interested.
Terms: Pays royalty. Offers advance.

N: ODD GIRLS PRESS, P.O. Box 2157, Anaheim CA 92814-0157. (800)821-0632. Fax: (419)735-2084. E-mail: publisher@oddgirlspress.com. Website: www.oddgirlspress.com. Estab. 1995. Publishes trade paperback originals. **Publishes 25% of books from first-time authors; 95% from unagented writers.** Averages 4 titles/year.
Needs: Fantasy, feminist, gay/lesbian, historical, literary, mystery, poetry, science fiction, suspense, western, young adult. All fiction must be lesbian-related. "We are looking for well-written material submitted in a professional manner following our guidelines. As a feminist press, we only accept writing by women."
How to Contact: Submit complete ms. Accepts simultaneous submissions. Responds in 1 month to queries; 3 months to mss.
Terms: Pays 7-10% royalty on retail price. Publishes book 1 year after acceptance of ms. Book catalog free; ms guidelines for #10 SASE.
Advice: "Our books are read by a wide range of readers, working class to academic. Our goal is to publish fiction and nonfiction covering topics of interest to contemporary lesbians. We will not accept mss written by men, even if the protagonist is lesbian or bisexual. We are looking for authors who know how to write and whose mss are not works in progress but finished books. Our editors work closely with the authors to polish mss and keep the author's voice intact."

N: A: O: ONE WORLD BOOKS, Ballantine Publishing Group, Inc., 1540 Broadway, 11th Floor, New York NY 10036. (212)782-8378. Fax: (212)782-8442. E-mail: adiggs@randomhouse.com. **Contact:** Anita Diggs, senior editor. Publishes hardcover, trade and mass market paperback originals and trade paperback reprints. **Publishes 50% of books from first-time authors; 5% from unagented writers.** Averages 24 titles/year.
Needs: "All One World Books must be specifically written for either an African-American, Asian or Hispanic audience. Absolutely no exceptions!" Adventure, comic books, confession, erotica, ethnic, historical, humor, literary, mainstream/contemporary, multicultural, mystery, regional, romance, suspense, strong need for commercial women's fiction. No poetry. Recently published *Bittersweet*, by Freddie Lee Johnson III.
How to Contact: *Agented submissions only. Accepts simultaneous submissions. Responds in 1 month to queries; 2 months to mss.*
Terms: Pays 7½-15% royalty on retail price. Offers $40,000-200,000 advance. Publishes book 18 months after acceptance of ms.
Advice: Targets African-American, Asian and Hispanic readers. All books must be written in English.

N: ♣ ○ © ORCA BOOK PUBLISHERS LTD., P.O. Box 5626, Station B, Victoria, British Columbia V8R 6S4 Canada. (250)380-1229. Fax: (250)380-1892. E-mail: orca@orcabook.com. Website: www.orcabooks.com. Publisher: R.J. Tyrrell. Estab. 1984. **Contact:** Ann Featherstone, children's book editor. Publishes hardcover and paperback originals. Books: quality 60 lb. book stock paper; illustrations. Average print order: 3,000-5,000. First novel print order: 3,000-5,000. Plans 3-4 first novels this year. Averages 35-30 total titles. Sometimes comments on rejected mss.

Needs: Contemporary, juvenile (5-9 years), literary, mainstream, young adult/teen (10-18 years). Looking for "contemporary fiction." No "romance, science fiction."
How to Contact: Query first, then submit outline/synopsis and 1 or 2 sample chapters. SASE. Agented fiction 20%. Responds in 2 weeks to queries; 2 months to mss. Publishes Canadian authors only.
Terms: Pays royalties of 10%; $1,500 average advance. Sends galleys to author. Publishes ms 6 months-1 year after acceptance. Guidelines available for SASE; book catalog for 8½×11 SASE.
Advice: "We are looking to promote and publish Canadians."

ORIENT PAPERBACKS, A Division of Vision Books Pvt Ltd., Madarsa Rd., Kashmere Gate, Delhi 110 006 India. Phone: +91-11-386-2201 or +91-11-386-2267. Fax: +91-11-386-2935. E-mail: orientpbk@vsnl.com. Website: www.orientpaperbacks.com. **Contact:** Sudhir Malhotra, editor. Averages 10-15 novels or story collections/year. "We are one of the largest paperback publishers in S.E. Asia and publish English fiction by authors from this part of the world."
Needs: Length: 40,000 words minimum.
How to Contact: Send cover letter, brief summary, 1 sample chapter and author's bio data. "We send writers' guidelines on accepting a proposal."
Terms: Pays royalty on copies sold.

OUGHTEN HOUSE FOUNDATION, INC., P.O. Box 1826, Coarsegold CA 93614. (937)767-9368. Fax: (937)767-1210. E-mail: info@oughtenhouse.com. Website: www.oughtenhouse.com. **Contact:** Dr. Robert J. Gerard, senior acquisitions editor (alternative health and self-help). Publishes trade paperback originals. Averages 2 titles/year.
Needs: Humor, spiritual.
How to Contact: Query with SASE. Does not accept simultaneous submissions. Responds in 3 months to queries.
Terms: Ms guidelines online.
Advice: "We are oriented toward spirituality and alternative medicine/health. It must be unique and substantial."

OUR CHILD PRESS, P.O. Box 4379, Philadephia PA 19118-8379. Phone/fax: (610)722-9111. E-mail: ocp98@aol.com. Website: www.ourchildpress.com. **Contact:** Carol Hallenbeck, CEO. Estab. 1984. Publishes hardcover and paperback originals and reprints.
• Received the Ben Franklin Award for *Don't Call Me Marda*, by Sheila Welch.
Needs: Especially interested in books on adoption or learning disabilities. Recently published *Things Little Kids Need to Know*, by Susan Uhlig.
How to Contact: Does not accept unsolicited mss. Send query letter. Responds in 2 weeks to queries; 2 months to mss. Accepts simultaneous submissions. Sometimes comments on rejected mss.
Terms: Pays royalties of 5% minimum. Publishes ms up to 6 months after acceptance. Book catalog available free.

PETER OWEN PUBLISHERS, 73 Kenway Rd., London SW5 ORE England. Phone: 44+ 020 7373 5628. Fax: 44+ 020 7373 6760. E-mail: admin@peterowen.com. Website: www.peterowen.com (includes complete backlist, book catalog plus ordering information). **Contact**: Antonia Owen, editorial director/fiction editor. "Independent publishing house from 1951. Publish literary fiction from around the world, from Russia to Japan. Publishers of Shusaku Endo, Paul and Jane Bowles, Hermann Hesse, Octavio Paz, Colette, etc." Averages 4 fiction titles/year. Titles distributed through Central Books, London, and Dufour Editions, USA.
Needs: Does not accept short stories, only excerpts from novels of normal length. Recently published *Hermes in Paris*, by Peter Vansittart (literary fiction); *Doubting Thomas*, by Atle Naess (translated literary fiction); *Lady Jean*, by Noel Virtue (fiction).
How to Contact: Query by post or e-mail with synopsis and/or sample chapter or submit through agent (preferred). Send SASE (or IRC).
Terms: Pays standard royalty. Average advance. Book catalog available for SASE, SAE with IRC or on website.
Advice: "Be concise. It helps if author is familiar with our list. New fiction is very hard to sell in the U.K.; it is also hard to get it reviewed. At the moment we are publishing less fiction than nonfiction."

RICHARD C. OWEN PUBLISHERS INC., P.O. Box 585, Katonah NY 10536. Fax: (914)232-3903. Website: www.rcowen.com (includes guidelines, book-of-the-month sample book, teacher development). **Contact:** Janice Boland, director of children's books. "We believe children become enthusiastic, independent, life-long readers when supported and guided by skillful teachers who choose books with real and lasting value. The professional development work we do and the books we publish support these beliefs." Publishes paperback originals. **Published 15 previously unpublished writers within the last year.** Distributes titles to schools via mail order. Promotes titles through website, database mailing, reputation, catalog, brochures and appropriate publications—magazines, etc.
Needs: Picture books. "Brief, strong story line, real characters, natural language, exciting—child-appealing stories with a twist. No lists, alphabet or counting books." Also seeking mss for upcoming anthologies of short, snappy stories and articles for 7-8-year-old children (2nd grade). Subjects include humor, careers, mysteries, science fiction, folktales, women, fashion trends, sports, music, mysteries, myths, journalism, history, inventions, planets, architecture, plays, adventure, technology, vehicles. Recently published *Mama Cut My Hair*, by Lisa Wilkinson (fiction, debut author); *Cool*, by Steven Morse (fiction, debut author); and *Author on My Street*, by Lisa Brodie Cook (fiction).
How to Contact: Send for ms guidelines, then submit full ms with SASE. No fax or e-mail queries. Responds in 1 month to queries; 2 months to mss. Accepts simultaneous submissions, if so noted.

Terms: Pays royalties of 5% on wholesale price; Books for Young Learners Anthologies and picture storybooks: flat fee for all rights. Publishes ms 3 years after acceptance. Guidelines available for SASE with 52¢ postage.

Advice: "Send entire ms. Write clear strong stories with memorable characters and end with a big wind up finish. Write for today's children—about real things that interest them. Read books that your public library features in their children's room to acquaint yourself with the best modern children's literature."

N ◯ ◎ PALARI PUBLISHING, P.O. Box 9288, Richmond VA 23227-0288. (804)883-6112. Fax: (804)883-5234. E-mail: palaripub@aol.com. Website: www.palari.net (includes writer's guidelines). **Contact:** David Smitherman, fiction editor. Estab. 1998. Small publisher specializing in southern mysteries and nonfiction. Publishes hardcover and paperback originals. **Published 2 new writers within the last year.** Averages 4 total titles, 2 fiction titles/year. Distributes titles through Baker & Taylor, Ingram, Amazon, mail order and website. Promotes titles through book signings, direct mail and the Internet. Member, Publishers Marketing Association.

Needs: Adventure, erotica, gay, historical, horror, lesbian, literary, mainstream, mystery/suspense, thriller/espionage. Recently published *We're Still Here* (cultural); and *Face Time* (Hollywood, gay).

How to Contact: Accepts unsolicited mss. Query with outline/synopsis and 3 sample chapters. Accepts queries by e-mail and fax. Include estimated word count, 1 page bio, Social Security number and list of publishing credits. Send SASE or IRC for return of ms or send disposable copy of ms and SASE for reply only. Responds in 1 month to queries; 2 months to mss. Accepts simultaneous and electronic submissions. Often comments on rejected mss.

Terms: Pays royalties. Publishes ms within 1 year after acceptance. Guidelines available on website.

Advice: "Send a good bio. I'm interested in a writer's experience and unique outlook on life."

PANTHEON BOOKS, Imprint of The Knopf Publishing Group, A Division of Random House, Inc., 299 Park Ave., New York NY 10171. (212)751-2600. Fax: (212)572-6030. Website: www.pantheonbooks.com. Editorial Director: Dan Frank. Senior Editors: Deborah Garrison, Shelley Wagner. Executive Editor: Erroll McDonald. **Contact:** Adult Editorial Department. Estab. 1942. "Small but well-established imprint of well-known large house." Publishes hardcover and trade paperback originals and trade paperback reprints. Averages 75 total titles, about 25 fiction titles/year.

Needs: Quality fiction and nonfiction. Published *Crooked Little Heart*, by Anne Lamott.

How to Contact: Does not accept unsolicited mss. Query with cover letter and sample material. Send SASE or IRC for return.

Terms: Pays royalties; offers advance.

N PANTHER CREEK PRESS, P.O. Box 130233, Spring TX 77393-0233. E-mail: panthercreek3@hotmail.com. Website: www.panthercreekpress.com. **Contact:** Bobbi Sissel, editor (literary); Jerry Cooke, assistant editor (mystery); William Laufer, assistant editor (collections). Estab. 1999. "Mid-size publisher interested in Merchant-Ivory type fiction." Publishes paperback originals. Books: 60 lb. white paper; docutech-printed; perfect-bound. Average print order: 1,500. Average first novel print order: 1,500. **Published 4 debut authors within the last year.** Plans 5 first novels next year. Averages 6 total titles, 4-5 fiction titles/year. Distributes titles through Baker & Taylor, Amazon.

Imprint(s): Enigma Books, Jerry Cooke, editor (mystery).

Needs: Ethnic/multicultural, experimental, humor/satire, literary, mystery/suspense (amateur sleuth), regional (Texana), short story collections. Recently published *The Caballeros of Ruby, Texas*, Cynthia Leal Massey (literary); *Under a Riverbed Sky*, by Christopher Woods (literary collection); and *Killing Daddy: A Caprock Story*, by Sandra Gail Teichmann (literary experimental novel).

How to Contact: Does not accept unsolicited mss. Send query letter. Accepts queries by e-mail. Include estimated word count, brief bio and list of publishing credits with submission. Send either SASE for return of ms or disposable ms and SASE for reply only. Responds in 3 weeks to queries; 5 weeks to mss. Considers simultaneous submissions.

Terms: Pays royalties of 10% and 5 author's copies. Sends galleys to author. Publishes ms 1 year after acceptance. Guidelines and catalog available on website.

Advice: "We would enjoy seeing more experimental work, but 'shock' narrative does not interest us. We don't want to see thrillers, fantasies, horror. The small, thoughtful literary story that large publishers don't want to take a chance on is the kind that gets our attention."

◎ PAPYRUS PUBLISHERS & LETTERBOX SERVICE, P.O. Box 27383, Las Vegas NV 89126-1383. (702)256-3838. Website: www.booksbyletterbox.com. Managing Editor: Anthony Wade. **Contact:** Geoffrey Hutchison-Cleaves, editor-in-chief; Jessie Rosé, fiction editor. Estab. London 1946; USA 1982. Mid-size independent press. Publishes hardcover originals. Books: audio. Average print order 5,000. Averages 3 total titles/year. Promotes titles through mail, individual author fliers, author tours.

Imprint(s): Letterbox Service; Difficult Subjects Made Easy.

How to Contact: "Not accepting right now. Fully stocked."

Advice: "Don't send it, unless you have polished and polished and polished. Absolutely no established author sends off a piece that has just been 'written' once. That is the first draft of many!"

◎ PEACHTREE PUBLISHERS, LTD., 1700 Chattahoochee Ave., Atlanta GA 30318. (404)876-8761. Fax: (404)875-2578. Website: www.peachtree-online.com (includes writer's guidelines, current catalog of titles, upcoming promotional events, behind-the-scenes look at creating a book). President: Margaret Quinlin. **Contact:** Helen Harriss, fiction editors. Estab. 1977. Independent publisher specializing in children's literature, nonfiction and regional guides.

Publishes hardcover and paperback originals and hardcover reprints. First novel print run 3,000. **Published 2 new writers within the last year.** Averages 18-20 total titles, 1-2 children's fiction titles/year. Promotes titles through review copies to appropriate publications, press kits and book signings at local bookstores.
Imprint(s): Freestone and Peachtree Jr.
Needs: Young adult and juvenile fiction. "Absolutely no adult fiction! We are seeking YA and juvenile works including mystery and historical fiction, of high literary merit."
How to Contact: Accepts unsolicited mss. Query, submit outline/synopsis and 3 chapters, or submit complete ms with SASE. Responds in 6 months to queries; 6 months to mss. Accepts simultaneous submissions. Do not fax or e-mail queries, manuscripts or submissions
Terms: Pays in royalties. Sends galleys to author. Free writer's guidelines. Publishes ms 2 years after acceptance. Book catalog available for 5 first-class stamps.
Advice: "Check out our website or catalog for the kinds of things we are interested in."

PEDLAR PRESS, P.O. Box 26, Station P, Toronto, Ontario M5S 2S6 Canada. (416)534-2011. Fax: (416)535-9677. E-mail: feralgrl@interlog.com. **Contact:** Beth Follett, editor (fiction, poetry). Publishes hardcover and trade paperback originals. **Publishes 50% of books from first-time authors; 100% from unagented writers.** Averages **Publishes 4 titles/year.**
Needs: Erotica, experimental, feminist, gay/lesbian, humor, literary, picture books, poetry, short story collections. Recently published *Mouthing the Words*, by Camilla Gibb.
How to Contact: Query with SASE or submit proposal package including 5 sample chapter(s), synopsis. Accepts simultaneous submissions. Responds in 1 month to queries; 6 months to mss.
Terms: Pays 10-15% royalty on retail price. Offers $400-800 advance. Publishes book 1 year after acceptance of ms. Book catalog for #10 SASE; ms guidelines for #10 SASE.
Advice: "We select manuscripts according to our taste. Be familiar with some if not most of our recent titles."

PELICAN PUBLISHING COMPANY, Box 3110, Gretna LA 70054-3110. (504)368-1175. Website: www.pelicanpub.com (includes writer's guidelines, featured book, index of Pelican books). **Contact**: Nina Kooij, editor-in-chief. Estab. 1926. "We seek writers on the cutting edge of ideas. We believe ideas have consequences. One of the consequences is that they lead to a bestselling book." Publishes hardcover and paperback originals and reprints. Books: hardcover and paperback binding; illustrations sometimes. Buys juvenile mss with illustrations. Distributes titles internationally through distributors, bookstores, libraries. Promotes titles at reading and book conventions, in trade magazines, in radio interviews, print reviews and TV interviews.
- *The Warlord's Puzzle*, by Virginia Walton Pilegard was #2 on *Independent Bookseller*'s Book Sense 76 list. *Dictionary of Literary Biography* lists *Unforgotten*, by D.J. Meador as "one of the best of 1999."
Needs: Juvenile fiction, especially with a regional and/or historical focus. No young adult fiction, contemporary fiction or fiction containing graphic language, violence or sex. Also no "psychological" novels. Recently published *The Loki Project*, by Benjamin King (adult historical fiction); and *There Was an Ol' Cajun*, by Deborah Ousley Kadair (children's tale, debut author).
How to Contact: Does not accept unsolicited mss. Send query letter. May submit outline/synopsis and 2 sample chapters with SASE. "Not responsible if writer's only copy is sent." Responds in 1 month to queries; 3 months to mss. Comments on rejected mss "infrequently."
Terms: Pays royalties of 10% and 10 contributor's copies; advance considered. Sends galleys to author. Publishes ms 9-18 months after acceptance. Catalog of titles and writer's guidelines for SASE.
Advice: "Research the market carefully. Check our catalog to see if your work is consistent with our list. For ages 8 and up, story must be planned in chapters that will fill at least 90 double-spaced manuscript pages. Topic for ages 8-12 must be Louisiana related and historical. We look for stories that illuminate a particular place and time in history and that are clean entertainment. The only original adult work we might consider is historical fiction, preferably Civil War (not romance). Please don't send three or more chapters unless solicited. Follow our guidelines listed under 'How to Contact.' "

PENGUIN PUTNAM BOOKS FOR YOUNG READERS, (Division of Penguin Putnam Inc.), 345 Hudson St., New York NY 10014. (212)366-2000. E-mail: online@penguinputnam.com. Website: www.penguinputnam.com. Estab.1838. Publishes hardcover and paperback.
Imprint(s): Dial Books for Young Readers; Dutton Children's Books; Dutton Interactive; Phyllis Fogelman Books; Grosset & Dunlap; Paperstar; Philomel; Planet Dexter; Platt & Munk; Playskool; Price Stern Loan; PSS; Puffin Books; G P Putnam's Sons; Viking Children's Books; Frederick Wayne.

PENGUIN PUTNAM INC., (Subsidiary of Pearson plc), 375 Hudson St., New York NY 10014. (212)366-2717. E-mail: online@penguinputnam.com. Website: www.penguinputnam.com. Estab. 1838. "The company possesses perhaps the world's most prestigious list of best-selling authors and a backlist of unparalleled breadth, depth, and quality." Publishes hardcover and paperback originals and reprints.
Imprint(s): Viking (hardcover); Dutton (hardcover); Viking Studio (hardcover); The Penguin Press (hardcover); DAW (hardcover and paperback); G P Putnam's Sons (hardcover and children's); Riverhead Books (hardcocver and paperback); Jeremy P Tarcher (hardcover and paperback); Grosset/Putnam (harcover); Ace/Putnam (hardcover); Boulevard (hardcover and paperback); Putnam (hardcover); Price Stern Sloan Inc (hardcover, paperback and children's); Marian Wood Books (hardcover); Avery; BlueHen (hardcover); Viking Compass (hardcover); Penguin (paperback); Penguin Classics

(paperback); Plume (paperback); Signet (paperback); Signet Classics (paperback); Onyx (paperback); Roc (paperback); Topaz (paperback); Mentor (paperback); Meridian (paperback); Berkley Books (paperback); Jove (paperback); Ace (paperback); Perigee (paperback); Prime Crime (paperback); HPBooks (paperbacks); Penguin Compass (paperback); Dial Books for Young Readers (children's); Dutton Children's Books (children's); Viking Children's Books (children's); Puffin (children's); Frederick Warne (children's); Philomel Books (children's); Grosset and Dunlap (children's); Wee Sing (children's); PaperStar (children's); Planet Dexter (children's).

PERFECTION LEARNING CORP., 10520 New York Ave., Des Moines IA 50322-3775. (515)278-0133. Fax: (515)278-2980. E-mail: sthies@plconline.com. Website: www.perfectionlearning.com (includes writer's guidelines, names of editors, book catalog). **Contact:** Sue Thies, editorial director. "We are an educational publisher of hi/lo fiction and nonfiction with teacher support material." **Published 10 new writers within the last year.** Publishes 50-75 total titles/year, fiction and nonfiction. Distributes titles through sales reps, direct mail and online catalog. Promotes titles through educational conferences, journals and catalogs.

Imprint(s): Cover-to-Cover; Sue Thies, editorial director (all genres).

Needs: Hi/lo mss in all genres. Readability of ms should be at least two grade levels below interest level. "Please do not submit mss with fewer than 4,000 words or more than 30,000 words." Published *Tall Shadow*, by Bonnie Highsmith Taylor (Native American); *The Rattlesnack Necklace*, by Linda Baxter (historical fiction); and *Tales of Mark Twain*, by Peg Hall (retold short stories).

How to Contact: Accepts unsolicited mss. Query with outline/synopsis and 3-4 sample chapters or submit complete ms with a cover letter. Accepts queries by e-mail and fax. Include 1-page bio, estimated word count and list of publishing credits. Send SASE or IRC for return of ms or send a disposable copy of ms and SASE for reply only. Responds in 3 months. Accepts simultaneous submissions.

Terms: Publishes ms 6-8 months after acceptance. Guidelines available on website; book catalog for 9×12 SASE with $2.31 postage.

Advice: "We are an educational publisher. Check with educators to find out their needs, their students' needs and what's popular."

THE PERMANENT PRESS, 4170 Noyac Rd., Sag Harbor NY 11963-2809. (631)725-1101. Fax: (631)725-8215. Website: www.thepermanentpress.com (includes catalog, updates, ordering info). **Contact**: Judith and Martin Shepard, publishers. Estab. 1977. Mid-size, independent publisher of literary fiction. Publishes hardcover originals. Average print order: 1,500. First novel print order: 1,500. **Published 4 new writers within the last year.** Averages 12 fiction titles/year. "We keep titles in print and are active in selling subsidiary rights." Distributes titles through Ingram, Baker & Taylor and Brodart. Promotes titles through reviews.

Needs: Accepts any fiction category as long as it is a "well-written, original full-length novel." Recently published *Walking the Perfect Square*, by Reed Farrell Coleman (mystery); *Lydia Cassat Reading the Morning Paper*, by Harriet Scott Chessman (fiction); *Fresh Eggs*, by Rob Levandoski (fiction); and *The Foodtaster*, by Ugo DiFonte (fiction, debut author).

How to Contact: Accepts unsolicited mss. Query with no more than 2 chapters. No queries by fax. Send SASE for return of ms or send disposable copy with SASE for reply. Responds in 3 weeks to queries; 4 months to mss. Accepts simultaneous submissions.

Terms: Pays royalties of 5-15%. Standard advance: $1,000. Sends galleys to author. Publishes ms up to 2 years after acceptance. Book catalog available for $3.

Advice: "We are looking for good books, be they tenth novels or first ones, it makes little difference. The fiction is more important than the track record. Send us the beginning of the story, it's impossible to judge something that begins on page 302. Also, no outlines—let the writing present itself."

DAVID PHILIP PUBLISHERS, P.O. Box 23408, Claremont 7735 South Africa. Fax: (21)6743358. E-mail: russell.martin@dpp.co.za.

Needs: "Fiction with Southern African concern or focus. Progressive, often suitable for school or university prescription, literary, serious."

How to Contact: Send synopsis and 1 sample chapter.

Terms: Pays royalties. Write for guidelines.

Advice: "Familiarize yourself with list of publisher to which you wish to submit work."

PHILOMEL BOOKS, Imprint of the Children's Division of Penguin Putnam Inc., 345 Hudson St., New York NY 10014. (212)414-3610. **Contact**: Patricia Lee Gauch, editorial director; Michael Green, senior editor. Estab. 1980. "A high-quality oriented imprint focused on stimulating picture books, middle-grade novels, and young adult novels." Publishes hardcover originals. Averages 25 total titles, 5-7 novels/year.

Needs: Adventure, ethnic, family saga, fantasy, historical, juvenile (5-9 years), literary, preschool/picture book, regional, short story collections, translations, western (young adult), young adult/teen (10-18 years). Looking for "story-driven novels with a strong cultural voice but which speak universally." No "generic, mass-market oriented fiction." Published *The Long Patrol*, by Brian Jacques; *I Am Morgan LeFay*, by Nancy Springer; and *Betty Doll*, by Patricia Palacco.

How to Contact: No unsolicited mss. Query first or submit outline/synopsis and first 3 chapters. Send SASE or IRC for return of ms. Agented fiction 40%. Responds in 10 weeks to queries; up to 4 months to mss. Accepts simultaneous submissions. Sometimes comments on rejected ms.

Terms: Pays royalties, negotiable advance and author's copies. Sends galleys to author. Publishes ms anywhere from 1-2 years after acceptance. Guidelines available for #10 SASE; book catalog for 9×12 SASE.

Advice: "We are not a mass-market publisher and do not publish short stories independently. In addition, we do just a few novels a year."

N THE PHOENIX GROUP, P.O. Box 20536, San Jose CA 95160. (877)594-9076. Fax: (877)594-9076. E-mail: info@tpgpub.com. Website: www.tpgpub.com. **Contact:** June Rouse, editor (holistic, self-help, spiritual), Vita Goins, assistant editor (mystery, suspense, thrillers). Publishes trade paperback, mass market paperback and electronic originals. Averages 1-3 titles/year.

Needs: Adventure, experimental, mystery, science fiction, spiritual, suspense.

How to Contact: Submit proposal package including 3 sample chapter(s), synopsis. Does not accept simultaneous submissions. Responds in 6 weeks.

Terms: Pays 8-25% royalty on retail price. Book catalog and ms guidlines free or online.

PIANO PRESS, P.O. Box 85, Del Mar CA 92014-0085. (858)481-5650. Fax: (858)755-1104. E-mail: pianopr ess@aol.com. Website: www.pianopress.com (includes company description, product line, ordering information and writer's guidelines). **Contact:** Elizabeth C. Axford, M.A., editor (short stories/picture books). Estab. 1999. "Piano Press is an independent publisher. We publish books, songbooks and CDs on music-related topics only, as well as some poetry." Books: medium weight paper; mimeo/offset printing; comb, spiral, saddle stitched or perfect-bound; music manuscripts and music graphics as illustrations. Average print order: 1,000-5,000. Averages 1-10 total titles, 3 fiction titles/year. Member, SCBWI, PMA, ASCAP, NARAS and MIC. Distributes titles through wholesale distribution, Baker & Taylor.

Needs: Children's/juvenile (preschool/picture book, music related only), ethnic/multicultural (music), short story collections. "Looking for short stories on music-related topics only. Also short stories and/or essays for our annual anthology, *The Art of Music—A Collection of Writings.*" Writers may submit and/or enter annual contest. See Contests & Awards. Recently published *Merry Christmas, Happy Hanukkah—A Multilingual Songbook & CD*; *The Musical ABC*; *Music and Me*; and *Strum a Song of Angels*.

How to Contact: Accepts unsolicited mss. Send query letter. Accepts queries by e-mail. Include estimated word count, brief bio, list of publishing credits and music background. Send SASE or IRC for return of ms or send disposable copy of ms and SASE for reply only. Responds in 3 months to queries; 6 months to mss. Accepts simultaneous and electronic submissions. Sometimes comments on rejected mss.

Terms: Pays author's copies or royalties. Sends galleys to author. Publishes ms 6-18 months after acceptance. Guidelines and book catalog available free for #10 SAE and first-class postage.

Advice: "We feel there is a need for more original writings on music-related topics. Work should be complete, original, fresh and legible. Typewritten manuscripts only, please. Please do not send non-music related material."

N PIÑATA BOOKS, Imprint of Arte Publico Press, University of Houston, Houston TX 77204-2174. (713)743-2841. Fax: (713)743-2847. Website: www.arte.uh.edu. **Contact:** Nicolas Kanellos, director. Estab. 1994. "We are dedicated to the publication of children's and young adult literature focusing on U.S. Hispanic culture." Publishes hardcover and trade paperback originals. **Published new writers within the last year.** Averages 10-15 total titles/year.

Needs: Adventure, juvenile, picture books, young adult. Published *Trino's Choice*, by Diane Gonzales Bertrand (ages 11-up); *Delicious Hullabaloo/Pachanga Deliciosa*, by Pat Mora (picture book); and *The Year of Our Revolution*, by Judith Ortiz Cofer (young adult).

How to Contact: Does not accept unsolicited mss. Query with synopsis, 2 sample chapters and SASE for reply. Responds in 1 month to queries; 6 months to mss. Accepts simultaneous submissions.

Terms: Pays royalties of 10% on wholesale price. Average advance: $1,000-3,000. Publishes ms 2 years after acceptance. Guidelines and book catalog available on website or with #10 SASE.

Advice: "Include cover letter with submission explaining why your manuscript is unique and important, why we should publish it, who will buy it, relevance to the U.S. Hispanic culture, etc."

PINEAPPLE PRESS, P.O. Box 3899, Sarasota FL 34230-3899. (800)746-3275. Fax: (941)351-9988. E-mail: info@pineapplepress.com. Website: www.pineapplepress.com (includes searchable database of titles, news events, featured books, company profile, and option to request a hard copy of catalog). **Contact:** June Cussen, executive editor. Estab. 1982. Small independent trade publisher. Publishes hardcover and paperback originals. Books: quality paper; offset printing; Smyth-sewn or perfect-bound; illustrations occasionally. **Published new writers within the last year.** Averages 20 total titles/year. Distributes titles through Pineapple, Ingram and Baker & Taylor. Promotes titles through reviews, advertising in print media, direct mail, author signings and the World Wide Web.

Needs: Historical, literary, mainstream, regional (most fiction is set in Florida). Recently published *At the Edge of Honor*, by Robert Macomber (novel).

How to Contact: No unsolicited mss. Query with outline, brief synopsis and sample chapters. Send SASE or IRC for reply. Responds in 3 months. Accepts simultaneous submissions.

Terms: Pays royalties of 6½-15% on net price. Advance is not usually offered. "Basically, it is an individual agreement with each author depending on the book." Sends galleys to author. Publishes ms 18 months after acceptance. Book catalog available for 9×12 SAE with $1.24 postage.

Advice: "Quality first novels will be published, though we usually only do one or two novels per year. We regard the author/editor relationship as a trusting relationship with communication open both ways. Learn all you can about the publishing process and about how to promote your book once it is published. A query on a novel without a brief sample seems useless."

PIPERS' ASH LTD., Church Rd., Christian Malford, Chippenham, Wiltshire SN15 4BW United Kingdom. Phone: 01249 720563. Fax: 0870 0568916. E-mail: pipersash@supamasu.com. Website: www.supamasu.com (includes catalog and guidelines). **Contact:** Manuscript Evaluation Desk. Estab. 1976. "Small press publisher. Considers all submitted manuscripts fairly—without bias or favor." This company is run by book-lovers, not by accountants. Publishes hardcover and paperback originals and reprints. **Published 12 new writers within the last year.** Averages 12 fiction titles/year. Distributes and promotes titles through direct mail and the Internet.

Needs: Adventure, children's/juvenile (adventure), literary, romance (contemporary, romantic suspense), science fiction (hard science/technological, soft/sociological), short story collections, translations, western (frontier saga, traditional), young adult/teen (adventure, fantasy/science fiction). Currently emphasizing stage plays. Planning anthologies: short stories, science fiction, poetry. "Authors are invited to submit collections of short stories and poetry for consideration for our ongoing programs." Recently published *Jessica A.*, by Phyllis Wyatt (war-time romance); *Recitable Rhymes*, by Alan Millard (poetry); *Tales from Thailand* (travel adventure).

How to Contact: Accepts unsolicited mss. Query with synopsis and first chapter. Accepts queries by e-mail, fax and phone. Include estimated word count. Send SASE or IRC for return of ms or send disposable copy of ms and SASE for reply only. Responds in 1 week to queries; up to 3 months to mss. Accepts electronic submissions and disk. Always comments on rejected mss.

Terms: Pays royalties of 10% and 5 author's copies. No advance. Sends galleys to author. Publishes ms 2 months after acceptance. Guidelines available on website; book catalog A5 SASE and on website.

Advice: "Study the market! Check your selected publisher's catalogue."

PIPPIN PRESS, 229 E. 85th Street, Gracie Station Box 1347, New York NY 10028-0010. (212)288-4920. Fax: (732)225-1562. **Contact:** Barbara Francis, publisher; Joyce Segal, senior editor. Estab. 1987. "Small, independent children's book company, formed by the former editor-in-chief of Prentice Hall's juvenile book division." Publishes hardcover originals. Books: 135-150 GSM offset-semi-matte paper (for picture books); offset, sheet-fed printing; Smythe-sewn binding; full color, black and white line illustrations and half tone, b&w and full color illustrations. Averages 5-6 titles/year. Distributes titles through commission sales force. Promotes titles through reviews, trade convention exhibits, as well as book fairs.

Needs: Juvenile only for ages 4-12. "At this time, we are especially interested in historical novels, 'autobiographical' novels, historical and literary biographies and humor." Recently published *A Visit from the Leopard: Memories of a Ugandan Childhood*, by Catherine Mudibo-Pinang (juvenile autobiography, middle readers; debut author); *Abigail's Drum*, by John A. Minahan (juvenile historical, middle readers; debut author); and *The Spinner's Daughter*, by Amy Littlesugar (juvenile fiction, young readers; debut author).

How to Contact: Does not accept unsolicited mss. Send query letter with SASE or IRC for reply. Responds in 3 weeks to queries. Sometimes comments on rejected mss.

Terms: Pays royalties. Sends galleys to author. Publication time after ms is accepted "depends on the amount of revision required, type of illustration, etc." Guidelines available for #10 SASE.

PLEASANT COMPANY PUBLICATIONS, Subsidiary of Pleasant Company, 8400 Fairway Place, Middleton WI 53528. (608)836-4848. Fax: (608)828-4768. Website: www.americangirl.com (includes writer's guidelines, names of editors, press releases, e-store including book list). **Contact:** Submissions Editor. Estab. 1986. Midsize independent publisher. "Moving in new directions, and committed to high quality in all we do. Pleasant Company has specialized in historical fiction and contemporary nonfiction for girls 7-12 and is now actively seeking strong authors for middle-grade contemporary fiction, historical fiction and fantasy for all ages." Publishes hardcover and paperback originals. Averages 30-40 total titles, 30 fiction titles/year.

Imprints: The American Girls Fiction (contemporary fiction); American Girls Library (crafts/nonfiction); Girls of Many Lands (historical fiction).

Needs: Children's/juvenile (historical, mystery, contemporary for girls 8-12). "Contemporary fiction submissions should capture the spirit of contemporary American girls and also illuminate the ways in which their lives are personally touched by issues and concerns affecting America today. We are looking for thoughtfully developed characters and plots, and a discernible sense of place." Stories must feature an American girl, aged 10-13; reading level 4th-6th grade. No first-romance stories. Recently published *The Night Flyer*, by Elizabeth McDavid Jones (historical fiction); *Smoke Screen*, by Amy Goldman Koss (contemporary fiction); and *The Secret Voice of Gina Zhang*, by Dori Jones Yang (contemporary fiction).

How to Contact: Accepts unsolicited mss. Accepts queries by fax and e-mail. Submit complete ms with cover letter for contemporary fiction. Include list of publishing credits. "Tell us why the story is right for us." Send SASE or IRC for return of ms or send disposable copy of ms and SASE for reply only. Agented fiction 5%. Responds in up to 4 months to queries; 4 months to mss. Accepts simultaneous submissions.

Terms: Advance against royalties. Publishes ms 3-12 months after acceptance. Guidelines available for SASE.

Advice: "No picture book submissions, no doll proposals."

N O PLEXUS PUBLISHING, INC., 143 Old Marlton Pike, Medford NJ 08055-8750. (609)654-6500. Fax: (609)654-4309. E-mail: jbryans@infotoday.com. **Contact:** John B. Bryans, editor-in-chief. Estab. 1977. Publishes hardcover and paperback originals. **Publishes 70% of books from first-time authors; 90% from unagented writers.** Averages 4-5 titles/year.
Needs: Mysteries and literary novels with a strong regional (southern NJ) angle. Recently published *Down Barnegat Bay: A Nor'easter Midnight Reader,* by Robert Jahn.
How to Contact: Query with SASE. Accepts simultaneous submissions.
Terms: Pays 10-15% royalty on net receipts. Offers $500-1,000 advance. Book catalog and ms guidelines for 10×13 SAE with 4 first-class stamps.

N O A PLUME, (formerly Dutton Plume), Division of Penguin Putnam Inc., 375 Hudson St., New York NY 10014. (212)366-2000. Website: www.penguinputnam.com. **Contact:** Rosemary Ahern, editor-in-chief (literary fiction). Estab. 1948. Publishes paperback originals and reprints. **Published new writers within the last year.**
Needs: "All kinds of commercial and literary fiction, including mainstream, historical, New Age, western, thriller, gay. Full length novels and collections." Recently published *Girl with a Pearl Earring,* by Tracy Chevalier; *Liar's Moon,* by Philip Kimball; and *The True History of Paradise,* by Margaret Cezain-Thompson.
How to Contact: Agented mss only. Send query with SASE. "State type of book and past publishing projects." Accepts simultaneous submissions. Responds in 3 months.
Terms: Pays in royalties and author's copies; offers advance. Sends galleys to author. Publishes ms 12-18 months after acceptance. Book catalog available for SASE.
Advice: "Write the complete manuscript and submit it to an agent or agents."

N POLYCHROME PUBLISHING CORPORATION, 4509 N. Francisco, Chicago IL 60625. (773)478-4455. Fax: (773)478-0786. E-mail: polypub@earthlink.net. Website: www.polychromebooks.com. Estab. 1990. Publishes hardcover originals and reprints. **Publishes 50% of books from first-time authors; 100% from unagented writers.** Averages 4 titles/year.
Needs: Ethnic, juvenile, multicultural (particularly Asian-American), picture books, young adult. "We do not publish fables, folktales, fairytales or anthropomorphic animal stories." Recently published *Striking It Rich: Treasures from Gold Mountain; Char Siu Bad Boy.*
How to Contact: Submit synopsis and 3 sample chapters, for picture books submit whole ms. Accepts simultaneous submissions. Responds in 8 months to mss.
Terms: Pays royalty. Offers advance. Publishes book 2 years after acceptance of ms. Book catalog for #10 SASE; ms guidelines for #10 SASE.

N PONCHA PRESS, P.O. Box 280, Morrison CO 80465. (303)697-2384. Fax: (303)697-2385. E-mail: info@poncha press.com. Website: www.ponchapress.com. **Contact:** Barbara Osgood-Hartness, editor-in-chief. Publishes hardcover and trade paperback originals. **Publishes 100% of books from first-time authors; 100% from unagented writers.** Averages 2-3 titles/year.
Needs: Literary, mainstream/contemporary. Recently published *The Gold of El Negro,* by Michael C. Haley; *Gemini,* by Michael Burns.
How to Contact: Writers should consult website for submission guidelines. Query with SASE. Accepts simultaneous submissions. Responds in 1 month to queries; 3 months to mss.
Terms: Pays royalty on retail price. Publishes book 9 months after acceptance of ms. Book catalog and ms guidelines on website; ms guidelines online.
Advice: "Only finished and polished manuscripts. No first drafts or proposals for unwritten work."

N O O PONDER PUBLISHING INC., P.O. Box 23037, RPO McGillivray, Winnipeg, Manitoba R3T 5S3 Canada. (204)269-2985. Fax: (204)888-7159. E-mail: service@ponderpublishing.com. Website: www.ponderpublishing. com (includes title information, distribution information, book excerpts, reader survey, website survey, romance/relationship column, writing contest information, editorial staff, contact information). **Contact:** Mary Barton, senior editor (romance); Pamela Walford, assistant editor (romance). Estab. 1996. "Small, independent publisher. Our submissions team is always on the lookout for diamonds in the rough, writers with a unique voice. We feel we've taken the best of formula romance and mainstream romance and combined them into a short, fast-paced, entertaining read." Publishes paperback originals. Books: groundwork paper; mass market format printing; perfect binding. Average print order: 5,000-15,000. First novel print order: 3,000-5,000. **Published 1 new writer within the last year.** Averages 2 total titles, 2 fiction titles/year. Member, Small Publishers Association of North America. Distributes titles through four major American and one Canadian distributor. Promotes titles through advertising, the Internet, trade shows and newsletter.
Needs: Romance (contemporary, futuristic/time travel, romantic suspense). "We are looking for a variety of voices and styles, anything unique, for our Ponder Romance line. We like light, highly entertaining story lines that are as

---

 A BULLET INTRODUCES COMMENTS by the editor of *Novel & Short Story Writer's Market* indicating special information about the listing.

enjoyable as the romance." Recently published *Oh Susannah*, by Selena Mindous; *Autumn's Eve*, by Jordanna Boston; and *Sand Pirates*, by Ellis Hoff (all romance). Upcoming 2003 releases, *Reluctant Roulette*, by Ellis Hoff (romance); and *Can't Buy Me Love*, by Amy Lillard (first fiction, romance).

How to Contact: Accepts unsolicited mss. Query with outline/synopsis and 3 sample chapters. Include estimated word count, brief bio and list of publishing credits. Send IRC for return of ms or send disposable copy of ms and IRC for reply only. Responds to queries; responds in 5 months to mss. Accepts simultaneous submissions. Often comments on rejected mss.

Terms: "Contracts are confidential and negotiable. We pay signing bonuses (as opposed to advances) in addition to royalties." Does not send galleys to author. Publishes ms 1-3 years after acceptance. Guidelines available for SASE and $1 postage (Canadian).

Advice: "Read our books. They are unique to the genre in a way that the writer's guidelines cannot fully convey. Ponder romances go right down the middle between category and mainstream romance."

THE POST-APOLLO PRESS, 35 Marie St., Sausalito CA 94965. (415)332-1458. Fax: (415)332-8045. E-mail: tpapress@dnai.com. Website: www.dnai.com/~tpapress/ (includes excerpts, catalog, reviews and ordering links). **Contact:** Simone Fattal, publisher. Estab. 1982. Specializes in "women writers published in Europe or the Middle East who have been translated into English for the first time." Publishes paperback originals. Book: acid-free paper; lithography printing; perfect-bound. Average print order: 1,000. First novel print order: 1,000. **Published new writers within the last year.** Averages 2 total titles/year. Distributes titles through Small Press Distribution, Berkeley, California. Promotes titles through advertising in selected literary quarterlies, SPD catalog, ALA and ABA and SF Bay Area Book Festival participation.

Needs: Literary, spiritual, translations. No juvenile, horror, sports or romance. "Many of our books are first translations into English." Recently published *Some Life*, by Joanne Kyger; *Where the Rocks Started*, by Marc Atherton (debut author, novel); and *Happily*, by Lyn Hejinian.

How to Contact: "The Post-Apollo Press is not accepting manuscripts or queries currently due to a full publishing schedule."

Terms: Pays royalties of 6½% minimum or by individual arrangement. Sends galleys to author. Publishes ms 1½ years after acceptance. Book catalog available free.

Advice: "We want to see serious, literary quality, informed by an experimental aesthetic."

PRAIRIE JOURNAL PRESS, Prairie Journal Trust, P.O. Box 61203, Brentwood Postal Services, Calgary, Alberta T2L 2K6 Canada. E-mail: prairiejournal@yahoo.com. Website: www.geocities.com/prairiejournal/ (includes guidelines, subscription information and home page). **Contact**: Anne Burke, literary editor. Estab. 1983. Small-press, noncommercial literary publisher. Publishes paperback originals. Books: bond paper; offset printing; stapled binding; b&w line drawings. **Published new writers within the last year.** Averages 2 total titles or anthologies/year. Distributes titles by mail and in bookstores and libraries (public and university). Promotes titles through direct mail, reviews and in journals.

● Prairie Journal Press authors have been finalists for The Journey Prize in fiction.

Needs: Literary, short stories. No romance, horror, pulp, erotica, magazine type, children's, adventure, formula, western. Published *Prairie Journal Fiction, Prairie Journal Fiction II* (anthologies of short stories); *Solstice* (short fiction on the theme of aging); and *Prairie Journal Prose*. "Our new series *Prairie Annals* is 8½×11, stapled, soft cover, full color art."

How to Contact: Accepts unsolicited mss. Query first and send Canadian postage or IRCs and $8 for sample copy, then submit 1-2 stories with SAE and IRCs (sorry, no US stamps). Responds in 6 months or sooner. Occasionally comments on rejected mss if requested.

Terms: Pays 1 author's copy; honorarium depends on grant/award provided by the government or private/corporate donations. Sends galleys to author. Book catalog available free to institutions; SAE with IRC for individuals. "No U.S. stamps!"

Advice: "We wish we had the means to promote more new writers. We look for something different each time and try not to repeat types of stories if possible. We receive fiction of very high quality. Short fiction is preferable although excerpts from novels are considered if they stand alone on their own merit."

PUCKERBRUSH PRESS, 76 Main St., Orono ME 04473. (207)866-4868. **Contact:** Constance Hunting (fiction). Estab. 1971. "Small independent trade publisher, unique because of editorial independent stance." Publishes paperback originals and paperback reprints. Books: perfect-bound, illustrations. Average print order 500. Average first novel print order 500. Averages 2-3 total titles, 1-2 fiction titles/year. Titles distributed through Amazon.com, Baker & Taylor, Barnes & Noble.

Needs: Literary. Recently published *Cora's Seduction*, by Mary Gray Hughes (short stories); *The Crow on the Spruce*, by C. Hall (Maine fiction); *Night-Sea Journey*, by M. Alpert (poetry).

How to Contact: Accepts unsolicited mss. Submit complete ms with cover letter. Accepts phone queries. Include a brief bio and a list of publishing credits with your submissions. Agented fiction: 0%. Responds in 2 weeks to queries; 2 months to mss. Often comments on rejected mss. Sometimes charges for critiques; "$50 per hour for thorough critique." Pays in royalties of 10-15%. Sometimes sends galleys to author. Guidelines available for SASE; book catalog for large SASE and 34¢ postage.

Advice: "Be true to your vision, not to fashion."

PUDDING HOUSE PUBLICATIONS, 60 N. Main St., Johnstown OH 43031. (740)967-6060. E-mail: pudding @johnstown.net. Website: www.puddinghouse.com (includes staff, departments, photos, guidelines, books for direct and wholesale purchase, publications list, writing games, poem of the month, Unitarian Universalist poets page, calls, etc.). **Contact:** Jennifer Bosveld, editor (short short stories only). Estab. 1979. "Small independent publisher seeking outrageously fresh short short stories." Publishes paperback originals. Books, chapbooks, broadsites: paper varies; side stapled; b&w illustrations. **Published new writers within the last year.** Promotes titles through direct mail, conference exhibits, readings, workshops.

Needs: Experimental, literary, the writing experience, liberal/alternative politics or spirituality, new approaches. Recently published *In the City of Mystery*, by Alan Ziegler (short short stories); and *Karmic 4-Star Buckaroo*, by John Bennett (short short stories).

How to Contact: Accepts unsolicited mss. Submit complete ms with cover letter and ample SASE. Include short bio and list of publishing credits. Send SASE for return of ms. Responds immediately unless traveling. No simultaneous submissions. Sometimes comments on rejected mss for various fee, if close.

Terms: Pays in author's copies. Sends galleys to author for chapbooks. Publishes ms 2-24 months after acceptance. Guidelines available free for SASE. Publication list available.

Advice: "Be new!"

PUFFIN BOOKS, Imprint of Penguin Putnam Inc., 345 Hudson St., New York NY 10014-3657. (212)414-2000. Website: www.penguinputnam.com. **Contact:** Sharyn November, senior editor; Kristin Gilson, executive editor. "Puffin Books publishes high-end trade paperbacks and paperback reprints for preschool children, beginning and middle readers, and young adults." Publishes trade paperback originals and reprints. Averages 175-200 titles/year.

Needs: Picture books, young adult novels, middle grade and easy-to-read grades 1-3. "We publish mostly paperback reprints. We do only a small number of original novels. We do not publish original picture books." Published *A Gift for Mama*, by Esther Hautzig (Puffin chapter book).

How to Contact: Does not accept unsolicited mss. Send query letter with SASE or IRC for reply. Responds in 3 months to mss. Does not accept simultaneous submissions.

Terms: Royalty and advance vary. Publishes ms 18 months after acceptance. Book catalog available for 9 × 12 SASE with 7 first-class stamps; send request to Marketing Department.

Advice: "Our audience ranges from little children 'first books' to young adult (ages 14-16). An original idea has the best luck."

G.P. PUTNAM'S SONS, Imprint of Penguin Putnam Inc., 375 Hudson St., New York NY 10014. (212)366-2000. Fax: (212)366-2666. Website: www.penguinputnam.com. Publisher: Neil Nyren. Vice President: Marian Woods. **Contact:** Acquisitions Editor. Publishes hardcover and trade paperback originals. Published new writers within the last year.

Imprint(s): Putnam, Riverhead, Jeremy P. Tarcher.

Needs: Adventure, literary, mainstream/contemporary, mystery/suspense. Recently published *The Bear and the Dragon*, by Tom Clancy (adventure).

How to Contact: Does not accept unsolicited mss. *Agented submissions only.* Responds in 6 months to queries. Accepts simultaneous submissions.

Terms: Pays variable royalties on retail price. Advance varies.

QUIXOTE PRESS, 1854 345th Ave., Wever IA 52658. (800)571-2665 or (319)372-7480. Fax: (319)372-7485. E-mail: heartsntummies@hotmail.com. **Contact:** Bruce Carlson, president. Quixote Press specializes in humorous regional folklore and special interest cookbooks. Publishes trade paperback originals and reprints. **Published mostly new writers within the last year.**

Needs: Adventure, ethnic, experimental, humor, short story collections, children's. Published *Eating Ohio*, by Rus Pishnery (short stories about Ohio); *Lil' Red Book of Fishing Tips*, by Tom Whitecloud (fishing tales); *How to Talk Hoosier*, by Netha Bell (humor); *Cow Whisperer*, by Skip Holmes (humor); and *Flour Sack Bloomers*, by Lucy Fetterhoff (history).

How to Contact: Query with synopsis and SASE. Responds in 2 months. Accepts simultaneous submissions.

Terms: Pays royalties of 10% on wholesale price. No advance. Publishes ms 1 year after acceptance. Guidelines and book catalog available for #10 SASE.

Advice: "Carefully consider marketing considerations. Audience is women in gift shops, on farm site direct retail outlets. Contact us at *idea* stage, not complete ms. stage. Be receptive to design input by us."

RAINBOW BOOKS, INC., P.O. Box 430, Highland City FL 33846. (863)648-4420. Fax: (941)647-5951. E-mail: rbibooks@aol.com. **Contact:** Besty A. Lampe, editorial director. Estab. 1979. Publishes hardcover and trade paperback originals. Averages 12-15 titles/year.

Needs: "We're looking for well-written mystery manuscripts that lend themselves to series development. We do not publish short story collections. We do not publish Christian fiction." Recently published *Medical School is Murder*, by Dirk Wyle (fiction); and *Dem Bones Revenge*, by Kris Neri (cozy mystery).

How to Contact: "Request writer's guidelines in writing." Does not accept unsolicited mss. Query with synopsis and first chapter. Send SASE or IRC for reply. Responds in 1 month to queries and proposals; 2 months to mss. Accepts simultaneous submissions.

Terms: Pays royalties of 6-12% on retail price. Offers advance. "Aggressively pursues subrights sales." Publishes ms 1 year after acceptance.

Advice: "Be professional in presentation of queries and manuscripts, and always provide a return mailer with proper postage attached in the event the materials do not fit our list. In mystery fiction, we don't want to see books with gratuitous violence, drugs or international intrigue."

N RAINCOAST BOOK DISTRIBUTION LTD., 9050 Shaughnessy St., Vancouver, British Columbia V6P 6E5 Canada. Publisher: Michelle Benjamin. **Contact:** Lyn Henry, executive editor. Publishes hardcover and trade paperback originals and reprints. **Publishes 10% of books from first-time authors; 50% from unagented writers.** Averages 60 titles/year.

Imprints: Raincoast Books, Polestar Books (fiction, poetry, literary nonfiction), Press Gang (lesbian and feminist nonfiction).

Needs: Literary, short story collections, young adult. Recently published *Mount Appetite*, by Bill Gaston; *Love and Other Ruins*, by Karen X. Tulchinsky.

How to Contact: *No unsolicited mss.*

Terms: Pays 8-12% royalty on retail price. Offers $1,000-6,000 advance. Publishes book within 2 years after acceptance of ms. Book catalog for #10 SASE.

◯ ◎ Ⓐ RANDOM HOUSE BOOKS FOR YOUNG READERS, Random House Children's Books, A Division of Random House, Inc., 201 E. 50th St., New York NY 10022. (212)751-2600. Fax: (212)782-9698. Website: www.randomhouse.com/kids. Vice President/Publisher: Kate Klimo. **Contact:** Heidi Kilgras, editorial director (Step into Reading); Jennifer Dussling, senior director (Stepping Stones); Jim Thomas, senior editor (fantasy).

Needs: "Random House publishes a select list of first chapter books and novels, with an emphasis on fantasy and historical fiction." Chapter books, middle-grade, young adult. Recently published *A to Z Mysteries*, by Ron Roy (chapter books); the Junie B. Jones series; the Magic Tree House series; and *Lady Knight*, by Tamora Pierce.

How to Contact: Agented fiction only. No unsolicited mss. No queries by fax. Responds in up to 4 months. Accepts simultaneous submissions but must be indicated as such.

Advice: (for all imprints) "We look for original, unique stories. Do something that hasn't been done before."

◪ RANDOM HOUSE CHILDREN'S BOOKS, (Division of Random House, Inc.), 1540 Broadway, New York NY 10036. (212)782-9000. Fax: (212)782-9452. Website: www.randomhouse.com/kids. Estab. 1925. "Producing books for preschool children through young adult readers, in all formats from board books to activity books to picture books and novels, Random House Children's Books brings together world-famous franchise characters, multimillion-copy series, and top-flight, award-winning authors and illustrators."

Imprint(s): Alfred A. Knopf Books for Young Readers; Bantam Books for Young Readers; Crown Books for Young Readers; David Fickling Books; Delacorte Press Books for Young Readers; Disney Books for Young Readers; Doubleday Books for Young Readers; Dragonfly Books; Laurel-Leaf Books; Lucas Books; Golden Books; Random House Books for Young Readers; Sesame Workshop (formerly Children's Television Workshop); Wendy Lamb Books; Yearling Books.

◪ RANDOM HOUSE, INC., (Division of Bertelsmann Book Group), 1540 Broadway, New York NY 10036. (212)782-9000. Fax: (212)302-7985. E-mail: editor@randomhouse.com. Website: www.randomhouse.com. Estab. 1925. "Random House has long been committed to publishing the best literature by writers both in the United States and abroad." Publishes hardcover and paperback originals and reprints.

Imprint(s): Alfred A. Knopf; Anchor Bible Commentary; Anchor Bible Dictionary; Anchor Bible Reference Library; Anchor Books; Ballantine Books; Bantam Hardcover; Bantam Mass Market; Bantam Skylark; Bantam Starfire; Bantam Trade Paperback; BDD Audio Publishing; Bell Tower; Children's Classics; Children's Media; Clarkson Potter; Crescent Books; Crimeline; Crown Books for Young Readers; Crown Publishers, Inc; CTW Publishing; Currency; Del Rey Delacorte Press; Dell; Dell Laurel-Leaf; Dell Yearling; Delta; Derrydale; The Dial Press; Discovery Books; Domain; Doubleday; Doubleday Bible Commentary; Doubleday/Galilee; Doubleday/Image; Dragonfly Books; DTP; Everyman's Library; Fanfare; Fawcett; First Choice Chapter Books; Fodor's; Grammercy Books; Harmony Books; House of Collectibles; Island; Ivy; Knopf Books for Young Readers; Knopf Paperbacks; Library of Contemporary Thought; Living Language; Main Street Books; The Modern Library; Nan A. Talese; The New Jerusalem Bible; One World; Pantheon Books; Picture Yearling; Princeton Review; Random House; Random House Children's Publishing; Random House Large Print Publishing; Random House Reference & Information Publishing; Shocken Books; Sierra Club Adult Books; Spectra; Strivers Row; Testament Books; Three Rivers Press; Times Books; Villard Books; Vintage Books; Wings Books.

◪ THE RANDOM HOUSE TRADE PUBLISHING GROUP, (Division of Random House, Inc.), 1540 Broadway, New York NY 10036. (212)782-9000. Fax: (212)302-7985. Website: www.randomhouse.com/atrandom. Estab. 1925. "The flagship imprint of Random House, Inc." Publishes hardcover and paperback trade books.

Imprint(s): Random House Trade Books; Villard Books; The Modern Library; Strivers Row; Random House Trade Paperbacks.

N ◐ RAVENHAWK™ BOOKS, The 6DOF Group, 7739 Broadway Blvd., #95, Tucson AZ 85710. (520)886-9885. Fax: (520)886-9885. E-mail: ravenhawk6dof@yahoo.com. Website: www.ravenhawk.biz (includes general overview of company and book catalog). **Contact:** Carl Lasky, publisher (all fiction). Estab. 1998. "Small, independent, literary press most interested in provocative and innovative works." Publishes hardcover and paperback originals. Books: 50 or 60 lb. paper; traditional, POD, e-book printing. First novel print order: 1,000. **Published 1 new writer within the last year.** Plans 3 first novels this year. Averages 6-8 total titles, 3-4 fiction titles/year. Member, SPAN. Distributes titles through Ingram, Baker & Taylor, Amazon, Borders, Barnes & Noble.

Needs: Children's/juvenile (adventure, animal, easy-to-read, fantasy, mystery, series), fantasy (space fantasy, sword and sorcery), horror (dark fantasy, futuristic, psychological, supernatural), humor/satire, literary, mainstream, mystery/suspense (amateur sleuth, cozy, police procedural, private eye/hardboiled), psychic/supernatural, religious (religious mystery/suspense, religious thriller), romance (contemporary, romantic suspense), science fiction (hard science/technological, soft/sociological), short story collections, thriller/espionage, young adult/teen (adventure, easy-to-read, fantasy/science fiction, horror, mystery/suspense, problem novels, series). Planning anthology of Damon Shiller Mysteries. Solicited material only. Published the Chaz Trenton Trilogy.

How to Contact: Does not accept unsolicited mss. "Submissions through acknowledged agents lists or by invitation only." Send query letter by postal mail only. Include estimated word count, brief bio and list of publishing credits. Send disposable copy of ms and SASE for reply only. Agented fiction 10%. Responds in weeks to queries; months to mss. Accepts simultaneous submissions. No e-mail or disk submissions. Sometimes comments on rejected mss.

Terms: Pays royalties of 45-60% "calculated from gross retail sales not net." No advances. "Author receives royalties 30 days after we receive payment from distributors, consumers or bookstores." Sends galleys to author. Publishes ms up to 18 months after acceptance. Guidelines available for SASE; book catalog on website only.

Advice: "Write dynamic prose utilizing a multi-dimensional edge (conflict). Persistence. Although the majority of elitists that control the publishing industry won't admit it, it really is a crap shoot out there. Don't ever give up if you believe in yourself. Courage."

RECONCILIATION PRESS, P.O. Box 3709, Fairfax VA 22038. (703)691-8416. Fax: (703)691-8466. E-mail: publisher@reconciliation.com. Website: www.reconciliation.com (includes historical fiction series, study guides and online stories). **Contact:** John Jenkins, publisher. Estab. 1997. "Small publisher to home school and Christian school market. Online serial historical novels." Publishes paperback originals and online series. **Publishes 2 new writers/year.** Publishes 2 new first novels/year. Averages 4 total titles, 4 fiction titles/year.

Needs: Historical (general, era: Christian American 19th and 20th century), young adult/teen (historical). Recently published *Cry of the Blood*, by J.L. Jenkins (historical fiction); *The Gift*, by K. O'Hara (historical fiction); and *Fool's Gold*, by E. Stobbe (historical fiction).

How to Contact: Query with outline/synopsis and 2 sample chapters. Accepts queries by e-mail. Include estimated word count, brief bio and list of publishing credits. Send disposable copy of ms and SASE for reply only. Responds in 2 weeks to queries; 2 months to mss. Accepts electronic submissions. Often comments on rejected mss.

Terms: Pays royalties of 7-30%. Publishes ms 3-6 months after acceptance.

RED DEER PRESS, MacKimmie Library Tower, Room 813, 2500 University Dr., NW, Calgary, Alberta T2N 1N4 Canada. (403)220-4334. Fax: (403)210-8191. E-mail: rdp@ucalgary.ca. Website: www.reddeerpress.com. **Contact:** Dennis Johnson, managing editor; Aritha van Herk, fiction editor. Estab. 1975. Publishes adult and young adult hardcover and paperback originals "focusing on books by, about, or of interest to Western Canadians." Books: offset paper; offset printing; hardcover/perfect-bound. Average print order: 5,000. First novel print order: 2,500. Averages 14-16 total titles, 1 fiction title/year. Distributes titles in Canada, the US, the UK, Australia and New Zealand.

Imprint(s): Northern Lights Books for Children, Northern Light Young Novels.

● Red Deer Press has received numerous honors and awards from the Book Publishers Association of Alberta, Canadian Children's Book Centre, the Governor General of Canada and the Writers Guild of Alberta.

Needs: Contemporary, experimental, literary, young adult. No romance or horror. Published *Great Stories of the Sea*, edited by Norman Ravvin (anthology); *A Fine Daughter*, by Catherine Simmons Niven (novel); *Great Stories from the Prairies* (anthology); *The Kappa Child*, by Hiromi Goto (novel); and *The Game*, by Teresa Toten (nominated for the Governor General's Award).

How to Contact: *Canadian authors only.* Does not accept unsolicited mss in children's and young adult genres. Query first or submit outline/synopsis and 2 sample chapters. Send SASE or IRC. Responds in 6 months. Accepts simultaneous submissions. Final mss must be submitted on Mac disk in MS Word.

Terms: Pays royalties of 8-10%. Advance is negotiable. Sends galleys to author. Publishes ms 1 year after acceptance. Book catalog available for 9 × 12 SASE.

Advice: "We're very interested in literary and experimental fiction from Canadian writers with a proven track record (either published books or widely published in established magazines or journals) and for manuscripts with regional themes and/or a distinctive voice. We publish Canadian authors exclusively."

RED DRESS INK, an imprint of Harlequin, 300 E. 42nd St., 6th Floor, New York NY 10017. Website: www.reddressink.com. **Contact:** Margaret Marbury, associate senior editor. "We launched Red Dress Ink to provide women with unique and irreverent stories that reflect the lifestyles of today's modern women." Publishes trade paperback originals. **Regularly publishes new writers.**

Needs: Wants "compelling, entertaining women's fiction with attitude. Stories should be fresh and depict women coping with the sometimes difficult aspects of modern life. The dialogue should be sharp and true-to-life, and the style of writing highly accessible. Settings should be urban in North America or well-known international locations." Length: 90,000-110,000 words. Recently published *On the Verge*, by Ariella Papa; *Fishbowl*, by Sarah Mlynowski; and *Burning the Map*, by Laura Caldwell.

How to Contact: Accepts unsolicited mss. "All material must be typewritten, double-spaced and on a reasonably heavy bond paper. Computer-generated material is acceptable, but it must be letter quality and pages must be separated." Submit complete ms with cover letter. Writers must include SASE or IRC for return of ms. No e-mail or disk submissions.

Terms: Pays royalties and advance. Sends galleys to author. Guidelines available for SASE or on website.

RED HEN PRESS, P.O. Box 3537, Granada Hills CA 91394. (818)831-0649. Fax: (818)831-6659. E-mail: editor@ redhen.org. Website: www.redhen.org. **Contact:** Mark E. Cull, publisher/editor (fiction); Katherine Gale, poetry editor (poetry, literary fiction). Estab. 1993. Publishes trade paperback originals. **Publishes 10% of books from first-time authors; 90% from unagented writers.** Averages 10 titles/year.

Needs: "We prefer high-quality literary fiction." Ethnic, experimental, feminist, gay/lesbian, historical, literary, mainstream/contemporary, poetry, poetry in translation, short story collections.

How to Contact: Query with SASE. Accepts simultaneous submissions. Responds in 1 month to queries; 3 months to mss.

Terms: Publishes book 1 year after acceptance of ms. Book catalog and ms guidelines available via website or free.

Advice: "Audience reads poetry, literary fiction, intelligent nonfiction. If you have an agent, we may be too small since we don't pay advances. Write well. Send queries first. Be willing to help promote your own book."

RED SAGE PUBLISHING, INC., P.O. Box 4844, Seminole FL 33775-4844. Phone/fax: (727)391-3847. E-mail: alekendall@aol.com. Website: www.redsagepub.com (includes authors and guidelines). **Contact:** Alexandria Kendall, editor (romance, erotica); Claire Richards, editor (romance, erotica). Estab. 1995. Publishes "romance erotica or ultra-sensual romance novellas written by romance writers. Red Sage is the leader in the publishing industry for erotic romance." Publishes paperback originals. Books: perfect binding. **Published 4 new writers within the last year.** Averages 1 total title, 1 fiction title/year. Distributes titles through Baker & Taylor, Amazon, Barnes & Noble, Borders and independent bookstores as well as mail order. Promotes titles through national trade publication advertising (*Romantic Times, Writerspace*), author interviews and book signings.

● Red Sage Publishing received the Fallot Literary Award for Fiction.

Imprint(s): The *Secrets* Collections (romance, ultra-sensual), edited by Alexandria Kendall.

Needs: Romance (ultra-sensual) novellas for *The Secrets Volumes: The Best of Romance Erotic Fiction* anthology. Length: 20,000-30,000 words. Writers may submit to anthology editor. Recently published *Insatiable*, by Chevon Gael; and *Strictly Business*, by Shannon Hollis.

How to Contact: Accepts unsolicited mss. Query with outline/synopsis and 10 sample pages. Include estimated word count and list of publishing credits if applicable. Send SASE or IRC for return of ms. Responds in 3 months. Sometimes comments on rejected ms.

Terms: Pays advance and royalty. Sends galleys to author. Publishes ms 1-2 years after acceptance. Writer's guidelines for SASE.

Advice: "Know what we publish and send what you think is better!"

REGAN BOOKS, HarperCollins, 10 E. 53rd St., New York NY 10022. (212)207-7400. Fax: (212)207-6951. Website: www.harpercollins.com. **Contact:** Judith Regan, president/publisher; Cal Morgan, editorial director. Estab. 1994. Publishes hardcover and trade paperback originals. Averages 75 titles/year.

Needs: Adventure, comic books, confession, erotica, ethnic, experimental, fantasy, feminist, gay/lesbian, gothic, hi-lo, historical, horror, humor, juvenile, literary, mainstream/contemporary, military/war, multicultural, multimedia, mystery, occult, picture books, plays, poetry, poetry in translation, regional, religious, romance, science fiction, short story collections, spiritual, sports, suspense, western, young adult.

How to Contact: No unsolicited mss. *Agented submissions only.* Accepts simultaneous submissions.

Terms: Pays royalty on retail price. Offers variable advance. Publishes book 1 year after acceptance of ms.

RENAISSANCE HOUSE, 9400 Lloydcrest Drive, Beverly Hills CA 90210. (310)358-5288. Fax: (310)358-5282. Website: www.renaissancehouse.net. **Contact:** Sam Laredo, publisher; Raquel Benatar, editor. Publishes hardcover and trade paperback originals. **Publishes 25-30% of books from first-time authors; 75% from unagented writers.** Averages 30 titles/year.

Needs: Fantasy, juvenile, multicultural, picture books, legends; fables. Recently published *The Spirits of the Mountain*, by Raquel Benatar.

How to Contact: Query with SASE. Accepts simultaneous submissions. Responds in 2 months.

Terms: Pays 5-10% royalty on net receipts. Book catalog free.

RENDITIONS, Research Centre for Translation, Institute of Chinese Studies, Chinese University of Hong Kong, Shatin, New Territories, Hong Kong. Phone: 852-26097399. Fax: 852-26035110. E-mail: renditions@cuhk.edu. hk. Website: www.renditions.org (includes sections about Research Centre for Translation, the Chinese University of Hong Kong, *Renditions* magazines, Renditions Paperbacks, Renditions Books, forthcoming, ordering information and related sites). **Contact:** Dr. Eva Hung, editor. Academic specialist publisher. Averages 2 fiction titles/year. Distributes titles through local and overseas distributors and electronically via homepage and Amazon.com. Promotes titles through homepage, exchange ads with *China Now* and *China Review International* and paid ads in *Feminist Bookstore News* and *Journal of Asian Studies* of AAS.

Needs: Will only consider English translations of Chinese fiction, prose, drama and poetry. Fiction published either in semiannual journal (*Renditions*) or in the Renditions Paperback series. Recently published *Hong Kong Stories: Old Themes New Voices*, by Eva Hung, editor; and *Traces of Love and Other Stories*, by Eileen Chang; and *City Women: Contemporary Taiwan Women Writers*, edited by Eva Hung.

How to Contact: For fiction over 5,000 words in translation, sample is required. Sample length: 1,000-2,000 words. Send sample chapter. "Submit only works in our specialized area. Two copies of translation accompanied by two copies of original Chinese text." Accepts fax and e-mail requests for information and guidelines.

Terms: Pays royalties for paperback series; honorarium for publication in *Renditions*.

⌨ ◎ RESOURCE PUBLICATIONS, INC., 160 E. Virginia St., Suite #290, San Jose CA 95112-5876. (408)286-8505. Fax: (408)287-8748. E-mail: info@rpinet.com. Website: www.rpinet.com/ml/. **Contact:** Acquisition Director. Estab. 1973. Publishes paperback originals. **Publishes 30% of books from first-time authors; 99% from unagented writers.** Averages 12-18 titles/year.

Needs: Fables, anecdotes, faith sharing stories; stories useful in preaching or teaching.

How to Contact: Query with SASE. Responds in 10 weeks to queries.

Terms: Pays 8% royalty (for a first project). Offers $250-1,000 advance. Book catalog online; ms guidelines online.

Advice: "We are publishers and secondarily we are book packagers. Pitch your project to us for publication first. If we can't take it on on that basis, we may be able to take it on as a packaging and production project."

◑ ◎ REVELL PUBLISHING, Subsidiary of Baker Book House, P.O. Box 6287, Grand Rapids MI 49516-6287. (616)676-9185. Fax: (616)676-9573. E-mail: lhdupont@bakerbooks.com or petersen@bakerbooks.com. Website: www. bakerbooks.com. **Contact:** Sheila Ingram, assistant to the editorial director; Jane Campbell, editorial director (Chosen Books). Estab. 1870. Midsize publisher. "Revell publishes to the heart (rather than to the head). For 125 years, Revell has been publishing evangelical books for personal enrichment and spiritual growth of general Christian readers." Publishes hardcover, trade paperback and mass market originals and reprints. Average print order: 7,500. **Published new writers within the last year.** Averages 60 total titles, 8 fiction titles/year.

Imprint(s): Spire Books.

Needs: Religious/inspirational (general). Published *Triumph of the Soul*, by Michael R. Joens (contemporary); *Daughter of Joy*, by Kathleen Morgan (historical); and *Blue Mist on the Danube*, by Doris Eliane Fell (contemporary).

How to Contact: "We are no longer taking unsolicited manuscripts. All manuscripts received will be returned to sender without a review." Recommends submitting mss to The Writer's Edge (www.writersedgeservice.com) or the Evangelical Christian Publishers Association's online service, First Edition (www.ecpa.org/FE). Both services charge writers a fee to post proposals/mss. "We subscribe to both these services and regularly review the proposals which appear there, as do many other Christian publishers." Accepts agented material. Agented fiction 20%. Queries (*not* proposals) by unrepresented writers should be by e-mail only. Responds in 3 weeks to queries; 2 weeks to mss. Accepts simultaneous submissions. Sometimes comments on rejected mss.

Terms: Pays royalties. Sends galleys to author. Publishes ms 1 year after acceptance. Guidelines available for SASE.

⌨ ◎ REVIEW & HERALD PUBLISHING ASSOCIATION, 55 W. Oak Ridge Dr., Hagerstown MD 21740. (301) 393-4050. **Contact:** Jeannette R. Johnson, acquisitions editor. "The Review & Herald Publishing Association nurtures a growing relationship with God by providing products that teach and enrich people spiritually, mentally, physically and socially as we near Christ's soon second coming. We belong to the Seventh-Day Adventist denomination." Publishes hardcover and paperback originals and reprints. Averages 40-50 titles/year.

Needs: Adventure, historical, humor, juvenile, mainstream, religious.

How to Contact: Query with synopsis and 3 sample chapters. Responds in 1 month to queries; 2 months to mss. Agented fiction: 5%. Accepts simultaneous submissions.

Terms: Pays royalties of 7-16%. Offers advance of $500-1,000. Publishes ms 18-24 months after acceptance. Catalog and guidelines available for 10×13 SAE.

◐ RISING TIDE PRESS, P.O. Box 30457, Tucson AZ 85751-0457. (520)888-1140. Fax: (520)888-1123. E-mail: milestonepress@earthlink.net. Website: www.risingtidepress.com (includes book catalog, writer's guidelines, about our authors, annual award information, monthly specials). **Contact:** Debra S. Tobin and Brenda J. Kazen. Estab. 1988. "Independent women's press, publishing lesbian and feminist nonfiction and fiction." Publishes paperback trade originals. Books: 60 lb. vellum paper; sheet fed and/or web printing; perfect-bound. Average print order: 5,000. First novel print order: 3,000. **Published 4-5 new writers within the last year.** Averages 12 total titles/year. Distributes titles through Ingram, Bookpeople, Baker & Taylor, Alamo Square, Marginal (Canada), Turnaround (UK) and Banyon Tree (Pacific Basin). Promotes titles through magazines, journals, newspapers, *PW*, Lambda Book Report, distributor's catalogs, special publications and Internet.

Needs: Lesbian adventure, contemporary, erotica, fantasy, feminist, romance, science fiction, suspense/mystery, western. Looking for romance and mystery. Recently published *One Summer Night*, by Gerri Hall (first novel, romance); *Taking Risks*, by Judith McDaniel (poetry); and *Deadly Butterfly*, by Diane Davidson (mystery). Seeking "coming out stories" and stories about growing up in a gay household for anthologies.

How to Contact: Accepts unsolicited mss. Query with 1-page outline/synopsis and SASE. Responds in 3 months to mss.

Terms: Pays 10% royalties. Publishes ms 6-18 months after acceptance. Guidelines available for #10 SASE.

Advice: "Outline your story to give it boundaries and structure. Find creative ways to introduce your characters and begin the story in the middle of some action and dialogue. Our greatest challenge is finding quality manuscripts that are well plotted and not predictable, with well-developed, memorable characters."

RIVER OAK PUBLISHING, Eagle Communication International, 2448 E. 81 St., Suite 4800, Tulsa OK 74317. (918)523-5600. Fax: (918)523-5644. Website: www.riveroakpublishing.com. **Contact:** Jeff Dunn, editorial director. Publishes hardback, trade paperback, mass market originals and reprints. Averages 40-50 titles/year.

Needs: Adventure, fantasy, historical, humor, mystery, religious, romance, spiritual, sports, western.

How to Contact: Submit query with SASE. Accepts simultaneous submissions. Responds in 1 month to queries; 6 months to mss. Agented fiction: 20%. Guidelines available for #10 SASE.

Terms: Pays royalty on wholesale price. Offers negotiable advance. Publishes ms 18 months after acceptance.

ROC, Imprint of New American Library, A Division of Penguin Putnam, Inc., 375 Hudson St., New York NY 10014. (212)366-2000. Website: www.penguinputnam.com. **Contact**: Laura Anne Gilman, executive editor; Jennifer Heddle, editor. "Roc tries to strike a balance between fantasy and science fiction. We're looking for books that are a good read, that people will want to pick up time and time again." Publishes mass market, trade and hardcover originals. Averages 36 total titles/year.

Needs: Fantasy, horror, science fiction. Recently published *The Pillars of the World*, by Anne Bishop; and *The Peshawar Lancers*, by S.M. Stirling.

How to Contact: Discourages unsolicited mss. Query with synopsis and 1-2 sample chapters. Send SASE or IRC for reply. Responds in 3 month to queries. Accepts simultaneous submissions.

Terms: Pays royalty. Advance negotiable.

RONSDALE PRESS, 3350 W. 21 Ave., Vancouver, British Columbia V6S 1G7 Canada. (604)738-4688. Fax: (604)731-4548. E-mail: ronhatch@pinc.com. Website: www.ronsdalepress.com (includes guidelines, catalog, events). **Contact**: Ronald B. Hatch, president/editor; Veronica Hatch, editor (YA historical). Estab. 1988. Ronsdale Press is "dedicated to publishing books that give Canadians new insights into themselves and their country." Publishes hardcover and paperback originals. Books: 60 lb. paper; photo offset printing; perfect binding. Average print order: 1,500. First novel print order: 1,500. **Published new writers within the last year.** Averages 3 fiction titles/year. Distributes titles through General Distribution. Promotes titles through ads in BC Bookworld and Globe & Mail, and interviews on radio.

Needs: Literary. Published *The City in the Egg*, by Michel Trembly (novel); *Jackrabbit Moon*, by Sheila McLeod Arnepoulos; and *Daruma Days*, by Terry Watada (short stories).

How to Contact: *Canadian authors only.* Accepts unsolicited mss. Submit outline/synopsis and at least first 100 pages. Accepts queries/correspondence by e-mail. Send SASE or IRC for return of ms. Short story collections must have some previous magazine publication. Responds in 2 weeks to queries; 2 months to mss. Sometimes comments on rejected mss.

Terms: Pays royalties of 10%. Provides author's copies. Sends galleys to author. Publishes ms 6 months after acceptance.

Advice: "We publish both fiction and poetry. Authors *must* be Canadian. We look for writing that shows the author has read widely in contemporary and earlier literature. Ronsdale, like other literary presses, is not interested in mass-market or pulp materials."

ROYAL FIREWORKS PUBLISHING, 1 First Ave., P.O. Box 399, Unionville NY 10988. (845)726-4444. Fax: (845)726-3824. E-mail: rfpress@frontiernet.net. Website: www.rfpress.com. **Contact:** William Neumann, editor (young adult); Myrna Kemnitz, editor (education). Estab. 1977. Publishes trade paperback originals and reprints. **Publishes 30-50% of books from first-time authors; 98% from unagented writers.** Averages 75-140 titles/year.

Needs: Young adult. "We do novels for children from 8-16. We do a lot of historical fiction, science fiction, adventure, mystery, sports, etc. We are concerned about the values." No drugs, sex, swearing. Recently published *Hitler's Willing Warrior*, by H. Gutsche (young adult fiction).

FOR EXPLANATIONS OF THESE SYMBOLS,
SEE THE INSIDE FRONT AND BACK COVERS OF THIS BOOK.

How to Contact: Submit complete ms. Does not accept simultaneous submissions. Responds in 3 months to mss.
Terms: Pays 5-10% royalty on wholesale price. Publishes book 9 months after acceptance of ms. Book catalog for $2.08; ms guidelines for #10 SASE.
Advice: Audience is comprised of gifted children, their parents and teachers, and children (8-18) who read.

RUMINATOR BOOKS, 1648 Grand Ave., St. Paul MN 55105. (651)699-7038. Fax: (651)699-7190. E-mail: books@ruminator.com. Website: www.ruminator.com. **Contact:** Pearl Kilbride. Publishes hardcover originals, trade paperback originals and reprints. **Publishes 60% from unagented writers.** Averages 8-10 titles/year.
Needs: Literary, adult fiction. Recently published *Facing the Congo*, by Jeffrey Tayler; *The Last Summer of Reason*, by Tahar Djarat; *An Algerian Childhood* (anthology).
How to Contact: Query with SASE or submit proposal package including outline, sample chapter(s), SASE. Accepts simultaneous submissions. Responds in 4 months to proposals.
Terms: Royalty varies. Offers varying advance. Publishes book 12-18 months after acceptance of ms. Book catalog for 9×12 SAE with 2 first-class stamps; ms guidelines for #10 SASE.

ST. MARTIN'S PRESS LLC, (Subsidiary of Holtzbrinck Publishers Holdings LLC), 175 Fifth Ave., New York NY 10010. (212)674-5151. Fax: (212)420-9314. E-mail: inquiries@stmartins.com. Website: www.stmartins.com. Estab.1952. Publishes hardcover, trade paperback, and mass market originals.
Imprint(s): Thomas Dunne Books; Golden Adult; Golden Guides; Griffin; Minotaur; Priddy & Bricknell; Stonewall Inn; Truman Talley Books; Whitman Coin Books and Products.

SALVO PRESS, P.O. Box 9095, Bend OR 97708. Phone/fax: (541)330-8746. E-mail: salvopress@hotmail.com. Website: www.salvopress.com (includes book catalog, writer's guidelines, author pages, sample chapters, author tours and links). **Contact:** Scott Schmidt, publisher (mystery, suspense, thriller & espionage). Estab. 1998. "We are a small press specializing in mystery, suspense, espionage and thriller fiction. We plan on expanding into science fiction and literary fiction. Our press publishes in hardcover and trade paperback and e-book format." Publishes paperback originals and e-books. Books: 5½×8½ or 6×9 paper; offset printing; perfect binding. **Published 3 new writers within the last year.** Averages 3 fiction titles/year.
Needs: Adventure, literary, mystery/suspense (amateur sleuth, police procedural, private eye/hardboiled), science fiction (hard science/technological), thriller/espionage. Recently published *Strong Conviction*, by Trevor Scott (mystery/thriller); *Bound to Die*, by Brian Lutterman (first fiction, thriller); and *Kafka's Fedora*, by A.J. Adler (mainstream).
How to Contact: Does not accept unsolicited mss. Send query letter. Accepts queries by e-mail; no queries by fax. Include estimated word count, brief bio, list of publishing credits "and something to intrigue me so I ask for more." Send SASE or IRC for return of ms or send disposable copy of ms and SASE for reply only. Agented fiction 15%. Responds in 3 weeks to queries; 1 month to mss. Accepts simultaneous submissions. Sometimes comments on rejected mss.
Terms: Pays royalties of 10-15%. No advance. Sends galleys to author. Publishes ms 9 months after acceptance. Guidelines and book catalogs available on website.

SARABANDE BOOKS, INC., 2234 Dundee Rd., Suite 200, Louisville KY 40205-1845. Fax: (502)458-4065. E-mail: sarabandeb@aol.com. Website: www.SarabandeBooks.org (includes authors, forthcoming titles, backlist, writer's guidelines, names of editors, author interviews and excerpts from their work and ordering and contest information). **Contact**: Sarah Gorham, editor-in-chief; Kirby Gann, fiction editor. Estab. 1994. "Small literary press publishing poetry and short fiction." Publishes hardcover and paperback originals. **Published new writers within the last year.** Averages 9 total titles, 3-4 fiction titles/year. Distributes titles through Consortium Book Sales & Distribution. Promotes titles through advertising in national magazines, sales reps, brochures, newsletters, postcards, catalogs, press release mailings, sales conferences, book fairs, author tours and reviews.
Needs: Short story collections, 250 pages maximum, 150 pages minimum. "Sarabande does not publish genre fiction." Recently published *Georgia Under Water*, by Heather Sellers (short stories); *What We Won't Do*, by Brocke Clarke (short stories); and *Bread for the Baker's Child*, by Joseph Caldwell (novel).
How to Contact: Submit in September only. Query with outline/synopsis and 1 sample story or 10-page sample. Include 1 page bio, listing of publishing credits. Send SASE or IRC for reply. Responds in 3 months to queries; 6 months to mss. Accepts simultaneous submissions.
Terms: Pays in royalties, author's copies. Sends galleys to author. Guidelines available (for contest only) for #10 SASE or on website; book catalog available.
Advice: "Make sure you're not writing in a vacuum, that you've read and are conscious of your competition in contemporary literature. Have someone read your manuscript, checking it for ordering, coherence. Better a lean, consistently strong manuscript than one that is long and uneven. Old fashioned as it sounds, we like a story to have good narrative, or at least we like to be engaged, to find ourselves turning the pages with real interest."

SCHERF BOOKS, Subsidiary of Scherf, Inc., P.O. Box 80180, Las Vegas NV 89180-0180. (702)243-4895. Fax: (702)243-7460. E-mail: ds@scherf.com. Website: www.scherf.com (includes book catalog). **Contact:** Dietmar Scherf (all fiction). Estab. 1990. "Small publisher concentrating on selective titles. We want to discover the next John Grisham, Danielle Steel, Nora Roberts, Tom Clancy, Michael Crichton, Ernest Hemingway, Anne Rice, Stephen King, etc. Based on our parent company we have vast resources and are known to get behind our books and authors just like a major publishing house would." Publishes hardcover and paperback originals. Average print order: 2,500-50,000. First novel print order: 2,500-20,000. Plans 10 first novels this year. Averages 2-4 total titles, 2 fiction titles/year. Distributes titles through Ingram Book Company, Baker & Taylor, Amazon.com and through most Internet bookstores. Promotes titles through advertisements, Internet, direct mail and PR.

Needs: Adventure, ethnic/multicultural (general), family saga, horror (dark fantasy, futuristic, psychological, supernatural), literary, mainstream, mystery/suspense, religious (inspirational, religious mystery/suspense, religious thriller), thriller/espionage, young adult/teen (adventure, easy-to-read, mystery/suspense, series).

How to Contact: Does not accept or return unsolicted mss. Send query letter. Include estimated word count and 1-paragraph bio. Send SASE for return of ms or send disposable copy of ms and SASE for reply only. Responds in 1 month to queries; up to 4 months to mss. Accepts simultaneous submissions. Sometimes comments on rejected mss.

Terms: Pays royalties of 5-10%. Offers negotiable advance. Sends galleys to author. Publishes ms 12-18 months after acceptance.

Advice: "We're concentrating on novels. There are many manuscripts out there, but it is difficult to find an excellent piece of work. But once we find that certain exceptional novel, we're getting behind it full throttle. Write the greatest book possible about a story that you love and are truly excited about. Learn some writing skills, especially grammar, characterization, dialogue or strong narrative qualities, plot, etc. A great story is a beginning, but the writer has to have excellent writing skills. Read books from authors that you like, but develop your own unique voice."

SCHOLASTIC CANADA LTD., 175 Hillmount Rd., Markham, Ontario L6C 1Z7 Canada. (905)887-7323. Fax: (905)887-3643. Website: www.scholastic.ca. **Contact:** Editors. Publishes hardcover and trade paperback originals. Averages 30 titles/year.

Imprint(s): North Winds Press; Les Éditions Scholastic (contact Sylvie Andrews, French editor).

Needs: Children's/juvenile, young adult. Recently published *The Promise of the Unicorn*, by Vicki Blum (juvenile novel).

How to Contact: *Accepts agented submissions only.*

Terms: Pays royalties of 5-10% on retail price. Average advance: $1,000-5,000 (Canadian). Publishes ms 1 year after acceptance. Book catalog available for 8½×11 SAE with 2 first-class stamps (IRC or Canadian stamps only).

SCHOLASTIC INC., 555 Broadway, New York NY 10012-3999. (212)343-6100. Website: www.scholastic.com (includes general information about Scholastic). **Contact:** Jean Feiwel, senior vice president/publisher, Book Group Scholastic Inc. Estab. 1920. Publishes books for children ages 4-young adult. "We are proud of the many fine, innovative materials we have created—such as classroom magazines, book clubs, book fairs, and our new literacy and technology programs. But we are most proud of our reputation as 'The Most Trusted Name in Learning.' " Publishes juvenile hardcover picture books, novels and nonfiction. Distributes titles through Scholastic Book Clubs, Scholastic Book Fairs, bookstores and other retailers.

Imprint(s): Blue Sky Press; Cartwheel Books; Arthur A. Levine Books; Mariposa; Scholastic Press; Scholastic Trade Paperbacks; Scholastic Reference.

SCHOLASTIC PRESS, Imprint of Scholastic Inc., 557 Broadway, New York NY 10012. (212)343-6100. Fax: (212)343-4713. Website: www.scholastic.com (includes information for teachers, parents and children, games/contests and information for children as well as book and author information—no guidelines online). **Contact:** Elizabeth Szabla, editorial director (picture books, middle grade, young adult); Dianne Hess, executive editor (picture books, middle grade, young adult); Tracy Mack, executive editor (picture books, middle grade, young adult); Lauren Thompson, senior editor (picture books, middle grade); Kate Egan, editor (picture books, middle grade and young adult novels). Publishes hardcover originals. **Published new writers within the last year.** Promotes titles through trade and library channels.

Needs: Juvenile, picture books, novels. Wants "fresh, exciting picture books and novels—inspiring, new talent." Recently published *The Three Questions*, by Jon J. Muth; *A Corner of the Universe*, by Ann M. Martin; *The Dinosaurs of Waterhouse Hawkins*, by Barbara Kerley, illustrated by Brian Selznick; and *Indigo*, by Alice Hoffman.

How to Contact: Does not accept unsolicited mss. Agented submissions only. Responds in 6 months to submissions from SCBWI members and previously-published authors. No fax queries.

Terms: Pays royalty on retail price. Royalty and advance vary. Publishes ms 18 months after acceptance.

Advice: "Be a big reader of juvenile literature before you write and submit!"

SCIENCE & HUMANITIES PRESS, P.O. Box 7151, Chesterfield MO 63006-7151. (636)394-4950. Fax: (636)394-1381. E-mail: pub@sciencehumanitiespress.com. Website: www.sciencehumanitiespress.com. **Contact:** Dr. Bud Banis, publisher. Publishes trade paperback originals and reprints, and electronic originals and reprints. **Publishes 25% of books from first-time authors; 100% from unagented writers.** Averages 20-30 titles/year.

Imprints: Science & Humanities Press, BeachHouse Books, MacroPrintBooks (large print editions), Heuristic Books, Early Editions Books.

Needs: Adventure, fantasy, historical, humor, literary, mainstream/contemporary, military/war, mystery, plays, poetry, regional, religious, romance, science fiction, short story collections, spiritual, sports, suspense, western, young adult.

How to Contact: "Brief description by e-mail." Accepts simultaneous submissions. Responds in 1 month to queries; 3 months to mss.

Terms: Pays 8% royalty on retail price. Publishes book 6-12 after acceptance of ms. Book catalog online; ms guidelines online.

Advice: Sales are primarily through the Internet, special orders, reviews in specialized media, direct sales to libraries, special organizations and use as textbooks. "Our expertise is electronic publishing for continuous short-run in-house production rather than mass distribution to retail outlets. This allows us to commit to books that might not be financially successful in conventional book store environments and to keep books in print and available for extended periods of time. Books should be of types that would sell steadily over a long period of time, rather than those that require rapid rollout and bookstore shelf exposure for a short time. We consider the nurture of new talent part of our mission but enjoy experienced authors as well. We are proud that many of our books are second, third and fourth books from authors who were once our first-time authors. A good book is not a one-time accident."

Ⓐ SCRIBNER, Imprint of Simon & Schuster, 1230 Avenue of the Americas, New York NY 10020. (212)698-7000. Publishes hardcover originals. Averages 70-75 total titles/year.
Imprint(s): Rawson Associates; Lisa Drew Books.
Needs: Literary, mystery/suspense. Recently published *From a Buick 8*, by Stephen King; *The Constant Gardener*, by John Le Carré; and *War in a Time of Peace*, by David Halberstam.
How to Contact: *Agented fiction only*. Responds in 3 months to queries. Accepts simultaneous submissions.
Terms: Pays royalties of 7½-15%. Advance varies. Publishes ms 9 months after acceptance.

Ⓝ Ⓛ SCRIVENERY PRESS, P.O. Box 740969-1003, Houston TX 77274-0969. (713)665-6760. Fax: (713)665-8838. E-mail: books@scrivenery.com. Website: www.scrivenery.com (includes writer's guidelines, catalog of books, sample chapters, interactive message boards, unique database of bookstores and more). **Contact:** Leila B. Joiner, editor (literary fiction); Chris Coleman, editor (mainstream and historical fiction). Estab. 1999. "As a newer publisher, we are actively seeking new mainstream/literary novels and collections for publication as trade paperback originals. As our backlist grows, we anticipate our requirements will become more stringent regarding unpublished wrtiers." Publishes hardcover and paperback originals and paperback reprints. Books: 60 lb. acid free paper; direct CTP printing; perfect-bound; line art and gray scale illustrations. Average print order: 2,000. First novel print order: 1,000. **Published 3 new writers within the last year.** Plans 3 first novels this year. Averages 10 total titles/year. Member, Publishers Marketing Association. Distributes all titles through Ingram Book Group, Ingram International and Baker & Taylor.
Needs: Adventure, experimental, historical (general, pre-WWII), literary, mainstream, mystery/suspense, regional, short story collections, thriller/espionage, translations. "We need polished, literate work that could be construed as a crossover between genre and literary fiction." Short story anthology in planning for 2001/2002. Recently published *Good King Sauerkraut*, by Barbara Paul (mystery); *A Journey to the Interior*, by E.A. Blair (historical); and *Cleaning Up the Mess*, by Paul F. Ferguson (collection/literary).
How to Contact: Does not accept unsolicited mss; will return unopened. Query with outline/synopsis and 3 sample chapters. Include estimated word count, brief bio, list of publishing credits and genre/target market. Send SASE or IRC for return of ms or send disposable copy of ms and SASE for reply only. Agented fiction 50%. Responds in 2 months to queries; 3 months to mss. Accepts simultaneous submissions.
Terms: Pays royalties of 8½-15%. Average advance: seldom offered. Sends galleys to author. Publishes ms 6-12 months after acceptance. Guidelines available free for #10 SASE or on website; book catalogs for $2 or on website.
Advice: "Scrivenery Press is open to unpublished talent, but not writers new to the craft. Polish your manuscript as best you can; expect to be judged against seasoned pros. Submit material in industry-standard format, but be aware we will need electronic word processor files for the final manuscript. If you send us a simultaneous submission, please note that in your cover letter."

Ⓞ Ⓞ SEAL PRESS, Imprint of Avalon Publishing Group, 300 Queen Anne Ave. N. #375, Seattle WA 98109. Fax: (206)285-9410. E-mail: Leslie.Miller@avalonpub.com. Website: www.sealpress.com. **Contact:** Ingrid Emerick, editor/publisher; Leslie Miller, senior editor; Christina Henry, managing editor. Estab. 1976. "Midsize independent feminist book publisher interested in original, lively, radical, empowering and culturally diverse books by women." Publishes trade paperback originals. Books: 55 lb. natural paper; Cameron Belt, Web or offset printing; perfect binding; illustrations occasionally. Averages 20 total titles/year. Titles distributed by Publishers Group West.
Imprint(s): Adventura (womens travel, outdoor adventure); Live Girls (pop culture/feminist).
Needs: Feminist, gay/lesbian, literary, multicultural. Recently published *Valencia*, by Michelle Tea (fiction); *Navigating the Darwin Straits*, by Edith Forbes (fiction); and *Bruised Hibiscus*, by Elizabeth Nunez (fiction).
How to Contact: Does not accept unsolicited mss. Query with outline/synopsis and 2 sample chapters. Does not accept e-mail queries. Send SASE for reply. Responds in 2 months to queries.
Terms: Pays royalties of 7-8% on retail price. Average advance: $2,000-10,000. Publishes ms 18 months after acceptance. Guidelines and book catalog available online.

Ⓞ Ⓞ Ⓞ SERENDIPITY SYSTEMS, P.O. Box 140, San Simeon CA 93452. (805)927-5259. E-mail: bookware@thegrid.net. Website: www.s-e-r-e-n-d-i-p-i-t-y.com (includes guidelines, sample books, writer's manuscript help, catalog). **Contact:** John Galuszka, publisher. Estab. 1985. "Electronic publishing for IBM-PC compatible systems." Publishes "electronic editions originals and reprints." Books on disk. **Published new writers within the last year.** Averages 36 total titles, 15 fiction titles/year (either publish or distribute).
Imprint(s): Books-on-Disks™ and Bookware™.

Needs: "Works of fiction which use, or have the potential to use, hypertext, multimedia or other computer-enhanced features. We cannot use on-paper manuscripts." No romance, religion, New Age, children's, young adult, occult. "We only publish book-length works, not individual short stories." Recently published *The Blue-Eyed Muse*, by John Peter (novel).

How to Contact: Query by e-mail. Submit complete ms with cover letter and SASE. *IBM-PC compatible disk required.* ASCII files required unless the work is hypertext or multimedia. Send SASE or IRC for return of ms or send disposable copy of ms and SASE for reply only. Responds in 2 weeks to queries; 1 month to mss. Often comments on rejected mss.

Terms: Pays royalties of 25%. Publishes ms 2 months after acceptance. Guidelines available on website.

Advice: "We are interested in seeing multimedia works suitable for Internet distribution. Would like to see: more works of serious literature—novels, short stories, plays, etc. Would like to not see: right wing adventure fantasies from 'Tom Clancy' wanna-be's."

SEVEN STORIES PRESS, 140 Watts St., New York NY 10013. (212)226-8760. Fax: (212)226-1411. E-mail: info@se venstories.com. Website: www.sevenstories.com. **Contact**: Daniel Simon and Jill Schoolman, editors. Estab. 1995. "Publishers of a distinguished list of authors in fine literature, journalism, contemporary culture and alternative health." Publishes hardcover and paperback originals and paperback reprints. Average print order: 5,000. **Published new writers within the last year.** Averages 20 total titles, 10 fiction titles/year. Distributes through Publishers Group West (US).

Needs: Literary. Plans anthologies. Ongoing series of short story collections from other cultures (e.g., *Contemporary Fiction from Central America; from Vietnam*, etc.) Recently published *A Place to Live and Other Selected Essays of Natalia Ginzburg*; *American Falls*, by Barry Gifford; and *The Incantation of Frida K.*, by Kate Brauerman.

How to Contact: Query with outline/synopsis and 1 sample chapter. Include list of publishing credits. Send SASE or IRC for reply. Agented fiction 60%. Responds in 1 month to queries; 4 months to mss. Accepts simultaneous submissions. Sometimes comments on rejected mss.

Terms: Pays standard royalty; offers advance. Sends galleys to author. Publishes ms 1-2 years after acceptance. Free guidelines and book catalog.

Advice: "Writers should only send us their work after they have read some of the books we publish and find our editorial vision in sync with theirs."

N ◐ ◉ SILHOUETTE DESIRE, a Harlequin book line, 300 E. 42nd St., 6th Floor, New York NY 10017. (212)682-6080. Fax: (212)682-4539. Website: www.eharlequin.com. **Contact:** Joan Marlow Golan, senior editor. "Sensual, believable and compelling, these books are written for today's woman. Innocent or experienced, the heroine is someone we identify with; the hero is irresistible." Publishes paperback originals and reprints. Books: newspaper print; web printing; perfect-bound. **Regularly publishes new writers.**

Needs: Romance. Looking for novels in which "the conflict is an emotional one, springing naturally from the unique characters you've chosen. The focus is on the developing relationship, set in a believable plot. Sensuality is key, but lovemaking is never taken lightly. Secondary characters and subplots need to blend with the core story. Innovative new directions in storytelling and fresh approaches to classic romantic plots are welcome." Manuscripts must be 55,000-60,000 words.

How to Contact: Accepts unsolicited mss. Send query letter or submit complete ms with cover letter. Send SASE or IRC for return of ms or send disposable copy of ms and SASE for reply only. No simultaneous, multiple or disk submissions.

Terms: Pays royalties and advance. Guidelines available for SASE or on website.

N ◐ ◉ SILHOUETTE INTIMATE MOMENTS, a Harlequin book line, 300 E. 42nd St., 6th Floor, New York NY 10017. (212)682-6080. Fax: (212)682-4539. Website: www.eharlequin.com. **Contact:** Leslie Wainger, executive senior editor. "Believable characters swept into a world of larger-than-life romance are the hallmark of Silhouette Intimate Moments books. These books offer you the freedom to combine the universally appealing elements of a category romance with the flash and excitement of mainstream fiction." Publishes paperback originals and reprints. Books: newspaper print; web printing; perfect-bound. **Regularly publishes new writers.**

Needs: Romance (contemporary). Looking for "novels that explore new directions in romantic fiction or classic plots in contemporary ways, always with the goal of tempting today's demanding reader. Adventure, suspense, melodrama, glamour—let your imagination be your guide as you blend old and new to create a novel with emotional depth and tantalizing complexity." Manuscripts must be approximately 80,000 words.

How to Contact: Accepts unsolicited mss. Send query letter or submit complete ms with cover letter. Send SASE or IRC for return of ms or send disposable copy of ms and SASE for reply only. No simultaneous, multiple or disk submissions.

Terms: Pays royalties and advance. Guidelines available for SASE or on website.

N ◐ ◉ SILHOUETTE ROMANCE, a Harlequin book line, 300 E. 42nd St., 6th Floor, New York NY 10017. (212)682-6080. Fax: (212)682-4539. Website: www.eharlequin.com. **Contact:** Mary-Theresa Hussey, senior editor. "Our ultimate goal is to give readers vibrant love stories with heightened emotional impact—books that touch readers' hearts and celebrate their values, including the traditional ideals of love, marriage and family." Publishes paperback originals and reprints. Books: newspaper print; web printing; perfect-bound. **Regularly publishes new writers.**

Needs: Romance (contemporary traditional). Looking for "talented authors able to portray modern relationships in the context of romantic love. Although the hero and heroine don't actually make love unless married, sexual tension is vitally important. Writers are encouraged to try creative new approaches to classic romantic and contemporary fairy tale plots." Manuscripts must be approximately 53,000-58,000 words.

How to Contact: Accepts unsolicited mss. Send query letter or submit complete ms with cover letter. Send SASE or IRC for return of ms or send disposable copy of ms and SASE for reply only. No simultaneous, multiple or disk submissions.

Terms: Pays royalties and advance. Guidelines available for SASE or on website.

SILHOUETTE SPECIAL EDITION, a Harlequin book line, 300 E. 42nd St., 6th Floor, New York NY 10017. (212)682-6080. Fax: (212)682-4539. Website: www.eharlequin.com. **Contact:** Karen Taylor Richman, senior editor. "Whether the sensuality is sizzling or subtle, whether the plot is wildly innovative or satisfyingly traditional, the novel's emotional vividness, its depth and dimension, clearly label it a very special contemporary romance." Publishes paperback originals. Books: newspaper print; web printing; perfect-bound. **Regularly publishes new writers.**

Needs: Romance (contemporary). "Sophisticated, substantial and packed with emotion, Special Edition demands writers eager to probe characters deeply to explore issues that heighten the drama of living, loving and creating a family, to generate compelling romantic plots. Subplots are welcome, but must further or parallel the developing romantic relationship in a meaningful way." Manuscripts must be approximately 76,000-80,000 words.

How to Contact: Does not accepts unsolicited mss. Send query letter with cover letter. Send SASE for return of ms. No simultaneous, multiple, e-mail or disk submissions.

Terms: Pays royalties and advance. Guidelines available for SASE or on website.

SILVER DAGGER MYSTERIES, The Overmountain Press, P.O. Box 1261, Johnson City TN 37605. (423)926-2691. Fax: (423)232-1252. E-mail: beth@overmtn.com. Website: www.silverdaggermysteries.com (includes submission guidelines, book catalog, author bios, links, touring schedules, newsletter). **Contact:** Alex Foster, acquisitions editor (mystery). Estab. 1999. "Small imprint of a larger company. We publish Southern mysteries. Our house is unique in that we are a consortium of authors who communicate and work together to promote each other." Publishes hardcover and paperback originals and reprints. Books: 60 lb. offset paper; perfect/case binding. Average print order: 2,000-5,000; first novel print order: 2,000. **Published 6 new writers within the last year.** Averages 15 fiction titles/year. Member, PAS. Distributes titles through direct mail, Ingram, Baker & Taylor, Partners, trade shows.

  • Julie Wray Herman was nominated for the Agatha Award for *Three Dirty Women & the Garden of Death*.

Needs: Mystery/suspense (amateur sleuth, cozy, police procedural, private eye/hardboiled), young adult/teen (mystery/suspense). Publishes *Magnolias & Mayhem*, an anthology of Southern short mysteries. Submissions "closed—editor solicits prior to contract signing." Recently published *Killer Looks*, by Laura Young; *Haunting Refrain*, by Ellis Vidler; and *Justice Betrayed*, by Daniel Bailey.

How to Contact: Does not accept or return unsolicited mss. Query with outline/synopsis and first 3 chapters. Does not accept queries by fax or e-mail. Include estimated word count, brief bio and list of publishing credits. Send SASE or IRC for return of ms. Agented fiction 30%. Responds in 1 month to queries; 3 months to mss.

Terms: Pays royalties of 15%. Sends galleys to author. Publishes ms up to 2 years after acceptance. Guidelines and book catalogs available on website.

Advice: "We are very author friendly from editing to promotion. Make sure your book is 'Southern' or set in the South before taking the time to submit."

SILVER MOON PRESS, 160 Fifth Ave., New York NY 10010. (212)242-6499. Fax: (212)242-6799. **Contact:** Hope Killcoyne, managing editor. Publishes hardcover originals. **Publishes 60% of books from first-time authors; 70% from unagented writers.** Averages 5-8 titles/year.

Needs: Historical, multicultural, biographical. Recently published *Thunder on the Sierra*, by Kathy Balmes; *Raid at Red Mill*, by Mary McGahan.

How to Contact: Query with SASE or submit proposal package including 1-3 sample chapter(s), synopsis. Accepts simultaneous submissions. Responds in 2 months to queries; 3-6 months to mss.

Terms: Pays 7-10% royalty. Offers 500-1,000 advance. Publishes book 18 months after acceptance of ms. Book catalog for 9×12 SASE; ms guidelines for #10 SASE.

SIMON & SCHUSTER, 1230 Avenue of the Americas, New York NY 10020. (212)698-7000. Website: www.simonsays.com.

Imprints: *Simon & Schuster Adult Publishing Group*: Simon & Schuster, Scribner (Scribner, Lisa Drew, Simple Abundance Press), The Free Press, Atria Books, Kaplan, Touchstone, Scribner Paperback Fiction, S&S Librow en Espanol, Simon & Schuster Source, Wall Street Journal Books, Pocket Books (Pocket Star, Washington Square Press, MTV Books, Sonnet Books, Star Trek, The New Folger Shakespeare, VH-1 Books, WWF Books). *Simon & Schuster Children's Publishing:* Aladdin Paperbacks, Atheneum Books for Young Readers (Anne Schwartz Books, Richard Jackson Books) Little Simon (Simon Spotlight, Rabbit Ears Books & Audio), Margaret K. McElderry Books, (Archway Paperbacks, Minstreal Books), Simon & Schuster Books for Young Readers.

SIMON & SCHUSTER ADULT PUBLISHING GROUP, (formerly Simon & Schuster Trade Division, Division of Simon & Schuster Inc.), 1230 Avenue of the Americas, New York NY 10020. (212)698-7000. E-mail: ssonline@simonsays.com. Website: www.simonsays.com. Estab. 1924.

Imprint(s): H&R Block; Lisa Drew Books; Fireside; The Free Press; Pocket Book Press; Rawson Associates; Scribner; Scribner Classics; Scribner Paperback Fiction; Scribner Poetry; S&S—Libros en Espanol; Simon & Schuster; Simon & Schuster Source; Simple Abundance Press; Touchstone; Wall Street Journal Books.

SIMON & SCHUSTER CHILDREN'S PUBLISHING, (Division of Simon & Schuster Inc.), 1230 Avenue of the Americas, New York NY 10020. (212)698-7200. E-mail: ssonline@simonsays.com. Website: www.simonsays.com. Estab. 1924.
Imprint(s): Aladdin Paperbacks; Atheneum Books for Young Readers; Little Simon; Margaret K. McElderry Books; Rabbit Ears; Simon & Schuster Books for Young Readers; Simon Spotlight.

GIBBS SMITH, PUBLISHER/PEREGRINE SMITH, P.O. Box 667, Layton UT 84041. (801)544-9800. Fax: (801)544-5582. E-mail: info@gibbs-smith.com. Website: www.gibbs~smith.com/. **Contact:** Gail Yngve, editor (poetry); Suzanne Taylor, senior editor (children's); Madge Baird, editorial director (western, humor); Linda Nimori, editor. Estab. 1969. Small independent press. "We publish books that make a difference." Publishes hardcover and paperback originals and reprints. Averages 40-60 total titles, 1-2 fiction titles/year.
● Gibbs Smith is the recipient of a Western Writers Association Fiction Award. Publishes the winner of the Peregrine Smith Poetry Contest (accepts entries only in April).
Needs: Only short works oriented to gift market. Publishes *The Peregrine Reader*, a series of anthologies based upon a variety of themes. Recently published *A Strong Man*, by Carol Lynn Pearson.
How to Contact: Send query letter or short gift book ms directly to the editor. Send SASE or IRC for return of the ms. Agented fiction 50%. Responds in 1 month to queries; 4 months to mss. Accepts simultaneous submissions. Sometimes comments on rejected mss.
Terms: Pays royalty depending on the book. Provides 10 author's copies. Sends galleys to author. Publishes ms 1-2 years after acceptance. Guidelines and book catalog available for #10 SASE and $2.13 in postage.

SNOWAPPLE PRESS, P.O. Box 66024, Heritage Postal Outlet, Edmonton, Alberta T6J 6T4 Canada. (780)437-0191. **Contact:** Vanna Tessier, editor. Estab. 1991. "We focus on topics that are interesting, unusual and controversial." Small independent literary press. Publishes hardcover and paperback originals. Books: non-acid paper; offset printing; perfect binding; illustrations. Average print order: 500. First novel print order: 500. Plans 1 first novel this year. Averages 3-4 total titles, 1-2 fiction titles/year. Distributes titles through bookseller and library wholesalers. Promotes titles through press releases and reviews.
Needs: Adventure, children's/juvenile (adventure, fantasy, mystery), experimental, historical, literary, mainstream/contemporary, short story collections, translations, young adult/teen (adventure, mystery/suspense). Published *Thistle Creek*, by Vanna Tessier (short stories); *The Last Waltz of Chopin*, by Gilberto Finzi, translated by Vanna Tessier (novel).
How to Contact: Does not accept unsolicited mss. Query with 1-page cover letter. Include estimated word count, 300-word bio and list of publishing credits. Send SASE with sufficient IRCs. Responds in 1 month to queries; 3 months to mss. Accepts simultaneous submissions.
Terms: Pays honorarium; provides 10-25 author's copies. Sends galleys to author. Publishes ms 12-18 months after acceptance.
Advice: "Query first with proper SASE and IRCs to obtain guidelines."

SOFT SKULL PRESS INC., 100 Suffolk St., Basement, New York NY 10002. (212)673-2502. Fax: (212)673-0787. E-mail: misshorse@softskull.com. Website: www.softskull.com. **Contact:** Sander Hicks, editor. Estab. 1992. "A small press combining the ferocity of the zine scene, the power of punk and the speed of the modern copy shop. Especially interested in authors under 35." Publishes hardcover and paperback originals. Books: 55 lb. paper; offset printing; cloth/paperback binding; illustrations. Average print order: 3,000; first novel print order: 3,000. **Published 8 new writers within the last year.** Plans 2 first novels this year. Averages 10 total titles, 6 fiction titles/year. Member, SPAN, PMA, Small Press Center and Union of Progressive Presses. Distributes titles through PGW.
Needs: Experimental, historical, literary, mainstream/contemporary, multicultural, short story collections. "We are inundated with 'drug and rock & roll' novels. We love left-of-center political material." Publishes *What the Fuck: The Avant Porn Anthology*. Recently published *Outline Of My Lover*, by Douglas A. Martin (gay/experimental); *Ripe Tomatoes*, by Nora Ruth Roberts (political satire); and *Document Zippo*, by L.A. Ruocco (experimental).
How to Contact: Accepts unsolicited mss. Query with SASE or submit proposal package including 1 sample chapter and synopsis. Include estimated word count. Send SASE or IRC for return of ms or send disposable copy of ms and SASE for reply only. Agented fiction 50%. Responds in 2 months to queries; 3 months to mss. Does not accept simultaneous submissions.
Terms: Pays royalties of 7-9%. Average advance: $100-15,000. Sends galleys to author. Publishes ms 6 months after acceptance. Guidelines available free for SASE; book catalogs free or on website.
Advice: "Make the commonplace extraordinary. Don't be afraid to be political, even radical. Know our list before submitting. We are interested in challenging and aggressive literature. No mainstream genre material, but cutting edge books that thwart genre expectations can be cool. We are moving away from 'drug and rock' novels. We may start looking at experimental or New Wave science fiction, urban fantasy, absurdist stuff."

SOHO PRESS, INC., 853 Broadway, New York NY 10003. (212)260-1900. Fax: (212)260-1902. E-mail: soho@sohopress.com. Website: www.sohopress.com (includes writer's guidelines and book catalog). **Contact:** Juris Jurjevics, editor (literary, mainstream novels); Laura Hruska, editor (literary fiction, literary mysteries); Bryan Derendorf, editor (literary fiction). Estab. 1986. "Independent publisher known for sophisticated fiction, mysteries set abroad, women's interest (no genre) novels and multicultural novels." Publishes hardcover originals and paperback reprints. Books: acid free paper; perfect binding; halftone illustrations. First novel print order: 5,000. **Published 5 new writers within the last year.** Plans 4 first novels this year. Averages 40 total titles, 34 fiction titles/year. Distributes titles through Farrar Straus & Giroux in the US, Hushion House in Canada, Turnaround in England.

Imprint(s): Soho Crime, edited by Laura Hruska: procedurals set abroad.

Needs: Ethnic/multicultural, literary, mystery/suspense (police procedural), translations. Recently published *A Working Stiff's Manifesto*, by Iain Levison; *A Loyal Character Dancer*, by Qin Xialong; *Latitudes of Melt*, by Joan Clark; *He Kills Coppers*, by Jake Arnott; and *Murder in the Sentier*, by Cara Black. Publishes various mystery series.

How to Contact: Does not accept unsolicited mss. Query with outline/synopsis and the first 3 sample chapters. Include estimated word count, brief bio and list of publishing credits. Send SASE or IRC for return of ms or send disposable copy of ms and SASE for reply only. Agented fiction 65%. Responds in 3 months to queries; 2 months to mss. Accepts simultaneous submissions. No e-mail or disk submissions. Sometimes comments on rejected mss.

Terms: Pays royalties of 10-15%. Offers advance. Sends galleys to author. Publishes ms up to 18 months after acceptance. Guidelines available for SASE and on website; book catalogs for $1 or on website.

N **◐** **◎** **SOUNDPRINTS,** Division of Trudy Corporation, 353 Main Ave., Norwalk CT 06851. Fax: (203)846-1776. E-mail: soundprints@soundprints.com. Website: www.soundprints.com. **Contact:** Chelsea Shriver, assistant editor. Estab. 1988. Publishes hardcover originals. **Published 4 new writers within the last year.** Averages 12-14 total titles/year.

Needs: Juvenile. "Most of our books are under license from the Smithsonian Institution and are closely curated fictional stories based on fact. We never do stories of anthropomorphic animals." Recently published *Bumblebee at Apple Tree Lane*, by Laura Gates Galvin; *Sockeye's Journey Home: The Story of a Pacific Salmon*, by Barbara Gaines Winkelman.

How to Contact: Query with SASE. Responds in 1 month to queries. Accepts simultaneous submissions.

Terms: Makes outright purchase. No advance. Publishes ms 2 years after acceptance. Guidelines available for #10 SASE; book catalog on website.

Advice: "Our books are written for children from ages 4-8. Our most successful authors can craft a wonderful story which is derived from authentic wildlife facts. First inquiry to us should ask about our interest in publishing a book about a specific animal or habitat. When we publish juvenile fiction, it will be about wildlife and all information in the book *must* be accurate."

◐ **SOUTHERN METHODIST UNIVERSITY PRESS,** P.O. Box 750415, Dallas TX 75275-0415. (214)768-1433 (acquisitions). Fax: (214)768-1428. **Contact:** Kathryn M. Lang, senior editor. Estab. 1936. "Small university press publishing in areas of film/theater, Southwest life and letters, religion/medical ethics and contemporary fiction." Publishes hardcover and paperback originals and reprints. Books: acid-free paper; perfect-bound; some illustrations. Average print order: 2,000. **Published 2 new writers within the last year.** Averages 10-12 total titles, 3-4 fiction titles/year. Distributes titles through Texas A&M University Press Consortium. Promotes titles through writers' publications.

Needs: Literary novels and story collections. "We are always willing to look at 'serious' or 'literary' fiction." No "mass market, science fiction, formula, thriller, romance." Recently published *In Paterson*, by Miriam Levine (novel); and *Blessings on the Sheep Dog*, by Gerda Saunders (short stories).

How to Contact: Accepts unsolicited mss. Query with outline/synopsis and 3 sample chapters. Send SASE or IRC for return of ms. Responds in 3 weeks to queries; up to 1 year on mss. Sometimes comments on rejected mss.

Terms: Pays royalties of 10% net, negotiable small advance, 10 author's copies. Publishes ms 1 year after acceptance. Book catalog available free.

Advice: "We view encouraging first time authors as part of the mission of a university press. Send query describing the project and your own background. Research the press before you submit—don't send us the kinds of things we don't publish." Looks for "quality fiction from new or established writers."

◐ **◎** **⚑** **SPECTRA BOOKS,** Subsidiary of Random House, Inc., 1540 Broadway, New York NY 10036. (212)782-8771. Fax: (212)782-9523. Website: www.bantamdell.com. **Contact:** Anne Lesley Groell, senior editor. Estab. 1985. Large science fiction, fantasy and speculative fiction line. Publishes hardcover originals, paperback originals and trade paperbacks. Averages 60 fiction titles/year.

● Many Bantam Spectra Books have received Hugos and Nebulas.

Needs: Fantasy, literary, science fiction. Needs include novels that attempt to broaden the traditional range of science fiction and fantasy. Strong emphasis on characterization. Especially well written traditional science fiction and fantasy will be considered. No fiction that doesn't have at least some element of speculation or the fantastic. Published *Storm of Swords*, by George R. Martin (medieval fantasy); *Ship of Destiny*, by Robin Hobb (nautical fantasy); and *Antarctica*, by Stanley Robinson (science fiction).

How to Contact: Query with 3 chapters and a short (no more than 3 pages double-spaced) synopsis. Send SASE or IRC for return of ms. Agented fiction 90%. Responds in 6 months. Accepts simultaneous submissions if noted.

Terms: Pays in royalties; negotiable advance. Sends galleys to author. Guidelines available for #10 SASE.

Advice: "Please follow our guidelines carefully and type neatly."

◐ **◎** **SPINSTERS INK,** Hovis Publishing Company, P.O. Box 22005, Denver CO 80222. (303)761-5552. Fax: (303)761-5284. E-mail: spinster@spinsters-ink.com. Website: www.spinsters-ink.com (includes online catalog, writer's guidelines, author interviews, staff list, chat rooms, excerpts from books, discussion forums). **Contact:** Sharon Silvas.

Estab. 1978. Small women's publishing company growing steadily. "We are committed to publishing works by women writing from the periphery: fat women, Jewish women, lesbians, poor women, rural women, women of color, etc." Publishes paperback originals and reprints. Books: 60 lb. acid-free natural paper; photo offset printing; perfect-bound; illustrations when appropriate. Average print order: 3,000. Average first novel print order: 3,000. **Published 3 new writers within the last year.** Plans 2 first novels this year. Averages 12 total titles, 10 fiction titles/year. Distributes titles through Words Distributing.

Needs: Feminist, lesbian, mystery (amateur sleuth, private eye/hardboiled), science fiction (soft/sociological), short story collection, thriller/espionage. Wants "full-length quality fiction—thoroughly edited novels which display deep characterization, theme and style. We *only* consider books by women. No books by men, or books with sexist, racist or ageist content." Published *Voices of the Soft-bellied Warrior*, by Mary Saracino (memoir); *The Elegant Gathering of White Snows*, by Kris Radish (fiction); *Booked for Murder*, by Val McDermid; *The Kanshou*, by Sally Miller Gearhart (science fiction/fantasy, the Earthkeep series). Publishes the Earthkeep series.

How to Contact: Send query letter. No faxed or e-mailed queries. Include estimated word count, brief bio and list of publishing credits. Agented fiction: 10%. Responds in 3 months to queries; 3 months to mss. Accepts simultaneous submissions. No e-mail or disk submissions. Occasionally comments on rejected mss.

Terms: Pays negotiable royalties. Publishes ms 18 months after acceptance. Guidelines and book catalog available on website.

Advice: "Send a thorough query letter; we only accept work that is top quality."

STARBURST PUBLISHERS, P.O. Box 4123, Lancaster PA 17604. (717)293-0939. Fax: (717)293-1945. E-mail: starburst@starburstpublishers.com. Website: www.starburstpublishers.com (includes writer's guidelines, authors, titles, editorial information, catalog, rights, distribution, etc.). **Contact:** Editorial Director. Estab. 1982. Midsize independent press specializing in inspirational and self-help books. Publishes trade paperback and hardcover originals. **Published new writers within the last year.** Averages 10-15 total titles/year. Distributes titles through all major distributors and sales reps. Promotes titles through print, radio, and major distributors.

Needs: Religious/inspirational: Adventure, contemporary, fantasy, historical, horror, military/war, psychic/supernatural/occult, romance (contemporary, historical), spiritual, suspense/mystery, western. Wants "inspirational material."

How to Contact: Accepts unsolicited mss. Query with outline/synopsis and 3 sample chapters. Accepts queries by e-mail (no attachments). Include bio. Send SASE or IRC for return of ms. Agented fiction less than 25%. Responds in 1 month to queries; 2 months to manuscripts. Accepts electronic submissions via disk and modem, "but also wants clean double-spaced typewritten or computer printout manuscript."

Terms: Pays royalties of 6-16%. "Individual arrangement with writer depending on the manuscript as well as writer's experience as a published author." Publishes ms up to one year after acceptance. Guidelines available for #10 SASE. Book catalog available for 9×12 SAE and 4 first-class stamps.

Advice: "50% of our line goes into the inspirational marketplace; 50% into the general marketplace. We are one of the few publishers that has direct sales representation into both the inspirational and general marketplace."

STARCHERONE BOOKS, P.O. Box 303, Buffalo NY 14201-0303. (716) 885-2726. E-mail: ted@starcherone.com. Website: www.starcherone.com. **Contact:** Theodore Pelton, publisher. Estab. 2000. One-person operation on part-time basis. Publishes paperback originals and reprints. Books: acid-free paper; perfect-bound; occasional illustrations. Average print order: 600. Average first novel print order: 1,000. **Published 3 new writers within the last year.** Averages 1-2 total titles, 1-2 fiction titles/year. Member, CLMP. Titles distributed through website, Amazon, independent bookstores.

Needs: Comics/graphic novels, erotica, experimental, gay, lesbian, literary, short story collection, translations. Recently published *Black Umbrella Stories*, by Nicolette de Csipkay (debut author, short stories); *The Voice in the Closet*, Raymond Federman (experimental); *Endorsed by Jack Chapeau*, by Theodore Pelton (debut author, short stories).

How to Contact: Accepts unsolicited mss. Send query letter or submit complete ms with cover letter. Accepts queries by e-mail. Include brief bio and list of publishing credits. Send SASE from return of ms or disposable ms with SASE for reply only. Responds in 2 months to queries; 6 months to mss. No simultaneous submissions.

Terms: Pays based on "individual arrangement with author depending on book." Sends galleys to author. Publishes ms 6-12 months after acceptance. Guidelines and catalog available on website.

Advice: "Become familiar with our interests in fiction. We are interested in new strategies for creating stories and fictive texts. Do not send genre fiction unless it is unconventional in approach."

STEEPLE HILL, Harlequin Enterprises, 300 E. 42nd Street, 6th Floor, New York NY 10017. Website: www.harlequin.com. Editorial Director: Tara Gavin. Senior Editor: Tracy Farrell. **Contact:** Ann Leslie Tuttle, Melissa Endlich, acquisitions editors; and all Silhouette/Harlequin Historicals editors. Estab. 1997. Publishes mass market paperback originals.

Imprint(s): Love Inspired.

Needs: Inspirational romance. Recently published *A Mother at Heart*, by Carolyne Aarsen.

How to Contact: Accepts unsolicited mss. Send query letter or submit synopsis and 3 sample chapters. Send SASE or IRC for reply.

Terms: Pays royalty. Guidelines available for #10 SASE.

Advice: "Drama, humor and even a touch of mystery all have a place in this series. Subplots are welcome and should further the story's main focus or intertwine in a meaningful way. Secondary characters (children, family, friends, neighbors, fellow church members, etc.) may all contribute to a substantial and satisfying story. These wholesome tales of romance include strong family values and high moral standards. While there is no premarital sex between characters, a vivid, exciting romance that is presented with a mature perspective, is essential. Although the element of faith must clearly be present, it should be well integrated into the characterizations and plot. The conflict between the main characters should be an emotional one, arising naturally from the well-developed personalities you've created. Suitable stories should also impart an important lesson about the powers of trust and faith."

STONE BRIDGE PRESS, P.O. Box 8208, Berkeley CA 94707. (510)524-8732. Fax: (510)524-8711. E-mail: sbp@stonebridge.com. Website: www.stonebridge.com (includes complete catalog, contact information, related features, submission guidelines and excerpts). **Contact:** Peter Goodman, publisher. Estab. 1989. "Independent press focusing on books about Japan in English (business, language, culture, literature, animation)." Publishes paperback originals and reprints. Books: 60-70 lb. offset paper; web and sheet paper; perfect-bound; some illustrations. Averages 6 total titles/year. Distributes titles through Consortium. Promotes titles through Internet announcements, special-interest magazines and niche tie-ins to associations.

Imprint(s): Rock Spring Collection of Japanese Literature, edited by Peter Goodman.

● Stone Bridge Press received a Japan-U.S. Friendship Prize for *Life in the Cul-de-Sac,* by Senji Kuroi.

Needs: Japan-themed. No poetry. "Primarily looking at material relating to Japan. Mostly translations, but we'd like to see samples of work dealing with the expatriate experience." Also Asian- and Japanese-American. Recently published *Ash,* by Holly Thompson (debut author, literary); and *Japanese Yoga,* by H.E. Davey.

How to Contact: Accepts unsolicited mss. Query with 1-page cover letter, outline/synopsis and 3 sample chapters. Accepts queries by e-mail and fax. Send SASE or IRC for return of the ms. Agented fiction 25%. Responds in 1 month to queries; up to 1 year to mss. Accepts simultaneous submissions. Sometimes comments on rejected ms.

Terms: Pays royalties, offers negotiable advance. Publishes ms 18-24 months after acceptance. Catalog available for 2 first-class stamps.

Advice: "As we focus on Japan-related material there is no point in approaching us unless you are very familiar with Japan. We'd especially like to see submissions dealing with the expatriate experience. Please, absolutely no commercial fiction. No poetry. No fantasy, science fiction or romance."

SUNSTONE PRESS, P.O. Box 2321, Santa Fe NM 87504-2321. (505)988-4418. **Contact:** James C. Smith, Jr. Estab. 1971. Midsize publisher. Publishes hardcover and paperback originals. First novel print order: 2,000. **Published new writers within the last year.** Averages 16 total titles, 2-3 fiction titles/year.

● Sunstone Press published *Ninez,* by Virginia Nylander Ebinger which received the Southwest Book Award from the Border Regional Library Association.

Needs: Western. "We have a Southwestern theme emphasis. Sometimes buy juvenile mss with illustrations." No science fiction, romance or occult. Published *Apache: The Long Ride Home,* by Grant Gall (Indian/Western); *Sorrel,* by Rita Cleary; and *To Die in Dinetah,* by John Truitt.

How to Contact: Accepts unsolicited mss. Query first or submit outline/synopsis and 2 sample chapters with SASE. Responds in 2 weeks. Accepts simultaneous submissions.

Terms: Pays royalties of 10% maximum and 10 author's copies. Publishes ms 9-12 months after acceptance.

TAB BOOK CLUB, (TEEN AGE BOOK CLUB), Scholastic Inc., 557 Broadway, New York NY 10012. **Contact:** Greg Holch, senior editor.

Needs: "TAB Book Club publishes novels for young teenagers in seventh through ninth grades. At the present time these novels are all reprints from Scholastic's trade division or from other publishers. The Tab Book Club is not currently publishing original novels."

How to Contact: "We are not looking at new manuscripts this year."

Advice: "The books we are publishing now are literary works that we hope will become the classics of the future. They are novels that reveal the hearts and souls of their authors."

NAN A. TALESE, The Doubleday Broadway Publishing Group, A Division of Random House, Inc., 1540 Broadway, New York NY 10036. (212)782-8918. Fax: (212)782-9261. Website: www.nanatalese.com. **Contact:** Nan A. Talese, editorial director. "Nan A. Talese publishes nonfiction with a powerful guiding narrative and relevance to larger cultural trends and interests, and literary fiction of the highest quality." Publishes hardcover originals. Averages 15 titles/year.

Needs: Literary. Looking for "well written narratives with a compelling story line, good characterization, and use of language. We like stories with an edge." Published *The Blind Assassin,* by Margaret Atwood; *Atonement,* by Ian McEwan; and *Great Shame,* by Thomas Keneally.

READ 'THE BUSINESS OF FICTION WRITING' section for information on manuscript preparation, mailing tips, rights and more.

How to Contact: Agented fiction only. Responds in 1 week to queries; 2 weeks to proposals and mss. Accepts simultaneous submissions.

Terms: Pays royalty on retail price, varies. Advance varies. Publishes ms 1 year after acceptance.

Advice: "We're interested in literary narrative, fiction and nonfiction—we do not publish genre fiction. Our readers are highly literate people interested in good story-telling, intellectual and psychologically significant. We want well-written material."

TATTERSALL PUBLISHING, P.O. Box 308194, Denton TX 76203-8194. (940)565-0804. Fax: (940)320-8604. E-mail: cwood@tattersallpub.com. Website: www.tattersallpub.com (current and backlist titles, works in progress, ordering, FAQ, writer's guidelines, links). **Contact:** Cheryl Wolfe, associate editor (fantasy, science fiction, mystery/suspense, historical, humor/satire). Estab. 1994. "Tattersall publishing began in 1994 as a self-publishing venture and has grown into a thriving small independent publisher with national distribution." Publishes hardcover originals and paperback originals. Books: 70 lb. paper; offset printing; perfect or smyth-sewn binding. Average print order: 1,000; first novel print order: 1,000. **Published 2 new writers within the last year.** Averages 3 total titles, 2 fiction titles/year. Distributes titles through Biblio Distribution.

• "Temporarily suspending acquisitions; check website for notice of reopening to submissions."

Needs: Fantasy (contemporary supernatural), historical (no family sagas), humor/satire, mystery/suspense (amateur sleuth, cozy), and science fiction (soft/sociological). Recently published *The Mendelian Threshold*, by Robert Humphrey (sociological science fiction); *Longhorns & Short Tales*, by Newcomb/Balmer (humor); *Rockhand Lizzie*, by Gerald Stone (historical).

How to Contact: Does not accept unsolicited mss. Often comments on rejected mss.

Advice: "I'm publishing less fiction but am open to considering exciting new things. I generally publish in paperback due to up-front costs, but will place an extraordinary book in hardcover. E-publishing and books on CD-ROM are the latest thing, but until there's an industry standard, we'll continue to produce books the old-fashioned way. Content-wise, it's a world of specialization, even in fiction. Find the niche market you like and write for it. Try the 'big guys' first, and use whatever feedback you get to improve your ms. (Who knows, they might buy it for real money!) Then impress me with your professionalism—follow the guidelines I've chosen and pretend you're applying for the best job of your life. Spelling and grammar and punctuation are **important**—the English language has rules that make our communication effective. (You can break rules for effect. But *know* them before you break them!)"

THIRD WORLD PRESS, P.O. Box 19730, Chicago IL 60619. (773)651-0700. Fax: (773)651-7286. E-mail: TWPress3@aol.com. Publisher/Editor: Haki Madhubuti. **Contact:** Gwendolyn Mitchell, editor. Estab. 1967. Black-owned and operated independent publisher of fiction and nonfiction books about the black experience throughout the Diaspora. Publishes hardcover and paperback originals and reprints. Plans 1 first novel this year, as well as short story collections. Averages 20 total titles each year. Average first novel print order 15,000 copies. Distributes titles through Partners, Baker & Taylor and bookstores. Promotes titles through direct mail, catalogs and newspapers.

Needs: Ethnic, feminist, historical, juvenile (animal, easy-to-read, fantasy, historical, contemporary), preschool/picture book, literary, mainstream, short story collections, and young adult/teen (easy-to-read/teen, folktales, historical), African-centered, African-American materials. Recently published *In the Shadow of the Son*, by Michael Simanga. "We primarily publish nonfiction, but will consider fiction by and about blacks."

How to Contact: Accepts unsolicited mss in July only. Query with SASE or submit outline/synopsis and 5 sample chapters and synopsis. Responds in 6 weeks to queries; 5 months to mss. Accepts simultaneous submissions. Accepts computer printout submissions.

Terms: Individual arrangement with author depending on the book, etc. Publishes ms 18 months after acceptance.

THISTLEDOWN PRESS, 633 Main St., Saskatoon, Saskatchewan S7H 0J8 Canada. (306)244-1722. Fax: (306)244-1762. E-mail: tdpress@thistledown.sk.ca. Website: www.thistledown.sk.ca (includes guidelines, catalog, teaching materials). Editor-in-Chief: Patrick O'Rourke. **Contact:** Jesse Stothers, editor. Estab. 1975. Publishes paperback originals—literary fiction, young adult fiction, poetry. Books: quality stock paper; offset printing; perfect-bound; occasional illustrations. Average print order 1,500-2,000. First novel print order: 1,000-1,500. **Published new writers within the last year.** Averages 12 total titles, 6-7 fiction titles/year. Promotes titles through intensive school promotions, online, advertising, special offers.

• Thistledown's *Prisoner in a Red-Rose Chain*, by Jeffrey Moore won the Commonwealth Writers Prize for Best New Book.

Needs: Literary, experimental, short story collections, novels.

How to Contact: Does not accept unsolicited mss. Query first with SASE or IRC for reply. Accepts queries by e-mail and fax. "We *only* want to see Canadian-authored submissions. We will *not* consider multiple submissions." Accepts photocopied submissions. Responds in 2 months to queries. Publishes anthologies. "Stories are nominated." Published *Japanese Baseball & Other Stories*, by W.P. Kinsella (short fiction); *Ariadne's Dream*, by Tess Fragoulis (novel); *A Traveller Came By: Stories About Dying*, by Seán Virgo (short fiction). Also publishes The Mayer Mystery Series (mystery novels for young adults) and The New Leaf Series (first books for poetry and fiction—Saskatchewan residents only).

Terms: Pays standard royalty on retail price. Publishes ms 1-2 years after acceptance. Guidelines and book catalog available for #10 SASE.

Advice: "We are primarily looking for quality writing that is original and innovative in its perspective and/or use of language. Thistledown would like to receive queries first before submission—perhaps with novel outline, some indication of previous publications, periodicals your work has appeared in. *We publish Canadian authors only.* We are continuing to publish more fiction and are looking for new fiction writers to add to our list. New Leaf Editions line is first books of poetry or fiction by emerging Saskatchewan authors. Familiarize yourself with some of our books before submitting a query or manuscript to the press."

[N] [icon] THORNDIKE PRESS, The Gale Group, 295 Kenney Memorial Dr., Waterville ME 04901. (207)859-1000. Fax: (207)859-1006. E-mail: Hazel.Rumney@gale.com. **Contact:** Hazel Rumney, editor (romance, western, women's fiction); Jamie Knoblock, editorial director. Estab. 1979. Midsize publisher of hardcover originals, reprints and paperback large-print *reprints*. Books: alkaline paper; offset printing; Smythe-sewn library binding. Average print order: 1,000. Publishes 112 total titles each year.
Imprint(s): Five Star, edited by Hazel Rumney.
Needs: Romance, western, women's. Has published *Friends and Enemies*, by Susan Oleksiw (mystery); *Desperate Acts*, by Jane Claudia Coleman (romance). "We want highly original material that contains believable motivation, with little repetitive introspection. Show us how a character feels, rather than tell us. Humor is good; clichés are not."
How to Contact: Submit proposal package with 3 sample chapters and synopsis. Responds in 3 months to queries and proposals; 4-6 months to mss. Accepts simultaneous submissions. Guidelines available for SASE.
Terms: Pays royalties on wholesale price. Offers advance: $1,000-2,000. Publishes ms 8 months after acceptance.

[icon] [icon] TIDEWATER PUBLISHERS, Imprint of Cornell Maritime Press, Inc., P.O. Box 456, Centreville MD 21617-0456. (410)758-1075. Fax: (410)758-6849. E-mail: cornell@crosslink.net. **Contact:** Charlotte Kurst, managing editor. Estab. 1938. "Tidewater Publishers issues adult nonfiction works related to the Chesapeake Bay area, Delmarva or Maryland in general. The only fiction we handle is juvenile and must have a regional focus." Publishes hardcover and paperback originals. **Published new writers within the last year.** Averages 7-9 titles/year.
Needs: Regional juvenile fiction only. Recently published *Chesapeake ABC*, by Priscilla Cummings and illustrated by David Aiken; and *Finding Birds in the Chesapeake Marsh*, by Zora Aiken and illustrated by David Aiken.
How to Contact: Query or submit outline/synopsis and sample chapters. Responds in 2 months.
Terms: Pays royalties of 7½-15% on retail price. Publishes ms 1 year after acceptance. Book catalog for 10×13 SAE with 5 first-class stamps.
Advice: "Our audience is made up of readers interested in works that are specific to the Chesapeake Bay and Delmarva Peninsula area."

[N] [icon] TILBURY HOUSE, PUBLISHERS, Herpswell Press, Inc., 2 Mechanic St., Gardiner ME 04345. (207)582-1899. Fax: (207)582-8227. E-mail: tilbury@tilburyhouse.com. Website: www.tilburyhouse.com. Publisher: Jennifer Elliot (New England, maritime, children's). **Contact:** Audrey Maynard, children's book editor. Estab. 1990. Publishes hardcover originals, trade paperback originals. Averages 10 titles/year.
Needs: Regional (New England). Recently published *Lucy's Family Tree*, by Karen Schreck.
Terms: Pays royalty. Book catalog free; ms guidelines online.

[N] TIMBERWOLF PRESS, INC., 202 N. Allen Dr., Suite A, Allen TX 75013. (972)359-0911. Fax: (972)359-0525. E-mail: submissions@timberwolfpress.com. Website: www.timberwolfpress.com. **Contact:** Carol Woods, senior editor. Publishes trade paperback originals. **Publishes 25% of books from first-time authors; 84% from unagented writers.** Averages 24-30 titles/year.
Needs: Fantasy, military/war, mystery, science fiction, suspense. "In addition to the p-book, we present each title in fully-cast, dramatized, unabridged audio theatre, available in the usual formats; and downloadable in all formats from our website. We also stream this audio in 30-minute episodes on our website. So our stories must maintain tension and pace. Think exciting. Think breathless. Think terrific story, terrific characters, terrific writing." Recently published *Blood & Iron*, by Dan MacGregor; *Book One of Bronwyn Etralogy: Palaces & Prisons*, by Ron Miller.
How to Contact: Query via e-mail only. Accepts simultaneous submissions. Responds in 1 month to queries; 3 months to mss.
Terms: Pays royalty on wholesale price. Offers industry standard advance or better. Publishes book 6 months after acceptance of ms. Book catalog and ms guidelines on website.
Advice: "We accept e-queries and e-submissions only: *submissions@timberwolfpress.com* And polish that query. Grammar, punctuation, and spelling are as important in e-queries and e-submissions as they are in p-queries."

[icon] [A] TOR BOOKS, Tom Doherty Associates, 175 Fifth Ave., New York NY 10010. (212)388-0100. Fax: (212)388-0191. E-mail: inquiries@tor.com. Website: www.tor.com. **Contact:** Patrick Nielsen Hayden, senior editor. Estab. 1980. Publishes hardcover and paperback originals, plus some paperback reprints. Books: 5 point Dombook paper; offset printing; Bursel and perfect binding; few illustrations. Averages 200 total titles/year, mostly fiction. Some nonfiction titles.
Imprint(s): Forge Books.
Needs: Fantasy, mainstream, science fiction, historical, adventure and horror. Published *The Path of Daggers*, by Robert Jordan; *1916*, by Morgan Llywelyn; *The Predators*, by Harold Robbins; and *Ender's Shadow*, by Orson Scott Card.
How to Contact: Agented mss preferred. Agented fiction 90%. No simultaneous submissions. Address manuscripts to "Editorial," *not* to the Managing Editor's office. Responds in 4 months to queries; 6 months to proposals.

Terms: Pays in royalties and advance. Writer must return advance if book is not completed or is unacceptable. Sends galleys to author. Publishes ms 1-2 years after acceptance. Free book catalog on request.

N **◎** **TORAH AURA PRODUCTIONS**, 4423 Fruitland Ave., Los Angeles CA 90058. (213)585-7312. Website: www.torahaura.com. **Contact:** Jane Golub. Estab. 1982. Publishes hardcover and trade paperback originals. **Publishes 2% of books from first-time authors; 100% from unagented writers.** Averages 25 titles/year; imprint publishes 10 titles/year.

Needs: Juvenile, picture books, religious, young adult. All fiction must have Jewish interest. No picture books.
How to Contact: Query with SASE. Reviews artwork/photos as part of ms package. Send photocopies. Accepts simultaneous submissions. Responds in 6 months to mss.
Terms: Pays 10% royalty on wholesale price. Offers advance. Publishes book 3 years after acceptance of ms. Book catalog free.

N **✿** **◎** **TRADEWIND BOOKS**, 2216 Stephens St., Vancouver, British Columbia V6K 3W6 Canada. (604)730-0153. Fax: (604)730-0154. E-mail: tradewindbooks@eudoramail.com. Website: www.tradewindbooks.com. **Contact:** Michael Katz, publisher (picturebooks, young adult); Carol Frank, art director (picturebooks); Tiffany Stone (acquisitions editor). Publishes hardcover and trade paperback originals. **Publishes 10% of books from first-time authors; 50% from unagented writers.** Averages 5 titles/year.

Needs: Juvenile. Recently published *Huevos Rancheros*; *The Jade Necklace*; *Aziz: The Storyteller*.
How to Contact: Query with SASE or submit proposal package including 2 sample chapter(s), synopsis. Accepts simultaneous submissions. Responds in 2 months to mss.
Terms: Pays 7% royalty on retail price. Offers variable advance. Publishes book 3 years after acceptance of ms. Book catalog and ms guidelines online.

N **◐** **TRICYCLE PRESS**, Subsidiary of Ten Speed Press, P.O. Box 7123, Berkeley CA 94707. (510)559-1600. Fax: (510)559-1637. Website: www.tenspeed.com. **Contact**: Nicole Geiger, publisher. Estab. 1993. "Tricycle Press is a children's book publisher that publishes picture books, board books, chapter books and middle grade novels. Likes its parent company Ten Speed Press, Tricycle Press has a reputation for books that are a bit outside the mainstream." Publishes hardcover and paperback originals and hardcover and paperback reprints. **Published 4 new writers within the last year.** Publishes 18-20 total titles, 15-17 fiction titles/year.

Needs: Children's/juvenile (adventure, historical, chapter books, mystery, preschool/picture book), young adult (middle grade novels). "One-off middle grade novels (no series)—quality fiction, 'tween fiction." Recently published *Oh, and Another Thing . . .*, by Karen Salmansohn ('tween fiction); and *Truth Is a Bright Star*, by Joan Price (middle grade adventure).
How to Contact: Accepts unsolicited mss. Query with outline/synopsis and 3 sample chapters. Include e-mail address, bio and list of publishing credits. Send SASE for return of ms or send a disposable copy and SASE for reply only. Agented fiction: 60%. Responds in 2-4 weeks to queries; 4-6 months to mss. Accepts simultaneous submissions.
Terms: Pays royalties of 7½-10% and author's copies. Offers negotiable advance. Sends galleys to author. Publishes ms 1 year after acceptance. Guidelines available for SASE and on website; book catalog for 9 × 12 SASE and $3 postage.

✿ **◐** **◎** **TURNSTONE PRESS**, 607-100 Arthur St., Winnipeg, Manitoba R3B 1H3 Canada. (204)947-1555. Fax: (204)942-1555. E-mail: editor@turnstonepress.mb.ca. Website: www.TurnstonePress.com (includes submission guidelines, new titles, selected backlist, excerpts and author tour information). **Contact**: Todd Besant, managing editor. Estab. 1976. "Turnstone Press is a literary press that publishes Canadian writers with an emphasis on writers from, and writing on, the Canadian west." Focuses on eclectic new writing, prairie writers, travel writing and regional mysteries. Books: offset paper; perfect-bound. First novel print order: 1,500. **Published 5 new writers within the last year.** Averages 12-15 total titles/year. Distributes titles through General Distribution Services (Canada and US). Promotes titles through Canadian national and local print media and select US print advertising.

 • *Summer of My Amazing Luck*, by Miriam Toews was nominated for the Stephen Leacock Award for Humor. Wayne Tefs, author of *Moon Lake*, won the Margaret Laurence Award for Fiction. *In the Hands of the Living God*, by Lillian Bouzane was longlisted for the Dublin IMPAC Literary Prize. *Sticks and Stones*, by Eileen Coughlan was shortlisted for the Arthur Ellis Award.
Imprints: Ravenstone.
Needs: Literary, regional (Western Canada), mystery, gothic, noir. "We will be doing only 4-5 fiction titles a year. Interested in new work exploring new narrative/fiction forms, travel/adventure/nature writing of a literary nature and writing that pushes the boundaries of genre." Recently published *This Place Called Absence*, by Linda Kwa (novel); and *Choke Hold*, by Todd Babiak (comic novel).
How to Contact: *Canadian authors only.* Accepts unsolicited mss. Query with 20-40 sample pages. Include list of publication credits. Send SASE or IRC for return of ms. Responds in 2 months to queries; up to 4 months to mss. Accepts simultaneous submissions if notified.
Terms: Pays royalties of 10% and 10 author's copies. Average advance: $500. Publishes ms 1 year after acceptance. Sends galleys to author. Book catalog available free with SASE.
Advice: "As a Canadian literary press, we have a mandate to publish Canadian writers only. Do some homework before submitting work to make sure your subject matter/genre/writing style falls within the publishers area of interest."

◐ ◎ **TYNDALE HOUSE PUBLISHERS INC.**, P.O. Box 80, Wheaton IL 60189. (608)668-8300. Website: www.tyndale.com. **Contact**: Anne Goldsmith, acquisitions editor (women's fiction, romance); Jan Stob, acquisitions editor (general fiction); Virginia Williams, acquisitions editor (children's products). Estab. 1962. Privately owned religious press. Publishes hardcover and paperback originals. First novel print order: 7,500-15,000. Averages 150 total titles, 30-40 fiction titles/year. **Published new writers within the last year.** Distributes titles through catalog houses, rackers and distributors. Promotes titles through print ads in trade publications, radio, point of sale materials and catalogs.
Imprint(s): HeartQuest; Anne Goldsmith, fiction editor (inspirational romance), Jan Stob, fiction editor (genre and mainstream inspirational fiction), and Virginia Williams, editor (inspirational children's fiction).
  • Three books published by Tyndale House have received the Gold Medallion Book Award. They include *The Last Sin Eater*, by Francine Rivers; *The Sword of Truth*, by Gilbert Morris; and *A Rose Remembered*, by Michael Phillips.
Needs: Religious (children's, general, inspirational, mystery/suspense, thriller, romance). "We primarily publish Christian historical romances, with occasional contemporary, suspense or standalones." Publishes anthologies (write for theme list). Recently published *Desecration*, by Tim LaHaye and Jerry Jenkins (general/inspirational); *North of Tomorrow*, by Cindy McCormick Martinusen (contemporary novel); *Lullaby*, by Jane Orcutt (contemporary novella); and *Out of the Shadows*, by Sigmund Brouwer (contemporary suspense).
How to Contact: Does not accept unsolicited mss. Queries with outline/synopsis and 3 sample chapters. Query by regular mail only. Include estimated word count, brief bio and list of publishing credits. Send SASE or IRC for return of ms or send disposable copy of ms and SASE for reply only. Agented fiction 80%. Responds in 2 months to queries; in up to 6 months to mss. Accepts simultaneous submissions. Never comments on rejected mss.
Terms: Pays royalties. Advance negotiable. Sends galleys to authors. Publishes ms 9 months after acceptance. Guidelines available for 9×12 SAE and $2.40 for postage or visit website.
Advice: "We are a religious publishing house with a primarily evangelical Christian market. We are looking for spiritual themes and content within established genres."

◐ ◎ **UCLA AMERICAN INDIAN STUDIES CENTER PUBLICATIONS**, UCLA, 3220 Campbell Hall, Box 951548, Los Angeles CA 90095-1548. (310)825-7315. Fax: (310)206-7060. E-mail: aiscpubs@ucla.edu. Website: www.sscnet.ucla.edu/esplaisc/index.html (contains submission guidelines, excerpts from books, catalog, ordering information). **Contact:** Duane Champagne, editor-in-chief. Estab. 1979. "Nonprofit publications unit at UCLA devoted to scholarship by and/or about Indian people; we produce numerous books, bibliographies, monographs, as well as the internationally recognized quarterly *American Indian Culture and Research Journal*, which contains academic articles, commentary, literature and book reviews." Publishes paperback originals and paperback reprints. Books: 60 lb. paper; perfect-bound; b&w illustrations. **Published 2 new writers within the last year.** Averages 4 total titles, 2-3 fiction titles/year. Member, PMA, SPD, bookpeople.
Needs: American Indian, literary, short story collections. Published *Comeuppance at Kicking Horse Casino*, by Charles Brashear (short stories).
How to Contact: Accepts unsolicited mss. Submit complete ms with cover letter. Accepts queries by e-mail. Include estimated word count and brief bio with submission. Send disposable copy of the ms plus SASE for reply only. Agented fiction: 0%. Responds in 1 month to queries; 4 months to mss. No simultaneous submissions, electronic submissions or submissions on disk.
Terms: Does not pay. Sends galleys to author. Publishes ms 8-12 months after acceptance. Guidelines not available; book catalogs free and on website.

◐ ◎ **UNITY HOUSE**, Unity School of Christianity, 1901 NW Blue Parkway, Unity Village MO 64065-0001. (816)524-3550 ext. 3190. Fax: (816)251-3552. E-mail: ~books@unityworldhq.org. Website: www.unityworldhq.org. **Contact:** Michael Maday, editor; Raymond Teague, associate editor. "We are a bridge between traditional Christianity and New Age spirituality. Unity School of Christianity is based on metaphysical Christian principles, spiritual values and the healing power of prayer as a resource for daily living." Publishes hardcover and trade paperback originals and reprints. **Published 4 new writers within the last year.** Averages 14 titles/year.
Needs: Spiritual, inspirational, metaphysical.
How to Contact: Query with synopsis and sample chapter. Responds in 1 month to queries; 2 months to mss.
Terms: Pays royalties of 10-15% royalty on net receipts. Publishes ms 13 months after acceptance of final ms. Guidelines and book catalog available free.

N ◆ ◎ **UNIVERSITY OF ALBERTA PRESS**, Ring House #2, Edmonton, Alberta T6E 2E1 Canada. (780)492-3662. Fax: (780)492-0719. E-mail: uap@ualberta.ca. Website: www.uap.ualberta.ca (includes full catalog, forthcoming titles, staff, media room, links). **Contact:** Leslie Vermeer, managing editor (all). Estab. 1969. Small independent publisher. "Academic publisher with small literary program." Publishes paperback originals and reprints. Books: acid free paper; sheet fed offset printed; perfect-bound. Average print order: 1,000. First novel print order: 1,000. **Published 1 new writer within the last year.** Plans 1 first novel this year. Averages 25 total titles, 2 fiction titles/year. Member, ACP, AAUP, ACUP, BPAA. Promotes titles through in-house marketing, external distributors for Canada, US, UK.
Needs: Ethnic/multicultural, experimental, feminist, literary, short story collections, translations. Recently published *Sawbones Memorial*, by Ross, Sinclair (Canadian literary novel); *Great Canadian War Stories*, by Whitaker, Muriel, ed. (short stories); and *Recurring Fictions*, by McGrath, Wendy (novel).

How to Contact: Accepts unsolicited mss. Does not return mss unless provided with SASE and ample postage (IRCs if ms mailed from US). Query with outline/synopsis and 3 sample chapters. Include estimated word count, brief bio and list of publishing credits. Send SASE or IRC for return of ms or send disposable copy of ms and SASE for reply only. Agented fiction less than 5%. Responds in 2 months. Accepts simultaneous submissions. No e-mail or disk submissions.

Terms: Pays royalties and advance. Amounts vary. Sends galleys to author. Publishes ms up to 1 year after acceptance. Guidelines available on website.

UNIVERSITY OF GEORGIA PRESS, 330 Research Dr., Athens GA 30602-4901. (706)369-6130. Fax: (706)369-6131. E-mail: books@ugapress.uga.edu. Website: www.uga.edu/ugapress (includes guidelines, catalog, contact information and mission statement). Estab. 1938. University of Georgia Press is a midsized press that publishes fiction *only* through the Flannery O'Connor Award for Short Fiction competition. Publishes 85 titles/year.

Needs: Published *Break Any Woman Down*, by Dana Johnson and *The Necessary Grace to Fall*, by Gina Ochsner, both recent award winners.

How to Contact: Guidelines available on website or for SASE. "No phone calls accepted."

Terms: Standard publishing contract. Publishes ms 1 year after competition judging. Competition guidelines for #10 SASE. Book catalog available free.

Advice: "Do not call editors with queries or ideas. *Always* submit them in writing."

UNIVERSITY OF IOWA PRESS, 119 W. Park Rd., Iowa City IA 52242-1000. (319)335-2000. Fax: (319)335-2055. Website: www.uiowa.edu/~uipress. **Contact:** Holly Carver, director; Prasenjit Gupta, acquisitions editor. Estab. 1969. Publishes hardcover and paperback originals. Publishes 35 titles/year. Average print run for a first book is 1,000-1,500.

Needs: Currently publishes the Iowa Short Fiction Award selections.

How to Contact: Competition guidelines on website. See Competition and Awards section for further information.

Terms: Pays 7-10% royalty on net receipts. Publishes ms 1 year after acceptance. Guidelines and book catalog available free.

UNIVERSITY OF MISSOURI PRESS, 2910 LeMone Blvd., Columbia MO 65201-8227. (573)882-7641. Fax: (573)884-4498. Website: www.system.missouri.edu.upress (includes authors, titles, book descriptions). **Contact:** Clair Willcox, editor. Estab. 1958. "Mid-size university press." Publishes paperback originals and reprints (short story collections only). Published new writers within the last year. Averages 65 total titles, 4 short story collections each year. Member, AAUP. Distributes titles through direct mail, bookstores, sales reps.

Needs: Short story collections. No children's fiction. Recently published *My Favorite Lies*, by Ruth Hamel (short story collection); *Boys Keep Being Born*, by Joan Frank (short story collection); *No Visible Means of Support*, by Dabney Stuart (short story collection).

How to Contact: Query first. Submit cover letter and sample story or two by mail only. Include bio/publishing credits. SASE for reply. Responds in 2 weeks to queries; 3 months to mss. Accepts simultaneous submissions. Sometimes comments on rejected ms.

Terms: Pays royalties of 6%. Sends galleys to author. Publishes ms 1-1½ years after acceptance. Book catalogs available free.

THE UNIVERSITY OF TENNESSEE PRESS, 110 Conference Center, Knoxville TN 37996-4108. (865)974-3321. Fax: (865)974-3724. E-mail: custserv@utpress.org. Website: www.utpress.org. **Contact:** Joyce Harrison, acquisitions editor (scholarly books); Jennifer Siler, director (regional trades, fiction). Estab. 1940. **Publishes 35% of books from first-time authors; 99% from unagented writers.** Averages 30 titles/year.

Needs: Query with SASE or submit synopsis, author bio. Recently published *The Marriage of Anna Maye Potts*, by DeWitt Henry.

How to Contact: Does not accept simultaneous submissions.

Terms: Pays negotiable royalty on net receipts. Book catalog for 12×16 SAE with 2 first-class stamps; ms guidelines for #10 SASE.

Advice: "Our market is in several groups: scholars; educated readers with special interests in given scholarly subjects; and the general educated public interested in Tennessee, Appalachia and the South. Not all our books appeal to all these groups, of course, but any given book must appeal to at least one of them."

UNIVERSITY OF TEXAS PRESS, P.O. Box 7819, Austin TX 78713-7819. Fax: (512)232-7178. E-mail: utpress@uts.cc.utexas.edu. Website: www.utexas.edu/utpress/. **Contact:** Theresa May, assistant director/editor-in-chief (social sciences, Latin American studies); James Burr, acquisitions editor (humanities, classics); Bill Bishel, acquisitions editor (sciences, Texana). Estab. 1950. **Publishes 50% previously unpublished writers/year.** Publishes 85 titles/year. Average print order for a first book is 1,000.

Needs: Latin American and Middle Eastern fiction only in translation. Published *Whatever Happened to Dulce Veiga?*, by Caio Fernando Abreu (novel).

How to Contact: Query or submit outline and 2 sample chapters. Responds in up to 3 months.

Terms: Pays royalty usually based on net income. Offers advance occasionally. Publishes ms 18 months after acceptance. Guidelines and book catalog available free.

Advice: "It's difficult to make a manuscript over 400 double-spaced pages into a feasible book. Authors should take special care to edit out extraneous material. Looks for sharply focused, in-depth treatments of important topics."

[N] VANDAMERE PRESS, AB Associates International, Inc., P.O. Box 17446, Clearwater FL 33762. (727)556-0950. Fax: (727)556-2560. **Contact:** Jerry Frank, senior acquistions editor. Estab. 1984. Publishes hardcover and trade paperback originals and reprints. **Publishes 25% of books from first-time authors; 90% from unagented writers.** Averages 8-15 titles/year.
Needs: Adventure, erotica, humor, mystery, suspense. Recently published *Cry Me a River*, by Patricia Hagan (fiction).
How to Contact: Submit 5-10 sample chapter(s), synopsis. Accepts simultaneous submissions. Responds in 6 months to queries.
Terms: Pays royalty. on revenues generated. Offers advance. Publishes book 1-3 years after acceptance of ms.
Advice: "Authors who can provide endorsements from significant published writers, celebrities, etc., will *always* be given serious consideration. Clean, easy-to-read, *dark* copy is essential. Patience in waiting for replies is essential. All unsolicited work is looked at, but at certain times of the year our review schedule will stop. No response without SASE."

[icons] VÉHICULE PRESS, Box 125, Place du Parc Station, Montreal, Quebec H2W 2M9 Canada. **Contact:** Simon Dardick, publisher/editor. Estab. 1973. Small publisher of scholarly, literary and cultural books. Publishes hardcover and paperback originals. Books: good quality paper; offset printing; perfect and cloth binding; illustrations. Average print order: 1,000-3,000. Averages 15 total titles/year.
Imprint(s): Signal Editions (poetry).
Needs: Feminist, literary, regional, short story collections, translations—"*by Canadian residents only.*" No romance or formula writing. Recently published *Rousseau's Garden*, by Ann Charney; and *Telling Stories: New English Stories from Quebec*, edited by Claude Lalumiere.
How to Contact: Send query letter or query with sample chapters. Send SASE or IRC for reply ("no U.S. stamps, please"). Responds in 3 months to mss.
Terms: Pays in royalties of 10-12%. "Depends on press run and sales. Translators of fiction can receive Canada Council funding, which publisher applies for." Sends galleys to author. Book catalog available for 9×12 SASE.
Advice: "Quality in almost any style is acceptable. We believe in the editing process."

[N] [icon] VERSUS PRESS, P.O. Box 170187, San Francisco CA 94117. E-mail: vs@versuspress.com. Website: www.v ersuspress.com (includes writer's guidelines, current list of books, interview series). **Contact:** John DeWitt, editor (fiction/literary); Don Waters, editor (fiction/literary). Estab. 1999. Small independent publisher. "Our primary goal is to provide a literary forum for emerging and recognized writers who carry messages that are at once renegade, progressive, urgent, political, but altogether needed." Publishes paperback originals. Books: 55 lb. natural paper; offset printed; perfect-bound. Average print order: varies. **Published 0 new writers within the last year.** Averages 2-3 total titles, 2 fiction titles/year. Distributes titles through Small Press Distribution, Baker & Taylor, Amazon.com, website.
Needs: Erotica, ethnic/multicultural, experimental, feminist, gay, glitz, humor/satire, lesbian, literary, mainstream, special interests: political, satire, urban fiction. Recently published *User*, by Blake Nelson (literary fiction/black humor); and *Grand Canyon, Inc.*, by Percival Everett (literary fiction/satire).
How to Contact: Accepts unsolicited mss. Query with outline/synopsis and 30 sample pages. Accepts queries by e-mail. Include estimated word count, brief bio and list of publishing credits. Send SASE or IRC for return of ms or send disposable copy of ms and SASE for reply only. Agented fiction 50%. Responds in 1 month. Accepts simultaneous submissions. No e-mail or disk submissions.
Terms: Pays royalties. Amounts vary. Sends galleys to author. Publishes ms 1 year after acceptance. Guidelines available on website; book catalog on website.
Advice: "Our main interest lies in novels (and nonfiction) that make necessary, socially aware critical comments and punctuates these comments with vivid prose."

[A] VIKING, Imprint of Penguin Putnam Inc., 375 Hudson St., New York NY 10014. (212)366-2000. Publisher: Clare Ferraro. **Contact:** Acquisitions Editor. Publishes a mix of literary and popular fiction and nonfiction. Publishes hardcover originals.
Needs: Literary, mainstream/contemporary, mystery, suspense. Published *Lake Wobegon Summer 1956*, by Garrison Keillor; *A Day Late and A Dollar Short*, by Terry McMillan; *A Common Life*, by Jan Karon; and *In the Heart of the Sea*, by Nathaniel Philbrick.
How to Contact: Agented fiction only. Responds in up to 6 months to queries. Accepts simultaneous submissions.
Terms: Pays royalties of 10-15% on retail price. Advance negotiable. Publishes ms 12-18 months after acceptance.

[icons] VIKING CHILDREN'S BOOKS, Imprint of the Children's Division of Penguin Putnam Inc., 345 Hudson St., New York NY 10014. (212)366-2000. Website: www.penguinputnam.com. Publisher: Regina Hayes. **Contact:** Melanie Cecka, Elizabeth Law. "Viking Children's Books publishes the highest quality trade books for children including fiction, nonfiction, and novelty books for pre-schoolers through young adults." Publishes hardcover originals. **Published new writers within the last year.** Publishes 80 books/year. Promotes titles through press kits, institutional ads.
Needs: Juvenile, young adult. Published *Someone Like You*, by Sarah Dessen (novel); *Joseph Had a Little Overcoat*, by Simms Taback (picture book); *See You Later, Gladiator*, by Jon Scieszka (chapter book).
How to Contact: Accepts unsolicited mss. For picture books, submit entire ms. Responds in 4 months to queries. SASE mandatory for return of materials.

Terms: Pays royalties 5-10% on retail price. Advance negotiable. Publishes ms 1 year after acceptance.
Advice: No "cartoony" or mass-market submissions for picture books.

[N] [A] VILLARD BOOKS, Random House, 299 Park Ave., New York NY 10171-0002. (212)572-2600. Website: www.atrandom.com. Publisher: Ann Godoff. Estab. 1983. Publishes hardcover and trade paperback originals. **Publishes 5% from unagented writers.** Averages 55-60 titles/year.
Needs: Commercial fiction.
How to Contact: *Agented submissions only.* Accepts simultaneous submissions.
Terms: Pays negotiable royalty. Offers negotiable advance.

[A] VINTAGE ANCHOR PUBLISHING, The Knopf Publishing Group, A Division of Random House, Inc., 299 Park Ave., New York NY 10171. Website: www.randomhouse.com. Vice President: LuAnn Walther. Editor-in-Chief: Martin Asher. **Contact:** Submissions Editor. Publishes trade paperback originals and reprints. Averages 200 titles/year.
Needs: Literary, mainstream/contemporary, short story collections. Published *Snow Falling on Cedars*, by Guterson (contemporary); and *Martin Dressler*, by Millhauser (literary).
How to Contact: Agented submissions only. Query with synopsis and 2-3 sample chapters. Responds in 6 months to queries. Accepts simultaneous submissions. No submissions by fax or e-mail.
Terms: Pays 4-8% royalty on retail price. Offers advance of $2,500 and up. Publishes ms 1 year after acceptance.

[globe] [pen] VISION BOOKS PVT LTD., Madarsa Rd., Kashmere Gate, Delhi 110006 India. (+91)11 3862267 or (+91)11 3862201. Fax: (+91)11 3862935. E-mail: orientpbk@vsnl.com. **Contact:** Sudhir Malhotra, fiction editor. Publishes 25 titles/year.
Imprint(s): Orient Paperbacks.
Needs: "We are a large multilingual publishing house publishing fiction and other trade books."
How to Contact: "A brief synopsis should be submitted initially. Subsequently, upon hearing from the editor, a typescript may be sent."
Terms: Pays royalties.

[○] [◎] VISTA PUBLISHING, INC., 422 Morris Ave., Suite One, Long Branch NJ 07740-5901. (732)229-6500. Fax: (732)229-9647. E-mail: info@vistapubl.com. Website: www.vistapubl.com (includes titles, authors, editors, pricing and ordering information). **Contact:** Carolyn Zagury, president. Estab. 1991. "Small, independent press, owned by women and specializing in fiction by nurses and allied health professional authors." Publishes paperback originals. **Published 3 new writers within the last year.** Plans 3 first novels this year. Averages 12 total titles, 6 fiction titles/year. Distributes titles through catalogs, wholesalers, distributors, exhibits, website, trade shows, book clubs and bookstores. Promotes titles through author signings, press releases, author speakings, author interviews, exhibits, website, direct mail and book reviews.
Needs: Adventure, humor/satire, mystery/suspense, romance, short story collections. Published *Never Be a Witness*, by Nancy Lamoureux (mystery); *Error in Judgement*, by Gary Birken (medical mystery); *The Golden Gate Park Murder*, by Pamela Hausman Hasting (murder mystery).
How to Contact: Accepts unsolicited mss. Query with complete ms. Accepts queries by e-mail but not by fax. Include bio. Send SASE or IRC for reply, return of ms or send disposable copy of ms and SASE for reply only. Responds in 2 months to mss. Accepts simultaneous submissions. Comments on rejected mss.
Terms: Pays royalties. Sends galleys to author. Publishes ms 2 years after acceptance. Guidelines and book catalog available for SASE.
Advice: "We prefer to read full mss. Authors should be nurses or allied health professionals."

WALKER AND COMPANY, 435 Hudson St., New York NY 10014. Fax: (212)727-0984. Publisher: George Gibson. Juvenile Publisher: Emily Easton. Juvenile Editor: Timothy Travaglini. **Contact:** Submissions Editor-Juvenile. Estab. 1959. Midsize independent publisher with plans to expand. Publishes hardcover and trade paperback originals. Average first novel print order: 2,500-3,500. Averages 70 total titles/year.
Needs: Juvenile: fiction, nonfiction, picture books. Recently published *IQ Does School*.
How to Contact: *Does not accept unsolicited mss.* Query with SASE. Query letter should include "a concise description of the story line, including its outcome, word length of story (we prefer 70,000 words), writing experience, publishing credits, particular expertise on this subject and in this genre. Common mistakes: Sounding unprofessional (i.e. too chatty, too braggardly). Forgetting SASE." Agented fiction 50%. Notify if multiple or simultaneous submissions. Responds in 3 months to queries. Publishes ms an average of 1 year after acceptance. Occasionally comments on rejected mss.
Terms: Negotiable (usually advance against royalty). Must return advance if book is not completed or is unacceptable.

[N] WALTSAN PUBLISHING, LLC, 5000 Barnett St., Fort Worth TX 76103-2006. (817)654-2978. E-mail: sandra @waltsan.com. Website: www.waltsan.com. **Publishes 95% of books from first-time authors; 95% from unagented writers.** Averages 10-20 titles/year.
Needs: "We look at all fiction." Full-length or collections equal to full-length only. Recently published *Shadows and Stones*, by Bernita Stark.
How to Contact: Query with SASE or submit proposal package including 3 sample chapter(s), synopsis or submit complete ms. Accepts simultaneous submissions. Responds in 1 month to queries; 2 months to mss.

Terms: Pays 20% royalty on wholesale price. Publishes book 9 months after acceptance of ms. Book catalog and ms guidelines online.

Advice: Audience is computer literate, generally higher income and intelligent. "When possible, authors record their manuscript to include audio on the CD. Check our website for guidelines and sample contract." Only publishes on CDs and other removable media.

WARNER ASPECT, Imprint of Warner Books, 1271 Avenue of the Americas, New York NY 10020. (212)522-7200. Website: www.twbookmark.com (includes each month's new titles, advice from writers, previous titles and interviews with authors, "hot news," contests). **Contact:** Betsy Mitchell, editor-in-chief. "We're looking for 'epic' stories in both fantasy and science fiction." Publishes hardcover, trade paperback, mass market paperback originals and mass market paperback reprints. **Published 2 new writers within the last year.** Publishes 30 total titles/year. Distributes titles through nationwide sales force.

Needs: Fantasy, science fiction. Published *The Naked God*, by Peter F. Hamilton (science fiction); *Parable of the Talents*, by Octavia Butler (fantasy); and *A Cavern of Black Ice*, by J.V. Jones (fantasy).

How to Contact: Agented fiction only. Responds in 3 months to mss. Does not accept simultaneous submissions.

Terms: Pays royalty on retail price. Average advance: $5,000 and up. Publishes ms 14 months after acceptance.

Advice: "Think epic! Our favorite stories are big-screen science fiction and fantasy, with plenty of characters and subplots. Sample our existing titles—we're a fairly new list and pretty strongly focused. Also seeking writers of color to add to what we've already published by Octavia E. Butler, Nalo Hopkinson, Walter Mosley, etc." Mistake writers often make is "hoping against hope that being unagented won't make a difference. We simply don't have the staff to look at unagented projects."

WARNER BOOKS, Time & Life Building, 1271 Avenue of the Americas, New York NY 10020. (212)522-7200. Website: www.twbookmark.com. **Contact:** (Ms.) Jamie Raab, senior vice president (general nonfiction and fiction); Rick Horgan, vice president/executive editor (general nonfiction and fiction, thrillers); Beth de Guzman, editorial director (fiction, romance); Caryn Karmatz Rudy, senior editor (fiction, nonfiction); Rob McMahon, senior editor (fiction, business, sports); Karen Koszto Inyik, senior editor (women's fiction). Publishes hardcover, trade paperback, mass market paperback originals, reprints and e-books. Warner publishes general interest fiction. Averages 250 total titles/year.

Imprint(s): Mysterious Press, Warner Aspect, Warner Faith, Walk Worthy; iPublish.

Needs: Fantasy, mainstream, mystery/suspense, romance, science fiction, thriller, horror. Recently published *Up Country*, by Nelson DeMille; and *A Bend in the Road*, by Nicholas Sparks.

How to Contact: Accepts agented submissions *only*.

WARNER BOOKS INC., (Subsidiary of AOL Time Warner Book Group), 1271 Avenue of the Americas, New York NY 10020. (212)522-7200. Fax: (212)522-7991. Website: www.twbookmark.com. Estab.1961. Publishes hardcover, trade paperback and mass market paperback originals and reprints.

Imprint(s): Aspect; Mysterious Press; Walk Worthy; Warner Business Books; Warner Vision.

WHITE MANE BOOKS, White Mane Publishing Company Inc., 63 W. Burd St., P.O. Box 152, Shippensburg PA 17257. (717)532-2237. Fax: (717)532-6110. E-mail: editorial@whitemane.com. Website: www.whitemane.com. **Contact:** Harold Collier, vice president; Alexis Handerahan, associate editor. Estab. 1987. Publishes hardcover, and trade paperback originals and reprints. **Publishes 50% of books from first-time authors; 75% from unagented writers.** Averages 60 titles/year; imprint publishes 12-18 titles/year.

Imprints: Burd Street Press (military history, emphasis on American Civil War); Ragged Edge Press (religious); White Mane Kids (historically based children's fiction).

Needs: Historical, juvenile (middle grade), young adult. Recently published *Send 'Em South: Young Heroes of History Series*, by Alan Kay.

How to Contact: Query with SASE. Accepts simultaneous submissions. Responds in 1 month to queries; 1 month to proposals; 3 months to mss.

Terms: Pays royalty on monies received. Offers advance. Publishes book 18 months after acceptance of ms. Book catalog and ms guidelines free.

WHITE PINE PRESS, P.O. Box 236, Buffalo NY 14201. Phone/fax: (716)627-4665. E-mail: wpine@whitepine.org. Website: www.whitepine.org (includes book catalog). **Contact:** Elaine LaMattina, editor (all fiction). Estab. 1973. Small, not-for-profit literary publisher. Publishes paperback originals. Books: text paper; offset printing; perfect binding. Average print order: 1,500. First novel print order: 1,500. Averages 8 total titles, 4 fiction titles/year. Distributes titles through Consortium Book Sales.

Needs: Ethnic/multicultural, feminist, literary, short story collections, translations. Recently published *Empire Settings*, by David Schmahmann (first fiction, novel); *Some Wine for Remembrance*, by Edmund Keeley (novel); and *River of Sorrows*, by Libertad Demitropoulos (novel in translation). Publishes the New American Fiction series.

How to Contact: Accepts unsolicited mss. Send query letter. "We do not accept queries via e-mail or fax." Include estimated word count and list of publishing credits. Send SASE or IRC for return of ms or send disposable copy of ms and SASE for reply only. Agented fiction 1%. Responds in 1 month to queries; 6 months to mss. Accepts simultaneous submissions. Sometimes comments on rejected mss.

Terms: Pays 100 author's copies. Sends galleys to author. Publishes ms 1-2 years after acceptance. Guidelines available free for SASE.
Advice: "Send query letter first detailing project. Stick to our guidelines. Don't telephone to see if we received it. We're interested in what's good, not what's trendy."

[N] [☺] ALBERT WHITMAN & CO., 6340 Oakton St., Morton Grove IL 60053-2723. (847)581-0033. Website: www.awhitman.com. **Contact:** Kathleen Tucker, editor-in-chief. "Albert Whitman publishes books for children on a variety of topics: holidays, special needs and problems like divorce." Publishes hardcover originals and paperback reprints. Averages 30 titles/year.
Needs: Children's fiction: picture books, adventure, ethnic, fantasy, historical, humor, mystery, holiday, concept books. No YA fiction. Currently emphasizing picture books; de-emphasizing folk tales and bedtime stories.
How to Contact: Submit complete ms for picture books; for longer works, query with outline and sample chapters. Agented fiction: 30%. Responds in 6 weeks to queries; 3-4 months to mss.
Terms: Pays 10% royalty for novels, 5% royalty for picture books. Offers advance. Publishes ms 18 months after acceptance. Guidelines available for #10 SASE. Catalog available for 8×10 SAE and 3 first-class stamps.

[N] [◑] WILDSIDE PRESS, P.O. Box 301, Holicong PA 18928-0301. E-mail: wildsidepress@yahoo.com. Website: www.wildsidepress.com (includes guidelines, sample contract, catalog, online store, message board). **Contact:** John Betancourt, publisher (all). Estab. 1989. "Wildside Press is a small press specializing in science fiction/fantasy, horror/mystery fiction and nonfiction." Publishes hardcover and paperback originals and hardcover and paperback reprints. Books: 60 lb. paper; varied printing; hardcover and trade paperback binding. **Published 0 new writers within the last year.** Plans 2 first novels this year. Averages 400 total titles, 350 fiction titles/year. Distributes titles through Ingram, Baker & Taylor, NACSCORP, catalog.
Needs: Fantasy (space fantasy, sword and sorcery), horror (dark fantasy, supernatural), mystery/suspense (amateur sleuth, cozy, police procedural, private eye/hardboiled), science fiction (hard science/technological, soft/sociological). Seeking to "reprint early novels by well-established current authors." Recently published *The Misenchanted Sword*, by Lawrence Watt-Evans (fantasy); *The Mark of Merlin*, by Anne McCaffrey (suspense); and *The Branch*, by Mike Resnick (science fiction).
How to Contact: Does not accept unsolicited mss. Will return unread in SASE. Prefers queries by e-mail. Include estimated word count, brief bio and list of publishing credits. Send SASE or IRC for return of ms or send disposable copy of ms and SASE for reply only. Agented fiction 30%. Responds in 1 week to queries; 2 months to mss. Accepts e-mail or disk submissions; query first.
Terms: Pays royalties of 3-8%. "Royalties only—no advance. Sends galleys to author. Publishes ms up to 1 year after acceptance. Guidelines available on website; book catalogs on website and for #11 envelope and 57¢ postage.
Advice: "Query via e-mail first. Don't waste our time—we really are looking for new and reprint work from well-established authors only. *No exceptions.*"

[N] WILLOWGATE PRESS, P.O. Box 6529, Holliston MA 01746. (508)429-8774. E-mail: willowgatepress@yahoo.com. Website: www.willowgatepress.com. **Contact:** Robert Tolins, editor. Publishes trade paperback and mass market paperback originals. **Publishes 50% of books from first-time authors; 100% from unagented writers.** Averages 3-5 titles/year.
Needs: Fantasy, gothic, historical, horror, humor, literary, mainstream/contemporary, military/war, mystery, occult, regional, science fiction, short story collections, sports. "We are not interested in children's, erotica, or experimental."
How to Contact: Query with SASE or submit outline, plus the first ten pages and ten pages of the aurthor's choosing. Do not send cash or check in lieu of stamps for return postage. Accepts simultaneous submissions. Responds in 2 months to queries; 6 months to mss.
Terms: Pays 5-15% royalty on retail price. Offers $500 advance. Publishes book 6 months after acceptance of ms. Book catalog and ms guidelines online.
Advice: "If a manuscript is accepted for publication, we will make every effort to avoid lengthy delays in bringing the product to market. The writer will be given a voice in all aspects of publishing, promotion, advertising and marketing, including cover art, copy, promotional forums, etc. The writer will be expected to be an active and enthusiastic participant in all stages of the publication process. We hope to attract the finest writers of contemporary fiction and to help generate similar enthusiasm in them and in their readers. Please don't send cash or a check in lieu of stamps for return postage."

[◐] [◎] WILSHIRE BOOK CO., 12015 Sherman Rd., North Hollywood CA 91605-3781. (818)765-8579. Fax: (818)765-2922. E-mail: mpowers@mpowers.com. Website: www.mpowers.com (includes types of books published). **Contact:** Melvin Powers, publisher; Marcia Powers, senior editor (adult fables). Estab. 1947. "You are not only what you are today, but also what you choose to become tomorrow." Looking for adult fables that teach principles of psychological growth. Publishes trade paperback originals and reprints. **Published 7 new writers within the last year.** Averages 15 titles/year. Distributes titles through wholesalers, bookstores and mail order. Promotes titles through author interviews on radio and television.
Needs: Allegories that teach principles of psychological/spiritual growth or offer guidance in living. Min. 30,000 words. Published *The Princess Who Believed in Fairy Tales*, by Marcia Grad; *The Knight in Rusty Armor*, by Robert Fisher. Allegories only. No standard novels or short stories.
How to Contact: Accepts unsolicited mss. Query with synopsis, 3 sample chapters and SASE or submit complete ms with cover letter. Accepts queries by e-mail. Responds in 2 months.

Terms: Pays standard royalty. Publishes ms 6 months after acceptance.

Advice: "We are vitally interested in all new material we receive. Just as you hopefully submit your manuscript for publication, we hopefully read every one submitted, searching for those that we believe will be successful in the marketplace. Writing and publishing must be a team effort. We need you to write what we can sell. We suggest that you read the successful books mentioned above or others that are similar: *Greatest Salesman in the World*, *Illusions*, *Way of the Peaceful Warrior*, *Celestine Prophecy*. Analyze them to discover what elements make them winners. Duplicate those elements in your own style, using a creative new approach and fresh material, and you will have written a book we can successfully market."

N **⊘** **WIND RIVER PRESS**. E-mail: submissions@windriverpress.com. Website: www.windriverpress.com. **Contact:** Katherine Arline, editor (mainstream, travel, literary, historical, short story collections, translations). Estab. 2002. "Wind River Press publishes full-length electronic and Print on Demand paperback titles." Publishes paperback originals and reprints and electronic books. Averages 4 total titles, 4 fiction titles/year. Distributes and promotes titles through Ingrams, Baker & Taylor, Bowkers, Amazon.com, US and international book reviewers. "Wind River Press works closely with the author to develop a cost-effective production, promotion and distribution strategy."

Needs: Historical, literary, mainstream, short story collections. Plans anthology of works selected from Wind River Press's magazines (*Critique* and *The Paumanok Review*). Recently published *Payback*, by Elisha Porat (short story collection in translation); and *Icy Current, Compulsive Course*, by Gaither Stewart (short story collection).

How to Contact: Accepts unsolicited mss. Send query letter by e-mail. Include estimated word count, brief bio and list of publishing credits. Send submission by e-mail unless previously instructed otherwise. Agented fiction 5%. Responds in 3 weeks to queries; 2 months to mss. Accepts simultaneous submissions. Always comments on rejected mss.

Terms: Pays royalties of 10% minimum; negotiable maximum depending on formats. Individual arrangement depending on book formats and target audience. Sends galleys to author. Publishes ms 6 months after acceptance. Guidelines and book catalog available on website.

Advice: "If you dislike self-promotion and a hands-on approach, this probably isn't the right press for you. When you submit a query to this or any other press, please also include a statement of how you intend to promote the book. The first concern is, of course, the quality of the work, but in a small press environment, a thorough understanding of the author's ability to follow through with business aspects of a book can improve the likelihood of acceptance."

⊘ **WINDSTORM CREATIVE LIMITED**, (formerly Pride and Imprints), 7419 Ebbert Drive SE, Port Orchard WA 98367. Website: www.windstormcreative.com. **Contact:** Ms. Cris Newport, senior editor. Estab. 1989. Publishes paperback originals and reprints. **Published new writers within the last year.** Averages 50 total titles/year.

Needs: Contemporary, fantasy, gay/lesbian/bisexual, historical, science fiction, young adult. No children's books, horror, "bestseller" fiction, spy or espionage novels, "thrillers," any work which describes childhood sexual abuse or in which this theme figures prominently. Recently published *Bones Become Flowers*, by Jess Mowry (contemporary fiction); *Annabel and I*, by Chris Anne Wolfe (lesbian fiction); *Journey of a Thousand Miles*, by Peter Kasting (gay fiction); *Puzzle from the Past*, by Mike and Janet Golio (young adult).

How to Contact: "You *must* visit the website, follow the guidelines and use our mailing label. All submissions which don't follow these guidelines will be destroyed unopened." Responds in 6 months to mss.

Terms: Pays royalties of 10-15% on wholesale price. Publishes ms 1-2 years after acceptance. Guidelines online only.

Advice: "Go to the website."

◎ **WIZARDS OF THE WEST COAST**, (formerly TSR, Inc.), Wizards of the Coast, P.O. Box 707, Renton WA 98057-0707. (425)226-6500. Website: www.wizards.com. **Contact:** Pete Archer, editorial director. Estab. 1974. "We publish shared-world fiction set in the worlds of Dungeons & Dragons, Magic: The Gathering, and Legend of the Five Rings." Wizards of the Coast publishes games as well, including the Dungeons & Dragons® role-playing game. Books: standard paperbacks; offset printing; perfect binding; b&w (usually) illustrations. Averages 50-60 fiction titles/year. Distributes titles through St. Martin's Press.

Imprint(s): Dragonlance® Books; Forgotten Realms® Books; Magic: The Gathering® Books; Legend of the Five Rings Novels.

Needs: Fantasy, science fiction, short story collections. Recently published *Dragons of a Lost Star*, by Margaret Weis and Tracy Hickman (fantasy); *Servant of the Shard*, by R.A. Salvatore (fantasy); and *Apocalypse*, by J. Robert King (fantasy). "We currently publish only work-for-hire novels set in our trademarked worlds. No violent or gory fantasy or science fiction."

How to Contact: Request guidelines first, then query with outline/synopsis and 3 sample chapters. Agented fiction 65%. Responds in 4 months to queries. Accepts simultaneous submissions.

Terms: Pays royalties of 4-8% on retail price. Average advance: $4,000-6,000. Publishes ms 1 year after acceptance. Guidelines available for #10 SASE.

⊕ **◎** **THE WOMEN'S PRESS**, 34 Great Sutton St., London EC1V 0LQ England. Website: www.the-womens-press.com. **Contact:** Editorial Dept. Publishes approximately 50 titles/year.

Needs: "Women's fiction, written by women. Centered on women. Theme can be anything—all themes may be women's concern—but we look for political/feminist awareness, originality, wit, fiction of ideas. Includes literary fiction, crime, and teenage list *Livewire*."

Terms: Writers receive royalty, including advance.

Advice: Writers should ask themselves, "Is this a manuscript that would interest a feminist/political press? What makes the work unique? What are its selling points? Who would want to read it? Is it double-spaced and on one side of the paper only? Have I enclosed return postage?"

◎ **WOODLEY MEMORIAL PRESS**, English Dept., Washburn University, Topeka KS 66621. (785)234-1032. E-mail: zzlaws@washburn.edu.Website: www.washburn.edu/reference/woodley-press (includes writer's guidelines, editors, authors, titles). **Contact:** Robert N. Lawson, editor. Estab. 1980. "Woodley Memorial Press is a small, nonprofit press which publishes book-length poetry and fiction collections by Kansas writers only; by 'Kansas writers' we mean writers who reside in Kansas or have a Kansas connection." Publishes paperback originals. Averages 2 titles/year.
Needs: Contemporary, experimental, literary, mainstream, short story collection. Published *Gathering Reunion*, by David Tangeman (stories and poetry); *The Monday, Wednesday, Friday Girl*, by Stuart Levine (short stories); and *Rudolph, Encouraged by His Therapist*, by Eugene Bales (satiric stories).
How to Contact: Kansas authors should query before sending ms. Accepts unsolicited mss. Submit complete ms with cover letter. Accepts queries by e-mail. Responds in 2 weeks to queries; 2 months to mss. Usually comments on rejected ms.
Terms: "Terms are individually arranged with author after acceptance of manuscript." Publishes ms about 1 year after acceptance. Guidelines available on website.
Advice: "We only publish one work of fiction a year, on average, and definitely want it to be by a Kansas author. We are more likely to do a collection of short stories by a single author."

🐾 ◎ ◎ **WORLDWIDE LIBRARY**, Division of Harlequin Books, 225 Duncan Mill Rd., Don Mills, Ontario M3B 3K9 Canada. (416)445-5860. **Contact:** Feroze Mohammed, senior editor/editorial coordinator. Estab. 1979. Large commercial category line. Publishes paperback originals and reprints. Averages 72 fiction titles/year. "Mystery program is reprint; no originals please."
Imprint(s): Worldwide Mystery; Gold Eagle Books.
Needs: "Action-adventure series and future fiction."
How to Contact: Query with outline/synopsis/series concept or overview and sample chapters. Send SAE with International Reply Coupons or money order. Responds in 10 weeks to queries. Accepts simultaneous submissions.
Terms: Advance and sometimes royalties; copyright buyout. Publishes ms 1-2 years after acceptance.
Advice: "Publishing fiction in very selective areas."

◐ **WRITERS DIRECT**, Imprint of Titlewaves Publishing, Book Division of H&S Publishing, 1351 Kuhio Highway, Kapaa HI 96746. (808)822-7449. Fax: (808)822-2312. E-mail: rs@hshawaii.com. Website: www.bestplacesonearth.com (includes book catalog). **Contact:** Rob Sanford, editor. Estab. 1985. "Small independent publishing house founded and run by published authors." Publishes hardcover and paperback originals and reprints. Books: recycled paper; digital printing; perfect binding; illustrations. **Published 4 new writers within the last year.** Averages more than 6 total titles, 2 fiction titles/year.
Needs: Adventure, humor/satire, literary, mainstream, New Age/mystic, psychic/supernatural, regional (Hawaii), religious (children's religious, inspirational, religious mystery/suspense, religious thriller), thriller/espionage.
How to Contact: Accepts unsolicited mss. Query with first chapter *only*. Include estimated word count, why author wrote book and marketing plan. Send SASE for return of ms or send disposable copy of ms and SASE for reply only. Responds in 1 month to queries; 3 months to mss. Accepts simultaneous submissions. Sometimes comments on rejected mss.
Terms: Pays royalties of 15-35%. Sometimes sends galleys to author. Book catalog for legal-size SASE.
Advice: "Do what you do best and enjoy most. Your writing is an outcome of the above."

🐾 ◐ **YORK PRESS LTD.**, 152 Boardwalk Dr., Toronto, Ontario M4L 3X4 Canada. (416)690-3788. Fax: (416)690-3797. E-mail: yorkpress@sympatico.ca. Website: www3.sympatico.ca/yorkpress. **Contact:** Dr. S. Elkhadem, general manager/editor. Estab. 1975. "We publish scholarly books and creative writing of an experimental nature." Publishes trade paperback originals. **Published new writers within the last year.** Averages 10 titles/year.
Needs: "Fiction of an experimental nature by well-established writers." Published *The Moonhare*, by Kirk Hampton (experimental novel).
How to Contact: Query first. Responds in 2 months.
Terms: Pays royalties of 10-20% royalty on wholesale price. Publishes ms 6 months after acceptance.

Ⓝ **ZEBRA BOOKS**, Imprint of Kensington Publishing Corp., 850 Third Ave., 16th Floor, New York NY 10022. (212)407-1500. Website: www.kensingtonbooks.com. **Contact:** Michaela Hamilton, editor-in-chief; Ann La Farge, executive editor; Kate Duffy, editorial director (romance); John Scognamiglio, editorial director; Amy Garvey, editor; Karen Thomas, editor (African-American fiction and nonfiction); Elaine Sparber, editor (health); Bruce Bender, managing director(Citadel); Margaret Wolf, editor; Richard Ember, editor; Bob Shuman, editor; Miles Lott, editor. Publishes hardcover originals, trade paperback and mass market paperback originals and reprints. Averages 600 titles/year.
Needs: Zebra Books is dedicated to women's fiction, which includes, but is not limited to romance.
How to Contact: Send synopsis and sample chapters with SASE. Accepts simultaneous submissions. Please no queries.
Terms: Publishes book 18 months after acceptance of ms. Book catalog online.

Contests & Awards

In addition to honors and, quite often, cash prizes, contests and awards programs offer writers the opportunity to be judged on the basis of quality alone without the outside factors that sometimes influence publishing decisions. New writers who win contests may be published for the first time, while more experienced writers may gain public recognition of an entire body of work.

Listed here are contests for almost every type of fiction writing. Some focus on form, such as short stories, novels or novellas, while others feature writing on particular themes or topics. Still others are prestigious prizes or awards for work that must be nominated, such as the Pulitzer Prize in Fiction. Chances are no matter what type of fiction you write, there is a contest or award program that may interest you.

SELECTING AND SUBMITTING TO A CONTEST

Use the same care in submitting to contests as you would sending your manuscript to a publication or book publisher. Deadlines are very important, and where possible, we've included this information. At times contest deadlines were only approximate at our press deadline, so be sure to write or call for complete information. To locate a contest based on its monthly deadline, turn to the Deadline Index at the back of this book.

Follow the rules to the letter. If, for instance, contest rules require your name on a cover sheet only, you will be disqualified if you ignore this and put your name on every page. Find out how many copies to send. If you don't send the correct amount, by the time you are contacted to send more, it may be past the submission deadline. An increasing number of contests invite writers to query by e-mail, and many post contest information on their websites. Check listings for e-mail and website addresses.

One note of caution: Beware of contests that charge entry fees that are disproportionate to the amount of the prize. Contests offering a $10 prize, but charging $7 in entry fees, are a waste of your time and money.

If you are interested in a contest or award that requires your publisher to nominate your work, it's acceptable to make your interest known. Be sure to leave the publisher plenty of time, however, to make the nomination deadline.

AIM MAGAZINE'S SHORT STORY CONTEST, AIM Magazine, P.O. Box 1174, Maywood IL 60153. (708)344-4414. Website: www.aimmagazine.org. **Contact:** Ruth Apilado, associate editor. This annual award is for short stories that embodies our goals of furthering the brotherhood of man by way of the written word. Award: $100 and publications. Competition receives 20 submissions per category. Judge: Staff members. No entry fee. Guidelines available anytime. Accepts inquiries by e-mail and phone. Entries should be unpublished. Contest open to everyone. Length: 4,000 word or less. Winners are announced in the autumn issue and notified by mail on Sept 1. List of winners available for SASE.

ALABAMA STATE COUNCIL ON THE ARTS INDIVIDUAL ARTIST FELLOWSHIP, 201 Monroe St., Montgomery AL 36130-1800. (205)242-4076, ext. 224. Fax: (334)240-3269. E-mail: randy@arts.state.al.us. Website: www.arts.state.al.us. **Contact:** Randy Shoults, Literature program manager. "To recognize the achievements and potential of Alabama writers." Annual. Competition receives 25 submissions annually. Judge: independent peer panel. No entry fee. Guidelines available January 2003. For guidelines, fax, e-mail, visit website. Accepts inquiries by fax, e-mail and phone. Deadline: March 1, 2003. "Two copies of the following should be submitted: a resume and a list of published works with reviews, if available. A minimum of ten pages of poetry or prose, but no more than twenty pages. Please label each page with title, artist's name and date. If published, indicate where and the date of publication." Winners announced in June and notified by mail. List of winners available for SASE, fax, e-mail or visit website.

ALASKA STATE COUNCIL ON THE ARTS CAREER OPPORTUNITY GRANT AWARD, Alaska State Council on the Arts, 411 West 4th Ave., Suite 1E, Anchorage AK 99501-2343. (907)269-6610. Fax: (907)269-6601. E-mail: aksca_info@eed.state.ak.us. Website: www.aksca.org. **Contact:** Director. Grants help artists take advantage of impending, concrete opportunities that will significantly advance their work or careers. Professional artists working in the literary arts who are requesting support for unique, short-term opportunities are eligible. Awards up to $1,000. Deadline: applications must be received by the first of the month preceding the month of the proposed activity. Alaskan residents only. Guidelines available on website. Accepts inquiries by fax, phone and e-mail.

N **©** **AMERICAN ASSOCIATION OF UNIVERSITY WOMEN AWARD IN JUVENILE LITERATURE**, North Carolina Literary and Historical Association, 4610 Mail Service Center, Raleigh NC 27699-4610. (919)733-9375. Fax: (919)733-8807. E-mail: michael.hill@ncmail.net. **Contact:** Michael Hill, awards coordinator. Award's purpose is to "select the year's best work of literature for young people by a North Carolina writer." Annual award for published books. Award: cup. Competition receives 10-15 submissions per category. Judge: three-judge panel. No entry fee. Guidelines available July 15, 2002. For guidelines, send SASE, fax, e-mail or call. Accepts inquiries by fax, e-mail, phone. Annual deadline: July 15. Entries should be previously published. Contest open to "recipients of North Carolina (three year minimum)." Winners announced October 15. Winners notified by mail. List of winners available for SASE, fax, e-mail.

N **AMERICAN MARKETS NEWSLETTER SHORT STORY COMPETITION**, American Markets Newsletter, 1974 46th Ave., San Francisco CA 94116. Fax: (415)753-6057. E-mail: sheila.oconnor@juno.com. **Contact:** Sheila O'Connor, publisher/editor. Award is to "give short story writers more exposure—all entries are considered for worldwide syndication whether they win or not." Biannual competition for short stories. Award: 1st place, $250; 2nd place, $100; 3rd place: $50, and worldwide syndication for all eligible entries whether they win or not. Judge: editor of American Markets Newsletter. $7.50 per entry; $12 for 2; $16 for 3; $20 for 4; and $4 each entry thereafter. For guidelines, send SASE, fax, or e-mail. Accepts inquiries by fax and e-mail. Deadline: June 30 and December 31. Published or previously unpublished entries are actively encouraged. Add a note of where and when previously published. Contest open to all. Length: 2,000 words or fewer. "All kinds of fiction are considered—we especially want women's pieces—romance, twist in the tale, but all will be considered." Winners announced "within 3 months of deadlines" and notified by mail if they include SASE.

▢ **SHERWOOD ANDERSON SHORT FICTION AWARD**, *Mid-American Review*, Dept. of English, Bowling Green State University, Bowling Green OH 43403. (419)372-2725. Fax: (419)372-6805. Website: www.bgsu.edu/midam ericanreview. **Contact:** Michael Czyzniejewski, editor-in-chief. Annual. "Contest is open to all writers. It is judged by a well-known writer, e.g., Peter Ho Davies or Melanie Rae Thon. Editors choose the top five entries, then the winner is selected by judge and guaranteed publication in the spring issue of *Mid-American Review*, plus $500. All entrants receive a copy of the issue in which the winners are printed." Competition receives 300-400 submissions. $10 fee per story (up to 5,000 words). Guidelines available in November for SASE, by e-mail or on website. Judge: Dan Chaon in 2002, TBA in 2003. Deadline: October 1. Unpublished material. Winners announced in Spring issue and notified before end of year by phone or mail. List of winners available for SASE, e-mail or visit website. "Everyone who is interested in our contest should be sure to follow our guidelines, firstly, and then mail us your best story. Anyone can win the contest—anyone who enters."

SHERWOOD ANDERSON WRITER'S GRANT, Sherwood Anderson Foundation, 216 College Rd., Richmond VA 23229. (804)282-8008. Fax: (804)287-6052. E-mail: mspear@richmond.edu. Website: www.richmond.edu/~journ alm/comp.html. **Contact:** Michael M. Spear, foundation co-president. Award to "encourage and support developing writers." Annual award for short stories and chapters of novels. Award: range $5,000 to $10,000. Entries are judged by a committee established by the foundation. See website for entry mail address; varies from year to year. No entry fee. Guidelines available on website. Accepts inquiries by e-mail. Annual deadline: April 1. Published or previously unpublished entries. "The contest is open to all struggling writers in the United States." No word length specifications. "Send in your best, most vivid prose that clearly shows talent." Winners announced in mid-summer each year and notified by phone. List of winners available by visiting website.

N **✿** **©** **ANNUAL ATLANTIC WRITING COMPETITION**, Writers' Federation of Nova Scotia, 1113 Marginal Rd., Halifax, Nova Scotia B3H 4P7 Canada. (902)423-8116. Fax: (902)422-0881. E-mail: talk@writers.ns.ca. Website: www.writers.ns.ca. **Contact:** Monika Sormova, executive assistant. Award's purpose is to "provide feedback to emerging writers and create a venue for their work to be considered against that of other beginning authors." Annual award to residents of Atlantic Canada for short stories and novels as well as children's literature, poetry and essay. Prize: In Canadian money—Novel: $200, $150, $100; Writing for Children: $150, $75, $50; Short Story: $100, $75, $50. Competition receives 25-100 submissions per category; about 300 entries total/year. "Judged by a jury of professionals from the field of literature/writing—authors, librarians, publishers, teachers." In Canadian dollars, $25 fee for novel entry ($20 for WFNS members); other categories, $15 ($10 for members). Guidelines available by SASE or visit website. Accepts inquiries by e-mail, phone. Annual deadline: "first Friday in August each year." Entries should be unpublished. To be eligible, writers must be residents of Atlantic Canada, older than 16 and not extensively published in the category they are entering. Length: story 3,000 words maximum, novel 100,000 maximum, children's writing 20,000 maximum. Writers "must use pseudonym; use 8½ × 11 white paper; entries must be typed and double-spaced. 2002 winners announced March 2003. Winners notified by mail late February 2003. List of winners available by visiting website. Press release sent to media.

ANNUAL FICTION CONTEST, Women In The Arts, P.O. Box 2907, Decatur IL 62524. (217)872-0811. **Contact:** Vice President. Annual competition for essays, fiction, fiction for children, plays, rhymed poetry, unrhymed poetry.

Award: $15-30. Competition receives 50-100 submissions. Judges: professional writers. Entry fee $2 per submission. Unlimited entries. Guidelines available for #10 SASE. No entries returned. Do not submit drawings for any category. Double-space prose. Entries must be typed on 8½×11 white paper and must be titled. Do not put your name on any page of the manuscript. Do put your name, address, telephone number, e-mail and titles of your entries on a cover sheet. Submit one cover sheet and one check, with all entries mailed flat in one envelope. Do not staple. All entries will be subject to blind judging. Entries that do not comply with the rules may be disqualified. Deadline: November 1 annually. Published or previously unpublished submissions. Open to anyone. Entries must be original work of the author. Entries must be titled. No entries published by WITA; author retains rights. Word length: essay, up to 1,500 words; fiction, up to 1,500 words; fiction for children, up to 1,500 words (do not submit drawings); play, one act only; rhymed poetry, up to 32 lines; unrhymed poetry, up to 32 lines. Winners announced March 15 annually. Winners notified by mail. "Send a perfect manuscript—no typos, Liquid Paper or holes from 3-ring binders."

ANNUAL JUVENILE-FICTION CONTEST, Women In The Arts, P.O. Box 2907, Decatur IL 62524. (217)872-0811. **Contact:** Vice President. Annual competition for essays, fiction, fiction for children, plays, rhymed poetry, unrhymed poetry. Award: $15-30. Competition receives 50-100 submissions. Judges: professional writers. Entry fee $2 per submission. Unlimited entries. Guidelines available for #10 SASE. Deadline: November 1 annually. Published or previously unpublished submissions. Open to anyone. "Entries must be original work of the author." Word length: 1,500 words maximum for fiction, essay, fiction for children; one act for plays; up to 32 lines for poetry. "Entrants must send for our contest rules and follow the specific format requirements." Winners notified by March 15.

N ANNUAL NOVEL-IN-PROGRESS CONTEST, The Catskill Colony Inc., P.O. Box 26, S. Fallsburg NY 12779. Winter address: 40 W. 86th St., 8A, New York NY 10024-3605. (845)434-8047. E-mail: tkennedyea@aol.com. Website: www.writerscolony.freeservers.com. **Contact:** Teresa Kennedy, founder. Competition's purpose is to "foster genuine talent and promote awareness of the colony's programs. We are not here to encourage bad writing, only to help good writers get published." Annual award for novels. Prize: "Free tuition at the Catskill Colony's Writers Bootcamp held in July. Possible cash prize depending on number of entries." Judging: "A panel of authors, agents and editors from the New York publishing community." $45 entry fee. Guidelines available by e-mail or on website. Accepts inquiries e-mail. Deadline: March 1. Entries should be unpublished. Contest open to "anyone, published or unpublished. No category or genre restrictions. Entries are judged solely on publication potential and literary merit."

O ANTHOLOGY ANNUAL CONTEST, P.O. Box 4411, Mesa AZ 85211-4411. (480)461-8200. E-mail: info@anthology.org. Website: www.anthology.org. **Contact:** Sharon Skinner, contest coordinator. Annual competition for short stories. Awards: 1st Prize $150, *Anthology* t-shirt, 1-year subscription; 2nd Prize, *Anthology* t-shirt, 1-year subscription; 3rd Prize, 1-year subscription. All prize-winning stories are published in January/February of following year. Judge: panel of local writers and *Anthology* staff. Entry fee $5/short story. Maximum number of entries: 5/writer. "All stories submitted to contest are eligible to be printed in upcoming issues of *Anthology*, regardless of finish, unless author specifies otherwise. We ask for one-time rights. All copyrights are held by their original owner." Guidelines available in January for SASE. 2002 deadline: August 31. Any subject, any genre. Length: 5,000 words maximum. Winners announced in January 2003 and notified by mail. List of winners available for SASE.

ANTIETAM REVIEW LITERARY AWARD, *Antietam Review*, 41 S. Potomac St., Hagerstown MD 21740. (301)791-3132. Fax: (240)420-1754. E-mail: winnie@washingtoncountyarts.com. Website: http://washingtoncountyarts.com/index3.html. **Contact:** Winnie Wagaman, managing editor. Annual award to encourage and give recognition to excellence in short fiction. "We consider only previously unpublished work. We read manuscripts between June 1 and September 1." Award: $100 for the story; publication in *Antietam Review* with citation as winner of Literary Contest; and 2 copies of magazine. Competition receives 100 submissions. "We consider all fiction mss sent to *Antietam Review* Literary Contest as entries for inclusion in each issue. We look for well-crafted, serious literary prose fiction under 5,000 words." $10 fee for each story submitted. Make checks payable to *Antietam Review*. Guidelines available for #10 SASE. Accepts inquiries by phone. Deadline: September 1 (entries accepted June through September only). Winners announced in January and notified by phone and mail.

N ✿ O ANVIL PRESS INTERNATIONAL 3-DAY NOVEL WRITING CONTEST, Anvil Press, 204-A 175 E. Broadway, Vancouver, British Columbia V5T 1W2 Canada. (604)876-8710. Fax: (604)879-2667. E-mail: subter@portal.ca. **Contact:** Brian Kaufman, managing editor. Annual prize for best novel written in 3 days, held every Labor Day weekend. Award: Offer of publication with percentage of royalties. Competition receives 400-500 submissions. Judges: Anvil Press Editorial Board. $35 entry fee. Guidelines available June 1 for SASE fax, e-mail, or visit website. Accepts inquiries by fax and e-mail. Deadline: Friday before Labor Day weekend. "Runner up categories may not be offered every year. Please query." Winners announced November 30 and notified by phone and mail. List of winners available November 30 for SASE or on website. "This is a short novel and should contain all the ingredients found in any good novel: character development, a strong story plot line and dramatic action. Don't think of a movie treatment or TV-style scenario and read past winners!"

ARIZONA COMMISSION ON THE ARTS CREATIVE WRITING FELLOWSHIPS, 417 W. Roosevelt St., Phoenix AZ 85003-1326. (602)229-8226. Fax: (602)256-0282. E-mail: pmorris@ArizonaArts.org. Website: www.ArizonaArts.org. **Contact:** Paul Morris, public information and literature director. Fellowships awarded in alternate years to Arizona fiction writers and poets. Award: $5,000-7,500. Competition receives 120-150 submissions. Judges: Out-of-state writers/editors. Guidelines available on website. Accepts inquiries by fax and e-mail. Deadline: September 12. Arizona resident poets and writers over 18 years of age only. Winners announced by March 2001 and notified in writing. List of winners available on website.

ARROWHEAD REGIONAL ARTS COUNCIL INDIVIDUAL ARTIST CAREER DEVELOPMENT GRANT, Arrowhead Regional Arts Council, 101 W. Second St. Suite 204, Duluth MN 55802-2086. (218)722-0952 or (800)569-8134. Fax: (218)722-4459. E-mail: aracouncil@aol.com. Website: www.aracouncil.org. **Contact:** Robert DeArmond, executive director. Award to "provide financial support to regional artists wishing to take advantage of impending, concrete opportunities that will advance their work or careers. Applicants must live in the seven-county region of Northeastern Minnesota." Award is granted 3 times a year. Competition open to short stories, novels, story collections and translations. Award: up to $1,000. Competition receives 15-20 submissions per category. Judge: ARAC Board. No entry fee. Guidelines now available. For guidelines send SASE, fax, e-mail or phone. Accepts inquiries by mail, fax, e-mail and phone. Deadlines: July 26, 2002; November 29, 2002; and April 25, 2003. Entries should be unpublished. Winners announced June 20, 2002 and notified by mail. List of winners available by phone.

THE ART OF MUSIC ANNUAL WRITING CONTEST, Piano Press, P.O. Box 85, Del Mar CA 92014-0085. (858)481-5650. Fax: (858)755-1104. E-mail: Eaxford@aol.com. Website: www.pianopress.com. **Contact:** Elizabeth C. Axford. "Piano Press is looking for poems, short stories and essays on music-related topics only." Award: First, second, and third prizes in each of 3 age-groups. Prizes include cash and publication in the annual anthology *The Art of Music- A Collection of Writings*. Judge: Panel of published writers. Entry fee $20/short story, essay or poem. Guidelines and entry form available on website, by SASE or by e-mail. Deadline: June 30. Contest open to all writers. Poems may be of any length and in any style, single-spaced and typed; short stories and essays should be no longer than five double-spaced, typewritten pages."Make sure all work is fresh and original. Music related topics *only*." Winners announced on September 1 and notified by mail. List of winners available for SASE or visit website.

ARTIST TRUST ARTIST FELLOWSHIPS; GAP GRANTS, Artist Trust, 1402 Third Ave., Suite 404, Seattle WA 98101-2118. (206)467-8734. Fax: (206)467-9633. E-mail: info@artisttrust.org. **Contact:** Heather Dwyer, program director. Artist Trust has 3 grant programs for generative artists in Washington State; the GAP and Fellowships. The GAP (Grants for Artist's Projects) is an annual award of up to $1,400 for a project proposal. The program is open to artists in all disciplines. The Fellowship grant is an award of $6,000 in unrestricted funding. Fellowships for Craft, Media, Literature and Music are awarded in odd numbered years, and Fellowships for Dance, Design, Theater and Visual Art will be awarded in even numbered years. Competition receives 600 (GAP) submissions; 500 (Fellowship). Judges: Fellowship—Peer panel of 3 professional artists and arts professionals in each discipline; GAP—Interdisciplinary peer panel of 5 artists and arts professionals. Guidelines available in December for GAP grants and in April for Fellowship; send SASE. Accepts inquiries by fax and e-mail. Deadline: late February (GAP), mid-June (Fellowship). Winners announced December (Fellowship), May (GAP) and notified by mail. List of winners available by mail.

ASF TRANSLATION PRIZE, American-Scandinavian Foundation, 58 Park Ave., New York NY 10016. (212)879-9779. Fax: (212)686-2115. E-mail: ahenken@amscan.org. Website: www.amscan.org. **Contact:** Publishing office. Estab. 1980. "To encourage the translation and publication of the best of contemporary Scandinavian poetry and fiction and to make it available to a wider American audience." Annual competition for poetry, drama, literary prose and fiction translations. Award: $2,000, a bronze medallion and publication in *Scandinavian Review*. Competition receives 20-30 submissions. Competition rules and entry forms available with SASE and by fax. Accepts inquiries by fax, phone and e-mail. Deadline: June 1, 2003. Submissions must have been previously published in the original Scandinavian language. No previously published translated material. Original authors should have been born within past 200 years. Winners announced in Winter 2002 and notified by mail. List of winners available for SASE. "Select a choice literary work by an important Scandinavian author, which has not yet been translated into English."

THE ISAAC ASIMOV AWARD, International Association for the Fantastic in the Arts and *Asimov*'s magazine, School of Mass Communications, U. of South Florida, 4202 E. Fowler, Tampa FL 33620. (813)974-6792. Fax: (813)974-2592. E-mail: rwilber@chuma.cas.usf.edu. **Contact:** Rick Wilber, administrator. "The award honors the legacy of one of science fiction's most distinguished authors through an award aimed at undergraduate writers." Annual award for short stories. Award: $500 and consideration for publication in *Asimov's*. Winner receives all-expenses paid trip to Ft. Lauderdale, Florida, to attend conference on the Fantastic in mid-March where award is given. Competition receives 100-200 submissions. Judges: *Asimov*'s editors. Entry fee: $10 for up to 3 submissions. Guidelines available for SASE. Accepts inquiries by fax and e-mail. Deadline: December 15. Unpublished submissions. Full-time college undergraduates only. Winners announced in February and notified by telephone. List of winners available in March for SASE.

♣ ◐ ◎ **ASTED/GRAND PRIX DE LITTERATURE JEUNESSE DU QUEBEC-ALVINE-BELISLE**, Association pour l'avancement des sciences et des techniques de la documentation, 3414 Avenue du Parc, Bureau 202, Montreal, Quebec H2X 2H5 Canada. (514)281-5012. Fax: (514)281-8219. E-mail: info@asted.org. Website: www.asted. org. **Contact:** Micheline Patton, president. "Prize granted for the best work in youth literature edited in French in the Quebec Province. Authors and editors can participate in the contest." Annual competition for fiction and nonfiction for children and young adults. Award: $500. Deadline: June 1. Contest entry limited to editors of books published during the preceding year. French translations of other languages are not accepted.

◐ ◎ **THE ATHENAEUM LITERARY AWARD**, The Athenaeum of Philadelphia, 219 S. Sixth St., Philadelphia PA 19106-3794. (215)925-2688. Fax: (215)925-3755. E-mail: erose@PhilaAthenaeum.org. Website: www.PhilaAthenae um.org. **Contact:** Ellen L. Rose, circulation librarian. Annual award to recognize and encourage outstanding literary achievement in Philadelphia and its vicinity. Award: A certificate bearing the name of the award, the seal of the Athenaeum, the title of the book, the name of the author and the year. Competition receives 8-10 submissions. Judged by committee appointed by Board of Directors. Guidelines available for SASE, by fax, by e-mail and on website. Accepts inquiries by fax, e-mail and phone. Deadline: December. Submissions must have been published during the preceding year. Nominations shall be made in writing to the Literary Award Committee by the author, the publisher or a member of the Athenaeum, accompanied by a copy of the book. The Athenaeum Literary Award is granted for a work of general literature, not exclusively for fiction. Juvenile fiction is not included. Winners announced spring 2003 and notified by mail. List of winners available on website.

N ◯ **AUTHORS IN THE PARK/FINE PRINT CONTEST**, P.O. Box 85, Winter Park FL 32790-0085. (407)658-4520. Fax: (407)275-8688. E-mail: authorsinthepark@earthlink.net. **Contact:** David Foley. Annual competition. Award: $1,000 (1st Prize), $500 (2nd Prize), $250 (3rd Prize). Competition receives 200 submissions. Guidelines available for SASE. Read guidelines before sending ms. Deadline: April 31. Word length: 5,000 words maximum. Winners announced in short story collection, *Fine Print*.

◯ **AWP AWARD SERIES IN POETRY, CREATIVE NONFICTION AND SHORT FICTION, AWP/ Thomas Dunne Books Novel Award**, The Associated Writing Programs, Mail Stop 1E3, George Mason University, Fairfax VA 22030. (703)993-4301. Fax: (703)993-4302. E-mail: awp@gmu.edu. Website: http://awpwriter.org. **Contact:** Katherine Perry. Annual award. The AWP Award Series was established in cooperation with several university presses in order to publish and make fine fiction, nonfiction, and poetry available to a wide audience. The competition is open to all authors writing in English. Awards: $2,000 plus publication for short story collection; $10,000 advance plus publication by Thomas Dunne Books for novel, an imprint of St. Martin's Press. In addition, AWP tries to place mss of finalists with participating presses. Competition receives 700 novel and 400 short fiction submissions. Novels are judged by editors at Thomas Dunne Books. Short fiction is judged by a leading author in the field (2002—Frederick Busch). Entry fee $20 nonmembers, $10 AWP members. Contest/award rules and guidelines available in late summer 2001for business-size SASE or visit our website. No phone calls please. Mss must be postmarked between January 1-February 28. Only book-length mss in the novel and short story collections are eligible (60,000 word minimum for novels; 150-300 pages for story collections). Open to all authors writing in English regardless of nationality or residence. Manuscripts previously published in their entirety, including self-publishing, are not eligible. No mss returned. Winners announced in August and notified by phone. Send SASE for list of winners or visit website.

◯ ◎ **AWP INTRO JOURNALS PROJECT**, Mail Stop 1E3, George Mason University, Fairfax VA 22030. (703)993-4308. Fax: (703)993-4302. E-mail: awp@gmu.edu. Website: www.awpwriter.org. **Contact:** Supriya Bhatnagar, publications manager. "This is a prize for students in AWP member university creative writing programs only. Authors are nominated by the head of the creative writing department. Each school may nominate no more than one work of nonfiction, one work of short fiction and three poems." Annual competition for short stories, nonfiction and poetry. Award: $50 plus publication in participating journal. 2002 journals included *Puerto del Sol*, *Quarterly West*, *Mid-American Review*, *Willow Springs*, *Bellingham Review*, *Shenandoah*, *The Journal*, *Crab Orchard Review*, *Tampa Review* and *Hayden's Ferry Review*. Judges: In 2002, Mary Anne Samyn (poetry), Aaron Roy Even (short fiction), Dinty Moore (creative nonfiction). Guidelines available in Fall 2002 for SASE or on website. Accepts inquiries by e-mail, fax and phone. Deadline: December 1. Unpublished submissions only. Winners announced spring notified by mail in late spring/early summer. A list of winners will be available for SASE or on website.

AWP PRAGUE SUMMER SEMINARS FELLOWSHIP, Associated Writing Programs, MS 1E3, George Mason University, Fairfax VA 22030. (703)993-4308. Fax: (703)993-4302. E-mail: awp@gmu.edu. Website: http://awpwriter.o rg. **Contact:** Supriya Bhatnagar, editor. Award to "grant fellowships to promising writers so they can attend the Prague Summer Seminars." Annual award for short stories, poetry, creative nonfiction or novel excerpts. Award: tuition to summer seminars (but not transportation). Competition receives 200-250 submissions in fiction and poetry. Judge: published writers in each field. $5 entry fee. Guidelines available in fall; send SASE or visit website. Accepts inquiries by e-mail and phone. Deadline: December 2002. Entries should be previously unpublished. Contest open to "any writer writing in English who has yet to publish a first book. Length: 20 pages maximum. Winners announced Spring 2003 and notified by phone. A list of winners will be available for SASE and on website.

N ◎ **BABRA AWARDS**, Bay Area Book Reviewers Association, %*Poetry Flash*, 1450 Fourth St. #4, Berkeley CA 94710. (510)525-5476. Fax: (510)525-6752. E-mail: babra@poetryflash.org. Website: www.poetryflash.org. **Con-**

tact: Joyce Jenkins, executive director. Award's purpose is "to celebrate books published by Northern California authors in poetry, fiction, nonfiction and children's literature." Annual award for novels, short story collections. Prize: "Publicity (from a professional publicist), $100, certificate and reading at awards ceremony. $1,000 for lifetime achievement award." Competition receives 60-100 submissions per category. Judge: "Members of the association, active book reviewers and book review editors." No guidelines. Accepts inquiries by fax, e-mail, phone. Deadline: December 1. Entries should be published in the calendar year, e.g. 2003. Contest open to "authors living in Northern California." Winners notified April 2003. List of winners available for SASE, fax, e-mail or on website.

BAKELESS LITERARY PUBLICATION PRIZES, Bread Loaf Writers' Conference Middlebury College, Middlebury College, Middlebury VT 05753. (802)443-2018. E-mail: bakeless@middlebury.edu. Website: www.middlebury.edu/~blwc. **Contact:** Ian Pounds, contest coordinator. "To promote new writers' careers." Annual competition for novels and story collections. Award: publication by Houghton Mifflin, some advanced money, full fellowship to attend Bread Loaf Writers' Conference. Submit as many entries as you want. Judges: Jay Parini (fiction). $10 fee per entry. Guidelines for SASE and e-mail. Accepts inquiries by e-mail and phone. 2002 deadline: November 15. Entries should be unpublished. "Contest open to writers writing in English." Length: 200-450 pages. "Be certain the work is as close to being done as possible." Winners notified by mail with SASE. List of winners available by visiting website.

◐ **EMILY CLARK BALCH AWARDS**, *The Virginia Quarterly Review*, One West Range, Box 400223, Charlottesville VA 22904-4223. **Contact:** Staige D. Blackford. Annual award "to recognize distinguished short fiction by American writers." For stories published in *The Virginia Quarterly Review* during the calendar year. Award: $500.

[N] ◐ MILDRED L. BATCHELDER AWARD, Association for Library Service to Children/American Library Association, 50 E. Huron St., Chicago IL 60611. (312)280-2163. Fax: (312)944-7671. E-mail: alsc@ala.org. Website: www.ala.org/alsc. **Contact:** Meredith Parets, program coordinator. To encourage international exchange of quality children's books by recognizing US publishers of such books in translation. Annual competition for translations. Award: Citation. Judge: Mildred L. Batchelder award committee. Guidelines available February 1 by phone, mail or e-mail. Deadline: December 31. Books should be US trade publications for which children, up to and including age 14, are potential audience. Winners announced in January and notified by phone. List of winners available by website, phone, fax, SASE.

[N] THE BEACON CONTEST, First Coast Romance Writers, P.O. Box 32465, Jacksonville FL 32237. E-mail: dianah2o@aol.com. Website: www.FCRW.com. **Contact:** Heather Waters, contest coordinator. Award to "provide published authors with a chance at greater success." Annual competition for novels. Award: a lighthouse pennant. Judge: finalists are read by book retailers. $25 entry fee. Guidelines available June. For guidelines, send SASE or e-mail. Accepts inquiries by e-mail. Deadline: February 1, 2003. Entries should be published (romance genre; 3 autographed copies of book; not returned; must be copyrighted 2002). Contest open to writers of all romance categories. Winners announced May 2003 and notified by mail. List of winners available for SASE or visit website.

◐ **GEORGE BENNETT FELLOWSHIP**, Phillips Exeter Academy, 20 Main St., Exeter NH 03833-2460. Website: www.exeter.edu. **Contact:** Charles Pratt, coordinator, selection committee. "To provide time and freedom from monetary concerns to a person contemplating or pursuing a career as a professional writer. The committee favors applicants who have not yet published a book-length work with a major publisher." Annual award of writing residency. Award: A stipend ($10,000 at present), plus room and board for academic year. Competition receives approximately 130 submissions. Judges are a committee of the English department. Entry fee $5. Application form and guidelines available for SASE and on website. Deadline: December 1. Winners announced in March and notified by letter or phone. List of winners available in March. All entrants will receive an announcement of the winner. "Stay within a few pages of the limit (we won't read more anyway). Trust us to recognize that what you are sending is a work in progress (you have the chance to talk about that in your statement). Hope, but don't expect anything. If you don't win, some well-known writers have been in your shoes—at least as many as have won the Fellowship."

[N] BEST LESBIAN EROTICA, Cleis Press, P.O. Box 4108, Grand Central Station, New York NY 10163. E-mail: tristan@puckerup.com. Website: www.puckerup.com. **Contact:** Tristan Taormino, series editor. Submit short stories, novel excerpts, other prose; poetry will be considered, but poetry is not encouraged. Accepts both unpublished and previously published material will be considered. Include cover page with author's name, title of submission(s), address, phone/fax, and e-mail. All submissions must be typed and double-spaced. Also number the pages. Length: 5,000. You may submit a maximum of 3 different pieces of work. Submit 2 hard copies of each submission. No e-mail submissions will be accepted; accepts inquiries by e-mail. All submissions must include a SASE or an e-mail address for response. No mss will be return.

◐ ◎ **"BEST OF OHIO WRITERS" CONTEST**, *Ohio Writer Magazine*, P.O. Box 91801, Cleveland OH 44101. (216)421-0403. Fax: (216)791-1727. E-mail: pwlgc@msn.com. **Contact:** Gail and Stephen Bellamy, editors. Award "to encourage and promote the work of writers in Ohio." Annual competition for short stories. Awards: $150 (1st Prize), $50 (2nd Prize). Competition receives 200 submissions. Judges: "a selected panel of prominent Ohio writers." $15 entry fee for first submission, $2 for each additional entry (includes subscription to *Ohio Writer* magazine). Guidelines available after January 1 for SASE, fax or e-mail. Accepts inquiries by e-mail and phone. Deadline: July 31.

Unpublished submissions. Ohio writers only. Length: 2,500 words. "No cliché plots; we're looking for fresh, unpublished voices." Winners announced November 1 and notified by mail. List of winners available November 1 for SASE or e-mail.

N **◎** **DORIS BETTS FICTION PRIZE**, North Carolina Writers' Network, 3501 Hwy. 54 W., Studio C, Chapel Hill NC 27516. (919)967-9540. Fax: (919)929-0535. E-mail: mail@ncwriters.org. Website: www.ncwriters.org. **Contact:** Lisa Robinson Bailey, program coordinator. Award to "encourage and recognize the work of emerging and established North Carolina writers." Annual competition for short stories. Awards: $150 1st Place, $100 2nd Place, $50 3rd Place. Competition receives 100-150 submissions. Judges change annually. Entry fee $8 for NCWN members; $12 for nonmembers. Guidelines available in July for SASE or on website. Deadline: March 1. Unpublished submissions. "The award is available only to legal residents of North Carolina or out-of-state NCWN members." Word length: 6 double-spaced pages (1,500 words maximum). Winners announced in June and notified by phone and letter. List of winners available for SASE.

N **BINGHAMTON UNIVERSITY JOHN GARDNER FICTION BOOK AWARD**, Binghamton University Creative Writing Program, P.O. Box 6000, Binghamton NY 13902-6000. (607)777-6134. Fax: (607)777-2408. E-mail: mgillan@binghamton.edu. Website: www.english.binghamton.edu/cwpro. **Contact:** Maria Mazzioni Gillan, director. Award's purpose is "to serve the literary community by calling attention to outstanding books of fiction." Annual award for novels, short story collections. Prize: $1,000. Competition receives approximately 500 submissions per category. Judge: "Rotating outside judges." Guidelines available for SASE and on website. Accepts inquiries by e-mail. 2002 deadline was March 1. Entries should be published in book form. Winners announced in summer. List of winners available for SASE and on website.

◑ **IRMA S. AND JAMES H. BLACK CHILDREN'S BOOK AWARD**, Bank Street College, 610 W. 112th St., New York NY 10025-1898. (212)875-4450. Fax: (212)875-4558. E-mail: lindag@bnkst.edu. Website: http://streetcat.bnkst.edu/html/isb.html. **Contact:** Linda Greengrass, award director. Annual award "to honor the young children's book published in the preceding year judged the most outstanding in text as well as in art. Book must be published the year preceding the May award." Award: Press function at Harvard Club, a scroll and seals by Maurice Sendak for attaching to award book's run. Judges: adult children's literature experts and children 6-10 years old. No entry fee. Guidelines available by SASE, fax, e-mail, or on website. Accepts inquiries by phone, fax and e-mail. Deadline: December 15. Expects to receive about 150 fiction entries for 2002 competition. "Write to address above. Usually publishers submit books they want considered, but individuals can too. No entries are returned." Winners notified by phone in April and announced in May. A list of winners will be available on website.

N **⊕** **BLACK HILL BOOKS SHORT STORY COMPETITION**, Black Hill Books, P.O. Box 23, Knighton, Powys, Wales LD7 1WS United Kingdom. Phone/fax: 01588-640551. E-mail: blackhillbooks@hotmail.com. Website: http://guynsmith.com. **Contact:** Jean Smith, competition manager. Annual award for short stories. Two sections: Adult Stories/Children's Stories prizes in each are £50, £25, £10. Total prize money £170. All 6 winning stories will be published in *Graveyard Rendezvous*. Competition receives "several hundred" submissions per category. Judge: well-known published authors. £3 entry fee per story (US $7). For guidelines, send SASE, fax or visit website. Accepts inquiries by fax, e-mail, phone. Deadline: April 26, 2003. Contest open to all writers. Length: 2,000 words. Enter "well written stories with good plot and good characterization." Winners announced in July. Winners notified by mail. List of winners available for SASE.

N **⊕** **◓** **◎** **JAMES TAIT BLACK MEMORIAL PRIZES**, Department of English Literature, University of Edinburgh, David Hume Tower, George Square, Edinburgh EH8 9JX Scotland. Phone: 44 0131 650 3619. Fax: 44 0131 650 6898. E-mail: s.strathdee@ed.ac.uk. Website: www.ed.ac.uk/englit/jtbint.htm. **Contact:** Sheila Strathdee, Department of English Literature. "Two prizes are awarded: one for the best work of fiction, one for the best biography or work of that nature, published during the calendar year: October 1st to September 30th." Annual competition. Award: £3,000 each. Competition receives approximately 150 submissions. Judge: Professor John Frow, Dept. of English Literature. Guidelines for SASE or SAE and IRC. Guildlines available Sept. 30. Deadline: September 30. Previously published submissions. "Eligible works are those written in English and first published in Britain in the year of the award. Works should be submitted by publishers." Winners announced in January and notified by phone, via publisher. Contact Department of English Literature for list of winners or check website. Accepts inquiries by fax, e-mail, phone.

FOR EXPLANATIONS OF THESE SYMBOLS,
SEE THE INSIDE FRONT AND BACK COVERS OF THIS BOOK.

THE BLACK WARRIOR REVIEW LITERARY AWARD, P.O. Box 862936, Tuscaloosa AL 35486-0277. (205)348-4518. E-mail: david.goldberg@ua.edu. Website: www.webdelsol.com/bwr. **Contact:** David Goldberg. "Determined by independent judges, the award grants $500 to a fiction writer whose work has been published in the previous fall and spring issues. All works of fiction included in these issues considered." Winners listed in fall issue. Accepts inquiries by fax and e-mail.

BOARDMAN TASKER PRIZE, Pound House, Llangennith, Swansea, Wales SA3 1JQ United Kingdom. Phone/fax: 44-1792-386-215. E-mail: margaretbody@lineone.net. Website: www.boardmantasker.com. **Contact:** Margaret Body, honorary secretary. "To reward a book which has made an outstanding contribution to mountain literature. A memorial to Peter Boardman and Joe Tasker, who disappeared on Everest in 1982." Award: £2,000. Competition receives 20 submissions. Judges: A panel of 3 judges elected by trustees. Guidelines available in January by fax, by e-mail, for SASE or on website. Deadline: August 1. Limited to works published or distributed in the UK for the first time between November 1 and October 31. Publisher's entry only. "May be fiction, nonfiction, poetry or drama. Not an anthology. Subject must be concerned with a mountain environment. Previous winners have been books on expeditions, climbing experiences; a biography of a mountaineer; novels." Winners announced in November and notified by phone or e-mail. List of winners available for SASE, by fax, e-mail and on website. "The winning book needs to be well written and to reflect an appreciation and knowledge of and a respect for the mountain environment."

BOOK PUBLISHERS OF TEXAS AWARD, Holy Cross Hall 304, St. Edwards University, 3001 S. Congress Ave., Austin TX 78704-6489. **Contact:** Paula Mitchell Marks, secretary. "Award to honor the best book written for children or young people that was published the year prior to that in which the award is given." Annual competition for children's literature. Award: $50. Competition receives approximately 40 submissions. Judges: Committee selected by TIL. Guidelines available after June for SASE. Accepts inquiries by e-mail and fax. Deadline: January 8, 2002. Previously published submissions from January 1 through December 31 of the year prior to the award. "To be eligible, the writer must have been born in Texas or have lived in the state for two years at some time, or the subject matter of the work must be associated with Texas." Winners announced April 15, 2002 and notified by phone. List of winners available on website.

BOOK SENSE BOOK OF THE YEAR AWARD, Book Sense, 828 S. Broadway, Tarrytown NY 10591. (914)591-2665. Fax: (914)591-2720. E-mail: info@bookweb.org. Website: www.bookweb.org. **Contact:** Jill Perlstein, director marketing services. "Independent booksellers vote for the books they most enjoyed handselling in the previous year." Annual award for "fiction, nonfiction, children's illustrated, children's literature and rediscovery." Award: $2,000. Judge: "Independent bookseller members of the American Booksellers Association." No entry fee. No guidelines. Accepts inquiries by fax, e-mail, phone. All entries should be previously published. Only books first nominated for the Book Sense 76 list are eligible. Member booksellers nominate books; writers may not submit their own work. Winners announced "at the Celebration of Bookselling at BookExpo America each spring." Winners notified by mail, phone or e-mail and at the Celebration of Bookselling immediately. List of winners available by visiting website.

BOSTON GLOBE-HORN BOOK AWARDS, *Horn Book Magazine, Inc.*, 56 Roland St., Suite 200, Boston MA 02129. (617)628-0225. Fax: (617)628-0882. E-mail: info@hbook.com. Website: www.hbook.com. **Contact:** Anne Quirk, marketing director. Annual award. "To honor excellence in children's fiction or poetry, picture and nonfiction books published within the US." Award: $500 and engraved silver bowl first prize in each category; engraved silver plate for the 2 honor books in each category. Competition receives 1,000 submissions. No entry fee. Guidelines available after January 31 for SASE, fax, e-mail, or on website. Accepts inquiries by fax and e-mail. Entry forms or rules for SASE. Deadline: May 15. "Children's and young adult books published in the U.S. between June 1, 2002-May 31, 2003 can be submitted by publishers." Winners announced in July and notified by phone. List of winners available in July on website, for SASE, by fax and by e-mail.

BOSTON REVIEW SHORT STORY CONTEST, *Boston Review*, E53-407, MIT, Cambridge MA 02139. (617)253-3642. E-mail: review@mit.edu. Website: http://bostonreview.mit.edu. **Contact:** Rob Mitchell. Annual award for short stories. Award: $1,000. Processing fee $15. Deadline: September 1. Unpublished submissions. Competition receives 500 entries. No restrictions on subject matter. Guidelines available in September 2001 for SASE, by e-mail or on website. Accepts inquiries by e-mail. Word length: 4,000 words. Winning entry published in December issue. All entrants receive a 1-year subscription to the *Boston Review* beginning with the December issue. Stories not returned. Winners announced December 1 and notified by mail.

BOULEVARD SHORT FICTION CONTEST FOR EMERGING WRITERS, *Boulevard Magazine*, PMB 325, 6614 Clayton Rd., Richmond MO 63117. (314)862-2643. Fax: (314)862-2982. E-mail: ballyman@hotmail.com. Website: www.richardburgin.com. **Contact:** Richard Burgin, editor. Annual competition for short stories. Award: $1,500. Competition receives 2 submissions per category. Judges: *Boulevard*'s editors. $15 fee per entry which includes a year's subscription to *Boulevard*. Guidelines available September 2002 for SASE or fax. Accepts inquiries by e-mail, fax, phone. Deadline: December 15, 2002. Entries should be unpublished. Open to: "Writers who have not yet published a book of fiction, poetry or creative nonfiction with a nationally distributed press are welcome." Length: 7,500 words. "Be familiar with *Boulevard Magazine*." Winners announced in the Spring Issue of *Boulevard Magazine* and notified by mail or phone in February/March.

◢ ◎ **BRAZOS BOOKSTORE (HOUSTON) AWARD (SINGLE SHORT STORY)**, Holy Cross Hall 304, St. Edwards University, 3001 S. Congress Ave., Austin TX 78704-6489. **Contact:** Paula Mitchell Marks, secretary. Award to "honor the writer of the best short story published for the first time during the calendar year before the award is given." Annual competition for short stories. Award: $750. Competition receives approximately 40-50 submissions. Judges: panel selected by TIL Council. Guidelines for SASE. Accepts inquiries by e-mail. Deadline: January 14. Previously published submissions. Entries must have appeared in print between January 1 and December 31 of the year prior to the award. "Award available to writers who, at some time, have lived in Texas at least two years consecutively or whose work has a significant Texas theme. Entries must be sent directly to the three judges. Their names and addresses are available from the TIL office. Include SASE. Winners announced April 15 and notified by phone."

THE BRIAR CLIFF REVIEW POETRY & FICTION CONTEST, *The Briar Cliff Review*, Briar Cliff University, 3303 Rebecca St., Sioux City IA 51104-2324. (712)279-5321. Fax: (712)279-5410. E-mail: currans@briarcliff.edu. Website: www.briarcliff.edu/bcreview. **Contact:** Tricia Currans-Sheehan, editor. Award "to reward good writers and showcase quality writing." Annual award for short stories and poetry. Award: $500 and publication in spring issue. Competition receives 100-125 submissions. Judges: editors. "All entries are read by at least 3 editors." $10 entry fee. Guidelines for SASE. Deadline: submissions between August 1 and November 1. Previously unpublished submissions. Word length: 5,000 words maximum. "Send us your best work. We want stories with a plot." Winners announced December or January and notified by phone or by letter around December 20. List of winners available for SASE sent with submission. "Send us your *best*. We want stories with a plot."

N ⊕ **THE BRIDPORT PRIZE**, Bridport Arts Centre, South Street, Bridport, Dorset DT6 3NR United Kingdom. (01308)459444. Fax: (01308)459166. E-mail: info@bridport-arts.com. Website: www.bridportprize.co.uk. **Contact:** Frances Everitt, administrator. Awarded to "promote literary excellence, discover new talent." Annual competition for short stories. Award: £3,000 sterling (1st prize), £1,000 sterling (2nd prize), £500 sterling (3rd prize) plus various runners-up prizes and publication of approximately 10 best stories in anthology. Judge: One judge for short story (in 2002, Tobias Hill); one judge for poetry (in 2002, Jo Shapcott). £5 sterling entry fee. Guidelines available January 2002; send SASE or visit website. Accepts inquiries by fax, e-mail and phone. 2002 deadline: June 30. Entries should be unpublished. Contest open to anyone. Length: 5,000 words maximum for short stories; 42 lines for poetry. Winners announced in October of year of contest and notified by mail or phone in September. List of winners available for SASE.

ARCH & BRUCE BROWN FOUNDATION, The Arch & Bruce Brown Foundation, PMB 503, 31855 Date Palm Dr., Suite 3, Cathedral City CA 92234. E-mail: archwrite@aol.com. Website: www.aabbfoundation.org. **Contact:** Arch Brown, president. Contest for "gay-positive works based on history." Annual contest; type of contest changes each year: short story (2004); playwrighting (2002); novel (2003). Award: $1,000 (not limited to a single winner). No entry fee. For guidelines, send SASE or visit website. 2002 deadline: November 30. Entries should be unpublished. Contest open to all writers. Winners announced Spring and notified by mail. List of winners available for SASE or visit website.

N ✉ ◯ ◎ **BURNABY WRITERS' SOCIETY ANNUAL COMPETITION**, 6584 Deer Lake Ave., British Columbia V5G 3T7 Canada. (604)444-1228. E-mail: lonewolf@portal.ca. Website: www.bws.bc.ca. Annual competition to encourage creative writing in British Columbia. "Category varies from year to year." Award: $200, $100 and $50 (Canadian) prizes. Receives 400-600 entries for each award. Judge: "independent recognized professional in the field." Entry fee $5. Guidelines available for SASE or on website. Contest requirements after March for SASE. Deadline: May 31. Open to British Columbia authors only. Winners announced in September and notified by phone, mail or e-mail. List of winners available for SASE.

◯ ◎ **BUSH ARTIST FELLOWS PROGRAM**, (formerly Bush Artist Fellowships), Bush Foundation, E-900 First Nat'l Bank Building, 332 Minnesota St., St. Paul MN 55101-1387. (651)227-5222 or (800)605-7315. Fax: (651)297-6485. E-mail: kpolley@bushfound.org. Website: www.bushfoundation.org. **Contact:** Kathi Polley, program assistant. Award to "provide artists with significant financial support that enables them to further their work and their contribution to their communities. Fellows may decide to take time for solitary work or reflection, engage in collaborative or community projects, or embark on travel or research." Annual grant. Award: $44,000 for 12-18 months. Competition receives 400-500 submissions. Literature (fiction, creative nonfiction, poetry) offered every other year. Next offered 2003 BAF. Applications available August 2002. Accepts inquiries by phone, fax and e-mail. 2002 deadline: October. Must meet certain publication requirements. Judges: a panel of artists and arts professionals who reside outside of Minnesota, South Dakota, North Dakota or Wisconsin. Applicants must be at least 25 years old, and Minnesota, South Dakota, North Dakota or Western Wisconsin residents. Students not eligible. Winners announced in Spring 2003 and notified by letter. List of winners available in May and sent to all applicants.

◯ ◎ **BYLINE SHORT FICTION & POETRY AWARDS**, P.O. Box 5240, Edmond OK 73083-5240. Phone/fax: (405)348-5591. E-mail: mpreston@bylinemag.com. Website: www.bylinemag.com. **Contact:** Marcia Preston, executive editor/publisher. "To encourage our subscribers in striving for high quality writing." Annual awards for short stories and poetry. Award: $250 in each category. Competition receives approximately 200 submissions in each category. Judges are published writers chosen by the *ByLine* staff. Entry fee $5 for stories; $3 for poems. Guidelines available for SASE. Accepts inquiries by e-mail and phone. Postmark deadline: November 1. "Judges look for quality writing, well-drawn characters, significant themes. Entries should be unpublished, not have won money in any previous contest and be suitable for publication in *ByLine*. Winners notified by mail and phone in January and announced in February issue, accompanied by photo and short bio. List of winners available for SASE, read magazine or visit website. Open to subscribers only."

CALIFORNIA BOOK AWARDS, The Commonwealth Club of California, 595 Market St., San Francisco CA 94105. (415)597-4846. Fax: (415)597-6729. E-mail: bookawards@commonwealth.org. Website: www.commonwealthcl ub.org. **Contact:** Barbara Lane, book awards manager. Annual competition for novels and story collections. Award: $2,000 (1st Prize); $300 (2nd Prize). Competition receives 400 submissions. Judges: panel of jurors. Guidelines available in July 2001 by e-mail, on website or for SASE. Accepts inquiries by phone and e-mail. Deadline: December 31. Previously published submissions that appeared in print between January 1 and December 30. "Writers must have been legal residents of California when manuscript was accepted for publication. Enter as early as possible—supply three copies of book." Winners notified in June by phone, mail or through publisher and announced in summer. List of winners available for SASE or on website.

JOHN W. CAMPBELL MEMORIAL AWARD FOR THE BEST SCIENCE-FICTION NOVEL OF THE YEAR; THEODORE STURGEON MEMORIAL AWARD FOR THE BEST SCIENCE FICTION SHORT FICTION, Center for the Study of Science Fiction, English Dept., University of Kansas, Lawrence KS 66045. (785)864-3380. Fax: (785)864-1159. E-mail: jgunn@ku.edu. Website: www.ku.edu/~sfcenter. **Contact:** James Gunn, professor and director. "To honor the best novel and short science fiction of the year." Annual competition for short stories and novels. Award: Certificate. "Winners' names are engraved on a trophy." Campbell Award receives approximately 200 submissions. Judges: 2 separate juries. Accepts inquiries by e-mail and fax. Deadline: December 31. Entries must be previously published. "Ordinarily publishers should submit work, but authors have done so when publishers would not. Send for list of jurors." Entrants for the Sturgeon Award are selected by nomination only. Winners announced in July. List of winners available for SASE.

CANADA COUNCIL GOVERNOR GENERAL'S LITERARY AWARDS, Canada Council for the Arts, 350 Albert St., P.O. Box 1047, Ottawa, Ontario K1P 5V8 Canada. (613)566-4414, ext. 5576. E-mail: joanne.laroc que-poirier@canadacouncil.ca. **Contact:** Writing and Publishing Section. "Awards of $15,000 each are given annually to the best English-language and best French-language Canadian work in each of seven categories: children's literature (text) and children's literature (illustration), drama, fiction, poetry, nonfiction and translation." Canadian authors, illustrators and translators only. Books must be submitted by publishers (4 copies must be sent to the Canada Council) and accompanied by a Publisher's Submissions Form, available from the Writing and Publishing Section. Self-published books are not eligible.

CAPTIVATING BEGINNINGS CONTEST, *Lynx Eye*, 542 Mitchell Dr., Los Osos CA 93402. (805)528-8146. Fax: (805)528-7876. E-mail: pamccully@aol.com. **Contact:** Pam McCully, co-editor. Annual award for stories "with engrossing beginnings, stories that will enthrall and absorb readers." Award: $100 plus publication, 1st Prize; $10 each for 4 honorable mentions plus publication. Competition receives 600-700 submissions. Judges: *Lynx Eye* editors. Entry fee $5/story. Guidelines available for SASE or by e-mail. Accepts inquiries by e-mail and phone. Unpublished submissions. Length: 7,500 words or less. "The stories will be judged on the first 500 words." Guidelines available year round for SASE. Accepts inquiries by e-mail and phone. Deadline: January 31. Winners announced March 15 and notified by mail. List of winners available March 31 for SASE.

RAYMOND CARVER SHORT STORY CONTEST, HSU English Dept., 1 Harpst St., Arcata CA 95521. (707)826-5946, ext. 1. Fax: (707)826-5939. E-mail: carver@humboldt.edu. Contact: Student Coordinator. Annual award for previously unpublished short stories. Award: $1,000 and publication in *Toyon* (1st Prize). $500 and honorable mention in *Toyon* (2nd Prize). Honorable mention in *Toyon* (3rd Prize). Competition receives 400 submissions. Entry fee $10/story. Guidelines available June 1 for #10 SASE. Deadline: January 10. For US citizens only. Send 2 copies of story; author's name, address, phone number and title of story on separate cover page only. Story must be no more than 6,000 words. For notification of receipt of ms, include self-addressed, stamped postcard. For Winners List include SASE. For a copy of the *Toyon*, send $5 in a separate envelope to *Toyon*, HSU English Dept., 1 Harpst St., Arcata CA 95521. "Follow directions and have faith in your work." Winners announced June 1 and notified by mail. List of winners available June 1.

CELTIC VOICE WRITING CONTEST, Bardsong Press, P.O. Box 775396, Steamboat Springs CO 80477-5396. (970)870-1401. Fax: (970)879-2657. E-mail: celts@bardsongpress.com. Website: www.bardsongpress.com. **Contact:** Ann Gilpin, editor. Annual competition for short stories. Award: cash awards for category winners; publication for winners and honorable mentions. Judges: selected guest judges. $10 fee per entry. Guidelines available January 1, 2003 for SASE, e-mail or on website. Accepts inquiries by e-mail. Deadline: September 30, 2003. Entries should be unpublished. Open to all writers. "We are looking for work that reflects the ageless culture, history, symbolism, mythology and spirituality that belongs to Celtic heritage. Following the guidelines specifications closely will give the greatest chance to do well in the competition. Let your imagination soar freely." Winners announced in January 2004 and notified by mail or e-mail. List of winners available for SASE.

THE CHELSEA AWARDS, P.O. Box 773, Cooper Station, New York NY 10276-0773. E-mail: rafoerster@aol.c om. **Contact:** Alfredo de Palchi. Annual competition for short stories. Award: $1,000 and publication in *Chelsea* (all entries are considered for publication). Competition receives 300 submissions. Judges: the editors. Entry fee $10 (for which entrants also receive a subscription). Guidelines available for SASE. Deadline: June 15. Unpublished submissions. Absolutely no simultaneous submissions. Manuscripts may not exceed 30 typed pages or about 7,500 words. The stories must not be under consideration elsewhere or scheduled for book publication within 8 months of the competition deadline. Include separate cover sheet; no name on ms. Mss will not be returned; include SASE for notification of results. Winners announced August 15 and notified by telephone. "No submissions or notification will be sent or responded to by e-mail."

CHICAGO LITERARY AWARDS, *Another Chicago Magazine*, 3709 N. Kenmore, Chicago IL 60613-2901. E-mail: editors@anotherchicagomag.com. Website: www.anotherchicagomag.com. **Contact:** Editor. "To award excellence in fiction and poetry writing." Annual competition for short stories and poetry. Award: $1,000 and publication in *Another Chicago Magazine*. Competition receives 400 submissions. Judge: Diane Wakoski (poetry). $10/story; length: 6,500; $10/set of 3 poems; length: 300 lines total. Checks payable to Left Field Press. No previously published work eligible; if work is under consideration elsewhere, *ACM* must be notified and work must be withdrawn upon acceptance elsewhere. "No names on mss; include cover page with name, address, titles, word count for fiction and line count for poetry. No mss returned." Winners announced April 1, 2002. Include SASE for notification of winners; SAS postcard for acknowledgement of entry. No certified mail please.

◻ ◎ **CHICANO/LATINO LITERARY CONTEST**, Dept. of Spanish & Portuguese, University of California-Irvine, Irvine CA 92697-5275. (949)824-5443. Fax: (949)824-2803. E-mail: CLLP@uci.edu. Website: www.humanities. hnet.uci.edu/spanishandportuguese/contest.html. **Contact:** Barbara Caldwell, coordinator. Annual award for different genre each year; novels (2003), short stories (2004), poetry (2005) and drama (2006). Award: Usually $1,000. Guidelines available in January for SASE or on website. Deadline: June 1. Accepts inquiries by fax, phone and e-mail. Unpublished submissions only. Winners notified by letter in October. A list of winners will be available on website.

⊕ ◻ **THE CHILDREN'S BOOK AWARD**, Federation of Children's Book Groups, The Old Malt House, Aldbourne, Marlborough, Wilts SN8 2DW England. Award to "promote good quality books for children." Annual award for short stories, novels, story collections and translations. Award: "Portfolio of children's writing and drawings and a magnificent trophy of silver and oak." Judges: Thousands of children from all over the United Kingdom. Guidelines for SASE or SAE and IRC. Deadline: December 31. "Work must be published in the U.K. during the current year."

◎ **CHILDREN'S WRITERS FICTION CONTEST**, Stepping Stones, P.O. Box 8863, Springfield MO 65801-8863. (417)863-7369. E-mail: verwil@alumni.pace.edu. **Contact:** V.R. Williams, coordinator. Award to "promote writing for children by encouraging children's writers and giving them an opportunity to submit their work in competition." Annual competition for short stories and translations. Award: $260 and/or publication in *Hodge Podge*. Competition receives 160 submissions. "Judged by Goodin, Williams, Goodwin and/or associates. Entries are judged for clarity, grammar, punctuation, imagery, content and suitability for children." Entry fee $8. Guidelines available for SASE or e-mail. Accepts inquiries by phone and e-mail. Deadline: July 31. Previously unpublished submissions. Word length: 1,500 words. "Work submitted on colored paper, book format is not acceptable. Stories should have believable characters." Winners announced in September and notified by mail. List of winners for SASE. "To avoid disqualification of entry, contestants must follow guidelines. If possible, the child should be the main character in the story. Stories about animals or inanimate objects should have a purpose. Children should enjoy the story, but also learn from it."

◻ **THE CHRISTOPHER AWARDS**, The Christophers, 12 E. 48th St., New York NY 10017-1091. (212)759-4050. Fax: (212)838-5073. E-mail: awards1@christophers.org. Website: www.christophers.org. **Contact:** Judith Trojan, program manager. Annual award "to encourage authors and illustrators to continue to produce works which affirm the highest values of the human spirit in adult and children's books." Published submissions only. Award: Bronze medallion. "Award judged by a panel of juvenile reading and subject experts. Juvenile works are 'children tested.'" No entry forms or submission fees. "Potential winners are nominated and reviewed throughout the year by panels of media professionals, members of the Christopher staff and by specially supervised children's reading groups. Friends of The Christophers are also encouraged to nominate titles." For guidelines send 6x9 SASE or fax. Accepts inquiries accepted by fax, e-mail and phone. Two deadlines: June 1 and November 1 every year. Books may be submitted any time in between as well. Winners chosen in January and notified by mail and phone late January. "Awards are presented at a black-tic gala on the third Thursday in February in New York City." List of winners available for SASE, by fax or visit website. Example of book award: *I Love You, Blue Kangaroo!*, by Emma Chicester Clark (children's book category 2000).

◻ **CNW/FFWA FLORIDA STATE WRITING COMPETITION**, Florida Freelance Writers Association, P.O. Box A, North Stratford NH 03590. (603)922-8338. Fax: (603)922-8339. E-mail: danakcnw@ncia.net. Website: www.writers-editors.com. **Contact:** Dana K. Cassell, executive director. Award "to recognize publishable writing." Annual competition for short stories and novels. Awards: $100 (first place), $75 (second place), $50 (third place). Competition receives 50-100 submissions in short story/novel division. Total 400-500 in all divisions. Judges: published authors, teachers, editors. Entry fee ($5-20) varies with membership status. Guidelines available for SASE or on website. Deadline: March 15. Previously unpublished submissions. Winners will be notified by mail by May 31. List of winners available for SASE or visit website.

COLORADO BOOK AWARDS, Colorado Center for the Book, 2123 Downing St., Denver CO 80205. (303)839-8320. Fax: (303)839-8319. Website: www.ColoradoBook.org. **Contact:** Chris Citron, executive director. "To celebrate the excellence of Colorado writers." Annual competition for novels. Award: $250, plaque and speaking appearances. Competition receives more than 200 submissions. Judges: 5 judges in each of the 10 categories. $45 fee per entry. Guidelines for SASE or fax. Accepts inquiries by fax. Deadline: January 15, 2003. Entries should be published in preceding year. Contest open to Colorado residents. Winners announced Fall of each year and notified by mail. List of winners available for SASE or fax.

THE COMMONWEALTH WRITERS PRIZE, The Commonwealth Foundation, %Book Trust, Book House, 45 East Hill, London SW18 2QZ England. (020)8516-2973/2. Fax: (020)8516-2978. E-mail: kate@booktrust.org.uk or tarryn@booktrust.org.uk. Website: www.oneworld.org/com_fnd/contents.html. **Contact:** Kate Mervyn Jones, prizes manager or Tarryn McKay, prizes administrator. "This award was set up to recognise and reward the diverse talent within the Commonwealth. It awards well estblished as well as first-time novelists, and is unique in the fact that the overall Best Book winner has an audience with HM the Queen." Annual prize for short stories (published as a collection) and novels. Award: Regional winners £1,000, Overall Best First Book £3,000 and Overall Best Book £10,000. Number of submissions varies. Judge: Regional judges for 2003 include Dr. Walter Perera, Professor Margery Fee and others. The judging criterion is confidential. No entry fee. "For guidelines either request direct from Book Trust, or ask publisher to contact us." Accepts inquiries by fax, e-mail, phone and post. "The deadline for entry November 15; any books we are advised of that are not published by this date must be first submitted in proof form, with originals following before December 31." Entries must be first published during the preceding year. Contest open to all fiction writers from Commonwealth countries. Length: Open. Writers may submit their own fiction only if it is published and with the publisher's consent. Regional winners announced in February and the overall winners in April. "Publishers will be notified of regional win, and winners are invited to a week long festival of literature, including the gala award dinner when the overall winners are announced." List of winners "should be in the papers, or contact us for a press release."

DANA AWARD IN SHORT FICTION, 7207 Townsend Forest Court, Browns Summit NC 27214-9634. (336)656-7009. E-mail: danaawards@pipeline.com. Website: www.danaawards.com. **Contact:** Mary Elizabeth Parker, chair. Award "to reward work that has been previously unrecognized in the area of fiction. All genres, including literary/mainstream, and speculative fiction. No work for or by persons under 16. "Let authors be aware work must meet standards of literary complexity and excellence. Character development, excellence of style are as important as the plot line." Award: $1,000. Competition receives 300 submissions annually. Entry fee $10/short story. Make checks payable to Dana Awards. Guidelines for SASE, by e-mail or on website. Accepts inquiries by e-mail and phone. Unpublished submissions, not under contract to any publisher. "See 'What We're Looking For' on our website for submission tips." Word length: No longer than 10,000 words, 3,000 word average preferred. Postmark deadline: October 31. Winners announced March and notified by phone, then by letter or e-mail. Send SASE with submission to receive competition results letter.

DANA AWARD IN THE NOVEL, 7207 Townsend Forest Court, Browns Summit NC 27214-9634. (336)656-7009. E-mail: danaawards@pipeline.com. Website: www.danaawards.com. **Contact:** Mary Elizabeth Parker, chair. Award to "reward work that has not yet been recognized, since we know from firsthand experience how tough the literary market is." Annual competition for novels. Award: $1,000. Competition receives 300-400 submissions annually. Judges: nationally-published novelists. $20 fee for each submission. Guidelines for SASE, e-mail or on website by March. "See website under 'What We're Looking For' for submission tips." Accepts inquiries by e-mail. Postmark deadline: October 31. Unpublished submissions and not under contract to be published. Novelists should submit first 50 pages only of a novel either completed or in progress. No novels for or by children/young adults. In-progress submissions should be as polished as possible. Multiple submissions accepted, but each must include a separate $20 entry fee. Make checks payable to Dana Awards. Winners announced March-April and notified by phone, mail, or e-mail. List of winners available late spring for SASE, e-mail, or on website. Send SASE with submission to receive competition results letter.

MARGUERITE DE ANGELI PRIZE, Delacorte Press Books for Young Readers, 1540 Broadway, New York NY 10036. (212)782-8633. Fax: (212)782-9452. Website: www.randomhouse.com. "To encourage the writing of fiction for middle grade readers (either contemporary or historical) in the same spirit as the works of Marguerite de Angeli." Open to US and Canadian writers who have not previously published a novel for middle-grade readers. Annual competition for first novels for middle-grade readers (ages 7-10). Award: One BDD hardcover and paperback book contract, with $1,500 cash prize and $3,500 advance against royalties. Competition receives 350 submissions. Judges: Editors of Delacorte Press Books for Young Readers. "The judges reserve the right not to award a prize." Send SASE, fax, or visit website for guidelines; available in August. Submit between April 1 and June 30 *only*. Deadline: Submissions must be postmarked by June 30. Previously unpublished (middle-grade) fiction. Length: 80 pages minimum, 144 maximum. Manuscript: 8½×11, white paper; 12 pt font; double-spaced; consecutively numbered pages with title. Include cover letter (with title; author's name, address and phone number) and plot summary. Do not submit art. Winners announced by October 31 and notified by phone. List of winners available by SASE or on website.

DEAD METAPHOR PRESS CHAPBOOK CONTEST, Dead Metaphor Press, P.O. Box 2076, Boulder CO 80306-2076. **Contact:** Richard Wilmarth. Award to "promote quality writing." Annual competition for prose and poetry. Award: 20 copies. Books assigned ISBN numbers and distributed by Small Press Distribution. Sample chapbook: $6. Competition receives 100-125 submissions, 40 of which are prose. Judge: Richard Wilmarth. Entry fee $12. Make checks payable to Dead Metaphor Press. Guidelines available for SASE in November. Deadline: October 31. Maximum length: 24 pages. Winners announced in January, publication in summer. List of winners available for SASE. Editor advises, "Keep it short and don't tell lies."

DEBUT DAGGER, Crime Writers' Association, % website. Website: www.thecwa.co.uk. Competition to stimulate new crime writing. Annual competition for first 3,000 words of novel and 500 word outline. Award: £250 cash, silver pin and free tickets for prize ceremony. Entry fee: £10. Guidelines available April/May on website. Deadline: Mid-August. Entries should be unpublished. Contest open to anyone who has not had a novel published in any genre. Winners announced October and notified by phone.

DELAWARE DIVISION OF THE ARTS, 820 N. French St., Wilmington DE 19801. (302)577-8284. Fax: (302)577-6561. E-mail: kpleasanton@state.de.us. Website: www.artsdel.org **Contact:** Kristin Pleasanton, coordinator. "To help further careers of emerging and established professional artists." Annual awards for Delaware residents only. Awards: $10,000 for masters, $5,000 for established professionals; $2,000 for emerging professionals. Competition receives 100 submissions. Judges are out-of-state professionals in each division. Entry forms or rules available after January 1 for SASE. Accepts inquiries by fax and e-mail. Deadline: August 1. Winners announced in December and notified by mail.

DAVID DORNSTEIN MEMORIAL CREATIVE WRITING CONTEST FOR YOUNG ADULT WRITERS, Coalition for the Advancement of Jewish Education, 261 W. 35th St., Floor 12A, New York NY 10001. (212)268-4210. Fax: (212)268-4214. E-mail: cajeny@caje.org. Website: www.caje.org. **Contact:** Operations Coordinator. Purpose of award is "to perpetuate the memory of a CAJE Conference Assistant who lost his life in the explosion of PAN AM flight 103. He was a lover of short stories, which he both read and wrote, and this prize perpetuates that aspect of his life." Annual award for short stories. Award: $1,000 split between up to 3 winners. If only 1 winner, writer receives $1,000. If 2 winners, first place $750, second place $250. 3 winners, first $700, second $200, third $100. Judge: "Lay committee with relevant expertise." No entry fee. For guidelines, send e-mail, visit website or call. Accepts inquiries by fax, e-mail, phone. Deadline: end of December 2002. Entries should be unpublished. "Must be on a Jewish theme or topic." Authors aged 18-35 by December 31 of competition year are eligible. Length: 5,000 words maximum. Winners announced by June 30. Winners notified by mail. List of winners available on website.

JACK DYER FICTION PRIZE, *Crab Orchard Review*, English Dept., Southern Illinois University, Carbondale IL 62901-4503. (618)453-6833. E-mail: jtribble@siu.edu. Website: www.siu.edu/~crborchd. **Contact:** Jon Tribble, managing editor. Award to "reward and publish exceptional fiction." Annual competition for short stories. Award: $1,000 and publication. Competition receives approximately 200 submissions. Judges: pre-screened by *Crab Orchard* staff; winner chosen by genre editor. Entry fee $15; year's subscription included. Guidelines available after January for SASE or on website. Deadline: March 15. Submissions accepted February 1 to March 15 *only*. Previously unpublished submissions. Word length: 6,000. "Please note that no stories will be returned." Winners announced by August 15 and notified by mail. List of winners available for SASE or on website.

EATON LITERARY ASSOCIATES' LITERARY AWARDS PROGRAM, Eaton Literary Associates, P.O. Box 49795, Sarasota FL 34230-6795. (941)366-6589. Fax: (941)365-4679. E-mail: eatonlit@aol.com. Website: www.eatonliterary.com. **Contact:** Richard Lawrence, vice president. Biannual award for short stories and novels. Award: $2,500 for best book-length ms, $500 for best short story. Competition receives approx. 2,000 submissions annually. Judges are 2 staff members in conjunction with an independent agency. Guidelines for SASE, fax, e-mail or on website. Accepts inquiries by fax, phone and e-mail. Deadline: March 31 for short stories; August 31 for book-length mss. Winners announced in April and September and notified by mail. List of winners available for SASE, fax, e-mail or on website.

EMERGING LESBIAN WRITERS FUND AWARDS, Astraea Lesbian Action Foundation, 116 E. 16th St., 7th Floor, New York NY 10003. (212)529-8021. Fax: (212)982-3321. E-mail: info@astraea.org. Website: www.astraea.org. **Contact:** C.J. Griffin, program associate. Award to "recognize and encourage new/emerging lesbian writers and poets." Annual competition for fiction and poetry. Award: $10,000 (one time only grantees). Competition receives 400 submissions. Judges: Established writers/poets (2 each category). $5 entry fee. Guidelines for SASE or e-mail (application form required). Deadline: March 8. Previously published submissions. U.S. residents only. Write for guidelines. "Must have at least one published work. No submissions accepted without application form." Winners announced in July and notified by mail and phone. List of winners available by visiting website.

THE EMILY CONTEST, West Houston Chapter Romance Writers of America, 5603 Chantilly Lane, Houston TX 77092. E-mail: ellen_watkins@juno.com. Website: http://www.poboxes.com/whrwa. **Contact:** Ellen Watkins, Emily contest chair. Purpose is "to help people writing romance novels learn to write better books and to help them make contacts in the publishing world." Annual competition for novels. First-place entry in each category receives the Emily brooch; all finalists receive certificates. Competition receives 40-60 submissions per category. First round judges are published authors and experienced critiquers. Final round judges (for finalists) are editors at a major romance publishing house. $15 entry fee for WHRWA members, $25 for non-members. Guidelines available July 2002. For guidelines, send SASE, e-mail or visit website. Accepts inquiries by e-mail. Contest open to all unpublished romance writers. Length: first 35 pages of novel. "We look for dynamic, interesting romantic stories with a hero and heroine readers can relate to and love. Hook us from the beginning and keep the excitement level high." Winners announced February 2003 and notified by mail or phone. List of winners available for SASE or visit website.

VIRGINIA FAULKNER AWARD FOR EXCELLENCE IN WRITING, *Prairie Schooner*, P.O. Box 880334, University of Nebraska, Lincoln NE 68588-0334. (402)472-0911. Fax: (402)472-9771. E-mail: eflanagan2@unl.edu. Website: www.unl.edu/schooner/psmain.htm. **Contact:** Hilda Raz, editor. "An award for writing published in *Prairie Schooner* in the previous year." Annual competition for short stories, essays, novel excerpts and translations. Award: $1,000. Judges: Editorial Board. Guidelines for SASE or on website. Accepts inquiries by fax and e-mail. "We only read mss from September 1 through May 31." Work must have been published in *Prairie Schooner* in the previous year. Winners announced in spring issue and notified by mail in February or March. List of winners will be published in spring *Prairie Schooner*.

FISH SHORT STORY PRIZE, Fish Publishing, Durrus, Bantry, Co. Cork, Ireland. Phone: (00)353-27-61246. E-mail: info@fishpublishing.com. Website: www.fishpublishing.com. **Contact:** Clem Cairns, editor. Award to "discover, encourage, and publish new literary talent." Annual competition for short stories. Award: First prize $1,200 and publication; second prize one week residence at Anam Cara Writers Retreat, Ireland and publication. Competition receives 1,200 submissions per category. Judge: Entries are shortlisted to approximately 100. These are sent to independent judges, who are well-known writers. "Top 18 stories will be published in an anthology." $15 entry fee. Guidelines available in July. Accepts inquiries by e-mail and phone. For guidelines, send SASE, e-mail or visit website. Deadline: November 30. Entries should *not* be previously published. Contest open to everybody. Length: 5,000 words or fewer. "Send your most finished, polished work." Don't be afraid of originality. Winners announced March 17 and notified in February. List of winners available for SASE, e-mail, or visit website.

DOROTHY CANFIELD FISHER AWARD, Vermont Dept. of Libraries, 109 State St., Montpelier VT 05609-0601. (802)828-3261. Fax: (802)828-2199. E-mail: ggreene@dol.state.vt.us. Website: http://mps.k12.vt.us/msms/dcf/dcf.html. **Contact:** Grace Greene, children's services consultant. Estab. 1957. Annual award. "To encourage Vermont schoolchildren to become enthusiastic and discriminating readers and to honor the memory of one of Vermont's most distinguished and beloved literary figures." Award: Illuminated scroll. Publishers send the committee review copies of books to consider. Only books of the current publishing year can be considered for next year's master list. Master list of titles is drawn up in March each year. Children vote each year in the spring and the award is given before the school year ends. Submissions must be "written by living American authors, be suitable for children in grades 4-8, and have literary merit. Can be nonfiction also." Accepts inquiries by e-mail. Deadline: December 1. Winners announced in April and notified by mail and phone. Call, write or e-mail for list of winners.

FLORIDA FIRST COAST WRITERS' FESTIVAL NOVEL, SHORT FICTION & POETRY AWARDS, Writers' Festival & Florida Community College at Jacksonville, FCCJ North Campus, 4501 Capper Rd., Jacksonville FL 32218-4499. (904)766-6559. Fax: (904)766-6654. E-mail: hdenson@fccj.edu. Website: www.fccj.org/wf/. **Contact:** Howard Denson and Brian Hale, festival contest directors. Conference and contest "to create a healthy writing environment, honor writers of merit and find a novel manuscript to recommend to New York publishers for 'serious consideration.'" Annual competition for short stories and novels. Competition receives 65 novel, 150-250 short fiction and 300-600 poetry submissions. Judges: university faculty and freelance and professional writers. Entry fees $30 (novels), $10 (short fiction), $5 (poetry). Guidelines available in the fall for SASE. Accepts inquiries by fax and e-mail. Deadlines: December 1 for novels; January 2 for poetry and short fiction. Unpublished submissions. Word length: none for novel; short fiction, 6,000 words; poetry, 30 lines. Winners announced at the Florida First Coast Writers' Festival held in May.

FLORIDA STATE WRITING COMPETITION, Florida Freelance Writers Association, P.O. Box A, North Stratford NH 03590-0167. (603)922-8338. Fax: (603)922-8339. E-mail: danakcnw@ncia.net. Website: www.writers-editors.com. **Contact:** Dana K. Cassell, executive director. "To offer additional opportunities for writers to earn income and recognition from their writing efforts." Annual competition for short stories and novels. Award: varies from $50-100. Competition receives approximately 100 short stories; 50 novels; total 400-500 entries in all categories. Judges: authors, editors and teachers. Entry fee from $5-20. Guidelines for SASE. Deadline: March 15. Unpublished submissions. Categories include short story and novel chapter. "Guidelines are revised each year and subject to change. New guidelines are available in summer of each year." Accepts inquiries by fax and e-mail. Winners announced May 31 and notified by mail. List of winners available for SASE marked "winners" and on website.

TO RECEIVE REGULAR TIPS AND UPDATES about writing and Writer's Digest publications via e-mail, send an e-mail with "SUBSCRIBE NEWSLETTER" in the body of the message to newsletter-request@writersdigest.com

[N] O H.E. FRANCIS SHORT STORY AWARD, Ruth Hindman Foundation, University of Alabama, English Department, Patricia Sammon, Huntsville AL 35899. E-mail: MaryH71997@aol.com. Website: www.uah.edu/colleges/liberal/english/whatnewcontest.html. **Contact:** Patricia Sammon, chairperson. Annual short story competition to honor H.E. Francis, retired professor of English at the University of Alabama in Huntsville. Award: $1,000. Competition receives approximately 500 submissions. Judges: distinguished writers. $15 fee per entry. Guidelines available for SASE and on website. Accepts inquiries by e-mail. Deadline: December 31. Unpublished submissions. Winners announced March and notified by mail. List of winners available for SASE.

[O] [O] THE JOSETTE FRANK AWARD, Children's Book Committee at Bank St. College, 610 W. 112th St., New York NY 10025-1895. (212)875-4540. Fax: (212)875-4759. E-mail: bookcom@bnkst.edu. Website: www.bankstreet.edu/bookcom. **Contact:** Alice B. Belgray, committee chair. Annual award "to honor a book, or books, of outstanding literary merit in which children or young people deal in a positive and realistic way with difficulties in their world and grow emotionally and morally." Only books sent by publishers for review are considered. Books must have been published within current calendar year. Award: Certificate and cash prize. Competition receives approximately 2,000 submissions. Accepts inquiries by e-mail and fax. Deadline: November 15. Winners announced in March and notified through their publishers and by mail.

[globe] [O] [O] MILES FRANKLIN LITERARY AWARD, Permanent, 35 Clarence St., Sydney NSW 2000 Australia. Phone: 8295 8191. Fax: 8295 8093. E-mail: linda.ingaldo@permanentgroup.com.au. Website: www.permanentgroup.com.au. **Contact:** Linda Ingaldo, awards administrator. Award "for the advancement, improvement and betterment of Australian literature." Annual award for novels. Award: AUS $28,000 (in 2001), to the author "of the novel which is of the highest literary merit for the year and which presents Australian life in any of its phases." Competition receives 60 submissions. Judges: David Marr, Dagmar Schmidmaier, Professor Elizabeth Webby, Hilary McPhee and Father Ed Campion (in 2002). $50 AU entry fee. Guidelines available in November; send SASE, fax or e-mail. Accepts inquiries by fax, phone and e-mail. Deadline: Second Friday in December. Contest open to previously published submissions. "The novel must have been published in the year prior to competition entry and must present Australian life in any of its phases." Winners announced June and notified by phone. List of winners for SASE.

[N] [blip] FREEFALL MAGAZINE FICTION & POETRY CONTEST, FreeFall magazine, 922 Ninth Ave. SE, Calgary, Alberta T2G 0S4 Canada. Phone/fax: (403)264-4730. E-mail: awcs@telusplanet.net. Website: www.alexandrawriters.org. **Contact:** Sherring Amsden, managing editor. Award established "to encourage the submission of quality work in fiction and poetry and give it recognition." Annual competition for short stories and poetry. Prize: 1st place, $200; 2nd place, $100. Judge: *FreeFall*'s editor and assistant editors. $10 entry fee. 2003 Guidelines available in March. For guidelines, send SASE, e-mail or visit website. Deadline: October 1, 2002. Entries should be unpublished. "Open to all writers over 18 years from any region, genre, ethnicity, etc." Length: 3,000 words maximum. "Carefully read and follow contest rules and guidelines for manuscript submission. Include signed contest entry form with payment." Winners announced December 2003. Winners notified by mail and e-mail in December. List of winners available for SASE, by e-mail or visit website.

JEROME FUNDED RETREAT, New York Mills Arts Retreat, 24 N. Main Ave. P.O. Box 246, New York Mills MN 56567. (218)385-3339. Fax: (218)385-3366. E-mail: nymills@kulcher.org. Website: http://www.kulcher.org. **Contact:** Heather Price, coordinator. "The purpose is to reward writers and other artists of merit with a financial stipend and a one-month getaway." Biannual competition for short stories, novels or story collections. Award: "one-month of retreat at our small-town facility including a $1,500 stipend." Competition receives 35-50 submissions per category. Judge: "All entries are juried together at the same time by a panel of five professionals in diverse art forms." No entry fee. Guidelines available year round. For guidelines, send SASE, fax, e-mail or visit website. Accepts inquiries by fax, e-mail, phone. Deadlines: April 1 and October 1 annually. Contest open to US citizens. Length: 12 pages or fewer. "Our stipend retreat awards require a community outreach proposal. It is very important that entries have strong educational value." Winners announced 2 months following each deadline and notified by phone.

THE FUNNY PAPER COMPETITION, F/J Writers Service, P.O. Box 22557, Kansas City MO 64113-0557. E-mail: felix22557@aol.com. Website: http://www.angelfire.com/biz/funnypaper. **Contact:** F.H. Fellhauer, editor. Award to "provide readership, help, and the opportunity to write for money to budding authors of all ages." Competition for short stories, fillers, jokes, poems, cartoons held 4 times/year. Award: $5-100. Competition receives 50-100 submissions per category. Judge: editors and selected assistants. No entry fee. Guidelines in every issue. For guidelines, send SASE or visit website. Accepts inquiries by e-mail. No deadline (unused entries are held for next contest). Entries should be unpublished, or published only if we are advised where and when. Contest open to all writers. Length: 1,000 words maximum. Winners announced in each issue and notified by mail on publication.

THE JOHN GARDNER FICTION CONTEST, *Harpur Palate*, English Dept., Binghamton University, Box 6000, Binghamton NY 13902-6000. E-mail: tfinley@binghamton.edu (for contest queries only). Website: http://harpurpalate.binghamton.edu/contests.shtml. **Contact:** Fiction Editor, *Harpur Palate*. "John Gardner—novelist, poet, translator, dramatist, and teacher—helped found the creative writing program at Binghamton University. In honor of his dedication to the development of writers, *Harpur Palate* hosts the Annual John Gardner Memorial Prize for Fiction." Annual award. Prize: $500 and publication in *Harpur Palate*. Entry fee: $10/story; make checks payable to *Harpur Palate*. "You may send as many stories as you wish, but please send each story in a separate envelope along with the entry fee." Entries should be previously unpublished. "Stories may be in any genre but should not exceed 8,000 words. Don't sacrifice character for plot or plot for character. Stories that have the best chance of winning take risks with genre and style. Please include your name and contact information in the cover letter *only*." All entrants receive a copy of the issue with the winning story. Make sure your entry fee is paid by a check (drawn on U.S. bank) or money order.

THE JANE GESKE AWARD, *Prairie Schooner*, 201 Andrews Hall, P.O. Box 880034, Lincoln NE 68588-0334. (402)472-0911. Fax: (402)472-9771. E-mail: eflangan2@unl.edu. Website: www.unl.edu/schooner/psmain.htm. **Contact:** Hilda Raz, editor-in-chief. Annual award "to honor work published the previous year in *Prairie Schooner* including fiction, essays and poetry." Award: $200. Competition is judged by the editorial staff of *Prairie Schooner*. No entry fee. For guidelines send SASE or visit website. "Only work published in *Prairie Schooner* in the previous year is considered." Work is nominated by the editorial staff. Winners announced in the spring issue and notified in February or March by mail.

N◎ GIFT OF FREEDOM AWARD, A Room Of Her Own Foundation, P.O. Box 778, Placitas NM 87043-0778. E-mail: info@aroomofherownfoundation.org. Website: www.aroomofherownfoundation.org. **Contact:** Darlene Chandler Bassett, president and founder. Awards purpose is "to provide very practical help, both materially and in professional guidance and moral support, to women who need assistance in making their creative contribution to the world." Annual award for short stories, novels, short story collections. Prize: Up to $50,000, payable over a two-year period in installments based upon the needs of the recipient. Judging: "Awarding panel will be composed of members of AROHO's Board of Directors, Advisory Council and volunteers from a wide variety of backgrounds. Each award is based upon merits of the application. $15 processing fee. For guidelines, send e-mail or visit website. 2002 deadline May 30, 2002. "Our next deadline will be in Fall of 2002." Entries may be either unpublished or previously published. Contest open to "U.S. female writers." Writers should submit 2 essays, each 5 double-spaced pages. "The successful applicant will have a well articulated project concept and a clear plan for how it may be accomplished." Winners announced in Fall. Winners notified by mail, phone. List of grant winners posted on website.

◐ GLIMMER TRAIN'S FALL SHORT-STORY AWARD FOR NEW WRITERS, Glimmer Train Press, Inc., 710 SW Madison St., Suite 504, Portland OR 97205-2900. (503)221-0836. Fax: (503)221-0837. Website: www.glimmertrain.com (includes writers' guidelines and a Q&A section for writers). **Contact:** Linda Swanson-Davies, fiction editor. Contest offered for any writer whose fiction hasn't appeared in a nationally-distributed publication with a circulation over 5,000. "We want to read your original, unpublished short (1,200-8,000 words) story." $12 reading fee. Make your submissions online (www.glimmertrain.com) by September 30. Winners will be notified and results will be posted by January 2. Winner receives $1,200, publication in *Glimmer Train Stories* and 20 copies of that issue. First/second runners-up receive $500/$300, respectively, and consideration for publication."

◐ GLIMMER TRAIN'S FICTION OPEN, Glimmer Train Press, Inc., 710 SW Madison St., Suite 504, Portland OR 97205-2900. (503)221-0836. Fax: (503)221-0837. Website: www.glimmertrain.com (includes writers' guidelines and a Q&A section for writers). **Contact:** Linda Swanson-Davies, contest director. Contest for short story, open to all writers. Award: First place $2,000, publication in *Glimmer Train Stories* (circ. 13,000) and 20 copies of that issue. First/second runners-up receive $1,000/$600 respectively and consideration for publication. "We want to read your original, unpublished short story. No theme or word count limitations. $15 reading fee. Make your submissions online (www.glimmertrain.com) by June 30. Winners will be notified and results will be posted by October 15."

◐ GLIMMER TRAIN'S SPRING SHORT-STORY AWARD FOR NEW WRITERS, Glimmer Train Press, Inc., 710 SW Madison St., Suite 504, Portland OR 97205-2900. (503)221-0836. Fax: (503)221-0837. Website: www.glimmertrain.com (includes writers' guidelines and a Q&A section for writers). **Contact:** Linda Swanson-Davies, contest director. Contest offered for any writer whose fiction hasn't appeared in a nationally-distributed publication with a circulation over 5,000. "We want to read your original, unpublished short (1,200-8,000 words) story. $12 reading fee. Make your submissions online (www.glimmertrain.com) by March 31. Winners will be notified and results will be posted by July 1. Winner receives $1,200, publication in *Glimmer Train Stories* and 20 copies of that issue. First/second runners-up receive $500/$300, respectively, and consideration for publication."

◉ GOLD MEDALLION BOOK AWARDS, Evangelical Christian Publishers Association, 1969 East Broadway Rd. #2, Tempe AZ 85282. (480)966-3998. Fax: (480)966-1944. E-mail: jmeegan@ecpa.org. Website: www.ecpa.org. **Contact:** Doug Ross, president. Award to "recognize quality/encourage excellence." Annual competition for 20 categories including fiction. Award: Gold Medallion plaque. Competition receives approximately 50 submissions in the fiction category. Judges: "Two rounds of judges—first round primarily Christian bookstore owners, managers and book buyers; second round primarily editors, book reviewers, industry leaders and selected Christian bookstore leaders. First round will determine five finalists in each of the 20 categories. Second round judges the finalists in each category." Entry fee of $300 for non-members. Guidelines available annually in October. Accepts inquiries by fax and e-mail. Deadline: December 1. Previously published submissions appearing during the calendar year preceding the year in which the award are to be presented. Entries must be submitted by the publisher. Winners announced annually in July at the Annual Gold Medallion Book Awards Banquet. List of winners available by contacting the ECPA offices.

N GREAT BEGINNINGS, Utah Romance Writers of America, 6678 S. Cristobal St., Salt Lake City UT 84121. (801)944-8277. E-mail: atreader@aol.com. Website: www.utahrwa.com. **Contact:** Alice Trego, chapter president. Annual competition for novels. Award: First place receives a plaque and 2nd through 4th place receive certificates. Competition receives 100 submissions per category. Judges: experienced, published and unpublished authors and editors in the final round. $10 entry fee. Guidelines available January 1. For guidelines, send SASE, e-mail or visit website. Accepts inquiries by e-mail. Deadline: March 17, 2003. Entries should be unpublished. Contest is open to both unpublished authors, and to published authors sumbitting unpublished, uncontracted works. Length: 3 ms pages. Winners are announced on May 12, 2003 and notified by mail, phone, e-mail on May 12, 2003. List of winners available for SASE, e-mail or visit website.

◯ **THE GREAT BLUE BEACON SHORT-SHORT STORY CONTEST**, *The Great Blue Beacon: The Newsletter for Writers of All Genres and Skill Levels*, 1425 Patriot Dr., Melbourne FL 32940-6881. (321)253-5869. E-mail: ajircc@juno.com. **Contact:** A.J. Byers, editor/publisher. Award to "recognize outstanding short-short story." Annual award for short-short stories. Award: $50 (1st prize); $25 (2nd prize); $10 (3rd prize), plus publication of winning entry in *The Great Blue Beacon*. Judges: outside panel of judges. Entry fee $5 ($4 for subscribers). Guidelines available periodically when announced. For guidelines send SASE or e-mail. Accepts inquiries by e-mail. Deadline: TBA. Entries should be previously unpublished. Open to all writers. Length: 1,000 words or fewer. Winners announced two months after contest deadline. Winners notified by SASE or e-mail. List of winners available for SASE or by e-mail.

◐ ◎ **GREAT LAKES BOOK AWARDS**, Great Lakes Booksellers Awards, 208 Franklin St., Grand Haven MI 49417. (616)847-2460. Fax: (616)842-0051. E-mail: glba@books~glba.org. Website: www.books~glba.org. Award to "recognize and reward excellence in the writing and publishing of books that capture the spirit and enhance awareness of the region." Annual competition for fiction, children's and nonfiction. Award: $500 plus bookstore promotion. Competition receives approximately 90 submissions. Five judges each category. No entry fee. Guidelines available. Deadline: May 31, 2003. Writer must be nominated by members of the GLBA. Winners announced August 2003.

◐ **GREAT PLAINS STORYTELLING & POETRY READING CONTEST**, P.O. Box 492, Anita IA 50020-0492. Phone/fax: (712)762-4363. E-mail: bobeverhart@yahoo.com. Website: www.oldtimemusic.bigstep.com. **Contact:** Robert Everhart, director. Estab. 1976. Annual award "to provide an outlet for writers to present not only their works but also to provide a large audience for their presentation *live* by the writer. Attendance at the event, which takes place annually in Avoca, Iowa, is *required*." Awards: $50 (1st Prize); $25 (2nd Prize); $15 (3rd Prize); $10 (4th Prize); $5 (5th Prize). $5 entry fee. Entry forms available at contest only. Guidelines available in August by SASE or e-mail. 2002 deadline: August 26. Contest takes place over Labor Day Weekend. Previously published or unpublished submissions.

THE JUDY & A.C. GREENE LITERARY FESTIVAL CONTEST, The Living Room Theatre of Salado, P.O. Box 1023, Salado TX 76571-1023. (254)947-3104. E-mail: lrts@direcway.com. Website: http://vrm.com/~lrts. **Contact:** Dr. Raymond Carver, director/producer. "The purpose of the festival is development of unpublished works by Texas writers. The Festival seeks unpublished literary works which may be adapted by staff of the Living Room Theatre for dramatic performance with two to five actors using lecture stands but no other theatrical elements." Annual competition for short stories, novels, story collections. Award: 1st prize $1,500; 3 finalists $250 each. Competition receives about 50 submissions. Judge: contest/festival staff. $20 entry fee. Guidelines available in October on website. For guidelines, send SASE, e-mail or visit website. Accepts inquiries by e-mail or phone. Deadline: March 1. Entries must be unpublished. Contest open to Texas residents or former residents. Length: 30-60 minutes reading aloud time. "No poems or discursive writing." Finalists announced in May and notified by mail or e-mail. List of winners available on website. "Material will be read aloud by 2-4 performers at festival. Emphasize dialog, plot, character. Short stories and plays will be adapted to readers theatre format."

◯ **THE GREENSBORO REVIEW LITERARY AWARDS**, English Dept., 134 McIver Bldg., UNC-Greensboro, P.O. Box 26170, Greensboro NC 27402-6170. (336)334-5459. E-mail: tlkenned@uncg.edu. Website: www.uncg.edu/eng/mfa. **Contact:** Terry Kennedy, managing editor. Annual award. Award: $500. Competition receives 1,000 submissions. Judged by editors of *Greensboro Review*. Guidelines for SASE or on website. Accepts inquiries by e-mail. Deadline: September 15. Unpublished submissions. "All manuscripts meeting literary award guidelines will be considered for cash award as well as for publication in *The Greensboro Review*." Winners notified by mail, phone or e-mail. List of winners published in the Spring issue of *The Greensboro Review*.

GULF COAST POETRY AND SHORT FICTION AWARDS, Gulf Coast: a Journal of Literature and Fine Art, University of Houston, Dept. of English, Houston TX 77204-3012. (713)743-3223. Fax: (713)743-3215. E-mail: gulfcoast@gulfcoast.uh.edu. Website: www.gulfcoast.uh.edu. **Contact:** Pablo Peschiera, managing editor. "To showcase excellent contemporary writing that pays attention to craft and language." Annual competition for short stories. Award: $300-500. Competition receives 100 submissions. $15 fee per entry. Guidelines available in Fall 2002 for SASE. Accepts inquiries by phone. Deadline: February 15. Entries should be unpublished. Contest open to all. Length: 6,000. "Provide a short cover letter and enter what you consider to be your best work." Winners notified by mail or phone in May. List of winners available for SASE.

▩ ◎ **HAMMETT PRIZE**, International Association of Crime Writers/North American Branch, P.O. Box 8674, New York NY 10116-8674. (212)243-8966. Fax: (815)361-1477. E-mail: mfrisque@igc.org. **Contact:** Mary A. Frisque, executive director, North American Branch. Award established "to honor a work of literary excellence in the field of crime writing by a U.S. or Canadian author." Annual award for novels, story collections by one author and also nonfiction. Award: trophy. Competition receives about 200 submissions per category. "Eligible books are read by a committee of members of the organization. The committee chooses five nominated books, which are sent to three outside judges for a final decision. Judges are outside the crime writing field." No entry fee. For guidelines, send SASE or e-mail. Accepts inquiries by e-mail. Deadline: December 1, 2002. Entries should be previously published. To be eligible "the book must have been published in the U.S. or Canada during the calendar year. The author must be a U.S. or Canadian citizen or permanent resident." "Nominations announced in January; 2002 winner will be announced in June 2003." Winners notified by mail, phone and at awards ceremony. List of winners available for SASE.

N HEART OF THE WEST WRITERS CONTEST, Utah Romance Writers of America, 6678 S. Cristobal St., Salt Lake City UT 84121. (801)944-8277. E-mail: atreader@aol.com. Website: www.utahrwa.com. **Contact:** Teresa Versey, chapter president. Annual competition for novels. Award: First place winners will recieve a golden locket, second through fourth place winners receive certificates. Competition receives 80 submissions per category. Judge: published and experienced, unpublished authors in the first round; editors in the second round. $25 entry fee. Guidelines available April 1. For guidelines, send SASE, e-mail or visit website. Accepts inquiries by e-mail. Deadline: July 15, 2003. Entries should be unpublished. Contest open to unpublished authors, and to published authors submitting unpublished, uncontracted work. Length: 20 ms pages. Winners are announced in November 2003 and notified by mail, phone and e-mail. List of winners available for SASE, e-mail or visit website.

DRUE HEINZ LITERATURE PRIZE, University of Pittsburgh Press, 3400 Forbes Ave., 5th Floor, Eureka Building, Pittsburgh PA 15260. (412)383-2456. Fax: (412)383-2466. E-mail: press@pitt.edu. Website: www.pitt.edu/~press. Annual award "to support the writer of short fiction at a time when the economics of commercial publishing make it more and more difficult for the serious literary artist working in the short story and novella to find publication." Award: $15,000 and publication by the University of Pittsburgh Press. "It is imperative that entrants request complete rules of the competition by sending an SASE before submitting a manuscript." Submissions will be received only during the months of May and June. Postmark deadline: June 30. Manuscripts must be unpublished in book form. The award is open to writers who have published a book-length collection of fiction or a minimum of three short stories or novellas in commercial magazines or literary journals of national distribution. Winners announced in February and notified by phone or mail. List of winners available for SASE sent with manuscript.

ERNEST HEMINGWAY FOUNDATION/PEN AWARD FOR FIRST FICTION, PEN New England, P.O. Box 400725, North Cambridge MA 02140. (617)499-9550. Fax: (617)353-7134. E-mail: awards@pen-ne.org. Website: www.pen-ne.org. **Contact:** Mary Louise Sullivan, awards coordinator. Annual award "to give beginning writers recognition and encouragement and to stimulate interest in first books of fiction among publishers and readers." Receives 130 submissions. Award: $7,500. Novels or short story collections must have been published during calendar year under consideration. Entry form or rules for SASE, e-mail or on website after September. Deadline: December 15. "The Ernest Hemingway Foundation/PEN Award For First Fiction is given to an American author of the best first-published book-length work of fiction published by an established publishing house in the US each calendar year." Winners will be announced in March. List of winners available by e-mail or on website.

LORIAN HEMINGWAY SHORT STORY COMPETITION, P.O. Box 993, Key West FL 33041-0993. (305)294-0320. Fax: (305)292-3653. E-mail: calico2419@aol.com. Website: www.shortstorycompetition.com. **Contact:** Carol Shaughnessy, co-director. Award to "encourage literary excellence and the efforts of writers who have not yet had major-market success." Annual competition for short stories. Awards: $1,000 (1st Prize); $500 (2nd Prize); $500 (3rd Prize); honorable mentions. Competition receives approximately 850 submissions. Judges: A panel of writers, editors and literary scholars selected by author Lorian Hemingway. Entry fee $10 for each story postmarked by May 1, 2003; $15 for each story postmarked between May 1 and May 15, 2003. Guidelines available January 15 by e-mail, phone, on website or for SASE. Accepts inquiries by SASE, fax, e-mail or visit website. Deadline: May 1-15, 2003. Unpublished submissions. "Open to all writers whose fiction has not appeared in a nationally distributed publication with a circulation of 5,000 or more." Word length: 3,000 words maximum. "We look for excellence, pure and simple—no genre restrictions, no theme restrictions—we seek a writer's voice that cannot be ignored." Winners announced at the end of July during Hemingway Days Festival and notified by phone prior to announcement. List of winners available by e-mail or visit website. "All entrants will receive a letter from Lorian Hemingway and a list of winners by October 1."

HIGHLIGHTS FOR CHILDREN, 803 Church St., Honesdale PA 18431. (570)253-1080. Fax: (570)251-7847. E-mail: eds@highlights-corp.com. Website: www.highlights.com. **Contact:** Marileta Robinson, senior editor. Award "to honor quality stories (previously unpublished) for young readers and to encourage children's writers." Award: Three $1,000 awards plus publication in *Highlights*. Competition receives 1,500 submissions. Judges: *Highlights* editors. No entry fee. Guidelines available July for SASE or on website. Accepts inquiries by phone. Deadline: February 28, 2003. Entries should be unpublished. Length: 500 words maximum for beginning readers (to age 8) and 900 words for more advanced readers (ages 9 to 12). No minimum word length. No entry form necessary. Submit *only* between January 1 and February 28 to "Fiction Contest" at address above. "No violence, crime or derogatory humor. Obtain a copy of the guidelines, since the theme changes each year." Nonwinning entries returned in June if SASE is included with ms. Winners announced in June and notified by phone or letter. List of winners will be sent with returned mss. "All other submissions will be considered for purchase by *Highlights*."

THE ALFRED HODDER FELLOWSHIP, The Council of the Humanities, Princeton University, Joseph Henry House, Princeton NJ 08544-5264. E-mail: humcounc@princeton.edu. Website: www.princeton.edu/~humcounc. **Contact:** Cass Garner, department manager. "This fellowship is awarded for the pursuit of independent work in the humanities. The recipient is usually a writer or scholar in the early stages of his or her career, a person 'with more than ordinary learning' and with 'much more than ordinary intellectual and literary gifts.' " Traditionally, the Hodder Fellow has been a humanist outside of academia. Candidates for the Ph.D. are not eligible. Award: $51,000. The Hodder Fellow spends an academic year in residence at Princeton working independently. Competition receives 300 submissions. Judges: Princeton Committee on Humanistic Studies. Guidelines available for SASE. Deadline: November 1. Winners are announced and notified in March. Applicants must submit a résumé, a sample of previous work (10 page maximum, not returnable), and a project proposal of 2 to 3 pages. Letters of recommendation are not required. List of winners available on website.

N THEODORE CHRISTIAN HOEPFNER AWARD, *Southern Humanities Review*, 9088 Haley Center, Auburn University AL 36849. Co-editors: Dan R. Latimer or Virginia M. Kouidis. Annual award "to award the authors of the best essay, the best short story and the best poem published in *Southern Humanities Review* each year." Award: $100 for the best short story. Judges: Editorial staff. Only published work in the current volume (4 issues) will be judged.

PEARL HOGREFE FELLOWSHIP, The Pearl Hogrefe Fund and Department of English, 203 Ross Hall, Iowa State University, Ames IA 50011. (515)294-2477. Fax: (515)294-6814. E-mail: englgrad@iastate.edu. Website: www.engl.iast ate.edu. **Contact:** Kathleen Hickok, graduate studies coordinator. "To provide new Iowa State University M.A. students with writing time." Annual competition for manuscript sample of 25 pages, any genre. Award: $1,000/month for 9 months and full payment of tuition and fees. Competition receives 60-75 submissions. Judges: the creative writing staff at Iowa State University. Guidelines available by e-mail. Accepts inquiries by fax, e-mail, phone. Deadline: February 1. Either published or unpublished submissions. "No restrictions, except the applicant cannot hold or expect to receive a master's degree in English or creative writing during the current year." Winners announced and notified by phone on April 1.

THE WINIFRED HOLTBY MEMORIAL PRIZE, The Royal Society of Literature, Somerset House, Strand, London WC2R 1LA United Kingdom. E-mail: info@rslit.org. Website: http://www.rslit.org. **Contact:** Julia Abel Smith. Award for "regional fiction, i.e., fiction with a strong sense of a particular place." Annual competition for novels. Award: £1,000. Competition receives 60 submissions per category. Judge: 3 judges, who are as yet unchosen. No entry fee. Guidelines available by e-mail, fax, phone or on website from September 2002 onwards. Accepts inquiries by fax, e-mail, phone. Deadline: December 15, 2002. Entries should be previously published. Contest open to citizens of the Commonwealth who may enter and only publishers can submit books. Publishers must nominate work. Winners are announced June 2003 and notified by phone in May. List of winners available by fax or e-mail.

L. RON HUBBARD'S WRITERS OF THE FUTURE CONTEST, P.O. Box 1630, Los Angeles CA 90078. (323)466-3310. Fax: (323)466-6474. E-mail: contests@authorservicesinc.com. Website: www.writersofthefuture .com. **Contact:** Contest Administrator. Estab. 1984. Quarterly. Foremost competition for new and amateur writers of unpublished science fiction or fantasy short stories or novelettes. Awards $1,000, $750, $500 in quarterly prizes, $4,000 annual Grand Prize. "Contest has four quarters. There shall be three cash prizes in each quarter. In addition, at the end of the year the four first-place, quarterly winners will have their entries rejudged, and a Grand Prize winner shall be determined." Judged by panel of professional authors. No entry fee. Entrants retain all rights. Guidelines available for #10 SASE, by e-mail and on website. Quarterly deadlines: September 30, December 31, March 31, June 30. Year closes September 30. Entries should be unpublished. Contest open to "those who have not professionally published a novel or short novel, or more than one novelette, or more than three short stories, in any medium. Professional publication is deemed to be payment, and at least 5,000 copies or 5,000 hits." Limit 1 entry per quarter. Length: up to 17,000 words. Manuscripts: white paper, blank ink; double-spaced; typed; each page appropriately numbered with title. Include cover page with author's name, address, phone number as well as estimated word count and the title of the work. Winners contacted quarterly.

INDIANA REVIEW FICTION PRIZE, *Indiana Review*, Ballantine Hall 465, 1020 E. Kirkwood Ave., Bloomington IN 47405-7103. (812)855-3439. Fax: (812)855-4253. E-mail: inreview@indiana.edu. Website: www.indiana.edu/ ~inreview/ir.html. **Contact:** Danit Brown, fiction editor. Annual. Contest for fiction in any style and on any subject. Award: $1,000, publication in the *Indiana Review* and contributor's copies (1st place). Each entrant will receive the prize issue. Competition receives over 500 submissions. Judges: *Indiana Review* staff and outside judges. $12 entry fee. Guidelines available in December for SASE. Accepts inquiries by fax, e-mail or phone. Deadline: October 28, 2002. All entries considered for publication. Cover letter must include name, address, phone number, and title of story. Entrant's name should appear only in the cover letter, as all entries will be considered anonymously. Manuscripts will not be returned. No previously published works, or works forthcoming elsewhere, are eligible. Simultaneous submissions

---

SENDING TO A COUNTRY other than your own? Be sure to send International Reply Coupons (IRC) instead of stamps for replies or return of your manuscript.

acceptable, but in event of entrant withdraw, contest fee will not be refunded. Length: 40 pages maximum, double spaced. Winners announced by December 2002 and notified by mail. List of winners available for SASE. "We look for a command of language and structure, as well as a facility with compelling and unusual subject matter. It's a good idea to obtain copies of issues featuring past winners to get a more concrete idea of what we are looking for."

INDIVIDUAL ARTIST FELLOWSHIP, Louisiana Division of the Arts, P.O. Box 44247, Baton Rouge LA 70804-4247. (225)342-8180. Fax: (225)342-8173. E-mail: arts@crt.state.la.us. Website: www.crt.state.la.us/arts.org. **Contact:** Dabne Liebke, literature program director. Annual grant for short stories, novels, poetry and/or nonfiction. Award: $5,000. Individual Artist Fellowship Program receives 20-25 applications. "Peer panel reviews applications through a blind review of samples of work only. Only finalists' application packets are studied in full." Guidelines and application available on website, by fax or phone. Deadline: March 1, 2003. Entries may be unpublished or previously published. Contest open to Louisiana residents residing in-state for part 2 years. "Students enrolled in arts-related degree or certificate granting program at grant deadline are ineligible to apply." Length: 30 pages of text (duplex 15 sheets of paper double-sided). "Save flowery language for sample. Always submit recent work. Address evaluation criteria." Winners notified in June by letter or phone. List of winners available for SASE, fax, e-mail or visit website.

INDIVIDUAL ARTIST FELLOWSHIP, Nebraska Arts Council, 3838 Davenport, Omaha NE 68131-2329. (402)421-3627. Fax: (402)595-2334. E-mail: swise@nebraskaartscouncil.org. Website: www.nebraskaartscouncil.org. **Contact:** Suzanne Wise, program manager. Award to "recognize outstanding achievement by Nebraska writers." Competition every third year for short stories and novels. Award: $5,000 Distinguished Achievement; $1,000-2,000 Merit Awards. Competition receives 70-80 submissions per category. Judges: panel of 3. 2002 deadline for literature: November 15. Published or previously unpublished submissions. Nebraska residents only. Length: 50 pages.

INDIVIDUAL ARTIST FELLOWSHIP/MINI FELLOWSHIP, Kansas City Commission, 700 SW Jackson St., Suite 1004, Topeka KS 66603-3761. (785)296-3335. Fax: (785)296-4989. E-mail: kac@arts.state.ks.us. Website: www.arts.state.ks.us. **Contact:** Karen Brady, program consultant II. "Awards are based on artistic merit and recognize sustained achievement and excellence." Fellowships awarded every other year in fiction, poetry and playwriting. Mini-fellowships awarded annually. Award: $5,000 (fellowship); $500 (mini-fellowship). Competition receives 40-50 fellowship submissions; 10-15 mini-fellowship submissions (fiction, poetry, playwriting). Judges: panel of writers, editors, educators and publishers from Kansas. For guidelines fax, e-mail, visit website or call. Accepts inquiries by fax, e-mail or phone. Deadline: October 18, 2002 for playwriting fellowship and all categories of mini-fellowship. Fiction and poetry fellowship have 2003 deadline. Entries may be unpublished or previously published year; do not submit "work completed prior to 1999." Contest open to Kansas residents. Undergraduate or graduate degree-seeking students are ineligible. Length: 30 pages/mss for fiction and playwriting; 20 pages/mss for poetry. "Follow guidelines for application explicitly." Winners announced in February each year and notified by mail or phone. List of winners available by fax or e-mail.

INDIVIDUAL ARTIST MINI-GRANT, Louisiana Division of the Arts, P.O. Box 44247, Baton Rouge LA 70804-4247. (225)342-8180. Fax: (225)342-8173. E-mail: arts@crt.state.la.us. Website: www.crt.state.la.us/arts. **Contact:** Dabne Liebke, literature program director. "Artist mini-grants are designed to encourage artistic development and to support the realization of specific artistic ideas." Biannual grant competition. Award: $500. "The Artist Mini-Grant Program awards approximately 15 mini-grants each year." Guidelines and appliaction available by fax, phone and on website. 2002 deadlines: August 1 and December 1. Entries should be unpublished or previously published. Writers may apply twice/year each year but are only eligible for one grant/year. Contest open to Louisiana residents who have lived in-state for the past 2 years. "Students enrolled in arts-related degree or certificate program at grant deadline are ineligible to apply." Length: 30 pages of text (15 sheets of paper, double-spaced). Sample work should always be recent material. Winners notified by phone.

INTERNATIONAL READING ASSOCIATION CHILDREN'S BOOK AWARDS, Sponsored by IRA, P.O. Box 8139, 800 Barksdale Rd., Newark DE 19714-8139. (302)731-1600. Annual awards given for a first or second book. Four IRA Children's Book Awards at US$500 each will be offered for an author's first or second published book. Awards will be given for fiction and nonfiction in 3 age categories: primary (preschool-age 8), intermediate (age 9-13), young adults (age 14-17). This award is intended for newly published authors who show unusual promise in the children's book field. Books from any country and in any language copyrighted during the 2002 calendar year will be considered. Entries in a language other than English must include a one-page abstract in English and a translation into English of one chapter or similar selection that in the submitter's estimation is representative of the book. Entries must be received by November 1, 2002. For guidelines with specific information write to Executive Office, International Reading Association, PO Box 8139, Newark, DE 19714-8139, USA. E-mail: exec@reading.org.

IOWA SCHOOL OF LETTERS AWARD FOR SHORT FICTION, THE JOHN SIMMONS SHORT FICTION AWARD, Iowa Writers' Workshop, 102 Dey House, 507 N. Clinton St., Iowa City IA 52242-1000. Annual awards for short story collections. To encourage writers of short fiction. Award: publication of winning collections by University of Iowa Press the following fall. Entries must be at least 150 pages, typewritten, and submitted between August 1 and September 30. Stamped, self-addressed return packaging must accompany manuscript. Rules for SASE. Iowa Writer's Workshop does initial screening of entries; finalists (about 6) sent to outside judge for final selection. "A different well-known writer is chosen each year as judge. Any writer who has not previously published a volume of prose fiction is eligible to enter the competition for these prizes. Revised manuscripts which have been previously entered may be resubmitted."

THE IOWA SHORT FICTION AWARD, University of Iowa Press, 100 Kuhl House, Iowa City IA 52242-1000. (319)335-2000. Fax: (319)335-2055. Website: http://www.uiowa.edu/~uipress. **Contact:** Holly Carver, director. Award to "give exposure to promising writers who have not yet published a book of prose." Annual competition for story collections. Award: Publication only under Press's standard contract. Competition receives 300-400 mss. Judge: "Senior Iowa Writers' Workshop members screen manuscripts; published fiction author of note makes final two selections." No entry fee. For guidelines, send SASE or visit website. Accepts inquiries by fax, phone. Deadline: Entries accepted during August and September. "Individual stories can have been previously published (as in journals) but never in *book* form." Stories in English. Length: "at least 150 word-processed, double-spaced pages; 8-10 stories on average for manuscript." Winners announced January following competition and notified by phone in January.

N IRONWEED PRESS FICTION PRIZE, Ironweed Press, Inc., P.O. Box 754208, Parkside Station, Forest Hills NY 11375. (718)544-1120. Fax: (718)268-2394. E-mail: IWPress@aol.com. **Contact:** Jin Soo Kang, special projects editor. Prize established "to promote and award excellence in fiction among emerging writers." Annual award for novels and story collections. Award: $2,500 prize, publication as trade paperback. Judge: A panel of three judges (editors, agents, writers). $25 entry fee. Guidelines available November 28, 2002. Send SASE. Deadline: June 27, 2003. "The manuscript may contain published material, provided that the work as a whole has not been previously published." Contest open to all writers. Length: minimum of 20,000 words. Winner announced November 3, 2003. Winner notified by mail or phone prior to announcement. List of winners available for SASE.

○ ◎ JOSEPH HENRY JACKSON AWARD, Intersection for the Arts/The San Francisco Foundation, 446 Valencia St., San Francisco CA 94103-3415. (415)626-2787. Fax: (415)626-1636. E-mail: info@theintersection.org. Website: www.theintersection.org. **Contact:** Kevin B. Chen, program director. Award "to encourage young, unpublished writers." Annual award for short stories, novels and story collections. Award: $2,000 and certificate. Competition receives 150-200 submissions. Entry form and rules available in mid-October for SASE. Deadline: January 31. Unpublished submissions only. Applicant must be resident of northern California or Nevada for 3 consecutive years immediately prior to the deadline date. Age of applicant must be 20 through 35. Work cannot exceed 100 double-spaced, typed pages. "Submit a serious, ambitious portion of a book-length manuscript." Winners announced June 15 and notified by mail. "Winners will be announced in letter mailed to all applicants."

N ◎ JAPAN FOUNDATION ARTIST FELLOWSHIP PROGRAM, 152 W. 57th St., 39th Floor, New York NY 10019. (212)489-0299. Fax: (212)489-0409. E-mail: info@jfny.org. Website: www.jfny.org/jfny. **Contact:** Yuika Goto, program assistant: . "This program provides artists and specialists in the arts with the opportunity to pursue creative projects in Japan and to meet and consult with their Japanese counterparts." Annual competition. Several artists fellowships from two to six months' duration during the 2003 Japanese fiscal year (April 1, 2003-March 31, 2004) are available to artists, such as writers, musicians, painters, sculptors, stage artists, movie directors, etc.; and specialists in the arts, such as scenario writers, curators, etc. Benefits include transportation to and from Japan; settling-in, research, activities and other allowances and a monthly stipend. See brochure for more details. Competition receives approximately 30-40 submissions. Judges: Foundation staff in Japan. Guidelines available after August by fax or e-mail. Accepts inquiries by fax, phone and e-mail. Deadline: December 1, 2002. Work should be related to Japan. Applicants must be accredited artists or specialists. Affiliation with a Japanese artist or institution is required. Three letters of reference, including one from the Japanese affiliate must accompany all applications. Winners announced in April and notified by mail. List of winners available by phone.

◐ ◎ JAPANOPHILE SHORT STORY CONTEST, *Japanophile*, P.O. Box 7977, Ann Arbor MI 48107-7977. (734)930-1553. Fax: (734)930-9968. E-mail: jpnhand@japanophile.com. Website: www.japanophile.com. **Contact:** Susan Aitken, editor. Estab. 1974. Annual award "to encourage quality writing on Japan-America understanding." Award: $100 plus possible publication. Competition receives 200 submissions. Entry fee: $5. Send $7 for sample copy of magazine. Guidelines available by August for SASE, e-mail or on website. Accepts inquiries by fax and e-mail. Deadline: December 31. Prefers unpublished submissions. Stories should involve Japanese and non-Japanese characters, maximum 5,000 words. Winners notified in March and notified by mail. List of winners available in March for SASE.

◐ ◎ JESSE JONES AWARD FOR FICTION (BOOK), Holy Cross Hall 304, St. Edwards University, 3001 S. Congress Ave., Austin TX 78704-6489. **Contact:** Paula Mitchell Marks, secretary. "To honor the writer of the best novel or collection of short fiction published during the calendar year before the award is given." Annual award for novels or story collections. Award: $6,000. Competition receives 30-40 entries per year. Judges: Panel selected by TIL Council. Guidelines available in July 2001 for SASE. Accepts inquiries by fax and e-mail. Deadline: January 8, 2002. Previously published fiction, which must have appeared in print between January 1 and December 31 of the prior year. "Award available to writers who, at some time, have lived in Texas at least two years consecutively or whose work has a significant Texas theme." Winners announced April 15, 2002 and notified by phone or mail. List of winners available on website.

○ **JAMES JONES FIRST NOVEL FELLOWSHIP**, Wilkes University, Wilkes-Barre PA 18766. (570)408-4530. Fax: (570)408-7829. E-mail: english@wilkes.edu. Website: www.wilkes.edu/humanities/jones.edu. **Contact:** J. Michael Lennon, English department professor. Award to "honor the spirit of unblinking honesty, determination, and insight into modern culture exemplified by the late James Jones, author of *From Here to Eternity* and other prose narrations of distinction," by encouraging the work of an American writer who has not published a book-length work of fiction. Annual award for unpublished novel, novella, or collection of related short stories in progress. Award: $6,000 for first prize; $250 honorarium for runner-up. Receives approximately 600 applications. Application fee: $20 payable to Wilkes University. Guidelines available after June 1, by e-mail or for SASE. Accepts inquiries by e-mail. Deadline: Postmark March 1. Unpublished submissions. Award is open to American writers. Word length: 50 double-spaced pages and a two-page thematic outline. "Name, address, telephone number and e-mail address (if available) on title page only." Winners announced on or near September 1 and notified by phone.

KATHA: INDIAN AMERICAN FICTION CONTEST, *India Currents* Magazine, P.O. Box 21285, San Jose CA 95148. (408)274-6966. Fax: (408)274-2733. E-mail: editor@indiacurrents.com. Website: www.indiacurrents.com. **Contact:** Vandana Kumar, managing editor. Award "to encourage creative writing which has as its focus India, Indian culture, Indian-Americans and America's views of India." Annual competition for short stories. Awards: $300 (1st Prize), $200 (2nd Prize), $100 (3rd Prize), 2 honorable mentions. Competition received 50 submissions last year. Judges: "A distinguished panel of Indian-American authors. Guidelines for SASE, e-mail, or on website. Accepts inquiries by e-mail and phone. Deadline: December 31. Unpublished submissions only. Length: 3,000 words maximum. Winners announced on April 1 and notified by mail. List of winners available for SASE. "Write about something you have experienced personally or do extensive research, so that you can write knowledgebly."

○ ◎ **EZRA JACK KEATS/KERLAN COLLECTION MEMORIAL FELLOWSHIP**, University of Minnesota, 113 Andersen Library, 222-21st Ave. S., Minneapolis MN 55455. (612)624-4576. Fax: (612)625-5525. E-mail: clrc@tc.umn.edu. Website: http://special.lib.umn.edu/clrc/. Award to provide "travel expenses to a talented writer and/or illustrator of children's books who wishes to use the Kerlan Collection for the furtherance of his or her artistic development." Annual competition for books of children's literature. Award: $1,500. Competition receives approximately 10 submissions. Judges: panel of non-Kerlan Collection staff; area professionals, educators, etc. Guidelines available after November for 55¢ SASE. Accepts inquiries by fax, phone and e-mail. Deadline: early May. Accepts unpublished and previously published submissions. Winners announced mid June and notified by phone and letter. List of winners available for SASE.

Ⓝ ○ ◎ **ROBERT F. KENNEDY BOOK AWARDS**, 1367 Connecticut Ave. NW, Suite 200, Washington DC 20036. (202)463-7575. Fax: (202)463-6606. E-mail: info@rfkmemorial.org. Website: www.rfkmemorial.org. **Contact:** Director of the Book Award. Endowed by Arthur Schlesinger, Jr., from proceeds of his biography, *Robert Kennedy and His Times*. Annual. "To award the author of a book which most faithfully and forcefully reflects Robert Kennedy's purposes." For books published during the calendar year. Award: $2,500 cash prize awarded in the spring. Guidelines available in the fall. Accepts inquiries by fax and e-mail. Deadline: January 31, 2003. Looking for "a work of literary merit in fact or fiction that shows compassion for the poor or powerless or those suffering from injustice." Four copies of each book submitted should be sent, along with a $25 entry fee and entry form (available on website). Winners announced Spring 2003 and notified by phone. List of winners available by phone, fax or e-mail.

Ⓝ ○ ◎ **KENTUCKY ARTS COUNCIL, KENTUCKY ARTISTS FELLOWSHIPS**, Old Capitol Annex, 300 W. Broadway, Frankfort KY 40601. (888)833-2787. Fax: (502)564-2839. E-mail: heather.lyons@mail.state.ky.us. Website: www.kyarts.org. **Contact:** Heather Lyons, individual artist program director. "To encourage and assist the professional development of Kentucky artists." 10-15 writing fellowships offered every other (or even-numbered) year in fiction, poetry, playwriting. Award: $7,500. Competition receives approximately 175 submissions. Judges are out-of-state panelists (writers, editors, playwrights, etc.) of distinction. Open only to Kentucky residents (minimum one year). Entry forms available for *Kentucky residents in July 2002*." Accepts inquiries by fax and e-mail. Deadline: September 15, 2002. Winners announced December 2002 and notified by mail.

◍ **KIRIYAMA PACIFIC RIM BOOK PRIZE**, Kiriyama Pacific Rim Institute, 650 Delancey St., Suite 101, San Francisco CA 94107. (415)777-1628. Fax: (415)777-1646. E-mail: jeannine@pacificrimvoices.org. Website: www.pacificrimvoices.org/. **Contact:** Jeannine Cuevas, prize manager. Annual competition for full-length books, fiction or nonfiction. Award: $30,000 divided equally between authors of one fiction and one nonfiction work. Competition receives 300 submissions. Judges: 2 panels of 5 judges (one panel for fiction and one for nonfiction). Guidelines available in February. Accepts inquiries by phone, mail, fax and e-mail. Deadline: July 1. All works should be published. Published entries must have appeared in print between October 1, 2002 and October 31, 2003. "The prize is open to publishers/writers world wide. Entries must concern the Pacific Rim. Writer must be nominated by publisher. Writers should prompt their publishers to do so." Winners announced Fall of 2003 and notified by phone.

Ⓝ ⊕ **KOREAN LITERATURE TRANSLATION AWARD**, The Korean Literature Translation Institute, 149-1, Pyeong-Dong, Jongno-Gu, Seoul 110-102, South Korea. Phone: 82-2-732-1442. Fax: 82-2-732-1443. E-mail: info@ltikorea.net. Website: www.ltikorea.net. **Contact:** Yun Hyong-sik. Biannual competition for translations of Korean Literature. Award: $20,000 grand prize, 3 work-of-merit prizes of $30,000; one special prize of $10,000 for publishers. Guidelines available in May by mail or on website. Accepts inquiries by fax and e-mail. Deadline: August 15. "Texts to be considered include quality translations of Koren literature published during the period from January 1, 1998 to December 31, 2002." Winners announced in early October and notified by telephone, fax or mail. List of winners available in October.

LAURIE, Smoky Mountain Romance Writers, P.O. Box 70268, Knoxville TN 37938. Phone/fax (call first): (865)922-7700. E-mail: skunkoml@aol.com. Website: www.smrw.org. **Contact:** Deborah Ledgerwood, contest coordinator. Award to "honor excellence in romance fiction." Annual competition for novels. Award: First place in each category wins a Laurie pendant and finalist and winner receive certificates. "We accept 50 entries maximum for each category." Judge: Finalists are judged by an acquisitions editor. $25 entry fee. Guidelines available November. For guidelines, send SASE, e-mail or visit website. Accepts inquiries by e-mail. Deadline: March 1. Entries should be unpublished. Contest open to Romance Writers of America members. Length: 5-page synopsis, prologue, and first chapter (not to exceed 30 pages). Winners announced May 19 and notified by phone and e-mail May 20. List of winners available by e-mail or visit website.

THE LAWRENCE FOUNDATION AWARD, *Prairie Schooner*, 201 Andrews Hall, P.O. Box 880334, Lincoln NE 68588-0334. (402)472-0911. Fax: (402)472-9771. E-mail: eflanagan2@unl.edu. Website: www.unl.edu/schooner/psmain.htm. **Contact:** Hilda Raz, editor-in-chief. Award "to honor and recognize the best short story published in *Prairie Schooner* in the past year." Annual competition for short stories. Award: $1,000. Judge: The editorial staff of *Prairie Schooner*. "Only work published in *Prairie Schooner* in the previous year is considered." Work is nominated by editorial staff. Winners announced in the Spring issue and notified by mail in February or March.

LAWRENCE FOUNDATION PRIZE, *Michigan Quarterly Review*, 3032 Rackham Bldg., Ann Arbor MI 48109-1070. (734)764-9265. E-mail: mgr@umich.edu. Website: www.umich.edu/~mgr. **Contact:** Doris Knight, administrative assistant. "An annual cash prize awarded to the author of the best short story published in *Michigan Quarterly Review* each year." Annual competition for short stories. Award: $1,000. Competition receives approximately 500 submissions. "Stories must already be published in *Michigan Quarterly Review*; this is not a competition in which manuscripts are read outside of the normal submission process." Guidelines available for SASE or on website. Accepts inquiries by e-mail and phone. Deadline: September. Winners announced in December and notified by phone or mail.

URSULA K. LE GUIN PRIZE FOR IMAGINATIVE FICTION, *Rosebud*, P.O. Box 459, Cambridge WI 53523. (608)423-4750. E-mail: JrodClark@smallbytes.net. Website: www.rsbd.net. **Contact:** Roderick Clark, publisher or John Lehman, associate publisher. This biennual competition is to select the very best imaginative short story entered. Award: $1,000 and publication in *Rosebud*. Competition receives 200-250 entries per category. Judge: a panel of 2-3 pre-judges and Ursula K. Le Guin is final judge. Entry fee is $10. Guidelines available in the fall on website or for SASE. Deadline: September 31, 2003. Entries should be previously unpublished. Contest open to anyone. Winners announced in mid-spring of each year and notified by mail, phone, or e-mail. List of winners available for SASE.

LEAGUE OF UTAH WRITERS CONTEST, League of Utah Writers, 4621 W. Harman Dr., West Valley City UT 84120-3752. (801)964-0861. Fax: (801)964-0937. E-mail: crofts@numucom.com. Website: www.luwrite.com. **Contact:** Dorothy Crofts, membership chair. "The annual LUW Contest has been held since 1935 to give Utah writers an opportunity to get their works read and critiqued. It also encourages writers to keep writing in an effort to get published." Annual competition for short stories and novels. Award: 34 categories, cash award of $30/$20/$10; children's book category, $50/$25/$15; full length book category $100/$50/$25; published writers category. Competition receives 10-100 submissions/category. Judges: professional judges who are paid for their services. Entry fee $3-6, short story; $5-12, full length book. Guidelines available January 2000 for SASE. Accepts inquiries by fax, e-mail and phone. Deadline: June 15, 2003. Both published and previously unpublished submissions. Published submissions must have appeared in print between June 2002 and June 2003. "We do have separate categories for speculative fiction, children's and teen's besides our full length book category on any subject." Word length: 1,500 words maximum, short short story; 3,000 words maximum, short story; 4,000 words maximum, speculative fiction; 90,000 word maximum, full length book; 3,000 words maximum children's story; 3,000 words maximum, teen story; 5,000 words maximum, Agnes Burke White/Leroy Meager Short Story. "Read the contest rules and guidelines. Don't skim over them. Rules change and are revised from year to year. Don't forget to enclose your entry fee when mailing your entries." Winners will be announced at the Annual Writers Round-up in September. List of winners available at Round-up or for SASE.

LIFETIME ACHIEVEMENT AWARD, Native Writers' Circle of the Americas, English Department, University of Oklahoma, Norman OK 73019-0240. (405)325-6231. Fax: (405)325-0831. E-mail: Geary.Hobson_1@ou.edu. **Contact:** Geary Hobson, director. Award to "honor the most respected of our Native American writers. Our award is the only one given to Native American authors by Native American authors." Annual competition. Author's lifetime work as a writer. Award: $1,000. Accepts inquiries by fax, phone, e-mail. Writers are voted on for the award by fellow American Indian writers. Writer must be nominated. 2002 deadline: March 15. Results announced March 20; winners notified by phone initially, then by e-mail.

LILITH ANNUAL FICTION AWARD, Lilith Magazine, 250 W. 57th St., Suite 2432, New York NY 10107. (212)757-0818. Fax: (212)757-5705. E-mail: lilithmag@aol.com. Website: www.lilithmag.com. **Contact:** Yona Zeldis McDonough, fiction editor. "*Lilith*, the award-winning independent Jewish women's magazine is offering its second annual prize in Jewish feminist fiction. We're looking for vibrant, compelling and original stories with heart, soul and chutzpah, short stories that illuminate issues central to the lives of contemporary Jewish women." Annual award for short stories. Award: $250, publication in *Lilith* and one year subscription. $15 entry fee. Make checks payable to *Lilith Magazine* or include credit card information. For guidelines, send SASE, e-mail, visit website or call. Accepts inquiries by fax, e-mail, phone. Deadline: December 1, 2002. Entries should be unpublished. Contest open to all writers. Manuscripts should be double spaced, 2,500 words or less, with name and contact information on a separate cover sheet. "Electronic submissions, in Microsoft Word, welcome. Does not return mss. Winners announced January or February 2003. Winners notified by phone.

LITERAL LATTÉ FICTION AWARD, *Literal Latté*, 61 E. 8th St., Suite 240, New York NY 10003. (212)260-5532. E-mail: litlatte@aol.com. Website: www.literal-latte.com. **Contact:** Edward Estlin, contributing editor. Award to "provide talented writers with three essential tools for continued success: money, publication and recognition." Annual competition for short stories. Award: $1,000 (1st Prize); $200 (2nd Prize); $100 (3rd Prize); up to 7 honorable mentions. Competition receives 400-600 submissions. Judges: the editors. Entry fee $10 ($15 includes subscription) for each story submitted. Guidelines available for SASE, by e-mail or on website. Accepts inquiries by e-mail. Deadline: mid-January. Previously unpublished submissions. Open to new and established writers worldwide. Word length: 6,000 words maximum. "The First Prize Story in the First Annual *Literal Latté* Fiction Awards has been honored with a Pushcart Prize." Winners notified by phone. List of winners available in late April for SASE or by e-mail.

◎ LITERALLY HORSES-REMUDA POETRY/SHORT STORY CONTEST, *Literally Horses*, 208 Cherry Hill St., Kalamazoo MI 49006-4221. (616)345-5915. E-mail: literallyhorses@aol.com. Website: www.literallyhorses.com. **Contact:** Laurie A. Cerny, publisher. Award to "promote/recognize horse/western lifestyle related poetry and short stories." Annual competition for short stories and poetry. Award: $100 first place short story; $75 first place poetry; honorable mention prizes in each category. "Anticipate at least 100 entries." Judge: a panel of judges—including *Literally Horses* publisher. $9.95 entry fee covers 3 poems or one short story (includes a 1-year subscription). Guidelines available August 1, 2002. For guidelines, send SASE. Deadline: July 31, 2003. Entries can be previously published. Contest open to anyone. Length: 3,500 words. "Make sure the topic has something to do with horses; racing, driving, riding, showing, backyard horse, etc. Also, cowboy/western lifestyle theme oriented is OK. Something different. Inspirational." Winners announced Fall 2002. List of winners available for SASE.

◻ LONG FICTION CONTEST INTERNATIONAL, White Eagle Coffee Store Press, P.O. Box 383, Fox River Grove IL 60021-0383. (847)639-9200. E-mail: wecspress@aol.com. Website: http://members.aol.com/wecspress. **Contact:** Frank E. Smith, publisher. To promote and support the long story form. Annual award for short stories. "Entries accepted from anywhere in the world; story must be written in English." Winning story receives A.E. Coppard Award—publication as chapbook plus $500, 25 contributor's copies; 40 additional copies sent to book publishers/agents and 10 press kits. Entry fee $15 US, ($10 for second story in same envelope). Must be in US funds. Competition receives 200 entries. Guidelines available in April by SASE, e-mail or website. Accepts inquiries by e-mail. Deadline: December 15. Accepts previously unpublished submissions, but previous publication of small parts with acknowledgements is OK. Simultaneous submissions OK. No limits on style or subject matter. Length: 8,000-14,000 words (30-50 pages double spaced) single story; may have multiparts or be a self-contained novel segment. Send cover with title, name, address, phone; second title page with title only. Submissions are not returned; they are recycled. "Previous winners include Adria Bernardi, Doug Hornig, Christy Sheffield Sanford, Eleanor Swanson, Gregory J. Wolos and Joe Hill. SASE for most current information." Winners announced March 30 and notified by phone. List of winners available March 30 for SASE or on website. "Write with richness and depth."

◻ ◎ THE LONGMEADOW JOURNAL LITERARY COMPETITION, c/o Robert and Rita Morton, 6750 Longmeadow Ave, Lincolnwood IL 60710. (312)726-9789. Fax: (312)726-9772. **Contact:** Robert and Rita Morton. Award to "stimulate the young to write." Annual competition for short stories. Award: $175 (1st Prize); $100 (2nd Prize); 5 prizes of $50. "We publish a total of 20 stories and also Honorable Mention winners' names." Competition receives 700 submissions. Judges: Robert and Rita Morton. Guidelines for SASE or fax. Accepts inquiries by fax. Award for "short story writers between the ages of 10-19." Word length: 3,000 words or less. Winners notified by December 31, 2002.

◖ LOS ANGELES TIMES BOOK PRIZES, *L.A. Times*, 202 W. First St., Los Angeles CA 90012. (213)237-5775. E-mail: tom.crouch@latimes.com. Website: www.latimes.com/bookprizes. **Contact:** Tom Crouch, administrative coordinator. Annual award for books published between January 1 and December 31. Award: $1,000 cash prize in each of the following categories: fiction, first fiction (the Art Seidenbaum Award), young adult fiction and mystery/thriller. In addition, the Robert Kirsch Award recognizes the body of work by a writer living in and/or writing on the American West. Entry is by nomination of juries—no external nominations or submissions are accepted. Juries appointed by the *L.A. Times*. No entry fee. "Works must have their first U.S. publication during the calendar year." Writers must be nominated by committee members. "The Times provides air fare and lodging in Los Angeles for the winning authors to attend the awards ceremony held in April as part of the *Los Angeles Times* Festival of Books."

⬛ ◻ LSU/SOUTHERN REVIEW SHORT FICTION AWARD, *The Southern Review*, 43 Allen Hall, LSU, Baton Rouge LA 70803-5005. (225)578-5108. Fax: (225)578-5098. E-mail: bmacon@lsu.edu. Website: www.LSU.edu/thesouthernreview. **Contact:** John Easterly. Award "to recognize the best first collection of short stories published in the U.S. in the past year." Annual competition. Award: $500, possible reading. Competition receives approx. 35-40 submissions. Judges: A committee of editors and faculty members. Guidelines for SASE. Deadline: January 31. Submissions must have been published between January 1 and December 31 of previous year. Only books published in the US.

THE HUGH J. LUKE AWARD, *Prairie Schooner*, 201 Andrews Hall, P.O. Box 880334, Lincoln NE 68588-0334. (402)472-0911. Fax: (402)472-9771. E-mail: eflanagan2@unl.edu. Website: www.unl.edu/schooner/psmain.htm. **Contact:** Hilda Raz, editor-in-chief. Award "an annual cash prize to honor work published in the previous year in *Prairie Schooner*, including essays, fiction and poetry." Award: $250. Judge: Competition is judged by the editorial staff of *Prairie Schooner*. No entry fee. For guidelines, send SASE or visit website. "Only work published in *Prairie Schooner* in the previous year is considered." Work is nominated by the editorial staff. Winners announced in the Spring issue and notified by mail in February or March.

MAIL ON SUNDAY/JOHN LLEWELLYN RHYS PRIZE, % Booktrust, Book House, 45 East Hill, London, SW18 2QZ England. Phone: 020-856-2973/2. Fax: 020-8516-2978. E-mail: susy@booktrust.org.uk or tarryn@booktrust.org.uk. Website: www.booktrust.org.uk. **Contact:** Kate Mervyn Jones, prizes manager or Tarryn McKay, prizes administrator. "The prize was set up by Jane Oliver, the widow of John Lewellyn Rhys, a young writer killed in action in World War II. It is awarded to a writer aged 35 and under and brings to light new and exciting talent." Annual award for short stories, novels, non-fiction and poetry. £500 to shortlisted authors and £5,000 to winner. Number of submissions varies. No entry fee. "For 2003 guidelines either request direct from Booktrust, or ask publisher to contact us by SASE, fax, e-mail or website." Accepts inquiries by fax, e-mail, phone and post. Deadline: end of June/July. Entries must be published during year preceding award. Open to any author who is a British or Commonwealth citizen. Writers may submit their own fiction only if it is published, with consent of the publisher. Publishers will be notified of winners by September. "The shortlist and winner should be in the papers, or contact us for a press release by SASE, fax, e-mail or website."

MALICE DOMESTIC GRANT, % Shirley Smith, 5562 Brittany Court, Frederick MD 21703. (301)293-0020. Fax: (301)797-7567. E-mail: ssmith811@aol.com. Grants Chair: Shirley Smith. Given "to encourage unpublished writers in their pursuit—grant may be used to offset registration, travel or other expenses relating to attending writers' conferences, etc., within one year of award." Annual competition for novels and nonfiction. Award: $500. Competition receives 35-50 submissions. Judges: the Malice Domestic Board. Guidelines for SASE. Accepts inquiries by e-mail. Deadline: December. Unpublished submissions. "Our genre is loosely translated as mystery stories of the Agatha Christie type, that is 'mysteries of manners.' These works usually feature amateur detective characters who know each other. No excessive gore or violence." Submit plot synopsis and 3 chapters of work in progress. Include résumé, a letter of reference from someone familiar with your work, a typed letter of application explaining qualifications for the grant and the workshop/conference to be attended or the research to be funded. Winners announced in May and notified by e-mail and phone. List of winners for SASE.

THE MAN BOOKER PRIZE FOR FICTION, (formerly Booker Prize), Booktrust, Book House, 45 East Hill, London SW18 2QZ England. Phone: 020 8516 2973 or 020 8516 2972. Fax: 020 8516 2978. E-mail: kate@booktrust.org.uk or tarryn@booktrust.org.uk. Website: www.themanbookerprize.com. **Contact:** Kate Mervyn Jones, prizes manager; Tarryn McKay, prizes administrator. Award to the best novel of the year. Annual competition for novels. Award: £50,000. Each of the short-listed authors receive £2,500. Guidelines available for SASE, fax, e-mail or website. Judges: five judges appointed by The Booker Prize Foundation. Deadline: July. Announcement of winners October/November. Publisher will be notified. Only published submissions eligible; must be a full length novel written in English by a citizen of the Commonwealth or Republic of Ireland. List of winners available for SASE, by fax, e-mail or website.

WALTER RUMSEY MARVIN GRANT, Ohioana Library Association, 274 E. First Ave., Suite 300, Columbus OH 43201. (614)466-3831. Fax: (614)728-6974. E-mail: ohioana@sloma.state.oh.us. **Contact:** Linda Hengst. "To encourage young unpublished (meaning not having a book published) writers (30 years of age or under)." Annual competition for short stories. Award: $1,000. Guidelines for SASE. Deadline: January 31. Open to unpublished authors born in Ohio or who have lived in Ohio for a minimum of five years. Must be 30 years of age or under. Up to six pieces of prose may be submitted; maximum 60 pages, minimum 10 pages double spaced, 12 pt type.

MASSACHUSETTS CULTURAL COUNCIL ARTIST GRANTS PROGRAM, Massachusetts Cultural Council, 10 St. James Ave., Boston MA 02116. (617)727-3668. Fax: (617)727-0044. E-mail: mcc@art.state.ma.us. Website: www.massculturalcouncil.org. **Contact:** Stella Aguirre McGregor, program manager, Artists Department. Artist Grant Program discipline categories rotate biennially. "Unrestricted cash rewards of $12,500 and $1,000 provide direct

---

TO RECEIVE REGULAR TIPS AND UPDATES about writing and Writer's Digest publications via e-mail, send an e-mail with "SUBSCRIBE NEWSLETTER" in the body of the message to newsletter-request@writersdigest.com

support to artists in recognition of exceptional work." Judges: "Independent peer panels comprised of artists and arts professionals of diverse stylistic perspectives review applications in an anonymous process." No entry fee. Guidelines, application forms and support materials instructions available on website. Deadline: Playwriting/New Theater Works, December 16, 2002; Fiction and Poetry, tbd, December 2003. Contest open to residents of Massachusetts aged 18 or older who have lived in-state at least 2 years prior to application. "The Artist Grants Program is highly competitive. Submit your strongest work—you do not need to submit a work-in-progress." Winners announced June 2002 and notified by mail, phone. List of winners available by visiting website.

◻ **THE MASTERS AWARD**, Titan Press, P.O. Box 17897, Encino CA 91416-7897. Website: www.titanpress.info. "One yearly Grand Prize of $1,000, and four quarterly awards of 'Honorable Mention' each in either 1) fiction; 2) poetry and song lyrics; 3) nonfiction." Judges: 3 literary professionals, TBA. $15 entry fee. Awards are given on March 15, June 15, September 15 and December 15. Any submission received prior to an award date is eligible for the subsequent award. Submissions accepted throughout the year. Fiction and nonfiction must be no more than 20 pages (5,000 words); poetry no more than 150 lines. All entries must be in the English language. #10 SASE required for guidelines. "Be persistant, be consistent, be professional."

MARY McCARTHY PRIZE IN SHORT FICTION, Sarabande Books, P.O. Box 4456, Louisville KY 40204. (502)458-4028. Fax: (502)458-4065. E-mail: sarabandeb@aol.com. Website: www.sarabandebooks.org. **Contact:** Kirby Gann, managing editor. "To publish an outstanding collection of stories and/or novellas, oe a short novel (less than 300 pages)." Annual competition for story collections and novella/novella collections. "The Mary McCarthy Prize in Short Fiction includes a $2,000 cash award, publication of a collection of stories, novellas, or a short novel, and a standard royalty contract." Competition receives 800-1,000 submissions per contest. Each year this contest is judged by a well-established writer. Past judges include Amy Hempel, Barry Hannah, and Rosellen Brown. Judge in 2003: Heather McHugh. $20 entry fee. Guidelines currently available. Deadline: February 15, 2003. "The collections themselves must be unpublished, but published individual stories are okay." Contest open to any writer of English (no translations) who is a citizen of the US. Length: 150-300 pages. "Read past contest winners to see the quality of writing we seek: *The Baby Can Sing*, by Judith Slater; *Head*, by William Tester; *What We Won't Do*, by Brock Clarke. Keep in mind that our final judge changes each year." Winners announced July 2003 and notified by mail or phone in May or June. List of winners available for SASE.

◻ **THE JOHN H. McGINNIS MEMORIAL AWARD**, *Southwest Review*, P.O. Box 750374, 307 Fondren Library West, Southern Methodist University, Dallas TX 75275-0374. (214)768-1037. Fax: (214)768-1408. E-mail: swr@mail.smu.edu. Website: www.southwestreview.org. **Contact:** Elizabeth Mills, senior editor. Annual awards (fiction and nonfiction). Judges: *Southwest Review*'s editor-in-chief and senior editor. Stories or essays must have been published in the *Southwest Review* prior to the announcement of the award. Awards: $1,000. Pieces are not submitted directly for the award but for publication in the magazine. Guidelines available for SASE and on website. Winners announced in first issue of the year. Winners notified in January by mail, phone, e-mail.

◼◻◉ **MCKNIGHT ARTIST FELLOWSHIPS FOR WRITERS, Administered by the Loft**, The Loft, Pratt Community Center, 1011 Washington Ave. S., Minneapolis MN 55416. (612)379-8999. Website: www.loft.org. Program Coordinator: Jerod Santek. "To give Minnesota writers of demonstrated ability an opportunity to work for a concentrated period of time on their writing." Annual awards of $10,000; 2 in poetry and 3 in creative prose; 2 awards of distinction of $20,000. Competition receives approximately 125-175 submissions/year. Judges are from out-of-state. Entry forms or rules available in October for SASE "or see website." Deadline: November. "Applicants *must* be Minnesota residents and must send for and observe guidelines." Winners announced by May 1 and notified by phone or mail. List of winners available in August for SASE.

◙ **MID-LIST PRESS FIRST SERIES AWARD FOR SHORT FICTION**, Mid-List Press, 4324-12th Ave. South, Minneapolis MN 55407-3218. (612)822-3733. E-mail: guide@midlist.org. Website: www.midlist.org. **Contact:** Lane Stiles, publisher. To encourage and nurture short fiction writers who have never published a collection of fiction. Annual competition for fiction collections. Award: $1,000 advance and publication. Competition receives 300 submissions. Judges: manuscript readers and the editors of Mid-List Press. $30 entry fee. Guidelines available in February for SASE or on website. Deadline: July 1. Previously published or unpublished submissions. Word length: 50,000 words minimum. "Application forms and guidelines are available for a #10 SASE or visit our website." Winners announced in January and notified by phone and mail in January. Winners' list published in *Poets & Writers* and *AWP Chronicle*; also available by SASE, e-mail or on website.

◻ **MID-LIST PRESS FIRST SERIES AWARD FOR THE NOVEL**, Mid-List Press, 4324-12th Ave. South, Minneapolis MN 55407-3218. (612)822-3733. E-mail: guide@midlist.org. Website: www.midlist.org. **Contact:** Lane Stiles, publisher. To encourage and nurture first-time novelists. Annual competition for novels. Award: $1,000 advance and publication. Competition receives approximately 500 submissions. Judges: manuscript readers and the editors of Mid-List Press. $30 entry fee. Guidelines available in July for SASE or on website. Deadline: February 1. Unpublished submissions. Word length: minimum 50,000 words. "Application forms and guidelines are available for a #10 SASE, or visit our website." Winners announced in July and notified by phone and mail. Winners' list published in *Poets & Writers* and *AWP Chronicle*; also available by SASE, e-mail or on website.

MILKWEED EDITIONS NATIONAL FICTION PRIZE, Milkweed Editions, 1011 Washington Ave. S., Suite 300, Minneapolis MN 55415-1246. (612)332-3192. Fax: (612)215-2550. E-mail: editor@milkweed.org. Website: www.-milkweed.org. **Contact:** Elisabeth Fitz, first reader. Annual award for a novel, a short story collection, one or more novellas, or a combination of short stories and novellas. Award: $5,000 cash advance as part of any royalties agreed upon at the time of acceptance. Contest receives 3-5000 submissions per category. Judged by Milkweed Editions. Guidelines available for SASE or check website. Accepts inquiries by e-mail and phone. Deadline: "Rolling—but 2003 winner chosen by October 2002." "Please look at previous winners: *Hell's Bottom, Colorado*, by Laura Pritchett; *The Empress of One*, by Faith Sullivan; *Falling Dark*, by Tim Tharp; *Montana 1948*, by Larry Watson; and *Aquaboogie*, by Susan Straight—this is the caliber of fiction we are searching for. Catalog available for $1.50 postage, if people need a sense of our list." Winners are notified by phone and announced in November. See catalog for winners.

MILTON CENTER FELLOWSHIP, The Milton Center, MN 2nd, Newman University, 3100 McCormick, Wichita KS 67213. (316)942-4291, ext. 326. Fax: (316)942-4483. E-mail: miltonc@newmanu.edu. Website: www.newmanu.edu/MiltonCenter. **Contact:** Essie Sappenfield, program director. Award to "help new writers of Christian commitment complete first book-length manuscript." Annual competition for fiction or poetry. Competition receives 20 submissions. Judges: Milton Center staff. Entry fee $15. Guidelines for SASE or e-mail. Deadline: March 15. Submit novel or book of stories: proposal and 3 chapters; poetry: 12-15 poems and proposal.

MIND BOOK OF THE YEAR, Granta House, 15-19 Broadway, London E15 4BQ England. **Contact:** Ms. A. Brackx. "To award a prize to the work of fiction or nonfiction which outstandingly furthers public understanding of the causes, experience or treatment of mental health problems." Annual competition for novels and works of nonfiction. Award: £1,000. Competition receives approximately 50-100 submissions. Judges: A panel drawn from MIND's Council of Management. Deadline: December. Author's nomination is accepted. All books must be published in English in the UK.

MINNESOTA STATE ARTS BOARD/ARTIST ASSISTANCE FELLOWSHIP, Park Square Court, 400 Sibley St., Suite 200, St. Paul MN 55101-1928. (612)215-1600. Fax: (612)215-1602. E-mail: msab@arts.state.mn.us. Website: www.arts.state.mn.us. **Contact:** Amy Frimpong, artist assistance program officer. "To provide support and recognition to Minnesota's outstanding literary artists." Annual award for fiction writers, creative nonfiction writers and poets. Award: up to $8,000. Competition receives approximately 150 submissions/year. Deadline: October. Previously published or unpublished submissions. Application guidelines available in mid-June by e-mail, phone or on website. Accepts inquiries by phone, fax and e-mail. A list of winners available by e-mail and on website. *Minnesota residents only.*

MISSISSIPPI REVIEW PRIZE, University of Southern Mississippi/Mississippi Review, P.O. Box 5144 USM, Hattiesburg MS 39406-5144. (601)266-4321. Fax: (601)266-5757. E-mail: rief@netdoor.com. Website: www.mississippireview.com. **Contact:** Rie Fortenberry, managing editor. Annual award to "reward excellence in new fiction and poetry and to find new writers who are just beginning their careers." Award: $1,000 plus publication for the winning story and poem; publication for all runners-up. Entry fee $15/story or group of 3 poems (includes copy of issue). Entries should be previously unpublished. No manuscripts returned. Guidelines available for SASE, e-mail or on website. Accepts inquiries by e-mail or phone. Deadline: August 31. Winners notified in January. List of winners and runners-up for SASE.

THE MISSOURI REVIEW EDITORS' PRIZE CONTEST, 1507 Hillcrest Hall, Columbia MO 65211. (573)882-4474. Fax: (573)884-4671. Website: www.missourireview.org. **Contact:** Contest Coordinator. Annual competition for short stories, poetry and essays. Award: $2,000 for fiction and poetry, $2,000 for essay and publication in *The Missouri Review*. Competition receives more than 1,800 submissions. Judges: *The Missouri Review* editors. $15 entry fee (checks payable to *The Missouri Review*). Each fee entitles entrant to a one-year subscription to *The Missouri Review*, an extension of a current subscription, or a gift subscription. Guidelines available June for SASE. Deadline: October 15. Outside of envelope should be marked "Fiction," "Essay," or "Poetry." Enclose an index card with author's name, address, and telephone number in the left corner and, for fiction and essay entries only, the work's title in the center. Entries must be previously unpublished and will not be returned. Page length restrictions: 25 typed, double-spaced, for fiction and essays, 10 for poetry. Winners announced in January and notified by phone and mail. List of winners available for SASE. "Send fully realized work with a distinctive voice, style and subject."

MODEST CONTEST, *New Stone Circle*, 1185 E. 1900 North Rd., White Heath IL 61884. (217)762-5801. Fax: (217)398-4096. E-mail: m-hays@uiuc.edu. **Contact:** Mary Hays, fiction editor. Award "to encourage good writing." Annual competition for short stories. Awards: $100 (1st Prize). All contestants receive a copy of the contest issue. Competition receives approximately 100 submissions. Judge: Mary Hays. Entry fee $10. Guidelines available for SASE or e-mail. Deadline: June 1. Unpublished submissions. Winners announced in November and notified by mail.

MONEY FOR WOMEN, Money for Women/Barbara Deming Memorial Fund, Inc., Box 630125, Bronx NY 10463. **Contact:** Susan Pliner, administrator. "Small grants to individual feminists in the arts." Biannual competition. Award: $500-1,500. Competition receives approximately 150 submissions. Judges: Board of Directors. Guidelines and required application available for SASE. Deadline: December 31, June 30. Limited to US and Canadian citizens. Length: 25 pages. May submit own fiction. "Only for feminists in the arts." Winners announced five months after deadline and notified by mail.

MONTANA ARTS COUNCIL INDIVIDUAL ARTIST FELLOWSHIP, 316 N. Park Ave., Room 252, Helena MT 59620. (406)444-6430. **Contact:** Arlynn Fishbaugh, executive director. Biennial award of $5,000. Competition receives about 80-200 submissions/2 years. Panelists are professional artists. Contest requirements available for SASE or e-mail at mac@state.mt.us. Deadline: April 1, 2003. Restricted to residents of Montana; not open to degree-seeking students.

MOONLIGHT & MAGNOLIA FICTION WRITING CONTEST: SF, F, H, Genre Writing Program, P.O. Box 180489, Richland MS 39218-0489. (601)825-7263. E-mail: hoover59@aol.com. **Contact:** K. Mark Hoover, contest administrator. This annual award is for short stories that recognizes and encourage new and unpublished writers throughout the South while rewarding excellence in genre writing. Award: $250 (1st prize); $100 (2nd prize); $50 (3rd prize); top ten finalist receive certificates suitable for framing. Entries must be in competition format. Judges: In 2002, Richard Parks; changes annually. Entry fees $7.50/story; $2.50/additional entry. Guidelines available for SASE or by e-mail. Accepts inquiries by e-mail. Deadline: December 15, 2002. Open to unpublished writers and those who have not published more than 2 stories in a nationally-distributed publication with a circulation over 5,000. Length: 10,000 words. "We are open to multiple submissions but please send only your best work. Southern writers are encouraged to participate, but the contest is world-wide. Regional contestants will not be given preference during judging." Winners will be announced January 31, 2003 and notified by mail, phone, or e-mail. List of winners available for SASE or by e-mail.

MOTA EMERGING WRITERS CONTEST, *Mota*, Triple Tree Publishing, P.O. Box 5684, Eugene OR 97405. (541)338-3184. Fax: (541)484-5358. E-mail: liz@tripletreepub.com. Website: www.tripletreepub.com. **Contact:** Liz Cratty, publisher. Purpose is "to seek out new, unpublished fiction writers." Annual award for short stories. Award: 1st prize, $100 and publication in *Mota*; 2nd prize, $50 and considered for publication; 3rd prize, $25 and considered for publication. Competition receives 200 submissions per category. Judge: "A panel of professional fiction authors and volume guest editor." $12 entry fee per entry. For guidelines, send SASE or visit website. Deadline: November 1. Entries should be unpublished. Contest open to "writers who are unpublished or have fewer than five short stories sold." Length: 8,000 words. "Know the volume theme. For 2002 it was Truth. For 2003 it is Courage. Write strong fiction with compelling characters and unusual problems." Winners announced in December. Winners notified by phone and mail. List of winners available for SASE or visit website.

THE NATIONAL CHAPTER OF CANADA IODE VIOLET DOWNEY BOOK AWARD, The National Chapter of Canada IODE, 254-40 Orchard View Blvd., Toronto, Ontario M4R 1B9 Canada. (416)487-4416. Fax: (416)487-4417. Website: www.iodecanada.com. **Contact:** Sandra Connery, chair, book award committee. "The award is given to a Canadian author for an English language book suitable for children 13 years of age and under, published in Canada during the previous calendar year. Fairy tales, anthologies and books adapted from another source are not eligible." Annual competition for novels, children's literature. Award: $3,000. Competition receives 100-120 submissions. Judges: A six-member panel of judges including four National IODE officers and two non-members who are recognized specialists in the field of children's literature. Guidelines for SASE. Accepts inquiries by fax and phone. Deadline: December 31. Previously published January 1, 2002 and December 31, 2002. "The book must have been written by a Canadian citizen and must have been published in Canada during the calendar year." Word length: Must have at least 500 words of text preferably with Canadian content. Winner announced in May and notified by phone.

NATIONAL OUTDOOR BOOK AWARDS, Association of Outdoor Recreation and Education and Idaho State University, P.O. Box 8128, Pocatello ID 83209. (208)282-3912. Fax: (208)282-4600. E-mail: wattron@isu.edu. Website: www.isu.edu/outdoor/. **Contact:** Ron Watters, chairman. Award "honors outstanding writing and publishing in the outdoor field." Annual competition includes awards for novels and story collections. Award: Extensive national publicity, including display of all submitted titles at the International Conference on Outdoor Recreation and Education; announcement of winning titles to the media; reviews, cover scans and publisher links of winning titles on Association website; use of award medallion and logo on book covers and promotions. Competition receives from 30-50 submissions in "Literature" category. Judge: nationwide panel includes book reviewers, columnists, authors, academics and trade representatives. A $65 application fee should accompany each nominated title. Guidelines available in April for SASE, by e-mail, fax, phone or on website. Accepts inquiries by fax, e-mail, phone. Award nominations open in April and are due September 1st of the award year. Entries should be previously published. "Must be bound; galleys not acceptable. Must have been released after June 1 of the previous year. Contest open to authors of any nationality, but books must be in English. Length: open. Fictional works should be entered in the "Literature" category. Winners announced "early November at the International Conference on Outdoor Recreation and Education" and notified by mail in early November. List of winners available by visiting website.

NATIONAL READERS' CHOICE AWARDS, Oklahoma Romance Writers of America, HC 68, Box 33, Kingston OK 73439. Phone/fax: (580)564-1105. E-mail: wfergus@swbell.net. Website: www.okrwa.com. **Contact:** Willena Ferguson, coordinator. Purpose of contest is "to provide writers of romance fiction a competition where their published novels are judged by readers." Annual award for novels. "There is no monetary award, just an annual awards banquet hosted at the Annual National Romance Writers Convention." Total annual entries between 390-425. Of the 12 categories, the least received is in novella category and the largest is the long contemporary category." Judge: "Readers in all 50 states." $25 entry fee. Checks payable to NCRA. No limit to number of entries, but each title may be entered in only one category. The 12 categories include traditional series (50-60,000 words); short contemporary series (fewer than 70,000); long contemporary series (more than 70,000); single title contemporary; short historical (100,000 or less); long historical (more than 100,000); Regency (50,000 or more); romantic suspense (50,000 or more); inspirational (50,000 or more); novella (approximately 25,000); erotic romance (50,000 or more). For guidelines, send SASE, e-mail or visit website. Entry form required; available on website. Deadline: November 20, 2002 for forms and fees (send to above address). Deadline for books receipt is January 11, 2003. Five copies of each entry must be mailed to category coordinator; contact information for coordinator will be provided by November 15. All entries must have "an original copyright date of 2002 or a first U.S. printing date of 2002 as evidenced by the copyright page or a letter from the publisher. Entry must have been available for sale in United States sometime during 2002." E-books accepted if publisher is recognized by RWA or is a member of EPIC or AED; submit a hard copy—perfect- or spiral-bound book galleys (no 3 ring binders) with ISBN—and also "e-disk and form of the book." E-books must also have evidenced 2002 copyright page. "Entries will be accepted from authors, editors, publishers, agents, readers, etc.—from whomever wishes to fill out the entry form, pay the entry fee and supply number of copies." 2001 Winners announced in July 2002. Winners notified by phone, if not at awards ceremony, in July 2002. List of winners will be mailed, also available by e-mail.

◐ NATIONAL WRITERS ASSOCIATION ANNUAL NOVEL WRITING CONTEST, National Writers Association, 3140 Peoria St., PMB 295, Aurora CO 80014. (303)841-0246. Fax: (303)841-2607. **Contact:** Sandy Whelchel, director. Annual award to "recognize and reward outstanding ability and to increase the opportunity for publication." Award: $500 (1st Prize); $300 (2nd Prize); $100 (3rd Prize). Award judged by editors and agents. $35 entry fee. Judges' evaluation sheets sent to each entry with SASE. Contest rules and entry forms available with SASE. Opens December 1. Deadline: April 1. Unpublished submissions, any genre or category. Length: 20,000-100,000 words.

THE NEBRASKA REVIEW AWARD IN FICTION, The Nebraska Review, University of Nebraska at Omaha, Omaha NE 68182-0324. (402)554-3159. E-mail: jreed@unomaha.edu. **Contact:** James Reed, managing editor. Award to "recognize short fiction of the highest possible quality." Annual competition for short stories. Award: publication plus $500. Competition receives 400-500 submissions. Judges: staff. $15 entry fee for each story submitted. Guidelines for SASE. Accepts inquiries by e-mail, phone. Deadline: November 30. Previously unpublished submissions. Length: 5,000 words. Winners announced March 15 and notified by phone, e-mail and/or mail in February. List of winners for SASE.

N: ◐ NESFA SCIENCE FICTION/FANTASY SHORT STORY CONTEST, New England Science Fiction Association, P.O. Box 809, Framingham MA 01701-0203. (617)625-2311. Fax: (617)776-3243. E-mail: info@nesfa.org. Website: www.nesfa.org. **Contact:** D. Snyder, short story contest chair. Contest to encourage people to write science fiction and fantasy short stories. Annual competition for short stories. Award: plaque and $50 of NESFA merchandise. Competition receives 20-50 submissions. Judges: well-known, professional science fiction and fantasy writers. Contest guidelines available for SASE, by e-mail or on website. Accepts inquiries by fax and e-mail. Deadline: November 15. Unpublished submissions. Limited to writers who have had no fiction published. Length: 7,500 words or fewer. "Read a lot of science fiction and fantasy. Write using good grammar. Have a plot, a beginning, middle and end." Winners announced at annual conference in February and notified by mail. List of winners will be sent to all entrants at the end of February.

◑ NEUSTADT INTERNATIONAL PRIZE FOR LITERATURE, *World Literature Today*, 110 Monnet Hall, University of Oklahoma, Norman OK 73019-4033. **Contact:** Robert Con Davis-Undiano, director. Biennial award to recognize distinguished and continuing achievement in fiction, poetry or drama. Awards: $50,000, an eagle feather cast in silver, an award certificate, and a special issue of *World Literature Today* devoted to the laureate. "We are looking for outstanding accomplishment in world literature. The Neustadt Prize is not open to application. Nominations are made only by members of the international jury, which changes for each award. Jury meetings are held in the fall of even-numbered years. Unsolicited manuscripts, whether published or unpublished, cannot be considered."

NEW CENTURY WRITERS AWARDS, New Century Writer LLC, 32 Alfred St., Suite B, New Haven CT 06512-3927. (203)469-8824. Fax: (203)468-0333. E-mail: newcenturywriter@yahoo.com. Website: www.newcenturywriter.org. **Contact:** Jason J. Marchi, executive director. "To discover and encourage emerging writers of fiction, screenplays and stage plays, and to provide cash awards, sponsor writing fellowships, and promote our best writers to agents, producer in the film industry, and editors in the publishing industry. Also to educate via the quarterly educational newsletter, *The Anvil*." Five annual competitions for short stories, novels/novellas, screenplays, stage plays and TV scripts. Prizes: $3,000; $1,000; $500; and four $100. Also, awards 1 or 2 Ray Bradbury Fellowships to *Zoetrope* Short Story Writer's Workshop in Belize worth $5,000 each. Publishes best 10 stories in nationally distributed anthology (lists best novels/novellas). Best stories also considered for publication in *Futures* and *Verbicide*. Competitions receive 2,000 submissions. Judged initially by published writers, editors, produced film makers and other film industry professionals. Past judges include editors of *Zoetrope*, Juliana Gribbins of McGraw Hill, Bari Evins of Debra Hill Entertainment, Lisa Lindo of ACMA Talent & Literary. $30 fee per entry (screenplay, stage play, novel excerpt); $15 for one short story, $20 for two short stories; $3 per poem under 100 lines. Guidelines available July 15 for 9×12 SASE, fax, e-mail or on website. Accepts inquiries by mail only. Deadline: January 31 for short stories (sometimes extended); March 30 for novels/novellas/excerpts; May 30 for poetry; July 31 for screenplays and stage plays. Short stories and poetry may have appeared in publications with circulation of under 10,000; all other entries must be unpublished. "All genres accepted. We have a diverse group of alliance companies with different tastes." Contest open to all writers. "Submit your best writing. Take the time to go over your work one more time. You do not have to be Hemingway, just tell a good, solid story." Winners notified by mail in June/July "for earlier contests and December for screenplays and stage plays." List of winners available by visiting website or send SASE.

NEW ENGLAND WRITERS SHORT, SHORT FICTION CONTEST, New England Writers, P.O. Box 483, Windsor VT 05089-0483. (802)674-2315. E-mail: newvtpoet@aol.com. Website: http://hometown.aol.com/newvtpoet/myhomepage/business.html. **Contact:** Frank Anthony, president. Competition for publication in annual *Anthology of New England Writers*. Annual competition for short stories. Marjory Bartlett Sanger Award: $300. Competition receives 150 submissions. 2002 fiction judge: Reeve Lindbergh. 2003 fiction judge: TBA. $6 entry fee; 2 or more entries $5 each. Guidelines available for SASE, by e-mail, on website in November. Accepts inquiries by e-mail or phone. Deadline: June 15 postmark. Unpublished submissions. Length: 1,000 words maximum. "Strive for originality taken from your own life experience, not others." Winners announced at annual N.E.W. conference in July. Winners notified by mail or phone right after conference. List of winners available for SASE.

NEW HAMPSHIRE STATE COUNCIL ON THE ARTS INDIVIDUAL ARTIST FELLOWSHIP, 40 N. Main St., Concord NH 03301-4974. (603)271-2789. Fax: (603)271-3584. E-mail: info@nharts.state.nh.us. Website: www.state.nh.us/nharts. **Contact:** Julie Mento, artist services coordinator. Fellowship "recognizes artistic excellence and professional commitment of professional artists in literature who are legal/permanent residents of the state of New Hampshire." Guidelines available on website. Accepts inquiries over phone and e-mail. 2002 deadline was May 3.

NEW JERSEY STATE COUNCIL ON THE ARTS PROSE FELLOWSHIP, P.O. Box 306, Trenton NJ 08625. (609)292-6130. Website: www.njartscouncil.org. Annual grants for writers of short stories, novels, story collections. Past awards have ranged from $5,000-12,000. 2001 awards averaged $8,000. Judges: Peer panel. Guidelines available on website. Deadline: mid-July. For either previously published or unpublished submissions completed within past 2 years. "Previously published work must be submitted as a manuscript." Applicants must be New Jersey residents. Submit copies of short fiction, short stories or prose not exceeding 15 pages and no less than 10 pages. For novels in progress, a one-page synopsis and sample chapter should be submitted.

NEW LETTERS LITERARY AWARD, UMKC, 5101 Rockhill Rd., Kansas City MO 64110-2499. (816)235-1168. Fax: (816)235-2611. E-mail: EzraA@umkc.edu or newsletters@umkc.edu. Website: www.umkc.edu/newsletters. **Contact:** Aleatha Ezra, contest coordinator. Award to "discover and reward unpublished work by new and established writers." Annual competition for short stories. Award: $1,000 and publication. Competition receives 400-600 entries/year. Entry fee $10. Judges: past judges include Joyce Carol Oates (poetry), Marilyn Hacker (poetry), Rosellen Brown (fiction), Michael Dorris (fiction). Guidelines available in January for SASE, by e-mail and on website. Accepts inquiries by phone and e-mail. Deadline: May 20. Submissions must be unpublished. Length requirement: 5,000 words or less. Winners notified by personal letter in September. List of winners available for SASE and on website.

NEW MILLENNIUM WRITING AWARDS, P.O. Box 2463, Knoxville TN 37901-2463. (423)428-0389. Fax: (865)428-2302. E-mail: DonWilliams7@att.net. Website: www.mach2.com/books or www.WritingAwards.com. **Contact:** Don Williams, editor. Award "to promote literary excellence in contemporary fiction." Biannual competition for short stories. Award: $1,000 and publication in *New Millennium Writings*. Judges: Novelists and short story writers. Entry fee: $16. Guidelines available year round for SASE and on website. Accepts inquiries by e-mail. Deadline: mid-June and mid-November. Unpublished submissions. Length: 1,000-6,000 words. "Provide a bold, yet organic opening line, sustain the voice and mood throughout, tell an entertaining and vital story with a strong ending. *New Millennium Writings* is a forward-looking periodical for writers and lovers of good reading. It is filled with outstanding poetry, fiction, essays and other speculations on subjects both topical and timeless about life in our astonishing times. Our pages brim with prize-winning essays, humor, full-page illustrations, writing advice, poetry from writers at all stages of their careers. First timers find their works displayed alongside well-known writers as well as profiles and interviews with famous authors such as John Updike, Sharyn McCrumb, Lee Smith, Howard Nemerov, Norman Mailer, Madison Smartt Bell, William Kennedy, David Hunter, Cormac McCarthy, Shelby Foote and more!" Winners announced October and April and notified by mail and phone. All entrants will receive a list of winners, plus a copy of the annual anthology. Send letter-sized SASE with entry for list.

NEW YORK STATE EDITH WHARTON CITATION OF MERIT, (State Author), NYS Writers Institute, Humanities 355, University at Albany, Albany NY 12222. (518)442-5620. **Contact:** Donald Faulkner, associate director. Awarded biennially to honor a New York State fiction writer for a lifetime of works of distinction. Fiction writers living in New York State are nominated by an advisory panel. Recipients receive an honorarium of $10,000 and must give two public readings a year.

JOHN NEWBERY AWARD, American Library Association (ALA) Awards and Citations Program, Association for Library Service to Children, 50 E. Huron St., Chicago IL 60611. (312)280-2163. Fax: (312)944-7671. E-mail: alsc@ala.org. Website: www.ala.org/alsc. **Contact:** Meredith Parets, program coordinator. Annual award. Only books for children published in the US during the preceding year are eligible. Award: Medal. Entry restricted to US citizens-residents. Judges: 2003 Newbery Award Selection Committee. Guidelines available on website, by fax, phone or e-mail. Accepts inquiries by fax and e-mail. Deadline: December 31. Winners announced January 27 and notified by phone. List of winners available in February on website.

NFB WRITERS' FICTION CONTEST, The Writers' Division of the National Federation of the Blind, 1203 S. Fairview Rd., Columbia MO 65203-0809. (573)445-6091. **Contact:** Tom Stevens, president of division. Award to "encourage members and other blind writers to write fiction." Annual competition for short stories. Award: four prizes of $50, $35, $20, $10, plus honorable mentions and possible publication in *Slate & Style*. Competition receives 25 submissions. Entry fee $5 per story. Guidelines available in August for SASE. Deadline: June 1, 2003. Unpublished submissions. Word length: 2,000 words (maximum). "Send a 150-word bio with each entry. Please, no erotica." Winners announced July 15 and notified by letter. List of winners available in July for SASE. "Be a serious contestant. Too many entries received with a multitude of spelling and grammatical errors."

THE NOMA AWARD FOR PUBLISHING IN AFRICA, P.O. Box 128, Witney, Oxon 0X8 5XU United Kingdom. (44)1993-775235. Fax: (44)1993-709265. E-mail: maryljay@aol.com. **Contact:** Mary Jay. Sponsored by Kodansha Ltd. Award "to encourage publication of works by African writers and scholars in Africa, instead of abroad as is still too often the case at present." Annual competition for a new book in any of these categories: Scholarly or academic; books for children; literature and creative writing, including fiction, drama and poetry. Award: $10,000. Competition receives approximately 140 submissions. Judges: A committee of African scholars and book experts and representatives of the international book community. Chairman: Walter Bgoya. Guidelines for SASE. Deadline: February 28. Previously published submissions. Submissions are through publishers only. Maximum number of entries per publisher is 3. Winners announced October and notified through publishers. List of winners available for SASE.

NORTH CAROLINA ARTS COUNCIL FELLOWSHIP, 221 E. Lane St., Raleigh NC 27699-4632. (919)715-1519. **Contact:** Deborah McGill, literature director. Grants program "to encourage the continued achievements of North Carolina's writers of fiction, poetry, literary nonfiction and literary translation." Biannual awards: Up to $8,000 each. Council receives approximately 300 submissions. Judges are a panel of editors and published writers from outside the state. Writers must be over 18 years old, not currently enrolled in degree-granting program, and must have been a resident of North Carolina for 1 full year as of the application deadline. Deadline: November 1, 2002.

NOVELLA PRIZE, *The Malahat Review*, University of Victoria, P.O. Box 1700 Stn CSC, Victoria, British Columbia V8W 2Y2 Canada. (250)721-8524. Fax: (250)472-5051. E-mail: malahat@uvic.ca. Website: www.malahatreview.com. **Contact:** Marlene Cookshaw, editor. Purpose: "To promote the writings of novellas." Biannual competition for novellas. Prizes: $500 plus payment for publication at our regular rate of $30/magazine page. Competition receives 100 submissions. Judges: "A 'blind' panel of judges/editors." editorial board and select judges. Entry fee: $30 in Canada; $40 Canadian; includes one year subscription. Guidelines available for SASE or on website. Accepts inquiries by e-mail or phone. Deadline: March 1, 2004. Entries should be unpublished. Contest open to all writers. Length: 30,000 words. Winners notified by mail 2-3 months after deadline.

THE NTH LITERACY AWARD, *comfusion*, 304 S. 3rd St., San Jose CA 95112. (408)981-7999. Fax: (707)523-0669. E-mail: info@comfusionreview.com. Website: www.comfusionreview.com. **Contact:** Jaime Wright, editor-in-chief. Award's purpose is "to showcase the work of our readers and initiate a bit of healthy competition." Annual award for short stories. Award: 1st prize, $150; 2nd prize, $75; 3rd prize, $50 plus publication in our summer issue. Competition receives approximately 100 submissions per category. Entries "judged blind by the editors of *comfusion*." $10 entry fee per entry (includes 2 issue subscription to *comfusion*). Make checks payable to Lotus Foundation. For guidelines, send SASE, e-mail or visit website. Accepts inquiries by e-mail. Deadline: December 31. Entries should be unpublished. "Please place title only on manuscript, with a separate cover sheet which includes title, name, address, e-mail and phone number (optional)." Contest open to all writers. Length: 5,500 words maximum. "Enter your best work. Polished pieces only." Winners announced February 1. Winners notified by mail and e-mail in January 15. List of winners available by e-mail and on website.

NTPWA ANNUAL POETRY & FICTION CONTEST, North Texas Professional Writers' Association, P.O. Box 563, Bedford TX 76095-0563. (817)428-2822. Fax: (817)428-2181. E-mail: through website. Website: www.ntpwa.org. **Contact:** Secretary of NTPWA. Award "to recognize and encourage previously unpublished writers." Annual competition for short stories, novels and poetry. Fiction awards: $75 (1st Prize), $35 (2nd Prize). Poetry awards: $75 (1st Prize),

**FOR EXPLANATIONS OF THESE SYMBOLS,
SEE THE INSIDE FRONT AND BACK COVERS OF THIS BOOK.**

$35 (2nd Prize). Judges: Published writers. Entry fee: $5 fiction, $5/2 poems. Guidelines available in March by e-mail or for SASE. Accepts inquiries by e-mail. Deadline: May 31, 2003. Unpublished submissions. Length: 20 pages (fiction); 30 lines (each poem). Winners announced July 31, 2003. List of winners available for SASE. "Chapbooks of winner's work available for $5 each. We find writers are not using proper manuscript style. We grade on this."

N ◯ O! GEORGIA! WRITING COMPETITION, O! GEORGIA TOO! WRITING COMPETITION, Humpus Bumpus, P.O. Box 1303, Roswell GA 30077-1303. (770)781-9705. Fax: (770)781-4676. E-mail: paulcossman@ mindspring.com. Website: www.humpusbumpus.com. **Contact:** Ms. Dani McLain, program coordinator. Mission: to "identify and publish new writers in order to help them launch their writing careers." Annual competitions for adults and students (K-12th grade). Guidelines available for SASE, fax, e-mail and on website. Judges: 3 judges for fiction and nonfiction, 3 judges for poetry; all are professors or published authors. Award: publication in trade paperback book sold at Humpus Bumpus Books and other stores. Contest receives 350-400 submissions. Entry fee: $10. Guidelines available on website or phone. Deadline: February 15. Winners announced June 30 and notified by mail. List of winners available for SASE. "Be original creative and fresh. Have good character development, good imagery, (good grammar and spelling)."

◯ THE FLANNERY O'CONNOR AWARD FOR SHORT FICTION, The University of Georgia Press, 330 Research Dr., Athens GA 30602-4901. Fax: (706)369-6131. E-mail: emontjoy@ugapress.uga.edu. Website: www.uga. edu/ugapress. **Contact:** Emily Montjoy, award coordinator. Annual award "to recognize outstanding collections of short fiction. Published and unpublished authors are welcome." Award: $1,000 and publication by the University of Georgia Press. Competition receives 330 submissions. Guidelines for SASE or on website. Accepts inquiries by mail only. Deadline: April 1-May 31. "Manuscripts cannot be accepted at any other time." $20 entry fee. Ms will not be returned. Winners announced in November and notified by mail. List of winners for SASE, fax, e-mail or on website.

◯ FRANK O'CONNOR FICTION AWARD, *descant*, Dept. of English, Texas Christian University, Box 297270, Fort Worth TX 76129. (817)257-6537. Fax: (817)257-6239. E-mail: descant@tcu.edu. Website: www.eng.tcu.edu/journ als/descant/index.htm. **Contact:** David Kuhne, editor. Estab. 1979 with *descant*; earlier awarded through *Quartet*. Annual award to honor the best published fiction in *descant* for its current volume. Award: $500 prize. Competition receives 500-1,000 submissions. Judge: *descant* fiction editors. No entry fee. Guidelines available for SASE or on website. 2002 deadline: April 1. Winners announced August and notified by phone in July. A list of winners will be available for SASE. "About 12 to 15 stories are published annually in *descant*. Winning story is selected from this group." Also offers the Sandra Brown Award for Short Fiction. Prize: $250. Send SASE for guidelines.

N ◎ OHIOANA AWARD FOR CHILDREN'S LITERATURE, ALICE WOOD MEMORIAL, Ohioana Library Association, 274 E. First Ave., Columbus OH 43201. (614)466-3831. Fax: (614)728-6974. E-mail: ohioana@slo ma.state.oh.us. **Contact:** Linda Hengst, director. Competition "to honor an individual whose body of work has made, and continues to make, a significant contribution to literature for children or young adults." Annual award of $1,000. Guidelines for SASE. Accepts inquiries by fax and e-mail. Deadline: December 31 prior to year award is given. "Open to authors born in Ohio or who have lived in Ohio for a minimum of five years." Winners announced in August and September and notified by letter in May. Entrants can call or e-mail for winner.

N ◯ ◎ OHIOANA BOOK AWARDS, Ohioana Library Association, 274 E. First Ave., Suite 300, Columbus OH 43201. (614)466-3831. Fax: (614)728-6974. E-mail: ohioana@sloma.state.oh.us. **Contact:** Linda R. Hengst, director. Annual awards granted (only if the judges believe a book of sufficiently high quality has been submitted) to bring recognition to outstanding books by Ohioans or about Ohio. Five categories: Fiction, Nonfiction, Juvenile, Poetry and About Ohio or an Ohioan. Criteria: Books written or edited by a native Ohioan or resident of the state for at least 5 years; two copies of the book MUST be received by the Ohioana Library by December 31 prior to the year the award is given; literary quality of the book must be outstanding. Awards: Certificate and glass sculpture (up to 6 awards given annually). Each spring a jury considers all books received since the previous jury. Award judged by a jury selected from librarians, book reviewers, writers and other knowledgeable people. No entry forms are needed, but they are available July 1, 2000. "We will be glad to answer letters asking specific questions." Winners announced in August or September and notified by mail in May.

◎ OKLAHOMA BOOK AWARD, Oklahoma Center for the Book, 200 NE 18th, Oklahoma City OK 73105-3298. (405)681-8871. Fax: (405)525-7804. E-mail: gcarlile@oltn.odl.state.ok.us. Website: www.odl.state.ok.us/OCB. **Contact:** Glenda Carlile, executive director. Award to "recognize Oklahoma authors or books written about Oklahoma in the pervious year." Annual competition for novels and story collections. Award: Medal. Competition receives 25-30 submissions for fiction and nonfiction. Judges: a panel of 5 judges for each of 5 categories (fiction, nonfiction, children/ young adult, poetry and design/illustration). Guidelines available mid-July for SASE, fax, e-mail or website. Accepts inquiries by fax, e-mail and phone. Deadline: January 8. Previously published submissions appearing between January 1 and December of the previous year. "Writers much live or have lived in Oklahoma or book must have an Oklahoma theme. Entry forms available after August 1. Mail entry along with 6 copies of book." Winners announced at book award ceremony March 9. Results available by phone after March 13.

N ◯ THE CHRIS O'MALLEY PRIZE IN FICTION, *The Madison Review*, 7123 Helen C. White Hall, Dept. of English, University of Wisconsin, 600 North Park St., Madison WI 53706. (608)263-0566. Website: http://mendota.en

glish.wisc.edu/~MadRev/. **Contact:** Jason Harklerode and Hillary Schroeder, fiction editors. Award to "recognize emerging writers." Annual award for short stories. Award: $500; publication; 2 issues. Competition receives 150-200 entries. Judges: "Entries go though an initial screening by staff members; final decision is made by editors." Entry fee $5. Guidelines for SASE. Deadline: entries only accepted during September. Previously unpublished submissions. Length: 9,000 words maximum. Winners announced January 2003. Winners notified by phone by December 25, 2002.

○ ORANGE BLOSSOM FICTION CONTEST, *The Oak*, 1530 Seventh St., Rock Island IL 61201. (309)788-3980. **Contact:** Betty Chezum Mowery, editor. "To build up circulation of publication and give new authors a chance for competition and publication along with seasoned writers." Award: Subscription to *The Oak*. Competition receives approximately 75 submissions. Judges: published authors. Entry fee six 37¢ stamps. Guidelines available in December for SASE. Word length: 500 words maximum. "May be on any subject, but avoid gore and killing of humans or animals." Deadline: April 1. Winners announced mid-April and notified by mail. "Material is judged on content and tightness of writing as well as word lengths, since there is a 500-word limit. Guidelines for other contests available for SASE."

⊕ ◎ ORANGE PRIZE FOR FICTION, Orange pcs, %Booktrust, Book House, 45 East Hill, London SW18 2QZ England. (020)8516-2973/2. Fax: (020)8516-2978. E-mail: susy@booktrust.org.uk or tarryn@booktrust.org.uk. Website: www.orangeprize.co.uk or www.booktrust.org.uk. **Contact:** Kate Mervyn Jones, prizes manager or Tarryn McKay, prizes administrator. "This award was set up to find and reward the very best in women's fiction writing." Annual competition for novels only. Award: £30,000 and a "Bessie" statue to the winner. Number of entries varies. Judges have not been confirmed for 2003. No entry fee. Guidelines available by SASE, fax, e-mail or website. Authors should "either ask their publisher to contact Booktrust, or request a form directly themselves. However, entries must be made through publisher." Accepts inquiries by fax, e-mail, phone and post. Entries should be previously published novels by women, all nationalities. Must be published in the UK by a UK publisher. Length: full-length novel. Publishers will be notified of entry. Winner should be announced in the papers "or contact us for press release." Longlist announced in March; shortlist announced in April; winner announced in June. List of winners available by fax, e-mail or website.

ℕ ◎ OREGON BOOK AWARDS, Literary Arts, Inc., 219 NW 12th Ave., Suite 201, Portland OR 97209. (503)227-2583. Fax: (503)243-1167. E-mail: la@literary-arts.org. Website: www.literary-arts.org. **Contact:** Kristy Athens, program coordinator. Annual award for outstanding authors of fiction, poetry, literary nonfiction, young readers and drama. Award: $1,000 in each category. Competition receives 20 submissions per genre. Judges: out-of-state experts. Guidelines available in February for SASE and on website. Accepts inquiries by fax and e-mail. Deadline: May 31. Limited to Oregon residents. Winners announced in November and notified at an awards ceremony. List of winners available in November.

◎ DOBIE PAISANO FELLOWSHIPS, Dobie House, 702 E. Dean Keeton St., Austin TX 78705. (512)471-8542. Fax: (512)471-9997. E-mail: aslate@mail.utexas.edu. Website: www.utexas.edu/ogs/Paisano. **Contact:** Audrey N. Slate, director. Annual fellowships for creative writing (includes short stories, novels and story collections). Award: 6 months residence at ranch; $2,000 monthly living stipend. Competition receives approximately 100 submissions. Judges: faculty of University of Texas and members of Texas Institute of Letters. $10 entry fee. Application and guidelines available after July 1, 2002 by fax, e-mail and on website. Accepts inquiries by fax, e-mail and phone. "Open to writers with a Texas connection—native Texans, people who have lived in Texas at least two years, or writers with published work on Texas and Southwest." Deadline: January 31, 2003. Winners announced in May and notified by telephone followed by mail. A list of winners will be available on website.

THE PATERSON FICTION PRIZE, The Poetry Center at Passaic County Community College, One College Boulevard, Paterson NJ 07505-1179. (973)684-6555. Fax: (973)523-6085. E-mail: mgillan@pccc.cc.nj.us. Website: www.pccc .cc.nj.us/poetry. **Contact:** Maria Mazziotti Gillan, director. Award to "encourage recognition of high-quality writing." Annual competition for books of short stories and novels. Award: $1,000. Competition expects 500 submissions this year. Judge: A different one every year. Guidelines available for SASE or on website. Deadline: March 15, 2003. Winners announced in July and notified by mail. List of winners available for SASE or visit website.

○ PEARL SHORT STORY PRIZE, *Pearl* Magazine, 3030 E. Second St., Long Beach CA 90803-5163. Phone/fax: (562)434-4523. E-mail: mjohn5150@aol.com. Website: www.pearlmag.com. **Contact:** Marilyn Johnson, fiction editor. Award to "provide a larger forum and help widen publishing opportunities for fiction writers in the small press; and to help support the continuing publication of *Pearl*." Annual competition for short stories. Award: $250, publication in *Pearl* and 10 copies. Competition receives approximately 100 submissions. Judges: Editors of *Pearl* (Marilyn Johnson, Joan Jobe Smith, Barbara Hauk). $10 entry fee per story. Includes copy of magazine featuring winning story. Guidelines for SASE or visit website. Accepts inquiries by e-mail or fax. Deadline: May 15. Unpublished submissions. Length: 4,000 words maximum. Include a brief biographical note and SASE for reply or return of manuscript. Accepts simultaneous submissions, but asks to be notified if story is accepted elsewhere. All submissions are considered for publication in *Pearl*. "Although we are open to all types of fiction, we look most favorably upon coherent, well-crafted narratives, containing interesting, believable characters and meaningful situations." Winners announced and notified by mail in August. List of winners available for SASE, fax, e-mail or on website.

◯ ◎ **WILLIAM PEDEN PRIZE IN FICTION**, *The Missouri Review*, 1507 Hillcrest Hall, University of Missouri, Columbia MO 65211. (573)882-4474. Website: www.missourireview.org. **Contact:** Speer Morgan, Evelyn Somers, Hoa Ngo, editors. Annual award "to honor the best short story published in *The Missouri Review* each year." Submissions are to be previously published in the volume year for which the prize is awarded. Award: $1,000. No application process; all fiction published in *The Missouri Review* is automatically entered.

◑ ◎ **PEN CENTER USA WEST LITERARY AWARD IN FICTION**, PEN Center USA West, 672 S. LaFayette Park Place, #42, Los Angeles CA 90057. (213)365-8500. Fax: (213)365-9616. E-mail: awards@penusa.org. Website: www.penusa.org. **Contact:** Awards Coordinator. To recognize fiction writers who live in the western United States. Annual competition for published novels and story collections. Award: $1,000, plaque, and honored at a ceremony in Los Angeles. Competition receives 125 submissions. Judges: panel of writers, booksellers, editors. $25 fee for each book submitted. Guidelines available in July for SASE, fax, e-mail or on website. Accepts inquiries by fax, phone and e-mail. Deadline: December 20. Books published between January 1 and December 31 of 2002. Open only to writers living west of the Mississippi. All entries must include 4 non-returnable copies of each submission and a completed entry form. Winners announced in May and notified by phone and mail. List of winners available for SASE or on website.

◎ **PEN NEW ENGLAND/L.L. WINSHIP AWARD**, P.O. Box 400725, N. Cambridge MA 02140. (617)499-9550. Fax: (617)353-7134. E-mail: awards@pen-ne.org. Website: www.pen-ne.org. **Contact:** Mary Walsh, coordinator. Award to "acknowledge and praise a work of (published 2001) fiction, nonfiction or poetry with a New England topic and setting and/or by an author whose main residence is New England." Annual competition for novels and poetry. Award: $2,500. Competition receives 150 submissions. Five judges. Guidelines available in early October for SASE. Accepts inquiries by fax, e-mail and website. Deadline: December 15, 2002. Previously published submissions that appeared between January 1 and December 31 of the preceeding year. Winners announced mid-March and notified through publisher or PEN-NE Executive Board member. List of winners available in April by fax or phone.

◑ ◎ **PEN/BOOK-OF-THE-MONTH CLUB TRANSLATION PRIZE**, PEN American Center, 568 Broadway, New York NY 10012. (212)334-1660. E-mail: jm@pen.org. **Contact:** John Morrone, awards coordinator. Award "to recognize the art of the literary translator." Annual competition for translations. Award: $3,000. Deadline: December 15. Previously published submissions within the calendar year. "Translators may be of any nationality, but book must have been published in the US and must be a book-length literary translation." Books may be submitted by publishers, agents or translators. No application form. Send three copies. "Early submissions are strongly recommended."

▨ **THE PERALTA PRESS WRITING AWARDS**, The Peralta Press, 555 Atlantic Ave., Alameda CA 94501. Website: www.peraltapress.org. **Contact:** Jay Rubin, editor. Annual award for short stories. Prize: $250 plus publication. Receives approximately 50 entries. Judge: panel of English instructors. Entry fee: $10. Guidelines available in January for SASE and on website. Entries should be unpublished. Contest open to all writers. Results announced January 2003. Winners notified by mail. For list of winners, include SASE with submission or visit website.

◎ **PEW FELLOWSHIP IN THE ARTS**, 230 S. Broad St., Suite 1003, Philadelphia PA 19102. (215)875-2285. Fax: (215)875-2276. E-mail: pewarts@mindspring.com. Website: www.pewarts.org. **Contact:** Melissa Franklin, director; Christine Miller, program associate. "The Pew Fellowships in the Arts provides financial support directly to artists so that they may have the opportunity to dedicate themselves wholly to the development of their artwork for up to two years. A goal of the Pew Fellowships in the Arts is to provide such support at a critical juncture in an artist's career, when a concentration on artistic development and exploration is most likely to contribute to personal and professional growth." Annual fellowship is awarded in three of 12 fields. Award: up to 12 $50,000 fellowships/year. Competition receives 100-200 submissions per category. Judges: a panel of artists and arts professionals. Application and guidelines available in late August for SASE and on website. Accepts inquiries by SASE, fax, phone, website. Contest open to residents of Bucks, Chester, Delaware, Montgomery or Philadelphia counties aged 25 or older who have lived in-county for at least 2 years. No students. Winners announced June 2003 and notified by mail. List of winners will be mailed to entrants.

MARY ANN PFENNINGER LITERARY AWARD, GEM Literary, 4717 Poe Rd., Medina OH 44256-9745. (330)725-8807. E-mail: gemlit@earthlink.net. Website: www.gembooks.com. **Contact:** Darla Pfenninger, agent. Award to "honor unpublished authors in memory of the founder of the company and an author." Annual award for novels or story collections. Award: literary representation and cash awards for top three winners, as well as certificates for top ten. Competition receives 100 submissions. Judge: local and company readers give point values. Readers are assigned by genre; synopsis required. $20 entry fee plus return postage. Guidelines available July for SASE, e-mail or visit website. Accepts inquiries by e-mail. Deadline: June 30. Entries should be unpublished but will accept self-published, or e-books. Contest open to anyone over the age of 18. Winners announced in August 28 and notified by mail or webpage. List of winners available for SASE, e-mail, or visit website. Submit "thought-provoking stories with unique characters, well written, with a sense of humor."

◯ ◎ **JAMES D. PHELAN AWARD**, Intersection for the Arts/The San Francisco Foundation, 446 Valencia St., San Francisco CA 94103-3415. (415)626-2787. Fax: (415)626-1636. E-mail: info@theintersection.org. Website: www.theintersection.org. **Contact:** Kevin B. Chen, program director. Annual award "to author of an unpublished work-in-progress of fiction (novel or short story), nonfictional prose, poetry or drama." Award: $2,000 and certificate. Competition receives more than 160 submissions. All submissions are read by three initial readers (change from year to year) who forward ten submissions each on to three judges (change from year to year). Judges are established Bay Area writers with extensive publishing and teaching histories. Rules and entry forms available after October 15 for SASE. Deadline: January 31. Unpublished submissions. Applicant must have been born in the state of California, but need not be a current resident; must be 20-35 years old. Winners announced June 15 and notified by letter.

N ◯ ◎ PLAYBOY COLLEGE FICTION CONTEST, *Playboy* Magazine, 680 N. Lake Shore Dr., Chicago IL 60611. (312)751-8000. Website: www.playboy.com. Award "to foster young writing talent." Annual competition for short stories. Award: $3,000 plus publication in the magazine. Competition receives 1,000 submissions. Judges: Staff. Guidelines available for SASE or on website. Deadline: January 1. Submissions should be unpublished. No age limit; college affiliation required. Stories should be 25 pages or fewer. "Manuscripts are not returned. Results of the contest will be sent via SASE." Winners announced in February or March and notified by letter. List of winners available in February or March for SASE or on website.

◯ ◎ POCKETS FICTION WRITING CONTEST, *Pockets Magazine*, Upper Room Publications, P.O. Box 340004, Nashville TN 37203-0004. (615)340-7333. Fax: (615)340-7267. (No submissions.) E-mail: pockets@upperroo m.org (no submissions). Website: www.upperroom.org/pockets. **Contact:** Patricia McIntyre, editorial assistant. The purpose of the contest is to "find new freelance writers for the magazine." Annual competition for short stories. Award: $1,000 and publication. Competition receives 600 submissions. Judged by *Pockets* staff and staff of other Upper Room publications. Guidelines available for #10 SASE or on website. Accepts inquiries by e-mail and fax. No entry fee or entry form required. Submissions must be postmarked between March 1 and August 15. Deadline: August 15. Former winners may not enter. Unpublished submissions. Word length: 1,000-1,600 words. "No historical fiction, fantasy or talking animals." Winner announced November 1 and notified by mail. "Send SASE with 4 first-class stamps to request guidelines and a past issue."

◎ MARY RUFFIN POOLE AWARD FOR BEST WORK OF FICTION, North Carolina Literary and Historical Association, 4610 Mail Service Center, Raleigh NC 27699-4610. (919)733-9375. Fax: (919)733-8807. E-mail: michael.h ill@ncmail.net. **Contact:** Michael Hall, awards coordinator. "Presented annually to best first published book-length work of fiction." Annual competition for novels and story collections. Award: $1,000 and an engraved plate. Competition receives 5-10 submissions per award category. Judge: three judge panel. Guidelines available July 1, 2002 for SASE, fax, e-mail or call. Deadline: July 15, 2003. Entries should be previously published (3 copies). Contest open to residents of North Carolina, minimum residency of 3 years. Winners notified by mail in October. List of winners available for SASE, fax or e-mail.

◯ KATHERINE ANNE PORTER PRIZE FOR FICTION, *Nimrod International Journal of Prose and Poetry*, University of Tulsa, 600 S. College, Tulsa OK 74104-3189. (918)631-3080. Fax: (918)631-3033. E-mail: nimrod@utulsa .edu. Website: www.utulsa.edu/NIMROD. **Contact:** Francine Ringold, editor-in-chief. "To award promising writers and to increase the quality of manuscripts submitted to *Nimrod*." Annual award for short stories. Award: $2,000 (1st Prize), $1,000 (2nd Prize) plus publication and two contributors copies. Competiton receives approximately 500 entries/year. Judge varies each year. Past judges: Ron Carlson, Anita Shreve, Mark Doty, Gordon Lish, George Garrett, Toby Olson, John Leonard and Gladys Swan. $20 entry fee. Guidelines available after January for #10 SASE or by e-mail. Accepts inquiries by e-mail or by phone. Deadline: April 30. Previously unpublished manuscripts. Length: 7,500 words maximum. "Must be typed, double-spaced. Our contest is judged anonymously, so we ask that writers take their names off of their manuscripts. Include a cover sheet containing your name, full address, phone and the title of your work. Include a SASE for notification of the results. We encourage writers to read *Nimrod* before submission to discern whether or not their work is compatible with the style of our journal. Single issues are $10 (book rate postage included)." Winners announced in July and notified by mail. List of winners available for SASE with entry.

POTOMAC REVIEW FIFTH ANNUAL SHORT STORY CONTEST, Montgomery College, Paul Peck Humanities Institute, 51 Mannakee St., Rockville MD 20850. (301)610-4100. Fax: (301)738-1745. E-mail: mgolden@mc.cc.md. us. Website: www.montgomery.edu/potomacreview. **Contact:** Myrna Goldenberg, executive editor. Annual competition for short stories. Award: $500 and publication for each winner in the fall 2003 issue. Competition receives more than 50 submissions. Judge: A top, independent writer. "No fee per se but submittor asked take $18 year's subscription." Guidelines will be in the fall-winter 2003 issue, website, or send SASE for guidelines or order sample copy ($5 ppd). Deadline: January-March 31. Previously unpublished submissions. There are no limitations of style or provenance. Word length: up to 3,000 words. Winners announced by summer via SASE. "We seek thoughtful, provocative, insightful work."

◎ PRAIRIE SCHOONER READERS' CHOICE AWARDS, *Prairie Schooner*, 201 Andrews Hall, P.O. Box 880334, Lincoln NE 68588-0334. (402)472-0911. Fax: (402)472-9771. E-mail: eflanagan2@unl.edu. Website: www.unl. edu/schooner/psmain.htm. **Contact:** Hilda Raz, editor-in-chief. Awards to "honor work published the previous year in *Prairie Schooner*, including poetry, essays and fiction." Award: $250 each. "We usually award 4-8 of these." Judge: the editorial staff of *Prairie Schooner*. No entry fee. For guidelines, send SASE or visit website. "Only work published in *Prairie Schooner* in the previous year is considered." Work is nominated by the editorial staff. Winners announced in the Spring issue and notified by mail in February or March.

THE PRESIDIO LA BAHIA AWARD, The Sons of the Republic of Texas, 1717 8th St., Bay City TX 77414. (979)245-6644. Fax: (979)244-3819. E-mail: srttexas@srttexas.org. Website: www.srttexas.org. **Contact:** Janet Hickl, administrative assistant. "To promote suitable preservation of relics, appropriate dissemination of data, and research into our Texas heritage, with particular attention to the Spanish Colonial period." Annual competition for novels. Award: "A total of $2,000 is available annually for winning participants, with a minimum first place prize of $1,200 for the best published book. At its discretion, the SRT may award a second place book prize or a prize for the best published paper, article published in a periodical or project of a nonliterary nature." Judges: recognized authorities on Texas history. Guidelines available in June for SASE, by fax, e-mail or on website. Accepts inquiries by mail, fax and e-mail. Entries will be accepted from June 1 to September 30. Previously published submissions and completed projects. Competition is open to any person interested in the Spanish Colonial influence on Texas culture. Winners announced December and notified by phone and mail. List of winners available for SASE.

PRISM: Futuristic, Fantasy and Paranormal Sub-Genre Chapter of Romance Writers of America. E-mail: scarlet@vampire-books.com. Website: www.romance-ffp.com. **Contact:** Michele Hauf, contest coordinator. Award to "recognize excellence in paranormal romances and paranormals with a strong romantic theme." Annual award for novels. Award: "PRISM award for 1st place in 5 novel categories as well as novellas and short stories, certificates for 2nd and 3rd place in each category." Competition receives approximately 50 submissions. Judges: "Entries judged on a scale of 1-10 in 4 categories (FF&P elements, writing & style, emotional impact, romance elements); judged by published authors and readers." Entry fee $30. Guidelines available on website or by e-mail. Entries must be previously published submissions that appeared between January 2002-December 2002. "Books must be romances with paranormal elements (i.e., futuristic/fantasy, time travel, or paranormal), or be paranormals with strong romance theme. We accept both print and e-book entries. Romance must be central to the story, but the story must contain paranormal elements." Winner announced July 2003 and notified by mail or e-mail and on website.

PRISM INTERNATIONAL SHORT FICTION CONTEST, *Prism International*, Dept. of Creative Writing, University of British Columbia, Buchanan E462-1866 Main Mall, Vancouver, British Columbia V6T 1Z1 Canada. (604)822-2514. Fax: (604)822-3616. E-mail: prism@interchange.ubc.ca. Website: www.prism.arts.ubc.ca. **Contact:** Billeh Nickerson, editor. Award: $2,000; five $200 runner-up prizes. Competition receives 400-500 submissions. Deadline: January 31. Entry fee $22 plus $5 reading fee for each story; 1 year subscription included. Guidelines available May for SASE, fax, e-mail, or visit website. Accepts inquiries by fax, phone and e-mail. Winners announced in July and notified by mail. List of winners available for SASE or on website. "Read a few back issues of *PRISM International*, and then send us something brilliant!"

PULITZER PRIZE IN FICTION, Columbia University, 709 Journalism Bldg., Mail Code 3865, New York NY 10027-6902. (212)854-3841. Fax: (212)854-3342. E-mail: pulitzer@www.pulitzer.org. Website: www.pulitzer.org. **Contact:** Professor Sig Gessler, administrator. Annual award for distinguished short stories, novels and story collections *first* published in US in book form during the year by an American author, preferably dealing with American life. Award: $7,500 and certificate. Competition receives about 200 submissions. Guidelines and entry forms available in May 2002 for SASE, by phone, fax, e-mail and on website. Accepts inquiries by fax, phone and e-mail. Deadline: Books published between January 1 and June 30 must be submitted by July 1; books published between July 1 and October 31 must be submitted by November 1; books published between November 1 and December 31 must be submitted in galleys or page proofs by November 1. Submit 4 copies of the book, entry form, biography and photo of author and $50 handling fee. Open to American authors. Winners announced April 7 and notified by telegram. A list of winners will be available for SASE, fax, e-mail or on website.

PUSHCART PRIZE, Pushcart Press, P.O. Box 380, Wainscott NY 11975. (516)324-9300. **Contact:** Bill Henderson, president. Annual award "to publish and recognize the best of small press literary work." Previously published submissions, short stories, poetry or essays on any subject. Must have been published during the current calendar year. Award: Publication in *Pushcart Prize: Best of the Small Presses*. Deadline: December 1. Nomination by small press publishers/editors only.

QUARTERLY WEST NOVELLA COMPETITION, University of Utah, 200 S. Central Campus Dr., Room 317, Salt Lake City UT 84112-9109. (801)581-3938. Website: www.chronicle.utah.edu/QW/QW.html. **Contact:** Margot Schilpp or Lynn Kilpatrick, editors. Biennial award for novellas. Award: 2 prizes of $500 and publication in *Quarterly West*. Competition receives 300 submissions. Guidelines for SASE. Accepts inquiries by phone. Deadline: Postmarked between October 1-December 31. Winners announced in late May and notified by phone. List of winners available for SASE.

QUINCY WRITERS GUILD ANNUAL CREATIVE WRITING CONTEST, P.O. Box 433, Quincy IL 62306-0433. (217)885-3327. E-mail: chillebr@adams.net. Website: www.quincylibrary.org/guild.htm. **Contact:** Carol Hillebrenner, treasurer. "A contest to promote new writing." Annual competition for short stories, nonfiction, poetry. Awards: Cash for 1st, 2nd, 3rd Place entries; certificates for honorable mention. Competition receives approximately 150 submissions. Judges: Writing professionals not affiliated with Quincy Writers Guild. Entry fee $4 (fiction and nonfiction, each entry); $2 (poetry each entry). "Guidelines are very important." Guidelines available after July for SASE, by e-mail or on website. Accepts inquiries by e-mail or post. Deadline: April 1. Unpublished submissions. Word length: fiction and nonfiction, 2,000 words; poetry, 2 pages maximum, any style. No entry form is required. Entries accepted after January 1. Winners announced June and at July annual meeting and notified by mail in late June. List of winners available after July for SASE or by e-mail. "2003 is the last year for QWG's writing contest. We appreciate all those who have entered our contest and hope we've encouraged good writers."

DAVID RAFFELOCK AWARD FOR PUBLISHING EXCELLENCE, National Writers Assn., 3140 S. Peoria #295, Aurora CO 80014. (303)841-0246. Fax: (303)841-2607. E-mail: sandywrter@aol.com. Website: http://www.nation alwriters.com. **Contact:** Sandy Whelchel, executive director. Award to "assist published authors in marketing their works and promoting them." Annual award for novels, story collections. Award: $5,000 value promotional tour and services of a publicist. Judges: publishers and agents. $100 entry fee. Guidelines available for SASE, e-mail or on website. Accepts inquiries by fax, e-mail, phone. Deadline: May 1 annually. Entries should be previously published. Contest open to anyone with a published book in the English language. Winners are announced in June at the NWAF Conference and notified by mail or phone. List of winners available for SASE or visit website.

🌊 ◎ **SIR WALTER RALEIGH AWARD**, North Carolina Literary and Historical Association, 4611 Mail Service Center, Raleigh NC 27699-4610. (919)733-9375. **Contact:** Michael Hill, awards coordinator. "To promote among the people of North Carolina an interest in their own literature." Annual award for novels. Award: Statue of Sir Walter Raleigh. Competition receives 8-12 submissions. Judges: University English and history professors. Guidelines available in August for SASE. Accepts inquiries by fax. Deadline: July 15, 2002. Book must be an original work published during the 12 months ending June 30 of the year for which the award is given. Writer must be a legal or physical resident of North Carolina for the three years preceding the close of the contest period. Authors or publishers may submit 3 copies of their book to the above address. Winners announced October and notified by mail. List of winners available for SASE.

◎ **THE REA AWARD FOR THE SHORT STORY**, Dungannon Foundation, 53 W. Church Hill Rd., Washington CT 06794. (860)868-9455. Website: www.reaaward.org. **Contact:** Elizabeth Rea, president. Annual award "sponsored by the Dungannon Foundation, the Rea Award was established in 1986 by Michael M. Rea to honor a living U.S. or Canadian writer who has made a significant contribution to the short story form. Award cannot be applied for. The recipient is nominated and selected by an annually appointed jury." Award: $30,000. Judges: 3 jurors. Award announced in spring annually. Winners available on website.

🌐 **REAL WRITERS/THE BOOK PL@CE SHORT STORY AWARDS**, (formerly Real Writers Short Story Competition), *REAL Writers* Support and Appraisal Services for Aspiring Writers, P.O. Box 170, Chesterfield, Derbyshire, S40 1FE United Kingdom. Phone/fax: (+44)01246-238492. E-mail: info@real-writers.com. Website: www.real-writers.com. **Contact:** Lynne Patrick, coordinator. Award to "provide a regular outlet for short fiction." Annual competition for short stories. Award: One prize of £2,500 ($3,500); ten category prizes of £100 each, including dedicated prizes for international and online entries. Winners published in an anthology, and runners-up are considered for publication in a leading magazine for writers. 2001 competition received 3,000 submissions. Judge: Winners selected for a shortlist by a senior editor from a major publishing house; Diane Pearson of Transworld in 2001, Francesca Liversidge of Bantam in 2002. Shortlist chosen by an experienced panel. £5 or $10 entry fee; optional critique for extra fee. Guidelines available May 2002 for SASE, e-mail or visit website. Accepts inquiries by fax, e-mail, phone. Deadline: September 30, 2002. Entries must be unpublished. Contest open to anyone. Length: 5,000 words. Winners announced February 2002 and notified by phone or mail. List of winners posted on website.

🅽 **REFLECTIONS SHORT FICTION AWARD**, *Reflections Literary Journal*, Piedmont Community College, P.O. Box 1197, Roxboro NC 27573. (336)599-1181, ext. 428. E-mail: thrasht@piedmont.cc.nc.us. **Contact:** Tami Sloane Thrasher, editor. "This annual contest is designed to encourage and reward authors writing quality short fiction." Annual award for short stories. Prize: publication, $250 award and 5 contributor's copies. "New contest—expect approximately 100 entries." Judge: each entry is evaluated and ranked by *Reflections* editorial panel, usually consisting of between 6-10 readers. Judges read for appropriateness for publication in *Reflections* and for overall literary quality. $10 reading fee per story; "the fees are used exclusively for advertising and publication costs of the journal." For guidelines, send SASE or e-mail. Accepts inquiries by e-mail. Deadline: December 31 annually. Entries should be unpublished. Contest open to all writers. Length: 5,000 words maximum. "Writers submitting work appropriate for *Reflections* will more than likely be more successful than writers who are unfamiliar with our journal and our readership." Winners announced in March. Winners notified by mail. List of winners available for SASE or by e-mail.

◎ **REGIONAL BOOK AWARDS**, Mountains & Plains Booksellers Association, 19 Old Town Square, Suite 238, Ft. Collins CO 80524. (970)484-5856. Fax: (970)407-1479. E-mail: lisa@mountainsplains.org. Website: www.mountains plains.org. **Contact:** Lisa Knudsen, director. Purpose: "to honor outstanding books set in the Mountains and Plains

---

MARKET CONDITIONS are constantly changing! If you're still using this book and it is 2004 or later, buy the newest edition of *Novel & Short Story Writer's Market* at your favorite bookstore or order from Writer's Digest Books by calling 1-800-448-0915.

regions." Annual competition for one children's book and three adult books in fiction, non-fiction and poetry/art. Award: $500 and framed copy of Regional Book Awards Poster. "There are two panels of judges, one for adult books and one for children's. Each panel consists of 3-5 persons selected by the Awards Committee." Guidelines available for SASE, fax, e-mail, visit website or call. Deadline: November 1. Entries should be previously published. The book must be published for the first time within the year under consideration, November 1 through October 31. Contest open to all; "however, should relate to our region." Winners announced January 2003 and notified by phone December 2003. List of winners available by visiting website.

LOUISE E. REYNOLDS MEMORIAL FICTION AWARD, the new renaissance, 26 Heath Rd., #11, Arlington MA 02474-3645. (781)646-0118. **Contact:** Louise T. Reynolds, editor-in-chief. Award established to "honor *tnr*'s founding manager, Louise E. Reynolds; to recognize and reward *tnr*'s writers; to promote quality writing in independent literary magazines." Award is for fiction, including bilingual translations. Prize: $500; $250; $125; one $50 honorable mention. Program receives 350-450 submissions a year. Judges: Independent and new each volume. "We usually ask writers or critics who are familiar with *tnr*." $16.50 entry fee required; subscribers pay $11.50; entrants from outside US pay $18, subscribers pay $13. Guidelines available for SASE or e-mail. Deadline: January 2-June 30 and September 1-October 31. Accepts inquiries by e-mail. Entries should be unpublished. "All fiction submissions are tied into award program." Only fiction published in a 3-issue volume of *tnr* is considered for award. Contest open to all writers of serious or quality or literary fiction. Length: 3-36 pages; double-spaced. Winners announced after publication of the third issue in a volume of *tnr*. Winners notified by mail within 1 month of publication. List of winners available for SASE/IRC or e-mail.

N ● THE MARY ROBERTS RINEHART AWARDS, Mail Stop Number 3E4, English Dept., George Mason University Creative Writing Program, 4400 University Dr., Fairfax VA 22030-4444. (703)993-1185. E-mail: wmiller@gmu.edu. **Contact:** William Miller, director. Annual award in fiction, nonfiction, and poetry by unpublished writers (that is, no book publications, and no previously published work may be submitted to this competition). Award: Three awards, one in each category each year (about $2,000 each). Competition receives approximately 125 submissions. Guidelines for SASE or e-mail. Accepts inquiries by e-mail and phone. Deadline: November 30. Writers must be nominated by a sponsoring writer, writing teacher, editor, or agent. Winners announced in Spring and notified by mail. List of winners available for SASE.

N ○ RIVER CITY WRITING AWARD IN FICTION, *River City*, Dept. of English, The University of Memphis, Memphis TN 38152. (901)678-4591. Awards Coordinator: Thomas Russell. "Annual award to reward the best short stories." Award: $1,500 (1st Prize); $350 (2nd Prize); $150 (3rd Prize). Competition receives approximately 600 submissions. Judge: To be announced (published author). Entry fee $12 which includes a subscription to *River City*. Guidelines available with SASE. Deadline: March 1. Unpublished fiction. Open to all writers. Word length: 7,500 maximum. Winners announced in June and notified by phone and mail.

◐ ◎ SUMMERFIELD G. ROBERTS AWARD, The Sons of the Republic of Texas, 1717 8th St., Bay City TX 77414. (409)245-6644. Fax: (979)244-3819. E-mail: srttexas@srttexas.org. Website: www.srttexas.org. **Contact:** Janet Hickl, administrative assistant. "Given for the best book or manuscript of biography, essay, fiction, nonfiction, novel, poetry or short story that describes or represents the Republic of Texas, 1836-1846." Annual award of $2,500. Competition receives 10-20 submissions. Competition is judged by a panel comprised of winners of the last three years' competitions. Guidelines available after June for SASE, by fax, e-mail or on website. Accepts inquiries by fax and e-mail. Deadline: January 15. "The manuscripts must be written or published during the calendar year for which the award is given. Entries are to be submitted in quintuplicate and will not be returned." Winners announced March and notified by mail or phone. List of winners available for SASE.

N ○ THE SANDSTONE PRIZE IN SHORT FICTION, Ohio State University Press, 1070 Carmack Rd., Columbus OH 43210-1002. (614)292-6930. Fax: (614)292-2065. E-mail: ohiostatepress@osu.edu. Website: www.ohiostatepress.org. **Contact:** Lee Martin, fiction editor. Competition for short stories or novellas. Award: $1,500; publication under standard book contract; invitation to direct a creative writing workshop at Ohio State; public reading. Judges: Independent judge. Entry fee $20 payable to the Ohio State University. Guidelines on website. Open to all writers in English, published or unpublished; Ohio State students or employees are ineligible. Deadline: January 31. Manuscript: "Must be typed double-spaced on white paper, about 300 words per page, one side only, pages numbered consecutively. Crisp photocopies are fine." Include "cover sheet with name, street and e-mail addresses, phone number(s); acknowledgements page with publication history for any previously published works; title page giving the title and approximate word count; a table of contents page listing only the stories and/or novellas by page numbers." Length: 150-300 typed pages (approximately 40,000-80,000 words); as part of collection, novellas less than 125 pages (approximately 35,000 words). Manuscripts not returned. Winners announced in May. Include SASE with ms for results.

MARJORY BARTLETT SANGER SHORT FICTION CONTEST, The Anthology of New England Writers, 151 Main St., Box 483, Windsor VT 0508-0483. (802)674-2315. E-mail: newvtpoet@aol.com. Website: www.hometown.aol.com/newvtpoet/myhomepage/index.html. **Contact:** Dr. Frank Anthony or Susan C. Anthony, co-directors. "To discover individual writing of integrity and timelessness." Annual competition for short stories. Award: $300; three to five $30 honorable mentions. Judge: Reeve Lindbergh. $6 one fiction entry fee; $5 two or more entries. Guidelines for SASE, e-mail, visit website or call. Deadline: June 15. Entries should be unpublished. Contest open to all writers. Length: 1,000 words. "Send your best work." Winners notified by mail or phone in July after conference. List of winners available for SASE.

THE SCARS/CC&D EDITOR'S CHOICE AWARDS, Scars Publications and Design/Children, Churches & Daddies Magazine, 829 Brian Court, Gurnee IL 60031-3155. E-mail: ccandd96@aol.com. Website: http://scars.tv. **Contact:** Janet Kuypers, editor/publisher. Award to "showcase good writing in an annual book." Annual competition for short stories. Award: publication of story/essay and one copy of book. $13 entry fee per written piece. For guidelines, visit website. Accepts inquiries by e-mail. Deadline: "Revolves for appearing in different upcoming books as winners." Entries may be unpublished or previously published. Contest open to anyone. Length: "We appreciate shorter works. Shorter stories, more vivid and more real storylines in writing have a good chance." Winners announced at book publication, online and notified by mail when book is printed. List of winners available for SASE or e-mail.

◻ ◎ **SCIENCE FICTION WRITERS OF EARTH (SFWoE) SHORT STORY CONTEST**, Science Fiction Writers of Earth, P.O. Box 121293, Fort Worth TX 76121-1293. (817)451-8674. E-mail: sfwoe@flash.net. Website: www.flash.net/~sfwoe. **Contact:** Gilbert Gordon Reis, SFWoE administrator. Purpose "to promote the art of science fiction/fantasy short story writing." Annual award for short stories. Award: $200 (1st Prize); $100 (2nd Prize); $50 (3rd Prize). First place story is published by *Altair—Magazine of Speculative Fiction*. *Altair* also pays 1¢/word to the author of the winning story on publication. "If *Altair* is unable to publish the winning story, SFWoE will place the story on their website for 180 days and pay the author $75 in addition to the $200 prize money." Competition receives approximately 240 submissions/year. Judge: Author Edward Bryant. Entry fee $5 for first entry; $2 for additional entries. Guidelines available after November for SASE, e-mail, or print from website. Accepts inquiries by e-mail and phone. Deadline: October 30. Submissions must be unpublished. The author must not have received payment for a published piece of fiction. Stories should be science fiction or fantasy, 2,000-7,500 words. "Visit our website and read the winning story in our online newsletter to know what the judge looks for in a good story. Contestants enjoy international competition." Winners announced January 31 and notified by phone or e-mail. "Each contestant is mailed the contest results, judge's report, and a listing of the top ten contestants." Send separate SASE for complete list of the contest stories and contestants (or print from website).

N ◎ **SCRIPTAPALOOZA**, Final Draft Inc., 7775 Sunset Blvd. PMB #200, Hollywood CA 90046. (323)654-5809. E-mail: info@scriptapalooza.com. Website: www.scriptapalooza.com. **Contact:** Mark Andrushko, president. Annual competition for screenwriting. Award: first prize, $10,000. Top three will be considered by major production companies. Ten runners-up have loglines submitted to same production companies. Top 30 entries receive software. Competition receives 1,000-2,000 submissions. $40-50 entry fee. Guidelines available now. For guidelines, send SASE, e-mail or visit website. Accepts inquiries by e-mail, phone. Deadline: January 2 (earlybird deadline $35); March 1 (first deadline $40); April 15 (final deadline $45). No pornography accepted. Length: 80-140 pages (proper screenwriting format). Winners announced August 15 and notified by mail, phone.

N ◎ **SCRIPTAPALOOZA TV**, 7775 Sunset Blvd. PMB #200, Hollywood CA 90046. (323)654-5809. E-mail: info@scriptapalooza.com. Website: www.scriptapaloozatv.com. **Contact:** Mark Andrushko, president. Award to "discover talented writers who have an interest in American television writing." Biannual competition for TV spec scripts and pilots. Award: $500 to top three winners in each category (total $1,500) plus software, production company consideration and possible pitch meetings. Competition receives 400-500 submissions in each category. Judge: Three founders of the company—Mark Andrushko, Genevieve Cibor and Kelli Bennett. $35 entry fee. Guidelines available now. For guidelines, send SASE, visit website. Accepts inquiries by e-mail, phone. Deadline: May 15, 2002 and November 15, 2002. Entries should be unpublished. Contest open to any vwriter 18 years or older. Length: standard television format whether one hour, one-half hour or pilot. "Pilots whould be fresh and new and easy to visualize. Spec scripts should be current with the shows, up-to-date storylines, characters, etc." Winners announced February 15 and August 15 and notified by mail, phone as soon as possible. List of winners available by visiting website.

◻ ◎ **SEVENTEEN MAGAZINE FICTION CONTEST**, *Seventeen Magazine*, 1440 Broadway, 13th Floor, New York NY 10018. (212)407-9700. Fax: (212)407-9899. Website: www.seventeen.com. **Contact:** Attn: Fiction Contest Rules. Awarded to "honor best short fiction by a young writer." Competition receives 1,000-2,000 submissions. Guidelines for SASE. Rules published in late fall issue. Contest for 13-21 year olds. Deadline: April 30. Submissions judged by a panel of outside readers, former winners and *Seventeen*'s editors. Cash awarded to winners. First-place story published in 2003 issue. Winners notified by mail. List of winners available for SASE.

◖ ◎ **SFWA NEBULA® AWARDS**, Science-Fiction and Fantasy Writers of America, Inc., 532 La Guardia Place #632, New York NY 10012-1428. President: Michael Capobianco. Annual awards for previously published short stories, novels, novellas, novelettes. Science fiction/fantasy only. "No submissions; nominees upon recommendation of members only." Deadline: December 31. "Works are nominated throughout the year by active members of the SFWA."

◎ **FRANCES SHAW FELLOWSHIP FOR OLDER WOMEN WRITERS**, The Ragdale Foundation, 1260 N. Green Bay Rd., Lake Forest IL 60045-1106. (847)234-1063, ext. 205. E-mail: ragdaleevents@aol.com. Website: www.ragdale.org. **Contact:** Sylvia Brown, director of programming and marketing. Award to "nurture and support older women writers who are just beginning to write seriously." Annual competition for short stories, novels and poetry.

Award: 6 weeks free residency at Ragdale, plus domestic travel. Competition receives 760 submissions. Judges: a panel of four anonymous women writers. Guidelines available for SASE. Accepts inquiries by fax or e-mail. Deadline: February 1. Previously unpublished submissions. Contest open to females over 55. Length: 20 pages/12 short poems. "Make your letter of application interesting, covering your desire to write and the reasons you have been thwarted to this point." Winners announced in April and notified by phone.

SHORT GRAIN CONTEST, Box 67, Saskatoon, Saskatchewan S7K 3K1 Canada. (306)244-2828. Fax: (306)244-0255. E-mail: grain.mag@sasktel.net. Website: www.grainmagazine.ca. ("E-mail entries not accepted.") **Contact:** Jennifer Still, business administrator. Annual competition for postcard stories, prose poems, dramatic monologues and creative non-fiction. Awards: 3 prizes of $500 in each category. Competition receives approximately 900 submissions. Judges: Blind judging; Tim Lilbern (prose poem), Anne Fleming (postcard story), Eugene Stickland (monologue). Query first. $25 basic entry fee includes one-year subscription. US and International entries in US dollars. US writers add $4 US postage. International writers add $6 US postage. Guidelines available by fax, e-mail, on website, for SASE or SAE and IRC. Deadline: January 31. Unpublished submissions. Contest entries must be either an original postcard story (a work of narrative fiction written in 500 words or less) or a prose poem (a lyric poem written as a prose paragraph or paragraphs in 500 words or less), a dramatic monologue (a self-contained speech given by a single character in 500 words or less) or creative nonfiction (a creative, nonfiction prose piece in 5,000 words or less). Winners announced April and notified by phone, e-mail and mail. List of winners available for SASE by e-mail, fax, on website.

SIDE SHOW 8TH SHORT STORY CONTEST, Somersault Press, 404 Vista Heights Rd., El Cerrito CA 94530. E-mail: jisom@atdial.net. **Contact:** Shelley Anderson, editor. Award "to attract quality writers for our 300-odd page paperback fiction anthology." Awards: $100 (1st Prize); $75 (2nd Prize); $50 (3rd Prize); $5/printed page paid to all accepted writers (on publication). Competition receives approximately 1,000 submissions. Judges: The editors of *Side Show*. $10 entry fee (includes recent issue of *Side Show*). No guidelines or restrictions on length or style. No genre, essays or novels. For informational leaflet, send SASE or e-mail. Accepts inquiries by e-mail. Sample copy for $10 plus $2 postage. Multiple submissions (in same mailing envelope) encouraged (only one entry fee required for each writer). Will critique if requested. "No deadline. Book published when we accept 20-30 stories." Winners notified before printing and announced upon publication.

SKIPPING STONES HONOR AWARDS, P.O. Box 3939, Eugene OR 97403-0939. (541)342-4956. Fax: (541)342-4956. E-mail: skipping@efn.org. Website: www.efn.org/~skipping. **Contact:** Arun N. Toké, executive editor. Award to "promote multicultural and/or nature awareness through creative writings for children and teens." Annual competition for short stories, novels, story collection, poetry and nonfiction. Award: honor certificates; seals; reviews; press release/publicity. Competition receives 125 submissions. Judges: "A multicultural committee of teachers, librarians, parents, students and editors." $50 entry fee ($25 for small/low income publishers/self-publishers). Guidelines for SASE or e-mail and on website. Accepts inquiries by e-mail, fax and phone. Deadline: January 15 annually. Previously published submissions that appeared in print between January 2001 and January 2003. Writer may submit own work or can be nominated by publisher, authors or illustrators. "We seek authentic, exceptional, child/youth friendly books that promote intercultural/international/intergenerational harmony and understanding through creative ways. Writings that come out of your own experiences/cultural understanding seem to have an edge." Winners announced April and notified through press release, personal notifications and by publishing reviews of winning titles. List of winners available for SASE, e-mail or on website.

THE BERNICE SLOTE AWARD, *Prairie Schooner*, 201 Andrews Hall, P.O. Box 880334, Lincoln NE 68588-0334. (402)472-0911. Fax: (402)472-9771. E-mail: eflanagan2@unl.edu. Website: www.unl.edu/schooner/psmain.htm. **Contact:** Hilda Raz, editor-in-chief. Award to "recognize the best work by a beginning writer published in *Prairie Schooner* in the previous year, including stories, essays and poetry." Award: $500. Judge: Competition is judged by the editorial staff of *Prairie Schooner*. No entry fee. For guidelines, send SASE, or visit website. "Only work published in *Prairie Schooner* in the previous year will be considered." Work is nominated by the editorial staff. Winners announced in the Spring issue and notified by mail in February or March.

KAY SNOW CONTEST, Willamette Writers, 9045 SW Barbur Blvd., Suite 5-A, Portland OR 97219-4027. (503)452-1592. Fax: (503)452-0372. E-mail: wilwrite@teleport.com. Website: www.willamettewriters.com. **Contact:** Bill Johnson, office manager. Award "to create a showcase for writers of all fields of literature." Annual competition for short stories; also poetry (structured and nonstructured), nonfiction, juvenile and student writers and screenwriters. Award: $300 (1st Prize) in each category, second and third prizes, honorable mentions. Competition receives approximately 400 submissions. $500 Liam Cullen Memorial Award for best overall entry to the contest. Judges: nationally recognized writers and teachers. $15 entry fee, nonmembers; $10, members; students free. Guidelines for #10 SASE, fax, e-mail or website. Accepts inquiries by fax, phone and e-mail. Deadline: May 15 postmark. Unpublished submissions. 2 poems with maximum 5 double-spaced pages per entry fee. Winners announced August and notified by mail and phone. List of winners available for SASE. Prize winners will be honored at the two-day August Willamette Writers Conference. Press releases will be sent to local and national media announcing the winners, and excerpts from winning entries may appear in our newsletter.

SOCIETY OF CHILDREN'S BOOK WRITERS AND ILLUSTRATORS GOLDEN KITE AWARDS, Society of Children's Book Writers and Illustrators, 8271 Beverly Blvd., Los Angeles CA 90048. (323)782-

1010. **Contact:** Mercedes Coats, chair. Annual award. "To recognize outstanding works of fiction, nonfiction and picture illustration for children by members of the Society of Children's Book Writers and Illustrators and published in the award year." Published submissions should be submitted from January to December of publication year. Deadline: December 15. Rules for SASE. Award: Statuette and plaque. Looking for quality material for children. Individual "must be member of the SCBWI to submit books."

◻ ◎ **SOCIETY OF CHILDREN'S BOOK WRITERS AND ILLUSTRATORS WORK-IN-PROGRESS GRANTS,** 8271 Beverly Blvd., Los Angeles CA 90048. (323)782-1010. **Contact:** SCBWI. Annual grant for any genre or contemporary novel for young people; also nonfiction research grant and grant for work whose author has never been published. Award: $1,500 (1st Prize), $500 (2nd Prize). Work-in-progress. Competition receives approximately 180 submissions. Judges: Members of children's book field—editors, authors, etc. Guidelines for SASE. Deadline: February 1-May 1. Entries must be unpublished. Applicants must be SCBWI members.

N ◎ SOUTH CAROLINA ARTS COMMISSION AND THE POST AND COURIER SOUTH CARO-LINA FICTION PROJECT, 1800 Gervais St., Columbia SC 29201. (803)734-8696. Website: www.state.sc.us/arts. **Contact:** Sara June Goldstein, program director for the literary arts, "This annual writing competition calls for previously unpublished short stories of 2,500 words or less. The stories do not need to be Southern, nor do they need to be set in South Carolina, although such stories are acceptable for consideration. Up to 12 short stories will be selected for publication; each writer whose work is selected will receive $500 from *The Post and Courier*, which purchases first publication rights. Stories will also be published electronically by posting them on *The Post and Courier* website, which links to the Art Commission's website. The applicant must be a legal resident of South Carolina and be 18 years of age or older at the time of application." Deadline: January 15. Guidelines and application available on website.

N ◎ SOUTH CAROLINA ARTS COMMISSION ANNUAL PROJECTS FOR INDIVIDUAL ARTISTS GRANTS, 1800 Gervais St., Columbia SC 29201. (803)734-8696. Website: www.state.sc.us/arts. **Contact:** Sara June Goldstein, program director for the literary arts. "This category is designed to support specific arts activities that promote individual artists' professional development or career advancement. Projects that promote excellence in an arts discipline and make such excellence accessible for general community-wide audiences are also encouraged. Annual project grants are awarded to help pay actual project costs; ordinary living expenses during the project cannot be supported with SCAC funds. The applicant must be a practicing artist in literature; be a legal resident of the U.S. and South Carolina with a permanent residence in the state for 6 months prior to the application date and throughout the grant period; not be a degree-seeking, full-time student during the grant period; and be 18 years of age or older at the time of application." Deadline: April 1 for twelve-month period July 1-June 30. "Requests must be over $1,000 and no more than $5,000. Match is 1:2 (applicant:SCAC), and 100% of applicant's match must be cash." Guidelines and application available on website.

N ◎ SOUTH CAROLINA ARTS COMMISSION INDIVIDUAL ARTIST FELLOWSHIPS, 1800 Gervais St., Columbia SC 29201. (803)734-8696. Website: www.state.sc.us/arts. **Contact:** Sara June Goldstein, program director for the literary arts. "Fellowships recognize and award the artistic achievements of South Carolina's exceptional individual artists. Fellowship awards are made through a highly competitive process and are based on only one criterion: artistic excellence. The fellowship awards bring recognition that may open the doors to other resources and employment opportunities. The applicant must be a legal resident of the U.S. and South Carolina with a permanent residence in the state for two years prior to the application date and throughout the fellowship period; be a practicing individual artist; not be a degree-seeking, full-time student during the award period; and be 18 years of age or older at the time of application." Deadline: October 1, 2002 for fiscal year 2004 award categories including Poetry and Prose (fiction or creative nonfiction). Award: $5,000 per fellowship. Guidelines and application available on website.

N ◎ SOUTH CAROLINA ARTS COMMISSION QUARTERLY PROJECTS FOR ARTISTS GRANTS, 1800 Gervais St., Columbia SC 29201. (803)734-8696. Website: www.state.sc.us/arts. **Contact:** Sara June Goldstein, program director for the literary arts. "This category is designed to support specific arts activities that promote individual artists' professional development or career advancement. Projects that promote excellence in an arts discipline and make such excellence accessible for general community-wide audiences are also encouraged. Quarterly project grants are awarded to help pay actual project costs; ordinary living expenses during the project cannot be supported with SCAC funds. The Arts Commission will not review or fund quarterly project grants applications from a resident of a county that has a subgranting arts council. The applicant must be a practicing artist in literature; be a legal resident of the U.S. and South Carolina with a permanent residence in the state for 6 months prior to the application date and throughout the grant period; not be a degree-seeking, full-time student during the grant period; and be 18 years of age or older at the time of application." Deadline: May 15 for the July-September quarter; August 15 for the October-December quarter; November 15 for the January-March quarter; February 15 for the April-June quarter. "Applicant may request up to $1,000 per award. Match is 1:2 (applicant:SCAC), and 100% of the applicant's match must be cash." Guidelines and application available on website.

◎ **SOUTH DAKOTA ARTS COUNCIL,** 800 Governors Dr., Pierre SD 57501-2294. (605)773-3131. E-mail: sdac@stlib.state.sd.us. Website: www.sdarts.org. **Contact:** Dennis Holub, executive director. "Individual Artist Grants (up to $3,000) and Artists Collaboration Grant (up to $6,000) are planned for the fiscal year 2003 through 2004." Guidelines and application available on website and by mail. Deadline: March 1. Grants are open only to residents of

South Dakota. Students pursuing an undergraduate or graduate degree are ineligible. Applicants must submit application form with an original signature; current résumé no longer than 5 pages; appropriate examples of artistic work (see guidelines); up to 5 pages additional documentation (see guidelines); SASE with adequate postage for ms return (if desired).

N **☐** **◎** **SOUTHERN HEAT CONTEST**, Romance Writers of America—East Texas Chapter (RWA-ETC), P.O. Box 131322, Tyler TX 75713-1322. E-mail: JanWJE@aol.com. Website: www.home.earthlink.net/~ralsobrook/rwaetc.htm. **Contact:** Wanda J. English, contest coordinator. Send entries to Southern Heat Contest, Wanda English, 4439 CD 4105 North, Overton TX 75684. Competition established "to bring talented unpublished writers to the attention of editors who buy the type of fiction they write. Competition motto is 'Today's contest winners are tomorrow's published authors.' " Annual award for romance novels with five categories: historical, contemporary, paranormal/futuristic, mainstream/single title, inspirational. Award: $15 (1st Prize); $10 (2nd Prize); certificates to first, second, third places and honorable mention in all categories. Winner in each category has complete ms read by judge/editor. Competition receives 5-30 submissions per category. First round judged by published authors who provide extensive critiques. Final round judged by editors of major publishing houses (Berkley/Jove, Pocket, etc.). Entry fees: $15 RWA-ETC members, $20 RWA members and $25 for all others. Guidelines available in June for SASE or e-mail. Deadline: August 15. Entries should be unpublished. Published authors may submit entry in category in which they are not previously published. Entrants must be over 18 years of age. Length: Submit first 10 ms pages plus 5-page synopsis. "Editors like an intriguing 'hook' that is appropriate to category and strong brief summary (synopsis)."

◖ **THE SOUTHERN REVIEW/LOUISIANA STATE UNIVERSITY SHORT FICTION AWARD**, *The Southern Review*, 43 Allen Hall, Louisiana State University, Baton Rouge LA 70803-5005. (225)578-5108. Fax: (225)578-5098. E-mail: bmacon@lsu.edu. Website: www.lsu.edu/thesouthernreview. **Contact:** John Easterly, associate editor. Annual award "to recognize the best first collection of short stories by an American writer published in the United States during the past year." Award: $500, possible campus reading. Competition receives 40-60 submissions. Judges: committee of editors and faculty members. Guidelines available for SASE. Accepts inquiries by fax and e-mail. Deadline: January 31. Two copies to be submitted by publisher or author. Winner announced summer and notified by mail or phone.

N **◎** **SPUR AWARDS**, Western Writers of America, Inc., 1012 Fair St., Franklin TN 37064. Phone/fax: (615)791-1444. E-mail: TNcrutch@aol.com. Website: www.westernwriters.org. **Contact:** Awards Coordinator. Purpose of award is to "reward quality in the fields of western fiction and nonfiction." Annual award for short stories and novels as well as poetry and nonfiction. Prize: trophy. Competition receives 25-30 submissions per category. No entry fee. Guidelines for 2003 competition available in August 2002. Send SASE. Deadline: December 31, 2002. Entries must be published in contest year. Contest open to all writers. Winners announced annually in summer. Winners notified by mail. List of winners available for SASE.

☐ **◎** **WALLACE E. STEGNER FELLOWSHIP**, Creative Writing Program, Stanford University, Stanford CA 94305-2087. (650)725-1208. Fax: (650)723-3679. E-mail: gay-pierce@forsythe.stanford.edu. Website: www.stanford.edu/dept/english/cw. **Contact:** Gay Pierce, program administrator. Annual award for short stories, novels, poetry and story collections. Five fellowships in fiction ($22,000 stipend plus required tuition of approximately $6,000). Competition receives 700 submissions. $50 entry fee. Guidelines available in July for SASE, by e-mail and on website. Accepts inquiries by phone and e-mail. Deadline: December 1. For unpublished or previously published fiction writers. Residency required. Word length: 9,000 words or 40 pages. Winners announced April and notified by telephone in mid-March. List of winners will be on website.

N **◎** **STONY BROOK $1,000 SHORT FICTION PRIZE**, Department of English, Humanities Bldg., State University of New York, Stony Brook NY 11794-5350. (516)632-7400. E-mail: Carolyn.McGrath@stonybrook.edu. Website: www.sunysb.edu/fictionprize. **Contact:** Carolyn McGrath, director. Award "to recognize excellent undergraduate fiction." Annual competition for short stories. Award: $1,000. Competition receives 150-200 submissions. Judges: Faculty of the Department of English & Creative Writing Program. No entry fee. Guidelines for SASE or on website. Accepts inquiries by e-mail. Deadline: March 7, 2003. Unpublished submissions. "Only undergraduates enrolled full time in American or Canadian colleges and universities for the academic year 2002-2003 are eligible. Proof required. Students of all races and backgrounds are encouraged to enter." Word length: 7,500 words or less. Winners notified by phone; results posted on website 2003.

❦ **☐** **SUB-TERRAIN ANNUAL SHORT STORY CONTEST**, *sub-TERRAIN Magazine*, P.O. Box 3008, Vancouver, British Columbia V6B 3X5 Canada. (604)876-8710. Fax: (604)879-2667. E-mail: subter@portal.ca. Website: www.anvilpress.com. **Contact:** Brian Kaufman, managing editor. Award "to inspire writers to get down to it and struggle with a form that is condensed and difficult. To encourage clean, powerful writing." Annual award for short stories. Award: $500 and publication. Runners-up also receive publication. Competition receives 150-200 submissions. Judges: An editorial collective. Entry fee $20 for one story, $5 extra for each additional story (includes 3-issue subscription). Guidelines available in November for SASE. "Contest kicks off in November." Deadline: May 15. Unpublished submissions. Length: 2,000 words maximum. Winners announced in July issue and notified by phone call and press release. "We are looking for fiction that has MOTION, that goes the distance in fewer words. Also, originality and a strong sense of voice are two main elements we look for."

⬤ **TALL GRASS WRITERS GUILD LITERARY ANTHOLOGY/CONTEST**, Outrider Press, 937 Patricia, Crete IL 60417-1375. (708)672-6630 or (800)933-4680 (code 03). Fax: (708)672-5820. E-mail: outriderpr@aol.com. Website: www.OutriderPr.com. **Contact:** Whitney Scott, senior editor. 2003 competition to collect diverse writings by authors of all ages and backgrounds on the theme of family gatherings: "You're Invited." Open to poetry, short stories and creative nonfiction. Award: publication in anthology; free copy to all published contributors. $1,000 in cash prizes. Competition receives 850 submissions. Judges: Jim W. Brown (prose), Maureen Seaton (poetry). Entry fee $16.50; $12 for members. Guidelines and entry form available for SASE, by fax, e-mail and on website. Accepts inquiries by e-mail. Deadline: February 28, 2003. Unpublished and published submissions. Word length: 2,500 words or less. Maximum 2 prose, 8 poetry entries per person. Include SASE. Winners announced in June. "Must include e-mail address and SASE for response."

N ⊚ TAMARACK AWARD, *Minnesota Monthly*, 10 S. Fifth St., Suite 1000, Minneapolis MN 55402. (612)371-5800. Fax: (612)371-5801. E-mail: editor@mnmo.com. Website: www.minnesotamonthly.com. **Contact:** Sarah Tieck, associate editor. Purpose of award is "to honor excellence in short fiction. Annual award for short stories. Award: $400. Number of entries varies. Judge: "Entries are judged anonymously by editorial staff." No entry fee. For guidelines, send SASE, e-mail or visit website. 2002 deadline: postmarked by May 26, 2002. Entries should be unpublished. Contest open to "residents of Minnesota, North Dakota, South Dakota, Iowa, Wisconsin and Michigan." Length: 1,000-3,000 words. "You may submit only one manuscript. Please type and double space the manuscript. Also, number the pages. Submit one clean copy. Please do not put your name on the manuscript; judging is anonymous. Include a cover sheet with your name, address, daytime and evening phone numbers and total word count of story." Manuscripts will not be returned. "Stories are judged on artistry, originality, structure and plotting. A human quality and a level of inspiration are valued over especially dark and violent themes. Obscene themes and language are inappropriate." Winners announced in November issue of *Minnesota Monthly*. Winners notified prior to publication by mail, phone and e-mail.

SYDNEY TAYLOR MANUSCRIPT COMPETITION, Association of Jewish Libraries, 315 Maitland Ave., Teaneck NJ 07666. (201)862-0312. Fax: (201)862-0362. E-mail: rkglasser@aol.com. Website: www.jewishlibraries.org. Award to "deepen the understanding of Judaism for all children by helping to launch new writers of children's Jewish fiction." Annual competition for novels. Award: $1,000. Competition receives 25 submissions. Judges: 5 children's librarians. Guidelines and release forms available on website and for #10 SASE. Accepts inquiries by fax and e-mail. Deadline: December 1. Previously unpublished submissions. "Children's fiction for readers 8-11 years with universal appeal and Jewish content. Writer must not have a previously published fiction book." Word length: 64 page minimum-200 page maximum, double-spaced. Winners announced April 1 and notified by phone or e-mail. List of winners available on website.

⊚ TEDDY BOOK AWARD, Writers League of Texas, 1501 W. 5th St., Suite E-2, Austin TX 78703-5155. (512)499-8914. Fax: (512)499-0441. E-mail: awl@writersleague.org. Website: www.writersleague.org. **Contact:** Stephanie Sheppard, executive director. Award established "to honor an outstanding book for children published by a member of the Writers' League of Texas." Annual competition for novels. Award: $1,000. Competition receives 25-50 submissions. $10 per entry fee. Guidelines available in January for SASE, fax, e-mail, visit website or call. Deadline: May 31. Accepts inquiries by fax, e-mail or phone. Entries should be previously published children's book by Writers' League of Texas member during period of June 1 to May 31. Winners announced September 2003 and notified at ceremony.

N ⊘ ⊚ TENNESSEE ARTS COMMISSION LITERARY FELLOWSHIP, 401 Charlotte Ave., Nashville TN 37243-0780. (615)741-1701. Fax: (615)741-8559. E-mail: dennis.adkins@state.tn.us. **Contact:** Dennis Adkins, communications director. Award to "honor promising writers." Annual award for fiction or poetry. Award: $5,000. Competition receives approximately 30 submissions. Judges are out-of-state jurors. Previously published and unpublished submissions. Writers must be previously published writers and residents of Tennessee. Length: 15 ms pages. Write for guidelines. Accepts inquiries by fax and e-mail. This year's award is for prose.

N TEXAS REVIEW PRESS BOOK COMPETITIONS, Texas Review Press, English Department, Box 2146, Sam Houston State University, Huntsville TX 77341-2146. (936)294-1992. Fax: (936)294-3070. Website: www.shsu.edu/~www_trp. **Contact:** Barbara Miles, managing editor; Paul Ruffin, director. The *Texas Review* has two annual competitions for fiction: the George Garrett Fiction Prize for a book of stories or short novel and the *Texas Review* Novella Prize for novellas. Competitions receive approximately 125 submissions. Judges: final judges are George Garrett and X. J. Kennedy. Entry fee $20. Guidelines available for SASE. Accepts inquiries by fax and e-mail. Deadline: George Garret Fiction Prize, September 15; *Texas Review* Novella Prize, October 15. Previously unpublished submissions. Word length: George Garret Fiction Prize, up to 250 pages; *Texas Review* Novella Prize, up to 150 pages. "Get your hands on previous winners and read them, but notice their diversity—we are not looking for the same thing twice." Winners announced by mail, time varies and notified by phone.

THOUGHT MAGAZINE WRITER'S CONTEST, *Thought Magazine*, P.O. Box 117098, Burlingame CA 94011-7098. E-mail: ThoughtMagazine@yahoo.com. Website: www.geocities.com/ThoughtMagazine. **Contact:** Kevin J. Feeney, publisher. "To recognize and publish quality writing in the areas of short fiction, poetry, and short nonfiction and to identify and give exposure to writers who have not yet been published in a national magazine." Award: 1st prize-$75 plus publication in *Thought Magazine*; 2nd prize-$50 plus publication in *Thought Magazine*. "All submissions are considered for publication in *Thought Magazine*." Competition receives 100 submissions per category. "Entries are judged by the editors and a panel of judges consisting of published writers and academics." $5 entry fee/story or essay or 3 poems. Accepts inquiries by e-mail. Deadlines: April 15 and August 15. Entries should be unpublished. Contest open to all writers. Length: fiction maximum of 3,000 words. Poetry maximum of 100 lines. Include name, address, phone number and/or e-mail. "We are not interested in extreme violence or pornography. May be helpful to review a back issue available for $6." Winners announced 1 month after deadlines and notified by phone or e-mail. List of winners available with SASE.

THREE OAKS PRIZE FOR FICTION, Story Line Press, Three Oaks Farm, P.O. Box 1240, Ashland OR 97520-0055. (541)512-8792. Fax: (541)512-8793. E-mail: mail@storylinepress.com. Website: www.storylinepress.com. **Contact:** Three Oaks Competition. Annual prize for novels and story collections. "The winner receives $1,500 cash sponsored by Bloomsbury Books of Ashland, Oregon, and publication of the winning entry by Story Line Press. Judge: Robert McDowell, publisher. $25 entry fee. Guidelines available for SASE, e-mail or on website. Deadline: April 30 annually. Entries should be unpublished, "except if published in literary journals or anthologies." Length: "Although there is no minimum or maximum requirements for length, the page count must be reasonable." Winners announced 6-8 weeks after deadline and notified by phone. "A press release announcing the winner along with a letter from the publisher is sent to all entrants who supply an SASE for contest results. If for some reason the contestant does not receive this, they may contact us by phone, fax, e-mail or mail."

THURBER HOUSE RESIDENCIES, Thurber House, 77 Jefferson Ave., Columbus OH 43215-3840. (614)464-1032. Fax: (614)228-7445. E-mail: thurberhouse@thurberhouse.org. Website: www.thurberhouse.org. **Contact:** Trish Houston, residency director. "Four writers/year are chosen as writers-in-residence, one for each quarter." Award for writers of novels, story collections and poetry collections. Award: $6,000 stipend and housing for a quarter in the furnished third-floor apartment of James Thurber's boyhood home. Competition receives over 60 submissions. Judges: Residencies Advisory panel. Guidelines available in August for SASE. To apply, send letter of interest and curriculum vitae. Deadline: December 1. "The James Thurber Writer-in-Residence will teach a two-week, graduate level intensive workshop/seminar in the Creative Writing Program at The Ohio State University; participate in a writing residency with a community agency; and offer a public reading in this newly redesigned residency. Candidates should have national visibility in poetry, fiction, or creative nonfiction, substantial book publications, and teaching experience." Winners announced in April and notified by mail. List of winners available in May for SASE.

THE THURBER PRIZE FOR AMERICAN HUMOR, Thurber House, 77 Jefferson Ave., Columbus OH 43215-3840. (614)464-1032. Fax: (614)280-3645. E-mail: humor@thurberhouse.org. Website: www.thurberhouse.org. **Contact:** Elizabeth Jewell, director of literary programs. Award "to give the nation's highest recognition of the art of humor writing." Biennial competition for books of humor. Award: $5,000; Thurber statuette. Up to 3 Honor Awards may also be conferred. Judges: Well-known members of the national arts community. Entry fee $25/title. 2003 competition guidelines available in January for SASE. Accepts inquiries by phone and e-mail. Deadline: April 1, 2003. Published submissions or accepted for publication in US for first time. No reprints or paperback editions of previously published books. Word length: no requirement. Primarily pictorial works such as cartoon collections are not considered. Work must be nominated by publisher. Winners announced in December 2003 and notified by phone. A list of winners available on website.

TICKLED BY THUNDER ANNUAL FICTION CONTEST, Tickled By Thunder, 14076-86A Ave., Surrey, British Columbia V3W 0V9 Canada. (604)591-6095. E-mail: info@tickledbythunder.com. Website: www.tickledbythunder.com. **Contact:** Larry Lindner, editor. "To encourage new writers." Annual competition for short stories. Award: 50% of all fees, $150 minimum (Canadian), 1 year's (4-issue) subscription plus publication. Competition receives approximately 30 submissions. Judges: The editor and other writers. Entry fee $10 (Canadian) per entry (free for subscribers but more than one story requires $5 per entry). Guidelines available for SASE, e-mail, website. Accepts inquiries by e-mail. Deadline: February 15. Unpublished submissions. Word length: 2,000 words or less. Winners announced in May and notified by mail. List of winners available for SASE.

JOHN TIGGES WRITING CONTEST, Loras College, 1450 Alta Vista, Dubuque IA 52004-0178. (563)588-7139. Fax: (563)588-4962. E-mail: cneuhaus@loras.edu. Website: www.loras.edu/conted. **Contact:** Chris Neuhaus, secretary of continuing education. This annual award encourages and recognizes aspiring writers as well as seasoned professionals. Prizes given for fiction, nonfiction, and poetry. Awards: $100 and publication in *Julien's Journal*, Dubuque area magazine (1st prize, fiction prize); $50 (2nd prize); and $25 (3rd prize). Poetry and nonfiction receive same monetary awards. First place in both are published in Dubuque *Telegraph Herald*. Entry fee: $5/entry. Written critiques available for contest entries, additional $15 per critique. "All requests for critiques must include SASE." Guidelines available February 2003. Accepts inquiries by fax, e-mail, or phone. Deadline: Must be "in-hand by" April 7, 2003. Entries should be unpublished. Length: fiction and nonfiction, 1,500 words—subject and style open; poetry, 40 lines maximum. Winners announced at the Sinipee Writer's Workshop, April 26, 2003 and notified by mail, first week in May.

TOWSON UNIVERSITY PRIZE FOR LITERATURE, College of Liberal Arts, Towson University, Towson MD 21252-0001. (410)704-2128. Fax: (410)704-6392. E-mail: snordhoffklaus@towson.edu. **Contact:** Beverly Leetchy, dean, College of Liberal Arts. Annual award for novels or short story collections and poetry, previously published. Award: $1,000. Competition receives 5-10 submissions. Requirements: Must be a Maryland resident. Guidelines available spring 2003 for SASE. Accepts inquiries by fax, phone and e-mail. Deadline: June 15. Winners announced December and notified by letter. List of winners available by calling or writing Sue Ann Nordhoff-Klaus.

[N] [©] ROBERT TRAVER FLY-FISHING FICTION AWARD, *Fly Rod & Reel Magazine,* P.O. Box 370, Camden ME 04843-0370. (207)594-9544. Fax: (207)594-5144. E-mail: pguernsey@flyrodreel.com. Website: www.flyrodreel.c om. **Contact:** Paul Guernsey, editor-in-chief. "The Traver Award is given annually for a work of short fiction that embodies an implicit love of fly-fishing, respect for the sport and the natural world in which it takes place and high literary values." Award: $2,500 and publication. Competition receives approximately 200 submissions. Judges: Members of John D. Voelker Foundation and *Fly Rod & Reel* editorial staff. Accepts inquiries by fax, e-mail, phone. Deadline: March 30. Include SASE. Winner announced in late summer/early fall publication and notified by mail upon publication.

[○] TROUBADOURS' SHORT STORY CONTEST, Troubadours' Writers Group, P.O. Box 138, Woodstock IL 60098-0138. E-mail: ghstwnl@aol.com. Website: http://home2.owc.net/~mason/troubadours.html. **Contact:** Carla Fortier, contest coordinator. Contest "for those who enjoy writing competitions and/or appreciate feedback from judges." Annual competition for short stories. Award: $75 (1st prize); $50 (2nd prize); $25 (3rd prize); each entry is given a written critique, which is returned to the author with SASE; winners are offered the opportunity to have their stories published in *The Lantern.* Competition receives 100 submissions. Judges: 2002 was Eleanor Taylor Bland, author of the Marti MacAlister mystery series. $5 entry fee per story; multiple entries OK if each is accompanied by $5 fee. Guidelines available for SASE, by e-mail or on website. Accepts inquiries by e-mail. Deadline: postmarked March 1. Unpublished submissions. Length: 1,500 words maximum. "Follow the format guidelines and enter a complete story with a beginning, middle and end. No poetry, vignettes, personal reminiscences or essays." Judges look for "a well-conceived storyline that revolves around characters in conflict with themselves or others. Writing should grab reader's attention and display a vitality of language and style through a balanced use of dialogue and narrative." Winners announced before July and notified by mail. List of winners enclosed with critique in author's SASE. Also available on website.

[◑] [©] STEVEN TURNER AWARD, The Texas Institute of Letters, Center for the Study of the Southwest, Flowers Hall 327, Southwest Texas State University, San Marcos TX 78666. (512)448-8702. Fax: (512)245-7462. E-mail: mb13@swt.edu. Website: www.english.swt.edu/css/TIL/index. **Contact:** Paula Mitchell Marks, secretary. "To honor the best first book of fiction published by a writer who was born in Texas or who has lived in the state for two years at some time, or whose work concerns the state." Annual award for novels and story collections. Award: $1,000. Judges: Committee. Guidelines available in July for SASE. Accepts inquiries by e-mail. Deadline: January 14. Previously published submissions appearing in print between January 1 and December 31. Winners announced in April and notified by phone. List of winners available on website.

[◐] [©] MARK TWAIN AWARD, Missouri Association of School Librarians, 3912 Manorwood Dr., St. Louis MO 63125. Phone/fax: (314)416-0462. E-mail: masl@il.net. Website: www.maslonline.org. **Contact:** Alice Neal. Estab. 1970. Annual award to introduce children to the best of current literature for children and to stimulate reading. Award: A bronze bust of Mark Twain, created by Barbara Shanklin, a Missouri sculptor. A committee selects pre-list of the books nominated for the award; statewide reader/selectors review and rate the books, and then children throughout the state vote to choose a winner from the final list. Books must be published two years prior to nomination for the award list. Publishers may send books they wish to nominate for the list to the committee members. "Books should be 1) of interest to children in grades 4 through 8; 2) written by an author living in the US; 3) of literary value which may enrich children's personal lives." Accepts inquiries by fax and e-mail. Winners announced in May and notified in April by phone. List of winners available.

[N] [○] THE MARK TWAIN AWARD FOR SHORT FICTION, *Red Rock Review,* NSSW English Dept., J2A, 3200 E. Cheyenne Ave., N. Las Vegas NV 89030-4296. (702)651-4005. Fax: (702)651-4639. Website: www.ccsn.nevada. edu/english/redrockreview/index.html (includes contest guidelines and general submissions guidelines). **Contact:** Rich Logsdon, editor. Award to "find and publish the best available works of short fiction." Annual competition for short stories. Awards: $1,000 and publication. Competition receives 250-300 entries. Judges: Pre-judging by magazine staff and readers; winner selected by guest judge (guest judge for 2001 contest was Douglas Unger). Entry fee: $10. Guidelines available November 1, 1999 for SASE. Accepts inquiries by fax and e-mail. Deadline: October 31, 2002. Previously unpublished submissions. Word length: 3,500 words or less. "Author's name should not appear anywhere on manuscript. Submissions should include cover page with author's name, address and phone. No simultaneous submissions. Writing should grab the reader's attention early and show a freshness of language and voice." Winners announced Spring 2003 and notified by phone. List of winners available for SASE.

SENDING TO A COUNTRY other than your own? Be sure to send International Reply Coupons (IRC) instead of stamps for replies or return of your manuscript.

N ⊕ ○ ◎ UPC SCIENCE FICTION AWARD, Universitat Politècnica de Catalunya Board of Trustees, gran capità 2-4, Edifici NEXUS, 08034 Barcelona Spain. Phone: 34 93 4016343. Fax: 34 93 4017766. E-mail: consell.soc ial@upc.es. Website: www.upc.es/op/english/sciencefiction/sciencefiction.htm. **Contact:** Anna Serra, secretary. "The award is based on the desire for integral education at UPC. The literary genre of science fiction is undoubtedly the most suitable for a university such as UPC, since it unifies the concepts of science and literature." Annual award for short stories: 1,000,000 pesetas (about $10,000 US). Competition receives 140 submissions. Judges: Professors of the university and science fiction writers. Guidelines available January 2001 by mail, e-mail, fax, phone, or website. Deadline: September 14. Previously unpublished entries. Length: 70-115 pages, double-spaced, 30 lines/page, 70 characters/line. Submissions may be made in Spanish, English, Catalan or French. The author must sign his work with a pseudonym and enclose a sealed envelope with full name, a personal ID number, address and phone. The pseudonym and title of work must appear on the envelope. Winners announced December 2002 and notified by phone November 2002. List of winners sent to all entrants; also available by mail and on website.

VERY SHORT FICTION SUMMER AWARD, *Glimmer Train Stories*, 710 SW Madison St., Suite 504, Portland OR 97205. (503)221-0836. Fax: (503)221-0837. Website: www.glimmertrain.com (includes writers' guidelines and Q&A section for writers). **Contact:** Linda Swanson-Davies, editor. Annual award offered to encourage the art of the very short story. "We want to read your original, unpublished, very short story (2,000 words or less). $10 reading fee. Make your submissions online (www.glimmertrain.com) by July 31. Winners will be notified and Top 25 places will be posted by November 1." Awards: $1,200 and publication in *Glimmer Train Stories* and 20 author's copies (1st Place); $500 (2nd Place); $300 (3rd Place).

VERY SHORT FICTION WINTER AWARD, *Glimmer Train Stories*, 710 SW Madison St., Suite 504, Portland OR 97205. (503)221-0836. Fax: (503)221-0837. Website: www.glimmertrain.com (includes writer's guidelines and a Q&A section for writers). **Contact:** Linda Swanson-Davies, editor. Award offered to encourage the art of the very short story. "We want to read your original, unpublished, very short story (2,000 words or less). $10 reading fee. Make your submissions online (www.glimmertrain.com) by January 31. Winners will be notified and Top 25 places will be posted by May 1." Awards: $1,200 and publication in *Glimmer Train Stories* and 20 author's copies (1st Place); $500 (2nd Place); $300 (3rd Place).

○ ◎ VIOLET CROWN BOOK AWARD, Writers' League of Texas, 1501 W. Fifth St., Suite E-2, Austin TX 78703-5155. (512)499-8914. Fax: (512)499-0441. E-mail: awl@writersleague.org. Website: www.writersleague.org. **Contact:** Stephanie Sheppard, executive director. Award "to recognize the best books published by Writers' League members over the period June 1 to May 31 in fiction, nonfiction and literary categories." Award: Three $1,000 cash awards and trophies. Competition receives approximately 100 submissions. Judges: A panel of judges who are not affiliated with the Writers' League or Barnes & Noble. Entry fee $10. Guidelines after January for SASE, fax, e-mail or website. Accepts inquiries by fax, e-mail or phone. Deadline: May 31. "Entrants must be Writers' League members. League members reside all over the U.S. and some foreign countries. Persons may join the League when they send in entries." Publisher may also submit entry in writer's name. Winners announced September and notified by phone and mail. List of winners available for SASE. "Awards are co-sponsored by Barnes & Noble Booksellers. Special citations are presented to finalists."

○ ◎ WALDEN FELLOWSHIP, Coordinated by: Extended Campus Programs, Southern Oregon University, 1250 Siskiyou Blvd., Ashland OR 97520-5038. (541)552-6901. Fax: (541)552-6047. E-mail: friendly@sou.edu. Website: www.sou.edu/walden. **Contact:** Brooke Friendly, arts coordinator. Award "to give Oregon writers the opportunity to pursue their work at a quiet, beautiful farm in southern Oregon." Annual competition for all types of fiction and creative nonfiction. Award: 3-6 week residencies. Competition receives approximately 30 submissions. Judges: Committee judges selected by the sponsor. Guidelines for SASE and on website. Accepts inquiries by fax and e-mail. Deadline: End of November. Oregon writers only. Word length: maximum 30 pages prose, 8-10 poems. Winners announced in January and notified by mail. List of winners available for SASE and on website.

◐ ◎ EDWARD LEWIS WALLANT MEMORIAL BOOK AWARD, 3 Brighton Rd., West Hartford CT 06117. Sponsored by Dr. and Mrs. Irving Waltman. **Contact:** Mrs. Irving Waltman. Annual award. Memorial to Edward Lewis Wallant offering incentive and encouragement to beginning writers, for books published the year before the award is conferred in the spring. Award: $500 plus award certificate. Judges: A panel of 3 literary critics. Books may be submitted for consideration to Dr. Sanford Pinsker, Department of English, Franklin & Marshall College, P.O. Box 3003, Lancaster PA 17604-3003. Deadline: December 31. "Looking for creative work of fiction by an American which has significance for the American Jew. The novel (or collection of short stories) should preferably bear a kinship to the writing of Wallant. The award will seek out the writer who has not yet achieved literary prominence." Winners announced January-February and notified by phone.

◐ ◎ WESTERN HERITAGE AWARDS, National Cowboy and Western Heritage Museum, 1700 NE 63rd St., Oklahoma City OK 73111-7997. (405)478-6404. Fax: (405)478-4714. **Contact:** M.J. Van Deuenter, director of publications. Annual award "to honor outstanding quality in fiction, nonfiction and art literature." Submissions are to have been published during the previous calendar year. Award: The Wrangler, a replica of a C.M. Russell Bronze. Competition receives 350 submissions. Entry fee $35. Guidelines available by SASE, fax or e-mail. Entry forms and rules available October 1 for SASE. Accepts inquiries by fax and e-mail. Deadline: November 30. Looking for "stories that best capture the spirit of the West. Submit five actual copies of the work." Winners announced March 1 and notified by letter. List of winners available by SASE, fax or e-mail. "All work must be published by a legitimate, professional publishing company. Self published works are disqualified and the entry fee is not returned. Entries should have a broad appeal to those interested in the West, western history and the western lifestyle."

WHITING WRITERS' AWARDS, Mrs. Giles Whiting Foundation, 1133 Avenue of the Americas, New York NY 10036-6710. Website: www.whitingfoundation.org. **Contact:** Barbara K. Bristol, director, writer's program. Annual award for writers of fiction, poetry, nonfiction and plays with an emphasis on emerging writers. Award: $35,000 (10 awards). Candidates are submitted by appointed nominators and chosen for awards by an appointed selection committee. Direct applications and informal nominations not accepted by the foundation. List of winners available October 30 by request and on website.

WILD VIOLET FICTION CONTEST, *Wild Violet*, 6599 Overheart Lane, Colombia MD 21045. E-mail: wildvio letmagazine@yahoo.com. Website: www.wildviolet.net. **Contact:** Amanda Cornwell, co-editor. Award's purpose is "to reward well-written fiction." Annual award for short fiction. Prize: $100 and publication in *Wild Violet* for first place; publication in *Wild Violet* for second and third place. Judge: "An independent panel of judges to be announced on the website." $5 entry fee. For guidelines, send e-mail or visit website. Accepts inquiries by e-mail. Deadline: March 1, 2003. Entries should be unpublished. "Contest open to any writer of any background." Length: 10,000 words. "Read previous issues of *Wild Violet* to get an idea of the type of fiction that interests this publication." Winners announced May 2003. Winners notified by e-mail. List of winners available for e-mail or visit website.

LAURA INGALLS WILDER AWARD, American Library Association/Association for Library Service to Children, 50 E. Huron St., Chicago IL 60611. **Contact:** Malore Brown, executive director. Award offered every 2 years; next year 2003. "To honor a significant body of work for children, for illustration, fiction or nonfiction." Award: Bronze medal. Authors must be nominated by ALSC members. Judge: Award committee. Guidelines available for SASE, fax, e-mail and on website. Deadline: December 1, 2002. Winners notified by phone and announced at press conference during the ALA Midwinter Meeting on January 27, 2003.

WISCONSIN ARTS BOARD INDIVIDUAL ARTIST PROGRAM, 101 E. Wilson St., First Floor, Madison WI 53702. (608)264-8191. Fax: (608)267-0380. E-mail: mark.fraire@arts.state.wi.us. Website: www.arts.state. wi.us. **Contact:** Mark J. Fraire. Biennial awards for short stories, poetry, novels, novellas, drama, essay/criticism. Awards: 5 awards of $8,000. Competition receives approximately 250 submissions. Entry forms or rules available in August upon request. Accepts inquiries by fax and e-mail. Deadline: September 15 of even-numbered years (2000, 2002 etc.). Wisconsin residents only. Students are ineligible. Winners announced in late December and notified by mail.

WISCONSIN INSTITUTE FOR CREATIVE WRITING FELLOWSHIP, University of Wisconsin—Creative Writing, English Department, 600 N. Park St., Madison WI 53706. Website: http://creativewritingwisc.edu. Competition "to provide time, space and an intellectual community for writers working on first books." Six annual awards for short stories, novels and story collections. Awards: $25,000/9-month appointment. Competition receives 500 submissions. Judges: English Department faculty. Guidelines available for SASE; write to Ron Kuka or check website. Deadline: February. Published or unpublished submissions. Applicants must have received an M.F.A. or comparable graduate degree in creative writing and not yet published a book. Limit 1 story up to 30 pages in length. No name on writing sample. Two letters of recommendation and vita or resume required.

PAUL A. WITTY SHORT STORY AWARD, International Reading Association, P.O. Box 8139, 800 Barksdale Rd., Newark DE 19714-8139. (302)731-1600, ext. 293. Fax: (302)731-1057. E-mail: jbutler@reading.org. Website: www.reading.org. **Contact:** Janet Butler, public information associate. Annual award given to the author of an original short story published for the first time in 2002 in a periodical for children. Award: $1,000. "The short story should serve as a literary standard that encourages young readers to read periodicals." For guidelines write to Executive Office or e-mail exec@reading.org. Deadline: December 1, 2002. Published submissions.

WORLD FANTASY AWARDS, World Fantasy Awards Association, P.O. Box 43, Mukilteo WA 98275-0043. E-mail: sfexessec@aol.com. Website: www.worldfantasy.org. **Contact:** Peter Dennis Pautz, president. Award to "recognize excellence in fantasy literature worldwide." Annual competition for short stories, novels, story collections, anthologies, novellas and life achievement. Award: Bust of HP Lovecraft. Competition receives approximately 600 submissions. Judge: Panel. Guidelines available for SASE. Deadline: June 30. Published submissions from previous calendar year. Word length: 10,000-40,000 novella; 10,000 short story. "All fantasy is eligible, from supernatural horror to Tolkienesque to sword and sorcery to the occult, and beyond." Winners announced November 1 at annual convention. List of winners available November 1.

WORLD'S BEST SHORT SHORT STORY CONTEST, English Department Writing Program, Florida State University, Tallahassee FL 32306-1580. (850)644-2640. E-mail: southeastreview@english.fsu.edu. Website: www.englis h.fsu.edu/southeastreview. **Contact:** Ed Tarkington, fiction editor. Annual award for short-short stories, unpublished, under 300 words. Prizewinning story gets $300 and a crate of Florida oranges; winner and finalists are published in *The Southeast Review*. Competition receives approx. 5,000 submissions. Entry fee $5 for up to 3 entries. Guidelines on website. Deadline: April 15. Open to all. Length: 300 words maximum. Winners are announced on June 15 and notified by mail between July 1 and August 1.

WRITE YOUR HEART OUT™, Ponder Publishing Inc., P.O. Box 23037, RPO McGillivray, Winnipeg, Manitoba R3T 5S3 Canada. (204)269-2985. Fax: (204)888-7159. E-mail: service@ponderpublishing.com. Website: www.ponderpublishing.com. **Contact:** Pamela Walford, assistant editor. "We are looking for potential Ponder Romances, and we felt the contest would be incentive for writers to pen something specifically for us since the mss do no have to be in a complete state." Awards: $500 cdn (grand prize); $100 cdn (2nd prize); and 10 consolation prizes (detailed critiques). Receives 100 entries per category. "Judged by our entire submissions team. Assistant Submissions Editors, Sr. Submission Editor, and Assistant & Sr. Editors. Entry fee: $10 U.S. & international; $15 Canadian. Guidelines now available for SASE, e-mail or visit website. Accepts inquiries by fax and e-mail. Deadline: April 30, 2003 (midnight). Entries must be unpublished. Open to anyone with romance mss. Length: First 3 chapters and 2 page synopsis. "Read our Ponder Romances. They are unique to the romance market." Winners announced September 1, 2003 and notified by phone before September 1, 2003. List of winners available by visiting website or include $1 extra with entry fee.

THE WRITERS BUREAU POETRY AND SHORT STORY COMPETITION, The Writers Bureau, Sevendale House, 7 Dale St., Manchester M1 1JB England. (+44)161 228 2362. Fax: (+44)161 228 3533. E-mail: comp@writersbureau.com. Website: www.writersbureau.com/resources.htm. **Contact:** Angela Cox, competition secretary. Annual competition for short stories and poems. Award: £1,000 (1st Prize), £400 (2nd Prize), £200 (3rd Prize), £100 (4th Prize), 6 awards of £50 (5th Prize). Judges: Alison Chisolm and Iain Pattison. £4 fee per entry. Guidelines available April 2003. For guidelines, send SASE, fax, e-mail, visit website or call. Accepts inquiries by fax, e-mail, phone. Deadline: July 31, 2003. Entries should be unpublished. Contest open to anyone. Length: 2,000 words. Winners announced September 30, 2003 and notified by mail. List of winners available for SASE or visit website.

WRITER'S DIGEST ANNUAL WRITING COMPETITION, (Short Story Division), *Writer's Digest*, 4700 E. Galbraith Rd., Cincinnati OH 45236. (513)531-2690, ext. 1328. E-mail: competitions@fwpubs.com. Website: www.writersdigest.com. **Contact:** Contest Director. Grand Prize $1,500 cash and your choice of a trip to New York City to meet with editors and agents or a trip to the 2003 Maui Writer's Conference. Other awards include cash, reference books and certificates of recognition. Names of grand prize winner and top 10 category winners are announced in the November issue of *Writer's Digest*. Top entries published in booklet ($6). Rules and entry form available by sending SASE to *Writer's Digest* Annual Writing Competition, in January through May issues of *WD* or online. Deadline: May 31. Entry fee $10 per manuscript. All entries must be original, unpublished and not previously submitted to a *Writer's Digest* contest. Length: 4,000 words maximum genre and mainstream fiction, 2,000 for children's fiction. No acknowledgment will be made of receipt of mss nor will mss be returned. Three of the ten writing categories target short fiction: mainstream/literary, genre and children's fiction.

WRITER'S DIGEST INTERNATIONAL SELF-PUBLISHED BOOK AWARDS, *Writer's Digest*, 4700 E. Galbraith Rd., Cincinnati OH 45236. (513)531-2690, ext. 1328. E-mail: competitions@fwpubs.com. Website: www.writersdigest.com. **Contact:** Contest Director. Award to "recognize and promote excellence in self-published books." Annual competition with 9 categories: mainstream/literary fiction; genre fiction, nonfiction, inspirational (spiritual, New Age), life stories, children's and young adult books, reference books, poetry and cookbooks. Grand prize: $2,500 plus an ad in *Publishers Weekly* and promotion in *Writer's Digest* as well as a 1-year membership in Publishers Marketing Association. Category winners receive $500 and promotion in *Writer's Digest*. Both grand prize and category winners receive guaranteed distribution to bookstores and libraries through Baker & Taylor and guaranteed review in *Midwest Book Review*. Judges: Final judges are successful self-published authors and book editors. Entry fee $100 for first entry; $50 for each additional entry. Guidelines available for SASE and online. Deadline: December 16. Published submissions. Author must have paid full cost of publication and book must have been published in year of contest or two years prior.

WRITERS' FILM PROJECT, The Chesterfield Writers Film Project, 1158 26th St., PMB 544, Santa Monica CA 90403. (213)683-3977. E-mail: info@chesterfield-co.com. Website: www.chesterfield-co.com. **Contact:** Ed Rugoff, administrator. Award "provides up to 5 yearly stipends of $20,000 to promote and foster talented screenwriters, fiction writers and playwrights." Annual competition for short stories, novels and screenplays. Award: 5 $20,000 awards sponsored by Paramount Pictures. Judges: Mentors, panel of judges. Entry fee $39.50 US dollars for each submission. Guidelines available for SASE or on website. Deadline: May 15, 2002. Published or previously unpublished submissions. "Program open to all age groups, race, religion, educational level etc. Past winners have ranged in age from early 20's to late 50's."

WRITERS' FORUM SHORT STORY COMPETITION, Writers International Ltd., P.O. Box 3229, Bournemouth BH1 1ZS United Kingdom. Phone: (44) 1202 589828. Fax: (44) 1202 587758. E-mail: writingl@globalnet.co.uk. Website: www.worldwidewriters.com. **Contact:** Zena O'Toole, editorial assistant. "The competition aims to promote the arts of short story writing. Prizes range from a minimum of £150 to £250 in each issue with an annual trophy and a cheque for £1,000 for the best story of the year. The competition is open to all nationalities, but entries must be in English." Reading fee: £10 (subscribers to *Writers' Forum*. Judges: a panel provides a short list to the editor.

WRITERS' JOURNAL ANNUAL FICTION CONTEST, Val-Tech Media, P.O. Box 394, Perham MN 56573-0394. (218)346-7921. Fax: (218)346-7924. E-mail: writersjournal@lakesplus.com. Website: www.writersjournal.com. **Contact:** Leon Ogroske, publisher/managing editor. Award: $50 (1st Place); $25 (2nd Place); $15 (3rd Place). Publishes prize winners and selected honorable mentions. Competition receives approximately 250 submissions/year. Entry fee $5 each. Unpublished submissions. Entry forms or rules available for SASE. Deadline: January 30 annually. Maximum length is 2,000 words. "Writer's name must not appear on submission. A separate cover sheet must include: name of contest, title and writer's name, address, and telephone number (e-mail address if available)." Winners announced and notified June 30 by mail. A list of winners is published in July/August issue and posted on website.

◯ ◎ **WRITERS' JOURNAL ROMANCE CONTEST**, Val-Tech Media, P.O. Box 394, Perham MN 56573-0394. (218)346-7921. Fax: (218)346-7924. E-mail: writersjournal@lakesplus.com. Website: www.writersjournal.com. **Contact:** Leon Ogroske, editor. Award: $50 (1st Prize); $25 (2nd Prize); $15 (3rd Prize); publishes prize winners plus honorable mentions. Competition receives 350 submissions. Entry fee $5/entry. No limit on entries per person. Guidelines available for SASE. Deadline: July 30, annually. Unpublished submissions. Word length: 2,000 words maximum. Winners announced in January/February issue and notified by mail and winners list published in *Writers' Journal Magazine* and on website. "Enclose #10 SASE for winner's list."

🌐 **WRITESPOT AUTUMN SHORT STORY COMPETITION**, WriteSpot Publishers International, P.O. Box 221, The Gap Queensland 4061 Australia. Phone: (07)3300-1948. E-mail: frontdesk@writersspot.com. Website: www.writersspot.com. **Contact:** Coordinator. "The competition is to allow writers a creative outlet. It is also used as a source for stories to be included in upcoming anthologies." Two competitions are held annually. Competition for short stories. Award: $750.; $250; $100; $50; Encouragement Award $50 value (for entrants under 18); publication also offered on up to 12 selected stories. Competition receives 100+ submissions. Judges: six members of the Publications Committee. $8 single entry fee; $12 two entries; $5 each three or more entries. Guidelines are available now and will appear on website one month prior to the opening of the competition; send SASE, e-mail, visit website or call. Accepts inquiries by e-mail and phone. Accepts inquiries by e-mail or phone. Deadline: May 30, 2003. Open to entries from February 3 to May 30. Entries should be previously unpublished. Contest open to all ages and locations. Length: 5,000 words maximum. "Work may be of any theme and should display flair and originality." Winners announced June 27, 2003. Winners notified by phone and e-mail. List of winners send SASE, e-mail or visit website.

🌐 **WRITESPOT SPRING SHORT STORY COMPETITION**, WriteSpot Publishers International, P.O. Box 221, The Gap Queensland 4061 Australia. Phone: (07)3300-1948. E-mail: frontdesk@writersspot.com. Website: www.writersspot.com. **Contact:** Coordinator. "The competition is to allow writers a creative outlet. It is also used as a source for stories to be included in upcoming anthologies." Two competitions are held annually. Competition for short stories. Award: $750.; $250; $100; $50; Encouragement Award $50 value (for entrants under 18); publication also offered on up to 12 selected stories. Competition receives 100+ submissions. Judges: members of the Publications Committee. $8 single entry fee; $12 two entries; $5 each three or more entries. Guidelines are available now and will appear on website one month prior to the opening of the competition; send SASE, e-mail, visit website or call. Accepts inquiries by e-mail and phone. Competition opens August 1, 2003. Deadline: November 14, 2003. Entries should be previously unpublished. Contest open to all ages and locations. Length: 5,000 words. "Work may be of any theme and should display flair and originality." Winners announced December 6, 2002. Winners notified by phone and e-mail. List of winners send SASE, e-mail or visit website.

🅽 ◯ ◎ **YOUNG READER'S CHOICE AWARD**, Pacific Northwest Library Association, 3738 W. Central, Missoula MT 59804. **Contact:** YRCA Chair. Annual award "to promote reading as an enjoyable activity and to provide children an opportunity to endorse a book they consider an excellent story." Award: Silver medal. Judges: Children's librarians and teachers nominate; children in grades 4-12 vote for their favorite book on the list. Guidelines for SASE. Deadline: February 1. Previously published submissions. Writers must be nominated by children's librarians and teachers. No unsolicited submissions.

◩ **ZOETROPE SHORT STORY CONTEST**, 916 Kearny St., San Francisco CA 94133. (415)788-7500. Fax: (415)989-7910. Website: www.all-story.com. Annual competition for short stories. Award: $1,000 (1st Prize); $500 (2nd Prize); $250 (3rd Prize). 2001 judge: Robert Olen Butler. Entry fee $10. Guidelines available on website. Unpublished submissions. Word length: 5,000 words maximum. "Please mark envelope clearly 'short fiction contest.'" Winners notified in December. A list of winners will be posted on website and printed in February issue.

Resources

Conferences & Workshops

Why are conferences so popular? Writers and conference directors alike tell us it's because writing can be such a lonely business—at conferences writers have the opportunity to meet (and commiserate) with fellow writers, as well as meet and network with publishers, editors and agents. Conferences and workshops provide some of the best opportunities for writers to make publishing contacts and pick up valuable information on the business, as well as the craft, of writing.

The bulk of the listings in this section are for conferences. Most conferences last from one day to one week and offer a combination of workshop-type writing sessions, panel discussions and a variety of guest speakers. Topics may include all aspects of writing from fiction to poetry to scriptwriting, or they may focus on a specific area such as those sponsored by the Romance Writers of America for writers specializing in romance or the SCBWI conferences on writing for children's books.

Workshops, however, tend to run longer—usually one to two weeks. Designed to operate like writing classes, most require writers to be prepared to work on and discuss their work-in-progress while attending. An important benefit of workshops is the opportunity they provide writers for an intensive critique of their work, often by professional writing teachers and established writers.

Each of the listings here includes information on the specific focus of an event as well as planned panels, guest speakers and workshop topics. It is important to note, however, some conference directors were still in the planning stages for 2003 when we contacted them. If it was not possible to include 2003 dates, fees or topics, we have provided information from 2002 so you can get an idea of what to expect. For the most current information, it's best to send a self-addressed, stamped envelope to the director in question about three months before the date(s) listed.

FINDING A CONFERENCE

Many writers try to make it to at least one conference a year, but cost and location count as much as subject matter or other considerations when determining which conference to attend. There are conferences in almost every state and province and even some in Europe open to North Americans.

To make it easier for you to find a conference close to home—or to find one in an exotic locale to fit into your vacation plans—we've divided this section into geographic regions. The conferences appear in alphabetical order under the appropriate regional heading.

Note that conferences appear under the regional heading according to where they will be held, which is sometimes different than the address given as the place to register or send for information. The regions are as follows:

Northeast (page 515): Connecticut, Maine, Massachusetts, New Hampshire, New York, Rhode Island, Vermont

Midatlantic (page 521): Washington DC, Delaware, Maryland, New Jersey, Pennsylvania

Midsouth (page 524): North Carolina, South Carolina, Tennessee, Virginia, West Virginia

To find a conference based on the month in which it occurs, check out our new Conference Index at the back of this book.

LEARNING AND NETWORKING

Besides learning from workshop leaders and panelists in formal sessions, writers at conferences also benefit from conversations with other attendees. Writers on all levels enjoy sharing insights. Often, a conversation over lunch can reveal a new market for your work or let you know which editors are most receptive to the work of new writers. You can find out about recent editor changes and about specific agents. A casual chat could lead to a new contact or resource in your area.

Many editors and agents make visiting conferences a part of their regular search for new writers. A cover letter or query that starts with "I met you at the Green Mountain Writers Conference," or "I found your talk on your company's new romance line at the Moonlight and Magnolias Writer's Conference most interesting . . ." may give you a small leg up on the competition.

While a few writers have been successful in selling their manuscripts at a conference, the availability of editors and agents does not usually mean these folks will have the time there to read your novel or six best short stories (unless, of course, you've scheduled an individual meeting with them ahead of time). While editors and agents are glad to meet writers and discuss work in general terms, usually they don't have the time (or energy) to give an extensive critique during a conference. In other words, use the conference as a way to make a first, brief contact.

SELECTING A CONFERENCE

Besides the obvious considerations of time, place and cost, choose your conference based on your writing goals. If, for example, your goal is to improve the quality of your writing, it will be more helpful to you to choose a hands-on craft workshop rather than a conference offering a series of panels on marketing and promotion. If, on the other hand, you are a science fiction novelist who would like to meet your fans, try one of the many science fiction conferences or "cons" held throughout the country and the world.

Look for panelists and workshop instructors whose work you admire and who seem to be writing in your general area. Check for specific panels or discussions of topics relevant to what you are writing now. Think about the size—would you feel more comfortable with a small workshop of eight people or a large group of 100 or more attendees?

If your funds are limited, start by looking for conferences close to home, but you may want to explore those that offer contests with cash prizes—and a chance to recoup your expenses. A few conferences and workshops also offer scholarships, but the competition is stiff and writers interested in these should find out the requirements early. Finally, students may want to look for conferences and workshops that offer college credit. You will find these options included in the listings here. Again, send a self-addressed, stamped envelope for the most current details.

Northeast (CT, MA, ME, NH, NY, RI, VT)

THE BLUE MOUNTAIN CENTER, Blue Mountain Lake, New York NY 12812-0109. (518)352-7391. **Contact**: Harriet Barlow, director. Residencies for established writers. "Provides a peaceful environment where residents may work free from distractions and demands of normal daily life." Residencies awarded for 1 month between June 19 and November 1 (approx.). For more information, send SASE for brochure.
To Apply: Send for brochure. Application deadline: February 1.

BREAD LOAF WRITERS' CONFERENCE, Middlebury College, Middlebury VT 05753. (802)443-5286. Fax: (802)443-2087. E-mail: blwc@mail.middlebury.edu. Website: www.middlebury.edu/~blwc. **Contact:** Noreen Cargill, administrative manager. Estab. 1926. Annual. Conference held in late August. Conference duration: 11 days. Average attendance: 230. For fiction, nonfiction and poetry. Held at the summer campus in Ripton, Vermont (belongs to Middlebury College).
Costs: In 2002, $1,850 (included room and board).
Accommodations: Accommodations are at Ripton. Onsite accommodations included in fee.
Additional Information: Conference information available January 2003. Accepts inquiries by fax and e-mail.

GOTHAM WRITERS' WORKSHOP, WritingClasses.com (online division), 1841 Broadway, Suite 809, New York NY 10023-7603. (212)974-8377. Fax: (212)307-6325. E-mail: office@write.org. Website: www.WritingClasses.com. **Contact:** Dana Miller, director of student affairs. Estab. 1993. "Classes are held throughout the year. There are four terms, beginning in January, April, June/July, September/October in 2002." Workshop duration: 10-week, 1-day, and online courses offered. Average attendance: approximately 1,300 students per term, 5,000 students per year. Offers craft-oriented creative writing courses in fiction writing, screenwriting, nonfiction writing, memoir writing, novel writing, children's book writing, playwriting, poetry, songwriting, mystery writing, science fiction writing, romance writing, television writing, sketch comedy and business writing. Also, Gotham Writers' Workshop offers a teen program, private instruction and classes on selling your work. Site: Classes are held at various schools in New York City as well as online at www.WritingClasses.com. View a sample online class on the website.
Costs: Ten-week and online courses—$420 (includes $25 registration fee); one-day courses—$150 (includes $25 registration fee). These fees are before any discounts. For information regarding our discounts, please contact us for a catalog. Meals and lodging not included.
Additional Information: "Participants do not need to submit workshop material prior to their first class." Sponsors a contest for a free 10-week online creative writing course (value=$420) offered each term. Students should fill out a form online at www.WritingClasses.com to participate in the contest. The winner is randomly selected. For brochure send e-mail, visit website, call or fax. Accepts inquiries by SASE, e-mail, phone, fax. Agents and editors participate in some workshops.

N GREAT RIVER ARTS, P.O. Box 639, Walpole NH 03608. (603)756-3638. Fax: (603)756-3302. E-mail: grai@sover.net. Website: www.greatriverarts.org. **Contact:** Amelia Farnum, public relations. Estab. 1999. Year-round workshops. Duration: 3-4 days. Average attendance: 5-6 per class. "This season we are offering screenwriting, Art and the Children's Book and The Community of Stories, a course exploring the stories inherent in community through memoir and interview writings." Site: Walpole, NH. "We use a conference center called Alyson's Orchard which is, indeed, a working apple orchard located on the shores of the Connecticut River." 2002 workshops included Screenwriting and Reading and Discussion with Charles Simic. 2002 speakers included Greg Blair (screenwriter), Charles Simic, Laurie Alberts, Douglass Whynott, Eileen Christelow, Lesle Lewis.
Costs: 2002 rates were $600-800. Does not include lodging or meals.
Accommodations: Provides list of area hotels.
Additional Information: Participants may need to submit material prior to arrival depending on course. Brochures for 2003 available in February/March 2003 by e-mail, phone, fax and on website. Accepts inquiries by e-mail, phone, fax.

GREEN MOUNTAIN WRITERS CONFERENCE, 47 Hazel Street, Rutland VT 05701. (802)775-5326. E-mail: ydaley@adelphia.net. Website: www.vermontwriters.com. **Contact:** Yvonne Daley, director. Estab. 1999. Annual. Conference to be held August 4-8, 2003. Average attendance: 40. "The conference is an opportunity for writers at all stages of their development to hone their skills in a beautiful, lakeside environment where published writers across the genres share tips and give feedback." Conference held at an old dance pavillion on a 5-acre site on a remote pond in Tinmouth, VT. Past features include: Place in story—The Importance of Environment; creating character through description, dialogue, action, reaction, and thought; The collision of real events and imagination. 2002 panelists/lecturers included Yvonne Daley, Sally Johnson, Jeffrey Lent, Reeve Lindbergh, Ursula Smith, Abigail Stone and Verandah Porche.
Costs: In 2001 cost was $375 (including lunch, snacks, beverages).
Accommodations: Transportation can be had at cost from area airports. Offers list of area hotels and lodging.
Additional Information: Participants mss can be read and commented on at a cost. Sponsors contests. Requirements: Free tuition, no lodging ($500); reading cost fee: $15. Essays plus 3 poems or 10 pages of fiction/non-fiction. Essays

should say why the writer wants to attend conference. Length: 1,000 words. Brochures available February, 2001 or on website before then. Brochures for SASE, e-mail, website or call. Accepts inquiries by SASE, e-mail, phone. Editors participate in conferences. "We aim to create a community of writers who support one another and serve as audience/mentors for one another. Participants often continue to correspond and share work after conferences." Further information available on website, by e-mail or by phone.

N. THE GYPSY DANCES: A WORKSHOP FOR YOUR CHARACTERS!, 995 Chapman Rd., Yorktown NY 10598. (914)962-4432. E-mail: emily@emilyhanlon.com. Website: www.thefictionwritersjourney.com. **Contact:** Emily Hanlon. Estab. 2003. One-time conference. Conference held May 1-4, 2003. Average attendance: 10-20. "Using fiction writing techniques, we will spend these four days exploring new characters or deepening our relationship to old characters by inviting them to step out and play." Site: "Bethany House is a retreat center in the Southern Catskills of New York State, about 2 hours north of NYC. It is set on a picturesque lake with plenty of grounds to walk on." Workshop led by Emily Hanlon, novelist.
Costs: 2002 prices: $375 for early registration; $425 regular fee.
Accommodations: "There is a bus from New York City to Highland Mills. In addition, Bethany House is close to Stewart Airport." Offers overnight lodging at Bethany House. All rooms are private. Price included in overall costs.
Additional Information: "Participants need to talk to Emily Hanlon on the telephone." Brochures available by e-mail, by phone, on website.

HOFSTRA UNIVERSITY SUMMER WRITERS' CONFERENCE, 250 Hofstra University, UCCE, Hempstead NY 11549. (516)463-5016. Fax: (516)463-4833. E-mail: uccelibarts@hofstra.edu. Website: www.hofstra.edu (under "Academics/Continuing Education"). **Contact:** Kenneth Henwood, director, Liberal Arts Studies. Estab. 1972. Annual (every summer, starting week after July 4). Conference held July 8-19, 2002. Average attendance: 65. Conference offers workshops in fiction, nonfiction, poetry, juvenile fiction, stage/screenwriting and, on occasion, one other genre such as detective fiction or science fiction. Workshops in prose and poetry for high school student writers are also offered. Site is the university campus, a suburban setting, 25 miles from NYC. Guest speaker is Rebecca Wolf, *Fence* editor. "We have had the likes of Oscar Hijuelos, Robert Olen Butler, Hilma and Meg Wolitzer, Budd Schulberg and Cynthia Ozick."
Costs: Non-credit: approximately $410 per workshop or $630 for two workshops. Credit: Approximately $1,100/workshop (2 credits) undergraduate and graduate; $2,100 (4 credits) undergraduate and graduate. "Continental breakfast and lunch are provided daily. Tuition also includes cost of the banquet."
Accommodations: Free bus operates between Hempstead Train Station and campus for those commuting from NYC. Dormitory rooms are available for approximately $350 for the 2 week conference.
Additional Information: "All workshops include critiquing. Each participant is given one-on-one time of ½ hour with workshop leader. We submit work to the Shaw Guides Contest and other Writer's Conferences and Retreats contests when appropriate." Conference information available March 2000. Accepts inquiries by fax, e-mail.

IWWG MEET THE AGENTS AND EDITORS: THE BIG APPLE WORKSHOPS, % International Women's Writing Guild, P.O. Box 810, Gracie Station, New York NY 10028-0082. (212)737-7536. Fax: (212)737-9469. E-mail: iwwg@iwwg.com. Website: www.iwwg.com. **Contact:** Hannelore Hahn, executive director. Estab. 1976. Biannual. Workshops held second weekend in April, and the second weekend in October. Average attendance: 200. Workshops to promote creative writing and professional success. Site: Private meeting space of the City Athletic Club, mid-town New York City. Saturday: One day writing workshop. Sunday morning: open house/meet the authors, panel discussion with eight recently published Guild authors. Sunday afternoon: open house/meet the agents, independent presses and editors.
Costs: $130 for the weekend.
Accommodations: Information on transportation arrangements and overnight accommodations available.
Additional Information: Accepts inquires by fax, e-mail.

N. IWWG SUMMER CONFERENCE, % International Women's Writing Guild, P.O. Box 810, Gracie Station, New York NY 10028-0082. (212)737-7536. Fax: (212)737-9469. E-mail: iwwg@iwwg.com. Website: www.iwwg.com. Executive Director: Hannelore Hahn. Estab. 1977. Annual. Conference held annually from the 2nd Friday to the 3rd Friday in August. Average attendance: 450, including international attendees. Conference to promote writing in all genres, personal growth and professional success. Conference is held "on the tranquil campus of Skidmore College in Saratoga Springs, NY, where the serene Hudson Valley meets the North Country of the Adirondacks." Seventy different workshops are offered everyday. Overall theme: "Writing Towards Personal and Professional Growth."
Costs: $775 for week-long program, includes room and board.
Accommodations: Transportation by air to Albany, NY or Amtrak train available from New York City. Conference attendees stay on campus.
Additional Information: Conference information available for SASE. Accepts inquires by fax, e-mail.

CAN'T FIND A CONFERENCE? Conferences are listed by region. Check the introduction to this section for a list of regional categories.

KEY WEST LITERARY SEMINAR, 4 Portside Lane, Searsport ME 04974. (888)293-9291. E-mail: keywest@mint.n
et. Website: www.keywestliteraryseminar.org. **Contact:** Miles Frieden, executive director. Estab. 1981. Annual. Spirit
of Place: American Literary Landscapes January 10-20, 2002. Workshop duration: 7 days. Average attendance: 400.
Costs: $400 plus tax.
Accommodations: Provides list of area hotels or lodging options.
Additional Information: For brochure send e-mail, visit website or call. Accepts inquiries by e-mail, phone. Agents
and editors participate in conference.

THE MACDOWELL COLONY, 100 High St., Peterborough NH 03458. (603)924-3886. Fax: (603)924-9142. E-
mail: info@macdowellcolony.org. Website: www.macdowellcolony.org. **Contact:** Admissions Coordinator. Estab. 1907.
Open to writers, composers, visual artists, film/video artists, interdisciplinary artists and architects. Includes main
building, library, 3 residence halls and 32 individual studios on over 450 mostly wooded acres, 1 mile from center of
small town in southern New Hampshire. Available up to 8 weeks year-round. Provisions for the writer include meals,
private sleeping room, individual secluded studio. Accommodates variable number of writers, 10 to 20 at a time.
Costs: "There are no residency fees. Grants for travel to and from the Colony are available based on need. The
MacDowell Colony is pleased to offer grants up to $1,000 for writers in need of financial assistance during a residency
at MacDowell. At the present time, only artists reviewed and accepted by the literature panel are eligible for this grant."
To Apply: Application forms available. Application deadline: January 15 for summer (May-August), April 15 for fall
(September-December), September 15 for winter/spring (January-April). Writing sample required. For novel, send a
chapter or section. For short stories, send 2-3. Send 6 copies. Brochure/guidelines available; SASE appreciated.

MANHATTANVILLE COLLEGE SUMMER WRITERS' WEEK, School of Graduate and Professional Studies,
2900 Purchase St., Purchase NY 10577-2131. (914)694-3425. Fax: (914)694-3488. E-mail: gps@mville.edu. Website:
www.manhattanville.edu. **Contact:** Ruth Dowd, R.S.C.J., dean, School of Graduate and Professional Studies. Estab.
1982. Annual. Conference held June 24-28, 2002. Average attendance: 110. Workshops include children's literature,
journal writing, creative nonfiction, personal essay, poetry, screenwriting, fiction, travel writing and short fiction. The
Conference is designed not only for writers but for teachers of writing. Students do intensive work in the genre of their
choice. Manhattanville is a suburban campus 30 miles from New York City. The campus centers around Reid Castle,
the administration building, the former home of Whitelaw Reid. Workshops are conducted in Reid Castle. A major
author is featured as guest lecturer during the Conference. Past speakers have included such authors as Toni Morrison,
Andy Bienen, Gail Godwin, Richard Peck and poet Mark Doty.
Costs: Conference cost was $560 in 2001 plus $30 fee.
Accommodations: Students may rent rooms in the college residence halls. More luxurious accommodations are
available at neighboring hotels. In the summer of 2002 the cost of renting a room in the residence halls was $40 per
night.
Additional Information: Conference information available March 15, 2003. For brochure send e-mail, visit website,
call or fax. Accepts inquiries by SASE, e-mail, fax, phone.

NEW ENGLAND WRITERS CONFERENCE, P.O. Box 483, 151 Main St., Windsor VT 05089-0483. (802)674-
2315. E-mail: newvtpoet@aol.com. Website: http://hometown.aol.com/newvtpoet/myhomepage/profile.html. **Contact:**
Dr. Frank or Susan Anthony, co-directors. Estab. 1986. Annual. Conference held third Saturday in July. Conference
duration: 1 day. Average attendance: 150. The purpose is "to bring an affordable literary conference to any writers who
can get there, and to expose them to emerging excellence in the craft." Site: The Grace Outreach Building, 1 mile
south of the Dartmouth campus, Hanover NH. Offers panel and seminars by prominent authors, agents, editors or
publishers; open readings, contest awards and book sales/signings. 2002 featured guests included Reeve Lindbergh
(fiction, memoir); Lloyd Goodwin, Avis Smalley, April Ossman and William W. Cook.
Costs: $20 (includes lunch). No pre-registration required.
Accommodations: Provides a list of area hotels or lodging options.
Additional Information: Sponsors poetry and fiction contests as part of conference (award announced at conference).
Conference information available in May. For brochure send SASE or visit website. Accepts inquiries by SASE, e-mail,
phone.

ODYSSEY, 20 Levesque Lane, Mont Vernon NH 03057-1420. Phone/fax: (603)673-6234. E-mail: jcavelos@sff.net.
Website: www.sff.net/odyssey. **Contact:** Jeanne Cavelos, director. Estab. 1995. Annual. Workshop to be held June 16
to July 25, 2003. Attendance limited to 20. "A workshop for fantasy, science fiction and horror writers that combines
an intensive learning and writing experience with in-depth feedback on students' manuscripts. The only workshop to
combine the overall guidance and in-depth feedback of a single instructor with the varied perspectives of guest lecturers
and the only such workshop run by an editor." Conference held at Southern New Hampshire University in Manchester,
New Hampshire. Previous guest lecturers included: Harlan Ellison, Ben Bova, Dan Simmons, Jane Yolen, Elizabeth
Hand, Craig Shaw Gardner, Terry Brooks, Patricia McKillip and John Crowley.
Costs: In 2002: $1,280 tuition, $367 housing (double room), $25 application fee, $350 food (approximate), $55 process-
ing fee to receive college credit.
Accommodations: "Workshop students stay at Southern New Hampshire University townhouses and eat at college."
Additional Information: Students must apply and include a writing sample. Students' works are critiqued throughout
the 6 weeks. Workshop information available in October. For brochure/guidelines send SASE, e-mail, visit website, call
or fax. Accepts inquiries by SASE, e-mail, fax, phone.

PERSPECTIVES IN CHILDREN'S LITERATURE, University of Massachusetts, Amherst MA 01003-3035. (413)545-1116 or (413)545-4325. E-mail: childlit@educ.umass.edu. Website: www.unix.oit.umass.edu/~childlit. **Contact:** Jane Pierce, coordinator. Estab. 1970. Annual. Conference duration: 8:30-4:00 p.m. Average attendance: 300-500. Conference is for teachers, librarians, writers, illustrators, parents, and students. Location: Isenberg School of Management classroom building. Previous presenters have included Julius Lester, Gail Carson Levine, Jane Dyer, Liza Ketchem, Jane Yolen, Rich Michelson, and more.
Costs: $60, general admission; $55, students.
Additional Information: Conference Information is available by January: send SASE, e-mail, visit website or call. Accepts inquiries by SASE, e-mail, phone. Agents and/or editors participate in conference.

THE PUBLISHING GAME, Peanut Butter and Jelly Press, P.O. Box 590239, Newton MA 02459. E-mail: Conference@PublishingGame.com. Website: www.PublishingGame.com. **Contact:** Alyza Harris, manager. Estab. 1998. Conference held monthly, in different locales across US; Boston, November 19, 2002; New York City, December 8, 2002; Philadelphia, January 26, 2003; Washington, DC, January 30, 2003; Boca Raton, February 2003; New York City, March 31, 2003; Boston, April 27, 2003; San Francisco, May 18, 2003; Los Angeles, May 25, 2003; Toronto, June 22, 2003; Boston, July 20, 2003; New York City, August 3, 2003; Boston, September 7, 2003. Conference duration: 9 a.m to 5 p.m. Average attendance: 20 writers. "A one-day workshop on self-publishing your book, creating a publishing house and promoting your book to bestsellerdom!" Site: "Elegant hotels across the country. Boston locations alternate between the Four Seasons Hotel in downtown Boston and The Inn at Harvard in historic Harvard Square, Cambridge." Fiction panels in 2003 include Propel Your Novel from Idea to Finished Manuscript; How to Self-Publish Your Novel; Craft the Perfect Book Package; How to Promote Your Novel; Selling Your Novel to Bookstores and Libraries. Workshop led by Fern Reiss, author and publisher.
Cost: $195.
Accommodations: "All locations are easily accessible by public transportation." Offers discounted conference rates for participants who choose to arrive early. Offers list of area lodging.
Additional Information: Brochures available for SASE. Accepts inquiries by SASE, e-mail, phone, fax but SASE preferred. Agents and editors attend conference. "If you're considering self-publishing your novel, or you've sold it to a publisher but would like to sell more copies, this conference will teach you everything you need to know to succesfully self-publish and self-promote your work."

"REMEMBER THE MAGIC" IWWG ANNUAL SUMMER CONFERENCE, International Women's Writing Guild, P.O. Box 810, Gracie Station, New York NY 10028-0082. (212)737-7536. Fax: (212)737-9469. E-mail: dirhahn@aol.com. Website: www.iwwg.com. **Contact:** Hannelore Hahn. Estab. 1978. Annual. Conference held August 10-17 2001. Duration of conference 1 week. Average attendance: 500. The conference features 70 workshops held every day on every aspect of writing and the arts. Saratoga Springs, 30 minutes from Albany NY and 4 hours from New York City, is blessed with every type of recreation. The town itself is a Victorian paradise, offering gingerbread houses and antique shops galore. Famous for its mineral springs, conference attendees may take baths at Spa Park. Conference attendees may also avail themselves of the famous Saratoga racing season, offering "race breakfasts" at 7:00 a.m. as well as ballet and music performances scheduled at the Saratoga Arts Festival. Workshop topics at previous conferences have included Promoting Your Book; Self-Publishing; The Art of Fiction Writing and One-Act Playwriting.
Costs: $880 for 7 days single, inclusive of meals and lodging.
Accommodations: Accommodations in modern, air-conditioned and non-air-conditioned dormitories—single and/or double occupancy. Equipped with spacious desks and window seats for gazing out onto nature. Meals served cafeteria-style with choice of dishes. Variety of fresh fruits, vegetables and salads have been found plentiful . . . even by vegetarians. Conference information is available in January. For brochure send SASE, e-mail, visit website or fax. Accepts inquiries by SASE, e-mail, phone or fax. "The conference is for women only."

SCBWI MIDYEAR CONFERENCE, NYC, (formerly SCBWI Conference in Children's Literature, NYC), 8271 Beverly Blvd., Los Angeles CA 90048. (323)782-1010. Fax: (323)782-1892. E-mail: conference@scbwi.org. Website: www.scbwi.org. President: Stephen Mooser. Estab. 1975. Annual. Conference held in February. Average attendance: 600. Conference is to promote writing for children: picture books; fiction; nonfiction; middle grade and young adult; meet an editor; meet an agent; financial planning for writers; marketing your book; children's multimedia; etc. Site: Manhattan.
Costs: See website for current cost.
Accommodations: Write for information; hotel names will be supplied.
Additional Information: Conference information available for SASE.

SCBWI/HOFSTRA CHILDREN'S LITERATURE CONFERENCE, Hofstra University, University College of Continuing Education, Hempstead NY 11549. (516)463-5016. Website: www.hofstra.edu/writers. **Contact:** Connie C. Epstein, Adrienne Betz and Marion Flomenhaft, co-organizers. Estab. 1985. Annual. Conference to be held April 12, 2003. Average attendance: 200. Conference to encourage good writing for children. "Purpose is to bring together various professional groups—writers, illustrators, librarians, teachers—who are interested in writing for children. Each year we organize the program around a theme. Last year it was Finding Your Voice." The conference takes place at the Student Center Building of Hofstra University, located in Hempstead, Long Island. "We have two general sessions, an editorial panel and five break-out groups held in rooms in the Center or nearby classrooms." Previous agents/speakers have included: Paula Danziger and Anne M. Martin and a panel of children's book editors who critique randomly selected first-manuscript pages submitted by registrants. Special interest groups are offered in picture books, nonfiction and submission procedures with others in fiction.

Cost: $70 (previous year) for SCBWI members; $78 for nonmembers. Lunch included.

N. SEACOAST WRITER'S ASSOCIATION SPRING AND FALL CONFERENCES, 59 River Rd., Stratham NH 03885-2358. Fax: (603)772-2720. E-mail: riverrd@tiac.net. **Contact:** Pat Parnell, conference director. Annual. Conferences held in May and October. Conference duration: 1 day. Average attendance: 50. "Our conferences offer workshops covering various aspects of fiction, nonfiction and poetry." Site: White Pines College in Chester, NH.
Costs: $50.
Additional Information: "We sometimes include critiques. It is up to the speaker." Spring meeting includes a contest. Categories are fiction, nonfiction (essays) and poetry. Judges vary from year to year. Conference information available for SASE April 1 and September 1. Accepts inquiries by SASE, e-mail, fax, phone.

STATE OF MAINE WRITERS' CONFERENCE, 16 Foley Ave., Saco MA 04072. (800)330-4975. **Contact:** Jeff Belyea. Estab. 1941. Annual. Conference held in August. Conference duration: 4 days. Average attendance: 40. "We try to present a balanced as well as eclectic conference. There is quite a bit of time and attention given to poetry but we also have children's literature, travel, novels/fiction and other issues of interest to writers. Our speakers are publishers, editors, illustrators and other professionals. Our concentration is, by intention, a general view of writing to publish. We are located in Ocean Park, a small seashore village 14 miles south of Portland. Ours is a summer assembly center with many buildings from the Victorian Age. The conference meets in Porter Hall, one of the assembly buildings which is listed on the National Register of Historic Places. Within recent years our guest list has included Lewis Turco, Amy MacDonald, Jeffrey Aronson, Wesley McNair, John N. Cole, Betsy Sholl, Denis Ledoux, John Tagliabue, Roy Fairfield, Oscar Greene and many others. We usually have about 10 guest presenters a year."
Costs: $90-100 includes the conference banquet. There is a reduced fee, $50, for students ages 21 and under. The fee does not include housing.
Accommodations: An accommodations list is available. "We are in a summer resort area and motels, guest houses and restaurants abound."
Additional Information: "We have a list of about nine contests on various genres. The prizes, all modest, are awarded at the end of the conference and only to those who are registered." Send SASE for program guide and contest announcements.

N. STONECOAST WRITERS' CONFERENCE, University of Southern Maine, 37 College Ave., Gorham ME 04038. (207)780-5617. **Contact:** Barbara Hope, conference director. Estab. 1979. Annual. Conference held in mid-July. Conference duration: 10 days. Average attendance: 90-100. "Conference concentrates on fiction, poetry, popular fiction and creative nonfiction. Freeport, Maine, is the site of the conference. Workshops are at the University of Southern Maine Stone House Conference Center." Past speakers include Joyce Johnson, Manette Ansay, Jonathan Lethem, David Huddle, Colin Harrison and David Bradley.
Costs: $510 includes tuition.
Accommodations: Accommodations provided in university housing.
Additional Information: Scholarships available for various groups.

N. ⊕ THE TUSCANY WORKSHOPS, 817 West End Ave., #11D, New York NY 10025. (212)666-6505. Fax: (212)666-7103. E-mail: jmworks@angel.net. Website: www.tuscanyworkshops.com. **Contact:** Susan Jenkins, registrar. Estab. 1995. Two annual conferences. 2001 conference held June 3-16 (in Tuscany); September 15-22 (on Cape Cod). Average attendance: 8. Conference focuses on fiction writing. Site: A 2,000-acre estate in Tuscany, with swimming and horseback riding; a day's drive from Florence, Assisi and Pisa. Novelist Susan Schwartz Senstad is scheduled to participate as a faculty member.
Costs: Tuscany, $2,950; Cape Cod, $1,500. Accommodation, 3 meals/day, tuition, ground transportation, the estate's own wine, housekeeping, classes, critiques, lectures and readings, use of projectors and lightboxes, delivery and pickup of processing, use of printers, paper, duplicating service, and guided field trips.
Accommodations: Cost for both Tuscany and Cape Cod is inclusive for shared or individual accommodations (five 18th-century farmhouses, all with double bedrooms and shared bathrooms. Main building for workshops, readings, lectures and slide shows.)
Additional Information: Submit fiction sample (max. 15 pages) with registration. Conference information available January. For 2003 brochure send e-mail, visit website, call or fax. Accepts inquiries by e-mail, phone, fax. Agents and editors participate in conference.

N. VERMONT STUDIO CENTER, P.O. Box 613, Johnson VT 05656. (802)635-2727. Fax: (802)635-2730. E-mail: writing@vermontstudiocenter.org. Website: www.vermontstudiocenter.org. **Contact:** Kevin Cummins, writing program coordinator. Retreat estab. 1984. Ongoing residencies. Conference duration: From 2-12 weeks. "Most residents stay for 1 month." Average attendance: 53 writers and visual artists/month. "The Vermont Studio Center is an international creative community located in Johnson, Vermont, and serving more than 500 American and international artists and writers each year (50 per month). A Studio Center Residency features secluded, uninterrupted writing time, the companionship of dedicated and talented peers, and access to a roster of 2 distinguished Visiting Writers each month. All VSC Residents receive three meals a day, private, comfortable housing, and the company of an International

community of painters, sculptors, poets, printmakers, and writers. Writers attending residencies at the Studio Center may work on whatever they choose—no matter what month of the year they attend." Visiting writers include Melanie Rae Thon and Larry Woiwode (December 2002); Alexander Theroux and John Keeble (January 2003); Rikki Ducornet and Charles Baxter (April 2003); Andrei Codrescu and Michelle Cliff (July 2003); John Yau and Antonya Nelson (September 2003); Jane Hamilton and Sharon Doubiago (December 2003).
Costs: "The cost of a 4-week residency is $3,300. Many applicants receive financial aid."
Accommodations: Accommodations provided.
Additional Information: Conferences may be arranged with visiting writers of the resident's genre. If conference scheduled, resident may submit up to 15 pages of ms. "We have competitions for Full Fellowships three times a year. The deadlines are February 15, June 15, and October 1. Writers should submit manuscripts of 15 pages. Application fee is $25." Writers encouraged to visit website for more information. May also e-mail, call, fax.

WESLEYAN WRITERS CONFERENCE, Wesleyan University, Middletown CT 06459. (860)685-3604. Fax: (860)685-2441. E-mail: agreene@wesleyan.edu. Website: www.wesleyan.edu/writing/conferen.html. **Contact:** Anne Greene, director. Estab. 1956. Annual. Conference held one week at the end of June. Average attendance: 100. For fiction techniques, novel, short story, poetry, screenwriting, nonfiction, literary journalism, memoir. The conference is held on the campus of Wesleyan University, in the hills overlooking the Connecticut River. Meals and lodging are provided on campus. Features readings of new fiction, guest lectures on a range of topics including publishing and daily seminars. "Both new and experienced writers are welcome."
Costs: In 2001, day rate $725 (including meals); boarding students' rate $845 (including meals and room for 5 nights).
Accommodations: "Participants can fly to Hartford or take Amtrak to Meriden, CT. We are happy to help participants make travel arrangements." Overnight participants stay on campus.
Additional Information: Manuscript critiques are available as part of the program but are not required. Participants may attend seminars in several different genres. Scholarships and teaching fellowships are available, including the Jakobson awards for new writers of fiction, poetry and nonfiction and the Jon Davidoff Scholarships for journalists. Accepts inquiries by e-mail, phone, fax.

THE WRITER'S VOICE OF THE WEST SIDE YMCA, 5 West 63rd St., New York NY 10023. (212)875-4124. (212) 875-4184. E-mail: wswritersvoice@ymcanyc.org. **Contact:** Fanon Howell, associate director. Estab. 1981. Workshop held four times/year (summer, spring, winter and fall). Workshop duration: 1-12 weeks, two hours one night/week. Average attendance: 15. Workshop on "fiction, poetry, writing for performance, non-fiction, multi-genre, playwriting and writing for children." Workshop held at the Westside YMCA.
Costs: $325/workshop.
Additional Information: For workshop brochures/guidelines send SASE, e-mail, visit website, call or fax. Accepts inquiries by SASE, e-mail, fax, phone. "The Writer's Voice of the Westside Y is the largest non-academic literary arts center in the U.S."

[N] WRITING AS A MYTHIC JOURNEY, 995 Chapman Rd., Yorktown NY 10598. (914)962-4432. E-mail: emily @emilyhanlon.com. Website: www.thefictionwritersjourney.com. **Contact:** Emily Hanlon. Estab. 2001. Annual. Conference held November 6-9, 2003. Average attendance: 10-20. "Using all forms of writing, including fiction, poetry and journaling, we will explore the writer's journey as a myth in which you are the hero/heroine. In the workshop, we embrace a most ancient tradition of the storyteller. Like the shaman, the storyteller is one who travels safely to the other side and returns with healing and transforming messages for ourselves and others. The workshop is open to anyone-regardless of writing experience—who is looking to explore the spiritual journey of the Inner Writer." Site: Bethany House, a retreat center in the southern Catskills about 2 hours north of New York City. Workshops led by Emily Hanlon.
Costs: 2002 prices were $375 for early registration; $425 regular fee. Includes lodging and meals.
Accomodations: Private rooms in Bethany House.
Additional Information: "Participants need to speak to Emily Hanlon on the telephone." Brochure available on website. Accepts inquiries by e-mail, phone.

[N] WRITING, CREATIVITY AND RITUAL: A WOMAN'S RETREAT, 995 Chapman Rd., Yorktown Heights NY 10598. (914)926-4432. E-mail: emily@emilyhanlon.com. Website: www.thefictionwritersjourney.com. **Contact:** Emily Hanlon. Estab. 1998. Annual. Retreat held September 2002. Average attendance: 20 is the limit. Retreat for "fiction, memoir, creative nonfiction and the creative process." Location varies. "I try to find places conducive to creativity and the imagination. September 2002, Tuscany, Italy." The theme of the retreat is "the passion and risk of the creative journey. Writing emphasis on the writer's voice through opening to characters that come from the writer's unconscious."
Costs: 2002 fees: $2,600-3,000 depending on choice of room. Includes workshop, room and all meals plus a bus fee for four days of touring, including Florence and Assissi.
Additional Information: Conference information free and available. Accepts inquiries by e-mail, phone. "This retreat is open only to women. Enrollment is limited to 20. More than just a writing workshop or conference, the retreat is an exploration of the creative process through writing—3-hour writing workshps daily, time to write on a villa high in the Tuscan hills. Four days of traveling/touring Florence and Tuscany."

YADDO, Box 395, Saratoga Springs NY 12866-0395. (518)587-0746. Fax: (518)584-1312. E-mail: yaddo@yaddo.org. Website: www.yaddo.org. **Contact:** Admissions Committee. Estab. 1926. "Those qualified for invitations to Yaddo are

highly qualified writers, visual artists, composers, choreographers, performance artists and film and video artists who are working at the professional level in their fields. Artists who wish to work collaboratively are encouraged to apply. An abiding principle at Yaddo is that applications for residencies are judged on the quality of the artists' work and professional promise." Provisions include room, board and studio space. No stipends are offered. Site includes four small lakes, a rose garden, woodland. Two seasons: large season is mid-May-August; small season is October-May (stays from 2 weeks to 2 months; average stay is 5 weeks). Accommodates approximately 16 writers in large season. **Costs:** No fee is charged; residency includes room, board and studio space. Limited travel expenses are available to artists accepted for residencies at Yaddo.
To Apply: Filing fee is $20 (checks to Corporation of Yaddo). Two letters of recommendation are requested. Applications are considerd by the Admissions Committee and invitations are issued by April (deadline: January 15) and September (deadline: August 1). Conference information available for SASE (55¢ postage), by e-mail, fax or phone and on website. Accepts inquiries by e-mail, fax, SASE, phone.

Midatlantic (DC, DE, MD, NJ, PA)

BALTIMORE WRITERS ALLIANCE CONFERENCE, P.O. Box 410, Riderwood MD 21139-0410. (410)377-5265. Fax: (410)377-4507. E-mail: hdiehl@bcpl.net. Website: www.baltimorewriters.org. **Contact:** Barbara Diehl. Estab. 1993. Annual. Conference held in November. Conference duration: 1 day. Average attendance: 150-200. Conference focuses on "many areas of writing and getting published." Site: Towson University. Panels featured in the 2001 conference include short fiction, romance novel, general fiction. Donna Boetig, Mary Joe Putney, Allegra Bennett and 20 plus others participated as speakers.
Costs: $75, includes food.
Accommodations: Provides a list of area hotels or lodging options "if asked."
Additional Information: Conference information is available August/September. For brochure e-mail, visit website or call. Accepts inquiries by e-mail and phone. Online registration available. Agents and editors participate in conference.

BOOKTOWNS OF EUROPE WRITERS WORKSHOPS, P.O. Box 1626, West Chester PA 19380. (610)486-6687. Fax: (610)486-0204. E-mail: info@booktownwriters.com. Website: www.booktownwriters.com/. **Contact:** Lenore M. Scallan, workshops coordinator. Estab. 1995. 3-4 per year. Conferences due to be held July 14-20, 2002, France; July 21-27, 2002, Germany; July 28-August 3, 2002, The Netherlands; August 5-10, 2002, Norway; December 8-14, 2002, Ireland. 2003 dates available August 2002. Average attendance: under 12 per site. "Booktowns of Europe focuses on the book-length project. We remove writers from daily distractions, provide a learning vacation atmosphere in the small villages and towns of western Europe, offer intensive support for all fiction and non-fiction topics: autobiography, biography, business, history, romance, sci-fi, self help, sports, etc. (no poetry, erotica or script-writing)." Site: offer 5-6 sites/year throughout Europe. Panels planned for next conference include two daily sessions - a morning writing assignment related to the location, and an afternoon session reviewing the morning session's results. Lenore M. Scallan and Bruce Mowday are scheduled to participate as faculty members.
Costs: $1,600 for entire package, including transportation between transfer city and workshop site; full tuition; all course materials; one half-hour private conference with workshop leader; six nights accommodation with daily breakfast and dinner; one afternoon/evening excursion.
Accommodations: All accommodations are comfortable, two-star European, double occupancy, first-come first-served. 10% discount for full-time students (with university ID) and seniors, plus group discounts for groups of six or more. Accommodations are limited.
Additional Information: A 10-page sample chapter, excerpt and/or full treatment for the book project with a $25 fee may be submitted 60 days prior to workshop for a technical and potential marketing evaluation. The submission will be returned with a marked copy and one-page evaluation sheet at the start of the workshop program. Conference information for SASE. "The workshop environment, while intense, offers plenty of private time opportunity for participants to write. They also have free time to explore the unique distinctions of each site. One additional option: a free-ranging post-dinnertime evening discussion in which town 'locals' often take part. Attendance is not required, but these open discussions often become the most memorable parts of the workshop experience.

THE COLLEGE OF NEW JERSEY WRITERS' CONFERENCE, English Dept., The College of New Jersey, P.O. Box 7718, Ewing NJ 08628-0718. (609)771-3254. Fax: (609)637-5112. E-mail: write@tcnj.edu. **Contact:** Jean Hollander, director. Estab. 1980. Annual. Conference will be held April 2003. Conference duration: 9 a.m. to 10:30 p.m. Average attendance: 600-1,000. "Conference concentrates on fiction (the largest number of participants), poetry, children's literature, play and screenwriting, magazine and newspaper journalism, overcoming writer's block, nonfiction books. Conference is held at the student center at the college in two auditoriums and workshop rooms; also Kendall Theatre on campus." The focus is on various genres: romance, detective, mystery, TV writing, etc. Topics have included "How to Get Happily Published," "How to Get an Agent" and "Earning a Living as a Writer." The conference usually presents twenty or so authors, plus two featured speakers, who have included Arthur Miller, Saul Bellow, Toni Morrison, Joyce Carol Oates, Erica Jong, Alice Walker, Joseph Heller, John Updike, Anna Quindlen, etc.
Costs: General registration $50, plus $10 for each workshop. Lower rates for students.
Additional Information: Conference information available by mail, e-mail, fax, phone.

N HIGHLIGHTS FOUNDATION FOUNDERS WORKSHOPS, 814 Court St., Honesdale PA 18437. (570)253-1172. Fax: (570)253-0179. E-mail: contact@highlightsfoundation.org. Website: www.highlightsfoundation.o rg. **Contact:** Maggie Ewain. Estab. 2000. Workshops held seasonally in March, April, May, June, September, October, November. Conference held June 20-27, 2003. Duration: 3-7 days. Attendance limited to 10-14. Conference focuses on children's writing: fiction, nonfiction, poetry, promotions. "Our goal is to improve, over time, the quality of literature for children by educating future generations of children's authors." Site: Highlights Founders' home in Boyds Mills, PA. Faculty/speakers in 2002 included Joy Cowley, Patricia Lee Crouch, Carolyn Yooler, Andrea Early, Rebecca Lay Dotlich, Kent L. Brown, Jr. and Peter Jacobi.

Costs: 2002 costs ranged from $795-995, including meals, lodging, materials.

Accommodations: Coordinates pickup at local airport. Offers overnight accommodations. "Participants stay in guest cabins on the wooded grounds surrounding Highlights Founders' home adjacent to the house/conference center."

Additional Information: "Some workshops require pre-workshop assignment." Brochure available for SASE, by e-mail, on website, by phone, by fax. Accepts inquiries by phone, fax, e-mail, SASE. Editors attend conference. "Applications will be reviewed and accepted on a first-come, first-served basis, applicants must demonstrate specific experience in writing area of workshop they are applying for—writing samples are required for many of the workshops.

N HIGHLIGHTS FOUNDATION WRITING FOR CHILDREN, 814 Court St., Honesdale PA 18431. (570)253-1192. Fax: (570)253-0179. E-mail: contact@highlightsfoundation.org. Website: www.lighlightsfoundation.o rg. **Contact:** Kent L. Brown. Estab. 1985. Annual. Conference held July 12-17, 2003; July 17-24, 2004; July 16-23, 2005. Average attendance: 100. Focuses on all genres of children's writing. Site: Chautauqua Institution. "Few cars are allowed on the grounds making for peaceful, idyllic surroundings. Architecture reflects the charm of the late 19th century. "Panels planned include Characterization, Writing Dialogue, Point of View, Developing a Plot, Think Pictures, etc. 2002 speakers included Sandy Asher, Barbara Barstow, Pat Broderick, Kent Brown, Mary Lou Carney, Joy Cowley, George Ford, Dayton Hyde, Jerry Spinelli, Eileen Spinelli and Lawrence Pringle.

Costs: In 2002, $1900 with meals, gate pass, conference supplies included. Lodging and transportation extra.

Accommodations: Coordinates pickup from local airports, Jamestown and Buffalo. Coordinates locating lodging. "Accommodations available on the grounds—inns, hotels, guesthouses." $330-695 per week.

Additional Information: Participants must submit ms if participating in ms program. Brochures available December 2002 by SASE, e-mail, phone, fax or on website. Accepts inquiries by SASE, e-mail, phone, fax. Agents and editors attend conference.

MONTROSE CHRISTIAN WRITER'S CONFERENCE, 5 Locust St., Montrose Bible Conference, Montrose PA 18801-1112. (570)278-1001 or (800)598-5030. Fax: (570)278-3061. E-mail: mbc@montrosebible.org. Website: www.montrosebible.org. **Contact:** Donna Kosik, MBC Secretary/Registrar. Estab. 1990. Annual. Conference held in July, 2002. Average attendance: 75. "We try to meet a cross-section of writing needs, for beginners and advanced, covering fiction, poetry and writing for children. It is small enough to allow personal interaction between conferences and faculty. We meet in the beautiful village of Montrose, Pennsylvania, situated in the mountains. The Bible Conference provides hotel/motel-like accommodations and good food. The main sessions are held in the chapel with rooms available for other classes. Fiction writing has been taught each year."

Costs: In 2002 registration (tuition) was $120.

Accommodations: Will meet planes in Binghamton NY and Scranton PA; will meet bus in Great Bend PA. Information on overnight accommodations is available. On-site accommodations: room and board $170-255/conference; $38-$57/ day including food.

Additional Information: "Writers can send work ahead and have it critiqued for $30." The attendees are usually church related. The writing has a Christian emphasis." Conference information available March 2002. For brochure send SASE, visit website, e-mail, call or fax. Accepts inquiries by SASE, e-mail, fax, phone.

N THE NEW JERSEY SOCIETY OF CHRISTIAN WRITERS FALL SEMINAR, P.O. Box 405, Millville NJ 08332-0405. (856)327-1231. Fax: (856)327-0291. E-mail: daystar405@aol.com. Website: www.njscw.com. **Contact:** Dr. Mary Ann Diorio. Estab. 1992. Annual. Conference held Saturday, November 1, 2003. Average attendance: 30. Conference focus varies annually; in 2003, it will be fiction. Site: Ramada Inn meeting room in Vineland NJ. Guest Speaker will be Gayle Roper, Christian Novelist.

Costs: $75.

Accommodations: Provides list of area hotels for guests who chose to arrive the night before.

Additional Information: Brochure available in July 2003 by e-mail, phone, fax and on website. Accepts inquiries by e-mail, phone, fax.

N OUTDOOR WRITERS ASSOCIATION OF AMERICA ANNUAL CONFERENCE, 158 Lower Georges Valley Rd., Spring Mills PA 16875. (814)364-9557. Fax: (814)364-9558. E-mail: eking4owaa@cs.com. Website: www.o waa.org. **Contact:** Eileen King, meeting planner. Estab. 1927. Annual. Conference held June 22-26, 2002, in Charleston, WV. Average attendance: 800-950. Conference concentrates on outdoor communications (all forms of media). Featured speakers have included Don Ranley, University of Missouri, Columbia; US Forest Service Chief Dale Bosworth; Nina Leopold Bradley (daughter of Aldo Leopold); Secretary of the Interior, Bruce Babbitt.

Costs: $175 for nonmembers; "applicants must have prior approval from Executive Director." Registration fee includes cost of most meals.

Accommodations: List of accommodations available after April. Special room rate for attendees.

Additional Information: Sponsors contests, "but all is done prior to the conference and you must be a member to enter them." Conference information available April 2002. For brochure visit website, send e-mail, call or fax. Accepts inquiries by e-mail, fax.

WILLIAM PATERSON UNIVERSITY SPRING WRITER'S CONFERENCE, English Dept., Atrium 232, 300 Pompton Rd., Wayne NJ 07470-2103. (973)720-3067. Fax: (973)720-2189. E-mail: parrasj@wpunj.edu. Website: http://euphrates.wpunj.edu/WritersConference. **Contact:** Dr. John Parras. Annual. Conference held April. Conference duration: 1 day. Average attendance: 100-125. Several hands-on workshops are offered in many genres of creative writing, critical writing and literature. Includes reading by nationally recognized author. Site: William Paterson University campus. 2003 keynote speaker: Russell Banks. Past faculty has included Yusef Komunyakaa, Joyce Carol Oates, Yusef Komunyakaa, Susan Sontag and Jimmy Santiago Braca.
Costs: $30 (2002) includes 2 workshops, plenary readings, meals.
Accommodations: Conference information is available November/December. For brochure send e-mail, visit website, call or fax. Accepts inquiries by SASE, e-mail, phone and fax. Agents and editors participate in conference.

PENNWRITERS CONFERENCE, RR #2, Box 241, Middlebury Center PA 16935. Website: www.pennwriters.org. Estab. 1987. Annual. Conference held the third weekend of May. Average attendance: 100. "We encompass all genres and will be aiming for workshops to cover many areas, including fiction (long and short), nonfiction, etc." Past workshops held in Harrisburg and Pittsburgh. Theme for 2002 was "Unlocking the Mysteries of Writing." Speakers included S.J. Rozan and Tamar Myers. Theme for 2003: "Write Here, Write Now."
Costs: Approximately $130 for members.
Accommodations: Special rate of $82/night if reservation is made by April 20.
Additional Information: Sponsors contest. Published authors judge fiction in 2 categories, short stories and Great Beginnings (novels). For conference information send SASE. Accepts inquiries by fax and e-mail. "Agent/editor appointments are available on a first-come, first serve basis."

N. PHILADELPHIA WRITERS' CONFERENCE, P.O. Box 7171, Elkins Park PA 19027-0171. (215)782-1059. E-mail: delamarg@juno.com or pwc@pwcgold.com. Website: www.pwcgold.com. **Contact:** Gloria T. Delamar. Estab. 1949. Annual. Conference held June 6-8,2003. Average attendance: 150. Conference covers many forms of writing, "novel, short story, genre fiction, nonfiction book, magazine writing, juvenile, poetry." Site: Entire wing of Independence Mall Holiday Inn. 2002 workshop leaders include Marilyn Tyner, Gregory Frost, Madeleine Costigan, Vivien Grey, Simone Zelitch, Juliana Baggott.
Costs: In 2002, conference was $180 ($160 early registration); does not include meals or lodgings. Friday night buffet $30; Saturday buffet $30.
Accommodations: "Hotel offers discount for early registration." In 2002, special conference rate was $139/night.
Additional Information: Sponsors contest. "Length generally 2,500 words for fiction or nonfiction. First prize in addition to cash and certificate gets free tuition for following year." Also offers ms critique. Brochures available usually in January for SASE, by e-mail and on website. Accepts inquiries by e-mail and SASE. Agents and editors attend conference. 2002 guest editors and agents included Juris Jurjevics, Soho Press; Dan Simon, Seven Stories Press; Lynn Rosen, Running Press; Samantha Mandok, Berkley Publishing Group; Toni Lopopolo, Toni Lopopolo Literary Agency; Meredith Bernstein, Meredith Bernstein Literary Agency; Jim Fitzgerald, Carl Wahn Agency; Lucienne Diver, Spectrum Literary Agency.

N. SANDY COVE CHRISTIAN WRITERS CONFERENCE, 60 Sandy Cove Rd., North East MD 21901-5436. (800)234-2683. Fax: (410)287-3196. E-mail: info@sandycove.org or james@jameswatkins.com. Website: www.sandycove.org. **Contact:** Jim Watkins, director of conference. Estab. 1982. Annual. Conference held October 5-9, 2003. Average attendance: 150. Focus is on "all areas of writing from a Christian perspective such as: periodicals, devotionals, fiction, juvenile fiction, Sunday School curriculum, screenwriting, self-publishing, Internet writing, etc." Site: "Sandy Cove is conveniently located mid-way between Baltimore and Philadelphia, just off I-95." Located on 206 acres of woodland, near headwaters of the Chesapeake Bay. 2002 panels include historical, juvenile, women's, beginner writer. Faculty: Christy Allen Scannel, Bonnie Brechbill, Michael Davis, Sharon Ewell Foster, Lisa Halls Johnson, Curtis Lundgren, Doug Newton, Kristi Rector, John Riddle, Kathy Scott, Olivia Seaton, Brian Taylor, Claudia Tynes, Jim Watkins, Carol Wedeven.
Costs: In 2002, costs were full package: $624 per person, single room occupancy or $490 per person double room occupancy—includes lodging, meals, materials, seminars, sessions, private appointments and 2 ms evaluations; day guest package: $356 per person, excluding lodging.
Accommodations: No arrangements for transportation. "Hotel-style rooms, bay view available. Suites available for additional fee."

VISIT THE WRITER'S MARKET WEBSITE at www.writersmarket.com for hot new markets, daily market updates, writers' guidelines and much more.

Additional Information: "For manuscript evaluations, participants may submit their manuscripts between six and two weeks prior to the conference. One copy should be sent in a 9×12 manila envelope. Include a self-addressed, stamped postcard if you want confirmation that it arrived safely." 2003 brochure available in April 2003 by e-mail, phone, or fax. Accepts inquiries by e-mail, phone, fax. Editors and publishers participate in conference. Also offers 1 day student training for high school and college age as well as a writer's retreat—24 hours of uninterrupted writing and mentoring.

WINTER POETRY & PROSE GETAWAY IN CAPE MAY, 18 North Richards Ave., Ventnor NJ 08406-2136. (609)823-5076. E-mail: wintergetaway@hotmail.com. Website: www.wintergetaway.com. **Contact:** Peter E. Murphy, founder/director. Estab. 1994. Annual. Workshop held January 17-20, 2003. Average attendance: 175. "Open to all writers, beginners and experienced over the age of 18. Prose workshops meet all day Saturday and Sunday and on Monday morning. Participants choose one workshop from among the following choices: short story (beginning and advanced), memoir, creative nonfiction, novel, drama, poetry, photography, story telling and pottery. Classes are small so each person receives individual attention for the new writing or work-in-progress that they are focusing on. The workshops are held at the Grand Hotel on the oceanfront in historic Cape May, New Jersey." 2002 speakers included Julianna Baggott, Michael Steinberg, Terese Svoboda, Stephen Dunn, Donna Perry, Mimi Schwartz, Robbie Clipper Sethi, and Richard Weems.
Costs: Cost for 2003 is $400 which includes breakfast and lunch for three days, all workshop session and evening activities, and a double room. Dinners are not included. Participants may choose a single room at an additional cost. Some workshops require additional material fees. Commuters who make their own arrangements are welcome. A $25 early bird discount is available if full payment is made by November 15.
Accommodations: "Participants stay in comfortable rooms, most with an ocean view, perfect for thawing out the muse. Hotel facilities include a pool, sauna and a whirlpool, as well as a lounge and disco for late evening dancing."
Additional Information: "Individual critiques may be available to prose writers at an additional cost. Work in progress should be sent ahead of time." For conference information (after September 15) send e-mail, visit website or call. Accepts inquiries by SASE, e-mail, phone. "The Winter Getaway is known for its challenging and supportive workshops that encourage imaginative risk-taking and promote freedom and transformation in the participants' writing."

WRITING FOR PUBLICATION, Villanova University, Villanova PA 19085-1099. (610)519-4618. Fax: (610)519-4623. E-mail: ray.heitzmann@villanova.edu. **Contact:** Dr. Ray Heitzmann, director. Estab. 1975. Annual. Conference dates vary, held in spring. Average attendance: 15-20 (seminar style). Conference covers marketing one's manuscript (fiction, nonfiction, book, article, etc.); strong emphasis on marketing. Conference held in a seminar room at Villanova University (easy access, parking, etc.). Panels include "Advanced Writing for Publication," "Part-time Writing," "Working With Editors." Panelists include Ray Heitzman, and others.
Costs: $450 (graduate credit); $100 (non-credit) plus $10 registration fee.
Accommodations: List of motels/hotels available, but most people live in area and commute. Special arrangements made on an individual basis.
Additional Information: Critiques available. Voluntary submission of manuscripts. Conference information available in late Fall. Brochures available for SASE, e-mail, fax or phone. Accepts inquiries by SASE, e-mail, phone, fax. "Workshop graduates have been very successful." Emphasis: Non-fiction.

Midsouth (NC, SC, TN, VA, WV)

[N] AEC CONFERENCE ON SOUTHERN LITERATURE, (formerly Chattanooga Conference on Southern Literature), c/o Arts & Education Council, P.O. Box 4203, Chattanooga TN 37405-0203. (423)267-1218 or (800)267-4232. Fax: (423)267-1018. E-mail: srobinson@artsedcouncil.org. Website: www.artsedcouncil.org. **Contact:** Susan Robinson, executive director. Estab. 1981. Biennial. Conference held April 24-26, 2003. Average attendance: 1,000. Conference on fiction, non-fiction, drama and poetry. Conference held in downtown Chattanooga on the campus of the University of Tennessee and in the historic Tivoli Theatre. 2003 speakers listed on website.
Costs: $50 (covers conference registration only).
Accommodations: "Radisson Read House Hotel offers a special rate for conference attendees." Shuttle service provided from the Radisson Read House Hotel to the University of Tennessee at Chattanooga.
Additional Information: Conference brochures with schedule available in January 2003. For brochure send SASE e-mail, visit website, call. Accepts inquiries by phone, SASE, e-mail.

AMERICAN CHRISTIAN WRITERS CONFERENCES, P.O. Box 110390, Nashville TN 37222. (800)21-WRITE. Fax: (615)834-7736. E-mail: regaforder@aol.com. Website: www.ACWriters.com (includes schedule). **Contact:** Reg Forder, director. Estab. 1981. Annual. Conference duration: 2 days. Average attendance: 100. To promote all forms of Christian writing. Conferences held throughout the year in over 2 dozen cities. Usually located at a major hotel chain like Holiday Inn.
Costs: Approximately $169 plus meals and accommodation.
Accommodations: Special rates available at host hotel.
Additional Information: Conference information available for SASE, e-mail, phone or fax. Accepts inquiries by fax, e-mail, phone, SASE.

BLUE RIDGE MOUNTAIN CHRISTIAN WRITERS CONFERENCE, P.O. Box 128, Ridgecrest NC 28770. (828)669-3596. E-mail: rhawkin@lifeway.com. Website: www.ridgecrestconferences.com. **Contact:** Robin Hawkins. Estab. 1999. Annual. Conference held April 6-11, 2003. Average attendance: 200. All areas of Christian writing, specializing in scriptwriting. Site: LifeWay Ridgecrest Conference Center. "Companies represented this year include Focus on the Family, Guidepost Books, LifeWay Christian Resources, Boardman & Holman, Tyndale, Walk Worth Press, Act One, Lawson Falle Publishing of Greeting Cards, Hartline Marketing and others."
Costs: Tuition, accommodations and 12 meals, $444-645. Off-campus rate is $325.
Accommodations: LifeWay Ridgecrest Conference Center.
Additional Information: Sponsors contests in published and unpublished categories for poetry and lyrics, articles and short stories, novels and novellas, and scripts. Award includes trophy and $200 scholarship toward next year's conference. Contest entry fee: $10/entry. For brochure, send e-mail, call or fax. Accepts inquiries by e-mail, phone, fax. Agents, film and television producers and consultants participate in conference.

CHRISTOPHER NEWPORT UNIVERSITY WRITER CONFERENCE, 1 University Place, Center for Community Learning, Newport News VA 23606-2988. (757)594-7158. Fax: (757)594-8736. E-mail: LDCurry@CNU.edu. Website: www.CNU.edu/ccl. **Contact:** Lisa Curry, director community learning. Estab. 1981. Conference held February 28-March 1, 2003. Duration: Friday evening and Saturday day. "This is a working conference, There is one keynote Saturday morning. Friday evening and Saturday morning consist of breakout sessions in fiction, nonfiction, poetry, juvenile fiction and publishing." Site: Christopher Newport University, Newport News, VA. 2002 panels included Publishing, Proposal Writing, Internet Research and various breakout sessions. 2002 faculty included Gregory Donovan, Pat Vermillion, Mary Montagu Sikes and keynote speakers Sam Horn and Rita Mae Brown.
Costs: $60, $45 senior citizen, $30 students; includes lunch. Agent/editor appointments for $10.
Accommodations: Provides list of area hotels.
Additional Information: Sponsors contest. "Entries must be unpublished. Fiction—3,000 words; juvenile fiction— 2,500 words. Typewritten, removeable cover sheet with name, title, category, phone, e-mail. No faxes. Submit only one piece in each category. No extra fee. Free critique. Winners' pieces and critiques published in a small booklet." Prizes: $100 for first, $50 for second, $30 for third. Contest entries should be submitted in February to the contact address provided above. Brochure available in December by e-mail, fax, phone and on website. Accepts inquiries by e-mail, phone. Agents and editors participate in conference.

THE COMPLETE WRITER INTENSIVE WRITERS' CAMP, Jones Brehony Seminars in partnership with Island Path Seminars, P.O. Box 878, Ocracoke Island NC 27960. (877)708-7284. E-mail: islandpath@ocracokenc.net. Website: www.jonesbrehony.com. **Contact:** Ruth Fordon or Ken DeBarth. Estab. July 2001. Conference held April. Conference duration: 6 days. Average attendance: under 20. Conference focuses on fiction, nonfiction, publishing. Site: Ocracoke Island, NC. Panels include Understanding the Publishing Industry and How to Make it Work for You, Letting the Muse Flow: Exploring and Manifesting Your Creativity as a Writer, Building the Container: Strategies and Discipline to Capture Your Creative Flow, Techniques of Fiction.
Costs: Workshop and breakfast, lunch, 2 dinners—$1,425; workshop and breakfast, lunch, 2 dinners and lodging— $1,675. Discounts for early registration. Fees include "16 hours of structured class time, 14 hours of intensive writing exercises with 1:1 mentoring, evening speakers—published authors and a publisher/editor, all handout materials, two post-workshop conference calls to report on your goals, T'ai chi and sunrise by the ocean, 50% off one bicycle for the week, 50% off one massage from a certified massage therapist."
Accommodations: Those not staying in the guest house receive 10% off other accommodations.
Additional Information: Brochure available by e-mail for SASE. Accepts inquiries by SASE, e-mail and phone. Agents and editors attend conference.

CREATIVE WRITING BY THE SEA, P.O. Box 15313, Wilmington NC 28408-5313. (910)397-0906. Fax: (910)397-9473. E-mail: Peg@Retreats4Women.com. Website: www.Retreats4Women.com. **Contact:** Peg Schroeder, president. Estab. 2001. Annual. Conference held April 2003. Duration: 6 days. Average attendance: 11. Conference's purpose it "to nurture female fiction writers at all levels of experience." Site: Bald Head Island, NC. "We are the exclusive occupants of a luxurious inn where all activities take place." Workshops led by Jill McCorkle.
Costs: In 2002, $2,255 included individual and group writing sessions, 5 nights luxurious accommodations, 1 full-body massage, daily yoga class, all gourmet meals.
Accommodations: "We provide ferry passage to the island as well as electric carts and bicycles for on-island transportation. Cars are restricted on the island. We also will make shuttle arrangements to the ferry from the airport." Lodging provided.
Additional Information: "Participants are invited, but not required, to submit manuscripts in advance. Maximum 25 pages, typed, double-spaced." Brochures available in September 2002 for e-mail, by phone. on website. Accepts inquiries by e-mail, phone, fax. Editors participate in workshops. "Our retreat is restricted to eleven women, ages 30 or better. It is an opportunity to immerse one's self in writing while the Side Trip's staff caters to all needs. The retreat takes place on semitropical Bald Head Island, NC."

GALACTICON, KAG SPRING BREAK, 5465 Hwy. 58, #502, Chattanooga TN 37416-1659. (423)326-0339. E-mail: galacticon@vei.net. Website: www.thewebfool.com/galacticon/. **Contact:** Clara Miller, programming director. Estab. 1999. Annual. Conference held March 21-23, 2003. Average attendance: 200-250. Conference focuses on "science fiction/fantasy: novels, short stories, poetry (when we have poets for panels), music (filk and folk)." Site:

"Hotel with function space." 2003 schedule TBA. "In the past we have had panels on Novel vs. Short Story; Writing for Special Markets; Building Your World and/or Universe; Alternate Worlds; Choosing a Publisher; Preparing a Manuscript; Writing With Another Author; Self-Publishing; Comparative Religions." Guest speakers: "Literary GoH: P.M. Griffin, Filk GoH: Emerald Rose, KAG GoH: Lawrence Schoen of the Klingon Language Institute."
Costs: "All published authors 1 free membership; Adults at the door: $35 (over 12); Children at the door: $20 (6 to 12); Children under 6 free."
Accommodations: "Staff will arrange pick up at airport and/or bus station (Chattanooga, TN). Offers overnight accommodations at Ramada Inn South. Hotel rooms at Ramada Inn South are single and/or double: $54 plus tax/night; king: $79 plus tax/night."
Additional Information: "Con Suite with real food. 2002 featured a 'Targ' (Klingon pig) roast with trimmings. Included in membership: Dealers Room, Slave Auction and Charity Auction. We have raised $345 (2001) and $280 (2002) for Make A Wish Foundation." Brochures available for SASE, by e-mail, phone or on website. For further inquiries, contact by mail, e-mail or phone. "We have a very knowledgeable and supportive attendees. We love to read, write, draw and sing. We have special programming for 6 to 12 year old with introductions to writing (they make a book) and costuming. They have their own masquerade."

HIGHLAND SUMMER CONFERENCE, Box 7014, Radford University, Radford VA 24142-7014. (540)831-5366. Fax: (540)831-5004. E-mail: jasbury@radford.edu. Website: www.radford.edu/~arsc. Chair, Appalachian Studies Program: Dr. Grace Toney Edwards. **Contact:** Jo Ann Asbury, assistant to director. Estab. 1978. Annual. Conference held first 2 weeks of June 2002. Conference duration: 2 weeks. Average attendance: 25. Three hours graduate or undergraduate credit. "The HSC features one (two weeks) or two (one week each) guest leaders each year. As a rule, our leaders are well-known writers who have connections, either thematic or personal, or both, to the Appalachian region. The genre emphasis depends upon the workshop leader(s). In the past we have had as guest lecturers Nikki Giovanni, Sharyn McCrumb, Gurney Norman, Denise Giardinia, George Ella Lyon, Jim Wayne Miller, Wilma Dykeman and Robert Morgan. The Highland Summer Conference is held at Radford University, a school of about 9,000 students. Radford is in the Blue Ridge Mountains of southwest Virginia about 45 miles south of Roanoke, VA."
Costs: "The cost is based on current Radford tuition for 3 credit hours plus an additional conference fee. On-campus meals and housing are available at additional cost. In 2002 conference tuition was $409 for instate undergraduates, $526 for graduate students."
Accommodations: "We do not have special rate arrangements with local hotels. We do offer accommodations on the Radford University Campus in a recently refurbished residence hall. (In 2002 cost was $19-28 per night.)"
Additional Information: "Conference leaders typically critique work done during the two-week conference, but do not ask to have any writing submitted prior to the conference beginning." Conference information available after February, 2002 for SASE. Accepts inquiries by e-mail, fax.

N LOST STATE WRITERS CONFERENCE, P.O. Box 1442, Greeneville TN 37744. (423)639-4031. Fax: (423)639-6748. E-mail: tamarac@xtn.net. Website: www.loststatewriters.com. **Contact:** Tamara Chapman, director. Estab. 1998. Biennial. Conference held September 2004. Duration: 3 days. Average attendance: 300. Conference focuses on "fiction, nonfiction, travel writing and TV/Radio writing though poetry workshops are included." Theme for 2002 conference was "The Role of Place." Site: "Historic Morgan Inn and Conference Center in the historic district of downtown Greenville, Tennessee." 2002 faculty included Lee Smith, writer; Charles Wright, writer; Sheila Kay Adams, singer/musician/writer; Hal Crowther, journalist/essayist; Betsy Cox, writer; C. Michael Curtis, senior editor *Atlantic Monthly*.
Additional Information: Participants must submit any workshop material in early June. Sponsors contest. "Scholarship contest covers expenses of attending. No reading fee. Submit 5 pages, typed and double spaced, unpublished work." Brochures available in June for SASE and by e-mail. Accepts inquiries by SASE, e-mail, phone. Agents and editors attend conference.

NORTH CAROLINA WRITERS' NETWORK FALL CONFERENCE, P.O. Box 954, Carrboro NC 27510-0954. (919)967-9540. Fax: (919)929-0535. E-mail: mail@ncwriters.org. Website: www.ncwriters.org. **Contact:** Janet Wheaton, program and services director, NCWN. Estab. 1985. Annual. Average attendance: 450. "The conference is a weekend full of workshops, panels, readings and discussion groups. It endeavors to serve writers at all stages of development from beginning, to emerging, to established. We also encourage readers who might be considering writing. We try to have *all* genres represented. In the past we have had novelists, poets, journalists, editors, children's writers, young adult writers, storytellers, playwrights, screenwriters, etc. We take the conference to a different location in North Carolina each year in order to best serve our entire state. We hold the conference at a conference center with hotel rooms available."
Costs: "Conference registration fee is approximately $200 and includes two meals."
Accommodations: "Special conference hotel rates are available, but the individual makes his/her own reservations."
Additional Information: Conference information available September 1, 2002. For brochure e-mail us with your mailing address, visit website, fax or phone. Accepts inquiries by SASE, phone, fax, e-mail.

N POLICE WRITERS ASSOCIATION CONFERENCE, P.O. Box 738, Ashburn VA 20146. (703)723-4740. E-mail: leslye@policewriter.com. Website: www.policewriter.com. **Contact:** Leslyeann Rolik, president. Estab. 1997. Annual. Conference held at various times around the year. Conference duration: 3 days. Average attendance: 50. Conference to "educate both experienced and novice fiction and nonfiction writers of police related work and networking,

networking, networking among writers, editors and agents." Held at a hotel conference center. Courses for 2002 included Writing Character-Driven Fiction, Point-of-View, Promoting Yourself on the Internet. 2002 speakers were Roger Fulton (nonfiction), Bonnie Hearn Hill (author and educator), Sarah Cortez (poetry).

Costs: $175-300 for 3 days.

Accommodations: Shuttle services included in conference fee. Special conference accommodations and prices available.

Additional Information: Sponsors a contest for police related stories up to 1,500 words in fiction and nonfiction. Entry fee is included in the registration fee. Conference brochures/guidelines available on website. Accepts inquiries by fax, e-mail. "The Police Writers Association sponsors this conference. Application for Association membership must be filed and accepted, and evidence of police affiliations or interest may be required."

SEWANEE WRITERS' CONFERENCE, 310 St. Luke's Hall, Sewanee TN 37383-1000. (931)598-1141. E-mail: cpeters@sewanee.edu. Website: www.sewaneewriters.org. **Contact:** Cheri B. Peters, creative writing programs manager. Estab. 1990. Annual. 2002 conference held July 16-28. Average attendance: 110. "We offer genre-based workshops in fiction, poetry, and playwriting, and a full schedule of readings, craft lectures, panel discussions, talks, Q&A sessions and the like. The Sewanee Writers' Conference uses the facilities of the University of the South. Physically, the University is a collection of ivy-covered Gothic-style buildings, located on the Cumberland Plateau in mid-Tennessee. Invited editors, publishers, and agents to structure their own presentations, but there is always opportunity for questions from the audience." 2002 faculty included John Casey, Daisy Foote, Debora Gregor, Barry Hannah, Andrew Hudgins, Mark Jarman, Diane Johnson, Randall Kenan, Romulus Linney, Margot Livesy, Jill McCorkle, Alice McDermott, Claire Messud, Dave Smith, Ellen Bryant Voigt.

Costs: Full conference fee (tuition, board, and basic room) is $1,325; a single room costs an additional $50.

Accommodations: Participants are housed in University dormitory rooms. Motel or B&B housing is available but not abundantly so. Dormitory shared housing costs are included in the full conference fee. Complimentary chartered bus service is available—on a limited basis—on the first and last days of the conference.

Additional Information: "We offer each participant (excepting auditors) the opportunity for a private manuscript conference with a member of the faculty. These manuscripts are due one month before the conference begins." Conference information available after February. For brochure send address and phone number, e-mail, visit website or call. "The conference has available a limited number of fellowships and scholarships; these are awarded on a competitive basis." Accepts inquiries by website, e-mail, phone, regular mail (send address and phone number).

SHEVACON, P.O. Box 416, Verona VA 24482-0416. (540)248-4152. E-mail: themecon@juno.com. Website: www.shevacon.org. **Contact:** Kevin Brown, treasurer. Estab. 1993. Annual. Conference held February 21-23, 2003. Average attendance: 400. Conference focuses on Writing (science fiction and fantasy, some horror), Art (science fiction and fantasy), Gaming (science fiction and fantasy). Fiction related panels included Stolen Stories: The Use of Historical Models; Blood on the Bulkhead: Is New Fiction Too Graphic?; Bad Guys We Want to Win: Writing Good Villains; Scare Me, Thrill Me: Is Horror More Difficult to Write than Fiction? Writer Guest of Honor is Hal Clement. Artist Guest of Honor is Daniel Trout.

Costs: $15 until October 31, 2003; $20 until February 1, 2002; $25 on site. "Meals are not included in the registration fee. Lodging is available at an extra fee."

Accommodations: "Shuttles from the airport are available; we do not have airline discounts." Offers overnight accommodations; "individuals must make their own reservations." Holiday Inn Roanoke Tanglewood. Convention rate $64/night.

Additional Information: Sponsors contest. "We will be awarding our first ever scholarship at our 2003 convention, keep an eye on our website for the entry requirements for the genres of Art and Writing." For brochure send SASE or visit website. Accepts inquiries by mail, e-mail or phone.

STELLARCON, Box 4, Brown Annex, Greensboro NC 27412. (336)294-8041. E-mail: info@stellarcon.org. Website: www.stellarcon.org. **Contact:** Tera Fulbright, convention manager. Estab. 1976. Annual. Conference held March 14-16, 2003. Average attendance: 500. Conference focuses on "general science fiction and fantasy (horror also) with an emphasis on literature." Site: Radisson Hotel in High Point, NC. Guest speakers include Jennifer Roberson, Jody Lynn Nye, Bill Fawcette, Stephen Mark Rainey.

Costs: $30 registration—if received before February 1; $40 at door registration. Does not include meals/lodging.

Accommodations: "Lodging is available at the Radisson." $75/night.

Additional Information: "If participating in the writer's workshop, please contact Tera Fulbright ahead of time to reserve space." Accepts inquiries by e-mail. Agents and editors participate in conference.

VIRGINIA FESTIVAL OF THE BOOK, 145 Ednam Dr., Charlottesville VA 22903. (434)924-6890. Fax: (434)296-4714. E-mail: vabook@virginia.edu. Website: www.vabook.org. **Contact:** Nancy Damon, programs director. Estab. 1995. Annual. Festival held March 19-23, 2003. Average attendance: 15,700. Festival held to celebrate books and promote reading and literacy. Held throughout the Charlottesville/Albemarle area.

Costs: $35 for festival luncheon and $25 fee for reception (reception free for participating authors). "All other programs free and open to the public."

Accommodations: Overnight accommodations can be found on the web at www.travelingamerica.com.

Additional Information: "Authors must 'apply' to the festival to be included on a panel." Conference information is available on the website, e-mail, fax or phone. For brochure visit website. Accepts inquiries by e-mail, fax, phone. Agents and editors participate in conference. "The festival is a five-day event featuring authors, illustrators and publishing professionals. The featured authors are invited or write and inquire to participate. All attendees welcome."

WILDACRE WRITERS WORKSHOP, 233 S. Elm St., Greensboro NC 27401-2602. (800)635-2049. Fax: (336)273-4044. E-mail: judihill@aol.com. Website: www.Wildacres.com. **Contact:** Judith Hill, director. Estab. 1985. Annual. Workshop held first week in July. Workshop duration: 1 week. Average attendance: 110. Workshop focuses on novel, short story, poetry, creative nonfiction. Site: Beautiful retreat center on top of a mountain in the Blue Ridge Mountains of North Carolina. Panels planned for next workshop include 2 novel classes; 2 short story classes; 1 mystery/suspense class. Past faculty has included Gail Adam, Janice Eidus, John Dufresne and Clint McCown.
Costs: $480 (everything is included: workshop, manuscript critique, double room, all meals).
Accommodations: Vans available, $50 round trip.
Additional Information: "New people must submit a writing sample to be accepted. Those attending send their manuscript one month prior to arrival." Workshop information is available mid-January. For brochure send e-mail or visit website. Accepts inquiries by e-mail and phone. Agents and editors participate in conference.

N THE WRITERS' WORKSHOP, 387 Beaucatcher Rd., Asheville NC 28805. (828)254-8111. **Contact:** Karen Ackerson, executive director. Estab. 1984. Held throughout the year. Conference duration: 1-3 days. Sites are throughout the South, especially North Carolina. Past guest speakers include John Le Carré, Peter Matthiessen and Eudora Welty.
Costs: Vary. Financial assistance available to low-income writers. Information on overnight accommodations is made available.

Southeast (AL, AR, FL, GA, LA, MS, PR [Puerto Rico])

ALABAMA WRITERS' CONCLAVE, P.O. Box 230787, Montgomery AL 36123-0787. (334)244-8920. Fax: (334)215-0811. E-mail: poettennis@aol.com. Website: www.alabamapoets.org or www.newsouthbooks.com. **Contact:** Donna Jean Tennis, editor. Estab. 1923. Annual. Conference held for three days, the first week in August. 2003 conference dates are July 31-August 2. Average attendance: 75-100. Conference to promote "all phases" of writing. Held at the Ramsay Conference Center (University of Montevallo). "We attempt to contain all workshops under this roof."
Costs: Fees for 3 days are $50 for members; $70 for nonmembers (which includes membership). Lower rates for 1- or 2-day attendance. Meals and awards banquet additional cost.
Accommodations: Accommodations available on campus. $21 for single, $42 for double.
Additional Information: "We have 'name' speakers and workshops with members helping members. We offer open mike readings every evening. We sponsor a contest each year with a published book of winners." Conference brochures/guidelines available for SASE, by e-mail, on website. Accepts inquiries by SASE, e-mail. Membership dues are $15 and include a quarterly newsletter. Membership information from Donna Jean Tennis at above address. Conference is "laid-back, comfortable, inexpensive and always interesting and informative!"

ATLANTIC CENTER FOR THE ARTS, 1414 Art Center Ave., New Smyrna Beach FL 32168. (386)427-6975. Fax: (386)427-5669. E-mail: program@atlanticcenterforthearts.org. Website: www.atlanticcenterforthearts.org. **Contact:** Thea Boggs, program coordinator. Estab. 1977. Rotating calendar. Conference duration: 3 weeks. Average attendance: 20. "All formats—the development of work in progress in a collaborative environment with other disciplines."
Costs: Meals and lodging provided at no cost to accepted associates.
Accommodations: Offers overnight accommodations. Private room & bath at no cost.
Additional Information: Variable application materials and deadlines. Residency information is available on website. Accepts inquiries by e-mail or phone.

FLORIDA FIRST COAST WRITERS' FESTIVAL, 9911 Old Baymeadows Rd., FCCJ Deerwood Center, Jacksonville FL 32256-8117. (904)997-2726. Fax: (904)997-2746. E-mail: kclower@fccj.org. Website: www.fccj.org/wf. **Contact:** Kathleen Clower, conference coordinator. Estab. 1985. Annual. Festival held May 15-17, 2003. Average attendance: 300-350. All areas: mainstream plus genre. Held at Sea Turtle Inn on Atlantic Beach.
Costs: "Early bird special $200 for 2 days (including lunch and banquet) or $175 for 2 days (including lunch) or $90 for each day; pre-conference workshops extra."
Accommodations: Sea Turtle Inn, (904)249-7402 or (800)874-6000, has a special festival rate.
Additional Information: Sponsors contests for short fiction, poetry and novels. Novel judges are David Poyer and Lenore Hart. Entry fees: $30, novels; $10, short fiction; $5, poetry. Deadline: December 1 for novels, short fiction, poems. Conference information available January 2003. For brochures/guidelines visit website, e-mail, fax, call. Accepts inquiries by e-mail, phone, fax. E-mail contest inquiries to hdenson@fccj.org.

FLORIDA SUNCOAST WRITERS' CONFERENCE, University of South Florida, Division of Workforce and Professional Development, 4202 E. Fowler Ave., MHH116, Tampa FL 33620-6756. (813)974-2403. Fax: (813)974-5732. E-mail: mglakis@admin.usf.edu. Website: www.conted.usf.edu/flcenter.htm. **Contact:** Martha Lakis, conference coordinator. Estab. 1970. Annual. Held February 6-8, 2003. Conference duration: 3 days. Average attendance: 350-400. Conference covers poetry, short story, novel and nonfiction, including science fiction, detective, travel writing, drama,

TV scripts, photojournalism and juvenile. "This is a working writers' conference, targeting categories and mechanics of writing and being published. Designated one of the 'Top 10 Workshops/Conferences for Writers' by *Writer's Digest*." Features panels with agents and editors. Guest speakers have included Lady P.D. James, William Styron, David Guterson, John Updike, Joyce Carol Oates, Wally Lamb, Frank McCourt, Francine Prose and Jane Smiley.
Costs: Call for verification.
Accommodations: Special rates available at area hotels. "All information is contained in our brochure."
Additional Information: Participants may submit work for critiquing. Extra fee charged for this service. Conference information available in October; request by e-mail, fax, phone. Accepts inquiries by e-mail, fax, phone.

FUN IN THE SUN: THE WRITE STUFF, P.O. Box 17756, Plantation FL 33318. (305)663-5779. E-mail: FRWConference@aol.com. Website: www.frwriters.org. **Contact:** A. Leitman, conference chair. Estab. 1986. Biannual. Conference held February 21-23, 2003. Average attendance: 130-150. "Focus is more on fiction writing. Although the conference focuses on romance writing, the workshops are useful to writers in all genres." Site: DoubleTree Guest Suites Galleria, Fort Lauderdale FL. "Workshops include topics on the art, craft and business of writing and there will be an editor/agent panel. There will also be editor/agent appointments; a live and silent auction; and an author booksigning event open to the public, in which all published authors attending the conference can participate." Faculty include Nancy J. Cohen, literary agent; Roberta Brown; Nicole Burnham; Chris Jackson; Leslie Kelly; Roxanne St. Claire; Carol Stephenson; Patricia Waddell and keynote speaker Suzanne Brockmann.
Costs: $145-175; member discounts and group rates available. Includes Friday night dessert tables; Saturday breakfast, lunch and snacks; Sunday breakfast; registration materials; attendance at all workshops and events.
Accommodations: Hotel provides shuttle to/from airport. "Driving directions from major freeway will be posted on our website." Offers overnight accommodations at conference site with special rates available. "Guest suites for up to six are $153/night; guest suites for up to 8 are $213/night."
Additional Information: "Ours is the longest-running conferences of any RWA chapter." Brochures available in July for SASE, by e-mail, by phone or on website. Accepts inquiries by SASE, by e-mail, by phone. Agents and editors participate in conference. Agents include Barbara Collins Rosenberg, Susannah Taylor, Roberta Brown, Pattie Steele-Perkins, and a representative from The Literary Group. "Editors will be listed on our website as they are confirmed."

HAMBIDGE CENTER, P.O. Box 339, Rabun Gap GA 30568. (706)746-5718. (706)746-9933. E-mail: center@hambidge.org. Website: www.hambidge.org. **Contact:** April Hawkins. Estab. 1934. Workshops/residencies held year round. Application deadlines: October 1 for February-August residencies; May 1 for September-December residencies. Residencies are from 2 weeks-2 months. Average attendance: 8 residents. "Creative artists in all disciplines use uninterrupted time to create (writers included!)." Facility is located on "650 acres in north Georgia mountains. Rural, beautiful, private cottage/studios. Dinner served February-December. On National Register of Historic Places."
Costs: $125/week.
Accommodations: "Artists stay in one of eight residence cottage-studios. Each living area is private and equipped with kitchen and bath facilities." Accommodations vary for workshops.
Additional Information: "Must submit an application ($20 application fee) and samples of work. Work is reviewed by a panel of professionals in each field." Workshop brochures/guidelines available on website or upon request with SASE. Accepts inquires by e-mail, fax, phone.

HOW TO BE PUBLISHED WORKSHOPS, P.O. Box 100031, Birmingham AL 35210-3006. (205)907-0140. E-mail: mike@writing2sell.com. Website: www.writing2sell.com. **Contact:** Michael Garrett. Estab. 1986. Workshops are offered continuously year-round at various locations. Workshop duration: 1 session. Average attendance: 10-15. Workshop to "move writers of category fiction closer to publication." Workshop held at college campuses and universities. Themes include "Marketing," "Idea Development" and manuscript critique.
Costs: $49-79.
Additional Information: "Special critique is offered, but advance submission is not required." Workshop information available on website. Accepts inquiries by e-mail.

KEY WEST WRITERS' WORKSHOP, 5901 College Rd., Key West FL 33040. (305)296-9081. Fax: (305)292-2392. E-mail: weinman_i@firn.edu. Website: www.firn.edu/fkcc/kwww.htm. **Contact:** Irving Weinman, director. Estab. 1996. Held 5 weekends/season (January-March). Workshop duration: 5 weekends. Average attendance: 10-12 participants in each workshop. Workshop focuses on fiction and poetry. Past guests include John Ashbery (poetry), Sharon Olds (poetry), Joy Williams (fiction), Carolyn Forché (poetry) and Robert Stone (fiction). Roxanna Robinson, Robert Stone, Edmund White are scheduled to conduct 2003 fiction workshops.
Costs: $300 per workshop.
Accommodations: Provides a list of area hotels or lodging options.
Additional Information: "It's very competitive; many more applicants than places. Early application is essential." Workshop information is available now. For brochure send SASE, e-mail, visit website, call, fax. Accepts inquiries by SASE, e-mail, phone, fax. High standards. "Informal, intimate, intense."

MOONLIGHT AND MAGNOLIAS WRITER'S CONFERENCE, 615 Red Maple Lane, Alpharetta GA 30044. E-mail: info@georgiaromancewriters.org. Website: www.georgiaromancewriters.org. Estab. 1982. **Contact:** Denise Houser. Annual. Conference held November 1-3, 2002 in Dawsonville, GA. Average attendance: 100. "Conference focuses on writing of women's fiction with emphasis on romance. Includes agents and editors from major publishing houses. Workshops have included: beginning writer track, general interest topics, and professional issues for the published author, plus sessions for writing for children, young adult, inspirational, multicultural and Regency. Speakers have included experts in law enforcement, screenwriting and research. Literacy raffle and advertised speaker and GRW member autographing open to the public. Published authors make up 25-30% of attendees." Brochure available for SASE in June.

Costs: $100 GRW member/$125 nonmember for conference registration. $195.02/person/day for accommodations (includes all meals). Other rates available for double, triple and quad occupancies.

Additional Information: Maggie Awards for excellence are presented to unpublished writers. The Maggie Award for published writers is limited to Region 3 members of Romance Writers of America. Deadline for published Maggies is April 18. Deadline for unpublished Maggies unpublished is June 1. Entry forms and guidelines available on website. Published authors judge first round, category editors judge finals. Guidelines available for SASE in spring.

NATCHEZ LITERARY AND CINEMA CELEBRATION, P.O. Box 1307, Natchez MS 39121-1307. (601)446-1208. Fax: (601)446-1214. E-mail: carolyn.smith@colin.edu. Website: www.colin.edu/NLCC. **Contact:** Carolyn Vance Smith, co-chairman. Estab. 1990. Annual. Conference held February 17-23, 2003. Average attendance: 3,000. Conference focuses on "all literature, including film scripts." Site: 500-seat auditorium, 1,200 seat auditorium, various sizes of break-out rooms. Theme will be "Exploration and Discovery Then and Now: Saluting the Bicentennial of the Louisiana Purchase." Scholars will speak on Welty, Faulkner, others in many areas of writing. Speakers will include Rex Reed, Clay Jenkinson, Clifton Taulbert and many others.

Costs: "About $100, including a meal, receptions, book signings, workshops. Lectures/panel discussions are free."

Accommodations: "Groups can ask for special assistance. Usually they can be accommodated." Call (800)647-6724."

Additional Information: "Participants need to read selected materials prior to attending writing workshops. Thus, pre-enrollment is necessary." Conference information is available in the Fall 2002. For brochure send SASE, e-mail, visit website, call or fax. Accepts inquiries by SASE, e-mail, phone and fax. Agents and editors participate in conference.

N OXFORD CONFERENCE FOR THE BOOK, Center for the Study of Southern Culture, The University of Mississippi, University MS 38677-1848. (602)915-5993. Fax: (662)915-5814. E-mail: aabadie@olemiss.edu. Website: www.olemiss.edu/depts/south. **Contact:** Ann J. Abadie, associate director. Estab. 1993. Annual. Conference held April 10-13, 2002. Average attendance: 300. Focus: "The conference celebrates books, writing and reading and deals with practical concerns on which the literary arts depend, including literacy, freedom of expression and the book trade itself. Each year's program consists of readings, lectures and discussions. Areas of focus are fiction, poetry, nonfiction and— ocasinnally—drama. We have, on occasion, looked at science fiction and mysteries. We always pay attention to children's literature." Site: University of Mississippi campus. Annual topics include Submitting Manuscripts/Working One's Way into Print; Finding a Voice/Reaching an Audience; The Endangered Species: Readers Today and Tomorrow. In 2002, panelists included Fiona McCrae, Amy Hundley, Carol Houck Smith, Rick Moody, Aishah Rahman, Natasha Trethewey, Tim Gautreaux, Richard Flanagan, Glora Jean Pinkney, Darcy Steinke, Steve Yarborough, David Galef.

Costs: "The conference is open to participants without charge."

Accommodations: Provides list of area hotels.

Additional Information: Brochures available in February 2003 by e-mail, on website, by phone, by fax. Accepts inquiries by e-mail, phone, fax. Agents and editors participate in conference.

N MARJORIE KINNAN RAWLINGS: WRITING THE REGION, P.O. Box 12246, Gainesville FL 32604. (888)917-7001. Fax: (352)373-8854. E-mail: shakes@ufl.edu. Website: www.writingtheregion.com. **Contact:** Norma M. Homan, executive director. Estab. 1997. Annual conference held in July 23-27, 2003. Conference duration: 5 days. Average attendance: 100. Conference concentrates on fiction, writing for children, poetry, nonfiction, drama, screenwriting, writing with humor, setting, character, etc. Conference held at historic building, formerly the Thomas Hotel.

Costs: $355 for 5 days including meals; $335 "early bird" registration (breakfast and lunch); $125 single day; $75 half day.

Accommodations: Special conference rates at area hotels available.

Additional Information: Optional trip and inner at Rawling Home at Crosscreek offered. Evening activities and banquets also planned. Manuscript consultation on an individual basis by application only and $100 additional fee. Sponsors essay contest for registrants on a topic dealing with Marjorie Kinnan Rawlings. Call for brochures/guidelines. Accepts inquiries by fax, e-mail.

SCBWI SOUTHERN BREEZE FALL CONFERENCE, "Writing and Illustrating for Kids," P.O. Box 26282, Birmingham AL 35260. E-mail: jskittinger@bellsouth.net. Website: www.southern-breeze.org. **Contact:** Jo Kittinger, co-regional advisor. Estab. 1992. Annual. Conference held in October. One-day Saturday conference. Average attendance: 125. "All Southern Breeze SCBWI conferences are geared to the production and support of quality children's literature." Keynote speakers TBA.

Costs: About $60 for SCBWI members, $75 for non-members, plus lunch (about $6). Individual critiques are available for additional fees.

Accommodations: "We have a room block with a conference rate. The conference is held at a nearby school If we can get an airline discount, we publish this in our newsletter and on our webpage."

Additional Information: "The fall conference offers 30 workshops on craft and the business of writing, including a basic workshop for those new to the children's field." Manuscript critiques are offered; manuscripts must be sent by deadline. Conference information is included in the Southern Breeze newsletter, mailed in September. Brochure is available for SASE, by e-mail or visit website for details. Accepts inquiries by SASE or e-mail. Agents and editors attend/participate in conference.

SCBWI SOUTHERN BREEZE SPRING CONFERENCE, "Springmingle '03," P.O. Box 26282, Birmingham AL 35260. E-mail: jskittinger@bellsouth.net. Website: www.southern-breeze.org. **Contact:** Jo Kittinger, regional advisor. Estab. 1992. Annual. Conference held January 31-February 2. Expected attendance: 100. "All Southern Breeze SCBWI conferences are geared to the production and support of quality children's literature." Event is held "in a hotel in one of the 3 states which compose our region: Alabama, Georgia or Mississippi." Springmingle'03 will be in Gulf Shores, AL. Springmingle'03 will focus on picture books. Speakers will be Charlesbridge art director, Susan Sherman; Dona Brooks, editorial director at Penguin Putnam; and Sylvia Williams, librarian.
Costs: "About $100; SCBWI non-members pay $10-15 more. Sometimes 1 or 2 meals are included."
Accommodations: "We have a room block with a conference rate in the hotel conference site. Individuals make their own reservcations. If we can get an airline discount, we publish this in our newsletter and on our webpage."
Additional Information: There will be ms critiques available this year for an additional fee. Manuscripts must be sent ahead of time. Conference information is included in the Southern Breeze newsletter, mailed in January. Brochure is available for SASE, by e-mail or visit website for details. Accepts inquiries by SASE, e-mail.

SCBWI/FLORIDA ANNUAL FALL CONFERENCE, 2158 Portland Ave., Wellington FL 33414. E-mail: barcafer @aol.com. **Contact:** Barbara Casey, Florida regional advisor. Estab. 1985. Annual. Conference duration: 2 days. Average attendance: 80. Conference to promote "all aspects of writing and illustrating for children." Time and location TBA.
Costs: $200 for SCBWI members, $230 for non-SCBWI members. Ms and art evaluations, $30.
Accommodations: Special conference rates on-site.
Additional Information: Accepts inquiries by e-mail.

N. **SILKEN SANDS CONFERENCE**, Gulf Coast Chapter RWA, P.O. Box 1815, Ocean Springs MS 39566. (228)875-3864. E-mail: mcnabbf@bellsouth.net. Website: www.GCCRWA.com. **Contact:** Fran McNabb, conference chair. Estab. 1995. Annual. Conference held April 25-27, 2003. Average attendance: 200. Focuses on romance fiction including paranormal, inspirational, romantic suspense, category. Site: White Sands Resorts located directly on the white sand beach of the Gulf of Mexico in Gulf Shores, AL. "We have workshops planned for both the beginning and experienced writer in areas of writing technique as well as paranormal, inspirational, romantic suspense and category." 2003 panelists include Katherine Sutcliffe, keynote speaker; Gayle Wilson, kickoff speaker; Robin Wells; Janet Lee Barton; Cheryl Lawallen; Sherry Cobb South; Elizabeth Smith; Beth White; Jay Sagel.
Costs: $125 includes "all workshops, editor/agent appointments, 2 breakfasts, lunch, banquet and welcoming luau. Raffle tickets can be purchased to win a critique from an editor or agent along with a 15 minute sitting."
Accommodations: Provides overnight accommodations. "Rooms at the White Sands Resort ar $74.95 and $104.95 (Gulf Front) plus tax until April 9, 2003. After that the rooms will be subject to the Hotel's Rack Rate. One night's room and tax are required for each reservation made."
Additional Information: Brochures available September 2002 for SASE, e-mail, phone or on website. Accepts inquiries by SASE, e-mail, phone. Agents and editors participate in conference. "The conference is noted for its relaxed, enjoyable atmosphere where participants can immerse themselves in the total writing experience from the moment they arrive. The white sand beaches of the Gulf Shore offer the perfect location to stroll along the beach in the moonlight or soak up the warm spring sunshine between conference activities."

SLEUTHFEST, 6056 NW 65th Dr., Coral Springs FL 33067. (954)782-8872. E-mail: RWymer55@aol.com. Website: www.mwa-florida.org. **Contact:** Anne K. Walsh, registration. Estab. 1990. Annual. Conference held March 13-16, 2003. Average attendance: 240. This is "a conference for working mystery writers with emphasis on the craft of writing, forensics and police procedure, as well as contact with top editors and agents and other writers." Site: "Deerfield Beach/ Boca Raton Hilton with free parking, shuttle access to beaches, shopping and dining in Boca Raton." 2003 panels TBA. Guest speakers include Daniel Keyes (*Flowers for Algernon*); Jeremiah Healy; Sue Grafton; Barbara Parker (*Suspicion of Betrayal*); Harlan Coben; Elaine Uets (*Doc in the Box*); police and legal experts, editors and agents.
Costs: $150 members/$165 nonmembers (early registration); $165/180, includes keynote lunch, welcome cocktail party Saturday and Sunday breakfast.
Accommodations: Hotel has shuttle from Lauderdale airport. Offers overnight accommodations provided by the Deerfield Beach/Boca Raton Hilton; special conference rate $149.
Additional Information: Conference information is available August 2002. For brochure send SASE, e-mail or visit website. Accepts inquiries by SASE and e-mail. Agents and editors participate in conference. "Editor appointment is included in the cost of registration. Appointments available on a first come, first served basis." National Shooting Sports Foundation instructs participants on the use and handling of over 20 types of firearms during a special outing. Cost included in conference fee.

N. **SOUTH FLORIDA WRITERS' CONFERENCE**, P.O. Box 571013, Miami FL 33257-1013. Phone/fax: (305)233-8680. E-mail: greenfie@hotmail.com. **Contact:** Henry Greenfield, director. Estab. 1993. Annual. Conference held May 16-18, 2003. Average attendance: 125. Conference focuses on short fiction, novels, poetry, juvenile, nonfiction, freelancing, playwriting, screenwriting, self-promotion, publication, e-books. Site: Barry University main campus.

"Tropical setting, university-type classrooms, theaters, cafeteria, housing." 2003 panels include stage & play reading and individual ms evaluation with agents, editors, authors. 2002 panelists included Adrian Peever, Barbara Nightingale, Jeff Herman, Joyce Sweeny, Judith Welsh, Mandy Greenfield, Lois Blume.

Costs: Provides overnight accommodations; double $59/night with meals, single $69/night with meals.

Additional Information: "Individual evaluations are $35. Manuscript of 20 pages or less or 3 poems due April 15, 2003. Fee includes 15 minutes with agent, editor or author." Sponsors contest. "Judges are professional writers. 2002 prizes were $3,200 for plays, novels, short fiction, poetry, nonfiction, juveniles. Deadline is usually in April." Brochures/guidelines available October 2002 by SASE, by e-mail. Accepts inquiries by SASE, by e-mail, phone, fax. Agents and editors participate in conference.

SOUTHEASTERN WRITERS ASSOCIATION, P.O. Box 774, Hinesville GA 31310-0774. (912)876-3118. E-mail: rube774@coastalnow.net. Website: www.southeasternwriters.com. **Contact:** Harry Rubin, treasurer. Estab. 1975. Annual. Conference held June 16-22, 2002. Average attendance: 75 (limited to 100). Conference offers classes in fiction, nonfiction, basic writing skills, poetry, etc. Site: Epworth-by-the-Sea, St. Simons Island, GA. Most classes are related to fiction writing.

Costs: 2002 costs: $250 early bird registration, $290 after April 15. $70 daily tuition.

Accommodations: Offers overnight accommodations. 2002 rate was $534 for the week, including motel-type room and board (3 meals/day).

Additional Information: Sponsors contests for humor, Southern regional literary fiction, limericks, fiction, short fiction/poetry/essay of 1,200 words maximum about the holiday season. Up to 3 mss may be submitted for evaluation. Judged by the instructors. Conference information available on website. Accepts inquiries for SASE, e-mail, phone. Agents and editors participate in conference.

N SOUTHERN LIGHTS, P.O. Box 8604, Jacksonville FL 32239-8604. (352)687-3902. E-mail: LBarone21@aol.com. Website: www.angelfire.com/fl/Romancewriting. **Contact:** Laura Barone, president. Estab. 1995. Annual. Conference held May. Conference duration: 2 days. Average attendance: 100. The focus of the conference is fiction writing. Site: Holiday Inn Baymeadows, which is "close to beaches, local attractions and shopping." Past panels included plotting, character development, sexual tension, avoiding contrivances, and editor/agent appointments. Cheryl Anne Porter (St. Martins, Harlequin), Vicki Heinze (St. Martins, Silhouette, Kensington), Katherine Garbera (Silhouette Desire), Lorna Tedder (Silhouette, Kensington), Jennifer Weis (editor, St. Martins Press), and Marge Smith (Harlequin, Silhouette, Kensington) participated in 2000.

Costs: $65 fee includes lunch; $55/night hotel.

Accommodations: "If request is made early we can arrange pickup at airport." Offers overnight accommodations at a special room rate at the conference site.

Additional Information: Conference information is available March. For brochure send SASE, e-mail, visit website, or call. Accepts queries by SASE, e-mail, phone. Agents and editors participate in conference.

N TOUCH OF SUCCESS WRITER'S CONFERENCE, P.O. Box 194, Lowell FL 32663. (352)867-0463. Website: http://touchofsuccess.com. **Contact:** Bill Thomas, director. Estab. 1983. Annual. Conference held March 22-29, 2003. Duration: 5 days. Average attendance: 8. Conference focuses on photojournalism, nonfiction, fiction. Site: "Author's Chalet in ancient storybook forest plus portions on a pontoon boat floating down a magical pristine Withlacoochee River." Workshops led by Bill Thomas, fiction and nonfiction author.

Costs: $495 plus lodging.

Accommodation: Arranges pickup at airport by van. Provides list of area lodging.

Additional Information: Brochures available in November/December 2002 by SASE, phone or on website. Accepts inquiries by SASE and phone. "This is a basic nuts and bolt conference which also includes intensive sessions on marketing to publishers, self-publishing, obtaining an agent."

TENNESSEE WILLIAMS/NEW ORLEANS LITERARY FESTIVAL, 938 Lafayette St., Suite 328, New Orleans LA 70113. (504)581-1144. Fax: (504)523-3680. E-mail: info@tennesseewilliams.net. Website: www.tennesseewilliams.net. **Contact:** Shannon Stover, executive director. Estab. 1987. Annual. Conference held March 26-30, 2003. Average attendance: "10,000 audience seats filled." Conference focuses on "all aspects of the literary arts including editing, publishing, and the artistic process. Other humanities areas are also featured, including theater and music." Site: "The festival is based at historic Le Petit Theatre du Vieux Carré and continues at other sites throughout the French Quarter." In 2002, a few panels included Tennessee's Women; Collective Rhythms and Common Threads: the Short Story Cycle; Moonlight, Magnolias and Malevolence: Stereotypes of Southern Literature; *On the Road* with Jack Kerouac; New Orleans Goes to War; Aspects of Power: Politics and Sports. Past speakers include Michael Cunningham, Melissa Bank, Rick Bragg, Tim Gautreaux, Emily Toth, Wally Lamb.

Costs: "Ticket prices range from $5 for a single event to $45 for special event. Master classes are $35 per class. Theatre events are sold separately and range from $10-21."

Accommodations: "Host hotel is the Monteleone Hotel."

Additional Information: "In conjunction with the University of New Orleans we sponsor a one-act play competition. Entries are accepted from September 1 through December 15, 2001. There is a $15 fee which must be submitted with the application form. There is a $1,000 cash prize and a staged reading at the 2002 festival, as well as a full production of the work at the 2003 festival." Conference information is available in late January. For brochure send e-mail, visit website or call. Accepts inquiries by e-mail and phone. Agents and editors participate in conference.

**WRITE IT OUT**, P.O. Box 704, Sarasota FL 34230-0704. (941)359-3824. Fax: (941)359-3931. E-mail: rmillerwio @aol.com. Website: www.writeitout.com. **Contact:** Ronni Miller, director. Estab. 1997. Workshops held 2-3 times/year in March, June, July and August, 2002. Duration: 5-10 days. Average attendance: 4-10. Workshops on "fiction, travel writing, poetry, memoirs." Workshops held across the United States as well as in Italy in a Tuscan villa, in Bermuda at a hotel or in Cape Cod at an inn. Theme: "Landscape—Horizon." Past speakers included Arturo Vivante, novelist. **Costs:** 2002 fees: Italy $1,595; Bermuda $495; Cape Cod $550. Price includes tuition, room and board in Italy, all other locations just tuition. Airfare not included.
Additional Information: "Critiques on work are given at the workshops." Conference information available year round. For brochures/guidelines e-mail, fax, phone or visit website. Accepts inquiries by fax, phone, e-mail. Workshops have "small groups, option to spend time writing and not attend classes with personal appointments made with instructors for feedback."

WRITING STRATEGIES FOR THE CHRISTIAN MARKET, 2712 S. Peninsula Dr., Daytona Beach FL 32118-5706. (904)322-1111. Fax: (904)322-1111*9. E-mail: romy14@juno.com. Website: www.amyfound.org. **Contact:** Rose-mary Upton. Estab. 1991. Independent studies with manual. Includes Basics I, Marketing II, Business III, Building the Novel. Critique by mail with SASE. Question and answer session via e-mail or U.S. mail. Critique shop included once a month, except summer (July and August). Instructors include Rosemary Upton, novelist; Kistler London, editor.
Costs: $30 for manual and ongoing support.
Additional Information: "Designed for correspondence students as well as the classroom experience, the courses are economical and include all materials, as well as the evaluation of assignments." Those who have taken Writing Strategies instruction are able to attend an on-going monthly critiqueshop where their peers critique their work. Manual provided. For brochures/guidelines/newsletter send SASE, e-mail, fax or call. Accepts inquiries by fax, e-mail. Independent study by mail only offered at this time.

WRITING TODAY—BIRMINGHAM-SOUTHERN COLLEGE, Box 549003, Birmingham AL 35254-9765. (205)226-4921. Fax: (205)226-3072. E-mail: dcwilson@bsc.edu. Website: www.bsc.edu. **Contact:** Annie Green, director of special events; Dee Wilson, assistant director of special events. Estab. 1978. Annual. Conference held March 7-8, 2003. Average attendance: 400. "Writing Today provides a quality event that is far more affordable than other conferences its size and quality. The conference presents writers, editors, agents and other literary professionals from around the country to conduct workshops on a variety of literary styles and topics tailored to meet the needs of writers at every stage of development. The conference is sponsored by Birmingham-Southern College and is held on the campus in classrooms and lecture halls." Previous speakers have included Eudora Welty, Edward Albee, James Dickey, Erskine Caldwell, Ray Bradbury, Pat Conroy, John Barth, Ernest Gaines and Joyce Carol Oates.
Costs: $120 for both days. This includes lunches, reception and morning coffee and rolls.
Accommodations: Attendees must arrange own transportation. Local hotels and motels offer special rates, but participants must make their own reservations.
Additional Information: "We usually offer a critique for interested writers. We have had poetry and short story critiques. There is an additional charge for these critiques." Conference brochures and registration forms available in March for SASE, e-mail or on website. Accepts inquiries by SASE, e-mail or fax. Sponsors the Hackney Literary Competition Awards for poetry, short story and novels. Guidelines available for SASE.

Midwest (IL, IN, KY, MI, OH)

ANTIOCH WRITERS' WORKSHOP, P.O. Box 494, Yellow Springs OH 45387. E-mail: info@antiochwritersworks hop.com. Website: www.antiochwritersworkshop.com. Estab. 1984. Annual. Conference held in early July. Duration: 1 week. Average attendance: 80. Workshop concentration: poetry, nonfiction and fiction. Workshop located downtown in the village of Yellow Springs. Speakers have included Sue Grafton, Imogene Bolls, George Ella Lyon, Herbert Martin, John Jakes, Virginia Hamilton, William Least Heat-Moon, Sena Jeter Naslund and Natalie Goldberg.
Costs: Tuition is $500 (approximate)—lower for local and repeat—plus meals.
Accommodations: "We pick up attendees free at the airport." Accommodations made through a village host program and area hotels. Cost is $150 for week (village host program).
Additional Information: Offers mss critique sessions. Conference information are available after March on website.

THE COLUMBUS WRITERS CONFERENCE, P.O. Box 20548, Columbus OH 43220. (614)451-3075. Fax: (614)451-0174. E-mail: AngelaPL28@aol.com. Website: www.creativevista.com. **Contact:** Angela Palazzolo, director.

Estab. 1993. Annual. Conference held in September. Average attendance: more than 200. "The conference covers a variety of fiction and nonfiction topics presented by writers, editors and literary agents. Writing topics have included novel, short story, children's, young adult, poetry, historical fiction, science fiction, fantasy, humor, mystery, playwriting, screenwriting, magazine writing, travel, humor, cookbook, technical, queries, book proposals and freelance writing. Other topics have included finding and working with an agent, targeting markets, time management, obtaining grants, sparking creativity and networking." Speakers have included Lee K. Abbott, Sarah Willis, Sheree Bykofsky, Rita Rosenkrantz and Mark D. Ryan as well as many other professionals in the writing field.

Costs: Early registration fee for Friday afternoon sessions is $70; otherwise fee is $85. Full conference early registration fee is $189 (Friday afternoon sessions, dinner, after-dinner program, Saturday program and meals); otherwise fee is $209. Early registration for the Saturday program (includes continental breakfast, lunch, and afternoon refreshments) is $154; otherwise fee is $174. Friday night dinner and program is $38.

Additional Information: Call, write, e-mail or send fax to obtain a conference brochure, available mid-summer.

[N] IMAGINATION, Cleveland State University, Division of Continuing Education, 2344 Euclid Ave., Cleveland OH 44115. (216)687-4522. **Contact:** Dan Chaon, director. Estab. 1990. Annual. Conference lasts 5 days and is held late June/early July. Average attendance: 60. "Conference concentrates on fiction, poetry and nonfiction. Held at Mather Mansion, a restored 19th century mansion on the campus of Cleveland State University." Past themes have included Writing Beyond Realism and Business of Writing. E-mail, fax or mail for brochure after January.

[N] INDIANA UNIVERSITY WRITERS' CONFERENCE, 464 Ballantine Hall, Bloomington IN 47405-7103. (812)855-1877. Fax: (812)855-9535. E-mail: writecon@indiana.edu. Website: http://indiana.edu/~writecon. **Contact:** Amy Locklin, director. Estab. 1940. Annual. Conference/workshops held from June 23-28, 2002. Average attendance: 115. "Conference to promote poetry, fiction and nonfiction." Located on the campus of Indiana University, Bloomington. "We do not have themes, although we do have panels that discuss issues such as how to publish. We also have classes that tackle just about every subject of writing. Mark Doty, Molly Giles, Andrew Hudgins, Paul Lisicky, Manuel Luis Martinez, Michael Martone, Erin McGraw, Reginald McKnight, Roger Mitchell, Lucia Perrillo, Karen Volkman are scheduled for 2002 workshops and panels.

Costs: Approximately $300; does not include food or housing. This price does *not* reflect the cost of taking the conference for credit. "We supply conferees with options for overnight accommodations. We offer special conference rates for both the hotel and dorm facilities on site."

Additional Information: "In order to be accepted in a workshop, the writer must submit the work they would like critiqued. Work is evaluated before accepting applicant. Scholarships are available determined by an outside reader/ writer, based on the quality of the manuscript." Conference information available annually in January. For brochures/ guidelines send SASE, visit website, e-mail, or call. Accepts inquiries by SASE, e-mail, phone. Application deadline is in early May. Apply early as workshops fill up quickly. "We are the second oldest writer's conference in the country. We are in our 60th year."

[N] [◎] KARITOS FESTIVAL OF CHRISTIAN ARTISTS & WRITERS, 1116 State St., B21, Lemont IL 60439. E-mail: editor@karitos.com. Website: www.karitos.com. **Contact:** Chris Wave, managing editor. Estab. 1996. Annual. Conference held in June. Conference duration: Thursday-Saturday night. Average attendance: 600-800. "Karitos is a celebration and teaching weekend for Christian artists and writers. Writing Division includes all genre. Although we generally do not teach any classes in romance. Neither do we solicit editors specializing in romance. All work must be from a Christian world view." Site: "Venue changes each year but we remain committed to Chicago area." 2002 fiction panels included "Writing Historical Fiction" and "Balancing Character and Plot." 2002 Faculty Members: John Desjarlais, Dr. Jill Pelaez Baumgaertner, Dr. Susan Bergman, Chris Wave.

Costs: In 2001, $40.

Accommodations: Provides list of area hotels/lodging options.

Additional Information: "*Karitos Review* is published 1-2 months prior to festival. Work accepted must be submitted through the website to the editor. We are looking for work with a Christian world view and with literary merit. It does not have to be religious. We are currently paying in copies." Conference information for 2003 is available in January of 2003; send e-mail or visit website. Accepts inquiries by e-mail. Editors participate in conference. "Our readership is multicultural and primarily Evangelical. Each year the festival has a theme but the writing does not need to reflect this theme. We do not publish romance or anything anti-Christian. We do publish thoughtful work reflecting an author's struggle with his faith."

[N] KENTUCKY WRITER'S WORKSHOP, 1050 State Park Rd., Pineville KY 40977. (606)337-3066. Fax: (606)337-7250. E-mail: Dean.Henson@mail.state.ky.us. Website: www.pinemountainpark.com. **Contact:** Dean M. Henson, special events coordinator. Estab. 1995. Annual. Workshop held March 28-29, 2003. Average attendance: 30-40. Focuses on fiction, poetry, short stories, essays. Site: Pine Mountain State Resort Park (a Kentucky State Park). 2002 Panels included Writing for 16 and Under; Grist for the Mill (transforming personal experiences into fiction); The Writing Commitment; Adult Novel Writing. 2002 Panelists included Martha Bennett Stiles, children's author; James Baker Hall, former poet laureate of Kentucky; Jenny Davis, novelist.

Costs: Registration fee is $30.

Accommodations: Offers overnight lodging. Rates vary seasonally; call for updated rates.

Additional Information: Brochures available 2 months in advance by e-mail or phone. Accepts inquiries by SASE, e-mail, phone, fax. Agents and editors attend conference. "Our conference features Kentucky writers of note speaking and instructing on various topics in the writing endeavor. This workshop is designed to help developing authors to improve their writing craft."

KENYON REVIEW WRITERS WORKSHOP, The Kenyon Review, Kenyon College, Gambier OH 43022. (740)427-5207. Fax: (740)427-5417. E-mail: kenyonreview@kenyon.edu. Website: www.kenyonreview.org. **Contact:** David Lynn, director. Estab. 1990. Annual. Workshop held late June through early July. Workshop duration: 9 days. Average attendance: 40-50. Participants apply in poetry, fiction or creative nonfiction, and then participate in intensive daily workshops which focus on the generation and revision of significant new work. The conference takes place on the campus of Kenyon College in the rural village of Gambier, Ohio. Students have access to college computing and recreational facilities, and are housed in campus housing. Faculty: Fiction—Keith Banner, Nancy Zafris and Sharon Dilworth; Poetry—Linda Gregerson and Janet McAdams; Nonfiction—Rebecca McClanahan.
Costs: $1,650 including room and board.
Accommodations: The workshop operates a shuttle from Gambier to the airport in Columbus, Ohio. Offers overnight accommodations. Students are housed in Kenyon College student housing. The cost is covered in the tuition.
Additional Information: Application includes a writing sample. Admission decisions are made on a rolling basis beginning Februrary 1. Workshop information is available November 1. For brochure send e-mail, visit website, call, fax. Accepts inquiries by SASE, e-mail, phone, fax.

MAGNA CUM MURDER CRIME FICTION CONFERENCE, Ball State University, Muncie IN 47306. (765)285-8975. Fax: (765)747-9566. E-mail: kennisonk@aol.com. Website: www.magnacummurder.com. **Contact:** Kathryn Kennison, director. Estab. 1994. Annual. Conference held from October 25-27, 2002. Average attendance: 350. "The main focus is the crime fiction novel, but attention is also paid to short stories, true crime." Site: the Radisson Hotel Roberts and the Horizon Convention Center directly across the street. Past workshops have included plotting, characterization, getting published, historical, and ethics. Guest of Honor: Michael Connelly. International Guest of Honor: Francis Fyfield.
Costs: $175 includes reception, continental breakfast and boxed lunch, banquet.
Accommodations: Offers list of area hotels or lodging options.
Additional Information: Conference information available: e-mail, visit website, call, or fax. Accepts inquiries by e-mail, phone, or fax. Agents and/or editors participate in conference.

MAUMEE VALLEY FREELANCE WRITERS' CONFERENCE, Lourdes College, Franciscan Center, 6832 Convent Blvd., Sylvania OH 43560. (419)824-3707. Fax: (419)882-3987. E-mail: gburke@lourdes.edu. Website: www.lourd es.edu. **Contact:** Gloria Burke, conference coordinator. Estab. 1997. Annual. Conference held March 15, 2003. Average attendance: 70. "The purpose is to provide a venue for freelance writers in a variety of genres. "Sessions in 2002 included 'Bringing Characters Alive on the Page,' 'Writing Novel Query Letters,' 'Putting a Face With Your Story' (importance of pictures with your story) and 'Online Writing.' 2003 conference will include on-site agents, writing competition and bookstore." Keynote speaker for the 2002 conference was Barbara Kuroff, Editorial Director of Writer's Digest Market Books.
Costs: $69/person including continental breakfast and lunch.
Additional Information: Conference information is available in January. For brochure send SASE, e-mail, visit website, call, fax. Accepts inquiries by SASE, e-mail, phone, fax. Agents and editors participate in conference. "Evaluations show that this is a well planned, well organized conference. Every effort has been made to reach freelance writers in the Maumee Valley and Southeastern Michigan areas. We have had anywhere from 38-70 people in attendance; as the conference coordinator, it is my goal to reach for the 100+ mark—hopefully, in 2003."

MIDLAND WRITERS CONFERENCE, Grace A. Dow Memorial Library, 1710 W. St. Andrews, Midland MI 48640-2698. (989)837-3435. Fax: (989)837-3468. E-mail: ajarvis@midland-mi.org. Website: www.midland-mi.org/grac edowlibrary. **Contact:** Ann C. Jarvis, conference coordinator. Estab. 1980. Annual. Conference held June 8, 2002. Average attendance: 100. "The Conference is composed of a well-known keynote speaker and workshops on a variety of subjects including poetry, children's writing, freelancing, agents, etc. The attendees are both published and unpublished authors. The Conference is held at the Grace A. Dow Memorial Library in the auditorium and conference rooms. Keynoters in the past have included Dave Barry, Pat Conroy, Kurt Vonnegut, Peggy Noonan, Roger Ebert."
Costs: Adult—$50 before May 26, $60 after May 27; students, senior citizens and handicapped—$40 before May 26, $50 after May 26. A box lunch is available. Costs are approximate until plans for upcoming conference are finalized.
Accommodations: A list of area hotels is available.
Additional Information: Conference brochures/guidelines available April/May 2002. Call, e-mail or write to be put on mailing list. Accepts inquiries by e-mail, fax, phone.

MIDWEST WRITERS WORKSHOP, Dept. of Journalism, Ball State University, Muncie IN 47306. (765)285-5587. Fax: (765)285-5997. E-mail: info@midwestwriters.org. Website: www.midwestwriters.org. **Contact:** Earl L. Conn. Estab. 1974. Annual. Workshop to be held July 25-27, 2002. Average attendance: 150. Conference held at New Alumni Center, Ball State University.
Costs: $240 for 3-day workshop; $65 for 1-day Intensive Session including opening reception, hospitality room and closing banquet.

Accommodations: Special hotel rates offered.

Additional Information: Critiques available. Conference brochures/guidelines are available for SASE.

N̄ THE MINISTRY OF WRITING: AN ANNUAL COLLOQUIUM, Earlham School of Religion, 228 College Ave., Richmond IN 47374. (765)983-1423. Fax: (765) 983-1688. E-mail: billbr@earlham.edu. Website: http://esr.earlha m.edy/centerpage.html. **Contact:** Rita Cummins, secretary. Estab. 1990. Annual. Conference held October 24-25, 2003. Average attendance: 42. Focuses on "the written word as an important part of the ministry." 2002 keynote speaker was Phil Gulley.

Costs: In 2002, $455 until October 1; $65 after October 1. Costs included all plenary sessions, workshops, Saturday lunch, refreshments. Friday evening reception for additional $15.

Accommodations: Transportation to and from airport by arrangement only. No overnight accommodations available. Offers list of area lodging.

Additional Information: Guidelines available mid-July by e-mail, on website, by phone or by fax. Accepts inquiries by e-mail, phone, fax.

MISSISSIPPI VALLEY WRITERS CONFERENCE, 1629 Second Ave., Suite 2, Rock Island IL 61201. (309)762-8985. E-mail: bjelsner@midwestwritingcenter.org. Website: www.writingcenter.org. **Contact:** B.J. Elsner, conference director. Estab. 1973. Annual. Conference held first week in June; in 2003, June 1-16. Average attendance: 80. "Conference for all areas of writing for publication." Conference held at Augustana College, a liberal arts school along the Mississippi River. Conference workshops included Basics for Beginners, Ann Boaden; Juvenile Manuscript Seminar, Mel Boring; Novel Basics, R. Karl Largent; Short Story, H.E. Francis; Pitch Your Book, Matthew Clemens.

Costs: $25 for registration; $50 for 1 workshop; $90 for two; plus $40 for each additional workshops; $25 to audit.

Accommodations: In 2002, accommodations were available at Erickson Hall on the Augustana College campus. Cost for 6 nights was $100; cost for 15 meals an additional $125.

Additional Information: Conferees may submit mss to workshop leaders for personal conferences during the week. Cash awards are given at the end of the conference week by workshop leaders based on mss submitted. Conference brochures/guidelines are available in January for SASE, on website, by e-mail. "Conference is open to the beginner as well as the polished professional—all are welcome."

OAKLAND UNIVERSITY WRITERS' CONFERENCE, 221 Varner Hall, Rochester MI 48309-4401. (248)370-3125. Fax: (248)370-4280. E-mail: gjboddy@oakland.edu. Website: www.oakland.edu/contin-ed/writersconf/. **Contact:** Gloria J. Boddy, program director. Estab. 1961. Annual. Conference held in October 2002. Average attendance: 400. Held at Oakland University. Each annual conference covers all aspects and types of writing in 36 concurrent workshops on Saturday. Major writers from various genres are speakers for the Saturday conference. Individual critiques, one-day writers' retreats and hands-on writing workshops are conducted Friday. Areas: poetry, articles, fiction, short stories, playwriting, nonfiction, young adult, children's literature. Keynote speaker in 2002: Marge Piercy.

Costs: 2002: Conference registration: $95; lunch, $10; individual ms, $68; writing workshop, $58.

Accommodations: List is available.

Additional Information: Conference information available after August 2002. For brochures/guidelines send SASE, visit website, e-mail, fax, call. Accepts inquiries by e-mail, fax, phone, SASE.

OPEN WRITING WORKSHOPS, Creative Writing Program, Dept. of English, Bowling Green State University, Bowling Green OH 43403-0215. (419)372-8370. Fax: (419)372-6805. E-mail: mmcgowa@bgnet.bgsu.edu. Website: http://personal.bgsu.edu/~wmayo/wshop.html. **Contact:** Mary McGowan, creative writing secretary. Estab. Spring 1999. Twice per academic year (fall and spring). Workshop held Spring, 2001: Date to be determined. Workshop duration: 1 day. Average attendance: 15-20/workshop. Intensive manuscript-based workshops in fiction and poetry. The open worksh ops are open to writers of all levels of achievement. Workshops are lead by creative writing program faculty who read, comment on and distribute mss ahead of time. Beginning or advanced—each ms is addressed on its particular merits. Wendell Mayo (fiction; Director of Creative Writing Program), John Wylam (Poetry; Advisor to BFA Writing Program), Karen Craigo (poetry; Poetry Editor, *Mid American Review*) aer scheduled to participate.

Costs: $50/person per ms. Does not include meals, lodging.

Accommodations: No. We provide parking on campus.

Additional Information: Participants need to submit workshop material prior to conference. Fiction: 1 story, 15 pages double-spaced maximum; send 2 copies. Poetry: 3 poems, a total of 100 lines for all 3, send 2 copies. "Deadlines are set about 3 weeks before the workshops. This gives us time to copy all the mss and mail to all participants with detailed instructions." For brochure send SASE, e-mail, visit website, call, fax. Accepts inquiries by SASE, e-mail, phone, fax. Editors participate in conference. "This is a no-nonsense workshop whose purpose is to 'open' doors for writers who are writing in comparative isolation. We provide guidance on preparation of mss for publication as well."

GARY PROVOST'S WRITERS RETREAT WORKSHOP, % Write It/Sell It, 2507 S. Boston Place, Tulsa OK 74114. (918)583-1471. Fax: (918)583-7625. E-mail: wrwwisi@cox.net. Website: www.writersretreatworkshop.com. **Contact:** Gail Provost Stockwell, director. Executive Director: Lance Stockwell. Estab. 1987. Workshop held May 23-June 1, 2003. Average attendance: 30. Focus on fiction and narrative nonfiction books in progress. All genres. Site: Marydale Retreat Center in Erlanger, KY (just south of Cincinnati, OH). "The Writers Retreat Workshop is an intensive learning experience for small groups of serious-minded writers. Founded by the late Gary Provost, one of the country's leading writing instructors and his wife Gail, an award-winning author, the WRW is a challenging and enriching adventure. The goal of the WRW core staff and visiting agents/editors/authors is for students to leave with a solid understanding of the marketplace as well as the craft of writing a novel. In the heart of a supportive and spirited community of fellow writers, students learn Gary Provost's course and make remarkable leaps in their writing, editing and marketing skills."

Costs: $1,695 for 10 days which includes all tuition, food and lodging (discount for past participants), consultations and course materials. The Marydale Retreat Center is 5 miles from the Cincinnati airport and offers shuttle services.

Additional Information: Participants are selected based upon the appropriateness of this program for the applicant's specific writing project. Participants are asked to submit a brief overview and synopsis before the workshop and are given assignments and feedback during the 10-day workshop. Workshop information available by mid-November 2002. For brochures/guidelines call 1-800-642-2494, e-mail or visit website. Accepts inquiries by e-mail, phone, SASE.

N READERS AND WRITERS HOLIDAY CONFERENCE, Central Ohio Fiction Writers (COFW), P.O. Box 1981, Westerville OH 43086-1981. E-mail: sargtaz@yahoo.com. Website: www.cofw.org. **Contact:** Patricia Sargeant-Matthews, conference director. Estab. 1990. Annual. Conference held October 5-6, 2002. Average attendance: 120. "Welcomes all genres of fiction, including romance, mystery, women's fiction and science fiction/fantasy." Site: Wyndham Dublin Hotel, Dublin, OH. Free workshop on October 4, "Honing Your Editor/Agent Pitch," presented by Silhouette Intimate Moments author Catherine Mann and Leisure Historical Romance author Winnie Griggs; editor and agent appointments; and a meet-the-authors bookfair. Guest speakers include *USA Today* bestselling, contemporary romantic comedy author Jennifer Crusie, whose recent releases include *Fast Women* and *Faking It*; Rita award-winning historical romance author Barbara Samuel (aka contemporary romance author Ruth Wind); Penguin Putnam editor, Cindy Hwang; literary agent Barbara Collins Rosenberg of the Rosenberg Group.

Costs: $70 non-COFW members, $60 COFW members; a Friday night networking dinner is $18 paid with registration.

Accommodations: "The Wyndham Dublin Hotel has reserved a block of rooms for attendees at a discounted rate of $79 per day. To make your reservations, call the hotel directly at (614)764-2200 or toll-free at (800)WYNDHAM and ask for COFW conference rate."

Additional Information: Registration form and additional information available on website or by e-mail.

N RETREAT FROM HARSH REALITY, Mid-Michigan RWA Chapter, 6845 Forest Way, Harbor Springs MI 49740. E-mail: ptrombley@voyager.net. Website: www.midmichigamrwa.com. **Contact:** Pam Trombley, retreat chair. Estab. 1985. Annual. Conference held April 25-27, 2003. Average attendance: limited to 50. Conference focuses on romance and fiction writing. Site: The W.K. Kellogg Biological Station Conference Center, on Gull Lake (Michigan) is the former summer home of cereal manufacturer and philanthropist W.K. Kellogg and one of the most picturesque estates in southwestern Michigan. This quiet country atmosphere lends itself to a productive and relaxing weekend. "We do not have panels. Emphasis is on one speaker and her or his expertise." Ruth Ryan Langan, *New York Times* and *USA Today* bestselling author, is scheduled speaker for 2003.

Costs: Fees range from $45 (Saturday only, lunch only) to $205 (weekend package, all meals, single room).

Accommodations: On-site rooms offer view of lake, kitchenette, twin beds. Handicapped rooms available.

Additional Information: Published author critique offered, 50 pages maximum, $15. Open to MMRWA members or retreat attendees. Conference information available February 2003. For brochure send SASE, e-mail, visit website, phone, fax. Accepts inquiries by SASE, e-mail, phone, fax. "Dress is casual—sweatshirts and jeans. One-on-one conversation with speaker and attendees is emphasized. A chance to relax, talk writing, learn and share ideas. We have a book sale and author signing. We also have a book basket raffle and auction fundraiser for the Kalamazoo YWCA Domestic Violence Program."

N ROPEWALK WRITERS' RETREAT, 8600 University Blvd., Evansville IN 47712. (812)464-1863. E-mail: ropewalk@usi.edu. **Contact:** Linda Cleek, conference coordinator. Estab. 1989. Annual. Conference held in June. Average attendance: 42. "The week-long RopeWalk Writers' Retreat gives participants an opportunity to attend workshops and to confer privately with one of four or five prominent writers. Historic New Harmony, Indiana, site of two nineteenth century utopian experiments, provides an ideal setting for this event with its retreat-like atmosphere and its history of creative and intellectual achievement. At RopeWalk you will be encouraged to write—not simply listen to others talk about writing. Each workshop will be limited to twelve participants. The New Harmony Inn and Conference Center will be headquarters for the RopeWalk Writers' Retreat. Please note that reservations at the Inn should be confirmed by May 1." 2002 faculty included Tim Cahill, Lynn Emanuel, Gary Gildner, Michael Martone, Karen Shepard.

Costs: $495 (2002), includes breakfasts and lunches.

Accommodations: Information on overnight accommodations is made available. "Room-sharing assistance; some low-cost accommodations."

Additional Information: For critiques submit mss approx. 6 weeks ahead. Brochures are available after January 15.

N SKYLINE WRITERS CONFERENCE, P.O. Box 33343, N. Royalton OH 44133. Website: www.skylinewriter.com. **Contact:** Constance Davis, conference director. Estab. 1983. Annual. Conference held August 24, 2002. Average attendance: 50-60. Features fiction, nonfiction, poetry, children's, science fiction, and inspirational. Conference held in Ridgewood United Methodist Church.

Costs: In 2002, $55 (non-members); $55 (members); $40 half day. Includes continental breakfast, full buffet lunch, snacks and 6 workshops.

Additional Information: Includes literary contest, 2 mss in two of the following categories: fiction, nonfiction, children's and poetry. Contest entrants receive written critiques of their work. "We are totally non-profit, supported only by members and attendees of conference." Brochures available for SASE or on website.

WALLOON WRITERS' RETREAT, P.O. Box 304, Royal Oak MI 48068-0304. Phone/fax: (248)589-3913. E-mail: johndlamb@ameritech.net. Website: www.springfed.org. **Contact:** John D. Lamb, director. Estab. 1999. Annual. Conference held September 27-30, 2001. Average attendance: 50. Focus includes fiction, poetry, creative nonfiction. Michigania is owned and operated by the University of Michigan Alumni Association. Located on Walloon Lake. Attendees stay in spruce paneled cabins and seminars are held in a large conference lodge with Fieldstone fireplaces and dining area. Features and faculty includes Joyce Maynard (The Terror of the Blank Page); Jacquelyn Mitchard (When Fiction Outs the Truth); Keith Taylor (short stories); and Michael Moore & Ben Hamper (panel discussions).
Costs: Single occupancy is $550, $475 (3 nights, 2 nights). $275 no lodging.
Accommodations: Shuttle rides from Traverse City Airport. Offers overnight accommodations. Provides list of area lodging options.
Additional Information: Optional: Attendees may submit 3 poems or 5 pages of prose for conferences with a staff member. Brochures available Mid-June by e-mail, on website or by phone. Accepts inquiries by SASE, e-mail, phone. Editors participate in conference. "Walloon Lake in Northern Michigan is the same lake that Ernest Hemingway spent the first 19 years of his life at his family's Windemere Cottage. The area plays a role in some of his early short stories. Notably in a couple of his Nick Adams stories."

[N] [◎] WRITER'S DIGEST SCHOOL, 4700 E. Galbraith Rd., Cincinnati OH 45236. (800)759-0963. Fax: (513)531-0798. E-mail: wds@fwpubs.com. Website: www.writersdigestschool.com. **Contact:** Registrar. Estab. 1920s. Correspondence course; ongoing. Conference duration: "Most courses offer a self-paced term of up to two years. We have courses in Getting Started in Writing (fiction and nonfiction), Fundamentals of Fiction, Novel Writing Workshop, Writing and Selling Short Stories, Grammar Composition." Faculty consists of up to 80 instructors, all published writers and/or editors.
Costs: Course prices range from $179-439.
Additional Information: Conference information is available by e-mail and on website. Accepts inquiries by e-mail or phone.

[N] [◎] WRITERS ONLINE WORKSHOPS, 4700 E. Galbraith Rd., Cincinnati OH 45236. (800)759-0963. Fax: (513)531-0798. E-mail: wdwowadmin@fwpubs.com. Website: www.writersonlineworkshops.com. **Contact:** Stephanie Steele, director. Estab. 2000. Online workshop; ongoing. Conference duration: From 4 to 14 weeks. Average attendance: 10-15 per class. "We have workshops in fiction, nonfiction, memoir, poetry and proposal writings." Site: Internet-based, operated entirely on the website. 2003 fiction-related courses include Fundamentals of Fiction, Focus on the Novel, Focus on the Short Story, Creating Dynamic Characters, Writing Effective Dialogue, Writing the Novel Proposal, Creativity & Expression (fiction and nonfiction).
Costs: 6-week workshop, $179; 12-week, $299; 14-week, $349.
Additional Information: Information always available on website. Accepts inquiries by e-mail and phone.

WRITE-TO-PUBLISH CONFERENCE, 9731 N. Fox Glen Dr., Suite 200, Niles IL 60714-4222. (847)299-4755. Fax: (847)296-0754. E-mail: lin@wtpublish.com. Website: www.wtpublish.com. **Contact:** Lin Johnson, director. Estab. 1971. Annual. Conference held from June 4-7, 2003. Average attendance: 225. Conference on "writing all types of manuscripts for the Christian market." Site: Wheaton College, Wheaton, IL.
Costs: $350.
Accommodations: Accommodations in campus residence halls or discounted hotel rates. Costs $190-$240.
Additional Information: Optional critiquing available. Conference information available in February 2002. For brochures/guidelines visit website, e-mail, fax or call. Accepts inquiries by e-mail, fax, phone.

North Central (IA, MN, NE, ND, SD, WI)

INTERNATIONAL MUSIC CAMP CREATIVE WRITING WORKSHOP, 1725 11th St. SW, Minot ND 58701. Phone/fax: (701)838-8472. E-mail: joe@internationalmusiccamp.com. Website: www.internationalmusiccamp.com. **Contact:** Joseph T. Alme, executive director. Estab. 1956. Annual. Conference held June 22-28, 2003. Average attendance: 15. "The workshop offers students the opportunity to refine their skills in thinking, composing and writing in an environment that is conducive to positive reinforcement. In addition to writing poems, essays, and stories, individuals are encouraged to work on their own area of interest with conferencing and feedback from the course instructor." Site: International Peace Garden on the border between the US and Canada. "Similar to a University Campus, several

---

CAN'T FIND A CONFERENCE? Conferences are listed by region. Check the introduction to this section for a list of regional categories.

dormitories, classrooms, lecture halls and cafeteria provide the perfect site for such a workshop. The beautiful and picturesque International Peace Garden provide additional inspiration to creative thinking." Professor Joseph Ringen from Minot State University is the instructor.

Costs: The cost including meals and housing is $200.

Accommodations: Airline and depot shuttles are available upon request. Housing is included in the $200 fee.

Additional Information: Conference information is available in September. For brochure visit website, e-mail, call or fax. Accepts inquiries by e-mail, phone and fax. Agents and editors participate in conference.

IOWA SUMMER WRITING FESTIVAL, 100 Oakdale Campus, W310, University of Iowa, Iowa City IA 52242-1802. (319)335-4160. E-mail: iswfestival@uiowa.edu. Website: www.uiowa.edu/~iswfest. **Contact:** Amy Margolis. Estab. 1987. Annual. Festival held in June and July. Workshops are one week or a weekend. Average attendance: limited to 12/class—over 1,500 participants throughout the summer. "We offer workshops across the genres, including novel, short story, poetry, essay, memoir, humor, travel, playwriting, screenwriting, writing for children and more. All levels." Site is the University of Iowa campus. Guest speakers are undetermined at this time. Readers and instructors have included Lee K. Abbott, Susan Power, Joy Harjo, Gish Jen, Abraham Verghese, Robert Olen Butler, Ethan Canin, Clark Blaise, Gerald Stern, Donald Justice, Michael Dennis Browne, Marvin Bell, Hope Edelman, Lan Samantha Chang.

Costs: $425/week; $175, weekend workshop. Discounts available for early registration. Housing and meals are separate.

Accommodations: "We offer participants a choice of accommodations: dormitory, $29/night; Iowa House, $69/night; Sheraton, $84/night (rates subject to changes)."

Additional Information: Conference information available in February. Accepts inquiries by fax, e-mail.

SINIPEE WRITERS' WORKSHOP, Continuing Education Loras College, Dubuque IA 52004-0708. (563)588-7139. Fax: (563)588-4962. E-mail: cneuhaus@loras.edu. Website: www.loras.edu. **Contact:** Chris Neuhaus, secretary of continuing education. Estab. 1985. Annual. Workshop held April 26, 2003. Average attendance: 40-50. The conference provides general information for writers on how to get published. There are several speakers at each workshop, usually someone for fiction, poetry, nonfiction and either a publisher, editor or agent. The conference is held in the Alumni Campus Center on the Loras College campus. The Campus Center is handicapped accessible. Speakers for 2003 are TBA. 2002 speakers include Shirley Damsgaard, Larry Goldberg, Pam Kress, Jim Shaffer and Kathryn Struck.

Costs: $65 ($70 at the door); discount available for senior citizens and students.

Accommodations: Provides a list of area hotels or lodging options.

Additional Information: Sponsors the John Tigges Writing Contest for short fiction, nonfiction, poetry as part of workshop. Requirements: $5 entry fee/$15 additional fee for written critique. Poetry must not exceed 40 lines and short fiction and nonfiction entries must be 1,500 words or less. Style and subject are open and work by aspiring writers as well as seasoned professionals is welcome. Deadline: Must be received by April 7, 2003. Workshop information is available February 2003. For brochure send e-mail, call, fax.

UNIVERSITY OF NORTH DAKOTA WRITERS CONFERENCE, Box 7209 UND, Grand Forks ND 58202-7209. (701)777-2768. Fax: (701)777-2373. E-mail: James_McKenzie@UND.nodak.edu. Website: www.undwritersconference.org. **Contact:** James McKenzie, director. Estab. 1969. Annual. Conference held March 18-22, 2002. Average attendance: 800/day. Covers all genres, focused around a specific theme. The conference is a regional cultural and intellectual festival that puts nationally known writers in intimate and large audience contact with other writers and the student, academic and general public. Almost all events take place in the campus memorial union which has a variety of small rooms and a 1,000 seat main hall. Fiction writers in 2002 included David Treuer, Michael Martone and Ursula Hegi as writer in residence.

Costs: Free, open to the public.

Accommodations: Offers overnight accommodations. "Campus residence halls are available at very good prices." Also provides a list of area hotels or lodging options.

Additional Information: Conference information is available January 31, 2001. For brochure send SASE, e-mail, visit website, call, fax. Accepts inquiries by SASE, e-mail, phone, fax.

WISCONSIN REGIONAL WRITER'S ASSOCIATION CONFERENCES, 510 W. Sunset Ave., Appleton WI 54911-1139. (920)734-3724. E-mail: wrwa@lakeside.net. Website: www.wrwa.net. **Contact:** Patricia Boverhuis, vice president. Estab. 1948. Annual. Conferences held in May and September "are dedicated to self-improvement through speakers, workshops, and presentations. Topics and speakers vary with each event." Average attendance: 100-150. "We honor all genres of writing. Spring conference is a one-day event featuring the Jade Ring Banquet and awards for six genre categories." Keynote speaker at the 2001 Fall conference was Ellen Kort, Wisconsin's first poet laureate. Spring 2002 conference site was be the Holiday Inn, Manitowoc, WI. Agents and editors participate in each conference.

Costs: $40-75.

Accommodations: Provides a list of area hotels or lodging options. "We negotiate special rates at each facility. A block of rooms is set aside for a specific time period."

Additional Information: Award winners receive a certificate and a cash prize. First place winners of the Jade Ring contest receive a jade ring. Must be a member to enter contests. For brochure, call, write, e-mail or visit website.

N WRITING TO SELL, Minneapolis Writers Conference, Box 24356, Minneapolis MN 55424. **Contact:** Herb Montgomery, board member. Estab. 1985. Annual conference held in August for 1 day. Average attendance: 100. Conference about writing to sell.

Costs: $85.

Additional Information: Brochure available in May for SASE.

N WRITING WORKSHOP, P.O. Box 65, Ellison Bay WI 54210. (920)854-4088. E-mail: clearing@theclearing.org. **Contact:** Michael Schneider, executive director. Estab. 1935. Annual. Average attendance: 16. "General writing, journal, poetry as well as fiction and nonfiction." Held in a "quiet, residential setting in deep woods on the shore of Green Bay."

Costs: $650 for double; includes lodging, meals, tuition.

Accommodations: "Two to a room with private bath in rustic log and stone buildings with meals served family-style."

South Central (CO, KS, MO, NM, OK, TX)

N THE AFRICAN AMERICAN BOOK CLUB SUMMIT, PMB 120, 2951 Marina Bay Dr., Suite 130, League City TX 77573. (866)875-1055. E-mail: pwsquare@pageturner.net. Website: www.summitatsea.com. **Contact:** Pamela Walker Williams, literary events chairman. Estab. 2000. Annual. Conference held October 20-27, 2002 on board the Carnival ship Victory; October 19-26, 2003 on board the Carnival ship Elation. Average attendance: 200. "The purpose of the conference is to bring authors and readers together. Aspiring writers will have an opportunity to discuss and obtain information on self-publishing, marketing and writing fiction." Site: on board cruise ship. "The ship Victory is one of the largest cruise ships afloat. Pool, jacuzzi, restaurant, bar, spa, room service, wheelchair accessible, fitness center, children's facilities, air conditioning." In 2002, panels include Workshops: Having What Matters; Creating Successful and Saleable Stories; Character, Conflict and Dialogue; How to Market and Self-Publish Your Own Book. Panelists include Dr. Jewell Parker Rhodes, Monique Greenwood, Timmothy McCann, Travis Hunter, Tracey Price Thompson, Nichelle Tramble, Dr. Monica Anderson, Tajuna Butler.

Costs: 2002 fees: for inside cabin, $996; for outside, $1186. Includes cruise, conference, on board meals, port charges and gratuities.

Accommodations: "Participants have the option to add airfare and/or shuttle service." Provides a list of area accommodations for people who chose to arrive early.

Additional Information: Brochures available on website. Accepts inquiries by e-mail, phone, fax. Agents and editors attend conference.

AGENTS! AGENTS! AGENTS . . . & EDITORS TOO!, 1501 W. Fifth St., Suite E-2, Austin TX 78703-5155. (512)499-8914. Fax: (512)499-0441. E-mail: awl@writersleague.org. Website: www.writersleague.org. **Contact:** Stephanie Sheppard, executive director. Estab. 1994. Annual. Conference held Summer 2003. Conference duration: 3 days. Average attendance: 220. The conference's purpose is to help writers "learn about the business of writing, and get the most up-to-date information about the writing industry." Site: Austin, Texas. 2002 topics included Agents & Editors: The Current Market for Fiction, The Current Market for Nonfiction; Exploring Audiobooks; Realistic Dialogue; Electronic Publishing; Genre Panels; Small Press; The Author-Editor Relationship; Writing Treatments That Sell; Taking Care of Business Matters for Writers; Ways to Market Your Writing; The Agony and Ecstasy of Self-Publishing. Agents in 2002: Sheree Bykosfky, Julia Castiglia, Jim Donovan, Nancy Ellis-Bell, Lawrence Jordan, Jim Hornfischer, Marcy Posner, David Hale Smith, Andrew Stuart. Editors in 2002: George Hodgman, Stephanie Land, Julia Pastore, Darryl Wimberley. Authors in 2002: Suzy Spencer, Karen Stolz, Jim Gramon, Don Webb, Mindy Reed, Greg Garrett, Bonnie Orr, Susie Flatan, Diane Fanning, Stacey Hasbrook, Joan Hall, Paula Hamilton, David Marion Wilkinson, Vanessa Leggett.

Costs: In 2002, $195 members; $240 nonmembers; $50 optional workshops.

Accommodations: Hotel offers special conference rate.

Additional Information: "The Writers' League of Texas sponsors a manuscript contest in conjunction with the annual agents and editors conference. For guidelines, please SASE or send an e-mail. Entry fees for 2002 were $20 and $35. Finalists receive a critique from a published author. Winners will be announced at the agents conference. There are no monetary prizes nor is there any offer for publication. Deadline for entry is approximately three to four months prior to conference." Conference information is available December 2002. For brochure send SASE, e-mail, visit website, call or fax. Accepts inquiries by SASE, e-mail, phone and fax. "As a bonus for attending the conference, participants will be offered a ten-minute consult with the agent or editor of their choice. For those that desire a consult, early registration is encouraged."

N ASPEN SUMMER WORDS WRITING RETREAT AND LITERARY FESTIVAL, 110 E. Hallam St. #116, Aspen CO 81611. (970)925-3122. Fax (970)925-5700. E-mail: info@aspenwriters.org. Website: www.aspenwriters.org. **Contact:** Julie Comins, executive director. Estab. 1976. Annual. Writing retreat and literary festival held in late June in Aspen, CO. Duration: 5 days. Average attendance: writing retreat, 50; literary festival, 1,500. Writing retreat for fiction, creative nonfiction and poetry; literary festival for craft lectures, industry talks, round table discussions and readings. 2002 festival featured Pam Houston, Mark Salzman, Larry Watson, Chip Kidd (fiction); Hilary Black and Jordan Pavlin (editors); Suzanne Gluck, Elizabeth Sheinkman, Jody Hotchkiss (agents).

Costs: $350/retreat; $135/festival; $460/both; $25/private meetings with agents and editors.

Accommodations On-campus housing $110/night single; $55/night double. Off campus rates vary. Free shuttle.

Additional Information: Manuscripts must be submitted prior to conference for review by faculty. Brochures available for SASE and on website.

N̄ AUTHOR'S VENUE FALL SEMINAR, 600 Central Ave. SE, Suite 235, Albuquerque NM 87102. (505)244-9337. Fax: (800)853-7655. E-mail: info@authorsvenue.com. Website: www.AuthorsVenue.com. **Contact:** Suzanne Spletzer, executive director or Stephanie Dooley, director of events. Estab. 2001. Annual. 2002 conference held October 3-6. Average attendance: 100. Conference focuses on mystery, romance and nonfiction and "provides education and publication opportunities for writers." Site: "The incredible Glen Eryie Castle & Conference Center in Colorado Springs, CO. 800-acre wildlife refuge." Panels planned for next conference include "Agents' panel, general session, editor/agent appointments." Panels from 2002 seminar's Mystery Track include The Investigation, The Criminal Justice System, Police Procedure, Inside the Criminal Mind, Trends in the Mystery Market, Forensics, Everything You Wanted to Know About Writing but Were Afraid to Ask. 2002 faculty members include Alton Gansky (mystery author), Estelle Sobel (nonfiction author) and police officers/federal agents; literary agents Sheree Bykofsky, Nancy Ellis, Anna Ghosh; editors from Penguin Putnam, Intrigue Press and others.
Costs: 2002 registration fee, $180 until August 15, $230 until September 30, $280 onsite. Includes 1 lunch and editor/agent.
Accommodations: "Travel arrangements can be made by contacing Carlson Wagonlit Travel at (800)809-0388 or e-mailing wpgtvl@flash.net." Offers overnight accommodations. "Three night's lodging: $290-450 (depending on room and single or double occupancy. Includes breakfast and lunch for entire stay."
Additional Information: Participants must submit material prior to arrival "if choosing to have a manuscript consultation. Send first 25 pages (double-spaced one inch margins, 12 pt font) and a one-page single spaced synopsis to the Author's Venue offices by August 1, 2002." Brochure available by e-mail, on website, by phone, fax. Accepts inquiries by mail, e-mail, phone and fax.

N̄ BAY AREA WRITERS LEAGUE CONFERENCE, P.O. Box 58007, Houston TX 77058. E-mail: info@bawl.org. Website: www.bawl.org. **Contact:** Conference Chair. Estab. 1989. Annual. Conference held May 9-10, 2003. Avergae attendance: 100. Conference focuses on "novice writers, all genres." Site: "University classroom building in a nature preserve." 2003 panels and speakers TBA.
Costs: $125 for two days, $75 for one day, $60 for students.
Accommodations: Does not provide list of area hotels.
Additional Information: Sponsors contest for high school students, unpublished authors, published authors. Fiction categories include Novel (synopsis and 20 pages) and Short Story (5,000 words). Requires $15 entry fee. Brochures/guidelines available January 2003 for SASE, by e-mail and on website. Accepts inquiries by SASE, e-mail. Agents and editors participate in conference.

COLORADO GOLD CONFERENCE, The Renaissance Hotel, Denver South, 10250 E. Costilla Ave., Denver CO 80207. (303)331-2608. E-mail: conference@rmfw.org. Website: www.rmfw.org. **Contact:** Diana Rowe Martinez, conference coordinator. Estab. 1983. Annual. Conference held September 13-15, 2002. Average attendance: 300-350. Conference focuses on commercial fiction writing. Site: The Renaissance Hotel, Old Stapleton, Denver. Panels planned for next conference covers every aspect of novel length fiction from the basics of the writing craft to promoting a book in print. "We have published authors addressing a variety of craft topics as well as professionals speaking on topics of interest to writers in every genre. A full list of faculty/panels/guest speakers/editors and agents can be found by requesting a brochure via e-mail or RMFW phone number or by visiting the web at www.rmfw.org/."
Costs: Registration before June 30, $169; after June 30, $189; late registration after August 30, $209.
Accommodations: "Please send an e-mail to inquire about any transportation needs. Discounted rooms are $59/night. Reservations must be made before August 24, 2001. Call the Renaissance at (800)654-4810 and indicate that you will be attending the Colorado Gold Conference."
Additional Information: "There is an opportunity to read to editors and agents during a Friday workshop. There is a $20 fee and slots are on a first come, first served basis. Participation in the Friday workshop does require an early submission of material to the workshop coordinator. Full details are in the registration brochure. Participants may—at no cost—sign up for one on one meetings with editors and agents. Again, details are in the brochure. Complete details are found on our website. The finalists are judged by an editor or agent seeking manuscripts in the contestant's category—mainstream, mystery, romance and science fiction/fantasy." Conference information is available. For brochure send e-mail, visit website or call. Accepts inquiries by SASE, e-mail and phone. Agents and editors participate in conference.

COLORADO MOUNTAIN WRITERS' WORKSHOP, P.O. Box 85394, Tucson AZ 85754. (520)206-9479. E-mail: mfiles@pimacc.pima.edu. Website: www.sheilabender.com. **Contact:** Meg Files, director. Estab. 1999. Annual. Conference to be held June 24-28, 2002. Average attendance: 30. Focuses on fiction, poetry, and personal essay. Conference is held on the campus of Colorado Mountain College, Steamboat Springs, Colorado. Features personal writing. Faculty includes Meg Files, Sheila Bender, and Jack Heffron.
Costs: $300.
Accommodations: Offers overnight lodging in on-site dormitory $308 (6 nights, also meals).
Additional Information: Brochures available November, 2001 for SASE, e-mail, website, fax or call. Accepts inquiries for SASE, e-mail, fax, phone. Editors participates in conferences. The conference is designed to lift writers, novice or experienced, to the next level. It offers writers isolation, intimacy, and inspiration. Daily activities include craft talks, small group workshops, readings, and ms consultations, as well as writing time.

EMINENCE AREA ARTS COUNCIL SHORT STORY WORKSHOP, P.O. Box 551, Eminence MO 65466-0551. (573)226-5655. E-mail: hilma@socket.net. **Contact:** Hilma Hughes, administrator. Estab. 1989. Annual. Workshop held April 17-19, 2003. Average attendance: 12 (maximum 15). "The Short Story Workshop focuses on fiction of any genre." Site: "Museum and Art Gallery conference room. We have large tables with chairs for participants. There is already a large screen TV and VCR for the leaders to use. Both facilities are available and the museum is accessible to the physically challenged." Workshop centers on the process of writing—participants leave with a finished short story. Workshop led by Dr. Tam Nordgren in 2003.
Costs $40.
Accommodations: Provides list of area lodging.
Additional Information: Participants should bring work-in-progress for critique by workshop director. Brochures available in January 2003 by e-mail or phone. Accepts inquiries by e-mail or phone. "We are a small rural community on the scenic Riverways. The workshops are an excellent opportunity to rest, relax, and get away from the rush of daily life. Many participants have valued this part if the experience as much as the learning and writing process."

FORT BEND WRITERS GUILD WORKSHOP, 12523 Folkcrest Way, Stafford TX 77477-3529. (281)498-5025. E-mail: rapdunit@ev1.net. Website: http://fortbendwritersguild.tripod.com. **Contact:** Roger Paulding. Estab. 1997. Biannual. Workshop held March 15, 2003, October 4, 2002. Average attendance: 75. Workshop focuses on fiction (novels) and screenwriting. Site: Holiday Inn.
Costs: $50 (including buffet lunch).
Additional Information: Sponsors a contest. Submit for novel competition—first 10 pages plus one page synopsis, entry fee $10; screenplay—treatment of 5-7 pages plus 3-5 pages of opening, total entry 10 pages, $10 each; short story—10 pages complete, $10 each. "Judges are published novelists." For brochure send SASE or e-mail. Accepts inquiries by SASE and e-mail.

GLORIETA CHRISTIAN WRITERS' CONFERENCE, Glorieta Conference Center, P.O. Box 8, Glorieta NM 87535-0008. (800)797-4222. Fax: (505)757-6149. E-mail: bdaniel@lifeway.com. Website: www.lifeway.org/Glorieta. **Contact:** Brian Daniel, events director. Estab. 1997. Annual. Conference held October 15-19, 2002. Average attendance: 250. Conference focuses on "beginners, professionals, fiction, poetry, screenwriting, writing for children, drama, magazine writing, nonfiction books." Site: "Conference center with hotels and dining hall with buffet-style meals." Plans "continuing course for fiction writers and numerous one-hour workshops" for 2002 conference. 2001 speakers included Liz Curtis Higgs and T. Davis Bunn.
Costs: $500-600, depending on housing preference. Includes tuition, hotel room and 12 meals.
Additional Information: Sponsors a contest with entries judged by published authors and editors. Guidelines available upon request. Conference information is available in Spring 2002. For brochure send e-mail, visit website, call or fax. Accepts inquiries by e-mail, phone and fax. Agents and editors participate in conference.

GOLDEN TRIANGLE WRITERS GUILD, 4245 Calder, Beaumont TX 77706. (409)898-4894. Advisor: D.J. Resnick. E-mail: gtwg@juno.com. Estab. 1983. Annual. Conference held during third weekend in October. Attendance limited to 350. Held at the Hilton Hotel on IH10 at Washington in Beaumont, Texas.
Costs: $210-235 before October 2nd; $235-260 after October 2nd. Cost includes meals and 1 year membership.
Accommodations: Special conference rates available at Holiday Inn (Beaumont).
Additional Information: Sponsors a contest. Attendance required. Preliminary judging done by published authors and/or specialists in each specific genre. Final judging done by editors and/or agents specializing in each specific area.

GREENVILLE CHRISTIAN WRITER'S CONFERENCE, P.O Box 8942, Greenville TX 75404-8942. (903)450-4944. E-mail: info@tuppence.org. Website: www.greenvillechristianwriters.com. **Contact:** James H. Pence, conference director. Estab. 1998. Annual. Conference scheduled for October 25, 2003. Average attendance: 50. "Christian fiction, non-fiction, magazine articles, greeting cards, e-publishing." Site: Ridgecrest Baptist Church in Greenville, Texas. Panels planned for next conference include writing fiction that sells. Guest speakers for 2000 included Reg Grant, novelist, emmy winning producer; Becky Freeman, bestselling Christian author; Jim Pence, novelist, The Osmosis Project 2003, Tyndale House, author of How to Do Everything with HTML.
Costs: $100; $75 before October 1. Includes lunch.
Accommodations: Offers list of area hotels and lodging options.
Additional Information: Conference information available January 2002; send SASE, e-mail, visit website, or call. Accepts inquiries by SASE, e-mail, or phone. "The Greenville Christian Writers' Conference is a small conference where both new and experienced writers can interact with published authors. We have informative workshops and opportunities for personal consultations."

MARKET CONDITIONS are constantly changing! If you're still using this book and it is 2004 or later, buy the newest edition of *Novel & Short Story Writer's Market* at your favorite bookstore or order from Writer's Digest Books by calling 1-800-448-0915.

N **MISSOURI WRITERS GUILD ANNUAL CONVENTION**, 505 W. 34th St., Joplin MO 64804. (816)361-1281. E-mail: vjones@joplin.com. Website: www.vedaboydjones.com. **Contact:** Veda Boyd Jones, president. Annual. Conference to be held April 4-5, 2003 in Jefferson City at the Capitol Plaza Hotel. Average attendance: 100+. Annual Convention brings members together to visit, network, meet agents, learn, and receive any awards from the annual contests. Our members have work published as novels, poetry, magazine articles, children's books, etc. Features important tips for submitting fiction to a publisher, ins and outs of self-publishing, honoring KC area authors at Friday night reception, banquet, and art to show-off the words.
Accommodations: Offers overnight accommodations.
Additional Information: Submit workshop materials prior to arrival. Sponsors contest. To enter, one must be a MWG member. Brochures available by e-mail. Accepts inquiries by e-mail. Agents and editors participate in conference.

N **THE NEW LETTERS WEEKEND WRITERS CONFERENCE**, University of Missouri-Kansas City, College of Arts and Sciences Continuing Ed. Division, 4825 Troost, Room 215, Kansas City MO 64110-2499. (816)235-2736. Fax: (816)235-5279. Website: www.umkc.edu/CE/College. **Contact:** James McKinley. Estab. in the mid-70s as The Longboat Key Writers Conference. Annual. Runs during June. Conference duration is 3 days. Average attendance: 75. "The New Letters Weekend Writers Conference brings together talented writers in many genres for lectures, seminars, readings, workshops and individual conferences. The emphasis is on craft and the creative process in poetry, fiction, screenwriting, playwriting and journalism; but the program also deals with matters of psychology, publications and marketing. The conference is appropriate for both advanced and beginning writers. The conference meets at the beautiful Diastole conference center of The University of Missouri-Kansas City."
Costs: Several options are available. Participants may choose to attend as a non-credit student or they may attend for 1-3 hours of college credit from the University of Missouri-Kansas City. Conference registration includes continental breakfasts, Saturday and Sunday lunch. For complete information, contact the University of Missouri-Kansas City.
Accommodations: Registrants are responsible for their own transportation, but information on area accommodations is made available.
Additional Information: Those registering for college credit are required to submit a ms in advance. Ms reading and critique is included in the credit fee. Those attending the conference for non-credit also have the option of having their ms critiqued for an additional fee. Accepts inquiries by phone, fax.

NIMROD ANNUAL WRITERS' WORKSHOP, *Nimrod*, University of Tulsa, 600 S. College Ave., Tulsa OK 74104. (918)631-3080. Fax: (918)631-3033. E-mail: nimrod@utulsa.edu. Website: www.utulsa.edu/nimrod. **Contact:** Francine Ringold, PhD, editor-in-chief. Estab. 1978. Workshop held annually in October. Workshop duration: 1 day. Average attendance: 100-150. Workshop in fiction and poetry. "Prize winners (Nimrod/Hardman Prizes) conduct worksh ops as do contest judges. Past judges: Rosellen Brown, Stanley Kunitz, Toby Olson, Lucille Clifton, W.S. Merwin, Ron Carlson, Mark Doty, Anita Shreve and Francine Prose."
Costs: Approximately $50. Lunch provided. Scholarships available for students.
Additional Information: *Nimrod International Journal* sponsors *Nimrod*/Hardman Literary Awards: The Katherine Anne Porter Prize for fiction and The Pablo Neruda Prize for poetry. Poetry and fiction prizes: $2,000 each and publication (1st prize); $1,000 each and publication (2nd prize). Deadline: must be postmarked no later than April 30. Guidelines available for SASE.

OKLAHOMA WRITERS FEDERATION CONFERENCE, P.O. Box 2654, Stillwater OK 74076-2654. (405)408-2141. E-mail: wileykat@ionet.net. Website: www.owfi.net. **Contact:** Moira Wiley, president, or Lou Mansfield, treasurer. Estab. 1968. Annual. Conference held the first weekend of May every year. Average attendance: 250-300. Conference covers all genres, fiction, poetry, nonfiction. Site: "Our conference is held at the Embassy Suites Hotel. It has 6 floors. Everything, all meetings are contained within the hotel."
Costs: Full conference, $100; one day only, $50; authors' banquet, $30; awards banquet, $30 (2000 fees).
Accommodations: The hotel provides a shuttle to and from airport. Embassy Suites room rates have been $79. Guests of the hotel get free buffet breakfast.
Additional Information: "The annual OWFI contest is open only to paid-up members. It features competitions for cash prizes in 28 unpublished ms categories and awards 4 trophies for the best books published during the previous calendar year. A $20 entry fee entitles participants to enter as many categories as they want, but they may enter no single category more than once. Since the contest's purpose is to encourage writers to produce professionally acceptable mss, the contest rules are very explicit, and contestants must follow them closely. Categories include mainstream novel; contemporary romance novel; historical romance novel; mystery/suspense novel; Western novel; science fiction/fantasy/horror novel; nonfiction book; picture book; middle reader book; and young adult book." For brochures/guidelines send SASE, e-mail, visit website, call. Accepts inquiries by SASE, e-mail, phone. Agents and editors participate in conference.

ROCKY MOUNTAIN BOOK FESTIVAL, 2123 Downing St., Denver CO 80205. (303)839-8320. Fax: (303)839-8319. E-mail: ccftb@compuserve.com. Website: www.coloradobook.org. **Contact:** Christiane Citron, executive director. Estab. 1991. Annual. Festival held in March. Average attendance: 10,000. Festival promotes published work from all genres. Held at Denver Merchandise Mart. Offers a wide variety of panels. Approximately 200 authors are scheduled to speak at the next festival. "Please submit a copy of book, bio and publicity material for consideration."
Costs: $4 (adult); $2 (child).
Additional Information: Brochures/guidelines available. Accepts inquiries by e-mail, fax.

ROCKY MOUNTAIN CHILDREN'S BOOK FESTIVAL, 2123 Downing St., Denver CO 80205-5210. (303)839-8320. Fax: (303)839-8319. E-mail: ccftb@compuserve.com. Website: www.coloradobook.org. **Contact:** Christiane Citron, executive director. Estab. 1996. Annual festival held in March as part of the Rocky Mountain Book Festival. Festival duration: 2 days. Average attendance: 10,000. Festival promotes published work for and about children/families. Open to the public. Held at Denver Merchandise Mart. Approximately 100 authors speak annually. Past authors include Ann M. Martin, Sharon Creech, Nikki Grimes, T.A. Barron, Laura Numeroff, Jean Craighead George and Jane Yolen.
Costs: $2 children, $4 adults.
Accommodations: "Information on accommodations available."
Additional Information: Send SASE for brochure/guidelines. Accepts inquiries by fax, e-mail.

ROMANCE WRITERS OF AMERICA NATIONAL CONFERENCE, 3707 FM 1960 West, Suite 555, Houston TX 77068. (281)440-6885, ext. 27. Fax: (281)440-7510. E-mail: info@rwanational.com. Website: www.rwanational.com. Executive Director: Allison Kelley. **Contact:** Jane Detloff, office manager. Estab. 1981. Annual. Conference held July 16-19, 2003. Average attendance: 1,500. Over 100 workshops on writing, researching and the business side of being a working writer. Publishing professionals attend and accept appointments. Keynote speaker is renowned romance writer. Conference will be held in New York City in 2003, in Dallas 2004, in Reno 2005.
Costs: In 2002, early registration $350 for RWA members/$425 nonmember; late registration, $400 for RWA members/$475 nonmember.
Additional Information: Annual RITA awards are presented for romance authors. Annual Golden Heart awards are presented for unpublished writers. Conference brochures/guidelines and registration forms are available for SASE and on website in May. Accepts inquiries by SASE, e-mail, fax, phone.

N SAN JUAN WRITERS WORKSHOP, P.O. Box 841, Ridgway CO 81432. (970)626-4125. E-mail: lepatter@ttacs.ttu.edu. Website: http://homepage.mac.com/inkwellliterary. **Contact:** Jill Patterson, director. Estab. 2002. Annual. Workshop held May, June, July 2003. Duration: 3 days. Average attendance: 40. Focuses on "fiction, poetry, creative nonfiction in each session. Sessions focus on Christian writers, women writers, literature of place and advanced writers." Site: "Community Center in beautiful mountain valley town of Ouray, Colorado." 2002 panels included Christian fiction, setting in fiction, advanced fiction writing. Panelists in 2002 included Albert Haley, Pam Houston, Melanie Rae Thon.
Costs: $450, includes breakfast and lunch daily.
Accommodations: Offers shuttle to/from airport in Montrose, CO. Provides list of area hotels.
Additional Informations: Participants must submit workshop material—10-20 pages of prose—by April 1, 2003. Brochure available January 1, 2003 by SASE, e-mail or on website. Accepts inquiries by SASE, e-mail, phone. "There are social activities, including mountain cookout, champagne brunch and readings."

SHORT COURSE ON PROFESSIONAL WRITING, University of Oklahoma, Journalism, 860 Van Vleet Oval, Norman OK 73019-0270. (405)325-4171. Fax: (405)325-7565. E-mail: jmadisondavis@ou.edu. Website: http://jmc.ou.edu/shortcourse. Estab. 1938. Annual conference held in early June. Average attendance: 200. Conference focuses on writing for publication—all commercial markets.
Costs: $230.
Accomodations: Provides special rates.
Additional Information: "Critiques are optional, but we provide them. Manuscripts must be submitted ahead of time." Brochures available by mail or on website. Accepts inquiries by fax, e-mail. "We have sixty years of success with editors, agents and authors. Many successful writers were 'discovered' at the Short Course."

SOUTHWEST LITERARY CENTER OF RECURSOS DE SANTA FE, 826 Camino de Monte Rey, Santa Fe NM 87505. (505)577-1125. Fax: (505)982-7125. E-mail: litcenter@recursos.org. Website: www.recursos.org or www.santafewritersconference.org. **Contact:** Literary Center Director. Estab. 1984. Annual. 2002 conference held July 31-August 5. Conference duration: 5 days. Average attendance: 50 people. "The Santa Fe Writers Conference offers intimate workshop-style conferences in fiction, poetry and creative nonfiction." Site: "very pleasant and close to downtown Santa Fe and the historic plaza." Faculty: Scott Russell Sanders, Laura Kasischke, Kevin McIlvoy in 2002; in 2003, Robert Boswell, Tony Hoagland, Antonya Nelson, Steve Orlen.
Costs: $675 (conference, no residence); $925 (conference and residence—double occupancy); $1125 (conference, residence and single room). Meals included. Scholarships may be available.
Additional Information: Brochure available by e-mail, fax, phone and on website.

SOUTHWEST WRITERS CONFERENCE, 8200 Mountain Rd. NE, Suite 106, Albuquerque NM 87110-7835. (505)265-9485. Fax: (505)265-9483. E-mail: swriters@aol.com. Website: www.southwestwriters.org. **Contact:** Conference Chair. Estab. 1983. Annual. Conference held in September. Average attendance: about 400. "Conference concentrates on all areas of writing and includes preconference sessions, appointments and networking." Workshops and speakers include writers and editors of all genres for all levels from beginners to advanced. 2002 keynote speaker was Debbie Macomber. 2001 keynote speaker was Catherine Ryan Hyde, author of *Pay It Forward*.
Costs: $365 and up (members), $425 and up (nonmembers); includes conference sessions and 2 luncheons.
Accommodations: Usually have official airline and discount rates. Special conference rates are available at hotel. A list of other area hotels and motels is available.

Additional Information: Sponsors a contest judged by authors, editors and agents from New York, Los Angeles, etc., and from major publishing houses. Eighteen categories. Deadline: May 1. Entry fee is $29 (members) or $39 (nonmembers). Conference information available in April 2001. For brochures/guidelines send SASE, visit website, e-mail, fax, call. Accepts inquiries by SASE, e-mail, fax, phone. "An appointment (10 minutes, one-on-one) may be set up at the conference with editor or agent of your choice on a first-registered/first-served basis."

SPRING AND FALL WORKSHOPS AND CLASSES, 1501 W. Fifth St., Suite E-2, Austin TX 78703-5155. (512)499-8914. Fax: (512)499-0441. E-mail: awl@writersleague.org. Website: www.writersleague.org. **Contact:** Stephanie Sheppard, executive director. Biannual. Workshops held in March, April, May, September, October and November. Workshops held weekends; classes held one evening/week and lasts 2-8 weeks. Average attendance: 20 for workshops; 12 for classes. "Classes and workshops provide practical advice and guidance on various aspects of fiction, creative nonfiction and screenwriting." Site: Writers' League of Texas resource center. "There are two multipurpose classrooms, a library, three offices and a workroom." Some classes are by e-mail. "Topics for workshops and classes have included E-Publishing; Creative Nonfiction; Screenwriting Basics; Novel in Progress; Basics of Short Fiction; Technique; Writing Scenes; Journaling; Manuscript Feedback; Essays; and Newspaper Columns." Instructors include: Marion Winik, Emily Vander Veer, Susan Rogers Cooper, Bonnie Orr, Jan Epton Seale, Susan Wade, Lila Guzman, Laurie Lynn Drummond, Darryl Wimberly, Patricia Wynn, Joan Neubauer, Graham Shelby, John Pipkin, Mindy Reed and Ann McCutchan.
Costs: Workshops $50; Classes $5-225.
Additional Information: Conference information is available in January and August. For brochure send SASE, e-mail, visit website, call or fax. Accepts inquiries by SASE, e-mail, phone and fax.

SPRING MUSE MAGIC RETREAT, P.O. Box 272, Tinnie NM 88351. Telephone/fax: (505)653-4437. E-mail: mystic springs@magicplace.com. Website: www.guardians.nativeland.com. **Contact:** Deborah Vanderleelie, director. Estab. 1999. Annual. Workshop held in May. Average attendance: 20-30. "Conference sessions cover poetry, fiction, nonfiction and journaling. Workshops are geared towards achieving deeper levels of creativity for all writers." Site: A guest ranch featuring large casitas (homes) fully equipped. Catering is also available. All homes and cabins have decks and grills. The ranch is surrounded by national forest and is nestled in the pines of The Capitan Mountains. Past sessions covered meditation writing, journaling and creative expression. Also included "Circle of Souls" discussion forum where all attendees shared on-site writing.
Costs: $295-395; also offers couples packages for $495 (2000 rates). Fee covered 2 nights' lodging, meals and all workshops.
Accommodations: Offers overnight accommodations, included in price of conference. If staying more nights than are included in conference package, room rental is $59-89/night.
Additional Information: Conference information is available on website only. Accepts inquiries by e-mail, phone. Editors participate in conference.

STEAMBOAT SPRINGS WRITERS GROUP, P.O. Box 774284, Steamboat Springs CO 80477. (970)879-8079. E-mail: MsHFreiberger@cs.com. **Contact:** Harriet Freiberger, director. Estab. 1982. Annual. Conference held July 2002. Conference duration: 1 day. Average attendance: 30. "Our conference emphasizes instruction within the seminar format. Novices and polished professionals benefit from the individual attention and the camaraderie which can be established within small groups. A pleasurable and memorable learning experience is guaranteed by the relaxed and friendly atmosphere of the old train depot. Registration is limited." Steamboat Arts Council sponsors the group at the restored train depot.
Costs: $35 before June 1, $45 after. Fee covers all conference activities, including lunch. Lodging available at Steamboat Resorts. Optional dinner and activities during evening preceding conference.
Additional Information: Available April 2002. Accepts inquiries by e-mail, phone, mail.

TAOS INSTITUTE OF ARTS, 108 Civic Plaza Dr., Taos NM 87571. (505)758-2793. Fax: (505)737-2466. E-mail: tia@taosnet.com. Website: www.tiataos.com. Estab. 1988. Annual. Workshops held June-October 2001. Workshop duration: 1 week. Average attendance: 12 students maximum/workshop. Covers novel and short story writing, nonfiction, poetry, travel writing, mystery writing, the business of publishing, children's book writing, free-association writing. Workshops take place in a variety of locations in Taos. 2002 faculty included US poet laureate Billy Collins, Robert Westbrook, Ben Bova, Joan Cavanaugh, Levin Romero.
Costs: $435 ($40 registration fee and $395 tuition). Meals, lodging, etc., are separate.
Accommodations: Provides a list of area hotels or lodging options.
Additional Information: In Westbrook's workshops, participants may send 1 chapter (20-page limit). In Ben Bova's writing workshops, participants must send writing sample before acceptance. Deadline at least 2 weeks prior to workshop. Conference information available February 2003. For brochure send e-mail, call. Accepts inquiries by SASE, e-mail, phone, fax.

TELLURIDE WRITERS CONFERENCE, P.O. Box 2189, 100 W. Pacific St., Telluride CO 81435-2189. (970)728-4519. Fax: (970)728-3340. E-mail: akennedy@telluride.lib.co.us. Website: www.telluride.lib.co.us. **Contact:** Ann Kennedy, program coordinator. Estab. 2001. Annual. Conference held May 17-18, 2003. Average attendance: 50. Focuses on fiction, nonfiction, essays, short stories. Site: Public Library Program Room. In 2002, panels included How to Get Published, How to Self Promote Once Published, Do You Need an Editor?, Do You Need an Agent?, When Do

You Approach a Publisher Directly?, Should You Self-Publish? 2002 faculty include Bruce Holland Rogers, fiction writing instructor and author; Michelle Curry Wright, novelist; Patricia Calhoun, magazine/newspaper editor; Sandra Bond, literary agent; P. David Smith, publisher.

Costs: $35 for Saturday presentations and panel discussion; $20 individual Sunday session with panelist (20 minute duration).

Accommodations: "Conference held during shoulder season to take advantage of inexpensive lodging." Provides attendants with list of area lodging.

Additional Information: Attendants not required to submit material prior to arrival, "though it would be nice to bring a sample of writing along if attending any of the individual sessions on Sunday." Brochures available in February/March 2003 by e-mail, phone, fax or on website. Accepts inquiries by e-mail, phone, fax. Agents and editors participate in conference. "Telluride is a gorgeous mountain town in Southwest Colorado. Hard to get to, hard to leave. Unpublished authors will get the most out of our conference."

TEXAS CHRISTIAN WRITERS' CONFERENCE, First Baptist Church, Houston TX 77024-2199. (713)686-7209. E-mail: martharexrogers@aol.com. **Contact:** Martha Rogers. Estab. 1990. Annual. Conference held August 3, 2002. Conference duration: 1 day. Average attendance: 60-65. "Focus is on all genres." Site: First Baptist Church fellowship center and classrooms. Panels planned for 2001 conference book proposal, 2002 creating character plate, point of view. Cecil Murphey, DiAnn Mills, Dennis Hensley and Dinella Kimura are scheduled to participate.

Costs: $60 members of IWA, $75 non-members, discounts for seniors and couples, meal at noon, continental breakfast, and breaks.

Accommodations: Offers list of area hotels or lodging options.

Additional Information: Open conference for all interested writers. Sponsors a contest for short fiction; categories include articles, devotionals, poetry, short story, book proposals, drama. Fees: $8 member, $10 non-member. Conference information available send SASE or e-mail. Accepts inquiries by SASE or e-mail. Agents participate in conference.

MARK TWAIN CREATIVE WRITING WORKSHOPS, University House, 5101 Rockhill Rd., Kansas City MO 64110-2499. (816)235-1168. Fax: (816)235-2611. E-mail: BeasleyM@umkc.edu. Website: www.umkc.edu/newsletters. **Contact:** Betsy Beasley, administrative associate. Estab. 1990. Annual. Conference held first 3 weeks of June, from 9:30 to noon each weekday morning. Average attendance: 40. "Focus is on fiction, poetry, and literary nonfiction." Site: University of Missouri-Kansas City Campus. Panels planned for next conference include the full range of craft essentials. Professor James McKinley and Robert Stewart are scheduled to participate.

Costs: Fees for regular credit and non-credit courses.

Accommodations: Offers list of area hotels or lodging options.

Additional Information: Submit workshop six poems/one short story prior to arrival. Conference information is available in March by SASE, e-mail, or on website. Accepts inquiries by SASE, e-mail, phone, or fax. Editors participate in conference.

UNIVERSITY OF NEW MEXICO'S TAOS SUMMER WRITERS CONFERENCE, Dept. of English, Humanities 255, University of New Mexico, Albuquerque NM 87131-1106. (505)277-6248. Fax: (505)277-2950. E-mail: taoscon f@unm.edu. Website: www.unm.edu/~taosconf. **Contact:** Sharon Oard Warner, director. Estab. 1999. Annual. Conference held July 12-18, 2003 (weekend workshops July 12-3, week-long workshop July 13-18). Average attendance: 150. Conference offers both weekend and week-long workshops for beginning and experienced writers. Workshop size is a maximum of 12, which allows for both group support and individual attention. We offer workshops in novel writing, short story writing, screenwriting, poetry, creative nonfiction, travel writing, and in special topics, such as historical fiction, memoir and revision. Workshops and readings are all held at the Sagebrush Inn Conference Center, part of the Sagebrush Inn, an historic hotel and Taos landmark since 1929.

Costs: Week-long workshop tuition is $475, includes a Sunday evening Mexican buffet dinner, a Friday evening barbecue, and evening museum tour. A weekend workshop tuition is $225.

Accommodations: We offer a discounted car rental rate through the Sagebrush Inn. Offers overnight accommodations. Participants may choose to stay at either the Sagebrush Inn or the adjacent Comfort Suites. Conference participants receive special discounted rates $59-99 per night. Room rates at both hotels include a full hot breakfast.

Additional Information: "Participants do not submit mss in advance. Instead, they bring copies to distribute at the first meeting of the workshop." Sponsors contest. "We offer four merit-based scholarships, the Taos Resident Writer Award and one D. H. Lawrence Fellowship. Scholarship awards are based on submissions of poetry and fiction." They provide tuition remission; transportation and lodging not provided. To apply, participants submit 10 pages of poetry or fiction along with registration and deposit. Applicants should be registered for the conference. The Fellowship is for emerging writers with one book in print or press, provides tuition remission and the cost of lodging. Brochures available late January-early February 2003. For brochures send e-mail, visit website, call or fax. Accepts inquiries by SASE, e-mail, phone, fax. "The conference offers a balance of special events and free time. If participants take a morning workshop, they'll have afternoons free, and vice versa. We've also included several outings, including a tour of the Harwood Arts Center and a visit to historic D. H. Lawrence Ranch outside Taos."

UNIVERSITY OF THE NATIONS SCHOOL OF WRITING AND WRITERS WORKSHOPS, YWAM Woodcrest, P.O. Box 1380, Lindale TX 75771-1380. (903)882-WOOD [9663]. Fax: (903)882-1161. E-mail: writingscho oltx@compuserve.com. Website: www.ywamwoodcrest.com. **Contact:** Carol Scott, School of Writing. Estab. 1983.

Annual. Conference held September 26-December 17, 2002. School of Writing lasts 12 weeks, individual workshops last 1 week each. Average attendance: 6-12. Site: "We are located in East Texas about 90 miles east of Dallas. Our campus is on 107 acres of wooded area."
Costs: "Interested parties should double check fees for School of Writing as housing/food costs may vary. 2002 School of Writing costs are $50 registration fee; $2,700 tuition/food/housing plus $50 book fee." Send for information on 1-week workshop costs.
Accommodations: "We can pick up students at Tyler Airport or Mineola Amtrack train station. Otherwise, we can assist in arranging shuttle service from Dallas. Costs vary depending on number of people. Housing is dormitory-style with several students sharing a common room and shower area (one for men, one for women). Married students or families housing will vary and is arranged on an as needed basis."
Additional Information: For brochure send e-mail, visit website or call. Send request. Accepts inquiries by e-mail, phone, fax or send request. Editors participate in conference. "If a student desires credit for a workshop or plans to attend the full School of Writing they must meet University of the Nations prerequisite (usually just the Discipleship Training School). Although we are associated with the *Youth With A Mission* missionary organization we welcome inquiries and attendees from all backgrounds, not just missionaries."

WINTER WRITERS CONFERENCE, 1501 W. 5th St., Suite E-2, Austin TX 78703-5155. (512)499-8914. Fax: (512)499-0441. E-mail: awl@writersleague.org. Website: writersleague.org. **Contact:** Stephanie Sheppard, executive director. Estab. 1999. Annual. Conference held Winter 2003. Conference duration: 3 days. Average attendance: 125. "The purpose of the conference is to bring writers together to explore the craft of writing. The 2002 conference featured Ann Patchett and focused on fiction. The 2001 conference featured Lee Gutkind and focused on creative nonfiction." Site: Austin, Texas. Topics for 2002 included short story markets, young adult and children's fiction, mystery writing, historical fiction, publishing tips, narrative techniques, character development, book to film, self-publishing options, editing advice. In addition to Ann Patchett, presenters in 2002 included Mark Dunn, Janice Woods Windle, Kathi Appelt, Diane Gonzales Bertrand, Sharon Kahn, Karen Stolz, Lori Aurelia Williams, Darryl Wimberley and Patricia Wynn.
Costs: 2002 conference was $135 for members. Included lunch on Saturday and a continental breakfast on both Saturday and Sunday.
Additional Information: Conference information is available December 2002. For brochure send SASE, e-mail, visit website, call or fax. Accepts inquiries by SASE, e-mail, phone and fax.

WRITER'S RETREATS, 906 Chelsey Lane, Durango CO 81301-3408. (970)247-5327. E-mail: thunder@animas.net. Website: www.manuscriptdevelopment.com. **Contact:** Michael Thunder. Estab. 1998. Duration: 1-2 weeks. Average attendance: 1 individual. Focus is on fiction and screenwriting. Site: Smiley School, Durango, Colorado, "beautiful mountain environment."
Costs: $750 coaching fee. Meals and lodging are dependent on the writer's taste and budget.
Accommodations: Provides a list of area hotels or lodging options.
Additional Information: "These writer's retreats are geared toward vision questing, a project or project development. Usually writers stay one week and receive 10 hours of one-on-one coaching. The rest of their time is spent writing." For brochure send e-mail, visit website or call. Accepts inquiries by SASE, e-mail and phone. Agents and editors participate in conference.

WRITERS WORKSHOP IN SCIENCE FICTION, English Department/University of Kansas, Lawrence KS 66045-2115. (785)864-3380. Fax: (785)864-1159. E-mail: jgunn@ku.edu. Website: www.ku.edu/~sfcenter. **Contact:** James Gunn, professor. Estab. 1985. Annual. 2002 workshop held June 24-July 7. Average attendance: 15. Conference for writing and marketing science fiction. "Housing is provided and classes meet in university housing on the University of Kansas campus. Workshop sessions operate informally in a lounge." The workshop is "small, informal and aimed at writers on the edge of publication or regular publication." Past guests include: Frederik Pohl, SF writer and former editor and agent; John Ordover, writer and editor; and Kij Johnson and Christopher McKittrick, writers.
Costs: Tuition: $400. Housing and meals are additional.
Accommodations: Several airport shuttle services offer reasonable transportation from the Kansas City International Airport to Lawrence. During past conferences, students were housed in a student dormitory at $12/day double, $22/day single.
Additional Information: "Admission to the workshop is by submission of an acceptable story. Two additional stories should be submitted by the end of June. These three stories are copied and distributed to other participants for critiquing and are the basis for the first week of the workshop; one story is rewritten for the second week. The Workshop offers a 3-hour session manuscript critiquing each morning. The rest of the day is free for writing, study, consultation and recreation." Conference information available December 2000. For brochures/guidelines send SASE, visit website, e-mail, fax, call. Accepts inquiries by SASE, phone, fax, e-mail. "The Writers Workshop in Science Fiction is intended for writers who have just started to sell their work or need that extra bit of understanding or skill to become a published writer."

N YOUTH WITH A MISSION'S SCHOOL OF WRITING, P.O. Box 1380, Lindale TX 75771-1380. (903)882-9663. Fax: (903)882-1161. E-mail: info@ywamwoodcrest.com. Website: www.ywamwoodcrest.com. **Contact:** Carol Hatheway Scott, school leader. Estab. 1986. Annual. Conference held 25 September-16 December, 2003. Duration: 7 one-week workshops or 12-week school (includes 7 week workshops interspersed with 'project weeks'). Average attendance: 10-15. Seven one-week workshops include nonfiction narrative, editing your writing, fiction that lives, marketing your writing, writing screenplays, writing on a theme (book length), writing magazine articles as well as a one-day workshop in poetry. Site: "Woodcrest has 107 acres of creative possibilities. Two buildings on the site at present." Faculty members include Janice Rogers, Elaine Wright Colvin, Brian Godawa, Roger Palms, Sandra Tompkins, Carol Hatheway Scott.

Costs: $20 registration (non-refundable), $175 tuition first week and $125 each additional week, $174 food/housing per week. "Book fee depends on class."

Accommodations: "We offer pick-up in Tyler, Texas (airport or bus station)." Offers overnight accommodation; dorm style rooms.

Additional Information: Brochure available for SASE, e-mail, phone, fax or on website. Accepts inquiries by SASE, e-mail, phone, fax. Editors attend conference.

West (AZ, CA, HI, NV, UT)

N: AUTHOR'S VENUE JOURNEY CONFERENCE, 600 Central Ave. SE, Suite 235, Albuquerque NM 87102. (515)244-9337. Fax: (800)853-7655. E-mail: info@authorsvenue.com. Website: www.AuthorsVenue.com. **Contact:** Suzanne Spletzer, executive director. Estab. 2001. Annual. Conference held April 24-27, 2003. Average attendance: 200. Conference focuses on fiction, nonfiction and screenwriting. Established "to provide education and publication opportunities for writers." Site: Hyatt Regency in Lake Tahoe, NV. Panels planned for next conference include Agents' Panel, Screenwriters Marketing Panel, Coaches Panel. 2003 faculty members include Gregg Levoy, author of *Callings*; Richard Walter, Professor UCLA TV & film school; Milton Kahn, publicist; John Baker, editorial director, *Publishers Weekly*; Blythe Camenson, author of *Your Novel Proposal*; Katherine Sands, literary agent; Pat Lobrutto, Tor editor. Sponsored by *The Writer* Magazine.

Costs: $350 until March 1, 2003; $299 until October 1, 2002; $450 after March 1 and on site.

Accommodations: Offers overnight accommodations at Hyatt Regency, $119 per night.

Additional Information: Participants must submit material for manuscript consultations prior to arrival, deadline: March 1. Manuscript consultations are $175 for 30 minutes with an editor or agent. For brochure, inquiries contact by e-mail, phone, fax, mail or visit website. "A great experience for professional writers."

N: © AUTHOR'S VENUE SCREENWRITERS INSTITUTE, 600 Central Ave. SE, Suite 235, Albuquerque NM 87102. (515)244-9337. Fax: (800)853-7655. E-mail: executivedirector@authorsvenue.com. Website: www.Authors Venue.com. **Contact:** Suzanne Spletzer, executive director or Stephanie Dooley, director of events. Estab. 2001. Annual. Conference held April 24-27, 2003. Average attendance: 50 screenwriters. Conference's purpose is to provide "education in screenwriting, connecting with professionals and producers." Offers Academy class taught by Academy Award winning or nominated writer. Site: Hyatt Regency in Lake Tahoe, NV. Panels include marketing screenplays panel, scene structure, dialogue. Faculty includes Richard Walter, professor at UCLA TV and Film School.

Costs: $299 until October 1, 2002; $350 until March 1, 2003; $450 after March 1, 2003 and onsite. Academy class, additional $150.

Accommodations: Offers overnight accommodations at Hyatt, $119 per night.

Additional Information: Academy class participants must bring screenplays to read and discuss. Accepts inquiries contact by mail, e-mail, phone, fax. Editors, agents, producers attend conference. Further guidelines available on website.

BIG BEAR WRITER'S RETREAT, P.O. Box 1441, Big Bear Lake CA 92315-1441. (909)585-0059. Fax: (909)266-0710. E-mail: duffen@aol.com. **Contact:** Mike Foley, director. Estab. 1995. Biannual. Conference held May 2003. Conference duration: 3 days. Average attendance: 15-25. Site: "A small intimate lodge in Big Bear, California, San Bernardino mountains of Southern California." Themes for 2002 included Bringing Depth to Characters, Creating Strong Hooks, Finding a New Creativity, Embracing Yourself as a Writer. Retreat is hosted annually by Mike Foley, editor, Dream Merchant Magazine and Tom Foley, Ph.D., artistic psychologist.

Costs: $550, includes meals and lodging.

Accommodations: Offers overnight accommodations. On-site facilities included in retreat fee.

Additional Information: Prior to arrival, submit a fiction or nonfiction sample, 10 double-spaced pages maximum. Conference information is available March 2002. For brochure send SASE, e-mail, call or fax. Accepts inquiries by SASE, e-mail, phone and fax. Editors participate in conference. "This is unlike the standard writers conference. Participants will live as writers for a weekend. Retreat includes workshop sessions, open writing time and private counseling with retreat hosts. A weekend of focused writing, fun and friendship. This is a small group retreat, known for its individual attention to writers, intimate setting and strong bonding among participants."

BLACK WRITERS REUNION AND CONFERENCE, P.O. Box 700065, Dallas TX 75370-0065. E-mail: bwrc@bl ackwriters.org. Website: www.blackwriters.org/conference. **Contact:** Tia Shabazz, conference chairperson. Estab. 2000. Annual. Conference held August 21-24, 2003, at Sheraton Gateway Hotel, Los Angeles, CA. Conference duration: 3 days. Average attendance: 400-500. Conference focuses on the craft of writing, publishing, poetry and the genres of romance, Christian fiction, fiction, television, playwriting, screenwriting. Site: "Touring conference; held in a different city and state each year." 2001 workshops included What's Wrong with My Manuscript; Dialogue; Point of View; Plot and Characterization; How to Get Published; Writing for Television; Writing the Sequel; Writing Outside the Box; Ideas, Theme and Premise; Writing Christian Fiction; Starting Your Writing Career; Editing; Self-Publishing; E-Publishing; Writer's Journey; How to Turn a Novel into a Film; Publicity; Marketing Strategies; Profitable Writing; Playwriting; The Power of Packaging; Building Better Interview Skills; Literary Legalities. 2001 panelists included Jewell Parker Rhodes, Donna Hill, Tananarive Due, Rochelle Alers, Brenda Jackson, Steven Barnes, Robert Fleming, Gwynne Forster, Angela Benson, Sandra Kitt, Tonya Marie Evans, Deirdre Savoy, Carol Taylor, Donna Williams, Ta'Shia Asanti, Mack Smith, Sara Freeman Smith, Margie Walker.
Costs: $175-275. Includes reception, banquet dinner, brunch and admission to all workshops and Gold Pen Awards Banquet.
Accommodations: Offers overnight accommodations. Negotiated rate of $89/night at the hosting Sheraton Gateway Hotel.
Additional Information: Sponsors an essay contest (500 words) for high school and college students. Essays are judged by committee. For brochure visit website. Accepts inquiries by e-mail. Agents and editors participate in conference.

JAMES BONNET'S STORYMAKING: THE MASTER CLASS, P.O. Box 841, Burbank CA 91503-0841. (818)567-0521. Fax: (818)567-0038. E-mail: bonnet@storymaking.com. Website: www.storymaking.com. **Contact:** James Bonnet. Estab. 1990. Conference held May, July, October 2002; February, May 2003. Conference duration: 2 days. Average attendance: 40. Conference focuses on fiction, mystery and screenwriting. Site: In 2002, Sportsmen's Lodge, Studio City, California. Panels planned for next conference include High Concept, Anatomy of a Great Idea, the Creative Process, Metaphor, The Hook, The Fundamentals of Plot, Structure, Genre, Character, Complications, Crisis, Climax, Conflict, Suspense and more. James Bonnet (author) is scheduled to participate as speaker.
Costs: $300 per weekend.
Accommodations: Provides a list of area hotels or lodging options.
Additional Information: For brochure send SASE, e-mail, visit website, call or fax. Accepts inquiries by SASE, e-mail, phone and fax. "James Bonnet, author of *Stealing Fire From the Gods*, teaches a story structure and storymaking seminar that guides writers from inspiration to final draft."

N **◎** **BOUCHERON**, 507 S. 8th St., Philadelphia PA 19147. Website: www.bconvegas2003.org. Conference held October 16-19, 2003. The Boucheron is "the world mystery and detective fiction event." Site: Riviera Hotel, Las Vegas, NV. Speakers and panelists scheduled include James Lee Burke, Ian Rankin, Ruth Rendall, S.J. Rozan.
Costs: $175 registration fee covers writing workshops, panels, reception, etc.
Accommodations: "The Riviera Hotel convention rate will be $115 per night. No reservations will be accepted until late October 2002."
Additional Information: Sponsors Anthony Award for published mystery novel; ballots due prior to conference. Information available on website.

N **BYU WRITING FOR YOUNG READERS WORKSHOP**, 399 HCEB, Brigham Young University, Provo UT 84602. (801)378-8925. Website: http://ce.byu.edu/cw/writing. **Contact:** Susan Overstreet. Estab. 2000. Annual. Workshop held July 7-11, 2003. Average attendance: 100. Conference focuses on "all genres for children and teens." Site: Brigham Young University's Harmon Conference Center. 2002 Faculty included Eve Bunting, Tony Johnston, Tim Wynne-Jones, John H. Ritter, Alane Ferguson, Lael Little, Laura Torres, Gloria Skurzynski.
Costs: $399 conference fee and closing banquet.
Accommodations Provides list of area hotels.
Additional Information: Brochures available in March by phone and on website. Accepts inquiries by SASE, e-mail, Phone. Agents and editors participate in conference.

CANYONLANDS WHITEWATER WRITERS RIVER TRIP/CANYONLANDS FIELD INSTITUTE, P.O. Box 68, Moab UT 84532. (435)259-7750. Fax: (435)259-2335. E-mail: cfiinfo@canyonlandsfieldinst.org. Website: www.canyonlandsfieldinst.org. **Contact:** Office Manager. Estab. 1998. Annual. Conference held last week of July. Conference duration: 6 days. Average attendance: 15. "Enjoy four days of instruction and critique as well as private time to do some of your own writing down Westwater Canyon of the Colorado River. You'll also learn about the fascinating geology, ecology and history of this beautiful canyon and run both mild and exciting rapids (class I-III riverstretch)." Site: "This workshop/river trip begins with an evening motel stay and introductory seminar in Grand Junction, Colorado. Our five-day, four-night river trip follows." Past faculty: Scott Russell Sanders, Alison Hewthorne Deming.
Costs: $950, $450 deposit. Includes meals, instruction, boating gear and first night's hotel stay.
Additional Information: Brochures available, send SASE, e-mail, visit website, call or fax. Accepts inquiries by SASE, e-mail, phone and fax.

▨ ◎ DESERT DREAMS CONFERENCE: REALIZING THE DREAM, 1066 E. Hope St., Mesa AZ 85203. (623)910-0524. E-mail: desertdreams2002@cs.com. Website: www.desertroserwa.org. **Contact:** Carrie Weaver, conference coordinator. Estab. 1986. Biennial. Conference held March 1-2, 2002. Next conference Spring 2004. Average attendance: 250. Conference focuses on romance fiction. 2002 site: Fiesta Inn in Tempi, AZ. Panels at 2002 conference include Plotting, Dialogue, Manuscript Preparation, Website Design, Synopsis, Help for the Sagging Middle. Keynote speaks in 2002, Stella Cameron and David Freeman. Other guest speakers were Lisa Gardner, Carolyn Greene, Denise Domning, Pamela Kaye Tracy. Guest editors from St. Martin's Press, Harlequin, Bantam Bell, Spectrum Literary Agency. **Costs:** $135 (includes lunch).
Accommodations: "Fiesta Inn provides shuttle service to airport." $129/night at Fiesta Inn. Mention conference to receive special rate.
Additional Information: Sponsors contest as part of conference. For brochure, inquiries, contact by e-mail, phone, fax, mail or visit website. Agents and editors participate in conference.

DESERT WRITERS WORKSHOP/CANYONLANDS FIELD INSTITUTE, P.O. Box 68, Moab UT 84532. (435)259-7750 or (800)860-5262. Fax: (435)259-2335. E-mail: cfiinfo@canyonlandsfieldinst.org. Website: www.canyonlandsfieldinst.org/. **Contact:** Office Manager. Estab. 1984. Annual. Held in October. Conference duration: 5 days. Average attendance: 30. Concentrations include fiction, nonfiction, poetry. Site is at a ranch near Moab, Utah. "Theme is oriented towards understanding the vital connection between the natural world and human communities." Faculty panel has included in past years Ann Zwinger, Pam Houston, Linda Hogan, Christopher Merrill, Terry Tempest Williams and Richard Shelton.
Costs: TBA. Includes meals, instruction, field trip, lodging.
Accommodations: At a guest ranch, included in cost.
Additional Information: Brochures are available for SASE. Accepts inquiries by phone, fax, e-mail. "Participants may submit work in advance, but it is not required. Student readings, evaluations and consultations with guest instructors/ faculty are part of the workshop. Desert Writers Workshop is supported in part by grants from the Utah Arts Council and National Endowment for the Arts. A partial scholarship is available. College credit is also available for an additional fee."

IWWG EARLY SPRING IN CALIFORNIA CONFERENCE, International Women's Writing Guild, P.O. Box 810, Gracie Station, New York NY 10028-0082. (212)737-7536. Fax: (212)737-9469. E-mail: iwwg@iwwg.com. Website: www.IWWG.com. **Contact:** Hannelore Hahn, executive director. Estab. 1982. Annual. Conference held second weekend in March. Average attendance: 80. Conference to promote "creative writing, personal growth and empowerment." Site: Bosch Bahái School, a redwood forest mountain retreat in Santa Cruz, California.
Costs: $345 for weekend program with room and board ($325 for members); $90 per day for commuters ($80 for members), $170 for weekend program without room and board ($150 for members).
Accommodations: Accommodations are all at conference site.
Additional Information: Conference information is available after August. For brochures/guidelines send SASE. Accepts inquiries by e-mail, fax.

LEAGUE OF UTAH WRITERS ROUND-UP, 4621 W. Harman Dr., W.V.C. UT 84120-3752. Phone/fax: (801)964-0861. E-mail: crofts@numucom.com. Website: www.luwrite.com. **Contact:** Dorothy Crofts, membership chairman. Estab. 1935. Annual. Conference held in September 2002. Conference duration: 2 days, Friday and Saturday. Average attendance: 200. "The purpose of the conference is to award the winners of our annual contest as well as instruction in all areas of writing. Speakers cover subjects from generating ideas to writing a novel and working with a publisher. We have something for everyone." Conference held at hotel conference rooms and ballroom facilities with view of lakeside for awards banquet. 2002 themes included Essays, Mystery, Writing for Magazines. Speakers include Mary Higgins Clark, mystery; Jennie Dunham, agent; Andy Whelchel, publisher; Skip Gregory, scriptwriting; Ron Carter, sequel and research; Carolyn Campbell, writing controversy; Bob Meyer, fiction.
Costs: 2002 costs: $125 for LUW members ($100 if registered before August 31); $160 for nonmembers (fee includes 4 meals).
Accommodations: Shuttle service is available from Salt Lake International Airport to Salt Lake Airport Hilton. List of hotel/motel accommodations available. Special hotel rate for conference attendees $79.
Additional Information: Opportunity for writers to meet one-on-one with literary agent from New York. Sponsors contests for eight fiction categories, three open to nonmembers of League. Word limits vary from 1,500 to 90,000. Conference brochures/guidelines available for SASE, e-mail, fax, phone and on website after May 2003. Accepts inquiries by fax, e-mail, SASE, phone.

▨ LOS ANGELES WRITERS CONFERENCE, 1010 Westwood Blvd., Los Angeles CA 90024. (310)825-9415. Fax: (310)206-7382. E-mail: writers@unex.ucla.edu. Website: www.uclaextension.org. **Contact:** Rick Noguchi. Estab. 1997. Annual. Conference held February 6-9, 2003. Average attendance: 150-200. Conference on creative writing, fiction, memoir. Located in UCLA Extension classrooms at 1010 Westwood Village Center. Instructors include Susan Taylor Chehak, Hope Edelman, Jerrilyn Farmer, Simon Levy and Leslie Spirson.
Costs: $625 before November 30; $525 after November 30.
Accommodations: Information on overnight accommodations is available.
Additional Information: Conference brochures available late September.

N̤ MAUI WRITERS CONFERENCE & RETREAT, Box 1118, Kihei HI 96753. (808)879-0061. Fax: (808)879-6233. E-mail: writers@maui.net. Website: http://mauiwriters.com. Estab. 1992. Annual. Conference held Labor Day weekend, August 28-September 1, 2003. Retreat held August 22-27, 2003. Average attendance: 1,200 conference, 200 retreat. Conference covers fiction, nonfiction, screenwriting, playwriting, children's books. Site: Outrigger Wailea Resort, "Four Diamond Resort on the beach in Maui, Hawaii." 2003 conference schedule includes "dozens of speakers, panels and workshops cover all aspects of writing and publishing fiction." Speakers from 2002 conference include Steve Martini, Billie Letts, John Saul, Elizabeth George, Dorothy Allison, Terry Brooks.

Costs: In 2002, conference was $495-695 depending when you sign up; retreat was $895-995 also depending when you sign up.

Accommodations: Offers "heavily discounted rates at Outrigger Wailea Resort, Grand Wailea Resort and Maui area condos."

Additional Information: Sponsors a contest. Submit 12 pages of fiction. Judged by NY Times bestselling author. Over $4,000 in cash prizes available. Must be attendee to participate. Guidelines/brochure available throughout the year. Send a request by letter, e-mail, fax or visit website. Accepts inquiries by phone, fax, e-mail or mail. "More than 50 agents and editors attend conference."

N̤ MORMON WRITERS' CONFERENCE, P.O. Box 51364, Provo UT 84605-1364. (801)579-8330. E-mail: dmichael@wwno.com. Website: www.aml-online.org. **Contact:** Dr. Michael Martindale, conference chair. Estab. 1999. Annual. Conference held November. Conference duration: one day, usually first Saturday of the month. Average attendance: 150. The conference will cover anything to do with writing by, for, or about Mormons, including fiction, nonfiction, theater, film, children's literature. Site: Thanksgiving Point, Lehi, UT. "Plenary speeches, panels and instructional presentations by prominent authors and artists in the LDS artistic community."

Costs: $50 including catered lunch with pre-registration. AML member and student discounts available.

Additional Information: For brochures/guidelines send SASE, e-mail, visit website. Accepts inquiries by SASE, e-mail.

◎ MOUNT HERMON CHRISTIAN WRITERS CONFERENCE, P.O. Box 413, Mount Hermon CA 95041-0413. (831)335-4466. Fax: (831)335-9413. E-mail: slist@mhcamps.org. Website: www.mounthermon.org. **Contact:** David R. Talbott, director of adult ministries. Estab. 1970. Annual. Conference held April 11-15, 2003 and April 2-6, 2004. Average attendance: 450. "We are a broad-ranging conference for all areas of Christian writing, including fiction, children's, poetry, nonfiction, magazines, books, educational curriculum and radio and TV scriptwriting. This is a working, how-to conference, with many workshops within the conference involving on-site writing assignments. The conference is sponsored by and held at the 440-acre Mount Hermon Christian Conference Center near San Jose, California, in the heart of the coastal redwoods. Registrants stay in hotel-style accommodations, and full board is provided as part of conference fees. Meals are taken family style, with faculty joining registrants. The faculty/student ratio is about 1:6 or 7. The bulk of our faculty are editors and publisher representatives from major Christian publishing houses nationwide."

Costs: Registration fees include tuition, conference sessions, resource notebook, refreshment breaks, room and board and vary from $850 (economy) to $915 (deluxe), double occupancy (2002 rates).

Accommodations: Airport shuttles are available from the San Jose International Airport. Housing is not required of registrants, but about 95% of our registrants use Mount Hermon's own housing facilities (hotel-style double-occupancy rooms). Meals with the conference are required and are included in all fees.

Additional Information: Registrants may submit 2 works for critique in advance of the conference, then have personal interviews with critiquers during the conference. No advance work is required however. Conference brochures/guidelines are available in December by calling (888)MH-CAMPS. Accepts inquiries by e-mail, fax. "The residential nature of our conference makes this a unique setting for one-on-one interaction with faculty/staff. There is also a decided inspirational flavor to the conference, and general sessions with well-known speakers are a highlight." Brochures/registration forms available in December 2001 on website, by e-mail, fax or phone.

PASADENA WRITERS' FORUM, 620 W. Huntington Dr. #216, Arcadia CA 91007-3427. (626)445-0704. E-mail: mbrucker@nccf.org. **Contact:** Meredith Brucker, coordinator. Estab. 1954. Annual. Conference held in March. Average attendance: 200. "For the novice as well as the professional writer in any field of interest: fiction or nonfiction, including scripts, children's, humor and poetry." Conference held on the campus of Pasadena City College.

Costs: $100 for one-day conference.

Additional Information: Brochure upon request, no SASE necessary. "Pasadena City College also periodically offers an eight-week class 'Writing for Publication'."

PIMA WRITERS' WORKSHOP, Pima Community College, 2202 W. Anklam Rd., Tucson AZ 85709-0170. (520)206-6974. Fax: (520)206-6020. E-mail: mfiles@pimacc.pima.edu. **Contact:** Meg Files, director. Estab. 1988. Annual. Conference held in May. In 2003, May 23-25. Average attendance 200. "For anyone interested in writing—beginning or experienced writer. The workshop offers sessions on writing short stories, novels, nonfiction articles and books, children's and juvenile stories, poetry and screenplays." Sessions are held in the Center for the Arts on Pima Community College's West Campus. Past speakers include Michael Blake, Ron Carlson, Gregg Levoy, Nancy Mairs, Linda McCarriston, Jerome Stern, Connie Willis, Larry McMurtry, Barbara Kingsolver and Robert Morgan.

Costs: $65 (can include ms critique). Participants may attend for college credit, in which case fees are $87 for Arizona residents and $215 for out-of-state residents. Meals and accommodations not included.

Accommodations: Information on local accommodations is made available, and special workshop rates are available at a specified motel close to the workshop site (about $60/night).

Additional Information: Participants may have up to 20 pages critiqued by the author of their choice. Mss must be submitted 3 weeks before the workshop. Conference brochure/guidelines available for SASE. Accepts inquiries by e-mail. "The workshop atmosphere is casual, friendly, and supportive, and guest authors are very accessible. Readings, films and panel discussions are offered as well as talks and manuscript sessions."

SAN DIEGO STATE UNIVERSITY WRITERS' CONFERENCE, SDSU College of Extended Studies, 5250 Campanile Drive, San Diego State University, San Diego CA 92182-1920. (619)594-2517. E-mail: extendedstd@sdsu.e du. Website: www.ces.sdsu.edu. **Contact:** Kevin Carter, coordinator, SDSU extension programs. Estab. 1984. Annual. Conference held on 3rd weekend in January. Conference duration: 2 days. Average attendance: approximately 375. "This conference is held in San Diego, California, at the Doubletree Hotel, Mission Valley. Each year the SDSU Writers Conference offers a variety of workshops for the beginner and the advanced writer. This conference allows the individual writer to choose which workshop best suits his/her needs. In addition to the workshops, editor/agent appointments and office hours are provided so attendees may meet with speakers, editors and agents in small, personal groups to discuss specific questions. A reception is offered Saturday immediately following the workshops where attendees may socialize with the faculty in a relaxed atmosphere. Keynote speaker is to be determined."

Costs: Approximately $280 (2002). This includes all conference workshops and office hours, coffee and pastries in the morning, lunch and reception Saturday evening. Editor/agent appointments extra fee.

Accommodations: Doubletree, Mission Valley, (800)222-TREE. Conference rate available for SDSU Writers Conference attendees. Attendees must make their own travel arrangements.

Additional Information: Editor/Agent sessions are private, one-on-one opportunities to meet with editors and agents to discuss your submission. For more information, e-mail, fax, call or send a postcard to above address. No SASE required.

N SANTA BARBARA CHRISTIAN WRITERS CONFERENCE, P.O. Box 42429, Santa Barbara CA 93140. (805)684-9593. **Contact:** Opal Dailey, director. Estab. 1997. Conference held October 4, 2003. Conference duration: 1 day. Average attendance: 60-70. Site: Westmont college, "liberal arts Christian College. Beautiful campus in the Montecito Foothills at Santa Barbara, CA."

Costs: $59 for 2001 includes continental breakfast, lunch and afternoon snack.

Additional Information: Conference information available May 2002. For brochure, send SASE or call. Accepts inquiries by SASE and phone. Agents and editors participate in conference.

THE WILLIAM SAROYAN WRITER'S CONFERENCE, P.O. Box 5331, Fresno CA 93755-5331. Phone/fax: (559)224-2516. E-mail: law@pacbell.net. **Contact:** Stephen Mettee, conference chair. Estab. 1991. Annual. Conference held March 28-30, 2003. Conference duration: "Friday noon to Sunday noon." Average attendance: 150. Conference on "how to write and how to get published." The conference is held at Piccadilly Inn which is "close to the airport, other hotels and all workshops in one section of the hotel." 2002 speakers included Harlan Ellison, Dan Millman, Loren Estleman, Leonard Tourney.

Costs: 2000 fees: $225 for all workshops (choice of 39), most meals, critique sessions, one-on-ones with agents, editors, etc. Overnight accommodations listed in brochure. On-site accommodations approximately $80/night.

Additional Information: Conference information available February. For brochures/guidelines visit website, e-mail, fax or call. Accepts inquiries by fax, SASE, phone, e-mail. The conference is "small, intimate—easy to talk with agents, editors, etc."

SCBWI/NATIONAL CONFERENCE ON WRITING & ILLUSTRATING FOR CHILDREN, 8271 Beverly Blvd., Los Angeles CA 90048. (323)782-1010. Fax: (323)782-1892. E-mail: scbwi@scbwi.org. Website: www.scbwi.o rg. **Contact:** Lin Oliver, executive director. Estab. 1972. Annual. Conference held in August. Conference duration: 4 days. Average attendance: 650. Writer and illustrator workshops geared toward all levels. Covers all aspects of children's magazine and book publishing.

Costs: Approximately $375; includes all 4 days and one banquet meal. Does not include hotel room.

Accommodations: Information on overnight accommodations made available.

Additional Information: Manuscript and illustration critiques are available. Brochure/guidelines available for SASE or visit website.

SOUTHERN CALIFORNIA WRITERS' CONFERENCE, 4406 Park Blvd., Suite E, San Diego CA 92116. (619)282-2983. E-mail: WeWrite@WritersConference.com. Website: www.WritersConference.com. **Contact:** Michael Steven Gregory, executive director. Estab. 1986. Annual. Conference held February 14-17, 2003. Conference duration: 4 days. Average attendance: 250. Conference focuses on facilitating mainstream fiction, nonfiction to market. Emphasis is on reading and critiquing conferees' manuscripts. Site: Holiday Inn Hotel & Suites, located in historic Old Town, San Diego, approximately 2 miles from Sea World. Panels planned for next conference include Fulfilling a Story's Promise; Sustaining Narrative Drive; Writing the Synopsis That Sells; and over 3 dozen workshops with extensive read-and-critiques, agents' panel and more. Gayle Lynds, Jerry Hannah, Bill Johnson, Mark Clements, Larry Brody and Mary Koski are scheduled to participate.

Costs: $275, which includes all workshops and events, including Saturday evening's banquet. Day rates available.

Accommodations: Hotel lodging discount available to conferees. Shuttle service to San Diego airport. Approximately $118-130/night.

Additional Information: Sponsors contest. 250-word "Topic" competition is announced the opening day of conference. Advance submission critiques are also available, followed by one-on-one consultation. Conference information is available in September. For brochure send e-mail, visit website, call or fax. Accepts inquiries by SASE, e-mail, phone and fax. Agents and editors participate in conference.

SQUAW VALLEY COMMUNITY OF WRITERS WORKSHOPS, P.O. Box 1416, Nevada City CA 95959-1416. (530)274-8551. Fax: (530)274-0986. E-mail: svcw@oro.net. Website: www.squawvalleywriters.org. **Contact:** Brett Hall Jones, executive director. Estab. 1969. Annual. Conference held in August. Conference duration is 7 days. Average attendance: 120. "The Fiction Workshop assists talented writers by exploring the art and craft as well as the business of writing." Offerings include daily morning workshops lead by writer-teachers, editors, or agents of the staff, limited to 12-13 participants; seminars; panel discussions of editing and publishinng; craft colloquies; lectures; and staff readings. Past themes and panels included "Personal History in Fiction," "Narrative Structure," "Roots" and "Anatomy of a Short Story." Past faculty and speakers included Michael Chabon, Mark Childress, Janet Fitch, Richard Ford, Karen Joy Fowler, Lynn Freed, Molly Giles, Sands Hall, James D. Houston, Louis B, Jones, Al Young.

Costs: Tuition is $650, which includes six dinners.

Accommodations: The Community of Writers rents houses and condominiums in the Valley for participants to live in during the week of the conference. Single room (one participant): $400/week. Double room (twin beds, room shared by conference participant of the same sex): $285/week. Multiple room (bunk beds, room shared with two or more participants of the same sex): $185/week. All rooms subject to availability; early requests are recommended. Can arrange airport shuttle pick-ups for a fee.

Additional Information: Admissions are based on submitted manuscript (unpublished fiction, a couple of stories or novel chapters); requires $25 reading fee. Submit ms to Brett Hall Jones, Squaw Valley Community of Writers, P.O. Box 1416, Nevada City CA 95959. Deadline: May 10. Notification: June 10. Brochure/guidelines available February by phone, e-mail or visit website. Accepts inquiries by SASE, e-mail, phone. Agents and editors attend/participate in conference.

N TMCC WRITERS' CONFERENCE, TMCC Community Services, 4001 S. Virginia St., RTMA 1, Reno NV 89502. (775)829-9010. (775)829-9032. E-mail: kberry@tmcc.edu or mikecroft@aol.com. Website: http://commserv.tmcc.edu. Estab. 1990. Annual. Conference held March 27-30, 2003 for Track A which includes critique workshops; March 29-30, 2003 for Track B. Average attendance: 125. Conference focuses on fiction (literary and mainstream), poetry, marketing to agents, publishers. Site: John Ascuaga's Nugget Hotel/Casino Resort—facilities include indoor pool, spa, numerous restaurants, celebrity showrooms, casino, sportsbook. "We strive to provide a well-rounded even for fiction writers and poets. We will have a panel discussion for one hour." Panelists include Sands Hall, novelist; Roy Parvin, short story writer; Andrea Wolf, screenwriter; Molly Fisk, poet; Calla Devlin, marketing department HarperCollins.

Costs: 4-day Track A $369; 2-day Track B $109 before February 28, $119 after. "Scholarships based on merit and finanacial need are awarded every December."

Accommodations: Hotel shuttle service from Reno airport available. Overnight accommodations available at site for conference rate of $90/night.

Additional Information: If participating in Track A, attendee should submit first chapter (20 pages maximum) by January 21. Brochures available November 2002 by e-mail, phone, fax or on website. Accepts inquiries by e-mail or phone. Agent will participate in conference. "This conference features an informal, friendly atmosphere where questions are encouraged. A 'Meet the Presenters' session allows for participants to mix with event speakers. No host lunches with presenters (limited to first 10 sign-ups per event) will also be held. The 4-day Track A keeps each critique group small— no more than 12 participants in each group."

N UCLA EXTENSION WRITERS' PROGRAM, 10995 Le Conte Ave., #440, Los Angeles CA 90024-2883. (310)825-9415 or (800)388-UCLA. Fax: (310)206-7382. E-mail: writers@uclaextension.org. Website: www.uclaextension.org/writers. **Contact:** Cindy Lieberman, conference coordinator. Estab. 1891. Courses held year-round with one-day or intensive weekend workshops to 12-week courses. Conference held February 6-9, 2003. A 9-month Master Class is also offered every fall. "The diverse offerings span introductory seminars to professional novel and script completion workshops. The annual Los Angeles Writers Conference and a number of 1, 2 and 4-day intensive workshops are popular with out-of-town students due to their specific focus and the chance to work with industry professionals. The most comprehensive and diverse continuing education writing program in the country, offering over 500 courses a year including: screenwriting, fiction, writing for young people, poetry, nonfiction, playwriting, publishing and writing for interactive multimedia. Courses are offered in Los Angeles on the UCLA campus and in the 1010 Center in Westwood

Village as well as online over the internet. Adult learners in the UCLA Extension Writers' Program study with professional screenwriters, fiction writers, playwrights, poets, nonfiction writers, and interactive multimedia writers, who bring practical experience, theoretical knowledge, and a wide variety of teaching styles and philosophies to their classes."

Costs: Vary from $90 for a one-day to $2,850 for the 9-month Master Class.

Accommodations: Students make own arrangements. The program can provide assistance in locating local accommodations.

Additional Information: Los Angeles Writers Conference information available October. For brochures/guidelines/guide to course offerings, visit website, e-mail, fax or call. Accepts inquiries by e-mail, fax, phone. "Some advanced-level classes have manuscript submittal requirements; instructions are always detailed in the quarterly UCLA Extension course catalog. An annual fiction prize, The James Kirkwood Prize in Creative Writing, has been established and is given annually to one fiction writer who has produced outstanding work in a Writers' Program course."

[N] [◎] VALLEY BIBLE CHRISTIAN WRITERS SEMINAR, 1477 Willow Ave., Hercules CA 94547. (510)799-3171. Fax: (510)799-3174. E-mail: vbcwrites@yahoo.com. Website: www.valleybible.org. **Contact:** Sandy Ormeo, seminar coordinator. Estab. 2001. Annual. Conference held September 27-28, 2002. Average attendance: 300. "We try to offer most genres. We offer unique panel classes and product demos." Site: "Our brand new campus has a worship center (1,200 seat auditorium, 10 classrooms, a bookstore and library). The Family Life Center has a 500 seat auditorium and 6 classrooms." 30 minutes from San Francisco, 15 minutes from Six Flags Marine World. 2001 keynote speaker was Lorraine Snelling (Bethany House). Other faculty members include Donna G. Albrecht, Bill Edmunds, Bill Nesbit, Denella Kimura.

Costs: $89. Offers a "Bring-a-Friend" rate; 25% off, $135 for both. Includes continental breakfast as well as coffee, drinks, snacks throughout.

Accommodations: Provides a list of area hotels/lodging options.

Additional Information: "We offer a limited number of manuscripts for critique by a professional faculty member." For brochure send e-mail, call, fax or visit website. For inquiries, contact by mail, e-mail, phone and fax. Agents attend/participate in conference.

VOLCANO WRITERS' RETREAT, P.O. Box 163, Volcano CA 95689-0163. (209)296-7945. E-mail: khexberg@volcano.net. Website: www.volcano.net/~khexberg. **Contact:** Karin Hexberg, director. Estab. 1998. Four times/year. Weekend retreats held in January, April and October. Duration: 3 days. "Summer Camp" held in July/August. Duration: 5 days. Average attendance: 20-25 (limited). Retreat for writing "fiction, poetry, essay, memoir." Held at the St. George Hotel. Hotel is 150 years old and located in the most picturesque of all the gold country towns, Volcano.

Costs: 2002 fees: weekend, $268-293; summer camp, $394-449 (including lodging and some meals).

Accommodations: Most attendees stay at the site although individuals may make other arrangements.

Additional Information: "Absolutely no critiquing. The purpose of this retreat is to create a non-competitive, non-judgmental, safe atmosphere where we are all free to write the worst stuff in the world." Brochures/guidelines for SASE. Accepts inquiries by e-mail.

WRANGLING WITH WRITING, Society of Southwestern Authors, P.O. Box 30355, Tucson AZ 85751. (520)546-9382. E-mail: wporter202@aol.com. Website: www.azstarnet.com/nonprofit/SSA. **Contact:** Penny Porter, director. Estab. 1971. Annual. Conference held January 24-25, 2003. Attendance: limited to 350. Conference "to assist writers in whatever ways we can. We cover all areas." Held at the Holiday Inn with hotel rooms available. Keynote speakers for 2002 conference were Elmore Leonard, Jacqueline Mitchard, Alan Dean Foster, Donald Maas. Plus 36 workshops for all genres of writing.

Costs: $235; includes meals.

Accommodations: Holiday Inn Pala Verde in Tucson. Information included in brochure available for SASE.

Additional Information: Critiques given if ms sent ahead. Sponsors short story contest (2,500 words or less) separate from the conference. Deadline May 31. Awards given September 21. Brochures/guidelines available after November for SASE, e-mail, fax, phone call or on website. Accepts inquiries by e-mail, fax, phone, SASE.

[N] WRITE FROM THE HEART, 9827 Irvine Ave., Upper Lake CA 95485. Phone/fax: (707)275-9011. E-mail: Halbooks@HalZinaBennett.com. Website: www.HalZinaBennett.com. **Contact:** Hal. Offered 4 to 6 times a year. Conference held October 11-13, 2002. Duration: 3-5 days. Average attendance: 20-30. "Open to all genres, focusing on accessing the author's most personal and individualized sources of imagery, characterization, tensions, content, style and voice." Site: Varies; in October 2002, held at Josephine Taylor center, at the foot of California's Mt. Shasta. Panels include Creativity and Life Experiences: Sourcing Story and Character from What You Have Lived. Speaker: Hal Zina Bennett.

Costs: $170-190 for 3 days (not including meals).

Accommodations: No arrangements for transportation. Provides list of area hotels.

Additional Information: Brochures available in October 2002 for 2003 information. Request by SASE, e-mail, phone, fax or on website. Editors participate in conference. "Hal is a personal writing coach with over 200 successfully published clients, including several bestsellers. His own books include fiction, nonfiction, poetry, published by mainstream as well as smaller independent publishers."

WRITER'S CONSORTIUM, P.O. Box 976, Fallbrook CA 92088-0976. Phone/fax: (760)451-1669. E-mail: carolroper @writersconsortium.com. Website: www.writersconsortium.com. **Contact:** Carol Roper. Estab. 1995. Ongoing seminars

monthly. Seminar duration: 2 days. Average attendance: up to 16. "Writers learn in a peaceful, creative environment unrestrained by the demands of everyday obligation. To write in a compelling way, writers need more than technique, writers need to know themselves. Only then can we write from a compelling sense of truth." Site: "Fallbrook, California is a small, friendly town, famous for its avocados, 50 miles north of San Diego's Lindbergh Field and 90 miles south of Los Angeles. The town boasts respected art galleries, several excellent restaurants, and four championship golf courses nearby. There are nature preserves to enjoy." Panels planned for upcoming workshops include Creativity and Spirituality; Discovering Your Muse; Creative Intuition; Personal Powers; A Return to Innocence. Award-winning writer, Carol Roper facilitates one and two day workshops.
Costs: $90-100/weekend; includes meals. Individual feedback and/or instruction available at $50/hour.
Accommodations: Nearby motels and bed & breakfasts. See website at www.writersconsortium.com.
Additional Information: Unpublished or unproduced writers must submit a 5-page writing sample with registration. For brochure send e-mail, visit website, call. Accepts inquiries by SASE, e-mail, phone.

WRITERS@WORK, P.O. Box 540370, North Salt Lake UT 84054-0370. (801)292-9285. E-mail: lisa@writersatw ork.org. Website: www.writersatwork.org. **Contact:** Lisa Peterson, program administrator. Estab. 1985. Annual. Conference held June 22-27, 2003. Duration: 6 days. Average attendance: 250. Focuses on fiction, nonfiction, poetry. Site: Westminster College Campus. 2002 panels included Publishing 101; Speculative Fiction: Modern Implications and Craft; The Writer in the Work: Authorial Distance Across the Genre; Blank Page Workshop. 2002 panelists included Nancy Stauffer Cahoon, Robert Boswell, Rikki Ducornet, Teresa Jordan, Carol Houck Smith, Jewell Parker Rhodes.
Costs: $395 adults, $225 young writers (ages 15-19). Meals and lodging not included in costs.
Accommodations: Provides residential suites on Westminster Campus; $150/duration of conference.
Additional Information: Sponsors contest. Guidelines available in December. Brochure available in December for SASE, e-mail, phone or on website. Accepts inquiries by SASE, e-mail, phone. Agents and editors participate in conference.

WRITING FOR YOUNG READERS WORKSHOP, 348 HCEB, BYU, Provo UT 84602-1532. (801)378-2568. Fax: (801)378-8165. E-mail: susan_overstreet@byu.edu. Website: http://ce.byu.edu/cw/writing. **Contact:** Susan Overstreet, coordinator. Estab. 2000. Annual. Workshop held July 14-17, 2003. Average attendance: limited to 100. Workshop focuses on fiction for young readers: picture books, book-length fiction and general fiction. "Mornings are spent in small group workshop sessions with published author." Site: Conference Center at Brigham Young University in the foothills of the Wasatch Mountain range. 2002 faculty included Eve Bunting, Lael Little, Tim Wynn-Jones and Alane Ferguson.
Costs: $389, includes final banquet.
Accommodations: Local lodging, airport shuttle. Lodging rates: $55-85/night.
Additional Information: Participants must bring at least one manuscript in progress to the workshop. Conference information is available April 15, 2003. For brochure visit website, call or fax. Accepts inquiries by e-mail, phone and fax. Editors participate in conference.

YOSEMITE WINTER LITERARY CONFERENCE, P.O. Box 230, El Portal CA 95318. (209)379-2646. Fax: (209)379-2486. E-mail: info@yosemite.org. Website: www.yosemite.org. **Contact:** Beth Pratt, vice president. Estab. 2001. Annual. Conference held February 23-27, 2003. Average attendance: 100. "Through workshops, panel discussions, readings and informal sessions, participants will debate and explore the literary landscape of California, the Sierra Nevada and the American West with a distinguished group of writers, publishers, artists, photographers and scientists." Site: Ahwahnee Hotel in Yosemite National Park. 2002 panels included Workpoints, Fiction Workshops, American Indian Storytelling, Inside the Writers Studio, Writing from Life, A Writer's Sense of Place. 2002 faculty included Francisco Alarcon, Karen Joy Fowler, Gerald Haslam, Jane Hirschfield, Pam Houston, Maxine Hong Kingston, Malcom Margolin, David Max Masumoto, Louis Owens, Al Young.
Costs: In 2002, $535 fee included opening reception, dinner banquet, park entrance fee.
Accommodations: No arrangements for transportation. Offers overnight lodging at the Ahwahnee Hotel, $1,450 for four nights, or Yosemite Lodge, $472 for four nights.
Additional Information: Brochures available in Fall 2002 by e-mail, phone, fax or on website. Accepts inquiries by e-mail, phone, fax. Editors participate in conference.

Northwest (AK, ID, MT, OR, WA, WY)

CENTRUMS PORT TOWNSEND WRITERS' CONFERENCE, Box 1158, Port Townsend WA 98368-0958. (360)385-3102. Fax: (360)385-2470. E-mail: lizzy@centrum.org. Website: www.centrum.org. **Contact:** Sam Hamill. Estab. 1974. Annual. Conference held mid-July. Average attendance: 180. Conference to promote poetry, fiction, creative nonfiction "featuring many of the nation's leading writers." The conference is held at a seaside 700-acre state park on the strait of Juan de Fuca. "The site is a Victorian-era military fort with miles of beaches, wooded trails and recreation facilities. The park is within the limits of Port Townsend, a historic seaport and arts community, approximately 80 miles northwest of Seattle, on the Olympic Peninsula." There will be 5 guest speakers in addition to 10 fulltime faculty.
Costs: Approximately $375-475 tuition and $345-425 room and board.

Accommodations: "Modest room and board facilities on site." Also list of hotels/motels/inns/bed & breakfasts/private rentals available.

Additional Information: Brochures/guidelines available for SASE or on website. "The conference focus is on the craft of writing and the writing life, not on marketing."

CLARION WEST WRITERS' WORKSHOP, 340 15th Ave. E., Suite 350, Seattle WA 98112-5156. (206)322-9083. E-mail: info@clarionwest.org. Website: www.clarionwest.org. **Contact:** Leslie Howle, administrator. Estab. 1983. Annual. Workshop held June 22-August 1, 2003. Average attendance: 17. "Conference to prepare students for professional careers in science fiction and fantasy writing. Held at Seattle Central Community College on Seattle's Capitol Hill, an urban site close to restaurants and cafes, not too far from downtown." Deadline for applications: April 1. Faculty: 6 teachers (professional writers and editors established in the field). "Every week a new instructor—each a well-known writer chosen for the quality of his or her work and for professional stature—teaches the class, bringing a unique perspective on speculative fiction. During the fifth week, the workshop is taught by a professional editor."

Costs: Workshop: $1,400 ($100 discount if application received by March 1). Dormitory housing: $1,000, meals not included.

Accommodations: Students are strongly encouraged to stay on-site, in dormitory housing at Seattle University. Cost: $1,000, meals not included, for 6-week stay.

Additional Information: "Students write their own stories every week while preparing critiques of all the other students' work for classroom sessions. This gives participants a more focused, professional approach to their writing. The core of the workshop remains science fiction, and short stories, not novels, are the focus." Conference information available in fall 2002. For brochures/guidelines send SASE, visit website, e-mail or call. Accepts inquiries by e-mail, phone, SASE. Limited scholarships are available, based on financial need. Students must submit 20-30 pages of ms with $25 application fee to qualify for admission. Dormitory and classrooms are handicapped accessible.

N CRAFTING YOUR NOVEL: FROM IDEA TO BOOK, % Peggy Staggs, 6000 Plantation Dr., Boise ID 83701. E-mail: jmcurry@boisestate.edu. Website: www.robinleehatcher.com/cbc. **Contact:** Catherine Mulvany, conference chair. Estab. 1998. Conference held every 2 years (next conference October 11-12, 2002). Conference duration: 1 day. Average attendance: 50-75. "Romance fiction is our main focus since we are a chapter of Romance Writers of America (Coeur du Bois Chapter)." Site: Owyhee Plaza Hotel in downtown Boise, Idaho. 2002 speakers include Carolyn Greene, Tami Cowden, Sue Swift, Adrianne Lee, Christy Yorke, Evan Fogelman.

Costs: 2002 fee, $75 prior to September 15; $85 after (includes reception and lunch).

Accommodations: The hotel operates a free airport shuttle. Overnight accommodations available. Special conference rate offered at the Owyhee Plaza Hotel.

Additional Information: Sponsors contest for book-length romantic fiction published the year preceeding the conference—"The Heart of Romance Readers' Choice Award"—which is judged by readers who do not belong to RWA. Conference information is available June 2002. For brochure send SASE, e-mail, visit website or call. Accepts inquiries by SASE, e-mail, phone. Agents and/or editors participate in conference.

THE GLEN WORKSHOP, Image, 3307 Third Ave. W., Seattle WA 98119. (206)281-2988. Fax: (206)281-2335. E-mail: glenworkshop@imagejournal.org. Website: www.imagejournal.org. Estab. 1991. Annual. Workshop held August 2002. Workshop duration: 1 week. Average attendance: 100-140. Workshop focuses on "fiction, poetry and spiritual writing, essay, memoir. Run by *Image*, a literary journal with a religious focus. The Glen welcomes writers who practice or grapple with religious faith." 2002 conference held in Santa Fe, NM and featured "presentations and readings by the faculty." 2002 faculty included Robert Clark (fiction); Greg Martin (nature writing); Emilie Griffin (spiritual writing); Mark Jarman and Kate Daniels (poetry).

Costs: $500-800, including room and board; $300-375 for commuters (lunches only).

Accommodations: Arrange transporatation by shuttle. (15) Accommodations included in conference cost.

Additional Information: Prior to arrival, participants may need to submit workshop material depending on the teacher. "Usually 10-25 pages." Conference information is available in February. For brochure send SASE, e-mail, visit website, call or fax. Accepts inquiries by SASE, e-mail, phone and fax. "Like *Image*, the Glen is grounded in a Christian perspective, but its tone is informal and hospitable to all spiritual wayfarers."

HAYSTACK WRITING PROGRAM, PSU Summer Session, P.O. Box 1491, Portland OR 97207-1491. (503)725-4186. Fax: (503)725-4840. E-mail: snydere@pdx.edu. Website: www.haystackpdx.edu. **Contact:** Elizabeth Snyder. Estab. 1968. Annual. Program runs from mid-July through first week of August. Workshop duration varies; one-week and weekend workshops are available throughout the four-week program. Average attendance: 10-15/workshop; total program: 400. "Haystack Program takes place during the summer on the sparkling Oregon coast and gives registrants an opportunity to get away from the demands of their daily lives, to reflect and renew, to network with others in their field and re-inspire their creative strengths." Past instructors have included William Stafford, Ursula K. LeGuin, Craig Lesley, Molly Gloss, Karen Joy Fowler, Tom Spanbauer, Sallie Tisdale.

Costs: Approximately $435/course weeklong; $150 (weekend). Does not include room and board.

Accommodations: Attendees make their own transportation arrangements. Various accommodations available including: B&B, motel, hotel, private rooms, camping, etc. A list of specific accommodations is provided.

Additional Information: Free brochure available after March. Accepts inquiries by e-mail and fax. University credit (graduate or undergraduate) is available.

N 🔘 **HEART TALK**, Women's Center for Ministry, Western Seminary, 5511 SE Hawthorne Blvd., Portland OR 97215-3367. (503)517-1931 or (800)547-4546, ext. 1931. Fax: (503)517-1889. E-mail: wcm@westernseminary.edu. Website: www.westernseminary.edu/women/. **Contact:** Kenine Stein, administrative assistant. Estab. 1998. Annual (alternates speaking/writing conferences). 2002 speaker's conference held March 14-16, 2003. Writer's conference held March 15, 2003 with Robin Jones Gunn as keynote speaker. Conference duration: writing, 1 day; speaking, 3-4 days. Average attendance: 100. "Heart Talk is designed for women beginning to write for publication/or speak publically. It provides inspirational training for Christian women." Previous writer's conference covered fiction, writing your life story, getting published, opportunities in the marketplace, writing words that matter, etc. Topics may range from writing for children to novels. Site: "Western Seminary has a chapel, small and large classrooms to accommodate various size groups. The campus has a park-like atmosphere with beautiful lawns, trees, and flowers. The squirrels are at home in this peaceful setting." Previous writing conference "featured speakers Sally Stuart and Eva Gibson. Each featured speaker leads workshops, along with Elsie Larson, Sandy Snavely and Karan Gleason."
Costs: $45 in 2001; included box lunch.
Additional Information: Conference information available in December by e-mail, phone, fax and on website. For inquiries, contact by mail, e-mail, phone. Conference "is open to Christian women who desire to begin to write for publication."

N 🔘 **HEDGEBROOK**, 2197 Millman Rd., Langley WA 98260. (360)321-4786. Fax: (360)321-2171. Website: www.hedgebrook.org. Retreat estab. 1988. Two annual sessions: June-November residencies (application deadline: March 15, 2002), January-May residencies (application deadline: October 1, 2002). "Six writers are in residence at one time." Retreat purpose: "Hedgebrook provides writing residencies to women, published or not, of all ages and from diverse backgrounds at its retreat on Whidbey Island in Washington state. Applicants are selected, based on peer-reviewed writing samples and project questionnaire, and offered residencies ranging from one week to six months." Site: 48-acre retreat; each writer assigned her own cottage. Meals prepared from organix garden.
Costs: No cost. "To support a diversity of women writers, the Hedgebrook stipend program provides financial support to meet expenses, such as loss of wages, child or elder care, travel or rent that would prevent a woman from accepting a residency." To qualify for stipend, applicants must be low-income women without a college degree or low-income women aged 55 or over. Must have gross annual income no more than 200% of federal poverty guidelines.
Additional Information: Application: "To apply for residency, and to request a stipend form and application, please send a self addressed, stamped envelope to 2197 E. Millman Rd., Langley WA 98260." Applications/brochures also available from website.

N **IDAHO WRITERS LEAGUE CONFERENCE**, 467 N. 3200 E., Lewisville ID 83431-5019. (208)754-4347. E-mail: writejoy@srv.net. Website: www.idahowritersleague.com. **Contact:** Joyce Lindstrom, state president. Estab. 1940. Annual. Conference held September 26-28, 2002. Usually last weekend in September. Average attendance: 50-90. Focuses on "all forms of writing." Site: In 2002, Shilo Inn in Idaho Falls. "Chapters take turns hosting the conferences and it's moved yearly around the state." 2002 panels included poetry, characterization, selling your fiction, children's literature, writing articles. 2002 speakers included Trudy Harris, children's author; Robert Kirby, feature writer for the *Salt Lake Tribune*; Patti Sherlock, author; Patricia Kempthorne, Idaho's first lady.
Costs: $100 includes 2 continental breakfasts, 2 luncheons, 1 banquet on Saturday night.
Accommodations: Provides list of area lodging.
Additional Information: Sponsors 2 contests; one for work written on a particular theme with various categories in fiction/nonfiction/poetry/children's fiction and the other contest for the first 30 pages/2 chapters of a novel. Open to Idaho Writer's League members only. Brochures and contest guidelines available July 15 for e-mail and on website. Accepts inquiries by SASE, e-mail, phone. Editors and agents sometimes attend conference.

N **NORTHWEST BOOKFEST**, P.O. Box 28129, Seattle WA 98118. (206)378-1883. Fax: (206)378-1882. E-mail: nicolet@nwbookfest.org. Website: www.nwbookfest.org. **Contact:** Nicole Turgeon, director of programming. Estab. 1994. Annual. Conference held October 19-20, 2002. Conference duration: 2 days, Saturday and Sunday. Average attendance: 28,000. "Northwest Bookfest is a literary festival for a region that's passionate about the written word. Over 200 local and national authors, 200 book and literacy-related exhibitors and literary activities for the entire family. All genres are represented." Site: Sand Point Magnuson Park. "We'll have over 20 fiction-related panels to be defined by volunteers and staff as authors are invited to attend."
Costs: "Bookfest is free to the public, with a $5 suggested donation, which is used to fund grants to literacy organizations throughout the region."
Accommodations: Volunteer provided transportation is available. Provides list of area hotels/lodging options. "There are Bookfest rates offered at many area hotels."
Additional Information: "Interested authors should send books or other publicity information to Nicole Turgeon, Director of Programming, at above address." Brochures available by e-mail, phone, fax and on website in early fall, after authors are confirmed. Accepts inquiries by e-mail, phone and fax. Agents and editors attend/participate in conference.

N **PACIFIC NORTHWEST WRITERS CONFERENCE**, P.O. Box 2016, Edmonds WA 98020-9516. (425)673-2665. Fax: (425)771-9588. E-mail: pnwa@melbycameronhull.com. Website: www.pnwa.org. **Contact:** Sue Palmason, association executive. Annual. Conference held July 24-27, 2003. Average attendance: 300. Site: "Newly renovated, technologically advanced hotel and conference center, located near SeaTac Airport." 2002 panels included Publishing 101; Opening Lines that Grab; "And the winner is . . .": The Inside Scoop on Literary Contests; Make a Long Story

Short: How to Craft an Effective Short Story; other panels on genre writing, publishing, screenwriting, creativity. Critique Workshops available for additional fee. Workshops include mainstream fiction, romance, mystery, science fiction/fantasy, screenwriting. 2002 panelists included Sheree Bykofsky, agent; Kimberly Cameron, agent; Donald Maas, agent; Cynthia Black, editor at Beyond Words Publishing; Maggie Crawford, editor at Pocket Books; Jennifer Heddle, editor at Penguin Putnam's New American Library; Jill Schoolman, editor at Seven Stories Press; Jean Auel, author; Chris Vogler, author; Janice Johnson, author; Carol Orlock, author; Eric Witchey, author.
Costs: Members, $400; nonmembers, $450. Some meals included. Additional fee for critique workshops.
Accommodations: Hotel shuttle to and from airport available. Offers discounted rate for overnight lodging; $119/ night in 2002.
Additional Information: Participants in critique workshops must submit 10 pages of current work-in-progress with completed registration form and workshop fee. Offers contest with eight fiction categories: The Stella Cameron Romance Genre Contest, playwriting, screenwriting, adult genre novel, adult non-genre novel, juvenile/YA novel, adult short story, juvenile short story/picture book. Entry requirements vary with category. Guidelines for contest available late fall 2002; brochure for conference available winter 2003. E-mail, call, fax or visit website for brochure/guidelines. Accepts inquiries by e-mail, phone, fax. Agents and editors participate in conference.

PORTLAND STATE UNIVERSITY HAYSTACK WRITING PROGRAM, PSU Summer Session, P.O. Box 1491, Portland OR 97207. (503)725-4186. Fax: (503)725-4840. E-mail: snydere@pdx.edu. **Contact:** Elizabeth Snyder. Estab. 1968. Annual. Conference held from mid-July to early August in one-week sessions meeting Monday through Friday; some weekend workshops. Average attendance: 10-15/class. Conference offers a selection of writing courses including fiction, nonfiction, poetry, essay and memoir—taught by well-known writers in small-group sessions. Classes are held in the local school with supplemental activities at the beach, community lecture hall, and other areas of the resort town. University credit available.
Costs: $185 (weekend)-$435 (weeklong). Participants locate their own housing and meals.
Accommodations: Housing costs are $50-400/week. Camping, bed and breakfasts and hotels are available.

SAGEBRUSH WRITERS WORKSHOP, P.O. Box 1255, Big Timber MT 59011-1255. Phone/fax: (406)932-4227. E-mail: sagebrsh@ttc-cmc.net. **Contact:** Gwen Petersen, director. Estab. 1990. Annual. Workshop held March 23-24, 2002. Average attendance: 30-35. "Each year, the workshop has a different focus. For 2002, romantic suspense." Conference features "intensive personal instruction, good food, advance critiques, well published authors/instructors, agents/editors, book sales and signings, readings." Site: Crazy Mountain Museum, Big Timber, MT.
Costs: $190, includes Saturday evening banquet dinner, Sunday lunch, all snack breaks.
Accommodations: Offers shuttle from airport by arrangement with Sagebrush. Provides a list of area hotels and/or lodging options.
Additional Information: "Submissions optional but encouraged—up to 15 pages." Workshop information is available January 2002. For brochure send SASE, e-mail, call or fax. Accepts inquiries by SASE, e-mail, phone and fax. Agents and editors participate in conference.

SITKA CENTER FOR ART AND ECOLOGY, P.O. Box 65, Otis OR 97368. (541)994-5485. Fax: (541)994-8024. E-mail: info@sitkacenter.org. Website: www.sitkacenter.org. **Contact:** Amy Buringrud, associate director. Estab. 1970. Annual workshop program. "Our workshop program is open to all levels and is held annually from late May until late November. We also have a residency program from September through May." Average attendance: 10-16/workshop. A variety of workshops in creative processes, including book arts and other media. The Center borders a Nature Conservancy Preserve, the Siuslaw National Experimental Forest and the Salmon River Estuary, located just north of Lincoln City, Oregon.
Costs: "Workshops are generally $50-300; they do not include meals or lodging."
Accommodations: Does not offer overnight accommodations. Provides a list of area hotels or lodging options.
Additional Information: Brochure available in February of each year by SASE, phone, e-mail, fax or visit website. Accepts inquiries by SASE, e-mail, phone, fax.

SITKA SYMPOSIUM ON HUMAN VALUES & THE WRITTEN WORD, P.O. Box 2420, Sitka AK 99835-2420. (907)747-3794. Fax: (907)747-6554. E-mail: island@ak.net. Website: www.islandinstitutealaska.org. **Contact:** Carolyn Servid, director. Estab. 1984. Annual. Conference held in June. Conference duration: 1 week. Average attendance: 60. Conference "to consider the relationship between writing and the ideas of a selected theme focusing on social and cultural issues." The Symposium is held in downtown Sitka. Many points of visitor interest are within walking distance. The town looks out over surrounding water and mountains. Guest speakers have included Alison Deming, Scott Russell Sanders, Rina Swentzell, Barry Lopez, William Kittredge, Gary Snyder, Margaret Atwood, Terry Tempest Williams, Robert Hass, Richard Nelson and Linda Hogan.
Costs: $300.
Accommodations: Accommodation rates are listed on Symposium brochure.
Additional Information: Ms critiques (individually with faculty) are available for people submitting work before May 20. Conference brochures/guidelines are available for SASE. Accepts inquiries by e-mail and fax.

Ⓝ SOUTH COAST WRITERS CONFERENCE, P.O. Box 590, 29392 Ellensburg Ave., Gold Beach OR 97444. (541)247-2741. Fax: (541)247-6247. E-mail: scwc@southwestern.cc.or.us. Website: www.southwestern.cc.or.us or www .southwestern.cc.or.us/scwriters. **Contact:** Janet Pretti, coordinator. Estab. 1996. Annual. Conference held February 14-

15, 2003. Workshops held Friday prior to conference, conference on Saturday. Average attendance: 100. "We try to cover a broad spectrum: fiction, historical, poetry, children's, Nature." Site: "Conference is held in the local high school. Pre-conference activities are held at the Event Center on the Beach." 2002 panels included Character Building, Emotions, Description, Fiction Basics, Juvenile Novels, Writing Novels in Spare Time, Poetry: Writing Myth and Magic, Writing Action Poems, Historical Research, Voice. 2002 presenters included Linda Barnes, Candice Flavilla, Judy Fleagle, Jerry Holcomb, Maragret P. Kirk, Phillip Margolin, Tom McAllister, Sylvia Mullen-Tohill.

Costs: $45 for Saturday conference, $25 each for pre-conference Friday workshops. No lodging, meals included.

Accommodations: Provides list of area hotels.

Additional Information: Sponsors contest. "Southwestern scholarship-open to anyone. Entry should be essay, short story, memoir or poetry between 750-1,000 words. Eva Douglass-Starett Memorial Scholarship-open to women 40 years old or older. Essay, memoir, short story (no poetry) between 750-1,000 words." Judged by conference planning committee and English professors. Brochures available by e-mail, phone, fax and on website. Accepts inquiries by e-mail, phone, fax. Agents and editors attend conference. "We try to keep our conference small, with a small-town feel and excellent presenters. Sponsored by Southwestern Oregon Community College."

WHIDBEY ISLAND WRITERS' CONFERENCE, P.O. Box 1289, Langley WA 98260. (360)331-6714. E-mail: writers@whidbey.com. Website: www.whidbey.com/writers. **Contact:** Celeste Mergens, director. Annual. Conference held February 28-March 2, 2003. Conference held in "a state-of-the-art high school and at local homes by the sea on Whidbey Island. A variety of informative classes and hands-on interactive writing workshops are offered. Expert panel discussions are held where agents and editors share inside details, devulge what they are looking for and offer important how-to's in skill building sessions." Presenters include Pattiann Rogers, Elizabeth George, Andrew Pham, Richard Lederer, Bruce Coville, Paula Danziger, Marian Dane Bauer, Eva Shaw, Susan Wiggs and others.

Costs: $325, including luncheons and receptions. Early bird and volunteer discounts available.

Accommodations: "We have an accommodations hotline available through the Langley Chamber of Commerce. When making lodging reservations please mention the conference to receive a participant discount."

Additional Information: "If registrant desires an agent/editor consultation, they must bring the first five pages for a chapter book or youth novel or entire picture book idea with a written one-page synopsis." Conference information available July 15. For brochures/guidelines send SASE, visit website, e-mail or call. Accepts inquiries by SASE, phone, e-mail.

WILLAMETTE WRITERS CONFERENCE, 9045 SW Barbur, Suite 5-A, Portland OR 97219-4027. (503)452-1592. Fax: (503)452-0372. E-mail: wilwrite@teleport.com. Website: www.willamettewriters.com. **Contact:** Bill Johnson, office manager. Estab. 1968. Annual. Conference held in August. Average attendance: 400. "Willamette Writers is open to all writers, and we plan our conference accordingly. We offer workshops on all aspects of fiction, nonfiction, marketing, the creative process, etc. Also we invite top notch inspirational speakers for keynote addresses. Recent theme was 'The Writers Way.' We always include at least one agent or editor panel and offer a variety of topics of interest to both fiction and nonfiction writers and screenwriters." Recent editors, agents and film producers in attendance have included: Donald Maass, Donald Maass Literary Agency; Jeff Herman, The Jeff Herman Agency, LLC; Mark Ryan, Web Brand Agency Group; Claire Eddy, Tor/Forge Books; Rachel Kahan, Crown Publishers; Mira Son, Avalon Books; Frederick Levy, Marty Katz Productions; Julian Fowles, Asparzc-Katz Productions; Christopher Vogler, *The Writer's Journey.*

Costs: Cost for 2-day conference including meals is $250 members; $285 nonmembers.

Accomodations: If necessary, these can be made on an individual basis. Some years special rates are available.

Additional Information: Conference brochures/guidelines are available in May for catalog-size SASE, e-mail, fax, phone or on website. Accepts inquiries by fax, e-mail, phone, SASE.

WRITE ON THE SOUND WRITERS' CONFERENCE, 700 Main St., Edmonds WA 98020-3032. (425)771-0228. Fax: (425)771-0253. E-mail: wots@ci.edmonds.wa.us. **Contact:** Frances Chapin, cultural resources coordinator. Sponsored by Edmonds Arts Commission. Estab. 1986. Annual. Conference held October 5-6, 2002. Conference duration: 2 days. Average attendance: 160. "Conference is small—good for networking—and focuses on the craft of writing rather than publishers and editors. Edmonds is a beautiful community on the shores of Puget Sound, just north of Seattle."

Costs: $85 for 2 days, $50 for 1 day (1999); includes registration, morning refreshments and 1 ticket to keynote lecture.

Additional Information: Brochures available August 1, 2002. Accepts inquiries by e-mail, fax.

N̲ WRITERS STUDIO, 42 N.E. Graham St., Portland OR 97212. (503)287-2150. Fax: (503)287-2150. E-mail: Jesswrites@juno.com. Website: http://writingoutthestorm.homepage.com. **Contact:** Jessica Morrell. Estab. 1998. "Every year I teach a variety of one day and weekend workshops in Portland, Oregon, and at the Oregon Coast. Subjects range from Creative Nonfiction to Finetuning Fiction. At this time my schedule for 2003 is not finalized because I will be a guest speaker at a number of writing conferences though I will be teaching workshops with Marian Pierce the first weekends in March, June and October." *Writing Out the Storm*, author Jessica Morrell and short story writer Marian Pierce are scheduled to participate as faculty.

Costs: "Price ranges from $60-225."

Accommodations: Provides a list of area hotels or lodging options.

Additional Information: For brochure send e-mail, call. Accepts inquiries by SASE, e-mail, phone, fax.

WRITERS WEEKEND AT THE BEACH, Ocean Park Retreat Center, Ocean Park WA 98640. (360)665-6576. E-mail: etchinson@pcifier.com. Website: www.birdieetchison.com. **Contact:** Birdie Etchison or Patricia Rushford. Estab. 1992. Annual. Conference held February 21-23, 2003. Duration: "Two nights, one full day and one morning." Average attendance: 50-60. "Ours is a retreat for writers with an emphasis on poetry, fiction, nonfiction." Site: "Everything is on one main lodge. Wooded setting— view of the Pacific Ocean." Panels and speakers TBA.
Costs: $165 includes food, lodging and seminars.
Accommodations: Offers overnight lodging on-site.
Additional Information: Brochures available in October 2002 on website. Accepts inquiries by SASE, e-mail, phone. Editors and agents sometimes participate in conference.

Canada

BLOODY WORDS MYSTERY CONFERENCE, 12 Roundwood Court, Toronto, Ontario M1W 1Z2. Phone/fax: (416)497-5293. E-mail: soles@sff.net. Website: www.bloodywords.com. **Contact:** Caro Soles, chair. Estab. 1999. Annual. Conference held June 7-9, 2002. Average attendance: 300. Focus: Mystery/true crime/forensics, with Canadian slant. Purpose: To bring readers and writers of the mystery genre together in a Canadian setting. Site: Delta Chelsea Inn, Gerrard St., Toronto. Conference includes a workshop and 2 tracks of panels, one on factual information such as forensics, agents, scene of the crime procedures, etc. and one on fiction, such as "Death in a Cold Climate," "Murder on the Menu," "Elementary, My Dear Watson," and a First Novelists Panel. Past guests included William Deverell and Loren D. Estleman with Donald Maass as a guest agent and Joan Hall Houey, an experienced writer/editor.
Costs: 2002 fee: $150 (included the banquet and all panels, readings, dealers room and workshop).
Accommodations: Offers hotel shuttle from the airport. Offers block of rooms in hotel; list of optional lodging available. Call Delta Chelsea Inn for special conference rates (1-800-CHELSEA).
Additional Information: Sponsors short mystery story contest—4,000 word limit; judges are experienced editors of anthologies; fee is $5 (entrants must be registered). Conference information is available now. For brochure visit website. Accepts inquiries by e-mail and phone. Agents and editors participate in conference. "This is a conference for both readers and writers of mysteries, the only one of its kind in Canada. We also run 'The Mystery Café,' a chance to get to know 15 authors, hear them read and ask questions (half hour each)."

BOOMING GROUND, Buch E-462, 1866 Main Mall, Creative Writing Program, UBC, Vancouver, British Columbia V6T 121 Canada. (604)822-2469. Fax: (604)822-3616. E-mail: bg@arts.ubc.ca. Website: www.arts.ubc.ca/bg. **Contact:** Andrew Gray, director. Estab. 1998. Annual. Conference held July 5-11, 2003. Average attendance: 70. Conference on "fiction, poetry, non-fiction, drama." Conference held at "Green College, a residential college at the University of Columbia, overlooking the ocean." 2002 panels included "The Writing Life" and "Paths to Publication." 2002 panelists included Martha Sharpe, Gary Ross, Thomas Wharton, Esta Spalding.
Costs: 2001 fees were $650 (Canadian). Meals and accommodation separate. Some scholarships available.
Accommodations: "Information on overnight accommodations is available and students are encouraged to stay on-site at Green College." On site accommodations: $442 and $478 (Canadian) for 7 nights.
Additional information: "Workshops are based on works-in-progress. Writers must submit manuscript with application for jury selection." Conference information available February 2003. For brochures/guidelines send SASE, visit website, e-mail, fax or call. Accepts inquiries by SASE, phone, fax, e-mail. "Classes are offered for writers at all levels—from early career to mid-career."

GOD USES INK ANNUAL WRITERS' CONFERENCE, P.O. Box 487, Markham, Ontario L3P-3R1 Canada. (905)471-1447. Fax: (905)471-6912. E-mail: conference@thewordguild.com. Website: www.thewordguild.com. **Contact:** N.J. Lindquist, director. Estab. 1984. Annual. Conference to be held June 12-14, 2003. Average attendance: 125. Hosted by The Word Guild, an association of Canadian writers and editors who are Christian. "The annual conference is our means of helping to develop writers of all levels and genres. The 2002 theme was 'Write with power and grace.' We have a very busy three days, with plenary addresses from a keynote speaker, six different continuing classes of five hours each, a variety of workshops, panels, a manuscript critiquing service, and opportunities to meet with both Canadian and US editors. The conference is also a great opportunity to get to know other writers, from beginner to professional." The conference is held at a "retreat center tucked away in the city of Guelph, Ontario, about 40 miles west of Toronto, 100 miles from Buffalo, and 200 miles from Detroit." Offers overnight accommodation. Additional information available on website. Brochures available each February by e-mail, website, call or fax. Accepts inquiries by SASE, e-mail, phone, fax.

HUMBER SCHOOL FOR WRITERS SUMMER WORKSHOP, Humber College, 205 Humber College Blvd., Toronto, Ontario M9W 5L7 Canada. (416)675-5084. Fax: (416)675-1249. E-mail: writers@humberc.on.ca. Website: www.humber.ca//~writers/. **Contact:** Joe Kertes, dean, School of Creative and Performing Arts. Annual. Workshop held July 2003. Duration: 1 week. Average attendance: 100. Focuses on fiction, poetry, creative nonfiction. Site: Humber College's north campus in Toronto. Panels cover success stories, small presses, large presses, agents. Faculty: Stevie Cameron, Wayson Choy, Bruce Jay Friedman, Isabel Huggan, John Metcalf, Kim Moritsugu, Tim O'Brien, Olive Senior.
Costs: Workshop fee is $779 Canadian ($491 US).
Accommodations: Provides lodging. Residence fee is $332 Canadian ($204 US).

Additional Information: Participants "must submit sample writing no longer than 15 pages approximately 3 weeks before workshop begins." Brochures available mid-December for e-mail, phone, fax. Accepts inquiries by e-mail, phone, fax. Agents and editors participate in conference.

⬛ 🍁 MARITIME WRITERS' WORKSHOP, Extension & Summer Session, UNB Box 4400, Fredericton, New Brunswick E3B 5A3 Canada. Phone/fax: (506)474-1144. E-mail: k4JC@unb.ca. Website: www.unb.ca/extend/writers/. Coordinator: Rhona Sawlor. Estab. 1976. Annual. Workshop held July 7-13, 2002. Average attendance: 50. "We offer small groups of ten, practical manuscript focus. Novice writers welcome. Workshops in four areas: fiction, poetry, screenwriting, writing for children." Site is University of New Brunswick, Fredericton campus.
Costs: $350, tuition; $135 meals; $125/double room; $145/single room (Canadian funds).
Accommodations: On-campus accommodations and meals.
Additional Information: "Participants must submit 10-20 manuscript pages which form a focus for workshop discussions." Brochures are available after March. No SASE necessary. Accepts inquiries by e-mail and fax.

⬛ 🍁 MINI WRITING CAREER, 103 Barton Ave., Toronto, Ontario M6G 1P8 Canada. (416)531-4851. E-mail: janejim@sympatico.ca. Website: http://miniwritingcareer.com. **Contact:** Jane Finley-Young. Estab. 2002. Seasonal-Fall, Winter, Summer. Duration: varies, offers a one-week intensive workshop and several courses once a week lasting four months. Conference focuses on fiction-short story *or* novel. "We developed this course with a *finished product* in mind. We help beginners write their raw material, move it into fiction and go through vigorous editing process to produce a finished product. Then we have a launch (public reading)." Site: 1-week intensive held in Nova Scotia at the Tatamagouche Centre; regular courses held in Toronto. Longer courses: "We will spend the first 6 sessions experimenting with different forms of generating new material. Techniques such as Proprioceptive Writing, Clustering, timed writes, writing using music and poetry will be used as you find out what you have to say and how you want to say it. We help you make the leap into fiction and we help you 'plump up' your work in order to come up with a first draft. Homework will be assigned for each class. The following 6 sessions will be spent revising. Discussion of voice, plot, character, dialogue, point of view and place will aid us in this process. We will do 2 collective edits of your piece. There will be a 'publication' of all the finished works and a public reading where, of you wish, you will do a reading of your piece." Similar arrangement for 1-week intensive.
Costs: Intensive, $895 (includes all meals and lodging); longer, ongoing courses in Toronto, $680.
Accommodations: Offers overnight accommodations for Intensive, or provides list of area hotels.
Additional Information: Brochures available by e-mail, phone and on website. Accepts inquiries by SASE, e-mail, phone.

🍁 SAGE HILL WRITING EXPERIENCE, Box 1731, Saskatoon, Saskatchewan S7K 3S1 Canada. Phone/fax: (306)652-7395. E-mail: sage.hill@sasktel.net. Website: www.lights.com/sagehill. **Contact:** Steven Ross Smith. Annual. Workshops held in August and October. Program duration 10-21 days. Attendance: limited to 36-40. "Sage Hill Writing Experience offers a special working and learning opportunity to writers at different stages of development. Top quality instruction, low instructor-student ratio and the beautiful Sage Hill setting offer conditions ideal for the pursuit of excellence in the arts of fiction, poetry and playwriting." The Sage Hill location features "individual accommodation, in-room writing area, lounges, meeting rooms, healthy meals, walking woods and vistas in several directions." Seven classes are held: Introduction to Writing Fiction & Poetry; Fiction Workshop; Nonfiction Workshop; Writing Young Adult Fiction Workshop; Poetry Workshop; Poetry Colloquium; Fiction Colloquium; Playwriting Lab.
Costs: $775 (Canadian) includes instruction, accommodation, meals and all facilities. Fall Poetry Colloquium: $975.
Accommodations: On-site individual accommodations located at Lumsden 45 kilometers outside Regina. Fall Colloquium is at Muenster, Saskatchewan, 150 kilometers east of Saskatchewan.
Additional Information: For Introduction to Creative Writing: A five-page sample of your writing or a statement of your interest in creative writing; list of courses taken required. For intermediate and colloquium program: A resume of your writing career and a 12-page sample of your work plus 5 pages of published work required. Application deadline is May 1. Guidelines are available after January for SASE, e-mail, fax, phone or on website. Accepts inquiries by SASE, phone, e-mail and fax. Scholarships and bursaries are available.

🍁 SUNSHINE COAST FESTIVAL OF THE WRITTEN ARTS, Box 2299, Sechelt, British Columbia V0N 3A0 Canada. (604)885-9631 or (800) 565-9631. Fax: (604)885-3967. E-mail: info@writersfestival.ca. Website: www.writersfestival.ca. **Contact:** Gail Bull. Estab. 1982. Annual. Festival held August 7-10, 2003. Average attendance: 9,500. One of the longest-running Canadian writers festivals, the Sunshine Coast Festival "tries to represent all genres." Held in a "500 seat pavilion set in the beautiful Rockwood Gardens in the seaside town of Sechelt, B.C." 1999 speakers included Margaret Atwood, Arthur Black, Andreas Schroeder, Bill Richardson, Anne Petrie and Margo Button.
Costs: Individual events, $12; Festival pass, $175; student discounts. Meals and lodging are not included.
Accommodations: Information on overnight accommodations is available.

SENDING TO A COUNTRY other than your own? Be sure to send International Reply Coupons (IRC) instead of stamps for replies or return of your manuscript.

Additional information: Conference brochures/guidelines available in May for SASE, on website, by e-mail, fax or phone. Accepts inquiries by fax, e-mail, SASE, phone.

⬙ SURREY WRITERS' CONFERENCE, (formerly A Writer's W*O*R*L*D), 12870 72nd Ave., Surrey, British Columbia V4P 1G1 Canada. (640)594-2000. Fax: (604)590-2506. E-mail: phoenixmcf@aol.com. **Contact:** Rollie Koop, principal. Estab. 1992. Annual. Conference held in fall. Conference duration: 3 days. Average attendance: 350. Conference for fiction (romance/science fiction/fantasy/mystery—changes focus depending upon speakers and publishers scheduled), nonfiction and poetry. "For everyone from beginner to professional." Conference held at Sheraton Guildford. Guest lecturers included authors Diana Gabaldon, Don McQuinn and Daniel Wood; agents and editors.
Accommodations: On request will provide information on hotels and B&Bs. Conference rate, $90. Attendee must make own arrangements for hotel and transportation.
Additional Information: "A drawing takes place and ten people's manuscripts are critiqued by a bestselling author." Writer's contest entries must be submitted about 1 month early. Length: 1,000 words fiction, nonfiction, poetry, young writers (19 or less). 1st Prize $250, 2nd Prize $125, 3rd Prize $75. Contest is judged by a qualified panel of writers and educators. Write, call or e-mail for additional information.

⬙ THE VANCOUVER INTERNATIONAL WRITERS FESTIVAL, 1398 Cartwright St., Vancouver, British Columbia V6H 3R8 Canada. (604)681-6330. Fax: (604)681-8400. E-mail: alee@writersfest.bc.ca. Website: www.writers fest.bc.ca. Estab. 1988. Annual. Held in October. Average attendance: 11,000. "This is a festival for readers and writers. The program of events is diverse and includes readings, panel discussions, seminars. Lots of opportunities to interact with the writers who attend." Held on Granville Island—in the heart of Vancouver. Two professional theaters are used as well as Performance Works (an open space). "We try to avoid specific themes. Programming takes place between February and June each year and is by invitation."
Costs: Tickets are $10-20 (Canadian).
Accommodations: Local tourist info can be provided when necessary and requested.
Additional Information: Festival information available on website. Accepts inquiries by e-mail, fax. "A reminder—this is a festival, a celebration, not a conference or workshop."

⬙ THE VICTORIA SCHOOL OF WRITING, Box 8152, Victoria, British Columbia V8W 3R8 Canada. (250)598-5300. E-mail: vicwrite@islandnet.com. Website: www.islandnet.com/vicwrite. **Contact:** Ruth Slavin, director. Conference held the third week in July annually. "Five-day intensive workshop on beautiful Vancouver Island with outstanding author-instructors in fiction, poetry, historical fiction and nonfiction, humour, children's lit."
Cost: $575 (Canadian).
Accommodations: On site.
Additional Information: Workshop brochures available. Accepts inquiries by e-mail and phone.

[N] ⬙ ⬙ ◎ WRITING WITH STYLE, The Banff Centre, Banff, Alberta T1L 1H5 Canada. (403)762-6100. E-mail: arts_info@banffcentre.ca. Website: www.banffcentre.ca/arts. **Contact:** Office of the Registrar. Semiannual. Writing workshop. "This writing program is offered to developing writers who may or may not be published." Conference held September and April, 2003. Duration: 1 week. Average attendance: 30-40 participants. "Each faculty member is a writer of a different genre which may include short fiction, poetry, memoir, children's fiction, science fiction, crime writing, mystery, etc." Site: "The Banff Centre is a centre for creative excellence where professional and developing artists engage in formal and informal dialogues with peers and mentors for the purpose of advancing their creative practices. As inspirational as it is beautiful, the mountain setting (in Banff National Park) is a unique feature of the Centre." September faculty genres include short fiction, memoir, poetry, mystery. September 2002 faculty (all Canadian writers): Sharon Butala and Trevor Herriot, memoir; Rhea Tregebov, poetry; Peter Robinson, mystery; Dianne Warren and Audrey Thomas, short fiction; Robert Sawyer, science fiction.
Costs: Workshop fee: $357 Canadian plus 7% GST. Meal plan: $120 or $154 (2002 rates—expect slight increase in 2003).
Accommodations: Offers overnight accommodations. Accommodation fee: $336 (single occupany room only option). "Onsite only, hotel style which also serve as private work spaces. Computers should be brought along for private use. Public computers available on campus."
Additional Information: "At time of application writers must submit writing samples and statement of expectations. Application deadline for September: May 10, 2002." Application fee: $50 Canadian. Brochure currently available for e-mail and on website. For inquiries, contact by SASE, e-mail, phone, fax. "Other more advanced writing programs are also offered at The Banff Centre."

International

🌐 ART WORKSHOPS IN GUATEMALA, 4758 Lyndale Ave. S, Minneapolis MN 55409-2304. (612)825-0747. Fax: (612)825-6637. E-mail: info@artguat.org. Website: www.artguat.org. **Contact:** Liza Fourré, director. Estab. 1995. Annual. Workshops held year-round. Maximum class size: 10 students per class. Workshop titles include: Fiction Writing: Shaping and Structuring Your Story with Gladys Swan (March 29-April 7, 2003), Creative Writing: From Journal to Finished Form with Laurie O'Brien (July 20-29, 2002), New Directions in Travel Writing with Richard Harris (February 27-March 8, 2003), and Creative Writing: Voice of the Soul with Sharon Doubiago (April 12-21, 2003).

Costs: $1,825 (includes tuition, air fare to Guatemala from USA, lodging and ground transportation).
Accommodations: All transportation and accommodations included in price of conference.
Additional Information: Conference information available now. For brochure/guidelines visit website, e-mail, fax or call. Accepts inquiries by e-mail, phone, fax.

⊕ **THE ARVON FOUNDATION LTD. WORKSHOPS**, Totleigh Barton Sheepwash, Beaworthy, Devon EX21 5NS United Kingdom. Phone: 00 44 14 09231338. E-mail: t-barton@arvonfoundation.org. Website: www.arvonfoundati on.org. **Contact:** Helen Chaloner, national director. Estab. 1968 (workshops). Workshops held April through November at 3 centers. Workshops last 4½ days. Average attendance: 16/workshop. Workshops cover all types of fiction writing. "Totleigh Barton in Devon was the first Arvon centre. Next came Lumb Bank (Hebden Bridge, West Yorkshire HX7 6DF) and now, 12 courses at Moniack Mhor (Moniack, Kirkhill, Inverness IV 5 7PQ)." Totleigh Barton is a thatched manor house. Lumb Bank is an 18th century mill owner's home and Moniack Mhor is a traditional croft house. All are in peaceful, rural settings. In the three houses there are living rooms, reading rooms, rooms for private study, dining rooms and well equipped kitchens."
Costs: In 2002 course fee will be £385 which includes food, tuition and accommodation. For those in need, a limited number of grants and bursaries are available from the Arvon Foundation.
Accommodations: There is sleeping accommodation for up to 16 course members, but only limited single room accommodation (there are 8 bedrooms at Lumb Bank, 12 bedrooms at Moniack Mhor and 13 bedrooms at Totleigh Barton). The adjacent barns at Lumb Bank and Totleigh Barton have been converted into workshop/studio space and there are writing huts in the garden.
Additional Information: Sometimes writers are required to submit work. Check for details. Workshop brochure/ guidelines available for SASE.

[N] ⊕ **CREATIVE WRITING IN OAXACA, MEXICO**, 15474 Airport Rd., Nevada City CA 95959-9402. (530)265-8799. E-mail: dhanelin@hotmail.com. Website: www.creativewritingclasses.net. **Contact:** Donna Hanelin, teacher. Estab. 1997. Annual. Conference held July or August 2003; August 6-12 in 2002. Duration: 7-10 days. Average attendance: 6-12. Focuses on "literary fiction, poetry, autobiography and creative nonfiction. Purpose is to offer a retreat for writers with classes, consultations and group discussion available but optional." Site: Oaxaca, Mexico. "We meet in small villas or B&Bs around the city of Oaxaca. Class meetings typically take place in living rooms or roof-top gardens, or on site in various locations (ruins, craft villages, markets, etc) in Oaxaca." 2002 theme was "The Use of Rhythm and Image" in prose and poetry. Donna Hanelin leads workshop.
Costs: In 2002, $865 including 7 nights lodging, 2 meals daily, all teaching and private consultations and touring in Oaxaca.
Accommodations: "Included in the above fee is transportation to and from the Oaxaca airport. Participants need to arrange their own airfare." Offers overnight accommodations in small villas or Bed and Breakfasts around Oaxaca. Included in fee.
Additional Information: "Manuscripts over 35 pages need to be submitted in advance of retreat. Any workshop material that is used in discussion requires participants to bring copies." Brochures available in January 2003 for SASE, e-mail or by phone. Accepts inquiries by SASE, e-mail, phone. " 'Creative Writing in Oaxaca' is an intensive retreat designed to be of use to either experienced and beginning writers. Because we are in a different culture, awareness of and sensitivity to place are important. A statement of purpose is required of participants before acceptance."

[N] ⊕ **CREATIVITY AND THE JOURNEY INWARD: A WRITING RETREAT IN THE SACRED VAL-LEY OF PERU**, 995 Chapman Rd., Yorktown NY 10598. (914)962-4432. E-mail: emily@emilyhanlon.com. Website: www.thefictionwritersjourney.com. **Contact:** Emily Hanlon. Estab. 1997. Annual. Conference held July 6-18, 2003. Average attendance: 20-25. Conference focuses on "Using all forms of writing, including fiction, poetry and journaling to explore the writer's journey as our passion, our teacher and guide to our deeper truths. We combine this with a journey into the authentic spiritual heart of the Andes, land of the Inka and the Quechuan people of Pachamama, Mother Earth." Site: "Wilka T'ika (sacred flower) is a retreat center in the heart of the Sacred Valley of the Inca. Situated between Cusco and Machu Picchu, the guest house offers grace and comfort enhanced by the aura of the Andes." Panels include "fiction writing techniques, among others, to open to a deeper creativity and explore the imaginative possibilities inherent in such an ancient place." Workshops led by Emily Hanlon, novelist, and Carol Cumes, author/anthropologist.
Costs: "The final fee is not yet set, although it will be around $3300. This includes all workshops, hotels, transport in Peru, specially selected guides, all entrance tickets, workshops with healers and many but not all meals."
Accommodations: "We suggest travel agents to help with all the bookings and provide transportation once participant arrives in Cusco." Offers overnight accommodations. "The guest cottages are newly-built in traditional 16th century Spanish colonial style." Single and double rooms available, all with private baths.
Additional Information: "Participants need to speak to Emily Hanlon on the telephone and write a letter (or e-mail) as to why they want to come to the retreat, what draws them to it and what they desire to experience in terms of their writing." Brochures available on website, by e-mail, by phone. Accepts inquiries by e-mail, phone. "It is important for all participants to know that we are at very high altitudes. Cusco is 12,000 feet, Wilka T'ika is 9,000 feet and Machu Picchu is 7,000 feet. Time and concern are given to acclimating everyone to high altitudes, however people with special health concerns should contact their physician. There is moderate climbing at times. All in all, this is a most unique, once in a lifetime experience by anyone seeking to explore the relationship between their writing, creativity and the spiritual journey.

N! ⊕ **DINGLE WRITING COURSES**, Balneanig, Ballyferriter, Tralee, County Kerry, Ireland. Phone: 00 353 66 9154990. Fax: 00 353 66 9154992. E-mail: info@dinglewriting.com. Website: www.dinglewriting.com. **Contact:** Camilla Dinker. Estab. 1996. Annual. Conference held 3 or 4 weekends per year. Average attendance: 14. Creative writing weekends for fiction, poetry, memoir, novel, etc. Site: "Residential centre at Inch on the Dingle Peninsula." 2002 faculty include Cole Moreton, Carlo Geber, Paula Meehan, Claire Keegan.
Costs: $340 for a weekend (Friday evening to Sunday evening) includes all meals, accommodation, tuition.
Accommodations: "We arrange taxis on request; cost not included in fee." Provides overnight accommodations. "Large communal eating facility and workroom; snug; all rooms with individual tables and lamps." Also provides list of area lodging.
Additional Information: Some workshops require material submitted in advance. Brochures available May 2003 by e-mail, phone, fax or on website. Accepts inquires by e-mail, phone, fax.

N! ⊕ **INTERNATIONAL READERS THEATRE WORKSHOPS**, P.O. Box 17193, San Diego CA 92177. (619)276-1948. Fax: (858)576-7369. E-mail: RTInst@aol.com. Website: www.readerstheatre.net. **Contact:** Bill Adams, director. Estab. 1974. Workshop held July 14-27, 2002. Average attendance: 70. Workshop on "all aspects of Readers Theatre with emphasis on scriptmaking." Workshop held at Wellington Hall on King's College Campus in London.
Costs: "$1,495 includes housing for two weeks (twin accommodations), traditional English breakfast, complimentary mid-morning coffee break and all Institute fees."
Additional Information: "One-on-one critiques available between writer and faculty (if members)." Conference information available December 2002. For brochures/guidelines send SASE, visit website, e-mail, fax, call. Accepts inquiries by SASE, fax, phone, e-mail. Conference offers "up to 12 credits in Theatre (Speech) and/or Education from the University of Southern Maine at $137/unit."

⊕ **PARIS WRITERS WORKSHOP/WICE**, 20, Bd du Montparnasse, Paris, France 75015. (331)45.66.75.50. Fax: (331)40.65.96.53. E-mail: pww@wice-paris.org. Website: www.wice-paris.org. **Contact:** Rose Burke and Marcia Lebre, directors. Estab. 1987. Annual. Conference held June 29-July 4, 2002. Average attendance: 40-50. "Conference concentrates on fiction, nonfiction, creativity and poetry. Visiting lecturers speak on a variety of issues important to beginning and advanced writers. 2003 writers in residence are Alice Mattison (novel), Isabel Huggins (short fiction), Kerry Hardie (poetry) and Michael Steinberg (creative nonfiction). Located in the heart of Paris on the Bd. du Montparnasse, the stomping grounds of such famous American writers as Ernest Hemingway, Henry Miller and F. Scott Fitzgerald. The site consists of 4 classrooms, a resource center/library and private terrace."
Costs: €380—tuition only.
Additional Information: "Students submit 1 copy of complete ms or work-in-progress which is sent in advance to writer in residence. Each student has a one-on-one consultation with writer in residence." Conference information available late fall 2002. For brochures/guidelines visit website, e-mail, call or fax. Accepts inquiries by SASE, phone, e-mail, fax. "Workshop attracts many expatriate Americans and other English language students from all over Europe and North America. We can assist with finding a range of hotels, from budget to more luxurious accommodations. We are an intimate workshop with an exciting mix of more experienced, published writers and enthusiastic beginners."

N! ⊕ **TASMANIAN READERS' & WRITERS' FESTIVAL**, Tasmanian Writer's Centre, 77 Salamanca Place, Hobart, Tasmania 7005 Australia. Phone: 61 3 6224 0029. Fax: 61 3 6224 0029. E-mail: director@tasmanianwriters.org. Website: www.tasmanianwriters.org/festival-2003.htm. **Contact:** Joe Bugden, director. Estab. 1996. Annual. Conference held March 28-April 6, 2003. Average attendance: thousands. Focuses on fiction, nonfiction, poetry, history, playwriting, travel writing, etc. Site: Centre for the Arts, Hunter St., Hobart, Tasmania. 2003 panels still to be confirmed "but there will be an emphasis on island culture and writing the island." Panelists include writers from Denmark, Indonesia, Greece, Ireland, Canada, Australia and New Zealand.
Costs: "Most events in the 2003 festival will be free."
Accommodations: Provides list of area lodging.
Additional Information: Brochures available in January 2003 by e-mail or on website. Accepts inquiries by SASE, e-mail, phone. Agents and editors attend conference.

⊕ **TŶ NEWYDD WRITER'S CENTRE**, Llanystumdwy, Cricieth Gwynedd LL52 OLW, United Kingdom. Phone: 01766-522811. Fax: 01766 523095. E-mail: tynewydd@dial.pipex.com. Website: www.tynewydd.org. **Contact:** Sally Baker, director. Estab. 1990. Regular courses held throughout the year. Every course held Monday-Saturday. Average attendance: 14. "To give people the opportunity to work side by side with professional writers, in an informal atmosphere." Site is Tŷ Newydd, large manor house, last home of the prime minister, David Lloyd George. Situated in North Wales, Great Britain—between mountains and sea." Past featured tutors include novelists Beryl Bainbridge and Bernice Rubens.
Costs: £345 for Monday-Saturday (includes full board, tuition).
Accommodations: Transportation from railway stations arranged. Accommodation in Tŷ Newydd (onsite).
Additional Information: Conference information available after January by mail, phone, e-mail, fax or visit website. Accepts inquiries by SASE, e-mail, fax, phone. "We have had several people from U.S. on courses here in the past three years. More and more people come to us from the U.S. often combining a writing course with a tour of Wales."

Writing Programs

Every year, thousands of writers seek out opportunities to improve their craft through classes—whether pursuing an undergraduate or graduate degree in creative writing, enrolling in continuing education classes, or signing up for online writing programs. In addition to giving writers instruction in the technical elements of craft, these programs also give writers a chance to have their work critiqued, critique the work of others, and provide a supportive structure within which to work. As Tracy Chevalier, bestselling author of *Girl With a Pearl Earring*, says of her in-class writing experience: "That year gave me deadlines, a critical audience, and most of all the expectation that I would write all day, every day. It was the line in the sand that I need to draw in my life, between the old life where writing was a hobby and my new life where writing is primary."

Statistics show that the number of creative writing programs in colleges and universities nationwide is growing exponentially. Associated Writing Programs (AWP), a nonprofit organization based at George Mason University in Fairfax, Virginia, estimates that in the last decade the number of programs has nearly doubled. Master's in fine arts (MFA) programs alone have jumped from 55 in 1992 to 99 last year. Reports say that last year at the country's oldest MFA program, at the University of Iowa, there were some 700 applicants for 20 openings. A *Chicago Tribune* article quoted that program's director as saying Iowa was "harder to get into than Harvard Law School."

Competition notwithstanding, writing programs can be an important—even critical—part of a writer's development. Here we've compiled a list of contact information for AWP graduate and undergraduate programs throughout the country. Use this list as a starting point to contact a program or programs near you to find out about the curriculum and tuition, faculty, and financial aid opportunities.

Alaska

UNIVERSITY OF ALASKA ANCHORAGE, Department of Creative Writing & Literary Arts, 3211 Providence Dr., Anchorage AK 99508-8252. (907)786-4330. Fax: (907)786-1382. **Contact:** Ronald Spatz.

UNIVERSITY OF ALASKA AT FAIRBANKS, Box 757920, Fairbanks AK 99775-7920. (907)474-7031.

Alabama

AUBURN UNIVERSITY, English Department, 9030 Haley Center, Auburn AL 36849-5203. (334)844-9029. **Contact:** Frances Collins.

UNIVERSITY OF ALABAMA AT BIRMINGHAM, HB205, 1530 3rd Ave. S, Birmingham AL 35294. (205)934-4250. Fax: (205)975-8125. Website: www.uab.edu/english. **Contact:** Robert Collins.

UNIVERSITY OF ALABAMA AT TUSCALOOSA, Creative Writing Program, 103 Morgan Hall, Box 870244, Tuscaloosa AL 35487-0244. (205)348-0766. Fax: (205)348-1388. Website: http://bama.ua.edu/~writing/. **Contact:** Robin Behn.

UNIVERSITY OF NORTH ALABAMA, Department of English, Box 5175, Florence AL 35631-0001. (256)765-4494. **Contact:** Lynne Burris Butler.

Arizona

ARIZONA STATE UNIVERSITY, Creative Writing Program, English Department, Box 870302, Tempe AZ 85287. **Contact:** Karla Elling.

ARIZONA WESTERN COLLEGE, The Writing College, Yuma AZ 85364. (602)726-1000. **Contact:** David Coy.

NORTHERN ARIZONA UNIVERSITY, Writing Program, English Department, Box 6032, Flagstaff AZ 86011. (602)523-5651. Website: www.nau.edu. **Contact:** Dr. Allen Woodman.

PHOENIX COLLEGE, English Dept., 1202 W. Thomas Rd., Phoenix AZ 85013. (602)285-7368. **Contact:** Jed Allen.

Arkansas

LYON COLLEGE, P.O. Box 2317, Batesville AR 72503. (870)793-1766. Fax: (870)869-2119. **Contact:** Andrea Hollander Budy.

PULASKI TECHNICAL COLLEGE, 3000 West Scenic Dr., North Little Rock AR 72118.

UNIVERSITY OF ARKANSAS AT FAYETTEVILLE, Writing Program, English Department, Kimpel Hall 333, Fayetteville AR 72701. (501)575-4301. **Contact:** Molly Giles.

UNIVERSITY OF ARKANSAS AT PINE BLUFF, Department of English Speech and Drama, Pine Bluff AR 71611. **Contact:** Doris Norman Holmes.

UNIVERSITY OF CENTRAL ARKANSAS, 201 Donaghey Ave., Irby Room 105, Dept. of Writing, Conway AR 72035.

California

ANTIOCH UNIVERSITY AT LOS ANGELES, 13274 Fiji Way, Marina Del Rey CA 90292. (310)822-4824. **Contact:** Keith Rand.

CALARTS, 24700 McBean Pkwy., Valencia CA 91355. (661)253-7803. **Contact:** Jon Wagner.

CALIFORNIA COLLEGE OF ARTS AND CRAFTS, 1111 Eighth St., San Francisco CA 94107. (415)551-9251. Fax: (415)551-9215. **Contact:** John Laskey.

CALIFORNIA STATE UNIVERSITY AT CHICO, English & Writing, West 1st and Salem Sts., Chico CA 95929. (530)898-5125. Fax: (413)538-2138. **Contact:** Carole Oles.

CALIFORNIA STATE UNIVERSITY AT FRESNO, 5245 N. Backer, PB 98, Fresno CA 93740-8004. (559)278-2359. Fax: (559)278-7143. **Contact:** Connie Hales.

CALIFORNIA STATE UNIVERSITY LOS ANGELES, 5151 State University Dr., Los Angeles CA 90032. (323)343-4174. Fax: (323)343-6470. Website: www.calstatela.edu/academic/english/edeptwp/. **Contact:** Dr. Mary Bush.

CALIFORNIA STATE UNIVERSITY NORTHRIDGE, 1811 Nordehoff St., Northridge CA 91330-8248. (818)677-3433. **Contact:** Dorothy Barresi.

CALIFORNIA STATE UNIVERSITY SACRAMENTO, 6000 J St., Department of English, Sacramento CA 95819-6075. (916)278-6925. Fax: (916)278-5410. **Contact:** Dr. Joshua McKinney.

CHAPMAN UNIVERSITY, 1 University Dr., Orange CA 92866. (714)997-6750. Fax: (714)997-6697. Website: www.chapman.edu/comm/english. **Contact:** Mark Axelrod.

HUMBOLDT STATE UNIVERSITY, Department of English, Arcata CA 95521. (707)826-5919. Fax: (707)826-5939. **Contact:** Jim Dodge.

IDYLLWILD ARTS ACADEMY, 52500 Temecula Rd., P.O. Box 38, Idyllwild CA 92549. (909)659-2171. **Contact:** Donald A. Put.

LOYOLA MARYMOUNT UNIVERSITY, Loyola Blvd. at W. 80th St., Los Angeles CA 90045. (310)338-7668. Fax: (310)338-7727. Website: www.lmu.edu. **Contact:** Gail Wronsky.

MILLS COLLEGE, 5000 MacArthur Blvd., Oakland CA 94603. **Contact:** Tonianne Nemeth.

POINT LOMA NAZARENE UNIVERSITY, 3900 Lomaland Dr., San Diego CA 92106. (619)849-2670. Fax: (619)849-2566. Website: www.ptloma.edu/ljml/index.htm. **Contact:** Richard Hill.

SADDLEBACK COLLEGE CREATIVE WRITING PROGRAM, 2800 Marguerite Pkwy., Mission Viejo CA 92692. (949)582-4837. Fax: (949)347-1663. Website: www.saddleback.cc.ca.us. **Contact:** Shelba Cole Rossback.

SAINT MARY'S COLLEGE OF CALIFORNIA, P.O. Box 4686, Moraga CA 94575. (925)613-4088. Fax: (925)631-4471. Website: www.stmarys-ca.edu/academics/graduate/mfa. **Contact:** Christopher Sindt.

SAN DIEGO STATE UNIVERSITY, Dept. of English and Comparative Literature, 5500 Campanile Dr., San Diego CA 92182-8140. (619)594-5234. Fax: (619)594-4998. Website: www.rohan.sdsu.edu/dept/writing. **Contact:** Sandra B. Alcosser.

SAN FRANCISCO STATE UNIVERSITY, School of Humanities, 1600 Holloway Ave., San Francisco CA 94132. (415)338-1541. Fax: (415)338-7030. **Contact:** Nancy McDermid.

SAN JOSE STATE UNIVERSITY, English Department, San Jose CA 95192-0090. (408)924-4432. Fax: (408)924-4580. Website: www.sjsu.edu/depts/english/creativewriting.htm. **Contact:** Alan Soldofsky.

SONOMA STATE UNIVERSITY, English Department N-362, 1801 E. Cotati Ave., Rohnert Park CA 94928. (707)664-2140. Fax: (707)664-4400. **Contact:** Merle Williams.

STANFORD UNIVERSITY, Creative Writing, Dept. of English, Stanford CA 94305-2087. (650)723-0504. Website: www.stanford.edu/dept/english/cw/. **Contact:** Tobias Wolff.

UCLA EXTENSION WRITERS' PROGRAM, 10995 LeConte Ave., Room #440, Los Angeles CA 90024. (310)825-9638. Fax: (310)206-7382. Website: www.uclaextension.org/writers.

UNIVERSITY OF CALIFORNIA AT DAVIS, English Department Creative Writing, Davis CA 95616. (530)752-6117. **Contact:** Shirley Martin.

UNIVERSITY OF CALIFORNIA AT IRVINE, MFA Programs in Writing, Department of English & Literature, Irvine CA 92697-2650. (949)824-6718. Fax: (949)824-2916. Website: www.humanities.uci.edu/english. **Contact:** Geoffrey Wolff (fiction); James McMichael (poetry).

UNIVERSITY OF REDLANDS, 1200 E. Colton Ave., P.O. Box 3080, Redlands CA 92373-0999. (909)793-2121, ext. 2464. Fax: (909)748-6294. Website: www.redlands.edu. **Contact:** Patricia Geary.

UNIVERSITY OF SOUTHERN CALIFORNIA, Professional Writing Program, Waite Phillips Hall 404, Los Angeles CA 90089-4034. (213)740-3252. Fax: (213)740-5775. Website: www.usc.edu/dept/LAS/mpw/. **Contact:** James Ragan.

Colorado

COLORADO STATE UNIVERSITY, Creative Writing Program, 359 Eddy Building, Fort Collins CO 80523-3010. (970)491-6429. Fax: (970)491-7374. **Contact:** Marcia Aune.

LIGHTHOUSE WRITERS WORKSHOP, 817 27th St., Denver CO 80205. (303)297-1185. Fax: (303)292-9425. **Contact:** Andrea Dupree.

UNIVERSITY OF COLORADO BOULDER, 226 UCB, Boulder CO 80309-0146. (303)492-5213. Website: www.colorado.edu/english.

UNIVERSITY OF DENVER, English Department, Pioneer Hall, Denver CO 80208. (303)871-2885. Fax: (303)871-2853. **Contact:** Brian Evenson.

Connecticut

CENTRAL CONNECTICUT STATE UNIVERSITY, English Department, Willard Hall, 1615 Stanley St., New Britain CT 06050. (860)832-2762. Fax: (830)832-2784. **Contact:** Dr. J. Tom Hazuka.

CONNECTICUT COLLEGE, Creative Writing Program, 270 Mohegan Ave., New London CT 06320-4196. **Contact:** Charles Hartman.

SOUTHERN CONNECTICUT STATE UNIVERSITY, English Department, 501 Crescent St., New Haven CT 06515-1355. (203)392-6745. **Contact:** Tim Parrish.

TRINITY COLLEGE, 300 Summit St., Hartford CT 06106. (860)297-2464. Fax: (860)297-5258. **Contact:** J. Frederick Pfeil.

UNIVERSITY OF CONNECTICUT, 215 Glenbrook Rd. U-4025, Storrs CT 06269-4025. (860)486-2324. Fax: (860)486-1530. **Contact:** Jennifer Spinner.

Washington, D.C.

GEORGE WASHINGTON UNIVERSITY, 801 22nd St. NW, Washington DC 20052. (202)994-6180. Fax: (520)621-7397. **Contact:** David Aleavey.

GEORGETOWN UNIVERSITY, English Dept., Box 571131, Washington DC 20057-1131. (202)687-7435. Fax: (202)687-7483. **Contact:** James F. Slevin.

JOHNS HOPKINS UNIVERSITY, Arts & Sciences, 521 Rome, 1619 Massachusettes Ave. NW, Washington DC 20036-2280. (202)452-0758. Fax: (202)530-9857. **Contact:** David Everett.

Florida

EMBRY-RIDDLE UNIVERSITY, 600 S. Clyde Morris Blvd., Daytona Beach FL 32114. (904)226-6668. **Contact:** Steve Glassman.

FLORIDA ATLANTIC UNIVERSITY, Department of English, 777 Glades Rd., Boca Raton FL 33431. (561)297-2973. **Contact:** William Covino.

FLORIDA INTERNATIONAL UNIVERSITY, Biscayne Bay Campus, 3000 NE 151st St., North Miami FL 33181. (305)919-5857. Fax: (305)919-5734. **Contact:** Dr. Les Standiford.

FLORIDA STATE UNIVERSITY, English Dept., Box 1580, Tallahassee FL 32306-1580. (850)644-4230. **Contact:** Debra Brock.

STETSON UNIVERSITY, English Department, 421 N. Woodland Blvd., Unit 8300, DeLand FL 32720. (904)822-7729. E-mail: twitek@stetson.edu.

UNIVERSITY OF CENTRAL FLORIDA, 4000 Central Florida Blvd., Orlando FL 32816. (407)823-2267. Fax: (407)823-3300. **Contact:** Judith Hemschemeyer.

UNIVERSITY OF FLORIDA, English Department, P.O. Box 117310, Gainesville FL 32611-7310. (352)392-6650. Fax: (352)392-0860. Website: www.english.ufl.edu/programs/grad/index.htm. **Contact:** Padgett Powell.

UNIVERSITY OF MIAMI, Creative Writing English Dept., P.O. Box 248142, Coral Gables FL 33124. (305)284-2182. Website: www.as.miami.edu/english. **Contact:** Fred D'Aquilar.

UNIVERSITY OF SOUTH FLORIDA, CPR 107, Dept. of English, 4202 E. Fowler Ave., Tampa FL 33620. (813)974-9570. Fax: (813)974-2270. Website: www.cas.usf.edu/english/index.html. **Contact:** Rita Ciresi.

UNIVERSITY OF TAMPA, 401 W. Kennedy Blvd., Tampa FL 33606-1490. (813)253-6216. **Contact:** Donald Morrill.

Georgia

ARMSTRONG ATLANTIC STATE UNIVERSITY, Creative Writing, 11935 Abercon St., Savannah GA 31419-1997. (912)921-5633. **Contact:** James Smith.

BERRY COLLEGE, Department of English, Box 350, Mount Berry GA 30149-5010. (706)802-6723. Fax: (706)802-6722. Website: www.berry.edu/academic/hass/english/creative.html. **Contact:** Sandra Meek.

EMORY UNIVERSITY, Creative Writing Program, N209 Callaway Center, Atlanta GA 30322. (404)727-7999. Fax: (404)727-4672. **Contact:** Lynaa Williams.

GAINESVILLE COLLEGE DIVISION OF HUMANITIES, P.O. Box 1358, Gainesville GA 30503. (770)718-3674. Fax: (770)718-3832. **Contact:** Tom Sauret.

GEORGIA COLLEGE & STATE UNIVERSITY, Creative Writing Program, CBX 44, Milledgeville GA 31061. (478)445-3176. Fax: (478)445-5961. **Contact:** Martin Lammon.

GEORGIA PERIMETER COLLEGE, 2101 Womack Rd., Dunwoody GA 30338. (770)551-3166. Fax: (770)551-7471. **Contact:** Lawrence Hetrick.

GEORGIA SOUTHERN UNIVERSITY, Writing and Linguistics, Box 8026, Statesboro GA 30460. (912)681-0156. Fax: (912)681-0783. **Contact:** Eric Nelson.

GEORGIA STATE UNIVERSITY, English Department, University Plaza, Atlanta GA 30303-3083. **Contact:** John William Holman.

KENNESAW STATE UNIVERSITY, Creative Writing Program, 1000 Chastain Rd., Kennesaw GA 30144-5591. (770)423-6297. **Contact:** Dr. Laura Dabundo.

MACON STATE COLLEGE, Creative Writing Program, 100 College Station Dr., Macon GA 31206.

Idaho

BOISE STATE UNIVERSITY, 1910 University Dr., Boise ID 83725-1525. (208)425-1205. Fax: (208)426-4373. Website: http://english.boisestate.edu/mfa. **Contact:** Robert Olmstead.

LEWIS-CLARK STATE COLLEGE, 500 Eighth Ave., Lewiston ID 83501. (208)792-2050. Fax: (208)792-2324. **Contact:** Claire Davis.

UNIVERSITY OF IDAHO, English Dept., Brink Hall, Room 200, P.O. Box 441102, Moscow ID 83844-1102. (208)885-6156. Fax: (208)885-6157. Website: www.its.uidaho.edu/english/CW. **Contact:** Robert Wrigley.

Illinois

ART INSTITUTE OF CHICAGO, MFA in Writing, 37 South Wabash, Chicago IL 60603. (312)899-5094. **Contact:** Rebecca Targ.

BRADLEY UNIVERSITY, English Department, Peoria IL 61625. (309)677-2463. **Contact:** Margaret Carter.

COLUMBIA COLLEGE OF CHICAGO, Fiction Writing Program, 600 S. Greenview Ave., Chicago IL 60605-1996. (312)663-1600, ext. 7615. **Contact:** Deborah Roberts.

ILLINOIS STATE UNIVERSITY, Creative Writing Program, English Dept., Campus Box 4240, Normal IL 61790-4240. **Contact:** Lucia Getsi.

KNOX COLLEGE, Knox College Creative Writing, English Department, Box K-50, Galesburg IL 61401. E-mail: rmetz@knox.edu. Website: www.knox.edu. **Contact:** Robin Metz.

NORTHWESTERN UNIVERSITY, English Major in Writing, UH 215, Evanston IL 60208-2240. (847)491-7294. **Contact:** Mary Kinzie.

SOUTHERN ILLINOIS, English Department, Carbondale IL 62901. (618)453-5321. **Contact:** Beth Lordan.

UNIVERSITY OF ILLINOIS, English Department, 608 S. Wright St., Urbana IL 61801. (217)333-4137. **Contact:** Michael Van Wellenghen.

UNIVERSITY OF ILLINOIS AT CHICAGO, 601 S. Morgan St., Chicago IL 60607. (312)413-2229. Fax: (312)413-1005. **Contact:** Eugene Wildman.

Indiana

BALL STATE UNIVERISTY, Department of English, Muncie IN 47306. (765)285-8409. **Contact:** Tom Koontz.

DEPAUW UNIVERSITY, 3232 Asbury Hall, Greencastle IN 46135. (765)658-4672. **Contact:** Tom Chiarella.

INDIANA UNIVERSITY, Purdue at Indianapolis, Cavanaugh Hall 5U2L, 425 University Blvd., Indianapolis IN 46201. (317)274-9831. Fax: (317)278-1287. **Contact:** Karen Kovacik.

INDIANA UNIVERSITY, English Dept., Ballantine Hall, 1020 E. Kirkwood Ave., Bloomington IN 47405. (812)855-9539. Fax: (812)855-9535. Website: www.indiana.edu/~mfawrite/. **Contact:** David Wojahn.

PURDUE UNIVERSITY, Creative Writing English Dept., Heavilon Hall, West Lafayette IN 47906. (765)494-0344. Fax: (765)494-3780. **Contact:** Marianne Boruch.

UNIVERSITY OF EVANSVILLE, Creative Writing Program, 1800 Lincoln Ave., Evansville IN 47722-0001. (812)479-2968. Fax: (812)477-4079. **Contact:** Michael Carson.

UNIVERSITY OF NOTRE DAME, Creative Writing Program, 356 O'Shaughnessy Hall, Notre Dame IN 46556-0368. (219)631-7226.

WABASH COLLEGE, English Department, 301 W. Wabash Ave., P.O. Box 352, Crawfordsville IN 47933. **Contact:** Warren Rosenberg.

Iowa

IOWA STATE UNIVERSITY, 203 Ross Hall, Ames IA 50011. (515)294-3210. Fax: (515)294-6874. **Contact:** Fern Kupfer.

UNIVERSITY OF IOWA, Department of English, 308 EPB, Iowa City IA 52242. (319)335-0454. Fax: (319)335-2535. **Contact:** Paul Diehl.

UNIVERSITY OF IOWA WRITERS' WORKSHOP, 102 Dey House, 507 N. Clinton St., Iowa City IA 52242-1000. **Contact:** Frank Conroy.

UNIVERSITY OF NORTHERN IOWA, Creative Writing, English Department, 117 Baker Hall, Cedar Falls IA 50614-0502. (319)273-3782. Fax: (319)273-5807. Website: www.uni.edu/english/webfiles/cw. **Contact:** Grant Tracey.

Kansas

EMPORIA STATE UNIVERSITY, English Dept., Creative Writing, Box 4019, Emporia KS 66801-5087. (316)341-5216. Fax: (316)341-5547. Website: www.emoria.edu/cw/index.htm. **Contact:** Dr. Philip Heldrich.

KANSAS STATE UNIVERSITY, English Department, 107 Denison Hall, Manhattan KS 66506-0701. (785)532-6716. Fax: (785)532-2192. Website: www.ksu.edu/english/programs/cw.htm. **Contact:** Elizabeth Dodd.

UNIVERSITY OF KANSAS, Dept. of English, 3114 Wescoe Hall, Lawrence KS 66045. (785)864-4520. Fax: (504)862-8958. **Contact:** Lori Whitten.

WICHITA STATE UNIVERSITY, English Department, Box 14, WSU, Wichita KS 672600-0014. (316)978-3130. Fax: (316)978-3548. **Contact:** Phillip H. Schneider.

Kentucky

MOREHEAD STATE UNIVERSITY, Creative Writing Program, Box 645, Morehead KY 40351. **Contact:** Dr. Mark Minor.

MURRAY STATE UNIVERSITY, English Department, P.O. Box 9, Murray KY 42071-0009. (502)762-4730. Fax: (612)624-8228. **Contact:** Squire Babcock.

SPALDING UNIVERSITY, 851 S. Fourth St., Louisville KY 40203. (502)585-9911, ext. 2423. Fax: (502)585-5178. Website: www.spalding.edu. **Contact:** Sena Jeter Naslund.

UNIVERSITY OF LOUISVILLE, Creative Writing Program, English/Brigham Humanities 315, Louisville KY 40292. (502)852-6801. Fax: (502)852-4182. **Contact:** Jeffrey T. Skinner.

Louisiana

LOUISIANA STATE UNIVERSITY, English Department, Baton Rouge LA 70803-5001. (225)388-3124. **Contact:** Judy Kahn.

LOYOLA UNIVERSITY NEW ORLEANS, 6363 St. Charles Ave., CBX50, New Orleans LA 70118. (504)865-2474. Fax: (504)865-2284. **Contact:** John Biguenet.

McNEESE STATE UNIVERSITY, Department of Languages, Lake Charles LA 70609. (337)475-5594. **Contact:** Dr. Miller Jones.

TULANE UNIVERSITY, Department of English, 122 Norman Mayer Hall, New Orleans LA 70118. (504)865-5160. **Contact:** Janice Mulvihill.

UNIVERSITY OF LOUISIANA AT LAFAYETTE, English Department, Box 44691, Lafayette LA 70504. (337)482-5478. **Contact:** Jerry McGuire.

UNIVERSITY OF LOUISIANA AT MUNROE, English Department, 700 University Ave, Munroe LA 71209. (318)342-1520. **Contact:** William Ryan.

UNIVERSITY OF NEW ORLEANS, English Department, Lakefront, New Orleans LA 70118. **Contact:** James Knudsen.

XAVIER UNIVERSITY OF LOUISIANA, English Department, Palmetto St., New Orleans LA 70125. (504)485-5161. Fax: (504)485-7944. **Contact:** Patrice Melnick.

Maine

UNIVERSITY OF MAINE AT FARMINGTON, Roberts Learning Center, 270 Main St., Farmington ME 04938-1720. (207)778-7454. Fax: (207)778-7452. **Contact:** Wesley McNair.

Maryland

GOUCHER COLLEGE, Creative Writing Program, 1021 Dulaney Valley Rd., Towson MD 21204. (410)337-6285. Website: www.goucher.edu/cwpromo. **Contact:** Madison Smartt Bell.

LOYOLA COLLEGE, Writing Media Department, 4501 N. Charles St., Baltimore MD 21210-2697. (410)617-2528.

SALISBURY STATE UNIVERSITY, 1101 Camden Ave., Salisbury MD 21801. (410)453-6445. **Contact:** Kathy Shaeffer.

TOWSON UNIVERSITY, English Department, Towson MD 21252. **Contact:** Clarinda Harriss.

UNIVERSITY OF MARYLAND, 3119 Susquehanna Hall, UMCP, English Department, College Park MD 20742. (301)405-3820. Fax: (301)314-7539. Website: www.inform.umd.edu/ARHU/Depts/English. **Contacts:** Michael Collier and Stanley Plumly.

Massachusetts

BOSTON COLLEGE, Carney Hall, Chestnut Hill MA 02467. (617)552-3716. **Contact:** Suzanne Matson.

BRIDGEWATER STATE COLLEGE, Tillinghast Hall, English Department, Bridgewater MA 02325. **Contact:** Dr. Iain Crawford.

EMERSON COLLEGE, English Department, 120 Boyleston St., Boston MA 02116. **Contact:** John Skoyles.

HARVARD UNIVERSITY, Barker Center, 12 Quincy St., Cambridge MA 02138. (617)495-2103. Fax: (617)496-6031. Website: www.fas.harvard.edu/english. **Contact:** Brad Watson.

LARCOM PRESS, P.O. Box 161, Prides Crossing MA 01915. (978)927-8707. Fax: (978)927-8904. **Contact:** Ann Perrott.

MIT, Program in Writing and Humanistic Studies, 14E-303, Cambridge MA 02139-4307. (617)253-7894. Fax: (617)253-6910. **Contact:** James Paradis.

UNIVERSITY OF MASSACHUSETTS AT AMHERST, Bartlett Hall, English Department, Amherst MA 01003-0515. (413)545-5459. **Contact:** Donna Johnson.

UNIVERSITY OF MASSACHUSETTS AT DARTMOUTH, English Department, 285 Old Westport Rd., North Dartmouth MA 02747-2300. **Contact:** Edwin Thompson.

Michigan

ALPENA COMMUNITY COLLEGE, 666 Johnson St., Alpena MI 49707. (989)358-7559. (989)358-7250. **Contact:** Thomas Ray.

CENTRAL MICHIGAN UNIVERSITY, Dept. of English Language & Literature, Mt. Pleasant MI 48859. (989)774-3126. Fax: (989)774-1271. **Contact:** Eric Torgersen.

GRAND VALLEY STATE UNIVERSITY, Writing Department, 1 Campus Dr., Allendale MI 49401. (616)895-3209. Fax: (616)895-3545. Website: www.gvsu.edu/writing. **Contact:** Roger Gilles.

HOPE COLLEGE, English Department, 126 E. 10th St., Holland MI 49423. (616)395-7116. Fax: (616)395-7134. Website: www.hope.edu. **Contact:** Heather Sellers.

MICHIGAN STATE UNIVERSITY, Creative Writing Program/English, 201 Morrill Hall, East Lansing MI 48824-1036. (517)355-7570. Fax: (517)353-3755. **Contact:** Marcia Aldrich.

NORTHERN MICHIGAN UNIVERSITY, Department of English, 1401 Presque Isle Ave., Marquette MI 49855. (906)227-2711. Fax: (906)227-1096. **Contact:** John Smolens.

UNIVERSITY OF MICHIGAN AT ANN ARBOR, 3187 Angell Hall, Ann Arbor MI 48109-1003. (734)615-3710. Website: www.lsa.umich.edu/english/grad/graduate.htm. **Contact:** Nicholas Delbanco.

WESTERN MICHIGAN UNIVERSITY, English Department, 619 Sprau Tower, Kalamazoo MI 49008-5092. (616)387-2570. Fax: (616)387-2562. **Contact:** Michele C. McLaughlin.

Minnesota

AUGSBURG COLLEGE, 2211 Riverside Ave., Minneapolis MN 55454. (612)330-1646. Fax: (612)330-1646. **Contact:** Katherine Swanson.

COLLEGE OF ST. BENEDICT, 37 S. College Ave., Maine 216, St. Joseph MN 56374. (320)363-5399. Website: www.csbsju.edu/literaryarts. **Contact:** Mary Jane Berger.

HAMLINE UNIVERSITY, Graduate Liberal Studies, 845 Snelling, 1536 Hewitt Ave., St. Paul MN 55104-1284. (612)523-2047. Fax: (612)523-2490. **Contact:** Mary Francois Rockcastle.

MACALESTER COLLEGE, 1600 Grand Ave., St. Paul MN 55105-1899. (651)696-6516. **Contact:** Diane Glancy.

MINNESOTA STATE UNIVERSITY AT MOOREHEAD, 1104 7th Ave. S., Moorhead MN 56563. (218)236-2764. **Contact:** Virginia Klenk.

MINNESOTA STATE UNIVERSITY MANKATO, English Department, 230 Armstrong Hall, Mankato MN 56001. (507)389-2117. Fax: (507)389-5362. Website: www.mankato.msus.edu/dept/english. **Contact:** Richard Robbins.

SOUTHWEST STATE UNIVERSITY, Writing Center English Department, 1501 State St., Marshall MN 56258. (507)537-7155. Fax: (607)255-6661. **Contact:** Eileen Thomas.

UNIVERSITY OF MINNESOTA AT MINNEAPOLIS, 209 Lind Hall, 207 Church St. SE, Minneapolis MN 55455. (612)625-4360. **Contact:** Jill Christman.

WINONA STATE, Winona MN 55987-5838. (507)457-5440. Fax: (507)457-5440. **Contact:** David Robinson.

Mississippi

MISSISSIPPI STATE UNIVERSITY, Drawer E. MS 39762, Mississippi State MS 39762. (601)325-2317. Fax: (516)287-8125. **Contact:** Joyce Harris.

UNIVERSITY OF MISSISSIPPI, Dept. of English Box 1848, Bondurant Hall, University MS 38677. (662)915-7439. Website: www.olemiss.edu/depts/english. **Contact:** Joseph Urgo.

Missouri

CENTRAL MISSOURI STATE UNIVERSITY, Dept. of English and Philosophy, Martin 336, Warrensburg MO 64093. **Contact:** Rose Marie Kinder.

DRURY UNIVERSITY, 900 N. Benton Ave., Springfield MO 65802. (417)873-7220. Website: www.drury.edu. **Contact:** Randall Fuller.

LINCOLN UNIVERSITY, Department of English MLK Hall, 820 Chestnut, Jefferson City MO 65102-0029. (573)681-5195. Fax: (573)681-5040. **Contact:** Ginger Jones.

SOUTHEAST MISSOURI STATE UNIVERSITY, English Department, MS 2650, Cape Girdeau MO 63701-4799. (573)651-5188. **Contact:** Dr. Susan Swatwout.

SOUTHWEST MISSOURI STATE UNIVERSITY, English Department, 901 S. National, Springfield MO 65804. (408)280-2143. **Contact:** Michael Burns.

STEPHENS COLLEGE, English & Creative Writing, Campus Box 2034, Columbia MO 65215. (573)442-2211, ext. 4668. Fax: (573)876-7248. **Contact:** Judith Clark.

UNIVERSITY OF MISSOURI, Program in Creative Writing, 202 Tate Hall, Columbia MO 65211. (573)884-7773. **Contact:** Sherod Santos.

UNIVERSITY OF MISSOURI AT KANSAS CITY, Professional Writing Program, 5101 Rockhill Rd., Kansas City MO 541120-2499. **Contact:** James McKinley.

UNIVERSITY OF MISSOURI AT ST. LOUIS, MFA Program Department of English, 8001 Natural Bridge, St. Louis MO 63121. **Contact:** Mary Troy.

WASHINGTON UNIVERSITY, The Writing Program English Dept., One Brookings Dr., St. Louis MO 63130. (314)935-7130. Website: http://artsci.wustl.edu/~english/writing. **Contact:** Carolyn B. Smith.

WESTMINSTER COLLEGE, 501 Westminster Ave., Fulton MO 65251-1299. **Contact:** Wayne Zade.

Montana

UNIVERSITY OF MONTANA, Creative Writing Program, English Department, Missoula MT 59812. **Contact:** Susie Castle.

Nebraska

CREIGHTON UNIVERSITY, English Department, 2500 California Plaza, Omaha NE 68178. (402)280-5768. Fax: (402)280-2143. **Contact:** Mary Helen Stefaniak.

UNIVERSITY OF NEBRASKA AT KEARNEY, Thomas Hall #202, 905 W. 25th St., Kearney NE 68849-1320. (308)865-8299. Fax: (308)865-8411. Website: www.unk.edu/acad/english/home.html. **Contact:** Barbara Emrys.

UNIVERSITY OF NEBRASKA AT LINCOLN, English Department, 202 Andrews Hall, Lincoln NE 68588-0333. (404)472-9771. Website: www.unl.edu/english/html/creative.html. **Contact:** Linda Rossiter.

UNIVERSITY OF NEBRASKA AT OMAHA, Writer's Workshop, 60th & Dodge, Omaha, NE 68182-0324. E-mail: ahomer@mail.unomaha.edu. Website: www.unomaha.edu/~fineart/wworkshop/wrkshop.html.

Nevada

UNIVERSITY OF NEVADA, LAS VEGAS, 4505 Maryland Pkwy., Box 455011, Las Vegas NV 89154-5011. (702)895-3533. Fax: (702)895-4801. **Contact:** Douglas Unger.

UNIVERSITY OF NEVADA, RENO, Department of English 098, Reno NV 89557. (702)784-6689. **Contact:** Geri McVeigh.

New Hampshire

UNIVERSITY OF NEW HAMPSHIRE, English Department, 95 Main St., Durham NH 03824. (603)862-0261. Fax: (603)862-3565. **Contact:** Margaret Love Denman.

New Jersey

ROWAN UNIVERSITY, College of Communication, 201 Mullica Hill Rd., Glassboro NJ 08028-1701. **Contact:** Pat Birmingham.

RUTGERS UNIVERSITY, English Department Armitage Hall, 311 N 5th St., Camden NJ 08102-1405. **Contact:** Kathy Volk Miller.

New Mexico

INSTITUTE OF AMERICAN INDIAN ARTS, 83 Avan Nu Po Rd., Sante Fe NM 87505. (505)424-2364. Fax: (505)424-3030. Website: www.iaiancad.org. **Contact:** Jon Davis.

NEW MEXICO STATE UNIVERSITY, Box 3001, Dept. 3E, Las Cruces NM 88003-0001. **Contact:** Christopher Burnham.

UNIVERSITY OF NEW MEXICO, English Department, Humanities Bldg. 255, Albuquerque NM 87131. (505)277-5576. Fax: (505)277-5573. Website: www.unm.edu/~english. **Contact:** Sharon Warner.

New York

BINGHAMTON UNIVERSITY, English Department, P.O. Box 6000, Binghamton NY 13902-6000. (607)777-2169. Fax: (607)777-2408. Website: http://english.binghamton.edu. **Contact:** Maria Gillan.

BROOKLYN COLLEGE, 2900 Bedford Ave., Brooklyn NY 11210. (718)951-5195. **Contact:** Nancy Black.

CANISIUS COLLEGE, 2001 Main St., Buffalo NY 14208. (716)888-2662. **Contact:** Mick Cochrane.

COLUMBIA UNIVERSITY SCHOOL OF THE ARTS, 415 Dodge Hall, 2960 Broadway, New York NY 10027. (212)854-4392. **Contact:** Anna Delmoro.

CORNELL UNIVERSITY, Department of English, 250 Goldwin Smith Hall, Ithaca NY 14853. (607)255-7989. Fax: (607)255-6661. Website: www.arts.cornell.edu/english/graduate.html. **Contact:** Jenka T. Pfyfe.

EUGENE LANG COLLEGE, 66 West 12th St., New York NY 10011. (212)229-5617. **Contact:** Beatrice Banu.

HAMILTON COLLEGE CREATIVE WRITING, 198 College Hill Rd., Clinton NY 13323. (315)859-4369. **Contact:** Nat Strout.

ITHACA COLLEGE PARK HALL, Danby Rd., Ithaca NY 14850. (607)274-3138. Website: www.ithaca.edu. **Contact:** Marion MacCurdy.

NASSAU COMMUNITY COLLEGE, 6th Floor Tower, One Education Dr., Garden City NY 11530-6793. (516)572-7711.

NEW YORK UNIVERSITY, Creative Writing Room 310, 19 University Place, New York NY 10003-4556. (212)998-8816. Fax: (212)995-4864. Website: www.nyu.edu/gsas/program/cwp. **Contact:** Russell Carmony.

SAINT LAWRENCE UNIVERSITY, Program in Creative Writing, English Department Richardson Hall, Canton NY 13617. (315)229-5125. Fax: (315)229-5628. **Contact:** Dr. Robert Cowser.

SARAH LAWRENCE COLLEGE, Office of Graduate Studies, 1 Mead Way, Bronxville NY 10594. (914)395-2371. Website: www.slc.edu. **Contact:** Thomas Lux.

SOUTHAMPTON COLLEGE OF LONG ISLAND UNIVERSITY, Humanities, 239 Montauk Highway, Southampton NY 11968. (631)287-8420. Website: www.southampton.liu.edu. **Contact:** Robert Pattison.

STATE UNIVERSITY OF NEW YORK, 35 New Campus Dr., Brockport NY 14420-2211. **Contact:** Stan Rubin.

STATE UNIVERSITY OF NEW YORK AT GENESEO, English Department, One College Circle, Geneseo NY 14454-1451. (716)245-5272. **Contact:** David Kelly.

SYRACUSE UNIVERSITY, 401 Hall of Languages, 100 University Place, Syracuse NY 13244. (315)443-9482. Fax: (315)443-3660. Website: www-hl.syr.edu/depts/english/cwp/cwindex.htm. **Contact:** Dr. Brooks Haxton.

North Carolina

EAST CAROLINA UNIVERSITY, Writing Program, Greenville NC 27858-4353. (252)328-6380. **Contact:** Jim Holt.

ELON UNIVERSITY, CB 2252, Elon University NC 27244. **Contact:** Kevin Boyle.

NORTH CAROLINA STATE UNIVERSITY AT RALEIGH, Department of English, Box 8105, Raleigh NC 27695-8105. (919)515-4102. **Contact:** Sharon Johnson.

ST. ANDREWS COLLEGE, 1700 Dogwood Mile, Laurinburg NC 28352. **Contact:** Ron Bays.

UNIVERSITY OF NORTH CAROLINA AT ASHEVILLE, 1 University Heights, Language & Literature Dept., Asheville NC 28804-3299. **Contact:** Kim Manning.

UNIVERSITY OF NORTH CAROLINA AT CHAPEL HILL, Greenlaw CB 3520, Department of English, Chapel Hill NC 27599-3520. **Contact:** Marianne Gingher.

UNIVERSITY OF NORTH CAROLINA AT GREENSBORO, MFA Writing Program Department of English, 134 MacIver Bldg., P.O. Box 26170, Greensboro NC 27402-6170. (336)334-5459. Website: www.uncg.edu/eng/mfa. **Contact:** James L. Clark.

UNIVERSITY OF NORTH CAROLINA WILMINGTON, English Department, 601 S. College Rd., Wilmington NC 28403. (910)962-3748. Fax: (910)962-7461. **Contact:** Lorrie Smith.

WARREN WILSON COLLEGE, MFA Program for Writers, P.O. Box 9000, Asheville NC 28815-9000. (704)298-3325. **Contact:** Peter Turchi.

WESTERN CAROLINA UNIVERSITY, English Dept., CO 305, Cullowhee NC 28723. (828)227-7264. Fax: (828)227-7266. Website: www.wcu.edu/as/english. **Contact:** Dr. Brian Railsback.

North Dakota

UNIVERSITY OF NORTH DAKOTA, Department of English, P.O. Box 7209, Grand Forks ND 58202-7209. (701)777-3321. Fax: (701)777-2373. **Contact:** Ursula Hovet.

Ohio

ASHLAND UNIVERSITY, 401 College Ave., Ashland OH 44805. (419)289-5110. **Contact:** Joe Mackall.

BOWLING GREEN STATE UNIVERSITY, English Department, 226 East Hall, Bowling Green OH 43403. (419)372-8370. **Contact:** Larissa Szporluk.

CASE WESTERN RESERVE UNIVERSITY, English Department, 11112 Bellflower Rd., Cleveland OH 44106-7117. (216)368-2355. Fax: (216)368-5088. Website: www.cwru.edu. **Contact:** Mary Grimm.

CLEVELAND STATE UNIVERSITY, Creative Writing Program, Euclid Ave at East 24th St., Cleveland OH 44115. (216)687-4522. **Contact:** Neal Chandler.

DENISON UNIVERSITY, English Department, Creative Writing Program, Granville OH 43023. **Contact:** David Baker.

HIRAM COLLEGE, Department of English, P.O. Box 67, Hiram OH 44234. (330)569-5152. Fax: (330)569-5130. **Contact:** Joyce Dyer.

KENT STATE UNIVERSITY, English Department, P.O. Box 5190, 113 Satterfield Hall, Kent OH 44242-0001. (330)672-2067. Fax: (330)672-2567. Website: www.kent.edu/wick. **Contact:** Maggie Anderson.

MIAMI UNIVERSITY, 356 Bachelor Hall, Oxford OH 45056. (513)529-5221. Fax: (513)529-1392. Website: www.unit s.muohio.edu/gradschool. **Contact:** Steven Bauer.

OHIO STATE UNIVERSITY, English Department, Creative Writing Program, 421 Denney Hall, 164 W. 17th Ave, Columbus OH 43210-1370. (614)292-2242. Fax: (614)292-7816. Website: www.english.ohio-state.edu/areas/creative_w riting. **Contact:** Michelle Herman.

OHIO UNIVERSITY PROGRAM IN CREATIVE WRITING, Dept. of English Language & Literature, College of Arts & Sciences, Ellis Hall, Athens OH 45701-2979. (740)593-9938. Fax: (740)593-4181. Website: www.english.ohio u.edu/gradprogram/creativew.html. **Contact:** Darrell Spencer.

OTTERBEIN COLLEGE, English Department, Westerville OH 43081. (614)823-1560. Fax: (812)479-2320. **Contact:** Norman Cheney.

UNIVERSITY OF CINCINNATI WRITING PROGRAM, English Department, P.O. Box 21-069, Cincinnati OH 45221-0069. **Contact:** Jon Hughes.

UNIVERSITY OF TOLEDO, Department of English, 2801 W. Bancroft, Toledo OH 43606. (419)530-4408. Fax: (419)530-4440. **Contact:** Jane Bradley.

Oklahoma

CAMERON UNIVERSITY, 2800 W. Gore Blvd., Lawton OK 73505.

OKLAHOMA STATE UNIVERSITY, Creative Writing Program, English Department, 205 Morrill Hall, Stillwater OK 74078. (405)744-6148. Fax: (405)744-6326. **Contact:** Cecilia Austell.

UNIVERSITY OF CENTRAL OKLAHOMA, 100 North University Dr., Edmond OK 73034. (405)974-5632. Fax: (405)974-3832. **Contact:** Dr. Stephen Garrison.

UNIVERSITY OF OKLAHOMA, English Department, 760 Van Vleet Oval #113, Norman OK 73019-0240. (405)325-6647. Fax: (405)325-0831.

Oregon

CLACKAMAS COMMUNITY COLLEGE, 19600 S. Molalla Ave., Oregon City OR 97045. (503)657-6958, ext. 2372. **Contact:** Emily Orlando.

LEWIS & CLARK COLLEGE, English Department, 0615 SW Palatine Hill Rd., #58, Portland OR 97219.

LINFIELD COLLEGE, Department of English, 900 SE Baker, McMinnville OR 97128-6894. (503)434-2288. Fax: (503)434-2215. **Contact:** Barbara Drake.

MOVEO ANGELUS LITERARY ARTS, 31450 NE Bell Rd., Sherwood OR 97140. **Contact:** Priska von Beroldingen.

OREGON STATE UNIVERSITY, Creative Writing Program, English Department, 238 Moreland Hall, Corvallis OR 97331-5302. (541)737-1635. Fax: (541)737-3589. Website: www.orst.edu/dept/english/orw. **Contact:** Marjorie Sandor.

UNIVERSITY OF OREGON, Program in Creative Writing, 5243 University of Oregon, 144 Columbia Hall, Eugene OR 97403-1286. (541)346-3944. Fax: (541)346-0537. Website: http://darkwing.uoregon.edu/~crwrweb/. **Contact:** Ken Calhoon.

Pennsylvania

BLOOMSBURG UNIVERSITY, English Department, 400 E. Second St., Bloomsburg PA 17815. (570)389-3006.

BUCKNELL UNIVERSITY, Stadler Center for Poetry, Lewisburg PA 17837. (570)577-1853. Fax: (570)577-3760. **Contact:** Cynthia Hogue.

CARLOW COLLEGE, 3335 Fifth Avenue, Pittsburgh PA 15213. (412)578-6346. Fax: (412)578-8722. **Contact:** Patricia Dobler.

CARNEGIE MELLON UNIVERSITY, Creative Writing Program, English Department, Pittsburgh PA 15213-2890. (412)268-2850. **Contact:** Jim Daniels.

CHATHAM COLLEGE, Woodland Rd., Pittsburgh PA 15232. (412)365-1190. Fax: (412)365-1505. **Contact:** Jeffrey Thomson.

DICKERSON COLLEGE, English Department, P.O. Box 1773, Carlisle PA 17013. (717)245-1346. Fax: (717)254-1942. Website: www.dickinson.edu/departments/engl/cw_minor.html. **Contact:** Adrienne Sue.

KUTZTOWN UNIVERSITY, English Department, Creative Writing Program, Kutztown PA 19530. **Contact:** James V. Applewhite.

LYCOMING COLLEGE, Creative Writing Program, English Department, Williamsport PA 17701-5192. (570)321-4000. Fax: (570)321-4389. **Contacts:** G. W. Hawkes and Sascha Feinstein.

PENN STATE ERIE, The Behrend College School of Humanities & Social Sciences, Station Rd., Erie PA 16563. (814)898-6440. **Contact:** Dr. Diana Hume George.

PENNSYLVANIA STATE UNIVERSITY, University Park PA 16802-6200. (814)865-6382. Fax: (814)863-7285. **Contact:** Julia Kasdorf.

SUSQUEHANNA UNIVERSITY, Writer's Institute, Hassinger Hall, Selinsgrove PA 17870. (570)372-4164. Fax: (570)372-2774. Website: http://susqu.edu/writers. **Contact:** Dr. Gary Fincke.

TEMPLE UNIVERSITY, Creative Writing Program, 1020 Anderson Hall, Philadelphia PA 19122-6090. (215)204-2662. **Contact:** Dr. Alan Singer.

UNIVERSITY OF PENNSYLVANIA, Creative Writing Program, English Department, Philadelphia PA 19104-6273. **Contact:** Gregory Djanikian.

UNIVERSITY OF PITTSBURGH, Department of English 526-CL, Pittsburgh PA 15260. (412)624-6508. Fax: (412)624-6639. **Contact:** Lynn Emanuel.

UNIVERSITY OF PITTSBURGH AT BRADFORD, 300 Campus Dr., Bradford PA 16701-2896. (814)362-7590. Fax: (814)362-5094. Website: www.upb.pitt.edu. **Contact:** Nancy McCabe.

UNIVERSITY OF PITTSBURGH AT JOHNSTOWN, 450 Schoolhouse Rd., Johnstown PA 15904-2912. (814)269-7140. Fax: (814)269-7196. **Contact:** Dr. Carroll Grimes.

UNIVERSITY OF SCRANTON, English Department, Creative Writing, Scranton PA 18510. (717)941-7619. **Contact:** John Meredith Hill.

Rhode Island

BROWN UNIVERSITY, English Department, Box 1852, Providence RI 02912-1852. (401)863-3260. **Contact:** Forrest Gander.

PROVIDENCE COLLEGE, English Department, River Avenue, Providence RI 02918-0001. (401)865-2587. Fax: (401)865-1192. **Contact:** Susan Fournier.

RHODE ISLAND COLLEGE, 600 Mt. Pleasant Ave., Providence RI 02908. (401)456-8115. **Contact:** Thomas Cobb.

South Carolina

CONVERSE COLLEGE, 580 East Main St., Spartanburg SC 29302. (864)596-9099. Website: www.converse.edu. **Contact:** Rick Mulkey.

UNIVERSITY OF SOUTH CAROLINA, Creative Writing Program, Humanities Bldg., Columbia SC 29208. (803)777-2096. Fax: (803)777-9064. **Contact:** Kwame Dawes.

South Dakota

UNIVERSITY OF SOUTH DAKOTA, 212 Dakota Hall, 414 E. Clark, Vermillion SD 57069-2390. (605)677-5966. Fax: (605)677-5298. **Contact:** Brian Bedard.

Tennessee

DYERSBURG STATE COMMUNITY COLLEGE, 1510 Lake Rd., Dyersburg TN 38024. (901)286-3326. **Contact:** Larry Griffin.

RHODES COLLEGE, English Department, Palmer Hall, 3rd Floor, 2000 N. Parkway, Memphis TN 38112. (901)843-3979. Fax: (901)843-3728. Website: www.rhodes.edu. **Contact:** Tina Barr.

UNIVERSITY OF THE SOUTH AT SEWANEE, Creative Writing Program, SPO 735 University Ave., Sewanee TN 37383-1000. **Contact:** Cheri Peters.

UNIVERSITY OF MEMPHIS, Creative Writing Program, English Department, Patterson Hall Room 463, Memphis TN 38152. (309)341-7090. **Contact:** Thomas Russell.

Texas

ABILENE CHRISTIAN UNIVERSITY, Creative Writing Program, English Department, Abilene TX 79699. (915)674-2263. **Contact:** Beth Lana.

BAYLOR UNIVERSITY, Department of English, P.O. Box 97404, Waco TX 76798. (254)710-1768. Fax: (254)710-3894. **Contact:** Dr. William V. Davis.

HARDIN-SIMMONS UNIVERSITY, Box 15114, Abilene TX 79698. (915)670-1214. **Contact:** Robert Fink.

SAM HOUSTON STATE UNIVERSITY, Texas Review, English Department, Box 2146, Huntsville TX 77341-2146. (936)294-1992. Fax: (936)294-3070. Website: www.shsu.edu. **Contact:** Barbara Miles.

LAMAR UNIVERSITY AT BEAUMONT, Creative Writing, P.O. Box 10023, Beaumont TX 77710. (409)880-8558. Fax: (409)880-8591. **Contact:** Sam Gwynn.

MIDLAND COLLEGE MAIN CAMPUS, 3600 N. Garfield, Midland TX 79705-6397. **Contact:** Dr. Leslie M. Williams.

NORTH LAKE COLLEGE, 5001 N. MacArthur Blvd., Irving TX 75038-3899. (972)273-3551. **Contact:** Dr. Gary D. Swaim.

SOUTHERN METHODIST UNIVERSITY, Department of English, P.O. Box 0435, Dallas TX 75275. (214)768-4369. **Contact:** Jack Myers.

SOUTHWEST TEXAS STATE UNIVERSITY, Creative Writing Program, 601 University Dr., San Marcos TX 78666-4616. **Contact:** Tom Grimes.

TEXAS A&M UNIVERSITY, 4227 TAMU, College Station TX 77843-4227. (979)845-8316. Fax: (979)862-2292. Website: www-english.tamu.edu/cw/. **Contact:** James McCann.

TEXAS TECH UNIVERSITY, English Department, Box 43091, Lubbock TX 79409-3091. (806)742-2501. Fax: (806)742-2501. Website: http://english.ttu.edu. **Contact:** Madonne Meyer.

TRINITY UNIVERSITY, Department of English, 715 Stadium Dr., San Antonio TX 78212-7200. (512)736-7517. **Contact:** Peter Balbert.

UNIVERSITY OF HOUSTON, Creative Writing Program, 229 Roy Cullen Bldg., Houston TX 77204-3015. (713)743-3014. Fax: (713)743-3013. Website: www.uh.edu/cwp. **Contact:** Faith Venverloh.

UNIVERSITY OF NORTH TEXAS, English Department, P.O. Box 311307, Denton TX 76203-1307. (940)565-4670. Fax: (940)565-4355. **Contact:** Barbara A. Rodman.

UNIVERSITY OF ST. THOMAS, 3800 Montrose, Houston TX 77006. (713)525-3172. Fax: (940)565-4355. E-mail: englishstaff@stthom.edu. **Contact:** Janet Lowery.

UNIVERSITY OF TEXAS AT DALLAS, Box 830688 JD 3.1, Richardson TX 75083-0688. Website: www.utdallas. edu/~nelsen/creativity.html. **Contact:** Robert Nelsen.

UNIVERSITY OF TEXAS AT EL PASO, Bilingual MFA Program, % Dept. of English, El Paso TX 79968. (915)747-5529. Fax: (915)747-6214. **Contact:** Leslie Ullman.

UNIVERSITY OF TEXAS MICHENER CENTER, Department of English, Parlin Hall, 702 East Dean Keeton, Austin TX 78705. (512)471-1601. Website: www.utexas.edu/academic/mcw. **Contact:** James Magnuson.

UNIVERSITY OF TEXAS AT SAN ANTONIO, 6900 North Loop 1604 W., San Antonio TX 78249. (210)458-4374. Fax: (210)458-5366. **Contact:** Linda Woodson.

Utah

BRIGHAM YOUNG UNIVERSITY, English Department, 3146 JKHB, Provo UT 84602. (801)378-4939. Fax: (801)378-4720. Website: http://english.byu.edu. **Contact:** Sally T. Taylor.

UNIVERSITY OF UTAH, Department of English, Salt Lake City UT 84112-0494. (801)581-6168. Fax: (801)585-5167. Website: www.hum.utah.edu/english. **Contact:** Catharine Coles.

WESTMINSTER COLLEGE OF SALT LAKE CITY, 2840 S 1300 E., Salt Lake City UT 84105. (801)488-1654. **Contact:** Natasha Sajé.

Vermont

BENNINGTON COLLEGE, Writing Seminar, Route 67-A, Bennington VT 05201. (802)440-4452. Fax: (802)440-4454. E-mail: writing@bennington.edu. Website: www.bennington.edu. **Contact:** Liam Rector.

GODDARD COLLEGE, 123 Pitkin Rd., Plainfield VT 05663. (212)533-9209. Fax: (802)454-8301. Website: www.goddard.edu. **Contact:** Paul Selig.

VERMONT COLLEGE, MFA in Writing, Montpelier VT 05602. (802)828-8840. Fax: (802)828-8649. Website: www.tui.edu/vermontcollege. **Contact:** Louise Crowley, Administrative Director.

Virginia

HOLLINS UNIVERSITY, P.O. Box 9677, Roanoke VA 24020-1677. (540)362-6317. Fax: (540)362-6097. E-mail: creative.writing@hollins.edu. Website: www.hollins.edu/academics/academics.htm. **Contact:** R.H.W. Dillard.

JAMES MADISON UNIVERSITY, English Department, MSC 1801, Harrisonburg VA 22807. (540)568-6202. Fax: (540)568-2983. Website: www.jmu.edu/english. **Contact:** Annette Frederico.

GEORGE MASON UNIVERSITY, Creative Writing Program, English Department MSN 3E4, 4400 University Dr., Fairfax VA 22030-4444. (703)993-1180. Fax: (703)993-1161. Website: www.gmu.edu/departments/english. **Contact:** William Miller.

OLD DOMINION UNIVERSITY, Creative Writing Program, English Department, Hampton Blvd., Norfolk VA 23529. (757)683-4770. **Contact:** Dr. Michael Pearson.

ROANOKE COLLEGE, Salem VA 24153. (540)375-2380. **Contact:** Paul Hanstedt.

UNIVERSITY OF VIRGINIA, P.O. Box 400121, Charlottesville VA 22904. (434)924-6675. Fax: (434)924-1478. **Contact:** Lisa Russ Spaar.

VIRGINIA COMMONWEALTH UNIVERSITY, P.O. Box 842005, Richmond VA 23284-2005. (804)828-1329. Fax: (804)828-8684. Website: www.has.vcu.edu/eng/grad. **Contact:** Laura Browder.

VIRGINIA POLYTECHNIC INSTITUTE & STATE UNIVERSITY, Department of English, Shanks Hall, Blacksburg VA 24061-0112. (540)231-6146. Fax: (540)231-5692. **Contact:** Lucinda Roy.

Washington

EASTERN WASHINGTON UNIVERSITY, Creative Writing Program MS 1, Spokane Center, 705 W 1st Avenue, Spokane WA 99201. (509)623-4217. **Contact:** Anita O'Brien.

UNIVERSITY OF WASHINGTON, English Department, Box 351130, Seattle WA 98195. (206)543-2690. **Contact:** Susan Williams.

WASHINGTON STATE UNIVERSITY, Department of English, P.O. Box 645020, Pullman WA 99164-5020. (360)650-6846. **Contact:** Carol Westensee.

WESTERN WASHINGTON UNIVERSITY, Department of English, Bellingham WA 98225-9055. (360)650-6846. **Contact:** Kathleen Lundeen.

West Virginia

WEST VIRGINIA UNIVERSITY, English Department, P.O. Box 6296, 230 Stansbury Hall, Morgantown WV 26506-6296. (304)293-1307, ext. 451. **Contact:** James Harms.

WEST VIRGINIA WESLEYAN COLLEGE, Creative Writing Program, English Department, Buckhannon WV 26201-2995. (304)473-8701. Fax: (304)473-8864. **Contact:** Mark DeFoe.

Wisconsin

BELOIT COLLEGE, Creative Writing Program, English Department, Box 23, Beloit WI 53511-5596. (608)363-2308. **Contact:** Clint McCown.

CARDINAL STRITCH UNIVERSITY, 6801 North Yates Rd., Milwaukee WI 53217. (414)410-4193. (315)443-3660. **Contact:** Barbara Wuest.

LAKELAND COLLEGE, Creative Writing, English Department, Sheboygan WI 53062-0359. (920)565-1276. Fax: (920)565-1206. Website: www.lakeland.edu. **Contact:** Karl Elder.

MARQUETTE UNIVERSITY, P.O. Box 1881, Milwaukee WI 53201. (414)288-7179. Fax: (414)288-5433. Website: www.marquette.edu/english. **Contact:** C.J. Hribal.

UNIVERSITY OF WISCONSIN AT MADISON, English Department, Helen C. White Hall, 600 N Park St., Madison WI 53706. (608)263-3805. Fax: (608)263-3709. Website: http://polyglot.lss.wlsc.edu/english. **Contact:** Ronald Wallace.

UNIVERSITY OF WISCONSIN AT MILWAUKEE, English Department, P.O. Box 413, Milwaukee WI 53211. (414)229-6691. Fax: (414)229-2643. **Contact:** John Goulet.

UNIVERSITY OF WISCONSIN AT WHITEWATER, Department of Modern Language & Literature, 800 W. Main St., Whitewater WI 53190-2121. (262)472-1036. Fax: (262)472-1037. **Contact:** Donna Lewis.

Wyoming

UNIVERSITY OF WYOMING, P.O. Box 3353, Hoyt Hall 201, Laramie WY 82071-3353. (307)766-6452. Fax: (307)766-3189.

Canada

■ **GRANT MACEWAN COLLEGE**, 10700-104th Ave., RM 5-265N, Edmonton, Alberta T5J 452 Canada. (780)497-4712. Fax: (780)497-5308. E-mail: mcmannd@admin.gmcc.ab.ca. Website: www.artsci.gmcc.ab.ca. **Contact:** Don McMann.

Organizations

When you write, you write alone. It's just you and the typewriter or computer screen. Yet the writing life does not need to be a lonely one. Joining a writing group or organization can be an important step in your writing career. By meeting other writers, discussing your common problems and sharing ideas, you can enrich your writing and increase your understanding of this sometimes difficult, but rewarding life.

The variety of writers' organizations seems endless—encompassing every type of writing and writer—from small, informal groups that gather regularly at a local coffeehouse for critique sessions to regional groups that hold annual conferences to share technique and marketing tips. National organizations and unions fight for writers' rights and higher payment for freelancers, and international groups monitor the treatment of writers around the world.

In this section you will find state-, province- and regional-based groups. You'll also find national organizations including the National Writers Association. Sisters in Crime and the Western Writers of America are examples of groups devoted to a particular type of writing. Whatever your needs or goals, you're likely to find a group listed here to interest you.

SELECTING A WRITERS' ORGANIZATION

To help you make an informed decision, we've provided information on the scope, membership and goals of the organizations listed on these pages. We asked groups to outline the types of memberships available and the benefits members can expect. Most groups will provide additional information for a self-addressed, stamped envelope, and you may be able to get a sample copy of their newsletter for a modest fee.

Keep in mind joining a writers' organization is a two-way street. When you join an organization, you become a part of it and, in addition to membership fees, most groups need and want your help. If you want to get involved, opportunities can include everything from chairing a committee to writing for the newsletter to helping set up an annual conference. The level of your involvement is up to you, and almost all organizations welcome contributions of time and effort.

Selecting a group to join depends on a number of factors. As a first step, you must determine what you want from membership in a writers' organization. Then send away for more information on the groups that seem to fit your needs. Start, however, by asking yourself:

• Would I like to meet writers in my city? Am I more interested in making contacts with other writers across the country or around the world?

• Am I interested in a group that will critique and give me feedback on work-in-progress?

• Do I want marketing information and tips on dealing with editors?

• Would I like to meet other writers who write the same type of work I do or am I interested in meeting writers from a variety of fields?

• How much time can I devote to meetings and are regular meetings important to me? How much can I afford to pay in dues?

• Would I like to get involved in running the group, working on the group's newsletters, planning a conference?

• Am I interested in a group devoted to writers' rights and treatment or would I rather concentrate on the business of writing?

For More Information

Because they do not usually have the resources or inclination to promote themselves widely, finding a local writers' group is usually a word-of-mouth process. If you would like to start a writers' group in your area, ask your local libraries and bookstores if they sponsor writers' groups.

The Internet is also an excellent resource for finding or establishing a writers' group. Many commercial online services have writers' sections and clubs. Websites such as Coffeehouse for Writers (www.coffeehouseforwriters.com) have discussion boards, critique groups and even writing workshops available.

ASHLAND AREA CHRISTIAN WRITERS GUILD, 1552 County Rd. 995, Ashland OH 44805. (419)281-1766. E-mail: ohboy@bright.net. **Contact:** April Boyer, director. Estab. 1998. Number of members: up to 15. Types of membership: Professional, midrange, student. "Ashland Area serves any area within comfortable driving distance. Members are asked to respect our mission statement. Our purpose is to share any knowledge, experiences, fellowship, support and prayer that we can for one another in pursuing God-honoring or family-friendly markets to publish our product; one that we each believe is a gift from God and a responsibility. We are interdenominational, do not discuss denominational differences, but freely express our faith in God." Benefits include support and fellowship, education, occasional speakers at monthly meetings, quarterly newsletter, social events. Dues: "There is no fee, but a donation is encouraged to cover small expenses. Non-attending affiliates who receive the e-letter or newsletters are also encouraged to donate. Any amount is appreciated. A completed interest form is required to register for membership." Mail, e-mail, phone for more information.

ASSOCIATED WRITING PROGRAMS, Mail Stop 1E3, George Mason University, Fairfax VA 22030-9736. (703)993-4301. Fax: (703)993-4302. E-mail: awp@gmu.edu. Website: www.awpwriter.org (includes FAQ, membership information/ordering, award series guidelines, links to institutional members, AWP news). **Contact:** Membership Services. Estab. 1967. Number of Members: 5,000 individuals and 324 institutions. Types of membership: Institutional (universities); graduate students; individual writers; and *Chronicle* subscribers. Open to any person interested in writing; most members are students or faculty of university writing programs (worldwide). Benefits include information on creative writing programs; grants, awards and publishing opportunities for writers; job list for academe and writing-related fields; a job placement service for writers in academe and beyond. AWP holds an annual conference in a different US city every spring; also conducts an annual Award Series in poetry, short story collections, novel and creative nonfiction, in which winner receives $2,000 honorarium and publication by a participating press. AWP acts as agent for finalists in Award Series and tries to place their manuscript with publishers throughout the year. Manuscripts accepted January 1-February 28 only. Novel competition: winner receives publication by St. Martin's Press and $10,000 in royalties. Send SASE for new guidelines. Publishes *The Writer's Chronicle* 6 times/year; 3 times/academic semester. Available to members for free. Nonmembers may order a subscription for $20/year; $29/year Canada; call for overseas rates. Also publishes the *AWP Official Guide to Writing Programs* which lists about 330 creative writing programs in universities across the country and in Canada. *Guide* is updated every 2 years; cost is $28.45, which includes shipping and handling. Dues: $59 for individuals; $37 students (must send copy of ID); additional $62 for full placement service. AWP keeps dossiers on file and sends them to school or organization of person's request. Send SASE for information. Inquiries by fax and e-mail OK.

THE AUTHORS GUILD, 31 E. 28th St., 10th Floor, New York NY 10016. (212)563-5904. Fax: (212)564-5363. E-mail: staff@authorsguild.org. Website: www.authorsguild.org (includes publishing industry news, business, legal and membership information). Executive Director: Paul Aiken. **Contact:** John McCloskey, membership coordinator. Purpose of organization: membership organization of 8,000 members offers services and informational materials intended to help published authors with the business and legal aspects of their work, including contract problems, copyright matters, freedom of expression and taxation. Maintains staff of attorneys and legal interns to assist members. Group health insurance available. Qualifications for membership: book author published by an established American publisher within 7 years or any author who has had 3 works, fiction or nonfiction, published by a magazine or magazines of general circulation in the last 18 months. Associate membership (authors with a firm contract offered) and membership-at-large (available to established attorneys and literary agents) also available. First year's dues: $90. Different levels of membership include: associate membership with all rights except voting available to an author who has a firm contract offer from an American publisher. Workshops/conferences: "The Guild and the Authors Guild Foundation conduct several symposia each year at which experts provide information, offer advice, and answer questions on subjects of concern to authors. Typical subjects have been the rights of privacy and publicity, libel, wills and estates, taxation, copyright, editors and editing, the art of interviewing, standards of criticism and book reviewing. Transcripts of these symposia are published and circulated to members." The *Authors Guild Bulletin*, a quarterly journal, contains articles on matters of interest to published writers, reports of Guild activities, contract surveys, advice on problem clauses in contracts, transcripts of Guild and League symposia, and information on a variety of professional topics. Subscription included in the cost of the annual dues. Inquiries by mail, e-mail and fax OK.

N AUTHOR'S VENUE ENTERPRISES, LLC, 600 Central Ave. SE, Suite 235, Albuquerque NM 87102. (505)244-9337. Fax: (800)853-7655. E-mail: info@authorsvenue.com. Website: www.AuthorsVenue.com. **Contact:** Suzanne Spletzer, executive director. Estab. 2001. Type of memberships: Professional and Basic. Has a network chapter in New Mexico, Colorado, Arizona. "Author's Venue provides education and publication opportunities for writers." Publichses a "Twice monthly e-Newsletter for advanced, experienced authors. Includes updates on the manuscript connection and helpful articles." Sponsors conferences; "Annual Journey Conference sponsored by *The Writer* magazine. Fall Seminar for mystery, romance and nonfiction authors." Children's Writing seminar in January. Dues: "Manuscript Connection is $94." For further information, contact by mail, e-mail, fax, phone.

N BARD SOCIETY, 1358 Tiber Ave., Jacksonville FL 32207-8951. (904)398-5352. E-mail: frankgrn@attbi.com. **Contact:** Frank Green, director. Estab. 1979. Sponsors weekly workshop where "manuscripts are read aloud and critiqued anonymously." Duration: 3 hours. Average attendance: 12. "Workshop has seen the publication of more than 25 novels." Fee: "Voluntary sliding scale depending upon ability to contribute financially." Further information available by mail, e-mail, phone.

N BASKERVILLE HALL CLUB OF SWEDEN, The Moor, Byggmästarvägen 29, Bromma 16832 Sweden. Website: www.hem.passagen.se/bvhall. **Contact:** Anders Wiggsstrom, secretary. Estab. 1979. Number of members: 81. Type of memberships: Student. Organization's purpose is "to study Sherlock Holmes and his world." Dues: $12. For further information, contact by mail or e-mail.

BLOOMINGTON AREA CHRISTIAN WRITERS, 9576 W. State Rd. 48, Bloomington IN 47404-9737. (812)876-8265. E-mail: katadams55@aol.com. **Contact:** Kathi Adams. Estab. 1994. Number of members: 10. Types of membership: Professional, associate. Open to all. Purpose is to "encourage Christians in their writing, both fiction and nonfiction, and to give useful critique to their work." Benefits include resource sharing-books, tapes, magazines, etc. "Share expenses related to attending writers' conferences. Prayer and emotional support." Inquiries by mail, e-mail, phone.

N BURNABY WRITERS' SOCIETY, 6584 Deer Lake Ave., Burnaby, British Columbia V5G 3T7 Canada. (604)444-1228. E-mail: lonewolf@portal.ca. Website: www.bws.bc.ca. **Contact:** Heather Hiebert, editor. Estab. 1967. Number of members: 300. "Membership is regional, but open to anyone interested in writing." Benefits include monthly market newsletter; workshops/critiques; guest speakers; information on contests, events, reading venues, etc.; opportunity to participate in public reading series. Sponsors annual competition open to all British Columbia residents; Canada Council sponsored readings; workshops. Publishes *Burnaby Writers Newsletter* bimonthly (except July/August), available to anyone for $30/year subscription. Dues: $30/year (includes newsletter subscription); $20 seniors, students. Meets second Thursday of each month. Send SASE for information.

CANADIAN SOCIETY OF CHILDREN'S AUTHORS, ILLUSTRATORS AND PERFORMERS (CANSCAIP), 35 Spadina Rd., Toronto, Ontario M5R 2S9 Canada. (416)515-1559. Fax: (416)515-7022. E-mail: canscaip@interlog.com. Website: www.interlog.com/~canscaip (includes children's authors, seminar information, art collection—samples [traveling]). **Contact:** Nancy Prasad, executive secretary. Estab. 1977. Number of Members: 1,100. Types of membership: Full professional member and friend (associate member). Open to professional active writers, illustrators and performers in the field of children's culture (full members); beginners and all other interested persons and institutions (friends). International scope, but emphasis on Canada. Benefits include quarterly newsletter, minutes of monthly meetings, marketing opportunities, publicity via our membership directory and our "members available" list, jobs (school visits, readings, workshops, residencies, etc.) through our "members available" list, mutual support through monthly meetings. Sponsors annual workshop, "Packaging Your Imagination," held every fall. Publishes *CANSCAIP News*, quarterly, available to all (free with membership, otherwise $25 Canadian). Dues: professional fees: $60 Canadian/year; friend fees: $25/year; institutional $30/year. "Professionals must have written, illustrated or performed work for children commercially, sufficient to satisfy the membership committee (more details on request)." CANSCAIP National has open meetings from September to June, monthly in Toronto. CANSCAIP West holds bimonthly meetings in Vancouver. Also has a London, Ontario branch. Send SASE for information. Inquiries by fax and e-mail OK.

N CREATIVE WRITERS FELLOWSHIP, 500 W. Bluestem, Apt. H4, North Newton KS 67117-8014. (316)283-7224. E-mail: estherbg@southwind.net. **Contact:** Esther Groves, secretary. Number of Members: approximately 20. Type of memberships: Professional and associate. "Our mission is to support and encourage writers as they develop and persue their writing gifts." Dues: 50¢/meeting. For further information, contact by mail or e-mail.

N FICTION WRITER'S CONNECTION, 4808 Madison Court NE, Albuquerque NM 87110. (505)352-9490. E-mail: bcamenson@aol.com. Website: www.fictionwriters.com. **Contact:** Blythe Camenson, director. Estab. 1993. Number of members: more than 200. Types of memberships: Professional, associate, affiliate, student and senior. "FWC's function is to help writers improve their craft and learn how to get published." Publishes *FWC's Tidbits*, an online newsletter free to members. Sponsors occasional writing contests. Offers member free critiquing, free consultation, a members—only area at the website with information on agents, discounts on query letter writing, e-mail courses. Dues: $74, $69 for full-time students and seniors. For further information, contact by e-mail, phone.

GREATER CINCINNATI CHRISTIAN WRITERS' FELLOWSHIP, 5499 Yellowstone Dr., Fairfield OH 45014-3868. (513)858-6609. E-mail: wwriter@fuse.net. Website: www.gccwf.com. **Contact:** Wayne Holmes, director. Estab. 1991. Number of members: 20-30. Type of membership: Professional. Open to all. "We are a 'Christian writers' fellowship and specialize in the 'Christian market.' Our purpose is to train men and women with an interest in writing from a Christian perspective in the art of communicating God's Word through articles, books, poetry and other media. We do this through encouraging our members to network, by bringing in guest speakers knowledgeable in the publishing industry, and by helping one another outside of the structured setting." Benefits include newsletter, which gives members an opportunity to see their writing in print. The articles deal with an aspect of the writing life. "Our organization offers fellowship, friendship, learning, and sharing of knowledge." Free membership. E-mail for information.

N 🌐 **HISTORICAL NOVEL SOCIETY**, *Solander Magazine*, % Marine Cottage, The Strand, Starcross, Cevon EX6 8NY United Kingdom. E-mail: histnovel@aol.com. Website: www.historicalnovelsociety.com. **Contact:** Richard Lee, publisher. Estab. 1997. Number of members: 800. Types of memberships: professional, associate, affiliate. Organization's purpose is "to promote historical fiction in all ways." Publishes *Historical Novels Review* (reviews all new releases in UK and US) quarterly and *Solander Magazine* (authoratative articles on genre) 2/year. Sponsors annual conference in London, UK with top name speakers (6th October 2001). Members receive "payment for short stories (2/year; £100 or equivalent dollars for each)." Dues: £18 or $35 US. Contact by e-mail for more information.

N **HORROR WRITERS ASSOCIATION (HWA)**, P.O. Box 50577, Palo Alto CA 94303. E-mail: hwa@horror.org. Website: www.horror.org. **Contact:** Information. Estab. 1987. Number of Members: 900. Type of Memberships: Active—writers who have published a body of horror writing at verified professional pay rates. Associate—non-writing professionals including editors, artists, agents and booksellers. Affiliate—beginning writers and others interested in the horror genre. Sponsors the "Bram Stoker Awards" for excellence in horror writing. Publishes membership directory, handbook and monthly newsletter with market reports. Offers comprehensive website available to members only. Dues: $55/year (US); $65/year (overseas); $75/year family membership; $100/year corporate membership. Meets once a year. Send SASE for information or visit website.

INSPIRATIONAL WRITERS ALIVE!, 6038 Greenmont, Houston TX 77092. (713)686-7209. E-mail: mlrogersll@houston.com. **Contact:** Martha Rogers, president, State Board of Directors. Estab. 1990. Number of members: 125 in five chapters. Types of memberships: Professional, associate, affiliate. No membership restrictions. Purpose is to "promote creative writing to glorify God as a ministry of writers, to aid its members in perfecting their writing skills, and to assist members in finding markets for their work. We have five chapters in Texas: Pasadena/Main, Houston First Baptist, Humble, Amarillo, East Texas/ Jacksonville." Benefits include newsletter, guest speakers, critique groups. Sponsors Open Writing Competition, January 1-May 15. Categories: short story, article, poetry, devotional, book proposal, drama. Dues: $25/year. Inquiries by e-mail.

INTERNATIONAL ASSOCIATION OF CRIME WRITERS NORTH AMERICAN BRANCH, P.O. Box 8674, New York NY 10116-8674. (212)243-8966. Fax: (212)361-1477. E-mail: mfrisque@igc.org. **Contact:** Mary A. Frisque, executive director, North America. Estab. 1987. Number of members: 265. Type of membership: Professional. "IACW is an organization of professional writers who have formed national branches in order to encourage communication among writers of all nationalities and to promote crime writing as an influential and significant art form." Quarterly newsletter. Offers North American Hammett Prize annually "for the best work of literary excellence in the field of crime writing by a US or Canadian author or permanent resident." Benefits include "opportunities to attend conferences and festivals abroad, sponsored by foreign branches. Dues: $50/year. Inquiries by SASE or e-mail.

M **MANITOBA WRITERS' GUILD**, 206-100 Arthur St., Winnipeg, Manitoba R3B, 1H3 Canada. (204)942-6134 or (888)637-5802. Fax: (204)942-5754. E-mail: mbwriter@escape.ca. Website: www.mbwriter.mb.ca. Number of members: approximately 550. Type of memberships: Regular, student, senior and fixed income. Open to anyone: writers, emerging and established; readers, particularly those interested in Manitoba literature. "Membership is provincial in general, although we have members from across Canada, USA and the world." Benefits include special discounts on programs, goods and services; regular mailings of program notices; and *WordWrap*, published 6 times/year, featuring articles, regular columns, information on current markets and publications, announcements, and profiles of Manitoba writers. Programs include Mentor/Apprentice program, small resource center (2-staff, small resource library, nonlending); open workshops once a month in fall and winter; annual conference, usually April; online database of Manitoba Authors, www.mbwriter.mb.ca/mapindex; online database of freelance authors and editors called Career Corner. Dues: $50 regular; $25 seniors, students, fixed-income. Send SASE for information.

THE MYSTERY WRITERS' FORUM, 111 Baywood Avenue, Menlo Park CA 94025-2701. Phone/fax: (650)328-6828. E-mail: mysmaster@zott.com. Website: www.mysterywritersforum.com. **Contact:** Lauri Hart, administrator.

TO RECEIVE REGULAR TIPS AND UPDATES about writing and Writer's Digest publications via e-mail, send an e-mail with "SUBSCRIBE NEWSLETTER" in the body of the message to newsletter-request@writersdigest.com

Types of membership: Professional, associate, affiliate, student. Membership open to all. Purpose is to " provide a place for published and aspiring mystery writers to trade information on the technical aspects peculiar to the mystery genre. Volunteer specialists in law enforcement, private investigation, and various forensic specialties can be checked with for advice on technical issues." Website has threaded discussion forum. Benefits include critique opportunites, information on agents and publishers, opportunities for authors, conferences and convention information, support and encouragement from peers. Free membership. Information available by e-mail or on website.

MYSTERY WRITERS OF AMERICA (MWA), 17 E. 47th St., 6th Floor, New York NY 10017. (212)888-8171. Fax: (212)888-8107. E-mail: mwa_org@earthlink.net. Website: www.mysterywriters.org (includes information about the newsletter, awards and membership). **Contact:** Mary Beth Becker, administrative director. Estab. 1945. Number of Members: 2,600. Type of memberships: Active (professional, published writers of fiction or nonfiction crime/mystery/suspense); associate (professionals in allied fields, i.e., editor, publisher, critic, news reporter, publicist, librarian, bookseller, etc.); corresponding (writers qualified for active membership who live outside the US); affiliate (writers unpublished in the mystery field and those interested in the genre). Benefits include promotion and protection of writers' rights and interests, including counsel and advice on contracts, MWA courses and workshops, a national office, an annual conference featuring the Edgar Allan Poe Awards, the *MWA Anthology*, a national newsletter, regional conferences, insurance, marketing tools, meetings and research publications. Newsletter, *The Third Degree*, is published 10 times/year for members. Annual dues: $80 for US members; $60 for corresponding members.

THE NATIONAL LEAGUE OF AMERICAN PEN WOMEN, INC., Headquarters: The Pen Arts Building, 1300 17th St., NW, Washington DC 20036-1973. (202)785-1997. Fax: (202)452-6868. E-mail: NLAPW1@juno.com. Website: members.aol.com/penwomen/pen.htm. **Contact:** Bernice Reid, president. Estab. 1897. Number of Members: 5,000. Types of membership: Three classifications: Art, Letters, Music. Publication and payment for work is a membership requirement. "Professional to us means our membership is open to women who sell their art, writings, or music compositions. We have over 175 branches in the mainland US plus Hawaii and the Republic of Panama. Some branches have as many as 100 members, some as few as 10 or 12. It is necessary to have 5 members to form a new branch." Benefits include a bimonthly magazine and local and national competitions. "Our facility is The Pen Arts Building. It is a 20-room Victorian mansion. One distinguished resident was President Abraham Lincoln's son, Robert Todd Lincoln, the former Secretary of War and Minister of Great Britain. It has rooms available for Pen Women visiting the D.C. area, and for Board members." In session 3 times a year. There are Branch and State Association competitions, as well as Biennial Convention competitions. Offers a research library of books by members and histories of the organization. Sponsors awards biennially to Pen Women in each classification: Art, Letters, Music, and $1,000 award biennially in even-numbered year to non-Pen Women in each classification for women age 35 and over who wish to pursue special work in art, music or letters field. *The Pen Woman* is the membership magazine, published 6 times a year, free to members, $18 a year for nonmember subscribers. Dues: $40/first year for national organization, $30/year thereafter; from $5-10/year for branch membership and from $1-5 for state association dues. Branches hold regular meetings each month, September through May except in northern states which meet usually March through September (for travel convenience). Send SASE for information. Inquiries via e-mail or fax OK, but SASE preferred.

NATIONAL WRITERS ASSOCIATION, 3140 S. Peoria, #295, Aurora CO 80014. (303)841-0246. Fax: (303)841-2607. Website: www.nationalwriters.com (includes contests, job listings and all other services). **Contact:** Sandy Whelchel, executive director. Estab. 1937. Number of Members: 4,000. Types of memberships: Regular membership for those without published credits; professional membership for those with published credits. Open to: "Any interested writer, national/international plus we have 16 chapters in various states." Benefits include critiques, marketing advice, editing, literary agency, complaint service, research reports on various aspects of writing, 6 contests, National Writers Press—self-publishing operation, regular newsletter with updates on marketing, bimonthly magazine on writing-related subjects, discounts on supplies, magazines and some services. Sponsors periodic conferences and workshops; short story contest opens April, closes July 1; novel contest opens December, closes April 1. Publishes *Authorship Magazine* (quarterly publication available by subscription $20 to nonmembers). Dues: $65 regular; $85 professional. For professional membership, requirement is equivalent of 3 articles or stories in a national or regional magazine; a book published by a royalty publisher; a play, TV script or movie produced. Chapters hold meetings on a monthly basis. Inquiries by SASE, e-mail and fax OK.

NEW HAMPSHIRE WRITERS' PROJECT, P.O. Box 2693, Concord NH 03302-2693. (603)226-6649. Fax: (603)226-0035. E-mail: nhwp@nh.ultranet.com. **Cotnact:** Katie Goodman, executive director. Estab. 1988. Number of Members: 750. Type of Memberships: individual; senior/student. Open to anyone interested in the literary arts—writers (fiction, nonfiction, journalists, poets, scriptwriters, etc.), teachers, librarians, publishers, editors, agents, booksellers and readers. Statewide scope. Benefits include a bimonthly publication featuring articles about NH writers and publishers; leads for writers, new books listings; and NH literary news. Also discounts on workshops, readings, conferences. Dues: $35 for individuals; $20 for seniors and full-time students; $250 for underwriters in bimonthly publication. Send SASE for information. Inquiries by fax and e-mail OK.

NORTH CAROLINA WRITERS' NETWORK, P.O. Box 954, Carrboro NC 27510-0954. (919)967-9540. Fax: (919)929-0535. E-mail: mail@ncwriters.org. Website: www.ncwriters.org. (includes workshop and competition guidelines, links to other organizations, N.C. Literary Hall of Fame bios and more). **Contact:** Linda W. Hobson, executive director. Estab. 1985. Number of Members: 1,800. Open to: All writers, all levels of skill and friends of books and writing. Membership is approximately 1,600 in North Carolina and 200 in 33 other states and 12 other countries. Benefits include bimonthly newsletter; reduced rates for competition entry fees; discounted fees for fall and spring conferences, workshops, etc.; use of critiquing service; use of library and resource center; press release and publicity service; information database(s). Sponsors annual Fall Conference for Writers, statewide workshops, Blumenthal Writers & Readers Series, Randall Jarrell/Harperprints Poetry Chapbook Competition. Publishes the 24-page bimonthly *Writers' Network News*, and *North Carolina's Literary Resource Guide*. Subscription included in dues. Dues: $55/year individual, $30/year students enrolled full-time in a degree-granting program, and $40/year seniors 65 + and disabled. Events scheduled throughout the year. Send SASE for information.

ROMANCE WRITERS OF AMERICA (RWA), 3707 FM 1960 West, Suite 555, Houston TX 77068. (281)440-6885. Fax: (281)440-7510. E-mail: info@rwanational.com. Website: www.rwanational.com. **Contact:** Lori White, administrative assistant. President: Harold Lowry (aka Leigh Greenwood). Estab. 1981. Number of members: over 8,400. Type of Memberships: General, associate (for agents, editors, publishers), affiliate (booksellers, librarians). Open to: "Any person actively pursuing a writing career in the romance field." Membership is international. Benefits include annual conference, contests and awards, magazine, forums with publishing representatives, network for published authors, group insurance, regional newsletters and more. Dues: $75 plus $25 processing fee/new members; $75/renewal fee. Send SASE for information.

THE DOROTHY L. SAYERS SOCIETY, Rose Cottage, Malthouse Lane, Hurstpierpoint, West Sussex BN6 9IY, United Kingdom. Phone: (+44)1273 833444. Fax: (+44)1273 835988. E-mail: jasmine@sayers.org.uk. Website: www.sayers.org.uk. **Contact:** Christopher Dean, chairman. Estab. 1976. Number of members: 500. Type of membership: Student. Membership open to anyone with an interest in Dorothy Sayers' life-works. Purpose to "promote the study of the life, works, and thoughts of Dorothy Sayers, and to encourage performance of her plays, publication of her works, and to assist researchers." Annual conference in July/August usually in UK, to consider a particular work or aspect of Sayers' life and work. Benefits include access to society archives, advice and help to scholars, bimonthly newsletter. Dues: $28/year. Inquiries by SASE, e-mail, fax.

SCIENCE FICTION AND FANTASY WORKSHOP, 1193 S. 1900 East, Salt Lake City UT 84108-1855. (801)582-2090. Fax: (801)650-2168. E-mail: workshop@burgoyne.com. Website: www.burgoyne.com/pages/workshop. **Contact:** Kathleen Dalton-Woodbury, director/newsletter editor. Estab. 1980. Number of members: 300. Types of memberships: "Active" is listed in the membership roster and so is accessible to all other members; "inactive" is not listed in the roster. Open to "anyone, anywhere. Our scope is international although over 96% of our members are in the US." Benefits include "several different critique groups: short stories, novels, articles, screenplays, poetry, etc. We also offer services such as copyediting, working out the numbers in plant building (give us the kind of planet you want and we'll tell you how far it is from the sun, etc.—or tell us what kind of sun you have and we'll tell you what your planet is like), brainstorming story, fragments or cultures or aliens, etc." Publishes *SF and Fantasy Workshop* (monthly), free via e-mail or may be downloaded from above website. Membership is also free in e-mail. See website.

SCIENCE FICTION WRITERS OF EARTH, P.O. Box 121293, Fort Worth TX 76121-1293. (817)451-8674. E-mail: sfwoe@flash.net. Website: www.flash.net/~sfwoe (includes contest rules, entry form, judge's report, contest results, list of writers who entered contest, interviews with the winners, reviews of the top three stories, short bios of the top 10 contestants, newsletter with articles of interest to contestants and writers in general). **Contact:** Gilbert Gordon Reis, SFWoE administrator. Estab. 1980. Number of Members: 150-200. Open to: Unpublished writers of science fiction and fantasy short stories. "We have writers in Europe, Canada, Australia and several other countries, but the majority are from the US. Writers compete in our annual science fiction/fantasy short story contest. This allows the writer to find out where he/she stands in writing ability. Winners often receive requests for their story from publishers. Many winners have told us that they believe that placing in the top ten of our contest gives them recognition and has assisted in getting their first story published." Dues: One must submit a science fiction or fantasy short story to our annual contest each year to be a member. Cost is $5 for membership and first story. $2 for each additional ms. The nominating committee meets several times a year to select the top ten stories of the annual contest. Author Edward Bryant selects the winners from the top ten stories. Contest deadline is October 30 and the cash awards and results are mailed out on January 31 of the following year. Awards $200 1st prize, $100 2nd prize, $50 3rd prize. The first place story is published by *Altair*, magazine of speculative fiction, or placed on the SFWoE website. The author is paid $75, in addition to $200 1st prize, for placing their story on the website for 180 days. Inquiries by SASE, e-mail (no contest submissions) or from the Internet OK.

SHORT MYSTERY FICTION SOCIETY. E-mail: gmh2@rcn.com. **Contact:** G. Miki Hayden, president. Estab. 1995. Number of members: 350. "All fans and authors (even editors) welcome." Supports writers of short mystery fiction. "We sponsor the yearly Derringer Awards for best published short stories." Benefits include a daily e-mail digest; subscribe to Shortmystery-subscribe@yahoogroups.com. Free membership. Inquiries by e-mail.

SISTERS IN CRIME, Box 442124, Lawrence KS 66044-8933. (785)842-1325. E-mail: sistersincrime@juno.com. Website: www.sistersincrime.org. **Contact:** Beth Wasson, executive secretary. Estab. 1986. Number of Members: 3,200. The original purpose of this organization was to combat discrimination against women in the mystery field. Memberships are open to men as well as women, as long as they are committed to the organization and its goals. Offers membership assistance in networking and publicity.

"WE WANT TO PUBLISH YOUR WORK."

You would give anything to hear an editor speak those six magic words. So you work hard for weeks, months, even years to make that happen. You create a brilliant piece of work and a knock-out presentation, but there's still one vital step to ensure publication. You still need to submit your work to the right buyers. With rapid changes in the publishing industry it's not always easy to know who those buyers are. That's why each year thousands of writers, just like you, turn to the most current edition of this indispensable market guide.

Keep ahead of the changes by ordering *2004 Children's Writer's & Illustrator's Market* today! You'll save the frustration of getting manuscripts returned in the mail stamped MOVED: ADDRESS UNKNOWN, and of NOT submitting your work to new listings because you don't know they exist. All you have to do to order next year's edition — at this year's price — is complete the attached order card and return it with your payment. Lock in the 2003 price for 2004 — order today!

2004 Children's Writer's & Illustrator's Market will be published and ready for shipment in November 2003.

Turn Over for More Great Books to Help You Get Published!

Get Your Children's Stories Published
with Help from These Writer's Digest Books!

2003 Guide to Literary Agents
Your search for powerful representation and the perfect writer's contract begins here. Find the right agent to get your fiction, nonfiction or screenplay into the hands of the publishers who can make your dreams come true! With 100% updated listings of 570+ agents who sell what you write.
#10811-K/$23.99/400p/pb

The Writer's Guide to Crafting Stories for Children
This unique guide offers detailed information and an in-depth examination of storytelling and story structure. Using worksheets, exercises and checklists you'll discover how to capture and keep a young reader's attention, whether your topic is fact or fiction.
#10762-K/$16.99/192p/pb

Creating Characters Kids Will Love
Learn to develop vivid characters that come to life on the page and engage children. Includes characterization exercises, observation techniques and memory builders for incorporating experiences from your own childhood.
#10669-K/$16.99/208p/pb

Story Sparkers:
A Creativity Guide for Children's Writers
Fire up your imagination! These easy-to-apply techniques will give your creativity a refreshing boost. You'll learn how to assess each new idea and use it to its fullest potential. Includes a guide to determine which formats will best showcase your ideas.
#10700-K/$16.99/208p/pb

How to Write and Illustrate Children's Books
And Get Them Published
Advice and insider tips from some of the finest talents in children's publishing are collected in this must-have guide for success in writing and illustrating in the children's market. You'll find inspiring and insightful instruction from experts in the field to help you get your work published.
#10694-K/$19.99/144p/pb

Picture Writing:
A new approach to writing for kids and teens
Learn to create evocative characters, setting and plots fueled by the power of vivid description. You'll discover how to optimize the five senses, and how to recognize what type of descriptive words work best for various age groups.
#10755-K/$16.99/224p/pb
Will be shipped when available in December 2002

Books are available at your local bookstore, or directly from the publisher using the Order Card on the reverse.

WESTERN WRITERS OF AMERICA, Office of the Secretary Treasurer, 1012 Fair St., Franklin TN 37064-2718. Phone/fax: (615)791-1444. E-mail: tncrutch@aol.com. Website: www.westernwriters.org (includes membership information, authors' profiles and magazine articles). **Contact:** James A. Crutchfield, secretary/treasurer. Estab. 1953. Number of Members: 600. Type of Membership: Active, associate, patron. Open to: Professional, published writers who have multiple publications of fiction or nonfiction (usually at least three) about the West. Associate membership open to those with one book, a lesser number of short stories or publications or participation in the field such as editors, agents, reviewers, librarians, television producers, directors (dealing with the West). Patron memberships open to corporations, organizations and individuals with an interest in the West. Scope is international. Benefits: "By way of publications and conventions, members are kept abreast of developments in the field of Western literature and the publishing field, marketing requirements, income tax problems, copyright law, research facilities and techniques, and new publications. At conventions members have the opportunity for one-on-one conferences with editors, publishers and agents." Sponsors an annual four-day conference during fourth week of June featuring panels, lectures and seminars on publishing, writing and research. Includes the Spur Awards to honor authors of the best Western literature of the previous year. Publishes *Roundup Magazine* (6 times/year) for members. Available to nonmembers for $30. Publishes membership directory. Dues: $75 for active membership or associate membership, $250 for patron. For information on Spur Awards, send SASE. Inquiries by fax and e-mail OK.

WILLAMETTE WRITERS, 9045 SW Barbur Blvd., Suite 5A, Portland OR 97219. (503)452-1592. Fax: (503)452-0372. E-mail: wilwrite@teleport.com. Website: www.willamettewriters.com. **Contact:** Bill Johnson, office manager. Estab. 1965. Number of members: 900. "Willamette Writers is a nonprofit, tax exempt corporation staffed by volunteers. Membership is open to both published and aspiring writers. WW provides support, encouragement and interaction for all genres of writers." Open to national membership, but serves primarily the Pacific Northwest. Benefits include a writers' referral service, critique groups, membership discounts, youth programs (4th-12th grades), monthly meetings with guest authors, annual writing contest, community projects, library and research services, as well as networking with other writing groups, office with writing reference and screenplay library. Sponsors annual conference held the second weekend in August; quarterly workshops; annual Kay Snow Writing Contest; and the Distinguished Northwest Writer Award. Publishes *The Willamette Writer* monthly: a 12-page newsletter for members and complimentary subscriptions. Information consists of features, how-to's, mechanics of writing, profile of featured monthly speaker, markets, workshops, conferences and benefits available to writers. Dues: $36/year; includes subscription to newsletter. Meets first Tuesday of each month; board meeting held last Tuesday of each month. Inquiries by SASE, fax and e-mail OK.

THE WRITER'S CENTER, 4508 Walsh St., Bethesda MD 20815-6006. (301)654-8664. Fax: (301)654-8667. E-mail: postmaster@writer.org. Website: www.writer.org. Executive Director: Jane Fox. **Contact:** Sunil Freeman, assistant director. Estab. 1977. Number of Members: 2,800. Open to: Anyone interested in writing. Scope is regional DC, Maryland, Virginia, West Virginia, Pennsylvania. Benefits include newsletter, discounts in bookstore, workshops, public events, subscriptions to *Poet Lore*, use of equipment and annual small press book fair. Center offers workshops, reading series, equipment, newsletter and limited workspace. Sponsors workshops, conferences, award for narrative poem. Publishes *Writer's Carousel*, bimonthly. Nonmembers can pick it up at the Center. Dues: $40/year. Fees vary with service, see publications. Brochures are available for SASE. Inquiries by e-mail and fax OK.

★ WRITERS' FEDERATION OF NOVA SCOTIA, 1113 Marginal Rd., Halifax, Nova Scotia B3H 4P7 Canada. (902)423-8116. E-mail: talk@writers.ns.ca. Website: www.writers.ns.ca. **Contact:** Jane Buss, executive director. Estab. 1976. Number of Members: 600. Types of memberships: General membership, student membership, Nova Scotia Writers' Council membership (professional), Honorary Life Membership. Open to anyone who writes. Provincial scope, with a few members living elsewhere in the country or the world. Benefits include advocacy of all kinds for writers, plus such regular programs as workshops and publications, including directories and a newsletter. Sponsors workshops, 3 book awards, one annual competition for unpublished manuscripts in various categories; a writers-in-the-schools program, a manuscript reading service, reduced photocopying rates. Publishes *Eastword*, 6 issues annually, available by subscription for $35 (Canadian) to nonmembers. Dues: $35/year (Canadian). Holds an annual general meeting, several board meetings annually, two awards ceremonies. Send SASE or e-mail for information.

★ WRITERS GUILD OF ALBERTA, Percy Page Centre, 11759 Groat Rd., Edmonton, Alberta T5M 3K6 Canada. (780)422-8174. Fax: (780)422-2663. E-mail: mail@writersguild.ab.ca. Website: www.writersguild.ab.ca. **Contact:** Norma Lock, executive director. Estab. 1980. Number of Members: 750. Membership open to current and past residents of Alberta. Regional (provincial) scope. Benefits include discounts on programs offered; manuscript evaluation service available; bimonthly newsletter; contacts; info on workshops, retreats, readings, etc. Sponsors workshops 2 times/year, retreats 3 times/year, annual conference, annual book awards program (Alberta writers only). Publishes *WestWord* 6

MARKET CONDITIONS are constantly changing! If you're still using this book and it is 2004 or later, buy the newest edition of *Novel & Short Story Writer's Market* at your favorite bookstore or order from Writer's Digest Books by calling 1-800-448-0915.

times/year; available for $60/year (Canadian) to nonmembers. Dues: $60/year for regular membership; $20/year senior/ students/limited income; $100/year donating membership—charitable receipt issued (Canadian funds). Organized monthly meetings. Send SASE for information.

WRITERS INFORMATION NETWORK, P.O. Box 11337, Bainbridge Island WA 98110. (206)842-9103. Fax: (206)842-0536. E-mail: WritersInfoNetwork@juno.com. Website: www.bluejaypub.com/win. **Contact:** Elaine Wright Colvin, director. Estab. 1980. Number of members: 1,000. Open to: All interested in writing for religious publications/ publishers. Scope is national and several foreign countries. Benefits include bimonthly magazine, *WIN-Informer*, market news, advocacy/grievance procedures, professional advice, writers conferences, press cards, author referral, free consultation. Conferences advertised in *WIN-Informer* and on website. Dues: $35 US; $40 foreign/year in US equivalent funds. Holds meetings throughout the Pacific Northwest. Brochures are available for SASE. Inquiries by fax and e-mail OK.

WRITERS' LEAGUE OF TEXAS, (formerly Austin Writer's League), Writers' League of Texas, 1501 W. Fifth, E-2, Austin TX 78703. (512)499-8914. Fax: (512)499-0441. E-mail: awl@writersleague.org. Website: www.writersleague. org. **Contact:** Stephanie Sheppard, executive director. Estab. 1981. Number of Members: 1,600. Types of memberships: Regular, student/senior citizen, family. Monthly programs and use of resource center/library is open to the public. "Membership includes both aspiring and professional writers, all ages and all ethnic groups." Job bank is also open to the public. Public also has access to technical assistance. Partial and full scholarships offered for some programs. Of 1,600 members, 800 reside in Austin. Remaining 800 live all over the US and in other countries. Benefits include monthly newsletter, monthly programs, resource center/library-checkout privileges, discounts on workshops, seminars, classes, job bank, discounts on books and tapes, participation in awards programs, technical/marketing assistance, copyright forms and information, Writers Helping Writers (mentoring program). Center has 5 rooms plus 2 offices and storage area. Public space includes reception and job bank area; conference/classroom; library; and copy/mail room. Library includes 1,400 titles. Sponsors fall and spring workshops, weekend seminars, informal classes, sponsorships for special events such as readings, production of original plays, media conferences, creative writing programs for children and youth; Violet Crown Book Awards, Teddy Children's Book Award and newsletter writing awards. Publishes *Texas Writer* (monthly newsletter), sponsors with Texas Commission on the Arts Texas Literary Touring Program. Administers literature subgranting program for Texas Commission on the Arts. Membership/subscription: $50, $70 family membership. Monthly meetings. Send SASE for information.

THE WRITERS ROOM, INC., 10 Astor Place, 6th Floor, New York NY 10003-6935. (212)254-6995. Fax: (212)533-6059. E-mail: writersroom@writersroom.org. Website: www.writersroom.org (includes organization's background information and downloadable application). **Contact:** Donna Brodie, executive director. Estab. 1978. Number of Members: 200 fulltime and 170 part-time. Founded in 1978 to provide a "home away from home" for any writer who needs a place to work. Description: Large room with 35 desks separated by partitions, space for 370 writers each quarter; open 24 hours a day year-round; kitchen, lounge and bathrooms, storage for files and laptops, small reference library; monthly readings. Dues: $270-450 for 6 months, $50 application fee, $60 key deposit. Send SASE for application and background information. Inquiries by SASE, e-mail and fax OK or visit website.

THE WRITERS' WORKSHOP, 387 Beaucatcher Rd., Asheville NC 28805. Phone/fax: (828)254-8111. E-mail: writrwkshp@aol.com. **Contact:** Karen Ackerson, executive director. Estab. 1984. Number of Members: 1,250. Types of memberships: Student/low income $25; family/organization $65; individual $35. Open to all writers. Scope is national and international. Benefits include discounts on workshops, quarterly newsletter, critiquing services through the mail. Center offers reading room, assistance with editing your work. Publishes a newsletter; also available to nonmembers ($20). Offers workshops year-round in NC and the South; 2 retreats a year, 4 readings with nationally awarded authors. Contests and classes for children and teens as well. Advisory board includes Kurt Vonnegut, E.L. Doctorow, Peter Matthiessen, Reynolds Price and John Le Carré. Also sponsors international contests in fiction, memoirs, poetry and creative nonfiction. Brochures are available for SASE.

Publishers and Their Imprints

The publishing world is constantly changing and evolving. With all of the buying, selling, reorganizing, consolidating, and dissolving, it's hard to keep publishers and their imprints straight. To help you make sense of these changes, we offer this breakdown of major publishers (and their divisions)—who owns whom and which imprints are under each company umbrella. Keep in mind that this information is constantly changing. We have provided the websites to each of the publishers so you can continue to keep an eye on this ever-evolving business.

SIMON & SCHUSTER
(Viacom, Inc.)
www.simonsays.com

Simon & Schuster Audio
Pimsleur
Simon & Schuster Audioworks
Simon & Schuster Sound Ideas

Simon & Schuster Adult Publishing
Atria Books
The Free Press
Kaplan
PB Press
Pocket Books
Scribner
Simon & Schuster
Simon & Schuster Trade Paperback

Simon & Schuster Children's Publishing
Aladdin Paperbacks
Atheneum Books for Young Readers
Little Simon®
Margaret K. McElderry Books
Simon & Schuster Books for Young Readers
Simon Pulse
Simon Spotlight®

Simon & Schuster Interactive

Simon & Schuster International
Distican
Simon & Schuster Australia
Simon & Schuster UK

HARPERCOLLINS
www.harpercollins.com

HarperCollins General Books Group
Access Press
Amistad Press
Avon
Ecco
Eos
HarperAudio
HarperBusiness
HarperCollins
HarperEntertainment
HarperLargePrint
HarperResource
HarperSanFrancisco
HarperTorch
Perennial

PerfectBound
Quill
Rayo
ReganBooks
William Morrow

HarperCollins Children's Books Group
Avon
Greenwillow Books
HarperCollins Children's Books
HarperFestival
HarperTrophy
Joanna Cotler Books
Laura Geringer Books
Tempest

HarperCollins Australia

HarperCollins Canada

HarperCollins New Zealand

HarperCollins UK

Zondervan

RANDOM HOUSE, INC.
(Bertelsmann Book Group)
www.randomhouse.com

The Ballantine Publishing Group
Ballantine Books
Ballantine Reader's Circle
Del Rey
Del Rey/Lucas Books
Fawcett
Ivy
One World
Wellspring

Bantam Dell Publishing Group
Bantam Hardcover
Bantam Trade Paperback
Bantam Mass Market
Crimeline
Delacorte Press
Dell
Delta
The Dial Press
Domain
DTP
Fanfare
Island
Spectra

The Crown Publishing Group
Bell Tower
Clarkson Potter
Crown Business
Crown Publishers, Inc.
Harmony Books
Shaye Areheart Books
Three Rivers Press

The Doubleday Broadway Publishing Group
Broadway Books
Currency
Doubleday
Doubleday Religious Publishing
Doubleday/Image
Main Street Books
Nan A. Talese

The Knopf Publishing Group
Alfred A. Knopf
Everyman's Library
Pantheon Books
Schocken Books
Vintage Anchor Publishing

Random House Audio Publishing Group
Random House Audible
Random House Audio
Random House Audio Assets
Random House Audio Dimensions
Random House Audio Price-less
Random House Audio Road
Random House Listening Library

Random House Children's Books
Knopf Delacorte Dell Young Readers Group
Alfred A. Knopf
Bantam
Crown
David Fickling Books
Delacorte Press
Dell Dragonfly
Dell Laurel-Leaf
Dell Yearling Books
Doubleday
Wendy Lamb Books

Random House Young Readers Group
Beginner Books
Disney
First Time Books
Landmark Books
LucasBooks
Picturebacks
Sesame Workshop
Step into Reading
Stepping Stones

The Random House Information Group
Fodor's Travel Publications

Living Language
Princeton Review
Random House Espanol
Random House Puzzles & Games
Random House Reference Publishing

The Random House Trade Publishing Group

AtRandom
The Modern Library
Random House Trade Books
Random House Trade Paperbacks
Villard Books

Random House Ventures

ebrary
Random House Audible
Xlibris

Random House Diversified Publishing Group

Random House Large Print Publishing
Random House Value Publishing

Random House Worldwide

Random House Australia
Random House of Canada Ltd.
Random House UK
Transworld UK

PENGUIN PUTNAM, INC.
(Pearson plc)
www.penguinputnam.com

Penguin Putnam, Inc.

Avery
BlueHen Books
Dutton
G.P. Putnam's Sons
Jeremy P. Tarcher
New American Library
Penguin
Plume
Viking

Berkley Publishing Group

Ace Books
Berkley Books
Boulevard
Diamond Books
HPBooks
Jam
Jove
Perigee
Prime Crime
Riverhead Books (paperback)

Penguin Putnam Books for Young Readers

AlloyBooks
Dial Books for Young Readers
Dutton Children's Books
Frederick Warne
G.P. Putnam's Sons
Grosset & Dunlap
Philomel
Phyllis Fogelman Books
Paperstar
Planet Dexter
Platt & Munk
Playskool
Price Stern Sloan
PSS
Puffin Books
Viking Children's Books

AOL TIME WARNER BOOK GROUP
www.twbookmark.com

Time Warner Book Group

Aspect
Mysterious Press
Walk Worthy Press
Warner Books
Warner Faith
Warner Vision

Little, Brown and Company Adult Trade Books

Arcade Books
Back Bay Books
Bulfinch Press

Little, Brown and Company
Children's Publishing
Megan Tingley Books

HOLTZBRINCK PUBLISHERS (Germany)
www.vhpsva.com/bookseller/HBGenInfo.html

St. Martin's Press
LA Weekly Books
St. Martin's Griffin
St. Martin's Minotaur
St. Martin's Paperbacks
St. Martin's Press
St. Martin's Reference
St. Martin's Scholarly & Reference
Thomas Dunne Books
Truman Talley Books
Whitman

Picador USA
Picador USA

Tor/Forge
Forge
Orb

Tor
Tor Classics

Henry Holt
Edge Books
John Macrae Books
Metropolitan Books
Owl Books
Owlets
Redfeather Books

Farrar, Straus & Giroux
Aerial
Faber and Faber
Hill and Wang
Mirasol
Noonday
North Point Press
Sunburst

❖ Canadian Writers Take Note

While much of the information contained in this section applies to all writers, here are some specifics of interest to Canadian writers:

Postage: When sending an SASE from Canada, you will need an International Reply Coupon. Also be aware, a GST tax is required on postage in Canada and for mail with postage under $5 going to destinations outside the country. Since Canadian postage rates are voted on in January of each year (after we go to press), contact a Canada Post Corporation Customer Service Division (located in most cities in Canada) or visit www.canadapost.ca for the most current rates.

Copyright: For information on copyrighting your work and to obtain forms, write Copyright and Industrial Design, Phase One, Place du Portage, 50 Victoria St., Hull, Quebec K1A 0C9 or call (819)997-1936. Website: www.cipo.gc.ca.

The public lending right: The Public Lending Right Commission has established that eligible Canadian authors are entitled to payments when a book is available through a library. Payments are determined by a sampling of the holdings of a representative number of libraries. To find out more about the program and to learn if you are eligible, write to the Public Lending Right Commission at 350 Albert St., P.O. Box 1047, Ottawa, Ontario K1P 5V8 or call (613)566-4378 or (800)521-5721 for information. Website: www.plr-dpp.ca/. The Commission, which is part of The Canada Council, produces a helpful pamphlet, *How the PLR System Works,* on the program.

Grants available to Canadian writers: Most province art councils or departments of culture provide grants to resident writers. Some of these, as well as contests for Canadian writers, are listed in our Contests and Awards section. For national programs, contact The Canada Council, Writing and Publishing Section, P.O. Box 1047, Ottawa, Ontario K1P 5V8 or call (613)566-4338 for information. Fax: (613)566-4390. Website: www.canadacouncil.ca.

For more information: See the Organizations and Resources section of *Novel & Short Story Writer's Market* for listings of writers' organizations in Canada. Also contact The Writer's Union of Canada, 40 Wellington St. E, 3rd Floor, Toronto, Ontario M5E 1C7; call them at (416)703-8982 or fax them at (416)504-7656. E-mail: info@writersunion.ca. Website: www.writersunion. ca. This organization provides a wealth of information (as well as strong support) for Canadian writers, including specialized publications on publishing contracts; contract negotiations; the author/editor relationship; author awards, competitions and grants; agents; taxes for writers, libel issues and access to archives in Canada.

Printing & Production Terms Defined

In most of the magazine listings in this book you will find a brief physical description of each publication. This material usually includes the number of pages, type of paper, type of binding and whether or not the magazine uses photographs or illustrations.

Although it is important to look at a copy of the magazine to which you are submitting, these descriptions can give you a general idea of what the publication looks like. This material can provide you with a feel for the magazine's financial resources and prestige. Do not, however, rule out small, simply produced publications as these may be the most receptive to new writers. Watch for publications that have increased their page count or improved their production from year to year. This is a sign the publication is doing well and may be accepting more fiction.

You will notice a wide variety of printing terms used within these descriptions. We explain here some of the more common terms used in our listing descriptions. We do not include explanations of terms such as Mohawk and Karma which are brand names and refer to the paper manufacturer.

PAPER

acid-free: Paper that has a low or no acid content. This type of paper resists deterioration from exposure to the elements. More expensive than many other types of paper, publications done on acid-free paper can last a long time.

bond: Bond paper is often used for stationery and is more transparent than text paper. It can be made of either sulphite (wood) or cotton fiber. Some bonds have a mixture of both wood and cotton (such as "25 percent cotton" paper). This is the type of paper most often used in photocopying or as standard typing paper.

coated/uncoated stock: Coated and uncoated are terms usually used when referring to book or text paper. More opaque than bond, it is the paper most used for offset printing. As the name implies, uncoated paper has no coating. Coated paper is coated with a layer of clay, varnish or other chemicals. It comes in various sheens and surfaces depending on the type of coating, but the most common are dull, matte and gloss.

cover stock: Cover stock is heavier book or text paper used to cover a publication. It comes in a variety of colors and textures and can be coated on one or both sides.

CS1/CS2: Most often used when referring to cover stock, CS1 means paper that is coated only on one side; CS2 is paper coated on both sides.

newsprint: Inexpensive absorbent pulp wood paper often used in newspapers and tabloids.

text: Text paper is similar to book paper (a smooth paper used in offset printing), but it has been given some texture by using rollers or other methods to apply a pattern to the paper.

vellum: Vellum is a text paper that is fairly porous and soft.

Some notes about paper weight and thickness: Often you will see paper thickness described in terms of pounds such as 80 lb. or 60 lb. paper. The weight is determined by figuring how many pounds in a ream of a particular paper (a ream is 500 sheets). This can be confusing, however, because this figure is based on a standard sheet size and standard sheet sizes vary depending on the type of paper used. This information is most helpful when comparing papers of the same type. For example, 80 lb. book paper versus 60 lb. book paper. Since the size of the paper is the same it would follow that 80 lb. paper is the thicker, heavier paper.

Some paper, especially cover stock, is described by the actual thickness of the paper. This is expressed in a system of points. Typical paper thicknesses range from 8 points to 14 points thick.

PRINTING

letterpress: Letterpress printing is printing that uses a raised surface such as type. The type is inked and then pressed against the paper. Unlike offset printing, only a limited number of impressions can be made, as the surface of the type can wear down.

offset: Offset is a printing method in which ink is transferred from an image-bearing plate to a "blanket" and from the blanket to the paper.

sheet-fed offset: Offset printing in which the paper is fed one piece at a time.

web offset: Offset printing in which a roll of paper is printed and then cut apart to make individual sheets.

There are many other printing methods but these are the ones most commonly referred to in our listings.

BINDING

case binding: In case binding, signatures (groups of pages) are stitched together with thread rather than glued together. The stitched pages are then trimmed on three sides and glued into a hardcover or board "case" or cover. Most hardcover books and thicker magazines are done this way.

comb binding: A comb is a plastic spine used to hold pages together with bent tabs that are fed through punched holes in the edge of the paper.

perfect binding: Used for paperback books and heavier magazines, perfect binding involves gathering signatures (groups of pages) into a stack, trimming off the folds so the edge is flat and gluing a cover to that edge.

saddle stitched: Publications in which the pages are stitched together using metal staples. This fairly inexpensive type of binding is usually used with books or magazines that are under 80 pages.

Smythe-sewn: Binding in which the pages are sewn together with thread. Smythe is the name of the most common machine used for this purpose.

spiral binding: A wire spiral that is wound through holes punched in pages is a spiral bind. This is the binding used in spiral notebooks.

Glossary

Advance. Payment by a publisher to an author prior to the publication of a book, to be deducted from the author's future royalties.

All rights. The rights contracted to a publisher permitting a manuscript's use anywhere and in any form, including movie and book club sales, without additional payment to the writer.

Amateur sleuth. The character in a mystery, usually the protagonist, who does the detection but is not a professional private investigator or police detective.

Anthology. A collection of selected writings by various authors.

Association of Authors' Representatives (AAR). An organization for literary agents committed to maintaining excellence in literary representation.

Auction. Publishers sometimes bid against each other for the acquisition of a manuscript that has excellent sales prospects.

Backlist. A publisher's books not published during the current season but still in print.

Book producer/packager. An organization that may develop a book for a publisher based upon the publisher's idea or may plan all elements of a book, from its initial concept to writing and marketing strategies, and then sell the package to a book publisher and/or movie producer.

Cliffhanger. Fictional event in which the reader is left in suspense at the end of a chapter or episode, so that interest in the story's outcome will be sustained.

Clip. Sample, usually from a newspaper or magazine, of a writer's published work.

Cloak-and-dagger. A melodramatic, romantic type of fiction dealing with espionage and intrigue.

Commercial. Publishers whose concern is salability, profit and success with a large readership.

Contemporary. Material dealing with popular current trends, themes or topics.

Contributor's copy. Copy of an issue of a magazine or published book sent to an author whose work is included.

Copublishing. An arrangement in which the author and publisher share costs and profits.

Copyediting. Editing a manuscript for writing style, grammar, punctuation and factual accuracy.

Copyright. The legal right to exclusive publication, sale or distribution of a literary work.

Cover letter. A brief letter sent with a complete manuscript submitted to an editor.

"Cozy" (or "teacup") mystery. Mystery usually set in a small British town, in a bygone era, featuring a somewhat genteel, intellectual protagonist.

Cyberpunk. Type of science fiction, usually concerned with computer networks and human-computer combinations, involving young, sophisticated protagonists.

Electronic rights. The right to publish material electronically, either in book or short story form.

E-zine. A magazine that is published electronically.

Electronic submission. A submission of material by modem or on computer disk.

Experimental fiction. Fiction that is innovative in subject matter and style; avant-garde, non-formulaic, usually literary material.

Exposition. The portion of the storyline, usually the beginning, where background information about character and setting is related.

Fair use. A provision in the copyright law that says short passages from copyrighted material may be used without infringing on the owner's rights.

Fanzine. A noncommercial, small-circulation magazine usually dealing with fantasy, horror or science-fiction literature and art.

First North American serial rights. The right to publish material in a periodical before it appears in book form, for the first time, in the United States or Canada.

Flash fiction. See short short stories.

Galleys. The first typeset version of a manuscript that has not yet been divided into pages.

Genre. A formulaic type of fiction such as romance, western or horror.

Gothic. A genre in which the central character is usually a beautiful young woman and the setting an old mansion or castle, involving a handsome hero and real danger, either natural or supernatural.

Graphic novel. An adaptation of a novel into a long comic strip or heavily illustrated story of 40 pages or more, produced in paperback.

Hard science fiction. Science fiction with an emphasis on science and technology.

Hard-boiled detective novel. Mystery novel featuring a private eye or police detective as the protagonist; usually involves a murder. The emphasis is on the details of the crime.

High fantasy. Fantasy with a medieval setting and a heavy emphasis on chivalry and the quest.

Horror. A genre stressing fear, death and other aspects of the macabre.

Hypertext fiction. A fictional form, read electronically, which incorporates traditional elements of story-telling with a nonlinear plot line, in which the reader determines the direction of the story by opting for one of many author-supplied links.

Imprint. Name applied to a publisher's specific line (e.g. Owl, an imprint of Henry Holt).

Interactive fiction. Fiction in book or computer-software format where the reader determines the path the story will take by choosing from several alternatives at the end of each chapter or episode.

International Reply Coupon (IRC). A form purchased at a post office and enclosed with a letter or manuscript to a international publisher, to cover return postage costs.

Juvenile. Fiction intended for children 2-12.

Libel. Written or printed words that defame, malign or damagingly misrepresent a living person.

Literary fiction. The general category of fiction which employs more sophisticated technique, driven as much or more by character evolution than action in the plot.

Literary agent. A person who acts for an author in finding a publisher or arranging contract terms on a literary project.

Mainstream fiction. Fiction which appeals to a more general reading audience, versus literary or genre fiction. Mainstream is more plot-driven than literary fiction, and less formulaic than genre fiction.

Malice domestic novel. A mystery featuring a murder among family members, such as the murder of a spouse or a parent.

Manuscript. The author's unpublished copy of a work, usually typewritten, used as the basis for typesetting.

Mass market paperback. Softcover book on a popular subject, usually around 4×7, directed to a general audience and sold in drugstores and groceries as well as in bookstores.

Middle reader. Juvenile fiction for readers aged 8-13, featuring heavier text than picture books and some light illustration.

Ms(s). Abbreviation for manuscript(s).

Multiple submission. Submission of more than one short story at a time to the same editor. Do not make a multiple submission unless requested.

Narration. The account of events in a story's plot as related by the speaker or the voice of the author.

Narrator. The person who tells the story, either someone involved in the action or the voice of the writer.

New Age. A term including categories such as astrology, psychic phenomena, spiritual healing, UFOs, mysticism and other aspects of the occult.

Noir. A style of mystery involving hard-boiled detectives and bleak settings.

Nom de plume. French for "pen name"; a pseudonym.

Novella (also novelette). A short novel or long story, approximately 7,000-15,000 words.

#10 envelope. $4 \times 9\frac{1}{2}$ envelope, used for queries and other business letters.

Offprint. Copy of a story taken from a magazine before it is bound.

One-time rights. Permission to publish a story in periodical or book form one time only.

Outline. A summary of a book's contents, often in the form of chapter headings with a few sentences outlining the action of the story under each one; sometimes part of a book proposal.

Over the transom. A phrase referring to unsolicited manuscripts, or those that come in "over the transom."

Payment on acceptance. Payment from the magazine or publishing house as soon as the decision to print a manuscript is made.

Payment on publication. Payment from the publisher after a manuscript is printed.

Pen name. A pseudonym used to conceal a writer's real name.

Periodical. A magazine or journal published at regular intervals.

Plot. The carefully devised series of events through which the characters progress in a work of fiction.

Police procedural. A mystery featuring a police detective or officer who uses standard professional police practices to solve a crime.

Print on demand (POD). Novels produced digitally one at a time, as ordered. Self-publishing through print on demand technology typically involves some fees for the author. Some authors use POD to create a manuscript in book form to send to prospective traditional publishers.

Proofreading. Close reading and correction of a manuscript's typographical errors.

Proofs. A typeset version of a manuscript used for correcting errors and making changes, often a photocopy of the galleys.

Proposal. An offer to write a specific work, usually consisting of an outline of the work and one or two completed chapters.

Protagonist. The principal or leading character in a literary work.

Public domain. Material that either was never copyrighted or whose copyright term has expired.

Pulp magazine. A periodical printed on inexpensive paper, usually containing lurid, sensational stories or articles.

Query. A letter written to an editor to elicit interest in a story the writer wants to submit.

Reader. A person hired by a publisher to read unsolicited manuscripts.

Reading fee. An arbitrary amount of money charged by some agents and publishers to read a submitted manuscript.

Regency romance. A genre romance, usually set in England between 1811-1820.

Remainders. Leftover copies of an out-of-print book, sold by the publisher at a reduced price.

Reporting time. The number of weeks or months it takes an editor to report back on an author's query or manuscript.

Reprint rights. Permission to print an already published work whose rights have been sold to another magazine or book publisher.

Roman à clef. French "novel with a key." A novel that represents actual living or historical characters and events in fictionalized form.

Romance. The genre relating accounts of passionate love and fictional heroic achievements.

Royalties. A percentage of the retail price paid to an author for each copy of the book that is sold.

SAE. Self-addressed envelope.

SASE. Self-addressed stamped envelope.

Science fiction. Genre in which scientific facts and hypotheses form the basis of actions and events.

Second serial (reprint) rights. Permission for the reprinting of a work in another periodical after its first publication in book or magazine form.

Self-publishing. In this arrangement, the author keeps all income derived from the book, but he pays for its manufacturing, production and marketing.

Sequel. A literary work that continues the narrative of a previous, related story or novel.

Serial rights. The rights given by an author to a publisher to print a piece in one or more periodicals.

Serialized novel. A book-length work of fiction published in sequential issues of a periodical.

Setting. The environment and time period during which the action of a story takes place.

Short short story. A condensed piece of fiction, usually under 700 words.

Simultaneous submission. The practice of sending copies of the same manuscript to several editors or publishers at the same time. Some people refuse to consider such submissions.

Slant. A story's particular approach or style, designed to appeal to the readers of a specific magazine.

Slice of life. A presentation of characters in a seemingly mundane situation which offers the reader a flash of illumination about the characters or their situation.

Slush pile. A stack of unsolicited manuscripts in the editorial offices of a publisher.

Social fiction. Fiction written with the purpose of bringing about positive changes in society.

Soft/sociological science fiction. Science fiction with an emphasis on society and culture versus scientific accuracy.

Space opera. Epic science fiction with an emphasis on good guys versus bad guys.

Speculation (or Spec). An editor's agreement to look at an author's manuscript with no promise to purchase.

Speculative fiction (SpecFic). The all-inclusive term for science fiction, fantasy and horror.

Splatterpunk. Type of horror fiction known for its very violent and graphic content.

Subsidiary. An incorporated branch of a company or conglomerate (e.g. Alfred Knopf, Inc., a subsidiary of Random House, Inc.).

Subsidiary rights. All rights other than book publishing rights included in a book contract, such as paperback, book club and movie rights.

Subsidy publisher. A book publisher who charges the author for the cost of typesetting, printing and promoting a book. Also Vanity publisher.

Subterficial fiction. Innovative, challenging, nonconventional fiction in which what seems to be happening is the result of things not so easily perceived.

Suspense. A genre of fiction where the plot's primary function is to build a feeling of anticipation and fear in the reader over its possible outcome.

Synopsis. A brief summary of a story, novel or play. As part of a book proposal, it is a comprehensive summary condensed in a page or page and a half.

Tabloid. Publication printed on paper about half the size of a regular newspaper page (e.g. *The National Enquirer*).

Tearsheet. Page from a magazine containing a published story.

Theme. The dominant or central idea in a literary work; its message, moral or main thread.

Trade paperback. A softbound volume, usually around 5×8, published and designed for the general public, available mainly in bookstores.

Traditional fantasy. Fantasy with an emphasis on magic, using characters with the ability to do magic such as wizards, witches, dragons, elves, and unicorns.

Unsolicited manuscript. A story or novel manuscript that an editor did not specifically ask to see.

Urban fantasy. Fantasy that takes magical characters such as elves, fairies, vampires or wizards and places them in modern-day settings, often in the inner city.

Vanity publisher. See Subsidy publisher.

Viewpoint. The position or attitude of the first- or third-person narrator or multiple narrators, which determines how a story's action is seen and evaluated.

Western. Genre with a setting in the West, usually between 1860-1890, with a formula plot about cowboys or other aspects of frontier life.

Whodunit. Genre dealing with murder, suspense and the detection of criminals.

Work-for-hire. Work that another party commissions you to do, generally for a flat fee. The creator does not own the copyright and therefore cannot sell any rights.

Young adult. The general classification of books written for readers 12-18.

Zine. Often one- or two-person operations run from the home of the publisher/editor. Themes tend to be specialized, personal, experimental and often controversial.

Contest Index by Deadline

Our deadline index organizes all the contests listed in this edition by their monthly deadline. If a contest occurs multiple times during the year (quarterly, for example), its name and page number should appear under each appropriate monthly heading. Turn to the listing's page number for specific dates and other more detailed information.

Conference Index by Date

Our conference index organizes all conferences listed in this edition by the month in which they are held. If a conference bridges two months, you will find its name and page number under both monthly headings. If a conference occurs multiple times during the year (seasonally, for example), it will appear under each appropriate monthly heading. Turn to the listing's page number for exact dates and more detailed information.

Category Index

Our category index makes it easy for you to identify publishers who are looking for a specific type of fiction. Under each fiction category are magazines and book publishers looking for that kind of fiction. Publishers who are not listed under a fiction category either accept all types of fiction or have not indicated specific subject preferences. Also not appearing here are listings that need very specific types of fiction, e.g., "fiction about fly fishing only." To use this index to find a book publisher for your mainstream novel, for instance, go to the Mainstream/Contemporary section and look under Book Publishers. Finally, read individual listings *carefully* to determine the publishers best suited to your work.

For a listing of agents and the types of fiction they represent, see the Literary Agents Category Index beginning on page 135.

ADVENTURE

Magazines

CHILDREN'S/JUVENILE

Magazines

Book Publishers

COMICS/GRAPHIC NOVELS

Magazines

Book Publishers

Book Publishers

EXPERIMENTAL

Magazines

FAMILY SAGA

Magazines

Book Publishers

FANTASY

Magazines

Book Publishers

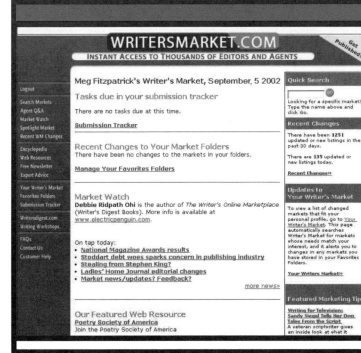

WRITERSMARKET.COM

Instant Access to Thousands of Editors and Agents

Sure, you already know *Writer's Market* is the essential tool for selling your writing — after all, a new edition has come out every year for almost a century! And now, to complement your trusty "freelance writer's bible," you can subscribe to WritersMarket.com! It's cool… it's quick…and it's $10 off the regular price!

Here's what you'll find at WritersMarket.com:

→ **EASY-TO-USE SEARCHABLE DATABASE** — Simply enter your search parameters, and voila! Zero in on potential markets in seconds.

→ **SUBMISSION TRACKER** — Have trouble remembering what you've sent to whom, or if you've heard back? The Submission Tracker does the work for you!

→ **PERSONALIZED MARKET LISTS** — Set up a personal profile and get news, new listings and market changes that match your interests…the second you sign on!

→ **MORE MARKETS** — Yes, there are 1,000+ pages in the book, but believe it or not, there are several hundred listings that just couldn't fit! You'll find even more markets and agents at WritersMarket.com, and we keep adding to the database whenever new listings become available!

→ **LISTINGS UPDATED DAILY** — It doesn't look good to address your query letter to the wrong editor or agent…and with WritersMarket.com, that will never happen again. You'll be on top of all the industry developments…as soon as they happen!

→ **LINKS TO WRITING RESOURCES** including a comprehensive library of writing tips, myriad fact books and dictionaries, media research, writing magazines, online workshops, and more!

WRITERSMARKET.COM

SUBSCRIBE TODAY AND SAVE $10!

03NSS

Book Publishers

GAY

Magazines

GLITZ

Magazines

Book Publishers

HISTORICAL

Magazines

HORROR

Book Publishers

HUMOR/SATIRE

Magazines

Book Publishers

LESBIAN

Magazines

Book Publishers

LITERARY

Magazines

Book Publishers

MAINSTREAM/ CONTEMPORARY

Magazines

Book Publishers

MILITARY/WAR
Magazines

Book Publishers

NEW AGE/MYSTIC/SPIRITUAL

Magazines

Book Publishers

ONLINE MAGAZINES

Magazines

Book Publishers

RELIGIOUS/INSPIRATIONAL

Magazines

Book Publishers

ROMANCE

Magazines

Book Publishers

SCIENCE FICTION

Magazines

Book Publishers

DISCOVER A WORLD OF WRITING SUCCESS

Are you ready to be praised, published, and paid for your writing? It's time to invest in your future with *Writer's Digest*! Beginners and experienced writers alike have been enjoying *Writer's Digest*, the world's leading magazine for writers, for more than 80 years — and it keeps getting better! Each issue is brimming with:

- Inspiration from writers who have been in your shoes
- Detailed info on the latest contests, conferences, markets, and opportunities in every genre
- Tools of the trade, including reviews of the latest writing software and hardware
- Writing prompts and exercises to overcome writer's block and rekindle your creative spark
- Expert tips, techniques, and advice to help you get published
- And so much more!

That's a lot to look forward to every month. Let *Writer's Digest* put you on the road to writing success!

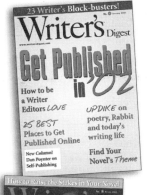

NO RISK!
Send No Money Now!

☐ **Yes!** Please rush me my 2 FREE issues of *Writer's Digest* — the world's leading magazine for writers. If I like what I read, I'll get a full year's subscription (12 issues, including the 2 free issues) for only $19.96. That's 67% off the newsstand rate! If I'm not completely happy, I'll write "cancel" on your invoice, return it and owe nothing. The 2 FREE issues are mine to keep, no matter what!

Name_____

Address_____

City_____

State_____ZIP_____

Annual newsstand rate is $59.88. Orders outside the U.S. will be billed an additional $10 (includes GST/HST in Canada.) Please allow 4-6 weeks for first-issue delivery.

www.writersdigest.com

T6CM3

Get  2 FREE TRIAL ISSUES of Writer's® Digest

Packed with creative inspiration, advice, and tips to guide you on the road to success, *Writer's Digest* will offer you everything you need to take your writing to the next level! You'll discover how to:

- Create dynamic characters and page-turning plots
- Submit query letters that publishers won't be able to refuse
- Find the right agent or editor for you
- Make it out of the slush-pile and into the hands of the right publisher
- Write award-winning contest entries
- And more!

See for yourself by ordering your 2 FREE trial issues today!

WESTERN

YOUNG ADULT/TEEN

Magazines

Book Publishers

General Index

Markets that appeared in the 2002 edition of *Novel & Short Story Writer's Market* but are not included in this edition are identified by a two-letter code explaining why the market was omitted: **(ED)**—Editorial Decision, **(NS)**—Not Accepting Submissions, **(NR)**—No (or late) Response to Listing Request, **(OB)**—Out of Business, **(RR)**—Removed by Market's Request, **(RS)**—Restructuring, **(TS)**—Temporarily Suspended, **(UC)**—Unable to Contact, **(UF)**—Uncertain Future.

Companies that appeared in the 2002 edition of *Novel & Short Story Writer's Market*, but do not appear this year, are listed in this General Index with the following codes explaining why these markets were omitted: (ED)—Editorial Decision, (NS)—Not Accepting Submissions, (NR)—No (or late) Response to Listing Request, (OB)—Out of Business, (RR)—Removed by Market's Request, (RS)—Restructuring, (TS)—Temporarily Suspended, (UC)—Unable to Contact, (UF)—Uncertain Future.

Companies that appeared in the 2002 edition of *Novel & Short Story Writer's Market*, but do not appear this year, are listed in this General Index with the following codes explaining why these markets were omitted: (ED)—Editorial Decision, (NS)—Not Accepting Submissions, (NR)—No (or late) Response to Listing Request, (OB)—Out of Business, (RR)—Removed by Market's Request, (RS)—Restructuring, (TS)—Temporarily Suspended, (UC)—Unable to Contact, (UF)—Uncertain Future.